W9-CTH-649

JE '87

Contemporary
Literary Criticism

Guide to Gale Literary Criticism Series

When you need to review criticism of literary works, these are the Gale series to use:

If the author's death date is: | **You should turn to:**

After Dec. 31, 1959
(or author is still living)

CONTEMPORARY LITERARY CRITICISM

for example: Jorge Luis Borges, Anthony Burgess,
William Faulkner, Mary Gordon,
Ernest Hemingway, Iris Murdoch

1900 through 1959

TWENTIETH-CENTURY LITERARY CRITICISM

for example: Willa Cather, F. Scott Fitzgerald,
Henry James, Mark Twain, Virginia Woolf

1800 through 1899

NINETEENTH-CENTURY LITERATURE CRITICISM

for example: Fedor Dostoevski, Nathaniel Hawthorne,
George Sand, William Wordsworth

1400 through 1799

LITERATURE CRITICISM FROM 1400 TO 1800
(excluding Shakespeare)

for example: Anne Bradstreet, Daniel Defoe,
Alexander Pope, François Rabelais,
Jonathan Swift, Phillis Wheatley

SHAKESPEAREAN CRITICISM

Shakespeare's plays and poetry

Antiquity through 1399

CLASSICAL AND MEDIEVAL LITERATURE CRITICISM

for example: Dante, Homer, Plato, Sophocles, Vergil,
the Beowulf poet

(Volume 1 forthcoming)

Gale also publishes related criticism series:

CHILDREN'S LITERATURE REVIEW

This ongoing series covers authors of all eras. Presents criticism on authors and author/illustrators who write for the preschool through high school audience.

CONTEMPORARY ISSUES CRITICISM

This two-volume set presents criticism on contemporary authors writing on current issues. Topics covered include the social sciences, philosophy, economics, natural science, law, and related areas.

ISSN 0091-3421

Volume 42

Contemporary Literary Criticism

Excerpts from Criticism of the
Works of Today's Novelists, Poets,
Playwrights, Short Story Writers, Scriptwriters,
and Other Creative Writers

Daniel G. Marowski
Roger Matuz
EDITORS

Robyn V. Young
ASSOCIATE EDITOR

Gale Research Company
Book Tower
Detroit, Michigan 48226

STAFF

Daniel G. Marowski, Roger Matuz, *Editors*

Robyn V. Young, *Associate Editor*

Sean R. Pollock, Jane C. Thacker, Debra A. Wells, *Senior Assistant Editors*

Kelly King Howes, Michele R. O'Connell, David Segal,
Thomas J. Votteler, Bruce Walker, *Assistant Editors*

Jean C. Stine, *Contributing Editor*

Melissa Reiff Hug, Thomas Ligotti, Jay P. Pederson,
Peter Wehrli, *Contributing Assistant Editors*

Jeanne A. Gough, *Production & Permissions Manager*

Lizbeth A. Purdy, *Production Supervisor*
Denise Michlewicz Broderick, *Production Coordinator*
Kathleen M. Cook, Maureen Duffy, Suzanne Powers,
Jani Prescott, *Editorial Assistants*

Linda M. Pugliese, *Manuscript Coordinator*
Donna Craft, *Assistant Manuscript Coordinator*
Jennifer E. Gale, Maureen A. Puhl, Rosetta Irene Simms, *Manuscript Assistants*

Victoria B. Cariappa, *Research Coordinator*
Maureen R. Richards, *Assistant Research Coordinator*
Daniel Kurt Gilbert, Kent Graham, Keith E. Schooley, Filomena Sgambati,
Vincenza G. Tranchida, Mary D. Wise, *Research Assistants*

Janice M. Mach, *Permissions Coordinator, Text*
Patricia A. Seefelt, *Permissions Coordinator, Illustrations*
Susan D. Battista, Margaret A. Chamberlain, Sandra C. Davis,
Kathy Grell, *Assistant Permissions Coordinators*
Mabel E. Gurney, Josephine M. Keene, Mary M. Matuz, *Senior Permissions Assistants*
Margaret A. Carson, H. Diane Cooper, Colleen M. Crane, *Permissions Assistants*
Eileen H. Baehr, Anita Ransom, Kimberly Smilay, *Permissions Clerks*

Special thanks to Carolyn Bancroft and Sharon Hall
for their assistance on the Title Index.

Frederick G. Ruffner, *Publisher*
Dedria Bryfonski, *Editorial Director*
Ellen T. Crowley, *Associate Editorial Director*
Laurie Lanzen Harris, *Director, Literature Criticism Division*
Dennis Poupard, *Senior Editor, Literary Criticism Series*

Library of Congress Catalog Card Number 76-38938
ISBN 0-8103-4416-5
ISSN 0091-3421

Computerized photocomposition by
Typographics, Incorporated
Kansas City, Missouri

Printed in the United States

Contents

Preface

Literary criticism is, by definition, "the art of evaluating or analyzing with knowledge and propriety works of literature." The complexity and variety of the themes and forms of contemporary literature make the function of the critic especially important to today's reader. It is the critic who assists the reader in identifying significant new writers, recognizing trends in critical methods, mastering new terminology, and monitoring scholarly and popular sources of critical opinion.

Until the publication of the first volume of *Contemporary Literary Criticism (CLC)* in 1973, there existed no ongoing digest of current literary opinion. *CLC,* therefore, has fulfilled an essential need.

Scope of the Work

CLC presents significant passages from published criticism of works by today's creative writers. Each volume of *CLC* includes excerpted criticism on about 50 authors who are now living or who died after December 31, 1959. More than 1,800 authors have been included since the series began publication. The majority of authors covered by *CLC* are living writers who continue to publish; therefore, an author frequently appears in more than one volume. There is, of course, no duplication of reprinted criticism.

Authors are selected for inclusion for a variety of reasons, among them the publication of a critically acclaimed new work, the reception of a major literary award, or the dramatization of a literary work as a film or television screenplay. For example, the present volume includes Walter Tevis, whose novels *The Hustler, The Man Who Fell to Earth,* and *The Color of Money* were adapted into critically acclaimed films; C. J. Koch, who cowrote the celebrated screen version of his novel *The Year of Living Dangerously;* and David Edgar, whose stage adaptation of Charles Dickens's novel *The Life and Adventures of Nicholas Nickleby* received much critical and popular attention. Perhaps most importantly, authors who appear frequently on the syllabuses of high school and college literature classes are heavily represented in *CLC;* James Baldwin and William Carlos Williams are examples of writers of this stature in the present volume. Attention is also given to several other groups of writers—authors of considerable public interest—about whose work criticism is often difficult to locate. These are the contributors to the well-loved but nonscholarly genres of mystery and science fiction, as well as literary and social critics whose insights are considered valuable and informative. Foreign writers and authors who represent particular ethnic groups in the United States are also featured in each volume.

Format of the Book

Altogether there are about 700 individual excerpts in each volume—with an average of about 14 excerpts per author—taken from hundreds of literary reviews, general magazines, scholarly journals, and monographs. Contemporary criticism is loosely defined as that which is relevant to the evaluation of the author under discussion; this includes criticism written at the beginning of an author's career as well as current commentary. Emphasis has been placed on expanding the sources for criticism by including an increasing number of scholarly and specialized periodicals. Students, teachers, librarians, and researchers frequently find that the generous excerpts and supplementary material provided by the editors supply them with all the information needed to write a term paper, analyze a poem, or lead a book discussion group. However, complete bibliographical citations facilitate the location of the original source as well as provide all of the information necessary for a term paper footnote or bibliography.

A *CLC* author entry consists of the following elements:

  • The **author heading** cites the author's full name, followed by birth date, and death date when applicable. The portion of the name outside the parentheses denotes the form under which the author has most commonly published. If an author has written consistently under a pseudonym, the pseudonym will be listed in the author heading and the real name given on the first line of the biographical and critical introduction. Also located at the beginning of the introduction to the author entry are any important name variations under which an author has written. Uncertainty as to a birth or death date is indicated by question marks.

• A **portrait** of the author is included when available.

• A brief **biographical and critical introduction** to the author and his or her work precedes the excerpted criticism. However, *CLC* is not intended to be a definitive biographical source. Therefore, *cross-references* have been included to direct the reader to other useful sources published by the Gale Research Company: *Contemporary Authors* now includes detailed biographical and bibliographical sketches on more than 86,000 authors; *Children's Literature Review* presents excerpted criticism on the works of authors of children's books; *Something about the Author* contains heavily illustrated biographical sketches on writers and illustrators who create books for children and young adults; *Contemporary Issues Criticism* presents excerpted commentary on the nonfiction works of authors who influence contemporary thought; *Dictionary of Literary Biography* provides original evaluations and detailed biographies of authors important to literary history; *Contemporary Authors Autobiography Series* offers autobiographical essays by prominent writers; and *Something about the Author Autobiography Series* presents auto-biographical essays by authors of interest to young readers. Previous volumes of *CLC* in which the author has been featured are also listed in the introduction.

• The **excerpted criticism** represents various kinds of critical writing—a particular essay may be normative, descriptive, interpretive, textual, appreciative, comparative, or generic. It may range in form from the brief review to the scholarly monograph. Essays are selected by the editors to reflect the spectrum of opinion about a specific work or about an author's literary career in general. The excerpts are presented chronologically, adding a useful perspective to the entry. All titles by the author featured in the entry are printed in boldface type, which enables the reader to easily identify the works being discussed.

• A complete **bibliographical citation** designed to help the user find the original essay or book follows each excerpt.

Other Features

• A list of **Authors Forthcoming in *CLC*** previews the authors to be researched for future volumes.

• An **Appendix** lists the sources from which material in the volume has been reprinted. It does not, however, list every book or periodical consulted during the preparation of the volume.

• A **Cumulative Author Index** lists all the authors who have appeared in *CLC, Twentieth-Century Literary Criticism, Nineteenth-Century Literature Criticism,* and *Literature Criticism from 1400 to 1800,* along with cross-references to other Gale series: *Children's Literature Review, Authors in the News, Contemporary Authors, Contemporary Authors Autobiography Series, Dictionary of Literary Biography, Something about the Author, Something about the Author Autobiography Series,* and *Yesterday's Authors of Books for Children.* Users will welcome this cumulated author index as a useful tool for locating an author within the various series. The index, which lists birth and death dates when available, will be particularly valuable for those authors who are identified with a certain period but whose death date causes them to be placed in another, or for those authors whose careers span two periods. For example, Ernest Hemingway is found in *CLC,* yet a writer often associated with him, F. Scott Fitzgerald, is found in *Twentieth-Century Literary Criticism.*

• A **Cumulative Nationality Index** lists the authors included in *CLC* alphabetically by nationality, followed by the volume numbers in which they appear.

• Beginning with Volume 40, in response to suggestions from many users and librarians, a **Cumulative Title Index** has replaced the Cumulative Index to Critics. The Cumulative Title Index lists titles reviewed in *CLC* from Volume 1 through the current volume in alphabetical order. Titles are followed by the corresponding volume and page numbers where they may be located. In cases where the same title is used by different authors, the author's surname is given in parentheses after the title, e.g., *Collected Poems* (Berryman), *Collected Poems* (Eliot). For foreign titles, a cross-reference is given to the translated English title. Titles of novels, novellas, dramas, films, record albums, and poetry, short story, and essay collections are printed in italics, while all individual poems, short stories, essays, and songs are printed in roman type within quotation marks; when published separately (e.g., T.S. Eliot's poem *The Waste Land*), the title will also be printed in italics.

Acknowledgments

No work of this scope can be accomplished without the cooperation of many people. The editors especially wish to thank the copyright holders of the excerpted essays included in this volume, the permissions managers of many book and magazine publishing companies for assisting us in securing reprint rights, and the photographers and other individuals who provided portraits of the authors. We are grateful to the staffs of the Detroit Public Library, the Library of Congress, the University of Detroit Library, the University of Michigan Library, and the Wayne State University Library for making their resources available to us. We also wish to thank Anthony Bogucki for his assistance with copyright research.

Suggestions Are Welcome

The editors welcome the comments and suggestions of readers to expand the coverage and enhance the usefulness of the series.

Authors Forthcoming in *CLC*

Contemporary Literary Criticism, Volumes 43 and 45, will contain criticism on a number of authors not previously listed and will also feature criticism on newer works by authors included in earlier volumes. Volume 44 will be a yearbook devoted to an examination of the outstanding achievements and trends in literature during 1986.

To Be Included in Volume 43

W. H. Auden (English-born American poet, critic, essayist, and dramatist)—Regarded as one of the preeminent poets of the twentieth century, Auden evidenced his strong political, social, and psychological orientations in verse centering on moral issues. His entry will include scholarly essays and recent reappraisals as well as reviews of *The English Auden: Poems, Essays, and Dramatic Writings, 1927-1939.*

John Betjeman (English poet and nonfiction writer)—Poet Laureate of England from 1972 until his death in 1984, Betjeman is best remembered for his literal, descriptive poetic style and his blend of humor and seriousness.

Rita Mae Brown (American novelist, poet, essayist, and scriptwriter)—Brown's fiction focuses upon strong female characters who are distinguished by their humor and their determination to succeed. Her recent novels include *Sudden Death* and *High Hearts.*

Dennis Brutus (South African poet, essayist, and critic)—Brutus is considered among the most significant contemporary South African poets. Well known for his participation in the anti-apartheid movement, he has lived in exile in England and the United States for over twenty years.

Zbigniew Herbert (Polish poet, dramatist, and essayist)—One of Poland's most important contemporary poets, Herbert often explores historical and political themes, focusing upon the conflict between ideals and reality. His recently translated works include *Report from the Besieged City,* a collection of verse, and *Barbarian in the Garden,* a volume of essays.

L. Ron Hubbard (American novelist, nonfiction writer, and short story writer)—Best known as the controversial author of *Dianetics* and the founder of the Church of Scientology, Hubbard was also a significant science fiction writer. His posthumously published fiction works include *The Enemy Within* and *An Alien Affair.*

Tama Janowitz (American short story writer, novelist, and journalist)—Janowitz became a literary celebrity with her short story collection *Slaves of New York,* in which she uses deadpan humor to chronicle the lives of bizarre characters who populate the art galleries, nightclubs, and restaurants of New York's Soho district.

Clarice Lispector (Ukrainian-born Brazilian novelist and short story writer)—Since Lispector's death in 1979, two of her works, *Family Ties* and *The Apple in the Dark,* have been reissued in English translation and two others, *The Foreign Legion* and *The Hour of the Star,* have been translated and published in the United States for the first time.

Nicholas Mosley (English novelist and nonfiction writer)—In his fiction, Mosley employs modernist narrative techniques to explore the underlying motives of human behavior. His recent novel, *Judith,* is the third of a projected six volumes detailing the lives of the characters in his complex work *Catastrophe Practice.*

Joe Orton (English dramatist, scriptwriter, and novelist)—Best remembered as the author of *What the Butler Saw* and other popular plays of the 1960s, Orton blended black humor, farce, and violence in his dramas to satirize archaic British moral standards.

Reynolds Price (American novelist, short story writer, essayist, poet, and dramatist)—A respected writer in several genres, Price is best known for his fiction, which is firmly rooted in the Southern tradition. Price's recent novel, *Kate Vaiden,* won the 1987 National Book Critics' Circle Award.

John Updike (American novelist, critic, and short story writer)—Among the most distinguished contemporary authors, Updike recently published *Roger's Version,* a novel that explores the spiritual conflicts of two men, one of whom seeks to prove the existence of God through the use of computers.

Kathy Acker (American novelist and scriptwriter)—Acker has attracted critical attention for her experimental novels *Great Expectations* and *Don Quixote,* in which she uses pornography, plagiarism, autobiography, and dream fragments to subvert literary conventions and to attack traditional social values.

Guillermo Cabrera Infante (Cuban-born novelist, short story writer, journalist, and critic)—In his recent novel, *Infante's Inferno,* Cabrera Infante continues his use of humorous wordplay and narrative experimentation for which he won international recognition with his earlier novel, *Three Trapped Tigers.*

Claude Gauvreau (Canadian poet, dramatist, critic, and novelist)—Gauvreau was a prominent member of Montreal's artistic community during the 1940s and 1950s. *The Entrails,* a translation of his early verse, has renewed interest in his experimental literary works, which were influenced by surrealism and automatism.

William Humphrey (American novelist, short story writer, and essayist)—Humphrey's fiction is usually set in the American Southwest and depicts families and individuals struggling to survive in an often hostile environment. His recent publications include *The Collected Stories of William Humphrey* and *Open Season: Sporting Adventures,* a volume of essays.

Joseph Kesselring (American dramatist and scriptwriter)—An author of popular Broadway comedies during the 1940s and 1950s, Kesselring is best remembered for his domestic farce *Arsenic and Old Lace.*

Ursula K. Le Guin (American novelist, short story writer, poet, and essayist)—A respected award-winning author of fantasy and science fiction, Le Guin is best known for her *Earthsea Trilogy.* Her recent works include *Always Coming Home* and *The Eye of the Heron.*

Thomas McGuane (American novelist, short story writer, scriptwriter, and essayist)—A leading contemporary American satirist, McGuane writes irreverent fiction that focuses on what he terms America's "declining snivelization." Works to be covered in his entry include the novels *Nobody's Angel* and *Something to be Desired* and the short story collection *To Skin a Cat.*

John Montague (American-born Irish poet, short story writer, and editor)—Montague's recent volumes of verse, *Selected Poems* and *The Dead Kingdom,* have secured his reputation as one of contemporary Ireland's leading poets.

Alice Munro (Canadian short story writer and novelist)—Munro writes humorous, well-crafted stories about the disturbing undercurrents that affect the ordinary lives of her characters, who inhabit a rural area in southwestern Ontario. Her recent collection, *The Progress of Love,* has attracted significant critical attention.

Lewis Nkosi (South African novelist, critic, and dramatist)—Nkosi, who has lived in exile in England, the United States, and Zambia for over twenty-five years, is well known for his essays on contemporary African literature. His first novel, *Mating Birds,* centers on a young Zulu man who is sentenced to die by the South African government for allegedly raping a white woman.

Charles Tomlinson (English poet, translator, and critic)—Considered one of England's most distinguished post-World War II poets, Tomlinson writes verse which displays his precise attention to detail and his concern with metaphysical themes. Tomlinson's recent collections include *The Flood* and *Notes from New York and Other Poems.*

Rex Warner (English novelist, nonfiction writer, poet, and translator)—Warner was a scholar of classical literature and history whose works are infused with allusions to ancient Greece. Warner's novels evidence his early interest in Kafkaesque techniques, his concern with contemporary political and social issues during the World War II era, and his later use of historical narratives to focus on universal themes.

James (Arthur) Baldwin

1924-

American novelist, essayist, dramatist, scriptwriter, short story writer, and author of children's books.

Baldwin is considered to be one of the most prestigious writers in contemporary American literature. Since the publication of his first and best-known novel, *Go Tell It on the Mountain* (1953), Baldwin has exposed the racial and sexual polarization of American society and has consistently challenged readers to confront and resolve these differences. Baldwin's influence and popularity reached their peak during the 1960s, when he was regarded by many as the leading literary spokesperson of the civil rights movement. His novels, essays, and other writings attest to his premise that the black American, as an object of suffering and abuse, represents a universal symbol of human conflict.

Much of Baldwin's work is loosely based on his childhood and adolescence. He was born into poverty in Harlem, a black district of New York City, and raised in a strict religious household headed by his stepfather, a storefront preacher who had migrated from New Orleans. As a junior high school student, Baldwin participated in his school's literary club; its academic advisor was Countee Cullen, a renowned poet of the Harlem Renaissance, which was a major literary and artistic movement of black Americans during the 1920s. In 1938 Baldwin began to preach at the Fireside Pentecostal Church in Harlem, where his sermons emphasized the vision of the apocalypse described in the Book of Revelations. After graduating from high school in 1942, Baldwin renounced the ministry and moved to New Jersey. He worked at several defense factories and witnessed violent confrontations between urban blacks and whites who had moved from the South in search of employment opportunities spawned by military-related industries. Baldwin returned to Harlem following his stepfather's death in 1943. During the next five years, he held a succession of menial jobs and began to write book reviews for such periodicals as *The Nation* and *The New Leader*. While working on *Go Tell It on the Mountain*, he met Richard Wright, the author of *Native Son,* who read his manuscript and became his mentor. Shortly after the publication of his first essay, "The Harlem Ghetto," in *Commentary* in 1948, Baldwin moved to Paris.

Baldwin was hailed by critics as a major novelist and a worthy successor to Ralph Ellison and Richard Wright following the publication of his semiautobiographical novel, *Go Tell It on the Mountain*. The book dramatizes the events leading to the religious confirmation of John Grimes, a sensitive Harlem youth struggling to come to terms with his confusion over his sexuality and his religious upbringing. Central to the novel is his family's legacy of brutality and hate, augmented by the destructive relationship between John and his stepfather, a fundamentalist preacher whose insecurities over his own religious commitment result in his abusive treatment of John and his emotional neglect of his family. Baldwin earned unanimous praise for his skillful evocation of his characters' squalid lives and for his powerful language, which some critics likened to a fire-and-brimstone oratory.

While most critics regarded *Go Tell It on the Mountain* as a cathartic novel in which Baldwin attempted to resolve the emo-

tional anguish of his adolescence, some critics viewed his next work, *Giovanni's Room* (1956), as one in which he confronts his homosexuality. The novel generated much controversy, for Baldwin was one of the first black writers to openly discuss homosexuality in his fiction. *Giovanni's Room,* which is set in Paris, tells the story of an ill-fated love affair between a white American student and an Italian bartender. Many critics were outraged by Baldwin's blunt language and his controversial topic, while others echoed David Littlejohn's assessment that it was "certainly one of the most subtle novels of the homosexual world." Baldwin's investigation of racial and sexual politics continues in the novel *Another Country* (1962), which provoked even more debate. Although it received largely negative reviews due to Baldwin's candid depiction of sex, some considered *Another Country* superior to *Giovanni's Room* in terms of thematic scope and descriptive quality. Baldwin's fiction of the late 1960s and 1970s was primarily influenced by his involvement in the civil rights movement. *Tell Me How Long the Train's Been Gone* (1968) centers on two brothers and their different approaches to escaping the ghetto; one finds success in the entertainment industry, while the other is nearly destroyed by racism and violence. *If Beale Street Could Talk* (1974) further examines blacks living in a hostile environment. In *Just above My Head* (1979), Baldwin returns to his earlier themes of religion and sexuality in a complex story of a homosexual gospel singer. Although these works were best-sellers, they signaled for most critics a decline in Baldwin's creative talents due to his reliance on didacticism.

Although Baldwin is best known as a novelist, his nonfiction works have received substantial critical acclaim. The essay "Everybody's Protest Novel," published in 1949, introduced him to the New York intelligentsia and generated much controversy for its attack on authors of protest fiction, including Richard Wright, who, Baldwin maintained, perpetuated rather than condemned negative racial stereotypes. While Baldwin viewed this piece as an exploration of the thematic options that black writers could follow, Wright considered it a personal affront and subsequently terminated his professional alliance with Baldwin. Nevertheless, critics praised Baldwin for his perceptive analysis of protest literature and for his lucid prose. Baldwin earned additional critical praise for the essays collected in *Notes of a Native Son* (1955) and *Nobody Knows My Name: More Notes of a Native Son* (1961). In these volumes, Baldwin optimistically examines the state of race relations in the United States and abroad in essays that range from poignant autobiographical remembrances to scholarly literary and social criticism. He also uses personal experience to address the problems artists face when drawn to political activism. Critics viewed Baldwin's next nonfiction work, *The Fire Next Time* (1963), as both a passionate plea for reconciliation between the races and as a manifesto for black liberation.

As racial tensions escalated in the mid-1960s, Baldwin's vision of America turned increasingly bitter and his prose more inflammatory. After the publication of *No Name in the Street* (1972), Baldwin was faulted for abandoning his deft powers of persuasion in favor of rhetoric and was accused by some of racism. Keneth Kinnamon summed up the change in Baldwin's attitude and literature during this period: "[The] redemptive possibilities of love seemed exhausted in that terrible decade of assassination, riot, and repression. . . . Violence, [Baldwin] now believes, is the arbiter of history, and in its matrix the white world is dying and the third world is struggling to be born. . . . Though love may still be a sustaining personal force, its social utility is dubious." Baldwin's recent nonfiction work, *The Evidence of Things Not Seen* (1985), is a lengthy treatise on the Atlanta child murders, which claimed the lives of more than twenty black children and young adults between 1979 and 1981. In this book, Baldwin combines straight reportage with an examination of the tragedy, perceiving the murders as a prelude to an apocalyptic confrontation between blacks and whites.

Baldwin's work has undergone substantial reevaluation since the publication of *The Price of the Ticket: Collected Nonfiction, 1948-1985* (1985). Many of the essays included in this volume help to explain Baldwin's viewpoints during various periods of his life and also illuminate the themes and ideas suggested in his fiction. In their reviews of this collection, critics generally complained that Baldwin's later commentaries are too heavily fraught with polemic and accusation. They agreed, however, that Baldwin's early essays endure as significant contributions to American literature and serve, according to David Sweetman, as "an irreplaceable record of the postwar years as suffered by so many."

(See also *CLC*, Vols. 1, 2, 3, 4, 5, 8, 13, 15, 17; *Contemporary Authors*, Vols. 1-4, rev. ed.; *Contemporary Authors New Revision Series*, Vol. 3; *Something about the Author*, Vol. 9; and *Dictionary of Literary Biography*, Vols. 2, 7, 33.)

JAMES CAMPBELL

In **"Everybody's Protest Novel"**, the essay which first brought the 24-year-old James Baldwin to the attention of the literary world in America, the author points out that two of the three prominent Negroes in Mrs Stowe's [*Uncle Tom's Cabin*] are black only in law, and are 'in all other respects as white as she can make them'. He is referring to the young married couple, Eliza and George. The former is 'a beautiful, pious hybrid, light enough to pass . . . differing from the genteel mistress who has overseen her education only in the respect that she is a servant'. George is darker, 'but makes up for it by being a mechanical genius'. Mrs Stowe's two protagonists do indeed put one in mind of little Oliver Twist, of whom it can be said that we have only Dickens's word for it that he is a working-class urchin; in all other respects he resembles the children of his intended bourgeois readers as much as can be.

The author-hero of *Go Tell It On The Mountain, Notes Of A Native Son* and *The Fire Next Time* is quite different. James Baldwin is very black. I am not, of course, referring to the irrelevant matter of the colour of his skin, but to his experience and the manner in which he expresses it through writing. We might call it 'soul'—a quality which Baldwin himself once described Ava Gardner as having more of than 'some black girls who are much, much whiter than Ava'. This possession, he would claim, has enabled him to withstand the terrible, at times near murderous, social, sexual and racial pressures of the white world. (p. 103)

He has, however, frequently suffered the accusation—most notably from the pen of Eldridge Cleaver—of being 'the white man's nigger', an Uncle Tom. And it is possible that, from a certain point of view, Baldwin's early political philosophy could be regarded as being submissive in its eagerness to form a truce with the white man. His politics were always conciliatory, he did not seek to avenge the wounds of his race—he does not believe that such a thing as violent revenge exists—his revenge 'would be to achieve a power which outlasts kingdoms'. His weapons in doing so would be love and the courage to face oneself and the world as they are. In 1949 he accused Mrs Stowe of a 'failure of perception' in drawing her portrait of slavery, and of leaving unanswered 'the only important question: what it was, after all, that moved her people to such deeds'. In 1963, in a letter to his nephew, he was pleading the same courage: 'we, with love, shall force our brothers to see themselves as they are, to cease fleeing from reality'. (pp. 103-04)

The early 'sixties were the years which brought Baldwin worldwide success with *Nobody Knows My Name* (1961) and *Another Country* (1962) which was a bestseller on both sides of the Atlantic. But it was *The Fire Next Time,* published the following year, which brought real recognition. It contains the essay **"Down At The Cross"** which begins with the story of Baldwin's days as a boy preacher, moving from there to a discussion of the rising Black Muslim movement, and it is laced throughout with a lucid analysis of black-white relations. The essay foresaw two possible conclusions to the struggle for human and civil rights in which Negroes were then engaged: chaos or reconciliation. In either case, the buck stopped at the feet of both races: 'If we—and now I mean the relatively conscious whites and the relatively conscious blacks, who must, like lovers, insist on, or create, the consciousness of others—do not falter in our duty now, we may be able . . . to end the racial nightmare.'

Following the success of *The Fire Next Time*, Baldwin was hailed by the white liberal establishment as a saviour, one who could solve what those same liberals liked to call 'the Negro problem' by lucid thoughts and elegant sentences alone. On the other wing, at the same time, a portion of the black militancy, chiefly represented by Cleaver, rejected him and accused him of perpetuating the self-contempt which for generations the whites had subtly forced Negroes to suffer. He was, ironically, being blamed with possessing the same 'whiteness' which he had so despised in Mrs Stowe's protagonists. (pp. 104-05)

When it appeared in 1972, *No Name In The Street* was not made welcome by the majority of critics. Saint James, it seemed, had become James X. Baldwin the saviour had turned into Baldwin the soldier. What they failed to notice was that he was still the preacher and the prophet, that his passion and rage were mingled with detachment, and that his gloomy prognostications were based on powerful observation and an understanding of the past which compelled their pessimism. Baldwin has never allowed wishful thinking to interfere with his judgements, but now the critics seemed incapable of separating these judgements from their own fastidious liberalism and a need to believe that, given time, everything would work out well. They had, however, fallen into the trap—as Baldwin would see it, a fatal, inescapable trap—of regarding their own history and the history of 'the wretched' in the same light:

> When the pagan and the slave spit on the cross and pick up the gun, it means that the halls of history are about to be invaded once again, destroying and dispersing the present occupants. These, then, can call only on their history to save them—that same history which, in the eyes of the subjugated, has already condemned them.

This shift in vision was not generally appreciated by reviewers, and *No Name In The Street* remains one of Baldwin's least read books. (pp. 105-06)

It must have been with the grimmest, most anguished satisfaction that the author of *The Fire Next Time* witnessed his prophesies coming true in the form of street riots and political assassinations. It would require a form of moral cowardice of which I believe him to be incapable, to sit back and say, with a grin or a grimace, 'I told you so.' It would also have seemed to have been a glaring irrelevance to have gone on prophesying, sooth-saying, lecturing, warning, no matter how eloquently one is capable of doing it, while the stage burned beneath one's feet and the walls came a-tumbling down. [*No Name In The Street*], however, an updated version of *The Fire Next Time*, appears to have been what the critics desired of Baldwin. (p. 107)

On the surface, *No Name In The Street* is a look back across the shoulder at the stormy 'sixties, but its real subject is the deceitful design which the architects and engineers of empires, and therefore of power, strive to impose between themselves and their labourers, and just how, in time, that design will work out. Baldwin is, perhaps, a true revolutionary, for he believes that an act of oppression does not end with the cowing of its victim. On the contrary, for an energy to have to be suppressed by force means that the enforcer does not understand that energy and therefore cannot control it: 'When this point is reached, however long the battle may go on, the victor can never be the victor.' As always, Baldwin's underlying theme

is the search for identity, and for a means to shape that identity into viable form, that it may survive the social and historical conditions forced upon it from without. If it is true, however, as I have said, that Baldwin never permits his emotion to interfere with his judgement, then that is not only the foundation of his moral courage, but also the basis of his right to be called a prophet. (pp. 107-08)

Whatever else he may have been throughout his career, Baldwin has always been a spokesman for those, black or white, prepared to pay the price of the delusions which their own imagination and egos bring them, and which society brings them. . . . He is no longer, if he ever was, simply a 'Negro writer': his despair is our despair, his vision our vision. This we ought to strive to understand, for, as he himself wrote sometime before the composition of *The Fire Next Time*, 'where there is no vision, the people perish'. (p. 110)

James Campbell, "Son of the Preacher Man: The Baptism of James Baldwin," in London Magazine, n.s. Vol. 19, Nos. 9 & 10, December, 1979 & January, 1980, pp. 103-10.

JONATHAN YARDLEY

When James Baldwin was a high-school student in Harlem, he had a brief conversation with his father that he later recalled as "the one time in all our life together when we had really spoken to each other." His father was a preacher, a stern and forbidding man who had encouraged his son's own apprenticeship in the pulpit but now sensed that the prodigy was becoming prodigal. "You'd rather write than preach, wouldn't you?" his father asked, to which the astonished youth replied honestly, "Yes."

This encounter, which Baldwin reports in his brilliant essay **"Notes of a Native Son,"** is significant not merely because it marks the moment when he committed himself to the writing that eventually made him famous, but because it reminds us that he has always been as much preacher as writer. . . . His prose has the rhythm, the rolling and irresistible cadences, of hellfire and brimstone; his expository method is that of the homily, a mixture of logic and passion that is both rational and emotive.

The subject of his sermons is almost always the life that black Americans live, but his real audience—his congregation, if you will—is white America. This is not to say that he has an insubstantial black readership—to the contrary, his following among black Americans is large and deservedly loyal—but that he has chosen to be the messenger of the downtrodden, and that in this role his words are directed principally to those whom he perceives as their oppressors. Depending on his mood and the aims he hopes to accomplish, these words can be angry, cajoling, contemptuous, witty, sarcastic, apocalyptic, compassionate; but they are always urgent, always intended to force the reader into a heightened awareness of the black situation and its potential ramifications for all America.

The more than four dozen essays collected in *The Price of the Ticket* display Baldwin in all his guises. They also, though quite unwittingly, provide painful evidence that since his great success in 1963 with *The Fire Next Time*—originally published the previous year in *The New Yorker* as **"Letter From a Region in My Mind"**—Baldwin's skills have steadily deteriorated; this conclusion is most unhappily confirmed by *The Evidence of Things Not Seen*, an excruciatingly slipshod meditation on the

Atlanta child murders. What has happened to Baldwin quite simply is that since he moved to a prominent position on the public stage, the preacher has taken over from the writer; for two decades his rhetoric has grown steadily more bombastic, grandiloquent and predictable, while the humor, sensitivity and self-mockery of the early essays have virtually disappeared.

So much has been written about Baldwin's work that it seems rather pointless to provide further exegesis of it here. Suffice it to say that reading his essays from the 1950s and early '60s for the first time in many years, I was struck as forcibly as ever not merely by their power and passion, which can be quite overwhelming, but also by their civility and restraint. The Baldwin of those years—the Baldwin whose essays were collected in *Notes of a Native Son* and *Nobody Knows My Name*— was a startling voice from a land called black America that white America scarcely knew, but he was a voice that sought to reason with us even as he exposed our hypocrisies and cruelties. He was angry, with ample reason, but he appealed to the decent and humane in us; he tried to make us understand that we were all in this business together, and that a genuinely egalitarian society served the self-interest of white America as well as black.

In the best of these essays—**"Many Thousands Gone," "The Harlem Ghetto," "Fifth Avenue, Uptown,"** [**"Notes of a Native Son"** and **"Nobody Knows My Name"**]—Baldwin wanted to submerge us in the squalor and despair of the ghetto, but he also wanted to interest us in the people who lived there and to make us realize that they were just like us, only with different skin color. He spared us almost nothing—the fury of **"Letter From a Region in My Mind"** is breathtaking—yet he reached out to us. Toward the end of *Notes of a Native Son*, contemplating the death of his father, he wrote:

> This was his legacy: nothing is ever escaped. That bleakly memorable morning I hated the unbelievable streets and the Negroes and whites who had, equally, made them that way. But I knew that it was folly, as my father would have said, this bitterness was folly. It was necessary to hold on to the things that mattered; blackness and whiteness did not matter; to believe that they did was to acquiesce in one's own destruction. Hatred, which could destroy so much, never failed to destroy the man who hated and this was an immutable law.

Unfortunately, though, it is a law whose effects Baldwin himself seems to have felt. When in the '60s he became one of the most prominent "spokesmen" for black America, he seems to have felt it necessary to move with the crowd rather than maintain the distance he had therefore kept from it—and the crowd was moving in the very directions Baldwin himself had deplored.... More and more frequently he issued insupportable blanket condemnations of whites: "Blacks are often confronted, in American life, with such devastating examples of the white descent from dignity; devastating not only because of the enormity of the white pretensions, but because this swift and graceless descent would seem to indicate that white people have no principles whatever."

That was published in 1976, in a pointless and discursive piece— a short book, actually—called *The Devil Finds Work*. Now, in his introduction to *The Price of the Ticket*, Baldwin goes further. "There was not, then," he writes, "nor is there, now, a single American institution which is not a racist institution."

In three decades have we made any progress toward a more egalitarian society? Of course we have. But Baldwin writes: "Spare me, for Christ's *and* His Father's sake, any further examples of American white progress. When one examines the use of this word in this most particular context, it translates as meaning that those people who have opted for being white congratulate themselves on their generous ability to return to the slave that freedom which they never had any right to endanger, much less take away."

Not merely is this twaddle, it is badly written twaddle: gassy, inflated, seat-of-the-pants rhetoric that has far less to say than its orotund phraseology at first leads one to believe. The same is true, though even more so, of the prose in *The Evidence of Things Not Seen*. This slender book ... is a piece of nonsense in the literal meaning of the word: it makes no sense at all. It is a tortured effort to squeeze out the required number of words, an effort that leads Baldwin into wild, and wildly irrelevant, speculations on everything from emasculation to "the European horror," which is to say white culture. The book is riddled with exclamation points and italics, names are dropped in every direction—as, alas, they also are in the later essays in *The Price of the Ticket*—and self-congratulation is everywhere.

For a writer of Baldwin's gifts, *The Evidence of Things Not Seen* is a pathetic embarrassment; certainly it is embarrassing to read. That he should have gone into so great a decline is a mystery, though the burdens and distractions of fame may well have had something to do with it. Whatever the case, the writer who gave us *Notes of a Native Son* is nowhere to be found in *The Evidence of Things Not Seen;* and if the writer who once warned us against hatred has not transformed himself into a racist, he is certainly putting on a good imitation of one. (pp. 3-4)

> Jonathan Yardley, "The Writer and the Preacher," in Book World—The Washington Post, October 27, 1985, pp. 3-4.

JOHN GROSS

A few pages into [*The Price of the Ticket*] you will come across the assertion that 'the mobs in the streets of Hitler's Germany were in those streets not only by the will of the German State, but by the will of the western world.' Can anything useful be learnt from someone who goes in for this kind of tub-thumping? If you didn't know who James Baldwin was, you might well decide that there was not much point in reading on.

You would be quite wrong, but the passage is a useful warning of problems that lie in wait elsewhere in the book. It is also a measure of how much Baldwin has changed, since it comes from the introduction—the most recent piece of writing (presumably) in a collection that spans nearly 40 years. There was a time when he chose his words more carefully.

The book brings together all his non-fiction, early, middle and recent. Along with work from two out-of-print collections, *Notes of a Native Son* and *Nobody Knows My Name*, it includes over 20 previously uncollected pieces and three long essays originally published as separate books, among them *The Fire Next Time*. There are memoirs, reviews, polemics, pieces that are impossible to classify—and it must also be said that there isn't an inert page in the book.

Baldwin is a good illustration, in fact, of the dictum that if you want to develop an effective style the first essential is to have something to say. And what that something is, as far as he is concerned, is plain enough. Even when he writes about other subjects, the issue of colour is never far away.

Nor is a sense of anger—but then he has something to be angry about. He was born into a world of stark prejudice: read his account, say, of being turned out of restaurants in New Jersey when he was working there as a teenager. . . . And that was relatively minor stuff; pressing down in the background was the whole burden of black American history.

Still, anger by itself would hardly have made a writer. Baldwin's best work is equally remarkable for the keen critical intelligence it displays. From the first, when he appeared on the scene analysing the culture of Harlem or teasing out the implications of *Uncle Tom's Cabin,* he has shown a subtle socio-literary touch. He is particularly adept at unmasking evasions and hidden assumptions, and he can be mordantly witty as well as eloquent.

From the mid-Sixties, however, a new kind of rhetoric begins to take over—more violent, more sweeping and, at its worst, a great deal more shrill. The turning point is most obviously marked in **"The Fire Next Time,"** a savage sermon . . . which turned into an apologia for Black Muslim theology (or demonology), and ends with a mixture of real threats and unreal demands. The white man's fears and longings, we are told, are projected onto the black man, and 'the only way he can be released from the Negro's tyrannical power over him is to consent, in effect, to become black himself.' . . .

Subsequently he was to write, often movingly, about Martin Luther King, Malcolm X and other victims or martyrs. But he also entered all too willingly into the Sixties escalation of verbal violence, the realm of easy apocalyptic menace; and on the whole he has been content to stay there.

If anything, the rhetoric has hardened. In 1967, he still sounded a little uneasy, or so it seems to me, about having compared Watts and Harlem to the Warsaw ghetto. As well he might have been. Why confuse the issue by dragging in such an unnecessary comparison? On the other hand his readers at the time may not have been fully alert to all its implications: for if the blacks of Watts and Harlem were the equivalent of the Warsaw Jews, someone else had to be the equivalent of the Nazis.

Five years later he was spelling it out loud and clear. In the long piece, **"No Name in the Street,"** published in 1972, he wrote that when he came to San Francisco and saw the flower children, already looking doomed, he couldn't help feeling that America, 'which, unhappily, I was beginning to think of as the Fourth Reich, would be forced to plough under the flower children—in all their variations—before getting round to the rest of the world.'

America as 'Amerika,' in other words; and though that particular ploy has gone out of fashion, Baldwin is still delivering the message it enshrines. . . .

Some readers may feel that putting up with excesses is a form of reparation which the white world owes a black writer. But words can have consequences, and Baldwin's work is not only powerful enough but disturbing enough to deserve the tribute of serious disagreement.

> *John Gross, "Black Man's Burden," in* The Ob-
> server, *November 24, 1985, p. 28.*

CLIVE DAVIS

James Baldwin carries a heavy burden. For the past 20-odd years, America's most famous black novelist has been obliged to put in overtime as his country's most famous black essayist, not to mention its most famous black political commentator—roles forced on him by the structure of American political and literary institutions. During a visit to London some months ago, he appeared on a cultivated TV chat show where the questioning revolved around his memories of the civil rights campaigns of the Sixties and where, no doubt for the thousandth time, he was asked to give his opinion on Whether Black Americans Have Made Any Real Progress and What Martin Luther King Was Really Like. There were, as far as I recollect, no questions about Baldwin's current work or his views on fiction in general. It would have been easy for idle viewers to have mistaken this slight, nervous man for a retired politician rather than a working writer.

The situation is, of course, partly of Baldwin's own making, if only because it is some six years since he published his last novel, *Just Above My Head,* a work which failed to allay suspicions that his best fiction had already been bound, printed and placed on the shelf. Baldwin has, in any case, always steered clear of being labelled as a novelist pure and simple, using his essays and journalism as a means of bolstering the civil rights movement. There is even a strong case for the argument that his prose style, with its dense semi-religious rhetoric, is better suited to the essay form than to fiction, more appropriate to the transmission of ideas than to characterisation. Future generations may well prefer *The Fire Next Time* to *Go Tell It On the Mountain.* The fact that such a choice arises is a testimony to Baldwin's versatility and energy.

The Price of the Ticket contains, according to the blurb, every important piece of nonfiction that Baldwin has written. . . . Although some of the pieces venture into the realms of cinema or (obliquely) homosexuality, the overwhelming majority are devoted to the American people's long and agonising struggle to come to terms with the fact that blacks might just be human after all.

Baldwin is remarkably consistent about what he caustically describes as 'the very last white country the world will ever see'. In his earliest essay, an anatomy of Harlem, he is mildly condescending about some aspects of ghetto life but has a far lower opinion of what is to be found beyond its boundaries. 'The white man's world,' he says, 'intellectually, morally and spiritually, has the meaningless ring of a hollow drum and the odour of slow death.' A quarter of a century later, in what is for my money his most profound work, *No Name in the Street,* Baldwin sees nothing to persuade him to change his mind. If anything, his judgment is even more damning—'as social and moral and political and sexual entities, white Americans are probably the sickest and certainly the most dangerous people, of any colour, to be found in the world today.'

The two quotations symbolise the strengths and weaknesses of this collection. Baldwin's analysis of American racism is eloquent and dignified. But read together, the essays tend to cancel themselves out, many of the shorter ones being, inevitably, reworkings of *The Fire Next Time* or *No Name in the Street,* with the same use of analogies with Nazi Germany and recollections about childhood events. I would gladly have exchanged a dozen of the minor articles for some of Baldwin's reflections on other themes—Europe or jazz, for instance, or the Arab-Israeli conflict.

Nevertheless, *The Price of the Ticket* still provides many memorable moments. Although there is immense passion in these pages, Baldwin seldom falls into the trap of making extravagant gestures. His has been a harsh life, yet he is still aware of his privileged position—he may be a nigger, but he is an affluent one. (p. 29)

Clive Davis, *"Notes of Native Sons," in* New States-man, *Vol. 110, No. 2853, November 29, 1985, pp. 29-30.*

TERRY TEACHOUT

"The failure of the protest novel," James Baldwin wrote in 1949, "lies in its rejection of life, the human being, the denial of his beauty, dread, power, in its insistence that it is his categorization alone which is real and which cannot be transcended." It was around this time that American critics first began to speak of Baldwin as a writer with the sensibility and detachment of a potentially first-rate artist; with the 1953 publication of *Go Tell It on the Mountain,* a beautifully written first novel about Harlem life, he proved them correct.

That book, together with the best of his early essays for *Commentary* and *Partisan Review,* quickly gave James Baldwin a well-deserved reputation as an outstandingly gifted writer—and the only black writer in America capable of staying out of what Lionel Trilling called in another connection "the bloody crossroads" between literary art and politics. Soon his name began to appear regularly in middlebrow magazines like *Harper*'s and the *New Yorker*.

But Baldwin's qualifications for playing the "Great Black Hope," as he later characterized his role, began to look a little more problematic with each passing year. He had, after all, abandoned Harlem for Paris with what looked suspiciously like enthusiasm. His ornate prose style reminded readers more of Henry James than of Richard Wright. And he was, though he did not advertise it at first, a homosexual. None of this seemed to have much to do with the kinds of things people like Martin Luther King, on the one hand, or Malcolm X, on the other hand, were saying in public. Younger and more militant blacks took elaborate pains to distance themselves from Baldwin; Eldridge Cleaver, in *Soul on Ice,* went so far as to accuse Baldwin of harboring a "shameful, fanatical, fawning, sycophantic love of the whites."

Eventually, perhaps in response to such criticism, the tone of Baldwin's work began to take on a raw, politicized stridency which had not previously been a part of his literary equipment. This stridency fatally compromised his standing as a writer of fiction; *Another Country* was the last of his novels to be taken at all seriously by the critics (and by no means all of them). But Baldwin's essays, early and late, have somehow remained impervious to revaluation—which makes it all the more useful to have this new volume of his "collected nonfiction."

The Price of the Ticket contains, complete and unabridged, *Notes of a Native Son; Nobody Knows My Name; The Fire Next Time; Nothing Personal; The Devil Finds Work; No Name in the Street;* and a couple of dozen previously uncollected articles of largely exiguous interest. The only important omissions are the autobiographical preface to *Notes of a Native Son* and Baldwin's latest book, an essay on the Atlanta child murders called *The Evidence of Things Not Seen.* [*The Price of the Ticket*] is a fat omnibus, clearly a gesture to posterity, and an attempt to consolidate Baldwin's shaky literary reputation. Times and

tastes have changed profoundly since Baldwin published his first important essay . . . forty-odd years ago, and so one inevitably wonders: does he still *sound* like a major writer? Is the literary value of his work compromised by his consuming obsession with race? Is his message as compelling as ever—or simply irrelevant?

Baldwin's first collection of essays, *Notes of a Native Son* (1955), was received with more or less uncritical admiration. . . . But *Notes of a Native Son* is likely to strike today's reader as uneven in a way that Baldwin's first novel, for all its flaws, is not. Baldwin spends the whole first part of the book searching for the right things to write about and the right tone in which to write about them. Though he is reasonably competent at it, straight reportage obviously does not become him; as for his initial attempts at literary criticism, these come out sounding hopelessly stilted.

What finally pulled Baldwin's nonfiction writing up to the level of the best parts of *Go Tell It on the Mountain* was his discovery, in a 1953 essay (also collected in *Notes of a Native Son*), **"Stranger in the Village,"** of the great good pronoun of his literary destiny: the concrete, liberating "I" which, as with Proust's "Marcel," would bring his idiosyncratic style into the sharpest focus. In this piece Baldwin finally learned to do in his writing what, as a budding young preacher in Harlem, he must have heard about in the cradle: to begin with anecdote and end in generalization:

> From all available evidence no black man had ever set foot in this tiny Swiss village before I came. I was told before arriving that I would probably be a "sight" for the village; I took this to mean that people of my complexion were rarely seen in Switzerland, and also that city people are always something of a "sight" outside the city. It did not occur to me—possibly because I am an American—that there could be people anywhere who had never seen a Negro.

With the simple but pregnant discovery of autobiography as a vehicle for social criticism, Baldwin had at last struck a workable balance between the two most characteristic aspects of his artistic personality, the fiery Harlem preacher and the urbane Parisian memorist. In the 1955 essays **"Equal in Paris"** and **"Notes of a Native Son,"** both written in the first person, it is the latter aspect which dominates; these two pieces, like *Go Tell It on the Mountain,* are devoid of an overtly political content, and the author's angry message emerges through stylish dramatized narrative rather than vague sermonizing. . . . (pp. 76-8)

"Equal in Paris" and **"Notes of a Native Son"** come close to justifying every word of praise ever uttered about *Notes of a Native Son.* On the other hand, Baldwin's second collection, *Nobody Knows My Name,* which also received high praise, contains nothing that comes anywhere near matching the remarkable quality of those two essays. Baldwin largely restricts himself here to reportage about the desperate condition of Southern blacks; while these articles are, as reportage, far more professional than their earlier counterparts in *Notes of a Native Son,* their literary value is strictly that of good celebrity journalism. And when Baldwin does use explicitly autobiographical material, the results, particularly in **"The Black Boy Looks at the White Boy,"** are diminished by a distressing new quality: an extreme, even mannered, self-consciousness.

Yet whatever may have been wrong with *Nobody Knows My Name,* readers of the November 17, 1962 *New Yorker* who opened their copies in order to read a report by James Baldwin on the Black Muslims called **"Letter from a Region in My Mind"** suddenly found in their hands the literary equivalent of a pinless grenade. The opening paragraph of this extraordinary essay, which quickly found its way between hard covers as *The Fire Next Time,* was riveting. . . .

Baldwin, describing the religion of his youth with incomparable vividness, concludes in *The Fire Next Time* that it is no longer sufficient. In light of the long history of racism, "whoever wishes to become a truly moral human being . . . must first divorce himself from all the prohibitions, crimes, and hypocrisies of the Christian church." He interprets the rise of the Black Muslims, who preach that Allah is black and the white man the devil, as the predictable outcome of the moral decadence of Christianity; though he rejects the simple-minded demonology and racial separatism of Elijah Muhammad and Malcolm X, he finds in it rough justice for the sins of the white man. (p. 78)

The Fire Next Time is not without its stylistic miscalculations, the worst of which is **"My Dungeon Shook,"** a four-page preface bearing the subtitle "Letter to My Nephew on the One Hundredth Anniversary of the Emancipation" and through whose resolute platitudes one slogs with dismay. But Baldwin's writing in the rest of *The Fire Next Time* is generally quite marvelous. It is, in fact, so good that something like an act of will is needed to ask the key question: what is being said here? What is being recommended?

"I was always exasperated by his notions of society, politics, and history," James Baldwin once said of Richard Wright, "for they seemed to me to be utterly fanciful." These harsh words are even more readily applicable to Baldwin himself, who is in a very real sense a man with neither politics nor philosophy. The political impact of his best work was previously achieved through implication alone; *The Fire Next Time* reveals that his specific responses to the condition of blacks in America are wholly emotional. (p. 79)

Despite its still formidable reputation as a central document in the struggle for equality, *The Fire Next Time* turns out to have little of interest to say about the question of racial politics. Its impact comes solely from the fact that it is so exquisitely written. And Baldwin's timing was immaculate. His passionate prophecies of impending doom scorched the collective consciousness of middle-class Americans in a way that no amount of sober analysis could have rivaled.

But *The Fire Next Time* was the last point at which the curve of James Baldwin's career intersected with the *Zeitgeist* of the Great Society. Public black rhetoric came to be dominated, just as Baldwin had predicted it would, by loveless images of violence. And Baldwin's response to this change was, to say the least, disheartening.

Though *The Fire Next Time* was full of the language of extremism, its message was not yet one of racial hate. That was still to come. In *No Name in the Street,* his 1972 sequel to *The Fire Next Time,* Baldwin's striking prose style, that arresting amalgam of Henry James and the Old Testament, remained largely intact. But the ends to which he now directed this style were another matter altogether. For even the most casual reading of *No Name in the Street* revealed that the literary control manifested in *The Fire Next Time* had now been coarsened by aimless, free-floating political hysteria. . . .

After a career spent dancing in and out of "the bloody crossroads," Baldwin had at last faltered. The lapse was to be permanent. Aside from *The Devil Finds Work,* an erratic and frequently embarrassing volume of autobiography masquerading as film criticism, he published only a handful of political essays after *No Name in the Street.* They are shocking in their abandonment of all pretense to literary detachment; in them Baldwin luxuriates in the foul rhetoric of zealotry that for more than a decade poisoned this country's political discourse. . . .

It is impossible to read the second half of *The Price of the Ticket* without feeling an intense sadness at the literary tragedy it embodies. And it is equally difficult to read the rest of the book without coming to feel that of its seven hundred pages one would willingly, even gratefully, part with all but *The Fire Next Time* and a handful of shorter essays. To revisit James Baldwin's nonfiction is to understand the full extent to which the trivializing claims of radical politics undermined the artistic career of the man about whom Edmund Wilson once said: "He is not only one of the best Negro writers that we have ever had in this country, he is one of the best writers that we have." (p. 80)

Terry Teachout, "Tragic Decline," in Commentary, *Vol. 80, No. 6, December, 1985, pp. 76-80.*

JAMES A. SNEAD

It may well be that 40 years from now James Baldwin will be called the finest American essayist of his generation. He has certainly been, over the last 40 years, the most prolific and most durable. The patented Baldwin style—comma-filled and intricately digressive with its asides, refinements, anecdotes, sudden tirades—builds over time into an almost Pentecostal routine of internal 'call-and-response.' With the appearance of *The Price of the Ticket,* the American reader can now reassess a body of writing that, better than any other, looks back on the stormy relations between white and black America from 1948 to 1985. . . .

Baldwin writes in the tradition of Montaigne, Emerson and Thoreau: His speculations never stray too far from autobiographical details. His "I" also (like the narrator of Ellison's *Invisible Man*) describes the "you." Baldwin invites us as readers to see ourselves mirrored in his inner states. With a blend of precision and extravagance unmatched in modern American essayists, Baldwin's eye documents exciting yet exacting times.

The fact is that Baldwin has seen and suffered much more than most—and has survived to tell the tale. His sheer ubiquity is amazing: In one extended recollection, **"No Name in the Street,"** we find Baldwin dodging racist policemen in Montgomery and Little Rock, writing in Beverly Hills a stillborn screen treatment of Malcolm X's autobiography, trading obscene oaths with a school chum over a Harlem fried-chicken dinner, visiting a wrongly accused black friend in a Hamburg prison, dining at the London Hilton with his British publishers. He seems to have been nearly everywhere, done nearly everything, and understood nearly everyone, from the lowliest chauffeur to highest luminaries of politics and culture. . . .

Baldwin's essays present three basic stances: (1) Baldwin, the artist/solitary, the *picaro* or outlaw whose behavior places him on the periphery of social definition and sanction; (2) Baldwin, the penitent sinner, whose confession also becomes our own, and (3) Baldwin, the prophetic visionary (a sort of latter-day

Amos, critical of the present, prescient about the future). Both his confessorial and prophetic stances underpin Baldwin's basically evangelical quest, despite his open break with the church as a youth.

Already in his first essay, **"The Harlem Ghetto"** (1948), we see that Baldwin cannot abide the easy platitudes and sterile subterfuges that cloak the truth of racial oppression. His exceptional candor is only possible because he has scrutinized himself. Baldwin has, more than any other writer of his generation, captivated the (normally white) American reader by speaking both as victimized and victimizer, exposing racism from within as economic and psychological self-interest.

Baldwin sees his role as unmasking the central delusions that white Americans still hold about blacks. Racial interaction in America, he says, fetters blacks with pervasive reproofs, and misleads whites into a false sense of superiority. "The price of the ticket" to such deceptive comfort is high, in psychological, economic, ethical and historical terms. Whites see the false front blacks present as "good racial relations." White Americans, to the extent that they accept the role of "white man," are controlled by the history they have repressed: "They are, in effect, still trapped in a history which they do not understand; and until they understand it, they cannot be released from it." "Incoherence" takes the place of morality: One is trapped by what one cannot face.

Yet, as Baldwin says admiringly about Bessie Smith, the artist can escape all "definitions by becoming herself. This is still the only way to become a man or a woman—or an artist." If the artist must tell the truth at all costs, then no one tells the truth more chillingly than Baldwin. (p. 1)

Baldwin is one of the last remaining American writers with a vision of what it might mean, individually and societally, to be whole: In an era of fragmentation and compartmentalization, that's saying quite a lot. Yet time is running out: one prophecy of these essays that grows more sinister as the years pass: "If we do not now dare everything, the fulfillment of that prophecy . . . is upon us: *God gave Noah the rainbow sign, No more water, the fire next time!*"

The Price of the Ticket remains, thankfully, incomplete: There are more essays to come. Baldwin's latest work, *The Evidence of Things Not Seen,* continues to challenge our most treasured sureties—here in a lengthy meditation on the Atlanta child murder case. . . .

Baldwin suffers from a few stylistic lapses during the essay: One senses that several all too painful issues—the intimation of black self-hatred; the unspoken subtleties of the New Racism of the '80s; the 'homosexuality' issue; the amorphous nature of the case itself—blunted Baldwin's attack here, and kept him from getting to the deeper psychological truth of the events involved. But Baldwin's moral challenge to us has never been keener. In the closing paragraphs, Baldwin sees, with St. Paul, "the evidence of things unseen" which is 'faith' in the ability of white society to change: "This is the only nation in the world that can hope to liberate—to begin to liberate—mankind." The prophet glimpses in the "evidence" of the present the unseen future: "I will not live to see anything resembling this hope come to pass. Yet I know that I *have* seen it—in fire and blood and anguish, true, but I have seen it." Reading Baldwin, one can almost see it too. The consistency of Baldwin's witness is impressive, but the intransigence of his listeners, and of racial oppression in general, remains troubling. (p. 6)

James A. Snead, "Baldwin Looks Back," in Los Angeles Times Book Review, *December 1, 1985, pp. 1, 6.*

DAVID SWEETMAN

When [*The Price of the Ticket*] begins in 1948 James Baldwin is a Negro, half way through he's Black and by the end he's Gay. For although this is his nonfiction—magazine articles, book reviews, speeches—it amounts to the autobiography of a man who witnessed and who finally was in himself a prime mover in the forty odd years of liberation for the West's minorities both racial and sexual. One is reminded of Sammy Davis: "I'm a one-eyed, Black Jew". Only James Baldwin isn't joking, much of the time it was too painful:

> And she did step a very short step closer, with her pencil poised incongruously over her pad, and repeated the formula: ". . . don't serve Negroes here."

> Somehow with the repetition of that phrase, which was already ringing in my head like a thousand bells of nightmare, I realized that she would never come any closer and that I would have to strike from a distance. There was nothing on the table but an ordinary watermug half full of water, and I picked this up and hurled it with all my strength at her. . . . I returned from wherever I had been, I *saw,* for the first time, the restaurant, the people with their mouths open, already, as it seemed to me, rising as one man, and I realized what I had done, and where I was, and I was frightened.

This book would not be easy for the White reader were it not that Baldwin writes so well you just go along with him—no doubt you want to know the outcome of that restaurant incident—he made it to the door just as a white friend of his came up who managed to misdirect the pursuing mob. It takes a special skill to turn a miserable racist encounter in New Jersey into a chase scene without losing the message. It is even more impressive that over the 52 articles in this collection, most of which concern the same fundamental issue of the black man in a white man's world, he never seems repetitious.

The reason goes beyond his undoubted skills as a writer and lies in his skill as a humane citizen—despite watching his father destroy himself with bitterness, despite the angst of growing up in Harlem and of meeting a world deliberately constructed to demolish such as himself, despite a life watching the destruction of those like Martin Luther King whom he supported, despite the betrayal of white politicians and the bleak moments of despair, despite all that and despite the quotation on the cover of the book to the contrary, James Baldwin is not motivated by "unquenchable rage". He is in truth the epitome of forgiveness.

I say this with some trepidation as from the first he trumpets his angry opposition to the forgiving figure of Uncle Tom, the gentle "nigger" who never throws a watermug at anyone. But there's forgiveness and forgiveness and while Baldwin has never sat back and taken whatever America has chosen to hand him, nor has he gone the way of his father, maddened by the confusions of impotent fury.

Why? He had a white school mistress who loved and helped in his early adolescence, there was a white editor who gave him his start writing book reviews, and towards whom he clearly feels great affection. But were they enough to enable him to hold to the faith that surfaces throughout this book: that there can never be a separation of black and white, that both are inextricably locked in what may at times seem like a dance of death but which in the end he defines as the struggle to sort out what being American is?

What keeps surfacing is the thought that there must be some other more powerful reason than these two good people. One can guess from having read *Giovanni's Room* that there must be a side to Baldwin's life that would provide other insights. But he seems to set his face against admitting us to that world and the only article—**"The Male Prison"** of 1954—to touch on the subject of homosexuality, is a not altogether sympathetic discourse on Gide's failings as a husband.

The very final piece—**"Here Be Dragons"** published this year at last makes clear that from his youth Baldwin moved in a parallel world where relations between black and white were of a different order from in the "straight" world—not necessarily better but different. In this world, after all, the whites too were persecuted for something over which they had absolutely no control and that presumably made them a little more understanding and understandable. It was a Spanish/Irish racketeer in Harlem who first took up the gawky black kid who believed that he was ugly, skinny and pop-eyed. . . .

Later there was a deep love affair with an Italian who presumably inspired [*Giovanni's Room*]. Perhaps it ought to have been one minority too many—one-eyed, black, Jew—but that skinny pop-eyed kid turned out to have broad shoulders. [*The Price of the Ticket*] has a nobility without any conscious pretentions to it. It is an irreplaceable record of the postwar years as suffered by so many, and for those on the white side of the tracks it contains moments that are almost too painful to read. At some point halfway through the book he calls being Black "a Cosmic joke" and that sudden brief moment of anguish produced a shudder of discomfort in this reader that made him groan aloud. We may thank God that Baldwin more often surmounts such judgements and that at the end he turns away from his beloved Bessie Smith—

> You can't trust nobody, you might as well be
> alone
> Found my long lost friend, and I might as well
> stayed at home.

to offer his own conclusions giving us all a little, just a little, more hope:

> We are a part of each other. Many of my countrymen appear to find this fact exceedingly inconvenient and even unfair, and so, very often, do I. But none of us can do anything about it.

> *David Sweetman, "Relations of a Different Order,"*
> *in* The Times Educational Supplement, *No. 3626,*
> *December 27, 1985, p. 17.*

NATHAN GLAZER

James Baldwin's collected nonfiction, *The Price of the Ticket*, appears simultaneously with his latest work of nonfiction, *The Evidence of Things Not Seen*, a small book on the trial of Wayne Williams, who was suspected of killing many black children and youths in Atlanta but put on trial only for two of these murders, as Baldwin reminds us again and again. It is a strange book. Little in it deals with either Atlanta, or the child killings, or the trial. (p. 40)

It is a very hard book to read. What we recall as the icy clarity of Baldwin's prose, the precision of his writing (he loves the word "precisely"), here melts and becomes somewhat muddy. The words are still there, the wonderful quotations from spirituals and blues and the Bible. But all one gets is the rush of anger and despair over the black situation, and what whites have done to make it so.

It was not always like this. Not that the tone of *The Evidence of Things Not Seen* is completely new—one finds the same in much of the writing collected in *The Price of the Ticket*. But that is just the problem. The black situation has changed. America has changed. Baldwin has not. Or, insofar as he has, it has been to get angrier and less precise about the targets of his anger, and to give up all hope, it seems, for black existence and the black future in America.

Which is strange indeed. His first pieces of writing date from 1948. A good deal has happened since then. Among other things, Baldwin tells us in *The Evidence of Things Not Seen,* we have had the only two presidents since perhaps Jefferson for whom "Blacks have had any human reality at all." But they are, "exquisitely, the exceptions that prove the rule." We leave out comment on the word "exquisitely," another Baldwin favorite. Why do they *prove* this rule? They are, after all, two of our last five presidents. (pp. 40-1)

The very first essay in [*The Price of the Ticket*], and Baldwin's first substantial piece of writing, is **"The Harlem Ghetto,"** from *Commentary* in 1948. I was on the editorial staff then; how he came to us I don't recall, but I do recall our pleasure that a remarkable young black writer—how remarkable we didn't yet know—had come to us. At that time, *Commentary* was a much more exclusively Jewish magazine than it would later become, and all we could think of suggesting to Baldwin was that he write about blacks and Jews. **"The Harlem Ghetto"** is much more than that. It exhibits a fully developed style as well as almost every theme that was to recur in Baldwin's nonfiction, and indeed many that were to be part of his fiction.

There is an immediate sense of the congestion and claustrophobia of Negro life in America, affecting every social class and every occupation. There are perceptive comments on the Negro press, in all its variants; on black leadership—political, lay, and clerical; observations on the difficulties of black intellectuals in relating to the black community, which were not so different from the difficulties Jewish intellectuals writing in *Commentary* then had in relating to the official Jewish community. (pp. 41-2)

And he describes the complex relationship between Negroes and Jews with remarkable sensitivity, by way of analysis of an archetypal sermon. It begins with the traditional accusation that the Jews killed Christ, "which is neither questioned nor doubted," but

> the term Jew actually operates to include all
> infidels of white skin. . . . The preacher begins
> by accusing the Jews of having refused the light
> and proceeds from there to a catalog of their
> subsequent sins and the sufferings visited upon
> them by a wrathful God.

But he is also describing "the trials of the Negro, while the sins recounted are those of the American republic." (p. 42)

There is much else in these few pages, which are worth re-reading today—one will of course notice wryly that the disappearance of the few Jews from Harlem has done nothing to improve matters. But my point is that this is a complex and subtle analysis of the relationship of Jew and Negro, of symbols and reality, in the ghetto. An incredibly distinctive voice came from a 24-year-old whose last formal education had been in a New York City high school. Where had he acquired that voice, so stinging and so elegant? It was a mystery, but a circle of editors, almost all Jewish, were ready to listen to, and publish, whatever he had to say.

It was not until the late 1950s that Baldwin broke away from the *New Leader-Commentary-Partisan Review-Encounter* connection, and began to publish in magazines and journals of wider circulation. The road to *Playboy*, which sent him to Atlanta to cover the story of the murdered children, was reached through the friendly and accepting channels of the New York intellectuals. And the notes of hope—particularly when Baldwin wrote from Paris, where he covered a Congress of Negro and African writers for *Encounter* in 1951, and compared French justice less than favorably with American in *Commentary* in 1950—were not completely absent even in his own writing. Consider the guarded optimism in his report from the Paris Congress:

> For what . . . distinguished the Americans from the Negroes who surrounded us, men from Nigeria, Senegal, Barbados, Martinique . . . was the banal and abruptly quite overwhelming fact that we had been born in a society, which, in a way quite inconceivable for Africans, and no longer real for Europeans, was open, and, in a sense which has nothing to do with justice or injustice, was free.

One will find nothing like this in Baldwin's writing since the civil rights revolution. Indeed, one would think, in the light of his blazing rhetoric since the early 1970s, that the movement had failed rather than succeeded. To Baldwin it *has* failed, as he writes in *The Evidence of Things Not Seen:* "Others may see American progress in economic, racial, and social affairs—I do not. I pray to be wrong, but I see the opposite, with murderous implications, and not only in North America."

One hesitates to resort to mere facts in dealing with such unqualified pessimism, and yet his very excess will lead many readers to involuntarily contrast what they think is happening in America with what Baldwin insists is the case. Consider the following (before the 1980 election): "[In] a couple of days, blacks may be using the vote to outwit the Final Solution." Or: "The educational system of this country is, in short, designed to destroy the black child. It does not matter whether it destroys him by stoning him in the ghetto or by driving him mad in the isolation of *Harvard*." And if one were to respond in amazement, "Black students are being destroyed *at Harvard?*" Baldwin would undoubtedly answer, "White students are being destroyed there, too." Little distinction is made among blacks—or among whites. Blacks are slaves, and have remained slaves. (But whites are slaves, too).

There is the same lack of specificity when Baldwin recurs (as he does on occasion) to the black-Jewish theme of his first essay. Between **"The Harlem Ghetto"** and **"Negroes are anti-Semitic because they are anti-White"**. . . , the voice becomes harder and harsher. The Jews are subsumed completely in the denunciation of white America ("the Negro is really con-

demning the Jew for having become an American white man''). One wants to protest, there are differences among Jews, and among whites. But it is all swept away in rhetoric. All this disables Baldwin from offering any precise or differentiated account of what goes on in America—and particularly of the panic over the murdered black children and the subsequent trial in Atlanta. For Baldwin, nothing has changed in America; it is as if he is frozen in a time capsule. The passage of time has only had the effect of dulling his perception of the distinctions and subtleties that were evident to him 30 years ago.

Writing of the Atlanta child killings and the trial of Wayne Williams, Baldwin draws parallels and makes references to scarcely relevant and distant events. It seems the 13th victim was a boy from the North, and it is this that "precipitated the [official] hue and cry." This reminds Baldwin of Emmett Till, another black boy visiting in the South from the North, who whistled at a white woman and was killed for it. But what indeed is the connection? That Atlanta's black establishment only takes account of Northern blacks, not its own native citizens? That Southern whites now as then kill black boys for uppityness? In Baldwin's mind there is a connection; in the reader's there can only be mystification. (pp. 42, 44)

Baldwin has become an accusing voice, but the accusation is so broad, so general, so all-embracing, that the rhetoric disappears into the wind. No one escapes, nothing is to be done, and we can only await "The Fire Next Time." There is enough that is badly amiss with blacks to justify gloom and foreboding, and yes, expectations of disaster. But just what is amiss? It is not, it cannot be, that blacks serve on juries, or become mayors or police chiefs or judges, or become middle class. Yet all this makes no difference to Baldwin at all, or makes things worse: he refuses to consider why, if such progress hasn't made a difference, it hasn't.

"I agree with the Black Panther position concerning black prisoners," he wrote in *No Name in the Street* in 1972. "Not one of them has ever had a fair trial. . . , white middle-class America is always the jury . . . and this fact is not altered, it is rendered even more implacable, by the presence of one or two black faces in the jury box." Is one wrong to detect here that kind of recent French philosophical logic that reverses traditional French clarity—the logic by which one demonstrates a point not *despite* the existence of opposite facts, but *because* of them? How could the situation be "rendered even more implacable" by the presence of black jurors? One grasps for an explanation. Because the blacks are forced to accept white logic? Because they are intimidated by whites? What? His friend is the mayor of Atlanta, the police chief is black, the judge is black—but all this to Baldwin is simply proof that the power still lies in white hands and whites are exclusively responsible for black distress. . . .

Baldwin is still worth reading, for many things: for the early essays in particular; for the rhetorical power of *The Fire Next Time*; for the snatches of autobiography, as in *The Devil Finds Work*, where he does make distinctions (and in which whites appear as individuals, not wrapped in an all-embracing thunder); for the wonderful analyses of the movies of the white world that a very sensitive and gifted young black boy saw (in the company sometimes of a white teacher or another white friend) 50 years ago, and for much else. But his vision of America seems increasingly to be shaped by projections made up of inner nightmares and crude leftist pictures of America. We have nightmares enough of our own, God knows, and the Atlanta child murders—which have been repeated again and again in recent years, with whites in all roles—are one of them. But I find little illumination now in a rhetoric that once struck me as sharp and precise, yet now wraps everything in darkness and disaster. (p. 44)

> *Nathan Glazer, "The Fire This Time," in* The New Republic, *Vol. 193, No. 27, December 30, 1985, pp. 40-2, 44.*

CHRISTOPHER HITCHENS

After I had finished [*The Evidence of Things Not Seen*], I was depressed enough to go back and look again at some of James Baldwin's early essays. To my relief, I found that they were as sharp and unsparing as I had remembered them. The author of *The Fire Next Time* used to know the difference between a polemic and a diatribe. With this effort, and its offhand, semi-mystical title, he has abandoned that distinction and others too.

The book concerns the rash of child murders which took place in Atlanta, Georgia—'the city too busy to hate'—between 1979 and 1981. . . . For [Baldwin] the case provides an occasion for a long, disjointed monologue about the fate of black people in white America.

There are occasional sparks of the old form. For Baldwin to say, as he does in closing, that blacks are 'between the carrot and the stick of the American Dream' strikes me as shrewd and well put. To say, as he does earlier, that 'the white man discovered the Cross by way of the Bible, but the black man discovered the Bible by way of the Cross' is to sacrifice a point to an epigram. And to say that 'the Western world is located somewhere between the Statue of Liberty and the pillar of salt' is to sound too much like one of those babbling evan-

gelists who have served the poor black (and the poor white) so ill.

We never really discover whether Baldwin thinks Williams was guilty, or whether he thinks his guilt was irrelevant given the wider incrimination of 'society.' And there is something bizarre about Baldwin's fixations on Williams in the first place. As the black critic Ishmael Reed has recently pointed out, 'both Williams and Baldwin were considered exceptional, both have fathers who abused them, both are gay, and both apparently have thought about committing murder from time to time.'

Baldwin has often said that he left the United States because he feared that, if he did not, he would either kill or be killed. What to say, then, about the case of a black man who has unleashed his rage—but on over two dozen black children? Baldwin gets over this problem by lavish use of generalisation. In order to follow him, you have to agree that Martin Luther King 'was *put to death*—he was *assassinated*—by the cowardice of the American people and the will of those who control whatever can be said to remain of the American Repubic' (his italics). There may just be an important particle of truth in that statement, but it is wholly obliterated by exaggeration and (someone has to say it) by hysteria. . . .

These are not good times for black America. But Baldwin has been in exile too long to offer much besides rhetoric. And even the rhetoric itself, which could be a contribution, has undergone a declension. Ishmael Reed says that the more sermons he preaches, 'the more he's going to resemble a literary ambulance-chaser.' A wounding comment but not, on the non-evidence of things not seen, an unjustified one.

> *Christopher Hitchens, "Sparks from an Old Fire," in* The Observer, *April 6, 1986, p. 26.*

Julian Barnes

1946-

English novelist, editor, and critic.

Barnes writes clever, humorous novels in which he examines such themes as obsession, self-discovery, and personal suffering. He has been praised for his assured tone, verbal proficiency, and irreverent wit. Barnes attracted wide critical attention with *Flaubert's Parrot* (1984), which ostensibly deals with the efforts of an amateur Flaubert enthusiast to authenticate the stuffed parrot Flaubert described in his novel *Un coeur simple*. Although some critics contended that *Flaubert's Parrot* lacks plot and emotion, many deemed the book an engaging marriage of fiction, biography, and literary criticism.

Barnes's first book, *Metroland* (1980), is the story of two youths in rebellion against a stifling society. While one retains his antagonism into adulthood, the other conforms to accepted social standards and finds family bliss in the suburbs. Although some reviewers faulted Barnes for unimaginatively dealing with commonplace subject matter, many praised his sincerity of tone and his perceptive accounts of the lives of his characters. In his second novel, *Before She Met Me* (1982), Barnes details the private obsessions of a middle-aged man who marries a former actress and becomes jealous of her previous onscreen love interests. According to Bill Greenwell, *Before She Met Me* consists of "a pattern of quips, apparently casual images, little incidents, all of which explore the battle between our rational and irrational selves, the perennial and unfathomable failure to reconcile our instincts, emotions, and intellect."

(See also *Contemporary Authors,* Vol. 102 and *Contemporary Authors New Revision Series,* Vol. 19.)

© Jerry Bauer

NICHOLAS SHRIMPTON

[Bohemianism] is deliciously mocked in Julian Barnes's first novel, *Metroland.* His heroes, as schoolboys, adopt the motto *épater la bourgeoisie.* But this grandiose ambition is promptly reduced to the level of 'epats', a thoroughly English field-sport in which the competitors attempt to shock respectable citizens for bets of sixpence a time. After this vision of the Decadence in short trousers, it is hard to take the idea of outrage too solemnly.

As the title suggests, however, the question of what it is to be bourgeois is also subjected to other forms of scrutiny. The central character, Christopher Lloyd, grows up in the suburbs of North-West London. He rejects this background but, unlike his schoolfriend Toni, eventually returns to it. Their discussions probe the problem of happiness. What is the distinction between contentment and capitulation? Are a wife and a family, a mortgage and a season ticket incompatible with sensibility and scepticism? Christopher's unfashionable assertions that they are not are handled with unusual sympathy, and the novel ends on a splendidly ambiguous reiteration of the colour symbolism which condemned suburbia in the opening chapters. . . .

The first section of [*Metroland*] is an exercise in the post-Portnoy school of adolescent self-revelation, the 'Look what a shit I am' movement of which Martin Amis has hitherto been the outstanding practitioner. Barnes handles it cleverly enough, but relies on individual jokes and particular sharp perceptions . . . to hold it together. In the second section, though his unpromising subject is that old war-horse, student life in Paris, he suddenly moves much deeper. The account of a boy's emergence from the self-absorption of adolescence is grippingly and sensitively done. There is a slight weakness for cultural name-dropping and the preoccupation, in a *Bildungsroman*, with school does somehow seem depressingly English. But if all first works of fiction were as thoughtful, as subtle, as well constructed and as funny as *Metroland* there would be no more talk of the death of the novel.

Nicholas Shrimpton, "Bourgeois v Bohemian," in New Statesman, *Vol. 99, No. 2558, March 28, 1980, p. 483.*

PAUL BAILEY

It was with keen anticipation that I approached [Barnes's] first novel, *Metroland,* and it is with a certain disappointment that I write about it. The book is neither daring nor imaginative: it traipses over well-worn territory, the territory of a thousand apprentice works, and arrives at the end of the trail decidedly short of fictional breath. We have been here before. **Metroland** is written in the first person by one Christopher Lloyd, who remembers his adolescence, the loss of his virginity, how he found true love, how he grew out of his strongest boyhood friendship, and so on. He remembers these common experiences and assumes that the reader will find them fascinating.

They are not. Novels written in the first person, novels intent on establishing the peculiar quality of a single life, survive when they set that life against a vivid background of other, possibly more interesting lives. There is a curious lack of people in **Metroland**, for all that their names are mentioned and some of their habits described. Christopher's parents, his brother and sister, are phantoms, and the French girl, Annick, who relieves him of his innocence, comes alive only as she departs from the narrative—before that she is little more than a convenience. The single rounded character in the novel is Christopher's Uncle Arthur, a mean old sod who uses his nephew shamelessly. Arthur actively dislikes Christopher, and seems to be alone in his contempt. Arthur's antipathy enlivens the otherwise self-congratulatory proceedings—his viewpoint, however jaundiced, provides some welcome shade.

Metroland is in three parts. In the first, Christopher is at school, an insubstantial place where he and his friend, Toni, go their Francophilic ways; in the second he is living in Paris in the late 1960s missing out on the students' demonstrations but finding himself instead; in the third he is back in suburbia—the Metroland of the title . . .—happily married to a sensible girl called Marion, and content (a mite too content, perhaps) with his lot.

Christopher leaves the privet hedges, tastes *la vie de Bohème,* but returns to the greenery refreshed and renewed. The narrow world of Part One is transformed into something like Paradise in Part Three. The intervention of Paris—the longed-for city of liberation—brings about this return to what Betjeman described as "the rows and rows of *Mon Repos*". Paris is not "real". The Home Counties are. It is a prig's progress. . . .

It is not Christopher's happiness one comes to dislike, it is his smugness. The lazy so-and-so never appears to have earned the right to it. His is not a civilized contentment, painfully gained. It comes in his Christmas stocking, along with Marion, after Annick has slipped through the hole in the toe. It is not made clear why the reader should laud his happy state.

There is, not surprisingly, a great deal of very good writing in **Metroland:** the book contains dozens of well-turned phrases. . . . It is not clear whether Julian Barnes intends us to dislike his hero, but I did. I liked Uncle Arthur, though, and enjoyed his company enough to wish that his creator would bother in his second novel to mingle more extensively with the bruised, to take more delight in their limited happiness.

Paul Bailey, *"Settling for Suburbia,"* in The Times Literary Supplement, *No. 4018, March 28, 1980, p. 345.*

TOM PAULIN

[In **Metroland,** Barnes] defines his narrative against a traditional subject. He takes the novel about growing up in a stifling society, writes it, and then instead of showing his protagonist defeated by suburban marriage and a mortgage he courageously and ironically presents Christopher basking in his suburban happiness. With a glance at Wallace Stevens he marries the aesthetic and the bourgeois. . . . [An] ironic allusion to Eliot's "in my end is my beginning" cleverly points to the circular form of the story which, in a very English way, locates Alexander Selkirk behind a privet hedge in Pinner. And so the myth which Defoe created in *Robinson Crusoe* is neatly reworked in **Metroland.**

There are several highly amusing comic scenes, a tight cartesian style, and many sharp unexpected reflections. There is, too, a fundamental decency which plays against the sometimes arid effort at narrative geometry and pure style. However, Barnes's treatment of Christopher's experience of growing up is flawed by his dedication to that ethic of privacy which the third section of the novel celebrates. His fictive symmetry—imaged in an electricity pylon and implied by the Eiffel Tower—cannot allow Christopher's relationship with Marion to be traced in any detail. As a couple they dovetail in a reassuringly neat manner which rather overlooks what Henry James terms "clumsy life." Also, the connection between private decency and that other world of salaries and anger is made in a most peculiar manner. Christopher works in publishing for a firm called Harlow Tewson:

> I've been an editor there for five years, with no regrets. It also doesn't make me feel shitty: we don't fight against making money, but we use good people, and we produce good books. . . .

The voice here is gruff in the face of possible accusations of sentimental complacency. It's a stiff-upper-lip tone resonant with British stoicism and it casts all irony aside. However, absolute irony is a scarifying knowledge to have to live with, and Christopher's kindly and witty decency is in certain ways preferable—it is gracefully civil and engagingly Horatian.

Metroland is a stimulating and interesting first novel which plays some extremely nimble tricks with the novel form. It touches on a myth of the Home Counties and historical absence, but it employs that myth rather as a structural device than as a groundswell of experience. Myths, after all, are the ghosts of experience and they tend to elude a logical and trim scepticism—though Barnes's vision of an aesthete metamorphosing into a suburban Crusoe has that combination of strangeness and recognition which is essential to myth. (p. 63)

Tom Paulin, *"National Myths,"* in Encounter, Vol. LIV, No. 6, June, 1980, pp. 58-63.

WILLIAM BOYD

[Barnes] combines the dual role of novelist and critic, although . . . in **Metroland** there is no happy meshing of the two professions. Anyone who is familiar with Barnes's polished acerbic reviews . . . will be surprised by his first novel. (p. 95)

Some reviewers of the book have sought to place it in the school of Amis (Martin) but in this case Barnes seems to me to share only the most superficial connections with that talented author. Indeed the occasions when he is most reminiscent of Martin Amis are in fact the least successful:

> The flat was as I'd left it, which means I'd half-arranged it. Reasonably tidy, but not obsessive either way. Books lying open as if in use . . . Lighting low and from the corners—for obvious reasons, but also in case some treacherous

spot had come into bud during the course of the film.

This, even in context, appears unnatural and strained-after, because the basic tone of the book is, despite a certain bluff knowingness, generally one of earnest sincerity. Barnes, instead of assuming the typical sneering stance of those writing about adolescence, takes up a position very similar to the one Graham Greene adopts in his autobiographical memoir *A Sort of Life*, where he reflects that

> There is a fashion today among many of my contemporaries to treat the events of their past with irony. It is a legitimate method of self defence. 'Look how absurd I was when young' forestalls cruel criticism but it falsifies history . . . Those emotions were real when we felt them. Why should we be ashamed of them?

This strikes me as being very close to Barnes's attitude in his novel. He details the environment and artefacts of his character's youth with faultless recall but, more importantly, he seems to respect the foibles and poses of adolescence and young manhood as things to be cherished and valued in their own right rather than merely being excuses for a few easy laughs; a fact which makes *Metroland* a rare and unusual first novel. (p. 96)

> William Boyd, ''Late Sex,'' in London Magazine, n.s. Vol. 20, No. 7, October, 1980, pp. 94-6.

BILL GREENWELL

Metroland is so effortlessly witty, so sure in its every squiggle and flourish, that the prospect of [Barnes's second novel] *Before She Met Me* produced in me an especially festive *frisson*. . . . The 'farcical bits' in *Metroland* are certainly sufficient to make it a hit. But when mulling it over . . . , after a compulsive speed-read, I registered much deeper satisfactions. It's not that Barnes is charging after the larger meanings, whatever they may be: leave that to the Heavy Brigade presently trampling up the fiction lists, *Earthly Powers* and all. There is a subtler sensibility in Barnes, in *Before She Met Me* as in *Metroland:* desire to disentangle the knots of the solitary self, to celebrate the pleasures of self-discovery unravelled in relationships, and to explore their vicious corollary—the terror of losing one's grip on independence. It's a common conundrum that captivates Barnes: to share is to sacrifice. His theme, if you like, is the silent siege laid *by* the self *for* the self. In *Before She Met Me,* in the private obsession of its protagonist, Graham Hendrick, the oil is boiling over the battlements on to the battering rams beneath.

Not that this is the initial impression. As the fingers flitter over its opening pages, the feeling is of having moved through Metroland to find, some years further on, Christopher revisited in Graham. Where we left Christopher settling down in the first novel, we find Graham in *Before She Met Me* settled, and beginning to settle up. Christopher we left in publishing, with, as his friend Toni puts it contemptuously, 'wife, baby, reliable job, mortgage, *flower* garden'. Graham we find at thirty-eight—

> fifteen years married; ten years in the same job; halfway through an elastic mortgage . . . he could feel the downhill slope already.

He is an academic, an historian, the only proper vestige of his earlier days being his friendship with Jack Lupton, who free-wheels as of old, a determinedly dissident, dilatory and cynical foil to Graham, but witty with it—Jack, it seems, is an older Toni.

But gradually, with an insidious brilliance, the new novel parts company with the old. Graham meets Ann, and ditches his first marriage for a second one, discovering again, with violent delight, the self that has been shuffled and lost in the deck of his first relationship. Now he is rescued, liberated from its tyranny. For Ann, resolutely independent, treats him with a respect he has long since denied himself. Yet it is not long before Graham is floundering, out of control, helpless with jealousy of everything and everyone in Ann's past—in the fifteen years he has 'lost'. Ann has frittered a few years on the fringe of the film world, a bit-part, B-movie starlet. Graham is gulled by his ex-wife Barbara into seeing one of her films. At first, he shrugs it off, but it triggers in him a violent obsession, in which he begins to visit every film she's appeared in, root out, map out her travels, conceiving terrible fantasies of vengeance against her former lovers, on or off the screen. (pp. 18-19)

Graham's breakdown is genuinely distressing, and subtly slow, so slow that we witness it with the same disbelief as Ann, as Jack, both helpless bystanders. Yet this is only superficially, although engrossingly, a novel about 'an unnerving version of . . . sexual jealousy', as the Cape flapdoodel suggests. There is a debate taking place beneath the surface of *Before She Met Me* about the warring factions of the human brain, a discussion smuggled into the substructure of the novel with wonderful ingenuity. . . . [This discussion is delivered through] a pattern of quips, apparently casual images, little incidents, all of which explore the battle between our rational and irrational selves, the perennial and unfathomable failure to reconcile our instincts, emotions and intellect. They are woven playfully, effortlessly, and surreptitiously into the fabric of the novel.

Which is why my money's on Barnes. The symbolism isn't thrust in the reader's face (as in, say, *The White Hotel*); it is gently persuasive. Moreover, Barnes's work is set down in a patch of simple reality, a familiar copse, not an impenetrable forest. It is a refreshingly recognisable place. . . .

And it's not that this second novel is flawless—Ann's film career is comically, but not convincingly contrived, and Jack's wife, Sue, is flimsily characterised, merely servicing the plot— it's simply that there is an irresistible blend of wit and intelligence in [Barnes's] work. (p. 19)

> Bill Greenwell, ''Flashback,'' in New Statesman, Vol. 103, No. 2665, April 16, 1982, pp. 18-19.

ANTHONY THWAITE

Julian Barnes is very witty . . . , but I'm reluctant to bracket enjoyment as something to be gained from *Before She Met Me* except by readers of tough sensibilities. . . . [The book presents an] elegantly hardboiled treatment of the nastier levels of obsession, full of controlled jokes when almost everything else has got out of control.

Graham is a university lecturer in history, who after 15 years of one marriage is now launched into what he calls 'the honey time' of a second, to Ann, with whom everything would be fine except for his retrospective jealousy—jealousy of all the sex she had, or he fancies she had, before they met. . . .

No Iago is necessary as partner to Graham's Othello: the monster grows by what it feeds on, self-fuelled, destructive and self-destructive.... For this professional student of the past, study becomes studdery, by fantasy built on hearsay.

The whole thing is extremely clever and conspicuously unpleasant, saving up what's most unpleasant for the end. Nimble verbal footwork, a succession of running gags and a tremendously winning assurance throughout don't, for me, quite compensate for the blind monomania one has to put up with in Graham's company; and a roguishly facetious novelist called Jack bulks much too large for my pleasure. I groaned every time he walked onto the page. When he walked off it I breathed again, though unsteadily.

> Anthony Thwaite, *"A Course in Creativity," in* The Observer, *April 18, 1982, p. 31.*

MARK ABLEY

The hero of Julian Barnes's first novel, *Metroland,* has the unnerving ability to detach himself from any experience and to observe his mixed reactions. Having lost his virginity he asks, "why didn't they tell you about the football fan in the back of your skull, the man with the rattle and the scarf who shouts Yippee and stamps his feet on the terraces?" When his insensitivity provokes his girlfriend to tears and anger, "the outburst gave me sudden jabs of pride: the pride of participation, and the pride of instigation." In his second novel, *Before She Met Me,* Barnes has taken this watchfulness and violent aloofness to a grim conclusion. Graham Hendrick, a mild-mannered historian at London University, becomes obsessed with his second wife's past.... Ann's previous affairs torment him, remove him from contact with everyday life. Nothing she does in the present can alter his fascination with her history. "What could account for such a shift in perceptions?", Graham wonders in a moment of relative lucidity. "What if your brain became your enemy?"

It's an interesting idea, and one that gives the imagination plenty of room to manoeuvre. But after a marvellous opening paragraph, *Before She Met Me* lurches downhill. It seems far better planned than realized, as if another draft or two could have made a world of difference. For most of the characters are paper-thin. Graham's first wife is a caricature, their daughter a virtual cypher. Ann, the former actress who unwittingly provokes his obsession, seems strangely inert, and her behaviour is scarcely more believable than that of her husband; even after a party at which his delusion brings him to demolish their French window with a garden fork, she refuses to admit that he might be jealous, still less mentally ill. The only character who has as much life as Barnes's strenuous prose is a middleaged novelist called Jack Lupton, who began his career as an earthy provincial realist and has all but turned into a latter-day Firbank. Windy, genial, sly and adulterous, Jack provides a much-needed contrast to the introspective Graham. But we know him as well after his second appearance as at the end. Only Graham is allowed to develop, and since the green-eyed monster soon dominates his temperament to the exclusion of everything else, he too becomes predictable: the only interest lies in seeing where his jealousy will lead.

Part of the trouble arises from the cleverness of Barnes's writing. He seems unable to resist any wry elaboration, any passing witticism. Some of these are very funny.... An occasional metaphor or sharp perception shows off another of the author's talents.... It takes more than intermittent felicities, however,

to make a convincing novel. What the preposterous plot requires is a certain intensity of feeling, and a prose that is able to convey sensuous and emotional force as well as adroit observations. Graham Hendrick is far distanced from the truth about his life; but we remain so distant from him, and from all the other characters, that their actions begin to seem insignificant as well as unlikely.

> Mark Abley, *"Watching Green-Eyed," in* The Times Literary Supplement, *No. 4125, April 23, 1982, p. 456.*

JOHN MELLORS

Before She Met Me is serious enough in intention and the author's performance is enthusiastic and vigorous. It is a study of obsessive jealousy, an illustration of an educated rational being's disintegration when illusion takes over from reality. However, the reader is entertained by the story without being convinced of its truth. Graham, a history teacher, enters into his second marriage with high hopes, feeling 'once more capable of folly and idealism'. Holding Ann's hand in an aeroplane he is happy with his 'neat, kind, unimprovable wife', easy 'in the face of love'. So far, so credible. But Julian Barnes proceeds to strain our credulity until it snaps. (pp. 133-34)

Graham becomes too much of a vehicle for his creator's cleverness. Barnes *is* clever, most of the time entertainingly so. He has, for instance, a waspish wit. Of the intelligent but not too well-informed Ann, he says that 'she could just about name the important members of the Cabinet; except that she was normally one Cabinet behind'. That is an amusing and appropriate remark. It fits with what we already know about Ann and adds to our belief in her reality. But when Graham confides in his friend, Jack, telling him of his jealousy of Ann's lovers 'before she met me' and of the intensity of his love for Ann, the author's ingenuity becomes too flamboyant to hold our confidence. Graham says that he loves Ann so much that when he clears the table at the end of a meal he eats the bits of gristle left on the side of her plate; he likes to think that food which might have been inside her stomach is now inside his instead. That makes me believe in the reality of Barnes sitting at his desk writing a novel about jealousy. It does not make me believe in the reality of Graham taking dishes into the kitchen to be washed. *Before She Met Me* is an ambitious book, promising much but in the end proving a disappointment. (p. 134)

> John Mellors, *"Bull's Balls," in* London Magazine, *n.s. Vol. 22, Nos. 1 & 2, April & May, 1982, pp. 133-36.*

DAVID COWARD

Flaubert's Parrot is an extraordinarily artful mix of literary tomfoolery and high seriousness. It deals ostensibly with the efforts of an amateur Flaubert enthusiast to identify the stuffed bird that served as a model for the parrot which hovers over the head of Félicité in the final paragraph of *Un Coeur simple.* Geoffrey Braithwaite, sixty-plus, widower, retired general practitioner and British down to his initials, commits himself to his quest with a self-deprecating yet embattled persistence. When the facts fail him, he widens the search. He writes learned notes about parrots in the work of Flaubert, ransacks the novels and correspondence for clues, and attempts to winkle out the mystery from the life and times, friends and enemies of a writer who hated intrusions into his private life. When this too fails,

Dr Braithwaite is led to wondering how the past—any past—may be truly grasped. . . .

[The] past is only one aspect of truth. What is truth? For instance, you can look at Flaubert from many angles and each angle will tell you something. . . . But all his angles do not add up to *an* angle. How many half-truths are needed to make the whole truth? The truth about Flaubert is uncertain and each certainty is certain to be undermined by a coincidence or an irony.

Why then does he persist? Dr Braithwaite fills his head with parrot squawkings because his mind is preoccupied by another, more immediate problem. He is a discreet and reticent man who does not find it easy to speak of himself. How shall he make a meaning of his married life, of his wife's death, if simple truths about jam and stuffed birds elude him? Mrs Braithwaite was a good wife but not faithful: no Emma Bovary, but a careless and bruisable suburban adulteress who never quite showed him up but ultimately let him down. Now it's over and he wonders what love is, what truth is, what the past is. Flaubert got it right but what precisely he got right Dr Braithwaite finds it difficult to say—and even Flaubert himself was never too sure. In one sense, the quest is a form of therapy. In another, it is a restatement of old questions. To look no further: what exactly is Flaubert's parrot?

It is, of course, the creature from Flaubert's story. Unless it is the sutffed bird at the museum in the Hôtel-Dieu at Rouen. Or that slightly less intimidating rival exhibit at the Croisset pavilion. That is, if it isn't the good doctor himself, *Flaubertus redivivus*. After all, he has a Flaubertian eye for irony and the grotesque, and he willingly embraces the Master's view that the human race is irredeemably stupid. Still, a coincidence or an irony all too easily knock him off his perch, and besides, he has a pawky individualism which makes him his own man. In that case, shall we say that the parrot is Life which repeats and mimics itself just as episodes in Flaubert's life parrot his work? If not, then it is Language: the choicest words are not much better than the chatter of this ''rare creature that makes human sounds'' and mocks with gaudy, ghastly parodies our attempts to move the stars to pity. . . . The clever reader will conclude that the parrot of the title is not any one of these, but all of them. There are as many parrots as there are readers. Or Flauberts.

Dr Braithwaite, who can be very sharp-tongued about critics, would not be satisfied with as little. He persists in his search for truth not as an intellectual exercise but out of personal need. In this sense he is that old-fashioned thing, a scholar who seeks knowledge for its own sake and for what it may do to make him wise. So very different from the modern version, the academic researcher who, self-regarding and self-advertising, churns out footnoted, deadening articles each constituting a professional leg-up and each banging another nail in the coffin of understanding. Dr Braithwaite would not be happy with the multi-parrot, multi-Flaubert theory, for not only does it dilute and disperse the truth he seeks but it stems directly from the unconquerable *bêtise* which Flaubert himself deplored. . . .

What then are we to think when the scrupulous scholar is careless with the date of Flaubert's earliest surviving composition? When the dictator of literature constructs a reworking of Louise Colet's view of Flaubert? When the exact stylist asks, anent the sexual irregularity of the nineteenth century, ''who shall escape whipping''? Mistakes or cods? For Dr Braithwaite is nothing if not playful. He devises programmes

for researchers (''Pets at Croisset'', ''The Ethics of English Governesses Abroad'') and sets an examination paper for his reader. He makes jokes and he plants seeds—an image, a quote, a thought—which sprout at a later point in his story, catching us unaware, hitting us with an artful coincidence or a prepared twist of irony: irony does not exist without an ironist. What then is the truth about Dr Braithwaite?

He is a man who sees quite clearly that the past is elusive and truth ungraspable: behind every parrot there is another parrot. Like Flaubert, he recognizes that the joke is on him and he accepts the fact with modesty and, if only for the sake of good manners, with dignity. Happiness lies in anticipation and in the memory of anticipated happiness. His quest ends in farce—the ironic thing about truisms is that they are true—but he has gained enough wisdom from the parrots he has scrutinized to know that the joke is cosmic, that it is played on him as it is played on Flaubert, Mrs Braithwaite, critics, curators and parrots. The quest's the thing. If he were a religious man, he would surely quote Pascal: he who seeks has found.

But while he is no creature of Pascal's are we to conclude that he is Julian Barnes's parrot? The author throws open the doors, disowns the translations from the French which are the work of an elderly general practitioner and then removes himself from the proceedings without even the faintest cry of ''Geoffrey Braithwaite, c'est moi''. Even so, there are unsevered umbilicals. Barnes's new novel develops themes and techniques from his two earlier books. The second, *Before She Met Me,* dealt with adultery-in-the-mind and despair. . . . Barnes's latest is an *After She Left Me,* and a *Vade-Retroland* for the clever-clever, the merely moody, the sardonic and the flip. But if it is non-Baudelairean and unashamedly Flaubertophile, it positively jangles with cross-fertilizing, self-seeding, memory-jogging, imagination-releasing resonances. Phrases, images, quotations, incidents recur, and come at you like your own memories.

Flaubert's Parrot is sober, elegant and wry. It works as literary detection, literary criticism and literary experiment. It tells good stories and deals with ideas empirically, in the British way, for this is a very Anglo-Saxon book. The modern British novel finds it easy to be clever and comic. Barnes also manages that much harder thing: he succeeds in communicating genuine emotion without affectation or embarrassment. Like the Julien of Flaubert's story, he has great compassion for the quietly desperate man whom he ferries between France and England, past and present, art and life, pessimism and stoicism. In an age which insists that every problem has an economic, political or technological solution, Barnes has the courage and good humour to remind us that there are questions to which there are no answers.

David Coward, ''The Rare Creature's Human Sounds,'' in The Times Literary Supplement, No. 4253, October 5, 1984, p. 1117.

TERRENCE RAFFERTY

[The narrator of *Flaubert's Parrot*], a retired, widowed doctor named Geoffrey Braithwaite, asks some pretty big [questions]: ''Does life improve?'' ''What knowledge is useful, what knowledge is true?'' and (his constant refrain) ''How do we seize the past?'' . . . Braithwaite is in the tradition of the worldly, cynical physicians we find in Chekhov or Graham Greene, and he knows his Flaubert cold, and yet, for all his knowledge, he can't come up with the answers he needs most. But he isn't pathetic or irritating, because Barnes knows enough to satisfy our curiosity as novel readers, which is all that matters: we know where Geoffrey Braithwaite is in this narrative, we feel the urgency of his interrogations, and so the mysteries that frustrate him are useful knowledge for us. We understand that the gaps in Braithwaite's knowledge aren't meant to be filled, that the dots on the map won't be connected, that his questions don't need answers because they're more than questions— they're the events of a first-person narrative, the graph of a singular human voice.

And Braithwaite's is a remarkably clear, straightforward voice. The convention of the criticism novel—including good ones, like *Pale Fire*— is that the narrator's critical activity is evasive, a way of delaying telling a story he doesn't want to tell (but invariably spills in the last few pages, after scattering small "inadvertent" revelations throughout the book). *Flaubert's Parrot* plays the what's-the-real-story? game, too, but plays it right out in the open.... Barnes has made [Braithwaite] smart and funny and perfectly self-aware (he even acknowledges our suspicion that he murdered his wife), so we're not tempted to flatter our intelligence by trying to anticipate him—we know he'll tell his story when he's ready to.

The real story—no surprise—is about Braithwaite's marriage and the death of his wife.... Too much correspondence between the narrator's Flaubert research and his summing up of his own life, and the novel would be just another overdetermined literary stunt, a donnish tour de force ...; too little, and the conceit is pointless—or pointedly arbitrary, which might be worse.... Instead of forcing the Flaubert material to match up one-to-one with the story of Geoffrey and Ellen, Barnes allows Flaubert to flower slowly as a metaphor in the course of the narrator's spiel, to gather resonance, *justness,* not from the details picked up by Braithwaite's wildly heterogeneous researches but from the patient accumulation of jokes, asides, confessions and questions that define a voice—and the tone of Geoffrey Braithwaite's voice is all we need to tell us what Flaubert means in this novel. The author of *Madame Bovary* is, for Braithwaite, an ideal of objectivity, the detached, eye-level gaze on death and adultery, on the fixed shadows of the past and the bright mess of the present. Braithwaite himself is like an amateur photographer taking pictures of his family, his love for his subjects inspiring a benign mania for precision.... (pp. 21-2)

Braithwaite's verbal footwork is a way of maneuvering for a true shot of his life with Ellen, a picture that's both honest and bearable: he takes too many steps, but he's more attractive than his master, who never showed his moves (and whose pursuit of exactness was surely inspired by a more abstract, less individual passion). *Flaubert's Parrot* is a minor classic, and one of the best criticism novels ever, because its critic/narrator has some dignity, because his choice of subject makes emotional sense and because the book has a lively, questioning spirit.... Barnes, in his offhand way, performs a couple of literary marriages straight out of critics' dreams: he's written a modernist text with a nineteenth-century heart, a French novel with English lucidity and tact. (p. 22)

> *Terrence Rafferty, "Watching the Detectives," in The Nation, Vol. 241, No. 1, July 6 & 13, 1985, pp. 21-2.*

JOHN UPDIKE

[If *Flaubert's Parrot*] is, as its dust jacket shyly claims, "a novel in disguise ... a novel that constantly surprises," it is the most strangely shaped specimen of its genre (that I have read) since Vladimir Nabokov's *Pale Fire*. On the other hand, if it is a biographical-critical treatise on a dead writer, it is the oddest and most whimsical such since Nabokov's *Nikolai Gogol.* ... [*Flaubert's Parrot* appeared in America] heavily garlanded by British praise ("An intricate and delightful novel"— Graham Greene. "Endless food for thought, beautifully written"—Germaine Greer. "Handsomely the best novel published in England in 1984"—John Fowles) and quickly acquired a headful of American posies as well ("I read it with a continuing chuckle"—Leon Edel. "Delightful and enriching"—Joseph Heller. "A gem"—John Irving. "*Flaubert's Parrot, c'est moi!*"—Fran Lebowitz). The book is indeed conceived with a dashing originality and does impart a great deal of odd data about Flaubert....

As an inventive and erudite treatise on Gustave Flaubert, *Flaubert's Parrot* is praiseworthy, hilarious in many of its details and yet serious in its search for clues to Flaubert's elusive and repellent character....

But as a novel? What is, indeed, the story, with its beginning, middle, and end, of *Flaubert's Parrot*? The self-abnegation of the loquacious narrator ... implies shame, something to hide. Dr. Braithwaite's unspoken secret, the motive for his tantalizing coyness, presses behind his screen of Flaubertian trivia, and occasionally pokes through. (p. 86)

The artistic strategy of *Flaubert's Parrot* employs the ancient magical technique of substitution; just as in *Pale Fire* Kinbote reads his own mad life into John Shade's poem on quite another subject, Braithwaite smuggles his own tragedy into the facts about Flaubert. The effect is ingenious but not, quite, moving. The blatant forestallment of revelation begins to nag as well as tease; as one disparate chapter of mock scholarship succeeds another—each chapter a fresh insult, as it were, to our natural curiosity concerning the shadowy Braithwaite—readerly fatigue and irritation set in. By the time the narrator comes clean, we are tired of his voice, by turns arch, quarrelsome, curt, cute, and implausibly literary. Braithwaite's wickedly witty list of types of novels he wants banned is surely a London culturati's, not a provincial physician's, and some of the metaphors are foppishly spun out.... Too many epigrams on art and life—"The past is autobiographical fiction pretending to be a parliamentary report," "Books are where things are explained to you; life is where things aren't"—keep reminding us that we are only reading a book. While the novel as a form certainly asks for, and can absorb, a great deal of experimentation, it must at some point achieve self-forgetfulness and let pure event take over. In *Flaubert's Parrot,* that point arrives too late, and brings too little. The attempt, I think, is to remind us that, as our narrator insists, "books are not life, however much we might prefer it if they were;" that is, real-life misfortune remains raw and rough, and resists sublimation by literature. But so much artifice in establishing the priority of the "real" feels artificial, and leaves us cold. Whatever we want from novels, we want more than conversation with the author, however engagingly tricksome. (p. 87)

> *John Updike, "A Pair of Parrots," in The New Yorker, Vol. LXI, No. 22, July 22, 1985, pp. 86-90.*

WENDY LESSER

Flaubert's Parrot is all head. Its author, British television critic Julian Barnes, describes the work as his third novel, but there is nothing particularly novelistic about this commentary—one might say rant—on Flaubert's life and work. Instead, it seems as if Barnes had a lot of things he wanted to say about Flaubert but couldn't bear to be trammeled by the constraints of either biography or literary criticism. Seating himself on the throne of fiction, he therefore felt free to throw stones at those two other structures without bothering to reinforce the transparent walls of his own refuge. The task Barnes set himself is not inherently impossible. Brecht, after all, created fictional biography in *Galileo,* while Nabokov's *Pale Fire* and Swift's *Tale of a Tub* are both successful (if self-mocking) examples of a marriage between fiction and literary criticism. But the sole fictional element in ***Flaubert's Parrot*** is the narrator, Geoffrey Braithwaite, ostensibly an elderly English doctor obsessed with Flaubert. Most of the time J.B. seems to forget that G.B. exists: we get little sense of any transmitting personality other than the author's. In only one chapter—the one where Braithwaite discloses the infidelities of his beloved late wife—does the book begin to suggest the novel it could have become. Here, in the reflections of a man who is simultaneously self-conscious and obtuse, we are given a vision of what that other doctor, Charles Bovary, might have felt if he had been capable of comprehending Emma's tragedy. But for the most part ***Flaubert's Parrot*** ranges from the petty to the merely clever. It has its amusing moments (particularly in the first and last chapters, which are about parrots), but it also has its points of extreme stupidity, notably in the chapter called "The Case Against," which sets up straw-man arguments against Flaubert and then flamboyantly knocks them down. The book purports to be anti-literary-critical, but I can't imagine that many non-critics—many people who simply read novels, that is—would be very interested in it. As a piece of writing, it shares Flaubert's worst flaws (his coldness, for instance, and his desire to be reductive) without possessing any of his overwhelming virtues. (pp. 470-71)

Wendy Lesser, "Bloated and Shrunken Worlds," in The Hudson Review, *Vol. XXXVIII, No. 3, Autumn, 1985, pp. 463-72.*

Ray(mond Douglas) Bradbury

1920-

(Has also written under pseudonyms of Douglas Spaulding and Leonard Spaulding) American short story writer, novelist, scriptwriter, poet, dramatist, nonfiction writer, editor, and author of children's books.

Regarded as an important figure in the development of science fiction, even though he does not write primarily in that genre, Bradbury was among the first authors to combine the concepts of science fiction with a sophisticated prose style. Often described as economical yet poetic, Bradbury's fiction conveys a vivid sense of place in which everyday events are transformed into unusual, sometimes sinister situations. In a career which has spanned more than forty years, Bradbury has written fantasies, crime and mystery stories, supernatural tales, and mainstream literature as well as science fiction. In all of his work, Bradbury emphasizes basic human values and cautions against unthinking acceptance of technological progress. His persistent optimism, evident even in his darkest work, has led some critics to label him as sentimental or naive. Bradbury, however, perceives life, even at its most mundane, with a childlike wonder and awe which charges his work with a fervent affirmation of humanity.

Bradbury began his career during the 1940s as a writer for such pulp magazines as *Black Mask, Amazing Stories,* and *Weird Tales.* The latter magazine served to showcase the works of such fantasy writers as H. P. Lovecraft, Clark Ashton Smith, and August Derleth. Derleth, who founded Arkham House, a publishing company specializing in fantasy literature, accepted one of Bradbury's stories for *Who Knocks?,* an anthology published by his firm. Derleth subsequently suggested that Bradbury compile a volume of his own stories; the resulting book, *Dark Carnival* (1947), collects Bradbury's early fantasy tales. Although Bradbury rarely published pure fantasy later in his career, such themes of his future work as the need to retain humanistic values and the importance of the imagination are displayed in the stories of this collection. Many of these pieces were republished with new material in *The October Country* (1955).

The publication of *The Martian Chronicles* (1950) established Bradbury's reputation as an author of sophisticated science fiction. This collection of stories is connected by the framing device of the settling of Mars by human beings and is dominated by tales of space travel and environmental adaptation. Bradbury's themes, however, reflect many of the important issues of the post-World War II era—racism, censorship, technology, and nuclear war—and the stories delineate the implications of these themes through authorial commentary. Clifton Fadiman described *The Martian Chronicles* as being "as grave and troubling as one of Hawthorne's allegories." Another significant collection of short stories, *The Illustrated Man* (1951), also uses a framing device, basing the stories on the tattoos of the title character.

Bradbury's later short story collections are generally considered to be less significant than *The Martian Chronicles* and *The Illustrated Man.* Bradbury shifts his focus in these volumes from outer space to more familiar earthbound settings. *Dan-*

© Thomas Victor 1986

delion Wine (1957), for example, has as its main subject the midwestern youth of Bradbury's semiautobiographical protagonist, Douglas Spaulding. Although Bradbury uses many of the same techniques in these stories as in his science fiction and fantasy publications, *Dandelion Wine* was not as well received as his earlier work. Other later collections, including *A Medicine for Melancholy* (1959), *The Machineries of Joy* (1964), *I Sing the Body Electric!* (1969), and *Long after Midnight* (1976), contain stories set in Bradbury's familiar outer space or midwestern settings and explore his typical themes. Many of Bradbury's stories have been anthologized or filmed for such television programs as "The Twilight Zone," "Alfred Hitchcock Presents," and "Ray Bradbury Theater."

In addition to his short fiction, Bradbury has written three adult novels. The first of these, *Fahrenheit 451* (1953), originally published as a short story and later expanded into novel form, concerns a future society in which books are burned because they are perceived as threats to societal conformity. In *Something Wicked This Way Comes* (1962), a father attempts to save his son and a friend from the sinister forces of a mysterious traveling carnival. Both of these novels have been adapted for film. *Death Is a Lonely Business* (1985) is a detective story featuring Douglas Spaulding, the protagonist of *Dandelion Wine,* as a struggling writer for pulp magazines. Bradbury has also written poetry and drama; critics have faulted his efforts in these genres as lacking the impact of his fiction.

While Bradbury's popularity is acknowledged even by his detractors, many critics find the reasons for his success difficult to pinpoint. Some believe that the tension Bradbury creates between fantasy and realism is central to his ability to convey his visions and interests to his readers. Peter Stoler asserted that Bradbury's reputation rests on his "chillingly understated stories about a familiar world where it is always a few minutes before midnight on Halloween, and where the unspeakable and unthinkable become commonplace." Mary Ross proposed that "Perhaps the special quality of [Bradbury's] fantasy lies in the fact that people to whom amazing things happen are often so simply, often touchingly, like ourselves." In a genre in which futurism and the fantastic are usually synonymous, Bradbury stands out for his celebration of the future in realistic terms and his exploration of conventional values and ideas. As one of the first science fiction writers to convey his themes through a refined prose style replete with subtlety and humanistic analogies, Bradbury has helped make science fiction a more respected literary genre and is widely admired by the literary establishment.

(See also *CLC*, Vols. 1, 3, 10, 15; *Contemporary Authors*, Vols. 1-4, rev. ed.; *Contemporary Authors New Revision Series*, Vol. 2; *Something about the Author*, Vol. 11; and *Dictionary of Literary Biography*, Vols. 2, 8.)

CHARLES LEE

Science-fictionist Ray Bradbury—ace practitioner of that special type of tale, the tall short story—is at his startling best in this collection of twenty-two yarns [*The Golden Apples of the Sun*].

Most of them are nightmare novelties, imaginative sprees that in turn terrorize or tantalize the mind. Mr. Bradbury offers feather-light fancies having to do with benevolent witches, delirious fantasies dealing with romantic dinosaurs, and fabulous conceits about rocket ships. He mixes murderers and mummified frogs, Chinese emperors and garbage collectors, time-machines and teenagers. Depending on his story, he is whimsical, poetical, allegorical, editorial, or macabre.

Everybody somehow expects Mr. Bradbury to take us forward in time for the purpose of jetting us through space with the pioneer settlers of Mars. And we are not surprised to whizz back through pre-history. . . . But what we may not expect is how he crosses those forward and backward thrusts into time with the present, as in his chill satire of mechanical uniformity in the year 2131 A. D., **"The Pedestrian."** . . .

The delicate poetry of **"The April Witch"** contrasts pleasantly with the boisterous humors of his teen-age piece, **"The Great Fire."** . . . Mr. Bradbury may strike some reader as too "tricky." But none will call him dull.

> *Charles Lee, "Terrorizing, Tantalizing," in* The New York Times Book Review, *March 22, 1953, p. 25.*

H. H. HOLMES

[Both] in science-fantasy and in realistic fiction, you'll find [in *The Golden Apples of The Sun*] some of the best and some of the worst short stories you're apt to read this year.

Of the twenty-two stories here collected, at most eight can be called "science fiction," ranging from the superb "The Wilderness," an addendum to *The Martian Chronicles* which provides a magnificent emotional refutation to Sir Charles Galton Darwin's thesis that man faces no more frontiers, down to the title story, as absurd a piece of scientific illiteracy as a first-class writer has ever perpetrated. Over half the volume is straight fiction, again highly varied in quality—often simple, perceptive, and moving, sometimes self-consciously quaint and condescending in its false naïveté. . . .

Obviously such a mixed book could be published only because of the importance of the author; and the best of the work here presented leaves no doubt that Bradbury is one of the most stimulating of the younger writers.

> *H. H. Holmes, "A Mixed Bag of Stories," in* New York Herald Tribune Book Review, *March 29, 1953, p. 12.*

MARY ROSS

A Medicine for Melancholy comprises twenty-two tales, most of them very brief, which range over time and our Earth as well as the Universe. Many of them pack a chuckle whereby the author is laughing not at his ability to confound the reader (though undoubtedly he often does just that) but with the reader at the endless variety of human wants and hopes and tastes and drives. Reading these wholly unusual tales will reward those who can bring to them some of the zest and nimbleness of imagination that has gone into the writing.

> *Mary Ross, "Tales Ranging the Universe," in* New York Herald Tribune Book Review, *March 29, 1959, p. 10.*

FREDERICK H. GUIDRY

Something about Mr. Bradbury's style—its terseness, its simplicity, or its flashes of imagery—invites a serious approach and arouses an eager expectancy of fresh insight into the human condition.

Although his modern parables do not always convey clear-cut meanings, their imaginative approach, suggestive of overtones of significance, keep the reader hunting for a message or moral.

This is true even in the most fanciful of the science-fiction tales that make up a large proportion of the 22 short stories in [*A Medicine for Melancholy*]. . . .

In stories about what it may be like to live on other planets, Mr. Bradbury is intrigued primarily by the mental aspects. Homesickness is depicted as a primary difficulty, even when space ships make regular trips. In **"The Strawberry Window"** a husband who has moved to Mars spends all his savings to send back for the loved front porch, the parlor furniture, and the old bed in a desperate bid to keep his wife from forcing a return to earth.

In **"Dark They Were, and Golden-eyed"** the thesis is that Mars irresistibly works on the visitor, first sapping the will and destroying the capacity to leave, then causing physical changes that make earthlings otherworldly in appearance.

The temptation is strong to search for hidden meanings, even though some of them may be as commonplace as those suggested by the cited examples. . . .

Readers should be warned that Mr. Bradbury's unorthodoxy, particularly in earth-bound episodes, leads occasionally to distasteful and morbid conclusions.

But when the author puts these themes aside, he is capable of storytelling flavored with humor, sentiment, suspense, and awe in a wide variety of settings.

> *Frederick H. Guidry, "Other Voices, Other Moons," in* The Christian Science Monitor, *June 4, 1959, p. 11.*

MARTIN LEVIN

[*The Machineries of Joy*] is like whiling away an afternoon in a dime museum—a good one, with top-drawer concessions that give the visitor his money's worth. Mr. Bradbury is a smooth pitchman for his versatile collection, luring you into each story with a well-thrown narrative hook, and then confronting you with whatever exhibit takes his fancy: a fungoid horror in **"Boys! Raise Giant Mushrooms In Your Cellar!"** a fat lady with a tattoo problem in **"The Illustrated Woman"**; an apocalyptic vision in **"The Vacation."**

One problem, not Mr. Bradbury's fault, is that one somehow expects each story to lead into the fantasy that made the author's reputation. Sometimes it does, as in a brilliant switch on Walter Van Tilburg Clark's "The Portable Phonograph" entitled **"To The Chicago Abyss,"** in which we are shown a terrifying future without name brands. And often as not it doesn't, as in **"A Flight of Ravens,"** which depicts the terrifying present of a couple of white collar slaves. Throughout *The Machineries of Joy,* fiction and fantasy alike, runs a horror of "the boxed and separate life within a mechanical hive" that people lead in cities. (pp. 38-9)

> *Martin Levin, in a review of "The Machineries of Joy," in* The New York Times Book Review, *February 16, 1964, pp. 38-9.*

STEPHEN HUGH-JONES

Why is Ray Bradbury so good? It is not—the conventional science fiction criterion—that his ideas are so striking. They tend to be no better than average; indeed many of these stories, as usual, are not SF at all and don't claim to be. It is partly a remarkable economy and delicacy of style; there aren't many people writing today who can say so easily exactly what they want to say. It is partly pure sentiment, that dogrose and cornflower sweetness common to so many American writers. This can be unspeakable corn, or not: Mr Bradbury sometimes teeters toward the borderline. [*The Machineries of Joy*] gave me a lot of pleasure, as must be evident, but also some unease. One story—the explorers of a new planet are promptly possessed by a resident intelligence—stands out: it is also the only one which is almost pure SF. Others, particularly those where a setting such as Mexico replaces an idea, are less impressive.

> *Stephen Hugh-Jones, "Bradburies," in* New Statesman, *Vol. LXVIII, No. 1749, September 18, 1964, p. 406.*

JOHN J. McLAUGHLIN

Much of the bulk of [Ray Bradbury's] fiction has been concerned with a single theme—the loss of human values to the machine. Now Bradbury has brought his message to a new medium, the theatre, and, typically, he has mustered all the resources of imagination, talent and ingenuity available to make the stage speak for him with the effectiveness of the printed page. . . . (p. 92)

[*The World of Ray Bradbury,* an evening of three one-act plays], represents more than dabbling in a new literary form for Bradbury. It is a full commitment to put time, energy and money into the theatre. (pp. 92-3)

Two of the three plays . . . , *The Pedestrian* and *The Veldt,* examine the future effects of two of our most proliferating machines: the automobile and the television set. One of the favorite techniques of science fiction writers is to take a contemporary problem and push it to its logical extreme. What happens, for example, when cars and TV sets insinuate themselves increasingly into our lives? Quite simple: no one walks any longer. So *The Pedestrian* is set in 1990—as are all three of the plays—when it is illegal to be out on the street at night on foot. . . .

In *The Veldt,* television is pushed to the point where it becomes a "complete environment"—a room where one is surrounded by three-dimensional pictures that reproduce any spot on earth with perfect realism. A man and his wife install such a TV playroom for their children and bustle them off to the room to keep them from under foot. But instead of duplicating the wonders of Egypt, the spectacle of Niagara, or any of the other enticements in the machine's repertory, the children keep the dial locked on a single ominous scene: an African veldt inhabited by lions that tear flesh from unidentified carcasses. The denouement is not too surprising. . . .

The final play, and in many ways the best of the three, deals with a theme that has concerned Bradbury for some time—mediocrity, and whether or not it has any value. In *To the Chicago Abyss* Bradbury sings a Whitmanesque song in praise of junk. The action takes place after an atomic holocaust when famine and dearth are so complete that remembering the affluent times of the past is forbidden. But an old man appears who cannot forget and cannot keep from talking. He remembers "the junk of a race-track civilization"—the cigarette packages, candy bars, the look of the dashboard on a Cadillac, and the sound of the Duncan sisters. He becomes a fugitive who is doomed because "somehow my tongue moves" and he is compelled to recite his catalogues. . . .

Bradbury buffs will recognize the plots of these plays because all three appeared originally as short stories. There is, of course, nothing new about adapting narrative material to the stage, but in the case of science fiction it presents several difficult problems. As a genre, science fiction combines the plot and moral tone of melodrama with the fantasy of romance, a combination which is a genuine literary novelty. The methods of melodrama are easily accommodated on the stage, but successful fantasy occurs more naturally in narrative fiction where the imagination can create worlds that never were. When fantasy is dramatized, it is usually combined with music, dance and comedy. . . . Film is much more congenial to science fiction than the stage because special-effects technicians are able to take the most fantastic imaginings of the writer and actually construct them from plastic or plasterboard. In a movie we don't have to use our imagination—the Martian landscape is there before our eyes.

How is a playwright to place science fiction on the stage? Will a bare stage and an appeal to the audience's imaginative powers be adequate for a play like *The Veldt*? Can we believe in such a machine without some hint of what it looks or sounds like? Bradbury's solution to these problems has been the same as the film maker's: turn it over to the technician. We are presented with a stunning array of futuristic projections and costumes, control panels with blinking lights, and a persistent sound track that bleeps and hums like a satellite orbiting around the balcony. (p. 93)

The sound is, on at least one occasion, terrifyingly effective: in the final scene of *The Veldt* where, sitting in the darkness amid horrifying screams, you hear lions about to spring into your lap. But for the most part the technical éclat intrudes upon the play—it becomes gimmicky rather than theatrical, crushing the drama rather than supporting it. The sounds, projections and costumes are attempts to *tell* us rather than to *suggest* what the future may be like. They are particularly obtrusive in the final play, *To the Chicago Abyss,* where Bradbury insists on actually showing the trivia his old man is describing—producing it magically by sleight of hand. . . . This is especially sad, for the play doesn't need the technical hokum; it is sensitively written and well acted and is quite able to get by on its own dramatic values.

Many of the defects of the three plays can be attributed to the difficulties a playwright is bound to encounter when he creates a theatre for his own work. . . . Taking into account inexperience, it is not too surprising that the theatrical balance, which one would expect to be weighted toward action and dialogue in a playwright's theatre, was instead shifted noisily in the direction of stagecraft. (pp. 93-4)

When asked recently whether he would do it the same way again, Bradbury refused to make excuses. "The final decisions were mine and I take full responsibility for what appears on the stage," he said. He did admit, however, that if he had learned anything from his first attempt to stage his own work it was "to trust the word." "You've got to believe in your own language," he said. But he is not defensive about his new theatre. "I don't think much of most of the theatre I see today," he said. "I'm not interested in writing an Albee play or a Baldwin play because it's the fashionable thing to do. I'm interested in experimenting with something different and in having fun doing it." (p. 94)

John J. McLaughlin, "Science Fiction Theatre," in The Nation, *Vol. 200, No. 4, January 25, 1965, pp. 92-4.*

JANE MANTHORNE

Ray Bradbury's stories cannot be half read. They compel the reader without pause to the final shock revelation, the neat twist, or the poetically just conclusion. Bradbury wraps fantasy in minuscule details of reality, so that the reader believes all and is ready for anything. Even in macabre tales such as **"Pillar of Fire,"** his rhythmic, word-savoring style makes poetry out of a dead man's emergence from the grave. These sixteen stories of science fiction and fantasy [in *S Is for Space*] offer proof of the range of Bradbury's art form from the Messianic theme of **"The Man"** to the mounting horror of **"Come into My Cellar,"** and the clear, sharp warning against conformity in **"The Pedestrian."** Bradbury suggests that Jules Verne was his father; H. G. Wells, his uncle; and Flash Gordon, one of his friends. No doubt about it!

Jane Manthorne, in a review of "S Is for Space," in The Horn Book Magazine, *Vol. XLIII, No. 1, February, 1967, p. 70.*

STANLEY REYNOLDS

Science fiction fans complain that snooty literary reviewers are ignoring a vital genre by failing to review SF. Well, no SF writer is more lauded than Ray Bradbury. His new volume of stories [*I Sing the Body Electric!*] comes with an amazing list of devotees—Graham Greene, Bertrand Russell, Christopher Isherwood, Bernard Berenson, Thornton Wilder, Ingmar Bergman, Nelson Algren and Gilbert Highet. I think, really, they must read Bradbury as great men were once said to relax with detective stories. Bradbury is pretentious, and in this collection gives full vent to his aspirations. There are stories here definitely aimed at being writing with a capital R. In some he almost brings it off. **"The Inspired Chicken Motel"** recreates the nomadic life of the Great Depression seen through an ordinary family rather than through the Okies of Steinbeck or Agee's *Let Us Now Praise Famous Men.* There is a genuine warmth and humanity about the story, but Bradbury ruins it, carrying the story a paragraph too far with a last sentimental belabouring of the point. This sentimentality runs amok in most of the tales, showing that under the still sparkling surface the treacle runs deep. (p. 452)

Stanley Reynolds, "British Caution," in New Statesman, *Vol. 79, No. 2037, March 27, 1970, pp. 451-52.*

ANALOG SCIENCE FICTION/SCIENCE FACT

Ray Bradbury is by no means the typical Analog reader's typical SF author, but he *is* the Literary Establishment's idea of what Mr. S.F. should be, and that makes his first new book in several years worthy of attention. Moreover, out of the seventeen stories and a poem in [*I Sing the Body Electric!*], seven are about as close to science fiction as Bradbury gets, these days. As for the others, three—including one of the best—seem to be spinoff from his stay in Ireland, . . . five are the Saroyanesque grotesques that we have had in other books, and a couple are out-and-out fantasies. . . .

The "body electric" of the title story is a robot grandmother, bought to care for motherless children, who gradually works her way into their affection and fulfills her function as a machine. I'm sure you know what it's like. . . .

There are two stories about Bradbury's own special Mars. The most elaborate is **"Lost City of Mars,"** where a lost robot city gives each visitor his real heart's desire. It is a city made to satisfy and sustain Martians—or men—that will not let them go. The better of the two—one of Bradbury's best—is **"Night Call, Collect."** In it, the last man on an abandoned Mars devises a plan to combat the loneliness of his last years . . . but the plan goes strangely wrong. (p. 165)

[One] of the Irish stories . . . is really one of Bradbury's gentlest and best "straight" stories. It is called **"The Cold Wind and the Warm,"** and it tells what happens when a flight of fairies—the kind who sun themselves on the Riviera and Fire Island—light for a moment in an Irish town.

Bradbury's "style for style's sake" attack is less evident here. He's getting older, and maybe mellower. I think it's his best collection in a long time. (p. 166)

A review of "I Sing the Body Electric!" in Analog
Science Fiction/Science Fact, Vol. LXXXV, No. 5,
July, 1970, pp. 165-66.

RALPH A. SPERRY

Ray Bradbury is a conventional writer: that is, for the most
part he adheres to literary conventions and, even if he did
propose some of them himself, among those his often overweening and more than occasionally vertiginous lyricism, by
now the reader can normally know what to expect out of a
Bradburian piece. But not in this instance. And immediately
I should warn you that less than half of the twenty-two stories
[in *Long after Midnight*] are even horror tales, let alone science
fiction; and I should also warn you that only five of the twenty-
two are any good at all. They happen to be superb.

Of those five, two in particular are tours-de-force. **"The Better
Part of Wisdom,"** the most sensitive, most restrained, most
graceful treatment of homosexuality I've ever read, ought to
be required reading for all gay writers. **"Have I Got a Chocolate
Bar For You!"** deals very subtly with a very subtle relationship
between a priest and a penitent. Neither of them relies in the
least on genre devices. Both of them, when they wax lyrical,
do so only in the most disciplined and appropriate ways. The
other three are each well planned, carefully written, and substantial in the points they make. **"The October Game,"** for
the satisfaction of Bradbury aficionados, is a horror story of
exquisite structure. But the other seventeen pieces. . . .

Many of them ought not to have been published in their present
form; they are so lax as to be nearly aimless. Some of them
ought never to have been published at all; they are not only
pointless but, alone, could never possibly be brought to any
point. And those few which might be considered technically
publishable are so literarily audacious as to be embarassing to
even the most ill-read. Bradbury dares to write, not like, but
as George Bernard Shaw; he dares to write as Thomas Wolfe.
He can't. It's painful. But, worse, **"Getting through Sunday
Somehow"** is a most unsubtle James Joyce ripoff, set in Dublin,
replete with pub scene and harp. And even worse than that,
"Interval in Sunlight" transcends the ripoff: it actually appears
to be a fictionalization of parts of Douglas Day's biography of
Malcolm Lowry.

This book is a poor return for the money, for the effort, and,
if you've liked Bradbury before, for the strain of trying to
maintain your appreciation of what he can do best in the face
of what he's done so horribly. The precious five good stories
in this collection amply demonstrate Bradbury didn't have to
do this whole book; even given them, don't you.

*Ralph A. Sperry, in a review of "Long after Mid-
night," in* Best Sellers, *Vol. 36, No. 9, December,
1976, p. 275.*

DAVID A. TRUESDALE

[*Long after Midnight*] contains 22 short stories many of which
are neither science fiction nor fantasy, but Bradbury remembering—in short vignettes or nostalgic mood pieces—about his
childhood experiences in Illinois. Some are particularly poignant and touching, several minor excursions in self-indulgent
sentimentality, while the majority of the stories can be lumped
into two fairly distinct categories: fantasy from the Weird Tales,
Other Worlds type markets of the early 1950s; and Ray perpetually attempting to resurrect a number of his favorite writers

or influences from the past, such as in **"The Parrot who Met
Papa"** and **"Forever and the Earth"** where Hemingway and
Thomas Wolfe are through different devices permitted to join
us once again—albeit in each case for only a short time.

If you like Bradbury you will like this new collection. My
personal opinion is that after reading through the whole book
without a break I came away tired of being hammered with
too-often gushy sentimentality time after time. . . . Reading a
few stories at a time would be a better way to approach Bradbury in this instance. Overall it is a fine collection.

*David A. Truesdale, in a review of "Long after Mid-
night," in* Science Fiction Review, *Vol. 7, No. 3,
July, 1978, p. 39.*

PETER STOLER

A father becomes his son, then takes the youngster's place in
his playground—a lower circle in Dante's hell. A fully auto-
mated house continues to function with mechanical mindlessness long after its inhabitants have been incinerated in a nuclear
holocaust. An electrical robot grandmother does more than
bake her grandchildren's favorite pies; she is a model of uncritical love. When the children grow old, she is on stand-by,
ready for their second childhoods. An uninhabited planet resists
earthlings who have come to settle it.

Only one mind could have produced these plots: that of Ray
Bradbury, author of the classic ***Martian Chronicles*** and the
gloomily prophetic ***Fahrenheit 451***. Bradbury has long been
considered one of the great long-distance runners of fantasy
and science fiction. But he is also a sprinter; his poignant and
ironic short stories have been anthologized for more than 30
years. Bradbury's latest book [*The Stories of Ray Bradbury*] is
a highly personal selection of those works: Martian adventures,
nostalgic reminiscences about small-town Midwestern life in
the '20s and '30s, and several evocative anecdotes about Ireland. But its best pieces remain the tales that made the author's
reputation: chillingly understated stories about a familiar world
where it is always a few minutes before midnight on Halloween, and where the unspeakable and unthinkable become commonplace.

Few writers can evoke this October country more trenchantly
than Bradbury. No reader of **"The Fog Horn"** can pass a
lighthouse without visualizing the sea creature listening in the
darkness. Parents who understand **"The Small Assassin,"** the
anecdote of a homicidal infant, will always wonder about the
Freudian undercurrents coursing through the minds of their
children.

Indeed, hypochondriacs might do well to skip **"Fever Dream"**
altogether. It describes the feelings of a youth who is certain
that his body is being taken over by bacteria. . . . (p. K14)

Though he manifestly prefers to write such hair-raisers, Bradbury is as entertaining on the sunny side of the street as he is
in the land of perpetual twilight. One of his stories shares the
delight of a poor Chicano who finds his life magically transformed by the purchase of a white suit. In the hilarious **"Anthem Sprinters,"** some rollicking Irishmen make a contest out
of their penchant for bolting out of a movie theater before the
playing of the national anthem at the end of a show. **"The
Picasso Summer"** acutely satirizes the dilemma of an art lover.
Strolling one evening, he stumbles upon the Master doodling
a huge mural in the French sand. Caught without a camera,
the tourist moves slowly up and down the beach, trying to

make a mental photograph of the masterpiece before a rising tide comes to wash it away.

Bradbury's spare, economical style reveals the consummate storyteller. But it conceals the moralist. Other science-fiction writers may celebrate technology; Bradbury warns readers to be wary of it. Other fantasists may admire power or cunning; Bradbury saves his praise for the fragile fabric of civilization, and extols the basic virtues of common sense and human affection.

Newcomers to Bradbury risk sensory overload by galloping through the book in the manner of the author's anthem sprinters. It is best to amble through this delightful collection. The volume, after all, contains 100 stories. A careful reader, consuming one a night, can make it last into the New Year. (pp. K14, K20)

Peter Stoler, "Sci-Fi Sprints," in Time, Vol. 116, No. 15, October 13, 1980, pp. K14, K20.

THOMAS M. DISCH

Ray Bradbury is America's Official Science Fiction Writer. . . .

To those familiar with the field, Ray Bradbury's figurehead status may seem hard to account for, if only because, as he himself notes, so small a part of his output may be called science fiction. . . .

Could the answer be sheer literary excellence? No. Only readers who would profess Rod McKuen to be America's greatest poet, or Kahlil Gibran its noblest philosopher, could unblushingly commend Mr. Bradbury's stories as literature. (p. 14)

["The Night" is] the first of 100 tales collected in *The Stories of Ray Bradbury*. Though published early in his career (1946), the vein of schmaltz evident in "The Night" recurs in Mr. Bradbury's work as regularly as he reaches for the unattainable. Early and late are meaningless distinctions in his output. Indeed, the secret of his success may well be that, like Peter Pan, he won't grow up. What's more, he knows it. This is from his Introduction:

> I was *not* embarrassed at circuses. Some people are. Circuses are loud, vulgar, and smell in the sun. By the time many people are fourteen or fifteen, they have been divested of their loves, their ancient and intuitive tastes, one by one, until when they reach maturity there is no fun left, no zest, no gusto, no flavor. Others have criticized, and they have criticized themselves, into embarrassment.

There's the choice—love Ray Bradbury, out there beyond embarrassment, or be enrolled among those loveless, zestless critics who never go to the circus. My own experience suggests other possibilities. I've been to the circus from time to time, invariably enjoyed the show, gasped, applauded, and *even so*, my ancient and intuitive taste tells me that Ray Bradbury's stories are meretricious more often than not. Because he's risked being loud, vulgar and smelly? No, because his imagination so regularly becomes mired in genteel gush and self-pity, because his environing clichés have made him nearly oblivious to new data from any source.

Consider this description (from "The Night"): "You smell roses in blossom; fallen apples lying crushed and odorous in the deep grass." Ordinarily apples don't fall when roses blos-

som, but in Mr. Bradbury's stories it's always Anymonth in Everywhereville. His dry-ice machine covers the bare stage of his story with a fog of breathy approximations. He means to be evocative and incantatory; he achieves vagueness and prolixity.

Perhaps it is élitist, these days, to discuss the prose style of any very popular writer. A readership in the millions proves that some sort of message is getting through. At a recent symposium of secondary-school teachers, I was assured that no s.f. writer is so teachable as Mr. Bradbury: even the least-skilled readers are able to turn his sentences into pictures in their heads. Inattentive, artless and very young readers are probably better able to construct agreeable daydreams out of Mr. Bradbury's approximative prose than if they were required to exercise their reading muscles more strenuously.

The Defense might argue that broad outlines, bright colors and stereotypical characters don't preclude the possibility of art, or at least of well-engineered amusement. Walt Disney and Norman Rockwell have endeared themselves to large audiences by such means. Indeed, there are other points of comparison even more pertinent. Like Disney, Mr. Bradbury has a knack of taming and sanitizing fairytales and myths so that even fauns and centaurs may be welcomed into the nursery. Like Rockwell, Mr. Bradbury celebrates the virtues and flavors of an idyllic, small-town American Way of Life, the myth on which a thousand suburbs have been founded.

Myths can serve various purposes: they can be decorative, a kind of literary Fourth of July bunting . . . ; they can be obfuscatory, a stop-gap lie to tell children before they're ready for the truth . . . ; or they can order complex emotional experience in the manner so well described by Bruno Bettelheim in his study of fairytales, *The Uses of Enchantment*. Some of Mr. Bradbury's more memorable tales achieve this last and largest purpose of myth-making—offering symbolically effective ways of thinking about the unthinkable.

Even as mythmaker, however, Mr. Bradbury's failures outnumber his successes. He summons spirits from the vasty deep, but they don't come. "The Black Ferris," one of only six stories collected for the first time in this volume, is representative of Mr. Bradbury at his worst. (pp. 14, 32-3)

There can be charm in art of . . . systematically false naïveté, and some few writers have managed to have it both ways, writing stories that are amusing to grown-ups and exciting to children: Hans Christian Andersen, A. A. Milne, Maurice Sendak. But Mr. Bradbury is not in their league. (p. 34)

Thomas M. Disch, "Tops in Brand-Name Recognition," in The New York Times Book Review, October 26, 1980, pp. 14, 32-4.

ORSON SCOTT CARD

Fifteen or 20 years ago, high school and college English teachers seized upon the work of Ray Bradbury. Ah! they cried in unison. Here is a science fiction writer whose work is *good!* Remarkably enough, however, the appeal of Bradbury's short stories has even survived the process of "required reading." Bradbury is that odd thing: a mid-20th-century writer whose literary output has been almost entirely short stories. Of his so-called novels, *Dandelion Wine* and *Something Wicked This Way Comes* were cobbled together from short stories; *Fahrenheit 451* was an unfortunate expansion of a fine novelette.

In recent years Bradbury seems to have contented himself with writing unprepossessing poetry and the odd article here and there. It takes a book like *The Stories of Ray Bradbury* to remind us that in his writing career he has already given us a body of work comparable to Poe's, to O. Henry's, to de Maupassant's. What's more, rereading these hundred stories also causes me to wonder why the illusion continues, even among science fiction readers, that Ray Bradbury is or ever has been a science fiction writer.

True, his early stories first appeared in the pulps during the late 1940s. But that was not because they belonged there—Bradbury was writing neither space opera nor nuts-and-bolts science fiction. In any reasonable world, the main stream of American letters would have seized instantly upon his work as a fresh voice, a new vision. Unfortunately, Bradbury began writing when the American short story establishment was already in the grip of the hardening of the arteries that would quickly lead to the paralysis we politely overlook today.

Ray Bradbury wrote about Mars, but even when he wrote the stories that later became *The Martian Chronicles* he knew that there never could be such a planet as he described. Rather he was setting his stories in the world of the dreams of a child growing up on Buck Rogers and John Carter. He was not writing science fiction. He was writing Ray Bradbury's child-like world:

It is a world of terrors, both named and nameless, that at once attract and repel.

It is a world of parents who are competent and kind, siblings who are eager to plunge into danger as long as you are close behind, tennis shoes that have miraculous powers.

It is a world where hope is the only possible philosophy, and is not disappointed.

Indeed, it is that very optimism, and not some imaginary genre, that sets off Bradbury's stories from most others. His ebullience borders on sentimentality, and if you do not read his stories in the correct frame of mind you are likely to detect cliché here and there, and mawkishness seeping through almost every tale.

For instance, the characters in **"I Sing the Body Electric"** are not particularly well-drawn. They are simply a boy and his siblings who have lost their mother. Their father arranges for them to choose a robot grandmother who is everything they want her to be. They become emotionally attached to the convincing fraud of an old lady. And then one day she, too, is "killed." This time, however, the machine they love can be resurrected easily—the faith of the children is restored, for their loved one can never be taken from them now. And more: when they are old, she will be able to come back to them and care for them as they retreat into a second childhood.

Maudlin? Yes, if you read it with emotional detachment, analyzing as you go. But Bradbury's stories resist such a reading.

It is not the characters he expects you to identify with. Rather, he means to capture you in his own voice, expects you to see through his eyes. And his eyes see, not the cliché plot, but the whole meaning of the events; not the scenes or the individual people, but yourself and your own fears and your own family and the answer, at last, to the isolation that had seemed inevitable to you. In short, if you will let him, Bradbury will give you a much better childhood than you ever had. He will

name all your nameless fears and bring them home and make you like them. (pp. 4-5)

Bradbury's stories do not all succeed, of course. His tributes to Hemingway only work if you feel toward Papa as too many people feel toward Elvis. Some of his stories are little more than an idea—what if the sea were a woman that coveted a man and regarded his wife as her rival? What if a dinosaur were still alive in the sea and thought a fog horn was a mating call? Other stories gush too much even for me.

But where he succeeds, where his voice and his subject matter and this particular reader find harmony, I find the stories have lived in me ever since that first reading. . . .

And most of all, the story Bradbury chose to lead off the collection of his own favorites among his work: **"The Night,"** which perhaps means so much to me because I'm just learning how much a parent is lost when a child is lost.

Indeed, that is Bradbury's magic: far more often than you will think possible, he will find the inexpressible things you most deeply know, and from then on the name of that thing will be his story. (p. 5)

> Orson Scott Card, *"From the Dark Carnival to the Machineries of Joy,"* in Book World—The Washington Post, *November 2, 1980, pp. 4-5.*

EDWARD J. GALLAGHER

The Martian Chronicles (1950) is one of those acknowledged science fiction masterpieces which has never received detailed scholarly study as a whole. Its overall theme is well known. Clifton Fadiman says that Bradbury is telling us we are gripped by a technology-mania, that "the place for space travel is in a book, that human beings are still mental and moral children who cannot be trusted with the terrifying toys they have by some tragic accident invented." Richard Donovan says that Bradbury's fear is that "man's mechanical aptitudes, his incredible ability to pry into the secrets of the physical universe, may be his fatal flaw." And from "we Earth Men have a talent for ruining big, beautiful things" to "science ran too far ahead of us too quickly, and the people got lost in a mechanical wilderness . . . emphasizing machines instead of how to run machines," *The Martian Chronicles* itself provides an ample supply of clear thematic statements.

The structural unity of the novel's twenty-six stories, however, is usually overlooked or ignored. Six of the stories were published before Bradbury submitted an outline for *The Martian Chronicles* to Doubleday in June 1949. Thus, while individual stories have been praised, discussed, and anthologized out of context, it has been widely assumed that the collection, though certainly not random, has only a vague chronological and thematic unity. (p. 55)

The Martian Chronicles may not be a novel, but it is certainly more than just a collection of self-contained stories. Bradbury, for instance, revised **"The Third Expedition"** for collection in the *Chronicles,* adding material about the first two expeditions and drastically changing the ending. *The Martian Chronicles* has the coherence of, say, Hemingway's *In Our Time.* The ordering of stories has a significance that goes beyond chronology and which creates a feeling of unity and coherence; thus it almost demands to be read and treated as though it were a novel. (p. 56)

To facilitate discussion, the twenty-six stories in *The Martian Chronicles* may be divided into three sections. The seven stories in the first section, from **"Rocket Summer"** to **"And the Moon Be Still as Bright,"** deal with the initial four attempts to successfully establish a footing on Mars. The fifteen stories in the second section, from **"The Settlers"** to **"The Watchers,"** span the rise and fall of the Mars colony; and the four stories in the final section, from **"The Silent Towns"** to **"The Million-Year Picnic,"** linger on the possible regeneration of the human race after the devastating atomic war.

Bradbury's purpose in this first group of stories is to belittle man's technological achievement, to show us that supermachines do not make supermen. The terse power of **"Rocket Summer"** is filtered through three humiliating defeats before man is allowed to celebrate a victory. In fact, "celebration," the goal men seek as much as physical settlement, is the main motif in this section. Bradbury uses it to emphasize the pernicious quality of human pride. The stories build toward the blatant thematic statement of **"And the Moon Be Still as Bright"**; but this story is artistically poor, since the section does not depend on it, either for meaning or for effect. Next to a sense of delayed anticipation, the strength of the section stems from a sense of motion; the stories of the three defeats are not repetitious of one another. Bradbury varies both style and tone in **"Ylla,"** **"The Earth Men,"** and **"The Third Expedition,"** increasing the intensity from the mellow and the comic to the savage. In this way, **"And the Moon Be Still as Bright"** serves a cohesive function as the climax of and clarification of views which we have already felt. Another significant motif in this section comes from the phantasmagoric atmosphere that Bradbury associates with Mars. This trapping, this "accident" of his fantasy, produces clashes of dream and reality, sanity and insanity, which serve functionally to underscore Bradbury's desire for us to view technology from a different perspective. (pp. 56-7)

The second section of *The Martian Chronicles,* the fifteen stories from **"The Settlers"** to **"The Watchers,"** spans the rise and fall of the Mars colony. Because of the large span of events, this section seems less taut, less focused and more discursive than the first section. Whereas the very short stories in the first section (**"Rocket Summer,"** **"The Summer Night,"** **"The Taxpayer"**) were stories in their own right, as well as introductions to the main stories about the three expeditions, here the nine very short stories seem burdened with the "history" of the settlement. As a result, the flow is a bit choppy. The most important stories in the section are **"Night Meeting"** and **"The Martian,"** and the purpose of the section is to point to mankind's hostility toward difference—toward otherness, another manifestation of human pride—as the factor which determines the quality of colonization. (p. 65)

The four stories [of the third section]—**"The Silent Towns,"** **"The Long Years,"** **"There Will Come Soft Rains,"** and **"The Million-Year Picnic"**—linger on the possible regeneration of the human race after a devastating atomic war and the consequent evacuation of Mars. Bradbury does not allow hope to come easy, and when it does, it comes almost grudgingly. Just as Bradbury filters the power of **"Rocket Summer"** through three unsuccessful expeditions, he squeezes optimism about a second beginning on Mars—a really new life—through three resounding defeats. **"The Silent Towns"** is a parody of the familiar new-Adam-and-Eve motif in science fiction, which comically thwarts notions of a new race of humans. **"The Long Years"** and **"There Will Come Soft Rains"** focus on the ma-

chines, the sons of men, which inherit the Earth. Both stories end with meaningless mechanical rituals which mock the sentience that gave them life. *The Martian Chronicles* does not turn upward until the last story, **"The Million-Year Picnic."** Only in the complete destruction of Earth, Earth history, and Earth values, plus the complete acceptance of a new identity, can hope be entertained. "It is good to renew one's wonder," says Bradbury's philosopher in the epigraph, "space travel has again made children of us all." In the context of game, vacation, and picnic, this last story entrusts the possibility of new life to a small band of transformed Earth children. (pp. 76-7)

Unless we pay close attention to the sermons of Spender [Bradbury's mouthpiece in **"And the Moon Be Still as Bright"**] and the symbolism of **"The Million-Year Picnic,"** it is easy to feel that in *The Martian Chronicles,* Bradbury is against space travel per se. Nothing could be further from the truth. Over and over again in his personal statements, Bradbury has stressed that space is our destiny. Speaking as Jules Verne in an imaginary interview, Bradbury says that the function of the writer is to push the wilderness back. "We do not like this wilderness, this material universe with its own unfathomable laws which ignore our twitchings. Man will only breathe easily when he has climbed the tallest Everest of all: Space. Not because it is there, no, no, but because he must survive and survival means man's populating all the worlds of all the suns." There is only one thing that can stop this journey—the wilderness in man himself. . . . (pp. 81-2)

The threat of atomic war, kept in the background and off stage in *The Martian Chronicles,* is more on Bradbury's mind than it might appear. "Today we stand on the rim of Space," he says; "man, in his immense tidal motion is about to flow out toward far new worlds, but man must conquer the seed of his own self-destruction. Man is half-idealist, half-destroyer, and the real and terrible thing is that he can still destroy himself before reaching the stars." Perhaps, he suggests, a book for his time would be one "about man's ability to be quicker than his wars." "Sometimes there is no solution, save flight, from annihilation. When reason turns murderously unreasonable, Man has always run. . . . If but one Adam and Eve reach Mars while the entire stagecraft of Earth burns to a fine cinder, history will have been justified, Mind will be preserved, Life continued."

Bradbury, then, comes not "to celebrate the defeat of man by matter, but to proclaim his high destiny and urge him on to it." The rocket is the conqueror of Death, the "shatterer of the scythe." The proper study of God is space. Bradbury—like Jonathan Edwards, for example—is truly a moralist. Edwards said that if you believe in the certainty of a hell, it makes good sense to scare people away from it. *The Martian Chronicles* is Bradbury's hellfire-and-brimstone sermon. (p. 82)

Edward J. Gallagher, "The Thematic Structure of 'The Martian Chronicles',' " in Ray Bradbury, *edited by Martin Harry Greenberg and Joseph D. Olander, Taplinger Publishing Company, 1980, pp. 55-82.*

SARAH-WARNER J. PELL

Imagery is not a new literary device. Aristotle lauded it as the most potent way to find similarities in dissimilar things. Bradbury is especially adept with imagery. His writing style brings galactic fantasy and an incredible imagination within the grasp of the reader, especially through the use of simile and metaphor. Unfortunately for readers of science fiction, not all authors are as able as Bradbury in using either the "tied" or the "free" image. (By this bit of technicality, I mean that the tied image has a meaning or associative value that is the same or nearly the same for all of us, while the free image has various values and meanings for different people.) (pp. 187-88)

If imagery is an index to able craftsmanship, of beauty and poetry of style, Bradbury qualifies as a master. In examining three works—*S Is for Space, The Martian Chronicles,* and *I Sing the Body Electric!*—all similes and metaphors used were extracted. Since the reading and revealing of these Bradbury classics continues to be a source of wonder and delight, there is no guarantee that a simile or metaphor will not have escaped, like the evanescent Martians. We are left with well over three hundred graphically original figures of speech. This imagery is marked by originality and imagination. Typically, it is tied, in that the metaphors and similes relate to common experiences of mankind. This is not to say that Bradbury will not make up his own original verb forms from existing nonverbs or simply from sound combinations suggesting his meaning.

How do we classify such a body of material? What can we say definitively about Bradbury? (p. 188)

Middletown, dreamtown America, untouched by violence, pestilence, famine, world wars, prejudice; the idyllic small-town American boyhood, never far from nature; an American boyhood of sounds, tastes, sights, feelings of birth, life, death, seasons—this is Bradbury's touchstone for the largest portion of his imagery.

As imaginary Martians with only our chronicles and two other slim volumes, let us look at Bradbury's Hometown, U.S.A. Could it be a small Midwestern town with "candy-cheeked boys with blue agate eyes" ...? We consistently find the denizens of this galactic hometown populating space. There is the fantasy trolley, "epaulets of shimmery brass cover it, and pipings of gold.... Within, its seats prickle with cool green moss." ... There are Civil War statues, wooden Indians, trains and twelve-year-old boys. There are seasons, "summer swoons," a "marble-cream moon," autumn leaves crackling and winter: "... panes blind with frost, icicles fringing every roof ... housewives lumbering like great black bears in their furs." ... (pp. 188-89)

Long metaphoric passages in the three novels populate Hometown, U.S.A. and its inhabitants, mainly through the eyes of youth.... How can we describe colonists to another planet? "They would come like a scatter of jackstones on the marble flats beside the canals" ..., or: "small children, small seeds ... to be sown in all the Martian climes."

What about machinery, computers, and rocket ships? Again, Bradbury metaphorically bonds science not only to the familiar hometown childhood but to nature as well. The beauty of nature abounds in Bradbury's imagery. Computers?—"a school of computers that chatter in maniac chorus ... a cloud of paper confetti from one titan machine, holes punched out to perhaps record his passing, fell upon him in a whispered snow." ... "Machines that trim your soul in silhouette like a vast pair of beautiful shears, snipping away the rude brambles, the dire horns and hooves to leave a finer profile." ... In addition to the skillful manipulation of simile and metaphor, these examples illustrate the connection to Earth's nature and times.

Rockets? Rockets can be either "flowers of heat and color" or pummeling objects. The following passage from *The Mar-*

tian Chronicles shows the Earthling and Martian picture series we used earlier for images tied to nature and small towns:

> The rockets came like drums, beating in the night. The rockets came like locusts, swarming and settling in blooms of rosy smoke ... men with hammers in their hands to beat the strange world into a shape that was familiar to the eye, to bludgeon away all the strangeness, their mouths fringed with nails so they resembled steel-toothed carnivores, spitting them into their swift hands....

So closely does Bradbury weave galactic travel and interplanetary settlement to experiences on Earth that the extracted metaphor does not seem to come from science-fiction literature. (p. 189)

Somehow, as we wander through space and future time with Bradbury, we remain tethered to the town and to nature. Twelve-year-old boys empty their pockets of treasures; this metaphor is used to describe alien machinery. Baseball is an important metaphorical vehicle: "He stared at the baseball in his trembling hand, as if it were his life, an interminable ball of years strung around and around and around, but always leading back to his twelfth birthday." ... Bradbury frequently uses boyhood games in his imagery, for instance, "the entire planet Earth became a muddy baseball tossed away." ...

As common as childhood games for Bradbury is the mirror: "Heat snapped mirrors like the brittle winter ice" ... or "In his bureau mirror he saw a face made of June dandelions and July apples and warm summer-morning milk" ... and, importantly: "The sand whispered and stirred like an image in a vast, melting mirror." ... This combination of the melting mirror brings us to another important image for Bradbury— melting: "The waves broke on the shore, silent mirrors, heaps of melting, whispering glass." ... Bradbury uses the simile of bones melting like gold, knees melting, a girl melting like a crystal figurine, melting like lime sherbet, people melting like metal, deserts melting to yellow wax, and spacemen, drained of rocket fever, melting through the floor. (p. 190)

People, star travelers—what are they like? How do they feel? "The world swarms with people, each one drowning, but each swimming a different stroke to the far shore," Bradbury tells us.... In imagery, Bradbury describes humans as great ships of men, red-shagged hounds, a chemist's scale, litmus paper, as an insect, a beetle, metallic and sharp, a hawk, "finished and stropped like a razor by the swift life he had lived" ..., a tobacco-smoking bear. He is remarkably gentle with the elderly, describing one man as a "blind old sheepherder-saint" ... and an old lady who "gestured her cane, like an ancient goddess." ... Withering apples in a bin and the hammer blows of the years shattering faces into a million wrinkles, describe the aging process as faces toll away the years. An old lady is viewed as "skittering quick as a gingham lizard." There are dry and crackling people and dried-apricot people. Remember the library, appearing in imagery several times. You know the librarian, Bradbury suggests:

> a woman you often heard talking to herself off in the dark dust-stacks with a whisper like turned pages, a woman who glided as if on hidden wheels.

> She came carrying her soft lamp of face, lighting her way with her glance. (*Sing* ...)

Maids or live-in sitters or teachers don't fare as well; they are characterized with this metaphor: ''. . . a crosscut saw grabbing against the grain. Handaxes and hurricanes best described them. Or, conversely, they were all fallen trifle, damp soufflé.'' . . . And, *some* people in groups . . . ''with everything well on its way to Safety, the Spoil-Funs, the people with mercurochrome for blood and iodine-colored eyes, come now to set up their Moral Climates and dole out goodness to everyone.'' . . . More hopefully for the human condition, however, ''good friends trade hairballs all the time, give gifts of mutual dismays and so are rid of them.'' . . .

In describing human emotion and thought, Bradbury again draws on nature. Adventure and excitement become dancing fire; rage is sour water in the mouth. Fear is a cold rock, a winter chill. Joy is a white blossom or a downpour of soft summer rain. Pain is a great impacted wisdom tooth. (p. 191)

Not knowing Bradbury at all, our Martian observer could detect an interest in photography, the theater, and, most certainly, science—simply through his use of imagery in these categories. As the famous author from Tau Ceti reveals his interest in geology through this startling metaphor, translated into Intergalactic—''The zxboric captain's thought weighed as the pstoralic cliffs with as many zenotropic caves of mystery''—so Bradbury centers similes around science; circuits; lubricating oil; eyes like small, blue electric bulbs; thoughts like gusts of pure oxygen; bitterness like black-green acid, as well as references to astronomy.

We can identify Shakespeare's influence in this image: ''they kept glancing over their shoulders . . . as if at any moment, Chaos herself might unleash her dogs from there.'' . . . Greek classics are evident in similes using the Fates, the Arcadian silo, Apollo's chariot, and the Delphic caves. We find similes whose vehicle is *Moby-Dick.* . . . [Other passages] reveal how the Hometown Library served to enrich the imagery. . . . (p. 192)

A last major category of metaphor and simile in the three novels we are discussing is Biblical or religious in nature. In general, the religious references are vengeful, negative ones. ''Oh, oh. Here he comes, Moses crossing a Black Sea of bile.'' . . . Helicopters and bus fares are likened to manna. Old Testament characters such as Delilah and Baal appear in simile. Metaphorically we find, ''One God of the machines to say, you Lazarus-elevator, rise up! You hovercraft, be reborn! And anoint them with leviathan oils, tap them with magical wrench and send them forth to almost eternal lives.'' . . . (p. 193)

Whether Martian or Earthling, science fiction fan or not, one comes away enriched by the creative language and style of Bradbury. He is a master of imagery, the implied analogy. In metaphorical use he most often compares both the qualities and the emotions evoked in humans by an ideal hometown and nature. He finds compelling similarities in dissimilar objects and events. He is a master of the simile, which is usually tied to earthly associations and is described concretely. As with the metaphor, hometown and nature are the most common vehicles employed in his construction of simile.

There is no doubt that, like it or not, after examining Bradbury's use of simile and metaphor in conducting us on our galactic tours, other science-fiction writing seems anemic and one-dimensional. Not only can we, the readers, tell a good bit about Bradbury—his childhood, hometown, relationship to nature and such disparate experiences and interests as theater, photography, science and religion—but Bradbury, using these stylistic forms of imagery, makes other worlds and far-flung reaches of space seem as understandable as our own back yards.

The adroit use of images seems to show that the author, with consummate skill and originality, makes his science fiction reach far beyond the banal, pedestrian ''pulp,'' beyond the stereotype ''blast-'em-up'' future fiction. Bradbury brought respectability to science fiction. Beyond this, his fertile imagination, as evidenced in his use of simile and metaphor, creates vivid images. To continue the juxtaposition of Martian and Earthling, the Martian grasps Hometown, U.S.A.—its sights, smells, sounds, tastes, and feelings—while the Earthling feels at home among the stars.

Two metaphors of Bradbury's seem to sum up the man and his style: ''. . . I leapt high and dove deep down into the vast ocean of Space.'' . . . But ''. . . I was tethered to heaven by the longest, I repeat, longest kite string in the entire history of the world!'' (pp. 193-94)

> Sarah-Warner J. Pell, ''Style Is the Man: Imagery in Bradbury's Fiction,'' in Ray Bradbury, *edited by Martin Harry Greenberg and Joseph D. Olander, Taplinger Publishing Company, 1980, pp. 186-94.*

DONALD WATT

''It was a pleasure to burn,'' begins Bradbury's *Fahrenheit 451*. ''It was a special pleasure to see things eaten, to see things blackened and *changed*.'' In the decade following Nagasaki and Hiroshima, Bradbury's eye-catching opening for his dystopian novel assumes particular significance. America's nuclear climax to World War II signalled the start of a new age in which the awesome powers of technology, with its alarming dangers, would provoke fresh inquiries into the dimensions of man's potentiality and the scope of his brutality. . . . The opening paragraph of Bradbury's novel immediately evokes the consequences of unharnessed technology and contemporary man's contented refusal to acknowledge these consequences.

In short, *Fahrenheit 451* (1953) raises the question posed by a number of contemporary anti-utopian novels. In one way or another, Huxley's *Ape and Essence* (1948), Orwell's *Nineteen Eighty-Four* (1948), Vonnegut's *Player Piano* (1952), Miller's *A Canticle for Leibowitz* (1959), Hartley's *Facial Justice* (1960), and Burgess's *A Clockwork Orange* (1962) all address themselves to the issue of technology's impact on the destiny of man. In this sense, Mark R. Hillegas is right in labeling *Fahrenheit 451* ''almost the archetypal anti-utopia of the new era in which we live.'' Whether, what, and how to burn in Bradbury's book are the issues—as implicit to a grasp of our age as electricity—which occupy the center of the contemporary mind.

What is distinctive about *Fahrenheit 451* as a work of literature, then, is not what Bradbury says but how he says it. With Arthur C. Clarke, Bradbury is among the most poetic of science fiction writers. Bradbury's evocative, lyrical style charges *Fahrenheit 451* with a sense of mystery and connotative depth that go beyond the normal boundaries of dystopian fiction. Less charming, perhaps, than *The Martian Chronicles, Fahrenheit 451* is also less brittle. More to the point, in *Fahrenheit 451* Bradbury has created a pattern of symbols that richly convey the intricacy of his central theme. Involved in Bradbury's burning is the overwhelming problem of modern science: as man's shining inventive intellect sheds more and more light on the truths of the universe, the increased knowledge he thereby acquires, if abused, can ever more easily fry his planet to a cinder. Burning as constructive energy, and burning as apocalyptic catastrophe, are the symbolic poles of Bradbury's novel. Ultimately, the book probes in symbolic terms the puzzling, divisive nature of man as a creative/destructive creature. *Fahrenheit 451* thus becomes a book which injects originality into a literary subgenre that can grow worn and hackneyed. It is the only major symbolic dystopia of our time.

The plot of *Fahrenheit 451* is simple enough. In Bradbury's future, Guy Montag is a fireman whose job it is to burn books and, accordingly, discourage the citizenry from thinking about anything except four-wall television. He meets a young woman whose curiosity and love of natural life stir dissatisfaction with his role in society. He begins to read books and to rebel against the facade of diversions used to seal the masses away from the realities of personal insecurity, officially condoned violence, and periodic nuclear war. He turns against the authorities in a rash and unpremeditated act of murder, flees their lethal hunting party, and escapes to the country. At the end of the book he joins a group of self-exiled book-lovers who hope to preserve the great works of the world despite the opposition of the masses and a nuclear war against an unspecified enemy.

In such bare detail, the novel seems unexciting, even a trifle inane. But Bradbury gives his story impact and imaginative focus by means of symbolic fire. Appropriately, fire is Montag's world, his reality. Bradbury's narrative portrays events as Montag sees them, and it is natural to Montag's way of seeing to regard his experiences in terms of fire. This is a happy and fruitful arrangement by Bradbury, for he is thereby able to fuse character development, setting, and theme into a whole. Bradbury's symbolic fire gives unity, as well as stimulating depth, to *Fahrenheit 451.*

Bradbury dramatizes Montag's development by showing the interactions between his hero and other characters in the book; the way Bradbury plays with reflections of fire in these encounters constantly sheds light on key events. Clarisse, Mildred, the old woman, Beatty, Faber, and Granger are the major influences on Montag as he struggles to understand his world. The figure of Clarisse is, of course, catalytic; she is dominant in Montag's growth to awareness. The three sections into which Bradbury divides the novel are, however, most clearly organized around the leading male characters—Beatty in Part One, Faber in Part Two, and Montag himself (with Granger) in Part Three. Beatty and Faber—the one representing the annihilating function of fire, the other representing the quiet, nourishing flame of the independent creative imagination—are the poles between which Montag must find his identity, with Mildred and Clarisse reflecting the same polar opposition on another level. The men are the intellectual and didactic forces at work on Montag, while the women are the intuitive and experiential forces. Beatty articulates the system's point of view, but Mildred lives it. Faber articulates the opposition's point of view, but Clarisse lives it. Fire, color, light, darkness, and variations thereof suffuse Bradbury's account of the interplay among his characters, suggesting more subtly than straight dialogue or description the full meaning of *Fahrenheit 451.* (pp. 195-97)

From its opening portrait of Montag as a singed salamander, to its concluding allusion to the Bible's promise of undying light for man, *Fahrenheit 451* uses a rich body of symbols emanating from fire to shed a variety of illuminations on future and contemporary man.

To be sure, the novel has its vulnerable spots. For one thing, Montag's opposition is not very formidable. Beatty is an ar-

ticulate spokesman for the authorities, but he has little of the power to invoke terror that Orwell's O'Brien has. The Mechanical Hound is a striking and sinister gadget; but for all its silent stalking, it conveys considerably less real alarm than a pack of aroused bloodhounds. What is genuinely frightening is the specter of that witless mass of humanity in the background who feed on manhunts televised live and a gamey version of highway hit-and-run. For another thing, the reader may be unsettled by the vagueness with which Bradbury defines the conditions leading to the nuclear war. Admittedly, his point is that such a lemming-like society, by its very irresponsibility, will ultimately end in destruction. But the reader is justifiably irritated by the absence of any account of the country's political situation or of the international power structure. The firemen are merely enforcers of noninvolvement, not national policy-makers. The reader would like to know something more about the actual controllers of Beatty's occupation. Who, we wonder, is guarding the guardians?

Probably a greater problem than either of these is what some readers may view as a certain evasiveness on Bradbury's part. Presumably, the controversies and conflicts brought on by reading books have led to the system of mass ignorance promulgated by Beatty. Even with this system, though, man drifts into nuclear ruin. Bradbury glosses over the grim question raised by other dystopian novelists of his age: if man's individuality and knowledge bring him repeatedly to catastrophe, should not the one be circumscribed and the other forbidden? Such novels as *A Canticle for Leibowitz, A Clockwork Orange,* and *Facial Justice* deal more realistically with this problem than does *Fahrenheit 451.* Although the religious light shining through Montag from the Bible is a fitting climax to the book's use of symbolism, Bradbury's novel does risk lapsing at the very close into a vague optimism.

Yet *Fahrenheit 451* remains a notable achievement in postwar dystopian fiction. . . . The book's weaknesses derive in part from that very symbolism in which its strength and originality are to be found. If *Fahrenheit 451* is vague in political detail, it is accordingly less topical and therefore more broadly applicable to the dilemmas of the twentieth century as a whole. Like the nineteenth-century French symbolists, Bradbury's purpose is to evoke a mood, not to name particulars. His connotative language is far more subtle, his novel far more of one piece, than Huxley's rambling nightmare, *Ape and Essence.* Though the novel lacks the great impact of *Nineteen Eighty-Four,* Kingsley Amis is right when he says that *Fahrenheit 451* is "superior in conciseness and objectivity" to Orwell's anti-utopian novel. If *Fahrenheit 451* poses no genuinely satisfying answers to the plight of postindustrial man, neither is the flight to the stars at the end of *A Canticle for Leibowitz* much of a solution. We can hardly escape from ourselves. By comparison with Bradbury's novel, *Facial Justice* is tepid and *A Clockwork Orange* overdone. On the whole, *Fahrenheit 451* comes out as a distinctive contribution to the speculative literature of our times, because in its multiple variations on its fundamental symbol, it demonstrates that dystopian fiction need not exclude the subtlety of poetry. (pp. 212-13)

> *Donald Watt, "Burning Bright: 'Fahrenheit 451' as Symbolic Dystopia," in* Ray Bradbury, *edited by Martin Harry Greenberg and Joseph D. Olander, Taplinger Publishing Company, 1980, pp. 195-213.*

TOM EASTON

[We] have a prime candidate for a "Rip-Off of the Year Award": *The Ghosts of Forever.* This oversized, $60 book contains five poems, a short story, and an essay on God in SF by Ray Bradbury, together with 35 illustrations by the Argentine artist Aldo Sessa. And that's all. . . . Bradbury's essay focuses on what he himself has done with God and SF. His poems are typical in flavor, but they are not his best; they lack the pith I have found and enjoyed in his work before. The short story is an abortion. Slickly done, it offends by illogic—on Mars, the natives alter their forms in accord with the dreams of human colonists; one night, a Martian enters the church and meets a priest as the crucified Christ; the priest takes the Martian as the Second Coming at first, but then accepts his explanation, although he refuses to release him until he promises to return next Easter in the same guise. Bradbury's priest is venal and self-deluded—he confuses image and reality and responds more to the image—and Bradbury seems to approve, to present him as an epiphany of faith.

> *Tom Easton, in a review of "The Ghosts of Forever," in* Analog Science Fiction/Science Fact, *Vol. CII, No. 3, March 1, 1982, p. 170.*

JACK HAND

[*Dinosaur Tales*] is only for those who must have everything published by Bradbury. Aside from the foreword by Ray Harryhausen and an introduction by Bradbury, there are only three new pieces among the six pieces collected here. Two of them, **"Lo, the Dear, Daft Dinosaur!"** and **"What If I Said the Dinosaur's Not Dead"** are doggerel verse which argue strongly against the existence of a viable SF poetry. The third, **"Besides a Dinosaur, Whatta Ya Wanna Be When You Grow Up?"** is a sentimental story that smells strongly of dandelion wine.

The strongest story in the book is the classic, **"The Fog Horn,"** which has been much anthologized and deals with the last dinosaur lured from the depths by a new and special fog horn, only to wreck the lighthouse when he discovers his love object is man-made. (p. 17)

> *Jack Hand, in a review of "Dinosaur Tales," in* Science Fiction & Fantasy Book Review, *No. 18, October, 1983, pp. 17-18.*

LAHNA F. DISKIN

Bradbury's gothic story [*Something Wicked This Way Comes*] . . . about children's sanctity and victory over evil is still appealing. In *Something Wicked This Way Comes* he gives us the Green Town not of summer as in *Dandelion Wine*—but of autumn when it is visited by a pair of underworlders who run a sinister carnival. The children are two boys whose names, Will Holloway and Jim Nightshade, are thematically symbolic. Born only minutes apart on Halloween and best friends, they are opposites. Together, however, they form a vulnerable yet invincible brotherhood. They combine bright simplicity and dark complexity. Like Bradbury's typical boys, they resist obedience to the orderly predictable existence of the adults in their lives. They frequent Rolfe's Moon Meadow. . . . There they are awed witnesses to the arrival of the Pandemonium Shadow Show run by Cooger and Dark who, as agents of Satan, afflict the weak and gullible.

With the Mirror Maze, the lunatic carousel and other diabolical amusements, the autumn demons thrive on human vanities, cravings and fantasies. Bradbury shows how the boys' salvation follows their "patterns of grace." Their ordeal in resisting the perverse attractions of the carnival proves their fortuity as in-

nocents. Unlike the adults who succumb, they withstand the atrocious marvels and destroy Cooger and Dark. In Bradbury's morality "play," Cooger and Dark perpetuate a fantasy world grotesque and lethal, because they symbolize time deranged. Their ministry of evil is defeated by children with enough goodness and joy.

> *Lahna F. Diskin, in a review of "Something Wicked This Way Comes," in* Science Fiction & Fantasy Book Review, *No. 18, October, 1983, p. 18.*

ANDREW ANDREWS

Although the "illustrated story" format in Bradbury's collection of his favorite own *Dinosaur Tales* is garish and unnerving, the collection as a whole is notable for his own spiffy reminiscences of his love of the beasts. While **"A Sound of Thunder"** and **"The Fog Horn"** bring us intensely believable milieus, braced with conviction, tales such as **"Besides A Dinosaur, Whatta Ya Wanna Be When You Grow Up?"** are mushy and cornball, made for only the most childish reader.

But don't be mistaken. Bradbury's enchanting obsession with the lore is alluring. He gets to you—in simple ways he shows you how to marvel over these awesome, startling creatures. There are poems that tell a strange rapture. And his happy-go-lucky writing is tarnished only by the paint-by-number running illustrations. Ignore them, but take in what Bradbury revels about.

> *Andrew Andrews, in a review of "Dinosaur Tales," in* Science Fiction Review, *Vol. 13, No. 1, February, 1984, p. 38.*

KATHLEEN MAIO

The pulp mystery magazines that flourished between the 1920s and the 1940s fostered one of the great formulas of detective writing, the hard-boiled school. School is an apt word, too. For it is in the pulps that many writers—including legendary figures like Dashiell Hammett and Raymond Chandler—learned and polished their craft. Ray Bradbury studied in that school. Although best known for haunting tales of science fiction, Bradbury apprenticed himself, in part, to the mystery pulps during the forties. *A Memory of Murder* . . . brings together for the first time Bradbury's early mystery tales.

It should surprise no one to learn that these are stories of "geeks" and demons rather than tough-guy private eyes. Bradbury gives us the interior monologue of a corpse and vengeful butchery among blind men. The opening story, **"The Small Assassin,"** is a truly shocking tale that gives new meaning to the phrase "post-partum depression." Although many of the stories are far from deathless classics, they will interest Bradbury fans, offering insights into the author's style and settings (like a carnival sideshow) used so effectively in later work. (p. 582)

> *Kathleen Maio, "Murder in Print," in* Wilson Library Bulletin, *Vol. 58, No. 8, April, 1984, pp. 582-83, 607.*

WILLIAM F. TOUPONCE

Ray Bradbury is known primarily as a writer of science fiction, fantasy, and children's literature, and he is especially noted for two books which he wrote during the 1950s, *Fahrenheit*

451 and *The Martian Chronicles*. When critics today discuss his work, it is usually in the context of genre theory. Not surprisingly, in view of certain aspects of surrealism in his writings that it is my purpose in this paper to present, Bradbury does not fare very well at the hands of these critics. He is often accused of narrative inconsistencies and poor knowledge of science (if not protofascist revulsion towards progress and technology). For example, the Marxist-structuralist critic Darko Suvin consigns Bradbury's writings to a monstrous and misshapen subgenre of real science fiction, ''science-fantasy,'' which according to him does not use scientific logic for a validation of the story's premises, but only as an excuse or rationalization that is later abandoned at the author's whim. Actually, and as I have demonstrated elsewhere, this is only the apparent truth about Bradbury's work. And it is at least ironic (especially when one considers that Suvin's poetics of science fiction claims to study *metamorphoses* of science fiction) that his generic logic of antinomies never allows him to consider the possibility that Bradbury's ''whims'' may be intended to direct the reader towards surrealist imaginings—or even surrational imaginings—to use a phrase coined by Gaston Bachelard that André Breton employed when he discussed surrealism's relationship to scientific knowledge.

In my opinion, Bradbury's work should be studied first for its rich imaginative vision, and secondarily for the way in which it links up with the larger literary movements of the twentieth century, surrealism and existentialism. While it is certainly relevant to take a generic approach to individual stories or novels, I would rate this approach last in terms of real value, for too often we find a critic using a text by Bradbury to exemplify a notion of what science fiction is, whereas another critic with a different set of conceptual schemata will cite the same text as an example of what science fiction is not. In short, at the current state of our knowledge of this genre and how it demands to be read, everyone is his own Aristotle. On the other hand, it has been obvious for some time now to writers of surrealist inspiration that such themes as telepathy (Bradbury's use of which in *The Martian Chronicles* still baffles theorists who are bent on creating a generic logic) and paranoia are a shared common interest with writers of science fiction.

Yet if the foreshadowing of an individual future and telepathic communication are themes essential to both surrealism and science fiction, the surrealist imagination surpasses the limits of any generic logic. Its basic structures of consciousness, and I would argue that they are delusion, dream and reverie, are expressed in many different literary forms. So if the concept of genre is going to be of use to us in discussing Bradbury's work, it must be modified to allow the claims of surrealism to overcome antinomies to be considered. I cannot give a precise account here of how this might be done, nor do I wish to. My simple aim is to measure the degree to which Bradbury approaches the central concerns of surrealism. In short, I believe we can achieve a more balanced view of Bradbury's work by arguing that he is a surrealist in science fiction and not vice versa. (pp. 228-29)

From the presentation in [Michel] Carrouges' book [*André Breton and the Basic Concepts of Surrealism*] it would seem that there was ample precedent for the acceptance of at least some science fiction writing as embodying authentic surrealist goals at the time when Bradbury's work was first translated in French. No French critic of the 1950s ever asserted that there was any influence of surrealism on Bradbury's work, however. Rather, he seems to have discovered surrealist territory entirely on his own and spontaneously, manifesting a kind of native American surrealism. Nor should this be surprising, since the surrealists have always said that the desires they speak of are eternal, and that every man has access to them. (p. 230)

The Martian Chronicles, which depicts the colonization and destruction of the nearly mystical and telepathic Martian civilization by successive waves of Earthmen, is not to be understood as a simple reflection of social and economic conditions. Yet it is nevertheless haunted by social upheavals which permit the reader's consciousness to have a glimpse of sudden fissures that accompany them. Cannily observing that many works of science fiction ostensibly about the future seem to offer us a retrospective glance as well, Carrouges explains that Bradbury's *Martian Chronicles* (and other works of science fiction; Carrouges here extends his argument to include the entire genre) expresses the guilt of the twentieth century's destruction of exotic and primitive civilizations. The ruins of Bradbury's Mars are a haunted domain, a dark mirror where the reader projects that which haunts him in his deepest secrets. . . . (pp. 230-31)

Carrouges' argument is cogent, if at times narrowly skirting a reductive stance, because it reveals that Bradbury's Mars is intended to haunt the reader in a surrealist fashion, speaking to him of his deepest desires and consequently liberating him from his deepest repressions. Bradbury's Martians thus represent our own lost oneiric being, the dreaming pole of our minds, which is normally suppressed by rationality. But outside of a short discussion of the relationship of telepathy and point of view, Carrouges does not discuss the novel's poetics. As interesting as this kind of analysis would be in terms of the central concerns of surrealism, for reasons of space I cannot offer it here. Let me simply draw on some observations made by another reviewer of Bradbury, Michel Deutsch, whose attempt to characterize Bradbury's imagination in a grouping of six of his works complements that of Carrouges' generic approach to one work. . . . His science fiction is . . . , according to Deutsch, characterized by . . . openness, which combines in a highly original alliance the ambiguities of the dream and the scientific hypothesis. But Bradbury is a surrealist for Deutsch primarily because of the situation of the object in his poetics, i.e., how Bradbury transforms those technological gadgets that populate his imaginary worlds. The future for Bradbury is essentially a poetic object, and his narratives unfold around them in an inspired surrealist vision. . . . (p. 231)

[Electric fireflies] begin a long list of objects gleaned by Deutsch from the writings of Bradbury and which seem to him to evince a marked turning away of the object from its functional use, liberating it and lending it a sort of sublimated quality which reaches an absolute stage in *The Martian Chronicles* (where golden fruit grows from crystal walls of houses that turn, like sunflowers, to follow the sun). But although Deutsch points out that they offer an oneiric support for the reader's own surrealist imaginings, he does not analyze them in a narrative context. . . . [Here] again we have an instance of a critic writing in a different literary milieu who strongly affirms Bradbury's affinity with surrealism. The contradictions manifestly committed by the author in his descriptions of Mars pose no problem, therefore, to Deutsch's understanding; it is not a question of astronomy, of pure scientific logic, but of the landscape of a dream. (p. 232)

Bradbury's own statements about the creative ambiance of his work approach surrealist notions of automatic writing and the waking dream. In giving his advice to other writers, like the surrealists he insists that all men have direct access to the marvelous if they will just try to make contact with the subconscious. Quoting Coleridge about the flow of the writing process and the streamy nature of association which thinking curbs and rudders, he declares a "Middle Way" which resolves for him the antinomies of writing "literary" as opposed to "commercial" fiction. He advises the aspiring writer to relax and concentrate on the unconscious message. This way of writing shorts out the mind's critical and categorizing activities, allowing the subconscious to speak. Then, he says, the writer will begin to see himself in his work in a kind of dreamlike state: "At night the very phosphorescence of his insides will throw long shadows on the wall." This oneiric atmosphere described by Bradbury is reminiscent of certain remarks made by Breton concerning the state of receptivity required of the surrealist writer. Bradbury describes his writing of science fiction as plunging into a wild meadow, if not a dizzying descent into the self. For Bradbury, writing is human desire let run, and the writer's sole task (although he allows for some revisions later) is first of all to enable self and world to interact in a state of "dynamic relaxation" and lucid reverie. He regards this way of writing, finally, as the only guarantee of authenticity:

> What do you think of the world? You, the prism, measure the light of the world; it burns through your mind to throw a different spectroscopic reading onto white paper than anyone else anywhere can throw.
>
> Let the world burn through you. Throw the prism light, white hot, on paper. Make your own individual spectroscopic reading.
>
> Then you, a new Element, are discovered, charted, named!

Prominent in this passage with its visual metaphor of the prism is the sense of surrealist discovery, suggesting, indeed, a parallel with scientific discovery: a new element is discovered, but not predicted beforehand. Self and world together make a new Element. At first glance, though, we may think that Bradbury is recommending that the writer become involved with visual images that he should try to transcribe—and this goes counter to Breton's strong rejection of the seeking of immediate enjoyment in one's images produced during the writing process. Breton feared that these images would block the flow of automatism, and he was convinced that Rimbaud and Lautréamont had no prior enjoyment of what they had still to describe. They did not understand the sibylline voices they listened to any better than we do when we first read them. In surrealism, Breton says, illumination comes afterwards.

But actually, the element most active in Bradbury's text is fire, and elsewhere in the same volume he expresses his idea more forcefully. During writing itself one must "explode—fly apart—disintegrate," just as in surrealism, a total disintegration of the mind is required to enter the avenues and dazzling zones of the marvelous. Even more revealing of Bradbury's surrealist desires, if one thinks of all the prestige that Breton gave to childhood and the manner in which children invest words and objects with a magical love, are these remarks concerning the writing of his semiautobiographical novel of childhood in an American small town, *Dandelion Wine:*

> . . . in my early twenties I floundered into a word-association process in which I simply got out of bed each morning, walked to my desk, and put down any word or series of words that happened along in my head.
>
> (pp. 232-33)

Written during the 1950s also, *Dandelion Wine* is arguably the purest surrealist text Bradbury has produced (in the same sense that it is free of any admixture of science fiction, gothic horror, etc.). Clearly, Bradbury's remarks in the passage describe the receiving of a linguistic message from the subconscious which is then later piloted and elaborated by the conscious mind in active cooperation with it. In short, the need to observe and to try to discern the play of dreamlike elements and the very subtle reintroduction of consciousness into the heart of automatism—just the very kind of intelligent surrealism advocated by Breton himself—lie at the heart of Bradbury's poetic practice. . . . *Dandelion Wine* is a text of pure reveries, organized by oneiric scenes of dandelion winemaking. This beneficial elixir becomes the substance of archetypal childhood which attracts the reader's own happy imagination. . . . [But] *Dandelion Wine* is not a work of science fiction. If it embodies surrealist structures of consciousness in their unadulterated form (no pun intended), that is because Bradbury is a surrealist in nearly everything he writes. . . . **"The Rocket Man"** (1951) . . . is one of Bradbury's earliest science fiction stories in which we can detect an interior world of magical preoccupations. Indeed, it deals—"innocently," to be sure—with several desires and central themes of surrealism. There is first of all the desire to fuse conscious and unconscious in a new concrete synthesis that leads to the possession of a world of marvels. But also, as in any attempt by surrealism to recover lost powers of imagination, there is the danger that the sun of rational awareness will destroy reverie. The mind must allow itself to be so strongly attracted, so rapidly borne along by the flow of automatism that it will dash after it in breathless pursuit with no desire to go back. (pp. 234-35)

The focus of the narrator's reverie towards childhood is his father's uniform, no utilitarian object to him, but one charged with the antinomies of light and dark. In his imagination it seems a dark nebula with little faint stars glowing through it. It is this object which is transformed in the story and which forms the pivot around which the narrative turns, for it lies directly on the axis of desire that organizes the characters and their roles. . . . The fabric of the cloth, its textuality as it were, organizes and constellates all the metaphors, those points of light along the boy's itinerary. It also functions phenomenologically as an unconscious complex, an organizer of psychic energy, for the nebula is mostly black, unconscious, although it bears within it points of light which offer the promise of conscious transformation if developed surrealistically into the worlds in themselves.

In this story the narrator tells how he wanted to become a rocket man like his father who travels among the distant stars and dangerous planets and who was seldom home on Earth. A basic Freudian question in the story revolves around whether or not the boy's desire will be defined by the mother, who wants to keep the father at home, or by the father through the mechanism of identification. But although this mechanism is set up in the story, the boy comes to define, through reverie, his own desire. The uniform is obviously involved in this play of desire because it is an object never displayed at home and which the boy wants to see. However, the boy's mother and father are both anxious that the boy not take up this life of sometimes intense loneliness and danger, but the boy, full of the allure of space travel and rockets, can only think of those faraway places his father visits.

At times the boy feels deprived and rejected because the father never brings him any gifts from these miraculous places. . . . At any rate, the Earthbound boy has to trade the ordinary objects he likes with other boys in order to get these surreal ones. One night, when the father has just returned from a tour of duty in the solar system and both parents are asleep in bed, the boy steals his father's travel case which contains his uniform, still smelling of metal and space, fire and time. He examines it in his own private world, apart from the parents. . . . (pp. 235-36)

If we examine this movement of reverie-consciousness a bit more closely, we discover that as the boy begins to knead the fabric of his dreams, the "dark stuff" in his warm hands, he smells traces of several worlds: Venus, Mars, Mercury—and we can assume here also the presence of the archetypal elements giving rise to many a surrealist cosmology; I mean, of course, fire, earth, and water. As olfactory images they bring about a released spontaneity of the imaginary in the boy's mind, the traces in the black fabric serving to generate an aspiration toward other worlds, functioning as passive syntheses of experiences the father has lived through and in which the boy desires to participate actively.

Once the boy touches matter imaginatively, he begins to materialize his desire. . . . The boy in our story has found that malleable matter which Bachelard says offers to the imagination a marvellous dynamic equilibrium between accepting forces and refusing forces. Through reverie, he has abolished the distance between himself and the objects of his desire, transforming self and world at the same time. A dynamic joy touches matter, kneads it, makes it lighter. The boy travels from microcosm to macrocosm, penetrating those magical crystals he has sublimated into "worlds themselves." A truly successful reverie, I might add, always develops this sense of cosmic participation both in Bachelard and Bradbury.

Since later on in the story the father's rocket falls into the sun, killing him, and the sun becomes a gaze almost impossible for the mother and son to avoid, we might be tempted to think that this story concludes with a defeat of the imagination. But on the contrary, Bradbury shows us their continuing desire to live in a world created and ordered by imagination: they have breakfast at midnight, go to all-night shows and go to bed at sunrise. Thus the sun of rationality (i.e., death) does not defeat man's desires. They transform a hostile world into a habitable one by their acts of imagination.

There are, of course, surrealist objects in the story of the sort Michel Deutsch mentions. But they are all asleep, significantly, along with the parents, in the passage I have chosen for analysis. One further, perhaps most important thing, argues for this story as an embodiment of surrealist imagination. Carrouges writes that if it were possible to come up with an objective standard for fidelity to surrealist concerns, he would be tempted to find it in the image of the *clair-obscur* (literally, clear-dark), the sense that there has to be a real and authentic encounter of the night and the day in the mind, between awareness and subconsciousness. And if it is this reciprocal presence of the dark worlds appearing in the clarity of the words or the layers of immanent brightness in the dark verbal fields which must be the authentic value of the surrealist image, then we have such an image in Bradbury's "black nebula," which bears luminous motes that are signs of the highest cooperation in them of the conscious and the subconscious. I would say that in almost all of Bradbury's writings this encounter takes place, but most certainly the story I have analyzed here. (pp. 236-38)

William F. Touponce, "Some Aspects of Surrealism in the Work of Ray Bradbury," in Extrapolation, *Vol. 25, No. 3, Fall, 1984, pp. 228-38.*

ROSS THOMAS

Venice. 1950.

Venice, California. Not Italy. Not Florida.

There is wet sand on the beach. And evil fog. And there are foghorns that moan like a brontosaurus with bronchitis. There is an old dead man in the green-scummed canal. There is a detective with a secret, perhaps unspeakable, vice. The detective's name is Elmo Crumley.

Crumley is tough and cynical and hardboiled, except at the core where he is as soft and gooey as a marshmallow toasted over a driftwood fire.

But Crumley is not our hero. He is our hero's new best friend. Our hero is a Young Writer. He writes for the pulps—for *Weird Tales* and *Amazing Stories*—and hopes, one suspects, to sell something eventually to Street & Smith's classy *Unknown,* which by 1950 was called *Unknown Worlds.* . . .

Comes now the fey part. For [*Death Is a Lonely Business*] is a very fey murder mystery. Loveable, cranky, crusty, wise-cracking characters abound. And our fey Young Writer is always with us, too, screaming out the window to all the world that he has just sold a story to *The American Mercury;* dashing across the street to answer the pay phone; riding the big red streetcars late at night; typing happily away—and rapidly, one suspects—on his 1935 typewriter.

But if you grow a bit tired of fey, how about a slice of quaint? There is a possible villain who has the body of a gorgeous young boy and the face of an evil old man. There is a blind man who grows rich betting on horses he can't see—although that may be more fey than quaint. There is an aging silent movie screen goddess who goes about in her Duesenberg disguised as her own chauffeur. There is an incompetent barber who once played with Scott Joplin. And there are a lot of dead and not overly interesting victims who for the most part die off stage.

But if neither fey nor quaint is your dish, what about sentimentality? For this is a very long and sentimental mystery. Our Young Writer hero's eyes mist over when they tear down the old beach motion picture house. The razing of the Venice rollercoaster makes him mourn. . . .

But the death toll continues to mount and there is none to believe the Young Writer's claim that something sinister is afoot. This is because all of the deaths are apparently from *natural causes*! Yet he believes. He senses. He feels. And he detects. God, how he detects. And finally, at long, long last, the murderer is revealed.

Ray Bradbury's writing remains as rich and ripe as ever. When describing a woman he has his Young Writer hero think of her as being "a lovely chess game carved and set in a store window when you were a kid. She was a freshly built girl's gym, with only the faintest scent of the noon tennis dust that clings to golden thighs."

And on writing itself, our Young Writer hero is convinced that "A day without writing was a little death . . . I would fight all the way with my Remington portable which shoots more squarely, if you aim it right, than the rifle of the same name."

As for the secret, unspeakable vice that has Detective Elmo Crumley in its thrall—well, he's a closet novelist.

Ray Bradbury has dedicated this novel, his first since *Something Wicked This Way Comes,* to—among others—Raymond Chandler, Dashiell Hammett, James M. Cain, and Ross Macdonald.

I am confident that each in his own way would have read it with deep interest.

> Ross Thomas, "*Homage to the Hard-Boiled,*" in Book World—The Washington Post, *November 3, 1985, p. 7.*

GEOFFREY O'BRIEN

[*Death Is a Lonely Business*] Ray Bradbury's first novel in 23 years can be read as a meditation on his own craft; not only is the anonymous hero a thinly veiled stand-in for the young Bradbury, penniless and love-starved as he writes his early fantasy classics for Dime Detective and Weird Tales, but the plot's tangle of murders and disappearances also turns out to be an oblique projection of the hero's imaginative processes. Just how that revelation occurs would be unfair to tell, because *Death Is a Lonely Business* is also a sort of fantastic detective story, dedicated to Hammett, Chandler, Cain and Ross Macdonald, and set against the appropriately dilapidated background of Venice, Calif., in the early 50's. Unfortunately, the hardboiled genre demands a minimal aura of reality to achieve its effects, whereas Mr. Bradbury's book is so dreamy and fog-laden that we never get our bearings. His too-calculatingly eccentric characters—a grotesquely fat opera singer, a piano-playing barber, a police detective who lives in a jungle of exotic flora—never seem more than counters in a tenuous allegorical game. In fact, the author's metafictional intrusions . . . appear designed to dismantle the apparatus of fantasy, laying bare the pulleys and wiring beneath. Ray Bradbury's most devoted readers, who are many, will enjoy this close-up of his mind . . . , but the final product is unlikely to supplant the more substantial make-believe of *R Is for Rocket* or *The October Country.*

> Geoffrey O'Brien, in a review of "*Death Is a Lonely Business,*" in The New York Times Book Review, *November 3, 1985, p. 26.*

PAUL BARBER

Off in the Virgo Cluster, and only a million light years from Andromeda, on a small planet encircling a small star, and at a particular (and possibly unique) conjunction of space and time, Ray Bradbury, the distinguished author of fantasy and science fiction, has written [*Death Is a Lonely Business*]—a splendid detective novel.

His readers will see from this that he is still engaged in his lifelong quest for a literary form that will stand still for the demands that he puts on it. There was never any doubt that straight sci-fi was not such a form: Bradbury is not a sci-fi writer from the mainstream . . . but a romantic. His interest is not so much in organizing and explaining as in finding, somehow, a means of breaking through the limitations of space and time and form, a way of saying the ineffable. It is for this reason that the very idea of a literary "form" seems out of place here: The rhetoric is always bursting its bounds, and where the characters can't go, the images will. But more on them later.

The novel is set in Venice, California, in a past that is evoked rather than defined—we are in the domain of poetry, not history—and it uses the conventions of the detective novel to create something that is profoundly, fundamentally different from the detective novel. A young novelist—he is not named, but the Bradbury fan will recognize the plots of his novels—finds that strange deaths are taking place in his circle of bizarre, outrageous and utterly fascinating friends, one of whom is a detective. This is no ordinary detective, of course, but another romantic—he has an African jungle retreat for a backyard, complete with sound effects—and it is he whom the hero involves in his attempts to unravel the mystery.

These attempts are certainly exciting—Bradbury is never dull—but the reader is advised not to expect a standard detective novel. . . .

This is because the ineffable turns out to be, well, hard to express in a detective novel. In the detective novel, as a rule, the hero pursues the villain principally by means of ratiocination, which he can do because it is assumed (a) that the villain has a motive and (b) that the motive is rational. But in Bradbury's novel, the villain's motives and actions simply do not make sense on any rational level (which is not to say that they do not make sense), and the hero's thought processes are intuitive, so that ideas arrive in gestalt form. This does not always work out well in narrative: As Aristotle (and more recently, De Saussure) pointed out, language cannot escape from its linearity. Events may take place all at once, but words cannot do so without sacrificing their meaning, which is why, in storytelling, the writer is obliged to resort to narrative devices of the "meanwhile, back at the ranch" variety. And while it is characteristic of Bradbury that he seeks to transcend such limitations, his attempts to do so are not always successful. In *Death Is a Lonely Business,* for example, there are many situations in which suddenly everything is revealed to the hero, in a moment, while nothing has been revealed to the reader. Indeed: The hero himself makes a revealing comment on his peculiar and distinctive data-processing mode when he says that ". . . years back I had pasted two gummed labels on my Underwood. One read: OFFICIAL OUIJA BOARD. The other, in large letters: DON'T THINK."

Fortunately for the reader, he did not impose on himself any sanctions against imagery, because that is one of Bradbury's great strengths. . . . And if the images are sometimes uneven . . . , it might be suggested, in Bradbury's defense, that we are looking at the defects of his virtues: He is, after all, always exploring, trying to raise the veil on the unknown. Being correct is not so important as being creative.

And in this, Bradbury succeeds splendidly. The unreconstructed rationalist may not like the novel, but it is hard to see how anyone could resist the sheer ecstatic vitality of his characters, such as Constance Rattigan, the reclusive silent film star, who finds new roles in her retirement, presenting herself as her own maid and her own chauffeur. And the portrayal of Venice is poetic, even sublime, with the three-dimensionality of fine description: Something tricky and inexplicable happens to the space-time continuum, so that, even if you were never there in the '50s, you are likely to feel that you remember Venice to have been just the way he describes it. The Ouija board, it seems, along with its prejudice against rationality, has a splendid knack for poetry, description and the creation of utterly memorable characters.

Paul Barber, in a review of "Death Is a Lonely Business," in Los Angeles Times Book Review, *November 17, 1985, p. 1.*

Richard (Gary) Brautigan

1935-1984

American novelist, poet, and short story writer.

Often considered a link between the Beat movement of the 1950s and the counterculture movement of the 1960s, Brautigan is best known for his novels *Trout Fishing in America* (1967) and *In Watermelon Sugar* (1968). In his novels, Brautigan employs lyrical prose, simple syntax, and a whimsical style while exploring such themes as death, sex, violence, betrayal, loss of innocence, and the power of imagination to transform reality. His early novels, *A Confederate General from Big Sur* (1964), *Trout Fishing in America,* and *In Watermelon Sugar,* are regarded as his most important works. They are generally seen as tragicomic pastorals in which Brautigan discards such traditional features of the novel as plot, characterization, and setting in favor of a more innovative approach utilizing metafictional techniques, imaginative prose, and a carefree style and surface texture that belie the somber nature of his concerns. While some critics contend that the many brief sketches included in Brautigan's novels are slight anecdotal fragments unconnected in either theme or style, others find them to be humorous vignettes that subtly interweave his central concerns and motifs.

While some critics maintain that Brautigan is an unclassifiable writer most closely allied with Kurt Vonnegut, Jr., he has also been associated with such American authors as Henry David Thoreau, Walt Whitman, Herman Melville, and Ernest Hemingway. He shares with these authors an interest in the American pastoral myth, a respect for nature and solitude, and a propensity for unadorned language. Brautigan, however, does not share these writers' beliefs in the authenticity of the pastoral tradition. According to Neil Schmitz, Brautigan ''does not write within the pastoral mode as an advocate of its vision'' but is instead ''an ironist critically examining the myths and language of the pastoral sensibility.''

Brautigan began writing poetry in San Francisco in the 1950s. His first collection, *The Pill versus the Springhill Mine Disaster* (1968), gathers his poems from 1957 through 1968. Characterized by an inventive use of language, fanciful analogies, and an offhand tone, Brautigan's poetry established his reputation as an imaginative writer. Usually slight in length and theme, Brautigan's poems in this collection are considered among his best. With subsequent volumes, including *Rommel Drives On Deep into Egypt* (1970), *Loading Mercury with a Pitchfork* (1975), and *June 30th, June 30th* (1978), critics found Brautigan's offhandedness annoying and his poetry's slightness ultimately unsatisfying. Brautigan stated that he began writing poetry in order to learn to construct sentences in preparation for writing novels.

Brautigan's first published novel, *A Confederate General from Big Sur,* is an account of the life of Lee Mellon, a comically perverse hero and resident of Big Sur who believes himself to be a general in the confederate army. Told in a series of thinly related episodes by a self-proclaimed student of theology who attempts to analyze the punctuation of the book of Ecclesiastes, the novel is, in one sense, a humorous exploration of rebellion. Although it is the second book Brautigan wrote, *A Confederate*

General from Big Sur has also been seen as an introduction to the themes and motifs he explores with more complexity and depth in *Trout Fishing in America.*

Widely regarded as the most important of Brautigan's novels, *Trout Fishing in America* exhibits many thematic and stylistic ties to Beat literature and anticipates the disillusionment experienced years later by the youth counterculture. The novel is a disjointed story of a man, a woman, and their child, who wander across America fishing trout streams while whimsically telling tales, writing letters, and sharing unusual recipes. Yet images of violence, environmental disintegration, and futility continually invade their idyllic adventures. Critics have described *Trout Fishing in America* as a tragedy in the pastoral mode filled with eulogistic imagery and written in a whimsical style that is purposefully inappropriate to the seriousness of Brautigan's subject matter. Terrence Malley stated: ''Ultimately, Brautigan is not writing a pastoral novel in *Trout Fishing in America.* Instead, he is writing an analysis of *why* the old pastoral myth of an America of freedom and tranquility is no longer viable.''

Brautigan's third novel, *In Watermelon Sugar,* has been called his most serious work of fiction. Recorded by a calm and nameless narrator, the book reflects, without intrusion of meaning or interpretation, the narrator's surreal experiences in a successful commune called iDEATH. Except for a band of renegades who have chosen to live a life of violence amid the forbidden ruins of a previous civilization, the inhabitants of iDEATH are content with their passive and unified existence. The rebels die in ritual mass suicide, while the commune continues on. This parable-like story, called a "religious tract" by Edward Halsey Foster, has been interpreted as Brautigan's prescription for survival in the twentieth century.

In his novels of the 1970s, including *The Abortion: An Historical Romance, 1966* (1971), *The Hawkline Monster: A Gothic Western* (1974), and *Dreaming of Babylon: A Private Eye Novel, 1942* (1977), Brautigan parodies various genres of popular fiction. Brautigan became more conventional in his use of plot and characterization in these works, and while they generated some serious critical attention, they are generally considered thematically and stylistically less significant than his first three novels. In *The Tokyo-Montana Express* (1980) and *So the Wind Won't Blow It All Away* (1982), Brautigan returns to the themes and style of *Trout Fishing in America*. In *The Tokyo-Montana Express*, which comprises short, semi-autobiographical observations on such topics as society, death, and aging, Brautigan attempts to recreate the comically evocative and unusual style of his early novels and extends the alternative vision of life he originally proposed in those works. *So the Wind Won't Blow It All Away* is a fictional recollection of a childhood spent wandering from town to town during the 1940s. Filled with eccentric characters, the novel culminates in the narrator's killing of his best friend in a shooting accident that symbolizes America's loss of innocence.

(See also *CLC*, Vols. 1, 3, 5, 9, 12, 34; *Contemporary Authors*, Vols. 53-56, Vol. 113 [obituary]; *Dictionary of Literary Biography*, Vols. 2, 5; and *Dictionary of Literary Biography Yearbook: 1980, 1984*.)

JOHN D. BERRY

Richard Brautigan's stories wear thin after a while. His strength is his originality, but after 13 years the inversions and unlikely extended metaphors that caught our attention in *Trout Fishing in America* have lost their force. Maybe our attention was more easily caught in the 1960s. . . .

Brautigan's new book, *The Tokyo-Montana Express,* is in the same mold as *Trout Fishing in America*. It consists of short, unrelated pieces, many of them less than a page long, which are little more than anecdotes and musings. . . . There's a focus now on aging that wasn't in *Trout Fishing,* and occasionally the daydreams are nasty. Most of the pieces are first-person, and they are all told from what seems to be a consistent point of view. In a prefatory remark, Brautigan says, "The 'I' in this book is the voice of the stations along the tracks of the Tokyo-Montana Express," but the narrator is a character who may or may not resemble the real-life author but certainly gives the illusion of doing so. He resembles earlier Brautigan narrators, especially in *Sombrero Fallout*. This narrator seems to live part of the time in a small town in Montana and spends a long while in Japan, and at some points he has a Japanese wife. (She has no name; she is simply "my wife" or "my Japanese wife.") The book seems to be the sum of the narrator's idle thoughts over a period of several months.

Most of those thoughts are inconclusive. The anecdotal pieces are best when they give some human insight; they are mildly amusing when the metaphor is funny or particularly well woven into the narrative; and the rest of the time they are dull. The stories with the most character are the longer ones: "Shrine of Carp" and "The Irrevocable Sadness of Her Thank You" are tiny moments of life in Japan that illuminate the people described, both narrator and object. The most memorable story is "The Menu/1965," which centers on one week's menu for the condemned men on Death Row in San Quentin, and the impact that menu has on the people the narrator shows it to. . . . But too many of the pieces are like "Marching in the Opposite Direction of a Pizza," in which the narrator sees the Japanese workers at a Shakey's Pizza Parlor in Tokyo leaving work: in another book, this might be a hook to hang either an irony or an amusing comment on, but in Brautigan's book this must stand alone.

Brautigan has kept his talent for turning phrases in unexpected ways. His prose can be evocative for a sentence or so—waking from nightmares, "my eyes tunnelled out of sleep at dawn"—but rarely, in this book, for more than a paragraph. He has a roving attention span, which fastens on a tiny object or a train of thought and examines it briefly, in very close focus, then drops it and passes on. It is the peculiar juxtaposition that interests him. . . . Brautigan spends most of his time describing things, and it is his unusual descriptions that catch our attention. But the interest lasts only as long as his descriptions stay fresh; after that, we look behind them for something more permanent. In *The Tokyo-Montana Express* the descriptions wilt after a while, and there is nothing behind them.

> *John D. Berry, "Taking a Ride with Richard Brautigan," in* Book World—The Washington Post, *October 19, 1980, p. 14.*

SUE M. HALPERN

The Tokyo-Montana Express is not a novel. It is a collection of vignettes held together by contrivance. At the outset Brautigan informs the reader:

> Though the Tokyo-Montana Express moves at great speed, there are many stops along the way. This book is those brief stations, some confident, others still searching for their identities. The "I" in this book is the voice of the stations along the tracks of the Tokyo-Montana Express.

It does not work. The "I" in this book is clearly the voice of Richard Brautigan—he often refers to himself by name—who is either extremely confused or attempting to disown this work.

The Tokyo-Montana Express is a peculiar travelogue that moves within the regions of the author's experience. There are pieces on Christmas trees, ghosts, Japan, Montana, light bulbs and candy wrappers. Despite the range, the reportage is flat and uninteresting. Perhaps this is a reflection of mind. Can this be too harsh an assessment of someone who writes, "umbrellas have always been a mystery to me because I can't understand why they appear just before it starts to rain"?

The vignettes are not all bad or boring, although many of them are. Many of them are brief, too—not more than a page—and this is not unrelated. When Brautigan takes the care to develop a story he can be entertaining and insightful, as in "The Good Work of Chickens," a revenge fantasy about people who abandon their dog in the middle of a harsh nowhere. Yet he rarely does this. At times, though, even his simple observations can be striking; these are usually in reference to death or beautiful women, where the contrasting image of an aging hippie is a sad, broken promise. All these pieces being equal, however, it is apparent that Brautigan does not know when he is good and when he is insipid. (pp. 416-17)

Sue M. Halpern, "A Pox on Dullness," in The Nation, *Vol. 231, No 13, October 25, 1980, pp. 415-17.*

BARRY YOURGRAU

[Here] comes *The Tokyo-Montana Express,* the ninth and newest of Brautigan's novels, a 131-station milk run of anecdotes, reminiscences, impressions and whimsies, set mostly in the late 70's (a few revisits to the 60's) and structured in the main by what I presume are the author's autobiographical experiences out at his country place in Montana (the winters are very cold; the author/persona keeps chickens and watches a lot of television) and in Tokyo, where the author appears to have spent a great deal of time musing on female strangers in the subways or holing up in his hotel room alone, reading of Groucho Marx's last days.

Now I have nothing against promulgations on a morsel. On occasion I can live with sentimentalism. But there are things in *The Tokyo-Montana Express* that belong in anybody's museum for the trivial and the goofily mawkish. For instance: "Spiders Are in the House" ("nice spiders protected from the wind") or "Cat Cantaloupe" (weird pet food!) or "The Last of My Armstrong Spring Creek Mosquito Bites" ("Good-bye, mosquito bites") or "Times Square in Montana" (stronger light bulbs in the barn!). I realize much of this is in the slight nature of the Brautigan animal, which diets on butterflies. But a number of these items strike me as just doodlings falsely promoted from the author's notebooks. Their only function seems to be to make the book fatter on the shelf.

On a more profound level I find myself exasperated by Brautigan's indirectness. For a writer who seems so intimate, he is really quite unrevealing and remote. He is now a longhair in his mid-40's, and across his habitually wistful good humor there now creep shadows of ennui and dullness and too easily aroused sadness. The telltales of an uneasy middle-aged soul peep darkly among the cute knickknacks of *The Tokyo-Montana Express:* dead friends, dead strangers in the papers and on the street, ghosts, regrets over wasted years, regrets over women, bad hangovers, loneliness, phone calls long after midnight. All these point toward hard, somber themes; but Brautigan's instrument is the penny whistle. So either he's trilling cutely, as in the moment of "The Man Who Shot Jesse James," when suddenly he finds his memory failing on who killed his boyhood hero, or he's tweeting melancholically under the bedclothes, as in "Tokyo Snow Story," or he's simply giving a maudlin squawk in the face of the human condition, "A Death in Canada." Whichever, the results are glancing and inadequate for the larger, intimated subject. One feels there is stormy stuff going on in the autobiography of Brautigan's "I"—but what, exactly? The author either can't or won't put us in the know. Brautigan's frail pipings are only random marginalia, quotes without a context; the revelations—the body of the text—are elsewhere.

Having said all this, I must admit that *The Tokyo-Montana Express* does yield its diminutive pleasures. Brautigan does have *something* going. His persona of the sweetly humorous, self-depreciating eccentric/naïf manages to survive as a genuine and pretty much first-hand article, despite its volatile preciousness. Coupled with a certain poetic temperament (nine books of poems among the author's opening credits), it can turn a piece beguilingly on a single image or figure—"Shrine of Carp," for instance. Brautigan can, in fact, sustain an amiably wistful atmosphere and he can demonstrate a bit of touch, a sly eye. "Homage to Groucho Marx," for example, is simply funny and nimbly fashioned; "Toothbrush Ghost Story" disposes of a love affair with a wry-detail or bathroom diplomacy.... I wish there were many more of these, and more like "Tire Chain Bridge," which quietly promotes a symbolette of the 60's—odd, resonant, low-key—through a happenstance of workmanly realism.

By comparison, Brautigan's signature work—*Trout Fishing in America*—works better. It's more of a whole, that first book. The nature and scale of its continuing subject—splashing around after fish—seem better attuned to Brautigan's temperament. It's pretty much a carefree (by which I don't mean tipsy) enterprise. Rereading it now after more than 10 years, I was pleasantly surprised to find that it has a certain tartness about it, a little bit of an edge. And the author's hippieness comes across really as a species of an abiding American voice—sort of Kool-Aid cracker-barrel.

Barry Yourgrau, "An Uneasy Middle-Aged Soul," in The New York Times Book Review, *November 2, 1980, p. 13.*

JAMES M. MELLARD

The pastoral/performative tradition to which Brautigan belongs has been extremely elastic, adaptable, and fluid. One can see in his work at some points strains of the lyrical novel, that sub-genre focusing upon the contents and shifting forms of consciousness and represented in the works of Bellow, Coover, Hawkes, Heller, Exley, and others, and in Brautigan's *In Watermelon Sugar.* At other points one can see the strain of authorially self-conscious metafictions—those fictions about the writing of fiction, represented currently in Nabokov's *Pale Fire,* Barth's *Lost in the Funhouse,* and, again, in Brautigan's *In Watermelon Sugar.* At yet other points one can see aspects of those fictions that convert the artistic process into a literary or metaphysical game of some sort, as in *Ada* and several other works of Nabokov, Coover's *The Universal Baseball Association, J. Henry Waugh, Prop.,* Don DeLillo's *End Zone,* Roth's *The Great American Novel,* and Updike's *The Centaur.* Brautigan touches this strain in *Trout Fishing in America* and in all his works that have their primary impulse in the parody or mimicking of popular, formulaic types: *The Abortion* and its parody of a "romance" such as *A Farewell to Arms; The Hawkline Monster,* a parody of the gothic and the western; and *Willard and His Bowling Trophies,* which parodies both pornography and the gangster genre of films such as *Bonnie and Clyde* and *Dillinger. A Confederate General from Big Sur* fits here, too, for it seems a parody of such bohemian or Beat works as Henry Miller's *Tropic* novels and Kerouac's *On the Road,* this latter especially. Brautigan does seem located at the very center of late modernist fiction, and he seems so not despite but because of his roots in the tradition of American naive or pastoral fiction that runs back through Malamud, Kerouac, Steinbeck, Faulkner, Hemingway, Fitzgerald, Anderson, Stein, Crane, Twain, and, according to Tanner [See *CLC,* Vol. 12], even beyond. Like his older but temporarily contemporary colleague Kurt Vonnegut, Jr., Brautigan does what the best pastoral writers have always done: he treats topical themes (which, in the tradition, are always universal) in the language of simple people so that the extremes, the best and worst, of our culture become more clearly visible.

In Brautigan every study must begin with *Trout Fishing in America* (1967). All those naive quirks and pastoral preoccupations that make his work significant and reveal his indebtedness to the tradition appear here. Perhaps the first traditional aspect of *Trout Fishing* that strikes one is point of view, the *pose* of the author. Because, as Walt Whitman had before him, Brautigan actually includes a photograph of himself with his work, the term pose applies literally as well as figuratively; the old-fashioned openness, directness, and rusticity of the author in the photograph seem clearly embodied in the prose. When Brautigan's first chapter "explains" the cover, unless we notice that he makes no mention of himself and the woman who shares the picture's space, he would not seem to be anything but direct in his style:

> The cover for *Trout Fishing in America* is a photograph taken late in the afternoon, a photograph of the Benjamin Franklin Statue in San Francisco's Washington Square.

> Born 1706—Died 1790, Benjamin Franklin stands on a pedestal that looks like a house containing stone furniture. He holds some papers in one hand and his hat in the other.

It seems a transparent prose, apparently interested only in the representation of the scene before us: at first glance here or in the next longish paragraph, wherein Brautigan explains the word "Welcome" appearing on the four sides of the statue and describes three almost leafless poplars and wet February grass, all the attention of the language appears to be directed toward the universe outside man, outside language, outside consciousness. All the interest seems horizontally directed toward depiction and narration.

But there is one disjunction in those two short paragraphs quoted above—the simile "like a house containing stone furniture." The simile here—and throughout Brautigan, as also in the whole tradition of colloquial/vernacular American literary style—introduces a movement away from the picture or the action and toward some vertex—a theme, idea, meaning. It raises all sorts of questions that we feel obliged to answer, but at this point there is virtually nothing to base our answers, so we read on, having slowed down the pace and prepared to pause again if similar vertical disjunctions recur. They do. We must pause again at "a tall cypress tree, almost dark like a room," and again at the church's "vast door that looks like a huge mousehole, perhaps from a Tom and Jerry cartoon." If Brautigan's prose remained horizontal and continued to point at the universe outside the book or outside language and man's consciousness, *Trout Fishing* would be one of the fastest reads in the history of the novel (perhaps only *The Old Man and the Sea* might match it outside Brautigan's canon). The novel reads slow and long, however, and the reason lies in these vertical dispersals of style. (pp. 155-57)

Trout Fishing in America is not *naively* naive, not a simple pastoral fiction; it is a subtle poetic novel by a lyrical poet, built upon the popular conventions of a widely shared tradition. As a lyrical novel, *Trout Fishing* will reveal its secrets to us not by analysis of "story"—what happens and what happens next—but, if at all, by meditative casts into the individual chapters, each a small deep pool whose meaning might perhaps rise to our best lures. (p. 157)

One of the pastoral themes in the tradition is the concern with man's fate, his *telos,* or end—his *death.* Death appears as a theme even in the opening chapter. That the theme appears is not surprising, but that it appears in such a disarming prose style may well be surprising to many readers. The clues are in those vertical dispersals. (pp. 157-58)

What we are left with, finally, is the traditional pastoral theme of *et in Arcadia ego:* even in Arcady or Eden—or America— there is death. (p. 158)

Two sets of related themes that thread their way through the whole book are sex and violence, death and excrement. Or are they sex and death, violence and excrement, sex and excrement, violence and death? The question seems always, where do we put the emphasis? Ultimately, it doesn't really matter, for each of the book's forty-seven sections interweaves these motifs. The book is one of the most mortifying experiences one could imagine, and yet it manifests a remarkably subtle wit and humor, both so pervasive that only two chapters ("The Salt Creek Coyotes" and "The Surgeon") have almost nothing humorous. What Brautigan has recognized is the way that sex and violence energize the conventions of humor, turn scatology into eschatology. They appear together everywhere in the American naive tradition that he continues. (pp. 158-59)

Because *Trout Fishing* is a popular traditional/lyrical novel, we can drop a line into any of its pools and might come up with a clear sense of the book's total meaning, a dominant theme drawing all the vertices together. At any given point in the book its main theme will be visible either in the text itself or in the activity that, implicitly, always lies behind it. In other words, we can often take the text at face value, or we can retreat to the transforming, metamorphic, metaphoric process of imaginative creation that underlies it. Individual chapters will often be about the disjunction between "reality" and "the world," with specific images concretely manifesting the grotesqueness of the world and other images illustrating the impact of mind, imagination, and creativity upon it. In the "Worsewick" episode, for example, the "bathtub" pool with all the dead trout, slime, and deerflies "says" one thing about the world, but Brautigan's language and the narrative structure his art imposes on the experience transform it into something different and not entirely repellent. The sheer playfulness of language conveys a rather cheerful message ("the medium *is* the message"), and the whole structure of the episode leads us from the most repellent-seeming of mundane activities to an act (ironically, it is *coitus interruptus* that achieves climactic revelation) that takes on cosmological significance, as Brautigan's similes take us from the age of the dinosaurs ("I did this by going deeper and deeper in the water, *like a dinosaur,* and letting the green slime and dead fish cover me over," he says of hiding his "hard on"), to the age of aeronautical technology ("like an airplane"), to the cosmic reaches of intergalactic space ("like a falling star"). Consequently, one would suggest that the book is not about reality, or that manifestation of it called "America," but about our knowledge of it, how we can cope with it and finally must make do with it. The process is at best tragi-comic, as the most profound pastoral art always is in its formulae of elegy, *ubi sunt,* or *et in Arcadia ego.*

The meta-narrative component of *Trout Fishing,* in contrast to most works in the tradition, we must extrapolate for ourselves from the discontinuous sections, but in doing so we see clearly how tragi-comic becomes the whole structure. While the book has frequently been called a "quest," a search for the "real" America to replace all the sham dreams, all the corrupted visions, an America for *Amerika*, it seems less to provide a quest than images manifesting the development of the artist. In other words, it seems not the *Bildungsroman*, but the *Künstlerroman*. In a general way the book's meta-narrative (reconstructed) moves, like the simpler *Bildungsroman*, from childhood to youth to maturity. "The Cover of Trout Fishing in America," of course, is the invitational prologue to the book, so the fact of the narrator's mature presence there does not interfere with the development that actually begins in the next two chapters, "Knock on Wood (Part One)" and "Knock on Wood (Part Two)," both of which concern the narrator's childhood initiation to "trout fishing in America." Initiation is disillusioning in a particularly modernist way for him, since the first trout stream and the magnificent waterfalls he sees turn out to be nothing more than a perceptual error, a "flight of wooden stairs leading up to a house in the trees." Modernist, too, is the way the ritual charm that he enacts—knocking on wood—has the effect not of confirming "reality" or protecting his fantasy or desire, but of revealing their unreality and impossibility. So the boy does the only thing that any modernist youth can do: he internalizes his dream and his reality: "I ended up by being my own trout and eating the slice of bread myself." . . . He becomes, in a word, the artist, and *Bildungsroman* metamorphoses into *Künstlerroman*, a portrait of the artist as a young (fisher) man.

"The Hunchback Trout" climaxes the series of episodes that includes the "Knock on Wood" sections, as well as "Grider Creek" and "Tom Martin Creek." These episodes show the various typal frustrations the young angler goes through before the glorious success of landing the hunchback trout. His success, however, is as much imaginative as sporting. Indeed, Brautigan's style intimates that the success is mainly literary, for the episode, more than most, is indicative of the role of style and language in *Trout Fishing.* . . . Narrating the day the "kid" "punched in" for work at the creek and landed the hunchback, he is able to match the incredible physical energy of the trout with the verbal, imaginative energy of the artist. . . . In the book, one has the impression that this episode marks not an end of innocence but a discovery of the one effective potency man has in an otherwise impermeable world. That potency, again sacramentally ingested, is the artist's. . . . (pp. 160-62)

In the last sequence of sections, the child-as-hero appears—or reappears. In *Trout Fishing,* as in pastoral generally, the positive, beneficent potentialities of the unfettered, phenomenologically uncluttered imagination belong to the child (or rustic or naif elsewhere in the tradition). Her anti-type here appears to be Trout Fishing in America Shorty. Shorty seems to be the emblematic, imaginative construct in the book who symbolizes all those other cripples—emotional, creative, psychopathic—who populate the book: "He was a legless, screaming middle-aged wino./He descended upon North Beach like a chapter from the Old Testament. He was the reason birds migrate in the autumn. They have to. He was the cold turning of the earth; the bad wind that blows off sugar." . . . The embodiment of universal negation, Trout Fishing in America Shorty belongs to the unimaginative "naturalism" of writers such as Nelson Algren, so the narrator and a friend decide to ship him to Chicago to Algren or, failing that, "if he comes back to San Francisco someday and dies," the narrator says, Shorty "should

be buried right beside the Benjamin Franklin statue in Washington Square." . . . (p. 165)

The child brings a fresh imagination to the world of *Trout Fishing in America.* That world is about as worn out as it can possibly be, but not merely because the landscapes are so depleted or trampled down or garbage-filled. It is worn out because the frame the angling Horatio Algering *mythos* has provided is now so inadequate. In its broadest configuration showing how the *mythos* can be replaced, the novel shows the narrator's becoming the creative, artistic imagination, not by denying the nugatory in our American existence but by transforming it. The always present and insistent dark vision accounts for much of the novel's length, for if the accounts of death and the epitaphs of one sort or another are eliminated, not much is left in *Trout Fishing.* The narrator here, as in any other pastoral work, especially one dealing with the theme of *et in Arcadia ego,* must simply adapt to the fact of decay and death even in Arcady, Eden, America—life itself. (p. 166)

Everything in *Trout Fishing in America* deserves its memorial, even when it has passed its usefulness (as in the Byronic and the Hemingway heroes) or was never of any use to begin with (Trout Fishing in America Shorty) or was genuinely antithetical to use (Jack the Ripper, John Dillinger, etc.). Trout Fishing in America—the old pastoral, Walden, Algerian, Gatsbean, Nick Adams dream—deserves its memorial, too, and receives it in what most critics have acknowledged as the purest, most extravagant expression of imagination in the book: "The Cleveland Wrecking Yard." . . . This chapter brings us full circle back to the opening chapters, for the two parts of "Knock on Wood" have foreshadowed the transformation of trout fishing in America into the artifacts of industrial, technological America. The boy's waterfall staircase now shows up in the "used plumbing department, surrounded by hundreds of toilets." . . . One can no longer market the myth as a fresh new product, but as an artist—a writer—Brautigan suggests that one can still find a way to use it: it can become the writer's medium and refresh his art: "I thought to myself what a lovely nib trout fishing in America would make with a stroke of cool green trees along the river's shore, wild flowers and dark fins pressed against the paper." . . . It may be gone now, but it was good in its time. *Requiescat in pace.* Rest in Peace, Trout Fishing in America *Peace. Trout Fishing* is a book filled with memorials and epitaphs, and their insistent presences suggest just how thoroughly it is permeated with the spirit of the elegy, the *ubi sunt,* and the *et in Arcadia ego* themes of pastoral art. The big question seems constantly to be how to cope—with the fact of death, with the passing of a cherished dream, with the ambiguities that surround one always. The myth upon which trout fishing rests as a real activity begins to seem inadequate in a social structure shot through with violence, fear, cruelty, overpopulation, and ecological disaster.

Brautigan seems very much to be working a stream of American literature represented by many novelists, but in some ways his themes seem best represented by the poetry and philosophy of Wallace Stevens. Stevens worked in the world—in that most mundane of professions, the insurance industry; still, he wrote poetry that illustrated the potency of the imagination in transforming the world, not by denying it but by using it. In *The Comedian as the Letter C,* Stevens begins with a pale, unimaginative hero voyaging into a new world, "a world without imagination." The tension in Stevens and Brautigan is always between the external reality and the faculty of imagination, but the result in both writers is that the best art comes from the combination of a phenomenological reality and an idealistic imagination: ''Nota: Man is the intelligence of his soil'' becomes ''Nota: his soil is man's intelligence.'' Both must interact if human beings are to bring order to chaos. Brautigan feels just as strongly as Stevens that reality must constantly be reinterpreted, the old myths replaced, revitalized, or stripped of their husks in order to lay bare the live core. But the job takes an artist's imagination, and we must all be artists. What *Trout Fishing in America* does, then, is to represent both the need and the expression of imagination, and Brautigan's portrait of a young trout fisherman thus becomes a portrait of the artist as well. (pp. 167-68)

> James M. Mellard, ''Brautigan's 'Trout Fishing in America','' in his The Exploded Form: The Modernist Novel in America, *University of Illinois Press, 1980, pp. 155-68.*

JOHN COOLEY

Trout Fishing in America is already something of a minor American classic, comparable, in both its stylistic achievement and intricate layering of themes, with works like *Miss Lonelyhearts, Winesburg, Ohio* and ''The Bear.'' More than a decade old now, it survived the peculiarities of the 1960s that it doubtless grew out of and spoke most directly to. It continues to grow in depth and meaning and to draw critical interest. It is a novel in the American tradition of stylistic innovation, presenting us with a voice both compelling and beguilingly original. *Trout Fishing* is a collection of tiny fictions or perhaps even prose poems, each highly wrought, like exquisitely handcrafted trout flies or lures, most of them with enough interest and hooking power to ''work'' by themselves. Yet the book, despite its very contemporary antiscale and antistory effects, also makes good narrative and thematic sense once rearranged for readings of plot, character, and theme. Along with these trendy, postmodernist techniques and themes which Brautigan incorporates so handily, there are many connections with the pastoral tradition. Rather like Vonnegut, he seems caught between twin impulses, to show the absurdity of life, and to pose suggestions for survival. One of his greatest achievements is the artful disguise of his ideas through a style and surface texture so imaginative that complex issues are handled deftly and lightly.

Also of interest has been the changing critical opinion of Brautigan's novel. Early criticism, such as Jack Clayton's essay (*North American Review* 11, 1971) said that *Trout Fishing* expressed the voice of an American subculture, ''giv[ing] people the assurance they can be free and part of a community of free people, *now*'' [see *CLC*, Vol. 12]. . . . Terrance Malley, in his book on Brautigan, has provided the most thoroughgoing discussion of *Trout Fishing* available (and imaginable), emphasizing the narrative and thematic order that underlies the apparent aimlessness of the novel [see *CLC*, Vol. 3]. Tony Tanner devotes a few pages of his *City of Words* to Brautigan, emphasizing the richness of the imagination at work in *Trout Fishing* [see *CLC*, Vol. 12]. He argues, quite convincingly, that Brautigan creates a pastoral fantasy, a verbal world not unlike a city (or country) of words—a way of maintaining one's sanity in modern America. Neil Schmitz, taking Tanner to task, emphasizes the ironic voice with which Brautigan invests his narrator, declaring that like Hawthorne, Brautigan ''does not write within the pastoral mode as an advocate of its vision'' [see *CLC*, Vol. 3]. Both are spokesmen for an ironic pastoral pessimism. Schmitz sees Brautigan as essentially ''an ironist

critically examining the myths and language of the pastoral sensibility that reappeared in the sixties.'' . . . Each of these essays illuminates aspects of Brautigan's pastoral, and, while seemingly disputatious, their varying interpretations are probably justifiable within the possibilities of this richly textured novel. To them I shall add a further hypothesis regarding Brautigan's use of the pastoral form.

''Trout Fishing in America'' is, as others have suggested, a person, a place, an outdoor sport, a cripple, a pen nib, and a book by Richard Brautigan. To these I will add that it is also a religion and a state of mind. In his highly stylized kaleidoscope of little fictions, Brautigan gives us disconcerting glimpses of a badly diseased American wilderness. The narrator, his woman friend, and their baby travel about from trout stream to trout stream, having the most unsettling experiences imaginable. In fact, *Trout Fishing* is filled with images of violence, environmental disintegration, and futility. It is a novel littered with both human and natural wreckage, the fallout of the twentieth century. There are trout streams for sale by the foot in a wrecking yard, trout killed with port wine, and coyotes killed with cyanide capsules. Brautigan gives hauntingly truthful images of an America in which one can buy and sell absolutely anything, not just the streams and trout, but even the waterfalls and the accompanying birds and insects. We see a country obsessed with commerce, with fishing equipment and camping paraphernalia, a cruel and dangerous parody of real outdoor experience. Through Brautigan's tough clarity we see a society so obsessed with commerce and profit that even the most resistant submit to the lure of ''fast bucks.'' Were he living today, Leonardo da Vinci would probably be turning out trout lures called ''the last supper,'' Brautigan fantasizes. He also hints at the extensive pseudo-naturalism that is another plague of our times. ''Jack the Ripper'' appears disguised as ''Trout Fishing in America,'' wearing ''mountains on his elbows and bluejays on the collar of his shirt.'' . . . ''The Ripper'' is clearly, in Brautigan's opinion, not the only embodiment of senseless violence and destruction posing as wholesome, rugged naturalness. From one point of view, *Trout Fishing* is so crammed with the details of a pastoral tragedy that one comes to feel that Brautigan is not writing a pastoral novel, but, as Malley puts it, ''an analysis of why the old pastoral myth of an America of freedom and tranquility is no longer viable'' [see *CLC*, Vol. 3]. . . . (pp. 413-15)

[It] is entirely likely that contemporary pastorals will be laden with images of the death of woods and stream, of the heart and spirit of wildness in America. What remains, for Brautigan and others, is more like a diseased garden contained within a machine. Unlike traditional pastorals, the tone of Brautigan's novel is hardly eulogistic or sentimental over wild America; it is a book that seems verbally high with puns, silliness, deadpan humor, clever turns of phrase, and amusing anecdotes. . . . If this were a book principally about the drawing, quartering, and selling of wild America, there would be a radical disjunction between its language and its theme. The reason one does not feel a grave inconsistency is that we unconsciously sense the two forces—the positive, inventive force of Brautigan's language, and the language of pastoral disintegration—merge with the unity of counterpoint to melody. (p. 415)

In contrast to Hemingway, Brautigan offers his readers no pastoral paradise. Thoreau argued that we can never get enough wilderness, but in *Trout Fishing* we can't get any. Nor have Brautigan or his narrator any solution to environmental deterioration. What Brautigan does offer is a state of mind, a state of the imagination so highly refined, so sharply pointed that it can transform experience. More than mere tonic of "kool aid," his book offers a way of imagining and experiencing so altered from the common paths of the mind that it may seem like a religious conversion. . . . He wishes to suggest that with an awakened imagination and an environmental consciousness one might *feel* like a religious convert.

The influence of Henry Thoreau hovers significantly behind this novel. This may seem unlikely, since Thoreau's argument for the virtues of wildness was made convincing by the directness of his statements and his unflinching integrity to principle. Brautigan proceeds mainly through indirection, fragmentation, hyperbole, and understatement. Of course Thoreau uses such techniques, but the two books provide a strikingly different reading experience. The great affinity between them lies in their turn inward. Both writers suggest that, as Thoreau puts it, we become "expert in home-cosmography." Despite the loving, painstaking detail devoted to making *Walden* real, foot by foot, season by season, it is for Thoreau a state of mind and thus a way of life rather than a specific place. Consequently, Thoreau could declare that he had other lives to live and urge each reader to create his or her own Walden. Thoreau wanted us to see that, like the "beautiful bug" trapped many years within an apple tree and then in a table plank, we too can emerge to a new and stunning life. In his own modestly unassuming way Brautigan seems "merely" to be demonstrating that stunning proposition.

Brautigan ties his fishing lures around the appropriately elusive figure of "Trout Fishing in America," perhaps an American expression of Eliot's "Fisher King." And that is one of the cantankerous pleasures of this slippery text; like slick jokes, allusions to Byron, Franklin, Thoreau, even Hemingway come slipping by and are frequently best ignored. TFA (as he will hereafter be called here) was probably a minor deity, a fishman perhaps, who possessed super-human powers but was also vulnerable to human pollution. . . . We also learn that to thousands of young Americans TFA has become synonymous with their opposition to nuclear testing and weapons proliferation. . . . Thus the spirit of TFA lives on as an inspiration toward nonviolence.

"Trout Fishing in America Terrorists" are a small group of sixth graders who hold TFA as inspiration in their battle for freedom of expression and freedom just to be sixth graders. (pp. 415-17)

This theme of pastoral conspiracy is stated another way by Neil Schmitz, when he speculates that "the setting of the modern pastoral is irrevocably the city it seeks to deny." . . . Metaphorically, this speculation rings true. One feels, in reading contemporary pastorals, that the garden is within the machine, or, as John Barth describes it in *Giles Goat Boy,* within the computer. In such an environment, conspiracies, gothic configurations, and clandestined meetings of armies in green, will be the necessary stock-in-trade of pastoral writing.

But Brautigan and his narrator offer more than the vague possibility of conspiracy. Brautigan gives ample evidence that he has been chosen by TFA as a disciple who has been given encouragement and guidance before the master's death. The most striking revelation of this relationship occurs in "Trout Fishing in America Nib." Here the narrator makes clear that his inspiration as writer comes not from Diana or any other mythological presence, but from TFA. He is allowed to use his mentor's gold nib pen. TFA warns, "Write with this but

don't write hard because this pen has got a gold nib and is very impressionable. After a while it takes on the personality of the writer." . . . We can speculate that Brautigan has inherited this pen and has followed the advice to write lightly. He has received through it the style of TFA himself. He writes with lightness and levity to protect the impressionable nib and preserve the line of inspiration.

This metaphor is carried a step further in a fascinating little episode called "Knock on Wood," which occurs when the narrator, still a youngster, goes fishing for the first time. His tackle consists of string, a bent pin, and doughballs from a slice of bread. But as he approaches the stream with bated breath and his "vaudevillian hook" baited with a doughball, be realizes something is very wrong. His waterfall is no more than a "flight of white wooden stairs leading up to a house in the trees." . . . This appears to be both a parody on the seemingly blind enthusiasm of trout fishermen as well as an indication of the narrator's commitment to TFA at an early age. Undaunted by his mistake, he says, "I ended up being my own trout and eating the slice of bread myself." . . . How much this sounds like Thoreau's observation, "It's not the berries that count, it's the experience." It also suggests that the pastoral virtues Brautigan gives expression to reside in the imagination rather than in the trout. Of course the reference to a "vaudevillian hook" charmingly suggests the technique Brautigan uses, the short, exquisitely tied little fictions, each capable of catching readers. "Knock on Wood" may thus be seen as a trial run for the narrator's craft and technique. Unable to catch fish, he hooks himself, (Thoreau puts it this way: "It would be nobler game to shoot oneself.") and in a stylized self-communion, Brautigan's narrator eats the bread himself. TFA has not missed a moment of this experience and recalls with amusement a similar incident of his own. ("I remember mistaking an old woman for a trout stream in Vermont, and I had to beg her pardon.")

So much is revealed in this little episode, the relationship of TFA to the narrator, the narrator's comically transforming experience, the implications of religious ritual, and the suggestion of a vaudevillian technique. Soon afterward, in "The Kool-Aid Wino," Brautigan gives further hints regarding his technique. One of the narrator's friends is kept from working by a rupture. Our young narrator brings his friend a nickel, and they set off to buy a package of kool-aid. Carefully they mix it in jars, but without sugar and at half-strength. The ceremony of mixing and drinking is exacting. His friend even turns off the water "with sudden and delicate motion like a famous brain surgeon removing a disordered portion of the imagination." . . . The two youngsters sit in the chicken house drinking the diluted and grape-flavored kool-aid, eating homemade bread covered with Karo syrup and peanut butter. It is another of Brautigan's little rituals; the "kool-aid wino" even resembles "the inspired priest of an exotic cult." It is here that Brautigan delivers what may be the most delightful and telling line of his novel. About the wino he says this: "He created his own kool-aid reality and was able to illuminate himself by it." . . . The young wino compensates for his injury, emblematic of all the injuries and sickness contained in the novel, by becoming addicted to kool-aid. It is merely the vehicle for creating a private reality through which one can illuminate and thus transform life.

As suggested above, Brautigan's "kool-aid reality" is reminiscent of Thoreau's "beautiful bug." Both are reminders of our powers locked within, of the spirit lives with which we can learn to illuminate ourselves. Like the ruptured child-priest, Brautigan also is a surgeon for diseased imaginations, providing the cool and therapeutic tonic of his imaginative fictions. Thus Brautigan invokes not so much the power of nature but of the imagination, under the influence of nature, to heal and transform. (pp. 417-19)

John Cooley, ''The Garden in the Machine: Three Postmodern Pastorals,'' in The Michigan Academician, Vol. XIII, No. 4, Spring, 1981, pp. 405-20.

MICHAEL MASON

Richard Brautigan is a writer whose mannerisms irritate many people, but these readers would be well advised to try him again in this new collection. It may sound odd to say that an author has arrived at a vision which is harmonious with his way of writing after a sequence of no fewer than eight novels, but it is a claim which can be pressed surprisingly far for Brautigan and *The Tokyo-Montana Express*. Two of the potentially irritating features of this writer's procedure are that he is laconic (affectedly so, for those in the irritated camp), and interested (perhaps self-indulgently or coyly) in a certain restricted range of experience: low-key, private sensations and ephemeral, minor constituents of the world. *The Tokyo-Montana Express* takes these tendencies as far as they have ever gone with the author. The book is an assemblage of about 130 short, sometimes extremely short, fragments with no easily discerned continuity. The book amounts, however, to a coherent mediation or investigation: united by a vision of things which is melancholy and alienated, and which is seeking an assuagement of these feelings.

The reader may soon sense that there is more design to the book's fragments than appears at first glance. Certain motifs establish themselves: animals, death, memories, dreams, snow and rain, food (and foodshops, restaurants, faeces, cooking), empty or vanished buildings (especially shops). One of the shortest pieces goes as follows:

> Once upon a time there was a dwarf knight who only had fifty words to live in and they were so fleeting that he only had time to put on a suit of armour and ride swiftly on a black horse into a very well-lit wood where he vanished forever. . . .

A different sort of consonance—this time involving Brautigan's typical brevity—is achieved in ''Her Last Known Boyfriend a Canadian Airman''. It concerns a gifted and beautiful Chinese girl from San Francisco whose life effectively ceases with the death of her young boyfriend in the war. She takes a job washing dishes in a restaurant. And that is all. She has been washing dishes, never talking about the past, for thirty-four years. The abruptness of the telling is right. There is a refusal by the text to take up more than a page and a half, and there has been an equivalent refusal by the nature of things to grant the Chinese girl a full life. When her boyfriend died ''she was a straight-A student'' at college. People couldn't understand why she washed dishes, because ''there were so many other things that she could have done''.

Variations on this phrase, formulations about ''things to do'', sound throughout *The Tokyo-Montana Express*. The ruling theme of the collection is, indeed, that of human purpose or intentness upon an aim (''The Purpose'' is the title of one fragment). There are many studies in obsession—for instance: an immi-

grant to America in 1851 (rather anachronistically described as a Czechoslovakian) who three times goes compulsively to California to seek gold, and dies there; a man staring at meat in a market; a man fixated on his wife's infidelity; a woman who works all her life to open a restaurant (which fails) and a man who does the same with a bar; a man obsessed about Japanese women's feet, and another who takes thousands of photographs of beautiful women in Tokyo; a female taxi-driver in Montana who is fascinated by ice-ages, and a male one in Japan whose cab is full of pictures of carp. . . .

Another group of fragments in *The Tokyo-Montana Express* concerns activity without true purpose: the Chinese dishwasher belongs with the bed-salesman who can't bring himself to look like ''somebody who sincerely wants to sell beds'', the butcher who similarly is more concerned about his cold hands than about selling meat, and the four pizza cooks having time off from Shakey's Pizza Parlour in Tokyo, about whom the author knows ''one thing for certain . . . they are not going to get a pizza.'' The cultural crossover here is interesting. Being ''sincere'' about beds—that is, about what you are commercially associated with—is a variety of apparent purposefulness very readily locatable in America. But Brautigan more commonly makes the American end of his ''express'' the land of aimlessness. Choosing Montana as a main setting facilitates this, of course, especially when the contrasting community is Tokyo (and there are several vignettes of commuting Japanese). One of the touchstone pieces in the book—and one of many about having ''nothing to do''—is ''Montana Traffic Spell''. It simply describes how the traffic is held up in a small Montana town when the author's friend cannot decide which way he feels like going at the only traffic light. . . .

There are three pieces in the collection which in a directly challenging fashion put the contrast between the small, transient and private, and what we normally regard as portentous and communally interesting. Food is a key notion in each of them. ''Light on at the Tastee-Freez'' is about the author's preoccupation with a light he sees in a closed milk-bar. . . . In a similar vein, ''A Different Way of Looking at President Kennedy's Assassination'' brackets together, perhaps implying that they are equally upsetting, the cancellation of pancakes from a menu and the shooting of Kennedy. And one of the longest pieces of all, ''The Menu/1965'', is about the author's visit to San Quentin, and his greater interest in the menu for Death Row inmates than in penological issues. . . .

This is the kind of thing which can bring on the allergic reaction to Brautigan, and there is nothing inadvertent in the provocation offered. But Brautigan is not, I think, glibly flourishing the idea of a shrugging, dismissive withdrawal from seriousness in such passages. Seriousness has its say in ''The Menu/1965'', when the author shows the Death Row bill-of-fare to a friend.

> ''It's so stark, so real,'' he said. ''It's like a poem, this menu alone condemns our society. To feed somebody this kind of food who is already effectively dead represents all the incongruity of the whole damn thing. It's senseless.'' . . .

Menu as menace. Brautigan wins hands down this confrontation with seriousness. The apparent disproportions in his vision of things—pancakes and the assassination of Kennedy, Tastee-Freez and Jimmy Carter—are there to suggest a correction to the opposite, more orthodox kind of disproportion in our attitudes. You can't *only* think of a beet and onion salad as a symbol of penological evil, and this goes for all the building-blocks of daily life. Moreover, Brautigan's mode is simply questioning, a proposed "different way of looking". After all, *The Tokyo-Montana Express* is full of obsessive people, and the author's high valuation of pancakes or Tastee-Freez (the name is flagrantly expressive of commercialism) may just be an internal version of what is seen from without in the man who stares at meat. Brautigan's description of the stations of his express is correct: "some confident, others still searching for their identities".

*Michael Mason, "The Pancakes and the President,"
in* The Times Literary Supplement, *No. 4074, May 1, 1981, p. 483.*

CHARLES HACKENBERRY

Richard Brautigan's longer works of fiction present various difficulties to reviewers and critics, and one of the most troublesome concerns their genre. Witness the problem of [John Clayton; see *CLC*, Vol. 12]: "*Trout Fishing in America* is not an anti-novel; it is an un-novel." Even less informative is [Robert Adams's] comment, which calls Brautigan's books "prose pieces (one can't call them novels or even fictions—they may well go down in literary history as Brautigans)." One might also speak, presumably, about Hemingways and Donnes as well. That each writer makes a form his own is well understood. What seems less clear is his debt to the tradition or traditions he chooses.

The difficulty of analyzing Brautigan's works of fiction and comparing them to similar works is complicated by his habit of projecting the outlines of various established forms upon his own: *The Hawkline Monster* (1974) is subtitled *A Gothic Western; Willard and His Bowling Trophies* (1975) is also *A Perverse Mystery; Sombrero Fallout* (1976) calls itself *A Japanese Novel.* His recent book-length fiction, *Dreaming of Babylon: A Private Eye Novel 1942* (1977), continues the practice. By examining the first of Brautigan's excursions into subtitling, *The Abortion: An Historical Romance 1966* (1971), I intend to explore here the degree to which the work is an actual romance and the degree to which it is not, obtaining from such an analysis an interpretation of the work that considers its form to be an essential part of its meaning.

In one sense, asserting that a book that has *An Historical Romance 1966* on its cover is indeed a generic romance seems a bit too easy, yet it needs saying. *Romance* is widely used, especially when dealing with popular fiction, to designate any kind of love story. That *The Abortion* is a love story, in addition to whatever else it is, only muddles the matter—as does a curious sentence on the cover of the paperback edition: "This novel is about the romantic possibilities of a public library in California." The effect of this ambiguity and funning is to hide the fact that many features of *The Abortion* show characteristics of the romance.

The theories of Northrop Frye, especially those which deal with myth and archetype, seem especially relevant to an explanation of the romance qualities of this work. . . . For example, Frye notices that one of the essential differences between the romance and the novel is a matter of characterization:

> The romance does not attempt to create "real people" so much as stylized figures which expand into psychological archetypes. It is in the romance that we find Jung's libido, anima, and

shadow reflected in the hero, heroine, and villain respectively. This is why the romance so often radiates a glow of subjective intensity that the novel lacks, and why a suggestion of allegory is constantly creeping in around its fringes.

The unnamed narrator of *The Abortion,* though distinguished by eccentric attitudes and gentleness, is never fully realized. While he is admirable for his view of humanity, a self-imposed isolation and his chosen role tend to reduce him in stature. This double nature is important for the construction of the story and will be discussed later. Estranged and remote, he lives a life apart, both in the depths of the library and in the labyrinthine rooms of the Mexican abortion doctor who performs the requested surgery on the relentlessly beautiful heroine, Vida. The stereotype of the mayhem-producing beautiful female has been traced from Katrina Van Tassel in "The Legend of Sleepy Hollow," Cecily Burns in George Washington Harris' *Sut Lovingood* tales, Eula Varner in *The Hamlet,* and Griselda of *God's Little Acre* to the public image of Marilyn Monroe. Vida, as a character name, has also been derived from the Latin *vita,* meaning life. If such interpretation is correct, the symbolic characterization thus produced tends not toward individualization but toward stylization and allegory. (pp. 24-6)

Identifying a shadow figure is more difficult. . . . *The Abortion* lacks an individual villain, but evil does exist in the narrative. The harshness of life outside the library is the shaping force on those who bring their pitiful volumes to be catalogued, and the strictures of law and society, as they prohibit abortion in America, necessitate the quest. (p. 26)

Much of the subjective intensity of *The Abortion* comes from the reader's recognition, probably at some deeply subliminal level, that the drama enacted in the romance has its counterpart in the history of the individual perceiving ego. Like members of the original audience at a classical Greek tragedy, we are not really very interested in the major turns of the plot, for we already know what must happen. Rather, we attend with a keen eye to see *how* the details will fall into place, to apprehend how the uncompromising universal law will influence this particular situation, these unusual people. Brautigan is interested in psychological insights at this level, and such struggle generates the unquestionable tension of the work. (p. 28)

Other characteristics of *The Abortion* also mark it as romance. Northrop Frye has suggested in the passage already quoted that the genre has an allegorical dimension. On one level, this story can easily so be read: "the library is a metaphor for America itself, and . . . its sequence of timid, strange, insecure librarians are the comic equivalents of American presidents." Even if such interpretation is valid, the allegory is still only partial; though the narrator is the thirty-fifth or thirty-sixth librarian, which corresponds to the numbering of presidents at the time the work was written (Cleveland's terms accounting for the confusion), the allegory is primarily peripheral. It is not a point-for-point allegory. While the library/America symbolism applies neatly for some levels of the story, the shaping force outside the library, which produces emotional cripples, must still be reckoned with—and it, too, is America.

Characterization and subjective intensity are but two of Frye's criteria for romance. One of his most important qualifications concerns plot, and here as well *The Abortion* stands close analysis: "The completed form of the romance is clearly the successful quest, and such a completed form has three main stages: the stage of the perilous journey and the preliminary minor adventures; the crucial struggle . . . and the exaltation of the hero.'' The preliminary adventures of *The Abortion* begin with the narrator's contact with those who bring manuscripts to him. (pp. 28-9)

The principal feature of these preliminary minor adventures, however, is the introduction of Vida into the narrative. Although she is present at the beginning of the tale, her history is gathered together in the first chapter of Book Two as a flashback which details the first meeting of the narrator and the nineteen-year-old heroine whose exquisite face does not match her voluptuous body, a further irony on the romance form, for the heroine's chief problem is her extraordinary beauty. Their first sexual experience provides the core of the initial adventures. While the perilous journey is certainly the trek to Tijuana, the peril, other than that associated with the abortion itself, is unusual, for it consists of nothing more than life in the outside world. . . . For his pains, the ''Library Kid'' as Foster calls him, is rewarded with a life that is richer than that of the narrow and confining subconscious. That he becomes a hero is, I believe, an authorial comment on the rarity of the completed transformation.

What Brautigan appears to have done in *The Abortion* is to construct a story in a traditional form, the romance, using its conventions, its abbreviated characterization, and its plot structure rooted in the emergence of the ego—while exaggerating and distorting romantic elements. . . . While *The Abortion* appears to be a genuine romance when viewed from the perspective of Frye's observations on the form as a genre and a vehicle for mythic content, the book is, at the same time, a minor-key parody of romance. (pp. 29-30)

One of the strongest elements which turns the tale toward parody is the object of the quest, the abortion. In terms of story values, it is entirely opposite to our expectations of the romance form. Brautigan's handling of the action, however, displays his balancing of romantic and parodic elements. (p. 31)

Brautigan has yet to receive the kind of critical attention he deserves. He is either praised to extremes by those who suppose they hear their own voice in his narrators or characters, or else he is dismissed as an opportunist who panders to popular taste for the money. Brautigan needs a re-evaluation, for his fiction has more complexity than has yet been seen, and rarely is he viewed in terms of the genres and modes that he selects and so often mingles. The subtitle for *The Abortion* asserts that the work is an *historical* romance. Normally, we would expect to find figures of history side by side with fictional characters, but we do not—unless the librarian/president symbolism is strained to an uncomfortable point. Furthermore, 1966 is too close to the date of composition of the work for the sort of candle-lit distancing that historical fiction usually trades on. Historical fiction, however, gets a lot of mileage from the differences between the setting of the story and the present; such, surely, is the nature of the point that Brautigan would make.

As a romance *The Abortion* may be interpreted as Richard Brautigan's record of how American idealism, in the course of a particular year, began to move outward into the light of day and away from its more self-conscious concerns. On one level, Brautigan's romance is his portrait of the peace movement's heroism and efficacy, its solution to the unwanted pregnancy of American intervention in Asia. Such interpretation rests heavily on the romance's capacity for allegory, but it is not an unlikely interpretation when viewed from the perspective

of the parodic elements of the work. To the degree that *The Abortion* is parody, it becomes a statement of self-doubt, a realization that the power of a minority, no matter how gentle and well-intentioned, is dependent on its activism. The ability to change the course of American thought is the point of difference between 1966 and the time of composition.

As in most of Brautigan's long fiction (one need only recall *In Watermelon Sugar* or *A Confederate General from Big Sur*), *The Abortion* is the story of a man strongly influenced by the literature he has read and obviously absorbed. To a large degree, the difficulties experienced by Brautigan's central characters are caused by their belief that life is—or ought to be—like literature. From Jesse of *A Confederate General from Big Sur* (1965) to the down-at-the-heels detective of *Dreaming of Babylon,* Brautigan presents characters who try to fashion their lives according to literary creation. In some works, the literary model is specific, as in *Dreaming of Babylon* and *Willard and His Bowling Trophies;* in others, the model is more general or has yet to be identified. Literary forms, Brautigan suggests, provide a framework for thought. They create, too, expectations for life—but *The Abortion* is a measure of how cockeyed a life based on these expectations can become if a too literal transposition is attempted. How and what we think are strongly influenced by these structures, but such thought is limited, perhaps limiting. The greatest strength of *The Abortion* is that it is not *just* parody. The work is also a testimony to the enduring truth of literary forms, however incomplete and imperfect—their power to shape human behavior and render psychological reality in dream-like sketches. (pp. 34-5)

Charles Hackenberry, ''Romance and Parody in Brautigan's 'The Abortion','' in Critique: Studies in Modern Fiction, *Vol. XXIII, No. 2, Winter, 1981-82, pp. 24-36.*

LONNIE L. WILLIS

In contrast to the respectable critical attention given to his novels of the sixties, *In Watermelon Sugar* (1967) and *Trout Fishing in America* (1967), Richard Brautigan's mid-seventies novel, *The Hawkline Monster* (1974), has received little attention beyond initial reviews. The novel probably merits notice if for no other reason than its resolution of some issues characteristic of Brautigan's earlier work. Unfortunately, the novel's pose as a ''Gothic Western'' has led some readers to view it as a mere parody of two popularized genres. Although it may be ''more of a parody than any of Brautigan's other fictions'' [see excerpt by Peter S. Prescott in *CLC*, Vol. 5], *The Hawkline Monster* continues Brautigan's serious concern with failed American dreams, with what has been defined in another context as his ''concern with the bankrupt ideals of the American past'' [see excerpt by Kenneth Seib in *CLC*, Vol. 1].

The Hawkline Monster investigates the failure of the American experience to harmonize expectation and reality, and it calls attention to illusions that have distorted the national vision. Professor Hawkline, the transplanted New England alchemist who attempts to create the synthetic resources for a better world in his Eastern Oregon laboratory, represents the American national design. When he fails in his idealistic purpose, he nevertheless continues to think ''right up to the moment the monster did that terrible thing to him that he would be able to correct the balance of The Chemicals and complete the experiment with humanitarian possibilities for the entire world.'' The Professor's idealism to the contrary, the novel fails to provide anything but a sense of doom for the American experiment. Customarily, Brautigan has been regarded as despondent but not ultimately without hope. While a "sense of failure and loss" pervades *Trout Fishing in America,* Brautigan is nevertheless "a legatee of an uncompromisingly idealistic strain of American writing that wills to redeem America through formal achievement" [see excerpt by David L. Vanderwerken in *CLC,* Vol. 5]. *The Hawkline Monster,* however, provides no more sense of uncompromising idealism than does Scott Fitzgerald's "The Diamond as Big as the Ritz," a story with which it shares not only a sense of futility but also more than a few similarities in organization and theme. Parallels between Fitzgerald's story and Brautigan's novel provides both a sense of tradition for Brautigan's skepticism and a source for his "monster." (pp. 37-8)

Brautigan, of course, can have arrived at his own attitudinal judgments about the failure of American experience without explicitly being influenced by Fitzgerald; however, his terminal skepticism about the national vision is an honest one that places him in a stream of "concern with the bankrupt ideas of the American past" that includes Fitzgerald and has its headwaters in Twain. Given a base for skepticism in "The Diamond as Big as the Ritz," Brautigan may also have found his monster close at hand.

Such a suggestion makes sense by placing *The Hawkline Monster* at the end of a line that begins with Twain's *The Gilded Age* which features a home more or less atop Sy Hawkins' "mountain full of coal" and continues through Fitzgerald's story about Braddock Washington's chateau on a "mountain full of diamonds" since *The Hawkline Monster* can be summarized as a short novel in which two gunmen travel through the West (at about the time that Fitzgerald's hero takes possession of his father's diamond) and come on a Victorian mansion constructed above ice caves as big as the Ritz. Faint echoes of *The Gilded Age* also occur in Brautigan's novel; when the Hawkline (Hawkins?) mansion is described as a house that "towered above them like a small wooden mountain covered with yellow snow," . . . beside which rises "a gigantic mound of coal," . . . one hears the echoes of both Twain and Fitzgerald, especially in concert with Brautigan's critical direction.

When Fitzgerald wishes to criticize American illusions about wealth in "The Diamond as Big as the Ritz," he dispatches his hero, young John T. Unger, on a journey into an isolated Montana valley where "the sunset lay between two mountains like a gigantic bruise from which dark arteries spread themselves over a poisoned sky." Amid such isolation the Washington chateau is discovered. . . . In like fashion when Brautigan proposes to criticize American illusions about its national design, he first posts his heroes, the cowboys Greer and Cameron, to travel into an isolated Oregon wilderness called the Dead Hills which "looked as if an undertaker had designed them from leftover funeral scraps," and their "road was very bleak, wandering like the handwriting of a dying person over the hills," and the Dead Hills "disappeared behind them instantly to reappear again in front of them and everything was the same and everything was very still." . . . In similar Western isolation Greer and Cameron are greeted at the Hawkline mansion. . . . In spite of expected dissimilarities of style and a tendency on Brautigan's part to fool around with comic interludes, the heroes of both tales find themselves in substantially the same country, the land of fantasy and fable—even myth. The perspective in both passages lies outside the real world's geography and time; where Fitzgerald translates into fable,

Brautigan translates into myth, though their comparable properties of the fabulous hint at relatedness. (pp. 38-40)

When Fitzgerald poses his protagonist's cheerful but blind idealism about wealth ("I like very rich people") against the dark practices of "the richest man in the world," Braddock Washington, the background is so fantasy-like as to be futuristic. His towers, fairyland, and aeroplanes resemble some kind of Art Nouveau science fiction. By allowing John Unger to watch the insular world of the "richest man" disintegrate during an attack by flying machines, Fitzgerald shows how the impingement of the outside technological world, grown so during Washington's isolation, creates an apocalypse which leaves John aware of his birth of consciousness about "the shabby gift of disillusion." Brautigan's apocalypse, however, takes place in a setting more reminiscent of the past, the Victorian mansion of the Hawkline family. Most of the gothic furniture is there, and in the basement laboratory lurks the monster. The destruction of the mansion, however, is futuristic, though brought about by a collusion between outside and inside forces. In the context of his own dream-like setting amid the Dead Hills of Oregon, Brautigan pits his heroes against the required "fabulous forces" in the form of the treacherous Hawkline monster which makes terrible noises in the basement and which "can change the very nature of reality to fit its mischievous mind." . . . When Greer and Cameron marshal their armaments, which also represent the technological world, "a 30:40 Krag, a sawed-off shotgun, a .38 and an automatic pistol," . . . and launch their attack against the Hawkline monster, the result is again an apocalyptic ending to a kind of insular world where illusions play like ghosts in the daytime. To effect the conclusion of their mission for Miss Hawkline, to destroy the monster that changes reality mischievously, they must also destroy its source, the Hawkline mansion itself; to bring this about they pour whiskey into the mixture of chemicals in which the monster resides. Sparks from the explosion catch the mansion afire, and the monster is turned into diamonds. Greer and Cameron rescue all the people who then stand "for a long time watching the house burn down." . . . (p. 44)

The most striking episode from "The Diamond as Big as the Ritz" which Brautigan parallels and which throws light on his own theme regarding failed dreams is the story's concluding impromptu picnic, where John Unger and the girls, Kismine and Jasmine, both just saved from the burning wreckage of the chateau, "spread the tablecloth and put the sandwiches in a neat pile upon it." The ironic discovery during this pastoral scene is that the two remaining handfuls of Washington diamonds, which the girls have saved, are mere rhinestones. That revelation leads Kismine to draw a parallel between the "diamonds" and the stars and to say that they make her feel "that it was all a dream, all my youth." Brautigan also explicates his theme most openly during the final episode of *The Hawkline Monster,* given the form of an impromptu picnic that brings together the protagonists, his two heroes, with the two sisters, Susan and Jane Hawkline. Brautigan's observations on this scene indicate clearly that one is here looking into the gothic future of the American experience: "The way everybody was sitting it looked as if they were at a picnic but the picnic was of course the burning of the house, the death of the Hawkline Monster and the end of a scientific dream. It was barely the Twentieth Century." . . . If what follows in the novel is, then, any indication of what Brautigan expects for America's future, it will be one of wasted expectations. In the next-to-last chapter Cameron dives into the lake created by the melting ice caves and returns with the "handful of blue diamonds" that are the final remains of the monster. His expectations hopeful, Cameron says, "We're rich." However, the final chapter, a summation of the major characters' latter histories resembling the conclusion of a Victorian novel, proves Cameron's hope to be a deception, for not only are the diamonds wasted but so are the lives of their owners. (p. 46)

As one looks back at the Fitzgerald picnic, one finds John making the following pronouncement of Kismine's suspicion that her youth, like diamonds, has been a dream: "It *was* a dream," he tells her. "Everybody's youth is a dream, a form of chemical madness." So, too, was Professor Hawkline's dream a form of "chemical madness," given to him by his creator as though Brautigan had been a visitor at Fitzgerald's picnic. Brautigan's reader, being aware that Professor Hawkline's dream is the dream of America, will perceive how unlikely the prospect is of maintaining the harmony of expectation and reality when the Hawkline monster's shadow falls between them. He will think with Eliot in "The Hollow Men": "Between the idea / And the reality / Between the motion / And the act / Falls the Shadow." Thus reads Richard Brautigan's final pronouncement on America's failed dream. (pp. 46-7)

Lonnie L. Willis, "Brautigan's 'The Hawkline Monster': As Big as the Ritz," in Critique: Studies in Modern Fiction, *Vol. XXIII, No. 2, Winter, 1981-82, pp. 37-47.*

EVE OTTENBERG

Grim, caustic, overly sentimental, peppered with incomprehensibly mixed metaphors, [*So the Wind Won't Blow It All Away*] seems determined to deprive its characters of any shred of well-being. Never exactly sunny to begin with, Mr. Brautigan has nonetheless nearly found his way out of the literary incoherence of the 1960's and landed in the middle of the current sullen trend. The results are not happy. *So the Wind Won't Blow It All Away,* though better than Mr. Brautigan's previous novels, aims so deliberately at putting the reader in a funk that by page five it has most definitely succeeded.

This rather elliptical, first-person memoir of an anonymous boy raised in poverty, unloved but tolerated by his welfare mother, shows the two of them shuffling from one depressing town to another in the Pacific Northwest circa 1947. There is a familiar assortment of local eccentrics: the old pensioner who lives in a waterside shack made of packing crates; the alcoholic guard of a sawmill, similarly housed in a shack in the middle of nowhere; the husband and wife who drive up to a pond every night, unload their furniture from their pickup truck, set up their living room by the water's edge and pass the night fishing. These people have little apparent relation to each other except that the boy knows them. He is obsessed with death, and a great deal of the novel is taken up with his morose thanatopsis. As a result, there is not sufficient space to develop the minor characters, and the reason why they do appear is never made clear.

The style is disconnected, chaotic, redolent of alienation. Everyone in the book has an acute case of the late 20th-century blues. The boy's mother, inexplicably terrified of the gas stove in her kitchen, passes night after night whispering, "Gas, gas, gas." The old pensioner has built a dock and a boat but for some reason never uses them. A gas station attendant, selling worms for fishing on the side, appears to have no other life. Meanwhile the narrator engages in some rather peculiar and disjointed humor, familiar from the avant-garde novels of a

decade or so ago: "My mother and my sisters won't be mentioned again because they are not really a part of this story. That of course is a lie. They will be mentioned later on. I don't know why I just told this lie." Neither does the reader, which leads inevitably to the thought that perhaps it should have been deleted. This happens with distressing frequency throughout the book; but even so, less frequently than in Mr. Brautigan's previous novels.

Ultimately, it turns out that there really is a cause for this novel's intensely disaffected tone. *So The Wind Won't Blow It All Away* does not merely meander from memory to memory, no matter how much it seems to; it has a climax, a horrible event that, retrospectively, accounts for the flat shell-shocked meaninglessness that precedes it. And if this well rendered, penultimate scene marks the direction in which Mr. Brautigan's fiction is going, then there is something to look forward to. As it is, I could not help thinking that the end is really the beginning, and the beginning is not there at all. (p. 47)

Eve Ottenberg, "Some Fun, Some Gloom," in *The New York Times Book Review, November 7, 1982, pp. 13, 47.*

DAVID MONTROSE

In literature at least, the American Dream has, over the decades, undergone a gradual transformation. At one time striving towards a golden future, its believers now more often look back sadly at a past that is irrecoverable except in memory. Certainly, this is true of [*So the Wind Won't Blow It All Away*], Richard Brautigan's latest novel, where the wistfulness that characteristically informs this author's work has deepened into melancholy, driving out most traces of his idiosyncratic humour. We have here no fantasy, few bizarre metaphors, no eccentric chapter headings.

Writing in 1979, the narrator—Brautigan himself or someone very like him—preserves in print recollections of a 1940s childhood for reasons summarized in the novel's leitmotif:

So the Wind Won't Blow It All Away
Dust . . . American . . . Dust

Two memories are of particular significance. One is a vivid mental snapshot of a fat, middle-aged husband and wife fishing at the local pond on a summer evening in 1947. They have brought their living room furniture with them: not only a couch to fish from, but an easy chair, end tables, a clock, framed pictures. For the narrator, the scene represents a lost America. . . . The second memory, revealed gradually, concerns the narrator's fateful decision one day to buy shells for his .22 rifle instead of a hamburger in the restaurant next to the gunshop. A short while later, on February 17, 1948 (a date inscribed on the mind), he kills his best friend, David, in a shooting accident. Slightly unhinged by the tragedy, the narrator for a time becomes (in the novel's only sustained comic episode) obsessed with hamburgers, believing that, as atonement for having made the wrong choice, he must find out everything about them. Searching for knowledge, he scours books, interviews short-order cooks and butchers. The narrator's childhood ended with David's death. His loss of innocence is directly equated with America's. He remembers, on the day of the accident, standing with his rifle before a filling station, waiting for David to arrive. Nobody paid any attention to him:

Needless to say, America has changed from those days of 1948. If you saw a twelve-year-old kid with a rifle standing in front of a filling station today, you'd call out the National Guard and probably with good provocation. The kid would be standing in the middle of a pile of bodies.

So The Wind Won't Blow It All Away sees the final demise of Brautigan's one-time optimism about the possibilities of life in contemporary America. It was, of course, always a qualified optimism. In the early novels—*A Confederate General from Big Sur, Trout Fishing in America, In Watermelon Sugar,* and *The Abortion*—which were suffused with the hippie ideals of the period, his individualistic characters had to seek their America outside the rat-race, usually in pastoral simplicity. Still, there was at least an America to be sought. Seven years (and three novels) later, with *Dreaming of Babylon,* the area of possibility shrank to the size of its hero's head: he could realize the good life—money, fame, beautiful women—only through the fantasy movies of his imagination. In the new novel, possibility is entirely absent from both present and future. America is located in an ever-receding stock of memories. . . .

Since his first three (and most interesting) novels, Brautigan's work has been increasingly weak on ideas. *So The Wind Won't Blow It All Away* reverses the process: though essentially a straightforward lament, it still represents the author's most substantial novel since *In Watermelon Sugar,* even if the untypical tone does make it a less purely enjoyable experience than most of the intervening titles. Potentially, the material is corny in the extreme, but Brautigan handles it well. In the main, he is content to tell a plain tale plainly; the style slips, briefly, only once. Brautigan is especially adept at evoking the everyday magic of childhood: when venturing into an unfamiliar part of the neighbourhood is a real exploit and the funerals leaving the undertaker's next door are a fascinating spectacle. The novel is by no stretch of the imagination a profound or major work. Nevertheless, Brautigan's departure from his customary mode might lead to greater things. After a run of variously disappointing books culminating in *The Tokyo-Montana Express,* a ragbag of brief sketches, revitalization is more likely in new fields than the well-ploughed furrow.

David Montrose, "Death of the Dream," in The Times Literary Supplement, *No. 4177, April 22, 1983, p. 399.*

ANN RONALD

As soon as I start to translate a Richard Brautigan novel into everyday prose, its words dissolve. When I try to pin down his imagery, *"so the wind won't blow it all away,"* it eludes me. *"dust . . . American . . . dust."* Like the fabled trout of his best-known work, sliding upstream just out of an angler's eager cast, the language of *So the Wind Won't Blow It All Away* floats transparently between Brautigan's imagination and mine.

Brautigan's narrator describes his task in an apparently straightforward manner. "As I sit here on August 1st, 1979," he explains, "my ear is pressed up against the past as if to the wall of a house that no longer exists." His goal is to invade that house of the imagination, to recreate the summer of 1947 when he was twelve years old and "the days of my childhood were running out, and every step I took was a step that brought me nearer to that February 17th, 1948, orchard where my childhood would fall apart just like some old Roman ruins of a childhood." Carefully, then, "like peeling an onion into a smaller and smaller circle with tears growing in my eyes until

the onion is no more, all peeled away and I stop crying," Brautigan's narrator unwinds his tragic past.

First his layered prose introduces an entire population of young and old eccentrics. The narrator becomes, in turn, the little boy who rises at dawn to watch early morning rituals at a funeral parlor next door, the grade-schooler who loses two playmates to death, and the twelve-year-old who is fascinated by hamburgers and guns. His companions, equally grotesque, range from the night watchman at a nearby sawmill, with his "thin beer-brittle physique," to an old man who carves docks and, when eating, dashes "stew down his beard like lava coming from a volcano." (p. 164)

Most of the time the boy wanders alone from encounter to encounter, seeking some friends and avoiding others, luring the reader into a nostalgic yet nightmarish past. "I can hear the sound of redwing blackbirds and the wind blowing hard against the cattails," the narrator recalls. "They rustle in the wind like ghost swords in battle and there is the steady lapping of the pond at the shore's edge, which I belong to with my imagination." My imagination meets the narrator, his boyhood self, and the 1940s' grotesques like the middle-aged fisherman at the shore's edge too. There I try to reconstruct Brautigan's world without making the implicit so explicit that the tragicomic evocation is destroyed.

So I choose not to explain the February day in 1948 when a childhood disintegrated. To learn about that event, "so the wind won't blow it all away," the reader must approach the rainswept apple orchard on his own. Suffice it to say that all our laughter turns to tears when baseball, Mom, apple pie, and Miss American Pie disappear into the American Gothic of Richard Brautigan's mind. (p. 165)

Ann Ronald, in a review of "So the Wind Won't Blow It All Away," in Western American Literature, *Vol. XVIII, No. 2, August, 1983, pp. 164-65.*

LARRY E. GRIMES

[In *Dreaming of Babylon: A Private Eye Novel 1942*] Brautigan makes formula fiction the playground of the fictive self. Hardly a novice to the art of re-visioning formula fiction, Brautigan had tinkered with the historical romance (*The Abortion*), the gothic novel and the western (*The Hawkline Monster*), and the mystery story (*Willard and His Bowling Trophies*) prior to *Dreaming of Babylon.* And like its predecessors, *Dreaming* is a spacey, comic tribute to its original.

Brautigan always touches base before he runs. *Dreaming* opens as should all good hard-boiled novels—with the private eye down at the heels of his gumshoes. A good news-bad news joke begins this first-person circular narrative. The good news is that on this day, 2 January 1942, C. Card, private eye, has been declared 4-F. The bad news is that he'd "gotten a case that [he] needed a gun for but [he] was fresh out of bullets." He is also fresh out of money and just about out of shelter. He is behind on his rent, and previously he has been forced to sell his car and to fire his secretary. As Card puts it (he usually talks in exaggerated hard-boiled similies),

> here I was with no bullets for my gun and no money to get any and nothing left to pawn. I was sitting in my cheap little apartment on Leavenworth Street in San Francisco thinking this over when suddenly hunger started working my stomach over like Joe Louis. Three good

right hooks to my gut and I was on my way to
the refrigerator.

                                                    (pp. 539-40)

Card's problems do not get particularly worse, although his
similes do. We have to put up with them as Card wanders from
police station to mortuary in his search for free bullets to fill
his gun. His quest for bullets and the slow turn of the clock
toward his scheduled rendezvous with his client are all we are
given to keep us going (speaking of hunger) for the first 114
pages, slightly more than half of the book. That and, of course,
Babylon.

Not only is Card a detective; he is also a dreamer. Beginning
with a fastball to the head, which ended his attempt to become
a big league player, Card has been subject to sudden "head
trips" to ancient Babylon. There Card is a baseball hero named
Samson Ruth. There he is the author of a private eye serial
featuring villain Dr. Abdul Forsythe and detective Ace Stag.
Ace is replaced later by detective Smith Smith in such classics
as "Smith Smith Versus the Shadow Robots."

Meanwhile, back in San Francisco, action intensifies and becomes both absurd and morbid in the second half of the novel.
Card meets his client, a petite, beer guzzling blonde woman
who never takes a piss. The blonde offers Card $1,000 to steal
the corpse of a hooker from the morgue. She tells Card she
has picked him for the job, rather than any one of a number
of better known detectives, because "you're the only one we
could trust to steal a body for us. . . . The other detectives
might have some scruples. You don't have any." . . . Card
acknowledges that she is right and that he isn't offended by
the charge. So much for the ethical attributes of the hard-boiled
hero.

Card has considerable difficulty stealing the body because a
pair of body-snatchers has been hired by the same lady to
compete with him. Morbid humor and hard-boiled perversity
dominate the scenes at the morgue as Card watches his cop
friend, Rink, interrogate the bungling body-snatchers. Even
Card has difficulty finding similes to fire the scene: "There
are no words to describe the expression on the hood's face
when Sergeant Rink pulled him out of the refrigerator. He
opened it up just a crack at first. You could only see the guy's
eyes. They looked as if Edgar Allan Poe had given them both
hotfoots." . . . (pp. 540-41)

There is violence, absurdity, and adventure enough in the last
forty pages of the novel. Card is chased around town by angry
blacks who threaten to make him into stew meat. He is forced
to hide the abducted corpse in his refrigerator. And, although
he keeps vigil, he is unable to retain his $1,000. Even worse,
at the cemetery he is caught by his mother and upbraided by
her for causing the death of his father. In retrospect, Card
concludes his narrative of 2 January 1942 with this observation:
"I was right back where I started, the only difference being
that when I woke up this morning, I didn't have a dead body
in my refrigerator." . . .

Both form and theme in *Dreaming* stretch the formula beyond
its usual shape by making it clear that there is a tension between
the facts of life and the meaning of life. Facts include no bullets
for one's gun and a corpse in one's refrigerator. They have no
intrinsic meaning. But Babylon has. It exists only because it
is an active extension of mind. Meaning, then, is connected
with Babylon, with the pure imagination, and not with objective fact. The implication for the formula is clear. According
to Brautigan, nothing meaningful is gained by taking murder

out of the drawing room and placing it in the streets. The real
and the meaningful are not synonyms. This is the case because,
at least in *Dreaming,* the world of facts is patently absurd—
guns but no bullets, refrigerators stocked with corpses.

So the world turns, accumulating facts but not revealing patterns. That being the case, a rich imagination, a lush fantasy
life, is to be preferred to a life of adherence to objective facts
of objectified codes. Card agrees. He is not, once you get past
the marginality and the similes, a very hard-boiled hero. He
is, rather, an unembroiled hero—detached from the world,
narcissistic. Card. Smith Smith. Ace Stag. Call him what you
will. He is more protean than daemonic. The fictive hero strikes
again. (p. 541)

> *Larry E. Grimes, "Stepsons of Sam: Re-Visions of*
> *the Hard-Boiled Detective Formula in Recent Amer-*
> *ican Fiction," in* Modern Fiction Studies, *Vol. 29,*
> *No. 3, Autumn, 1983, pp. 535-44.*

MARC CHENETIER

Ever since Richard Brautigan's remarkable irruption on to the
experimental, radical literary scene of the mid-1960s, his work
has come in for much the same kind of commentary. A poet
who had been hovering discreetly on the edges of the fifties
Beat Generation while he was in his twenties (Richard Brautigan was born in 1935, in Tacoma, Washington) had now
made it on his own, and emerged as the product-image-leader
of the Woodstock-generation sensibility. Firmly anchored,
therefore, amid the rolling fleet of sixties personalities—Her-
mann Hesse, Carlos Castañeda, Alvin Toffler, Charles Reich—
Brautigan could then be celebrated or damned, according to
the view one took of the whole 'hippie' tendency. His work
could be praised for its 'gentle' and 'zany' qualities, or else
condemned for its trendiness or naïveté. It is difficult for any
writer, when he is perched astride two self-conscious generations, in a culture highly sensitive to fashion and eager for
period pieces, not to become completely a product of his times;
and this happened to Brautigan.

No one can deny that Brautigan's first four works of fiction
stood as strong, eerie harmonics of a time when America was
supposed to be 'greening', when a new mood of questioning
prevailed, and youth was 'in'. Nor was Brautigan averse to
endorsing a stage in his career that not only brought him great
fame but also preserved for him a modicum of the youth he
had spent in a San Francisco still more strongly flavoured with
the spirit of North Beach than that of Haight-Ashbury. All this
was a powerful and popular characterization for its time, but
it was always insufficient. The peculiar, radical kind of writing
which was, from the start, Brautigan's hallmark cannot, and
should never have been, reduced to a set of vapid social themes,
or an innocent plucking of leaves away from what Pierre-Yves
Pétillon calls 'the artichoke heart of the Woodstock generation'.
Moreover, Brautigan's career certainly did not end when the
social phenomenon he was supposed to express subsided and
the sixties turned into something else. In fact, it has gone on
to display even more clearly the originality and the genuine
contribution of a fiction writer who . . . has always been much
more akin to the metafictionists of the seventies than to the
naïve flower-children of what I should like to call the pre-
Nixapsarian sixties.

Certainly, though, as long as Brautigan's productions were still
limited to the early poems (ending with *The Pill Versus the
Springhill Mine Disaster* (1968) and *Rommel Drives on Deep*

into Egypt (1970)) and to his first four novels (*A Confederate General from Big Sur* (1964), *Trout Fishing in America* (1967), *In Watermelon Sugar* (1968) and *The Abortion* (1971)), it could remain plausible—if not very satisfactory—to ignore the specific technical qualities of a highly experimental writer, and instead invest all one's critical capital in the study of his themes and subject-matter, or else set out in quest of the elusive, whimsical, half-hidden first-person narrator who seemed to stare out from the book covers in the guise of a John-Lennon-like idol. There was a strong body of cultural and social phenomena to turn to on the one hand, a seemingly weird author-as-personality on the other; the path towards critical label-mongering was more or less irresistible. So, by the seventies, when the time came for the academics to stand back and take stock, most of the critical studies that appeared in the USA were written in a haze of nostalgia or cultural evocation. They drew their arguments from past debates and decisions, calling up the lore of 'relevance and grooviness', all the nickel-and-dime cultural and metaphysical interrogations that invaded the sixties classrooms, and the columns of both the *Berkeley Barb* and *Time* magazine. Brautigan's own complexion and complexity apparently would not suffice; study after study gave evidence of what Roland Barthes used to call 'cosmetic' criticism. Naming was solving: 'funky' and 'young' became part of the critical vocabulary. At best Brautigan was disliked and dismissed, locked into that category reserved for 'minor' writers who have caught a mood or become a phenomenon. At worst he was venerated, covered from famed sombrero to surmised cowboy boot-tip with vague and empty adulation. In the end any censer kills, smothers and censors the iconic object much more surely than does total silence. Criticism becomes incantation; the author is masked and concealed by his followers.

Since then, this approach largely having had its day, it has mainly been replaced by what Cleanth Brooks used to call 'the heresy of paraphrase'. Criticism retells the matter of his work but loses sight of its essential spirit; no explanations are offered of the unique blend of inventions and devices that gives his fictions their particular and extraordinary flavour. Moreover, when Brautigan began to publish books that no longer fitted his received image, critical activity largely responded by discarding him. His next four novels were mostly panned by their reviewers; the celebrated 'easy vignettes' ('easy' as in 'easy rider' or 'five easy pieces'), which carried their all-important message to the sixties, were now read as merely easy in the sense of facile, and could therefore be readily discarded. Little attention was paid to the potential aesthetic pertinence of a fragmentary, self-questioning experimental activity, equivalents of which were in the meantime warmly praised when they came from the pen of Donald Barthelme, writing in the *New Yorker*. The sixties had taken its arts from the communes and the country; apparently the seventies and eighties had moved right back into town, among the condominiums, and our author had not. If criticism of Brautigan turned to anything now, it was to his themes, but with a similar poverty of discussion. The life-asserting, free-floating, liberated, funny hippie of the sixties was increasingly credited with a darkening vision, but this was just seen as another phenomenon of cultural history; the times they were a-changing. Brautigan was gradually discovered to be obsessed with the duality of an existence irretrievably divided between (as the critics liked to say) life and death, but these shadows in his work—though in fact they had always been there for the finding—were simply read as proof that the light of the sixties had faded into the night of the seventies. This explained why their primary mouthpiece had

grown sour, sad and gloomy. No one, still, cared to examine the craft of a writer whose continuing work made him ever harder to parody and deride; in the accepted view Brautigan was the voice of an era that had come and gone, his poems were mere nothings, and his prose was increasingly vacuous and 'irrelevant'.

It is not the purpose of this study to claim that Brautigan rivals Melville and Faulkner, that his trout dwarfs the white whale or his Confederate general outflanks the Sartorises. Neither do I plan to dismiss all thematic approaches to his work. However, the 'minor' status Brautigan is now accorded seems ridiculously inadequate if one is convinced, as much of the best Western criticism of the past thirty years has been, that, as Harry Levin put it in 1950, 'technicalities help us more than generalities'. Brautigan's misfortune is that he lost out on two counts: those who were really interested in his work have wielded either outdated or naïve critical weapons, while those with more sophisticated and useful tools of analysis have not chosen to concern themselves with a writer judged to be of slender repute and slight status. In a time when fiction writers have been increasingly pressed to make ponderous statements on the origin, nature, problems and future (if any) of fiction, Brautigan has never given a single long interview on his craft or ideas. He has tended to mock his own endeavours, refusing to take them as seriously as serious writers are expected to do. He has displayed in his work an undoubted irreverence for critical institutions, but without asserting that aggressive anti-intellectualism that would locate him in a time-honoured American literary tradition. For such reasons, Brautigan has been identified as a 'minor' writer; but other, more specifically literary, reasons have been advanced for regarding him in that light. An apparent thematic thinness has alienated philosophically inclined critics, while his very popularity has repelled many serious critical analysts. More classical critics have been disturbed by the gradual disappearance from his work both of predictable content and of traditionally dominant features of the novel (plot, character, setting); while his lack of explicit theoretical assertion has not won him the interest of those concerned with innovative developments in American fiction. Oddly placed, then, on the margins of 'metafiction' and 'post-modernism' (margins being where Brautigan likes to be), he has not been given full admission into that club—or, rather, as John Barth has so nicely put it, been 'clubbed into admission'.

So, at a time when the most theoretically interesting American writers have far more articles written about them than they have copies sold of their books, and when dubious bestsellers keep on bestselling despite their meagre literary qualities, this most contemporary of American writers sells millions of intelligently crafted books to engaged audiences in the midst of a near-total critical silence. Perhaps Brautigan is in fact so easily read that it is perverse to look for the intricate complexities of his craftsmanship. Certainly few have felt inclined to explore the inner workings of texts which are, on the surface, so easily 'consumed', even though they obviously resist traditional approaches. But, as I have tried to explain elsewhere, it is not only what Osip Brik called 'literary generals' who make for the advance of literature, and an assessment of Brautigan's contribution seems in order at the precise moment when public interest shows some signs of flagging, and the artificial nature of his reputation is beginning to fade. Detailed analyses of Brautigan's fiction are so few and far between that there are no lances to be tilted at anyone. Apart from the few stimulating theoretical discussions of his work which do exist (Tanner [see

CLC, Vol. 12], Pétillon and Pütz, in particular), there is really a large critical desert. (pp. 15-19)

For me, Brautigan, if a 'minor' writer, is a far more important miner than many recognized writers. If Boris Vian or Nathanael West are minor writers, Brautigan is indeed in very good company.... Mapping out a territory is as important as settling it, and one may prefer census-taking to sense-making: the actual weighing of the nuggets will be left to others. After all, I too am just another miner, dealing with the ores and pans; the scales of individual taste are for each reader of Brautigan's works to use. (p. 20)

> *Marc Chenetier, in his* Richard Brautigan, *Methuen, 1983, 96 p.*

EDWARD HALSEY FOSTER

In order to understand Richard Brautigan, it is important to remember a few things about the generation or age that made him its literary envoy to the rest of the world. It should be emphasized immediately that Brautigan had less in common with this generation than many—particularly those who did not bother to read his books—once assumed, but it was as a "hippie writer" that he was first read and popularized, and it is here that we should begin.

And if we are to recall that time, we might start with the moment when, according to the media, it all began: the so-called "summer of love." That summer can be dated from the Monterey International Pop Festival, held at the Monterey County Fairgrounds on 16-18 June 1967. Monterey is a short drive south from what was to be the center of the summer of love, the Haight-Ashbury district of San Francisco, and it seemed as if everyone in the "Hashbury" who could pay the admission and hitch a ride made the trip to Monterey that weekend to hear such new San Francisco bands as the Jefferson Airplane and Big Brother and the Holding Company.

But the Hashbury contingent found much more in Monterey than they expected. Monterey Pop was more than a festival of music by San Francisco groups; it was the deciding moment in the creation—with the media as midwife—of the counterculture. A new type of music—the San Francisco sound—was here established as the principal new form of popular music for American youth, and as the music spread from coast to coast, it brought with it the politics, the manner of dress, the customs, and the drugs that separated the hippie culture from the rest of the world. Just as poetry, a decade earlier, had bound the Beat generation together, so music—specifically the San Francisco sound or acid rock, as it was also called—bound a new generation together, gave it a shared interest and identity. (p. 1)

In 1967, Richard Brautigan was thirty-two, considerably older than most Americans who were making their way to San Francisco and Monterey Pop. He had published a few minor, soon-forgotten volumes of poetry, some copies of which were given away free, and in 1964 ... had published his novel *A Confederate General from Big Sur*. Some critics liked it, others didn't, and the public was overwhelmingly indifferent. Generally publicized as a novel of the Beat generation, it appeared long after the beats had ceased to interest the American public, and few critics saw any reason to arouse an interest again.

"Poor Beats!" wrote Malcolm Muggeridge in his review of the book for *Esquire*. "Mr. Brautigan has convinced me that we are better without them." An anonymous reviewer for *Playboy* decided that the book was "a surrealist synopsis of everything that was worth missing in the now-fading beat literary scene," and the distinguished critic Philip Rahv commented in the *New York Review of Books* that the novel was "only a series of improvised scenes in the manner of Jack Kerouac. It is pop-writing of the worst sort" [see *CLC*, Vol. 12]....

And it is here, among forgotten and forgettable beat writers, writing "in the manner of Jack Kerouac," that Brautigan might have remained were it not for the publication in 1967 of his *first* novel (first, that is, to be written, second to be published), *Trout Fishing in America*.... A few years earlier, a San Francisco book might have attracted—like a San Francisco band—very little attention or none at all. But things were changing. When the Hashbury's new arrivals sought out books that reflected and confirmed their way of life, they found *Trout Fishing in America*.... Brautigan's novel was soon as much a part of the counterculture as the Jefferson Airplane's *Surrealistic Pillow* and Big Brother and the Holding Company's *Cheap Thrills*.

But there was a paradox here, one which would soon lead those more interested in literature than in hippies to wonder if this new generation was really reading the book with real seriousness and attention. Written in 1960-61, its aesthetic design and its politics, insofar as they belong to any age, belong to the 1950s. It is far more a novel of the Beat generation than *A Confederate General from Big Sur*. *Trout Fishing in America* cultivates in its prose an attitude of emotional and intellectual detachment that was to be found at the very center of the existential, alienated culture characteristic of the hipsters and the beats of the 1950s, while *A Confederate General from Big Sur* is *about* people who cultivate this attitude. There is something almost voyeuristic about *A Confederate General from Big Sur*. In that novel, we are asked to watch people in the midst of their detachment from the conventional behavior and rewards (money, fame, social status, and so forth) of civilization, but in *Trout Fishing in America,* we are, in effect, asked to adopt this attitude for ourselves and, for the moment, see the world through its focus. The novel so solidly projects and insists on the ultimate truth and reliability of this attitude that had *Trout Fishing in America* been published at the same time as *A Confederate General from Big Sur,* it might well have been as emphatically dismissed by readers and the critics. (pp. 4-6)

In order to understand Brautigan's relation to American literature in general, it may help first to see him together with other writers from his part of the country, the Northwest. That region has, of course, never produced a literature to equal the literatures of New England and the South, but over the years since 1945, it has produced several popular and respected novelists and poets, including Tom Robbins, Ken Kesey, Philip Whalen, and Gary Snyder. These writers share a fascination with mystical, rather than objective or analytical, perceptions of experience. Their works are profoundly influenced by non-Western, or rather non-European, theories and attitudes: shamanism, primitivism, and Eastern quietism, especially as manifested in Taoism and Zen Buddhism. (pp. 13-14)

Kesey, Snyder, Whalen, Brautigan, and Robbins appear to have little use or respect for traditional Western rationality and have instead turned to Eastern and Amerindian mystical attitudes and theories of experience as foundations on which to build their literary visions. Whether or not it is appropriate to insist strictly on a regional, literary, or intellectual disposition (since their shared point of view is in turn shared by a number of prominent contemporaries such as Robert Bly, W. S. Merwin, and Allen Ginsberg—writers with few or no ties to the Northwest), the similarities between them do seem to be far more than coincidental. . . . If we cannot accurately speak of a "school" of northwestern writers, at least we can say that shared interests and attitudes do set their work off from much traditional American literature.

In the larger patterns of American literature, these writers have much less in common with Henry James, Saul Bellow, and John Updike than with Ralph Waldo Emerson, Henry David Thoreau, and Walt Whitman. They seem far closer to William Carlos Williams than to say, T. S. Eliot. They are not, in short, traditionalists; they do not fit comfortably into any European-American literary tradition. They seem, rather, iconoclasts, spiritual revolutionaries. (p. 14)

Brautigan shares with Snyder, Whalen, and other American writers influenced by Zen an aesthetic concern for the spontaneous and immediate. Such things matter, so to speak, and any attempt to create a sense of permanence only multiplies illusion: the illusions of experience are compounded by the illusion of permanence. There is little in Brautigan's work that is reflective, analytical, or strictly intellectual. Although what he writes is often startlingly unique, it never seems complex; it is plain, direct. With the simplest verbal gestures, he devises a world that is intensely felt but instantly perishable. This aesthetic realization would presumably be the result of considerable work, the result of careful working and reworking of language, yet the impression that the finished work gives is much the opposite. It does not seem as if it had been difficult to write, but we need only try to construct typical Brautigan sentences to see how difficult it is. Brautigan's language sounds as if it were easily put together; it is not.

Brautigan's method of composition, however, makes his work *sound* as if it were easily written. He says that he is an expert typist and with an electric typewriter can type out as much as a hundred words a minute. Speaking of his writings, he says that he gets "it down as fast as possible." For those who prefer the precision, craftsmanship, and complexities of the poem or sentence endlessly reworked, his writings can seem too easy, too simple. His language seems to have reached the page too soon; it should have benefited (or so the argument goes) from reflection and revision.

Brautigan's method of composition reminded Bruce Cook, historian of the Beat generation, of Kerouac's technique of spontaneous prose. . . . Kerouac said that he wished to record things exactly as they were at the moment that they happened, and to do that is, for anyone drawn to the Buddhist doctrine of impermanence, the best that one can do. Intellectual reflection, when motivated by a desire to identify principles and patterns underlying experience, leads only to a kind of mystification, the creation of a sense of permanence (the repeating principle or pattern) where there is none. (Indeed what we are doing in this paragraph—identifying certain patterns in Brautigan's prose—is exactly the sort of thing to be avoided.) To claim that things are set and permanent, just sitting there, unchanging, while the writer perfects his description, is to misconceive both nature and art. Since everything, except the void itself, is in an unending state of flux, all that the writer can do, working as fast as he can, is pinpoint a moment in that perpetual transition before it passes forever. As an aesthetic program, Kerouac's technique of spontaneous prose seems, therefore, an ideal extension of Brautigan's vision of experience. (pp. 17-19)

It does not really matter to most readers how Brautigan writes, what his techniques are, but Cook's suggestion of a parallel between Kerouac's technique and Brautigan's is important. In the end, of course, only the finished book matters—not how it came to be what it is—yet, at the least, this parallel helps us to place Brautigan historically, to suggest that, in terms of literary history, it may be as helpful to see him specifically as a writer of the Beat generation, sharing their techniques and literary theories, as it is to see him in relation to the literature of the Northwest, Eastern mysticism, and the nineteenth-century American tradition represented by Emerson, Whitman, and Thoreau. Brautigan, whom some have considered to be quite unlike anyone before or since, seems to be, on closer inspection, very much within specific literary and metaphysical traditions. (p. 19)

Edward Halsey Foster, in his Richard Brautigan, *Twayne Publishers, 1983, 142 p.*

WILLIAM L. STULL

Despite its crystal-clear surface, placid babble, and meandering course, Richard Brautigan's novel *Trout Fishing in America* (1967) offers the critical angler some tricky crosscurrents, deep holes, and big fish. Through the cool waters of Brautigan's book flow the main currents of American thought—individualism, progress, love, death, and escape. Like Hemingway's Big Two-Hearted River, Frost's West-Running Brook, and Eliot's strong brown god, Brautigan's trout streams carry the flotsam and jetsam of American dreams, the hopes and fears of innocents, explorers, and vagrants. . . . Again and again, Brautigan's characters cast into the waters only to come up with the detritus of America's past.

Brautigan's slim, unprepossessing book is, thus, far deeper and darker than early reviewers imagined it to be. *Trout Fishing* offers, to borrow terms from Roland Barthes, a network of references, ruses, and enigmas, the traces of a culture and its writing. During the 1970s, scholars steadily revealed the book to be a Sargasso Sea of American literature, filled with direct and indirect references to classic and contemporary writers. As Neil Schmitz observes, "To fish for trout, Brautigan knows, is to cast a lure like Thoreau (up into the pale) and handle the strike like Hemingway." Indeed, one of Brautigan's characters puts the matter succinctly when he quips, "Longfellow was the Henry Miller of my childhood." . . . The author has carefully stocked the streams of his book with fry scooped from Walden Pond, from Twain's Mississippi—even from Melville's ocean. For these reasons, Schmitz and other anglers have concluded, "One steps into the stream and inescapably enters the current of American literature."

The allusiveness of *Trout Fishing in America* is apparent even before one reaches the first page. On the cover of the book the author and a smiling lady friend pose before the Benjamin Franklin statue in San Francisco's Washington Square. His getup of striped vest, high-crowned felt hat, and droopy mustache recalls Mark Twain stepping off the stagecoach in *Roughing It*. Hers—boots, brass-buttoned jacket, lace headband—evokes Betsy Ross fallen on hard times. With these American icons, Brautigan opens a fish story that mentions not only Franklin's *Autobiography* . . . but also an eclectic range of American writing from *Walden* . . . and the *Journals* of Lewis and Clark . . . to Algren's *Neon Wilderness* . . . , Styron's *Set This House on Fire,* and Burroughs' *Naked Lunch*. . . . (pp. 68-9)

As Barthes writes, literary references, like all the "codes" that constitute literature, "create a kind of network, a *topos* through which the entire text passes. . . . Alongside each utterance, one might say that off-stage voices can be heard. . . ." Thus, while Brautigan's parallels, parodies, and pastiches are often comic, they also expand the structure of the fable at large, giving *Trout Fishing* considerable depth, breadth, and cultural resonance. Over the past decade, a score of scholars have gone fishing in Brautigan's waters, and few have come back without a catch. But because the evidence of the author's borrowing has appeared piecemeal, never comprehensively, it requires assessment. Moreover, a glance into the anglers' creels shows that, good as the fishing has been, a big one still lurks near the bottom of Brautigan's "trout stream of consciousness."

It was an Englishman, Tony Tanner, who first cast into *Trout Fishing in America* and pulled in a whale. He called attention to Brautigan's parody of John Talbot's epitaph in the seventh chapter of *Moby-Dick*. Where Melville's Talbot "at the age of eighteen, was lost overboard, / Near the Isle of Desolation, off Patagonia, / *November 1st, 1836*," Brautigan's "at the Age of Eighteen / Had His Ass Shot Off / In a Honky-Tonk / November I, 1936." . . . [This] indirect reference to *Moby-Dick* immensely broadens the scope of the episode and gives the comical epitaph a dying fall. Moreover, as Tanner writes, "Brautigan's echo is typically quiet and unobtrusive, yet indicative of how carefully his deceptively slight book is put together." Working the same hole, David L. Vanderwerken revealed larger structural parallels between Brautigan's book and Melville's, as well as debts to Benjamin Franklin's *Autobiography* [see *CLC*, Vol. 5].

Writing of Brautigan's first published novel, *A Confederate General from Big Sur* (1964), Gerald Locklin and Charles Stetler were struck by its indebtedness to two American classics: "What intrigues us most about Richard Brautigan's novel, *A Confederate General from Big Sur,* is its strong resemblance to *The Sun Also Rises* and *The Great Gatsby*" [see *CLC*, Vol. 12]. . . . Parallels with *Gatsby,* beyond Brautigan's nostalgia for "a fresh, green breast of the new world," have yet to be demonstrated in *Trout Fishing in America*. But in *Richard Brautigan,* the only full-length study to date, Terence Malley calls Brautigan's relationship to Hemingway "almost obsessive," and hints at "at least a dozen conscious or unconscious specific echoes of Hemingway" in *Trout Fishing.* As Malley points out, "Trout Death by Port Wine" owes its theme to *The Old Man and the Sea,* where the great marlin, like the trout killed by port, suffers an ignoble, "unnatural" death.

Similarly, Thomas Hearron has argued that Brautigan's work "is firmly rooted in the tradition of Twain and Hemingway" [see *CLC*, Vol. 5]. Like Malley, Hearron concentrates on major thematic links among *Trout Fishing, The Sun Also Rises,* and the Nick Adams stories. But the stylistic connection between Brautigan and Hemingway is, if anything, more striking. Again and again, sometimes in deferential imitation, sometimes in wry parody, Brautigan echoes Hemingway's crisp, laconic voice. This ambivalence is clear in "Trout Death by Port Wine," where the nameless narrator and a fishing buddy enjoy a day of fishing on Owl Snuff Creek. In plot characterization, and style, the episode exactly parallels the twelfth chapter of *The Sun Also Rises,* where Jake Barnes and Bill Gorton fish, drink, and banter in the Irati valley above Burguete. Brautigan's setting is the Pacific Northwest, but each of the streams in *Trout Fishing* has its source in the Michigan woods and carries the same waters as Hemingway's Big Two-Hearted River.

From the cover photograph of the Benjamin Franklin statue ("PRESENTED BY / H. D. COGSWELL / TO OUR / BOYS AND GIRLS / WHO WILL SOON / TAKE OUR PLACES / AND PASS ON."), to the final notice of "the passing of Mr. Good," . . . *Trout Fishing in America* is a haunted book, filled with graves and ghosts of America's past. Hemingway's long shadow falls across nearly every page, symbolizing a lost literary promise that parallels the lost grandeur of virgin forests and clear streams. In "The Last Time I Saw Trout Fishing in America," Brautigan explicitly links the passing of the American *genius loci* with the suicide of the country's foremost writer: "The last time we met was in July on the Big Wood River, ten miles away from Ketchum. It was just after Hemingway had killed himself there, but I didn't know about his death at the time. . . . Trout Fishing in America forgot to tell me about it. I'm certain he knew. It must have slipped his mind." . . . Thanks to the work of Malley and Hearron, few readers of *Trout Fishing in America* will suffer such lapses of memory in the future. (pp. 70-2)

Hearron and Malley alike argue for Mark Twain's influence on Brautigan. But while one senses that Twain's matter and manner are ubiquitous in *Trout Fishing,* pointing to specific borrowings is no easy matter. Malley suggests that Brautigan derives his "rambling, yarn-spinning narrative energy" from Twain, a generalization too true to be much good. Hearron traces a major thematic link between *Huckleberry Finn* and *Trout Fishing:* an obsession with ways of escape from bourgeois society. Like Huckleberry Finn, the narrator attempts to "light out for the Territory ahead of the rest," as does Trout Fishing in America himself. For Huck, the West offers at least a semblance of escape from Aunt Sally and the Widow Douglas. For Brautigan's protagonist, however, even in the wilderness there is the inevitable Coleman lantern, "with its unholy white light burning in the forests of America." . . . As the narrator ends his journey and comes home to Mill Valley, he ruefully admits that America is "often only a place in the mind." . . . Hearron shows that for Brautigan's narrator, the only escape left is inward, into the literary imagination. By taking up his golden "Trout Fishing in America Nib" and closing his book with a deliberately misspelled word, the narrator clenches his freedom. Except for imagination, however, all frontiers have been closed. (pp. 72-3)

Another scholar, Brad Hayden, has noted striking parallels between *Trout Fishing in America* and *Walden* [see *CLC*, Vol. 12]. Like *Walden, Trout Fishing* is episodic and ritualistic, following the protagonist's maturation over a single year. But Hayden rightly concludes that the differences between the books greatly outweigh the similarities. In particular, he contrasts the largely asocial world of *Walden,* centered on the individual, with the crowded landscape of *Trout Fishing,* a book bristling with social satire. Oddly, Hayden neglects to consider Brautigan's one direct reference to *Walden.* The chapter "A Walden Pond for Winos" confirms Hayden's thesis and reveals the depth of Brautigan's pessimism. The winos' Walden is, of course, Washington Square park, forested with "three poplar trees, almost leafless except for the top branches" . . . and dominated by the Benjamin Franklin statue. There, the narrator chats with two friends, "both broken-down artists from New Orleans," who have fallen into a dead-end dilemma: "They were either going to open up a flea circus or commit themselves to an insane asylum." . . . While the latter has its amenities, including "a dance once a week with the lady kooks, clean clothes, a locked razor and lovely young student nurses," . . . it is hardly the kind of refuge Thoreau envisioned. Deforested and filled with the dregs of society, Brautigan's Walden Pond for winos is among his darkest parodies.

Direct and indirect references to earlier American literature thus make *Trout Fishing in America* a far richer book than reviewers initially supposed. Where in 1971 John Clayton saw only flower-powered utopianism [see *CLC*, Vol. 12], subsequent readers have found a Spenglerian account of the decline of the West. Considering the angling, seining, and dredging scholars have done in Brautigan's waters, one might expect *Trout Fishing in America* to be as fished out as Tom Martin Creek.... But like the Grand Old Trout in Brautigan's third novel, *In Watermelon Sugar* (1968), one big fish has so far resisted the scholarly lures. Moreover, this last *Trout Fishing in America* allusion illuminates an episode that two of Brautigan's critics have singled out for special attention.

The novel's thirtieth chapter is entitled "Room 208, Hotel Trout Fishing in America": "Half a block from Broadway and Columbus is Hotel Trout Fishing in America, a cheap hotel. It is very old and run by some Chinese. They are young and ambitious Chinese and the lobby is filled with the smell of Lysol." . . . Its primer syntax notwithstanding, this description is dense with irony, symbolism, and allusion. Trout fishing in America—the rivers that Jefferson cataloged in *Notes on the State of Virginia* (1781-1782) and the fisheries St. John de Crèvecoeur extolled in *Letters from an American Farmer* (1782)—has dried up. It has become a skid-row tenement, managed by immigrants intent on covering the stench of its decay with a commercial disinfectant. But instead of cleansing the Augean lobby, "The Lysol sits like another guest on the stuffed furniture, reading a copy of the *Chronicle*, the Sports Section." So much for the American dream of endless resources and infinite perfectibility. (pp. 73-5)

Students of modern American literature will recall room 208 as a familiar address at another apartment hotel, a "nondescript affair" named the San Bernardino Arms. The San Bernardino, better known as the San Berdoo, is the home of Tod Hackett, the protagonist in Nathanael West's *The Day of the Locust* (1939). . . . Like the couple in Hotel Trout Fishing in America, Tod rents a third-floor room. But his thoughts and steps invariably linger on the second story, for "It was on that floor that Faye Greener lived, in 208." . . . Thus, just as the headstone in "Trout Fishing on the Bevel" marks the grave of Melville's John Talbot, so the door of "Room 208, Hotel Trout Fishing in America" opens into the apartment of West's lubricious *femme fatale*. In effect, Brautigan's and West's characters share rooms at the same cheap hotel, a stopping place, West points out, for "the people who come to California to die." . . . Like Brautigan's other allusions to earlier American

fiction, "Room 208" thus has a dark undercurrent beneath its light surface. (p. 76)

West's influence on Brautigan reaches well beyond matters of atmosphere and setting, however. In the same chapter of *The Day of the Locust,* sandwiched between the sketches of the San Berdoo and the Chateau, lies what may be the source of Brautigan's leitmotif in *Trout Fishing* at large. The passage describes one of Tod's artworks, a precursor of his apocalyptic painting *The Burning of Los Angeles:*

> Abe was an important figure in a set of lithographs called "The Dancers" on which Tod was working. He was one of the dancers. Faye Greener was another and her father, Harry, still another. They changed with each plate, but the group of uneasy people who formed their audience remained the same. They stood staring at the performers in just the way that they stared at the masqueraders on Vine Street. It was their stare that drove Abe and the others to spin crazily and leap into the air with twisted backs like hooked trout. . . .

West's closing simile, the dancers gyrating "like hooked trout," anticipates the controlling metaphor in Brautigan's book. With their collocations of room number, Lysol bottle, and trout imagery, the parallel chapters in West's and Brautigan's novels mark yet another spot where *Trout Fishing in America* runs with recycled waters. (p. 77)

The pervasive reference code in Brautigan's novel is likely to render any talk of a "last" *Trout Fishing in America* allusion premature, if not presumptuous. Like the big one that nearly got away in "Room 208, Hotel Trout Fishing in America," further allusions to American literature likely float in the depths of the text. As Brautigan's burned-out fisherman Alonso Hagen concludes in "a little Trout Fishing in America epitaph," "Somebody else will have to go / out there." . . . What finally matters is not the single catch but the fishing at large, and *Trout Fishing in America* proves to be well stocked—in Barthes's terms, "replete." There, as in those two classics of modernism, *The Waste Land* and *Ulysses*, each reference to earlier literature proves to be an exponent of a larger cultural code: a history, a style, or an ideology. Dark, deep, and teeming with remembrances of things past, Brautigan's "trout stream of consciousness" branches off the mainstream of American literature. (p. 80)

William L. Stull, "Richard Brautigan's 'Trout Fishing in America': Notes of a Native Son," in American Literature, *Vol. 56, No. 1, March, 1984, pp. 68-80.*

William S(eward) Burroughs

1914-

(Has also written under pseudonyms of William Lee and Willy Lee) American novelist, short story writer, nonfiction writer, essayist, scriptwriter, and editor.

An innovative and controversial author of experimental fiction, Burroughs is best known for *Naked Lunch* (1959), a surreal account of his fourteen-year addiction to morphine and other drugs. Intended, according to Burroughs, to be "necessarily brutal, obscene and disgusting," the novel was first published in Europe and aroused heated critical debate in the United States even before its American publication, which followed three years of court trials for obscenity. Although some reviewers denounced the book on moral grounds, condemning its graphic descriptions of drug injections, casual murders, and sadomasochistic homosexual acts, such writers as Mary McCarthy, Allen Ginsberg, and Norman Mailer lauded it as an experimental masterpiece notable for its radical break with traditional language and narrative. In *Naked Lunch* and his subsequent fiction, Burroughs uses addiction as a metaphor for the human condition, postulating a cosmic vision in which all human consciousness is addicted to some form of illusory gratification. As Burroughs stated, his major concern throughout his work has been "with addiction itself (whether to drugs, or sex, or money, or power) as a model of control, and with the ultimate decadence of humanity's biological potentials."

Burroughs is the grandson of the industrialist who modernized the adding machine and the son of a woman who claimed descent from Civil War General Robert E. Lee. In 1936, he received his bachelor's degree in English from Harvard University. In 1944, he began using morphine. During the 1950s, Burroughs, together with Allen Ginsberg and Jack Kerouac, helped found the Beat movement. The writers who became part of this group produced works which attacked moral and artistic conventions. Burroughs's addiction to increasingly harder substances, his unsuccessful search for cures, and his travels to Mexico to elude legal authorities are recounted in his first novel, *Junkie: The Confessions of an Unredeemed Drug Addict* (1953; republished as *Junky*). Written in the confessional style of pulp magazines under the pseudonym of William Lee, the novel received little critical notice. In 1957, Burroughs traveled to London to undergo a controversial drug treatment known as apomorphine. Following two relapses, he was successfully cured of his addiction.

Ostensibly the story of junkie William Lee, *Naked Lunch* features no consistent narrative or point of view. The novel has been variously interpreted as a condemnation of the addict's lifestyle, as an allegory satirizing the repressiveness of American society, and as an experiment in form, exemplified by its attacks upon language as a narrow, symbolic tool of normative control. Consisting of elements from diverse genres, including the detective novel and science fiction, *Naked Lunch* depicts a blackly humorous, sinister world dominated by homosexual madness, physical metamorphoses, and cartoon-like characters, including Dr. Benway, who utilizes grotesque surgical and chemical alterations to cure his patients. Escape from the imprisoning concepts of time and space are dominant themes in this work and in Burroughs's later fiction, reflecting the

© *Thomas Victor 1986*

addict's absolute need for drugs and his dependency on what Burroughs termed "junk time." Burroughs explained the book's title as "the frozen moment when everyone sees what is on the end of every fork."

Burroughs's unused writings from *Naked Lunch* make up the bulk of its sequels, *The Soft Machine* (1961), *The Ticket That Exploded* (1962), and *Nova Express* (1964). In these works, Burroughs, influenced by artist Brion Gysin, develops his "cut-up" and "fold-in" techniques, experiments similar in effect to collage painting. Collecting his narrative episodes, or "routines," in random order, Burroughs folds some pages vertically, juxtaposing these with other passages to form new pages. This material, sometimes drawn from the works of other authors, is edited and rearranged to evoke new associations and break with traditional narrative patterns. In the surrealistic, quasi-science fiction sequels to *Naked Lunch*, Burroughs likens addiction to the infestation of a malignant alien virus, which preys upon the deep-seated fears of human beings and threatens to destroy the earth through parasitic possession of its inhabitants. The title of *The Soft Machine*, a novel emphasizing sexuality and drugs as a means of normative control throughout history, indicates the innate biological device which allows the virus entry into the human body. Mind control through word and image is the subject of *The Ticket That Exploded*. In this novel and in *Nova Express*, Burroughs suggests a number of remedies to the viral infestation. Although he expresses a cautious optimism, the crisis remains unresolved, and humanity's fate is uncertain at the saga's end.

In 1970, Burroughs announced his intention to write a second "mythology for the space age." Although his recent novels have generally received less acclaim than *Naked Lunch* and its sequels, critics discerned a remarkably straightforward approach to these works, which rely less on cut-up strategies and horrific elements and more on complex, interrelated plots and positive solutions to escaping societal constraints. As Jennie Skerl noted, "In Burroughs's recent fiction, pleasure and freedom through fantasy balance the experience of repression, bondage, and death that the earlier works had emphasized." The universe of *The Wild Boys: A Book of the Dead* (1971) is similar to that of Burroughs's earlier books but is epic in proportion, encompassing galactic history and the whole of humanity in its scope. In this work, which again involves a destructive virus, a near-future Western society is fragmented into large totalitarian cities and vast unsettled regions. The cities are challenged by "the wild boys," a libertarian, homosexual society of nomadic gunfighters engaged in guerrilla warfare with the forces of control. The wild boys are led by Audrey Carsons, one of Burroughs's alter egos. Carsons also appears in two interrelated works, *Exterminator!* (1973) and *Port of Saints* (1975), which feature a similar blend of science fiction, juvenile novel, Western novel, and fairy tale. Time and space travel figure prominently in *Cities of the Red Night: A Boys' Book* (1981), in which detective Clem Snide traces the source of the alien virus to an ancient dystopian society. *The Place of Dead Roads* (1984) transfers the conflict to near-future South America, where descendents of the wild boys ally themselves with Venusian rebels in an escalating battle for galactic liberation.

Burroughs's recently published novel, *Queer* (1985), was one of his first literary attempts and is considered a companion piece to *Junkie*. According to Burroughs, the book was "motivated and formulated" by the accidental death of his wife in Mexico in 1951, for which Burroughs was held accountable. The novel centers once again on William Lee, chronicling a month of withdrawal in South America and his bitter, unrealized pursuit of a young American male expatriate. Harry Marten stated that the book functions as "neither a love story nor a tale of seduction but a revelation of rituals of communication which substitute for contact in a hostile or indifferent environment."

Burroughs is also well known for his nonfiction works. *The Yage Letters* (1963) contains his mid-1950s correspondence with Allen Ginsberg concerning his pursuit in Colombia of the legendary hallucinogen *yage*. Further correspondence to Ginsberg is collected in *Letters to Allen Ginsberg, 1953-1957* (1982). During the mid-1960s, Burroughs became an outspoken proponent of the apomorphine treatment, claiming that its illegal status in the United States was the result of a conspiracy between the Food and Drug Administration, police, and legal authorities. His arguments are presented in *Health Bulletin, APO 33: A Report on the Synthesis of the Apomorphine Formula* (1965) and *APO 33, a Metabolic Regulator* (1966). Burroughs's observations on literary, political, and esoteric topics appear in a collaborative venture with Daniel Odier, *Entretiens avec William Burroughs* (1969; revised and translated as *The Job: Interviews with William Burroughs)*, and in his recent collection, *The Adding Machine: Collected Essays* (1985). *The Third Mind* (1979), written in collaboration with Brion Gysin,

is a theoretical manifesto of their early "cut-up" experiments. Burroughs has also written a screenplay, *The Last Words of Dutch Schultz* (1970).

(See also *CLC*, Vols. 1, 2, 5, 15, 22; *Contemporary Authors,* Vols. 9-12, rev. ed.; *Contemporary Authors New Revision Series*, Vol. 20; *Dictionary of Literary Biography*, Vols. 2, 8, 16; and *Dictionary of Literary Biography Yearbook: 1981.*)

RICHARD KLUGER

Naked Lunch is an action painting of twisted forms and oozing substances, spectral fiends playing out hideous episodes like distended sick jokes, a hipster's medley on the 12-tone scale. . . .

[Burroughs] is an American novelist writing in an existentialist idiom that proclaims the essential absurdity of life and reduces it to a flash series of cruel and often pointless charades. Time and place and plot and character are all missing; yet none of this matters, by the standards invoked. What matters, as in all abstract art, are the effects created, and Burroughs' effects are stunning. He is a writer of rare power.

"I have no precise memory of writing the notes which have now been published under the title of *Naked Lunch*, the author says in the introduction; he was an opium addict at the time. This, while perhaps explaining the rarified limbo through which the book whirls, seems irrelevant, for the writing is precise and the imagery sharply evocative. . . . True, there is an overripe lushness about Burroughs' phantasmal landscape—recurring tonal words include "arabesques," "iridescent," "baroque" and "mosaic"—but it exists next to abundant, this-worldly references to Madison Avenue, P. J. Clarke's, the fluoridation debate and clinical descriptions of the dope-taking process. But the scene oscillates so swiftly between Burroughs' grotesque dream world and the topical, locatable one that the two mesh and, by the end, it all seems one surrealistic madhouse.

We have had some of this on the stage, of course. Genet is perhaps the closest in feeling, with his bizarre and often obtuse masques. . . . But where Genet is shrill . . . , Burroughs is often very funny and always absorbing. The best piece of sustained writing in the book is a chapter called "The County Clerk," which begins as a Kafkaesque exercise in civic fruitlessness but flowers into broad, almost predatory burlesque.

Other influences are detectable—Orwell in much of the political satire and Henry Miller, of course, in the eruption of four-letter words and an accompanying moral anarchy. But Burroughs constructs no systems like Orwell's, and the sex, most of it autoerotic and homosexual in context, seems just another ingredient in the stench of corruption overhanging the scene. For this paean to nihilism strikes me as more than the caterwaulings of a long-time addict, writing about addicts, for addicts and the beatnik fringe, which has embraced Burroughs as a genius. Of those who would dismiss the addicted as mankind's dispirited and worthless dregs, Burroughs seems to ask if there are not addictions worse than narcotics—if, in other words, the drugged are any worse off than the rest of us.

The title, we are told, is "the frozen moment when everyone sees what is on the end of every fork." It is not a pleasant sight. But William Burroughs calls our attention to it in a memorable way; his talent is something more than notorious. It may well turn out to be important.

Richard Kluger, "Panorama of Perversity," in Books, *November 25, 1962, p. 8.*

ALFRED CHESTER

Burroughs is actually Robbe-Grillet-Without-Tears. He is easier and more fun to read, very different in manner and technique, but his idea and effect are the same. According to literary legend, Allen Ginsberg, while visiting Burroughs in his Paris apartment sometime during the 1950's, found the floors littered with hundreds of sheets of paper that Burroughs had scrawled on while high on heroin. Ginsberg, it is said, gathered the papers together, read them with reverence, and put them into the form, or rather sequence, they now have [in *Naked Lunch*]. He needn't have bothered to sort them, since the book would have almost the same effect if he had shuffled the manuscript like a deck of cards. (p. 90)

Naked Lunch is no work of genius, but the first half of it is pleasantly readable without too much skipping, and the second half of it is pleasantly skippable without too much yawning. What has given Burroughs the air of genius, aside from the up-to-date erotic passages that stud the book, and aside from having his name connected with Ginsberg, Kerouac, and Corso, is that his implications are metaphysical, almost unique in an American, and that he follows the Europeans in his abandonment of the quest for a moral position. He is the first American novelist to be not merely childishly iconoclastic about his civilization, but to have turned his back upon it totally.

Though he reminds me of other writers, he falls short by comparison. In his tireless and tiresomely intellectual use of obscenities and in his shrieks of outrage, he is like an adolescent Henry Miller. In his savage political parodies, he is like a naive George Orwell. In his brutal sexual fantasies, he is like a timid Marquis de Sade. In his overpowering belief that the mention of petroleum jelly, baboons' behinds, and contraceptives will infallibly provoke laughter, no matter how many hundreds of times repeated, he is like a senile Joey Hirsch, the boy next door to me when I was ten.

But most of all he reminds me of Lewis Carroll. Whether or not Burroughs wrote his book in a narcotic trance, his debt to *Alice in Wonderland* is enormous, and to have got himself thus indebted is so right and so brilliant that it makes me wish I liked *Naked Lunch* better than I do. In attempting to write a novel that will pull the washplug out of the universe, that will wither with scorn and smear with muck all the works of man and God, what could be more superb or to the point than to take as one's method the method used in the most loved story of the English language?

Burroughs's rabbit hole is heroin, and like Alice he falls down, down, down—into a world of dreams. Unlike Alice's, his dreams are brief and unsustained, rarely lasting a page, often enough lasting barely more than a sentence or two. . . . Endless pairs of boys make love, breaking each other's neck for climax, dying, living, breaking, dying. It is all somehow a work of spite, a work of revenge. . . . Some of it is funny and some of it marvelously dirty, but it just goes on and on; it begins to sound like the whine of a girl who's been stood up. It begins to sound like a tantrum. (pp. 90-1)

If you take the trouble, you can probably relate the things and people and events in this book to your own life, just as we do

with *Alice,* although only two or three times does Burroughs approach the precision, wit, and truth of Carroll. . . .

Let us now make our adieux to Alice for we are returning to the 20th century where no good little girl belongs or is likely. We might as well also say goodbye to Burroughs, but not because he doesn't belong. We say goodbye because he isn't there, and I mean by this Burroughs the hero of the novel. He is a fantast created by narcotics, and his world is dreams in which he seldom figures. Who is the man? The man is no man, a receptacle of fantasies, like Robbe-Grillet's inferential man, who we presume has been created by narcotics. But this is only a presumption, since the author gives us no reason to believe that the dreamer isn't merely dreaming his own creation. It toils back upon itself. Life is a series of horrible and disconnected illusions which, alas, cannot even be relegated to the mind of a drug addict. The statement is absolute, the illusions are the whole of reality. But extend the implications further, to include yourself and myself. Who then are we, the dreamers who *may* not exist, or ghosts of the dream who then surely *do* not exist? And who then is dreaming us? (p. 91)

Alfred Chester, "Burroughs in Wonderland," in Commentary, *Vol. 35, No. 1, January, 1963, pp. 89-92.*

DONALD MALCOLM

It is tolerably easy to abominate William Burroughs' *Naked Lunch.* . . . Almost the entire contents of the book are offensive—hypothetically, at least—to what were called "the finer feelings" in the days when it was believed that the public came equipped with such a commodity. The work, moreover, has so little structure, being a mere hectic accumulation of anecdotes and fantasies, that it might as fittingly have been issued in a paper bag as between hard covers. On occasion, the writing falls to a level not commonly seen since the disappearance of those lurid pulp magazines whose covers featured an anguished beauty on the verge of ravishment by some unlikely purple cephalopod. Over considerable areas of narrative, to round off the indictment, the work is vastly more conspicuous for its pretensions than for its actual accomplishments. To concede all this is to find oneself in a poor position to argue with those authorities who would consign the book to immediate oblivion. And yet some attempt at argument, I think, ought to be made.

To discover the merit and interest of *Naked Lunch,* it is necessary only to decline to accept the book on its author's terms. By altering our expectations, we alter our judgments. It may be fruitful, then, to postpone our consideration of Mr. Burroughs' claims for the work and simply regard it as a raw document of personal history, as which it exerts a deal of fascination. Mr. Burroughs, by his computation, was for fifteen years an addict to opium and its multitudinous derivatives. The bulk of the work was written during this period, and when it specifically treats of an addict's life, and the single, appalling need that stains his every contact with the world, then we find the author in his strength. The book opens well, with a grittily realistic episode in a subway. The narrator, having jettisoned the telltale utensils of addiction (an eye dropper and spoon), eludes a pursuing narcotics detective by leaping aboard a departing train, in which he encounters a young "advertising exec. type fruit." Our anti-hero is prompt in his assessment of his mark ("You know the type comes on with bartenders and cab drivers, talking about right hooks and the Dodgers, call the counterman at Nedick's by his first name"), and he further observes that "A square wants to come on hip. . . . Talks about 'pod,' and smoke it now and then, and keeps some around to offer the fast Hollywood types." He regales his dazzled companion with an assortment of lurid, elliptical, and wandering anecdotes of addiction, and advances by degrees toward the touch, reflecting:

> He's a character collector, would stand still for Joe Gould's seagull act. So I put it on him for a sawski and make a meet to sell him some "pod" as he calls it, thinking, "I'll catnip the jerk." (Note: Catnip smells like marijuana when it burns. Frequently passed on the incautious or uninstructed.)

But no such appointment is reported, and the victim is never spoken of again. A peculiar air of disconnection has entered the narrative:

> I cut into the automat and there is Bill Gains huddled in someone else's overcoat looking like a 1910 banker with paresis and Old Bart, shabby and inconspicuous, dunking pound cake with his dirty fingers shiny over the dirt.

There is no conversation between the narrator and this pair; the sight of them merely reminds him of a gruesome anecdote of addiction, which he relates with mordant relish, and this is followed by

> So back downtown by the Sheridan Square Station in case the dick is lurking in a broom closet.

Disconnection increases as the narrator stocks up on heroin and flees New York. Other cities swim briefly into focus and then simply vanish from the field of vision. Chicago, St. Louis, New Orleans, Cuernavaca, Tangier loom and shimmer and evaporate. Addicts and perverts appear and disappear, recur and vanish, as insubstantial as images upon a screen. In this proffered view—flickering, intermittent, and often vivid—one makes out the addict's mode of life as Mr. Burroughs has known it. Toward the public, "the squares," the addict's attitude is usually and unabashedly predatory. With the police, he is wary and in great dread of arrest and its consequence, the withdrawal of drugs. With other addicts, he shares not so much a relationship as an acknowledgment of their mutual isolation. I find all this as interesting, and as fit a subject of interest, as the delvings of anthropologists into the lives of distant aborigines, who generally are quite as unlovable as the run of addicts, and even less articulate than Mr. Burroughs.

Fantasies begin to engulf the narrative. At their best, these fantasies continue—in another key—the theme of addiction, its preoccupations, and its anxieties. They often are grisly, but the subject, after all, is not a pleasant one, and the horrors are rendered with a ferocious jocundity that sometimes rises to effective style. As one delves further into the book, however, it becomes evident that Mr. Burroughs regards his fantasies not as personal property but as general parables of our time. Through a thickening welter of degradations and perversion, of bloody and pointless violence committed on the helpless, one dimly perceives the objects of the author's rage. His feelings about contemporary politics and science are transposed into visions of sadism and narcotism, relieved of all contact with reality, and discharged in lurid episodes that frequently are meant to nauseate the reader, and frequently do. These passages oblige us to suspend our appreciation of the work as a document and to confront it on the ground of its highest ambition. "The title," Mr. Burroughs writes, "means exactly what the words say: NAKED Lunch—a frozen moment when everyone sees what is on the end of every fork." Let us select for scrutiny an episode of which the author has observed, in his introduction:

> Certain passages in the book that have been called pornographic were written as a tract against Capital Punishment in the manner of Jonathan Swift's *Modest Proposal*. These sections are intended to reveal capital punishment as the obscene, barbaric, and disgusting anachronism that it is. As always the lunch is naked. If civilized countries want to return to Druid Hanging Rites in the Sacred Grove or to drink blood with the Aztecs and feed their Gods with blood of human sacrifice, let them see what they actually eat and drink. Let them see what is on the end of that long newspaper spoon.

It should be noted that Mr. Burroughs is speaking not of atrocities but of ordinary capital punishment as it is practiced in this country, among others. It is curious, then, to see him write of a "return" to ancient barbarities, as if the trend of the times were to extend the death penalty to an ever-increasing number of offenses, whereas the current of history long has been flowing, though with appalling sluggishness, in precisely the opposite direction. We may, however, ascribe this lapse of the historic sense in the author to the generosity of his anger, and proceed to examine the satire.

The first job is to find it. For a satire "in the manner of Jonathan Swift," the tract is singularly lacking in trenchancy. In fact, amid so general a preoccupation with death, rot, and brutality, one can ferret out the satire only by balancing probabilities and opting for the chapter in which hangings are most elaborate and doings likely to be called pornographic are most graphically rendered. This chapter is by way of being the scenario of a *cinéma bleu*, and begins with a couple of embranglements involving a boy and girl whose ideas of a good time may very well strike the judicious as bordering a little on the rococo. No injuries are reported. Next, the girl is withdrawn from play, her place being taken by another young man, a substitution that does not diminish the sexual complexities or relieve the hermetic atmosphere. Nevertheless, all participants remain in good health. At length, however, the girl returns to the corroboree, and assists one of the young men in the hanging of the other, taking her pleasure with the victim at the moment of execution. She then sets about devouring him, "her face covered with blood, eyes phosphorescent." The surviving youth assaults her, then proceeds to hang her and assault her again. Matters continue in this vein for several more pages, and involve violations and deaths by burning, by shotgun, and again by hanging, for the last of which a lewd sheriff is selling tickets. And that is the satire.

If, in the *Modest Proposal*, Swift had written exclusively and vividly of the slaughter, evisceration, and disjointing of infants for ragouts and fricassees, then Mr. Burroughs' claim to literary kinship might carry weight, but in fact Swift pursued a very different course, and the difference is instructive. The Dean of St. Patrick's assumed that the reader would find cannibalism horrible, and turned that spontaneous horror to intellectual account, directly and pointedly scoring off—among other things—the luxury of the rich, the brutality of the poor, the exactions of landlords, the dishonesty of shopkeepers, and the policies of the ruling party in England, which allowed Ireland no effective voice in the regulation of her own economy. Mr. Burroughs, by contrast, is so emphatically bent upon making horror stark upon the page that he accomplishes very little else. The only approach of his satire to its subject lies with the ticket-selling sheriff and the notion of the *cinéma bleu,* which rather vaguely imply that capital punishment exists to gratify the cravings of a sick public to gloat upon the infliction of death. There might have been something in this scheme if executions still were, as they used to be, a public spectacle, but contemporary executions tend to be decorous, dismal, and private occasions that offer small scope for a general morbid thrill, with the consequence that Mr. Burroughs' single satirical shaft misses its target by veritable parsecs. It is a poor sort of satire, I think, that attacks a real evil for unreal reasons, and allows the perpetrators—in this case every citizen who condones capital punishment—to declare, with perfect truth, ''This has nothing whatever to do with me.''

I am afraid that objections of this sort must be brought against the author's every attempt to rectify the world by the intensity of his visions of its sordidness. These visions remain entirely personal, and the point is missed. As *Naked Lunch* progresses, and the author calls for helping after helping of what amounts essentially to the same dish, it requires great patience not to be tempted to reply, at last, with all possible dignity, ''Sorry, I'm not your waiter.'' Interesting as Mr. Burroughs can be when he is dealing with the addicted life he has known, it is profitless to accompany him on his excursions into nightmare. A vividness of incident on the page is no substitute for a sense of experience in the mind, and a shrill tantrum is not as good as a clear thought. An obsessional dealing with violent irreality can be dangerous for a writer, in that it tends to lure him into sentences like these:

> One Friday ''Fats'' siphoned himself into The Plaza, a translucent-grey foetal monkey, suckers on his little soft, purple-grey hands, and a lamphrey disk mouth of cold, grey gristle lined with hollow, black, erectile teeth.

> Its hairless body was a strange and ghoulish blue, except for a broad band of white which encircled its protruding, single eye: an eye that was all dead white—pupil, iris, and ball.

The second of these sentences, in point of fact, was not written by William Burroughs at all but by an earlier fantast, named Edgar Rice Burroughs. This one can be found in an opus called *The Gods of Mars.* It makes one think. (pp. 114, 117-18, 120-21)

> Donald Malcolm, *''The Heroin of Our Times,''* in The New Yorker, Vol. XXXVIII, No. 50, February 2, 1963, pp. 114, 117-18, 120-21.

CAROLE COOK

I hear that one day . . . Burroughs returned to his hotel on one of the narrowest and most literary streets of Paris to find his artist friend Brion Gysin cracking up over a chance discovery that he christened the Cut-up Method—a writer's equivalent of the painter's collage technique, and a kind of contact point between words and pictures.

First of all, the Method provided a solution to a suitcase full of Burroughs's junk-dream writings, which were cut up into his *Nova Express/Soft Machine/Ticket That Exploded* trilogy. On the simplest level, *The Third Mind* (which is naturally made

of cut-ups) is the story of the collaboration and extraordinary friendship of two peripatetic geniuses. That part is quite clear.

But *The Third Mind* (which also includes further literary and graphic extensions of the Method) is like Hesse's Magic Theater: Not For Everybody. What it is depends not just on who is reading it, but when he is reading it and what he is looking for in it; successive readings will yield entirely different books. For example, the authors say their work can be put to such uses as mind expansion and time travel; it can be used as ''a manual of elementary illusion techniques,'' and as a key to decoding what other writers are *really* saying. In other words, it is theory, method, and object in one package—Zenbook, dreambook, and mirror of the reader's imagination.

The Third Mind has no genre and no literary predecessor. It is one of a kind, in a category of its own. . . . It's still several light-years ahead of its time.

> Carole Cook, in a review of ''The Third Mind,'' in Saturday Review, Vol. 6, No. 1, January 6, 1979, p. 56.

REGINA WEINREICH

> The trapdoor is closed on the secrets of Dr. Sax, he rumbles below. . . . in his own huge fantasies about the end of the world. ''The end of the world,'' he says, ''is Coming. . . .''
> —Jack Kerouac, *Dr. Sax* (1959)

William S. Burroughs's rumblings have surfaced in *The Third Mind,* with greater impact than Beat ally Kerouac could envisage at the creation of this fictive persona. . . .

In the East Village, anarchy consorts most happily with spectacle, even if the rumblings now span two decades. The connection of the literary avant-garde with the new wave in music is made explicit through *The Third Mind.* With antivalues so prominently in display, the avant-garde enters the media proper. The recent Nova Convention was attended by many Burroughs fanatics accustomed to hearing their prophet predict the survival of our Planet. But Nova conspirators agree: Never has his program appeared so clear, so refined, so—visible. (p. 73)

This hooplah in America masks the importance of *The Third Mind* as a provocative, philosophical document. Without the hype, in Europe, where its tenets have been known for two years (in the French, *Oeuvre croisees*), Burroughs is revered as a new Sartre. Burroughs and his collaborator, Brion Gysin, . . . contribute an idiom of consciousness to existentialist tradition—the cut-up.

Notice this example, a part of a percussive poem that reads something like a mantra:

PROCLAIM	PRESENT	TIME	OVER
PROCLAIM	PRESENT	TIME	
OVER	PROCLAIM	PRESENT	
TIME	OVER	PROCLAIM	
PRESENT	TIME		

The words dart off the page in pulsating word/images. Fixed on the page but not in syntactical position, they can be read in any combination. Meaning is conveyed in camera clicks. Words flash. As Burroughs explains, this typography attempts to bring word and image together, to bring writing closer to its origins (calligraphy and hieroglyphics), and to allow writing to catch up to painting, which is 50 years ahead through the use of montage. The word is thus invested with new powers: Reichian orgone, Joycean epiphany, orgasm—energy packed images in spurts. Wrested from the restrictions of the linear sentence, and thus free of cause-and-effect, the word conjures a variety of mind associations, dynamic deja vu.

And this is precisely how the urban mind flows; the cut-up is a manifestation of stream of consciousness, a literary montage of the mind cut constantly by random factors. Cut-ups emphasize the randomness of life. . . . *The Third Mind* suggests that coincidence is not only frequent, but patterned, "if people keep their eyes and ears open." These telepathic associations open the mind to the future.

The cut-up theory not only provides an alternative to linear thinking; to the sentence and the pervasive blandness of the straight-jacket novel, the cut-up is treason. But nonlinear prose calls attention to itself and is most difficult for the artist to defend. Far from promulgating a cult of unintelligibility—as he is often accused of doing—Burroughs has repeatedly tried to explain and justify his writing. . . . *The Third Mind* is a compilation rehash of prior literary theories, though in a more elegant form than these early underground pamphlets. Philosophy and experiments are included from early scrapbooks—grids, fold-ins, intersections, permutations, and illustrations—some dating back nearly 20 years. They are not ordered in sequential chapters, but are in interchangeable sections, a cut-up text.

The Third Mind, intended as a futuristic model for all the arts, further suggests their interdependence. All third minds are the interweavings of two autonomous systems of thought—for example, Burroughs and Gysin, the reader and the book. The third mind created in the collaboration is separate from each component. . . . The new consciousness opens the mind to Burroughsean literature.

Still, for all this expansion of the mind, Burroughs's initial paranoia about the end of the world requires more than his present rhetorical or aesthetic solution. Here I find the cut-up at its greatest disadvantage for writing: Word/image associations do not adequately overcome word/symbol associations, which tie us in time to the past. In Burroughs's obsession with the future, the past is to be cut loose at once. But without tradition, writing loses the innuendo of feeling; it looks thin. And the same is true for a social philosophy that implies survival without ideals.

Elsewhere, Burroughs has tackled this problem in his assertion that Darwinian theory, which only deals with natural selection and survival of the fittest, does not account for the development of language: "The word can as easily hinder survival when there is a symbol and what it refers to." Burroughs leaves the symbol to the "new mythology" he says he is creating in his novels. The word as we know it, he argues, is the manipulative tool of those in power to preserve it. Easily distorted by politicians and governments, history is impenetrable in linear Time. But even when Burroughs supplies the mental framework to transcend linear Time, it is naive to think the result will be directionless Space. Judging by the appeal of the most nihilistic in Burroughs—the indulgence of violence and the "bad boy" sensibility that marks so much of his most powerful fiction—he promulgates a cult of decadence too hermetic for Space.

The greater hope of *The Third Mind* is survival in art—to celebrate new collaborations, and thereby regenerate. . . . The world can't end if art continues. *The Third Mind* inspires the mind. (pp. 73-4)

Regina Weinreich, "The Dynamic Déjà Vu of William S. Burroughs," in The Village Voice, Vol. XXIV, No. 5, January 29, 1979, pp. 73-4.

ROBERT PETERS

[Letters collected in *Letters to Allen Ginsberg, 1953-1957*] transcend the trivia and chatter of most gatherings of letters; they should strike even jaded readers as important and stimulating.

Despite claims in the preface, Burroughs is hardly a De Quincey of junk. He was a talented, harrowed man who spent much of the '50s either on a quest for junk or for cures to enable him to kick it. These letters, reeking with pain, are particularly eloquent since they allow us to see the immense personal struggle Burroughs waged against hard dope, a battle he finally won. There are leavenings of humor throughout, too, often at Burroughs's expense. One passage offers the hilarious conjecture that President Ike was a junkie via an "Osmosis Recharge" he received from Burroughs. . . .

Many letters provided raw materials for important segments of *Naked Lunch,* the best American novel of its decade. These include withdrawal nightmares in which Lee (as Burroughs called himself in the novel) is tortured by Arabs and whole cities go up in flames . . . , [and] obsessions with knives, guns and general mayhem, often with a bizarre smear of sexuality and scatology.

Another Burroughs obsession, pederasty, appears throughout. His intense and prolonged affair with a young Arab is presented with charm and tenderness.

Some of his literary tastes are frankly expressed. He loathes Lionel Trilling and warns Ginsberg against him. . . . He is a bit sniffy about Paul Bowles, Truman Capote and Tennessee Williams. . . . And he exclaims over his own fondness for parody: "Neither in life nor in writing can I achieve complete sincerity."

Perhaps because Burroughs excised love passages written to Allen Ginsberg—as Ginsberg reports in his fine, affectionate introduction—the drift of the book is toward a pretty self-obsessed Burroughs. Moments of self-pity are as numerous as zits on an unwashed adolescent's face. He whines because he feels rotten and needs money, or because he's hocked his typewriter to buy junk. But, then, for his gift of *Naked Lunch* alone, we easily forgive self-indulgences. There is a weird grandeur in *Letters to Allen Ginsberg.*

Robert Peters, "Gifted Letters with a Weird Grandeur," in Los Angeles Times Book Review, September 19, 1982, p. 15.

SMALL PRESS REVIEW

Written from Tangiers, William Burroughs' letters to his young friend Allen Ginsberg [collected in *Letters to Allen Ginsberg, 1953-1957*] are not only the primary sources for *Naked Lunch,* but also a diaristic account of who was doing what, with whom, and when, when the Beat Generation was really on the road. Ginsberg's introduction to this volume fills in for his long-lost half of the correspondence and recollects his more than 30-year friendship with Burroughs. These "epistolary confessions" as Ginsberg calls them, provide a "self-portrait of the strange Burroughs that Kerouac and I knew, the gentle Melancholy Blue Boy, the proud elegant sissy, the old charmer, the intelligent dear.'' Or, as Burroughs himself puts it, ''the ancient saga of a moaning man of letters.'' . . .

[These letters] provide a source and resource for *Naked Lunch* itself, and a record of ''the transmutation of experience dated and in context'' into the fictions we have come to know as contemporary classics. Burroughs' voice emerges as querulous, moaning, sometimes petty and self-pitying, but always direct and engaging.

A review of ''Letters to Allen Ginsberg, 1953-1957,'' in Small Press Review, *Vol. 14, No. 10, October, 1982, p. 8.*

PERRY MEISEL

By now, Mr. Burroughs's early work may appear anachronistic, even though both *Naked Lunch* and the work of his subsequent middle phase—particularly *The Soft Machine* (1961), *The Ticket That Exploded* (1962) and *Nova Express* (1964)—have led to accolades from an enduring cult that heralds him as an American original and a major innovator in experimental fiction. To be sure, Mr. Burroughs's novels have all the markings of a studious infatuation with modern literature. Harvard-educated and a legendary cosmopolitan, he has pursued that infatuation as aggressively as he once pursued narcotics, and the pursuit has resulted in an almost textbook replica of the techniques of James Joyce's polylogues and T. S. Eliot's fragmented verse narratives throughout the novels on which his literary reputation has been based for 20 years.

With the publication of *Cities of the Red Night* in 1981, Mr. Burroughs entered a new phase, presenting his own vision with exactitude and originality. Gone was the slavish scrambling of syntax, sequence and sense. Instead, the novel presented two neat, clipped narratives—a detective story and an account of a young sailor's adventures in 1702. The book's climax comes when the two plots collide, and the collision is extraordinary. The stories join as the youngster from the 18th century eventually exchanges identities with the missing suburban boy from the present whom the novel's deadpan sleuth, Clem Snide, has been hired to find.

In fact, the two merge quite literally by means of a bizarre, quasi-medical procedure in which the head of one boy is transferred onto the body of the other, making Mr. Burroughs's long interest in telepathy or astral projection a physical as well as a psychic reality in his books. The key is time travel and conspiratorial cloning, technologies controlled by feuding cosmic cabals that link the Central Intelligence Agency and the Mafia with the wizards and sorcerers of mythical ''cities of the red night'' located somewhere near the Gobi Desert 100,000 years ago. The picture grows more complicated when intelligence from outer space is shown to have had a role in the manipulation of time by the ancients. . . .

Mr. Burroughs takes the premises of cosmic conspiracy and time travel a step further in his new novel, *The Place of Dead Roads,* continuing to fulfill a wish he expressed in *The Soft Machine,* to produce a mythology durable enough for the space age. In no way an attempt at generic science fiction, Mr. Burroughs's new novel, like *Cities of the Red Night,* is really an extension of his earlier work—but only now have his intentions become plain. Even *Naked Lunch* contained enigmatic allusions to star travel and cosmic struggle, but it was not until *The Soft Machine* and *Nova Express* that exchange of identities, interplanetary transit and galactic war between the forces of

tyranny and freedom became real activities rather than mere metaphors in the world Mr. Burroughs creates. *Cities of the Red Night,* his best novel, made all this especially convincing and absorbing because the prose was less ostentatiously surreal than before, so the reader experienced the kind of vertigo Mr. Burroughs's characters had to contend with. In *The Place of Dead Roads,* he adds to both the scope and the settings of his mythology.

The emergence of his new hero, Kim Carsons, is already foreshadowed in *Cities of the Red Night* by the appearance there of Audrey Carsons, who was originally Clem Snide, the detective. Late in the story, he is transmuted into a frontier rowdy who knows Wyatt Earp and the Clantons thanks to the artistry of time warping and identity transfer. As the names suggest, Mr. Burroughs is interested in the Old West as well as in time travel and interplanetary strife. Kim is a gunslinger, or ''shootist,'' who goes West in the 1880's to form a cowboy conspiracy Mr. Burroughs calls ''the Johnson family.'' The moniker is borrowed from Western lore and denotes the proverbial bond of honor among thieves and murderers.

Despite a largely naturalistic style and an often conventional mode of storytelling, *The Place of Dead Roads* slips and slides in time and place—almost unaccountably until one is again reminded that a transpersonal web links everything together. Like the boys in *Cities of the Red Night,* Kim and his Robin Hood outlaws are really agents in a vast organization; they are allied with Venusian political insurgents in a fight for galactic liberation. Time travel, space travel and cloning again account for the oddities in what is otherwise a predictably Beat picaresque novel. . . .

Wherever he is, Kim is connected to a network of Johnsons that spans time and space. He can travel more easily than Mr. Burroughs's earlier characters because the technology of the author's universe has progressed beyond the surgical time transport of *Cities of the Red Night.* . . . By implication, space and time travel need no longer be bound by the limitations of bodily form, psychological identity or even natural conception. Instead, in Mr. Burroughs's ideal state, ''identity'' consists of random particles drawn from the infinite reaches of space and time. Like the distortion of the name Kit Carson, everything in *The Place of Dead Roads* is a trifle out of focus, testimony to the presence of another point in time in another place always synchronous with the one the reader—or the characters—occupy. ''Kim's memory of his past life,'' the narrator says, is ''spotty. Sometimes he feels he is getting someone else's memories.'' (p. 8)

To imagine such a world is one thing; to represent it is another. The advance in technology in Mr. Burroughs's magnificent universe is not matched by similar advances in the writer's style. *Cities of the Red Night* had promised a new narrative strategy. It featured the cool flow of an almost hard-boiled realism, punctured only late in the story when the novel revealed its cosmic intentions. Mr. Burroughs then had good reason to use the Joycean mannerisms of his middle phase in an attempt to show how all things metamorphose into one another in the book's concluding sections.

In *The Place of Dead Roads,* Mr. Burroughs tries to play the two styles off against each other, and the result is a watery realism on the one hand and a now tiresome imitation of the Joycean approach on the other. If the former is too loose compared to the realistic portions of *Cities of the Red Night,* the latter is too mechanical. In retrospect, much of his writing seems like that. Joyce's apparently foolish puns and juxtapositions have an internal logic that detonates almost endless possibilities of meaning; Mr. Burroughs's use of such techniques is meretricious. Rather than build his world, as Joyce does, through montages that yield detail and density when scrutinized closely, too often he takes the short cut of simply swathing signs and images together to be strange and absurd. His justification is doubtless the Beat poet Brion Gysin's theory of "cut-ups," with which Mr. Burroughs has long been associated; it defines literary composition as the assemblage of bits and pieces of discourse at random.

In fact, his zaniest writing is still obliged to Joyce, and so is the bold idea behind it. Mr. Burroughs's time travel is a logical extension of Joyce's notion of metempsychosis, or the transmigration of souls, in *Ulysses*. As Joyce puts it, "we . . . weave and unweave our bodies . . . their molecules shuttled to and fro." The description elucidates Mr. Burroughs's ideas at least as well as Joyce's own. (pp. 8-9)

Too learned to be simply an example of what Lionel and Diana Trilling called the "modernism in the streets" of the Beat Generation, Mr. Burroughs's project is really a soft Modernism that relies on effect more than effectiveness, suggestion more than achievement. Unlike his late partisan and friend Jack Kerouac, he does not radiate the deep passion that commands attention, whatever the shortcomings of style.

Such overt and inescapable discipleship may well point to the ultimate irony of Beat, counterculture and many other brands of post-Modern esthetics. They are indebted to a modern tradition of revolt that inveighs above all against indebtedness, against the staleness of habit or convention. . . . Although kicking "junk" has symbolized kicking all habits for Mr. Burroughs ever since *Naked Lunch,* kicking the habit is the very habit of modern literature itself.

His is a position of untenable contradiction. As the stylistic impasses of *The Place of Dead Roads* suggest, his work as a whole is caught in an insoluble quandary. The very signature of his originality is the signature of someone else. While this may be the kind of truth his own fiction portrays to the extent that it can, it is also the truth that modern writers have the most difficulty accepting—unless (as great writers always do) one is willing to outsmart it. The decline of the avant-garde—at least of a Modernist or post-Modernist avant-garde—is already well under way, but Mr. Burroughs remains one of its more intriguing figures. (p. 9)

> *Perry Meisel, "Gunslinger in a Time Warp," in* The New York Times Book Review, *February 19, 1984, pp. 8-9.*

OLIVER CONANT

[*The Place of Dead Roads*] is a repellent novel that cannibalizes some of the stalest, least interesting formulas of mass entertainment—the ritual violence of subliterary Westerns, the body-snatching and "replicants" of '50s science fiction. Burroughs has used mass art in his writings before; in their very different ways, *Junkie* and *Naked Lunch* employed the idiom and attitude of hard boiled detective fiction as a means of rendering the underworld reality of drug addiction. No such purpose attaches to the Western and science fiction narratives in his latest offering, nor are they intended as satire or for some higher purpose—unless you believe Burroughs when he claims . . . that he "writes for the Space Age."

The "antihero" of this weary amalgam is Kim Carsons, really an all-purpose fantasy figure—a turn-of-the-century "shootist," and leader of homosexual robber bands. These bands go on rampages against those Burroughs refers to as the "shits of the world," the "bigoted ignorant basically frightened middle-class." The bands dress in "Shit Slaughter" uniforms, and carry out "Shiticides." (Their resemblance to Hitler's SS seems to bother Burroughs not at all. The excrementitiousness is representative.) The shoot-'em-ups are followed by invaders from Venus; the last third of the novel features Kim as an anti-Venusian agent.

The novel begins with the death of a William Seward Hall (the first two names are Burroughs' own), a writer of Western stories who uses the pseudonym "Kim Carsons." Apart from this obligatory and unrevealing postmodernist flourish, Burroughs shows far less interest in issues of authorship or identity than in avidly chronicling Kim's gunfights, his time and space travels, and most of all his endless copulations with a variety of partners, sometimes multiple ones. Homosexual reveries, as much as heterosexual ones, can make for fine fiction; here the sex is unvaryingly mechanical and repetitive. (p. 19)

While full of the breathless, ellipsis-strewn lyricism of Burroughs' earlier works, *The Place of Dead Roads* contains nothing so startling as, say, the line in *Naked Lunch* that impressed Norman Mailer: "Gentle reader, we see God through our assholes in the flashbulb of orgasm." In fact, the style is surprisingly and deplorably lax. I got off Burroughs' bus along about *The Ticket That Exploded,* but the naturalism of *Junkie* and the surrealism of *Naked Lunch* do demonstrate stylistic range.

The laxness of the new novel cannot be explained away as deliberate, as an avant-gardist's subversion of cliché. Rather, it suggests the author's exhaustion. His clichés, in contrast to the bureaucratic or scientist jargon spoofed in *Naked Lunch,* are his own. . . . Paris "is like a painting that moves," and we are told of "the narrow twisting streets" of an Arab town. None of this serves any satiric purpose; it is simply bad writing.

Strictly speaking, there are no ideas in *The Place of Dead Roads* either, only obsessive, private concerns of a pseudoscientific cast. Burroughs ruminates on mummification, cloning, viruses ("what we call evil is quite likely a virus parasite occupying a certain brain area"), and "gun-smithing." (He knows more, and is willing to write more, about hand guns, dum-dum bullets and hair triggers than one could ever hope to read outside of a small-arms manual.) In the past, Burroughs has given the impression of being at a number of weird forefronts; his ethnographic fantasies were diverting, and his knowledge of a vast variety of exotic drugs certainly tested. This time out he is content to present such startling observations as the following: "Recent research has established that dreaming is a biological necessity. If dream sleep, REM sleep, is cut off, the subject shows all the symptoms of sleeplessness. . . ."

There are, of course, scattered efforts at Deep Thinking: "We might say that the next radically new concept biologically speaking will be the transition from Time to Space." Elsewhere, Burroughs is less mysterious about what he thinks of as biological advance; he wishfully predicts the evolutionary triumph of young male homosexuals, who will be able to do without women through the use of "artificial wombs." Ultimately, Burroughs looks forward to the abolition of separate sexes, the production of "a-sexual offspring," and so on. Women, it goes without saying, have no part in the novel, except as the focus of fear and barely concealed loathing. (In *Naked Lunch* women were referred to as "gashes." No doubt for prudential reasons, Burroughs has dropped this objectionable usage, as well as the often cruelly funny characterizations of homosexuals found in both *Naked Lunch* and *Junkie*.)

Although nothing in *The Place of Dead Roads* ever quite rises to the level of an idea, there is diffused in it, however inchoately, a feeling about what the world is like that has several points of resemblance to the dopier aspects of '60s counterculture ideology—despite Burroughs' Nazoid touches. (pp. 19-20)

Apparently for Burroughs, as perhaps for the faithful who continue to buy his books, the world is a simple place, divided between a "them"—bigots, replicants, "arch conservatives"—and an "us." The saving remnant turns out to be those bold spirits willing to entertain, along with Burroughs, fantasies of

> a united space program . . . the earth becomes a space station and war is simply *out,* irrelevant, flatly insane in a context of research centers, space ports, and the exhilaration of working with people you like and respect toward an agreed-upon objective, an objective from which all workers will gain.

The imaginative poverty, the simplifying ideology, the violence and pornography that appear in Burroughs show him to be no more than an index to our unhappy contemporary culture. As if recognizing how little there is in *The Place of Dead Roads* that is in any way real or challenging—after all these years, and after so much of the freedom and license called for by the Beats has been sanctioned—Burroughs endeavors nevertheless to shock, or at least to sicken.

In this he succeeds, at least for me. I find shocking, even if dumb, his fulminations against England and the English. . . .

I find sickening the gratuitous gore involving humans that is directed at animals, too, notably horses and dogs. Television has numbed us to the violent ends of gunfighters, but the suffering of animals retains its power somehow. I will spare . . . [readers] lengthy quotations; suffice to say that the depth of Burroughs' bloody-mindedness surfaces in an extended and perfectly disgusting dog-shooting episode.

Burroughs' well-known "cut-up" technique, the more or less random assemblage of prose fragments, may have quickly become unreadable for all except his most devoted followers, yet it conveyed, most memorably in *Naked Lunch,* his singular vision of fragmentation and apocalypse, of an America given over to excess. The awfulness of the new novel, though, can hardly be attributed to its consecutive narrative. . . .

No, it is the distance Burroughs has put between himself and the desperation of drug addiction and the drug addict's world— a reality he was once intimately acquainted with—that explains the unreality of *The Place of Dead Roads* (where drugs are, as they say, "strictly recreational"). . . . [In a piece he wrote for the *New York Times*], Burroughs chided reviewers for pigeonholing him as the "writer of drug addiction," asserting, as he has many times in the past, that "from the beginning I have been . . . concerned, as a writer, with addiction itself (whether to drugs, or sex, or money, or power) as a model of control, and with the ultimate decadence of humanity's biological potentials. . . ."

We have seen what this talk of "biological potentials" amounts to. As for addiction, it seems to me far less easily assimilable to other kinds of human experience than Burroughs would have us believe. For evidence one could turn to Burroughs' own first books, in which he bore powerful witness (I do not say responsibly or humanly) to the uniqueness of the drug addiction experience. But even if it were so easily assimilable, the author of *The Place of Dead Roads* is not the man who could convince us. (p. 20)

Oliver Conant, "Burroughs Lost in Space," in The New Leader, *Vol. LXVII, No. 6, April 2, 1984, pp. 19-20.*

ALAN HOLLINGHURST

[*The Place of Dead Roads*] is a dizzying, sickening and ill-planned journey, and ostentatiously so; its global rangings teach us nothing about the world (or indeed about Venus), and observation, with extensive view, surveys not mankind but one man: William S. Burroughs.

The Dead Roads that meet at the Place are the roads leading away from the author's past addresses—Jane Street, called Larachi, Tangier, Arundel Terrace, SW13—roads he will never use again. Burroughs is seventy now, and the habitual nostalgia of his writing, with its recurrent memories of his St Louis adolescence, is sharpened here with an abhorrence of age, gruesomely exemplified in vignettes of Somerset Maugham and Beau Brummell, seen in their final squalid loss of self-control.

Kim Carsons, the novel's protagonist, is a further and more autobiographical manifestation of the Audrey Carsons of *The Wild Boys* and *Exterminator!*—a morbid, clever, obscene, sex-obsessed, malodorous, unliked youth. Though he shares characteristics with Burroughs (both are likened to a "sheep-killing dog"), his kinship to the author is more tellingly revealed in the collusive, manipulative way he is handled. . . . Kim is an ideally powerful agent sent out imaginatively by the ageing Burroughs into a corrupt world; by his shape-changing and transmogrifications he remains ever young and invincible; his psychopathic deeds are exercises of the author's savage indignation and kinky humour. And having given him preternatural skill and acuity, Burroughs cannot resist entering the story himself, speaking suddenly in the first person as a member of Kim's gang, secreting himself within the legend he has created.

This legend describes Kim's mobilizing of dissident elements in society to eliminate a self-righteous, religious, dogmatic and industrial establishment. At one level the plan, gorily vengeful, naively fantastic and rabidly misogynistic, is adolescent and absurd; but at another it assumes an ingenious and satirical logic. Based on the premise that humans only work to one-fiftieth of their potential, it advocates decentralization of power, the conserving of resources, intelligent assessment, the tapping of latent energy, *Vispassana* or self-awareness. Between these levels there is ideological strife: mind-expanding freedom from constraint is sought through means of totalitarian violence. The political terrain, like all aspects of Burroughs's work, is the scene of bafflingly personal struggles, which, though illogical and obscure, are presented with a surrealistic conviction that they make sense. . . .

In all this, traditional adolescent literature undergoes a perverse and relished corruption: the Westen and the fairy-tale are redeployed to sinister ritual ends. Cultic, talismanic power accrues to guns, knives, clothes, sexual acts; gestures have unspoken significance; ordinary words are codes. There are occasions when the effect is very similar to the ''Journal of an Airman'' in Auden's *Orators*, a resemblance intensified by Burroughs's use of a virus as the carrier of the church-going self-righteousness of the enemy. . . . Kim keeps a diary in which sex-scenes are entered in code. At its wittiest—and there are pages of unpredictable brio—Burroughs's writing here claims descent from Auden's symptomatic riddles, his ''handsome and diseased youngsters'' spreading their rumour horrifying in its capacity to disgust.

But Burroughs's writing is not, and has never aimed to be, so compact and laconic a medium. Its natural tendency is to virulent excess; though *The Naked Lunch* stands out for its mordant and prodigal invention, Burroughs's *oeuvre* tends to blur in retrospect, an effect intensified by the recurrence of characters and the obsessive repetitions of subject-matter. There is, for example, a set of phrases of erotic nostalgia—''late afternoon light'', ''drifting smoke'', ''phantom train whistles from lonely sidings'', ''whiff of carrion''—which Burroughs has told like a rosary in book after book: unpunctuated, trancelike, they reappear time and again in *The Place of Dead Roads*. And the descriptions of boys and sex, though uncontrollably frequent, revolve a minute repertoire of words and phrases with an effect that is both haunting and tiring.

The Place of Dead Roads shows clearly this obsessive, snagged attention to narrow areas; the prolonged verbal dwelling on the makes, calibres and designs of guns intensifies the fetishistic emotion with which they are regarded. Their handling becomes personalized, instinctive and supremely efficient: guns partake of the sex-magic which enshrouds the whole book in its empyreumatic smoke. Equally relentless is the stress on smell: Kim, like other boys of his kind, gives off a ''rank ruttish smell'' when aroused. His *smell brain* revels in the stink of the corruption which is the book's consistent practice. Early on we hear of a Parisian bartender who fashions a weapon from his breath, the smell of which induces ''vertiginous retching horror''. . . . Such olfactory nasties are outdone by the genetic mutations of Venus, where men turn into centipedes, and the land is rutted by shmunns, violent and repellent hogs which excrete through their skin. Here Kim cooks recipes from *La Cuisine de Peste*—''possum succumbed to climatic buboes . . . candied suckling armadilloes cooked in their own leprosy''— the esurient fantasies of Epicure Mammon given a further obscene twist. At one point, Burroughs picks up on a plague described in *The Unfortunate Traveller*, and he clearly identifies with Nashe as a journalist of atrocity: like all his books *The Place of Dead Roads* is stuffed with cruelty relished as spectacle. And in such passages his writing displays a Rabelaisian inventiveness and humour, a hallucinogenic vividness.

None the less it is not getting anywhere; it exemplifies inertia, in both senses of the word—it is static, and it goes on and on unstoppably. In particular it does not get into our sympathy. The most exquisite scene in the book describes Kim's sex with an incubus, and it is a fitting emblem of Burroughs's deliberate and satirical repudiation of human normality, contact and aspiration. . . . But Burroughs does not reach out to mortals; negative in everything else, he has no negative capability. His imaginative journeys really are made down dead roads, itineraries within the arid kingdom of his mind; Kim's murderous, fantastical progress is a parable of Burroughs's own subversive career. It is Burroughs's awareness of this that gives the novel, for all its self-indulgence and its chaotic vehemence, a valedictory mood.

Alan Hollinghurst, ''Travelling with Kim's Gang,'' *in* The Times Literary Supplement, *No. 4231, May 4, 1984, p. 486.*

OLIVER HARRIS

Like their author, the essays [in *The Adding Machine: Collected Essays*] are a minefield of misinformation, an eccentric collage of ambiguous provocations and disguises. Indeed, having long since abandoned any distinction between his life and his work, the Burroughs of these pieces is very much in persona. At the lectern or on stage, this avant-garde senior citizen—here at his most accessible—is a Demolition Man who cannot be dismissed.

Nothing if not extreme, his style is redolent of the same bitter odour as Swift's *A Modest Proposal*. And yet, beneath, there is a suffering melancholy, a naive charm and outrageous honesty: con man or idiot savant, Burroughs remains a genuine writer, an incorruptible genius. And the *truth* of his work? Well, as Nietzsche remarked, 'The falsity of an opinion is no objection to it'—what counts is whether it proves life-furthering. Apocalyptic visions may be commonplace, indeed ubiquitous, but then we just might be the generation the past has warned us about. The evidence looks good.

The collection opens with a retrospective, a literary autobiography which details the sources that have inspired his parodic offspring. The theme is taken up in another piece, **''Les Voleurs''**, where he eschews the 'fetish of originality' and makes plagiarism the ironic principle of creativity: coming out of the closet to join the ranks of mature poets who steal rather than borrow.

Burroughs's piracy extends beyond kidnapping the characters of other writers to the wholesale theft of his own work. Thus, **''Les voleurs''** closes with the call, 'We are not responsible. Steal anything in sight.'—words lifted straight from *Naked Lunch*. From this bizarre self-referential nature of the Burroughs oeuvre comes its haunting power to disturb and mutate. The B-side of his obsessive repetition is a tautological invulnerability: Burroughs is impervious to questions of common-or-garden accuracy.

Indeed, contradictions and mistakes run both within and across essays. For example, he quotes a sentence from Hemingway's ''The Snows of Kilimanjaro'' three times, each time differently, never correctly. It is surely a measure of Burroughs's anomalous genius that such errors are creative rather than detrimental: they further attest to his fiction's omnivorous refusal to be either defined or definitive. . . .

The function of writing is variously defined: as time travel, as sympathetic magic, as revealing the knowledge we hide from ourselves. . . . There are essays on civil defence, Freud, women (drily subtitled 'A Biological Mistake?'), immortality, mind control, even how to stop smoking. He reports on Genet, Conrad and Greene and writes superbly about Kerouac, Beckett and Proust. He reminisces about Paris, warns against the CIA practising its 'computerized black magic' and hails Nixon as a folk hero. Humankind is heckled for being a beached fish of a species, heading for disaster, while he rails against Jerry Falwell and 'Moron Majority' and welcomes space as the Final Frontier.

And yet, despite the range of subjects, they are written about in the same nasal voice, drawling along until each illustrative skit takes on independent life, blossoming into a Venus Fly

Trap for the unwary reader. So, *The Adding Machine* is inevitably another invitation into Burroughs's private universe, sent out from his present semi-retirement in Hicksville, Kansas, where he lives, like the Wizard of Oz, a frail figure behind the curtain of his sorcerer's prose, still frantically pulling levers to exorcise the daemons we cannot quite dismiss.

Oliver Harris, "The Magus," in New Statesman, *Vol. 110, No. 2849, November 1, 1985, p. 36.*

HARRY MARTEN

[*Queer* represents] an early fragment of a narrative in which we can see clearly the beginnings of the road that led to Mr. Burroughs's more fully realized, Boschlike portraits of chaos and decay in *Naked Lunch, Nova Express* and *The Soft Machine.*

A companion piece to *Junky* (1953), which was Mr. Burroughs's first and simplest effort to set down his experience as an addict, *Queer* moves in fits and starts to chronicle the "hallucinated month of acute withdrawal" of William Lee, the protagonist. Setting his tale amid the contradictions of a Mexico City and Latin America that are inviting one moment and menacing the next—where inanimate objects seem to spring shrieking to life while living beings just as suddenly appear "curiously spectral"—Mr. Burroughs renders a discomforting account of Lee's sexual pursuit of a disengaged American drifter named Eugene Allerton. It is neither a love story nor a tale of seduction but a revelation of self-protective rituals of communication that substitute for contact in a hostile or indifferent environment. . . .

"After withdrawal," Mr. Burroughs writes in his open and informative introduction, "the organism readjusts and stabilizes at a pre-junk level." In the last chapters of *Queer,* fragments uncomfortably yoked to the first two-thirds of the narrative, we discover Lee finally stabilized but still unstable, drifting south with Allerton toward the Amazon in a fruitless search for the hallucinogen yage. Like much of the action, it is a dead-end journey, marked only by short-circuited encounters, altercations and separation.

"The book is motivated and formed," Mr. Burroughs says, by "the accidental shooting death of my wife, Joan, in September 1951" (at Mr. Burroughs's own hands). This is the event that Lee, "knowing and yet not knowing, tries to escape," the action toward which he feels himself "inexorably driven." And while it is hard to grasp this in the text itself because it is "an event which is never mentioned, in fact is carefully avoided," the insight clarifies the brooding, ominous atmosphere that hovers increasingly over the disparate pieces of the text.

Finally, after only 130 pages, *Queer* just trails off, leaving its narrator much as we first found him, alone in a chaotic and sinister world, parading his coping mechanisms and still hoping to connect. Though it is neither wholly realized nor fully satisfying, it is good to have *Queer* in print for the first time, 33 years after its composition. A blueprint for many of Mr. Burroughs's themes, narrative techniques and characterizations, it helps us come to grips with the dark humor, violent energy and unsettling vision of this writer who has forced himself into our consciousness and seized a place in our literary history.

Harry Marten, "Mexican Specters," in The New York Times Book Review, *November 3, 1985, p. 22.*

CHRIS VINCENT

[*The Adding Machine*] displays Burroughs' characteristic sharpness, intelligence and humour. This is a fascinating book, both for the insights it affords into Burroughs' own style and method of writing (the celebrated "cut-up" technique) and for his assessment of other writers.

In these essays, Burroughs' oddities and inconsistencies are in evidence: the scholarly, gentlemanly figure in the lightweight suit and trilby hat who emerges from some of these pieces is at odds with the psychotic junkie from the urban wasteland, who drops helpful hints about carving up muggers on the subway, or coping with withdrawal symptoms. In the end, the quirkiness of Burroughs the personality fades into insignificance beside the coruscating brilliance of his writing.

Chris Vincent, in a review of "The Adding Machine: Collected Essays," in Tribune, *Vol. 49, No. 51, December 20, 1985, p. 8.*

BOB HALLIDAY

[*Queer*] is by no means [Burroughs'] best, but it will catch a lot of people off guard. *Queer* puts a human face on a mysterious author whose work has made him seem to be the most heartless tough guy in serious American fiction. . . .

Some of the most unnerving passages of Burroughs' novels draw their power from insect imagery, and there has always seemed to be something insect-like in the cold frenzy with which he unleashes the high-speed, super-corrosive visions that make his most successful writing so brutalizing. Anyone who reads it must wonder about the less public thoughts of a creative intelligence so harsh that a single drop of sentimentality would pollute and destroy it. *Queer* fills in some of the blanks. Chronologically it is Burroughs' second novel, written in 1952 following *Junky.* The circumstances surrounding its genesis are shocking. Burroughs attempts to describe them in an astonishing preface:

> When I started to write this [preface], I was paralyzed with a heavy reluctance, a writer's block like a strait jacket: "I glance at the manuscript of *Queer* and feel I simply can't read it. My past was a poisoned river from which one was fortunate to escape, and by which one feels immediately threatened, years after the events recorded.—Painful to an extent I feel it difficult to read, let alone write about. Every word and gesture sets the teeth on edge." . . .

One is not used to tears from Burroughs, and it is difficult to convey the poignancy his preface to *Queer* achieves when read with an awareness of his other work. "I am forced to the appalling conclusion that I would never have become a writer but for Joan's death," he writes, "and to a realization of the extent to which this event has motivated and formulated my writing . . . [T]he death of Joan brought me in contact with the invader, the Ugly Spirit, and maneuvered me into a lifelong struggle, in which I have had no choice except to write my way out."

Burroughs actually does seem to believe that some "invader" possessed him at the time of the shooting and forced him helplessly to kill Joan. This fact, considered in light of Burroughs' description of *Queer* as a work "motivated and formed" by the murder, will set off alarms in readers with a psychobiographical turn of mind. *Queer* is a purely homosexual work, an account of the narrator's intense infatuation with a young man named Eugene Allerton during a period of expatriate life in Mexico City. Was the "Ugly Spirit" an irresistible urge to blast away the heterosexual entrapments that kept him from experiencing a form of love which drew him much more powerfully?

If so, it was a double disaster. The account Burroughs gives in *Queer* of his passion for Allerton is a chronicle of humiliation, almost unrelievedly harrowing. (p. 6)

Although the narrative of *Queer* picks up roughly where *Junky* left off, Burroughs shifts gears abruptly. He tries to distance himself somewhat from the painful subject matter by switching from the first to the third person, but the style doesn't really suit him and threatens to go mushy. Furthermore, the narrator is no tough guy. The confident harshness of the earlier book disappears as Lee becomes increasingly infatuated with Allerton, and a palpable self-disgust takes its place. . . .

Lee eventually declares himself, gets Allerton drunk and takes him to bed. The predictable reaction takes place: the primarily straight Allerton is disgusted, but also realizes that he has the upper hand. He starts avoiding Lee, torturing him by traveling around town with a woman friend and making a quick exit whenever Lee appears on the scene. Lee tries to compensate by stepping up the attention-getting chatter and by making large gifts of money, further repelling Allerton. Finally he is driven to levels of despair that draw from Burroughs a kind of prose found nowhere else in his work: "[Lee's] throat began to ache, moisture hit his eyes, and he fell across the bed, sobbing convulsively. He pulled his knees up and covered his face with his hands, the fists clenched. Toward morning he turned on his back and stretched out. The sobs stopped, and his face relaxed in the morning light."

Lee manages to persuade Allerton to undertake a joint trip to South America in search of the drug, yage. He agrees to keep his sexual demands to a minimum, and Allerton tolerates him. But finally Allerton leaves, and when Lee is reunited with him in the book's final pages, it is only in the context of a bleak, self-detesting dream. . . .

Queer is a weak novel, with its stylistic careening and uneasy, confessional tone; it is certainly not the proper entry point into Burroughs' work. But readers who have lived for a while with his other books, particularly those written in the late '50s and early '60s, will find it fascinating and revealing. The preface contains some of the most affecting writing Burroughs has published in many years. Together they form an unprecedented personal revelation from one of the most controversial and influential writers of the past decades. (p. 7)

> Bob Halliday, "Mexican Joyride: The Apprenticeship of William Burroughs," in Book World—The Washington Post, *December 29, 1985, pp. 6-7.*

JENNIE SKERL

The publication of *The Wild Boys* in 1971 marked a new direction in Burroughs's writing, characterized by new thematic emphases, new imagery, and a new narrative style. *The Wild Boys* introduces a second metaphorical world, which replaces the Nova mythology of Burroughs's earlier work and which he continues to develop in the following works. The second mythology repeats Burroughs's three major themes—social criticism, the biological trap of sex and death, and the quest

of the writer to free himself and his readers from bondage; but the emphasis on politics, on sexual fantasy, and the writer's power is new, as is the attention given to man's positive potential for autonomy, regeneration, and creation.

Burroughs's second mythology, like the Nova myth, is constructed from autobiographical experience and popular culture, but he makes use of new materials from both sources. The most significant biographical material in the later works is childhood memories, and, in particular, the sexual fantasies of adolescence. Thus sexuality becomes the central metaphor of the later works, replacing the earlier addiction metaphor. In the recent fiction, pleasure and freedom through fantasy balance the experience of repression, bondage, and death. Sexual fantasy is linked to artistic creation as a source of and model for fiction—a different but powerful formulation of Burroughs's recurrent thesis that art can be made by everyone and that everyone is an artist. At the same time, Burroughs attaches greater importance to the ability of the *writer,* more than any other artist, to create new worlds and to writing as an art form that cannot be replaced by other media. (pp. 76-7)

Just as in his earlier works, Burroughs combines autobiographical and popular material to create a mythological world that informs all of his fiction from 1971 to 1981. In this second metaphorical world, however, the myth is developed through narrative rather than through cutups. For each of his three major themes—social criticism, the biological trap, and the writer's quest, Burroughs creates a fantasy that becomes one of the major narrative lines in the recent fiction and a metaphor in the myth.

An innovation in Burroughs's treatment of social criticism in the works since 1971 is the creation of utopian alternatives to the present social order so that his satirical fantasies now present both utopias and dystopias in conflict with each other, whereas his earlier fiction had contained extensive portrayals only of dystopias. Burroughs's utopian vision begins in *The Wild Boys* with the futuristic fantasy of "the wild boys"—an adolescent all-male hunting society. This creation evolves throughout the fiction of the next decade, as Burroughs incorporates the wild boys into various utopian and dystopian fantasies. (p. 78)

The plot of the myth is again an eternal battle between good and evil, but the opposing forces are now more clearly separated and polarized, leading to simpler images and action as well as to more violence as mutually exclusive realities attempt to destroy each other. More weight is given to the power of utopian fantasy to conquer dystopian reality. The wild boys can finally destroy a repressive civilization simply by ignoring or forgetting it. The individual can enter and control his dreams and thus free himself from his past, his own socially controlled ego, and the bondage of physical existence. Art can produce individual and social freedom, and everyone is an artist in that everyone can create alternative realities and control his own fantasies. The persona of the writer, however, has a limited power that qualifies the myth's simplicity. He is the ego that must remain—no matter how diminished—in order to have consciously controlled fantasy, that is, art; and as long as some ego remains, the reality principle must limit the pleasure principle. Burroughs's utopian fantasies exist in the past or in the future as alternative realities, but never succeed in conquering present reality. (p. 80)

The Wild Boys consists of eighteen relatively brief routines. . . . These routines consist largely of narrative sequences with fewer cutup passages than the trilogy [*The Soft Machine, The Ticket That Exploded,* and *Nova Express*]. *The Wild Boys* explicitly tells the reader that the book is a film montage in style and structure, thus clarifying and simplifying Burroughs's film metaphor. (p. 81)

The simplicity of character and image, combined with the explicit film metaphor, makes *The Wild Boys* a more accessible book than the works in the trilogy and establishes parallels with popular narratives such as comic books. But the corresponding demand upon the reader to see every narrative fragment and every personal identity as a transitory artifice or illusion requires a sophisticated reading of an apparently simple narrative.

The Wild Boys introduces all three major themes of the new mythology: social control versus revolt, the biological trap versus immortality, the writer's simultaneous freedom to create (and destroy) and his bondage to the past. These themes are presented primarily through the stories about the wild boys and Audrey Carsons. Other characters, both old and new, serve mainly as vehicles for social satire.

The story of the wild boys is the dominant narrative in the novel (hence the title), and thus makes revolt the dominant theme. The wild-boys story is a science-fiction fantasy set in the near future in which Burroughs imagines a breakdown of the current social order. Large portions of the Western world have reverted to savagery and chaos, and what remains of our civilization exists within walled enclosures where an elite rule through a totalitarian police state. The character of the future dystopia is based on the middle-class, middle-aged, midwestern America of Burroughs's youth, represented by the interminable racist bore, Colonel Greenfield. This dystopia is opposed by the wild boys, who are a utopian force: a tribe of youth without leadership or hierarchy. They are both an escape from a repressive civilization to a fantasy world of endlessly gratified desire, and a world-wide guerrilla force that recruits and trains youth to fight the totalitarian social order. (pp. 81-2)

The imagery and actions that describe the wild boys define them as embodiments of demonic energy. Physically they are young, naked males continually engaged in sex, violence, *and* practical jokes. Like traditional devils, they combine depravity and malicious glee. The wild boys are the demonic evil of repressed desire in our culture. They give free rein to the instinctual drives of *eros* and *thanatos* in forms society calls perverse and criminal, existing either in a chaotic whirlwind of murderous violence and orgiastic lust or else in the sated, drugged languor of fulfilled desire. They are savages in their totemistic organization into hunting packs, in their mutilation of corpses and cannibalism, and in their ritualistic use of drugs and sex to control the forces of life and death. They display the demonic behavior of the tribe living a dream-life beyond good and evil in which the individual has no consciousness that separates him from the group. The wild boys are immortal, for they have found the secret of bringing the dead back to life through orgiastic cult practices; hence they are free of parents, women, birth, and death. They exist in a state of ecstasy, represented by their enigmatic, dreamy smiles when they contemplate their actions, a smile that invites ironic comparison with the smile of Dante's Beatrice and of the Mona Lisa—two hallowed female icons that embody traditional Western values. In Burroughs's futuristic fantasy the image of a smiling boy becomes a popular icon that subverts the social order by recruiting more wild boys. This image of the smiling boy and its effect on others (creating more wild boys) is also a metaphor

for Burroughs's own subversive pop-art technique and expresses his belief that art can change consciousness to produce action.

The satanic immortality of the cult, the savagery of the tribe, the perverse gratification of instinctual desire, and the naked male body define the wild boys as embodiments of demonic energy; and it is as energy that they are best understood, not as characters. They are utopian as a *force*, not as literal images of the ideal community. . . . The wild boys represent the release of demonic energy in conscious fantasy, which Burroughs believes is a means of human liberation—both personal and social. By bringing the unconscious irrational desires of the individual and the group to consciousness and by playing with these forces in artistic structures, Burroughs seeks to free, understand, and regulate man's irrational desires. From this conscious playing with demonic energy Burroughs believes a new human and a new society can evolve. *The Wild Boys,* however, does not describe this new world: it ends on a note of conflict and disintegration as an unidentified narrator attempts to break conventional time barriers and join the wild boys in the fictional future. (pp. 82-3)

Burroughs's next major work, *Exterminator!,* continues in the style of *The Wild Boys:* more narrative, fewer cutups, explicit use of the film metaphor, greater simplicity of action and characterization. *Exterminator!* differs from *The Wild Boys* in that the narrative passages and cutups are shorter (most are a few pages), while characters, places, and themes are more numerous, ranging over the whole body of Burroughs's work and giving the book a kaleidoscopic quality. . . . The major theme throughout is the writer's quest for freedom, and *Exterminator!* is largely devoted to developing this storyline within the second mythology.

In *Exterminator!* Burroughs seems to illustrate in fiction his definition of art as aggressive action: "If I really knew how to write, I could write something that someone would read and it would kill them." . . . The writer in *Exterminator!* is equated with a (vermin) exterminator, a job that Burroughs once held. The exterminating writer kills off all of his characters and destroys their worlds. This "extermination" is singularly mild in its impact upon the reader because the explicit film metaphor and the cartoon level of characterization distance us from the characters and the acts of violence. Each character is an ephemeral image, not a fixed identity, an actor in the film the author has created from his own consciousness and whom he can painlessly destroy.

Furthermore, since all of the characters are presented as versions of Burroughs the writer, Burroughs directs the violence inward, toward himself and his fictions, rather than toward others. The autobiographical Audrey Carsons is described as a child who wants to be a writer and whose first story, "The Autobiography of a Wolf," expresses his fantasies of becoming an outlaw and escaping both social control and human form. Burroughs shows that all of his subsequent characters are transformations of Jerry the wolf, including Audrey himself, who is a later fictional creation. Transformation of characters is accompanied by transformation of stories, as stories within stories are told, ending in death or apocalypse. The ease with which the writer creates, transforms, and destroys his fictions encourages the reader to view "self," "reality," and "time" as equally transitory and illusory fictions, which we have the power to destroy or change. Fictional transformation is equated with immortality.

But the writer cannot finally disappear into his fictions. In the final routine, called "The End," Burroughs portrays a writer whose film is running out but who cannot imagine a life outside the film. Burroughs seems to be acknowledging that, although his art attacks conventional concepts of reality, it is still bound by those conventions. Similarly, Burroughs the man is tied to his temporal, physical existence and cannot be free of his own historical self. *Exterminator!* shows the power of the writer to create and destroy and thus the power of consciousness to play with the structures of reality, but bondage to "present time" remains. (pp. 84-5)

[*Port of Saints* shows Burroughs] returning to narrative as the basic form of the novel, for *Port of Saints* consists entirely of stories. Although some of the stories are typical Burroughs routines (satirical fantasies), most are nonsatirical narratives set in an imaginary past or future. For the first time Burroughs becomes a storyteller who develops his imaginary world through narrative transformation (that is, storytelling) rather than through juxtaposition (cutups). These stories are not, however, whole narratives. They tend to be episodes that are part of an implied, but not completed, plot. Also, the stories in *Port of Saints* are not narrated in a straightforward, conventional manner. Burroughs has fragmented the stories into very short passages and shuffled them together. Chapters organize groups of fragments under titles derived from popular song lyrics. The organization of the plot fragments is partly chronological, partly thematic, and partly arbitrary. *Port of Saints* is a collage of stories different in concept and structure from the montage of routines and cutups that provided the structure of Burroughs's novels from *Naked Lunch* to *Exterminator!* (p. 87)

The most important plot development in *Port of Saints* is the merger of the Audrey Carsons and the wild boys stories in a plot to rewrite history. In *Port of Saints,* Audrey becomes a wild boy and is part of a guerrilla action by the wild boys to "rewrite all the wrongs of history" through time travel, identity change, immunity from the cycle of birth and death, individual control of sex and dreams, and technological creativity. An example of how to rewrite history is given in the second chapter, "Numero Uno." The wild boys travel to a West Indian island in the year 1845 and act as technical advisers to black guerrillas fighting Portuguese and British colonialists. Using raw materials, technology, and knowledge available at the time, the wild boys invent a grenade and a gun that are technologically superior to existing European weapons, enabling the guerrillas to massacre the British troops sent to suppress the rebellion. The secret of their success is not present knowledge transported to the past, but inventive thinking that goes back to the beginning of firearms (the firecracker) and constructs weaponry on entirely different principles from the technology of existing weapons. The wild-boy intervention in the West Indies changes not only political history but technological history: science fiction changes the present by changing the past. This new plot development in *Port of Saints* and the numerous new narrative episodes that appear in this book stress the freedom-through-fantasy theme as both Audrey and the wild boys escape the past (both personal and historical) and the biological trap (the cycle of birth and death).

[*Cities of the Red Night*] is a culmination of Burroughs's second mythology of freedom through fantasy. Burroughs attempts in this novel to expand his mythological narratives to include the entire earth, all of its peoples, both sexes, and all of human history. The length and style of *Cities* also imply the intent to portray an all-encompassing mythology. *Cities* is longer than

any other Burroughs novel (over 300 pages) and contains more sustained narrative. Furthermore, the book's three interrelated plots thoroughly develop the three major themes of Burroughs's second myth. A retroactive utopia founded by eighteenth-century pirates is the basis for Burroughs's social criticism. A story about the dystopian cities of the red night focuses on the theme of the biological trap. And the writer's quest is conveyed through a contemporary detective story in which a private investigator uncovers the biological trap and finds he must rewrite history to escape it. (pp. 87-8)

Cities of the Red Night creates a science-fiction myth that explains all of human history as we know it and an alternative history that shows the power of fantasy. The cities of the title are an imaginary, prehistoric civilization portrayed in a science-fiction mode that satirizes contemporary Western society. The cities are a dystopia set in the past but mirroring the present. These prehistoric cities are also the source of the B-23 virus, a metaphor for the biological trap of sex and death. This virus in present time sets in motion a contemporary detective story that is gradually transformed into the writer's attempt to free mankind from bondage to the past. Burroughs contrasts his dystopian vision of the cities of the red night and their disastrous legacy to the present with a retroactive utopia that universalizes the wild-boy fantasy. He transforms the wild-boy plot to rewrite history into the story of a libertarian pirate society in eighteenth-century South America that overthrows Spanish rule and changes the course of history. The citizens who subscribe to "the Articles" of liberty fight a continual guerrilla war against the nation state and its methods of control. They create a society of small communes, loosely federated to share technology, expertise, and defense. This anarchist utopia is projected into present time, based on its imaginary historical origin. Thus Burroughs's dystopian cities and utopian communes are placed in conflict in the present as metaphors for opposing forces in contemporary society, and the writer-detective must resolve the conflict. (pp. 89-90)

In his fiction from *The Wild Boys* to *Cities of the Red Night* Burroughs continues to be an innovator who combines prophetic visions and experimental technique. He creates powerful imaginary worlds that critique present reality and that show the reader how to alter his consciousness and thus his world. (p. 91)

> *Jennie Skerl, in her* William S. Burroughs, *Twayne Publishers, 1985, 127 p.*

ADAM MARS-JONES

Queer is an unfinished novel dating from the 1950s, though its cover and blurb conspire to keep the punter in the dark about its fragmentary status. The narrative tails off in a series of ineffectual closures; but there is an impressive finish to each paragraph which makes up for the lack of a satisfactory overall shape. . . .

[Burroughs] sets up the hero of the narrative, William Lee, as a case history, a heroin addict experiencing withdrawal and the accompanying terrible efflorescence of sexuality. The effect of this is to diminish the test, since it is not Lee's predicament which is so remarkable, but the accommodation he makes to it.

Lee wants human rather than merely sexual contact. In Chapter Two we are told that he spends the night with a Mexican boy he picks up in a bar, but this information is conveyed without detail or emphasis. His emotional appetites focus, after a few false starts, on a young man called Eugene Allerton, who is curious, complaisant, and sometimes even responsive.

Allerton is no angel, but his relationship with Lee has a muffled intermittent tenderness which suggests that the effort on Lee's part is not altogether wasted. . . .

Lee registers every nuance of manipulativeness and rejection; but though his sensitivity is heightened, his priorities are shown to be authentic. A minor character, for instance, is described as showing "the ravages of the death process, the inroads of decay in flesh cut off from the living charge of contact".

In spite of its lurid title and its comic interludes, *Queer* has a tone of stoical vulnerability. Burroughs's later writings at their least persuasive display instead a cold frenzy. The relationship between the two modes is mysterious, but the introduction to *Queer* provides some indications.

The manuscript tails off after Lee and Allerton have made a trip to South America in search of the fabled drug Yage, which like some voodoo tincture can submit one person to the will of another. Burroughs's introduction explains something not in the foreground of the manuscript: the expedition effects Lee's stabilization from addiction, since in the remote places he visits no drugs are available, except for alcohol. . . .

The great merit of the later Burroughs is that his ideas, when they aren't lucid and instantly convincing, are preposterous and instantly dismissable; very little falls between these categories. So Burroughs attributes his wife's death to the eruption of a hieroglyphic virus which invaded him from the Egyptology department of the University of Chicago in 1939; he goes to some lengths to establish that this is not a metaphorical statement (possessing entities like nothing better than posing as metaphors).

One of the most striking sentences of the *Queer* manuscript records that "The court of fact had rejected Lee's petition", but it is only in fiction, apparently, that there can be no appeal. Burroughs backs up his version of events by citing cut-ups and comments—which he treats as oracular—from his friend Brion Gysin.

Cut-up is a legitimate device if its object is the avoidance of cliché, but like surrealism it has managed to generate its own style of cliché, its compulsory disruptions. To treat cut-ups, and a friend's casual comments, as sources of revealed truth is to add a silly mysticism to the silly demonology of the possession theory.

It's unappealing enough that a man should blame his wife's death in effect on the mummy's curse, worse that he should pose as the real casualty. Burroughs's subsequent life, apparently, has been one long struggle to escape from Control; many readers of *Queer* will feel that control (with the lower case, denoting merely human agency) is exactly what he achieved here, and, by abandoning the manuscript, rejected. In his later work, Burroughs stipulates an "algebra of need", in which one addiction substitutes for another. In *Queer,* needs have yet to be systematized, and Lee's feeling for Allerton substitutes for his heroin habit only as day, with all its bleakness, substitutes for night.

*Adam Mars-Jones, "Victims of the Mummy's Curse,"
in* The Times Literary Supplement, *No. 4333, April
18, 1986, p. 415.*

(John) Ramsey Campbell

1946-

(Has also written under pseudonyms of Montgomery Comfort, Carl Dreadstone, and Jay Ramsey) English novelist, short story writer, critic, and editor.

In the opinion of many leading critics of supernatural fiction, Campbell is the most prominent contemporary successor to a literary tradition which began with the eighteenth-century Gothic novel and later comprised the works of Edgar Allan Poe, Arthur Machen, M. R. James, and H. P. Lovecraft. Contrasting with the majority of modern works of horror and the supernatural, which have their closest artistic analogies in popular movies, television shows, and comic books, Campbell's fiction displays an artistry and imagination that is often compared to the classics of Gothic literature. Moreover, few contemporary horror writers have been as highly praised for their power and acuity in portraying what Jack Sullivan has termed, apropos of Campbell's work, the "grey and grubby modern world."

Campbell was born and grew up in Liverpool; the impersonal, often disintegrating urban landscape of that city serves as the background for much of his best work. Campbell's first published stories, however, suggest little of this later development. Collected in *The Inhabitant of the Lake, and Less Welcome Tenants* (1964), these pieces represent Campbell's effort to perpetuate H. P. Lovecraft's Cthulhu Mythos, a term coined by Lovecraft admirers which refers to his tales of cosmic legend. In his first volume, Campbell transplants the horrific elements of Lovecraft's stories to a fictional English setting while maintaining essentially Lovecraftian characters and supernatural phenomena. These stories, several of which were reissued in the collection *Cold Print* (1984), are considered to be among the best of their kind.

With his next collection, *Demons by Daylight* (1973), Campbell drew away from Lovecraft's influence and revealed a manner of storytelling that was an unexpected leap both in his personal evolution as a writer and in the history of supernatural horror fiction. Although supernatural writers of the 1950s and 1960s attempted to adapt the fundamental plots and themes of Gothic literature to a modern milieu, *Demons by Daylight* is recognized as the first book to realize this ambition without sacrificing the intensity and imaginative richness of traditional Gothicism. Such tales as "The Old Horns" and "The Sentinels" combine the banality of ordinary life and human relationships with the dreamlike quality that forms the basis for the masterpieces of supernatural fiction. This is achieved in Campbell's fiction by various means, most conspicuously through the perspective of extreme subjectivity from which his stories are narrated. By relating the incidents of a narrative from the most intimate level of his characters' consciousness, Campbell magnifies the natural doubts, dreams, and fears of human existence to the point where they merge with the supernatural. In "The Interloper," for instance, a schoolboy's fear of his instructor ultimately attains a fantastic dimension in a scenario of doom that is convincing more in the manner of a nightmare than in the mode of realistic fiction. This technique is heightened in effectiveness by a metaphorical prose style that sustains an atmosphere of poetic delirium. Such stories as "Ash" and "Litter," which appear in Campbell's second collection, *The*

© Jerry Bauer

Height of the Scream (1976), and "The Chimney" and "Mackintosh Willy," from *Dark Companions* (1982), are particularly successful studies of the menacing universe inhabited by his characters.

In addition to his short story collections, Campbell has written several novels of the supernatural, including *The Doll Who Ate His Mother* (1976), *To Wake the Dead* (1980), *The Nameless* (1981), *The Incarnate* (1983), and *Obsession* (1985). Critics have generally perceived Campbell's novels to be less striking than his short stories, although this opinion is offered with the understanding that shorter fictional forms are more suited to expressing the tenuous and often intense effects of supernatural horror and that the supernatural novel is seldom more than a qualified success. Nevertheless, Campbell's novels are praised for the same qualities of style and imagination which distinguish his short stories. *The Face That Must Die* (1979), a nonsupernatural work, is respected for its rigorous and violent narrative energy.

(See also *Contemporary Authors*, Vols. 57-60 and *Contemporary Authors New Revision Series*, Vol. 7.)

T. E. D. KLEIN

[The essay excerpted below was written in 1974.]

This is the story of how a young man crawled out from under H. P. Lovecraft's shadow, saw the sun, and wrote **Demons by Daylight** . . .

Back in 1969, after Arkham House had exhausted its supply of Lovecraft fiction and had run through three volumes of miscellaneous "Lovecraftiana" (juvenile efforts, fragments, "Lovecraft as Mentor," "Lovecraft in Providence," "Lovecraft and the New England Megaliths," et al), it dipped still further into the barrel and came out with *Tales of the Cthulhu Mythos,* a collection of pastiches in the Lovecraft tradition. (p. 19)

[The] best of the pastiches—i.e. the most faithful—were unaccountably the worst. One might almost conclude, in fact, that, as a literary form, the pastiche is really a close cousin to the translation (if temporal rather than spatial) and that it is, therefore, in the words of the adage, like a woman: the more beautiful, the less faithful; the more faithful, the less beautiful.

It isn't so surprising as it might seem, then, that of all the *Tales of the Cthulhu Mythos,* the most effective were those that departed most radically from the original Canon. The best of the lot—and certainly the most haunting—was a short piece called "Cold Print." The title itself, in its very understatement, stood out in contrast to all the Dwellers in Darkness, the Shadows from the Steeple, and the Shamblers from the Stars that proliferated throughout the book; and the story stood out even more.

It began, it's true, with one of those portentous epigraphs from a Forbidden Work—in this case something called the *Revelations of Glaaki,* Volume 12 (certainly the most unsavory title since *De Vermis Mysteriis*)—and, in fact, the quotation itself was even more portentous than most, claiming as it did that "even the minions of Cthulhu dare not speak of Y'golonac"—rather an arrogant assertion for a relative newcomer to make, reminding one of those billboard ads that heralded the movie *Mighty Joe Young:* "Mightier, More Terrifying Than *King Kong!!!*"

Happily, though, this unholier-than-thou air was dispelled by the story's opening sentence, in which a young schoolmaster with the disreputable name of Sam Strutt "licked his fingers and wiped them on his handkerchief." The tale went on to include such untraditional elements as sexual frustration, loneliness, and outright horniness; pornography of the kind known euphemistically as "discipline"; hints of homosexuality and pedophilia; allusions to Burroughs, Robbe-Grillet, Hubert Selby, Jr., and B-movies . . . ; but the commercialization of Christmas, and the despair that only a holiday can breed; throwaway images both comical and bleak ("Once he met the gaze of an old woman staring down at a point below her window which was perhaps the extent of her outside world. Momentarily chilled, he hurried on, pursued by a woman who, on the evidence within her pram, had given birth to a litter of newspapers . . ."); one reference to an obscure dabbler in the occult named Roland Franklyn; to say nothing of such un-Lovecraftian details as bus fumes, slush, snot, and dogshit; all capped by one of the most breathtakingly gruesome endings I have ever read.

Save for that memorable finale, and the fact that the story was miserably proofread, this was hardly the kind of thing one would expect to find in a volume of Lovecraftiana. It was much too good. It seemed a product of that lonely land somewhere between *New Grub Street* and the "New Town" of *Jubb* (two of the dozen or so indispensable British novels); it was a tale Lovecraft might have written if he'd had the benefit of an excellent editor, if he'd survived into the fifties—and if he'd been far, far more honest about himself.

The tale's author, one J. Ramsey Campbell, was listed in the back of the book. It was noted with old maidish redundancy, that he had "the same background as the popular Beatles—Liverpool, England," and that he had been born in 1946. . . . (pp. 19-20)

The note went on to mention two books of Campbell's; one, ***The Inhabitant of the Lake and Less Welcome Tenants,*** was, it declared, "published by Arkham House when he was but 18" . . . and the other, **Demons by Daylight,** was forthcoming. . . .

The former proved something of a let-down. Like Frank Utpatel's rather cartoony cover and end-paper maps, the tales seemed too eager to spell everything out. They told too much. So did the introduction, in which the young author announced, with bold naivete, his intention to create a new setting for the Cthulhu Mythos, the Arkham area having been "saturated." (God knows he was right about that!) He went on to describe each imaginary city in considerable detail, as well as the "esoteric volume" he intended to quote from—thereby saving readers much work, but also much pleasure, a mistake he was never to repeat. The effect was as if the bravado of "Cold Print"'s epigraph had found its way into the text. That story had been searingly honest about the secret urges of its protagonist; here, unfortunately, the Campbell of an earlier day was proving all too candid about his own authorial ambitions.

Throughout the book one was conscious of a deliberate striving after a Lovecraftian *corpus,* a deliberate dropping of names, a deliberate setting up of the horrors. Except for one understated little piece called "**The Will of Stanley Brooke,**" done largely in dialogue, the stories seemed filled with artifice; Campbell hadn't yet learned to cover his tracks.

That it was an extraordinary work for an 18-year-old boy to have produced was, of course, obvious in every line; but obviously, too, this was the work of a writer still laboring in Lovecraft's shadow. (p. 20)

In succeeding years other Arkham House editions were sent for, as finances and enthusiasms dictated. One by one the Derleth anthologies arrived, each with its spurious "unpublished Lovecraft" tale written by Derleth himself, testifying less to his modesty than to his marketing sense; and, each time, the first thing I looked for was the Campbell offering. He made, I believe, every volume.

They were a mixed bag. If no story ever excited me quite as much as "**Cold Print,**" largely because of that one's unusually evocative atmosphere, they were nevertheless far superior to those tales in the **Inhabitant** volume. "**The Church of High Street**" was, to be sure, an example of Early Campbell, bearing that period's distinguishing feature, the over-explicit first-person narrator; it seemed, in fact, to belong more to **Inhabitant** than "**The Will of Stanley Brooke,**" and no doubt preceded that tale. "**The Stone on the Island**" seemed heavy-handed, too, but the story did offer pleasant hints of things to come: a protagonist desperately alone, his alienation seeming to distort the workday world around him, rendering it surrealistic, dismal, absurd; the half-hearted passes at girls in the office; the office itself, convincingly dull, filled with obtuse people doing trivial things; and the conclusion, whose grisliness made up for whatever lapses the plot may have had.

"The Cellars," "Napier Court," "The Scar" (in a non-Arkham anthology)—the tales grew better and better with each new volume, more subtle and more difficult. **"Cold Print,"** I began to realize, had been a kind of Campbell Primer, containing nearly all the elements that distinguished these later stories. The Early Campbell was gone, and so was the *corpus* he'd tried to create; at last we were witnessing the formation of a genuine body of work, unified not by mere intention but by vision.

That observation, of course, is one calculated to embarrass any writer, and to Campbell himself I apologize for it; it sounds entirely too grandiose, too pretentious. Yet a vision there was, a sustaining one; and now that **Demons by Daylight** has at last been published, we can see that this vision of the universe— paranoiac, often confounding, always haunting, dreadful, unique—has been sustained throughout an entire book. (pp. 20-1)

One of the first things that strikes one about Campbell's stories in this new collection is that—following the trend of his earlier pieces—they are extremely difficult. (p. 21)

Still, being "difficult" is not necessarily a fault; and for horror, in fact, it is almost always a great virtue. Several years ago, when I was teaching school, a fellow teacher was charged with being "too difficult" for the students; the material he presented was, it was argued, "over their heads." I recall his reply: "I think it's important to give them a little more than they can handle," he said. "I like to remain a little beyond them."

For an English instructor this may or may not be true; but for a horror writer, it should probably be the rule. Writing horror stories must be rather like playing the Pied Piper; if the tune one pipes is too fast or difficult or subtle, the reader grows bored and drops out of the dance. If, on the other hand, the tune is too plodding and predictable, the reaction is the same: boredom, loss of attention. The trick, apparently, is to dance just a little ahead of the reader, teasing him, leading him on.

The risk, of course, is considerable: if one balks at making the slightest concession to the reader, one may end up with a kind of "horror tale as minimal art," akin to the most progressive of progressive jazz, the most abstract of abstract painting. In that case, as Kirby McCauley has pointed out, one runs the risk of writing stories for oneself alone; even if other readers might have the means to decipher them, no one will care to try.

Yet the other extreme presents an even graver danger: write a tale too easy to grasp and you allow the reader to realize he is more intelligent than the writer—something that, inexplicably, a brilliant man like Derleth permitted in his own dismayingly predictable Lovecraft pastiches.

Campbell, fortunately, seems to have mastered that trick of dancing just beyond our reach. Most of his stories have a hazy, dreamlike quality in which events are comprehensible when taken by themselves as discreet units, but in which they are piled upon one another so frantically that one gets lost in the swirl. Take, for example, the mad rush of images that we find at the beginning of **"The Lost"**:

> It was in Rudesheim that I had my first important insight into Bill's character. The previous night, outside Koblenz, we had caught a

bus in an unsuccessful attempt to find the town centre and when our three marks fare ran out had been abandoned in the country, by a filling station railed off by leaping brilliant rain. I'd been sure there had been hefty figures following us as we walked into the stinging darkness— but Bill had seen a bus heading back to our hotel: he hadn't wanted a fight. So we'd joined the rest of our coach party that morning. Chair-lifts were strung down a hillside of vineyards to Rudesheim; I stood up until Bill protested, although I had already seen that there could be no danger at all unless you fell on one of the vine-poles. Our courier led us down into Rudesheim, through the contorted cobbled streets of aproned women selling souvenirs, between tables full of tankards and huge packed laughing Germans, and into an inn. Here Bill revealed himself."

Quite an opening paragraph—by no means Campbell's best writing, of course, but typical of the way he buffets the reader with a succession of unrelated images, so that one finds oneself growing winded, a little punchy—and at the same time more susceptible to Campbell's attack. Or (to mix metaphors) one cries, "Slow down!" but the tour has moved on, back to Rudesheim.

The fact that all these incidents are crowded into a single paragraph (the journalist in me would run them down the page) makes the writing seem even more compressed and difficult than it really is; often entire conversations receive the same treatment, with considerable atmospheric effect, if technically improper. (pp. 21-2)

Add to this the fact that, whether or not Campbell intended it, the tales are almost totally lacking in line breaks, and you have something very confusing indeed. One example, from among dozens: In **"At First Sight,"** we follow the heroine onto a bus: "As she passed the seat where she'd seemed to see the face she stretched out her hand and touched the leather. It was cold as the stones of a well." The new paragraph begins immediately: "A glass was held toward her, half-full of some dark liquid." Huh? Where, on the bus? Coca-Cola vendor, perhaps? But no: "Her eye refused to look beyond the hand which held the glass. Then she saw that it was not a glass; it was a girl, struggling among her fingers, one bare arm thrust out beneath the thumb. Nor was it a hand which held her." And then a third paragraph: "Val sat up in bed." Etc. Somehow we've jumped from the bus seat into a bed, after having plunged through a most confusing dream. (p. 22)

The hand holding the glass that turns into a hand holding a girl . . . typifies another characteristic of Campbell's fiction: distorted images, seen always through the eyes of the protagonist, images that tend to shift and disappear as we try to understand them. "Their heads—no, they couldn't be heads," realizes one character. "On their shoulders were set huge paper masks like balloons, nodding horribly, their grinning mouths stretched wide as if bloated from within . . . Heads inflated by mud." That comes from a nightmare in **"The Old Horns"** . . . , but the images need not be confined to dreams. For example, in a city at night: "I saw a totem-pole striding toward me down a side street. It was a child stacked on his father's shoulders." In **"Concussion,"** a sentimental science fiction story reminiscent of Robert F. Young, based on a kind of "nostalgia for the present," we find: "A colossal green leper stood on the horizon; the Liver Clock, flaking off each second from the future.'' Or, from a pub scene in **''Made in Goatswood''**: ''His face swam forward through the yellow light like a shark closing for the kill.'' And a few lines down: ''Footsteps plodded up the stairs toward them. It was her father. Kim watched, unwillingly fascinated. The father took shape from the shadows, looming above them. The footsteps continued.'' It is as if we've been forced to look at the world through a fish-eye lens, or the spectacles of some astigmatic stranger. People dream even in daylight; they are prone to visions any place they go—city streets, even—and thus any place can be frightening. It's a world in which a totem-pole can come striding down the sidewalk toward you, and even after it's been ''explained away'' the surreal quality lingers. In short, it's a world in which anything can happen. Expect anything. Expect the worst.

What this leads to . . . is a kind of dreamlike paranoia that affects his characters' perceptions—not a new thing for horror stories, it's true, except that Campbell does it so much better, and he does it in *crowds* more often than not. In the paragraph I quoted from **''The Lost,''** one of the first things the narrator mentions is the ''hefty figures following us as we walked into the stinging darkness''; and later in that same tale, the narrator finds himself in a German tavern, staring at a girl at the bar: ''I was fascinated,'' he reports. ''She seemed to be with three overflowing men. She must have known when eyes were watching her wherever they were, just as I do, for she turned and stared at me . . . She said something to the man on her right, and he swung round trailing smoke, his cigar like a blackened gun-barrel, to train his gaze on me. I knew he was hostile; I always do.'' Admittedly the tale presents us with a patently insane narrator whose vision of the universe is deliberately distorted; but such distortion is the norm throughout this book. (And for all the narrator's paranoiac delusions, events bear out his philosophy: a mere flood of German curses provokes the longed-for murder of his companion.)

One effect of this distorted vision is that the reader becomes even [more] paranoiac than the protagonist: after reading several Campbell stories, one's ear grows extraordinarily sensitive to conversations overheard at the next table (something about that girl they found dead in the park . . .), and one learns to pay scrupulous attention to stray scraps of wind-tossed newspaper bearing ominous references to ''mutilations'' and ''police baffled . . .'' The ladies on the bus, one seat behind us, are talking about a series of murders, and we find ourselves nodding cynically—''Uh-huh, somebody's going to *get* it!''—aware as we are that Campbell is above all an economical writer . . . , and that half-heard conversations and muttered warnings are seldom inserted simply as window dressings; they are *clues* and, like as not, the protagonist—who ignores them—is going to wind up just as mutilated as the corpse the news vendor hinted of . . .

But stray snatches of barroom conversation are by no means required to raise the hackles of the veteran Campbell reader; simple code words are often enough. Shadows, gloom, an alley, a deserted park on an evening in February, a row of abandoned warehouses—we don't ask for much. A cave, perhaps, as in the brilliant **''End of a Summer's Day,''** but that's hardly necessary—a mere hint of underground passages, a dark doorway that might perhaps lead to catacombs, a trap-door in the floor of a basement . . . No need for elaboration, no need for mapping out the subterranean network of tunnels (a Campbell staple). Just give us the doorway, give us the trap-door, and we'll fill in the rest. After all, we've been here before.

Such is the cumulative power of the best horror fiction—Lovecraft's, Machen's, and certainly Campbell's. Each new tale gains drama and atmosphere from those that have gone before—which, of course, gives writers such as Campbell an immediate edge over newcomers to the field. Take a story by an unknown writer and, if it opens with a picnic on the beach, we'll be yawning by page two. After all, an ordinary summer's outing . . . What's scary about that? Who cares if the title is ''The Slime Monster'' or something equally lurid? Yet Campbell can rivet our attention with just such a scene, and we'll react with a shudder to every mention of dunes and mud-puddles—despite a title as innocuous as **''The Old Horns.''** (pp. 22-3)

Campbell's readers, then, become acutely sensitive to phrases that evoke atmosphere, as well as to carefully placed hints of imminent doom. As with most horror stories, the reader is customarily one step ahead of the protagonist, leading to a kind of reluctant fascination, the old ''Don't-go-in-there-you-fool'' syndrome—for, of course, the hero does go in there, and ultimately pays for it.

The fact that so many Campbell heroes end up dead suggests that Campbell's universe is not a particularly moral one; innocent people are just as prone to die as the guilty, and that Campbell Primer, **''Cold Print,''** ends on just such a note: ''Strutt's last thought was an unbelieving conviction that this was happening because he had read the *Revelations;* somewhere, someone had *wanted* this to happen to him. It wasn't playing fair, he hadn't done anything to deserve this—but before he could scream out his protest his breath was cut off . . .''

No, it isn't particularly fair; Campbell's obsessive young men and neurotically passive young women don't deserve to die. And yet, in a sense, all of them are guilty of *something*—an overweening curiosity, perhaps, or, as in Strutt's case, simply ''evil thoughts.'' I can't help but wonder (as one is supposed to wonder in essays like this) if such retribution isn't some sort of holdover from Campbell's Catholic upbringing; Catholicism is, after all, a religion that punishes one for sinful thoughts as well as sinful action. We are, in that case, all of us guilty.

Not that the Church represents any ''Force of Goodness'' in these stories. It seems, in fact, rather impotent, indeed quite fatuous, a collection of lithograph Jesuses and a herd of sheep trotting into a cathedral. (This image, from Bunuel's *The Exterminating Angel,* represents one of Campbell's many film references; for that matter, his very narrative makes frequent use of cinematic devices: a hideous face at the window, out of focus, is revealed as a friend; flash cuts to the details of a city street yield a kind of cinematic fragmentation, etc. Campbell has, in fact, written film criticism for the BBC.) (p. 23)

[The Good versus Evil] conflict doesn't even exist in these tales. There *is* no Force of Goodness to pit against Evil; we are given no heroic Dr. Armitages or Professor Rices to battle against Campbell's Yog-Sothoths. In fact, Campbell eschews Heroes of any kind; many of his creations are criminal, and the rest enjoy a stature no better than our own: they are weak, timid, and—if in love—selfishly so. Were they suddenly to receive ''magical powers,'' they'd certainly abuse them. They are, in short, refreshingly easy to identify with, after years of cool-eyed psychic investigators and aristocratic aesthetes.

Ironically, the only force arrayed against the sundry evils of the universe is the force of human stupidity. By that I mean the very blindness, insensitivity, slavishness to habit and dogma, that keeps Campbell's minor characters busy with their daily rounds in the office while the protagonist is going quietly mad from fear. The effect is, once again, very dreamlike, for if the reader customarily knows more than the main character, *he* in turn knows a great deal more than the minor ones, and therefore finds himself in that horrifyingly familiar world in which no one but him quite understands what's going on. Such paranoia reaches its height in **"The End of a Summer's Day,"** one of those perfect stories that, like Lovecraft's "Hypnos" and "Polaris," allows for two satisfactory sets of explanations, one quite natural, one less so. On the one hand it's the apotheosis of that infantile nightmare, "I'm screaming and no one's listening," and in fact it appears in the section Campbell labels "Nightmares." (Perhaps we should take him at his word.) At the same time, one can't help theorizing the existence of strange subterranean cults who, for reasons of their own, inhabit certain English caves where, every ten years or so, they trap a luckless tourist, substituting for him their previous captive—who, by this time, of course, is blind as a mole.

Exasperating as they are, these herds of common humanity with their heads stuck in their newspapers—muttering about "all this godlessness going round" and "Don't get involved" and other banalities—do constitute a kind of strength, running their sane little world in the midst of a mad universe. "What do you believe in?" asks a Campbell hero, and his girlfriend's father answers, quite seriously, "What's around me. Not politics disguised as panaceas, not poets trying to be philosophers. This house. My job. Reality." One senses a sort of wisdom here, in this middle-class sage; it's obvious that he speaks from long experience. Believe deeply enough in your slogans, and nothing can harm you . . . (One senses, too, Campbell's ambiguity toward the character; he's given him some good lines.) At any rate, it isn't the people like him who get hurt: it's the meddlesome few who learn, as in Lovecraft, More Than Mortals Were Meant to Know. They pay for it, these characters, in suffering and death; and those that aren't killed find their perceptions of the world forever altered.

If darkness is to be defeated, then, it won't be by any mystical Powers or Catholic saints; it will be by unimaginative men keeping their minds on their work, Thus, the slogan might run, "In Banality there is Strength"—but that doesn't really offer much protection. The title of this collection notwithstanding, there isn't any light in Campbell's world to hold back the darkness; and this fact does tend to make the tales inexorably grim and pessimistic. Lovecraft, at least, offered a wide variety of panaceas: Science, The Great Race, Childhood, Dreams, the very concept that "It's All in Your Mind" (a la *Kadath*) and hence not to be feared. In the world of M. R. James there's a kind of Victorian social stability to rescue us from the ancestral ghosts; one flees the cemetery or the swamp and returns to a comfortable seat by the fire. And Arthur Machen balances his pagan atrocities with hymns to pagan joy; to use Walter Van Tilburg Clark's phrase, Machen gives us both "the ecstasy and the dread." But in Ramsey Campbell's world, there is only the dread.

It's absurd, of course, to take a horror writer to task for writing horror, especially when he does it with such originality and grace; indeed, I think Campbell reigns supreme in the field today. Yet horror *per se* can be, in the end, somewhat limiting; and now that he has mastered it, one might hope for an occasional ray of light to alleviate the gloom. Black magic, by its existence, implies white magic; and while I'm not looking for a collection of fairy tales, it strikes me that an occasional vision of something beyond a glass of stout and a secretary's

knickers might add a needed dimension to the world Campbell has created. (pp. 23-4)

[Campbell] has changed the shape of the modern horror story; he has done for our own field what other young British writers are doing for science fiction. And for a one-time Lovecraft disciple to have done so is all the more impressive. . . . (p. 25)

T. E. D. Klein, "Ramsey Campbell: An Appreciation," in Nyctalops, *No. 13, May, 1977, pp. 19-25.*

STEPHEN KING

[Campbell] writes a cool, almost icy prose line, and his perspective on his native Liverpool is always a trifle offbeat, a trifle unsettling. In a Campbell novel or story, one seems to view the world through the thin and shifting perceptual haze of an LSD trip that is just ending . . . or just beginning. The polish of his writing and his mannered turns of phrase and image make him seem something like the genre's Joyce Carol Oates (and like Oates, he is prolific, turning out good short stories, novels, and essays at an amazing clip), and there is also something Oatesian in the way his characters view the world—as when one is journeying on mild LSD, there is something chilly and faintly schizophrenic in the way his characters see things . . . and in the things they see. (p. 331)

Good horror novels are not a dime a dozen—by no means—but there never seems to be any serious shortage of good ones, either. . . . But, maybe paradoxically, maybe not, good horror *writers* are quite rare . . . and Campbell is better than just good.

That's one reason fans of the genre will greet **The Parasite** with such pleasure and relief; it is even better than his first novel, of which I want to treat briefly here. Campbell has been turning out his own patented brand of short horror tale for some years now. . . . Several collections of his stories are available, the best of them probably being **The Height of the Scream**. A story you will not find in that book, unfortunately, is **"The Companion,"** in which a lonely man who tours "funfairs" on his holidays encounters a horror beyond my ability to describe while riding a Ghost Train into its tunnel. **"The Companion"** may be the best horror tale to be written in English in the last thirty years; it is surely one of half a dozen or so which will still be in print and commonly read a hundred years from now. Campbell is literate in a field which has attracted too many comic-book intellects, cool in a field where too many writers—myself included—tend toward panting melodrama, fluid in a field where many of the best practitioners often fall prey to cant and stupid "rules" of fantasy composition.

But not all good short-story writers in this field are able to make the jump to the novel. . . . Campbell made the jump almost effortlessly, with a novel as good as its title was off-putting: **The Doll Who Ate His Mother**. (pp. 331-32)

Campbell's novel begins with Clare Frayn's brother Rob losing an arm and his life in a Liverpool car accident. The arm, torn off in the accident, is important because somebody makes off with it . . . and eats it. This muncher of arms, we are led to suppose, is a shadowy young man named Chris Kelly. Clare—who embodies many of the ideas already labeled as "new American gothic" (sure, Campbell is British, but many of his influences—both literary and cinematic—are American)—meets a crime reporter named Edmund Hall who believes that the man who caused Rob Frayn's death was the grown-up version of a boy he knew in school, a boy fascinated with death and cannibalism. (p. 333)

Clare, Edmund Hall, and George Pugh, a cinema owner whose elderly mother has also been victimized by Kelly, join together in a strange and reluctant three-way partnership to track this supernatural cannibal down. Here . . . we feel echoes of the classic tale of the Vampire, Stoker's *Dracula*. And perhaps we never feel the changes of the nearly eighty years which lie between the two books so strongly as we do in the contrast between the group of six which forms to track down Count Dracula and the group of three which forms to track down "Chris Kelly." There is no sense of self-righteousness in Clare, Edmund, and George—they are truly little people, afraid, confused, often depressed; they turn inward to themselves rather than outward toward each other, and while we sense their fright very strongly, there is no feeling about the book that Clare, Edmund, and George must prevail because their cause is just. They somehow symbolize the glum and rather drab place England has become in the second half of the twentieth century, and we feel that if some or all of them do muddle through, it will be due more to impersonal luck than to any action of their own.

And the three of them do track Kelly down . . . after a fashion. The climax of the hunt takes place in the rotting cellar of a slum building marked for demolition, and here Campbell has created one of the dreamiest and effective sequences in all of modern horror fiction. In its surreal and nightmarish evocation of ancient evil, in the glimpses it gives us of "absolute power," it is finally a voice from the latter part of the twentieth century which speaks powerfully in the language which Lovecraft can be said to have invented. Here is nothing so pallid or so imitative as a Lovecraft "pastiche," but a viable, believable version of those Lovecraftian Elder Gods that so haunted Dunwich, Arkham, Providence, Central Falls . . . and the pages of *Weird Tales* magazine.

Campbell is good, if rather unsympathetic, with character (his lack of emotion has the effect of chilling his prose even further, and some readers will be put off by the tone of this novel; they may feel that Campbell has not so much written a novel as grown one in a Petrie dish): Clare Frayn with her stumpy legs and her dreams of grace, Edmund with his baleful thoughts of glory yet to come, and best of all, because here Campbell does seem to kindle real feelings of emotion and kindliness, George Pugh holding on to the last of his cinemas and scolding two teenage girls who walk out before the playing of the National Anthem has finished.

But perhaps the central character here is Liverpool itself, with its orange sodium lights, its slums and docks, its cinemas converted into HALF A MILE OF FURNITURE. Campbell's short stories live and breathe Liverpool in what seems to be equal amounts of attraction and repulsion, and that sense of place is one of the most remarkable things about *The Doll* as well. This locale is as richly textured as Raymond Chandler's Los Angeles of the forties and fifties or Larry McMurtry's Houston of the sixties. "Children were playing ball against the church," Campbell writes. "Christ held up His arms for a catch." It is a small line, understated and almost thrown away (like all those creepy, reaching gloves in *The Parasite*), but this sort of thing is cumulative, and at least suggests Campbell's commitment to the idea that horror exists in point of view as well as in incident.

The Doll Who Ate His Mother . . . is not as good as Campbell's *The Parasite* . . . but it is remarkably good. Campbell keeps a tight rein on his potentially tabloid-style material, even playing off it occasionally (a dull and almost viciously insensitive teacher

sits in the faculty room of his school reading a paper with a headline which blares HE CUT UP YOUNG VIRGINS AND LAUGHED—the story's blackly hilarious subhead informs us that *His Potency Came From Not Having Orgasms*). He carries us inexorably past levels of abnormal psychology into something that is much, much worse. (pp. 334-35)

[The picture Campbell draws of Liverpool] gives the reader the feeling that he is observing a slumbering, semisentient monster that *might* awake at any moment. His debt to [Fritz] Leiber seems clearer here than that to Lovecraft, in fact. Either way, Ramsey Campbell has succeeded in forging something uniquely his own in *The Doll Who Ate His Mother*. (p. 336)

> Stephen King, "Horror Fiction," in his Danse Macabre, *Everest House Publishers, 1981, pp. 241-360.*

JACK SULLIVAN

[The essay excerpted below was originally published in Whispers *by Jack Sullivan in 1982.]*

Writing about Ramsey Campbell in 1974, T.E.D. Klein expressed the hope that Campbell, having mastered horror, would in the future let in "an occasional ray of light to alleviate the gloom" [see excerpt above]. Since then, the light has not materialized; if anything, Campbell's recent fiction is darker than ever, an uninterrupted nightmare in which the setting, a grey and grubby modern world, is as frightening as the demonic force that assaults it.

What makes Campbell's uncompromising bleakness bearable, indeed more memorable than ever, is the quality of his prose. To some extent, this has always been the case. With the publication of *Demons by Daylight* (1973), Campbell established himself as the premier stylist in modern horror fiction, a writer whose stories were always worth reading, even the ones which did not work, because they were written with an intelligence and control completely beyond most of his contemporaries. *Demons by Daylight* signaled the arrival of a young writer whose works were worthy successors to LeFanu, M. R. James, and others whose tradition he inherited.

Many of the distinctive features of Campbell's style remain intact; he still writes fragmented, jagged images which dwell on the disorderliness of everyday life; he still distorts chronologies so that memories appear, then dissolve, like apparitions, exposing themselves as memories only by their sudden absence (*The Doll Who Ate His Mother* (1976) is the most extended development of this technique); he still disperses dreams into reality and sometimes omits calling a dream a dream—although never consistently enough to qualify as a full-blown "surrealistic" writer; and he still writes sentences which have a tangy musicality. Like the major horror writers of the past (Poe, Machen, and Blackwood in particular), Campbell pays close attention to the sound of his sentences, but he haunts us with music that has a dissonant, contemporary clang.

What distinguishes Campbell's recent short fiction is a new compression and intensity, a relentless Poe-like focus on a single obsessional motif. As Campbell has moved increasingly in the direction of psychological horror, his stories have become more unpleasant and downbeat, a series of pared-down images organized around a central obsession. This is not to say that Campbell has deserted the supernatural (except in his novel *The Face That Must Die* (1979)); indeed many recent tales, such as **"Call First"** and **"Down There"** are old fashioned ghoul and monster stories. But it is to say that Campbell is more concerned than ever with the psychology of the supernatural encounter and that his grimmest phantasms often spring as much from the psyches of his doomed heroes as from a malignant cosmos; the threatening apparition is all the more deadly in that it leaps from both places at once.

The most striking thing about this greater intensity is how high it raises the horror ante. Campbell's horror stories are more horrific than ever; they often begin on a more somber note than before and build toward something truly nightmarish ("**Loveman's Comeback,**" Campbell's notorious necrophilia story, seems to be almost a parody of this spectacular grimness); the horrifyingly quotable last lines tend to be even nastier now.

An extreme example of this tendency is "**Baby**" (1974) which is told from the point of view of a self-pitying derelict who spends the entire story staggering or "slithering grittily" through the slums of Liverpool (an even more unsavory Liverpool than Campbell's usual version), attempting to escape a familiar he has unleashed by bashing an old woman's head in with a metal bar. Unlike most of the stories in *Demons by Daylight* and *The Height of the Scream* (1976), "**Baby**" not only ends unpleasantly but begins that way as well: the stalking and killing of the old woman—perhaps the single most violent scene in Campbell's short fiction—is as harrowing as the supernatural pursuit which follows. Yet the entire story is so supercharged with intensity that there is no sense of anticlimax.

Campbell here eschews the LeFanu technique of subtle, incremental terror and adopts Poe's method of grabbing the reader by the throat in the first paragraph and never letting go. Also reminiscent of Poe is Campbell's use of a villainous protagonist, a departure from the LeFanu model in which an innocent victim is randomly persecuted. The Poe tradition is also apparent in Campbell's detailed exploration of psychological motive. . . . (pp. 79-80)

The style, however—with its jagged images and powerful verbs, its unique tautness and tension—is wholly Campbell's own. . . . Characteristically, there is a sparsely dispensed but memorable sense of wonder to counterbalance the grubbiness, especially in a brief description of the old lady's mysterious globes the killer discovers while scrabbling for her money:

> He convulsed as if with uncontrolled nausea.
> With his wrapped hand he swept all four globes
> off the photograph, snarling. They took a long
> time to fall. They took long enough for him to
> notice, and to stare at them. They seemed to
> be sinking through the air as slowly as dust,
> turning enormously like worlds, filling the whole
> of his attention. In each of them a faint image
> was appearing: in one a landscape, in another
> a calm and luminous face. . . . They were fall-
> ing slowly—yet he was only making a move
> towards them when the globes smashed on the
> floor, their fragments parting like petals. He
> heard no sound at all.

This moment of magic and poetry—in which the reader, character, and action become mercifully hypnotized and frozen—is all the more haunting in that it comes suddenly out of nowhere, vanishes just as quickly, and is never explained. Despite Campbell's recent interest in twisted psychological states, he is fundamentally animated by mystery and inexplicability, by forces which transcend psychology.

In "**The Chimney**" (1975), the psychological and supernatural are beautifully fused. The ingenious plot focuses on a child's paralyzing fear of something decidedly unjolly emerging from his chimney at Christmas. . . . (pp. 80-1)

Something does indeed crawl out of the chimney, something charred and shriveled instead of fat, but grinning nonetheless. The apparition apparently has something to do with the death of the narrator's father, which occurs ten years later in a fire, but Campbell typically refuses to act as a chaperone between fantasy and reality: the reader must sort the two out for himself. It's an indication of Campbell's maturity in the genre that the question we would expect the story to raise—the overworked Henry Jamesian dilemma of whether the apparition is real or hallucinated—never really materializes. The more gripping question, as the narrator puts it at the end, is whether "What emerged from the chimney was in some sense my father," and what the "sense" precisely is. "Maybe most of it was only fear," begins the narrator, in the first desperate sentence, "But not the last thing, not that. To blame my fear for that would be worst of all." The horror in "**The Chimney**" is the dilemma of whether the stunted, turnip-faced spectre is a premonition of death or whether, in some terrible and enigmatic way, the narrator's childhood vulnerability and panic evoked both it and the death. In either case, supernatural and psychological dread are one and the same. The story is like a romantic poem in which seeming polarities blend in a single vision. The apparition scenes give us all the otherworldly chills we could ask for, while the closely explored relationship between the narrator and his parents—the pathetic but touching attempts made by the parents to love each other and their child "in their own way" as their hostility reinforces his fears—gives us a tragedy that is all too worldly. "**The Chimney**" is as relentlessly dark as any recent Campbell, but it is also unexpectedly poignant. It is one of his most remarkable creations.

"**The Trick**" (1976), another holiday story told from the point of view of a terrified child, is somewhat less remarkable, and thoroughly cold-blooded. This time the season, appropriately enough, is Halloween. The child, a little girl, is haunted by a vicious monkey, presumably a familiar, and an equally vicious old lady, presumably the witch who controls it. The monkey, with its grinning malice and unremitting tenacity, seems to come hopping out of LeFanu's "Green Tea" (another unsparingly cruel story): it even speaks, as does LeFanu's monkey, in a voice we are never allowed to hear.

The witch, however, is a creature only Campbell could have created:

> The woman drew herself up rigidly; bony hands
> crept from her sleeves. The wizened apple turned
> slowly to Sandra, then to Debbie. The mouth
> was a thin bloodless slit full of teeth; the eyes
> seemed to have congealed around hatred. . . .
>
> Cars rushed by, two abreast. Shoppers hurried
> past, glancing at the women and the two girls.
> Debbie could seize none of these distractions;
> she could see only the face. It wasn't a fruit or
> vegetable now, it was a mask that had once
> been a face, drained of humanity. Its hatred
> was as cold as a shark's gaze. Even the small-
> ness of the face wasn't reassuring; it concen-
> trated its power.

A principle of cold hatred, the old lady appears not in a Halloween setting appropriate for traditional witches, but in a modern setting more horribly appropriate because it matches her coldness: "They muffled their footsteps, which sounded like a dream. The bleached street stood frozen around them, fossilized by the glare; trees cast nets over the houses, cars squatted, closed and dim. The ghost of the street made Debbie dislike to ask, but she had to know. "Do you think she put something funny in those sweets? Did you taste something?"" The entire story is organized with cold, corpse-like "fossilized" images. The doomed child is persuasively childlike in her dialogue and perceptions, but Campbell does not evoke her plight with the sense of compassion and tragedy so generously evident in "**The Chimney.**" The perspective is rather like that of "**Baby,**" even though the victim (again of a mysterious old lady) is an innocent child rather than a guilty homicidal derelict. In Campbell's colder stories, where everyone is subject to the same nightmarish conspiracies, such distinctions don't seem to matter. The girl is pursued with a ferocity that is chilling and perversely compelling precisely because it is so uncalled for. Hers is a suffering without catharsis, without meaning. Whatever illumination she may receive is denied the reader: at the end, the monkey speaks, "relishing each separate word," but we are not permitted to hear what he says.

This focus on random persecution places stories like "**The Trick**" in the austere tradition of LeFanu and Bierce. "**The Trick**" is a harrowing, bone-chilling story of the type which separates Campbell's unwavering admirers from those who find his work too dark. At its most extreme, Campbell's vision has limited his audience to a small set of connoisseurs. . . . [Campbell's] willingness to pull out all the stops, to be more overtly horrifying and less enigmatic, may well help him with a larger audience; and although he has maintained the integrity of his style, some of his plots, as we shall see, are of the proven variety favored by Stephen King.

Nevertheless, there are several recent stories which are even more unremittingly grim than those in *The Height of the Scream*. "**The Sneering**" (1976), for example (an inimitable Campbell title), goes about as far down as anyone in this genre has ever plummeted. It is not only a thoroughly depressing story, but a story entirely *about* depression, indeed a psychological ghost story in which depression becomes the apparition: "His depression stood over him, sneering." "It was as if an intruder were strolling through the house staring at the flaws, the shabbiness. The intruder stared at Emily, inert before the window; at Jack, who gazed sadly at her as he pretended to read. So much for their companionship." The demon which sneers at this pathetic couple is middle-age depression, a grim apparition indeed, which threatens not damnation but simple loneliness. . . . As in "**The Chimney,**" the supernatural and psychological merge at the furthest extremity of fear. "**The Sneering**" trembles on the brink of compassion: the miserable couple staring at the lonely highway from their shabby house, is drawn with absolute authenticity and with some sympathy. But the story itself is icy: Campbell not only kills both of them off, but dooms them, as in a LeFanu tale, to a possibly infinite cycle of further agony. In this context, the powerful finale is even more horrendous than it seems: "He pressed her face into his chest to hide her from what was upon them: the car, and the grinning face inflated with blood." What is also upon them is a lonely infinity in which the sneering face will become their own.

Stories like "**The Sneering**" leave us much like Jack—desolated, "appalled and inert." It is almost a relief to turn from them to stories like "**Down There**" and "**Call First,**" old-fashioned monster stories in the *Weird Tales* and E. C. horror

comics tradition, replete with ghoulish long-fingernailed crones in creaky houses and blob-like monstrosities oozing from elevators. "**Down There**" is fortissimo horror; it assaults the reader with a garish intensity and explicitness worthy of Poe's "The Facts in the Case of M. Valdemar" (another blob story), while maintaining the kind of stylistic control we have come to expect of Campbell.

The plot has a simplicity and single-minded purity increasingly typical of recent Campbell: a harried office worker begins to suspect that something lurks beneath her in the basement of the elevator shaft in her building. Whatever it is reminds her unpleasantly of rotting food. . . . "**Down There**" reeks consistently with images of rot and decay, from the "obese half-chewed sandwiches" left on windowsills by the janitor to the gigantic rotting food-like creatures who assault the heroine in her elevator at the end. . . . (pp. 82-5)

There is nothing quite like this in either *Demons by Daylight* or *The Height of the Scream*. It is as if Campbell, having abandoned Lovecraft after *The Inhabitant of the Lake* (1964) and struggled to find his own voice, now has the confidence and freedom to write what he pleases, including something whose texture has a Lovecraftian vileness. The voice and ambience are still wholly Campbell's. No one else could create an office—the kind millions of people toil in every day—that manages to be as sinister, "atmospheric," and malevolently alive as any haunted house: "Ranks of filing cabinets stuffed with blue Inland Revenue files divided the office down the middle; smells of dust and old paper hung in the air. Beneath a fluttering fluorescent tube, protruding files drowsed, jerked awake." This is the banality of evil with a vengeance; no one captures this theme in this or any other genre, better than Campbell.

One of the characteristics of these recent tales is thus their sheer variety and inventiveness. From the deeply personal resonances of "**The Chimney**" to the simple grisly fun of "**Down There,**" Campbell's stories offer increasingly unpredictable settings and plots: "**Call First,**" a wonderfully jolting homage to the E. C. horror comics, has a genuine haunted house and a creakingly conventional one at that; "**The Companion,**" a story which unleashes an almost Medieval apparition of death, has the next best thing, a spook house at a deserted carnival; "**Accident Zone,**" a more modernistic story, has a haunted highway; "**The Invocation,**" which has perhaps the most frightening ending of any Campbell story (no small statement), has an E. F. Benson-like slug creature called down accidentally from the clouds; "**First Foot**" (also known as "**Calling Card**"), the most radically telescoped Campbell story, has a living corpse called up from a river, his resurrection announced by an unsigned Christmas card received by the horrified heroine—"A Very Harried Christmas," reads the ghostly scrawl, "And No New Year."

What all these stories have in common is the same powerful intensity and condensation that now characterizes Campbell's short fiction. "**First Foot,**" in particular, has a sharpness of focus, a cutting of extraneous elements, a scalpel-like precision that signals what appears to be a new direction in his work. Transitional material that would be fragmented in earlier stories here disappears almost completely, leaving us with a series of drowning images of engulfing horror. Campbell's images have always been his greatest strength, and he is now offering them to us in a terrifyingly undiluted form. At his best, as he is in these stories, he writes what is surely the greatest short fiction of anyone in supernatural horror today.

As for T. E. D. Klein and the others who have been waiting nearly a decade for that elusive ray of light, Campbell seems perfectly willing to leave them grumbling and groping in the dark. (pp. 85-6)

Jack Sullivan, ''Ramsey Campbell: No Light Ahead,'' in Shadowings: The Reader's Guide to Horror Fiction, 1981-1982, *edited by Douglas E. Winter, Starmont House, 1983, pp. 79-86.*

T. E. D. KLEIN

Tales of violence and horror, it's said, offer readers a form of catharsis—and they evidently do the same for writers, judging from Ramsey Campbell's highly personal introduction to **The Face That Must Die,** a novel written, in part, from the point of view of a razor-wielding psychopath. Campbell's introduction recounts with almost painful candor the bloody breakup of his parents' marriage, his father's sudden absence, his mother's descent into madness, and his own reaction to it all: ''More than once I grew so frustrated that I ran at a wall of the room head first. I wasn't always sane myself.'' It's clear that writing a novel as savage as **Face** must have been, among other things, therapeutic—a kind of exorcism. . . .

[The] book's central character—called, wonderfully, Horridge—makes a quintessential spatter-film villain. Crippled in mind and body, he limps through Liverpool like a sex-hating Savonarola with a particular horror of homosexuality, savoring his own cunning and justifying his murderous behavior with the twisted logic of a paranoid who reads dark things in people's faces and finds hidden meanings in every word and name. He's the sort of man who, on visiting a pub, soon convinces himself that government agents are spying on him from the telly by the bar. Listening to him run through the inevitable list of crank grievances—gays, blacks, snooping police, young layabouts, etc.—I couldn't help thinking of the title character of Keith Waterhouse's brilliant novel *Jubb,* which, two decades earlier, examined so many of the same obsessions but turned them into comedy.

Ironically, what's most disturbing about **Face** is not the violence—that, after all, is purveyed by any number of writers these days—but Campbell's unremittingly bleak view of humanity, one that will be familiar to admirers of his short stories. Repulsive and bloody-minded as Horridge is, he's much more fun to read about than any of the ''normal'' characters Campbell gives us, and he's no more unpleasant than Peter, nominally the book's hero, a selfish, shallow fellow perpetually absorbed in drugs, comic books, and Conan. Nobody ends up looking very attractive here.

Humanity fares little better in Campbell's new novel, **Incarnate.** The world appears to be populated by an army of rude barmaids, sneering bosses, nasty ticket clerks, callous teachers, brutal policemen, sadistic customs inspectors, bad-tempered neighbors, and various menacing strangers. Everyone seems sullen, angry, spoiling for a fight. Children are invariably mistreated or, at best, ignored. Even one's own unconscious can betray one.

It's this last danger that forms the basis of the novel. The extremely tangled plot concerns five disparate Londoners who, 11 years before, had participated in a rather vaguely described Oxford experiment in ''prophetic dreaming.'' Recently, in their own individual ways, they've each begun to grow a little mad, and, unbeknownst to them, the unconscious material of their dreams has begun to take on tangible form: a mother begins lavishing affection on a strange, menacing little girl at the expense of her own daughter; a social worker finds herself playing hostess to a mysterious bedridden old woman; a sexually repressed, violence-prone male not unlike Horridge sees his secret spanking fantasies enacted on the television.

It's an annoying necessity in books of this type (and one Campbell handles with more finesse than anyone else I know) that, until the end, characters must be kept in ignorance of their own condition. For most of the way, therefore, the novel cuts back and forth among the five as their daily lives grow increasingly removed from reality. They never get in touch with one another, never answer letters, never simply sit down to compare notes and talk about their fears; though two of the women meet by chance and become friends, even working in the same building, they fail to recognize each other. When at last they all do come together, we're treated to glimpses of various dream worlds (including a dream London) and are witness to a clash of wills between characters real and unreal, the latter mutating, merging, and recombining like putty. It's a scene reminiscent of *Altered States* and Machen's *Novel of the White Powder,* and it's all pretty confusing.

But maybe that's the nature of the subject. Campbell has always been a skilfully impressionistic writer, locking us within his characters' distorted perceptions: ''Headless men were queuing in the market, or dwarfs in coats too big for them, and then he saw they were empty coats, hanging on the wire mesh.'' In this book, however, the distortions affect entire chapters; a detailed scene in a police station goes on for pages, rich in dialogue and description, but is revealed several chapters later to have been ''only a dream.'' The fact that such revelations inspire pleased surprise rather than irritation demonstrates the power of Campbell's spell.

T. E. D. Klein, ''On the Razor's Edge,'' in Book World—The Washington Post, *November 20, 1983, p. 12.*

DOUGLAS E. WINTER

Ramsey Campbell is Britain's finest living writer of horror fiction, and arguably the best short story talent ever to grace the field on either side of the Atlantic. His first book, **The Inhabitant of the Lake** (1964), was published . . . when Campbell was but eighteen years old. Since that time, more than two hundred of his short stories have seen print, as well as three major collections: **Demons by Daylight** (1973), **The Height of the Scream** (1976) and **Dark Companions** (1982); but since the mid-seventies, Campbell has worked with growing effectiveness in the novel form. His first novel, **The Doll Who Ate His Mother,** appeared in 1976, and was followed in the United States by three ambitious volumes: **The Parasite** (1980), **The Nameless** (1981) and, most recently, **Incarnate.** His second novel, **The Face That Must Die,** appeared in paperback in England in 1979, but did not find an American edition until late in 1983. . . .

The autobiographical introduction to **The Face That Must Die,** ''I Am It And It Is I,'' written especially for the American edition, is without doubt the most chilling—and honest—response to the question of what makes a horror writer that could be imagined. It is also one of Campbell's best pieces of writing. . . . The novel itself, placed in the ''definitive version'' for American publication by the restoration of a deleted chapter, is quintessential Campbell—its surreal urban landscapes and detailed portrayals of pathology overshadow the plot, which concerns a murderous madman with an affection for the slash of a straight razor. Although tentative in approach to a length at which Campbell was not yet accustomed to working, *Face* succeeds through its unremitting bleakness and the power of Campbell's portrayal of insanity.

Campbell's new novel, *Incarnate,* was published almost simultaneously with *Face,* and reflects a substantial maturation in Campbell's style and mastery of the novel form. It is also concerned with insanity and betrayal by the unconscious mind. Five people have participated in a vague university experiment involving "prophetic dreaming." Something dreadful—which Campbell refuses entirely to explicate—interrupts the experiment; eleven years later, reality begins to assume a dreamlike quality in the lives of each of the participants.

Incarnate is undoubtedly Campbell's best novel to date; his writing has never been more controlled— nor more daring in its intellectual challenges. Impressionistic and elliptical, Campbell's prose questions not only the perception of his characters, but of his readers as well, more fully capturing the aesthetics of nightmare than the work of any other writer living today, in or out of the horror field. Indeed, the distortions at the heart of this novel may well dishearten the casual reader—entire chapters of rich detail are later disclosed as mere dreams, and the reader, like the five subjects of the aborted experiment, cannot trust what he or she sees and feels.

Incarnate is filled with powerful, affecting writing. In a recent review of Campbell's *Dark Companions,* I wrote that Campbell's most recent short stories were "not simply frightening, but disturbing—the hallmark of a horror writer at the height of his powers." *Incarnate* confirms that those words apply to Campbell the novelist as well.

> *Douglas E. Winter, "The Long and Short of Ramsey Campbell," in* Fantasy Review, *Vol. 7, No. 2, March, 1984, p. 28.*

MICHAEL A. MORRISON

For my money, Ramsey Campbell writes scarier horror stories than any other living author. His literate, sophisticated short stories and novels worm their way into your consciousness and lurk there, waiting to zap you at odd moments with a jolt of unrefined terror. If you think this mere reviewer hyperbole, get a copy of Campbell's latest novel, *Obsession,* an ingenious, beautifully crafted tale rooted in the horrors of real life.

Even when they treat standard motifs of horror fiction, Campbell's novels are refreshingly free of hackneyed imagery and plot devices. *Obsession* is a case in point. Superficially, this novel seems to be a variant on the deal-with-the-devil story— a shopworn plot that has been rattling around as long as there have been horror stories. But *Obsession* is not a superficial book.

Campbell's wish-fulfillment nightmare begins in 1958, in the British coastal village of Seaward, with the predicaments of four teenage friends. Steve Innes is being persecuted by a sadistic English teacher. Jimmy Waters' father haunts the local betting shops, compulsively gambling away money he needs to run his cafe. Robin Laurel's mother is trying to keep secret the fact that Robin is illegitimate. And Peter Priest must contend with his grandmother. After being terrorized by thieves in her home, she moved in with Peter and his parents. But the old lady was unhinged by the break-in and now, browbeating

Peter's mother back into childhood and his father into withdrawal from the family, she is making of Peter's home life a suffocating, living hell.

One hot, stormy July afternoon Peter wanders to a cliff outside Seaward and broods. "He could see no end to [his plight]: it looked like the whole of his future. He shouted something, he didn't know what—a plea or a curse—into the storm that was sweeping toward him, jabbing at the black sea."

Later that afternoon, something answers Peter; he receives an anonymous letter that reads: "WHATEVER YOU MOST NEED I DO." He replies, and soon he and his three friends each have a chance to make a wish. They do, and their wishes are granted.

But "there was more to it than just wishing." Now, 25 years later, the four friends are still living in Seaward. Peter is a social worker, unsuccessfully trying to expiate his obsessive guilt over his grandmother's death. Steve is married, a partner in his father's shaky real estate business. Jimmy, too, is married; a policeman, he is relieved to be raising his family "away from city life and all that it threatened." And, after seven grueling years in medical school, Robin has set up a practice in her home, which she shares with her aging mother. Now, although they don't realize it, all four are beginning to pay dearly for their boons. . . .

Campbell's plot moves like a fine Swiss watch, impelling each of his characters toward a crossroads of right and wrong, an ineluctable moment of free choice in which they will confront their true selves—and in so doing, reveal themselves to us.

The unsparing bleakness of King's *Cujo* derived in part from its lack of a supernatural explanation for its uncomfortably real horrors. Unlike King, Campbell gives us a way out, leaving little doubt that there is at work in his novel a malefic supernatural power. But the supernatural element is kept off-stage, shrouded in ambiguity, and it affords little comfort. . . .

If *Incarnate* remains Campbell's best novel, *Obsession* could be his breakthrough to a wider readership. It is his best plotted and most accessible book, and his clear, beautifully cadenced prose is here free of the subjective ambiguities that have in the past alienated some readers.

In the introduction to *Cold Print,* Campbell says that he was made a writer by reading a book of stories by Howard Phillips Lovecraft. Indeed, Campbell's first book [*The Inhabitants of the Lake, and Less Welcome Tenants*] . . . revealed a talent all but buried under the influence of Lovecraft's brilliant, neurotic horror fiction. This new, superbly illustrated retrospective of Campbell's Lovecraftian tales [*Cold Print*] chronicles his emergence from the chrysalis of that influence.

The underlying premise of Lovecraft's stories is rich with menace: the survival from prehistory of immensely powerful, malevolent alien beings whose form and substance are beyond comprehension, beings that now lurk on the fringes of awareness, awaiting a chance to annihilate man and retake the universe. But most Lovecraftian pastiches fail utterly. Clogged with conventions established in Lovecraft's stories—shunned buildings in decaying, remote villages; arcane (imaginary) tomes of mythic lore with titles like *Necronomicon* and *Revelations of Glaaki;* a conveniently obtuse narrator—and bloated with adjectives like "eldritch," "blasphemous" and "unspeakable," they evoke giggles rather than shivers. The earliest tales in *Cold Print* are pastiches, drawn from [*The Inhabitant of the Lake*] . . . ; yet, in spite of considerable clutter and occasional attacks of adjectivitis, these journeyman's exercises have an undeniable power.

But it is the more recent stories in *Cold Print* that fascinate and frighten. "**The Faces at Pine Dunes**" and "**Cold Print**," for example, are mature horror stories of the first rank, devoid of Lovecraftian debris and told in Campbell's distinct voice. Finally, in "**The Voice of the Beach**"—the most original, terrifying realization of Lovecraftian themes I have ever read—Campbell solves the essential problem of how to represent the ineffable to a modern reader so as to evoke the terror and cosmic mystery of Lovecraft's best work.

In these stories and in novels like *Obsession*, Ramsey Campbell continues to break new ground, advancing the style and thematic content of horror fiction far beyond the work of his contemporaries. He writes of our deepest fears in a precise, clear prose that somehow manages to be beautiful and terrifying at the same time. He is a powerful, original writer, and you owe it to yourself to make his acquaintance.

> *Michael A. Morrison, "Deals with the Devil," in* Book World—The Washington Post, *May 25, 1985, p. 10.*

GARY WILLIAM CRAWFORD

Second perhaps only to Robert Aickman, Campbell is the best writer of horror fiction in Great Britain in the past fifteen years.

His fictional world is essentially Gothic, but his Gothic horrors have a modern setting. Like many a Gothic novel, there is an attitude of moral relativism, but in Campbell, one is tempted to say moral anarchy. His short fiction and novels reveal a modern culture that is essentially chaotic and amoral. Perhaps drawing his impetus from H. P. Lovecraft, Campbell's work presents a coherent philosophy: the universe is essentially hostile and man's position in it is that of victim, a victim of forces within himself and on the outside. Like Lovecraft's fictional world, Campbell's is highly atmospheric, but with a difference: his unique prose style is like no other in supernatural horror fiction. As in Ann Radcliffe's early Gothic novel *The Mysteries of Udolpho*, the main character in Campbell is essentially the setting, and his characters perceive their environment in a manner that can be summed up in one word: paranoia.

Like Emily in *The Mysteries of Udolpho*, Campbell's characters perceive reality in a distorted manner, as the images of Campbell's prose style are marked by mental collusion. It is also striking how very cinematic is Campbell's technique. There is, like the quick cutting of cinematic narrative, a sudden shift from image to image. Each sentence conveys one or more images in rapid succession, as in the externalization of internal thoughts.

There is essentially narrative dislocation, and, as Campbell has remarked, his fiction has been influenced by the films of Resnais and the novels of his collaborator Robbe-Grillet. The mental landscape thus created is the hallmark of the early Gothic novel, and one might even say that Campbell's Gothicism may be described as "urban Gothic." (pp. 13-14)

It is, above all, . . . Campbell's vision of the supernatural which reflects Campbell's Gothic origins. From one of Campbell's blackest stories, "**Potential**," to the potent evil of *The Doll Who Ate His Mother*, Campbell's urban Gothic world is one on which man is a victim of implacable evil. His characters are normal human beings, at least his protagonists are, who find a horrifying mental and material universe, within themselves and within others, and they are helpless victims. Sexuality, love, death, and dreams are some of the elements of Campbell's urban Gothicism, and the world in which they live seems itself potent with evil.

Campbell was no doubt influenced by Lovecraft's Gothicism, but his earliest short fiction is, for the most part, unoriginal. "**The Church in High Street**" and "**The Inhabitant of the Lake**" are patterned after Lovecraft and are remarkable only in that they were produced when Campbell was in his teens; they contain no trace of the quality of his later fiction.

"**The Cellars**" is, by contrast, an early tale of high quality that deals with an "urban" or "modern Gothic" theme that Campbell develops more fully later: implicit sexuality as a harbinger of death and decay. The story, while not as stylistically mature as Campbell's later work, conveys an atmosphere of death born of sexuality as a young man encounters with a girl friend a fungus in a murky warehouse cellar and begins to disintegrate physically after the encounter. Here, the city of Liverpool becomes a neo-Gothic realm as the horror of the universe is of implacable evil.

"**Before the Storm**" is a more realistic Cthulhu Mythos story which is noteworthy in that it reveals Campbell's concern with the cosmic Gothic realm of alien horror that courses under the mundane. By contrast, "**The Stocking**" is a well-developed psychological horror story with a realistic surface which develops its terror as an outgrowth of a relationship between a young man and a woman. Although not as powerful as "**The Cellars**," it develops a similar theme. "**Cold Print**," an effective Cthulhu Mythos story, reflects Campbell's maturing style, the hallmark of which is a carefully observed reality, but rich in imagery, and an attention to detail, usually of putrescence and filth, the elements of Campbell's "urban Gothicism." Although not a Cthulhu Mythos story, "**Napier Court**" shows further development in Campbell's use of narrative dislocation, another element of his neo-Gothic descriptive technique. In this tale, as in others, he blends dream and waking states, making no attempt to draw a line between the two, thus creating an effective atmosphere reminiscent of some of the masters of Gothic narrative. The tale is of a lonely young girl who struggles with her love for a young man with whom she has had a brief romantic encounter, while the reputedly haunted house in which she lives expresses metaphorically her inner tensions.

Campbell again equates sexual love and the supernatural in "**Concussion**." In this tale, Kirk Morris, an old man nearing death, meets a young girl who may be, Campbell suggests, a supernatural creature from the past. As in "**Napier Court**," a delicate blend of fantasy and reality conveys the typical Gothic isolation and alienation of Campbell's character.

As Campbell's fiction matured in the late 1960's, it depicted, for the most part, the struggle of ordinary people to find meaning in a modern, indeed, neo-Gothic world, devoid of humanity. Campbell's characters during this period are often civil servants and students who confront the supernatural in the harsh reality of the light of day. Like much of twentieth century literature, Campbell's mature stories deal with philosophical questions of the nature of reality; they present an "urban Gothic" vision of modern man and his coming to terms with the horrors of human experience. One of Campbell's darkest stories, "**Potential**," displays in concentrated form the themes of moral anarchy that Campbell weaves throughout the entire body of his fiction. The story narrates a young civil servant's first encounter with the youth culture of Liverpool. In a brief episode at a party where he expects to have his first drug experience, he finds himself taking part in a mind game during which he is taken in by a staged scene of torture and sadism and commits murder, thus realizing his potential for evil.

As Campbell's writing developed further in the 1970's, it became more potently terrifying. The later stories, unlike those of the 1960's, reveal Campbell's dexterity in creating an uncanny atmosphere of implicit supernaturalism, almost in the manner of M. R. James, Aickman, or De La Mare. (pp. 14-16)

For the most part, the supernatural horror tale is best exemplified in its short story or novella varieties. One can surely say, however, that Campbell's novels rise above the masses of horror novels one finds at the drug stores at the present time. His one saving grace in the novel form is his prose style, which is the essence of his urban Gothicism. A passage from the early chapters of Campbell's first, and perhaps most honest and non-commercial novel, *The Doll Who Ate His Mother,* exemplifies his technique. As Clare Frayn begins to piece together the clues that solve her brother's murder, her mind absorbs descriptive details, vivid, living images, like a confrontation with a monstrous, Gothic, evil in the city of Liverpool:

> . . . great feathers against the sky, conical leafy beehives as high as a house, swelling billows like smoke from a factory chimney, a bent old man scratching his armpit beneath a covering of shaggy lumps of dust. Beneath she could make out the winter patterns, thick vertical piping, candelabras sprouting candelabras sprouting candelabras, intricate webs of twigs gliding over one another and changing, all standing still against the sky—until a branch stood still almost into her face and she slipped on a twig. . . .

This is only one example of the kind of rich, fluid, almost cinematic imagery that inheres in Campbell's sentences. It is a highly atmospheric, descriptive style, neo-Gothic to be sure, as the great Gothic writers, even modern Lovecraft, give close attention to descriptive detail, creating a mental landscape—one of the hallmarks of great Gothic literature.

This is perhaps what saves Campbell's neo-Gothic novels. These books, however, do achieve a crescendo effect, which is largely because they are structured along the lines of the detective novel. One cannot help but think of the resemblance of *The Doll Who Ate His Mother* to Stoker's *Dracula,* because, in that novel, the evil character lives and walks among and becomes intimate with those who attempt to destroy him. Chris Kelley, is, like Stoker's vampire, a very human, victimized, yet potently evil creature whose innocence has been corrupted.

What places this novel higher than the works of King, for example, is its prose style. We see the world through Chris Kelley's mind and Clare Frayn's mind, and the two seem to meet at the novel's climax. The world through their minds is vivid, paranoical, rich in detail. One wonders who is the hunter or the hunted.

Campbell's second novel, *The Face That Must Die,* is clearly a psychological thriller somewhat like Bloch's *Psycho,* but again, Campbell's prose style raises it above the more psychotic killer-thrillers. We enter the psychotic mind and discover the paranoid world within, which is projected onto others, its victims. But again, one wonders who is the victim and who is the victimizer.

Campbell's *The Face That Must Die* is quite similar to his first novel, *The Doll Who Ate His Mother,* but this second novel was judged by the New York publishing establishment to be so horrifying they would not touch it, so it was published in America in a limited edition by a small press.

With *The Parasite* (published in Great Britain with a different ending as *To Wake the Dead*), Campbell solidifies his reputation as a horror novelist, although it may be the most prolix of his novels. The novel has many excellent points. First, it is narrated in the third person from the point of view of Rose Tierney, who discovers that she is inhabited by the parasitic form of an occultist Peter Grace. The increasingly paranoid quality of Rose's gradual initiation into the occult is well described as Rose's environment takes on the quality of a nightmare. Her perceptions are pointed and vivid, rich in detail. Her normal, happy life gradually disintegrates, and Campbell's description of her reality moves from beauty to horror, much as do the sublime landscapes Emily St. Aubert experiences in Radcliffe's *The Mysteries of Udolpho.*

Again, the novel is structured along the lines of the detective novel, as Rose discovers that she will give birth to the parasitic form of Peter Grace. Similarly, the elements of the supernatural mystery novel find form in Campbell's fourth novel, *The Nameless,* which is more tightly constructed than *The Parasite.* In this novel, Barbara Waugh pieces together the clues that led to the supernatural murder of her daughter. Again, Campbell's prose style, attention to detail, nuance, and character, and above all, atmosphere, raise this novel above most of the hack horror novels churned out at this time.

The Incarnate contains a highly original theme: a monstrous entity formed of a group dreaming experiment, and again, Campbell's style lifts it to the status of at least a modicum of artistry. In this novel, as in the others discussed here, Campbell's pen turns what could be quite banal into something one can truly enjoyably read. (pp. 17-19)

If Campbell has any flaws, [they lie] in the fact that his stories are at times almost too shocking, as in *The Face That Must Die.* He lacks the elegance and musicality of Aickman, and he is often poetic, but in a different manner than Aickman. It is a very harsh, shocking world that Campbell creates, and there is little truly beautiful or mysterious about Campbell. True, he can move from beauty to horror, but we do not find the idea of the sublime in Campbell, as we would, say in Ann Radcliffe. The sublime can lead to terror and awe, but occasionally, Campbell's paranoical world is a little too harsh. This is clearly what Campbell cannot do.

Taken as a whole, Campbell's works are surely the finest supernatural horror stories being produced in England at the present time. . . . (p. 19)

> *Gary William Crawford, "Urban Gothic: The Fiction of Ramsey Campbell," in* Discovering Modern Horror Fiction, *edited by Darrell Schweitzer, Starmont House, 1985, pp. 13-20.*

(Allen) Turner Cassity

1929-

American poet.

Cassity writes classically structured verse characterized by dense syntax, metered lines, and a formal tone. Although he is often associated with Yvor Winters's formalist school of poetry due to his concern with social and moral themes and his emphasis on conventional techniques, Cassity, unlike Winters, uses satire to irreverently expose the incongruities of history and international politics. Using diverse settings and subject matter, Cassity has consistently examined the topic of colonialism, centering on South African apartheid in several of his works. While some critics find his verse impersonal and recondite, others praise Cassity for the skill and discipline he brings to his craft.

In his first two collections, *Watchboy, What of the Night?* (1966) and *Steeplejacks in Babel* (1973), Cassity employs controlled, richly descriptive language to create what he terms "colonial pastorals" of locations from Mississippi to South Africa. His attacks on colonialism satirize politics and emphasize the fall of past empires. Some critics considered Cassity's third collection, *Yellow for Peril, Black for Beautiful: Poems and a Play* (1975), to be more accessible than his earlier work. While remaining understated and reserved, Cassity displays a deeper emotional involvement with his themes in this volume. Focusing on South Africa in the majority of these poems, Cassity also composed an unrhymed verse play concerning the death of Cecil Rhodes, a powerful diamond magnate and British statesman who was instrumental in establishing European rule in southern Africa during the late nineteenth century. By offsetting his formal style with wit and satire, Cassity pays mock tribute to his subject.

The Defense of the Sugar Islands: A Recruiting Post (1979) is a narrative sequence of short, rhymed poems relating the adventures of a young American soldier stationed in Puerto Rico during the Korean War. Although the tone is essentially humorous, Cassity also depicts cultural differences confronting those who travel to foreign lands. Timothy Steele noted that while "a number of the poems in the sequence . . . are fully realized in their own terms and the sequence possesses a general unity of impression," the frequent density of Cassity's syntax "on occasion results in obscurities and confusions." Cassity's recent collection, *Hurricane Lamp* (1986), continues his witty, erudite explorations of a wide range of subjects.

(See also *CLC*, Vol. 6; *Contemporary Authors*, Vols. 17-20, rev. ed.; and *Contemporary Authors New Revision Series*, Vol. 11.)

LAURENCE LIEBERMAN

While the oblique surface of Turner Cassity's poems [in *Watchboy, What of the Night?*] will repel many readers . . . , Cassity's poetry repays close study to a degree one could hardly have anticipated on first reading. The defense of an involuted and

Courtesy of Turner Cassity

esoteric poetry that risks obscurity (to all but professors, editors, and other poets—perhaps), in an age which places heavy emphasis on the virtue of readableness, is stated incisively in "**Ways of Feeling,**" a poem which discloses the author's temperament, as well as his artistic predilection:

> The fresh incision you, the drug, the knife.
> Mine is the threatened and surrounding life. . . .
>
> Who shows the sores becomes in time the leper.
> Who, his privacy his skill,
> Has learned their language, knows, if surgeons fail,
> An inexhaustible and cautious braille.

One finds a surprisingly high ratio of fully achieved poems in this book. There is no room here to take account of the cosmopolitan breadth of experience encompassed by these poems, but I'd like to sketch the aesthetics I feel are advanced by the succession of meticulously wrought couplets: A poem is a carefully polished diamond, excruciatingly chipped into shape. It is not mainly intent on virtues of communication or personal communion. It is a shaped artifact, a custom-made object. The chiseled phrasing and angular rhythms instill a solidity at the core, resembling metalwork or sculpture. A poem is worked into a ruthlessly formal, if impersonal, perfection. In a time that has given birth to the poetry of hysteria and confession, Cassity's poems return us to classical rigor and toughness. The individual word and phrase are jewels mounted securely in their settings. If many of the lines are opaque, even to the sensitive intelligence, none are brittle. If at times, the meticulous artisan who hammered these poems into shape forgets poems are made for readers, he never forgets they must be fashioned for survival. (pp. 396-97)

Laurence Lieberman, "Art in Transition," in Poetry, *Vol. CIX, No. 6, March, 1967, pp. 395-99.*

R. W. FLINT

Taciturnity is a welcome asset in a poet; Cassiturnity is that asset squared. And if I don't, like Richard Howard in his Note to *Yellow For Peril, Black For Beautiful,* go on about Cassity's capacity, Cassity's veracity, Cassity's sagacity, it is because I am too modest to make jokes at the expense of a name. The poet himself is not so inhibited:

> Arrogant and hilly,
> Insomniac and chilly.
> Who are fond of Roebling
> Find your views ennobling.
> Buffs of a different kidney
> Take up Quebec or Sydney.
>
>   (**"Against San Francisco"**)

A wit, a very palpable wit, the best in several years to present himself as such, a fitting last graduate of the Yvor Winters annex to the Scriblerus Club at Olde Stanford-by-the-sea. When one scans the Winters scripture for what years ago may have brought the two men together and occasioned such a lurid new coloring of the old flame, it is not the ex-Catholic's austere Platonizing of a J. V. Cunningham, nor the ex-Presbyterian's "tendency toward mysticism" of an Edgar Bowers, grave and accomplished as both unquestionably are. Not at all. But there may be a clue in Winters's declaration in *Primitivism and Decadence* that "the moral intelligence is merely the knowledge and evaluation of evil; and the moral intelligence is the measure of the man and of the poet alike." That was written in the earliest dawn of West Coast academic idealism and seems an observation with which Cassity, making his way between Millsaps College and Columbia by way of Stanford in the early fifties, may well have agreed. The first poem of his first book, *Watchboy, What of the Night,* ends as follows:

> Apartheid stares in classic pride
> Youth, knowing what the mirror utters,
> Will not hear now, on either side,
> Time running out in darkened gutters.

As uncompromisingly as Nadine Gordimer and her friends and with a luxuriant lyric wit that they can seldom afford, Cassity has shaped his neo-classic epigrammatic style around his support of Third World causes, South Africa (where he worked for the Transvaal Provincial Library) standing always at the center. How dependent the Augustan proprieties are on a concrete, lively, unequivocal sense of evil cannot be doubted when one remembers how Pope and Dryden sparkled in invective, how Corneille and Racine rose to their greatest heights in the *tirade.* Whether in poetry or the other arts, classic principles of construction irresistibly suggest some masterful secular goal. Now it is obviously something juicier than pure Kantian Reason that brings Cassity to the tropics. But merely being moral and stoically self-possessed, as Winters recommended, somehow lacked germinal potency detached from any clear line of action outside the universities. Cassity understood this, understood it

radically and soon. His travels to countless odd places started early and they had a beast in view, the expiring but still dangerous fact of colonialism. James Merrill was sharp in describing Cassity's verse as "an opera house in a jungle"; one wonders, though, if Merrill realized back then how *seria* the opera would turn out to be. In *Watchboy* about a third of the fifty poems deal with the ironies of colonialism. In *Steeplejacks in Babel* the count is over two-thirds, especially if the term is stretched to include all symptoms of that cultural conjunctivitis, that disease of the retina of which Cassity is now a foremost pathologist. Some people just call it travel.

Winters was afraid of impersonation, of all kinds of dramatic literature. Cassity not. *Yellow for Peril, Black for Beautiful* opens with twenty-four pages of page-long poems in rhymed couplets or simple stanzaic variations thereof. After which come thirty-eight pages of an unrhymed verse play, in comfortable six-stress lines, about the death of Cecil Rhodes. That Cassity had been brooding on the scene for some time is proved by **"A Ballade For Mr. Rhodes"** in *Steeplejacks* that contains the play *in nuce.* Everything here is demonstrated, nothing explained by the author stepping into or out of the action. Yet the energizing theme seems plain enough; that Rhodes, like his apologist Kipling . . . , was a homosexual aesthete with latent anti-Semitic tendencies. Raised a vicar's son at Bishop's Stortford in England and sickly by the standards of the time, Rhodes, according to Cassity, in his emotional life swung between an intense enjoyment of certain kinds of weather—the moment just before a thunderstorm—grandiose engineering, and the creation of a *Broederbond* of Anglophile males, "an all male family," the Great Man's only constructive notion of empire. All this is written so coolly, in such a perfect recapturing of the stale flatness of an empty idol's last hours, the tired recrimination and pointless comic funk of men drawn to Rhodes by their weaknesses, that it would require a very good performance and a very attentive audience to be effective on stage. Yet as a chamber play for the mind's eye it is extremely well done. It reeks with authenticity.

Howard is right about Cassity's "talent to amuse and his genius for being amused." He thinks that this book "gives off a certain preexplosive glow, satanic and suburban both." Certainly **"Spring in the Academy," "A Map of the Small Town,"** and **"Clay Bertrand is Alive and in Camelot"** (no need to quote after titles like those) extend his scorched-earth policy to Menckenesque lengths. Others, especially the Los Angeles poems, project a metaphysical glee for what used to be called slumming worthy of Miller's *Tropic of Cancer* or *Miss Lonelyhearts.* A poet to watch and await. (pp. 102-04)

R. W. Flint, "Exiles from Olympus," in Parnassus: Poetry in Review, *Vol. 5, No. 2, Spring-Summer, 1977, pp. 97-107.*

FRANCIS GOLFFING

Turner Cassity's eye . . . is for the geographically, historically, geopolitically given (or aborted). Yet his diagnoses or stock-takings have, from the start, been coded to a degree. The poems in his latest collection [*Yellow for Peril, Black for Beautiful*]— as subtle as ever in their prosody—tend to be less hermetic than the earlier work; instead, they bring to mind the surrealist acrobatics of Cocteau or Picabia; what controls his bizarre ballet are certain mock formalities, an upside-down classicism whose closest analogue may be found in the work of John Frederick Nims. The outrage Cassity commits, time and again, on common sense is condign punishment for the outrages the latter perpetrates with sinister regularity on the springs of the imagination. His *coq-à-l'âne* method is not strictly satirical, though satire is one of its resources (and provides, we are tempted to speculate, every now and then a convenient fall-back position, an excuse for strategic withdrawal). His verse is distinguished, both in the usual sense and in the sense of abounding in distinctions as careful as they are minute, sometimes to the point of captiousness.

Cassity's heartlessness is refreshing in an era which fancies either the casual, sleeveless mode or the heart-embroidered sleeve appropriately brought up-to-date. Which is to say that the comfort he provides his readers is cold: a banquet of piquant hors d'oeuvres which take away the appetite by extravagantly satisfying it. With one notable exception, or set of exceptions: in the poems dealing with his South African experience Cassity shows that he can command a more resonant kind of poignancy. Once things get under his skin—which does not happen very often to this well defended psyche—they are apt to pierce rather deeply, and mordant elegancies are for the nonce laid aside. What is kept is the habit of extreme notional complexity, elliptically presented in the smallest possible space. Witness such cunningly flat, unspectacular, understated poems as "**The Corpses at Zinderneuf**" and "**Catechism for Cape Malays.**" . . . [The] ring of finality is unmistakable; so is the sense of lesion or trauma: a sense usually overridden and neutralized through the exercise of non-sense, super-sense, or under-sense— open-ended strategies which invite the reader to have the last interpretive word. (pp. 178-79)

[This] is a book of admirable poetic contrivances . . . , the witty incongruities partake of the nature of Mannerist distortion, collage, or *trompe l'oeil.* No mean achievement, this, and most welcome in an age so largely marked by stupid seriousness; though—changing an earlier metaphor—too highly spiced and alembicated to be everybody's cup of tea. (p. 179)

> *Francis Golffing, "Four Faces of the Muse," in* The Southern Review, *Vol. XIV, No. 1, Winter, 1978, pp. 177-82.*

TIMOTHY STEELE

[Turner Cassity's *The Defense of the Sugar Islands*] concerns the experiences of a young American soldier stationed in Puerto Rico during the Korean War. More generally, the work deals with the problems men encounter when they live in an alien culture. Cassity, who has described himself as a writer of colonial pastorals, has addressed this subject before. Yet with the exception of his amusing *Silver out of Shanghai,* a narrative of some 2,000 lines of blank verse, this present effort is his most arresting treatment of the theme. The work is, in addition, interesting in that it provides an illustration of some of the potentials of the narrative sequence and of one of the most obvious difficulties the poet working in the form must overcome.

The sequence opens with a retrospective poem. The American, speaking in the present and no longer young, recalls his tour of duty in the army and the glamour military life once held for him. . . . But no sooner is this dashing figure conjured up than the speaker undercuts it. If blue serge becomes a soldier, it also "is for bellhops in a good hotel." (pp. 207-08)

The work then moves from the present back to the early fifties and to the young draftee in Puerto Rico. In the second poem

of the sequence, the poet again takes up the theme of living a lie, though here the context of the lie is public, not private. . . . The real defense, the real war, is half a world away, and the troops stationed in the Caribbean, and the natives themselves, lead lives determined not by the horrors and heroism of battle, but rather by "cane sugar, fraud, per diem checks." The young American finds in his surroundings a sultry beauty and ease, but that beauty and ease exact a toll. For in adapting to the exotic environment, he loses something of his natural character and vitality. And in the fourth poem of the sequence, he apostrophizes a chameleon and compares the lizard's existence to his own. . . . (p. 208)

The American subsequently tries to find sustenance in a relationship with another person, but this ultimately proves no more substantial than the "double language" of the commonwealth to which his government has sent him. . . . One person can only know another person imperfectly, and the emissaries of one culture can only understand the people and customs of another culture imperfectly. As a result, the man in love and the colonial on foreign soil are alike doomed to experience pain or feelings of failure. (pp. 208-09)

Eventually, the war ends, and the American returns to his homeland. Yet his eyes "have looked on loss"; he has been marked emotionally by his experience, and he must sustain the effects of the experience like "a living wound" for the rest of his life.

Such, then, is the basic structure of *The Defense of the Sugar Islands.* Before advancing a judgment of the work, we should note that a certain amount of backing and filling is inevitable in a narrative sequence. Ideally, each poem in the sequence should stand on its own merits, but I doubt if this ideal can be realized. . . . It can be argued that this condition indicates an inherent deficiency in the form: if the poet composing a sequence must perforce produce at least a few items that are to some extent shaped by a functional purpose, would he not be better off simply undertaking a long poem instead? Does not the poet embarking on a sequence run the risk of falling between two stools, and of attaining neither the even flow of the conventional extended work nor the concentration of the short poem? Yet it can also be argued that while the writer of the sequence is always in danger of assuming the limitations of both the long poem and the short, he can as well, if he is sufficiently talented, avail himself of certain virtues of each form while escaping certain restrictions of each. And it can be urged that it is possible to write a sequence characterized by a minimum of padding and by a breadth of treatment and tone unfeasible in the short poem—a sequence, in brief, like Cunningham's, in which a high percentage of the parts are individually distinctive and at the same time contribute to effective narrative development.

If one views Cassity's work in light of these latter considerations, I think one has to consider it successful. A number of the poems in the sequence (notably the first, the seventh, and the ninth) are fully realized in their own terms, and the sequence possesses a general unity of impression. Having passed this verdict, I must offer a couple of reservations. Some of Cassity's poems (here and elsewhere) are difficult, and I often have trouble following his thought. I believe the source of the problem is the frequent density of Cassity's syntax—a density which at times gives his work a richness of texture, but which on occasion results in obscurities and confusions. Consider, for instance, **"Lights Out,"** the third poem in the sequence:

> The sand is scented and the war remote.
> Hut, tent—the difference obscured, dissolved—
> Enjoy in netted calm the humming night.
> Laconic bugler, let the shining spit
> Hang on your mouthpiece, as, through honey valved,
> The shining insects quit the jasmine vine.
> Then, draining out of brass the drops of time,
> Quit you their sounding water-clock. Breathe here,
> Say rather, tongue your breath, as we whose dream
> Converts these cots to lanterns tongue the flame:
> Match after match, in each mosquito-bar,
> The two throats quiet and the warm smoke sweet.

I have read the passage from "Laconic bugler . . ." to the end of the poem many times, and the more I have read the passage, the further it has seemed to retreat from intelligibility. Those two throats in the last line—do they belong to the speaker and the bugler? Or to the "we" whose collective dream converts cots to lanterns? Is the dream real or figurative? (pp. 209-10)

If **"Lights Out"** is elliptical, the sequence as a whole suffers somewhat from ellipticalness. I wish, for one thing, I knew a little more about the relationships between the young American and some of the people mentioned in the sequence. I express this desire not out of a hunger after scandal, but instead because I sense that the connection between the private man and the public colonial—between the needs of the individual and the demands his profession places on him—is an issue central to Cassity's concerns. This issue is adeptly handled in *Silver out of Shanghai*, but in *The Defense* too much detail is withheld. There are only ten poems in the sequence, and three consist mostly of generalized statement. Though the statement is interesting, much of it refers to experiences that are but hinted at; we are provided, that is, with analysis of circumstances inadequately located, and the force of the sequence is thereby somewhat diminished.

This matter is crucial, and it calls attention to what is perhaps the greatest difficulty that someone composing a narrative sequence must face. The form requires a delicate balance of, on the one hand, well-chosen particulars and, on the other hand, apposite commentary on the particulars, and it takes a rare and versatile talent to achieve this balance. And while it seems to me that Cassity is not entirely successful in this regard, I hasten to add that if he errs, he errs in good company. [Robert Frost's] "The Hill Wife," for instance, provides an illustration of the same imbalance that afflicts *The Defense of the Sugar Islands*, though in Frost's case the imbalance results not from an insufficiency of particulars but from a weakness of commentary. . . . [The] conclusion of the poem is unsatisfactory; it is not especially (to use Aristotle's terms) probable or necessary. And the reason it isn't especially probable or necessary is that Frost, while sharply rendering the externals of the young woman's condition, neglects to give us any clear examination of her motives. (pp. 210-11)

Despite its arbitrary conclusion, "The Hill Wife" is an engaging work, and so is Cassity's sequence. And if Cassity is not always as clear about his subject as he might be, he always has a subject, which is more than one can say about most poets today. In addition, while Cassity's pentameters are from time to time a trifle unwieldy, he can handle the line with great grace when he wants to. (pp. 211-12)

Turner Cassity's work does not invite byzantine interpretation, but he is a genuine poet. He has written fine shòrt poems (e.g., **"Calvin in the Casino," "Carpenters,"** and **"Cartography Is an Inexact Science"**), and he has a gift for longer works. He has ideas, he has wit, he can writè delightfully well. And while some of his poems have an air of willed and brittle eccentricity, his best poems are accessible and moving. I hope he will continue to work in longer forms, and I hope, too, that the longer works he has already published will find a wider audience than they have hitherto. They deserve it. (p. 213)

Timothy Steele, "Curving to Foreign Harbors: Turner Cassity's 'Defense of the Sugar Islands'," in The Southern Review, *Vol. 17, No. 1, Winter, 1981, pp. 205-13.*

DANA GIOIA

Turner Cassity may be the most brilliantly eccentric poet in America. Just the "Contents" page of a Cassity book usually contains more poetry than the average contemporary volume (for no poet since Wallace Stevens has had such a flair for titles.) *Steeplejacks in Babel,* for instance, contains such provocative but never gratuitous titles as **"Pacelli and the Ethiop," "Leander of the Diving Board," "The Entrance of Winifred into Valhalla,"** and **"In the land of the great aunts."** Cassity is an unabashed virtuoso. His poems bristle with historical and cultural allusions, and he is never shy in displaying his gifts for rhyme and word play. The technical audacity, the recondite subjects he explores, and the sheer excitement of his language have made each book sparkle like a fireworks show. But at the same time, as much as I have enjoyed reading him, I have always regretted how few of his poems really showed all he was capable of. Too much of his work seemed arch and overwrought, its technique too brilliantly displayed for its own sake, and its exotic subjects too remote from his real concerns to have all the personal intensity he could have brought to them.

The Defense of the Sugar Islands, however, marks a real breakthrough for Cassity. In this ten-poem sequence, which tells the story of an American sailor stationed in the Caribbean during the Korean War, the execution is never anything less than brilliant, but Cassity does not let his virtuosity get the better of his material: for once the poems have as much emotional as intellectual force to them. The reason, I suspect, is that the protagonist is based on the poet himself rather than some figure from colonial history. In any event, Cassity has vividly recreated an island "where sand is scented and the war remote" and a young sailor caught between boredom and lust. The sequence develops in a series of scenes—the soldier trying on his new uniform before a mirror, a military funeral, etc.—each of which could stand alone as an individual poem, but which, taken together, constitute a fascinating portrait of a particular person, time and place. What impresses me most about this book is that Cassity is as adept at psychological realism as he is at high satire. And he can play the novelist without losing his poet's ear. *The Defense of the Sugar Islands* also shows the full range of Cassity's talents. He can still write comedy as well as ever but now manages lyric moments of uncharacteristic tenderness. . . . (pp. 496-97)

The Defense of the Sugar Islands . . . is the finest book Cassity has ever written, and one of the best new collections I have read all year. (p. 497)

Dana Gioia, "Poetry and the Fine Presses," *in* The Hudson Review, *Vol. XXXV, No. 3, Autumn, 1982, pp. 483-98.*

DONALD DAVIE

Turner Cassity is very markedly and self-consciously a writer of *verse*, in the sense that central to his awareness of what he is doing is the integrity of the verse-line, and particularly of the *turn* from one line into the next. This is not quite the same as saying, what is none the less true, that Cassity writes in meter—an alternative that, in the case of younger generations of American poets, is I think rather seldom considered. It's in a poem from his second collection, *Steeplejacks in Babel* . . . , that Cassity announces most defiantly his espousal of this alternative. But open defiance is not at all his way; and his act of defiance is conveyed, with characteristic obliquity, in a poem which overtly isn't about writing at all but about the harbor of Sydney, Australia:

Cruise ships are, for the young, all that which varies.
The aged disembark with dysenteries.
Always, it is middle age that sees the ferries.

They hold no promise. Forward or reverse
Impels them only to where what occurs,
Occurs. Such is, at least, the chance of being terse,

And is their grace. The lengthy liners, fraught
Sublimely, shrill for tugs. If they're distraught,
That is because the thoughts of youth are long, long
   thoughts—

Save those of gratitude. The slow, massed force
That frees them they will cast off in due course,
To learn, or not to learn, the ferries' sole resource:

How, in the crowding narrows, when the current
Runs in opposition and the torrent
Claws the wheel, to locate in routine, abhorrent

For the storm, the shore that makes it specious;
Where one calls the vicious, curtly, vicious,
And the scheduled ferry, not the cruise ship, precious.

                                                        (pp. 22-3)

Cassity's **"In Sydney by the Bridge,"** though invaluable as a sort of programmatic poem, represents him, just because it *is* programmatic, at less than his best. I'd define what is deficient about it by remarking that it could have been written by a poet who had never actually *been* in Sydney, New South Wales; or else (the same point the other way round) that we as readers have really no more sense of the scene of Sydney Harbour when we finish the poem than before we began reading it. Much better, to my mind, is a poem about Amsterdam which really *is* about that Dutch city. . . . It is of course a *paysage intérieur* as much as it is a *paysage* locatable on the map, and a season of the soul as much as it is a tourist season, or part of one. The double-meanings of "reflection" and "vision," to go no further, give to the reader so inclined sufficient provocation for allegorizing. But we should beware, I think, of allegorizing too promptly and too eagerly: Cassity is very much a world-wandering poet, a globetrotter, and although the places that he responds to have something in common (mostly, for instance, they are post-colonial places), still the sheer irreducible variety of visitable places and climates is something brought powerfully home to us as we read Cassity; and to some un-

Platonic minds, the compelling assurance of that available diversity is in itself a pleasure and a comfort.

There could hardly be a starker contrast to [Cassity's former teacher and mentor Yvor] Winters who, vividly though he responded to places and climates, never left the United States, and through much of his life could only with difficulty be lured more than 100 miles from San Francisco. (pp. 24-5)

[How] unlikely, and how impossible to account for in Winters's scheme of things, that one of the poets he schooled should by choice or chance spend many years in the Union of South Africa, and should give a more nuanced and affecting image of life in that strange society than has been given, to the best of my knowledge, by any English-speaking South African, whether black or white or yellow or brown! If that is Turner Cassity's achievement, or one of his achievements, it is hard to see how any of the currently influential American schools of criticism is able to come to terms with it, or to value it, any better than Wintersian criticism does. For a criticism which, whatever other disputes may divide it, still agrees to take as the central task of American poetry the defining of *American* identity, there is no way to account for an American poet whose most noble and moving verses are imagined as spoken by the ghost of President Paul Kruger hovering over his own effigy in Pretoria. . . . Confronted with this phenomenon, we either damn with faint praise ("Cassity is a limited poet, but . . . performs candidly within his range") [see excerpt by Jerome J. McGann in *CLC,* Vol. 6], or else, more disastrously, we decide that he can't be serious. Of this second way of turning the force of Cassity's challenge to our preconceptions Richard Howard has remarked [in his introduction to **Yellow for Peril, Black for Beautiful**], with fine distaste:

> Architecture, as Walt Whitman once observed, is what you do to a building when you look at it, and our transactions with this poet's oeuvre suggest that we turn a building into a "folly" when we don't look it at enough. It is our neglect which is playing the fool here, not Cassity's capacity, not Cassity's veracity, not Cassity's sagacity.

And yet even Mr. Howard sees an element of "the folly" in the extraordinary edifice that Cassity erected in 1970 on the pages of *Poetry* magazine, a narrative poem in twelve sections about a 1917 German airship expedition to South West Africa, story-line and *dramatis personae* both and all entirely solid and clear; or again, in the verse-play, **"Men of the Great Man,"** set around the death-bed of Cecil Rhodes. This last [poem] Mr. Howard describes as "a Lament for the Dead Hero which is this poet's own snarling version of the collapse of the Knights of the Grail—a kind of *Boys Own Parsifal,* wherein the Fellowship dissolves into . . . Rhodes scholarships!" This is certainly an accurate as well as admirably compact description of this play. And undoubtedly the decline of imperial grandeur to Rhodes scholarships calls for some sort of astonished exclamation mark. It would be a pity, though, if Mr. Howard's exclamation mark carried too much the implication of "What an amusing thing to have thought of writing about!"

Cassity himself, unfortunately, invites that sort of snickering reading. Too often his titles are arch and cute. The poem about Amsterdam, for instance, has the dandified title, **"A Somewhat Static Barcarolle."** It is a mannerism that we have been resigned to ever since Wallace Stevens, and I've never seen a convincing explanation of what purpose Stevens meant his dandified titles to serve. In Cassity's case very often they seem to signal only a nervous giggle. A more grievous case is his entitling his poem about the German dirigible, **"The Airship Boys in Africa"**—which certainly seems to imply that if we take the poem seriously (as for my part I certainly do—it is too well written for me to take it otherwise), we are making fools of ourselves.

And Cassity's giggle sounds elsewhere than in his titles. On his way to **"The Airship Boys in Africa,"** he had written for instance a poem in his first book, **"The Afterlives of Count Zeppelin"**. (Somewhere behind them both, I would guess, is Winter's solemn and impressive "Elegy. For the U.S.N. Dirigible, Macon.") The Count Zeppelin poem begins with a good joke, then deteriorates rapidly. . . . I haven't the heart to go on. . . . It should be clear that the self-consciously "wicked" outrageousness of the rhymes has taken hold of the poem and wrenched it out of any possibility of shapeliness; it is as if the Sydney Harbour ferry crashed full tilt into the pier on every second traverse—this verse never turns, it shudders to a stop, then painfully starts again. "Dandified" is hardly the word for this effect; yet the motive behind it seems the same—the compulsion to always astonish, outsmart, upstage any conceivable reader. And for this we now, thanks to Susan Sontag, have a better word than "dandified;" it is *camp*—not just an effect, but the sensibility which seeks out such effects and revels in them, a sensibility which since 1964. . . , we have no excuse for not defining quite precisely, and recognizing as a powerful strain in American poetry of our time. "Camp," I would say, is Turner Cassity's besetting temptation.

Twenty years ago Susan Sontag confessed to feeling very ambivalent about "camp.". . . Yet on the whole, despite misgivings, she welcomed "camp" as an ally in her polemic *Against Interpretation*. In this I think she was mistaken. None of us who are involved in institutions of allegedly higher learning can think that "interpretation" as she defined it is any less of a menace now than it was 20 years ago; the *interpreters,* bearing in upon the content of texts, operate in every classroom up and down the land, breeding there more of their own kind—that is to say, people who under the pretence of serving art in fact emasculate it, and *tame* it. But what stops these colleagues of ours in their tracks are not the "camp" texts which brazenly are more conerned with form than with content, but on the contrary texts which leave the interpreter with nothing to do precisely because their content is unchallengeably obvious, texts which in the most obvious way mean implacably just what they say. Ms. Sontag, wistfully yearning for just such an overt and undeviating art, found it only in the cinema; but if she had looked a little further, she would have found it in our poetry also—though in a sort of poetry which goes largely unregarded because it does not suit the vested interests of the institutionalized "interpreters", and also (it must be said) because our students are so obtuse about the resources of their native language that no content, however overt, is overt enough for them not to miss it or get it wrong. Turner Cassity, for one, has written such admirably overt poems. (pp. 26-9)

> *Donald Davie, "On Turner Cassity," in* Chicago Review, *Vol. 34, No. 1, Summer, 1983, pp. 22-9.*

FRANK J. LEPKOWSKI

Cassity's latest collection [**Hurricane Lamp**] is highly various, ranging from treatments of classical themes to travel notes from the world over. The poet is erudite and very skilled at the traditional versification he favors; he is dextrous as well at argument, at what in Pope's day was called wit. At times, the author is too witty by half; the conceit of likening a school crossing guard to the infamous Ilse Koch is jarringly inappropriate, and ruins an otherwise lovely poem. All too often a tone of brittle, mandarin playfulness predominates. This book is recommended, however, for the several fine poems that rise above raillery, among them **"Why Fortune Is Empress of the World," "Advice to King Lear," "The Alfano Ending,"** and the luminous, utterly gorgeous **"Promises, Promises."**

> *Frank J. Lepkowski, in a review of "Hurricane Lamp," in* Library Journal, *Vol. 111, No. 3, February 15, 1986, p. 183.*

JOHN ASH

Mr. Cassity's **Hurricane Lamp** arrived on my desk heavily draped with advance praise. To J. D. McClatchy his work suggests "a collaboration between William Empson and Noël Coward." Other names that come to mind are John Crowe Ransom and Yvor Winters. Donald Davie invokes the name of Baudelaire and describes the poems as *fleurs du mal*. This may be overstating the case (perhaps Mr. Davie was overalarmed by a single poem about a leather bar), but there is a distinctly 1890's, even Pre-Raphaelite air about some of Mr. Cassity's work. In terms of style there isn't much that suggests a date later than 1929. . . . [There] are times when Mr. Cassity's mannered language seems merely anachronistic and periphrastic, but this kind of formal, allusive and highly literary poetry has its own charms. I particularly like Mr. Cassity's habit of juxtaposing the exotic and the ordinary—as in **"Scheherazade in South Dakota"** and **"Maeterlinck in Ontario"**—and his sharp eye for eccentricity.

His insistence on formality does present problems, however. His regular meters and strict rhyme schemes can become rigid and monotonous. They can also drive him to ugly linguistic contortions—"Only ash may fully be implicit, / May in bright beginning fire be end." I find that difficult to unscramble. I am also unable to decide whether a man who begins a poem with the word "Implacablest" should be applauded for his daring or rebuked for his insensitive ear. But even in his failings Mr. Cassity shows his independence of mind. He may be overcontrolled, but he would never be guilty of the kind of maudlin and seemingly interminable free verse effusions that fill so many pages of contemporary American poetry magazines. At his epigrammatic best he combines elegance with an attractive pungency—"The random that we create creates us. / In overcrowded lifeboats, we draw lots."

> *John Ash, "A Brash Yankee and a Southern Dandy," in* The New York Times Book Review, *April 20, 1986, p. 19.*

(William) Robertson Davies

1913-

(Has also written under pseudonym of Samuel Marchbanks) Canadian novelist, essayist, dramatist, short story writer, editor, and critic.

Davies's reputation as a leading figure in Canadian literature was firmly established by his novels *Fifth Business* (1971), *The Manticore* (1973), and *World of Wonders* (1975), collectively known as *The Deptford Trilogy*. Like all of his fiction, these novels are densely plotted, well-crafted, and humorous while displaying Davies's knowledge in a wide range of subjects. Davies often directs his satirical humor towards Canadian provincialism, which he perceives as a hindrance to Canada's cultural development. While his novels are firmly rooted in realism and are presented in traditional forms, Davies introduces such elements as magic, supernatural events, and religious symbolism to underscore the mystery and wonder of life. His novels are infused with a Jungian sensibility which informs his characters' search for identity. Central to Davies's novels is his belief that a particular action may produce consequences of infinite possibility and irreversible effect. *The Deptford Trilogy*, for instance, is structured around the single act of a character throwing a snowball, an event that shapes the destiny of the trilogy's three protagonists.

Davies was a respected columnist, newspaper editor, and dramatist before he began writing the novels which would gain him international recognition during the 1950s. His first three novels, *Tempest-Tost* (1951), *Leaven of Malice* (1955), and *A Mixture of Frailties* (1958), comprise *The Salterton Trilogy*, which examines a small Canadian university town. *Tempest-Tost* recounts the attempts of Salterton's amateur theater group to stage Shakespeare's *Tempest*. The company's ineptitude and churlish behavior are the source of much of the novel's humor and represent factors limiting Canada's cultural growth. The plot of *Leaven of Malice* revolves around the placement in Salterton's local newspaper of a false engagement announcement linking a young man and woman from rival families. The pretentiousness of the two families is satirically exposed as they go to great extremes to humiliate each other. Love triumphs, however, and the couple eventually marry. *A Mixture of Frailties* concerns a young Salterton woman who travels to Europe to train as a singer. Her development from a rustic small-town girl to a sophisticated woman reflects Davies's belief that education and experience are important elements for a complete life.

The Salterton Trilogy was followed by Davies's acclaimed *Deptford Trilogy*. These novels focus on the individual's need to accept the irrational, unconscious side of the self in order to achieve completeness. *Fifth Business* reveals the seemingly inconsequential incident of a thrown snowball that ultimately alters the lives of three men. Dunstan Ramsey, who dodged the snowball, suffers remorse and guilt because the snowball that missed him struck a pregnant woman. He attempts to rationalize the experience through an interest in saints, magic, and psychology. *The Manticore* recounts the psychoanalysis of David Staunton, the son of the boy who threw the snowball. In this novel, Davies employs Jungian archetypes and ancient myths to unravel the mysteries of the subconscious which con-

tribute to Staunton's self-awareness. *World of Wonders* is the story of Paul Dempster, whose mother was hit by the snowball, causing his premature birth and her mental breakdown. Dempster's life is shaped by magic and illusion after he is kidnapped as a child by a carnival magician and eventually becomes the world-famous prestidigitator, Magnus Eisengrim. The dominant themes displayed in these novels are Davies's concern with the individual's quest for identity and the moral necessity to examine all facets of life. Of *The Deptford Trilogy*, Claude Bissell declared: "These novels comprise the major piece of prose fiction in Canadian literature—in scope, in the constant interplay of wit and intelligence, in the persistent attempt to find a pattern in this 'life of marvels, cruel circumstances, obscenities, and commonplaces.'"

Davies's reputation was further enhanced by his novels *The Rebel Angels* (1981) and *What's Bred in the Bone* (1985). *The Rebel Angels* centers around a group of professors at a Toronto university who serve as executors of the estate of Francis Cornish, a collector and patron of the arts. Among the eclectic subjects touched upon by Davies in this novel are the works of French satirist François Rabelais and Swiss alchemist Philippus Paracelsus, gypsy customs, and "filth therapy." *What's Bred in the Bone* explores the influence of external forces upon one man's life. Ostensibly a biography of Francis Cornish as narrated by two angels, *What's Bred in the Bone* also contains a frame story involving characters from *The Rebel Angels*. Like Davies's other novels, this work concerns the protagonist's pursuit of self-discovery and is infused with supernatural, psychological, and religious elements while being firmly rooted in realism. Davies also displays his diverse intellectual interests, discussing such subjects as art, embalming, and astrology. *What's Bred in the Bone* was described by D. J. Enright as "a fascinating story, beautifully organized, never drifting into inconsequence, its literal narrative and its metaphorical signals always in step, as with the best poetry."

Davies has also won praise for his work in other genres. In a series of newspaper articles and anecdotes on Canadian social and cultural themes, Davies introduced himself as Samuel Marchbanks, a curmudgeon who has been likened to Samuel Johnson and Canadian satirist Stephen Leacock. These essays were collected in *The Diary of Samuel Marchbanks* (1947), *The Table Talk of Samuel Marchbanks* (1949), and *Marchbanks' Almanack* (1967). Portions of these collections were edited and republished in *The Papers of Samuel Marchbanks* (1985). In these pieces, Davies is often humorously excessive in his bitter attacks on such topics as politicians, social movements, and mechanical appliances. Although known primarily as a novelist and satirist, Davies is also an important force in Canadian drama. He has authored over a dozen plays, including *Overlaid* (1948), *Fortune, My Foe* (1949), *A Jig for the Gypsy* (1954), and an adaptation of *Leaven of Malice* (1973), and has worked in such capacities as actor, director, and board member for several major Canadian theater companies.

(See also *CLC*, Vols. 2, 7, 13, 25; *Contemporary Authors*, Vols. 33-36, rev. ed.; and *Contemporary Authors New Revision Series*, Vol. 17.)

BRUCE KING

Robertson Davies's *Tempest-Tost* (1951) concerns the behaviour, manners and morals of an amateur theatre group in a provincial Ontario city. The group has chosen to perform Shakespeare's *Tempest,* which in such a cultural backwater is thought of as somewhat daring; 'pastoral' has not been produced previously by a local theatre group. Ironically, the play is relevant to the behaviour of the cast, as off stage the interaction of the actors has a parody resemblance to the main characters of the drama. A dull, pedantic university professor is the novel's Prospero; his daughter is an unloved Miranda, and the play's Ferdinand attempts to seduce the girl who acts the part of Ariel. While it is not necessary to recognise the similarities between the novel and the play, the analogies serve a triple function. They satirise, bringing out by contrast the narrow vision and weak passions of local life; they give a universal significance to otherwise petty behaviour in a small provincial city; they implicitly suggest that Shakespeare's 'pastoral' is grounded in continuing realities. The social comedy of the novel can, like *The Tempest,* alternatively be seen as a pleasant escape from the hard facts of life or as an embodiment of recurring, fundamental kinds of human behaviour. The author's amusement with the rivalries and snobberies of a provincial city is playful, but the novel is also highly satiric; *Tempest-Tost* reveals the hypocrisy, malice, pride and other evils of provincial Ontario. As in Shakespeare's play, literary

convention and stylisation make comedy out of what might otherwise be extremely unpleasant situations and behaviour.

Although *Tempest-Tost* makes use of the reader's literary and social sophistication, it also draws upon a specifically Canadian literary tradition. Indeed *Tempest-Tost* might be seen as a further development of Leacock's treatment of Ontario; amusement, fun and the pastoral sugarcoat social satire and an awareness, which Leacock preferred not to explore, of the darker side of life.

Davies has created from what might be character sketches a complete, self-sufficient little world, with its own social hierarchies. The local university, cathedral and Royal Military College represent the continuation of colonial culture in modern Canada. There is a continuity between manners, behaviour and morals which allows the reader to place and judge each character even though Davies's fictional world is more stylised, lighter in texture, and more obviously reliant upon types than that of the great nineteenth-century novelists. While manners, class and desire are noted, they are both exaggerated and simplified into caricature; the people in *Tempest-Tost* inhabit a community seemingly unthreatened by the radical anxieties of our century. As in many novels by R. K. Narayan, the conflicts of personalities and classes within provincial life appear mere foibles, but the author's tolerance is deceptive. The comedy is only possible because the characters, having already been judged, are sources of amusement. (pp. 200-01)

Although *Tempest-Tost* records in detail part of the social life of provincial Ontario, its perspective towards events and characters is sophisticated and cosmopolitan. It appears to belong to the English nineteenth-century tradition of the novel of social comedy, modified by Canadian humour, emphasis and subject-matter; but it also belongs to the 1950s when wit, judgement, order and tone were key terms of critical praise. . . . (p. 202)

Davies's novels examine what Canadians are and how they became that way. If *Tempest-Tost* makes Chekhovian comedy from the colonial haute bourgeoisie, Davies is aware that the real history of the country is in the small-town Protestants; raised in poverty they have made their cruel puritanism into a national character which lacks vitality and ambition and represses desire. The satire on Hector Mackilwraith, the calculating, reserved schoolmaster, who lives at the YMCA and eats at the Snak Shak, is Davies's first attempt to explore one of the main themes of *Fifth Business* (1970) and the *Deptford Trilogy*—the division of the Canadian soul between its puritan heritage and its hidden romantic aspirations. Beneath the seemingly settled views of the author there exists a radical streak which will come more to the surface in later novels. It is interesting that Margaret Atwood will also see Canadians as lamenting their fate, and urge them to discover what they are.

Tempest-Tost was followed by two further novels of Salterton, *Leaven of Malice* (1954) and *A Mixture of Frailties* (1958). There is a noticeable deepening of moral concern, an awareness of how breeding and environment influence behaviour. In *Leaven of Malice,* a false engagement notice is inserted in the Salterton evening newspaper stating that Pearl, the daughter of Professor and Mrs Walter Vambrace, will marry Solomon Bridgetower on 31st November. The announcement brings out the worst in the characters. Professor Vambrace and Mrs Bridgetower are selfishly possessive of their only children, look down socially upon each other's family, and regard the engagement notice as a humiliating plot against their dignity. Since 31st November does not exist as a date, Professor Vambrace threatens to sue the newspaper for defaming his daughter's character. Supposed friends of Mrs Bridgetower insinuate that she will lose face unless her son takes some legal action to protect the family name. A situation thus occurs when both Pearl and Solomon may go to court claiming each has been defamed by the other through the engagement notice. Eventually the two young people are brought together by their parents' attempts to keep them apart; and at the end of the novel they are indeed engaged to be married.

The announcement was inserted by a Mr Bevill Higgin, an immigrant singing teacher who carries with him a sense of being treated unjustly and who appeals to colonial prejudices of the local Canadians. Although Higgin, like Iago, is malicious, cunning, and has an unjustified sense of grievance, he is basically a catalyst for the malice in others. (pp. 203-04)

Although *Leaven of Malice* ends on a happy note, and therefore technically speaking is a comedy, it has shown the potential for evil that is available in a provincial Ontario city. Davies has kept to the conventions of social comedy, but his Salterton novels recognise the dark side of human nature under the trappings of local eccentricities. . . . The third novel of the [*Salterton Trilogy*], *A Mixture of Frailties,* shows Davies's growing concern with how the past influences the future. A dead mother has attempted to dictate to her son through her will, denying him his inheritance until he has produced a son to carry on the family name. Instead the money is used to train an uncultured local gospel singer as a concert artist. The novel indicates that education and experience, especially that gained abroad, are necessary for a fuller life than that found in Canada. The singer only begins to develop as a musician after a love affair with her teacher in Europe. (pp. 204-05)

While Davies's first three novels are known mostly within Canada, his [*Deptford Trilogy*] has been an international success. *Fifth Business* (1970), *The Manticore* (1972) and *World of Wonders* (1975) might be said to extend the Ontario novel to the world scene. The three books trace the history of several Canadian families from the early twentieth century to the present. Davies has broadened the scope of the usual family saga beyond a record of social changes to show the transformation of a representative Canadian from a provincial to involvement with the modern world and to show how fear of uncovering the truth about the Canadian past has prevented self-discovery and liberation.

If Davies's novels began as social satires of provincial Ontario society they progress to unmasking what is hidden beneath surface appearances and then to an implied statement about the need to accept and use the subterranean depths of the soul as part of growth towards wholeness. The particular and universal are explicitly shown to be related, in *The Manticore,* through Jungian archetypes and other myths that reveal the inner spiritual life and true self. Indeed, following on more subtly from *Tempest-Tost,* Davies explores the relationship of illusion and reality, dream and truth. *World of Wonders,* the third book in the *Deptford Trilogy,* suggests that man is half human, half animal; myths are summaries of experience, and a real world of 'wonder' exists below the surface of life, which can be found from the study of history, psychology and magic.

World of Wonders is essentially the biography of Magnus Eisengrim. Magnus's original name was Paul Dempster. The snowball which in *Fifth Business* Percy Boyd Staunton intended for Dunstan Ramsay instead hit Mary Dempster, bringing about Paul's premature birth and her craziness. After his

mother was discovered with a tramp, Paul's life became unbearable in their village and he escaped, only to become the captive of a sodomising circus magician. Years of degradation resulted in his evolution into the greatest modern magician and his change of name. He represents a hidden side of the Canadian character, which contrasts to Dunstan's grey, schoolmaster qualities. It is the discovery and acceptance of such opposites that, Davies seems to imply, is necessary for psychic health.

Although Davies's Jungianism and international canvas may seem unrelated to Canadian nationalism, except as a criticism of provincial attitudes, his novels are attempts to explore what makes Canadians tick. The snowball that Boyd Staunton denies having tossed may seem a peculiar incident around which to build the plot of three novels, but his sense of humiliation, vindictiveness and injustice, the craftiness of the narrator, Dunstan Ramsey, and their refusal to admit guilt are similar to the poverty and cruelties of the small town, part of the past which must be uncovered if deep currents in the national character are to be understood. Davies has spoken of Canada as having a northern mysticism behind the tight, puritanical appearance it offers the world. A concern with myth and Jungian archetypes has for several decades been a feature of Canadian literary culture, as can be seen from the critical theories of Northrop Frye, the poetry and plays of James Reaney and, more recently, the work of Margaret Atwood. The attraction of Jung to Canadian intellectuals is that his theories of archetypal polarities being at the core of the soul, and their suppression being the cause of psychic disturbance, might utilise the presence in Canada of such opposites as the English and French languages, British and American culture, the blandness expected of Canadian behaviour and the harsh realities of life in northern winters, or the divided loyalties sometimes felt by the settlers and immigrants.

World of Wonders raises some of these possibilities in explaining the attraction in the past of an out-of-date Englishness to many Canadians. . . . (pp. 205-07)

[*World of Wonders*] begins in rural poverty, petty provincial small-mindedness, and progresses to the international scene and Jungian psychology, and concludes with one of the most amazing fictional biographies in modern literature. It is significant of the need to give meaning and pattern to colonial and new national cultures that many of the writers from the Commonwealth use myth in their work. Davies's early novels may appear to be social comedies of a settled society, but in fact the tendency of his work is similar to that of Soyinka, Harris, Narayan and Hope, in seeing within myths profound realities which would give significance to the apparent lack of purpose in ordinary life. (pp. 208-09)

[Davies has a] fulness and largeness of narrative art. . . . To those who claim that he is writing about the past, his boyhood in post-Victorian Ontario, Davies replies that he is writing about real life, 'people who are still there', and a Canada which has rejected its past, but which has not yet accepted its future. That he has worked in the theatre and himself written plays is evident from the kinds of characters, dialogue and situations found in his novels. It is possible that his involvement with the theatre has contributed to his skill in representing the universal through local society.

Alongside Davies's sophistication and closeness to international culture there are similar anxieties and conflicts to those found throughout the new English literatures. The satire on settled Ontario in the early novels reflects a generational conflict and rejection of an established bourgeoisie during a period of social change when the economy and attitudes are being transformed and modernised. The portrayal of an early, poverty-stricken, rural Ontario in *Fifth Business* searches the past for the roots of present anxieties. Perhaps the main theme of Davies's trilogy is 'Who am I?' In each of his novels there is the uncovering and recognition of evil behind the apparent blandness of Canadian life. The experiencing of and conflict with evil brings about wondrous transformations which share characteristics with myth. If I understand correctly, Davies is showing that the mean-spirited puritanism and conventionality associated with Canada hide the evil, romance and longing of real lives. The early novels show passions repressed; but it is with the recognition of evil in *Leaven of Malice* and the need to experience life fully in *A Mixture of Frailties* that he found the perspective which shapes his later trilogy. Although he brings an international perspective to his novels, Davies is conscious of working within what has in recent decades become the tradition of Canadian thought and uses concepts that have since been used by many neonationalist writers. (pp. 209-10)

> *Bruce King, "Canada: Robertson Davies and Identity," in his* The New English Literatures: Cultural Nationalism in a Changing World, *St. Martin's Press, 1980, pp. 196-214.*

ANDREW ALLENTUCK

[*High Spirits*] succeeds in raising the ghost story to a high plane of civility: Davies's ghosts are not the dour, threatening creatures of 19th-century literature but jovial, literate spirits. The collection of ghosts, frog princes, and various other-worldly creatures offer, as Davies puts it, "a dietary supplement, a vitamin taken to stave off that most dreadful of modern ailments, the Rational Rickets."

In one of the stories, a Russian singer, famed for his low voice, is a student at the U of T and member of the college choir. He decides to correct the degenerate, bourgeois lyrics of The Messiah by substituting anti-bourgeois Soviet rhetoric. As punishment, the conductor gives him the evil eye and turns him into a frog. Kissed again into temporary manhood by the ladies of the orchestra, the student needs Nikita Khrushchev's royal buss (a.k.a. the proletarian kiss) for permanent salvation. Does the dead Comrade K. rescue the lad (or frog)? Does he/it still squat in amphibian repose? It's just one of the delightful dilemmas of this most civilized of spook books.

> *Andrew Allentuck, in a review of "High Spirits," in* Quill and Quire, *Vol. 49, No. 2, February, 1983, p. 34.*

PUBLISHERS WEEKLY

In *High Spirits,* Robertson Davies (author of the *Deptford Trilogy*) has collected 18 comic ghost stories, which he wrote for the annual Christmas party, or Gaudy Night, while master of Massey College in the University of Toronto. All of these tales are set at Massey College, and their content is somewhat limited by the occasion of Davies's original intended audience. Perhaps only a graduate student could fully savor certain stories, for example, **"The Ghost Who Vanished by Degrees,"** about a spirit who, unable to get his Ph.D. in life, returns to defend successfully his theses in a variety of subjects; or **"Dickens Digested,"** in which a bust of Dickens literally consumes an earnest American scholar. Yet a playful sensibility informs all the tales, which demonstrate Davies's facility for puns and his vivid imagination. . . . These witty little tales give insight into the making of ghost stories, while simultaneously showing the master at work. (pp. 58-9)

> *A review of "High Spirits: A Collection of Ghost Stories," in* Publishers Weekly, *Vol. 224, No. 11, September 9, 1983, pp. 58-9.*

DAVID STOUCK

Davies has attracted public attention throughout his career by his witty, often satiric observations on Canadian life and by his cultivation of a theatrical personality. The high esteem in which this author is held, however, has a more solid foundation in certain philosophical concerns which have informed Davies's writings for many years and which give his work as a whole a coherency of purpose and statement.

A list of Davies's subjects would be almost endless, for he has an insatiable interest in all manner of knowledge and information. In his plays we learn about such curious matters as Bohemian puppetry, jest books, Victorian photography, while in the novels we are made to consider such diverse subjects as hagiography, Jungian psychoanalysis, heraldry, and the stagecraft of the illusionist. What is impressive is the way Davies's out-of-the-way lore is made to yield real knowledge about human life.

Although there is great range and diversity to his interests, certain themes recur consistently in all of Davies's writings. As a Canadian Davies frequently attempts to define the essential character of life in Canada, pointing to those special traits of a people with a northern geography and limited political power. More generally, as a critic of contemporary manners, Davies is concerned with attacking the narrow-mindedness and philistinism of any society hostile to individuality and the imaginative life. In this regard Davies frequently aims his barbs at women, who, in his opinion, often embody the stultifying influences of conformity and self-righteousness. But the serious core of Davies's writing is a concern with the values of the carefully examined life. He has long been fascinated with Jung's theories of wholeness in human personality and with the importance of myth in explaining the patterns of individual lives. Davies has also been much attracted to the Swiss psychologist's idea that evil is an embodiment of the unlived life, those things that an individual has repressed in himself. In Davies's public voice there is an aristocratic disdain for the majority of people, but there is also admiration expressed for the individual who tries to understand his thoughts and feelings fully, who places feeling on the same plane of importance as reason, and whose life's goal is not the pursuit of happiness, but of self-knowledge. Indeed, we might say that the program of all of Davies's writing is the search for wisdom.

Davies's development as a writer began with the creation of Samuel Marchbanks, an irascible Johnsonian eccentric, whose scathing opinions on humankind were first voiced in the columns of the *Peterborough Examiner*. In 1947 Davies assembled the sketches in book form as *The Diary of Samuel Marchbanks*. The book's success resulted in a sequel, *The Table Talk of Samuel Marchbanks* (1949), and twenty years later *Samuel Marchbanks' Almanack* (1967). Marchbanks is a crusty old bachelor who lives alone in Skunk's Misery, Ontario, from which vantage point he passes judgment on society in general and on Canadians in particular. With typical comic acerbity he observes: "Most Canadians dislike and mistrust any great show of cheerfulness. If a man were to sing in the street he would probably end up in jail.'' Marchbanks believes Canadians are essentially puritans who frown on pleasure in any form. A Canadian woman, he says, ''is a dowdy and unappetizing mammal, who is much given to Culture and Good Works, but derives no sinful satisfaction from either,'' while ''the Canadian male is so hounded by taxes and the rigors of our climate that he is lucky to be alive,'' much less have sex appeal. It is the uncertainty of the weather, says Marchbanks, which ''makes Canadians the morose, haunted, apprehensive people they are.'' Ibsen's plays, he adds, reflect the Canadian spirit admirably, a favorite observation by Davies over the years. Marchbanks's own life as a Canadian is dramatized in his winter-long battle with his furnace and his struggle in summer with the weeds in his garden. Marchbanks is an admirer of eccentric individuality; he rails against the present, with its ideals of conformity and machine-age efficiency. He claims to be a democrat, but admits: ''The idea that a gang of anybodies may override the opinion of one expert is preposterous nonsense. Only individuals think, gangs merely throb.'' It has been suggested that Marchbanks's exaggerated and often outrageous observations represent a parody of Davies himself—his own iconoclastic spirit, arrogant misanthropy, and antifeminist feelings. The suggestion is fitting, for Davies comes to assert in his later critical writings that fictional characters often represent something the author has been forced to suppress in himself. The Marchbanks books are often reminiscent of Davies's favorite Canadian author, Stephen Leacock. They are sometimes ponderous and sometimes trivial, but for Davies they represent an important apprenticeship with the techniques of humor.

The second phase in Davies's development saw him turn to the theatre as a vehicle for comedy and for presenting his ideas and social comments. In the years 1947-54 he wrote and produced more than a dozen plays, several of them for the Peterborough Little Theatre. The published plays include *Overlaid* (1948), *Eros at Breakfast and Other Plays* (1949), *Fortune, My Foe* (1949), *At My Heart's Core* (1950), and *A Jig for the Gypsy* (1954). The subjects and settings of these plays vary greatly—*Fortune, My Foe* is about an immigrant from Prague who wants to start a puppet theatre in Canada, while *A Jig for the Gypsy* deals with politics and magic in nineteenth-century Wales—but a constant theme in the plays, indeed in all of Davies's writings, is the importance of art to civilization. Perhaps the liveliest and most amusing treatment of this theme is in the brief, one-act play *Overlaid*. Here Pop, an old Canadian farmer, and his middle-aged daughter, Ethel, argue as to how Pop should spend a $1,200 windfall from a paid-up insurance policy. Pop, who describes himself as ''the Bohemian set of Smith township, all in one man,'' dreams of going on a spree in New York City, where he would enjoy a gourmet dinner, sit in the front row at the Metropolitan Opera, and wind up at a night club show, perhaps giving fifty dollars for the stripper's brassiere. When his daughter, however, is persuaded to confide her inner dream of spending the money on a huge granite tombstone that would give solidity and dignity to the family name, Pop yields to what he calls her ''power of goodness'' and gives her the money. Pop's love of theatre and opera and his dream of a good time is ''overlaid'' by the tombstone; Davies wants the audience to view this very Canadian symbol of ''goodness'' in a negative light.

The conflict between the world of imagination and a sober, utilitarian environment is strongly emphasized in *At My Heart's Core,* which is set in the backwoods society of Upper Canada

in 1837. The central characters include the Strickland sisters—Catherine Parr Traill and Susanna Moodie—who were willing to sacrifice personal needs and comforts in order to achieve certain cultural goals. The play, however, develops another theme, one that becomes of central importance in Davies's later works. As in *Overlaid,* the central characters (the Strickland sisters and a third pioneer woman, Frances Stewart) are each brought to confess their innermost dreams. Mrs. Stewart admits a romantic regret for an aristocratic social life that she lost when she rejected a suitor in Ireland, Mrs. Traill admits an ambition to become an acknowledged botanist, and Mrs. Moodie confesses her desire to be a famous writer. Cantwell, the man who elicits these confidences, does so in order to betray the women publicly and revenge himself on their ''tight, snug, unapproachable little society,'' from which he and his wife are excluded. One of the minor characters in the play calls Cantwell the devil, pointing to an important idea in Davies's writing—namely, that we identify as evil any embodiment or open expression of our secret longings. To the three women in the play Cantwell is the devil incarnate because he has successfully tempted them to give voice to their repressed thoughts and wishes. In addition he has stolen their peace of mind by making them feel that their dreams can perhaps be realized. Davies's early plays are fascinating to read in the light of his later fictions, for one can trace in embryo the development of certain ideas that were to gain importance as he continued to write. But the plays are not wholly satisfying in themselves because characters are always secondary to ideas and remain very much one-dimensional types.

The third phase in Davies's work was the writing of three related novels about the social, moral, and artistic life of a small Ontario city called Salterton. These novels, published in the 1950s, are essentially comic and contain many lively and entertaining scenes, but like the early plays suffer from flatness of characterization. The plot of *Tempest-tost* (1951) turns on an outdoor production of Shakespeare's *Tempest* by Salterton's little theatre group, a plot rich in comic ironies because Shakespeare's play is served up in a bumbling amateur production. Davies's chief purpose in the novel is to satirize the cultural immaturity of Canada, where aesthetic standards must take second place to the ambitions and narrow-minded prejudices of the people. (pp. 197-201)

In *Leaven of Malice* (1954) Davies continues to make fun of Canadian provincialism, but in this deftly plotted comedy he probes that more serious theme—the nature and operation of evil. The plot turns on the repercussions which ensue when a false engagement announcement is placed in the Salterton newspaper. This bit of malice works in the community to bring all the major characters into a series of conflicts with each other. In accord with Davies's idea that evil is actually an expression of one's suppressed fears and wishes, the characters in the novel are shown to be freed by the false announcement and its implications. (pp. 201-02)

A Mixture of Frailties (1958), the third and most ambitious novel in the *Salterton Trilogy,* is a study of the development of an artist, a *Künstlerroman.* Although the novel begins and ends in Salterton and continually refers to its values, its focus is on Monica Gall, a young Salterton woman sent to England to train as an opera singer. Monica seems an unlikely heroine because of her family's working-class background and fundamentalist religion. The special interest of the novel, however, is the relationship between the artist and her life, how she gradually substitutes the universal values of art for the specific and limited values of her Salterton background. . . . In spite of its important themes, the novel is not wholly successful. The farcical tone of the Salterton scenes does not mesh with the serious portrait of the artist. The Canadian setting is the world of childhood and comedy, while England and Europe are the place of art, education, and wisdom. Unfortunately, Monica's consciousness does not comprehend and integrate both worlds fully.

In *A Mixture of Frailties* Monica's mentor, Sir Benedict, describes the theme of a certain opera as "the metamorphosis of physical man into spiritual man." This summary describes exactly the intent and achievement of *Fifth Business* (1970), an expansive and complex book which has been a bestseller and may be Davies's masterwork. The first of a trilogy of novels whose principal characters originate in the small Ontario town of Deptford, *Fifth Business* takes the form of a long letter written by a retired schoolteacher, Dunstan Ramsay, who is intent on revealing to the headmaster of the school that he is not the colorless person his colleagues always assumed him to be, that his life on the contrary has been wide-ranging and eventful. (pp. 202-03)

[The] unifying thread has been a lifetime involvement with two characters from his childhood, Boy Staunton and Mary Dempster. In the novel's opening scene, Ramsay, a boy of ten, ducks to avoid a snowball (containing a stone) thrown at him by his friend and rival, Boy Staunton. The snowball instead strikes pregnant Mary Dempster, the Baptist preacher's wife, who falls, gives birth to a son, Paul, prematurely, and is said to have been made "simple" by the accident. (p. 203)

The problems of tone and point of view that seriously mar *A Mixture of Frailties* are solved in *Fifth Business* by Davies's choice of Dunstan Ramsay as first-person narrator. In the earlier novel the characterization of Monica Gall is not large enough to unite the serious episodes concerning her development as an artist and the farcical treatment of Salterton. But Dunstan Ramsay is a narrator whose sensibility, similar to the author's, includes both satirical delight in the foibles of human nature and religious awe at the unfathomable mysteries of human experience. *Fifth Business* accordingly is a hybrid of unlikely literary modes—satire and romance. Such writing is not easily done, because the author is working with forms of experience that are poles apart. A romance portrays a hero's quest for some kind of ideal, while satire focuses on the incongruities that exist between a professed ideal and what actually happens. But satirical romance describes exactly the double nature of this book and its hero, and one of the most impressive feats in *Fifth Business* is the way Davies indulges the satirist's delight in human folly without ever destroying the solemn, religious mood of the hero's romantic quest. (p. 204)

The popular and critical success of *Fifth Business* encouraged Davies to explore the Deptford material in two more novels. *The Manticore* (1972) is narrated by Boy Staunton's son, David, who has had a nervous breakdown after his father's death and is undergoing therapy at the Jungian Institute in Zurich. David examines his life chronologically so that a completely different perspective is taken on many of the events narrated by Ramsay in *Fifth Business*. The novel, however, focuses on David's breakdown and the process of establishing a meaningful pattern for his life again. . . . *World of Wonders* (1975) is the story of Paul Dempster, known professionally as Magnus Eisengrim, and the consequences of the snowball thrown at the beginning of *Fifth Business* are viewed from yet another perspective. Magnus, now in his sixties, is a world-celebrated magician,

and Ramsay, as a historian, is making a record of his life which includes not only Paul Dempster's own account of his transformation into Eisengrim but the thoughts and reactions of important admirers such as the Swedish film director Jurgen Lind and the members of his film crew. Fascinating though they are, neither *The Manticore* nor *World of Wonders* is as successful as the first volume in the trilogy. The problem is that the wealth of information about Jungian analysis and the stagecraft of magic is not wholly integrated with the central character studies in these novels; it is interesting material, but not given the fully developed dramatic purpose that the study of the saints' lives is given in *Fifth Business*.

Davies's principal weakness in his plays and his novels is that Shavian propensity to explain his ideas at length rather than dramatize them fully through character and action. In *Fifth Business* both Padre Blazon and Liesl are splendid characterizations, but their conversations with Ramsay have a homiletic cast. The nature of Jungian analysis and the importance of magic are subjects presented even more clinically in the subsequent novels. However, to cite this flaw in Davies's writing is also to draw attention to his strength, which is that he is a writer with important ideas for us to consider. Davies's ideas have international origins and universal application, but as a comic writer Davies approaches humor in a peculiarly Canadian way. He sees satire, not as an agent to destroy the formal structures of society, but as a means of changing society for the better—as a leavening agent (to use one of his favorite metaphors) in creating a better and wiser world. The realm of wisdom is always Davies's vision and goal. (pp. 209-10)

> David Stouck, "Robertson Davies," in his Major Canadian Authors: A Critical Introduction, *University of Nebraska Press, 1984, pp. 197-212.*

H. R. PERCY

Samuel Marchbanks is the man for whom the word "curmudgeon" was coined and by whose attitudes and behaviour it is best defined. His opinions, acerbities, and misadventures were first dumped upon an unsuspecting public in the form of his *Diary* in 1947. His *Table Talk* followed in 1949 and in 1967 a freakish third shoe dropped, *Samuel Marchbanks' Almanack,* self-described as "an Astrological and Inspirational VADE MECUM" containing "Character Analyses, secrets of Charm, Health Hints, How to be a Success at Parties, Fortune-Telling by the Disposition of Moles on the Body and divers other arcane knowledge" as well as "the correspondence, Pensées, Musings, Obiter Dicta and Ruminations of the Wizard Marchbanks." This—all, of course, with the Davies tongue very far in the cheek—gives a fair idea of the delightfully zany but far from frivolous nature of the Marchbanks *oeuvre*, now in edited form appearing in one volume as [*The Papers of Samuel Marchbanks*].

Marchbanks has been and will long be a source of pleasure and cogent quotation to a sizeable band of devotees. This following is likely to increase, for although Marchbanks himself indignantly denies that his effusions are funny, at their flash-in-the-pan best they out-Leacock Leacock (who never learned that the quality of humour is not strained). They also occasionally out-whimsy Charles Lamb and out-irony Laurence Sterne. The popularity of this plump volume is assured: the reader can plow into it with the smug satisfaction of imbibing "literature" while being vastly entertained. For in this *mélange* of cranky and often outrageous opinion and speculation there

lies embedded much erudition, esoteric lore, and wisdom—
wisdom of a sort sometimes hard to swallow, and it is the very
relish of the churlish extravagance that carries down almost
unawares the bitter pill of truth.

In its grasshopper passage over the broad field of human thought
and experience the Marchbanks mind alights on a vast range
of topics and covers the full gamut of mood. Well-honed satire
and mordant commentary on the most profound moral, social,
and political questions are interspersed with the tirades of an
impractical man beset by the malevolent forces of a mechanized
age. The furnace in Marchbanks's basement is his cunning and
implacable enemy, symbolic of all the petty demands made by
the exigencies of everyday life on the time and attention of a
meditative man. Life is full of minor annoyances that have a
way of blossoming into major preoccupations, such as the
interminable lawsuit against the man who put a skunk in his
car. (p. 14)

All the qualities that make Marchbanks a delight and a surefire
success are present—though in vastly different proportions—
in Davies's new novel *What's Bred in the Bone:* erudition, wit,
irony, great narrative skill, and a surprising knowledge of such
arcane subjects as embalming, art restoration, astrology, and
the religious connotations of Renaissance art. Yet the frequent
excessive objectivity of the narration imparts a bloodless quality and prevents the book from being the triumph one anticipates. However bizarre and outrageous the Marchbanks characters may be, they are compellingly alive and capable of being
identified with. One knows them from within. Most of them
in *What's Bred in the Bone* remain emotionally aloof. Their
passions and conceits are posited with great eloquence and
insight, but only rarely do they induce a vicarious response in
the reader. (p. 15)

There are [some] fascinating narrative skeins, including the life
of Zadok Hoyle, who makes an astonishing death-bed revelation. Zadok is by far the richest and most finely drawn character in the book, and it is only when we imagine what Thomas
Hardy might have made of him that we realize how far the
book falls short of its great potential. It has a cold brilliance
that makes it eminently worth reading—and rereading—but it
is not the exciting brilliance of *Fifth Business.* It is a cerebral
rather than the emotional experience a truly great novel should
provide. (p. 16)

*H. R. Percy, "Between Earth and High Heaven,"
in* Books in Canada, *Vol. 14, No. 8, November,
1985, pp. 14-16.*

MICHIKO KAKUTANI

The moderns, says a character in Robertson Davies's new novel
[*What's Bred in the Bone*] "are painting the inner vision, and
working very hard at it when they are honest, which by no
means all of them are. But they depend only on themselves,
unaided by religion or myth, and of course what most of them
find within themselves is revelation only to themselves." Mr.
Davies, by contrast, adheres to rather a more old-fashioned
approach to art: drawing upon both Jungian myth and religious
allegory, he has created a rich oeuvre of densely plotted, highly
symbolic novels that not only function as superbly funny entertainments but that also give the reader, in his character's
words, a deeper kind of pleasure—delight, awe, religious intimations, "a fine sense of the past, and of the boundless depth
and variety of life."

In his latest—and perhaps most accomplished—novel to date,
Mr. Davies relates the tale of one Francis Cornish, a wealthy
Canadian provincial, who grows up to become a painter and
one of the world's foremost patrons of art. Mr. Davies, of
course, has rarely settled for telling a story straight-on—*Fifth
Business* took the form of a super-long letter of grievance; *The
Manticore* explored the personality of its hero through his ex-
periences in psychoanalysis—and this book is no exception.

Framed by the dilemmas of Cornish's biographer, the novel is
told largely from the omniscient perspective of two angels,
who have meticulously charted the artist's progress through
life. . . .

Angels, certainly, aren't the only manifestation of the marvelous—or incongruous—in this novel. Like the late G. K.
Chesterton, Mr. Davies possesses an essentially religious sensibility, and his fictions portray a world in which the miraculous
dwells side by side with the mundane. Indeed, his predilection
for Gothic incidents and all manner of outrageous plot tricks
speaks as much to his sense of fate's quirky methods of working, as to a nimble novelist's love of invention. In this book,
for instance, an elaborate artistic hoax, a deformed infant hidden in the attic of the family manse, intimations of inherited
madness and several highly contrived cases of mistaken paternity give Mr. Davies—and his angelic narrators—plenty of
opportunities to muse, at length, upon the questions of free
will and predestination, chance and fate, even as they supply
the reader with the makings of a deliciously readable story.

That story begins in the author's native Canada, and as he's
done in such previous works as *Leaven of Malice* and the *Deptford Trilogy,* Mr. Davies draws a sharp, satiric portrait of life
in the provinces—the stultifying, repressive atmosphere that
obtains in a small, isolated town obsessed with social and
religious standing. . . . [His] characters are clearly recognizable
comic types. But if Mr. Davies uses them to provide the novel
with some of its funnier moments, he has also managed to
invest them with a measure of sympathy that makes us like
them, even care.

As for Francis (who made a brief appearance in the author's
last novel, *The Rebel Angels*), he, too, seems familiar at first—
one of those sensitive, high-strung lads, destined to become
an artist. And on the surface, his adventures are fairly typical
Bildungsroman stuff: an awful childhood, a painful adolescence, a humiliating stint at boarding school, followed by emergence into manhood at Oxford, apprenticeship to an older artist
and a little-noticed career with M15 during World War II. With
these bare bones of a story line, Mr. Davies performs a lot of
energetic sleight of hand, twisting and turning a seemingly
predictable plot into an altogether remarkable—and ornate—
creation. . . .

In recounting Francis's coming of age as an artist, Mr. Davies
provides us with a fascinating account of a would-be painter's
career, buttressed with astonishingly detailed information on
painting and forgery techniques, and some wry musings on the
pretensions of the art world. In addition, he seems to want to
give us a psychological case study—in this case, as in *Fifth
Business,* one man's search to achieve the Jungian ideal of
creative development, "wholeness" and "completion." In what
ways, he asks, has Francis's repressed childhood affected his
career, and to what degree does it alter the larger, almost mythic
patternings in his life? How much power does his daimon—
who, incidentally, happens to be one of the angels, relating
the story at hand—wield in determining his fate?

Mr. Davies does not supply pat answers to such questions, but through lengthy philosophical debates between his hero and his mentors, he does goad the reader into thinking about these issues. Although his attempts to make Francis's life embrace various Jungian dialectics (between the anima and the animus, logos and eros, male and female) feel a bit strained and schematic at times, his story-telling remains so intelligent, so assured, that we barely notice and certainly never mind.

> *Michiko Kakutani, in a review of "What's Bred in the Bone," in* The New York Times, *November 6, 1985, p. C25.*

HEATHER HENDERSON

Robertson Davies's **What's Bred in the Bone** is an intricate spiritual drama that chronicles the making of a soul. Readers of Davies's **The Rebel Angels** will recall Francis Cornish, an art collector whose death is the beginning of the novel's intrigue. In the opening pages of **What's Bred in the Bone,** Cornish is back as the subject of a biography that a friend is having trouble writing. Cornish's two presiding spirits, the sentimental angel of biography, Lesser Zadkiel, and Cornish's artistic conscience and taskmaster, Daimon Maimas, swoop down to tell his story. Their tale moves between the inner and outer life of Cornish, who is also a painter and amateur spy, as he discovers his destiny and the secret life of a small town.

Blairlogie, Ont., the setting of the first half of the novel, is one of Davies's happiest creations. As the grandson of an Ottawa Valley lumber baron, Francis grows up occupying "the finest house in a small Canadian town about which a part of the community harbors the darkest mythical suspicions." The local rich boy is also the fledgling hero of Celtic myth, cursed (or blessed) with a mysterious conception, a double birth and a succession of guardians who "grind, shape and refine" his spirit. Blairlogie is no Eden: while it harbors such benevolent souls as Zadok Hoyle, the undertaker's assistant who introduces Francis to the solace of art, it is also full of bullies and gossips. . . .

In Francis's story, patterns cleverly repeat themselves and shadowy hints find fulfilment. Never loved by his mother, Francis seeks a female who will usher him into the world of imagination. At the same time, he learns his craft by sketching Zadok's deceased clients, seeing through mere flesh with spiritual eyes. Zadok prepares the way for the mature Francis's most powerful teacher, the skilled restorer, Tancred Saraceni. . . .

With Saraceni the novelist comes perilously close to polemic. His darts are aimed at those who paint—or write—only what they can see, abandoning the open text of myth for stunted, subjective expression. Saraceni offers Francis the choice of staying in Europe under his tutelage or returning to a country of "frozen art" to "paint winter lakes and wind-blown pine trees." In finding his own voice on Saraceni's terms, Francis paints himself into a corner with a single masterpiece that haunts him forever.

Fortunately for the novel, Francis's dead end is balanced by Davies's roguish energy and delight in subterfuge. Sparkling and erudite, he discusses Renaissance iconography and the forgery of 16th-century paintings with wit and assurance. Davies has fallen short of producing a book that encompasses all the world but he has found the soul of his native land, bathing it with radiant, symbolic imagination.

> *Heather Henderson, "Secrets of a Small Town," in* MacLean's Magazine, *Vol. 98, No. 46, November 18, 1985, p. 64.*

LARRY McCAFFERY

"What's bred in the bone will not out of the flesh," says the old English proverb that serves as an epigraph to this novel by the Canadian author Robertson Davies. Certainly what is bred in the bone of Mr. Davies's hero, the painter-art forger Francis Cornish, is a fascinating and volatile mixture of contradictory qualities. Focusing on the life and career of an artist irresistibly drawn to the methods and symbols of a bygone era, **What's Bred in the Bone** also explores perhaps the central problem facing contemporary artists: how to retain the old-fashioned virtues associated with great art of the past (chiefly, art's ability to instruct and console by providing a coherent system for interpreting the world and our role in it) in a century whose twin allegiances—to a heartfelt but potentially chaotic subjectivism or to dehumanizing rationality—pose equal dangers to the artist. Mr. Davies ambitiously plunges headlong into these deep divisions and creates both a hero and a novelistic form designed to reconcile these oppositions. In the end, however, Mr. Davies may have produced a masterpiece that is so tied to the codes and methods of an earlier era that it becomes an anachronism. (p. 6)

The first third of the novel, depicting Cornish's youth, is in many respects the most vivid and engaging section of the book, and it allows Mr. Davies to display his considerable skills as a caustic and amusing satirist of the pettiness and outmodedness of Canadian provinciality. As the envied rich kid growing up in a latter-day house of Atreus, Cornish experiences a childhood that is often traumatic and lonely, but is also peopled with a wondrous assortment of Dickensian characters: quirky relatives, monstrously insensitive schoolmates, dwarfs—and Zadok Hoyle, an embalmer and bootlegger who helps unlock for Cornish the secret beauty of the human body and demonstrates that artistry appears in many unlikely guises.

Once Cornish leaves home, the action slows somewhat, especially when Mr. Davies indulges his passion and lets his brilliant talkers talk too much and too often. But these are minor interruptions in what is basically a gripping, if highly contrived, narrative that eventually takes Cornish through encounters with espionage and Bavarian countesses, unsuccessful romances and dealings on the international art scene that have global repercussions. Mr. Davies manages to connect all these episodes to Cornish's central quests to understand the sources of conflict within himself and to discover the most suitable means to express his personal vision in painting.

Those familiar with Mr. Davies's **Deptford Trilogy** (**Fifth Business, The Manticore** and **World of Wonders**), which first brought him to attention in the United States during the 70's, will discover in **What's Bred in the Bone** many of the same elements found in his earlier works. Here too we see Mr. Davies blending realism with the conjuring illusions of art, employing classical allusions and symbols alongside esoteric references to astrology and alchemy, fusing comedy of manners with Gothic melodrama.

This odd mixture—part Trollope, part Samuel Johnson, part Nabokov—only partially obscures Mr. Davies's basically conservative, even elitist, views about life and art. These aristocratic preferences ultimately prevent him from creating a work that is Canadian in the way so many important contemporary works from Latin America seem recognizably Latin American in sensibility. Whereas such authors as Gabriel García Márquez, Carlos Fuentes, Manuel Puig and Julio Cortázar have joined European and Latin American ideas and styles, incorporating into their fiction the full range of their cultures' conflicting myths, voices, gestures and symbols, Mr. Davies has self-consciously written a novel that looks to Europe (and especially England) for its central motifs, symbols and methodology. This approach, elaborately mirrored and rationalized in Cornish's esthetic stance, is ultimately an ingenious but limiting evasion.

I call it an evasion because it appears to be founded on a nostalgia for the artistic principles of a different age—one in which the artist's inner vision of things could be presented within a coherent language of symbols shared by the community. Cornish finds such a language in the religious and mythic icons used by the great Renaissance painters; he eventually produces two masterpieces that derive from his own experience.

Mr. Davies's reliance on many of the conventions of the 19th-century novel, on an intricate series of literary and artistic allusions and most centrally on the symbolism and patterns of the Arthurian Grail legend and the biblical story of Jesus and Mary is based on a desire to find a system of interpretation he can share with his readers. Cornish and his creator both seek a means not simply to give artistic expression to life's pain, mystery and beauty, but to offer a means of interpreting them. And both suspect their belief that "art is a way of telling the truth" has been eroded by a world view dominated by skepticism and despair and the contemporary artistic emphasis on ambiguity, subjectivity, free play and art for art's sake.

But is our age really so devoid of potent symbols, patterns, terminology and systems of interpretation? There are dozens of such possibilities available to contemporary writers—those of science (dismissed here because it has only "a miserable vocabulary" and a "pallid pack of images to offer us"), medicine, economics, computer systems, various musical forms. It may be lamentable that many people today are more familiar with the symbols of the film *Star Wars* than with those of *Morte d'Arthur*, that the big bang, entropy and black holes grip our imaginations more fully than biblical creation myths or the Devil or that Bruce Springsteen's lyrics about fast cars, urban jungles and the promise of the open road speak to some more urgently about their longings and disappointments than classical poetry. But to ignore the emergence of contemporary myths and symbols, or to deny their power to move people and help them interpret their existence, is to risk being out of touch with one's age.

At one point in *What's Bred in the Bone,* Cornish is exhorted to "Wake Up! Be Yourself, not a bad copy of something else." The novel is certainly not a "bad copy" of anything; its intricate conception and intelligence are impressive on their own terms. But those terms also prevent the book from being the original it might have been. (pp. 6-7)

> *Larry McCaffery, "Painter, Forger, Miser, Spy,"*
> in The New York Times Book Review, *December 15, 1985, pp. 6-7.*

JACK BEATTY

Plot is the enemy of strong local effects in the novel, especially the novel that traces the whole life cycle of its major character.

The novelist may be rendering the character's youth and adolescence splendidly, but the plot demands that he move on to the fulfillments and disasters of adulthood. Consequently, instead of a good novel about childhood, too often we get a mediocre one covering the entire life of someone we lost interest in pages ago. For it is a rare writer who can capture the Plato to Nato of a life, as it were, with equal authority.

Robertson Davies, it pains me to say, is not of that company—at least not in [*What's Bred in the Bone*], which takes its main character, a Canadian art authority named Francis Cornish, from a marvelously conceived childhood to a feebly presented young manhood and a positively perfunctory old age. The setting is provincial Canada—Mr. Davies is our powerful neighbor-to-the-north's most distinguished man of letters. The time, in the best parts of the novel, is the Edwardian-Georgian era. The novel opens in the present, with a discussion among several of the late Francis Cornish's relatives and friends, one of whom, as his biographer, has unearthed a scandal: Francis Cornish, the scion of a prominent Canadian banking family, had been a forger of 16th-century paintings. This prologue gives way to another and, mercifully, briefer one, in which The Angel of Biography and Cornish's personal "daimon" engage in the sort of italicized chatter about character and fate that gets books thrown against walls. These supernal spirits show up throughout, and why should a device that's perfectly acceptable in Frank Capra movies seem so ludicrous in a novel?

Once the spirits are offstage the novel finds its richest vein, a portrait of Francis's early years in Blairlogie. . . .

The assured wry tone is characteristic of Mr. Davies when his talent is being released by his material (when it is being inhibited, his prose loses its voice). It is the right tone for the story of Blairlogie ("Altogether the town numbered 5000 carefully differentiated souls. . . . There were no Jews, blacks, or other incalculable elements") and of the McRory family, whose patriarch, Senator James Ignatius McRory, a timber magnate with high social ambitions for his daughter, Mary-Jim, sets the plot in gear. (p. 47)

Alas, Francis soon outgrows Blairlogie, and when he does Mr. Davies loses his imaginative footing. Francis goes to Oxford, becomes a part-time spy for British Intelligence, meets his share of (thinly) imagined Communists—one of whom, a young woman who has barely a breath of life on the page, becomes his wife and bears him another man's child. . . . Francis is just too passive a hero to sustain our interest in a book of this length. Thus under the influence of a sort of Berenson character—another vivid supporting player—Francis becomes an authority on 16th-century painting who rarely uses his authority (the McRory timber thousands having become the Cornish bank millions, Francis does not have to work) and an artist who even more rarely paints. He is a spy whose spying never comes to anything. His one possible love affair ends when his lady friend is killed in the Blitz. He develops a crush on a young art critic after the war, but this hint of the love that dare not speak its name leads nowhere. Francis does indeed fake several pictures, but what he's really faking is his life. Of Francis Cornish, both as man and fictional character, we may write this epitaph: his later life was unworthy of his childhood. (p. 48)

> *Jack Beatty, "Canada Dry," in* The New Republic,
> *Vol. 193, No. 27, December 30, 1985, pp. 47-8.*

D. J. ENRIGHT

Robertson Davies has for long been dealing in mysteries, deeper than anything in [Keri Hulme's] *The Bone People* and less restricted, less eccentric because central to Western myth and history, but always with clarity; and with—what is necessary to any mystery worth its name—a good substantial story. We might describe him as a Canadian Thomas Mann, though the chief justification for "Canadian," not meant as a limiting epithet, is that, like Mann, he is rooted in material reality, even in provincial life, however widely his branches spread. His *Deptford Trilogy,* consisting of *Fifth Business* (1970), *The Manticore* (1972), and *World of Wonders* (1975), a sustained achievement unparalleled in recent years, is rather more relaxed and more fantastical than his new novel, *What's Bred in the Bone.* New readers might begin with *The Rebel Angels* of 1982, with which the new novel is lightly linked.

That rare bird, an intellectual entertainer, Robertson Davies might more closely be compared with Borges, in that both of them carry coolness and common sense into realms supposedly inimical to, or irreconcilable with, those qualities. And, more significantly, in that both taletellers see what we call "chance" as part of the complex phenomenon of causality. Coincidence, says a supernatural commentator in *What's Bred in the Bone,* is "a useful, dismissive word for people who cannot bear the idea of pattern shaping their own lives." Everything means something, whether done or left undone; what evinces itself in the flesh is what has been bred in the bone.

This is nothing so simple as the doctrine of predestination, since a fair share is left to what we think of as "free will." The same card may be dealt out to various people, but how they use it, misuse it, or fail to use it, will depend to some degree on what was bred in the bone. A delicate balance of forces prevails, perceptible yet barely analyzable. (p. 16)

In *What's Bred in the Bone* we overhear at intervals conversations between the Angel of Biography, a member of the Recording Angel's staff, known as the Lesser Zadkiel, and Maimas, the personal daimon of Francis Cornish, the Canadian hero of the novel. The Lesser Zadkiel is a compassionate soul and even, as someone says, an angel of mercy, "though a lot of biographers aren't," whereas the Daimon Maimas declares that as a tutelary spirit it is not his job to protect softies; he is "the grinder, the shaper, the refiner." In one of their brief, pithy chats, and with the young Francis Cornish in mind, the milder angel deplores the breaking of hearts, but Maimas asserts that the important thing is to break the heart in such a way that when it mends it will be stronger than before. His job is to nudge Francis in the direction of the destiny he may have, he's not a guardian angel (sniff!) but a daimon, and his work is bound to seem rough at times. Like the Lesser Zadkiel, Maimas is a metaphor, as he remarks toward the end of the book, a metaphor in the service of the greater metaphors that have shaped Francis's life: "Saturn, the resolute, and Mercury, the maker, the humorist, the trickster." It was his task to see that these, the Great Ones, "were bred in the bone, and came out in the flesh."

But all this makes the novel sound more, or more explicitly, philosophical or theological than it is. It is that. But it is also a fascinating story, beautifully organized, never drifting into inconsequence, its literal narrative and its metaphorical signals always in step, as with the best poetry. Or, a comparison more germane, the greatest painting.

The plot of *What's Bred in the Bone* is complex and packed with incident and "coincidence"; to attempt to summarize it would be foolish. (pp. 16-17)

Whoever is concerned with the ineffable must be liberal in adducing the effable, and firm and exact in portraying it. The way to the infinite, Goethe observed, is by following the finite in as many directions as you can. Without clarity and cleanness of expression, and the persuasive authority they bring, no excursion into mystery will be more than merely mystifying. And those qualities rely on knowledge, simple knowledge if you like, but sound knowledge. Since Robertson Davies is usually so trustworthy, so precise and right, his rare inexactitudes—or what seem so—stand out the more. Would a young lady in the mid-1930s talk of something being "bang on"? The expression is believed to derive from bomber crews' slang in the Second World War and, according to Eric Partridge, was adopted by civilians as meaning "dead accurate" around 1954. Back home in Canada after the war, on page 414, Francis hears painters talking about dipping deep into their own unconscious, "a word that was new to Francis in this context"—although his mentor Saraceni had used it mockingly three times in his presence, in prewar Germany, on pages 333 and 334. Small matters, however.

In *Fifth Business* there is much out-of-the-way (yet pertinent) history and hagiology, along with technical insights into magic and illusionism; in *The Manticore* a sound grasp of Jungian theory; in *World of Wonders* a vivid account of a traveling carnival show, its freaks, jugglers, conjurers, and knife throwers. . . .

Merged with minor triumphs like the counterpointing of Catholics and Protestants in the Ottawa Valley town of Blairlogie, the dominant theme in the present novel is art, and the underworld of art, managed with what one would term expertise were it not that the experts make a sorry showing here. Francis is able to prove that a *Harrowing of Hell* purportedly painted by Hubertus van Eyck is a later forgery in that the monkey hanging by its tail from the bars of hell is not the traditional *Macacus rhesus* but a *Cebus capucinus* from the New World; and monkeys with prehensile tails were unknown in Europe in van Eyck's day. If "chance" had led Francis to the local zoo on the afternoon before the experts met in the Hague to sit in judgment, it was his innate perceptiveness that made the connection.

Francis's early training lay in drawing the corpses at the Blairlogie undertaker's, which also served as the local bootlegger's. Later he apprentices himself to the brilliant if faintly sinister Italian, Tancred Saraceni, a master restorer of old paintings, who keeps the Renaissance "in repair." (p. 17)

Like other "unworldly" characters in the book, Saraceni has a sharp eye for money. (A keen cinema-goer in his youth, Francis didn't care for Charlie Chaplin: "He was a loser.") Saraceni is Francis's earthly daimon, at least his guide and scurrilous guru, and he shows some kinship with the satanic visitant in Mann's *Doctor Faustus.* Francis observes that when he is in Saraceni's presence, and particularly when the Italian is discoursing on art's heedlessness of conventional morality, he feels like Faust listening to Mephistopheles. . . . (pp. 17-18)

Saraceni's disparaging views on modern art are shared by Francis, and by Robertson Davies too, one surmises, for they point up the novel's "meaning." In earlier times the inner vision with which all true painters are concerned "presented itself in a coherent language of mythological or religious terms," but now both mythology and religion have lost their power to move. . . .

Like Mann's, like Henry James's, Robertson Davies's people are both dismayingly and inspiringly intelligent; we feel humble, or underprivileged, beside them, but we believe in them. They have no need of streams-of-consciousness or similar latter-day devices to impress their high seriousness upon the reader, or make up for a poverty of story. Where the unconscious is concerned, and other mysteries factitious or genuine, they are able to be perfectly and unself-consciously conscious. Their author offers both pleasure and instruction. (p. 18)

D. J. Enright, "Worlds of Wonder," in The New York Review of Books, *Vol. XXXIII, No. 8, February 27, 1986, pp. 16-18.*

David Edgar

1948-

English dramatist, scriptwriter, and journalist.

The author of over forty original plays and television scripts, Edgar is also well known for his stage adaptations of works from other genres. Edgar's early works are agitprop plays written in collaboration with various "Fringe Theater" groups and are characterized by radical social and political views. Edgar's background in journalism and his association with Great Britain's counterculture contribute to the topical nature of his drama. He uses specific references to current events in order to comment on economic and political issues. Edgar's agitprop plays contain such elements of popular culture as rock music and vaudeville sketches, adhering to his intention to both entertain and educate the audience. Although sometimes faulted for didacticism and two-dimensional characters, Edgar's work has received much notice and popular acclaim. Steve Grant commented of the more obviously political plays: "Not only did they require a firm grasp of theatrical imagery, economy and factual research, they also represent a good deal that is best about both Edgar's own work and that of his contemporaries: the employment of journalistic criteria as a virtue and not a vice; an ability to tackle public subjects in a serious and uncompromisingly ideological manner; and the development of a brusque, immediate comic style."

Many of Edgar's early plays satirize political issues. *Tedderella* (1971), for example, lampoons former British Prime Minister Edward Heath in a retelling of the story of Cinderella; *Dick Deterred* (1974), mimicking the structure of Shakespeare's *Richard III*, parodies Richard Nixon and Watergate; and *The National Theatre* (1975) parodies former Prime Minister Harold Wilson in a speech appealing for national commitment during which burlesque dancers disrobe onstage. Other plays by Edgar deal more seriously with economic and political subjects and are characterized by their social realism. *The Case of the Worker's Plane* (1973) and *Events Following the Closure of a Motorcycle Factory* (1976) depict working-class struggles in a documentary fashion. *Destiny* (1975) equates conservative trends in England from 1947 to 1975 with the rise of fascism in post-World War I Europe. The epic scope of *Destiny* distinguishes it from Edgar's previous work and is repeated in *Maydays* (1983), which details the growth and eventual fragmentation of England's radical youth organizations. Malcolm Hay contended that *Maydays* "confirmed Edgar's stature as a dramatist capable of taking on big public themes. More striking still was the evidence *Maydays* provided of how, in skilled hands, the full resources of theatre—vivid stage images and spectacle, powerful dialogue and strong characterisation—can be used to elicit from audiences an attentive, indeed absorbed, response."

The most popular and acclaimed of Edgar's theatrical adaptations is *The Life and Adventures of Nicholas Nickleby* (1980), an ambitious, eight-hour production based on the novel by Charles Dickens. This work received a Tony Award and a New York Drama Critics' Circle Award and was well-received in both the United States and England. Two of his other noted adaptations, *The Jail Diary of Albie Sachs* (1978) and *Mary Barnes* (1978), are based on autobiographical accounts. *The*

Photograph by Mark Gerson

Jail Diary of Albie Sachs, dramatizing the repeated incarceration of a white Jewish lawyer in South Africa, comments on apartheid and illustrates the torture and boredom of solitary confinement. *Mary Barnes* concerns the unconventional treatment of a schizophrenic woman and raises questions about society's ability to cope with those who do not readily fit its structures. While these plays reflect the didacticism and public concerns of all of Edgar's work, they deemphasize political themes and project a more humanistic approach to the characters.

(See also *Contemporary Authors*, Vols. 57-60; *Contemporary Authors New Revision Series*, Vol. 12; and *Dictionary of Literary Biography*, Vol. 13.)

CATHARINE HUGHES

Young David Edgar's play [*Dick Deterred*] is the most successful theatrical attempt thus far to come to grips with Watergate. And, like the *Watergate Classics*, it has classical antecedents—in this case Shakespeare's *Richard III*. . . .

One of the first things you notice about Edgar's parody is its fidelity—an idea that may seem strange in this context. But, in its fancy, *Dick Deterred* blends a delightful mock-Elizabethan blank verse with contemporary allusions and slang, which rather remarkably manage almost consistently to rhyme or scan ("Greater love hath none in time of strife, / than to lay down his friends to save his life"). Or, to take another example, there's Eugene, Duke of Clarence, otherwise identified as the "Senator for Minnesota": "I go with lesser joy, / the Yippies are even now in Illinois." And Edgar certainly doesn't stop at *Richard III* in his Shakespearean redactions: "To bug or not to bug, that is the question. Whether it was nobler in the mind to suffer the slings and arrows of the *New York Times. . . .*"

Inevitably, there are some cheap shots and some fallbacks on the old jokes (though "Would you buy a used car from me?" happens to work pretty well in context) and much of the humor is obvious—once you've heard it. (Sir Ron Catesby, press secretary: "I must myself have knowledge of the truth if I am expected to deny it.") What sets *Dick Deterred* apart from other attempts to satirize Watergate is its consistency. Without suggesting it "rings true" to its facts, it rings true to its sources. . . .

What could be more obvious than, "A goat, a goat, my kingdom for another scapegoat"? Nothing, you might say—but how many of us would have thought of it? Even so, it does sometimes seem, at least at first glance, that the type of satire Edgar is attempting in *Dick Deterred* should be fairly easy to bring off. It clearly isn't. Otherwise we'd have far more of it, given the fact that the potential subjects are hardly in short supply.

Like other forms of political theatre, however, political satire requires a certain distancing if it is to avoid becoming simply an ineffectual servitor rather than an effective exponent of its point of view. It's not an easy trick, and Edgar brings it off with insight, gusto and a very appealing good humor. *Dick Deterred* is far less strained than *Macbird*, its most obvious recent forerunner, and it's hard to imagine American audiences not delighting in it. At least the ones who'd relish seeing a Richard who does wind up choked in his own tapes.

> Catharine Hughes, "Political Payoff," in America, Vol. 130, No. 15, April 20, 1974, p. 309.

JOHN BURGESS

David Edgar's new play [*Destiny*] spans two continents and nearly 30 years, from 1947 to the present day. There are several interlocking stories. The central action traces the odyssey of a provincial racist, one Sergeant Turner, who served with the army in India. Returned to England and civilian life, he opens a small antique business in a manufacturing town in the West Midlands, but is outraged to discover that the block of which his shop is part has been acquired by an Asian property company. Finding that his grievance awakes a sympathetic response within his small circle, he founds the Taddley Patriotic League— at first little more than a one-man protest movement, but which is absorbed into the neo-fascist Nation Forward Party. Turner is adopted as their candidate in a parliamentary by-election and polls quite a respectable proportion of the vote, but is utterly disoriented by the discovery that the wealthy businessmen funding Nation Forward are the real owners of the property company that caused all the trouble in the first place.

The sheer breadth of the play's scope is itself exhilarating and it's packed with telling social detail. Particularly enjoyable is

an episode in which the Taddley Patriotic League, all three of them, become affiliated to the Nation Forward Movement— the half-baked earnestness of the beleaguered little group is funny, nightmarish and entirely credible. There is another very fine scene later on, where a sweating Turner is grilled by his backers to make sure that he has the right answers off pat before he goes out canvassing. These are as fine as anything this author has done.

Occasionally in the past it was possible to feel that as a dramatist Edgar was more outraged by inconsistency than by injustice. If he could catch a public figure out contradicting himself, then that figure could be 'discredited' for all time. This dramaturgy of exposure sometimes meant that the plays were overburdened with facts which were never, in performance, as evocative as the structure required them to be. What were intended as depth charges went off as squibs: the audience simply found itself confirmed in the belief that politicians were people who said one thing and did another. *Destiny* marks a great step forward in that this remorseless eye for detail has at last found a satisfactory outlet in the action of the play itself. The local texture of the scenes is a sheer delight and often extremely witty.

But these individual pleasures are often achieved at the expense of a steadily developing action. Nearly two hours and a wealth of incident elapse between Turner's first encounter with the property company and his discovery of its true ownership— by which time the irony has been robbed of much of its impact. The audience is allowed to lose sight of the central fact about Turner: that here is a man stubbornly working against his own best interests. Towards the end of the play, one of the characters remarks that there is now twice as much British capital in India as there was before independence. Suddenly a whole new vista opens up. It's a great pity that no way was found to get the economic factors which underline the action more squarely into focus. This would have provided the necessary thread to guide the audience through the labyrinth of what is constantly threatening to become mere sociology. . . .

But a part of Edgar's strategy as a dramatist is to shock his audience into awareness by the uncanny accuracy of his predictions. This is the true function of the detail with which each scene is crammed: its purpose isn't to reassure by a naturalistic description of surfaces but to unsettle an audience by the exactness of its forecasting. It has a polemic edge—saying, in effect, 'If this can be foreseen, it can be altered'—which is blunted by the passage of time.

> John Burgess, in a review of "Destiny," in Plays and Players, Vol. 24, No. 3, December, 1976, p. 38.

ANTHONY CURTIS

[*Destiny*] follows the fortunes of its political Britons from the time of the break-up of the Empire in 1947 when they are serving in the army in India to the present when they are fighting a by-election. The main action concerns the fictional constituency of Taddley to the west of Birmingham in the late 1960s and early 1970s where the National Forward, a fascist organization with strong local roots is contesting the by-election. The play tracks kaleidoscopically the careers of a number of men British and Indian who return to Britain from the subcontinent and have to start again their lives in the days when the nation was being told it had never had it so good. One of these men, the former Sergeant Turner, sets up in the antique business with a small moderately prosperous shop but in Mr.

Edgar's words he suffers 'from a gross deficiency of greed' and his shop is taken over by the Metropolitan Investment Trust in those palmy days for developers and financiers. The seeds of his new political creed are thus implanted in Turner ... where they flourish.

Mr. Edgar succeeds in the difficult task of re-creating the political ambience at local level, the meetings in draughty halls bedecked by Union Jacks hung the wrong way up with a crackling public address system, the make-shift committee rooms in which hasty deals are hatched.... The aspect of British politics that depends on the enthusiasms, in this instance the embittered enthusiasms, of a few individuals has never been drawn so accurately before. If Bolt's master is Shaw, Edgar's is Galsworthy. He has a power of realism and a control in this disturbing play that was absent from his earlier work. He must now be considered one of the most impressive of our younger playwrights.

Anthony Curtis, in a review of "Destiny," in Drama, *No. 125, Summer, 1977, p. 58.*

JOHN COLEBY

[*Destiny*] is stuffed with ideas and arguments, down to earth, realistic. It makes you think about British fascism and gives you something of both sides of each question it asks. 'None of the characters in the play has ever existed.' is printed under the production credits. Fair enough, but most of them seem frighteningly, or in a few cases boringly, familiar. The play is somewhere between documentary and theatre-as-tract. David Edgar is concerned to transmit to us his view of the present state of our nation's affairs and how he thinks they might come out. He makes a cogent if inconclusive case; he has thought hard and clearly about his subject and how to present it in terms of theatre. It is never less than interesting, often enthralling, but it is not first rate theatre. There are so many characters involved in a complicated succession of events leading up to and including a Parliamentary by-election in the West Midlands that development has to be sacrificed to narrative. The ease with which the play was transferred to the small screen indicates that it may lack something of the humanity which can make a dramatic work uniquely theatrical.

John Coleby, in a review of "Destiny," in Drama, *No. 130, Autumn, 1978, p. 79.*

SALLY AIRE

[In *Mary Barnes*], David Edgar is concerned to show us not how to avoid creating a schizogenic family, but the rehabilitation of those damaged by one. If I am to take another of the piece's lessons to heart, I should of course not be throwing around psychiatric blanket terms such as schizophrenia, personality disorder, or even cure, convenient though these may be. For, whatever label you care to slap on Mary, the fact is that she was unacceptable as an adult in the society in which she was expected to live. Drug therapy, ECT and similar horrors are in the very first scene succinctly (and rightly) dismissed as facile treatments of symptoms and not of causes. Mary's therapy takes the form of a reliving of her infancy and childhood: in the shelter of a communal house of doctors and patients; until the physically reborn adult emerges, still an emotionally highwire person, but as whole as she is able to become.

The play itself (based by Edgar on a book by Mary Barnes and her psychotherapist, Joseph Berke) is at the same time cool and deeply compassionate. The politics (which necessarily go hand in hand with the doctors' approach to their work), do seem at times, however, to lie uneasily across the narrative.... I had some difficulty in differentiating between the individuals ..., and wondered if perhaps there was not one character too many here....

Significantly, in a piece which seems to demand from the audience a personal involvement in the restoration of Mary, although we are constantly and totally immersed in it (it is one of those rare pieces without a sag in the middle), we do remain rather in the position of concerned observers. This is due in part to the staging, which distances the piece, and in part to David Edgar's own objective, almost polemical approach to his source material.

Sally Aire, in a review of "Mary Barnes," in Plays and Players, *Vol. 26, No. 2, November, 1978, p. 19.*

PAUL ALLEN

[*Teendreams*] begins with a flash-forward: it depicts the suicide attempt of a teenage girl which is to be the pivotal point in the personal journey of a young feminist who, as the girl's teacher, has to come to terms with herself when she is accused of responsibility for the attempt. There is a sense in which all serious plays are didactic: they attempt to make some sort of shape and sense of the world in which they happen. *Teendreams* also wanders occasionally into the kind of didacticism that seeks to cover all points and arguments, and to defend itself in advance against the inevitable sectarian attacks of other groups involved in sexual or more conventionally Left-wing politics.

There is, for instance, a scene in which the heroine's flat becomes a refuge for an old friend who has just walked out on her husband. The heroine's boyfriend at first does the tactful thing (leaving the room to do the washing up) but later launches himself into an incredibly sententious speech about small-scale politics which totally depersonalises the woman's own experience and denies it any expression. The speech sat oddly on a character who had previously in the play showed, at the very least, a decent sensitivity. I was told afterwards that like much of the story-line the speech had actually happened (the play was written after extensive research, in collaboration with ... Susan Todd), but it seemed to be there just to make a point.

In fact it was a point which was made several other times anyway: it was part of the play's general defence against the charge that the feminist movement, or sexual politics as a whole, is some sort of sideshow distracting potential comrades from the main current of socialism. This is a subject worth arguing, but not worth getting obsessed with, in a play which despite its occasional repetition and occasional laboriousness does present a real and compelling story, does offer real characters as well as issues and is far too questioning to lapse into dull or ranting agit-prop. If it has a message, it is one of consolation to people disappointed that the revolution turns out not to be an overnight affair. The end sees the heroine and her friend getting on their glad rags for a night on the town, making the best of the progress that has been made, undefeated and having found a life they are able to lead.

The play is stretched over five different points in time, one of the slight passing echoes of David Edgar's *Destiny*. Instead of major public events providing the reference points we home-in on key personal moments in the teacher's life. That 'blissful dawn' of student revolt (whatever happened to the day which was meant to follow?) recalls 1968, and a reference to the Housing Finance Act (remember Fair Rents?) tells us it is 1972, but usually the most potent and ironic method of dating events comes from pop records used as part of the action or as bridges between scenes. Golden Oldies abound.

Paul Allen, "Teendreams," in Plays and Players,
Vol. 26, No. 6, March, 1979, p. 28.

EDWARD PIXLEY

[The context of *The Jail Diary of Albie Sachs*] is Capetown, S.A., 1963 and the infamous ninety-day detention law, permitting a person to be detained in solitary confinement for questioning, without charges, for up to ninety days and then, if he has refused to answer questions, he is set free and immediately rearrested. The drama, about a young white lawyer, Albie Sachs, and his survival of such detention, is adapted by David Edgar from Sach's own account of his lonely ordeal. . . .

How to survive the ninety days and how to resist the questioning are the problems that quickly emerge, problems aggravated by isolation, by lack of outside news, and mostly by Sachs's gnawing suspicion that his jealously guarded information is quite harmless to others, and his resistance, therefore, futile. At last, the resistance itself is what matters most, and we are drawn with fascination into the games he invents, the routines he establishes to stave off the oppressive boredom, culminating each day in the evening musical event, shared with an unseen whistler (an act of love in which neither ever lets the other down).

The play has a surface calm, maintained by this gentle man against the uncompromising interrogation. It is a protection, an effort to retain his humanness that sometimes borders on desperation, as seen in one of his survival games—naming all the United States in order, alphabetically, geographically, and then by major cities. The need to name each one intensifies as, almost imperceptibly in the background, we detect the sound of a lashing being administered to a black national. The game and background sound rise to a desperate shared climax: a scream from the national and Sachs's screaming realization that he could not remember "Birmingham, Alabama."

Imprisonment has instilled in Sachs a heightened consciousness, an attention to the detail of daily routine as well as to the habits and personalities of his jailers, an awareness that provides him both a detachment from and a sympathy with his persecutors. The interminable time allows him the luxury of patient discovery. One such discovery comes from reading the one book available in his early detention, the Bible. Here he discovers an existential affinity with Job's lonely obeisance to an omnipotent god, only to have his "born again Christian" jailer explain Job as a triumph in which Job, after blessing God, is rewarded for his fidelity. Sachs responds with ironic fascination to this polluted perception which justifies all prejudices, apartheid included, through the Bible.

Sachs's desperation grows as the isolation wears him down. He wonders where the heroes of the Nazi-resistance got their endurance. He sees himself as lacking their strength and heroism. Nor does the audience see him as a hero. Rather, we share in his very human routines for survival and his humanizing fascination with the jailers and the other, unseen, prisoners. But his nonheroics are ultimately the things of which heroes are made, and this gentle man's action seems to put

heroism within reach, a result of holding onto one's humanity. It is not a superhuman act; it is totally human, and that is the realization that finally rings through the play. (p. 419)

Its characters are authentic, its structure clear, its subject matter is current wherever oppression is an issue, and its action is vital wherever people doubt their ability to hold onto their humanity under duress. (p. 420)

Edward Pixley, in a review of "The Jail Diary of
Albie Sachs," in Theatre Journal, Vol. 31, No. 3,
October, 1979, pp. 419-20.

JOHN SIMON

The Jail Diary of Albie Sachs, which David Edgar has fashioned from the prison memoir of a young Jewish South African lawyer, Albert Sachs, is by its very ominous understatement one of the most powerful stage works to come out of South Africa, that cradle of social injustice and extraordinary playwriting. It is pitiful that it should take the brutality of apartheid to produce some of the most haunting drama of our time, but inspiriting that such drama gets written. . . .

Albie Sachs, jailed under the preposterous "90-days law," which allows the government to arrest and detain people without trial for indefinitely renewable three-month periods, was held in solitary confinement for nigh on six months, during which he was dragged from one jail to another, almost released only to be thrown back in, sometimes accorded a few comforts (books, writing materials) and sometimes not, and never tortured except by utter isolation. He was not quite a hero: Though long refusing to answer questions, he did make some concessions at last to get out. Rearrested two years later, he finally left the country in self-defense. Nevertheless, his stalling game did help others, and even his partial, as it were Brechtian, heroism inspired friends and confounded enemies. At one point in the play, Albie lies down on his cot and lets *us* stare in absolute silence at bare cell walls. Even this little proves acutely painful; then what about six months?

Sachs does not hate anyone: not a former Nazi prison commander who shows him some kindness, not various more or less obvious brutes merely executing orders, not the hand that holds the whip, even though he cringes hearing another, presumably black, prisoner being flogged next door. He hates only the whip itself and racism. Of such material, you cannot make heroes, only saints. But Albie is too sensual and unfanatical for a saint. Yet by hanging on to humor, sanity, and humanity under extremely trying circumstances, he proves himself something as good: a full human being. This brings this documentary drama that much nearer to us; so too does its humor, from black to childish but all of it invigorating and elating. . . .

If there is one flaw, it is that the last scene, though philosophically needed, is dramatically anticlimactic and should have been boiled down to one speech. No matter. *The Jail Diary of Albie Sachs,* though no circus, is as necessary as bread. (p. 109)

John Simon, "More Than We Deserve," in New
York Magazine, Vol. 12, No. 47, December 3, 1979,
pp. 109-10.

RONALD HAYMAN

Edgar's attitude to conventional bourgeois culture is articulated in his play *The National Theatre* (produced 1975), which is set in a dressing room occupied by three actresses. The first to arrive is Ella, who works through some lines from Chekhov's *Three Sisters* as if she is about to perform in it. But she changes into a very un-Chekhovian costume, and after the second girl, Marie, has arrived, it emerges that the three actresses are appearing in a striptease show. Though the play has moved tangentially away from *The Three Sisters,* it seems as though a disillusioned parallel is intended: the proprietor of the club is known as the Colonel. And the function of the play's title is not merely to mislead. The main point is that *louche* voyeurism is representative of the consumer attitude to the arts prevalent in bourgeois Britain. The play was written in the final phase of Harold Wilson's final stint as Prime Minister, and though he is not savaged as Heath was in Howard Barker's *Edward: The Final Days,* the closing sequence of **The National Theatre** introduces a parody of Wilsonian rhetoric when a character who had previously seemed to be an assistant stage manager talks into a microphone, appealing to the nation for austerity and restraint. 'Not a year for self, but a year for Britain.' The speech is counterpointed against a routine of vulgarly choreographed striptease to imply that creative energy is being misspent on catering for a minority of rich perverts and Japanese tourists in mackintoshes.

Meanwhile considerable tension is developed out of personal relationships. Marie, a working-class girl, has been having an affair with the Colonel, unaware of his preference for another girl-friend. Though Ella puts on an act of not being middle-class, her behaviour still accords with her accent. A failed actress, she goes on doing voice exercises and entertaining fantasies about success. Eileen, another working-class girl, arrives late with the bruises all over her body, having been raped by her husband. Her problem is how to camouflage the bruises for the striptease. At the climax Marie and Eileen are both sacked; Ella is kept on because of her classy accent. Not that she speaks during the show.

Like Margaretta D'Arcy, though, David Edgar is not interested in story for its own sake, and, like Howard Brenton, he sees it as his main duty to warn audiences that the possibility of a totalitarian Britain is not as remote as it was in 1948, when Orwell was writing *Nineteen Eighty-Four.* . . . David Edgar's 1973 play **Operation Iskra** was set in 1977, so it is already unproducible. After starting like a documentary set in the future, it develops into something more like a political thriller. Most of it is entertaining, with a few patches of dullness due to over-hasty incorporation of material Edgar discovered during his conscientious research into such subjects as legal infringements of liberty in Britain, and how to make your own bomb. Some of the violent climaxes—such as the explosion in the dress shop—are contrived without enough relevance to the rest of the action, but a considerable theatrical momentum is developed as the plot comes to grips with the theme of terrorism. The terrorists are all characterized sympathetically but fairly convincingly, and the conflict between them depends more on clashing personalities than clashing ideologies. David Edgar's 1976 play **Destiny** was prefigured most directly in the creation of the least convincing character, a Tory brigadier who lectures at a university and runs an anti-terrorist unit in the police force, covertly recruiting it from the army. Two of the girls who appear to be working for one side are secretly working for the other—here the writing owes a lot to espionage films—and the climax comes when the Brigadier is captured and finally shot by a terrorist splinter group. This scene suffers by comparison with Christopher Hampton's 1973 play *Savages,* which treats its killing with much more sensitivity.

Destiny is better integrated, never making sacrifices or compromises for the sake of immediate dramatic effect. Ambitiously conceived, painstakingly researched and ingeniously constructed, it is a disturbing piece of writing, which centres on an analysis of the factors that pressure people into joining the National Front (or the Nation Forward Party, as it is called in the play). The second scene of Act Two realistically reconstructs a meeting of a Midlands patriotic league which is about to join forces with Nation Forward. Heterogeneous grievances are voiced. The secretary of the league thinks that coloured schoolchildren will infect the whites by spreading parasitic worms. A middle-aged woman complains that the Young Conservatives 'often seem more socialist than the socialists themselves' and that there is no trade union to protect the people who have to live on fixed incomes. The wife of a polytechnic lecturer grumbles about mortgage rates and immigrant students who don't study seriously. A shop steward in a foundry voices his resentment of Indian immigrants who are competing for jobs with English factory workers. The sequence is quite convincing in its demonstration of the way disparate grievances like these can be raked together by a party that offers scapegoats and promises constructive action.

The play is aimed primarily at an audience which went neither to West End theatres in the Fifties nor to the Royal Court in the Sixties. It is a journalistic play, a dramatization of material yielded by the kind of research that might have gone into the preparation of a television documentary, and in so far as it succeeds in the theatre, it succeeds by setting up in rivalry to television, at the same time as taking advantage of the sense of community that didactic plays can offer an audience of believers. In the same way that *Comedians* can be fully effective only if the public is willing to accept the gospel of class hatred that Gethin preaches, **Destiny** depends on the audience's willingness to accept its prognosis. (pp. 107-10)

The imperial theme is presented very cleverly by starting the action in India on 15 August 1947 when British rule is coming to an end. The scene introduces an elderly colonel, a major, a sergeant, and an Indian servant. Back in England we meet the colonel's nephew, who becomes a Conservative candidate, the ex-sergeant, who becomes secretary of the patriotic league and later a Nation Forward candidate, and the ex-major, who is rejected as Conservative candidate and eventually attracted to Nation Forward. The Indian servant becomes an immigrant factory worker who will be active in picket-line brawling.

Some of the climaxes do not depend at all on personal relationships. There is a very effective scene in which the ex-sergeant, who has become an antique dealer, tries to argue with the Pakistani representative of a big property developer who has done a deal with the council over a compulsory purchase order, so that nothing can save the shop from being made into a zen macrobiotic luncheon take-away. There is another scene—possibly derived from Brecht's *Der aufhaltsame Aufstieg des Arturo Ui* . . . in which the Hitler character is coached in oratory by an actor—showing how Turner is rehearsed by the leaders of Nation Forward for his election speech. But the Labour Party candidate's relationship with his wife is developed, less convincingly, in terms of political disagreements. . . . (p. 111)

In fact none of the private relationships is developed as effectively as in **The National Theatre**. Certainly, temperamental clashes at a picket line are as legitimate a subject for drama as temperamental clashes in the drawing-room or the bedroom, but the characterization in **Destiny** suffers because David Edgar is more concerned to deploy the results of research than to explore material in the process of writing. The action is too schematic to admit any investigation of individuality, while his only interest in storytelling is to illustrate his thesis. . . .

[*Wreckers*] is rougher still, both in its aggressiveness and in its construction. Again, more energy seems to have gone into the research than into the writing, both, this time, being done collectively. The question of the relationship between law-breaking and immorality had arisen in *Destiny*, where the Labour candidate argues that since he is standing for election as a legislator, he is committed to believing in the validity of the laws and in the wrongness of breaking them. The sympathy of the play is with the man who equates this attitude with 'Defending our traditions. Preserve our way of life. Put Britain first. Wogs begin at Calais.' In *Wreckers* this question is central. (p. 112)

> *Ronald Hayman, "The Politics of Hatred," in his British Theatre Since 1955: A Reassessment, Oxford University Press, Oxford, 1979, pp. 80-128.*

MEL GUSSOW

In 1965, Mary Barnes, an English nurse diagnosed as a schiz-ophrenic, went to live in a "therapeutic community" in East London, an experimental clinic run by doctors seeking an alternate approach to mental illness. Placed in a "noncoercive environment," rather than being treated with drugs and shock therapy, encouraged to relive her youthful trauma, she underwent an emotional rebirth. Subsequently she was released from the home and became a professional artist. Her story was told in a book, *Mary Barnes: Two Accounts of a Journey Through Madness*, written by the patient and her doctor, Joseph Berke. That book is the basis of David Edgar's play *Mary Barnes*. . . .

As he did in *The Jail Diary of Albie Sachs*, his play about injustice in South Africa, . . . Mr. Edgar has taken a true story and turned it into a quasi-documentary dramatization. The subject is provocative, but the approach seems incomplete.

As demonstrated on stage, the evidence for Miss Barnes's recovery is not conclusive; nor are we convinced of the efficacy of the doctors' radical methods. The author's response might be that he is presenting a case history, not pleading a cause—in an interview he once spoke of the story's "dynamic ambiguity"—but the arc of this three-act play and our knowledge of the outcome lead us to expect more analysis and interpretation. . . .

However, as a map of a journey through a world of madness, *Mary Barnes* has its compelling moments. . . .

The play offers no solutions, which may be the author's principal intention. The chief doctor dismisses the idea that anything can be cured. "Curing is what one does to bacon" is one of his precepts. However, a change does come over Mary Barnes—and we are her witnesses.

> *Mel Gussow, "Stage: A Journey through Madness," in The New York Times, March 6, 1980, p. C21.*

STEVE GRANT

[Edgar] is the most prolific and in many ways the most representative playwright of his generation. So far he has written 37 stage plays, not counting radio and TV plays and collaborations. Many of these were agitprop pieces . . . on specific social and political issues of the early seventies, for example

Rent—or Caught in the Act, a Victorian melodrama parody about the Conservative Housing Finance Act and *The National Interest,* on the Industrial Relations Act.

Edgar's other areas of interest have included more complex and sometimes over-crammed living documentaries—*The Case of the Workers' Plane,* about Concorde and its workers, and *Events Following the Closure of a Motorcycle Factory,* about the closure of the Norton-Villiers-Triumph factory at Meriden. There are also brilliant parodies, such as *Dick Deterred,* a dynamic musical about Nixon, which was remarkably faithful to its source—*Richard III;* and *Tedderella,* a version of the Cinderella story involving Edward Heath and the Common Market Ball. Edgar has also presented more reflective, personalized studies of individuals at odds with the system: *Baby Love,* about a child-stealer who had lost her own baby, and *Excuses, Excuses,* dealing with the thorny motives of a factory arsonist. But since the great success of *Destiny* in 1976 Edgar has divided his time neatly between adaptation, as in *Mary Barnes* and *The Jail Diary of Albie Sachs,* for large subsidized theatres . . . , and more dramatized documentary or documentary drama. . . . (p. 135)

It would be deceptively easy to split Edgar's career into two separate halves, almost using two different clocks: the political activist and the 'serious' dramatist. However, Edgar, who spent some years as a journalist in Bradford, has no qualms about his more obviously political or ephemeral projects. Indeed, not only did they require a firm grasp of theatrical imagery, economy and factual research, they also represent a good deal that is best about both Edgar's own work and that of his contemporaries: the employment of journalistic criteria as a virtue and not a vice; an ability to tackle public subjects in a serious and uncompromisingly ideological manner; and the development of a brusque, immediate, comic style. Edgar believes that the major problem of his generation's writers is the attempt to merge the psychological drama of naturalism with its emphasis on individual free will and the more rigidly determinist theatre of his own agitprop past. The result would be a dynamic which shows people acting in relation to their social situation and exercising some choice. Obviously, as a Socialist, Edgar is also concerned with the quality of that choice.

In *Destiny*, Edgar's most ambitious play to date, he has attempted to create such a dynamic. His central character, Turner, is a man whose personal experience leads him into involvement with ultra-right-wing politics. This experience, however, is also of a business kind for Turner's crucial, personal crisis is the take-over of his small antique shop by a ruthless property conglomerate. (pp. 135-36)

The play begins in India on Independence Day, 1947, with a collection of army officers drinking scotch and preparing to leave. "Is it true they'll be able to come to England now, to live?" Sergeant Turner asks his Colonel. In the next scene we are in Taddley, a West Midlands town with an unsafe Tory majority and a pending by-election. Colonel Chandler, the town's MP and that old brand of paternalistic Tory also featured in Brenton's *Magnificence and Brassneck,* is dead. The nomination goes to his nephew Crosby, the new Tory man, "concerned, humane, constructive, with just the right note of apology in his voice". Meanwhile, Major Rolfe, old-style fire and brimstone, declares his faith in the army and his commitment to the lower middle class. . . .

Sergeant Turner, robbed of his business, comes under the influence of the ultra-right party Nation Forward, whose origins are shown in a brilliantly theatrical set piece: a group of people are gathered together and deliberately set up as members of an unspecified left-wing group. Only gradually do we realize that they are members of a British Nazi party gathered to celebrate Hitler's birthday. (p. 136)

One of the play's many strengths is its vast detail, the result of years of painstaking research into right-wing organizations. In a bitter struggle Nation Forward ditches its more populist, socially conscious arm and moves to a position of outright Nazism, world conspiracy and all. Turner becomes Taddley's Nation Forward candidate and is gradually forced into a position of outward anti-Semitism through the tutelage of Nation Forward's Cleaver. The play climaxes with the inter-weaving of two plot strands: the election and a strike at a local foundry over racial discrimination in piecework and promotion. The strike is led by Khera, the only Indian representative from the 1947 leaving party. The factory owner reluctantly employs the Nation Forward party to break the picket line. Violence ensues, an Indian worker is arrested and deported; the Labour candidate, despite supporting the strike, refuses to intervene on the grounds that it would be asking for the law to be broken and not changed, and the Tory wins the election, Nation Forward picking up 22% of the vote. At the climax of the play Turner discovers that the firm which took away his livelihood is owned by Rolfe who is busily engaged in forming a deal between Nation Forward and Big Business, which obviously parallels the situation in Germany at the time of Hitler's rise to power.

Destiny suffers . . . insofar as it is open to contrary interpretations according to the particular prejudices of the individual. It has been accused both of being a Marxist tract and of being so confused as to be capable of interpretation as an apologia for fascism. To some extent these points are valid. The best 'speeches' are often and deliberately put into the mouths of the characters of whose politics Edgar least approves. Rolfe, for example, has a profoundly moving monologue over the coffin of his son, killed in action in Belfast, and Cleaver has a similarly powerful speech about his own aged uncle, petrified that an Indian temple will be built over his grave. So, too, the weakest characters seem to be the most obviously sympathetic, particularly Clifton, the Labour candidate. Edgar himself has argued that in *Destiny* the plot devices are insufficiently powerful to support the undoubtedly impressive wealth of social detail and verbal power, as if his agitprop sense of construction has led to a skeletal framework for what is in effect an epic play. Indeed, the strike and the election never come close to grabbing our attention from the brilliant scenes involving Nation Forward, while Turner's realization that he has been duped and the Indian worker's comment that British capitalism has a bigger hold over India now than it did in 1947, are never really assimilated into the main thrust of the action. In spite of these flaws *Destiny* is an eloquent and important play. (pp. 136-38)

Destiny represents an important development in contemporary theatre insofar as it marks the 'promotion' of radical theatre to suitably large and prestigious settings. This is an event that Edgar, in common with Hare, Brenton and Howard Barker, considers to be of vital importance if the fringe is to consolidate its achievements and writers are to realize their full imaginative potential. *Destiny*'s other main importance lies in its complexity. It is the first political play of its kind to come to terms with the attractions of right-wing politics as well as their more obvious shortcomings. Edgar's own researches led him to a committed involvement with the Anti-Nazi League whose ac-

tive combatting of the National Front on Britain's streets has had an undoubted effect on the (hopefully permanent) decline of Britain's fascist organizations. *Destiny* has itself played a part in that process, while paradoxically it seems that Edgar's most solidly artistic achievement has had the greatest long-term political effect on the society he so obviously longs to improve. Edgar is a prodigious talent, ever willing to learn, highly self-critical and intent on writing plays until he drops. He may well prove to be the most enduring talent of his generation. (p. 138)

> Steve Grant, "*Voicing the Protest: The New Writers,*" *in* Dreams and Deconstructions: Alternative Theatre in Britain, *edited by Sandy Craig, Amber Lane Press, 1980, pp. 116-44.*

FRANK RICH

And so, after eight-and-a-half hours of *The Life & Adventures of Nicholas Nickleby,* we go home with an indelible final image.

The time is Christmas, and a grand Victorian happy ending is in full swing. Carolers are strewn three stories high about the stage, singing "God Rest Ye Merry Gentlemen." Families have been reunited, couples joined together, plot ends neatly tied. And our young picaresque hero, Nicholas, has vanquished the two enemies who have stalked him for five acts—his usurious uncle, Ralph, and the cruel Yorkshire schoolmaster, Wackford Squeers.

But is all right with the world? Not entirely. For as Nicholas sings along with everyone else, he spots, crouching far downstage center, a starving boy. At first our hero tries to ignore the sight, but he can't. So he walks over to the youth, lifts him up into the cradle of his arms, and then stands to face the audience.

As the singing and lights dim, Nicholas stares and stares at us—his eyes at once welling with grief and anger—and what do we feel? What we feel, I think, is the penetrating gaze of Charles Dickens, reaching out to us from the 19th century, imploring us to be like his hero at this moment—to be kinder, better, more generous than we are. "If men would behave decently, the world would be decent"—that's how Orwell distilled Dickens's moral vision. It's a vision that can still inflame us—and does—at the very end of [David Edgar's adaptation] . . . of Dickens' third novel. . . .

What does not fall into place, I must report, is a sustained evening of theater. We get an outsized event that sometimes seems in search of a shape. While the high points of this *Nicholas Nickleby* are Himalayan indeed, they are separated by dull passages which clog the production's arteries. The problem is not the length of the work per se—it's the *use* of that length. In adapting a long novel to the stage, the British playwright David Edgar has chosen a strategy that is as questionable as it is courageous.

Unlike so many stage and film adapters of Dickens, Mr. Edgar has gone whole hog: he gives us at least a glimpse of every plot development and character (over 50 of substance and 200 altogether) in the original book. But how is this possible, even in an adaptation of this length? Many of the characters in Dickens's novels—especially the subsidiary ones—are not revealed through dialogue or action, but by the steady accretion of the writer's vitally observed details. In the theater, those details can only be conveyed if each actor is given enough stage time to communicate them through performance—or if a narrator reads Dickens's descriptions aloud. While Mr. Edgar does use narration here (distributed cleverly among the entire cast), he generally uses it to fill in plot rather than to supply characterizations (except in the case of a few major figures). And eight-and-a-half hours is not enough time for all the minor characters to occupy center stage as they can in an 800-page novel.

So Mr. Edgar gives some of them short shrift. The milliner Manatalini and her profligate husband, the Keswigs family, the cameo-artist Miss La Creevy and the accountant Tim Linkinwater—among others—receive television's Masterpiece Theater treatment: they appear in proper costume, in animated tableaus, but they whisk away so fast that they blur. The difficulty is not that they don't measure up to the book—that's not required—but that they don't add up to anything much at all, whether one has read Dickens or not.

Individually, their brief scenes aren't bothersome, but, collectively, they pile up as dead weight—especially in the four-hour part one. There are two theoretical ways to solve this dilemma: to make *Nicholas Nickleby* twice as long as it is, or to cut some of these people out and take care of their plot functions (if any) by adding to the spoken narration. The latter, far more preferable route *can* be accomplished—if a scenarist is willing to exercise fully his right of esthetic selectivity.

When it is dealing with its major characters—those that do have the time to reveal all their human twists—*Nicholas Nickleby* is far more effective. . . .

Not surprisingly for a man of the stage, Mr. Edgar gives the fullest treatment by far to those supporting characters who belong to the fleabag acting troupe that Nicholas joins in Portsmouth. These provincial theatrical hams are all hilariously rendered, and their bowdlerized performance of *Romeo and Juliet* ends Part One on a high parodistic note that echoes the mechanicals' *Pyramus and Thisbe* in *A Midsummer Night's Dream*.

Interestingly enough, both the *Romeo and Juliet* and the production's brilliant crowning moment are the creations of Mr. Edgar. One wishes he had taken more such liberties, for these inventions are more Dickensian in spirit than many of the scenes in which he tries to be literally faithful to the book. Yet if this mammoth show recreates the breadth and plot of a Victorian novel without consistently sustaining its exhilarating mixture of pathos and comedy, one must treasure those instances when it does rise to the full power of Dickens's art. The rest of the time *Nicholas Nickleby* is best enjoyed—and, on occasion, endured—as a spectacular display of theatrical craft.

Frank Rich, "Stage: 'Nicholas Nickleby' Arrives as a Two-Part, 8 1/2 Hour Drama," in The New York Times, *October 5, 1981, p. C13.*

MYRON MAGNET

[How different is David Edgar's] eight-and-a-half-hour version of Charles Dickens's *Nicholas Nickleby* from the last "theatrical event of the decade," the Living Theater's *Paradise Now* of a dozen years ago. In those days the players demanded audience participation with a vengeance, aiming—by means of hostility mixed with earnest eroticism—to liberate viewers from the unfeeling armor of social life and so restore them, figuratively and literally stripped, to man's original openness and amity, all by 11 P.M. By contrast, in this decade's equally-heralded theatrical event, the actors personally touch the au-dience in the spirit of a diametrically opposed ideology, as they mingle with them at intermission, shaking hands and trading compliments in a show of ready civility that Dickens would wholeheartedly have endorsed. If the Living Theater celebrated two millenia of stage tradition by flinging down dramatic conventions one after another and dancing upon them, the Royal Shakespeare Company for its part affectionately claims that tradition as a rich inheritance. And here too it sounds an authentically Dickensian note, for the power of convention—especially theatrical convention—is second only to the power of civility among the central constructive forces of *Nicholas Nickleby*.

Dramatizations of *Nickleby* are nothing new: the first one opened even before the final serial installment of the novel was published late in 1839. But none can have been so loving and skillful as this. The wonderfully inclusive script compresses the novel's 900 pages with intelligence, sometimes with brilliance. . . . (p. 75)

But just as the first dramatization of *Nickleby*, which Dickens liked, introduced some lines so contrary to the work's world view that the actress who spoke them remembered the novelist snarling, "Cut them out," so this adaptation contains several obtuse additions, none more distorting than those tending to make the novel into a radical tract. Take, for instance, the scene where Nicholas, the young hero, appears for a job interview as private secretary to a windbag Member of Parliament, just when the MP is receiving a deputation of disgruntled constituents. All this the novel renders with heavy-handed jocularity: the MP has broken his promises to astonish the government and play the devil with everything; Nicholas turns down the job because the MP wants to put all his own duties on an underpaid secretary's shoulders; Parliament is dismissed as an inane collection of sanctimonious, self-interested nobodies. But in David Edgar's dramatization, the dignified voters charge their MP with betraying a pledge to take specific early-Victorian left-wing positions, and the scene closes with the MP shrilly accusing Nicholas of being a Chartist (a radical working-class political group of the 1830's and 40's which Dickens distrusted), while Nicholas calls him a "politician," in a tone and a context that seem to make that term the sneering equivalent of "class oppressor." Then, too, there is the play's closing tableau, with Nicholas sheltering in his arms a ragged, miserable Dotheboys Hall pupil, indignantly held up, one can only suppose, as testimony to systematic social injustice. In the novel, these abused boys have a quite different significance; but the impression the play gives of its hero as a crusader against social oppression is further underscored by the picture on the program and in the advertisements of an angry Nicholas raising his clenched fist in an apparently political gesture. All this, unfortunately, is not just a veneer. For by omitting certain key passages that add up to Dickens's own explanation of what *Nickleby* is about, the play ends up offering these radical gestures as its primary interpretation of the novel.

To be sure, the clenched fist is centrally important in Dickens's book, so much so that the villainous Squeerses mistakenly keep calling Nicholas "Mr. Knuckleboy." It is important, however, not as a political symbol but because *Nicholas Nickleby* is a novel not just "about" but indeed *obsessed* with aggression as an overwhelming human problem for which the book, try as it may, can find no wholly satisfactory solution. On almost every page of the novel, some act of violence occurs or threatens, and the play is appropriately punctuated by the thud of blows. People are quick to hate in *Nickleby*, and a random, spontaneous aggressiveness pervades both play and novel, from the shower of muffins that pelts the stockholders' meeting at the play's very start, through the young aristocrats who pull off door knockers and beat up policemen for fun, to the more menacing image of the champagne bottle turned into a lethal weapon at Lord Frederick's party. (pp. 75-6)

But what no viewer or reader of *Nickleby* can ever forget is the aggression of the two villains, Wackford Squeers and Ralph Nickleby, whose malevolent energy turns the wheels of the plot. Mr. Squeers is proprietor of one of those infamous Yorkshire schools, squalid warehouses for unwanted children—the illegitimate, the crippled, the retarded—schools whose advertisements assure parents or guardians in large letters of "No Vacations" for pupils. . . .

If anything, the play intensifies the sordid brutality of this concentration camp for boys simply by making the novel's vague, undifferentiated crowd into a collection of recognizably individual human victims with palpable flesh to hurt. From the moment Squeers enters the play, cuffing a weepy new pupil of Dotheboys Hall, he is a dynamo of violence, administering blows and whippings with hardly an intermission. . . .

Of *Nickleby*'s two principal embodiments of aggression, the second and more complex is Nicholas's uncle Ralph, the usurer. (p. 76)

"How people dupe themselves!" sneers Ralph in the play, summing up the world view that is inseparable from his cosmic aggression and that makes him so psychologically interesting and weighty a villain. Pretending to unflinching self-knowledge and unique truthfulness, he despises the world of self-deceivers, and his boast of authenticity further reinforces his aggression by confirming his refusal to accommodate himself to the concerns of others. Stifling all social emotions—for even to *feel* the wants and values of others would be to dilute the self-subsistent authenticity of his inner life—he is left only with feelings of hostility and belligerence. His suicide in the novel is an act of aggression against the whole universe; and having said he believes the reality of any pretty face is the grinning skull beneath it, he ends by choosing for himself the ultimate authenticity of death.

Not understanding this, the play's adaptor puts into Ralph's mouth some nonsensical last words about being "an outcast" (words also jarringly given to Smike) and so denatures his powerful final scene. . . . (pp. 76-7)

All this violence is terrible and Dickens, whose hatred of cruelty and injustice is palpable throughout *Nickleby,* deplores it—but not because it's political oppression, as the play's audience is led to conclude. Picking up this cue, the *New York Times* reviewer [Frank Rich], for example, saw in Smike "the perfect apotheosis of those oppressed souls Dickens championed." But, on reflection, surely a crippled half-wit would be a contemptuous symbol for the oppressed; and surely a school for repudiated middle-class boys, a school whose annual fee amounted to a laborer's yearly wage, makes for an unconvincing allegory for an oppressive social order.

Far from being the result of unjust social arrangements, violence in *Nickleby* is a consequence of the original, inborn nature of man, in which aggression forms a constituent instinct. . . . For Dickens, the state of nature is not holy but Hobbesian, the war of all against all. . . .

Certainly this isn't to say that men are without an endowment of finer feelings. But as Charles Cheeryble, Nicholas's Pick-

wickian fairy-godfather, explains in the novel but not in the play, these feelings "must be reared and fostered, or it is as natural that they should be wholly obscured, and that new feelings should usurp their place, as it is that the sweetest productions of the earth, left untended, should be choked with weeds and briars."

Only fragments of this explanatory framework are left standing in the play—as when the predacious Sir Mulberry Hawk, who shows that even sex can become merely another mode of aggression, flings the resisting Kate Nickleby down before him on a sofa while derisively counseling her to "be more natural— my dear Miss Nickleby, be more natural—do." Or there is Squeers instructing his famished pupils, with brutal humor, to "subdue your appetites, my dears, and you've conquered human natur." These pointers, along of course with the whole dramatic situation, leave Dickens's meaning still discernible, but regrettably more dimly so in the play than in the novel. (p. 77)

For retailoring human nature, who can compare with the Crummleses, that shabby troupe of strolling provincial actors who are the comic triumph of novel and play alike? Taming aggression is their stock-in-trade, in creaky melodramas like *The Mortal Struggle* or their hilarious pantomime of *The Indian Savage and the Maiden,* in which the civilizing power of love subdues wild ferocity. Nothing, though, can top the play Nicholas translates for them, involving a man who stabs his son, throws his wife and child out of the house, and relents in the end, when a clock striking ten interrupts his suicide by reminding him of a similar clock in his infancy, making him burst into tears, drop his gun, and become an exemplary citizen forever after. The Crummleses, in other words, can retailor even the villainy of a character like Ralph Nickleby. (Edgar's adaptation has them go on to give *Romeo and Juliet* a happy ending, in a hilarious and appropriate addition, partly deriving from Mr. Wopsle's travesty of *Hamlet* in *Great Expectations,* but owing infinitely more to the skill of the adaptor and the company, and to their consummate understanding of the tradition of their craft. . . .) . . .

All the conventions of this theater, and melodrama is made up of nothing but conventions, go to insure the triumph of justice over aggression, of right over brute force—like the conventions of society, but more dependable. And like the whole effort of human culture, the Crummles theater strives to hold up an ideal, however simple or fustian, of what life should be to be fully human. Surely these conventions and ideals retain their power undiminished; watching *Nicholas Nickleby,* itself a melodrama of the higher kind, the New York audience vehemently hisses the cruelty of Squeers and greets his downfall with tumultuous applause.

And how far *Nickleby*'s notion of a truly human existence is from Ralph Nickleby's grim authenticity. A fully human identity is necessarily stagy and contrived: how can it not be, if we live in a society and are continually playing to others? No wonder, from Nicholas disguised as "Mr. Johnson" to Mr. Mantallini with his kisses and poison bottle, everyone in *Nickleby* is always acting. And no wonder so theatrical a novel works so well on the stage. (p. 78)

Myron Magnet, "Why 'Nicholas Nickleby'?" in Commentary, *Vol. 72, No. 6, December, 1981, pp. 75-8.*

ROBERT ASAHINA

[Ironic] descriptive passages are the one important element that has been sacrificed in David Edgar's 500-page script [for *Ni-*

cholas Nickleby], which necessarily emphasizes dialogue—most of it quite faithful to the original. (At times the adaptation is so true to the written word that jokes get lost in the translation from eye to ear. When Nicholas is tutoring the Kenwigs family, Mr. Lillyvick, the children's uncle and the "collector of water rates," asks, "What is French for 'water'?" Nicholas replies, "L'Eau," and Lillyvick remarks, "Lo, eh? I thought as much." I was the only one in the theater who laughed—but I had read the book.) To be sure, throughout the play are scenes that mix conversation with narration, often in ways that are both revealing of and true to the spirit of Dickens. Nicholas' self-dramatizing tendency, for instance, is amusingly underscored when the character interrupts himself to address the audience, referring to himself in the third person. . . .

Too often, unfortunately, Edgar's fidelity to his source is actually a source of problems. Why bother including so many characters when their roles have shrunk so much that they are nearly unrecognizable? The lecherous Mantalini, for example, who pursues Kate Nickleby when she comes to work for his wife, the milliner, plays such a small part in the adaptation that he could just as easily have been left out. The time gained by eliminating other such minor characters and their subplots could have been used to beef up more important parts, like that of Sir Mulberry Hawk, whose lust for Kate and whose complicated relationship with the evil Ralph Nickleby are given short shrift. And elsewhere, the adaptation is only superficially faithful. When Nicholas leaves London with his constant companion, the loyal Smike, whom he has rescued from Dotheboys Hall, we are told in a snatch of narration that the fog over the city "clothes its schemes of profit." In the novel, the passage is much richer: "A dense vapour still enveloped the city they had left as if the very breath of its busy people hung over their schemes of gain and profit and found greater attraction there than in the quiet region above." No doubt Edgar simply had to edit to save valuable time. But since he is well-known as one of the self-avowed Leftists who emerged in Britain out of The Fringe movement of the late sixties, I cannot help suspecting that part of his motivation for changing the words was political.

Of course, Dickens' novel did have an explicit political purpose—to draw attention to the abuses of the notorious Yorkshire schools (of which Dotheboys Hall was a fictional version). "No vacations and no questions asked," the schools advertised in Dickens' time, and they served as little more than involuntary confinement for the blind, crippled, disfigured, retarded and illegitimate offspring of uncaring parents, as well as the children of credulous middle-class families desperately trying to educate them but lacking the resources for proper schooling. Dickens meant his audience to be as outraged as Nicholas is at Squeers's cruelty, so we should not be surprised that Edgar does likewise.

But sometimes he goes too far, as in the last scene, which ends with perhaps the most striking image of the entire play. In the background is the double wedding of Nicholas to Madeline Bray (like him, one of the beneficiaries of the charitable Cheeryble brothers) and Kate to Frank Cheeryble. As the couples celebrate to the tune of "God Rest Ye Merry, Gentlemen," a scrawny urchin—one of the refugees from Dotheboys Hall, who bears an uncanny resemblance to the recently deceased Smike—appears in the foreground. Nicholas alone notices him, and our hero advances forward, lifts the boy in his arms, and gazes solemnly at the audience as the lights dim for the last time. This is certainly a powerful note on which to close. But

is it Dickens or Edgar? More the latter than the former, I'm afraid. Indeed, the scene, which has been favorably noted by some critics as an improvement on the author, is actually an invention of the adaptor. Although Dickens can certainly be faulted for his political sentimentality, he typically erred on the side of unbelievably happy endings, not on the side of denouements charged with reformist passion.

That example might merely be a case of Edgar's exaggerating certain implicit tendencies in Dickens' writing. Elsewhere, however, the adaptor adds material that cannot even be said to be true to the spirit of the original. Some of this is harmless—for example, remarks apparently inserted for the sole purpose of twitting American audiences. . . . But other additions, though equally amusing, belong in another production, as when Crummles' troupe stages a hilarious play-within-the play, a version of *Romeo and Juliet* that would have done "Beyond the Fringe" proud (which is precisely the problem).

At other points, Edgar seems rather confused in his use of narration. When Nicholas and Smike arrive in London, along with their conversation we hear a description—"Wealth and poverty stood side by side"—that is straight out of the novel. All well and good, since our imagination needs some help in transforming what we see—the sole set of the production—into a teeming city. But why then does Edgar follow that line with "Streams of people apparently without end poured on and on"? After all, we can behold quite plainly the actors crowded and milling about in a pretty good imitation of a street scene. (pp. 93-5)

Robert Asahina, in a review of "Nicholas Nickleby," in The Hudson Review, *Vol. XXXV, No. 1, Spring, 1982, pp. 92-8.*

FRANK RICH

Although David Edgar has written some 40 other plays, chances are that he'll always be most remembered as the man who adapted *The Life and Adventures of Nicholas Nickleby* for the Royal Shakespeare Company. If you want to learn why, you'll find at least a partial answer in *Saigon Rose,* an earlier Edgar effort. . . .

[In *Saigon Rose*] Mr. Edgar is writing in his more usual mode—as a second-rung British political playwright whose most successful pre-*Nickleby* work was also an adaptation, *The Jail Diary of Albie Sachs.* Left entirely to his own devices in *Saigon Rose,* Mr. Edgar quickly writes himself into a jam.

His title refers to "a particularly virulent strain of gonorrhea mutated during the American involvement in Vietnam." His theme is the "Saigonization" of the British Empire. *Saigon Rose* is set in Scotland in the mid-70's, as American oil companies exploit the resources of the North Sea. Along with their ecology-transforming technology and petrodollars, the Americans also bring to tranquil Scotland their corrupting cultural and social values—which are symbolically heralded by a local outbreak of the poisonous Saigon Rose.

Mr. Edgar tries to make his strident ideological points indirectly, by containing them within the story of four drifting and disillusioned young people whose romantic entanglements are farcically altered by their unfortunate physical ailment. But the story hasn't been worked out, and most of the characters are agitprop types. Whenever the author wishes to get down to his serious business—whether to attack what he sees as industrial imperialism or to wax poetic about the lost revolutionary ideals of the Vietnam 60's—he brings the action to a halt and cranks up the appropriate soliloquies. For humor, there are burlesque gynecological examinations that take us back to the juvenile sex gags of England's latter day *Carry On* movies.

[The evening's only] intriguing element is the extent to which Mr. Edgar's failings in *Saigon Rose* recall those that accounted for the sluggish passages in *Nickleby*. These include frequent repetitions, the marching on and off of extraneous characters and an inability to organize farflung events into a tight dramatic shape. Lacking either Dickens or the Royal Shakespeare Company to bolster his slack dramaturgy this time, Mr. Edgar ends up with a play that makes two hours pass like roughly eight and a half.

> *Frank Rich, in a review of "Saigon Rose," in* The New York Times, *November 30, 1982, p. C13.*

RICHARD F. SHEPARD

[You get the idea of *Dick Deterred*] right from its punning name, a play on Shakespeare's *Richard III* which provides the format from which this takeoff takes off.

The book and lyrics for this clever political satire are by David Edgar, who adapted *Nicholas Nickleby* from novel to stage.... Mr. Edgar wrote the piece in Britain in 1974, while the Watergate scandal was still a burning issue....

It is a novel conceit.... There are, however, two drawbacks, both in terms of time. History—which like antiques, often changes function with time—has taken a toll. It is savage comedy that met its moment of history, but today it seems somewhat of an overkill for viewers who have lived through the 10 intervening years. Also, it tends to be overlong; once one has gotten the idea, the show, in its second half, tends to be overdrawn....

Dick Deterred lends itself to—and its comedic political commentary is better suited to—an informal cabaret surrounding, rather than the more formal confines of a theater. As it is, it is a bit too much of a good thing, somewhat late in going to press.

> *Richard F. Shepard, "'Dick Deterred', A Watergate Musical," in* The New York Times, *January 24, 1983, p. C14.*

DAVID IAN RABEY

David Edgar has been concerned to perceive, and engage the audience in, a sense of history which can provide a sense of causality, continuity and inspiration behind the disparate, initially bemusing pattern of 'isolation in a crowd' which is the only socially sanctioned image of so much daily life. (p. 49)

Edgar has proposed that 'we live in an age *defined* by a lack of any shared philosophical, religious or artistic assumptions' which therefore lacks 'any sense of history, of changing social circumstances, of political developments'.... Viewing his relationship with his audience in complex, sophisticated but realistic terms, Edgar thinks his plays should 'confront the audience with their own emotional response to a point that I call dynamic ambiguity', which is designed to stimulate and challenge rather than offer the comparatively easy options of simple identification, dissociation, facile optimism or tragic resignation, yet still advance a consistent and persuasive response to events which is strengthened, rather than undermined, by mod-

ulations of alienation and self-criticism, the final aim being 'to present recognizable reality within a context that makes clear its place in history'.

Edgar's early plays for touring groups sometimes evoked established popular or literary models in order to provide a basis of shared experience which could then be developed in less familiar, more challenging directions; notably in the use of thriller conventions in *Operation Iskra* (1973) and the presentation of the Watergate scandal in parodic Shakespearian history terms for *Dick Deterred* (1974). Edgar's work has also shown a similar efficiency in plays written for London West End theatre and small touring groups, and a clear-eyed view of the challenge represented by each.... Edgar agrees with David Hare's formulation that a play's potential power 'is not going to be in the things you are saying; it is in the interaction of what you are saying and what the audience is thinking'. *Destiny* (1976) is a highly successful response to this recognition in its direct approach to emergent British fascism, its attractions and its hideous results. It gains immediacy from its contemporary setting but also from Edgar's prefatory establishment of the historical processes creating the modern situation; the play's opening in India demonstrates how certain attitudes, beliefs and behaviour were legitimised, even encouraged, in certain characters by supposed national interests, and how the maintenance of the British Empire manipulated and geographically distanced fascistic impulses. Without this clear outlet, the middle-ranked and middle-class Turner is taught by the stronger members of a British Nazi party to redirect his aggression born of his uncertainty, into the service of their group in a local election. Another strength of the play is the broad political and social spectrum established around the local election in Taddley Heath and the fascinations and weaknesses given to the very human faces which collectively constitute this panorama, as befits Edgar's intention 'to create characters that the audience could relate to and in a way that they could confront in themselves' whilst always maintaining the firm objective 'to put the frighteners on the conventional play-going audience—people who might be attracted in the direction of fascism'. Certainly the unease and fear of the characters upon which Nation Forward builds its support are depicted with due sympathy and complexity, making their allegiance to the party all the more disturbing when we are made witness to the backstage manipulations of its leaders, who are themselves divided by their degrees of extremism. But the ignorance, bigotry and self-interest of the group do not in themselves allow the other characters to dissociate themselves completely from their sources, or dismiss them as the fuel of a cranky, peripheral phenomenon.... Characters who may have remained ciphers in a social spectrum are given rounded, humanised viewpoints in a comprehension which even extends to several of the fascist spokesmen; however, *Destiny* is not paralysed by its widespread understanding of its characters.... Easy responses and identifications were anticipated and criticised, forcing the audience to reassess their personal attitudes to the play's themes in a fresh, urgent, alienated light; which is not to say that such attitudes are left in a disrupted stasis. Having met and accommodated conventional, partial responses to Nation Forward, *Destiny* ends with a dramatically powerful confluence of their practice and theory: Turner's conspiring exploiters are revealed as the corporations which provide support for his political party, leaving the final word to a '*gentle, quiet, insistent*' voice over the final tableau:

> Only one thing could have stopped our Movement: if our adversaries had understood its prin-

ciple, and had smashed, with the utmost bru-
tality, the nucleus of our new Movement.
Slight pause.
Hitler. Nuremburg. Third of September, 1933.
Blackout.

Thus the quotation is offered for the digestion and response of
the audience a crucial moment before disclosing its source,
which provokes a more easy and instant response, then leaves
the attributed phrase and its author to acquire a more urgent
and relevant import in relation to the preceding events of the
play, and ends it on a typically well-crafted and effective note.

Certainly Edgar has demonstrated his ability to write plays that
are rich but uncompromising, self-critical and thereby more
realistic and confident in their assertions. He has managed to
create political drama which, in its quite unforgettable images
of isolated pain and collective strength, forces its audience to
confront the cost and value of an active role in history, and
thereby reassess their own role in the perception and dynamic
of that history. (p. 59)

> *David Ian Rabey, "Audience Engagement and Re-
> flexive History in the Plays of David Edgar," in
> Critical Quarterly, Vol. 25, No. 3, Autumn, 1983,
> pp. 49-60.*

PAUL ELLEN

Maydays may be too coolly ironic, too elegantly analytical, too
self-consciously structured for its own good. But it is not unimportant, and in two scenes near the beginning and end I think
we can see Edgar, fresh from his collaboration with Charles
Dickens, learning . . . to handle not just the scale but the breathtaking complexity of the true epic; and it is that complexity,
set against the realisation that politics is the one 'science' that
still believes an analysis can be absolutely and objectively
correct, which forms the core of the play.

Maydays starts in 1945 with a passionate affirmation of revolution as not only inevitable and ideologically desirable but
fun. It ends in the early Eighties with the man who made that
speech recruiting for the hard right. The plot, enough for a
thick novel which is not always an advantage, has two more
strands linked to personal journeys: that of a public schoolboy
who turns to Trotskyism and slides all the way back via 'quality' journalism, and that of a Russian soldier, dissident and
eventually exile.

In addition to the narrative structure Edgar goes in for a system
of using familiar phrases and ideas in the way well-organised
music will occasionally drop in a phrase or chord sequence to
pay off a development. Lenin's remark that 'a revolution is a
festival' is cleverly used first to exhilarate and then to depress;
Trotsky's reference to 'human dust' becomes more chilling
each time it becomes more personal, and it gets harder to find
anyone who has sustained a belief in individual freedom and
rights; Kronstadt and Red Barcelona recall Communist atrocities and become emblems of disillusion regularly repeated. . . .

Unfortunately Edgar has so much plot to get in that he has to
resort continually to the long, measured speech which, obligingly, nobody interrupts. Verbal smartness, gags about the
barmy sectarianism, party newspapers, the chronic inability
actually to organise anything, all lighten the narrative but leave
it somehow literary and earthbound. And in the long central
sections there are too few surprises in the perceptions: I agree
that Crowther might get finally turned off because his students

split their infinitives and spell fascism with an 'h' and thus
undervalue his standards and by extension himself, but I am
not overwhelmed at the news.

What is more encouraging is Edgar's vision of socialism as a
kind of baton being passed on in a relay race. It doesn't matter
if runners fall by the wayside or join another team if somebody
else takes over. If his view that the current runners are the
feminists is contentious because liberation—freedom—is not
a synonym for socialism, well, the point he is trying to make
is precisely that it ought to be.

But what lifts the whole play into a richer and headier dimension is the 'Russian' strand to the story, and those two scenes.
We have barely settled in our seats when we meet Lermontov
interrogating rebel Hungarians in 1956. In a scene bristling
with dramatic activity (and 13 people on stage) he gets a graphic
lesson in Communism from a prisoner he decides to release.
The prisoner takes a grenade, uses it to sear the body of a
Russian soldier, and Lermontov's response is to shoot his next
prisoner, a racist counter-revolutionary. All the issues whirl in
the air (Lermontov has also insulted his ill-educated woman
stenographer) in a scene lasting perhaps 15 minutes. . . .

It is no accident that Lermontov is so much more impressive
than Edgar's other characters. Nothing is certain around him,
least of all the language. He struggles for words which dry up
or come out in shooting streams. Everybody else in Edgar's
writing . . . has the fluency of the kind of river you sit beside
while thinking of something else. *Maydays* includes too much
and still misses things out (the bulk of the voters on either side
for a start) but it is still the richest and most expansive play
we have had about the difficulty of idealistic revolutionary
socialism. (p. 31)

> *Paul Ellen, "Passing the Baton," in New Statesman,
> Vol. 106, No. 2745, October 28, 1983, pp. 31-2.*

STEVE GRANT

Despite its massive scope, both geographically (Britain, Europe, America) and historically (1945-1980), [*Maydays*], David
Edgar's first original play since his award-winning *Destiny*, is
above all concerned with the political and personal history of
the '68 generation'. Its central character, . . . Martin Glass
(Glass/Mirror-geddit?) is very much of those times, which though
undoubtedly overvalued, were uniquely exhilarating. Not because of their 'revolutionary potential' but because of their
unique mix. Politics became a thing of Trotskyist theory, third
world practise, the brief flickering of student-worker unity in
France and even Britain; the cultural overlay of rock music,
drugs, casual sex, fully on tap for a generation of young people
fully benefiting from the Butler Education Act. At universities,
public-school boy met the daughter of unskilled labourer, sociology and socialism combined with anti-Vietnam demos and
student occupations, people played football in the Vice Chan-
cellor's office, tore up their exam-papers, lauded Che and Mao,
misspelled 'fascism' but knew Dylan's lyrics backwards. It
was all a massively enjoyable but over-rich repast, designed
to bring on eventual nausea. Ask the Angry Brigade. Or the
Czechs.

It is a period that Edgar, former student orator *par excellence*,
agit-prop playwright, political activist, has lived through. It is
a period which Edgar, social historian cum dramatist, has sought
to illuminate: the squabbles, the disillusionments, the recriminations, the wrongheadedness as much as the personal growth

and political integrity of his favoured characters. For Edgar, adapter of the marathon *Nicholas Nickleby,* careful interpreter of the experiences of Mary Barnes and Albie Sachs, has long nurtured his dramatic and rhetorical skills for the 'big public one', the play which puts on vivid, epic display both the politics and the people of post-war Britain, America and the Eastern Bloc.

The mention of *Nicholas Nickleby* is not without point, for *Maydays* has a particularly Dickensian turn of narrative coincidence. A rather whey-brained American girl student will just happen to have a boyfriend who is a militant anti-draft campaigner (blown up by his own bomb) and a Friedmanite economist father. Martin Glass remains close to a public-school teacher and former young Communist who conveniently becomes a disillusioned university professor harrassed by arrogant illiterate student yobs and moves finally to a position of Black Paper eminence as a Think Tank-cross between Kingsley Amis and Professor CB Cox. Even Glass who moves from CND schoolboy to Trot activist to right-wing lackey by the play's finale just so happens to have a country estate . . . next to Greenham Common—a fact which allows him not only to reunite with an old girlfriend/comrade but allows Edgar to concentrate his resources into an open-endedly optimistic final image of struggle and resistance.

Edgar the polemicist (marvellously so in *Destiny*) has also packed his dense narrative with several massively long speeches. He has been criticised for this, but not fairly, I think. Theatre is unrivalled in its capacity for intellectual feedback. Most of the speeches in question are magnificently rich in ideas and invective, notably . . . [Glass's] Damascus-style deconversion to Leftism at a trendy sub-Rowan-and-Martin party or Bob Peck's Russian dissident Lermontov doggedly and movingly refusing to become a puppet of right-wing anti-Sovietism, declining to accept some spurious award for his own personal witnessing of Stalinism's mistakes and wrongs: 'Yours are not gaolers' faces'—but perhaps the faces of the people who hire the gaolers'. Only in the case of a quite bafflingly long-winded monologue by . . . American economist Teddy Weiner is the spell really broken, particularly as [he] . . . delivers what is meant to be an unpleasantly conservative line in such rapturous tones.

The writer has been criticised . . . for certain omissions and distortions in his depictions of the Left in the late 60s and 70s and certainly there is far too much emphasis on the smaller, more insignificant Trotskyist factions, nothing about the wrangles within the Communist or Labour Parties, the leftwards drift of a Tony Benn or Arthur Scargill. That said, what *is* represented (though students in 1970 didn't spend *all* their time discussing politics; or rather only the ones that were avoided like the plague) is often bitingly accurate about the bigotry of the period—I too remember the SLL friends refused leave of absence (even when painfully ill) from newspaper-seller duty, or the brightsparks who wanted to burn TS Eliot's 'fascist' poetry or send their support to the 'ideologically correct' Khmer Rouge during their campaign of 'normalisation' in Cambodia.

However this is a point where Edgar the historian and Edgar the playwright are in confusion. A playwright chooses his characters carefully and *Maydays* possesses a heroine in the figure of . . . Amanda—a mother, a socialist, a survivor who is glimpsed at the finale camped out at Greenham Common and pushing the cause of the nameless, leaderless, permanent struggle against injustice. . . . But typically Amanda is a very *sympathetic* feminist. How representative is she? Amanda, for instance, would *never* want to ban transsexuals from a conference on the grounds

that by their very nature they were 'collaborators' with men (a true incident and surely 'Hurray for the Khmer Rouge' in a different form!). Are we any more certain about Amanda's assertions? And isn't Edgar's cry of 'Hats off' to resistance for its own sake as spurious and naive as the ideologies that have come before and been explored in depth? (pp. 17-18)

Maydays is not by any means a perfect play, in form, historical accuracy or personal or political insight, but it is a play by which all others on the theme of modern political history may well come to be judged. (p. 18)

Steve Grant, in a review of "Maydays," in Plays & Players, *No. 363, December, 1983, pp. 17-18.*

MALCOLM HAY

David Edgar has already established himself as one of the most accomplished and provocative playwrights working in England today.

The arrival of his latest stage play, *Maydays,* . . . confirmed Edgar's stature as a dramatist capable of taking on big public themes. More striking still was the evidence *Maydays* provided of how, in skilled hands, the full resources of theatre—vivid stage images and spectacle, powerful dialogue and strong characterisation—can be used to elicit from audiences an attentive, indeed absorbed, response to the discussion of issues which the majority of theatregoers probably find both knotty and forbidding.

The subject of *Maydays* is the politics of the extreme Left in Britain since the Second World War, and the shifts and accommodations and compromising of beliefs made by individuals over the course of time. Edgar's treatment of this subject makes it as compelling and exciting as the more private dramas which occupy most of our stages. (p. 13)

Edgar's first play, *Two Kinds of Angel,* written for two student actresses in June 1970, is not entirely characteristic of the work which was to follow. It is based on the contrasting attitudes of a young student revolutionary and a sexy actress and model. Edgar extends the action, and the frame of reference, by intercutting episodes from the revolutionary activities of Rosa Luxemburg and the last days of Marilyn Monroe, but the play lurches into melodrama and Edgar's own retrospective verdict is that he was 'relying on a series of fairly obvious effects culled from watching the wrong sorts of plays at an impressionable age'.

More typical of his work in the first three years were some of the plays he wrote for The General Will, a political theatre company set up in Bradford at that time. *The National Interest,* the first of Edgar's documentaries for The General Will, took as its theme the first twelve months' events under the recently elected Tory government. Written as a series of revue-like sketches, and parodying the government by presenting them as, for example, Chicago gangsters or light entertainers performing a cross-talk song, *The National Interest* is most interesting for the early glimpses it offers of Edgar's skill in using humour and parody of easily-recognised entertainment genres to illuminate social and political issues.

In much the same vein, *Rent, or Caught in the Act,* devised in 1972 for performance to tenants' groups, sought to explain the effects of an Act of Parliament (the Housing Finance Act) by presenting the information in the form of a Victorian melodrama, complete with a wicked landlord, a gallery of other villains, and an honest hero in a local councillor. (pp. 13-14)

The move towards a greater realism in style can be seen in plays like *Baby Love,* a concentrated study of a lonely and socially deprived young woman who kidnaps a child from outside a supermarket. The significance of *Destiny,* however, on which Edgar first started work in 1973, is that in its final version it represents a full-scale and remarkably successful, attempt to find a way of portraying realistic characters acting in relation to the social situations that affect their lives.

Destiny is an epic treatment of the rise of fascism in post-war Britain, starting in India in 1947, as a group of Army officers prepare to leave the newly independent country, then moving forward in time to trace the subsequent experiences and reactions of some of the characters and their descendants.

If the sheer detail about right-wing attitudes and thinking contained in *Destiny* is accurate and convincing, it is because the play was painstakingly researched. Edgar succeeds in creating believable people without delving into the intimacies of characters' personal lives. The audience remains ignorant of factors such as whether the shopkeeper turned Nation Forward candidate is married or single, or what the private as opposed to public behaviour of Edgar's characters is like. Significantly, much of the play is set in streets and public meetings, in a factory or on a picket line, rather than in enclosed domestic situations.

Edgar's ability in *Destiny* to work on a large scale, while still retaining a tight focus through his main characters on the central issue of how the seeds of fascism can take root and flourish, marks it out as possibly the single most important play in his development as a dramatist. Ironically, however, the three plays from Edgar's still considerable output of work between *Destiny* and *Maydays* in 1983 which attracted the most critical praise and public attention were all, as it happens, stage adaptations of books. (p. 14)

[The plot of *Maydays*] concerns the radical movements which many of Edgar's generation at one time or another embraced only, in many cases, to defect by changing sides politically. Edgar concentrates on three characters—a schoolteacher who moves from being a communist at the end of the war to espousing hardline authoritarian Toryism; one of his former pupils, who progresses (or regresses, according to the view point) from a commitment to revolutionary left-wing politics in the 1960s to working as a snidely disillusioned journalist; and a Russian dissident who takes refuge in the West and impinges on both their lives.

It is impossible in a few short paragraphs to convey the richness of social detail or the fascination . . . of watching the separate lines of action interweave, with parallels and contrasts between the behaviour of different characters subtly pointed through deliberate ironies and echoes running throughout the narrative.

Above all, Edgar succeeds in relating personal actions to political beliefs in a way which he avoided in *Destiny*. The play is truly epic in scope yet also intimate. What sticks in the mind are not just the big scenes which reflect Edgar's taste for spectacle—the arrival of the dissident at the airport, American protestors stopping a troop train, a nuclear alert at the Greenham Common missile base; the simple, everyday conversations which suddenly reveal the yawning gaps between individuals, the subtle and complex way in which people's ideas change, are so accurately chronicled that they become equally as striking and dramatic.

What also emerges very clearly is that Edgar is now very far removed from being a didactive propagandist. He remains a political playwright, he is still a socialist, but in *Maydays* he is harsh on revolutionary posturing and self-deception. (p. 16)

*Malcolm Hay, ''David Edgar: Public Playwright,''
in* Drama, *No. 151, 1st Quarter, 1984, pp. 13-16.*

Harlan (Jay) Ellison

1934-

(Has also written under pseudonyms of Lee Archer, Phil "Cheech" Beldone, C. Bird, Cordwainer Bird, Jay Charby, Robert Courtney, Price Curtis, Wallace Edmondson, Landon Ellis, Ellis Hart, E. K. Jarvis, Ivar Jorgensen, Al[an] Maddern, Paul Merchant, Clyde Mitchell, Nabrah Nosille, Bert Parker, Jay Solo, and Derry Tiger; has also written under joint pseudonym of Ellis Robertson and in collaboration with Henry Slesar as Sley Harson) American short story writer, scriptwriter, editor, novelist, nonfiction writer, and critic.

Ellison is a controversial award-winning author of speculative fantasy, or what he has termed "magic realism." Although he has consistently denied being an author of science fiction, Ellison's reputation largely rests upon his powerful stories written during the 1960s which utilize themes and elements common to both science fiction and fantasy. His stories reflect his highly personal, colloquial style through their authorial intrusions and asides. Writing in a prose rich with mythic allusions, Ellison typically centers on vulnerable heroes engaged in lethal conflict with forces of nature. These forces control the fates of his protagonists through fear and horror; from their experiences, Ellison's characters draw the moral strength to resist and defy their adversaries. Ellison maintains that humanity's greatest threat lies both in its subservience to elemental forces and in conformity to its own impersonal systems.

Ellison began his literary career in New York in the mid-1950s. Writing under many pseudonyms, Ellison sold approximately 150 short stories in various genres to magazines over a two-year period. His interest in authenticating the violence and amorality of street life led him to assume a false identity and join a street gang in the late 1950s. Ellison's gang adventures figure directly in his first novel, *Rumble* (1958; republished as *Web of the City*), and in the autobiographical narratives collected in *Memos from Purgatory: Two Journeys of Our Times* (1961). Ellison's short stories about street life appear in such collections as *The Deadly Streets* (1958), *The Juvies* (1961), and *Gentleman Junkie and Other Stories of the Hung-Up Generation* (1961). His first science fiction novel, *The Man with Nine Lives* (1960), was published together with his first collection of science fiction short stories, *A Touch of Infinity* (1960). The novel, which is based on Ellison's story "The Sound of the Scythe," links a plan for human colonization on an alien planet with a classic revenge story.

Ellison moved to Hollywood in the early 1960s. By 1963 he had established himself as a successful scriptwriter, contributing episodes to many television series, including "The Untouchables" and "The Outer Limits." Ellison received a Hugo Award for "City on the Edge of Forever," a script he wrote for "Star Trek." In the mid-1960s, Ellison began producing his most highly-regarded short stories. These works exhibit his characteristic concern with the individual's struggle against the conformity which limits satisfaction and cripples personal expression. Ellison received Nebula and Hugo Awards for "'Repent, Harlequin!' Said the Ticktockman," a short story included in the collection *Paingod and Other Delusions* (1965). This story centers on Everett C. Marms, a harlequin who, through continual tardiness and practical jokes, disrupts the

Photograph by Michael J. Elderman/Photoworks. Courtesy of Harlan Ellison

schedules and routines of a society whose actions are determined by a mechanical clock. Although Marms is finally caught and brainwashed, his rebellion against conformity has a damaging effect on the rigid automata of his society. The title story of Ellison's next collection, *I Have No Mouth and I Must Scream* (1967), earned him another Hugo Award. In this tale, a computer system called AM has achieved a humanlike consciousness and exterminates all but five humans, who serve as objects for the computer to torture and abuse. The protagonist demonstrates his moral superiority over AM by killing his four companions in order to release them from suffering and enslavement, but he is finally reduced to the state of a disembodied mind, which will be endlessly punished by the computer. His actions, like those of Everett C. Marms and other Ellison heroes who rebel against authority, have a limited yet potent effect upon the machinery of control.

In the mid-1960s, Ellison determined to edit an anthology of "magic realism" stories by diverse authors as a means of demonstrating the term's wide application to a variety of literary forms and of rejecting science fiction labels. Ironically, Ellison's anthology, *Dangerous Visions* (1967), resulted in his being called one of the leading American initiators of the "New Wave" in science fiction, which, according to some critics, introduced social, psychological, and literary content to the genre. The stories which appear in *Dangerous Visions* and its sequels, *Again, Dangerous Visions* (1972) and *The Last Dangerous Visions* (1976), were selected by Ellison according to their experimental or controversial nature. Prefaced by Ellison's introductions, they extended the limits of conventional fantasy to include such previously peripheral elements as sex and black humor. Ellison received special Hugo Awards for the first two collections. Ellison's own stories from this period move gradually away from science fiction concerns toward increasingly dark, personal expressions of mythic destruction, as in the short story collection *Love Ain't Nothing but Sex Misspelled* (1968). The essentially harmless rebellion of Everett C. Marms in "'Repent, Harlequin!' Said the Ticktockman" contrasts sharply with the anarchic Everyman hero of the title story from *The Beast That Shouted Love at the Heart of the World* (1969), who wreaks his revenge on a loveless, impersonal world through random violence and terrorism. Ellison received a Hugo Award for this story and a Nebula Award for *A Boy and His Dog,* a novella published in the same collection. Set in the aftermath of World War III, this work, which was also adapted for film, contrasts the free but perilous existence of a young man and his telepathic dog with the safe but rigidly structured ways of an underground society.

Ellison received two Hugo Awards for works collected in *Deathbird Stories: A Pantheon of Modern Gods* (1975), the first for his complex novella, *Adrift Just Off the Islets of Langerhans, Latitude 38° 54' N, Longitude 77° 00' 13" W,* and the second for the volume's title story, "The Deathbird." The latter tale, experimental in both subject matter and style, depicts in twenty-six numbered sections Satan's heroic attempts to awaken humanity to the notion that God is an insane tormentor responsible for the world's suffering. Ellison also received an Edgar Allan Poe Award for "The Whimper of Whipped Dogs," a crime story based on an actual murder, and won Hugo and Nebula Awards for a fantasy story, "Jeffty Is Five," about a child who does not age. The latter tale appears in the collection *Shatterday* (1980).

Ellison has published several nonfiction works. His essays on such topics as television and cinema, originally published in the *Los Angeles Free Press,* are collected in *The Glass Teat: Essays of Opinion on the Subject of Television* (1970) and *The Other Glass Teat: Further Essays of Opinion on Television* (1973). *Sleepless Nights on the Procrustean Bed* (1984) and *An Edge in My Voice* (1986) contain essays on a variety of topics, including Hollywood and American society.

(See also *CLC,* Vols. 1, 13; *Contemporary Authors,* Vols. 5-8, rev. ed.; *Contemporary Authors New Revision Series,* Vol. 5; and *Dictionary of Literary Biography,* Vol. 8.)

P. SCHUYLER MILLER

Theodore Sturgeon, who writes what may be the only "respectable" reviews of science fiction for a serious American magazine . . . , suggests in a brief introduction [to *I Have No Mouth and I Must Scream*] that Harlan may be writing out of the forces that are stirred up in less intense folk by LSD and its congeners. After all, as Aldous Huxley pointed out, the experiences that are currently tagged "psychedelic" have been felt for centuries and probably millennia without the use of drugs. (pp. 162-63)

But so much for the indescribable: how about the book?

You'll find it unlike anything else on the SF shelf, unless *Paingod* was. If the events and visions of these stories *are* psychedelic, most of the "trips" are bad ones. You'll be looking into an ugly world, as ugly as your worst nightmares. You may find some of the stories obscene, with an obscenity that has nothing to do with sex or the eliminative end of the alimentary tract, but drags out into view the perversions of the bruised and mangled human psyche. I'm tempted to say that it's like William Burroughs, except that at its wildest it makes sense—and in my book that makes it science fiction, which (in the same book) Burroughs' literary gymnastics are not. . . .

In "**I Have No Mouth and I Must Scream,**" a super-computer is playing obscenely with a few men and a woman, much as men play with other men when they have the power. In "**Big Sam Was My Friend**" you'll feel numbly that all the good will and fine intentions in the universe can't stand up against the brute unreason of tradition and revelation. "**Eyes of Dust**" is a bitter little parable on the sin of being ugly, even among other ugly persons.

"**World of the Myth**" is the closest to conventional science fiction in the book. . . . The insectlike creatures of another world are a kind of psychic laser—aimed at your own head. "**Lonely Ache**": A pure, horrible nightmare of self-hate and self-torment lived through moment by moment—a very bad trip without need of drugs. "**Delusion for a Dragon Slayer**": . . . a fantasy—*the* fantasy—about the man who can make his own Heaven and destroys it because he has no heaven in him. (Why wait till morning to hate yourself?) And finally, "**Pretty Maggie Moneyeyes,**" a grotesque legend of Las Vegas, the story of a haunted slot machine and a haunted man.

These stories wring you out—which is what Harlan Ellison intended. Writing them wrung him out. (p. 163)

        *P. Schuyler Miller, in a review of "I Have No Mouth
        and I Must Scream," in* Analog Science Fiction/
        Science Fact, *Vol. LXXXI, No. 4, June, 1968, pp.
        162-63.*

RICHARD RHODES

If you don't like his book of racy short stories [*Love Ain't Nothing But Sex Misspelled*], Harlan Ellison challenges on its jacket, "go find some cornball who'll tell you how nice everything is." William Price Fox does that in *Southern Fried Plus Six,* but it is Mr. Ellison who seems, by contrast, the cornball. *Love Ain't Nothing But Sex Misspelled* only pretends tough-mindedness: it reeks with fear. . . .

Harlan Ellison once joined a Brooklyn gang so that he could write more authentically about the real world. In his version of the human condition, abortions inevitably end in hemorrhage and death; bully writers prove themselves in all-night drinking bouts with callow Yale men; [and] a bitch-goddess's soul takes up residence in a slot machine. . . . (p. 36)

Only one of the 22 stories in *Love Ain't Nothing But Sex Misspelled,* avoids Grand Guignol. "**The Resurgence of Miss Ankle-Strap Wedgie**" appears to be an attempt at a novel about Hollywood. Its tone breaks halfway through, but for part of its length we are reading competent writing about authentic people, broken actors and actresses who cannot disentangle their lives from their illusions of success.

Ellison usually doesn't describe; he flails. He sets up his characters with minimal sympathy and then batters them down at each story's end. He apparently believes his inventions aren't worthy to act out their own lives, and regularly summarizes things for them to help them out:

"A man may truly live in his dreams, his noblest dreams, but only, *only* if he is worthy of those dreams." "She knew she had reached another junction of her existence. There *were* things worse than being ugly and lonely." . . . "For as he had believed in no god . . . no god believed in him."

Mom and Pop, a-settin' on the back porch eatin' Ho-Made Pie, couldn't have said it better. (pp. 36-7)

> *Richard Rhodes, "Life Is What You Make It," in* The New York Times Book Review, *June 30, 1968, pp. 36-7.*

ROBERT SCHOLES

Harlan Ellison (the ofay Ellison) has been officially designated by *The New Yorker* as the "chief prophet of the New Wave." Whatever that is. He may have come a long way from Painesville, O., but by any standard less matronly than *The New Yorker*'s he still has a long way to go before dipping so much as a toe in anything like a new wave. *Love Ain't Nothing But Sex Misspelled* is a collection of stories which Ellison says "took a lot of years and a lot of miles and a lot of emotions to write." (The quotation is from the jacket, written by the author himself, who does a lot of his own flacking. He is actually pretty good at it. The jacket is more interesting than the book.) Here is a sample of the prose produced by all those years, miles, and emotions:

> Tear loneliness across its pale surface; rend it totally and find the blood of need welling up in a thick, pale torrent. Let the horns of growth blare a message in rinky-tink meter. Turn a woman carrying all her years into a sloe-eyed gamine. . . .

As *The New Yorker* might have said in better days, Block That Metaphor. And block those clichés, and circumlocutions, and fake emotions. This paragraph is not intended as parody. It is straight sentiment, as close to truth or imagination as Mr. Ellison ever gets. On the jacket he warns "Mr. or Miss Square Face" not to buy the book. He says nothing about *Mrs.* Square Face. Perhaps it is for her that he has, as he so aptly puts it, got "down into the nitty-gritty."

It would be unfortunate if this sad book were to obscure the genuine resurgence of short fiction that we are experiencing. Far from replacing the short story, the nonfiction article has reinvigorated it in some important ways. A new hybrid form of fictionalized journalism is being developed brilliantly by writers as different as Tom Wolfe, Norman Mailer, and Terry Southern. . . . Both the parajournalists and the fabulators are creating literary works that are imaginatively equal to the enormities of our time.

Mr. Ellison, on the other hand, is offering warmed-over and watered-down combinations of F. Scott Fitzgerald, Raymond Chandler, and other writers from a past which seems all too remote. His unintentional parodies of the giants of the Twenties, Thirties, and Forties emphasize this very remoteness. But it is not just that his models are failing him. He is failing them

as well. Even the relatively simple good and bad guys of Dashiell Hammett and Chandler are beyond him. . . .

Another "new wave" has turned out to be just a ripple on the Ohio River.

> *Robert Scholes, " 'Rinky-Tink' Meter for Message," in* Saturday Review, *Vol. LI, No, 28, July 13, 1968, p. 32.*

P. SCHUYLER MILLER

Small wonder that Harlan is the principal U.S. prophet of the "New Thing" in science fiction—or speculative fantabulation, if you prefer. He needs new ways, new themes, new values—anything to shock his readers out of lethargy. In this collection from many sources [*The Beast That Shouted Love at the Heart of the World*], he does it as well as he ever has.

The title story won a "Hugo" award. This unexpurgated version is not so different from the magazine story as Harlan insists in his typical and revealing introduction. (I am sure some people read his books entirely for the introductions.) It gives the universe—the worn old SF universe of multiple alternate worlds—a structure that Dante might have appreciated. *A Boy and His Dog,* which closes the book, is also a little harsher, a little bit more ruthless than it was in the *New Worlds* version and in other reprints. It shows us a future in which ghetto culture—an evolved ghetto culture—has [survived] a nuclear holocaust. A few of the elite protected themselves underground.

"Shattered Like a Glass Goblin" is really fantasy, but it is probably the best story in the book—an evocation of the drug culture in terms of a bad trip that is somehow real. I'm told the story has put Harlan in the doghouse with the set who are accused of miscellaneous butchery in California. **"Along the Scenic Route"** does the same sort of thing for the drag-race culture by projecting a future in which rodders duel with their cars.

There are fifteen stories in the book, all of them experiences. **"Phoenix"** is, of all things, a trick-ending story about a grim future Earth. **"Asleep: With Still Hands"** shows a world in which war has been outlawed by a mental-control machine deep under the Sargasso. Two rival forces try to shut it off. (I think this is the least successful of the lot). (pp. 168-69)

"Try a Dull Knife" is another Los Angeles underground story—the same world that produced **"Glass Goblin." "The Pitll Pawob Division"**—very short, very alien. **"The Place with No Name"**—a nightmare about the pimp who rescued Prometheus. **"Run for the Stars"**—1957 *S.F. Adventures* yarn about the man sent out with a bomb in his stomach, still pure Ellison in its intensity. . . .

"Are You Listening?"—a parable, really, in which a nothing man becomes literally nothing. **"S.R.O."**—a show-spaceship docks in New York. **"Worlds to Kill"**—Earth invasion, by creatures as strange as any you've ever encountered. And that's it. Ideas. Ugly, nightmarish visions. Violence and more violence. It's the world Harlan sees around him. It's the universe he shows us. (p. 169)

> *P. Schuyler Miller, in a review of "The Beast That Shouted Love at the Heart of the World," in* Analog Science Fiction/Science Fact, *Vol. LXXXV, No. 6, August, 1970, pp. 168-69.*

PHILIP M. RUBENS

Ellison does much with myth and legend; his understanding of American Indian gods, in fact, is superlative. One wonders how far he has delved into primitive myth, legend, and religion. It is significant, for instance, that in some of the tales in *Deathbird Stories* he develops a set of circumstances, a group of characters, and a specific landscape that echo many of the traditional journeys to hell—from patristic literature to Norse myth. Ellison employs this framework to take the reader into new myths—new faiths needed to survive in an increasingly hostile world. (p. 378)

The main character in these descents is generally a sleeper who enters hell in a dream or as a doppelgänger. During the descent, the protagonist journeys through various levels of hell, often actively participating in the afflictions. This character is guided by an ambiguous figure who is sometimes not identifiably a "holy" person. Furthermore, the protagonist journeys through a violent, dark, and blasted landscape which is pervaded by a mountain. High in the mountain, the protagonist must face either a giant, whom he must outwit to survive, or some kind of erotic creature. All of these elements of the traditional descent into hell play an important role in Ellison's fiction. While many of Ellison's stories can be used to illustrate this point, four tales—"Delusion for a Dragon Slayer," *Adrift Just Off the Islets of Langerhans: Latitude 38° 54′N, Longitude 77° 00′ 13″W*, "The Place With No Name," and "The Deathbird"— aptly demonstrate something of the range and purpose of Ellison's use of the descent-into-hell motif.

"Delusion for a Dragon Slayer" contains many of the traditional elements of the descent and is based mainly on two ideas: the doppelgänger and postmortem consciousness. The latter technique generally depicts the workings of the human mind under extremely violent conditions—man's mental perceptions immediately before death. John Denney Crane maintains that there are four distinct phases to such an experience: time lag, extreme hypersensitivity, temporary reality, and physical death. In addition to a sense of postmortem consciousness, Warren Glazer Griffin, the protagonist, displays many of the qualities of a doppelgänger during his adventures. This concept, as Otto Rank points out, was created by primitive man's need to be reassured of immortality. To attain such assurance, man creates a spiritual self; but at some point man's attitude toward this other self changes from benevolent to malevolent. This, of course, means that the double could be a harbinger of death. Such an ambiguity has been assimilated into literature and finds expression as two opposing selves which, Rank claims, threatens the destruction of the individual. In this tale, the doppelgänger, which suggests the possibility of death, works to reinforce the postmortem consciousness device. Both are used to describe a descent into the self where man finds his own private hell.

Warren Glazer Griffin, the dragon-slayer, begins his adventure when he is crushed by a wrecking ball. His entire story occurs in the microseconds between life and death. As he runs along his well-worn track (rabbit warren?) to work, he realizes he will be late if he does not step out of his usual path. The wrecking ball he encounters while taking a shortcut sends him through a window (glazer, or one who makes windows) into a land of fantasy. Once in this land, he exhibits the hypersensitivity typical of the postmortem consciousness experience. He sees brilliant colors, hears acutely, and feels, rather than sees, the presence of obstacles. Furthermore, this land becomes the temporary reality Griffin (the dragon) uses to stave off

physical death. . . . Like many other doppelgänger manifestations, this one also exhibits an incredible amount of pride, a quality that brings about Griffin's destruction.

While Griffin's doppelgänger cavorts in his own psyche, he undergoes many of the traditional tasks of the descent into hell. First, he must overcome the sea and the reefs around the island (his plunge through the reef-bound coast is the first of many births in these tales). When he arrives at the island, he must defeat the mist-devil and win the love of the woman. In each of these encounters, Griffin falls short. His pride and hypersensitivity make him ignore the real dangers of the reef; therefore, he loses his ship and crew. (pp. 379-80)

In *Adrift Just Off the Islets of Langerhans*, Ellison depicts another descent into a psychic hell, the soul of a werewolf— a man cursed with eternal life. Instead of a psychic doppelgänger, however, Larry Talbot, the adventurer, has a literal, physical miniature who journeys into his body to find his soul. This miniature is an intriguing addition to descent literature. Robert Plank has made a persuasive study of such man-made figures. He claims that mechanical men, cyborgs and the like, can be traced to the Jewish golem, a creature made of clay and animated by either science or magic. In addition, Plank outlines a variety of motifs associated with these creations: the creature begins to function independently of the creator's will; there is a lack of communication; and, finally, either the creature or the builder is destroyed. These, of course, are all elements in Ellison's tale.

Talbot's journey in search of peace cannot begin until he learns the geographic coordinates for his soul from Mr. Demeter who serves as his initial guide to the underworld. Appropriately enough, Demeter's name recalls the goddess Demeter who, although she could not prevent Persephone's marriage to the god of the underworld, won for her daughter the right to return to earth periodically. Consequently, Persephone's character is ambiguous; she symbolizes both death and the rebirth of nature; and it is this cleansing rebirth through death that Talbot seeks through the mediation of Mr. Demeter and his microscopic double. (pp. 380-81)

[Having entered hell, Talbot] comes to the pancreatic sea on the shore of which he finds many of the memories of his childhood. . . . [The sea offers] access to Erebus, the judgment place. Talbot finds a boat (abandoned by Charon?) and sails toward the Islets of Langerhans. While becalmed near the island, he hears a radio broadcast about an old woman who was imprisoned by society because she was somehow different. The homunculus reacts by crying which breaks the calm and delivers him to the coordinates for his soul—Erebus.

In the center of hell, he discovers his soul—a smiling, meaningless Howdy-Doody button—and a large castle—the palace of Hades from Greek myth. Talbot will be judged here. . . . The resolution of the tale centers on Talbot's compassion for two old women—the one in the castle, the other a surrogate mother. He retreats into the hell of his own body with these two women to atone for the sins of the world. Unlike the previous adventurer, Talbot discovers that man can benefit from a view of his own soul even if it is not spotless—man *can* change; he *can* atone.

In these first two works, Ellison has shown a propensity to use the traditional framework of the descent into hell along with some closely related devices to comment on his perception of man's place in an inscrutable universe. The first tale, **"Delusion for a Dragon Slayer,"** shows the depth of Ellison's commitment to the psychological in terms of his use of doppelgängers and postmortem consciousness. It reveals what happens when man is not equal to his dreams, when he is flawed and cannot discern what must be done to correct his shortcomings. On the other hand, the second tale, *Adrift Just Off the Islets of Langerhans,* is a work fraught with possibility. The protagonist ventures into the self very much in terms of traditional descent literature and comes back with viable answers. Yet it is in two other tales, **"The Place With No Name"** and **"The Death-bird,"** that Ellison makes his most penetrating and perceptive analysis of the nature of man, God, Satan, good, and evil.

In **"The Place With No Name,"** Norman Mogart, the protagonist, while trying to escape from the police, runs into a shop kept by a very ambiguous fellow. This figure, like Mr. Demeter of the previous tale, has some magical abilities: "The little man shimmered, and changed form." . . . He also seems to be a holy figure. His name—"You can call me Simon. . . . Or Peter" . . .—recalls the apostle, Simon Peter. This guide-figure is also conspicuously absent in the tale as was Demeter in *Adrift Just Off the Islets of Langerhans* and the magician of **"Delusion for a Dragon Slayer."** This, however, is a typical occurrence in Ellison's descents.

When Norman escapes, he finds himself in *"another* body" in a junglelike setting. He also knows that he must locate a particular person—Prometheus—in "a place outside thought or memory," that other world of myth and legend. . . . [He] speculates on a variety of Indian religious beliefs, including the idea that Prometheus "was the bringer not of fire, but of lies; not the searing brand of truth, but the greater revelation of falsehood." . . . Even though he senses an ambiguity in his task, he continues to search for Prometheus.

Delirious with wandering and disease, Morgart begins to hallucinate; he sees the same brightly colored circles that plagued Warren Glazer Griffin. . . . [He] finds himself in a dormant volcano, a symbolic womb where he finds Prometheus [who is described in nonhuman terms]. . . . Mogart exchanges places with this half-fish/half-snake creature and is left to speculate on the meaning of it all throughout eternity. He eventually concludes that both Christ and Prometheus were aliens who had compassion for men and brought them knowledge. However, Ellison leaves the nature of such knowledge ambiguous—good *or* evil? . . . [In] this tale, the descent into hell, while approached in rather traditional terms, demonstrates the difficulty of finding answers to increasingly complex questions.

In the final work under consideration, **"The Deathbird,"** Ellison creates not only a descent into hell but an apocalyptic vision of despair and futility. The tale is told in a discursive style that at times seems to introduce irrevelant elements; however, since Ellison tells us that we can rearrange the work to suit our needs, a pattern can be discerned in the work. Significantly, Ellison prefaces the story with a disclaimer concerning the divinity of gods; instead, he maintains that man has the spark of life (the Hindu, *Atem*) and, as a consequence, may be God. . . . (pp. 381-83)

In the tale, Norman Stack, the protagonist, is awakened by a snakelike creature and brought to the blasted surface of the Earth. . . . While Stack journeys toward the lights in the mountains, flying devils try to snare him with their snakelike spores, a situation found in the *Vision of Drihthelm* (700 A.D.) and the *Vision of Furseus* (640 A.D.). . . . Stack does finally prevail over these terrors, but he must still confront the giant on the mountain.

When Stack actually faces the giant, he thinks of the Wizard of Oz, a fantasy character who spread terror and inspired awe through illusions. . . . Stack realizes at last that God is mad, a spoiled child who treats the Earth as little more than a toy. Unfortunately, he also realizes that it is too late for the snake, who is *really* man's friend; the Earth, which is dead; and man, who finds out too late that he is God.

The descent into hell in literature usually represents a kind of ritual initiation experience. Adventurers go to such places to learn about the gods, death, life, as well as the nature of good and evil. Most of these incidents contain specific characters, identifiable landscapes, and a general pattern of events. While Ellison's work includes many of these conventions, it also generally lacks quite a few. For instance, characters are usually conspicuously absent. Where is Satan? Charon? Persephone? Are the gods dead? . . . If the gods are gone, what can man hope for? Perhaps that is why Ellison wants man to journey into his soul, to go through that ritual birth into self-knowledge which will show man his real nature, his real worth—good or bad, human or god. (pp. 383-84)

> *Philip M. Rubens, "Descents into Private Hells: Harlan Ellison's 'Psy-Fi',"* in Extrapolation, *Vol. 20, No. 4, Winter, 1979, pp. 378-85.*

GEORGE R. R. MARTIN

[Ellison] is almost unique in being a major contemporary writer whose reputation rests in its entirety on his short stories and his frequent short-story collections. (p. 9)

[*Shatterday*] is the latest Ellison collection, featuring virtually all of his most recent material plus one older collaboration. Unfortunately, it is a long way from being one of his best.

The problem with being a short-story writer today is that you have to publish several collections to earn as much money as you might on a single strong novel. To make up each new collection, one either must duplicate material from previous collections, or use virtually everything one has written recently. Ellison chooses the latter course, and *Shatterday* is thus a pot-pourri of his recent work, good, bad, and indifferent.

When Ellison is writing at the top of his form, he is one of the great living American short story writers. **"Shatterday,"** represents Ellison at his best, a powerfully written, unforgettable fantasy about identity. **"Jeffty Is Five,"** a gentle, moving account of a boy who never grows up, is almost as good, and there are a few other strong stories to keep these two company.

Unfortunately, the rest of the book is not up to these standards. Some pieces, like **"Django"** and **"Shoppe Keeper"** and **"The Man Who Was Heavily Into Revenge,"** are only minor, but there are others, like **"How's the Night Life on Cissalda?,"** that are embarrassingly bad. Ellison has often raged against the science-fiction label that has haunted his career, preferring to be called just a writer, or at most a fantasist. He has a good point. He is a fantasist, really, and his best stories are set firmly in the here-and-now and partake strongly of the flavor of our times. On occasion he does write a marginal piece that uses some of the devices of sf, and could be so categorized, but almost invariably these are his weakest stories. This is certainly true in *Shatterday.*

Perhaps the most interesting story in the book—though not the most successful—is the longest, **"All the Lies That Are My Life,"** which is not science fiction, and not fantasy, but instead a sort of fictionalized autobiography or roman à clef about the death of a writer named Kercher O. J. Crowstairs, who very much resembles Harlan Ellison. . . . In his introductory note, Ellison stresses, "This is fiction, not personal memoir." . . . Ellison is clearly unhappy about those who read too much of him into his stories.

It is not a problem he is likely to escape. . . . As with Norman Mailer or Hunter S. Thompson, it is difficult to read the work now without being constantly aware of the author. This is emphatically so of **"All the Lies That Are My Life."** . . . Unfortunately, in this case the game provides the chief fascination of the story. Those who know Ellison or think they know Ellison may have a great time picking apart this tale and speculating about it. But read in a vacuum, solely as fiction, it is a flat failure. Kercher O. J. Crowstairs, as a fictional creation, is empty. He lives only as a shade of Harlan Ellison. (pp. 9, 11)

George R. R. Martin, "Scanning the Stars of the Short Story," in Book World—The Washington Post, January 25, 1981, pp. 9, 11.

ALGIS BUDRYS

Shatterday collects some of the best short stories of Ellison's recent period (1977 and up), including . . . **"Jeffty is Five,"** **"Alive and Well on a Friendless Voyage,"** and **"All the Lies That Are My Life."** Others were written as radio readings, or appeared in other obscure or ephemeral media, and so are not likely to be at all familiar. . . .

[Ellison] is a remarkable writer. As I've said on earlier occasions, the quintessential SF short story writer of his time, which falls after Bradbury's time. What I want to stress now is that part of that quintessence, which has many parts, lies in his burgeoning demand that he be treated as a writer, just plain a writer, some of whose work finds a home in SF media but all of which is in fact part of a larger literary construct. (p. 52)

[Ellison] has done something else that no one else—regardless of talent or empathy—had ever been able to do from his position. He has created an entire school of writers who now routinely operate from the position that it's all one set of standards, and who are accepted as such by a growing number of people who wouldn't have been caught dead taking that sci-fi stuff seriously. There are even inklings that in some literary quarters, we are for the first time being permitted to not be invariably perfect, without getting the whole of SF damned as a consequence.

Not all of the stories in this book, for instance, are excellent. Some of them verge on not being very good at all. So what? The *writer* is good; the good stories are good not only in themselves but as reflections of a good source. (pp. 52-3)

Ellison is the foremost voice of the New Romanticism, in which the illusion is that (A) lies are evil per se and (B) to call something a lie is to speak the truth. But sourness and dark ain't nothin' but sweetness and light sproinnged out. Until we have writers who fully understand their own motives, the New Romanticism is not intrinsically more truthful than the old. Yet it is refreshing, at the very least, and like any other powerful literature, produces more good work by mistake than some forms do by diligent application. (p. 53)

Algis Budrys, in a review of "Shatterday," in The Magazine of Fantasy and Science Fiction, Vol. 60, No. 6, June, 1981, pp. 52-3.

COLIN GREENLAND

[The British edition of *Shatterday*] omits all but one of [Ellison's] Introductions, which guard every story in the . . . original. They could have cut them all. One Ellison is enough without another doing the commentary. . . . In the one Introduction that survives Ellison describes his "mission": "I spend my life and miles of visceral material in a glorious and painful series of midnight raids against complacency." . . . Whether this is a true or even coherent account of his artistic motives does not matter. It establishes that Ellison is after the personal touch, preferably on an exposed nerve; he is compulsively hyperbolic; and if he offends it is with good will.

Ellison developed the habit of Introducing in *Dangerous Visions,* his large anthology of "taboo-breaking" science fiction, published in 1967. Even then many of the stories seemed somehow less tremendous than his fanfares and alarms proclaimed; something similar is the case now. Ellison does not employ suspense and revelation, a spring-loaded punchline, or any of the devices by which a narrative can literally shock its reader. Nor does he go in much for moral shock, the *frisson* of contemplating the unmentionable. Two stories about sex, for example, **"Would You Do It for a Penny?"** and **"How's the Night Life on Cissalda?"**, are respectively a seduction fantasy and an extended smutty joke: routine, even sexist. He is more often annoying than shocking; but he can certainly be personal.

The centrepiece of this collection is **"All the Lies that are My Life"**, twenty thousand words of fictional self-exposure for which Ellison adopts the unusual expedient of two personae: a rich, flamboyant SF writer and his somewhat less manic old friend, who narrates the story of the writer's death and peculiarly binding bequests. It takes restraint, not just ego, to do this at all well, and Ellison does it well enough. If the theme is how the dead actually do possess the living, the theme of **"Shatterday"**, whose protagonist is also subdivided, is how the living dispossess the dead. **"Shatterday"** begins like **"All the Lies"** in a characteristic flurry of wisecracks, then quiets and ends sombrely. It is the more effective story. In fact, and I doubt that this is only a prejudice of national character, Ellison's most successful and disturbing stories are those which are least exhibitionist, least coarsened by his preferred aggressive manner: **"Count the Clock that Tells the Time"**, about the limbo of human ineffectuality; **"All the Birds Come Home to Roost"**, in which an undeserving man is revisited by all the women he has ever coupled with, one by one, in reverse order: **"Opium"**, a suicide hallucination; and **"The Other Eye of Polyphemus"**, a graceful parable of Purgatory and a comforter who cannot identify his own desire. This last is Ellison writing as Hemingway—no fireworks, no trumpets, and it is the most accomplished and powerful piece in the book. Surely there is significance in that?

Colin Greenland, "The Personal Touch," in The Times Literary Supplement, No. 4136, July 9, 1982, p. 739.

DANIEL CARIAGA

[If Ellison] wants new labels, what about repetitive? Self-indulgent? Disingenuous? All these terms describe this collection of 20 stories and essays [*Stalking the Nightmare*], all previously published, though sometimes in different forms. Fantasist is Ellison's own self-description, and it applies, but the modifiers urban and sleazy might be added, more often than not. This writer's worlds are not pretty places, or locales of calm, hope or optimism; such worlds might be engrossing if presented credibly and in depth. Here, they become merely ghettos of terror, fear, competitiveness and despair. Still, Ellison's most unattractive quality is his flamboyant self-consciousness, which surfaces somewhere in every story, to its detriment.

> *Daniel Cariaga, in a review of "Stalking the Nightmare," in* Los Angeles Times Book Review, *October 24, 1982, p. 14.*

MICHAEL BISHOP

[Ellison's *Stalking the Nightmare*] contains three or four good recent stories, a few ghastly stories from the 1950s (scrupulous revision has merely thrown their ghastliness into high relief), and four personal essays of such wit, passion, or poignancy that they easily redeem the whole motley compilation.

Empiricist or supernaturalist? Where does Ellison stand? In a moving introductory fable ("**Quiet Lies the Locust Tells**"), the author's narrator declares, "I do not believe in Gods, but I ask God never to let Her [i.e., Ellison's elusive personification of all that cripples or destroys genuine creativity] discover a way of reading the inside of the people. If she ever finds a way to probe and drain the heart, or the head, then all hope will be lost." . . .

Ellison's up side gets play in the essay "**Saturn, November 11th**," which celebrates the triumph of the Voyager I mission in 1980, the formidable significance of this event, and the author's own involvement as "an eye-witness to history." The images sent back from Saturn placed everyone at the Jet Propulsion Lab in Pasadena in the fictional territory of the novel version of *2001: A Space Odyssey*. . . . These images were *real*, however, and the unexpected and mechanically unaccountable braiding of the planet's rings tied the conventional scientific wisdom of the astronomers into knots. As Ellison puts it in this delightful piece, "The celestial engineer has been cutting capers again."

When NASA officials discover that a moon postulated by a French astronomer in 1966 does not in fact exist, Ellison gloats: "I am not a science fiction writer, no matter how my work is mislabled by anal-retentive pigeon-holers; I have written so few stories that required a scientific education that I have nothing to apologize for." *Stalking the Nightmare* confirms this persnickety observation. Insofar as subject matter goes, "**Saturn, November 11th**" is atypical Ellison. It is representative, however, in that it shows a concern for minute and gritty documentation that appears even in the bleakest of the *contes cruels* elsewhere in this collection. In the stories optimism gives way to angst (with two or three exceptions), and the "celestial engineer" of this essay steps aside for demons, irreverent magi, hideous ghouls, troublesome jinn, and the unappeasable Eumenides of loneliness. Ellison's religion, if he has one, is survival with dignity.

"**Grail**," a phantasmagoric account of one man's search for True Love, is the best story in the book. . . . "**Grail**" was almost left out in favor of [another] story. . . . Because the cruelest *contes* in this collection are pseudo-science-fiction yarns that should have been permitted to molder in the pulps ("**Blank**

. . . ," "**Visionary**," "**Invasion Footnote**," "**Final Trophy**," "**Transcending Destiny**," and "**Tracking Level**," to cite the cruelest), I am extremely grateful to Ellison for his decision to substitute "**Grail**" for the ironically entitled "**Invulnerable**." The substitution is a mature parable, vintage 1981, and its theme transcends the fashions of the moment.

> *Michael Bishop, in a review of "Stalking the Nightmare," in* Book World—The Washington Post, *December 26, 1982, p. 6.*

ALGIS BUDRYS

Harlan Ellison says that if there is a person with a decent impulse, if there is a moment of love, the impulse and the moment are invariably sufficient to evoke crass crushing destruction by the way things *really* are. Except every scarce now and then, of course.

We love hearing it. In *Stalking the Nightmare*, we can hear it again.

Why do we want to? It's not true. Experience and observation show there is no correlation between arousing the envy of the gods and getting zapped. But we want to believe it's true. And so we have made, of a skilled writer with a personality that invites trouble, a spokesman for all of us who feel that goodness invites trouble.

On the face of it, *Stalking the Nightmare* is the latest collection from an extremely able short-story writer, whether considered in the SF universe or, more properly, measured against any such figure in English language writing. Gathered from sometimes obscure sources, dating often from the mid-1950s but provided with a good leavening of middle-period and recent Ellison, it slices through the author's career like a core sample. If you wanted just one Ellison book, for some reason, this would be the one. (p. 32)

Each new thing [Ellison] writes, no matter how ostensibly different from what has gone before, is all of a piece with a view of the universe as hostile and capricious. And the details of his actual life, as well as the apocrypha he feels obliged to add to its embellishment, appear as a role played in the grand composition of his life. He is his own hero, and in that sense is very much at one with the protagonists he has deployed in his written creations. And we love it.

We have always loved it. We cherish him now with an intensity that marks social esteem not for an individual but for what that individual triggers in us. . . . It had never previously occurred to me to detect a link between Ellison and Lovecraft, and Lovecraft's precursors and descendants, but if there is something to this construct, it explains the affinity between Ellison and Robert Bloch . . . and Stephen King. (p. 33)

> *Algis Budrys, in a review of "Stalking the Nightmare," in* The Magazine of Fantasy and Science Fiction, *Vol. 64, No. 6, June, 1983, pp. 32-3.*

STEPHEN ADAMS

After a one-paragraph prologue that explicitly states his moral, the narrator of Harlan Ellison's "**'Repent, Harlequin!' Said the Ticktockman**" says, "Now begin in the middle, and later learn the beginning; the end will take care of itself". . . . This disruption of ordinary chronology not only gains the reader's attention but it also dramatizes Ellison's theme, his protest against a rigid, tyrannizing sense of time. Message and medium come together. Just as the Harlequin disrupts various "normal" schedules, the narrator subverts the normal chronological order of his story.

Perhaps Ellison has yet another reason for initiating his story as he does. Beginning in medias res is a convention of the classical epic and a glance through "'Repent, Harlequin!'" reveals other epic conventions: catalogs, elaborate similes, an arming scene, launching of a ship, a dangerous woman, battles, single combat, a background of social disturbance, etc. Such features suggest that Ellison is tapping the epic genre, as well as science fiction and political fable, and that epic conventions in the story might be explored to shed light on its form and meaning.

More accurately, "'Repent, Harlequin!'" is not epic but mock-epic. It introduces epic conventions in order to parody them, twist them, turn them upside down. Thus, instead of being a long poem in twelve or twenty-four books, "'Repent, Harlequin!'" is a fairly short story of ten pages. Its protagonist, the unheroically named Everett C. Marm, proves an odd successor to Achilles, Odysseus, Aeneas, or the Christ of Milton's epics; he is a mousy, "ridiculous" rebel who dresses in motley, apologizes profusely, and has little apparent impact on the social order that he challenges. One by one Ellison introduces epic conventions only to subvert them.

If epics usually feature an arming scene, we watch the Harlequin "girding himself" for battle, dressing not in armor but "that ghastly clown suit" . . . . The epic launching of the ship appears equally diminished: "foof! air-boat, indeed! swizzle-skid is what it was, with a tow-rack jerryrigged" . . . . In place of bloody battles we find slapstick encounters that injure nothing but the smooth operation of social machinery and scheduling. For his first engagement, the Harlequin "skimmed over a slidewalk, purposely dropping a few feet to crease the tassels of the ladies of fashion, and—inserting thumbs in large ears— he stuck out his tongue, rolled his eyes, and went wugga-wugga-wugga." "It was a minor diversion," the narrator comments, twice in the same paragraph. . . . In other "battles," the Harlequin releases a load of jelly beans . . . , catches government agents in the net they were preparing for him . . . , and turns back an "assault" by workers sent to stop his subversive haranguing of shoppers. . . . (pp. 285-86)

Ellison also inverts epic seriousness and establishes a sense of oral delivery through slang and informal, colloquial expressions. . . . He comments explicitly on the moral of his story . . . and writes in an exuberant, anarchic, rebellious style that parallels the Harlequin's activities. . . . [Thus, the] narrator and the Harlequin merge in their aims and methods. The narrator accomplishes stylistically what the Harlequin sets out to do with his practical jokes: they both upset established rules (social or literary) and interject spontaneous, anarchic humor into an otherwise joyless, predictable, over-regulated world.

Why does Ellison bother with the epic trappings, especially when his setting is the nonheroic world of "'Repent, Harlequin!'"? Perhaps the contrast between tenor and vehicle is part of his message, as it is in all mock-epics. The inappropriateness of the epic conventions emphasizes the diminished state of the world that Ellison depicts.

Epic allusions prove most effective as a critical weapon because of generic expectations that we readers bring to the story. We expect an epic to define the culture from which it emerges and to transmit the values of that culture. "'Repent, Harlequin!'" does define a culture—a nightmare America of the future— but rather than celebrating its values, Ellison attacks them. American efficiency, time-consciousness, social organization, and cultural homogeneity all are here to be questioned. Through the Harlequin, Ellison celebrates values that he sees disappearing from, and subversive to, society: individuality, nonconformity, spontaneity, humor, playfulness. As the opening quotation from Thoreau's "Civil Disobedience" indicates, this "hero" serves society not by embodying it but by resisting it. . . . (pp. 287-88)

Because he is an individual, the Harlequin poses a threat to his society, as epic heroes often do. W.T.H. Jackson points out that epics frequently focus on an intruder hero, "careless of established institutions," who clashes with the king, the guardian of the social order. Clearly, the Ticktockman plays the kingly role in "'Repent, Harlequin!'" As the Master Timekeeper, "capable of revoking the minutes, the hours, the days and the nights, the years of your life," he controls all cardioplates; "And so, by this simple scientific expedient . . . the System was maintained. . . . It was, after all, patriotic". . . .

According to Jackson, "epics spring from violent social disturbance, when long-standing patterns of civilization are being challenged or overturned". . . . (p. 288)

As does most science fiction, "'Repent, Harlequin!'" concerns not so much the imagined time of the story (beyond 2389) as the time of its composition (1965). It clearly reflects the social upheaval of the mid-sixties and the strategies that some protesters used to challenge and change society. . . . "'Repent, Harlequin!'" expresses the hope that in a world containing awesome implements of destruction (the only "epic" feature of an otherwise diminished society), humor can serve as a weapon against the forces of conformity and repression, and that the bold, nonviolent assertion of individuality can make a difference.

But, as Jackson points out, "Any reader of epics knows that they rarely end in unqualified success for the principal character". . . . Again, Ellison plays with and inverts an epic convention. Marm gets neither the long nor glorious life of Achilles' choice; in the end he is destroyed. Yet, Ellison insists, "if you make only a little change, then it seems to be worthwhile". . . . That Marm has made a change is indicated by the Ticktockman's lateness at the conclusion and by the noise he makes in the final sentence of the story. . . . [He] ends up "going mrmee, mrmee, mrmee, mrmee" . . . ; this man-machine has been damaged.

"'Repent, Harlequin!'" concludes, then, with some ambivalence—with a defeat that is in a sense victory. Ambivalence is inescapably a feature of the mock-epic genre that Ellison experiments with. From one perspective, the epic conventions, as they are parodied and inverted, point to a diminished hero and society. The heroic conventions seem laughably inappropriate to mousy, apologetic, ineffective Everett C. Marm up against a banally evil social order. And yet the epic conventions do elevate Marm, just as *The Rape of the Lock* elevates Belinda and her world by the wealth of imagination and generic heightening that Pope bestows on them. By forcing us to consider Marm in the context of ancient heroic warfare, Ellison encourages us to revise our notion of heroism in the present. As a mock-epic, "'Repent, Harlequin!'" thus becomes an exercise in what Frost calls making the most of a diminished thing. (pp. 288-89)

Stephen Adams, "The Heroic and Mock-Heroic in Harlan Ellison's 'Harlequin'," in Extrapolation, *Vol. 26, No. 4, Winter, 1985, pp. 285-89.*

DON D'AMMASSA

The fact that [*An Edge in My Voice*] contains more than 500 pages of non-fiction by Harlan Ellison should in itself be sufficient incentive for people to run out and buy it. It consists of a series of columns he did over a period of three years, with some additional material, dealing with a variety of topics. . . . It is almost a redundancy to say that [the columns] are opinionated, inflammatory, controversial, and fascinating. You won't always agree with his opinions, but you'll certainly find them entertaining, perhaps maddening. The interactions between Ellison and various correspondents, and the saga of the mysterious man with no identity are particularly intriguing. This is an absolute must for his fans and enemies alike.

Don D'Ammassa, in a review of "An Edge in My Voice," in Science Fiction Chronicle, *Vol. 7, No. 4, January, 1986, p. 34.*

TOM EASTON

[*An Edge in My Voice*] is, of course, patent Ellison. Raging, fulminating, swearing against the follies of the modern world, this literary *agent provocateur* aims to wake people up, to make them think about their lives and their fellows, and he succeeds.

However, Ellison is not the perfectly clear-eyed observer he seems to claim he is. At least once, when a letter-writer takes him to task for his attack on De Palma's films, he demonstrates that he too wears blinders. The writer made a valid point comparing De Palma's *Blow Out* with *The French Connection*, calling the latter more evil because its characters are more blasé about the villainies around them, despite *Blow Out*'s sadistic antifeminism, and Ellison refused to recognize the point at all.

Still, Ellison remains as remarkable an essayist as he is a short-story writer.

Tom Easton, in a review of "An Edge in My Voice," in Analog Science Fiction/Science Fact, *Vol. CVI, No. 4, April, 1986, p. 179.*

George Faludy

1913-

(Born György Faludy) Hungarian-born Canadian poet, auto-biographer, translator, novelist, and biographer.

A Hungarian exile living in Canada, Faludy is probably most widely recognized in the West for his autobiography, *My Happy Days in Hell* (1962). This work chronicles his persecution under both the Nazi and Communist governments in Hungary and his experiences as an exile in France, North Africa, England, and the United States during and after World War II. Faludy was, however, well known in prewar Hungary for his poetry, most notably his free translations of such authors as François Villon and Heinrich Heine. Using detailed sensual imagery, irony, metaphor, and satire, Faludy writes verse ranging from simple love poems to vehement political diatribes denouncing what he perceives to be the evils of capitalism, totalitarianism, and imperialism. He imbues his poetry with what M. Travis Lane called a "proud vitality," professing his joy at being alive in spite of his life's many hardships.

Faludy began publishing his poems in periodicals and newspapers during the early 1930s. Strongly opposed to the Fascist regime then ruling Hungary, he expressed his opposition in a series of poems he wrote to masquerade as translations of the fifteenth-century French poet François Villon. These poems, actually composed by Faludy, became very popular in Hungary, but their political implications brought Faludy into conflict with the government. By 1938, facing arrest for "slandering a friendly nation," Faludy fled to Paris, where he remained for seven years, writing poems and translating literature into Hungarian. When France fell to the Nazis in 1940, Faludy escaped to North Africa; in 1941, he came to the United States. Although active in the Free Hungary Movement in America and a United States Army volunteer after the bombing of Pearl Harbor, Faludy refused the American citizenship offered him at the end of the war, choosing to return to Hungary, where he became literary editor of the official paper of the Social Democratic Party. After Faludy had published several books, including collections of his own poetry, his work began to be suppressed by the Communist government. In 1950, he was arrested and sentenced to twenty-five years in a prison camp. Despite the severe forced-labor conditions which caused the deaths of many prisoners, Faludy and a small group of intellectuals survived by reciting poetry and sharing lectures on various topics. The death of Stalin in 1953 eased tensions in Hungary, and many political prisoners, including Faludy, were released. Although he attempted to remain in Hungary, he was forced to leave in 1956. Fleeing to Vienna, then to London, Faludy finally settled in Toronto and has since become a Canadian citizen.

Faludy details his experiences in *My Happy Days in Hell,* an account of his eventful life as a literary celebrity turned political dissident and a chronicle of the tragedy of Hungary under Fascist and Communist dictatorships. While Irving Wardle found the book to be a "disconcertingly gay memoir of concentration-camp life," most critics admired the passion, humor, and dignity with which Faludy tells his tale. In a statement underscoring the paradox of the book's title, Bernard Bergonzi observed: "In this terrible yet light-hearted book [Faludy] shows

© Lütfi Özkök

what it means to persist in being human in a society run by the enemies of humanity.''

While Faludy's poetry has long enjoyed popular success in his homeland, few of his poems had been translated into English until the publication of *East and West: Selected Poems of George Faludy* (1978). Consisting of poems written between 1935 and 1975, the collection demonstrates the evolution of Faludy's poetry from the formalities of his early work to the accessibility of his later poems. Henry Kreisel observed that while Faludy's early poetry derives inspiration "from certain aesthetic concepts of late nineteenth century European poetry" and displays some "affinities, in suggestiveness, in poetic structure, and in the nature of the imagery, with the French symbolists," his later work exhibits "a loosening up of emotion . . . reflected not only in the discursive structure . . . , but above all in the rich colloquial quality of the language."

In *Learn This Poem of Mine by Heart* (1983) and *Selected Poems, 1933-1980* (1985), Faludy again warns of the dangerous effects of capitalism, technology, and consumerism on the West while continuing to condemn the totalitarian regimes of Eastern Europe. Characterized by Faludy's social and political consciousness, his imagination, and his lyrical language, these poems reflect his humanist beliefs and display his impatience with poverty, cruelty, and ignorance. According to Paul Stuewe,

Faludy's poetry draws its power from "the struggle to preserve humanistic values in an increasingly totalitarian world." Faludy has also published several other books, among them a historical novel, *Karoton* (1966), set in fourth-century Alexandria, and a well-received biography of the medieval scholar Erasmus.

(See also *Contemporary Authors,* Vols. 21-24, rev. ed.)

RAOUL ENGEL

My Happy Days in Hell is a brilliant and important book. It tells with frequent flashes of gaiety a story of terrible poignancy—the story of the liberal European intellectual trapped between fascism and communism, dispossessed and persecuted by both, his books confiscated and burnt first by the one and then the other, forced to leave his own country and yet unable to put down real roots anywhere else. In parallel, the tragedy of Hungary is also told—first under the fascist Horthy regime, later 'liberated' by the Russians, its nascent democratic institutions quickly crushed and replaced by the dictatorships of Rakosi, Nagy, and Kador.

Against this backdrop, front stage centre, stands George Faludy, a precociously gifted (and famous) young poet in pre-war Budapest; charming and sophisticated, vain and faintly cruel, his elegant but rarely profound poetry freely published throughout Hungary, he lived at the centre of a small glittering literary world. Then suddenly—and unaccountably, since he was never a political radical or activist—his books were seized, a warrant was issued, and he fled to Paris in the nick of time to avoid arrest. There, with his wife whom he loathed but didn't know how to abandon, he fell in with the dismal circle of Hungarian émigrés huddling together in bars and sleazy hotels. When France fell, he and a few friends managed to reach North Africa after a hair-raising series of adventures, told with dazzling pace and excitement.

But then the months spent in Casablanca, as well as in the desert with an improbable young Moroccan, dissolve into a highly romanticized fable, a succession of Arabian nights more reminiscent of *The Sheik* than Valentino himself. Not only does this part wholly fail to convince, but it clashes incongruously with the stark and harrowing realism of the second half of the book.

Mr Faludy spent the war years in the United States, at the personal invitation of President Roosevelt, and among good friends. Immediately afterwards, against all advice, he returned to Budapest filled with hope and confidence. Quickly, both were to be destroyed. As literary editor of a liberal newspaper, his freedom was steadily curtailed and his professional standards reduced to the moronic level demanded by the Party. Eventually he was denounced, arrested, and flung into a concentration camp identical in most respects to the German model. Five years of torture, hard labour, and near starvation followed, but also a deepening and refinement of his feelings for people—especially for his fellow prisoners, whom he depicts with insight and compassion.

My Happy Days in Hell makes one think of Arthur Koestler, inevitably. But it does more than chronicle the suffering and disillusionment of an idealist. Mr Faludy has experienced the European inferno, and has the talent to communicate its torments to us with humour, dignity, and passion.

> *Raoul Engel, in a review of "My Happy Days in Hell," in* The Listener, *Vol. LXVIII, No. 1755, November 15, 1962, p. 825.*

BERNARD BERGONZI

[*My Happy Days in Hell*] is immensely absorbing, Mr. Faludy's literary gifts are apparent, though he hasn't been well served by his translator. His experiences are described with a great sense of veracity, and sometimes in astonishing detail. Although he tells us a great deal about himself, the depths of his personality remain elusive. One has the feeling of being presented with a kind of Byronic persona: the author is always conscious of himself as a poet, he is basically gay, learned, vain, sexually susceptible, not particularly heroic but showing considerable resourcefulness when undergoing the horrors of imprisonment. If Don Juan had ended up in a Stalinist prison camp he might have written a similar book. For Mr. Faludy, being a poet is much more essentially part of his character than it could be for most West European poets; he grew up in a society where the poet could still be regarded as a *scop* or *jongleur,* and an embodiment of national consciousness rather than a representative of minority culture. Even the camp guards would urge him to recite to them. Certainly Mr. Faludy's vocation as a poet helped him to preserve a sense of identity; when deprived of writing implements he continued to compose poems in his head. Unlike his Marxist fellow-prisoners he had no ideological commitments, and therefore felt no need to argue tortuously about whether or how far the system had gone wrong. He was content to hate Communism for its inhumanity and leave the debate to others. Above all, he saw very clearly how Marxism destroyed the capacity for independent thought by making it impossible for the Communist victims of Stalinist terror to think in any other categories, so that they were quite unable to make any kind of intellectual rebellion. . . . (p. 769)

In such a world Faludy the apolitical poet kept his sanity and his grasp on human values. He underwent innumerable beatings and nearly died of starvation in the labour camp. But he survived and helped other prisoners to survive. In this terrible yet light-hearted book he shows what it means to persist in being human in a society run by the enemies of humanity. (p. 770)

> *Bernard Bergonzi, "Poetry and Terror," in* The Spectator, *Vol. 209, No. 7012, November 16, 1962, pp. 769-70.*

GEORGE JONAS

Long ago George Faludy received the highest possible compliment the Nazis and Communists can pay an author: all his books were burned, pulped, or confiscated by both regimes. Today many regard Faludy as the greatest living Hungarian poet, a distinction he would probably have achieved even if he had not been discovered by Hitler and Stalin. His censors were instrumental in spreading Faludy's fame at home and abroad, a fact Faludy readily acknowledges in his autobiography.

Fortunately *My Happy Days in Hell* is more than just an autobiography. It is impressive reportage, witty and thought-provoking, always readable and occasionally fascinating. Faludy's writing is not dulled by the facts or restricted to them;

he manages to create an atmosphere of almost frightening authenticity.

North American readers will be disappointed to find that Faludy, after discussing in detail his experiences in France and Africa during the war, writes next to nothing about the United States, where he lived for nearly five years as the personal guest of President Roosevelt. The last part of the book, Faludy's return to Hungary and his eventual imprisonment, are a literary precedent. From penny-dreadfuls to Orwell's *1984*, many works of fiction have been based on totalitarian prisons, but I believe few writers of Faludy's calibre have actually spent years in a Communist forced-labour camp—and survived to tell about it. This account alone makes the book well worth reading. (pp. 96-7)

> George Jonas, in a review of *"My Happy Days in Hell,"* in The Tamarack Review, *No. 26, Winter, 1963, pp. 96-7.*

RALPH G. ROSS

My Happy Days in Hell is a splendid book, to be neglected by any reader only at his intellectual peril. Aspects of Europe and North Africa during the Nazi conquests and the actions of people who become refugees not for the moment, but as a way of life, are wonderfully perceived, but the unforgettable story is that of a prison camp in which Faludy was interned in the days of Hungarian Stalinism.

What Faludy tells us strikes utterly true because it is almost uninventable. . . .

[Events from his life bring to Faludy's] mind the old Turkish occupation of Hungary, medieval heresy trials, or the conduct of a Roman proconsul. The European classical education and sense of history are used to explain what is happening as it happens, to see it in historical perspective, and even to anticipate consequences of the kind that are familiar from man's past.

Although in this way events cease to be brute facts and become intelligible patterns, and so more meaningful and more important, they also at times lose the searing impact of immediacy. As Faludy says about the fall of France, "Yet all this left me so completely untouched that I might have been listening to insignificant episodes of the Peloponnesian war."

> Ralph G. Ross, *"Paeans: To Mother, to Motherland,"* in New York Herald Tribune, *May 31, 1964, p. 4.*

IRVING WARDLE

George Faludy first came before the British public four years ago with a disconcertingly gay memoir of concentration-camp life [*My Happy Days in Hell*]. In *Karoton* he presents a fat novel of fourth-century Christianity that groans under the weight of research. Not that Mr. Faludy has entirely lost his ribaldry. His early Christians roam the streets at night snapping the members off the more outstanding specimens of Alexandrian statuary; and he presents an adulterous proconsul whose litter is equipped with a false bottom to facilitate infidelities *en route*. But most of the book is soberly attached to its fearsomely complex subject—the development of Catholicism in the multi-racial, multi-sectarian society of Alexandria at a time when the Empire itself was divided between five *augusti*.

One of the rulers, at any rate (Daja, the ex-herdsman), comes strongly to life; and so, fitfully, do other figures—a hedonistic poet, a silver-tongued old rhetorician, and (among the historical figures) the theologian Arius. Karoton himself, though—a passionate young convert plagued with lust—is vague both in himself and as a force in the narrative. Nor, in spite of the detail, does the book show how Christianity changed from a persecuted faith to a dominant creed; the two phases are simply exhibited one after the other. If any modern ideological parallel is intended, I missed it.

> Irving Wardle, *"A Death in the Family,"* in The Observer, *February 20, 1966, p. 27.*

BILL BYROM

Karoton is about fourth-century Alexandria. Its hero is an Arian who goes over to the Athanasian camp when Constantine succeeds in beating down his rivals. Its publisher commends it for its 'colour' and 'many good scenes': the usual feeble claims made for historical fiction. It is as if the book has special literary merit just because of its setting—an assumption which, I suspect, accounts for the ruin of many an Oxford and Alexandrian novel. And 'many good scenes' suggests that there are bits in-between which the reader need not bother about. On these terms, *Karoton* is a work of genius. On many others, it is boring and silly, the book of a bad film epic, no more. No Alexandrian novel is, of course, complete without sex, practised as variously as in Durrell. Characters are for ever lifting chlamys and parting peplos to reveal hidden fruits. It is entirely absurd, and for all the genuine re-creation of antiquity, it might as well have been set in Bournemouth 1966.

> Bill Byrom, *"An Oxford Novel,"* in The Spectator, *Vol. 216, No. 7183, February 25, 1966, p. 232.*

EDITH FARR RIDINGTON

George Faludy's *City of Splintered Gods* [published in Great Britain as *Karoton*] . . . is a subtle novel of real literary merit. Its setting is Alexandria just before and after the accession of Constantine; its main theme the Arian-Athanasian controversy. A wide variety of people, real and imaginary, are portrayed through incident and conversation. A number of rather startling sexual vignettes are casually thrown in, not just for sensation, but as an essential part of the background for this place and age. The book is full of lively little sketches of fourth century Alexandria, in many ways a city like Lawrence Durrell's twentieth century one; and there are bits of subtle, sometimes aphoristic writing.

> Edith Farr Ridington, in a review of *"City of Splintered Gods,"* in The Classical World, *Vol. 61, No. 6, February, 1968, p. 224.*

ROSEMARY AUBERT

East and West is, in a sense, the log-book of a 40-year odyssey. This selection of poems . . . draws from the work done between 1935 and 1975 by George Faludy, a Hungarian poet already well respected in his native country before political events made him an outcast and a wanderer. He has been by turns a prisoner of the Fascists and later the Communists; a soldier in the U.S. army in World War II; an exile in Morocco and elsewhere; and now, living in Toronto, a quiet man with some nearly silent admirers.

This collection . . . shows us a most remarkable poet. The sensual imagery—not only visual but olfactory and tactile—is a banquet. This is a poet to whom no detail, however minute, is undeserving of full and loving attention. And this is to say nothing of the sensitivity of the many delicate but powerful love poems, or of Faludy's ability to keep alive his joy at the very fact of existence despite his experience of the most degrading hardships. In one poem, a mouse, a pest he has unsuccessfully sought to exterminate, seems to regard the poet not with hatred but with a joyful gratitude that life has not been snuffed out. Life is all that matters. . . .

[In his notes, editor John Robert Colombo] remarks that much of the technical expertise of Faludy's work, his special use of rhythm, for example, has been necessarily lost in translation. What remains, however, serves as a reminder of what we can gain from exposure to the excellent work of some of our contemporary writers from other languages and cultures; those who live alongside us and those who, like Faludy, live among us.

Rosemary Aubert, in a review of "East and West: Selected Poems of George Faludy," in Quill and Quire, *Vol. 44, No. 10, July, 1978, p. 12.*

CHRISTOPHER LEVENSON

[In *East and West: Selected Poems of George Faludy*] it is apparent that Faludy, now 65, writes out of his whole life, a full life that has covered as much ground emotionally as it has geographically. Like Neruda, and in a way that few Canadian poets can equal, he comes across as a man whose grasp of the contemporary world is in several senses all-embracing: he is an experienced traveller, an experienced lover, a cosmopolitan. His subjects range from a moving sequence on his wife dying of cancer, through such historical projects as **"Lorenzo de Medici, about 1480"** and evocations of Western Australia or Morocco, to poems written from a Hungarian prison in the early 1950s. His poetry alternates, and indeed often mediates, between public and private worlds.

Even in translation it is clear that Faludy has a way with metaphor. In **"To Suzanne, from Prison,"** for instance, he thinks of how long he may have to remain in jail:

> And if it is ten or twenty years? I will endure it:
> My eyes will retreat in their sockets like train lamps
> You see at crossings streaming by the fields at night.
> My flesh will dangle from my bones like dough . . .

Sometimes this power grows merely fanciful, as when in **"Ave Luna, Morituri Te Salutant"** the young poet-persona views the pre-NASA moon as "Ophelia's mad breast floating naked / in the dark waters of the sky," or later as a "transcendental angel's rump / sitting tranquil / on heaven's latrine / Hercules' adolescent scrotum," while sometimes, especially in the love sonnets, which strike one as rather conventional and tawdry, a rhetorical strain surfaces that must surely be present also in the original. So too, in **"In the Reading Room of the British Museum,"** one finds a more overt didacticism than is generally acceptable in Canadian poetry. The museum's readers, he concludes, "will know that their lives have had a meaning / That they have not lived vainly, as have billions of others." But both rhetorical and didactic excesses may derive partly from the high status still accorded to the artist as seer in Hungary and indeed many other countries, a role with which Canadian poets are neither blessed nor cursed. (pp.14, 16)

Underlying all is a sense of inventiveness and energy, even in his surprisingly successful treatment of such a conventional motif as the *danse macabre,* Faludy's committed humanism—his impatience with poverty, cruelty, ingnorance, and the tyranny of petty bureaucrats, his boredom with amoral technologies, no less than his enjoyment of what is fully alive in man and nature—shines through even the less inspried translations and obviously springs from a life full of both thought and action, so that I for one am prepared to take on trust the linguistic control of the original and welcome his work as a powerful addition to the the Canadian literary scene. (p. 16)

Christopher Levenson, "A Meeting of the Twain," in Books in Canada, *Vol. 7, No. 9, November 16, 1978, pp. 14, 16.*

M. TRAVIS LANE

George Faludy has been a hero in the grand style of a protesting integrity, and he is, moreover, a better scholar and a better poet than most of us. Working on the translation of Faludy's poetry must have been a humbling experience for his translators. Nevertheless the several writers who have put into English some of Faludy's poems for *East and West: Selected Poems of George Faludy* . . . manage to convey a good deal of what must be Faludy's original proud vitality in their version of his verse. Although the translators use the serviceable, plain "international" style, in which language never commands particular attention to itself, Faludy's imagery controls and illuminates the language, making it strikingly rich and individual. . . . [Few] translators have done so well. The rhythms here are rarely weak, and insight and emotion are powerfully conveyed.

One of the strengths of Faludy's poetry is the education that lies behind it, the habit of thinking and of reading. Our own few "educated" poets (such as Ralph Gustafson) who write in this richly thoughtful manner are rarities among a multitude of poets who write as if they read nothing but each other, who handle a news event as if it were a novelty rattling loosely in a naive sensibility. But Faludy, as much in his love poems as in his satire, "connects" with the universe. (pp. 136-37)

Faludy has become a poet who can tell and rejoice in the full value of life without forgetting or underestimating the force of all that is wrong, ill, or contemptible in the human heart. So fresh is his capacity to express love, compassion, and hate that the vigour of his reactions is, in a few of the late poems, out of proportion to the experience. Philadelphia condemned for eternity because it has muggers or the Robarts Library stomped down for its architecture and atmosphere are inappropriate antagonists for Faludy. He is at his best against opponents his own size—the indifferent Creator, "master of peeps"; or a petty Devil with the face of Werner von Braun in poems such as **"Ave Luna, Morituri Te Salutant"** and **"Darwin's Rubber Plant"** which, now put into English, are among the finest philosophical poems in our language.

"Darwin's Rubber Plant," the simpler and shorter of the two, is a model of how complexities of emotional thought structure a poem. Faludy begins with a series of contrasts between what the Polynesian guide thinks should be the visiting poet's reactions and the poet-speaker's comparative uninterest in the famous rubber plant, his irritated sense of pleasure in the luscious garden and marine landscape admixed with a sense of poor timing, and his angry disappointment at finding himself in the sensuous dreamland of Pago-Pago "too late for marriage, too late for sex," with time only

> for a hurried shedding of clothing
> at some dry and frustrating orgy
> by the exhibitionism
> of this rude and naked landscape . . .

The guide insists on instructing the poet and shows how the rubber plant's fertilization depends on injuries done to the tough wall between stamen and pistil by a tiny parasite. Such absolute dependence seems "senseless and inane" to the poet. But as he raises the hard, phallic-shaped and unattractively coloured flower to his eyes, he sees through the parasite's pinprick holes a kaleidoscopic vision of the gorgeous, inane universe and of the naked being of its Creator. . . . (pp. 137-38)

This ambivalent and courageous applause for "the impresario" carries the poet through the poems of his subsequent imprisonments and through the prolonged dying of his wife. . . . Later in the same sequence the poet, perhaps somewhat awkwardly translated, declares:

> Today it is assumed that all we leave behind is a
>   carcass,
> more dead animal for the garbage heap.
> But five senses don't suffice to grasp
> the entirety of things. This is my only hope.

And five senses are not enough to explain the power of the poetry of George Faludy. (p. 139)

> *M. Travis Lane, "George Faludy: Master of Peeps,"*
> *in* The Fiddlehead, *No. 120, Winter, 1979, pp. 136-39.*

HENRY KREISEL

The earliest poems [in *East and West: Selected Poems of George Faludy*] dating from 1935, have a formal, even a somewhat stiff quality, at least so far as one can judge from the translations. . . . The poet who speaks here seems to derive his inspiration from the Parnassians and from certain aesthetic concepts of late nineteenth century European poetry. In some of the early poems there are also affinities, in suggestiveness, in poetic structure, and in the nature of the imagery, with the French symbolists, and with poets like the early W. B. Yeats. . . . Increasingly, as Faludy's poetry develops, there is a loosening up of emotion, and this is reflected not only in the discursive structure of the later poems, but above all in the rich colloquial quality of the language, which shines through even in translation. At the same time, as such poems as **"On My Father"** clearly demonstrate, Faludy maintains a tight discipline over the subject matter of the poems. Increasingly also, particularly from the 1940s onward, the poet himself moves into the centre of the poems and confronts the reality of the twentieth century world head-on.

Faludy is, in one sense, an autobiographical poet, and insofar as he is that, his is a poetry of experience. But his prime aim as a poet is not to explore the private sensibility, but on the contrary to use his own individual experience in an attempt to illuminate the experience of hundreds of thousands, perhaps even of millions of other human beings. . . .

In poems like [**"Poets Return"**], the individual experience is dwarfed by the communal experience, but Faludy never forgets that we are not talking about a million anonymous deaths, but about the deaths of single, unique individuals a million times repeated. The poet's voice, though it speaks in the first person singular, thus becomes a representative voice. It is a humanist voice raised during a period when the humanist vision seems to have been drowned in blood.

Sometimes the poet is himself the victim, for example in the moving prison poems **"Western Australia,"** **"Monologue on Life and Death,"** and **"To Suzanne, from Prison."** In these poems, written between 1950 and 1952 in various Hungarian jails, he steels himself to endure what must be endured, even if his imprisonment were to last for ten or twenty years. Yet he will return, even if it is "limping or crawling in the mud, with spreading cancer," so that he might once more sit beside his beloved Suzanne on a bench, and see her silver hair among the shafts of sunlight. But even if he must die, he would do so still professing her everlasting faithfulness.

At other times, as in **"Death of a Chleuch Dancer,"** written in Morocco in 1940, the poet is witness to a murder in a marketplace. He watches the blood, which "did not penetrate the dust, but lay and rippled," and it falls to him, a stranger in a strange land, to bear human witness and to remember the murdered dancer. How, he wonders, should he "honour his bittersweet memory?"

> I sat in the dust, destroyed,
>   beside his blood,
>   and beat the flies away.

Modern man confronts two kinds of reality. Human beings are specks in a vast and uncaring universe, never more concretely rendered than in the poems written in Morocco, Mauritania, Tangiers, and Khorb el-Ethel in 1940 and 1941, where men and women act out their lives, make love, are born and die, against an immense panorama of desert and rock, of earth and sky, of "galaxies, crystal nebulae, planets, even stars beyond stars." That is a reality that must be accepted. . . . The other reality is the inferno human beings make themselves. Faludy is of course primarily concerned with the man-made inferno of the twentieth century. This is an inferno with which we are unhappily only too familiar, and which Faludy renders in his prison poems, and in such poems as **"Song of the German Mercenaries,"** **"Ode to Stalin on his Seventieth Birthday,"** and **"The Execution of Imre Nagy."** And there is the ever-present threat of an unspeakable inferno yet to come, for "the future has claws, and they hold plutonium." That reality must be resisted. Against that reality the poet must raise his voice, even if it is drowned out, even if it is not heard.

The universe George Faludy tries to come to terms with is thus a post-humanist one, that has known the ideological terrors of the right and of the left, a world that has known Hiroshima, a world in which cities have been turned into jungles. It is a world in which the inhabitants no longer feel bound together. . . . How, given the monstrous forces ranged against us, can individuals assert their individuality? . . . It is possible to maintain one's integrity; it is possible to be courageous, to have "neither fears nor inhibitions / when attacking a Monster State" (**"Characteristics of G. F.,"**), and it is possible, "thanks to a faint post-scientific shiver of ethics," to refuse "to evolve into / a rat from the traps of Dr. B. F. Skinner" (**"Behaviorism"**). And it is possible to establish lasting friendships, and to commit oneself unreservedly, absolutely, to another, through all of life and to the end of life. . . . So, over against all the terrors, those cosmic ones over which we have no control, and those which we ourselves have fashioned, Faludy sets the power of the human spirit and the power of human endurance.

Faludy, it should be remembered, is not only a poet. He is also, among other things, a biographer of Erasmus. In the epilogue to his biography of Erasmus (*Erasmus of Rotterdam*, published in 1970), he speaks of "the persistent presence of humanism in our own time." He recognizes that this persistence is both complicated and controversial. He singles out Erasmus' pacifism and Erasmus' tolerance as the keys of that humanism, as well as Erasmus' belief that the self-destructive impulses of human beings can be restrained. "Modern humanism," says Faludy, "has also retained Erasmus' contempt for ideological quarrels and, perhaps above all, his belief that man is his own end and not a means—be it to the ends of totalitarian dictatorship or those of technocracy."

Faludy's mature poetry, direct, colloquial, emotional but never sentimental, above all accessible, is in itself a demonstration of the persistent presence of humanism in our own time.

This is in one sense a paradox, and it is all the more remarkable since the evidence of Faludy's own poems seems at times to belie even the glimmer of hope in the survival of humanity that must in the end be the underpinning of any serious profession of humanism. All one can say is that, when all is said and done, the love of life and the wonder of existence triumph over a more apocalyptic vision. A moralist like Faludy could not after all be so angry if he did not care. And so the persistent presence of humanism asserts itself. It may be embattled, it may at times be tenuous, but it clings tenaciously to life. (pp. 28-9)

> Henry Kreisel, "The Humanism of Faludy," in The Canadian Forum, *Vol. LVIII, No. 687, March, 1979, pp. 27-9.*

ALEXANDRE L. AMPRIMOZ

In 1937, at the age of 24, George Faludy published *The Ballads of Villon* in Hungarian. The book must have been popular in Budapest: in 1943 the Nazis burned its eleventh edition, in 1947 the Communists confiscated its fifteenth edition and the twenty-seventh edition was printed in Stockholm in 1976. Even if Faludy would have written only this book, he should at least have generated a minimum of curiosity among Canadian intellectuals had an English version of this text been available. (p. 94)

Several of Faludy's early poems are included in *East and West*. The most impressive of them is also the most Villonesque: **"Danse Macabre"** written in Budapest in 1935. Its English version . . . is just superb and captures both the essence and the rhythm of the French fifteenth century poet. Faludy, like Villon, can express with the force of simplicity, timeless, universal but hard truth. Each of the nine stanzas of **"Danse Macabre"** presents the death of a person, each representing a different social class, namely: The Emperor, The Doctor, The Child, The Harlot, The Banker, The Lady, The Alchemist, The Bishop and The Old Peasant. The last lines of the poem sculpt like a cold marble the universal evidence:

> —We go underground one and all
> years fly like minutes to amaze us
> by the spilt dewdrops of your blood
> be merciful to us Prince Jesus.

This conclusion, beyond its content and artistic quality, has a political message and comes from Faludy, the future member of the Social Democratic Party and Faludy, the outspoken critic of Fascism who, in 1937, signed another significant poem,

"Song of the German Mercenaries." Here again he shows how, in the end, death conquers even ill-reputed, cruel monstrous soldiers. True democracy is Faludy's only political ideal and throughout his whole life he has remained faithful to it. (pp. 95-6)

Faludy's democratic attitude derives very much from Villon who has always been 'a poet of the people', who has always believed that men were equal because they were equal in death. (p. 96)

[The] feeling that one derives by reading *East and West* is that one is reading Faludy and Faludy only. The translators are fine poets or people with a keen sense for poetry and they should be praised for their transparency, their ability to let the reader see the Hungarian poet; dream of the original.

Faludy's **"Wife"** is a great poem because it deals with a private situation, probably his own, and yet reveals something universal. His lines could be addressed to a lover, a mother and, had Paul Claudel written them, we would have no hesitation in understanding that they could constitute a prayer to The Holy Virgin Mary. One can imagine the young Faludy writing this poem in Paris, trying to transcend his suffering. In 1937 his book-length poem *Heine's Germany* had been banned in Hungary and in 1938 both his poems *At the Gates of Pompeii* and his 'translations' *An Anthology of European Poets* were burnt by the Nazis. Only his collection *Laudatur* escaped the hands of iconoclastic fanatics, but it will be burnt by the Communists in 1948. (pp. 96-7)

Death's avidity for the young inspires the poet. Here again Villon echoes in his work. . . . The constant presence of death in life makes you feel "closer to final truth", the only thing that really matters for the poet. [In **"Morocco"**] for the first time Faludy finds pleasure and aesthetic refinement by looking at the end of life. . . . (p. 97)

In the nocturnal poems the **"Danse Macabre"** atmosphere is evoked again. **"Twilight"**, a text written "after the fall of France", presents seven men as "seven corpses" and the rather standard description is enhanced by the casual allusion: "a stage set for some *Walpurgisnacht*". This makes the reader stop and realize that some of Faludy's poems, beyond their simplicity, open on a vast and deep imagery.

Literally speaking, the *Walpurgisnacht* begins on the evening of April 30th and ends at twilight on May 1st. In the Harz Mountains it is believed that every year on that night a witches' sabbath takes place on the Brocken peak. On a first level, the poem symbolically conveys a political message: France has fallen to the hands of the Nazi witches, the same evil spirits that burnt his books.

However **"Twilight"** is a little more subtle. On one hand the poet seems to be in a peaceful environment "reclining on the lawn chair of the garden". Also the presence of the words 'silence' and 'peace' indicate clearly the restful state of the night. There is however the awareness of a war that everyone is trying to ignore. . . . (p. 98)

On the other hand, the negative pole of the poem gravitates around the notion of the supernatural. There are in fact "ghosts in burnooses" who "appear and disappear on the street", there are also "shadows" who "creep over" the moon "like moss upon a tree". These images contribute to the creation of the sinister *Walpurgis Night* atmosphere. Before going further into the woods of symbols, another cultural stop seems appropriate.

Indeed through one of its allusions, **"Twilight"** echoes Paul Verlaine's poem "Nuit de Walpurgis Classique" and this parallel might clarify the ironical rhetoric deployed by Faludy. In the ghostly and rhythmic sabbath of the "Nuit de Walpurgis Classique" we are haunted by "feverish ghosts" and ethereal shapes "full of deep despair". The poet's intuition of the approach of his own disintegration dominates the text and Verlaine's world of dreams is also a world of death where the moonlight gives men the white-grey aspect of cadavers. As he did with Villon's poems, Faludy writes what Verlaine would have felt in 1940 in Morocco, had he been there. No imitation, no anxiety of influence here but simply the belief that there is a universal poet and that he has many lives. Verlaine was 22 when he wrote "Nuit de Walpurgis Classique", Faludy, 27, when he composed **"Twilight"**. In both poems we see the approach of death as the preparation of a grotesque event.... Both life and matter seem ready to fall, without grace from exhaustion. As Verlaine did, Faludy tells us that death is already contained in life and that our existence, like light between night and day is extremely precarious. It is not genial to state the obvious universal truth, but it is almost divine to incarnate such 'Vérité', through poetry. The method Faludy uses, perhaps unconsciously, is the one of Villon's "Ballade des contrevérités". In fact for Faludy, in Morocco there is anxiety only in a peaceful and natural but fenced-in place. As for Verlaine, it takes a ridiculously neat "Lenôtre garden" to express the same feelings. So, a closed-in space that should inspire security against the exterior night actually creates fear for the poet. More generally, every human concept implicitly contains its opposite. (pp. 98-9)

"Death of a Chleuch Dancer" is a less poetic but more dramatic illustration of reality as a 'danse macabre'. In it we witness the murder of a boy by "the man he had been unfaithful to". The intense sensuality of the Morocco poems balances their dark atmosphere. The search for sexual pleasure is only the wise consequence of the universal truth simply stated by the poet in **"The Final Night"**: "Do not mourn, do not tremble, do not rage against death! You will curse in vain."

From death to pleasure, the favourite transitional image is not a sensual one. It seems that with Faludy, situations must be absorbed by the mind first.... In turn, the solving of problems becomes a metaphorical process for sensuality illustrated by the images of chess. (p. 101)

[In **"Tense Night"**] sensuality continues to be associated with a mental game which also symbolized war and conflict.... The chess imagery associated to love and death [in **"Typhoid Epidemic"**] is more than a mere game; it reflects the poet's desire to reduce infinite mystery to bound reality. There is the vain hope, the mad challenge to play against death on an infinite board. But poems like **"The Desert"** and **"The Casbah"** assess in a direct and cutting way the insanity of the project.... Faludy is dealing ... with a fundamental problem. Man is puzzled by beauty and tries to solve the mystery by sexual possession; a method that provides very little cognitive experience and that requires the endless return of the body to its violent structures. Sensual knowledge then becomes the symbol of the impossibility of metaphysical performance.... Only the incarnation of truth could satisfy the poet.... But the chess player's intellectual integrity doesn't allow the poet to take the step beyond. He can only turn towards **"The Casbah"** "where life is sexual and death pleasurable."

Other images reveal the poet's desire to turn to vagueness of sexuality and death into tangible, hard, solid, evident matter.

One can read this type of process in the metallic metaphors associated with sensuality: "The sky is unfathomable tonight and has the keen smell of copper." Such a line creates its own self-illusion. The smell indicating the metallic presence would have one believe in the tangible solid presence that would stop the quest for love or truth—poets have a tendency to advantageously confuse both. (pp. 102-03)

The Morocco poems reveal a rare richness and an intensity that assert the sure talent of a poet who, at the time, hadn't yet reached thirty.

In 1941 President Roosevelt invited George Faludy to come to the United States. The poet lived there until 1946 when he returned to Hungary. During this period, the second edition of *At the Gates of Pompeii* was published and immediately pulped by the Communists.

Only five poems represent this period in *East and West*. **"Brothel-Going"** written in Newburg, Missouri, in 1943 evokes the experience of soldiers visiting whores. With humour and compassion the poet defends the innocence of young men. **"Aurora Borealis"** is an epiphany set in Alaska where Faludy discovers that the colours of the sky and the landscape remind him of a lover's skirt. **"A Pilot is Speaking"** treats of the absurdity of love and death and is vaguely reminiscent of American War Poetry. The poem is rather intense and gives a vivid account of the anatomy of survival.... Less dramatic but more ironical, **"French Intellectuals, 1946"** is quite typical of Faludy's insight:

> Look at these men of pale and intent faces,
> hear these women of no secular graces,
> in this land they live and prosper like weeds after a
>   train.
> They earn their living by singing the praises
> of Russia where they'd only earn a bullet in the brain.

Darwin's Rubber Plant in Samoa leads the poet to reflect upon the origin of life and matter, in a long poem [entitled **"Darwin's Rubber Plant"**] that ends with a revelation. The poet finally meets the creator he had refused to see during his youth or during his years in Morocco.... However the poem is more a metaphysical scream than the expression of religious submission. In fact Faludy's God is a divinity who "casts aside what he will not have". And the poet, along with "the fireworks" and "the planets" is part of the objects that are rejected. The "director of the fireworks" doesn't seem to care much for what he creates. God reveals himself to Faludy so the poet can "applaud him". The point of the poem can be transposed in the tangible world: it is not enough to create, one must learn not to abandon one's creation.

From 1946 to November 1956 Faludy lived in Hungary, mainly in prison and death-camps. Then he spent ten years in London. Both periods are poetically well-represented in *East and West*. During these twenty years his expression seems to have been immense—total. From personal experience and suffering to universal history, Faludy derived well-crafted poems. On this basis we feel that an English edition of his collected works is not only justified but needed.

Faludy emigrated to Canada and settled in Toronto in 1967. It is here that he found the opportunity to compose his work on humanism: *Erasmus of Rotterdam* (1970); it is here that he has brought together his *History of Humanism* to be published sometime in the near future; it is here that he has composed fine Canadian poems like **"Ave Luna, Morituri Te Salutant"** and **"Northern Summer"**. The young Faludy still lives in the poet and what he has brought here shouldn't be ignored as he is helping those who read him 'live their lives'. He is doing so by giving us a vision of our society that very clearly points out that the freedom of one man ends where that of another begins. . . . Faludy is one of our rare Canadian poets truly concerned with social and political conscience while retaining his artistic qualities. . . . (pp. 104-06)

> *Alexandre L. Amprimoz, "Reflection on the Young Faludy," in* The Antigonish Review, *No. 38, Summer, 1979, pp. 94-106.*

JOHN HAVELDA

George Faludy became an important figure on the literary scene of Budapest in the 1930's when his free translations of Villon's ballads appeared. After that, his work was published only to be banned by both fascist and communist regimes in his native land. Since his arrival in Canada in 1967, he has struggled for recognition as a poet despite the publication of *East and West* (1978), a selection of his poems in translation, his *Collected Poems* (1980) in Hungarian, and this second selection [*Learn This Poem of Mine by Heart*]. Of these sixty poems only two appeared in *East and West,* and those by different translators. . . . Immediately after the poems . . . is Faludy's Convocation Address upon being awarded an honorary doctorate from the University of Toronto—an eloquent statement about the power of learning to "somehow arm the spirit to the point that it could prevent the body's collapse," based on an account of how Faludy and some of his fellow prisoners in Hungarian concentration camps lectured on everything from Roman Law to *War and Peace* in order to keep alive a world from which they were isolated. Faludy argues that the death of one prisoner was due to his decision "to sleep rather than talk," and goes on to compare the mentality of those prisoners who were concerned with bodily survival alone, to that of the consumer societies of the world.

The danger of privileging comfort over culture is one of the main thematic concerns of the poems. In a poem written in 1940, the narrator paints a bleak picture of the capitalist democracies: "It looks as if we will stand in slag up to our ears and factory chimneys will smoke us with industrious happiness. We will be free to collect industrial junk / While fat hypocrites cook their profits from our souls." The same concern is echoed 32 years later: "There will be no cart, no place / To which to run—when the rotten basket / Of plenty crashes down upon our heads." Throughout the selection there are references to those who have rejected physical comfort: Erasmus of Rotterdam, Christ, Voltaire, and a Mr. Pang of Cathay who "taught himself to swim and loaded in a boat / his ten thousand and twenty six pieces of gold / and capsized the boat in the centre of the Yangtse / so his money would be of injury to no one."

While some of the poems present a powerful critique of the poisonous effect of technology and consumerism on the West, others attack the oppression of past and present regimes in Hungary. **"At the Hungarian Border"** describes Faludy's arrest after his invitation by the Hungarian authorities to return to his native land; and **"The Ballad of the Hell Hound"** focuses on the mentality of the servants of such regimes. . . . One of Faludy's main criticisms of the country from which he is exiled is its oppression of the writer. . . . Part of the function of these poems is revenge. In a recent interview, Faludy spoke about his reasons for writing his autobiography *My Happy Days in*

Hell: "Whenever I was beaten up . . . I thought, 'I will take my revenge: I will write you,' and this in Hungary is the worst that you can say to someone—that I will describe your character." However, his criticism of censorship, in the regimes under which he has suffered, at times rather insensitively belittles the achievements of writers still working in Hungary. . . . (pp. 98-100)

Although *Learn This Poem of Mine by Heart* suggests the range of Faludy's formal experiments—sonnets are juxtaposed with prosaic anecdotes, quatrains with Whitmanesque songs—many of the translations fail to convey the quality of the originals. . . . [However, the translators] hardly had an easy job. Hungarian has very little in common with Indo-European languages: its syntax and rhythm (the first syllable of every word in Hungarian is stressed) are completely different. As a result, some of the translations sink to the level of journalese. . . . Similarly, the English versions cannot begin to reproduce the important effects of rhyme in the poetry of a language whose plurals nearly all end in *-ak, -ek, -ok,* and *-uk.* . . .

Although these translations are weak in places, they are generally far superior to those in *East and West.* (p. 100)

Despite the improvements from *East and West,* the quality of the translations in *Learn This Poem of Mine by Heart* is still uneven. Occasionally their status as poetry is questionable. Although we should be grateful for the work of those translators who make Faludy's poetry accessible to English-speaking audiences, unless the quality of their work is consistently high, Faludy is never likely to get the attention he deserves. (p. 101)

> *John Havelda, "Co-Translations," in* Canadian Literature, *No. 103, Winter, 1984, pp. 98-101.*

PAUL STUEWE

Faludy's poetry [in *Learn This Poem of Mine by Heart*] derives much of its power from the struggle to preserve humanistic values in an increasingly totalitarian world. This is most evident in poems such as **"Starving,"** which describe life under fascist and communist regimes, where idealists are forced to become realists in the ultimate test of the concentration camp. . . .

But Faludy's insistence upon man as the measure also requires that he condemn such less dramatic and yet perhaps even more pervasive phenomena as the so-called progress of industrial civilization, which renders our cities "Concrete, glass and metal / on the outside. Inside we will have / nightmares, claustrophobia and fear" (**"I Play Chess with an Arab Professor"**). His values transcend political specificities and seek to remind us of the attractions of a world where "There would be long walks, crafts, / Impecuniousness would be appreciated, / As it had been upon a time" (**"Some Lines on the State of the Universe"**).

In contemporary North American society such notions often stand for nothing more than a kind of sentimental nostalgia for a world that never was, but in Faludy's case they represent a solid core of ideals and visions forged in some of our time's most traumatic experiences. *Learn This Poem of Mine by Heart* charts the development of these principles in verse that harries the truth with exhilarating passion, and faces consequences—including the author's candidly confessed inadequacies—with the classic courage of grace under pressure.

> *Paul Stuewe, in a review of "Learn This Poem of Mine by Heart," in* Books in Canada, *Vol. 13, No. 3, March, 1984, p. 31.*

CATHY MATYAS

[A] reader quickly learns about Faludy from the poems [in *Learn This Poem of Mine by Heart*]. . . . His life is his poetry, and the personal is the political. Poems like **"The Wild Duck"** and **"A Prisoner's Ode to a Fine Lady from the Past"** were written while Faludy was a political prisoner in Budapest, between 1950 and 1954. The latter poem was written in the cellar of the offices of the secret police, and it is an example of themes that have preoccupied Faludy for many years. **"A Prisoner's Ode to a Fine Lady from the Past"** is not only an indictment of the totalitarian governments of eastern Europe; it is also a sharp criticism of the passive West. This half of the hemisphere must accept its share of the blame for our impoverished society because of our material concerns and narrow vision. . . . (pp. 352-53)

Faludy's books have been banned by the Nazis and confiscated by the Communists. And yet, in spite of the oppressiveness of the regimes under which he has lived, Faludy has remained a writer who is consistent in his writing and his morals. Indeed, he has been hailed as Hungary's greatest living poet, a point of view which caused some agitation in *The Times Literary Supplement* between 1981 and 1982. In his foreword to *Learn This Poem of Mine By Heart*, George Mikes has included the series of letters to the *TLS* which debate Faludy's greatness. From amidst the critical wrangling, what sticks in my mind is Arthur Koestler's assessment of Faludy. "There is no doubt in my mind that Faludy belongs to the handful of contemporary Hungarian poets of international stature," he writes, "and that among those handful he is *primus inter pares.*"

Faludy was awarded an honorary doctorate by the University of Toronto in 1978, and his convocation address is also included in *Learn This Poem of Mine By Heart*. It provides some interesting insights into both the man and his work. In that address, Faludy speaks of "the survival of humanistic learning in a world where affluence has joined hands with destruction." . . . (p. 353)

[This] address and the sixty poems in *Learn This Poem of Mine By Heart* are not intended to console. Perhaps one can understand Faludy's psychology in terms of a line from **"Casablanca, Summer 1940"**—"better poems are written when I'm afraid"—but I really don't think it's that simple. And our understanding is not made any easier by the fact that there's a tendency, in this half of the world, to dismiss writers with Faludy's background as being inflicted with a kind of ethnic nostalgia. (p. 354)

There is a strong discursive element in *Learn This Poem of Mine By Heart* that I suspect would be minimal in the originals. Many of the poems seem less concerned with poetics than with relating an incident or telling a story. And yet, in spite of the disclaimers [on translation] by both Faludy and [editor John Robert] Colombo, one can't help but be captivated by some of the lines. One example is **"Remembering the Old Family Farmhouse,"** in which the author recalls the death of his grandfather:

> He told me that he would be departing soon
> and that he would leave no trace here on earth,
> because when a man dies all his things
> will be as if he had never been born.

> Only in one place does his being remain:
> on the beam of light that breaks free of him
> and eats right through the reaches of space
> in quick bites, each a million miles or more.
> Not a frame is lost from the film of the past:
> the film unrolls on the beam of light,
> flicking from one fixed star to another,
> as it projects the past of all our lives.

It seems to me that we should acknowledge the deficiencies of translation and get on with reaping from these poems the treasures Faludy has sown. (pp. 354-55)

Cathy Matyas, "Bett-er to Reid Faludy," in Essays on Canadian Writing, *No. 80, Winter, 1984-85, pp. 352-58.*

RAYMOND FILIP

George Faludy follows in the *wieszcz* tradition of Hungarian poets as "pillars of fire." He carries the distinction of having been persecuted by both Nazis and Soviets as a voice of freedom for the Magyar peoples. [*Selected Poems, 1933-1980*] is a must for English readers. . . .

[The translators] have rendered the graceful palatal glides of the love poems, as well as the vicious vowels and strident affricates of the diatribes, into a parallel Anglo world. It is a tribute to their workmanship as translators, or to Faludy's pure lyricism, that the images come across as clean as a laser beam through a transmission fibre.

As with Lithuanian, Latvian, Polish, and the poetry of other Eastern European Christian nations under oppression, Faludy's early verse equates the scourged mother country with Christ crucified. In **"Danse Macabre"** the final steps lead to death as a door to salvation. . . .

As in the Hungarian czardas dance, Faludy's poems often begin with slow melancholy steps that accelerate into a fiery climax. **"Ave Luna, Morituri Te Salutant"** is a case in point. From the luscious lunar imagery of the opening section, it builds to a dramatic denunciation of imperialism upon the moon through technological conquest. . . .

Faludy is more of a bibliophile than a technophobe. . . . He chooses Petronius as a model.

> . . . because he demonstrated, and I learned,
> that mere existence is a greater pleasure,
> hundredfold, than luxury or possessions;
> because, though he loved life, he did not grab it,
> and, even in the direst situations,
> conjured a paradise around himself.
> (Imprisoned by the Reds, I tried to ape him.)

And from Faludy, we can continue to learn that poverty and physical torment are not enough to destroy nobility of heart and mind. (p. 30)

Raymond Filip, "Pillars and Eye-Cons," in Books in Canada, *Vol. 15, No. 2, March, 1986, pp. 30-1.*

J(ürg) F. Federspiel

1931-

Swiss novelist, short story writer, poet, dramatist, journalist, scriptwriter, critic, and essayist.

A prolific writer and winner of many European literary awards, Federspiel explores themes of morality and death as they pertain to Western cultures. He writes in a terse prose style and occasionally employs black humor to convey his view of the absurd and arbitrary nature of humanity's fate. Only two of Federspiel's works have been published in the United States. In *Die Ballade von der Typhoid Mary* (1982; *The Ballad of Typhoid Mary*), an allegorical novel based on the actual case history of the infamous typhus carrier, Federspiel contrasts the optimism of late nineteenth-century America with the fate of the people who come in contact with Mary. The short stories contained in *An Earthquake in My Family* (1985) are taken from three untranslated collections. In these stories, Federspiel uses macabre and romantic elements to explore themes of alienation and human responsibility.

RICHARD EDER

For Thomas Mann it was tuberculosis and for Albert Camus it was bubonic plague. To evoke an image of spiritual rot, they used a real disease and wrote, respectively, *The Magic Mountain* and *The Plague*.

Now a Swiss writer, J. F. Federspiel, has constructed an icy fable around another epidemic. **The Ballad of Typhoid Mary** is a penitential vision of Western prosperity as the incubating phase of a mortal illness.

The story builds around history. The vast wave of immigration between the Civil War and the end of the 19th Century was a foundation of our country's wealth. The classic picture is of impoverished masses arriving in wretched conditions, undergoing hardship and exploitation, and eventually, in a generation or two, sharing in the wealth that they helped to create. . . .

The immigrant ships, crowded and festering, brought disease as well as hopes from Europe. Hence, health stations, quarantine and delousing powder. The precautions were not foolproof. There were periodic scares about epidemics that had managed to sneak in; periodic warnings about an itinerant servant or laborer who went from place to place spreading them.

Ballad, written sparely and elliptically, takes one such "Typhoid Mary" and devises an enigmatic life for her. It is told at second and third hand, each of these filters contributing both to create distance and to infuse a deliberate banality with a quality of legend. (p. 1)

Mary is beautiful, strongly sexed and willed, capable of ferocity and fierce attachments. Does she know what she is? What does she feel? It is a question that obsesses the narrator, and one he cannot fully answer. "What I imagine is this: nothing but a huge indifference," he writes. "The indifference

that attacks us all occasionally and that is now breaking in upon us as the latest and probably final spiritual plague."

In the second-remove narrative she is enigmatic, speaking little and obliquely. She is as touching as Job in her continual flights, as if her condition were a persecution; but she is never given Job's understanding. And she is frightening—as, indeed, Job was to those around him, because affliction is always frightening.

This fugitive figure, who drops from sight for years on end and invariably re-emerges to a cluster of typhoid deaths, serves as more than a curious and unsettling protagonist. The author's purpose goes beyond her.

Mary is the dark side of the Gilded Age, the hidden bill for a decades-long orgy of accumulation and spending, the crack in the edifice. She arrives in wealthy household after household as the very symbol of the good life: a splendid cook unbendingly devoted to her mission of seeing her patrons well fed. Affluence, at least of the kind that the West has adopted as its talisman of virtue over the past century, is a dream that becomes a nightmare.

Federspiel's book is laconic and put together with the greatest skill. Our disquiet mounts imperceptibly; something is winching us higher and higher, and we cannot see what it is. There is a bleakness to the writing, and the arbitrary quality of any parable. This is a chilly work, and perhaps too much so to be quite real. But it is a chill we catch. (p. 8)

> Richard Eder, "The Contagion of a Systemic Illness," in Los Angeles Times Book Review, December 18, 1983, pp. 1, 8.

MARK CALDWELL

J. F. Federspiel calls [*The Ballad of Typhoid Mary*] a ballad. And he's right. It's a ballad along the lines of "99 Bottles of Beer on the Wall"—you keep telling the same story over and over again with slight variations from verse to verse until the school bus driver pulls over and yells at you to stop. Federspiel's tale has more punch, though, since it's not about beer but eating, sex, disease, and death.

Also, of course, it's based on fact. Sometime in the 1860s or '70s, a young female immigrant typhoid carrier did rise out of the murk (Federspiel puts her on a plague-stricken North German passenger ship called the *Leibnitz*); she did, most of the time, call herself Mary Mallon; and she did hire herself out to various hapless New Yorkers as a cook. . . . Mary's stolid tumbril-like passage through life was epically destructive but morally and psychologically flat, the same thing happening over and over again. So [Federspiel is] constrained to dish up a sufficiently varied and compelling sequence of victims for Mary's lumbering innocence to kill off. (p. 4)

The very randomness of Mary's death-dealing progress through her adopted country guarantees Federspiel an automatic and unearned moral complexity—the guilty survive while the innocent perish, or vice versa, or everybody lives, or everybody dies.

But so what? The real test of Federspiel's success is the vigor with which we can imagine each new batch of potential victims, and it seems to me that entropy sets in as the book progresses. Early on, Mary spends an eerily idyllic and affectionate month tending a little mongoloid girl whose mysterious parents hope Mary's mortal gift will work on their unwanted offspring. The kid thrives and Mary gets fired. In later sequences, Federspiel tries to turn everything into an apocalyptic symbol of the American experience. There is, for instance, Mary's stint with Mr. Spornberg, who, compensating for sensory deprivation in childhood, has filled his apartment with hundreds of clocks. When typhus arrives to put him out of his misery, he and Mary join in a rather contrived and unpersuasive clock-bashing rampage—their attack on a world which has left them behind. . . .

All this ends when Dr. Josephine Baker (she really existed) arrives on the scene, clad not in ostrich feathers but righteousness and the epidemiological theories of Robert Koch, and arrests Mary. In the book, she's apprehended in the apartment of her anarchist friend, though in reality she was run to earth in a humdrum Park Avenue household. The change illustrates Federspiel's slightly overheated determination to gussy up the facts and pass them off as epiphanies. . . .

As we encounter her in the book, nothing in Mary's character lifts her above the mundane except the swarms of bacteria milling around in her innocent gallbladder. Only an onslaught of yellow journalism turned her from a competent domestic into a national scourge. Federspiel wants to contrast the flatness of her character with the hair-raising grotesqueness of her fate. But his narrative trickiness (the story is told by a dying doctor who leaves the manuscript to his daughter) and the flashiness

of his invented characters and situations frustrate that desire. Besides, even as fact the story can be outclassed. Mary wasn't the record-breaking typhoid carrier of all time: she was officially credited with only 51 cases and three deaths, whereas the champion, a dairy farmer, delivered the *salmonellae typhosae* in his cream and caused 409 cases and 40 deaths. Federspiel could have got a longer book out of that, if not a better one. (p. 5)

> Mark Caldwell, in a review of "The Ballad of Typhoid Mary," in VLS, No. 23, February, 1984, pp. 4-5.

J. THOMAS GILBOY

[In *The Ballad of Typhoid Mary*] Mr. Federspiel has served us a dish of the universal guilt of parasitism; his Mary parallels Strindberg's cook in *The Ghost Sonata*, who retorts to her employers, "You drain us of sap, and we drain you." The nagging ethical problem of why Mary never turned herself in after she recognized the pattern of death trailing her becomes, for the author, a struggle for survival between the well-to-do class and the subservient class.

Irony sustains this work, though characters are undeveloped. For instance, Mary is at once a destroyer and an indomitable spirit resolved to survive and be creative, though her thoughts and feelings are veiled. Mr. Federspiel has succeeded with a tricky narrative technique and in handling the contradictions of a life in partnership with disease. In the end, however, he does not satisfy the complete expectations potential in his technique and subject.

> J. Thomas Gilboy, in a review of "The Ballad of Typhoid Mary," in Best Sellers, Vol. 44, No. 1, April, 1984, p. 5.

MAUREEN HOWARD

An old account, used as counterpoint to the present, is put to us directly in *The Ballad of Typhoid Mary* . . . by the Swiss writer, J. F. Federspiel. He makes use of a contemporary narrator who tells the grisly tale of Mary Carduff, the most famous carrier of the deadly bacillus. Dr. Howard J. Rageet, a pediatrician who lives on Riverside Drive, is dying as he writes his version of the infamous Mary. He looks up from the manuscript, as it were, to tell us more directly of himself. It is a good intermingling of stories: Rageet (a stand-in for Federspiel, who spends some of each year on the Upper West Side of Manhattan) is witty, urbane, absolutely in charge as he heads to his end. He's terrific on New York: on a simple level Mary's immigrant story, which begins in 1868, allows the doctor to re-create the city with a touching vitality that displays his own sense of life. A subplot provides us with the fact that the doctor's grandfather was one of the enlightened medical men who tried to capture and quarantine Mary over the years when she practiced her death-dealing trade as a cook.

Still, we may rightly ask, why Typhoid Mary?—a catch phrase, in the age of modern medicine a mere reference, even something of a joke. We, after all, are safe from her ravages. But Rageet is dying: it is his final exercise to make her his character. For Mary he can invent households—of perverts, petty *petit bourgeois*, of crabbed families who deserve to die as well as decent folks who don't. Mary is his last case, and she is awful, moving and awful, like a tough little whore done by Brecht. Indeed, the humor of the *Ballad of Typhoid Mary* (it is shockingly funny at points) depends on techniques I read as Brecht-ian. The years flash by in headlines, history is a quick take of triumphs and disasters, yet the song goes by with its overkill, affronts us and entertains us. Mary is crafty but witless in her terrible innocence, a girlish Mother Courage, as much duped by, as cynically duping, her every contact. And it is quite within the dictates of epic theater that Rageet gives Mary, who is indifferent to sexual abuse, a sentimental attachment, a sort of *mariage blanc,* to an anarchist, as well as a pastoral interlude with a child who is a simpleton. Our blighted heroine is hired to fill the role of hit man. Miraculously, the adoring child does not die under Mary's touch. Not aware that another "solution" will be found, Mary is paid off handsomely by her anonymous employer.

A cruel world, indeed. If you don't laugh, you've got to cry—which is Dr. Rageet's attitude. Brecht used both history and legend to his advantage (the Hundred Years' War, the myth of the god Baal). What he gained was a comfortable distance from the facts in order to deliver his uncomfortable message. The material which Federspiel has chosen works for him in the same way, and while his rendering of Mary's life is a grand spectacle, the message, though ever so true, comes at the end of this brilliant parable with an undramatic thud:

> What thoughts might occur to an uneducated woman made to realize that she brings death to others but cannot choose her victims? What I imagine is this: nothing but a huge indifference. The indifference that attacks us all occasion-ally, and that is now breaking in upon us as the latest and probably the final spiritual plague.

> A specter is haunting the world: the specter of hopelessness.

What I see here is the novelist forcing both the maxim for our day and his narrator's hand. Rageet's tone, which has been poised and worldly without a moment's self-pity, is lost.

The failure lies in the doctor's re-creation of Mary—his use of her being far more ingenious and attractive than Federspiel's creation of his self-effacing narrator. Rageet, the dying man, remains underrealized; therefore the past dominates the present while the present instructs us rather too baldly on matters of ecology and capital punishment. The most moving lines of the novel come at the end of the doctor's manuscript:

> Tomorrow I'll try to describe Mary's motives—no, not the motives, there aren't any. But maybe I'll be able to imagine something.

> My imagination is growing dim. I don't need it anymore.

It is a powerful signing off. Mary has come to her end. So has Rageet, the master puppeteer. Unfortunately, we care more about the rendering of her case than we do about the doctor's own life and suicide, although I do see, in what I'd call an overreading, that Rageet is as powerless in facing our larger diseases as his grandfather was in attempting to contain Mary Carduff. (pp. x, xiii)

> *Maureen Howard, in a review of "The Ballad of Typhoid Mary," in* The Yale Review, *Vol. 74, No. 2, January, 1985, pp. x, xiii.*

KIRKUS REVIEWS

[The fourteen extremely uneven stories in *An Earthquake in My Family*] are all based on confrontations between a dis-gruntled first-person narrator and his gross, buffoonish, per-haps imaginary friend, Paratuga. In the title story, the narrator reads obsessively from the history of earthquakes, including the lootings in Managua and inhumane treatment of Chinese in San Francisco and Jews in Basel during times of general social deterioration that, in his opinion, may have brought on the quakes. Meanwhile, Paratuga, in drag, opens a wax mu-seum featuring dummies of the narrator's ancestors; a quake is threatened but never happens; and the narrator summarily concludes, "It takes an earthquake to reveal man's true na-ture."

In other stories, Paratuga introduces the narrator to **"Hitler's Daughter"** (really the child of refugees), and to a young Turk who has sexually tickled his three middle-aged wives to death. Earlier stories try "surprise" plot twists: a little girl who is dragged by fat repulsive aunts to her father's funeral happily witnesses them blown to bits by a sudden wind; a delinquent runs away from home, planning to beat and rob, but ends up charmed by the man who gives him a lift, buys him breakfast and tells stories of the South and adventure. Two standout stories, both concerned with the aftereffects of WW II, cannot, alas, redeem the rest. In **"The Sapper: A Romance,"** a little girl on an Alpine outing gets her foot stuck in the wires of a land mine; the crisis works a reconciliation between the uncle of the trapped girl and an unkempt, ex-demolitions-expert. In **"Oranges on Her Windowsill,"** a quiet story of repentance, a former Nazi returns to Paris to rent an apartment that was the scene of one of his war crimes.

Overall, the subject matter here is uniformly grim, the plots obscure; and the characters, a down-in-the-mouth lot, oddly predictable in their alienation. And the predominantly surreal stories read like a succession of throwaway lines, delivered with a flatness not even awkward translation can excuse.

> *A review of "An Earthquake in My Family," in* Kir-kus Reviews, *Vol. LIV, No. 4, February 1, 1986, p. 145.*

PUBLISHERS WEEKLY

Culled from [Federspiel's] three previous collections published in the '60s and '70s, [the stories in *An Earthquake in My Family*] display a characteristic eccentricity of vision and a way of lighting down anywhere for their setting—Occupied France during and immediately after the war, the Lower West Side of Manhattan—whatever scene seems right for situation and characters. In the first tale, set in Vichy France, a German deserter and his French mistress are seen in shadow through the recollections of their concierge; by deft touch a brutal, sinister atmosphere is evoked, and there it remains after Lib-eration. In **"Hitler's Daughter,"** one of a series featuring the chimerical Paratuga who resides, "fat, quarrelsome, insidi-ous" in the narrator's mind, his host is introduced to Emily Hitler, a "failed abortion" now employed in the stationery department of F. W. Woolworth. While making love, Emily tells all manner of curious tales in an extraordinarily florid vernacular, confident she will conceive an *Uebermensch*. These stories . . . are uniformly surehanded, quirky, driven by an idiosyncratic imagination, in tones ranging from dank to dark to bleakly comic.

A review of ''An Earthquake in My Family,'' in Publishers Weekly, *Vol. 229, No. 7, February 14, 1986, p. 69.*

JOHN BROSNAHAN

Extravagant and *grotesque* aptly describe the content and atmosphere of [the stories in *An Earthquake in My Family*]: an alienated teenager hits the road; a Jewish father and daughter try to escape from occupied France to the freedom of Switzerland during World War II; a man must turn to his bitterest enemy in order to rescue his niece. In each case, Federspiel highlights the psychological turmoil of his characters and illuminates their lives and world with lightning flashes of explosive revelation.

John Brosnahan, in a review of ''An Earthquake in My Family,'' in Booklist, *Vol. 82, No. 15, April 1, 1986, p. 1116.*

ANGELA CARTER

The often powerful and enigmatic stories gathered in *An Earthquake in My Family* originally appeared in German as long ago as the early 1960's. Not one of them was published later than 1973. This means the collection forms more of a prequel than a follow-up to the arrival in English of J. F. Federspiel's recent, cruel, memorable novel, *The Ballad of Typhoid Mary*. Presumably the selection has been made to show what else the distinguished Swiss writer can do besides making scrupulous inquiries into the morality of the typhoid carrier. As it turns out, that is just what he does best; he is most satisfying when he is most somber.

He is the poet of anxiety and obsession, touched by Surrealism, crackling with black humor, but these strengths can be grounded by a leaden whimsy and dissipate themselves in perverse eccentricity. The group of stories about the volatile Dr. Paratuga, who is more of an extended quirk than a man or an idea, are elaborately artificial, strenuously fey, with the ungainly sprightliness of an elephant's polka—like cruel parodies of magic realism. Yet this writer can achieve extraordinary effects and has the capacity to move the intellect as forcefully as the heart.

Mr. Federspiel is not a writer with a message of good cheer. He used a quotation from Thomas Wolfe for *Typhoid Mary*, ''Life is strange and the world is bad.'' This motto also applies in full measure to these earlier stories. Only the inmates of a lunatic asylum dare to speculate about happiness in **''The Man Who Brought Happiness.''** One madman believes himself to be the painter van Gogh, another madman. Insanity squared. This is a characteristically Federspiel paradox. The self-styled van Gogh defines happiness, modestly enough, as ''being able to bear everything and finding life good.'' Then they lock him up for the night and take the key away.

It seems that Mr. Federspiel spends a part of each year in New York, but his sensibility is that of the Northern European who regards with gentle amazement a country where the right to pursue happiness is written into the Constitution. Mr. Federspiel's is a pessimism of the intellect with a vengeance. But—another Northern European characteristic—he can certainly see the funny side of the sad trap of mortality, in which his characters so often find themselves caught in the most ludicrous positions.

For death comes often in these stories and in antic disguises. . . .

Mr. Federspiel writes with affectionate understanding and without sentimentality about children and adolescents, always the sign of a good heart. There is the boy Malaan in **''Prospects for an Expedition,''** who plans a violent and gratuitous crime only to be freed from the compulsion to perform it by the sheer liveliness of his intended victim. And there are the mountain children, dozens of them, in **''The Sapper: A Romance,''** who stumble upon a live, unexploded bomb and are saved.

This pastoral and restrained tale turns out, wonder of wonders, to depict a very fairish simulacrum of that ''promised village,'' where, in spite of all the squabbling and gossip and heavy drinking, people do take care of one another, almost out of habit, ask for neither gratitude nor love in return, are kind as simply as they breathe. All is not lost.

Some of the stories in *An Earthquake in My Family* are not so brilliant, but J. F. Federspiel is a very fine writer indeed.

Angela Carter, ''Missing the Titanic, Drowning in the Bath,'' in The New York Times Book Review, *April 6, 1986, p. 7.*

Dick Francis

1920-

(Born Richard Stanley Francis) Welsh-born English novelist, short story writer, autobiographer, and biographer.

A prolific author of suspense fiction, Francis is best known for his novels which focus on corruption in the sport of horse racing. He draws upon his many years as a professional jockey, as well as his experience as a newspaper correspondent and a World War II pilot, to create realistic settings in which the integrity of an organization or an individual is threatened. Physical and psychological pain are important elements in Francis's fiction; many of his protagonists have sustained injuries or must care for disabled dependents, while others have suffered career losses or divorces. When they become involved in criminal investigations, his characters often become victims of assault, torture, or attempted murder. Francis incorporates some of his personal attitudes into his novels, but he does not attempt to moralize or philosophize, preferring to allow his characters to stoically confront the turmoil in their lives. Although Francis has been faulted for shaping overly violent, formulaic novels and for creating idealized characters, he has been praised for his fast-moving plots, his unpretentious prose style, and for carefully researching his subjects. Francis has won several literary awards, including Edgar Allan Poe Awards for *Forfeit* (1968) and *Whip Hand* (1979), and his work is among the most commercially successful in the crime and mystery genre.

In his early fiction, Francis depicts the racing world with which he is so familiar. *Dead Cert* (1962), his first novel, is the story of a jockey who uncovers and eliminates a race-fixing scheme. This subject—the integrity of horse racing threatened by dishonest gamblers—resurfaces in *Forfeit,* which centers on a racing journalist whose invalid wife discovers a bookmaking scheme. *Odds Against* (1965) and *Whip Hand* are the only two of Francis's novels to share the same protagonist. These books involve Sid Halley, an ex-jockey who has become a private investigator and discovers unscrupulous elements in the racing field. *Reflex* (1980) is generally regarded as a successful departure from Francis's usual style. In this work, Francis concentrates less on detailing brutality and more on complex psychological character development. Other representative Francis novels about horse racing include *Nerve* (1964), *For Kicks* (1965), *Flying Finish* (1966), *High Stakes* (1975), and *Trial Run* (1978).

In several novels, particularly his later works, Francis portrays underworld activities in fields other than horse racing. For example, he investigates gold mining in *Smokescreen* (1972); art in *In the Frame* (1976); technology in *Twice Shy* (1981); high finance in *Banker* (1982); and the liquor industry in *Proof* (1985). Francis's novels about horse racing, however, as evidenced by his recent novel, *Break In* (1986), remain his most popular and critically successful books. John Welcome summed up the opinion of Francis's admirers by stating that "[Francis] has made racing into a microcosm of the contemporary world, with its flawed values and ruthless manipulation." Francis has also written a well-received autobiography, *The Sport of Queens* (1957), and *Lester—The Official Biography* (1986), a biography of the renowned English jockey, Lester Piggott. *Dead*

Cert was adapted for film, and *Odds Against* was the basis for the British television series "The Racing Game."

(See also *CLC,* Vols. 2, 22; *Contemporary Authors,* Vols. 5-8, rev. ed.; and *Contemporary Authors New Revision Series,* Vol. 9.)

BARRY BAUSKA

[The] whole point about Francis novels—indeed, about Mr. Francis himself—is that a person can do more than one thing well.

In a brief but very useful review of Francis' second novel (*Nerve,* 1964), Anthony Boucher hazarded the opinion that unlike several other celebrities who had tried (and failed) to create mysteries from their fields of specialization . . . Dick Francis seemed "an unusually intelligent suspense novelist," eminently capable of translating his experiences around steeplechase courses into stirring detective fiction. Since that time Mr. Francis has rated himself at the very solid pace of a novel a year, and in the process has more than vindicated Mr. Boucher's judgment. Indeed it is now reasonable to accept the *Times*

Literary Supplement reviewer's contention that "Mr. Francis (is) most people's present first choice as crime writer."

Presumably Dick Francis got there, as he has gotten everywhere else in his career, by a great deal of hard work. His account of first learning to ride . . . [in his autobiography *The Sport of Queens*] is most interesting for what it reveals about the young boy who went on first to become England's champion steeplechase jockey, and then to capture just about all of the stakes worth winning in the realm of detective fiction. . . . (p. 238)

[A] determination (to gut it out, regardless of the odds, until one gets it right) is a central feature of Francis' writings and entire career. In the autobiography, in talking about riding show horses as a youth, he describes the lessons he learned from an uncompromising father. . . .

The father's professional attitude took solid, if more gentle, hold in the son. Whether riding a donkey around the farm or a champion jumper around Aintree, or learning to fly a plane or doing his own writing for *The London Sunday Express*, Dick Francis has consistently pushed himself to do the new thing well. Just as that has meant, in his case, demonstrating capabilities both substantial and varied, so too do we find his protagonists—who are in one form or another versions of Francis himself—to be multi-talented individuals. In *Odds Against* (1965), Sid Halley, an ex-steeplechase jockey, wins over a most off-putting father-in-law by soundly trouncing him at chess; the central character in *Flying Finish* (1966) is, through no fault of his own, an Earl, but he also rides as an amateur steeplechase jockey, and (crucially, for the outcome of the novel) is an excellent small plane pilot as well. The hero of *Bonecrack* (1972), Neil Griffon, is by trade a dealer in antiques, but he fills in formidably as trainer of his father's stables when the old man is stricken ill. Sooner or later, of course, all Francis heroes—be they jockeys or trainers or transport pilots or actors or bloodstruck agents—must also of necessity become detectives.

In considering the make-up of the Francis hero it is interesting to examine Francis' attitude toward amateurism/professionalism. Clearly he has little interest in conduct or effort that might be considered "amateurish," nor in professionals who do not take their professions seriously. Just as clearly he greatly admires the true professional—the man who goes about his work with the confidence based on full knowledge of what is required and an awareness that he has the skills to attend to those demands. Francis' greatest affection, however, seems reserved for what might be called the "amateur professional"—the figure who does what he does (with all the talent and commitment of the true professional) for the love of the thing, and not for money. (p. 239)

Such a personality occupies the center stage of Francis' first novel, *Dead Cert* (1962): the narrator, Alan York, is an amateur steeplechase jockey who rides for the thrill and the challenge of racing. . . . York is a very good rider; he is also very much a gentleman (he tolerates, but does not really join in the rough humor of the other jockeys). What the gentleman finds, however, as the novel unfolds is that he is pitted against a set of characters who have no notion of gentlemanly rules at all, and it is their game he must play if he is to survive. Fairly early in the going York receives some preliminary schooling for what lies ahead when he submits to a grilling by the guardian aunt of a young lady whom both he and a professional jockey, Dane, are courting. . . .

A true gentleman, York neither embarrasses the awful aunt, nor undercuts his rival by laying the facts out before her. And by the novel's end, when Uncle George is revealed as the head of a vicious protection racket and the director of a savage manhunt to track down and kill York, our hero chooses not to turn him into the police, but instead tosses him a gun so that he may take the gentlemanly way out (obligingly, he does). . . . (p. 240)

One thing Francis heroes are not is James Bond types. To be sure, their abilities are considerable and diverse; they are extremely resourceful, always capable of rising to the crisis at hand. But at the same time they are usually—outside of their area of particular expertise, and at least on the surface—fairly ordinary people. In *Flying Finish* (1966) Henry Grey is described by a fellow worker (female) as a "prim, dim, sexless *nothing*. He's not alive." His own self-assessment is scarcely more exciting: "A repressed, quiet, 'good' little boy I had been: and a quiet, withdrawn, secretive man I had become. I was almost pathologically tidy and methodical, early for every appointment, controlled alike in behaviour, handwriting and sex." . . . But if Grey is no James Bond, he certainly can ride horses, fly planes, and—by the book's end—prove that he can shoot to kill if that is what he must do. . . . (pp. 240-41)

In another flying novel, *Rat Race* (1970), Matt Shore—"A flat matt name. Very suitable"—describes himself as being "as negative as wall paper." But the negative goes positive at the crucial moment, and Shore saves the day in what Newgate Callendar accurately describes as "an in-the-air rescue sequence that would make you really and truly angry if you had to put it down." A last instance of the hero who succeeds in spite of his appearances is David Cleveland (*Slay-Ride* 1973). Cleveland turns out to be Chief Investigator for the British Jockey Club, but his looks and demeanor lead just about everyone (except, of course, the reader) to write him off along the way. Cleveland is the sort of person whom people overlook or fail to wait on in restaurants, and whose name is invariably forgotten. None of that deters him, however, from solving a crime that had baffled the entire Norwegian police force.

Another feature of Francis heroes, particularly in more recent works, is that they have suffered wounds, either physical or psychological or both, which they must endure. Jonah Dereham (*Knockdown*, 1974) has taken so many falls in his steeplechasing career that he must be bound together with webbing (a fact that the villains of the piece do not ignore). Sid Halley (*Odds Against*) has a hand so badly crippled that he tries to keep it concealed in his pocket. Divorce, or separation from one's spouse, figures conspicuously in Francis' novels. For the author such a condition seems to stand for the ultimate psychological pain of dislocation (the heroes of *Rat Race, Blood Sport*, and *Odds Against* have all been left by their wives, and in *Enquiry* Kelly Hughes' wife is killed instantly in a car accident). There is also in Francis' world very often the spectre of a relative whose disabilities weigh heavy upon the central protagonist. In *Forfeit* (1968) James Tyrone's wife is a victim of polio, confined for life to an iron lung; in *Smokescreen* (1973) Ed Lincoln's daughter is retarded; and in *Knockdown*, Jonah Dereham's brother is a soggy, loutish alcoholic whose final fate gives that recent novel Francis' most poignant ending.

Such are the handicaps Francis' protagonists must bear . . . and endure and overcome. Because those protagonists really are romantic heroes, they never whine about these things; instead they bite the bullet, and go on with the business of living—often in a kind of Hemingwayesque fashion. The clearest manifestation of this is Sid Halley (*Odds Against*). Beginning life as a natural child (his father was killed before he was born), he rose to become, briefly, an outstanding steeplechase jockey. Then, abruptly, he suffered a crippling fall, which smashed his hand, his career, and his marriage. Halley does not complain about his fate, but it remains something he carries with him always. . . . (p. 241)

The crucial, if somewhat grotesque, turning point for Halley is his linking up with Zanna Martin, a woman who might have been quite attractive had not her beauty been blasted away in a childhood fireworks accident. . . . Much of the heroism of Francis' protagonists lies in their ability to transcend their handicaps and prevail over them; in the case of Halley and Miss Martin that comes to mean literally forcing themselves to emerge from their protective shadows.

It is clear from Francis' novels that the steeplechaser's gritty commitment to the 'chase (in spite of bumps and bruises and cracked collarbones—Francis sustained something like a dozen of those in his riding career) is reflected in the shaping of his protagonists. It is interesting, for example, that at the beginning of at least three works (*Odds Against, Rat Race,* and *Blood Sport*), the protagonists are seen "nursing their bruises," having consciously taken up positions of detachment from the world about them. Hurt by life in the past, Sid Halley, Matt Shore, and Gene Hawkins now stand carefully apart from it, stoically experiencing life at second-hand. Ultimately, however, the crises that inform each of these novels force them back into the fray (where, quite clearly, Francis feels they belong, and where they perform, naturally, extremely well).

Perhaps the most interesting of these particular novels is *Blood Sport* (1968), which features in Gene Hawkins, the closest Francis comes to drawing a Bond-like protagonist: An authentic British agent, he sleeps very lightly with his Luger tucked under his pillow; when awake he is a master of several Eastern European languages, and betrays a slightly annoying inclination to talk like Sam Spade or Philip Marlowe. . . . But beneath this slick surface Hawkins remains a Francis character through and through. "I look ordinary," he tells us at the beginning, and clearly he feels worse: "My work, of its nature, set me apart. And I had no one to go home to, to share with, to care for. The futility and emptiness had gone down to my roots, and nothing seemed to lie ahead but years and years more of what I was already finding intolerable." . . . His response to this life is simply to try to survive it: "One more day, I thought in the end. Anyone could manage just one more day. If one said that firmly enough every night, one might even finish the course." Ultimately it is his expertise at his profession, his ability to get the job taken care of cleanly, honestly and without resort to Bondian flashiness, that allows him to get through his day—the adventures of *Blood Sport*—and then to bed (alone).

If one were to envision the "typical" Dick Francis novel, it would go something like this: At the outset something has happened that looks wrong (a jockey is set down by a board of enquiry that seemed predetermined to find him guilty; a horse falls going over a final hurdle it had seemed to clear; horses perfectly ready to win consistently fail to do so). The narrator-protagonist (usually not a detective, but always inherently curious) begins to poke around to try to discover what has occurred. In so doing he inevitably pokes too hard and strikes a hornet's nest. The rest of the novel then centers on a critical struggle between the searcher-after-truth and the mysterious agent of evil, whose villainy had upset things in the first place, and is now turned full-bore upon the hero. In Fran-

cis' first novel [*Dead Cert*] this climaxes in a marvelous and protracted chase scene: the hero astride his gallant horse, Admiral, pursued and hemmed in by an entire fleet of taxis ("Marconicars") which are being directed in their manhunt by . . . [a] fanatical voice crackling through their radios. . . . That voice, in a variety of accents, has been the voice of a great many Francis villains: malicious, dangerously disturbed, and the source of an awful tension.

Sooner or later this creature will get his shot at the hero, and when he does he can be counted on to take it as nastily as possible. The sadism of the villain's revenge is especially prominent in several of the earlier works. In *Nerve* (1964), Rob Finn is hung up in an abandoned tack room, drenched with icy water, and left to die in the wintry night; in *Odds Against* (1965), Sid Halley's already crippled hand is smashed repeatedly with a poker; and in *Flying Finish* (1966), Henry Grey is compelled to serve as close-range target for young Billy's sadistic marksmanship. . . . (pp. 241-43)

Billy of course is just a hit man (perhaps more accurately, a near-miss man); he is not the controlling agent behind the scenes. Indeed one might say he hasn't the name for it, for in Francis' early works especially there was a tendency to tag the main villain with a hyphenated last name: George Ellery-Penn (*Dead Cert*), Maurice Kemp-Lore (*Nerve*), Mr. Rous-Wheeler (*Flying Finish*), Charles Carthy-Todd (*Rat Race*). In his last half-dozen efforts Francis has avoided tipping his hand in this manner, though there is still an occasional "villainous name" that crops up: Vjoersterod (*Forfeit*), Enso Rivera (*Bonecrack*).

There is not much to be gained from faulting Francis for such past flaws, since the whole evolution of his writing has been to improve. In part that improvement has meant moving steadily beyond such stark (indeed melodramatic) confrontations of Good and Evil as I have just been discussing. What I have described as the "typical" Dick Francis novel really applies best to his earliest works (*Nerve, Odds Against, Flying Finish*). In recent years, though the plots may run along similar lines, Francis' focus has been increasingly directed at the protagonist himself, and at considering what goes into the making not so much of a "hero" as of a good man. This line, traceable through *For Kicks* (1965), *Blood Sport* (1968), *Forfeit* (1968), *Rat Race* (1970), *Bonecrack* (1971), and *Knockdown* (1974), seems plainly the direction of Francis' future development as a novelist. In such works survival is still a key concept—"everyone lives on a precipice"—but it is no longer the ability / capacity to endure the villain's tortures, but rather the strength to prevail over one's own self-doubts and private fears. Surely it is not mere coincidence that as a focus of tension physical pain is being supplanted by psychological strain as Mr. Francis himself grows farther and farther away from his riding days. The result, of course, is that Dick Francis is becoming less a writer of thrillers and more a creator of literature—while remaining, as he always has been, splendidly readable. In shifting much of his emphasis from external (plot) tension to internal (psychological) stress, Mr. Francis is obviously working with more difficult materials. Not surprisingly, the transition has had some rocky moments; *Blood Sport* and *Rat Race*, for instance, are clearly flawed novels, especially in the early going, yet even they steadily build for the reader. And in *For Kicks, Bonecrack, Knockdown,* and *High Stakes* (all of which happen to be centrally concerned with horseracing, and are to my mind Francis' finest works) the author has achieved everything that could be asked of him: carefully controlled suspense, sensitive and convincing characterization, fine dramatic climaxes, and three almost perfect last pages.

In Anthony Boucher's initial review of *Nerve,* he wrote, "The author constructs his suspense to skillfully, builds his characters so firmly and, in short, writes so well that one's reaction is not, 'How can a great jockey write such a good novel?' but rather, 'How can such an excellent novelist know so much about steeplechasing?' That response is still there for anyone reading a Francis novel for the first time, and of course is one of the special pleasures for anyone who goes to the races himself. At the same time, for all the genuineness of the racing scene—the marvelous horses (Admiral, Template, Moon Rock, Lancat, River God), the smells of walking rings and the crush of betting crowds—it remains quite clear that the logical point of comparison to this jockey-turned-novelist has really never been a Lester Piggott or Gordon Richards or Willie Shoemaker, but rather a John Buchan or Dorothy Sayers, or in fact that noted doctor and spiritualist, Sir Arthur Conan Doyle. (p. 244)

> *Barry Bauska, "Endure and Prevail: The Novels of Dick Francis," in* The Armchair Detective, *Vol. 11, No. 3, July, 1978, pp. 238-44.*

PHILIP LARKIN

It was the late Edmund Crispin who recommended Dick Francis to me. "If you can stand the horse parts", he said, "the mystery parts are quite good." I found this an understatement in reverse. The horse parts, as everyone knows by now, are brilliant vignettes of a tiny portion of English life: the world of steeplechase racing. Novel by novel we meet the jockeys, the trainers, the owners (usually being taken for a ride in another sense), the bookmakers, the bloodstock agents, the sporting journalists. We learn what it is like to be a stable boy at a skinflint North Country trainer's, to ride in freezing February fog . . . , to be Clerk of a run-down course that wrong-doers are determined to close. But the mystery parts, if inevitably less realistic, arise naturally from the greed, corruption and violence that lie behind the champagne, big cars and titled Stewards; they concern horse-pulling and betting frauds, and lead to wads of used notes in anonymous envelopes, whispered warnings by telephone, and sudden hideous confrontations with big men in stocking masks.

These two elements are welded into adult reading by the Francis hero. Francis has no recurrent central character, no Bond or Marlowe; his heroes are jockeys, trainers, an owner who manufactures children's toys, a journalist, a Civil Service screener. But they tell the story in the first person, and they tend to sound alike; they are bachelors, or widowers, or separated: very twice-shy men, living in caravans or undistinguished flats. Sometimes they are handicapped psychologically (*Blood Sport*), physically (Sid Halley in *Odds Against* has a crippled hand) or circumstantially, in *Forfeit* living with a paralysed wife, in *Knock Down* with an alcoholic brother. Their narratives are laconically gripping, and graphic in a way that eschews Chandler's baroque images and Fleming's colour-supplement brand names. They combine unfailing toughness with infinite compassion.

There is a lot of pain in Francis novels, which puts some people off. Their heroes are beaten up thoroughly and in detail, taking days to recover; we are regularly reminded that steeplechase jockeys are used to breaking their bones and rapid recoveries. There can be pain for horses, as in *For Kicks* or *Flying Finish,* and pain between men and women, as when the hero in *Forfeit* has to perform the nightly routine of attending to his paralysed wife's physical needs when she has just learnt of his unfaith-

fulness to her. But there can be liberating happiness also: the loner heroes often find warmhearted unselfish women (Francis's women are usually as nice as his men, with the exception of a few fiendish bitches), and the love scenes, usually long deferred, are unpretentiously honest. *Bonecrack,* which I suppose I should under pressure nominate as my favourite, is a moving, original and exhilarating study of parallel escapes from parental domination.

It would perhaps be pushing it a little to say that each Francis novel is a different story enclosing the same story, but it seems like this at times, as if the whole sequence were an allegory of the suffering individual inside endless inimical environments. Francis gives colour to this by his perversely-uninformative titles. One can just remember that *Nerve* is about a jockey losing, or not losing, his nerve; *In the Frame* is about sporting pictures; *Flying Finish* is about horse transport by air. But what is *Rat Race*? *For Kicks*? *Risk*? They seem designed to throw the station-bookstall reader into an agony of indecision as he struggles to remember whether he has read them before. He needn't worry: they are all worth rereading.

The theme of the latest, *Reflex,* is, I suppose, photography. . . .

One hesitates to criticize a Francis novel, but *Reflex* displays in a less extreme form a defect of its predecessor *Whip Hand,* in which three themes proved in the end to have nothing to do with each other. Francis usually observes Chekhov's dictum that if there is a pistol hanging on the wall, sooner or later someone in the story must fire it, but in fact the sister search is irrelevant to the photography problem, and when she is found in unhappy circumstances the hero does nothing to rescue her. . . . I have a feeling that Francis is tending to put too many themes into his books at present to compensate for the lack of real dominance of any one, and is failing to relate them satisfactorily: this, coupled with a certain blandness in the writing, suggests there may be a limit to the number of imaginative thrillers to be derived from the steeplechase scene. One can't exactly complain about this: Francis has written a dozen superb novels in less than twenty years, but there have been occasions since 1972 when the vein has shown signs of being worked out. This is one of them.

> *Philip Larkin, "Four Legs Good," in* The Times Literary Supplement, *No. 4045, October 10, 1980, p. 1127.*

JEAN M. WHITE

By now, the racing metaphors have been exhausted in praise of the thoroughbred thrillers of Dick Francis, who has bred a string of sure-fire winners with galloping suspense down to the finish wire.

In *Twice Shy* . . . , Francis forsakes his jockey-heroes (the racing game still provides the back-drop) for the world of high technology and the men who manipulate computers for greedy ends. And he makes computer programming as thrilling and exciting as a horse race.

The Franciscan trademarks are all there: a devilishly clever, twisting plot; villains who are vicious and unreasoning bullies; violent, non-stop action; reluctant heroes who are both decent and flawed; colorful and convincing characters.

In *Twice Shy,* Francis offers two narrator-heroes—Jonathan and William Derry, brothers, who tell their stories with an interval of 14 years.

Jonathan is a 33-year-old physics teacher and expert marksman whose excitement comes in the classroom when a student shows a flash of intellectual passion over the mysteries of the universe. A friend in the computer business gives Jonathan three cassettes of Broadway musicals. When the friend is killed in a suspicious boat explosion, Jonathan finds the cassettes are tapes of a computerized handicapping system.

While his wife and friend's widow are held hostage, Jonathan traces the tapes to a feisty old widow, whose husband had worked out the system on paper. Jonathan cleverly manages to free his wife and fool the gambler-thugs. A raging bull of a man named Angelo is convicted of the murder of the cheap hustler who stole the original papers of the handicapping system.

Then comes a break of 14 years. William, the younger brother by 18 years, picks up the story.

Jonathan and his unhappy wife have moved to California for a fresh start. William, grown too tall for his boyhood dream of becoming a jockey, is managing a string of horses. When Angelo, freed from prison, seeks a man named Derry for revenge, he breaks into William's cottage, swinging a bat in a destructive swath.

William must now trace the long-forgotten tapes, before Angelo's fury is once more unleashed on the Derry brothers for an explosive showdown.

Twice Shy is another winner, although Francis is not so sure-footed as usual in breaking new ground as a suspense writer. The structure—with two narrators and an interval of 14 years—breaks the momentum of the novel. And one wishes Jonathan, a far more interesting and complex man than William, would have told the story to the end.

> *Jean M. White, in a review of "Twice Shy," in* Book World—The Washington Post, *April 18, 1982, p. 6.*

STANLEY ELLIN

In *Twice Shy,* Dick Francis again deals with English horse racing, a sport and business that he, once a successful jockey and later a racing journalist, obviously knows inside out. His protagonist, Jonathan Derry, is a thirtyish, gentle, reflective physics teacher whose avocation is rifle shooting and who has won medals in competitions. His acquaintance with horse racing, as the novel begins, is limited to trying to keep his teenage brother, William, aimed toward a university education and away from dreams of becoming a jockey. This acquaintance, however, intensifies when Jonathan suddenly finds himself in possession of a computer program worked out by a brilliant eccentric, Liam O'Rorke, and recorded on cassettes. The program provides a handicapping system bound to make money for the bettor using it if—a large if—he uses it properly.

Credit the author with having done his microchip homework well. A device such as a magical betting system can be pretty hard for the reader to swallow, but Francis, by means of a precise description of the system's limitations as well as its potential, makes it palatable. (pp. 13, 23)

Jonathan plans to get the cassettes to their rightful owner, O'Rorke's feisty widow. But Harry Gilbert, proprietor of a chain of betting shops, and his son Angelo, an almost psychopathically quick-on-the-trigger tough, plan to get the cassettes for themselves. The showdown between Jonathan and Angelo, handled with consummate skill by both Jonathan and

the author, winds up with Angelo in prison for the murder of the man who handed Jonathan the computerized system.

At this point, Francis undertakes a risky tour de force in narrative: a leap ahead to that time 14 years later when Angelo is released from prison with a rabid hunger for both vengeance and the betting system, and a shift in protagonist from Jonathan to his younger brother, William, who at 29 is a successful horse trainer. William, with Jonathan out of the picture, must now deal alone with Angelo. By subtly increasing the tempo and tension of the narrative, Francis handles this confrontation in fine style.

Jonathan and William Derry are among the author's most appealing characters. The computerized betting system actually makes sense, the story plausibly portrays integrity and decency under fire, and the writing is spare, clean and always effective. *Twice Shy* rates among the best of the Dick Francis canon, a novel bound to add numbers to his already huge audience. (p. 23)

> *Stanley Ellin, "Murderous Entertainment," in* The New York Times Book Review, *April 25, 1982, pp. 13, 23.*

T. J. BINYON

With [*Banker*] Dick Francis seems to have taken a quantum leap in a new direction. His hero-narrator, Tim Ekaterin, unlike those many predecessors crippled with psychic or physical wounds, is a bright, cheery individual; he's even described as a "child of the light" by another character. The only fly in his ointment is that he's deeply in love with the wife of a man who is gradually succumbing to Parkinson's disease: a reversal, this, of the situation in a much earlier novel, *Forfeit*. The difference in treatment shows the gigantic advance the author has made, as novelist, over the past fourteen years.

Ekaterin is a merchant banker; he persuades his fellow directors to put three million pounds into buying a stallion for a leading stud farm—an investment which, some time later, comes to look rather less sensible. . . . But not until some considerable time later, as—another departure from the earlier Francis—the action is not compressed into a short period, but stretched out over three whole years, during which a number of hares are started and red herrings dragged across the path while behind the scenes preparations are made for the dénouement. Nurtured on previous books, we know that something appallingly dreadful is going to happen: it does, but while we're waiting for it suspense whitens our hair. At the same time *Banker* preserves all the old Franciscan virtues: it's simply and strongly told, with a number of well-observed characters and a great deal of recondite information on a technical subject—we've recently had photography and computers; now it's pharmacology's turn. With each succeeding novel one is tempted to say that this must be his best yet: here the extension into a new form, the ease and confidence with which new problems of novelistic technique are dealt with, makes it necessary to repeat the statement once again.

> *T. J. Binyon, in a review of "Banker," in* The Times Literary Supplement, *No. 4158, December 10, 1982, p. 1378.*

EVAN HUNTER

It seems to me . . . that the most astonishing thing about [Dick Francis'] work is his ability to juggle three elements—mystery, horses and exotic information—in each of his novels and keep them suspended magically in the air. It is not easy to juggle a horse. It is even more difficult to ring in so many variations on horses while simultaneously keeping those other two elements airborne. In *Banker,* Mr. Francis' new novel, horses and exotic information are more heavily weighted than mystery, and perhaps die-hard fans may carp at the imbalance. But the author has written a brief introduction to allay their fears. . . . (p. 15)

If ever there was clear warning, this is it. Mr. Francis, in effect, is telling us that there will not be so much as a threat of violence until page 56, that there will not be a murder (and that offstage) until page 123 and that until he is ready to weave his various strands together we must be content to learn all about merchant banking (the exotic information) and the breeding and healing of thoroughbreds. Whether Mr. Francis' fans will sit still through all of this is something of a gamble. But he has always been one to take risks.

Tim Ekaterin, like most of Mr. Francis' heroes, is a sympathetic man in his 30's. He is also madly in love with his boss's wife. Here the chaste sex of Mr. Francis' earlier novels is even more noticeable in that his would-be lovers scarcely exchange more than glances, hand touches and an occasional discreet kiss. In reviewing *Twice Shy* (1982), one critic said that Mr. Francis "has grown too fond of his heroes." I don't know what that means. If a writer isn't fond of his heroes, he shouldn't be writing about them in the first place. It is easy to become as fond of Tim Ekaterin as Mr. Francis is. And when, early on, he convinces his banking board to invest heavily in a horse breeder whose future is predicated on the stud performance of a star race horse, we can only admire and applaud his courageous, offbeat stand—even if we know it will lead to heaps of trouble later on.

The trouble starts when the thoroughbred's progeny proves to be faulty—here a missing ear, there a malformed heart valve, here a deformed foot, there a foal born dead—and this is when the novel begins gaining true force and momentum. Unless someone can find out why and how the problem originated, the breeder will go bust, the bank will lose its sizable investment, and no one will be happy—except the culprit responsible. In getting to the bottom of the mystery, Tim has to learn a great deal about how horses are bred and treated for various illnesses. Since he is a banker and not a horse expert, his education necessitates a great many lessons that the casual reader may find tedious. I myself found them as fascinating as the expected violence that erupts toward the end of the book.

In *Twice Shy* Mr. Francis tried something daring for a thriller and succeeded admirably. In each of the novel's two sections separate heroes faced the same frightening villain 14 years apart. In *Banker* he has taken a similar risk. His new book *must* span three years because foals—like humans— aren't conceived and born overnight, and the "harmless-seeming seeds" Mr. Francis mentions in his introduction need time to germinate. That he manages to capture our attention and hold us spellbound over the course of those three years is further proof of his juggling skill. And when the unraveling finally does come, it comes with all the breathless pace we have come to expect of this superb writer.

I for one am very happy that Mr. Francis no longer rides horses. (pp. 15, 20)

Evan Hunter, "Who's Fooling with the Foal?" in The New York Times Book Review, March 27, 1983, pp. 15, 20.

CAROL FLAKE

Because Dick Francis was a jockey and because his plots move so quickly, one is tempted to handicap his books rather than review them, assigning each a speed rating and a weight allowance. When Mr. Francis is in form, he is better than a season at the races for providing an introduction to good horses and bad company. I shall try, however, to forgo the usual racing conceits, since he has been moving away from his usual race track settings and thoroughbreds make only a perfunctory appearance in *The Danger,* his new mystery/thriller. Typically, we meet Mr. Francis' sleuths as they awaken, groaning in a hospital room, or as they try to gather their wits in the dark after an unforeseen assault. Crime catches them unaware, leaves them off balance. As *The Danger* begins, Andrew Douglas, a kidnap consultant, watches in frustration as Italian police botch a ransom drop for his client, Paolo Cenci, a wealthy Bolognese businessman, whose daughter, Alessia, a famous jockey, has been abducted.

Alessia's is the first of several kidnappings that take Douglas from Italy to England and on to America. A partner in a low-profile firm that specializes in kidnap prevention and negotiation, he is an expert at reducing ransom demands. He also counsels the victims' families and comforts the victims themselves once they have been rescued. As usual, Mr. Francis has done his homework, and at times *The Danger* reads like a primer on the stages of emotional recovery that kidnap victims experience after their release.

Although Douglas knows nothing about horses, he fits the profile of a typical Dick Francis protagonist. He's youngish, self-contained, physically unremarkable, good at his trade, a loner but not a maverick. Criminals are always underestimating the courage and tenacity of Mr. Francis' quiet, colorless heroes, and wives and lovers are always underestimating their devotion. In fact, the hero's apparent detachment often enrages villains and loved ones alike, driving killers to violence and wives to shrillness. In the heat of pursuit, the hero inevitably takes a battering.

Douglas is Mr. Francis' iciest hero yet. . . . Unlike most of Mr. Francis' heroes, Douglas is sure of his emotions and sure of his professional calling. In that sense, he's a traditional hard-boiled hero. He has no messy domestic situation to resolve, no personal crises to overcome as he tries to track down the criminal mastermind who is disturbing the social order or violating the racing code. And, of all Mr. Francis' heroes, he seems the least baffled by women. His dispassionate sympathy is the perfect balm for Alessia's emotional wounds. . . .

Unfortunately, however, Douglas is one of the least compelling and least wittily drawn of Mr. Francis' heroes. Despite his achievements in derring-do, he seems dull and earnest. The villain, too, lacks Mr. Francis' usual inventiveness. The plot whizzes along at pot-boiler pace, but when we finally find out the identity of the kidnapper, it hardly seems to matter. *The Danger,* which has all along seemed part thriller, part mystery, becomes pure thriller.

In a final dramatic confrontation, Mr. Francis attempts to draw a parallel between hero and villain. Douglas stares at the kidnapper, "seeing the obverse of myself, seeing the demon born in every human. We organized, we plotted, and we each in our way sought battle." But Francis is no advocate of the doppelgänger theory of evil; one seldom senses any real affinity between the honest sleuth and the greedy criminal. As Douglas observes of the kidnapper, "Where he wantonly laid waste, I tried to rebuild.'' For Douglas, the line between good and evil is clearly drawn. In Mr. Francis' world, one never sympathizes with the villain or blames the social system in which he operates. Corruption is personal, not institutional. Capitalists deserve their wealth, royalty deserves its titles, and criminals deserve their punishment.

For Mr. Francis, the capacity for crime is like the unlucky number one draws in the lottery; some of us are born good, others bad. The hero of *Twice Shy,* attributed the violent disposition of a would-be murderer to the ''genetics of evil, the chance that bred murder, the predisposition which lived already at birth.'' Such a view of human fallibility may not work in a confessional, but it works serviceably for mystery novels in which one cannot, finally, account either for the hero's goodness or for the criminal's villainy. Moreover, in a novel like *The Danger,* one can breathe a sigh of relief at the end, knowing that order has been restored. . . .

Carol Flake, ''Logical Loner Seeks Italian Heiress,'' in The New York Times Book Review, *March 18, 1984, p. 12.*

THE NEW YORKER

Mr. Francis's new novel [*The Danger*] (his twenty-second), like its immediate predecessors, is twice the length of those novels (*Nerve, For Kicks, Odds Against*) with which he so compellingly introduced himself, it is twice as heavily plotted, and horse racing, the subject of all of his best work, has only a token presence. His practically faceless narrator, here called Andrew Douglas, is a star operative for a British anti-kidnap agency. We meet him in Italy, where he recovers the jockey daughter of a rich industrialist, follow him back to England, where he recovers the three-year-old son of the owner of a famous racehorse, and follow him finally to Washington, where he recovers the senior steward of the Jockey Club of England. The thirty-mile-an-hour gallop that Mr. Francis was once capable of is now no more than a jog trot.

A review of ''The Danger,'' in The New Yorker, *Vol. LX, No. 9, April 16, 1984, p. 161.*

JAMES MELVILLE

Dick Francis is not only one of the most popular crime writers of our times, he is also one of the finest, having for several years been that most happy of men—the author who can truthfully say that his best book is the one most recently published. Although horses and the world of racing are invariably involved at some stage in his narratives, he tends nowadays to choose different central themes, often highlighting some unusual profession or arcane specialization. Dick Francis has an unobtrusively stylish gift for conveying interesting background information at the same time as telling a good story, and he writes with humble, honest respect about believable, rounded characters who have not lost sight of the possibility of integrity, love, faith, courage and compassion.

He also handles the difficult first-person narrative technique with grace and skill, [in *Proof*] in the persona of Tony Beach, a wine merchant in a modest but comfortable way of business. He is a young widower, lonely, diffident and troubled in spirit, but possessed of a remarkable palate. His expertise leads to his being hired as a specialist consultant by an industrial investigation agency looking into a major case of fraudulent substitution of wines and spirits while simultaneously helping

the police to unravel a related murder. Although a modest and properly prudent hero, Tony is forced into a terrifying series of confrontations with men who have too much at stake to scruple over taking his or others' lives, culminating in his personal moment of truth and release. Dick Francis has once more cantered home ahead of the field, with what is another thoroughly good book.

James Melville, in a review of ''Proof,'' in British Book News, *October, 1984, p. 617.*

MARTY S. KNEPPER

Dick Francis is not a man afraid of risks. In fact, the secret of Francis' success, both as a British steeplechase jockey from 1946 to 1957 and as a writer of mystery/suspense fiction for the past two decades, seems to be his willingness to take risks.

Each time Francis mounted a horse for a race, as an amateur and later a professional National Hunt jockey, he knew he was taking psychological, physical and financial risks. With each win came euphoria. But there was always the possibility of losing a race, for any number of reasons, and disappointing the owner, the trainer, the fans (especially those with heavy bets on his horse), and, of course, himself. (p. 224)

For Francis, taking risks has also led to success in his writing. Ironically, one of his worst moments as a jockey—the mysterious fall of the Queen Mother's Devon Loch just as the horse was winning the 1956 Grand National at Aintree—led to Francis' taking up a writing career. Because of the huge amount of publicity surrounding the Devon Loch debacle and because of his fame as a jockey, publishers were eager to market an autobiography of Dick Francis. At this point in his life, by refusing the services of a ghost writer and choosing to write the book himself (with the editorial assistance of his wife, Mary), Francis took a second major career risk, a risk that led him to become, eventually, one of the foremost contemporary writers of mystery/suspense fiction.

When Dick Francis made this decision to take up writing, few gamblers would have wagered on his success. He had no experience as a writer, and his education was weak. . . . In spite of these handicaps, Francis completed his autobiography [*The Sport of Queens*], which is a fascinating account of his life and draws a detailed picture of British steeplechasing, and he chose to become a professional writer. (p. 225)

After four years as a journalist, Francis found he needed to supplement his income. Instead of choosing a safe job with financial security, he decided to take another risk, to write a mystery novel with a racing setting. This first novel, *Dead Cert,* appeared in 1962.

Since *Dead Cert,* Francis has gone on to write twenty more novels at an average rate of one a year. He has also written several short stories and edited anthologies of racing stories. Francis' novels are popular with critics and with the general public. *Forfeit* and *For Kicks* have won awards from the British Crime Writers' Association and the Mystery Writers of America, and reviewers have consistently praised his novels for their tight structure, imaginative use of racing plots and intriguing heroes. (pp. 225-26)

Francis' popular and critical success as a writer may seem, at first, to be due to the fact that he does *not* take risks. It is true that he has chosen to write in the hard-boiled mystery/suspense genre, which has its established conventions and its devoted fans. And he has chosen also to write primarily about the two subjects he knows best, racing and flying. (Francis was a pilot in World War II.) The seeds for many of his plots, it is also true, can be found in *The Sport of Queens*. . . . Violence sells books easily, and it is true that Francis' novels, especially his earlier novels, have scenes of excruciating, bone-cracking violence. What's more, Francis' heroes may, at first, seem to be carbon copies of each other, just one more example of the lonely knight walking down those mean streets—or, in this case, the lonely, compassionate jockey riding down those mean tracks.

A more careful analysis of Francis' twenty-one novels, however, suggests that he has, in fact, taken some rather amazing risks in his writing, and, in addition, one of the major themes in his books is risk-taking. For Francis the writer, like Francis the rider, success is the result of risk-taking.

The most obvious risk Francis has taken as a writer is to create a new hero for each novel. Most detective fiction authors create a series character . . . who is interesting enough and predictable enough that readers will buy book after book in a series just to see their hero in action one more time. The appeal of these heroes is precisely the fact that they do not change significantly from book to book. . . . Because Francis has chosen not to recycle the same detective character in every book, with the exception of the character Sid Halley who appears in two novels, *Odds Against* and *Whip Hand*, he cannot count on reader loyalty to a particular detective hero to sell his books. Yet, by creating different heroes, Francis has given himself a great deal of freedom—specifically, the freedom to create heroes with a wide variety of personalities, occupations and backgrounds and the freedom to show these different characters developing and changing as a result of the events in each book. By taking the risk of not using a series hero, Francis has managed to write novels with a depth of characterization most detective novels lack.

Critics have looked for the characteristics Francis' heroes share in an effort, perhaps, to suggest that they are, in actuality, literary clones with different names but the same essential identity. In support of this point of view, there is the fact that many of the heroes are orphans, and nearly all have some connection with horse racing. What's more, all of them, more or less, fit the description of Edward Link, hero of *Smokescreen:* "patient, powerful, punctual, professional and puritanical." . . . While there is some validity and usefulness in this approach, it tends to blind the reader to the important differences among Francis' heroes and to underestimate his achievement as a writer.

One quality in people Francis admires is professionalism, the ability to do a job well and to do it responsibly. By creating heroes in a wide variety of professions, Francis can explore this idea more fully than he could if all his heroes were private eyes. (In fact, only three of Francis' heroes are investigators, Sid Halley, David Cleveland in *Slayride* and Gene Hawkins in *Blood Sport*.) The rest represent a cross-section of occupations, some involved with racing and some not: jockey, horse trainer, bloodstock agent, stable lad, artist, journalist, pilot, accountant, physics teacher, photographer, banker, actor, toy inventor, farmer. In presenting his heroes, Francis always examines their professions in some detail: What are the rewards, the challenges, the responsibilities of the job? What qualities does it take to become an expert in the field? Two examples will illustrate this point. In *Smokescreen*, Francis writes about film acting. He shows how everyone expects Edward Link, an actor

featured in James Bond type adventure films, to be just like the characters he plays in the movies. Francis illustrates that actors have to deal, often, with egocentric directors, families who may resent long separations during on-location shooting, and publicity agents eager to exploit an actor's privacy to sell a film. He also demonstrates that actors need physical and mental endurance, keen observation and a willingness to reveal their innermost feelings to the camera. Because Edward Link is a private man, publicity events and exposing his emotions on film are difficult for him. In *Reflex*, Francis shows, in great detail, what skills are necessary for a person to be a professional photographer. Philip Nore spends much time in the novel in his darkroom, attempting to resolve the photographic mysteries created by George Millace by using different exposures, different chemicals and other tricks of the trade. Francis shows, too, that photographers face an interesting occupational hazard: the temptation to blackmail.

Francis also explores the issue of social class by having his heroes, and other characters, represent various social classes and various attitudes toward the class system in England. (pp. 226-28)

Francis also uses his heroes to examine the nature of relationships between men and women. . . . In presenting . . . a wide variety of relationships between women and men, Francis is a marked contrast to most hard-boiled detective fiction writers who rely, over and over, on the macho bachelor-*femme fatale* formula. . . . (pp. 228-29)

Many writers fail to give their detective heroes much of a life history, though the detectives may have colorful personalities. We do not, for example, know much about Hercule Poirot's upbringing or Lew Archer's family. Francis gives each of his heroes a family background which helps to explain their different attitudes and personalities and which gives his readers some sharp insights into the psychological dimensions of family life. . . .

From the desperately suicidal spy, Gene Hawkins, in *Blood Sport*, to the happy, carefree jack-of-all-racing-trades William Derry, in *Twice Shy*, Francis has clearly made his heroes very different people. Because Francis has taken the risk of creating heroes as individual human beings rather than a single fantasy hero, he has been able to explore, in some depth, class, the demands of various professions, family relationships, interactions between women and men, and other issues. Ironically, his strategy seems to have worked in his favor; readers eagerly await each new novel to see what kind of hero he will have this time.

The other major advantage of using different heroes rather than one hero, over and over, is that the author can allow the character to develop. Not only is each of Francis' heroes a unique person, but each hero, to some degree, changes as a result of his adventures so that he is not the same person at the end of the novel that he was at the beginning. (p. 229)

Unlike Francis, writers who have one repeating hero do not have the luxury of letting their characters grow and change. . . .

Besides taking the risk of not using a series hero, Francis' novels are particularly interesting because of the ways in which he violates the formulas for mystery fiction, the ways he foils readers' expectations. Francis' novels fall within the general parameters of the hard-boiled mystery/suspense novel, as described by John Cawelti, George Grella and others. Yet Francis breaks with writers such as Hammett, Chandler, Ross Macdonald and Spillane, especially in his portrayal of society, women and violence. Francis also surprises readers by his challenging of stereotypes, including the stereotype of the hard-boiled detective hero, and his treatment of unpleasant, painful or even taboo topics. (p. 230)

Although Francis' heroes are usually amateur detectives, they are not eccentric, celibate intellectuals like Sherlock Holmes. Rather, they are like Philip Marlowe and Lew Archer: shrewd men of action, essentially lonely, fairly ordinary men, except for their extraordinary toughness, their unswerving loyalty to a personal code of conduct (often at odds with society's rules), and their willingness to jeopardize their own safety to protect the innocent. (p. 231)

Although Francis writes about race tracks more than urban mean streets and although he is less cynical about modern civilization than some of the American hard-boiled mystery writers, he nevertheless portrays a world that is violent, in which greed leads to inhumane behavior, in which power, more often than virtue, is rewarded, in which the innocent suffer. Francis' world is not W. H. Auden's ''Great Good Place'' nor exactly Cawelti's ''glamorous high life of *Playboy* or . . . *Esquire*. Francis' novels are not just whodunits, how, why, where and when? His heroes must make moral choices, must resist temptation and refuse to be intimidated or bribed, must endure physical and psychological punishment. Often the identity of the criminal (or criminals) is revealed early, and the rest of the book is a battle of brain and brawn between hero and adversaries. (pp. 232-33)

What is also fascinating and challenging about Francis' novels is the way in which he challenges readers to reassess the assumptions about men, women and society that underlie the hard-boiled detective fiction conventions. He joins such writers as Robert Parker and Joseph Hansen in developing this genre beyond its earlier parameters.

One particularly pernicious and widespread tradition has been to use women characters to symbolize perverted values in modern society. The message in one hard-boiled mystery after another is that women cannot be trusted. . . . Women in hard-boiled mysteries are not allowed to be three-dimensional human beings. They are portrayed as flat and emotionless.

Francis' treatment of women characters is a notable contrast. No doubt influenced by the less misogynist traditions in British literature and by his wife, Mary, a woman undaunted by challenges (such as piloting an airplane), Francis develops his women as human beings as they exist in the real world, not nightmarish specters that haunt men's dreams or helpless, clutching, dependent creatures. For example, since women have relatively little power in the world of British steeplechasing, Francis does not, generally, make women his villains. This is not an indication he feels women are too pure or too unintelligent to be criminals. In *Blood Sport*, Yola Clive and her brother, Matt, are involved in horsenapping; in *Enquiry*, a mentally unbalanced Grace Roxford tries to kill Kelly Hughes. Francis shows bright women in all his novels, working the racing field and outside it: for example, Henrietta Craig, competent ''head lad'' in Griffons' Stables in *Bonecrack;* Sophie Randolph, an air traffic controller in *Knockdown;* Pen Warner, pharmacist in *Banker;* and Clare Bergen, the ambitious publishers' assistant in *Reflex*.

Another positive aspect of Francis' treatment of women is that he deals with problems women face as important human problems. In *Flying Finish*, Gabriella helps distribute birth control pills, which pilots and others smuggle into Catholic Italy. The pills are desperately needed by women exhausted physically and mentally by too many pregnancies. In *Twice Shy*, the problems of old and young women are examined. (p. 234)

Francis not only explores the problems women face, but he also challenges the validity of some of the more unfair stereotypes of women, stereotypes that pervade literature, not just hard-boiled detective fiction. In *Nerve*, Rob Finn's mother, Dame Olivia Cottin, is a dedicated professional pianist, a chic, totally unmaternal woman who has ignored Rob most of his life. Rather than presenting Dame Olivia in a negative light for her coldness and her rejection of the maternal role, Francis suggests that having a professional pianist for a mother can have its advantages. (p. 235)

Another stereotype is of the skinny, sexless old maid, not very interesting, not very competent, not very useful. Francis shatters this stereotype in *Risk* with his characterization of Hilary Pimlock, the headmistress of a girls' school in Surrey. When Hilary first meets Roland Britten, a thirty-one-year-old accountant and amateur jockey, he has just swum ashore and collapsed on the beach next to her, exhausted, afraid and pursued by angry men on a boat. She is visiting Minorca on holiday; he has just escaped from the boat on which he has been held captive, in solitary confinement, for many long days and nights. Hilary saves Ro by hiding him in her hotel room. After feeding and clothing Roland, Hilary, between forty-two and forty-six years old, with glasses, wrinkles and flat feet, makes Ro a sexual proposition. (p. 236)

Ro, intrigued by this straight-forward, unusual woman, grateful to her, yet not sexually attracted to her, summons what little energy he has and gives her a lab course in sex education. . . .

Hilary, no sex-starved spinster who craves repeat performances and no silly romantic who wants to marry Ro and give up her career, becomes Ro's ''rock,'' the woman in his life who defies categorization. . . . A deep bond of friendship, respect and love develops between them. (p. 237)

[Another of the characters, aware of the relationship,] is profoundly shocked, as perhaps are readers who cannot deal with a woman who does not fall into the stereotypes: a professional woman with nerves, brains, self-possession and common sense and yet with kindness; an older, single woman who can sleep with a man and yet who is not a ''dirty old woman'' or a suffocating, jealous mother figure; a woman who is capable of love but who prefers the single, celibate life. Hilary Pimlock is Francis' most intriguing and most fully developed female character, and she illustrates the degree to which Francis has rejected the stereotypes of women found repeatedly in hard-boiled mysteries.

Francis also challenges the macho image of the hard-boiled detective hero. On the surface, it may seem that Francis' heroes are the epitome of stereotypical manliness because they are competent in their professions, they are in good physical shape, and they are too stubborn to give in to intimidation tactics. However, Francis' heroes are not Mike Hammers or James Bonds. They suffer a great deal of violence but administer very little. For example, in *Nerve*, the psychologically unbalanced Maurice Kemp-Lore hangs Rob Finn from a harness hook in a cold, deserted stable and leaves him there, after having doused him with cold water; when Rob gets a chance at revenge, however, he sets Maurice free, after making sure he will harm no one again. Francis' heroes, unlike most hard-boiled heroes, prefer women with lively minds with whom they can have long-term relationships rather than women with beautiful bodies with whom they can have one-night stands. . . . These men are not afraid of commitment either, in the form of marriage, ongoing friendship or the sharing of living quarters. Francis' men have deep, very human feelings. This is a contrast to the image of stoicism presented by heroes like Sam Spade. Charles Todd's cousin, Donald Stuart, in *In the Frame,* is devastated for weeks after his wife is murdered; his tears are not presented as a sign of unmanliness. Jonah Dereham, in *Knockdown,* suffers from loneliness and unrequited love. In *Whip Hand,* Sid Halley abandons a case he is working on because he is afraid.

Francis' undercutting of the hard-boiled hero fantasy is most obvious in *Smokescreen* and *Whip Hand.* In the former, Francis emphasizes the contrast between Edward Link's false image, the film screen macho man, irresistible seducer of women and invincible fighter of men, and the reality, Link's ordinariness. In the novel, we see that Link is essentially a domestic man, faithful to his wife and concerned about his children. When events force Link to take on the macho role for real—when he is trapped in a car for days in the African desert, with no food and water, his arms handcuffed to the steering wheel—Link makes no miraculous escape a la James Bond. Instead, for pages, Francis describes Link's incredible physical and psychological suffering. Link is a survivor and a bright, resourceful man, but he is no macho superhero, and this is, in large part, the "message" of this detective novel.

In *Whip Hand,* Francis portrays a hero, Sid Halley, who does, to a large extent, possess the "manly" attributes of pride, stoicism and physical stamina. However, Francis reveals with devastating irony both the falsity of the hard-boiled hero image and its physical and psychological dangers. Sid is perceived by crooks in the racing world (Trevor Deansgate, Lucas Wainwright) as a dangerous, invincible superhero. We see Sid, however, grappling, for six long days in Paris, with his cowardice, and we see him agonizing over the hurt he feels because of his divorce from his wife, Jenny. The image, clearly, is exaggerated; the man behind the image is human. Yet because Sid has assimilated "masculine" values, to a great degree, we also see the consequences of living according to the macho code of behavior. His enemies, because they are convinced and afraid of his supposed power and invulnerability, are driven to desperate tactics to stop him: Deansgate, for example, threatens to maim Sid's one good hand. Also, Sid learns, from Jenny, that it is his competitiveness and his inability to communicate feelings that, in large measure, destroyed their marriage. . . . Ironically, Sid's macho stoicism saves his life, when Trevor Deansgate threatens to kill him, but it loses him his wife. Francis, like Amanda Cross, is fully aware of the consequences of the hard-boiled hero's code—especially the precipitation of violence and the suppression of one's feelings—and, rather than glorifying macho heroes, Francis presents androgyny as a more sane and humane alternative than extreme "masculinity" or extreme "femininity."

Readers are sometimes put off by Francis' many scenes of violence, torture and physical and psychological anguish. The significant difference between Francis and other hard-boiled writers is that Francis does not romanticize violence or make it exciting and titillating. In Francis' novels, pain hurts . . . intensely, and it does not go away in a page or two. Also, the heroes suffer the violence most often, forcing readers to feel the pain vicariously. What is more, violence in Francis' novels is not usually a matter of participation in gunplay and fistfights as much as it is a matter of enduring physical pain and psy-

chological torment over a long period of time. For example, when Edward Link is locked in a car at the end of *Smokescreen,* Francis makes him suffer for twenty full pages before he is rescued. During the days in the car, we feel the heat, the headaches, the boredom, the aching body, the parched throat, the hunger, the cramps, the stench (the result of no convenient bathroom facilities), the desperation, the anger, the desire for death. By presenting torture scenes like this realistically, which he does in many of the novels, Francis runs the risk of alienating readers who are used to having the criminals, not the heroes, suffer the effects of violence and who are used to reading about violence mystery formula, his realistic, detailed presentation of violence is, in itself, a critique of the romanticized violence in many hard-boiled detective books. Francis is not naive; he knows violence is part of the real world, as a result of greed, selfishness, psychological aberrations, sociological factors; and yet he will not advocate violence or suggest that choosing violence is an option that is without devastating consequences for both victim and victimizer.

In his portrayal of society, Francis also rejects the simple answers provided by many other hard-boiled mystery writers, that society is corrupt and that, to exist as a moral individual, one must disassociate oneself from the institutions of society and live as a loner. Indeed, in hard-boiled novels, corruption is rampant and false values (such as money and lust) have replaced more humane values (such as justice and love).

Francis' world is not the "Great Good Place" of the classic detective novel. He shows, repeatedly, greedy, unscrupulous people victimizing other people. In *Knockdown,* Pauli Teska and his confederates manipulate bidding at horse auctions so that they can gain huge commissions from owners paying inflated prices, and they try to run out of business honest owners, like Antonia Huntercombe, and honest agents, like Jonah Dereham. But, and this is a crucial difference, Francis' heroes are, on the whole, not anti-establishment types. Randall Drew, after all, works at the bidding of royalty in *Trial Run;* David Cleveland, in *Slayride,* is chief investigator for Britain's Jockey Club; Steven Scott, in *High Stakes,* has reaped the financial benefits of the capitalist system. Society, in Francis' world, is not inherently corrupt, though individuals may be. Whereas, in many hard-boiled mysteries, the hero seems to be the only unsullied character in his world, in Francis' novels, the hero has allies, including representatives of the establishment, who are supportive, like Sid Halley's father-in-law, Admiral Charles Roland, in *Odds Against* and *Whip Hand;* the Earl of October in *For Kicks;* and banker Charlie Canterfield in *High Stakes.* For Francis, the answer to the problems of modern society is not separation from it, but working within it.

Francis deals with problems that exist in modern society seriously and in some depth. He treats modern social and psychological problems, including some topics generally considered unpleasant or even taboo, by making them a major part of his novels, by making the hero involved, in a personal way, with these problems. In fact, most Francis novels have double plots intertwining, one plot dealing with the racing-related mystery and one plot dealing with a psychological or sociological problem the hero must work through. Gene Hawkins, in *Blood Sport,* for example, battles against his own very strong suicidal urges. Jonah Dereham must deal with an alcoholic brother in *Knockdown.* Sid Halley, in *Odds Against,* must learn to accept a physical disability, his smashed hand. In *Twice Shy,* Jonathan Derry and his wife cannot have children, a situation that is destroying their marriage. In *Reflex,* Philip Nore must deal with his abandonment by his mother, with his mother's drug addiction, and with his sister's involvement with an exploitative religious cult. In exploring these issues, Francis writes with seriousness, sympathy and sensitivity, never minimizing the problems or suggesting easy solutions. Just as Francis makes his readers *feel* the effects of brutal, violent behavior, he makes readers empathize with persons experiencing these problems. To read **Blood Sport,** for example, is to learn what it feels like to be lonely, paranoid and suicidal.

Francis, then, has written novels that are in the hard-boiled detective fiction tradition, but he has taken the risk of violating the conventions of the genre, even challenging the assumptions on which it is based. He does this by presenting women as human beings, not just *femmes fatales* or pathetic, helpless victims; by dealing seriously with women's problems; and by exposing as narrow and false some of the common stereotypes of women. Likewise, Francis calls into question the macho man stereotype many hard-boiled mysteries perpetuate, and he shows the physical and psychic dangers of the macho mentality. Unlike many hard-boiled mystery writers, Francis refuses to romanticize violence, and he does not blame social institutions for the injustices and abuses of power individuals cause. Social and psychological problems Francis treats seriously, making them central, not just part of the background; he does not shy away from dealing with painful, unpleasant realities. Francis, like Robert Parker and Joseph Hansen, is moving the hard-boiled mystery away from escapist formula fantasy and into the realm of serious literature about life.

Besides using many detective heroes instead of one and moving away from the hard-boiled mystery/suspense formula, Francis has taken other risks as a writer, risks that have paid off. One is creating endings that violate readers' expectations. Strict moralists, for instance, will object to Philip Nore, in **Reflex,** finding his true profession as a blackmailer, even a blackmailer on the side of "good." Romantics will find the endings of **Knockdown** and **Trial Run** disappointing, for the two women, Sophie Randolph and Lady Emma, refuse to settle down with the men who love them, Jonah Dereham and Randall Drew. Many persons may question the ethics of Angelo Gilbert's lobotomy at the ending of **Twice Shy.** Conventional people will perhaps disapprove of the ending of **Forfeit** in which James Tyrone and his wife, Elizabeth, agree to Ty's having an extramarital affair with a black woman, Gail Pominga, whom Ty cares for and respects.

Another risk Francis has taken is to move away from his areas of expertise (racing and flying, primarily) and to explore other subjects, other professions. He has, for instance, written about art (**In The Frame**), computers (**Twice Shy**), gold mining (**Smokescreen**), accounting (**Risk**) and the food industry (**Twice Shy**). When Francis decides to move into a new area, he does his homework well. . . . (pp. 238-43)

Francis has also taken risks with geographical settings. He has set his novels outside Britain in several cases: **Smokescreen** is set in South Africa; **Slayride,** Norway; **In The Frame,** Australia; **Blood Sport,** the United States; **Trial Run,** Russia. In each of these cases, Dick and Mary Francis have traveled to the locations for the books and researched social and political issues, history, geography, lifestyles, and other cultural information. The Russian setting in **Trial Run** was probably Francis' biggest risk. While the tone of the novel is depressing because of the details he gives about Russian life (the blank faces people must put on, the spying on each other, the cold, the bad food, the lack of freedom, the overwhelming government bureaucracy),

Francis does not present the Russian people as villains or victims, but, rather, as human beings, who live under a different political system. One of his most interesting characters is Mr. Chulitsky, an architect who is "an unwilling mental traitor," a dedicated Communist who suffers guilt because of his love of luxury and his sense of humor. . . . In **Trial Run,** Francis also cleverly contrasts the realities of life in Russia with Lady Emma's romantic ideas about socialism. In short, he uses the setting to paint a picture of another culture, but, while he decries terrorism, he does not explicitly condemn the Communist government of the U.S.S.R. Just as Harry Kemelman's insertion of Jewish materials enriches his mysteries, Francis' experimentation with subjects and settings adds an extra dimension to his novels.

Francis' recent books have been amazing because of their complexity of themes and structure. In the true spirit of adventure and risk-taking, he has not only examined new subject areas and geographical settings, but he has also experimented with multiple mysteries, with interrelated themes and with dual narrators. **Whip Hand,** for example, intertwines three separate plots: Lucas Wainwright and the horse-buying syndicates; Trevor Deansgate and the sabotaging of horses by inoculating them with a swine disease; and Nicholas Ashe and a phony charity solicitation racket. On top of this, Sid's relationships with two women (his ex-wife, Jenny, and a new friend/lover, Louise McInnes) and with two men (his partner, Chico Barnes, and his father-in-law, Admiral Roland) are explored. Besides all these characters, there are detailed portraits of minor characters: for example, young Mark Rammeleese and intrepid balloonist John Viking. All of this comes together, under Francis' expert manipulations, to become a well-integrated novel about love and courage.

Reflex deals with even more mysteries and subjects. Jockey and amateur photographer Philip Nore must solve the mystery of his past, the mystery of George Millace's personality and his death, the photographic mysteries he has inherited from Millace, and the mystery surrounding the universally disliked Ivor den Relgan's election to the position of racing steward. The novel deals also with heroin addiction, religious cults, homosexuality and homophobia, feminism, photography, and, of course, racing. What is more, Francis shows Philip's transformation from a passive, alienated, morally blasé boy to an active, caring, morally committed man. While this may seem like overkill—too many characters, plots and subjects—the novel works surprisingly well, except perhaps for too much emphasis on photography. The reason it works is that Francis is becoming more of a master, with each novel, at concise, detailed characterizations and at elaborate plotting.

Twice Shy is another complex, multi-faceted novel, and an even more successful experiment than **Reflex** because Francis uses the device of having two narrators, brothers Jonathan and William Derry, tell their stories, which take place fourteen years apart. Not only does this device allow Francis to bring in a number of subjects and issues, but it allows him to develop fascinating contrasts between the two heroes. . . . The book also explores the psychological aspects of gambling and, a favorite theme in Francis' novels, father-son relationships.

Francis' recent experiments in plotting have been risks—he certainly comes close to overburdening the reader with characters, issues, main plots, subplots, and technical information—but so far his risk-taking in this area has led him to push further and further the limits of the mystery form and to create books that are powerful and provocative.

Not surprising for a man who has chosen two risky professions, and who, most notably in his second profession has never been complacent, always experimenting and innovating, Francis' favorite subject in his novels is taking risks. Who, indeed, can speak with more authority on the subject? Francis presents positive images of risk-takers, he explores the reasons why people fear risk-taking and the consequences of not taking risks, and he examines, specifically, professional risk-taking and taking risks in human relationships.

A frequent plot pattern in Francis' novels is for a character who is in a nice, safe rut to find the courage to make a new, more satisfying life for himself or herself. Daniel Roke, in *For Kicks,* runs a successful stable in Australia and supports his orphaned siblings; yet his life is hard work and holds few psychic rewards. He has the satisfaction of working for others, but he has little else to make him happy. His home is a "prison." . . . When the Earl of October asks him to leave Australia and do undercover detective work in England, posing as a stable lad, Daniel agrees, although working as a stable lad holds little promise of being the good life. By risking his safety and his security, Daniel finds, ironically, through the utter brutality and degradation he must endure as a mistreated stable lad, that freedom lies within his own soul and that only by taking risks, and enduring hardships and danger for the cause of justice, can he be happy. At the end of the novel, Daniel accepts a permanent job as an undercover agent for the British government. Francis does not suggest that Daniel Roke will live happily ever after. In fact, the suicidal Gene Hawkins in *Blood Sport,* suffering from acute loneliness and paranoia, may be Daniel Roke a few years in the future. But Francis does suggest that for a person to be happy, to be sane, to. be free, to be challenged, risk-taking is essential. Throughout his novels, Francis presents the risk-takers with great admiration and approval: Hilary Pimlock, Jonah Dereham, Liam O'Rorke, Steven Scott, Rob Finn, Henry Grey, Clare Bergen and others.

Those characters who are too afraid to take risks are presented by Francis as tragic figures; he examines, in his novels, the causes and consequences of their cowardice. Crispin Dereham, in *Knockdown,* cannot adapt when life proves disappointing, and he becomes an alcoholic. Eunice Teller, in *Blood Sport,* has been brought up to be dependent and decorative, not useful and independent. She takes refuge in meaningless, self-destructive game-playing. Philip Nore, in *Reflex,* had so little stability in his life as a child, passed from one set of his mother's friends to another, that passivity and going along with other people's expectations has become a way of survival. For Maurice Kemp-Lore, in *Nerve,* his family's unreasonably high expectations for him to succeed, as they had all succeeded, as riders or racers of horses, leads him to develop a fear of failure and an uncontrollable anger at persons, like Rob Finn, who have succeeded in steeplechasing. Francis sympathizes with these characters who do not have the nerve to take risks in life, even the psychopathic Kemp-Lore, and he does not minimize their suffering: depression, anger, feelings of meaninglessness, self-hatred, boredom, alienation. In most cases, Francis shows these tragic characters beginning to transcend their pasts and learning to live fully. Often, it is the example of a risk-taking character that motivates them to change and grow.

One of Francis' particular fascinations is professional risk-taking. Sometimes the characters take on new, challenging vocations, as Daniel Roke does in *For Kicks* or Neil Griffon does in *Bonecrack.* More often, they move from being amateurs, or what Henry Grey, in *Flying Finish,* calls "shama-

teurs," to professionals. Henry Grey, William Derry, and Philip Nore, for example, are all characters who, at first, prefer the safe, amateur, temporary, no-real-commitment status. But they find the courage to make a commitment professionally, to flying, to managing a horse empire, and to photography, respectively. (pp. 243-46)

Risk-taking, for Francis, is important not only in people's work lives but also in their private lives as friends, lovers, spouses, relatives. Risks, Francis argues, are necessary to the building of honest communication, meaningful friendship, solid love. This means taking the risk of being real and open (rather than playing a safe role), having the guts to be assertive about needs and desires . . . , and having the self-confidence to allow other people to be free (rather than clinging dependently or controlling through manipulation).

In *Forfeit,* Elizabeth Tyrone, a bed-ridden, ninety-percent paralyzed woman, is dependent totally on her husband, James Tyrone—financially, physically, emotionally. If Ty ceases to care for her and leaves, if he does not provide twenty-four-hour care for her and pay for the machines she needs to breathe, she cannot live. Understandably, Elizabeth feels she must play the role of saint; she does not feel she can risk being herself. Although she cannot, for physical and psychological reasons, have sex with Ty, she is not confident enough in herself or in him to discuss honestly the strain this puts on their marriage. And, while she acknowledges to herself that she is probably not being fair in expecting sexual fidelity from Ty, she is too insecure to allow him the freedom to build emotional or sexual relationships outside their marriage. By the end of the novel, however, Elizabeth learns that she does not have to be a saint for Ty to love her; that communication and assertiveness on her part will strengthen, not weaken, their marriage; and that, if she allows Ty more freedom, she will free herself from anxiety, guilt and jealousy. For all human beings, even for a person as physically limited as Elizabeth, Francis argues, risk-taking is as essential to life as breathing.

Francis' own life, as a steeplechase jockey and as a writer, is a testimonial to risk-taking. As a jockey, he faced psychological, physical and financial risks, but he pursued this challenging career, finding both disappointment (losing the 1956 Grand National) and success (becoming Britain's Champion Jockey). As a mystery novelist, Francis has taken risks from the very beginning: by using different heroes instead of a series hero; by altering and adapting, and ultimately transforming and transcending the hard-boiled mystery/suspense formula; by exploring a wide variety of subjects and settings; and by experimenting with increasingly complex plots. In his novels, Francis has examined the subject of risk-taking from the point of view of those who have nerve (the Hilary Pimlocks and the Rob Finns) and those who lack it (the Eunice Tellers and Crispin Derehams). Francis taps the sympathy we feel for those persons who are defeated by life and the admiration we have for those who beat the odds, those who have the determination and daring to live fully, whether they are jockeys or pilots, accountants or inventors, headmistresses or invalids. Given his achievements so far, it is a safe bet that Dick Francis will continue to take risks in his writing and to write about risks— unless, of course, he decides to take up the challenge of a new profession. (pp. 246-47)

Marty S. Knepper, "Dick Francis," in Twelve Englishmen of Mystery, *edited by Earl F. Bargainnier, Bowling Green University Popular Press, 1984, pp. 222-48.*

CHARLES MONAGHAN

When Agatha Christie was translated to the great bookstore in the sky, there was much speculation in the publishing world about who would take her place as a mystery best seller. It is now clear that the mantle has fallen on the shoulders of Dick Francis. *Proof* is his 26th book, and every one of his recent efforts has had a healthy run on the best-seller lists and enormous paperback sales in a spectrum of languages.

Proof will undoubtedly have a comfortable springtime at the top of the charts. All the classic Francis elements are there in abundance. There are the protagonist darkened by personal tragedy, beautifully drawn cameos of English eccentrics, the horse-racing background and enough blood and guts spattered about for several books on surgery. . . . Over the years, he has taught his readers nearly everything there is to know about horse-racing. In *Proof,* there is a small encyclopedia of facts about booze. . . . I found all his information to be accurate and his judgment on wine and liquor to be sound. It is evident that not only has Francis done his homework but that he has quaffed a bottle or two in his time.

The gore starts to flow early in *Proof,* as a 10-ton horse van plows into a tentful of merrymakers, and barely begins to coagulate before Beach and a friend stop a couple of shotgun blasts. Sandwiched in there somewhere is a very nasty murder by plaster of Paris. Such mayhem not only captures the attention of the reader but is also part of the Francis technique. He establishes the beastliness of the villains and the general bloodiness of the world and then threatens to bring it all down on the head of the hero, of whom the reader has grown rather fond. You can't help but begin to fear for Tony Beach's safety—and Francis has you in his grip. This is genre writing, but Francis is a master of it. . . .

Though some of his novels predate the Iron Maiden's arrival at the center of Britain's political life, I see Dick Francis's stories as a reflection of the era of Margaret Thatcher. There is a spare-the-rod-and-spoil-the-child tone that erupts frequently. In *Proof,* Beach's friend McGregor says at one point: "It is fashionable to explain away all crime as the result of environment, always putting the blame on someone else, never the actual culprit. No one's born bad, all that sort of thing. If it weren't for poor housing, violent father, unemployment, capitalism, et cetera, et cetera. You've heard it over and over." (The fact is, of course, that no one has heard "it" even once as a full exculpation of violent criminal acts, except from the utterest of fools or, very properly, from lawyers defending their clients.) Since sentiments similar to McGregor's pepper books by Francis, I take them to be the author's own. He sets up a straw liblab and then knocks him down. Rampant Thatcherite grumpiness.

At any rate, Dick Francis wasn't hired to be a professor of philosophy or attorney general. We buy his novels for amusement, for story-telling, for suspense. He seems to get better at his craft all the time, and *Proof* may well be his best novel yet.

> *Charles Monaghan, "Vintage Dick Francis," in* Book World—The Washington Post, *March 17, 1985, p. 5.*

ROSS THOMAS

The first thing you learn about Tony Beach is that he's a grieving widower whose wife died six months ago. The second

thing you learn is that he owns a liquor store in a British suburb. And the third thing you learn is that Beach's grandfather and father were heroes in World Wars I and II respectively and were also gentlemen jockeys—although the son and grandson, alas, is neither. Thus in four pages Dick Francis gives us an emotionally wounded hero with a fairly unusual occupation and background, whose forebears, at least, had something to do with racing—an important ingredient in many a Francis novel. . . .

I found *Proof* to be formula writing at its most professional, showing that well-researched background can almost be made to compensate for a perfunctory mystery and less than gripping suspense. The style is patented Francis—serviceable, practiced and plain. As for Tony Beach, the liquor-store-owner hero, he finally discovers that not all acts of bravery are performed on battlefields and that he need no longer be haunted by either his father's Distinguished Service Order or his grandfather's Victoria Cross. This is a useful lesson for Beach, of course, but it is also one the reader will have been anticipating since the first few pages.

> *Ross Thomas, "Who Watered the Whisky?" in* The New York Times Book Review, *March 24, 1985, p. 13.*

THE NEW YORKER

Mr. Francis's audience grows with every new novel, and every new novel diminishes in quality. In [*Proof*], his twenty-fourth, he takes well over three hundred pages to tell us how his usual characterless narrator—here called Tony Beach, and a wine dealer by trade—discovers a scheme in which ordinary Scotch whiskey is bottled and sold as something better and vin ordinaire is bottled and labelled as St. Estèphe, St. Emilion, Nuits St. Georges, etc., and how Beach runs the crooks to justice. There is, for once, no sex. There is, as always, a horse race.

> *A review of "Proof," in* The New Yorker, *Vol. LXI, No. 9, April 22, 1985, p. 144.*

MARY FRANCES GRACE

One of the pleasures of following a regular writer through the years is the thrill of seeing him grow as a writer, watching him play with his craft, risk new types of characters, more dangerous villains, different lines of work for his protagonists.

Such a writer is Dick Francis, grown bolder and more sure of himself with each book he writes. Readers faithful to Francis know that they can always expect from him that best of pleasures, a good read. Francis's plots are always complex enough to tantalize, mystify, and satisfy; his pacing has always been exceptional, his books the hardest to put down. His protagonists are always resourceful and intelligent enough to tackle the problems that complicate their lives, yet they are very human and so both likable and credible.

Readers who have avoided Francis's books because he writes about horses and horse-racing no longer have an excuse to pass by his books. In *Proof,* as in his last few novels, the horses are very much kept in the wings. On center stage in *Proof* are wines and liquors, particularly fine Scotches, in the person of Tony Beach, a wine-shop owner recently widowed who still has not adjusted to the emptiness of his home and his life. In a rather convoluted way, he is taken on both by the police and by a private detective agency to act as an expert taster in a case involving a bizarre but common, these days, sort of counterfeiting: substituting cheaper wines or liquors for brands of far better quality.

Once again, Francis has done his homework admirably well: as Beach helps lead Detective Sergeant Ridger and Gerard McGregor closer to the person behind it all, we learn in a pleasantly unobtrusive way a great deal about wine and whiskey manufacturing and tasting. Francis has a deft way of scattering bits of knowledge into his characters' conversations without seeming to quote verbatim from whatever sources he's used. Such a talent is a rare gift that makes his books even more fun to read, as well as more believable. His characters know what they're talking about.

Part of what makes Francis's books so good are the changes that take place in his main characters: his protagonists grow, they are changed by what happens to them and by what, in the course of the novel, they choose to do. Because he is capable of such growth, Tony Beach, like Francis's other protagonists, is an interesting, living-and-breathing character who because he is so carefully and fully developed has earned our concern and our affection. (pp. 77-8)

"Paul Young," the man created by Francis to threaten all that is good in *Proof,* is a particularly evil and callous man who has so little feeling for other human beings as to make him almost subhuman. Beach meets Young early in *Proof* but is not able to connect the face with the man's real name, and so have all come clear, until the very end.

Francis's protagonists are always, at that end, threatened physically by the people they try to bring to some form of justice. Most suffer some kind of terrible beating, or a bad fall from a horse; we've read of an occasional kidnapping, or a shooting, or perhaps a knife in the back. But in *Proof,* Francis employs one of the least violent forms of aggression against his main character, which, of them all, is also the most horrifying—a particularly gruesome and horrible form of suffocation. Whether or not Francis has realized that horror bred from imagination and anticipation . . . is infinitely more effective than any number of torturings with iron pokers or beatings with chains and fists—whether or not he has realized this, the method works, and works well. Paul Young's techniques are the stuff of nightmares.

Francis has always done well by his minor characters, individuals interesting in their own right who fill in his backdrops without getting lost in the scenery. A few quick strokes, a few choice words, and a living, breathing human being serves a purpose and then quietly retires.

In *Proof,* one such character fascinated me—a young retarded man named Brian who works in Tony Beach's wine shop, lugging cartons, moving stock, helping deliver orders. Brian enjoys his job—if he is not paid, he damn well should be—and he has "learned a lot in the three or so months" he has been working. Brian does not read but recognizes bottles and labels once taught their names, and he knows "all the regular items by sight." He knows where things belong in the stockroom, which Beach has kept methodically organized since hiring him. . . .

Beach, in fact, wonders "how much one could teach him if one tried." . . . Tony Beach and Dick Francis deserve a special commendation for employing—in more than one sense—Brian.

One minor complaint, on Tony Beach's behalf: if some kind soul had been good enough to point out to him early on in *Proof* that rescuing dozens of people from the aftermath of a terrible traffic accident requires a great deal of courage, Beach might have come to terms with himself—and with his courageous father and grandfather—sooner. In one respect, this flaw adds to the fun of the book: Tony, we say, you're a fool, you're wonderfully brave. In any case, it would take many more flaws than this to spoil such a rare vintage as *Proof.* (p. 78)

Mary Frances Grace, in a review of "Proof," in The Armchair Detective, Vol. 19, No. 1, Winter, 1986, pp. 77-8.

CONNIE FLETCHER

[*Break In* is another] spirited winner by Dick Francis that sets the world of horse racing against another milieu, in this case, ruthless and sleazy journalism. Steeplechase jockey Kit Fielding's twin sister, Holly, and her husband, horse trainer Bobby Allardeck, suddenly find their business imperiled by nasty slurs printed in a gossip column. Fielding looks into the attacks, sensing that Bobby's powerful and soon-to-be-knighted father may be the intended target. Fielding's probes into a subtle, sophisticated, and very evil enemy involve two Fleet Street newspapers and a host of ruined businesses. Francis' complex, principled hero, his fully fleshed out supporting characters, and the story's fast pace combine to keep the reader turning pages. As always, the steeplechase scenes are described with nerve-wrenching, fence-by-fence accuracy.

Connie Fletcher, in a review of "Break In," in Booklist, *Vol. 82, No. 10, January 15, 1986, p. 706.*

PUBLISHERS WEEKLY

Francis's 25th thriller [*Break In*] is suavely handled and full of suspense. The narrator, Kit Fielding, wins handily as a steeple-chase jockey and enjoys the friendship of the princess who owns the horses he races. But trouble threatening his twin Holly and her husband Bobby Allardeck interrupts Kit's routine. As horse trainers, the Allardecks are about to go bankrupt after a scandal sheet prints the false report that they can't pay their debts. Determined to discover the motive for the attack, Kit enlists the help of people in the princess's circle, which includes her niece, Danielle. A romance develops between the jockey and Danielle, interrupted by villains sent to kill him. Thanks to Kit, the Allardecks' business is saved and he outwits the perpetrators of a shameful conspiracy. The love story, as well as the author's colorful descriptions of English jump racing and newspaper tycoons, add zest to the intricate novel.

A review of "Break In," in Publishers Weekly, *Vol. 229, No. 4, January 24, 1986, p. 64.*

MARILYN STASIO

Although much of the violence [in *Break In*] could be avoided if characters took elementary precautions and maybe even called the p-o-l-i-c-e (the word is rarely uttered aloud in a Francis novel), the author's clean, studied prose gets positively eloquent when he gives us action scenes, both on and off the track. I'd much rather read Mr. Francis on how it feels to get kicked in the head by a horse than yawn through one of his love scenes.

When Mr. Francis started dabbling in vintage wines and other areas beyond his racetrack expertise, there was some speculation that he was getting bored reliving 30-year-old memories and wanted to change literary batteries. After reading **Break In,** I'm not sure I agree. The vigor of the novel's racing-world background, its hero's cocky energy and the absolute lustiness of its horse racing scenes convey no whiff of ennui but rather the high spirits of a homecoming.

Kit says, "I feel alive on a horse." So long as it stays mounted, so does the book.

> *Marilyn Stasio, "Back on the Track," in* The New York Times Book Review, *March 16, 1986, p. 7.*

Brian Friel

1929-

Irish dramatist, short story writer, and scriptwriter.

Friel is one of contemporary Ireland's most respected dramatists. He is praised for his talent with dialogue and for his
exploration of the ways in which language can be used to shape
and distort reality. Friel's plays are often set in and around the
rural village of Ballybeg and depict the effects on individuals
of Irish social and cultural problems. Within this context, Friel
examines such universal themes as love, authority, and truth
versus illusion. Friel has used a variety of dramatic structures
and devices in presenting these concerns. Seamus Deane commented: "The anguish of the individual life passes over into
the communal life through violence, borne in language. The
exploration of that difficult transition, the discovery of a series
of dramatic forms in which it can be reconnoitred, is central
to [Friel's] achievement and part of the reason for his importance." Most of Friel's plays have enjoyed popular success in
Ireland, and several have had extended runs in London and on
Broadway.

Friel first gained recognition with *Philadelphia, Here I Come!*
(1964), which centers on Gar O'Donnell, a young Irishman
who recounts his failures and frustrations and speculates on
his future on the eve of his emigration to America. During the
play, an actor in the role of O'Donnell's alter ego articulates
emotions O'Donnell is unable to express and allows the audience to view both the inner and outer forces that have influenced his life. The introduction of a theatrical device into an
otherwise realistic setting is a common feature in Friel's plays,
helping to extend the implications of his themes. *The Loves of
Cass McGuire* (1966) centers on an embittered protagonist who
relates some of her failed hopes directly to the audience while
events in the play further her sense of despair. *Lovers* (1967)
consists of two one-act plays, *Winners* and *Losers*. In *Winners,*
a young couple envision a happy future together despite the
woman's unexpected pregnancy and the man's uncertain future. After they relate their hopes, two narrators inform the
audience that the couple will soon die tragically, ironically
commenting on both the delusions and the happiness associated
with their dreams. *Losers* is a comic farce concerning a couple
whose lovemaking is constantly interrupted by the woman's
invalid mother. The play climaxes with the symbolic portrayal
of old age's triumph over youthful love.

During the late 1960s, Friel began to make greater use of
political themes in his plays. *The Mundy Scheme* (1969) is a
satire of Irish politics involving a group of statesmen who
attempt to stimulate the economy and maintain their power by
offering Ireland as a vast international burial ground for human
corpses. In *The Freedom of the City* (1973), Friel examines
such issues as terrorism, political commitment, and proper and
improper uses of authority. This play concerns three politically
active Irish people who are mistakenly branded as terrorists
and are killed by English soldiers. Friel reveals how a series
of coincidences and misunderstandings contribute to the tragedy. One character in the play, a visiting psychologist, gives
a lecture on social unrest which ironically underscores the failure of rationalism in understanding the complexity of social
dynamics. *Translations* (1980), one of Friel's most important

© Victor Patterson

works, is set in nineteenth-century Ireland as British troops
arrive to survey the Ballybeg landscape and to anglicize Gaelic
placenames. Friel examines a number of themes related to the
act of translating, including the ways in which humans interpret
reality through language and action. While *Translations* won
wide acclaim, a companion piece, *The Communication Cord*
(1983), which updates *Translations* to a contemporary setting,
was not as well received.

In several plays, Friel explores the role of the artist in society.
Critics generally cite *Faith Healer* (1979), in which a faith
healer resembles an artist who uses his gift to soothe the pains
of life, as his most successful work in this mode. The play
consists of four monologues, two by the protagonist and two
by characters who question the validity of his practice, leading
the faith healer to contemplate whether his actions help people
or merely foster delusions. In addition to his plays, Friel is
respected as a short story writer. His stories, like his plays,
are set in the Ballybeg region and focus on isolated yet universal
human concerns. *The Saucer of Larks: Stories of Ireland* (1969)
collects stories from his two previous volumes, *The Saucer of
Larks* (1962) and *The Gold in the Sea* (1966).

(See also *CLC*, Vol. 5; *Contemporary Authors*, Vols. 21-24,
rev. ed.; and *Dictionary of Literary Biography*, Vol. 13.)

PATRICIA MacMANUS

A recurrent theme in [the eighteen stories that make up *The Saucer of Larks: Stories of Ireland*] by a decidedly gifted new Irish writer is the essential aloneness of individuals (though not necessarily loneliness), which, even in the midst of happiness, isolates yearning human being from yearning human being. But it's not a brooding analysis of man's ''plight'' that concerns Brian Friel; rather, he seeks to capture those moments of flashingly perceptive revelation—something akin to Joyce's ''Epiphanies''—that from time to time illumine the half-light of workaday living. Writing in a spare, Gaelic-inflected style, Friel makes of each of these tales a miniature drama, ranging through the comic, the tragi-comic, the nostalgic, the absurd; and his people step from the page with a frequently moving reality of their own, particularly the children who appear and re-appear throughout the series. . . . He's a good man with his pen, this Brian Friel, and worth your attention.

> *Patricia MacManus, in a review of ''The Saucer of Larks: Stories of Ireland,'' in* Books, *June 24, 1962, p. 7.*

THE TIMES LITERARY SUPPLEMENT

Many of [Friel's stories in *The Saucer of Larks*] are told through the eyes of children and even when he is concerned with adults, as in **''The Foundry House''**, it is to evoke a memory of things past. Virtue for him tends to reside in the clear candour of the child or in old people facing more final intimations of immortality. Where his adults appear, they tend to have power over children and old people but to be weak in their judgment of how to exercise it, drab because they must be prudent and worldly in comparison with the children who feel and the aged who suffer.

Mr. Friel has a delicate sense of place and humour. He has been brought up among ''characters'' and knows how to domesticate them to the somewhat limited range he has set himself. If the reader is left faintly dissatisfied it is perhaps because too many of the stories fall so neatly into the formula of slightly dotty recollection now so popular with the *New Yorker*. But this is an intelligent and pleasing book.

> *''Classical Sex,'' in* The Times Literary Supplement, *No. 3190, April 19, 1963, p. 261.*

THE TIMES, LONDON

[*The Blind Mice*] had an almost documentary touch for its first-night audience. In it there is the singlemindedness of Father Green who cannot, however, make a decision about a brother cleric, Father Chris Carroll, who has just returned home, a changed, tragic figure after five years' solitary confinement in communist China. He has come home a hero, a martyr for his faith, and the town is preparing to give him a hero's welcome. Chris knows he is not the man they think he is; he has not suffered physically but spiritually, and that is something not even his brother John, to whom he is attached, can understand, nor the mob, when they learn the truth. They are enraged and their hooliganism was something in which a Belfast audience, knowing of mob violence within its own streets the past few days, could well believe.

The characters, however, are not all against the spiritually wounded man, and it is in his ability to pit one against the other that Mr. Friel scores. John's devotion to his brother turns out to be a love-hate complex; in his fury his resentment at Chris's always having been the centre of family affection, with the best of everything offered him, is revealed.

There are, however, his devoted mother . . . and his uncomplicated father . . . who, though they do not probe deeply into motives, are unwavering in their regard for him, and there is, above all, the forthright remarks of [a] leftwinger . . . who had been the first to denounce him but in the face of mass hysteria rallies to his aid.

> *''Early Play by Brian Friel,'' in* The Times, *London, October 7, 1964, p. 8.*

WALTER KERR

Philadelphia, Here I Come is a funny play, a prickly play, finally a most affecting play, and the pleasure it gives is of a most peculiar kind. Author Brian Friel has set all of his cranky, fond, and obstinately shy people to searching for the one word that is everlastingly on the tip of everyman's tongue, and everlastingly not spoken. He has written a play about an ache, and he has written it so simply and so honestly that the ache itself becomes a warming-fire.

It has taken craft as well as truthfulness to do the trick. Hero [Gar O'Donnell] is a man with a misbegotten past, a yearning present, and a dubious future. He has failed to speak in time for the girl he loved. He cannot prod the father he shares his meals with to so much as ask if he happens to be tired of an evening. He is leaving the tiny town of Ballybeg to fly on a shiny jet to a possibly shinier America, but he already knows the American Irish he will share life with there. They have, for all their ceaseless chirping about ground-floor apartments and the latest in air-conditioning, less to say than the folk at home. ''It's the silence that is the enemy,'' our hero cries as he stands between two worlds knowing that he can enter neither.

But it is not [O'Donnell] who sounds the cry. In order to make his baffled man articulate, author Friel has given him an alter ego to slip about the stage with him, now in lockstep, now dancing away in spite, mocking his every thought and pouring out all of the invective and all of the imprisoned love that chokes him dry. . . . [The alter ego] is no mere Voice of Conscience to his strangled master; there is no trace here, you will be happy to know, of the woodenness O'Neill imposed upon his split central figure in *Days Without End*. Instead we are listening to the skipping, sassy, candid, tormenting back-talk all of us give ourselves when we know we are behaving like the chuckleheads we are, listening to the running argument we keep up with ourselves every furious, fumbled day of our lives. . . .

But the play is no wake for all of the solitary souls in the universe. For it has enough of the habit of poetry in it to slip inside solitariness and find the gentle fire, the suppressed fire, that is there. Playwright Friel can turn a scene inside out, without warning, and supply glancingly the moving truth you hadn't counted on. . . .

The play is without pretense and it never cheats, doing exactly what it means to do very simply and very well.

> *Walter Kerr, in a review of ''Philadelphia, Here I Come!,'' in* New York Herald Tribune, *February 17, 1966. Reprinted in* New York Theatre Critics' Reviews, *Vol. XXVII, No. 4, February 21, 1966, p. 369.*

STANLEY KAUFFMANN

"This is a great country for export," a man said to me once in Galway, "and what we export is young men." That is the theme of Brian Friel's play, *Philadelphia, Here I Come!* . . . , the familiar tale of youth setting out in the world, and in this case an Irish youth leaving a tiny village that has grown tinier. . . .

The agony of youthful frustration is familiar, and even the Irish version (through Frank O'Connor, Edna O'Brien and a flock of lovely others) is familiar by now, too. What Mr. Friel has to offer is not new insight but novelty—and not so novel at that: the idea of having his hero played by two actors. There is a public Gar, whom everyone sees, and a private Gar, seen only by the other one—a source of dialogues when alone, and of impudent comment when public Gar is in company.

Through this not-quite-novel novelty of view, we see the last night at home before Gar's departure. There are scenes of reminiscence: when he lacked the gumption to speak up for his girl, when his "American" aunt and uncle visited their old village and asked him to come live with them in Philly and be their filial love—with air-conditioning and a promise of a job.

There are scenes of the ritual and rote in the O'Donnell household: the tea, the schoolteacher's visit on the way to the pub, the canon's nightly call for supper and checkers, the affectionate nagging of the old housekeeper. . . . The texture of Gar's repetitious life is well woven. We know all the reasons why he wants to break out of this webby humdrum, all the fragments and snips of American jive and TV and film that have formed a transparent mosaic across his vision and all the reasons deeper than reason that at last tug at him when he must go.

And all this Mr. Friel has made recognizable and believable. But all this is also a little flat. His play, as a dramatic event, moves along mostly in one plane of intensity and progress, and as a lyric of poignancy, it lacks edge. Only toward the end, there is one scene like a micro-photograph of the familiar, scrutinizing so closely that the familiar becomes new. At two o'clock on that last morning, when the widowed father and his son cannot sleep and meet in the parlor, they try to reach across the long-frozen feelings between them, casting back and forth a thin filament of memory.

It snaps. They never embrace or exchange a really affectionate word. The awareness of that schism, unbridgeable, between the two, who see it, hate it, yet cannot even speak of it, is Mr. Friel's sharpest barb of the evening. . . .

There is considerable pleasantness, little poetry and insufficient power in his play. His Ballybeg household is drawn honestly enough, but it comes trailing a long line of novels and plays that deal with the same material: with Billy-Liar youths dreaming fantasies in drab bedrooms, mocking the clichés around them and finally feeling the ties that underlie even dislike.

Forty or 50 years earlier we might all, figuratively speaking, have been bowled over by Mr. Friel's candor and his theatrical devices. He has his own countrymen to blame, as well as a lot of other authors, if we now think his play is like his hero: amiable and appealing enough but unexciting.

Stanley Kauffmann, "An Irish Play," in The New York Times, *February 17, 1966, p. 28.*

HENRY HEWES

One reason Brian Friel's new Irish play, *Philadelphia, Here I Come!,* is so likable may be that it so honestly assesses two unsatisfactory civilizations: inhibited and materially impoverished Ireland and its opposite, America. The playwright's view seems to be that Ireland's tragedy is the constant emigration of its best young people, and that the Irish emigrant's tragedy is that his achievement elsewhere is rootless and disconnected. For the play's entire action is its protagonist's sometimes humorous, sometimes sad, search for any reason to stay where his roots are. . . .

While the author doesn't demonstrate a capacity for writing dialogue comparable to that of an O'Casey or a Behan ("You wait, says she, till the rosary's over and the kettle's on" is about as lyrical as he gets), his powers of observation permit him to recreate characters with telling accuracy. . . .

Furthermore, like *The Glass Menagerie*, this play expresses a tender awareness of how memory distills events, with the evening's nicest irony being that the uncommunicative father remembers his son through one past incident, while the lonely young man remembers his father through a different one. But the tragic fact is that neither can recall the other's incident.

Because it is such an honest piece of work the play ends inconclusively, and one feels that the playwright may have missed an opportunity to allow the private Gareth to stir us with a more passionate and poetic summing up. Nevertheless, *Philadelphia, Here I Come!,* achieves great poignancy without pretension and deserves to be widely appreciated. (p. 54)

Henry Hewes, "Going through Emigration," in Saturday Review, *Vol. XLIX, No. 10, March 5, 1966, pp. 54-5.*

THE TIMES LITERARY SUPPLEMENT

Mr. Friel can be seen as a valid inheritor of the Irish tradition of short-story writing. Perhaps the narrow horizons of Irish life encourage precision of focus; certainly everything [in *The Gold in the Sea*] has been watched closely. Mr. Friel does not seek specious effects. There is no fat in his writing, and no flannel. He relies heavily on dialogue, and this increases the impression of impersonality. His best field lies between the economical evocation of a habitual environment and some exceptional event that jolts it. The reorientation that follows such a nudge of the normal is of course a classic peripety of the form.

The stories in *The Gold in the Sea* that particularly convince are those concerning the kinds of sports which can dramatize social relationships and privately-nursed ambitions—fishing, pigeon-racing, cock-fighting. However we do not, finally, have much sense of a searching or transforming view of life behind these tales. Although they often impress, they remain disparate and self-contained, and thus their effect, when collected, is a muted one. The talent is there, but is not yet in full possession of its characteristic and identifying mode.

"Old Girls, Young Girls," in The Times Literary Supplement, *No. 3348, April 28, 1966, p. 361.*

WALTER KERR

The Loves of Cass McGuire is almost entirely populated with dreamers—old ones, young ones, some who should be busy about their middleaged chores but are ready to slip, ever so softly, into something nicer than life as it just happens to be right now. . . .

There is only one character in Mr. Friel's elusive game of musical shadows who cannot dream. She drinks. . . . [The title character has] had no loves, really. She has left Ireland 52 rattled years ago, she has come home at 70 to see her family again, and, with the help of a bottle, she keeps her Americanized head clear.

She still sounds like a child, with a voice like a penny-whistle, her tongue stuck sassily in the side of her mouth, and a red-and-white hair-ribbon tacked to the back of her neck. But she has led a life of false promises, waiting on tables and assorted men, and she does not propose to begin calling a spade a sunbeam.

In no time at all she has broken up the local pub, ticked off for her relatives the disloyal fellows she has lived with, disillusioned a teen-age lad and snapped her very quick fingers beneath the noses of a pretending world. Into the Eden [an old folks home] she must go quickly, bag and baggage, bottle and gaudy sequined jacket.

Before she goes, there is one thunderingly striking scene. For the whole of her 52 years away she has sent five dollars a week to her brother's family—to help things along a bit and perhaps to buy presents for the children. Now, in an uprush of brimming geniality, the brother has a surprise for her. He has been affluent all along, and he has saved every cent of the money. He is giving it back. It is all hers.

The news drops like the weight of centuries dead upon [Cass McGuire's] crumpling shoulders. Ashen, trying to wipe the creases in her forehead away as if they were so many cobwebs, she must grasp—in an instant—that the one gift she has given anybody, the one gesture in which she can take pride, has never really existed, has in fact been her own stupid dream. And, grasping the ugly truth, she is also expected to be grateful for it.

Mr. Friel writes the scene with casual force, letting the ache assert itself from inside the hearty benevolence of a gay family gathering. Indeed, line by line, Mr. Friel writes nearly everything well. Thoughtless cruelty is brushed in lightly: "Wouldn't you think at her age she wouldn't mind where she'd be?" The grubbing, grating ordinariness of [Cass McGuire's] past is sunk deep into her casual vocabulary: "Boy, the number of women I knew that went down with the cancer. You could pack Radio City with 'em."

What our author has not done this time around—the play that opened last evening is no match for last season's beguiling *Philadelphia, Here I Come!*—is to thread the lines together into a sustained, consistently moving pattern. He is very much concerned with patterns. The occasion as a whole is most freely arranged, so freely that [the title character] can chat with the audience any time she likes ("Listen, I wanted to be damn sure I was here when the curtain went up!"), freely enough to permit the actors to exchange roles now and then and the voices of the play to come streaming together like so many fragments of sound from echoing, isolated continents.

Sometimes the separate melodies mesh, sometimes sometimes they seem to drop away from one another quite out of breath and ready to ask directions from any stranger. The mood is unevenly distributed, the bits and pieces are not assimilated into one single, simple truth. In the end [the title character] gives up her candor and agrees to save herself with lies, too.

She comes home. But this is a rather easy, familiar, matter-of-fact ending for a play that truly wants to master the stage in an original fashion.

Walter Kerr, "Brian Friel's 'The Loves of Cass McGuire' Has Premiere," in The New York Times, *October 7, 1966, p. 36.*

RICHARD WATTS, JR.

In his second play [to be produced in the United States], Brian Friel again proves that he possesses the rueful imagination of the true Irish poet. His *The Loves of Cass McGuire* . . . contains much that is beautifully moving and a touch of humorous sharpness. Yet it must inevitably face comparison with Mr. Friel's *Philadelphia, Here I Come!* and there is no denying that it lacks the satisfying completeness of his unforgettable first comedy.

It is in a curious way the reverse of its predecessor. Where *Philadelphia, Here I Come!* dealt with youth on the eve of departing from Ireland, *The Loves of Cass McGuire* has to do with old age returning to its home land of Erin. And, where the earlier work indicated that his young hero was destined to encounter unhappy surroundings in America, the second one has its central character, a raffish old girl of 70 with a disreputable career behind her, end up in a home for the aged, together with several other wistful and dreaming exiles from life.

In both plays Mr. Friel employs a rather tricky device for his narrative. . . . Here the device might seem simpler, since it merely consists of having Cass McGuire step out of the action from time to time to address the audience and talk of the play as a play. But the fact is that the trick worked perfectly in the former, while in the second it appears a bit pointless and unnecessary.

It is when the author turns unashamedly to the lyric and emotional phase of his story that he is most successful. There is touching beauty in the scenes of an old man telling how his bride had been drowned during their honeymoon many years ago and an old woman describing romantic youthful travels that never actually took place, while Cass finally accepting her fate and showing kindness to the other inmates of the home becomes an appealing figure. Even the brother and sister-in-law who send Cass to the institution emerge as understandable and sympathetic.

When the play is being humorous, it can at times be amusing, but here, I think, trouble enters. It is Mr. Friel's intention to show what a rowdy old dame Cass had been, and it is a perfectly worthy aim. But, when she begins telling bawdy stories and tossing four-letter words about, I had less the impression of a good, earthy comic writer at work than of a serious professor trying to prove he is one of the boys. The two diverse aspects of the story somehow refuse to merge, the interest lessens, and the play must depend on its individual scenes of poetic compassion to show the quality that makes Brian Friel an exciting theater talent.

Richard Watts, Jr., "Cass McGuire Comes back to Erin," in New York Post, *October 7, 1966. Reprinted in* New York Theatre Critics' Reviews, *Vol. XXVII, No. 12, Week of October 10, 1966, p. 277.*

JOHN V. KELLEHER

Brian Friel's [stories in *The Gold in the Sea*] are set in western Ulster, divided between the Republic and Northern Ireland,

and the characters are nearly all Ulster Catholics. In one story a woman goes off to Cork to lead the gay life! From most, one gets the feeling of a society with short economic or social leeway, much like that reflected in the southern Irish stories of 20 or 30 years ago: not a poverty-stricken society, but one permitting few choices, restricted alike in the means for adventure and for sin.

Over the border in Donegal, Friel discovers magic. At home in Derry or Tyrone all is strictly for real, whether it be sorrow, envy, secret fantasy or plain fun. The stories have that down-to-earth, brass-tacks quality that was long one of the abiding attractions of Irish literature and that has been fading in the increasingly prosperous south.

Friel's style, if somewhat bald, is sturdy and direct; it fits his subjects and does not fail his moods. The one weakness of his technique is the tendency to rely on parallelisms, telling a story openly and at the same time mirroring the theme or characters in a set of images that are intended to illuminate the meaning or to add depth—just as he used two actors to illustrate facets of the same protagonist in his fine play, *Philadelphia, Here I Come!* Sometimes, as in "The Illusionists," the images are more obvious than the story. When the method really works, in "The Barney Game" for instance, it is because neither component is simple nor obvious, because there are large reserves in the story, not to be tapped on the first reading.

This is by no means the only story with adequate reserves. I had never read Friel's work in quantity before. I read it with respect. (p. 65)

John V. Kelleher, "Irish Portraits," in The New York Times Book Review, *October 16, 1966, pp. 64-5.*

ULICK O'CONNOR

Brian Friel, after his outstanding Broadway success with *Philadelphia Here I Come,* has returned to Dublin with a double bill, *Losers* and *Finders.* . . . *Losers* is perhaps the funniest play to be seen on the Irish stage for many a year. At times the audience were reduced to that state of chaotic disruption which only high comedy can bring on.

Losers tells of a middle-aged Irish bachelor who is prevented from pursuing a satisfactory courtship because of an interfering mother who rings a bell from her bed every time there is a lull in the conversation from the dining room downstairs where her daughter and the wooer are sitting. To thwart her manoeuvres, the frustrated Don Sean recites "Gray's Elegy" in between mouthfuls of kisses, thus assuaging the curiosity of the termagant above. This scene on the couch, with the bell ringing intermittently, has a Dali-esque quality, a surrealist version of the bedroom farce. Later he has his moment of triumph when he discovers that the mother's favourite saint, St. Philomena, has been abolished by the Pope. But he spoils his victory by succumbing to the "malaise Irlandaise", and in a drunken fit behaves so grossly towards the mother that she has him once more in her power when he returns to sobriety. . . .

Finders has only two characters, a schoolboy and a schoolgirl. We see them studying for the final examinations, lying on a hillside in Donegal. Their marriage will take place immediately . . . as the girl is pregnant. The fluctuations of young love are depicted a trifle sentimentally, and in between a picture of their family background emerges. Commentators at the side of the stage tell us in news-bulletin prose what happened to the pair after they left the hill that afternoon. We gather that they were drowned a few hours later while boating on a lake nearby.

This is the Greek device bravely attempted but only partially successful. . . .

Both pieces are perhaps essentially short stories jazzed up for the stage. But if they are slight dramatically, they are great value as entertainment. Anyway, why not translate literary modes for the stage? Mr. Friel, who is both a short-story writer and a dramatist, may have discovered something.

Ulick O'Connor, "Double Bill by Brian Friel," in The Times, *London, July 22, 1967, p. 7.*

DAN SULLIVAN

Lovers, the pair of one-act plays by Brian Friel . . . , makes an admirer of the author feel a little like the father of a very bright kid who has brought home an all B-plus report card. It's very good, but you know that there's more in him than that.

Let's emphasize the "very good." Mr. Friel's plays—the first one is called *Winners* [titled *Finders* in an earlier production] and the second *Losers*—add up to as pleasant an evening in the theater as you are likely to find this summer, and I will throw in the other seasons as well. . . .

Winners is about a very young couple, Mag and Joe, who are out for a day in the country three weeks before their wedding. There has been some embarrassment about the wedding. Mag is pregnant, and the news—especially since they're no more than 17—has not gone down well at home or at the rectory.

But, bygones be bygones. They love each other, the adults have been pacified and their future looks, if not bright, at least possible. On the crest of a hill overlooking their home town, she sprawls and gabs and he tries to (as much as you can with a woman around) study for his final exams.

Simultaneously, we learn from [the narrator], watching the two lovers from a spot somewhere to the side of the hill, that this is to be their last day on earth.

[The narrator's] dry recitation of the facts and figures that surround their death—time they were last seen in the village, depth of the water from which their bodies were taken—alternates with the girl's careless, confident talk of the future and the boy's imitations of some of the stuffier people in the village.

Our knowledge of what their future actually holds gives it all a double meaning, of course; his ambition to be somebody, her ideas about decorating the apartment. There is a chilling moment, for which we can doubtless credit Hilton Edwards, the director, when they roll down the hill giggling, and for the briefest instant their bodies assume the ungainly posture of the dead.

But the foreshadowing of calamity is, oddly, not disturbing or even unpleasant. Death, says Mr. Friel, will keep these lovers from being the losers that life almost surely would have made of them. Frozen in time before us, they play out their little day and disappear, "as if" [says the narrator] "nothing ever happened."

Winners is a lyric. *Losers* is a farce. . . .

[In *Losers* we get an] ample measure of laughter, some melancholy thoughts about the sadness of life in general and life in cleric-ridden, biddy-ridden Ireland in particular. Very good.

And yet . . . a little too familiar. *Winners* comes uncomfortably close to *Our Town* in its all-seeing narrator, its young lovers on the brink of an unknown future. Nor are the people in *Losers* fresh enough to be completely convincing—haven't we met this fake invalid mother, this shy bachelor, this man-hungry spinster in Irish literature before; are they not, in fact, precisely the people that we usually do meet?

A good story is a good story, and Mr. Friel has two of them to tell here. But were they newer stories, we would like them a little better.

> Dan Sullivan, "Art Carney and 'Lovers'," in The New York Times, *July 26, 1968, p. 21.*

ADRIAN RENDLE

Lovers is a marvellous double bill about young and old love which has enjoyed a huge success on Broadway and has already been acclaimed in Dublin. This is, perhaps, the most intuitive piece of playwriting I have encountered for some time and its success lies in its simplicity. *Lovers* is divided wryly into *Winners* and *Losers*—the titles of each of the plays. In *Winners* two young students meet on a hillside and bring their textbooks; they are Mag and Joe. It quickly transpires that Mag is pregnant and that they are going to get married. She is listless and loving whilst Joe is anxious, studious and eventually wild.

Their wonderful youth is the light of a gorse fire that will quickly burn itself out while on either side of the stage sit two narrators who factually relate circumstances of the accidental death by drowning on the very day we are watching the young lovers. This is superbly handled; it is as beautiful as any of the great love stories—a modern Romeo and Juliet caught out in the trivia of irrational disaster. The second play *Losers* tells of an older couple who in the course of the action re-tell their tragi-comic romance in which they spend frustrated hours waiting for the girl's old mother to die in her invalid bed above the courtyard. The old lady ruins their courtship by waiting for their conversation to stop and then selecting a delicious moment of silence in which to ring a loud, unfeeling handbell. To counteract this the lovers devise a system of the man reciting Gray's *Elegy* whilst trying to make love—a conversational voice keeping the intrepid bell silent. The result is hilarity and awfulness—a knife edge brilliantly honed by Mr. Friel. The end of the play shows the couple in retrospect with the Mother triumphant and the man suffering under the disgrace of having come home drunk and smashing the plaster saint in the invalid's bedroom. Hanna, his woman, has gone cold on him and he is left with a pair of binoculars to study the brick wall of the back yard. Gray's *Elegy* has come full circle—no words now, but with the Mother in control the handbell also is silent.

Brian Friel writes with a fantastic eye for human detail. . . . (pp. 67-8)

> Adrian Rendle, in a review of "Lovers—Winners and Losers," in Drama, *No. 93, Summer, 1969, pp. 67-8.*

RICHARD WATTS, JR.

Some plays experience difficulty in traveling. Brian Friel's *The Mundy Scheme* is an ironic satire on the venality of Ireland's political leaders, and in Dublin this summer it delighted Irish playgoers by the sharpness and pertinence of its sardonic implications. . . . [In its American production, *The Mundy Scheme*] had moments of effective humor but unfortunately lost most of its forceful sting.

In Dublin, when it began with the playing of the national anthem, "The Soldier's Song," went in for a glowing peroration on the martyrs of the long struggle for independence, and then proceeded to show the pettiness and self-serving of the present breed of leadership, the effect on the audience was electric. In New York, deprived of that background, it becomes parochial and you see that it is a quietly pleasant but mild and not very enlivening or striking comedy.

It deals with a scheme to divide great areas of Western Ireland into burial lots and sell them to foreigners, especially Americans, of Irish descent as their final resting place. The Prime Minister and his colleagues have got themselves in a mess at home and face the loss of their treasured offices. So when the Foreign Minister comes to them with the Mundy idea, they see a way to regain their popularity and, at the same time, line their pockets by buying up the property in secret.

Once the Mundy scheme, which seems a bit wild-eyed to begin with, has been hit upon, the Prime Minister and the other boys start trying to outsmart one another, which is the somewhat slender core of the play. This head man, bogusly genial fellow who addresses every one as "Great Heart," is the shrewdest of the crowd, and, although they use every trick to get ahead of him, they never have a chance. I think it is one of the weaknesses of the evening that they don't even give him a good battle. Only his old mother is able to bully him.

Since Mr. Friel is skillful in the use of words, *The Mundy Scheme* contains his characteristic touches of graceful and humorous writing. And no one can say the subject of the skulduggery of politicians is potentially without universal interest. But he has written it with an eye on Irish audiences and studiously given his story those parochial applications, and, though they can be bright, amusing and filled with shrewd observations of character, the tenuousness and some vagueness in the narrative keep getting in the way of proper enjoyment.

> Richard Watts, Jr., "The Wiles of Irish Politicians," in New York Post, *December 12, 1969. Reprinted in* New York Theatre Critics' Reviews, *Vol. XXX, No. 21, Week of December 8, 1969, p. 162.*

CLIVE BARNES

We have all seen the spectacle of characters in search of an author. Brian Friel's *The Mundy Scheme* . . . offered us the no less singular spectacle of scenes in search of a play.

Mr. Friel is a sensitive Irishman with the gift of blarney and an as yet unfulfilled talent for writing plays. The season before last he gave us a slight and graceful duet for people that he called *Lovers,* and in two earlier Broadway imports he has revealed a prolific and promising talent.

There are many virtues to being prolific, but consistency is rarely among them. *The Mundy Scheme* is too slight by half. It starts with a bright idea. The idea proves incapable of decent development. Political duplicity provides one or two brilliant scenes that prove that Mr. Friel is still alive and well and living in Dublin, and then the play fizzles out to an ending that even an amateur would call amateurish.

First for the bright idea. Mr. Friel has conceived of an Irish Government that proposes, through the happy conjunction of an enterprising Foreign Minister and an Irish-American philanthropist, a Mr. Mundy, to make the Emerald Isle the grave-yard of the Western world.

New York, Paris, London, such great urban centers have a real estate problem. Land values are high, the cost of burial prohibitive, and the space taken by an unproductive corpse positively antisocial. Why not have the corpses of the world emigrate, under strictly religious but tactfully ecumenical auspices, to the bogs of Western Ireland?

The idea is funny. But only momentarily funny. There has to be a kernel of possibility to comedy for it to work longer than it takes to deliver the punchline of a joke. Mr. Friel's idea has not got even a fantasy air of truth to it. If Manhattan wanted to export corpses they would be exported to the Jersey Meadows and Neil Simon would be writing a play about it.

What is worse, the idea cannot be expanded. It just does not lend itself to comic elaboration. Mr. Friel tries to improve the shining hour by adding all kinds of political finaglings. This helps a little. . . .

It would be unfair to reveal any further details of a plot that has so few further details to reveal. Suffice it to say, and needless to say it does not suffice, that all three of the principal conspirators are sent off to fates as vague as the logic in an Irish tavern. . . .

> Clive Barnes, "Friel's 'Mundy Scheme'," in The New York Times, December 12, 1969, p. 75.

ADRIAN RENDLE

It is perhaps not surprising to find that Brian Friel's play *Crystal and Fox* has not moved from the Irish stage in the same way as his other work. Not surprising because the life of Fox Melarky, the proprietor of a travelling show, does not readily assume the universal image of Friel's other characters. The tatty little road show led by a husband and wife team who eventually try to shield their son from a murder charge remains localized and a touch too sentimental. As always with Brian Friel there is some fine writing and the characters are well drawn. The piece is clearly intending to pose the question of the rights of personal freedom we may have at any given moment of our lives and contains a good dramatic twist at the end. . . .

> Adrian Rendle, in a review of "Crystal and Fox," in Drama, No. 101, Summer, 1971, p. 84.

DESMOND RUSHE

The political turbulence in the North of Ireland found its first dramatic outlet in the work of a major writer when Brian Friel's new play, *The Freedom of the City,* recently exploded on the stage. . . . In a setting starkly evocative of a claustrophobic ghetto covered with graffiti of sectarian politics, the stream of gas billowed from the rubble of a Derry street, while the air was filled with the noises of water cannon and rubber bullets. Then the bullets became real, and a woman and two young men lay dead. The time is a Saturday afternoon in February, 1970, after a banned civil rights march has been scattered, leaving three victims. But the date could have been Jan. 30, 1972, and the number of dead 13, because in its external trappings, Mr. Friel's play is a bitterly ironic documentary on Bloody Sunday, on disastrous overreaction by security forces, on the subsequent Widgery tribunal of inquiry and on the response to the killings by churchmen, politicians and people.

But into the ferment walks Dr. Philip Alexander Dodds, an American sociologist, to give a lecture on the subculture of poverty, and it quickly becomes apparent that Mr. Friel is using the Bloody Sunday situation merely as a frame. The canvas concentrates on the deprived, the poor, the have-nots, the ghetto-dwellers, and the play becomes a commentary on the social conditions that make a Bloody Sunday possible.

Dr. Dodds lectures on how ghetto life tends to perpetuate itself in a narrow, subjective way, whether in Derry or New York or London or Latin America. But once the ghetto-dwellers get an objective view of their conditions, they tend to break out of their subculture, and claim their share of the prosperity that has been denied them.

Mr. Friel's subculturists unwittingly escape from gas and rubber bullets by taking refuge in the mayor's parlor of Derry's Guildhall, the sacred symbol of oppressive rule. There is irony here, and there is added irony in the innocent fun they have while they wait for things to quiet down outside. They drink the mayor's liquor, ring up friends on the mayor's telephone, dress themselves in civic robes and confer on themselves the freedom of a city that has ground them into the dirt. Meanwhile, the British army is circulating reports that the Guildhall has been occupied by armed terrorists and is moving in its armed might to force a surrender.

The irony mounts, but a play does not live on irony alone, and while Mr. Friel is sincere, concerned and noble in his intentions, he is not altogether successful in giving them impact. When one strips *The Freedom of the City* of its deeply emotive and highly dramatic Bloody Sunday connotations, one is left with rather trivial fare, because unlike Sean O'Casey, who gave slum-dwellers like Juno a universal stature, Mr. Friel's characters remain identifiable only with their localized surroundings. He has failed to create identifiable prototypes of the universal ghettoland.

Which is both a pity and a disappointment, because apart from expatriate Samuel Beckett, Mr. Friel is Ireland's finest living playwright. (pp. 31-2)

> Desmond Rushe, "Dublin: Ferment Has Outlet on Stage," in The New York Times, March 1, 1973, pp. 31-2.

CLIVE BARNES

As long as Ireland has its troubles, Irish playwrights will tragically always have a subject matter. Brian Friel's *The Freedom of the City* . . . is set in Londonderry, Northern Ireland, in 1970, in the middle of the recent disturbances.

In his perhaps too luridly fictionalized story, three people have fled from a civil rights march. In an effort to get away from the rubber bullets and tear gas of the troops and police they take refuge by chance in the strangely deserted Guildhall. Here they find their way into the Lord Mayor's Parlor, or his inner office. They dress up in his ceremonial robes, drink his liquor and chat.

Somehow—we never learn how—the British troops discover the presence of "terrorists" in the Guildhall. It seems that they imagine there could be as many as 50 of them, all, according to the army, fully armed. They are called upon to surrender. The three of them, unarmed, with their hands above their heads, walk out and are promptly massacred by the British troops.

That is really the beginning of the play, for the play itself is the story of the whitewashing British Court of Inquiry. The evidence (brief and slender) is intercut with the scenes of the victims finding their way to the Guildhall and their behavior once inside.

Mr. Friel's concern is to draw an ironic contrast between what really happened and what is said to have happened. . . .

Mr. Friel seems to know more about writing plays than about constructing them. He has here, for example, at least two extremely successful set pieces, intended as commentaries. In one we have an American sociologist talking about "the sub-culture of poverty"—which turns out to be nonsense of the finest quality. Then, even better, we have an unctuous Dublin radio announcer describing, in a mixture of hearts, flowers and glycerine, the funeral of the martyrs.

As we know from his past work (particularly *Philadelphia, Here I Come* and *Lovers*) Mr. Friel has a handy, if obvious, hand with dialogue. The interplay between the two young men is nicely done, and Mr. Friel has described Lily with love and insight. To hear her talk about her mongoloid son is to listen to a real woman, and what could be better than her writing in a hotel guest book, after the one good meal of her life, "God, bless the Cook!" Someone ought to bless Lily.

Unfortunately for Mr. Friel, the play is not only rather slow in motion, but it is also perfectly predictable, and once a playwright has sacrificed the ace of surprise, he has to have a lot of other good cards in his hand. Here within five minutes of the play's opening we know exactly what is going to happen. Also, the playwright forgets that irony is much strengthened by likelihood. Can we really be expected to believe that the British Army would mobilize against these three people 22 tanks, two dozen armored cars, four water cannon and "a modicum of air cover"? The final finding of the court is far-fetched, indeed, impossible.

> *Clive Barnes, " 'The Freedom of the City,' about the Irish," in* The New York Times, *February 18, 1974, p. 32.*

SEAMUS HEANEY

[The essay excerpted below originally appeared in The Times Literary Supplement *on March 21, 1975.]*

[The title of Friel's play *Volunteers*] courts the stock response. Volunteers answer the call, rise to the self-sacrificing occasion and are noble in the cause, whether of Ireland or Ulster. The word has a sacral edge which blunts (nevertheless) to sancti-moniousness, and it is this potential sanctimoniousness that the play is intent on devastating. Misery and bravery can be ennobled from a distance—the armchair poets of the First World War are a good example—but one of the artistic imperatives is to say the truth as exactly as possible. The message implicit in Friel's play is explicit in Wilfred Owen's 'Apologia Pro Poemate Meo': 'These men are worth your tears. You are not worth their merriment.'

Like Owen's soldiers, and still more like his miners, Friel's internees are dug in—on an archaeological site. For five months they have been on daily parole to assist the excavation of a Viking site that is soon to be buried under a multi-storey hotel. They have volunteered for the job, have been ostracized by their fellow internees for their collaboration and on this last day of the dig they learn that they are to be violently punished,

probably killed, by their comrades back in the cells. They are trapped between political, economic and social realities and received ideas: victims, which is another word that Friel is intent on pursuing into accuracy. They come in under the in-different eye of a warder, work their stint under the supervision of a petty bourgeois foreman and go out under the shadow of violent death. What happens in between is a masque of anarchy.

The action—or, more precisely, the interaction—centres on Keeney, a man who has put an antic disposition on, for Viking Ireland, like Denmark, is a prison. He is a Hamlet who is gay, not with tragic Yeatsian joy but as a means of deploying and maintaining his anger.

Volunteers to a large extent depends on the various plays within the play initiated by, directed by and starring Keeney, a shower-off and a letter-down, who uses as a starting-point for much of his improvisation the skeleton of a murdered Viking, ex-posed *in situ,* a bony structure that can be fleshed with any number of possible meanings: a symbol, in fact, as is the thirteenth-century jug lovingly restored by the site foreman.

A number of reviewers simply refused to accept the dramatic kind that Friel has broken into, a kind that involves an alienation effect but eschews didactic address. As a playwright he has always been obsessed by the conflict between public and private selves, by games and disguises. . . . Double-talk and double-takes, time-shifts, supple dialogue and subtle exposures, these have been the life of his plays, but one occasionally sensed a tension between the vision and the form, as if a man whose proper idiom was free verse was being forced to realize himself in metrical stanzas.

In *Volunteers* he has found a form that allows his gifts a freer expression. Behind the writing there is an unrelenting despair at what man has made of man, but its expression from moment to moment on the stage is by turns ironic, vicious, farcical, pathetic. . . . The play is not a quarrel with others but a vehicle for Friel's quarrel with himself, between his heart and his head, to put it at its simplest. It is more about values and attitudes within the Irish psyche than it is about the rights and wrongs of the political situation, and represents a further digging of the site cleared in his *Freedom of the City.*

Still people yearn for a *reductio:* what does he mean? He means, one presumes, to shock. He means that an expert, hurt and shocking laughter is the only adequate response to a cal-loused condition (perhaps one should adduce Sassoon instead of Owen) and that no 'fake concern' (the phrase is the *Honest Ulstermans'*) should be allowed to mask us from the facts of creeping indifference, degradation and violence. And he means to develop as a playwright and to create, despite resistance, the taste by which he is to be enjoyed. (pp. 214-16)

> *Seamus Heaney, "Digging Deeper: Brian Friel's 'Volunteers'," in his* Preoccupations: Selected Prose, *1968-1978, Farrar, Straus, Giroux, 1980, pp. 214-16.*

RICHARD EDER

Brian Friel's new play uses a broken-down, itinerant Irish faith healer to construct a parable about the artist and his estranging art. *Faith Healer* is an intriguing and sometimes powerful piece of writing. But it doesn't seem well suited for the stage. . . .

The play is set out in four successive monologues; two by the faith healer, one by his wife, and one by his assistant. They tell three somewhat differing versions of the same story: their travels over the years through the back-country of Scotland and Wales, and the grisly ending that destroys them at a pub in Donegal.

The monologues do more than relate, in cryptic bits and pieces, the narrative of their wanderings, the sparsely attended gatherings, the occasional apparent healings, the frequent failures, the stink and misery of an itinerant poverty.

They contribute to the portrait of an artist and his burden. The wife tells of the alternating squalor and grandeur of being companion and lover to a man whose art—faith-healing in this case—comes and goes; who is human and unremarkable in its absence, and remarkable and inhuman when it is there.

The Cockney assistant, a practical factotum full of small bits of common sense and a large helplessness, has some comical observations about the artist as inspired fool. He tells of his two dogs. One is intelligent and helpful, but incapable of performing on the stage. The other is a performing genius—he plays ''Come Into My Garden, Maud'' on the bagpipes, practices all day, and is a mess in every other respect.

The faith healer himself is both artist and failed artist; Mr. Friel makes the two inseparable. Occasionally he has performed miraculous cures; most of the time he fails. But his monologues, a mixture of obsessive reminiscence and reflection, suggest that failure is a kind of relief.

He reflects that most people come to him not to be cured but to be confirmed in their certainty that they cannot be cured. Most of the time that is what they get. . . .

For him as well, as an artist, the burden of success was more terrible than that of failure. Success was an estranging mystery. And so when he goes home to Ireland and is challenged by four murderous drunks to cure a crippled man, there is a kind of satisfaction in knowing that he will fail and that they will kill him for it.

In a beautiful final passage, the faith healer recalls walking out of the pub and into the courtyard where his challengers and murderers wait for him. ''As I walked across that yard towards them, then for the first time I had a simple and genuine sense of homecoming,'' he says, speaking after his death. ''At long last I was renouncing chance.''

Mr. Friel's language is frequently beautiful, and his images can be both striking and stirring. The parable is an arresting one. On the stage . . . , though, it is more often an imprisoning one.

> Richard Eder, ''Friel's 'Faith Healer','' in The New York Times, *April 6, 1979, p. 3.*

BRENDAN GILL

People who complain of the scarcity in contemporary theatre of plays that are well written and well made had reason to be grateful last week for the arrival . . . of Brian Friel's *Faith Healer*. . . . In the arts, it is always a risky business to seem comfortably at home in the past, and it's true that Mr. Friel is sometimes a trifle too literary for his own good; a distinguished short-story writer as well as a playwright, he tells the intricate, curious tale of *Faith Healer* by means of three voices, but we are never unaware that the voices are his and that the suspense he creates is a result of the cleverest possible contrivance. His plot is more that of a novella than that of a play; it looks back

to the Henry James of ''A Bundle of Letters'' rather than forward to, say, the Sam Shepard of *Buried Child*.

There are but three characters in *Faith Healer*—Frank, an itinerant, hard-drinking Irishman, who possesses a gift for healing the maimed, the halt, and the blind, and who doesn't understand the nature of his gift; Grace, his patient mistress; and Teddy, his Cockney manager, who books Frank into seedy small-town theatres and halls as if he were a vaudeville act. Everything we learn about the three of them emerges in the course of four long soliloquies, delivered in sequence by Frank, Grace, Teddy, and Frank again. Each appears on the stage alone, and as much dramatic conflict as the play contains is related and not represented. Little by little, we discover that Frank is to meet a terrifying end, in the courtyard of a pub somewhere in Ireland; so artful is Mr. Friel that we cannot be sure what has befallen Frank until the last two words of the last soliloquy are spoken. (pp. 115-16)

> Brendan Gill, ''In Sunny Italy,'' in The New Yorker, *Vol. LV, No. 9, April 16, 1979, pp. 115-16.*

WILLIAM A RAIDY

Faith and doubt, the fire and water of philosophical life, stand like opposing armies to the psyche of Frank Hardy, a self-doubting, alcoholic 'healer' and the dark hero of Brian Friel's thrilling new play, *Faith Healer*. Perhaps he knows instinctively that men are not saved by faith but the want of it; perhaps he also knows that the tepid water of doubt may sometimes act as an emetic, making a man vomit out the fears at his innards.

Both are dangerous bits of knowledge to this seedy, boozing itinerant spellbinder who travels with his beatendown mistress and his ever-buoyant manager along the back roads of Wales, Scotland, and finally Ireland, his birthplace, selling 'cures' and show business fanfare. Frank, appearing in broken-down barns and chilly old churches rented for the evening, is not a religious evangelist justifying the ways of God to man. No, he has what his mistress calls 'this gift, this craft, this talent'.

He calls his meetings 'performances' and dreams of raising a sick princess up from death in a palace and going away with a purse of gold. Whatever this talent is, it eludes both the mistress and the would-be healer. Is he a charlatan, a mere mountebank, a mock miracle worker taking pennies from superstitious farmers in the shabby, bleak and derelict backwaters of rural Britain? Frank Hardy knows he has a special 'talent' and he has seen it work at his healing sessions under the tatty, faded banner that reads: 'The Fantastic Francis Hardy'. Lame men have got up and walked away. Frank realises, however, that most of the disfigured and halt who come to him are actually without real hope. Inwardly they want to be reassured of this hopelessness. Friel makes Hardy the symbol of the artist who has the talent to raise people from the animal level. But is he really an artist with a magic hand?

Just as these hopeless people secretly want the knowledge that absolutely nothing can help them to be reaffirmed, their 'healer' wants to know something too. In his drunken, falling apart state, he curiously enough knows that doubt of whatever kind can be ended by action alone. It is this action . . . his final action . . . that sits dead centre in the strange vortex of Friel's vastly theatrical play. (p. 34)

Faith Healer is an exciting, provocative and highly inventive drama. . . . (p. 35)

William A Raidy, "Fictions of a Healer," in Plays and Players, *Vol. 26, No. 9, July, 1979, pp. 34-5.*

CLIVE BARNES

The time is 1833. The place is County Donegal in Ireland. Thirty-five years earlier, staggered by the Irish resistance culminating in the bloody battle of Vinegar Hill in Wexford, the English had decided to try to cease its centuries long attempts to colonize Ireland, and to bring it into the same kind of political union that had so far proved moderately peaceful with Scotland and Wales.

Later, at the pressure of Daniel O'Connor, in 1800, the Act of Catholic Emancipation had been passed. It looked like a time of hope for Ireland and for England.

But then the English parliamentarians lost time and interest, and the suppression reasserted itself. British soldiers were sent out to re-map Ireland. The Gaelic names were given English equivalents.

Forgive the politics—Friel's [*Translations*] has to be set up. Among the young English officers is Lieutenant Yolland—a good-natured, good-looking romantic. He takes one look at Donegal and falls in love with it.

He also meets Maire after a dance and falls in love with her "always." He only speaks English. She only speaks Gaelic. Imagine a Romeo and Juliet who couldn't speak Italian. They manage. He reels off the Gaelic names from the maps he is studying. They pledge love in different tongues. They embrace.

That night he is murdered for his love, and the next morning she goes mad. The English soldiers pillage the countryside in revenge. You see the right translations never have been made—even now.

Friel is also concerned with the loss of national identity through language—the rejection of the Gaelic scholars and their so-called Hedge Schools, who could converse in Latin and Greek, and taught English. And technically he is absorbed by the idea of having two people talk in "English" while the audience has to know that one of them is really talking Gaelic—another translation.

This picture, this analysis, of Ireland at a time conceivably of hope deferred if not lost, is full of that Hibernian gift of transforming a foreign reality into a native poetry. Once more translation.

The play, produced in Derry at the end of last year, has a special importance in the history of the Irish drama. Since the great Anglo-Irish playwrights from Congreve to Shaw, or, dare one say, O'Casey, and the eternal monolith of Yeats, the Irish playwright has usually been a talent with a short fuse, a big explosion and a long silence.

After one early, overpraised success, Friel has seemed a playwright in waiting. The waiting is now over. This play gleams with that old bardic poetry translated—as they say—into style. (pp. 265-66)

Clive Barnes, "A Play Worthy of 'Translations'," in New York Post, *April 15, 1981. Reprinted in* New York Theatre Critics' Reviews, *Vol. XLII, No. 8, Week of April 20, 1981, pp. 265-66.*

FRANK RICH

It's not big news that Brian Friel, the Irish playwright, can write some of the most beautiful language to be heard in the contemporary theater. But in his new play, Mr. Friel has taken his love of words further still. Language is not just the dramatic currency of *Translations*—it is also the play's subject. What's more, the playwright has elevated his esthetic passion to a matter of life-and-death importance. Though *Translations* is a manifestly uneven piece of theater, it has something profound to say about how words can determine the fates of ordinary people, nations and even centuries of history.

The people of *Translations* . . . are peasants whose "ostentation of language is lacking in their material lives." They are residents of the tiny Irish hamlet of Baile Beag in 1833. It is four years after the Catholic Emancipation, and a contingent of now-friendly British redcoats has arrived for a seemingly benign task. New maps are to be drawn up of the countryside; Irish place names are to be translated into "standardized" English.

What does this mean for the lowly farmers of Baile Beag? On the surface, not much. This is, ostensibly, a good time for the Irish. Under the new laws of tolerance, they can worship in freedom. They no longer have to seek an education in their clandestine "Hedge Schools," but will soon be able to attend new, modern schools being built by the state. If the British want to rename every hill and dale, if they want to Anglicize the local language, that seems a small price to exact for the benefits they are giving the Irish in return.

As the evening progresses, it rapidly becomes clear that this price is not small at all. *Translations* consists of a series of homely anecdotes in which the townsfolk, now attending the final sessions of their outmoded hedge school, realize that by losing their language, they are facing "an eviction of sorts." As the boozy old schoolmaster . . . explains in one of Mr. Friel's most moving lines, "Civilizations can be imprisoned in a linguistic contour that doesn't match the language of fact."

Not everyone sees the Anglicization of Ireland as a cause for alarm, however. Even the schoolmaster, a proud literary nationalist, has gladly accepted an invitation to run the new English-speaking school that will supersede his informal classroom of 35 years. Though one of his sons . . . plans to resist the new regime, the other . . . has signed on with the invading British as a translator. One of his adult students, Maire . . . , views the Irish language as "a barrier to progress" and plans, in any case, to leave her homeland forever for America. Her fellow pupils—who range from a nearly mute farm girl . . . to an aged O'Casey-esque barroom bard . . .—hardly know what all the fuss is about.

But a society is changing, and Mr. Friel limns the upheavals with intimate humor. In the evening's most inspired scene, two erstwhile cross-cultural lovers exchange intimacies without comprehending a word the other is saying. The soon-to-emigrate Maire has fallen for one of the British soldiers, Lieutenant Yolland . . . , because she loves the sound of his foreign speech. She doesn't understand that Yolland is the one soldier who disapproves of his Government's mission; he loves the sound of *Maire's* speech and wants to settle with her in Ireland. As these two try to establish their doomed courtship without a common language, they somehow convince themselves that they are meeting on common ground. But there is no common ground. Their linguistic comedy of errors emblematizes the gap that has set even peace-craving British and Irish apart for generations.

As is frequently the case with Mr. Friel, this play's failures are of a structural nature. *Translations* flounders about at the outset of Act I, as the students arrive for lessons at their musty barn of a classroom. . . . Act III trails off into an underwritten apocalypse. The potentially wrenching relationships among the schoolmaster and his two sons are only vaguely sketched in; the minor students are also ill-defined. (p. 264)

Like so many other elements in *Translations,* [the] schoolmaster, too, could be more expansively written; the part is not as large as its importance to the drama. Yet it's hard to complain too angrily. Though one wishes that Mr. Friel's follow-through fully matched his intentions here, there are far worse playwriting sins than leaving the audience hungry for more. (p. 265)

Frank Rich, "'Translations' from Brian Friel," in The New York Times, *April 15, 1981, pp. 264-65.*

JOHN SIMON

As the very title of [*Translations*] indicates, the subject is language—or, rather, languages: the cleavage between people caused by unshared speech and the problems caused or exacerbated by their mutual incomprehension. Translation itself is a sort of transition: the bridge between sequestration and communion. But it is a bridge where structural weaknesses cause disturbances, from traffic bottlenecks to total collapse of the bridge, from comic mishaps to tragic misunderstandings. It is a fascinating subject, and Friel plays imaginatively with more forms of translation and mistranslation than you can shake a shillelagh at—even such translations as a foolish dreamer's translating himself, with the help of that great interpreter, poteen, into the age of Hellenic myth, and fancying himself Pallas Athene's bridegroom. . . .

The second act of *Translations,* whose haunting highlight is the scene in which Yolland and Maire make verbal love with the only words they have, and cherish, in common—Irish place names—is altogether engrossing. But it, too, is only a transition between the humdrum exposition of Act I and the deliberately low-key non-resolution of Act III. A splendid middle, then, flanked by unsatisfying extremities, the last scene even unpleasantly reminiscent of an O'Casey ending: Little people drunkenly or self-absorbedly unaware of the tragedy in their midst.

There are fine ironies scattered throughout the play, and the concentric translation metaphors expand with powerfully poetic impact. If only people learned a common language instead of wallowing in parochialism, or studying luxuriously useless dead languages (like the Irish peasantry), or not even studying them (like the English conquerors). For even a shared dead language could palliate the need for translation. Add to this the magisterial dramaturgic device of having Irish represented by English spoken with a brogue, while English is represented by brogueless English. Thus two people can talk at each other in essentially the same language (humanity) and not understand, while the audience is privileged to grasp both sides of this noncommunicating and realize how reconcilable the differences might be but for the linguistic wall. Still, the play feels far too much like a fragment from a novel, with too much missing at both ends to yield a fulfilling entity. (p. 59)

John Simon, "Unfinished Business," in New York Magazine, *Vol. 14, No. 17, April 27, 1981, pp. 59-62.*

MARTIN ESSLIN

Having insulted the Irish by putting on Howard Brenton's play, *The Romans in Britain,* which equated the Catholic population of Northern Ireland with naked, illiterate barbarian aborigines of a wild ancient Britain, the National Theatre has now redressed the balance: Brian Friel [in *Translations*] shows us a Gaelic-speaking community in County Donegal, around 1830, the members of which are able to converse in fluent Greek and Latin, quoting Homer and Virgil, proud of their native Irish tongue and despising English as a language particularly suited for the purposes of commerce, but without any poetry. The scene is a 'hedge school' one of those privately, and almost clandestinely established schools in which the rural population of Ireland endeavoured to keep alive with the country's ancient language and high culture.

How much more subtle and intelligent Brian Friel's approach to the Irish problem is than Brenton's clumsy pamphleteering! An ordinance survey mapping operation is being conducted in the school's area by English soldiers, Royal Engineers. One of the schoolmaster's sons, Owen, is acting as interpreter and helping with establishing the names of villages, hills and other features of the landscape. The English lieutenant in charge of this name-giving is unable to transliterate the subtle Irish sounds and so the region's place names are being radically and insensitively anglicized—a wonderful metaphor that for the process by which a culture is being obliterated by conquerors. Yet that self-same lieutenant, George Yolland, is enchanted by Ireland, wants to learn Erse and has fallen in love with a beautiful local girl, Maire, with whom the schoolmaster's other son, Manus, is also, but unhappily, in love.

In a subtle and beautiful scene—with echoes of Henry V and his Kate—George and Maire establish their mutual love for each other in spite of their inability to speak each other's languages, but are observed by a dumb girl whom Manus has helped to regain some ability to speak. She tells Manus that his girl is making love to another man; Manus is so devastated by seeing the scene, that he decides to leave the area. When George Yolland, the English lieutenant, disappears and must be presumed murdered, the next morning, suspicion is bound to fall on his disappointed rival. Some of the villagers know that the murder has in fact been committed by local Irish nationalist rebels. The English announce that unless the matter is cleared up the whole village will be dispossessed, the population evicted. As the play ends all we know is that the schoolmaster's other son Owen has gone to deal with the matter. Will he save the village by betraying the nationalists with whose cause he is in sympathy? We are left with that question.

It is this ending which, I feel, shows Brian Friel's subtlety and political intelligence: he has abundantly established the case for the Irish population's national feeling and yearning for freedom. He has also shown the undoubted mutual human attraction between at least some individuals on both sides of the national divide. And he brilliantly highlights the moral dilemma of those in Ireland who desire independence and national freedom but abhor violence in any form. . . .

It is, of course, the ultimate irony of the play that it is written entirely in English, in a convention by which we must believe that the Irish characters speak Erse, the English English, and the translator between them suggests what he is doing merely by paraphrasing the same sentence in different (English) words—which is, in itself, an extremely funny and effective device, as it makes us see what the interpreter suppresses, how he reduces the pompous bureaucratic language of the officers into homely commonsensical speech. Similarly the love scene between George and Maire gains its humour and poignancy from our hearing both sides of this mutually incomprehensible exchange. . . .

[*Translations* has] obvious merits: its political and moral integrity, and the subtlety of its construction, the ingenious way in which it modulates variations on the theme of language and communication between human beings: the speechlessness of dumb Sarah, for example, is sensitively brought in as another variation on the theme of language; and that it is her ability to speak that Manus has given her which destroys Manus' world is a masterstroke of dramatic irony, as, indeed, is the fact that her shock at what she has done again deprives her of the power of speech, probably for ever.

Translations is undoubtedly one of Brian Friel's best plays. It puts him in the very front rank of contemporary dramatists.

> *Martin Esslin, in a review of "Translations," in* Plays & Players, *No. 29, November, 1981, p. 36.*

CHARLES SPENCER

Brian Friel's new play *The Communication Cord* is described as a companion piece to his prize-winning *Translations* and as such it must be counted a disappointment. *Translations* was an immensely satisfying work, set 150 years ago in an Irish hedge school which made profound points with great delicacy about the differences, particularly of language which still divide the English from the Irish.

The Communication Cord brings us into the present. The scene is still the remote townland of Ballybeg in County Donegal and the fashionably rustic weekend cottage in which the action takes place might even be the old hedge school, radically converted, in which the farm labourers of *Translations* used to study their Greek texts.

Friel's interest in language and its shifting treacherousness also remains. The central character Tim Gallagher is a junior lecturer in linguistics . . . but without the ability to hold an ordinary conversation and the play's plot depends almost entirely on desperate lies and the breakdown of communication.

And while *Translations* showed the British annexing the Irish language, *The Communication Cord* shows the Irish middle classes taking over and sentimentalising the tradition of the peasantry. But despite these passing similarities of location and theme all, in the Yeatsian phrase, is changed, changed utterly: . . . a terrible farce is born.

That is perhaps unfair, as in the first half Friel organises his comedy with brisk efficiency and there were many occasions when I laughed immoderately. But every good farce depends on an increasingly fast and bewildering accumulation of confusion and after the interval the author seems to lose his touch. The jokes slow down, implausibilities mount up and there are too many obtrusive explanations in which the characters attempt to unravel what is going on. Despite a curtain line which quite literally brings the house down, laughter is in stubbornly short supply during most of the play's second hour. (p. 32)

False identities and misunderstandings quickly abound and Friel even steals Peter Shaffer's old trick of playing certain scenes as if they were in pitch darkness when the audience can of course see quite clearly.

But doubts about the play grow even in the dizziest and funniest scenes. Too many of the hurried explanations would clearly be audible to characters who are meant to remain in blissful ignorance and there are moments too when Friel appears to be trying—and failing—to make serious points about the nature of communication and Ireland's relationship with its own past.

Implausibility—the most dangerous threat to farce which relies on absolute logic however absurd the situation—reaches its damaging depths when a senator voluntarily chains himself to a wall. The vital suspension of disbelief is put under severe strain and the performances become increasingly shrill, desperate and unconvincing. (p. 33)

> *Charles Spencer, in a review of "The Communication Cord," in* Plays & Players, *No. 358, July, 1983, pp. 32-3.*

SEAMUS DEANE

A closed community, a hidden story, a gifted outsider with an antic intelligence, a drastic revelation leading to violence—these are recurrent elements in a Brian Friel play. They are co-ordinated in the pursuit of one elusive theme, the link between authority and love. Most of the people in Friel's drama are experts in the maintenance of a persona, or of an illusion upon which the persona depends. But their expertise, which most often takes the form of eloquence and wit, and which is a mode of defence against the oppressions of false authority, has no power to alter reality. So they become articulators of a problem to such a degree that the problem becomes insoluble, so perfectly etched are all its numbing complexities. To be gifted at all, an expert, is to be displaced, a commentator, not a participant, an outsider, not an insider. Yet the sense of displacement is acute in such figures and it is the more profoundly felt when it is expressed for them in the secret or hidden stories of others. The stories are tales of passion, thwarted and violent; the displacement is a condition of lucid weariness, often witty and cruel in its responses. The tension between the two embodiments of thwarted desire disrupts the closed community, undermines its sham system of authority and leads to various kinds of breakdown, individual and social. Friel's drama is concerned with the nervous collapse of a culture which has had to bear pressures beyond its capacity to sustain.

The closed community is that of the County Donegal village of Ballybeg, or of sectors within that generic community—monastic as in *The Enemy Within* (1962), psychological as in *Philadelphia, Here I Come!* (1964), sexual-familial as in *The Gentle Island* (1971) or *Living Quarters* (1977), political as in *The Freedom of the City* (1973) or *Volunteers* (1975). The cast of characters is tightly contained in a quarantined area, enclosed with the infection which is coming to a head on this particular moment, in this particular setting. The dramatic unities of time, place and action are strictly observed but the apparently effortless and often humorous registration of the details of provincial manners helps to disguise the structural tautness which gives these works their symmetry—although . . . *The Communication Cord* (produced in 1982) reveals more obviously than these others how strictly organized his plays are. The illness which plagues the small community is failure, cast in every conceivable shape, protean but always recognizable. The central failure is one of feeling and, proceeding from that, a failure of self-realization and, deriving from that, the seeking of a refuge in words or work, silence or idiocy, in exile or in a deliberate stifling of unrequitable desire. Every character has his or her fiction; every fiction is generated out of the fear of the truth. But the truth is nevertheless there, hidden in the story which lies at the centre of the play, a story which tells of how authority, divorced from love, became a sham. (pp. 166-67)

[In] *Volunteers,* the republican prisoners working on the archaeological site on which a new hotel is to be erected, provide us with an image of many of the characteristic political and economic forces in Irish society, all of them governed by corrupt authorities. Equally, in *Living Quarters* the Butler family, or in *The Gentle Island* the Sweeney family, or the central trio in *The Freedom of the City,* all provide us with this public display of existing conditions, of circumstances easily recognized as the sort which would make news—the return of Irish UN troops from a trouble spot, the mass departure of a community from an island, the official killings and inquiries of the Northern situation. Yet the recognizability of the conditions is one of Friel's naturalistic illusions. For the secret story—of Smiler in *Volunteers,* of Lily in *The Freedom of the City,* of Manus in *The Gentle Island,* challenges that recognizability and forces the audience to sense within it an element of mystery, a suppressed quotient of feeling. Clearly, these people are all victims of foul conditions. Their fate is predetermined and all their attempts to escape it are futile. Smiler's mock escape, Manus's invented story about the loss of his arm, Lily's fake reasons for being on the civil rights marches are all illusions, lies created to disguise a truth, their malevolent presence indicated by some physical deformity or mental affliction. The function of the hidden story, when it is uncovered, is to transform the stage as public exhibition area into the stage as private and sacral area. The recognizable social 'meaning' is constantly being undermined by another kind of significance which is more complex and cryptic. The shock·of the conclusion finally clarifies this cryptic element. Violence is not a manifestation of the pressures of specifically Irish conditions. In the conclusion we see death, individual death, the death of a way of life or of a social formation, finally confronted by people who have been escaping it all their lives. In the light of that, all authority fails, even the authority of love.

Still, our sympathy or our admiration tends to be given to the people who have no illusions, who are not locked into some conspiracy of discretion or of despair and who regard the world with a liberated and liberating intelligence. Keeney in *Volunteers,* Skinner in *The Freedom of the City,* Eamon in *Aristocrats,* Shane in *The Gentle Island,* are the most obvious examples. But Keeney and Skinner are killed, Shane is crippled for life, Eamon is bereft with the rest of the O'Donnell family. Further, they are all outsiders, but with an insider's knowledge of the society. They put an antic disposition on, partly as a mode of rejecting authority, partly as a mode of escaping responsibility. But, disengaged in this way, they become mere wordsmiths. Their language is gestural, being in effect nothing more than a series of mimicries, a ventriloquism by performers who run the risk of losing their own voices. The displacement of voice, the switching of vocabularies, always important in a Friel play, is a symptom of the splintering of authority, the failure of any one voice to predominate and become accepted as a standard. . . . Still, the moment has to come when the gesturing is laid aside and the voice of conviction, the true voice of feeling of, say, Skinner in *The Freedom of the City* is heard. . . . (pp. 168-69)

Such set speeches frequently occur in Friel's plays and they are not confined to the type Skinner represents. Sometimes their eloquence is out of character, although usually we feel that, at the point of crisis, the characters are able to draw on resources they never knew they had. But the explanatory, even hectoring voice which emerges, in a kind of authorial overdrive, and spells out 'what it's all about', turns the stage into a platform, the text into a lecture. Dr Dodds, the sociologist in *The Freedom of the City,* and the various experts called upon by the Widgery-like judge in that play, have similar moments of annunciation. It is sometimes difficult to distinguish between the voice of the truth-teller and that of the expert. Yet it is important to do so, since the expert is usually someone who knows everything but the truth. In this particular case, is Lily really marching on behalf of the poor, the outcasts of the earth, of whom her mongol child Declan is one? If so, the play is a political one in essence and the object of its complicated structure is the analysis of official injustice, the corruption that is inseparable from authority. Suppression and oppression are so frequently analysed in Friel's drama that it is not difficult to accept him as a political dramatist. But the point bears some further consideration.

Authority and love may be divorced, to the detriment of both, but there is at least the implication that they were once married. In *The Enemy Within,* St Colmcille discovers that his love for family and for country is beginning to undermine his vocation and his position as abbot in the island community of Iona. In order to give himself wholly to his work he has to destroy the enemy within himself—his fatal attraction to Ireland and home. This attraction has repeatedly led Colmcille into the position of seeming to lend his authority to bloody faction fights. So, with great difficulty and determination, he stifles it. So too in the dialogue between Public and Private Gar in *Philadelphia Here I Come,* the attraction of Ireland has to be subdued so that the place may be left. In *Faith Healer,* the attraction has to do with Francis Hardy's hope for a restoration of his strange gift; but it is also an attraction towards sleep and death. In *Translations,* there are two Irelands, two languages, two kinds of violence, and Owen, who has migrated to the new Ireland, is nevertheless pulled by his sentimental loyalties towards the one he has helped to bury. The unfortunate Lieutenant Yolland is his mirror image in this respect. In all of these cases the repudiation of Ireland carries with it a certain guilt, a sense of betrayal; but equally, to give in to the place is a form of suicide. Ireland is, of course, a metaphor in these contexts as well as a place. It is the country of the young, of hope, a perfect coincidence between fact and desire. It is also the country of the disillusioned, where everything is permanently out of joint, violent, broken. . . . It hardly needs saying that [in *Translations*] these two versions of the Irish psychic landscape are enunciated on the brink of violence—the '98 Rebellion and the disappearance of Yolland. On the hither side of violence is Ireland as paradise; on the nether side, Ireland as ruin. But, since we live on the nether side, we live in ruin and can only console ourselves with the desire for the paradise we briefly glimpse. The result is a discrepancy in our language; words are askew, they are out of line with fact. Violence has fantasy and wordiness as one of its most persistent after-effects.

Like Owen in *Translations,* we can thus give our love to the failed world (Ireland) but our respect to the conquering world (England). But if what can be respected is not loved, and what can be loved cannot be respected, there is little recourse for us but violence. Authority is denied for the sake of the failure that is loved; failure is mocked and hated for the sake of the authority it has lost. Skinner and Lily in *The Freedom of the City* are caught in the same dilemma as Owen or Hugh in *Translations.* They have two roles each. One is heroic, that of the oppressed natives in the Mayor's Parlour, later as murdered victims of British Army SLR bullets. The other is the sociologist's categorization of them as creatures of the 'culture of poverty', Bogsiders immersed in the stupor of their condition. Again it is the choice between paradise and ruin. Again it is a choice enforced by violence. Finally neither alternative allows one to live. The native condition, which is that of being human, not Irish, is almost destroyed; the foreign condition of an enforced identity, political or sociological, is also resisted. Struggle is the only action, crisis the only climate.

Such a politics is metonymic of a wider condition. The plays all work as parables in which the development of a particular action contributes to the representation of a general condition. Also, the propositions which abound in these plays and which seem to have a general import when they are directed outward at the audience in an oratorical *tour de force,* and thus seem to have meaning for the human condition as such, tend to narrow themselves into statements symptomatic of a particular person's plight, or of a culture's specific pressure. This ambivalence of scope in the language of these plays is most clearly manifest in **Faith Healer,** the play in which the device of metonymy is most openly used or at least most appropriately applied. If we cast the play into the form of a question and look to the text for an answer, we may ask, what is the gift of Francis Hardy and why does it necessarily lead to his death in Ballybeg? (pp. 169-72)

Hardy's gift is his essence and yet it is subject to chance; only by giving himself over to death does he renounce chance. In doing so he also renounces the gift. The certitude of death is preferable to the vicissitudes of life with (or without) the gift. His capacity to heal others, in other countries, and his incapacity to heal himself except by coming back to his own country, dying back into the place out of which his healing came in the first place, is a strange metonym for the gift in exile, the artist abroad. This association between gift and exile, creativity and death, is more purely stated here than elsewhere in Friel's work. The play throws no political shadow; it provides no action, only four monologues. It shows a man creating his own death by coming home out of exile.

It is the inevitability of death, finally realized, which makes the Faith Healer feel at peace in that last scene. The maimed body which he faces but cannot heal, the instruments in the tractor which will maim him, the 'black-faced macerated baby' buried in Scotland, the weekly parade of cripples who listen to the scratched record of Fred Astaire singing 'The Way You Look Tonight', are all semi-farcical, semi-tragic recognitions that perfection is a desire granted only on the other side of violence, through death. Thus Friel asserts the lethal quality of the gift, the urge to create wholeness out of distortions. So the gift, the stolen fire, is returned to death, to its source. But other things remain. The unique life of Francis Hardy is not repeatable, but as a parable its weight is inherited. It is this weight of inherited failure and the uniqueness of the individual response to it which are both made manifest on Friel's double stage, the exhibition area and the magic circle area. The anguish of the individual life passes over into the communal life through violence, borne in language. The exploration of that difficult transition, the discovery of a series of dramatic forms in which it could be reconnoitred, is central to his achievement and part of the reason for his importance. (p. 173)

Seamus Deane, ''Brian Friel: The Double Stage,'' *in his* Celtic Revivals: Essays in Modern Irish Literature, 1880-1980, *Faber & Faber, 1985, pp. 166-73.*

Zulfikar Ghose

1935-

Pakistani-born novelist, poet, nonfiction writer, short story writer, and autobiographer.

In his work Ghose often expresses the viewpoint of a culturally alienated individual. Born in Pakistan, Ghose was raised and educated in Bombay, India, and England and now lives in the United States. The variety of influences in Ghose's background is reflected in his fiction and poetry and contributes to the understanding and compassion evident in his work. Ghose has described himself as "an alien whose unconscious desire is to attach himself to a land with which he can claim an identity." This desire has led Ghose to such diverse locations as England, Brazil, and Texas.

The theme of cultural dislocation is dominant in Ghose's first novel, *The Contradictions* (1966), in which an English woman married to a civil servant is unable to find her place either in her homeland or in the unfamiliar society of India, where her husband is briefly stationed. In his next novel, *The Murder of Aziz Khan* (1967), Ghose broadens his range of characters and concerns to relate the story of a Pakistani farmer's unsuccessful attempt to resist a land acquisition scheme engineered by three corrupt brothers. Martin Tucker claimed that "if the novel is at one level a revelation of the corruption of Pakistani progress, it is on another and deeper level a restatement of the human condition and its quiet, insubordinate defiance of tragedy." A fascination with the enduring human spirit is also evident in Ghose's acclaimed Brazilian trilogy, which spans four centuries of Brazilian history. The first volume, *The Incredible Brazilian* (1972), recounts the adventures of Gregório, the son of a rich plantation owner, and provides a vivid portrait of seventeenth-century Brazil. Gregório is reincarnated in *The Beautiful Empire* (1975), which follows his life through a succession of triumphs and failures during the late 1800s, when Brazil was undergoing much change and development. The vision of Brazil as a tempestuous, vibrant environment is also present in the last volume of the trilogy, *A Different World* (1978), in which Gregório reappears as a revolutionary in a contemporary setting.

Ghose returns to an English locale in *Crump's Terms* (1976), a fanciful novel in which a schoolteacher reminisces on the events of his life in stream-of-consciousness prose that sometimes takes the form of a dialogue with his students. *Hulme's Investigations into the Bogart Script* (1981) is even more unconventional, combining a variety of narrative styles and techniques in an exploration of words and meaning. Larry McCaffery described the novel as "an utterly dreamlike progression where anything can happen within the boundaries of its chosen cliches, formulas, and language structures." Ghose's next two novels resemble *The Incredible Brazilian* in tone and locale. *A New History of Torments* (1982) is the story of a South American ranch family whose tranquility is permanently disturbed by a curse brought on by the father's affair with a young woman. *Don Bueno* (1984) also involves a family curse, and it too is a kaleidoscopic epic tale set in South America. In this novel, the men of the Calderón line are destined to kill their fathers and to be killed by their sons. Grace Ingoldby called Ghose's recent book, *Figures of Enchantment* (1986), "a phil-

osophical, poetic novel in which endurance raises itself as the quality that counts in a life where dreams, expectations, even the quest for knowledge, are revealed as mere stratagems to distract us from infinite despair."

In much of his poetry Ghose examines the theme of the outsider seeking his place in the world. *The Loss of India* (1964) focuses on the bittersweet nostalgia Ghose feels for his birthplace despite his fondness for his life in England. The poems in *Jets from Orange* (1967) similarly evoke impressions of movement and rootlessness and describe several diverse landscapes. In *The Violent West* (1972), Ghose records his observations of Texas, where he moved in 1969. *A Memory of Asia: New and Selected Poems* (1984) provides an overview of Ghose's poetry, evidencing his continuing attention to the difficulties of cultural alienation as well as nostalgic reflection.

Ghose has also published a collection of short stories, *Statement against Corpses* (1964), with B. S. Johnson, and an autobiographical prose work, *Confessions of a Native-Alien* (1965). *Hamlet, Prufrock, and Language* (1978) and *The Fiction of Reality* (1984) are volumes of criticism praised for their skillful and compelling presentation of ideas.

(See also *Contemporary Authors*, Vols. 65-68.)

P. N. FURBANK

Zulfikar Ghose shows what you can do by scrupulous cultivation of a small talent. His first volume [of poetry, *The Loss
of India*], is a gentle tour round his own personality, with a
good deal of looking in the mirror—studying his 'morose-
Ghose' face for Indian ancestors or his appearance to English
eyes. He is concerned, and not concerned, about belonging,
and floats comfortably in a permanent state of mild displacement; cool themes, most intelligently examined, in a fluctuating verse-rhythm, sometimes approaching syllabics, *that* suits
such gentle ruminations. I don't find the 'elegant savageness'
which Charles Causley has discovered in him—more of a shrug;
and on the whole his political ironies are his weakest thing.
The 'loss of India' is final for him, he has shrugged off post-
independence India as an impossible albatross-burden, and it
no longer provides, poetically speaking, a vital conflict for
him.

I notice one other minor weakness: irrelevant description—
concrete and 'vivid' evocations ('and his words foamed at his
mouth like lather / collected round a leak in a drainpipe') which
aren't vivid, or are so in a way that doesn't help the poem.

> *P. N. Furbank, in a review of "The Loss of India,"
> in* The Listener, *Vol. LXXII, No. 1863, December
> 10, 1964, p. 949.*

STEPHEN WALL

The loss of India: of that Zulfikar Ghose most complains [in
The Loss of India]. It coincides, it appears, with the loss of
his youth. He finds, however, a good deal of consolation in
England, parks especially—"There's an empathy between the
trees / and me in England, an air between / us that's constantly
beneficent". His poems mediate a rather owlish persona that
makes him seem at times like a refugee from *A Passage to
India,* and they are not helped by a style that cannot really
reconcile neo-Georgian ramblings with clumsy propositions.
His use of syllabics often makes his lines indistinguishable
from prose—the first sentences of **"Of Land and Love"** for
example, quite pleasant *as* prose—but such metrical inanition
confirms the general impression of debility. (p. 59)

> *Stephen Wall, "Brutalities Foreign and Suburban,"
> in* The Review, *No. 15, April, 1965, pp. 58-60.*

CHAIM BERMANT

[*Confessions of a Native-Alien*] is part autobiography, part
travelogue, with the former an exploration of self, the latter
of India. The author fails to reach the heartland of either, but
the quest is, on the whole, exciting.

Scenes reverberate in the mind long after one has put the book
down: the young boy struggling at his circumcision, unwilling
to yield his foreskin to his Muslim past; brothers, sisters, cousins and aunts, living on top of one another, noisy and quarrelsome, but tied to each other by tradition and need; grandmother fasting to establish dominion over her sons; the Hindu
festival of Divali, with its ceremonial blessing of account books.
Situations come to life through the very sequence of words. . . .

[Mr. Ghose] is perhaps more adept at describing than explaining. His main problem is one of identity. He is a Muslim, but
without the faith, a Pakistani who has never lived in Pakistan.
His education was split between a Catholic school in Bombay
and a grammar school in Chelsea. He feels a link with the sub-

continent, but no compulsion to live there. His predilections
are English, but not his roots. He is the eternal alien, a sort
of wandering Jew but without even the solace of Jewishness.

His constant endeavour to establish who or what he is, to
assemble the components of his being into some definable
entity, amounts to an obsession, and readers who have never
been bothered by the problem of identity may find it wearying.
I found it fascinating.

I was less fascinated by what might be termed Mr. Ghose's
secondary obsession. He falls in love as easily and makes love
as frequently as other men fall asleep, and every incident of
falling and making—which he appears almost to regard as
identical experiences—is diligently recorded. The second obsession may, of course, arise out of the first. If one cannot
find oneself, there can hardly be a happier way of staying lost.

> *Chaim Bermant, "Travelography," in* The Ob-
> server, *June 6, 1965, p. 27.*

THE TIMES LITERARY SUPPLEMENT

[In *Confessions of a Native-Alien,* Mr. Ghose] appears to have
three main interests: poetry, cricket and girls. No sensible
person ought to quarrel with his tastes and they could—combined with his basic search for a spiritual home—have been
worked up into a fascinating book. Unfortunately, Mr. Ghose
never really goes deeply enough into any of these themes and
for the most part his *Confessions,* especially the English part
of them, merely record a series of trivial occurrences, of only
personal relevance.

The early chapters about the difficulties of being a Pakistani
in India, a Muslim in a Hindu community, are much the best.
Mr. Ghose writes affectionately and well about his family and
he conveys refreshingly the romance and wonder of India, even
at its most maddening and ineffectual. Though he lacks V. S.
Naipaul's novelist's expertise and beady, sharp eyes, the heart
and vision that underlie his attitudes are more immediately
engaging.

Mr. Ghose is, *au fond,* wide-eyed and naive; his attempts at
sophistication, when conceit goes ill with innocence, are the
more engaging for this. And when he describes the very formidable problems he has had to face in finding a realistic
identity he is at once touching and interesting. What is missing
from his book is any real sense of character, any skill in the
treatment of scene and dialogue.

> *"No Home," in* The Times Literary Supplement, *No.
> 3303, June 17, 1965, p. 520.*

VENETIA POLLOCK

Zulfikar Ghose is a young Pakistani whose austere formal elegance of style reminded me that India belongs to a far older
civilisation than our own. Not that [*The Contradictions*] is primarily about India—the characters are English, their sojourn
in India is brief—but for a first novel it is so assured, so
meticulous and unyielding, it carries the distillation of centuries
within it. The concise almost stilted style with its clipped phrases
exactly matches the coldness of unawakened Sylvia. Even at
29, newly married to a much older Indian Civil Servant, she
is unsure of how to immerse herself in India but sees only the
"unapproachable with their poverty and disease, their deformity and hunger at the edge of the gutter." Nor does marriage
fulfil or release her. Back in England she becomes increasingly

introverted, communing alone with the Hampshire countryside. Four rasping shocks jolt Sylvia into life, each unexpected, symmetrically shaped to the plot and as amazing to the reader as to Sylvia.

As an exercise in novel writing this might win a prize with extra marks for efficiency and tidiness, but its coldness makes polite reading. I longed to be lured, for a little warmth and life. . . .

> Venetia Pollock, in a review of "The Contradictions," in Punch, Vol. CCLI, No. 6576, September 21, 1966, p. 454.

BILL BYROM

The Contradictions suffers, it must be said, a very great deal from the self-consciousness of the writing. In the hard prose, so pure of phrase and elegant of cadence, one senses a lack of spontaneity. Not that Mr Ghose is imitative, just that there is a jarring alertness in his paragraphs to effects of fluency and coldness. His prose isn't quite the real thing.

But the Indian scene, and especially the English presence, is sketched with fidelity. . . . [Mr Ghose's] purposes are high, intelligent, well-informed. He fails because he shies away from the experience of his characters too much, fearful no doubt of falsifying them. So the meaning remains peripheral and rarefied. Sylvia's conversation with her husband is full of generalisations which are not afterwards prosecuted to a significant point. And the novelist who intrudes at the end succeeds only in further removing Sylvia and the reader from the significance of the whole. The work dissolves in vague excuses about finding adequate figures for life, in a self-justifying aestheticism that altogether misses the real point of the novel. But Mr Ghose needs only temerity to write an astonishing novel. (p. 388)

> Bill Byrom, "Lonelyhearts," in The Spectator, Vol. 217, No. 7213, September 23, 1966, pp. 387-88.

THE TIMES LITERARY SUPPLEMENT

The debate in Zulfikar Ghose's poems [in *Jets from Orange*] is one between the sense of movement and the sense of roots—having them or needing them: "as if suspended mobility were my home". In **"One Chooses a Language"**, he is aware of his rootlessness, his continual sense of being foreign. Seasons and landscapes (in France, England, India, Pakistan) are the settings of many of his poems with the restless movement of jets above giving him an image not only of his own feeling of transit but also a more universal one of transitoriness. These are honest, tentative poems, marred only by a too frequent sense of enervation, if not exhaustion. The language is not always sharp enough to catch and fix effectively the persistent cloudiness of mood. The title poem [**"Jets from Orange"**] is fine, altogether more in focus than many of the others.

> "Oddly Elegant," in The Times Literary Supplement, No. 3428, November 9, 1967, p. 1059.

THOMAS LASK

[*The Murder of Aziz Khan*] can not only be read on two levels, but also can not be read otherwise if it is to be more than a cinematic excursion into the art of fiction.

Written in supple prose, with a fine economy of means and with touches that reflect the author's poetic cast of mind, it is nevertheless a story lurid and sensational in incident and with characters only a single dimension in depth. The villains are wholly evil; the good men, if not immaculate, are wholly innocent; the women are bundles of idle gossip and unfocused desire. Evil is on the side of the big battalions: the police power is venial, the government corrupt, the citizenry mendacious. The ruthless and the avaricious are in the saddle and ride mankind. Like the Vices in the medieval drama, the men and women are types and qualities. The characters do not develop; they progress, almost all into hells of their own making. . . .

The parallel to the decent homesteader on the Western plains with wife and nubile daughter, who stands up to the dishonest but powerful cattle barons will suggest itself to all moviegoers. The difference is that no gun slinger rides out of the purple sage to redress the balance. On the contrary, in ways typical of the fiction of the thirties, evil wins handily. It is a no contest.

The book is, however, not an entertainment, but a morality. . . . [Mr. Ghose's volume of poetry, *Jets from Orange*], is streaked with guilt: for the dialect he did not learn, the secularism that separates him from the older members of the family, the attraction he feels for things European and foreign. He cannot shake off his country, but he cannot live in it either.

His novel is a round in the battle with himself. A despairing self-hatred runs through it. He despises the ruthlessness of the new men, but has only contempt for the passivity of the old. The improvements may be necessary, but the methods are inhuman. . . .

Aziz Khan represents the old, wholesome attitudes. He has a loyalty to the land and the peasants who work it. But he is revealed as so passive, so superstitious, so stolid as to reach a point of paralysis. And the people in the town and the peasants in the field are shown as cowardly and corrupt. When a man is falsely accused of murder, witnesses are easily found to testify against him. When the land is taken from Aziz Khan, not a finger is lifted to help him. But it is easy to see that the author's disgust is a form of anger and his condemnation more a plea than an accusation.

The novel is not melodrama, for virtue doesn't triumph in the end. It is not tragedy since no character is large enough to engage our sympathy. It is another moving chapter in the war between two brothers and two societies, the pattern of whose history goes back at least to the days of Cain and Abel.

> Thomas Lask, "Love Letters Home," in The New York Times, January 25, 1969, p. 27.

SHANE STEVENS

The Murder of Aziz Khan, according to its publisher, is the first novel on Pakistan by a Pakistani ever to be published in the United States. It is also, I am happy to report, an attempt that is largely successful. Yet for all its success in presenting a view of Pakistani life in the mid-1950's, the novel is somehow curiously unrewarding.

In using the word unrewarding, I do not in any way suggest that author Zulfikar Ghose has failed in his purpose. He has, after all, taken the broad landscape of Pakistan as his canvas and has painted, in a succession of brilliant sketches, the story of an entrepreneur mercantile dynasty of irresistible force which meets the immovable object of a dirt farmer who will not sell his bit of land. So far so good—but this novel is a still larger undertaking. One soon realizes that Mr. Ghose has also attempted to tell of the changing of one social order for another, with all the moral corruption and brutal dislocation that such movements always entail.

Such ambition requires considerable talent, and this the author has. Yet it is perhaps in this very excess of talent that the novel may seem to stumble. Aziz Khan, the defeatist farmer who is indeed murdered but nonetheless alive at the novel's conclusion, is more a symbol of the land than a character in his own right. The Shah brothers, who rape, kill, corrupt officials, cause innocent people to be executed and murder to be committed, exist more as caricatures of a certain kind of new nation business vulture than as flesh-and-blood people. That is to say, the author has perhaps succeeded so well in presenting the various forces at war in a time of national chaos that his portrayal of some of the novel's characters has been made to suffer. Yet Mr. Ghose can excel in characterization; as indeed he does with his women, who are all too human and not meant to be symbolic of anything.

What we have, then, is a novel that is brilliantly conceived and successfully executed, though with an over-emphasis of characterization into mere representation. A novel that is, nonetheless, eloquent and tragic and, finally, important.

Zulfikar Ghose is to be congratulated. *The Murder of Aziz Kahn* is not the definitive novel of the first 20 years of Pakistan's existence. That remains to be written, perhaps, by Mr. Ghose. But in scope and power and intent, it has come awesomely close.

> Shane Stevens, "War to the Death in Pakistan," in The New York Times Book Review, *January 26, 1969, p. 38.*

MARTIN TUCKER

The publisher is advertising [*The Murder of Aziz Khan*] as "the first novel on Pakistan by a Pakistani ever to be published in the United States." This informational gimmick is an interesting but largely irrelevant bit of exotica. Although the novel has the hang of the humid, festering Pakistani city and its cool mansions, it could be set in a number of other lands. . . . What makes the novel curiously provocative and extraordinarily lingering is another combination of effects.

Some of these effects have, admittedly, to do with exotica for an American audience. The Shah brothers who run the vast, industrial combine in Kalapur have the dubious charm of unexpected vulgarity. As Pakistani businessmen they are much the same as American or German or Indian businessmen, prick their skin and they will howl for compensation. But Ghose is able to invest them with a local glamour; he has seized their accents and their paradoxical amalgam of cajolery and arrogance. Ghose has another appealing local and universal character in Aziz Khan, the farmer who will not sell his land to the Shah brothers, though they have aggrandized everything else about him. Aziz Khan is the eternal simple man. He envisions no symbol of posterity other than his family and the perennial provisions of this land. Khan is thus the traditional hero: he is as much Wordsworth's leech gatherer preaching resolution and independence as he is a relic in modern Pakistan. It is Ghose's achievement that Aziz Khan seems as much a real man as he does a symbol, particularly in the final chapters when he has been deprived of his land and his family, and he

walks wraith-like alongside the barbed wire that keeps him from entering his house.

It is partly this combination of old-fashioned stately rhythms and modern thematic counterparts that accounts for Ghose's success in provoking sympathy. Ghose has taken traditional themes and invested them in modern stock situations. The constant flow—it is never a shift or break—between the contemporary and the traditional gives his book an almost fable-like quality. And Ghose has contributed to this air by his use of the narrator's voice. In many instances he seems to stop the activity of the novel to comment on possible meanings.

There is more than a hint of E. M. Forster's tone in Ghose's narrators' voice. It is quiet, witty, insidious, and committed in its refusal to divide up human nature into convenient categories. Like Forster's commentary in his novels, Ghose's voice reveres the very thing it mocks. It is a reverence of mockery, an acceptance of the unexpected which all along, by definition of the nature of the universe, had been expected. (pp. 116-17)

Like Forster, Ghose is tantalized by and enmeshed in ironies. Though Aziz Khan is "murdered" at the end of the novel—in being stripped of everything that meant anything to him—the tone remains ironic. The Shah brothers are destroyed too—at least their smugness and security—and in working back, or forward, to the center-line, the narrator's voice suggests that meaningful values will reestablish themselves. Thus, if the novel is at one level a revelation of the corruption of Pakistani progress, it is on another and deeper level a restatement of the human condition and its quiet, insubordinate defiance of tragedy. For this reason, much more than for its local habitation by Pakistani, the novel is a significant contribution to the year's literature. (p. 118)

> Martin Tucker, in a review of "The Murder of Aziz Khan," in Commonweal, *Vol. XL, No. 4, April 11, 1969, pp. 116-18.*

THE TIMES LITERARY SUPPLEMENT

Zulfikar Ghose's two earlier books of verse, *The Loss of India* and *Jets from Orange,* were much concerned with the poet as travelling and rootless man. . . .

The Violent West marks Mr Ghose's removal to the United States in 1969, and so the landscapes of south Texas join those of the Punjab, Bengal, Provence and suburban England. Yet for all the careful notation and the accumulation of concrete detail, the effect is disappointingly ironed out into something too wistful, generalized and insipid to make much impact. This is partly due to Mr Ghose's tiresomely inert forms: for example, the first section of the new book consists of twelve poems written in a complex but unrewarding six-line syllabic stanza, with the rhymes so lightly stressed that they count for nothing and seem to have no function except to imprison the poet in a jail of his own making. When Mr Ghose tries something more spontaneous and casual (**"4 am Traffic"**, **"At a Difficult Time"**), one senses enervation rather than release. But there are a few poems which show that, taking a closer focus, Mr Ghose can produce work that is altogether sharper: **"A Private Lot"**, **"A Woman's Illness"**, **"Disfiguration"**. There is one poem, **"The Remove"**—about a Punjabi schoolmaster teaching in a London Secondary Modern—which is a small classic of adept and straight-faced social irony, and this seems to show that Mr Ghose has lighter gifts which he should not allow his more solemn sense of deracination to smother.

"Bedtime Initiations," in The Times Literary Supplement, *No. 3674, July 28, 1972, p. 873.*

PAUL WEST

[*The Incredible Brazilian*] is the first volume of a projected trilogy which, credibly enough, will track Gregório the hero through a series of incarnations beginning with the 17th century and ending in present day Brazil. It's a splendid idea thus to raid and exploit a nation's history for purposes of long-distance picaresque, but a better idea would be to vary the narrative mode over a thousand pages, shifting from the roustabout episodic to, say, voluminous Proustian excursus or an avalanche of epitomic fragments. Born in Pakistan and now resident in Texas, Ghose has lived in Brazil as well and, as this book shows, knows enough about it and isn't reluctant to draw a bold, often caricatural hand. Whether he *will* vary his narrative strategies, I don't know; I just wonder if we now need, or can stand, a trilogy that's all (as the blurb puts it) "brawling, bawdy, and picaresque" and if something standardized and inflexible won't ultimately afflict even this frisky hop-step-and-jump with sameness.

Son of a well-to-do planter, Gregório at 14 is effete, virginal, and corrigibly vain, and as you might expect, he chutzpahs through the novel shedding disqualifications while compiling and losing one fortune after another. Picaro here, picaro there, he's an everyman on greased skids, and his vicissitudes, his bounces-back, prefigure his incarnations to come. . . . [His] rotational semi-delirium of marking time while time marks him sets him apart from picaresque forebears. Like light traveling at its own peculiar speed, he doesn't seem to move at all.

Especially to the sexual episodes here, Ghose brings a juicy voracity for saliences: the nipples of the servant Aurelia, on whom Gregório's father has fathered a bastard, get snipped off by the betrayed wife and served, it's rumored, in father's meat; a young wife straddles a supine statue of Jesus in an empty church; and menstrual blood goes into the stew. To boot, Gregório is subjected to homosexual rape, a Brazilian Lawrence of Arabia, and then sold into slavery; but eventually, like a bubble in a sump, he surfaces. Becomes a leader. Discovers gold. Fetching up in Rio, he's there during its bombardment by the French, and suffers a heart attack when the Françoise he's in bed with turns out to be François. As it happens, that mutation only confirms the Byronic mood of the whole; the novel's last word is penis.

Brazil (where Donne said the sun dines) is as rich a presence here as our nonstop Gregório, and I particulary enjoyed Ghose's Janus-faced portrait of atavistic colonials copycatting the urbane ways of the Old World. Ghose's writing has momentum and verve, and in his chosen old-fashioned belly-thumping way he has made quite a meal on Brazil the luscious. But as yet only breakfast.

Paul West, "Picaro Here, Picaro There," in Book World—The Washington Post, *October 15, 1972, p. 8.*

JAMES R. FRAKES

[*The Incredible Brazilian*] is lukewarm picaresque with the fillip of a series of reincarnations for its rogue-hero: "I know that I am indestructible, who have, in one form or another, lived through four centuries . . . I once married a girl . . . who turned out to be my own great-granddaughter."

The Prologue, laced with mock-Defoe protestations of honesty and fake apologies for lack of artistry ("I shall have to neglect the graces of style which only a leisurely pace could afford opportunity for"), promises much more than the ensuing narrative supplies. For the voice in the Prologue is at least capable of irony and self-deflation, while the voice of the foppish Gregório . . . is almost calculatedly irritating and totally humorless. As he plunges up and down through the precipitous caste-levels of colonial Brazil, from the Portuguese aristocracy to blacks and Indians and back again, Gregório moves in constant wide-eyed wonder through mass slaughter, religious corruption, cannibalism, sodomy, transvestism, piracy and dyspepsia. Sated with bloody history and exhausted from ecstatic apostrophes to "the sound of Brazil," our retrospective narrator muses profoundly, "Finally, there is no reality; each one of us expresses his own version of the possibilities of experience, each one of us is, in the end, an approximation."

When he isn't panting over memories of his sexual initiation in the bed of his mother's black maid or indulging in leaden irony about the blessings of slavery, Gregório recalls (totally) and recounts (drearily) endless monologues by wayfarers and chance acquaintances—another picaresque convention reduced here to flatulence. I would like to believe that the grinding prose, pretentious rhetoric and crashing boredom are (as they would be in Henry James) dramatic devices to reveal the pomposity and essential shallowness of the first-person narrator. Maybe the next two volumes of Zulfikar Ghose's trilogy will nourish this naively trustful belief.

James R. Frakes, "Picarooning, Bike-Riding, Modern Youth, a Jersey Jerk," in The New York Times Book Review, *November 12, 1972, p. 64.*

JULIAN BARNES

The Native [published in the United States as *The Incredible Brazilian*], the first volume of Zulfikar Ghose's Brazilian trilogy, ended in melodramatic symbolism. Gregorio, pursuer of the Brazilian dream, was about to possess Françoise, a dishy servant, when he discovered that she was in fact a boy, and died of a heart attack. *The Beautiful Empire,* set two centuries later in the 1860s, contains a similar rise-and-fall story and a reincarnated Gregorio who uncomplicatedly explains on the first page that "Brazil expressed her story through me". This time, his experiences include the Paraguayan war, the revolution, the loss of his wife, and financial ruin when the rubber industry perishes and he fails to bounce back. It's the sort of zesty, colourful romance which tends to come in two versions—the one with endpaper maps, and the one with intellectual pretensions. This one doesn't have a map.

Instead, we are offered some stagey vignettes to illuminate the paradox of Brazil, plus some underplayed stuff on reincarnation to justify the trilogy's structure. Gregorio tells his story with unfeigned clumsiness: he apologises . . . that there is 'neither subtlety nor refinement to this prose'. Such a device can come off . . . but needs a great deal of dexterity; here, however, one cannot be sure which of a quantity of lumbering images Mr Ghose endorses.

Julian Barnes, "Neh?" in New Statesman, *Vol. 90, No. 2331, November 21, 1975, p. 650.*

NEIL HEPBURN

In the opening paragraph of [*The Beautiful Empire*], Mr Ghose's Incredible Brazilian, Gregório Peixoto da Silva Xavier, defiantly exclaims: 'How glorious was the 19th century!' And, of course, he is right. There is a good deal of envy in our contempt for Europeans in the age of empire, denied as we are the self-confidence and vigour with which they set about refashioning the world. But there is a good deal of justice, too; and, in this second instalment of his trilogy, Mr Ghose has chosen a most satisfying metaphor not only of the century's gloriousness, when the sun of European self-assurance climbed to its brief zenith, but also of the anomalies that seem, in a mere half-century, to have eclipsed that bright conviction. For the setting of Gregório's rise and fall is the Amazonian city of Manaos: once, for a moment of time, the densest concentration of wealth and ostentation on earth, and now, with its empty marble opera house 1,000 miles from anywhere, the nearest thing we have to the Ozymandian colossus.

Gregório's enterprise, in a Manaos on the threshold of mountainous fortune-making as the sole source of the world's rubber, is a fleet of waterborne brothels serving the inflamed gentry of the boom town, and he is soon rich. The apogee of his fortunes coincides quite naturally with the top of the city's monopoly power—but it is no mere natural event: for it gradually becomes clear that, reincarnated for the purpose, he is to take part in all the convulsive events that have left that vast land undisturbed as the epitome of adventure. It is he, indeed, who unknowingly helps the English botanist Wickham in the smuggling out of the *Hevea brasiliensis* seedlings which, maturing in Malaya, deal the deathblow to Manaos.

The 'beautiful empire' connotes at least four of Mr Ghose's concerns—Gregório's refulgent whore-mastership, Manaos as a locus of infection or growth-point of the European virus in the primaeval green body of Brazil, Brazil itself as the earthly paradise of European expectations, and, beneath it all, the 19th century as an era of inventive glory. Mr Ghose has a lot going for him: great narrative strength, excellently drawn characters, a central concern, never lost sight of, with the interaction of private gratification and public constraint and a respect for his material which is quite admirable. Gregório, a kind of Latin Flashman, is no flawless liberal touting a 20th-century conscience around the sybaritic excesses of Manaos society, but a wholly convincing 19th-century man, with a conscience that might smart under dishonesty but which judges the murder of Indians for their rubber-rich lands only a distasteful, not a disgraceful, business method. Our hindsight tells us these atrocities made Brazil more green hell than earthly paradise. Mr Ghose tells us, in many subtle ways, that there was no hindsight then, not much foresight, either; and that things have not changed for the better.

Neil Hepburn, "Twilight Emperors," in The Listener, *Vol. 94, No. 2436, December 11, 1975, p. 806.*

JOHN MELLORS

The enjoyment with which Zulfikar Ghose wrote *Crump's Terms* is so obvious and so infectious that the novel's many faults are easily forgiven. Much of the book is an old-fashioned stream of consciousness in which Crump, a schoolmaster in suburban Middlesex, his mind not entirely on the class in front of him, ranges over past journeys with his wife in Brittany, Provence, Spain and Berlin. Crump is a compulsive punster and adapter of quotations: 'Crumpoet', he sometimes calls himself. He deplores the Harrods-Habitat civilisation into which he thinks Western Europe, even his beloved France, is fast degenerating, and believes that futility is 'the final human condition'.

We are never quite sure how many of Crump's recollections and reveries are 'true'. . . . Did his wife really flee into East Berlin and ask for asylum and a job, although she could not speak any German? Was she looking for her vanished mother? Or reacting against Crump's cynicism? *Crump's Terms* is a messy, self-indulgent book; but, oddly enough, the self-indulgence is its saving grace, and the author's enthusiasms—his love of travel and his pleasure in playing with words—come over strongly. Many of his puns are best forgotten, but I shall remember his evocation of a cottage in Provence and of an almost deserted hotel in out-of-season Brittany.

John Mellors, "Life without Love," in The Listener, *Vol. 95, No. 2454, April 22, 1976, p. 518.*

FRANK PIKE

The central character of this contemporary picaresque of the mind [*Crump's Terms*] is Mike Crump, a west London schoolteacher whose pyrotechnic, free-associating pedagogic style engenders affectionate amused tolerance rather than illumination in his less intellectually agile pupils. The narrative is a sophisticated variant of stream-of-consciousness, a mosaic of internal and external events which seems in the end more arbitrary in arrangement than the author, impatient no doubt with the convention that one thing must come after another, may have hoped or intended. Much of the time the writing is good enough to be worth reading for its own sake—the classroom scenes, the thought processes of teacher and taught, are rendered with a humorously acute fidelity to the excitements and frustrations which are so much a part of that situation. Intercut with these is Crump's private life, most notably an extensive tour of Europe.

The obliqueness, the abrupt shifts in location, mood and time, often make severe demands on the reader's alertness. This is particularly true of the elusive, if haunting, personal-political dimension of a visit to East Berlin. Towards the end of the book Crump's coruscating classroom monologues become shrill denunciations of contemporary decadence, whether in poetry or in the gratuitous nudity in colour supplements; all this provokes in the reader rather too ready a sympathy for a pupil's "Sir, why are you telling us this?" Somehow the energy, the fluency, the manifest talent are not sufficient answer.

Frank Pike, "Class Struggle," in The Times Literary Supplement, *No. 3867, April 23, 1976, p. 481.*

NINA BAWDEN

The hero of *A Different World,* which completes Zulfikar Ghose's fascinating trilogy about Brazil, is a reincarnation. Gregório, who appears in the two earlier volumes, has many pasts and many futures, and is a symbol of his country's history. Born again in this century, into a period of political turmoil, he is, to begin with, just a young man absorbed in his own concerns. Revolutionary ideas are only part of his growing up and mean little more than a modern way of finding a sexual partner.

As he develops and becomes involved in urban terrorism, robbing banks and kidnapping ambassadors, he discovers that life is more complex. Power does not come to those who merit it, but to those who scheme for it, and when Governments change, all that happens is that a different person wears the boot that kicks the people.

The opening third of the book is the most successful. The narrative is gripping and concrete, the tone exuberant. After that, although the elegant prose is always a pleasure, events become subordinated to the windy tedium of political theory, too many profound truths are repeated too often, and the exuberance diminishes.

Nina Bawden, in a review of "A Different World,"
in The Times, *London, January 11, 1979, p. 9.*

VALENTINE CUNNINGHAM

A Different World is nuts on Brazil. At least its strutting narrator—'I, Gregório Peixoto da Silva Xavier . . . known the world over'—is keen on the 'idea' of Brazil. And keener still to keep that idea pure from the kind of internationalist uniformity that turns his family ranch into a cosmopolitan play-centre and invades Brazil with Leftism. So, plying the reader the while with his heavy line on the awfulness of nations mimicking each other—he has a habit of pomp and sentence too eagerly picked up from his dully thoughtful friends—Gregório takes to counter-insurgence and right-wing terror.

It's some relief that the novel refuses him a totally smoothed run. Casual suggestions about kidnapping ambassadors and their like, dropped only to keep him in with leftist groups, are embarrassingly fruitful. The police will misread his intentions. But though ambivalent success is all his Buy Brazilian politics are allowed to earn him, Gregório's incessant rhetoric against communist cant, Ché-ist tyrannies and other foreign barbarisms nevertheless holds his novelist's support. And disconcertingly so, for this emotionally defended Brazil is in practice denied the substance that might give its idea actuality. We can grant the error—we're exhorted to, anyway—of making Brazil a 'European idea'. But what does Gregório's Brazil amount to? A preciously wordy little, dimly perceived and vaguely put, whose major characters, especially Gregório of the many existences in Ghose's previous novels, are only verbose shadows. A feeble country of a baggy mind, alive only in minor characters like Rubirosa the pock-marked secret-policeman, in a mistress here, a whore there, and in bits of action on beaches and in brothels which could be anywhere.

Valentine Cunningham, "Going Places," in New Statesman, *Vol. 97, No. 2495, January 12, 1979, p. 54.*

LARRY McCAFFERY

[Practically] everything in Ghose's intriguing, phantasmagoric narrative [*Hulme's Investigations into the Bogart Script*] are blatantly rhetorical devices designed to manipulate and confound reader expectations. The nature of the reality of this book therefore depends not upon any correspondence with the real world but only upon the unfolding process of language appearing on the page. A description of Disneyland made by Hulme can thus provide a useful summary of much that we encounter in this novel: "The fantastic as living theatre. Comic book figures larger than life. Every image a representation of unreality."

Hulme's remarks suggest a great deal about Ghose's intentions here, for this narrative presents readers not with an image of the modern world so much as an image of its status in our imagination. Not surprisingly, then, this book is replete with images which have long haunted America's silver screens, dime novels, the juke boxes of neighborhood bars, our boob tubes. The assorted cowboys, Indians, gangsters, hookers, gun-slingers, and detectives who appear, shift shapes, and then disappear are familiar sorts, doing familiar kinds of things, spouting variations of the cliches we have heard before—though never quite in these bizarre contexts. Like Coover, Barthelme, Manuel Puig, and other writers anxious to explore the mythology of our popular culture, Ghose is well aware of the power of these representations of unreality to move us, to inform our judgments, to provide peculiar indices to our obsessions and fears. . . . And more importantly, Ghose shares with these writers a marvelous ear for the *language* of these forms and senses just when to push the familiar into new territories which unleash unexpected energies we long figured were exhausted. As Hulme explains while analyzing a story line constructed by the narrator from various familiar elements, the key to this kind of work depends entirely "on style. On performance."

Clearly Ghose's interests in *Hulme's Investigations* lie precisely in the direction of style and performance. Here there are no "characters" or "events" in the traditional sense; instead scenes, settings, temporal dimensions, and characters are magically transformed into variants, seemingly on the basis of broad associational or linguistic relationships. . . . Ghose's novel is an utterly dreamlike progression where anything can happen within the boundaries of its chosen cliches, formulas, and language structures. With logical continuity largely ignored, the sentences themselves become our chief focus as they unroll before us, with the narrative elements combining and recombining with an almost mathematical certitude that nevertheless retains a sense of freedom and verbal exuberance.

Beneath all this linguistic play—and implicit within the book's method of development—a number of important issues are momentarily washed up upon Ghose's verbal shores, only to be swept away by the next wave of wacky dialogue or lyrical descriptions of the lonely countrysides. What we sense as this book proceeds is an imagination straining to put words together into some coherent shape—a shape made available to the poet but not to those who rely only on traditional methods of using language. Underlying the book's methodology is the notion that all political, sociological, anthropological, psychological, and critical analyses—this review not excepted—are only rhetoric. The suggestion seems to be that language is still a potentially important means of perceiving significant relations, but that too often it rigidifies into jargon and other linguistic abuses which destroy its power. In deliberately undercutting and distorting the familiar shapes and contexts of language and narrative conventions, Ghose aims at creating new metaphors, fresher shapes, which are not based upon—or even concerned with—life-outside-of-language. Instead he creates his own world of language and meaning that is openly metaphorical, literary, figurative. Somewhat like Beckett's Molloy or the Unnamable, his narrator delights in generating new combinations of words and stories, not so much hoping that he can penetrate the barrier of language to some fabric of truth, but asking us to appreciate the strength, beauty, and utility of language as pure play and metaphor. The fun derived is well worth the effort.

Larry McCaffery, in a review of "Hulme's Investigations into the Bogart Script," in The American Book Review, *Vol. 4, No. 2, January-February, 1982, p. 6.*

ALAMGIR HASHMI

[In *Hulme's Investigations into the Bogart Script,* some] elements of familiar contemporary mythology and popular (Western) culture are recast in eight continuous, interminable scripts subtly phased into one another, with the characters and situations multiplying and re-creating themselves as if nature had been spawned by an intelligent camera. As narrative, the script is a clever device allowing the fisheye use of the familiar lens to achieve simultaneity and a reduced time-scale in which to make things happen; similarly, a good deal of stage direction, the commentary, can be incorporated into the story without hazard—in short, the functions and freedoms of "photographic memory," which can, at the same time, pick out the particular moment.

The narrator Walt reads a text in a London newspaper stating that, in connection with a recent kidnap-rape-murder case, "Inspector Hulme is leading the investigation into the extraordinary circumstances surrounding the case which involves such puzzlingly disparate factors as a desert tribe, jet-setting movie stars, and the world of art." Hulme's case was supposed to shuttle between London and Tunis. But the same Hulme turns out to be Walt's double, foil and collaborator when Walt himself is engaged in his criminal/human/artistic investigations on the American continent.

Foul perversions of sex-and-marriage, the craze for money, the futility of dogmas and the debasement of land and "nature" by human avarice and possessiveness are not all entirely new in Ghose as fit themes for fiction, but this novel, his seventh, marks an advance in storytelling and gives all that he touches a contemporary focus: "This is California, sweetie, it's the end of the world. Their fantasies, reality and scripts are all mixed up." The search for gold in the desert is a recurrent theme, and several strands of identity, time and place, immutable essences, come together at the end as Walt, upon being asked, "What have you found, gold?" replies to Rosemary with a positive (though noncommittal) "Maybe." How Walt finds it in the American earth is perhaps the main story.

> *Alamgir Hashmi, in a review of "Hulme's Investigations into the Bogart Script," in* World Literature Today, *Vol. 56, No. 3, Summer, 1982, p. 574.*

ALAN BOLD

[*A New History of Torments*] comes complete with clues to the cultural level of its contents: the title is derived from a poem by Neruda, and quotations by T. S. Eliot and César Vallejo introduce the two parts of the book. Plot, in such circumstances, is secondary to artistic performance, and character is a pretext for a text full of allegorical significance. . . .

The novel concerns the search for El Dorado; it begins by describing a line painted on the Equator and subsequently explores the Amazonian jungle and modern South American civilization. The main characters are blessed with great material wealth, but find it necessary to escape from the sordidly commercial present into the spiritually richer past. Jorge Rojas, a ranch-owner, is attached to his "eight thousand hectares of land enjoying best the view from the southeast corner that showed at a distance of some thirty kilometers, one of the peaks of the Andes which was always capped with snow." When he leaves this behind in order to indulge his sexual passion for a young woman, he thereby subjects his family to a curse that threatens the stability of the whole area.

The Rojas children, Rafael and Violeta, are archetypal innocents at large in an exotic world, and are taken from their land by Mark Kessel, an opportunist posing as a political and archaeological idealist. In return for a sixteenth-century map showing the way to El Dorado, Kessel has agreed to aid the cause of revolution in South America and he does so as ostentatiously as possible. He drives a golden Lincoln Continental whose upholstery is stuffed with gold bars, and his melodramatic entrance into the narrative steps up the symbolism. In his "golden beast" of a car he loses the way in a "dark and seemingly endless" forest; because of his fatal intervention Rafael and Violeta are separated and are only allowed to get back together in a disturbing incestuous climax. . . .

As the book unfolds, old legends and ancient myths begin to reassert themselves in the modern world of cars and canned music. The latter, Ghose's vision implies, is suffering from a lack of magic and enchantment, and it is a vision that makes *A New History of Torments* an exceptional novel.

> *Alan Bold, "In the Tracks of the Golden Beast," in* The Times Literary Supplement, *No. 4145, September 10, 1982, p. 981.*

GERALD JAY GOLDBERG

Botanically speaking, fiction writers fall into two major divisions—the Faulkners, rooted to one particular geographical patch, and the Nabokovs, or wandering tumbleweeds. The former are impossible to transplant. The latter thrive anywhere.

Zulfikar Ghose is an adaptable tumbleweed. . . .

The themes of rootlessness, disorder and alienation run deep in Ghose's novels, short stories and poems, and they are central to *A New History of Torments,* his labyrinthine latest novel. Brazil, where much of the book's action takes place, seems to have the fascination for him that the Congo had for Conrad (another tumbleweed); he has used it before in his picaresque novel, *The Incredible Brazilian,* published in 1972. The Brazil that Ghose's deracinated characters traverse, in which a hapless lad may be held in a pit and forced to stud any number of Amazons, is an exotic never-never land. As realism, it is no more convincing than the Africa of *Henderson the Rain King.* But realism is not what Ghose is after. (p. 214)

In the fiction of the rooted, the emphasis tends to be on character and self-exploration; Ghose gives us unlikely predicaments and external dangers. Sudden threats come with a mechanical regularity that borders on farce. No sooner does Rafael leave home than he is robbed at gunpoint. Violeta barely escapes being raped. Ignorant of each other's whereabouts, brother and sister find sanctuary for a time on neighboring estates. Pledged anything he desires by his host, Rafael marries the man's attractive daughter for whom "even the tips of his teeth had terrible longings," and is promptly betrayed by her. Violeta's bizarre agreement to be the first to sleep with the man her friend loves leads to her destruction.

A New History of Torments is a book in which the tail of plot often seems to be wagging the canine of character. The one character who almost transcends this limitation is Mark Kessel. He is a middle-aged idealist who has selflessly devoted his life to revolutionary causes in order to free the oppressed, only to discover belatedly the seductive joys of property and power. He assumes the role of oppressor with all the vim of the newly converted and, credibility aside, the transformation is riveting. Describing the thousand workers now in his employ, Kessel speaks enthusiastically, even gaily, of "slaves" and "chains"; he condemns his former revolutionary associates as "political thugs," and humanity itself as "the scum of mediocrities who populated the earth." One is, of course, reminded of Conrad's Kurtz—that other do-gooder—and his final advice on improving the lot of the Congo natives: "Exterminate all the brutes!"

Kessel, too, has murder on his mind. In a scheme to eliminate his nephew Jason, the rightful owner of Kessel's tobacco plantation, he sends the young innocent down the Amazon on a quest he cannot possibly survive. That Jason, his fate improbably linked to the Rojas family, actually lives to tell the tale is hard to believe. Nevertheless, the droll and dangerous events that befall this Brazilian Candide as he makes his laborious way from Manaus to Iquitos are, despite much wooden dialogue, the highlights of the novel. . . .

For all the disasters that mangle the Rojas family and the people around it, [Rafael and Violeta's mother] nevertheless believes that "all states of disorder [are] temporary." And so does the author. Not surprisingly, a tumbleweed dreams of a vanished Arcadia and yearns for lost roots. In the end, the parched land receives its ritual rain and the Rojas clan returns to the old homestead. That is, all except Violeta, who commits suicide when she discovers that the man she has slept with is, in fact, her brother.

One wonders what to make of a world where, though the father is the adulterer, the innocent daughter must be sacrificed to remove the curse from the family. Zulfikar Ghose makes of it *A New History of Torments* but, despite the novel's mythical trappings, it seems like the same old sexist history to me. (p. 215)

Gerald Jay Goldberg, "Tumbleweed Fiction," in The Nation, *Vol. 236, No. 7, February 19, 1983, pp. 214-15.*

HARRIET WAUGH

Don Bueno is set in South America, mostly in the Amazonian jungle. It follows the flight of the hero, Calderón, from the fate that awaits him—to be killed by his unknown son. His flight, both from the city and his successful business, starts soon after his girlfriend declares that she is pregnant. It is as though death has laid a hand upon his shoulder. It occurs to neither of them that the child might be a girl. Like some sort of mutant gene, fatherless boy has followed fatherless boy down generations of Calderón's forebears, with each son involuntarily avenging his fatherless state. Calderón moves through the jungle looking for peace within himself and sometimes, momentarily, finding it among strange grotesque people. He does not know his fate and is unable to accept the possibility that he has already killed his own father, although it is his act of patricide which bedevils him. In fact, he killed his father in a provincial town called Santa Rosa through accidentally stabbing him in a bar brawl. His father, drawn lemming-like to his fate, even pressed himself, in an obscene parody of an embrace, upon the point of the knife. If this sounds pretentious I can only say that the story grips one and that the writing is often fine: 'Soon he was overcome by pleasantness and felt dreamily that he was dissolving into the current of the still air that hung over the rosemary bushes. He sat there motionless

for a long time, losing sense of himself as if he were only the space between two tiny, thorn-like needles on a sprig of rosemary.' It is in such passages, showing a fusion of inner states with a transformed world, that Zulfikar Ghose's quality as a mystical writer lies.

Three stories are told. The first is that of Calderón's father. He is an urban criminal who abandons the mother of his child when Calderón is two, driven away by his strong repulsion for him. The second is Calderón's own story, which is woven throughout the other two. The third story concerns Calderón's son, Simon, an urban guerrilla brought up by an unloving mother. As long as the novel stays within its strange, dreamlike world, filled with portentous utterances such as, 'What a terrible thing destiny must be', it works extremely well. Only when the narrative attempts naturalism does it fall into banality, partly because Mr Ghose's characters are not strongly developed and are uninteresting until attacked by some premonition of disaster or mystical pain.

This is particularly true of women under 50. Mr Ghose has considerable difficulty in depicting them at all. Sometimes he gives them curves, and a few times he shows them coupling with a man, but they are stranger to him than the jungle beasts that disturb Calderón with their mating cries. There is a villainess who is so crudely drawn that even in a children's novel she would lack credibility. Leticia, the villainess, is the mother of Simon, Calderón's son. She is an emancipated woman who sneers at her lover's lack of sexual ardour. She is given to making pat psychological insights about others while treating her own child as though he were someone else's irritating and unattractive pet with whom she has reluctantly become encumbered. Finally, she builds Calderón's abandoned business into a vast Empire dedicated to the grossest and most destructive forms of commercialism. Six years after becoming a tycoon, her lust for vengeance against Calderón for deserting her takes her to an underworld witch. In other hands this character might have worked, but Mr Ghose seems to have poured all his scorn and dislike for the modern woman into this jerkily manipulated creation. This makes the last part of the novel, which to a great extent concerns itself with Leticia and the baldly described schoolboy tribulations of Simon, disappointing. Neither of them is given an inner self, and their outward shells are insufficiently substantial to carry the melodrama of a novel about predestination.

However, although *Don Bueno* is patchy, it is never dull, and Mr Ghose has a powerful imagination which more than makes up for the various limitations of this book.

Harriet Waugh, "Mystic Fumes," in The Spectator, *Vol. 251, No. 8108, December 3, 1983, p. 31.*

ALAMGIR HASHMI

Of Zulfikar Ghose's nine novels, [*Don Bueno*] specifically recalls his trilogy, *The Incredible Brazilian*. The three hundred years of Gregorio's life in those novels are here patterned as successive reincarnations of an ultra-Byronic hero who requisitions different bodies across four generations and is known in each life by the pious sobriquet of "Don Bueno." Not that each of these four "heroes" does not have a name of his own: they are Napoleon Calderon, Cesar Calderon, or Simon Bolivar Calderon—names that instantly set off historical echoes with insidious narrative relevance. Legend, however, takes over quickly, and their own personalities are subsumed under the pressure of circumstances in which they face (and partly create) as well as fulfill their individual but repetitive destiny. . . . People call them each "Seignior Good" or "Don Bueno" in their respective turn, in the fashion of a Greek chorus or E. M. Forster's *Esmiss Esmoor,* as fiction triumphs over social fact in a book whose real concerns are with obsession, destiny, and mystery.

The elements of surprise and clash of identity combine with brilliant metaphors piled one upon the other to accentuate the logical tensions of disparity in situ, suggesting the baroque as much as the *nouveau roman.* The protagonists conceal their real names and go through changes of identity, often keeping alive essences, shoring up fragments against (or for) their own ruin. They undergo searing conflicts of self and body. . . . The structure might even appear rigid, for beneath the rush of event and surprise can be traced a detailed, logical and dramatic plan. Ghose remains sufficiently detached to use cooking and meals often as a metaphor for the writer's craft, and he does not shirk from poking occasional fun at his own conventions—authorial complements to the well-constructed framework. Ghose also employs foils to help delineate character as well as provide a larger context and, sometimes, fun, as in the contrast between Cesar, a failure at sex and fatherhood, and the lusty, fertile cattle breeder Marcos.

There are few novels of such magnitude and poetic intensity, which can yet encompass the life of a whole society. In addition to human reincarnations, the birth cycle, and the incessant and unavoidable presence of evil—the South American forest, untempered ambition, et cetera—certain key images, phrases, and motifs reemerge through the shifting time sequence in which the narrative evolves. In the daring of its imaginative powers, the profundity of its moral and psychological insight, its structural resources and verbal resolutions, and the minute evocation of the deepest feelings, this novel is a masterpiece. Its sure, fine prose is an even greater pleasure.

> *Alamgir Hashmi, in a review of "Don Bueno," in* World Literature Today, *Vol. 59, No. 1, Winter, 1985, p. 158.*

K. S. NARAYANA RAO

The twenty new poems in part 1 of *A Memory of Asia* show a sensitive man with a keen awareness of nature: birds, trees, flowers, oceans, and volcanoes. The author is more sensitive to "living" nature than to other aspects, and there is a greater emphasis on visual than on auditory imagination and metaphors. The first poem ["**A Memory of Asia**"] strikes the keynote of an important theme: nostalgic memories of the poet's former homeland. It also deals with the elusive nature of memory, which plays on his mind like light and shade. The second piece, "**Notes toward a Nature Poem,**" is a key to another important theme of the volume: Ghose's sensitive reaction to nature. His poetic sensibility is more readily seen in a number of poems of this section than anywhere else.

The selections in part 2 are distinctly different. Almost all of them deal with Ghose's boyhood experiences in Bombay, and one cannot help thinking that the poet has a great attachment to the first of the four countries with which he has been associated in his life—namely India. Occasional poems on the theme of the alien in England lend a melancholic air. . . . It is interesting to note that this poet is also a critic . . . , and in

choosing the selections for the second part he has eschewed what he considers not really worthy of the reader's attention. There is also a sense of tolerance and objectivity when he rises above parochial political prejudices and declares, "Religion is irrelevant to grief: / you will not agree, nor will Pakistan." It is for this consciousness of universal themes that he should be congratulated.

> *K. S. Narayana Rao, in a review of "A Memory of Asia: New and Selected Poems," in* World Literature Today, *Vol. 59, No. 2, Spring, 1985, p. 317.*

VALENTINE CUNNINGHAM

For years now South America has been the novel's most potent continent—a riveting political new-found-land where daily oppressions come raw enough to jack up the most jaded appetite for concerned realism, but also a cornucopian version of what James Joyce labelled Who-found-land, a place inciting endless fabulation, dream-work enough to outlast a thousand-and-one nights. . . . [In *Figures of Enchantment*], Zulfikar Ghose, long a Brazil-nut, shows there's life in the South American Connection yet.

The figures that enchant Ghose's shanty-town dwellers and office drudges are lucky lottery numbers, cock-fight winnings, the impossible noughts they fantasise as appearing on the end of their nugatory stipends. These will be tickets, they imagine, to the paradise islands, the bliss of the colour-TV soaps than enliven the protracted grimness of their slums.

And Ghose sympathises, as who wouldn't, with his people's dreams of comfort and delight. But the folly of their efforts to gain Utopia also mightily bemuses his prim narrative. Whoring just turns beautiful girls into drudges, pimping gets their husbands shot dead in the gutter. Government statistician Gamboa, victim of corrupt civil administration, does get landed in a paradisal spot, but his particular Brave New World sours in the customary fashion, monkeyed about with by agents of the commercially powerful, not to mention a local version of Caliban, goatish beast-in-man. And being well-off to start with—as the careers of the wrinkled old birds paying hugely for young gigolos are meant to illustrate—is unsatisfactory too.

In fact, Vanity of Vanities is Ghose's wryly pervasive theme. It has him arranging moral vignettes as furiously as John Bunyan, and sounding off much of the time like Malcolm Muggeridge. Instructively bad ends come to almost everyone, especially those who profit financially by ministering to foolish human lusts.

> *Valentine Cunningham, "Dreams and Illusions," in* The Observer, *March 2, 1986, p. 29.*

GRACE INGOLDBY

The taunting image of 'a brightness elsewhere' is the dream which torments the two male characters of *Figures of Enchantment* and allows neither any rest. Gamboa, a clerk, imagines that money is the passport to this 'place'. A desperate Mr Small, he dreams of wealth with the passion of Raskolnikov but far from leading to promotion his anxious zeal is overlooked and all dreams are shattered when he is arrested in a political demonstration and unceremoniously dumped on a desert island where money is no currency at all. His fate is strangely linked with that of Frederico, his daughter's boyfriend of whom he thoroughly disapproved. Frederico's fate is controlled by a charm which takes him on an extravagant odyssey which 'with almost a perversely deliberate malevolence had given him not the life he sought but a parody of it that was vile and farcical.' Gamboa and Frederico meet again on the island where the possibilities of a fairy-tale ending for them hang enticingly just beyond their grasp. This is a philosophical, poetic novel in which endurance raises itself as the quality that counts in a life where dreams, expectations, even the quest for knowledge, are revealed as mere stratagems to distract us from infinite despair. (p. 31)

Grace Ingoldby, "Lives of Quiet Despair," in New Statesman, *Vol. 111, No. 2870, March 28, 1986, pp. 30-1.*

Herbert Gold

1924-

American novelist, short story writer, essayist, nonfiction writer, editor, and author of children's books.

In his fiction Gold examines human relationships within contemporary American settings. The nature of love, self-discovery, and the celebration of human possibility are among his principal themes. Gold's use of language is considered the most distinctive quality of his work. His reproduction of colloquial speech reinforces the realistic descriptions of his characters' lives and turns their mundane experiences into drama. An observer of the problems inherent in family situations and urban environments, Gold often satirizes his typically middle-aged, middle-class, professional protagonists, yet he treats them with compassionate understanding. Gold has said that his fiction "is an effort to master experience. . . . [To] make a vision not just of reality as it is, but as it should be."

Gold's earliest fiction is set in the midwest and is influenced by his Jewish heritage and his youth in Cleveland, Ohio. His first novel, *Birth of a Hero* (1951), profiles the midlife crisis of his characteristically unremarkable, conservative protagonist, while his next work, *The Prospect before Us* (1954; republished as *Room Clerk*), is a pessimistic study of outsiders who experience racism and rejection. *The Man Who Was Not with It* (1956; republished as *The Wild Life*) is considered by many critics to be Gold's best early work. This novel chronicles the passage to maturity of a carnival worker and morphine addict who comes to realize that being "with it" is not the sole aim of life. In *The Optimist* (1959), on the other hand, Gold's protagonist, an unethical politician whose drive for perfection alienates his wife, is unable to come to terms with himself. *Salt* (1963) explores the themes of friendship and commitment by focusing on three contemporary New Yorkers.

Gold moved to California in the late 1960s. Many of his later works, including *The Great American Jackpot* (1969), *Swiftie the Magician* (1974), and *Waiting for Cordelia* (1977), satirize the people and lifestyles of his adopted region. *Slave Trade* (1979) and *He/She* (1980) move away from satire and California settings; the former novel is a detective story set in Haiti, while the latter is a clinical delineation of the disintegration of a marriage. *True Love* (1982) and *Mister White Eyes* (1984) portray aging protagonists alternately fumbling for and avoiding love while making discoveries about themselves. Gold's recent novel, *A Girl of Forty* (1986), concerns the tempestuous relationship between the title character, her unstable son, and a San Francisco journalism professor.

Gold has also published books directly related to his Jewish upbringing. In *Fathers: A Novel in the Form of a Memoir* (1967) and *Family: A Novel in the Form of a Memoir* (1981), Gold blends fact and fiction while examining his relationship with his parents and their continuing influence on his life and work. In a related nonfiction work, *My Last Two Thousand Years* (1972), Gold discusses his Jewish background and analyzes its implications for a writer in the United States. In addition to his novels and memoirs, Gold has written several collections of stories and essays. *Love and Like* (1960) and *Lovers and Cohorts: Twenty-Seven Stories* (1986) include many

© Lütfi Özkök

of Gold's stories. *The Age of Happy Problems* (1962) collects essays on society and the art of writing. In *A Walk on the West Side: California on the Brink* (1981), Gold returns to his familiar role of cultural observer to examine unusual aspects of the California lifestyle.

(See also *CLC*, Vols. 4, 7, 14; *Contemporary Authors*, Vols. 9-12, rev. ed.; *Contemporary Authors New Revision Series*, Vol. 17; *Dictionary of Literary Biography*, Vol. 2; and *Dictionary of Literary Biography Yearbook: 1981*.)

HARVEY SWADOS

When Richard Aldington wrote *Death of a Hero* in 1929, the First World War had been over for ten years, and serious writers of the generation that had survived the carnage were still assessing its effects on their lives and their world. For Aldington, who conceived of his novel as both a threnody and an atonement, the death of a hero in the war was "sickening putrid cant." As the intelligentsia became radical during the Depression and the Popular Front came into being, the idea of the hero was revitalized: he was no longer a pathetic figure but a symbolic representative of the moral grandeur and eventual triumph of the proletariat. In the best novels—those of Malraux and Silone—he was profoundly expressive of the noblest aspirations of the time.

But now we are in another time, and Herbert Gold's **Birth of a Hero** can be read as a kind of signal indicating how far we have come. Although Mr. Gold is a young veteran, his hero is a fighter in neither imperial nor class conflict. He is not even young. He is a business-man-lawyer-commuter-family-man in a Cleveland suburb who conceives a heroism initially not as derring-do but more modestly as an interruption of established routine. There is no mention of war in this chronicle of the forty-sixth year of the fledgling hero, who was presumably too young for the first war and too old for the second; and as for the class struggle of yore, nothing could be more removed from the daily life of Reuben Flair, for whom the acquisition of a new car is an event pregnant with meaning and who accepts as his due a quiet nook in a stratified society that is slowly congealing, like a glossy but essentially tasteless dessert.

As the book opens, Flair is celebrating his forty-fifth birthday en famille. His son-in-law refers to him as the hero of the evening, and "the mocking word" is "spittle in Reuben Flair's face." But the opportunity for heroism is presented by the woman next door, a voluptuous and exotic female of uncertain years who believes that any man can be a hero, that "you can make yourself a hero for yourself," because, as she explains after seducing Flair, "you can learn from everyone. That's the miraculous part of you—in fact, that's what makes you a hero." (p. 283)

His heroism, however, is really tested when her brother Larry (who is not really her brother at all) comes to Flair's house and ensconces himself as a member of the Flair family. Larry Fortner, a kind of Mysterious Stranger, pushes Flair to the limits of his endurance by threatening to reveal the truth to Mrs. Flair, fornicating with the Negro maid, and goading Reuben to examine with the utmost candor his relations with Lydia and with his own family.

While Larry's brutally deliberate assault on the Flair household is resolved melodramatically, Flair's liaison with Lydia is terminated on a muted note that is wryly apropos; and Reuben himself has learned that "he was heroic not in freedom, which is the lie about heroes, but in submission freely given to a chosen responsibility, like a man."

I am afraid that this bald recital does not begin to summarize the factual layer of Mr. Gold's ingenious novel, much less the philosophical overtones with which it is somewhat too heavily weighted. (pp. 283-84)

But if it is true that Mr. Gold's novel has a special importance because it represents a turning point in the intellectuals' attitude toward the middle class (it is my guess that **Birth of a Hero** will fulfil the promise of its title in a special sense by being the first of a series of conservative novels attempting to anchor the unaffiliated intellectual to that middle-aged segment of American society which he has hitherto scorned above all others), it must not be overlooked that Mr. Gold writes with charm and talent. He understands the phenomena at which he is smiling, and he communicates adroitly his delighted recognition of the significance of such neglected rituals as the office party and the commuter's daily journey. If we are really at the beginning of a new era of conservatism, we can only hope that the writers who will choose to celebrate the heroic virtues of the middle-aged and the comfortably placed will be able to do

so with at least a portion of Mr. Gold's benevolent wit, radical perception, and intellectual vigor. (p. 284)

Harvey Swados, "A New Kind of Hero," in The Nation, *Vol. 173, No. 14, October 6, 1951, pp. 283-84.*

JAMES KELLY

Like Flaubert, Herbert Gold hangs his effects on a faithful reporting of sensations recorded by the five senses. He did it in **Birth of a Hero,** a satirical and spasmodically moving novel of a quietly desperate man caught in a middle-aged peccadillo. He does it again in this second novel [**The Prospect Before Us**], the story of a fat man who operates a fleabag hotel on Cleveland's skid row. What distinguishes Harry Bowers, Prop., from colleagues up and down Prospect Avenue is that he loves himself more than he loves money or love. And when a racial minority chooses his hotel as a test spot (the focal point of a rather unfocused novel), it's predictable that Bowers will flaunt local business precepts by going along. Take the problem raised in Laura Hobson's *Gentleman's Agreement,* assume that the Boniface and the unwelcome guest join forces to fight public opinion—and you have the pivotal idea of **The Prospect Before Us.**

Mr. Gold's new novel is not as soundly constructed as his first. Scenes are strung together necklace-style and motivation is not always clear or credible. Characters have labels and are stuck to them. It's a cerebral performance with a tangle of long, long thoughts, most of them entertainingly presented in colorful, runaway language. A high fidelity ear and eye are at work here. The candid conviction and jocular low humor of small encounters drawn from the author's own diary as a hotel night manager provide the right enveloping action. (p. 5)

To those already fascinated by the seedy side of the street **The Prospect Before Us** offers its own rewards. For this observer, however, Mr. Gold writes better than he plots. One looks forward to an easier wedding next time out. (p. 25)

James Kelly, "Fat Harry's Defiance," in The New York Times Book Review, *February 14, 1954, pp. 5, 25.*

ROBERT DONALD SPECTOR

By now Herbert Gold must be weary of criticism that praises his talents but denies his achievements, and yet it is not difficult to understand—if not altogether to condone—the critical reluctance to express whole-hearted approval of his work. To be sure, his novels have demonstrated a range of subject matter extending from adolescent to mature love, from sophisticated to Beat society, and from personal to social problems. At the same time, he has captured the American idiom in its seemingly infinite variety, and he has anatomized American mores in all their complexities. But yet . . . the author stands unlovingly between his work and the reader. His self-conscious rhetoric too often imposes an unbecoming smugness on the tone of his narrative and interferes with the emphatic possibilities of his characterization.

What, for example, is the purpose of the cast of characters that he uses to introduce **Therefore Be Bold?** It is no more than a launching pad for a series of wisecracks that fizzle and never leave the ground. He is so intent upon being clever that he ignores the gap that this artificial device creates between the ultimate seriousness of his account and the reader's emotional register. Granted that Gold is depending upon wit to balance the sentiment of his story about adolescent growing pains, but artifice is no substitute for the revelations that should come through art.

And yet . . . *Therefore Be Bold* is a superior novel. Its author knows what it means to be a young Jewish intellectual struggling not only against the external social prejudices but against the status-seeking values of his own family. But beyond that, Gold remembers the tumultuous period of all adolescence. His hero, Daniel Berman, fluctuates between his idealization of all young women and the adolescent desire for a physical conquest that is masked by a mysticism of its own.

Perhaps "all adolescence" as a generalization is too broad. Gold's adolescents are of the pre-World War II variety, and they create a nostalgia for an innocence of Andy Hardy vintage *sans* saccharine. . . . Alongside the sophistication of modern dating, with its reckless spending of money and morality, Gold's episodes have an almost antique quaintness. The rebellion of his characters is directed toward positive values, which the war that hovers ominously in the background of this novel helped to demolish. . . .

Despite his annoying rhetorical mannerisms, Herbert Gold is a craftsman who not only knows how adolescents feel, talk, and act, but, at his best, allows them to perform with genuine vitality for the reader. He appreciates the mélange of nobility and absurdity, selfishness and idealism that confuses their wisdom and illuminates their ignorance. Whatever the defects of *Therefore Be Bold,* with so much to praise, it would be unjust to laud his talents without also admiring his achievement.

> Robert Donald Spector, "Herbert Gold: His Gift, His Problem," in New York Herald Tribune Book Review, *October 16, 1960, p. 11.*

THE TIMES LITERARY SUPPLEMENT

"The writing of any story", says Mr. Gold, "unleashes personal energies and passions upon fantastical events." This is one of the many earnest statements which Mr. Gold appends to his collection of stories entitled *Love and Like,* anxious as he is to assure the reader about the circumstances in which he writes.

Clearly, here is a writer much concerned with the psychological mechanism of his talent, and, in spite of his critical success in America, nervous of being misunderstood. In fact, these stories are not so very difficult or striking, except in so far as they all reflect the vulnerability of personal relationships in present-day American society. The title story concerns a man on a visit to his children and divorced wife; memories of passion revive, but the least conversation shows him that this pent-up woman with her psychiatric jargon and her preconceived ideal man is someone he could never like. Many of Mr. Gold's stories revert to the theme that sexual love betrays—the university teacher providing "experience" for a pretty suburban sophomore, the shipboard lover who finds he has been used by a callous wife to goad her fat husband, the ordinary chap ruined by a cool and frantic beat generation girl. But among these pseudo-profound comments on erotic love are two or three stories about Jewish family relationships, and these, perhaps because they are more objective and spontaneous, are quite excellent.

> "Talents in Miniature," in The Times Literary Supplement, *No. 3080, March 10, 1961, p. 149.*

DELMORE SCHWARTZ

Although Herbert Gold's first collection of essays [*The Age of Happy Problems*] covers an extreme variety of subjects and is culled from periodicals as diverse as *The Hudson Review* and *Playboy,* it has a real unity based on the consistent point of view of a practising novelist very much concerned with the quality and character of American life. It is a book few admirers of the author's fiction will want to ignore, since, in addition to its intrinsic value, it has a direct bearing on his novels.

The title Gold gives to his collection of essays is, as one would expect, ironic. No problem is a form of happiness. . . .

Gold's genuine and persistent concern is to attack the refusal to face the reality of unhappiness, of failure and of genuine problems, and to attack particularly the assertion—in such forms of mass culture as TV dramas and popular fiction—that everyone in America is happy, or would be if only he could believe that all problems were happy problems. (p. 5)

[It is the] recognition and realization of selfhood which makes possible delight in love and work which is the heart of Gold's new book and, of course, of his fiction as well.

The book includes essays dealing with the problem of being an artist's wife; **"The Bachelor's Dilemma,"** which Gold believes to be a rejection of love; **"Divorce as a Moral Act"**—that is, as sometimes an unpleasant but desirable necessity, but at other times a self-indulgent and fatuous repetition of failure; **"The Mystery of Personality in the Novel,"** about contemporary fiction. Indeed, the scope of Gold's book—and perhaps its limitations—flow from his natural obsession with the vocation of the writer of fiction.

Thus he describes the American as hipster and as beatnik, a phenomenon he condemns (though with qualifications as to the talent of some of its best writers) as being just as much a denial of selfhood in its own way as much popular fiction; a blind pursuit of sensation for its own sake just as so much popular fiction is "upper middle soap opera."

The second half of the book subtitled "American Places," concerns such ports-of-call as [Paris, Cleveland, Haiti, Reno, Greenwich Village, and Miami]. . . . These are all American places because they are American resorts, and often desperate resorts. This is precisely Gold's point throughout the book: the traveler is motivated by a flight from selfhood and freedom and love.

It must be said again that the book is limited, quite naturally, by the novelist's interests—but it is also an important book for that very reason. It is full of perceptions that the sociologist, the anthropologist (especially if he is European) and the pure moralist often neglect: Nothing could be more important than a plea, concrete and realistic, for free selfhood, conscious and powerful, as the real source of work and love. (pp. 5, 17)

> Delmore Schwartz, "The Traveler's Flight," in The New York Times Book Review, *July 1, 1962, pp. 5, 17.*

DAVID BOROFF

It is already a truism that with the death of Hemingway and Faulkner, a new generation of writers seems to be coming into its own, no longer intimidated by those two awesome father-figures. Salinger and Updike, Bellow and Roth and Malamud—these are the names one hears. At the edge of this near-greatness stands Herbert Gold, an immensely gifted, dangerously facile writer, who seems to have created a special role for himself. Gold has emerged as a kind of literary hipster, far too cunning to be taken in by any hipster nonsense, but who in his unsentimental coolness, pitiless sense of the contemporary, and inside dopsterism has links with the type.

Even more important, Gold, like very few of our major writers, has tried to stretch language to meet the new requirements of our time. He has used an idiom that is highly permutable, strained perhaps, too shifty; but it reaches out to encompass new states of mind that writers in an easier time did not have to cope with. At its best, it is taut, keyed-up, nervously inventive; at its worst, it is merely artsy-smirky, a pushy, obtrusive prose. And it defines Gold's stance: the novelist as wiseguy.

None of Gold's five earlier novels has the pure ring of greatness. So much in the mainstream of contemporary life, Gold has nevertheless not been an architect of our consciousness. Somehow he misses the magical fusion of image and idea that stamps the major writer. Like Baldwin, he has taken recourse to essays and articles to explain himself. . . .

Herbert Gold's *Salt* is a New York novel. And if he is indeed an existentalist writer, then he has at last found the appropriate setting, for New York is the Holy City of existentialism where "everything is possible in this most impossible of worlds."

Salt deals with two friends, Peter Hatten and Dan Shaper. Peter is thirty-three years of age . . . and a sexual con-man. . . . He is joined in New York by Dan, a wounded veteran of the marital wars. Dan soon gets the hang of the make-out routines of New York, but, with a full share of human susceptibility, he falls in love with Barbara, one of Peter's castoffs. A natural spoiler, a midtown diabolist, Peter moves in on the girl once more. At this point the tone of the novel abruptly changes. There is a violent confrontation between the two men, and the story ends on a note of muted hopefulness.

But nothing could be more misleading than this synopsis. For the tone of a novel is its clearest declaration. And for most of *Salt* we are treated to an astringent portrait of the erotic whirlybirds of New York. (p. 45)

And Gold is at his best in this *milieu*. Nowhere has his prose been less quirky. The verbal nervousness has subsided into grace and easy motion. And the author reveals himself to be a superb satirist, murderously observant, joyously unillusioned, who can catch a glittering facet of New York in a glittering phrase. This is the best novel of the city in years. But Gold leaps to the portrayal of the inhuman city so gleefully that his upbeat ending is called seriously into question. His eye is too cold, his tongue too sharp. The existentialist voyagers ring true. The hearth-seekers do not. For a while one believes that out of all this emptiness and dry thrashing about some hipster revelation will emerge. There is a stir of disappointment when, at the end, the only answer is the mechanical one of love-love-love leavened by a tough-grained midcentury fatalism. The wiseguy has turned cautious.

Herbert Gold leaves us where we were before. There is a terrible emptiness everywhere. If the older generation of writers dealt with the loss of values, Goid's characters seem never to have had them. One is tempted to contrast *Salt* with Philip Roth's *Letting Go*. If Roth's characters agonize too much, Gold's don't feel enough. They are automatons of pleasure,

slaves of the transient itch, picturesque antiheroes in expensive clothing.

Gold is prodigiously talented—perhaps the most clever novelist in America today—but his new work confirms the suspicion many people have of a misspent creative vitality. (pp. 45-6)

David Boroff, "The Spice without the Savor," in Saturday Review, Vol. XLVI, No. 16, April 20, 1963, pp. 45-6.

DAVID L. STEVENSON

Herbert Gold's new novel, *Salt*, is a brilliant and corrosively comic fantasia on men and women caught alive in our time, who avoid "the prime questions of life on earth," and constantly mistake the "body's clamoring" for love. . . .

Salt is Herbert Gold's sixth novel, and his most significant one. It attains its compelling force, its power over us, as a deliberately stylized abstraction. It gives us, as does Saul Bellow's *The Adventures of Augie March* and Walker Percy's *The Moviegoer*, a look at modern man, tumbling through space and time, desperately reaching to possess the ultimately unpossessables of love and purpose. But the strength of Gold's novel lies in its oddly "unreal" quality. Its chief fumblers—its Peter, its Dan, its Barbara—are individualized types rather than characters whom we know and apprehend. They do not inhabit tangible reality so much as a state-of-mind, a moment-to-moment surrealistic consciousness of what Gold calls "that curious, lifting, floating, pleasurable anxiety" of contemporary existence.

These fumblers, these questers, are given to us with a leanness of tone and sentiment, a detachment at once bitter and humorous. Peter, in his lovemaking, for example, is described as driving "a runaway machine," with Barbara "a small animal caught under him on the highway." . . .

Yet at the novel's end, something startlingly like love and purpose appear with Dan's and Barbara's plans for marriage. The ending is an emotionally moving one, for it catches the reader with his own soft, tender, Oedipal feelings suddenly and rawly exposed. It is, I take it, the final irony of *Salt* that Dan and Barbara, and the reader, find themselves caught together in an ineluctable longing for a solace that does not exist.

David L. Stevenson, "Fumblers at Life," in The New York Times Book Review, April 28, 1963, p. 5.

RENATA ADLER

[The essay excerpted below was originally published in a slightly different form in The New Yorker, *June 22, 1963.]*

In satirizing the clichés of modern American life, Herbert Gold has fallen among the clichés of modern American satire. The worn, familiar targets—cynical Madison Avenue, opportunistic Wall Street, sterile suburbia, impersonal New York—are set up once again and duly re-assassinated. The mode of attack has become familiar, too. For years, there has been apparent—in works as disparate as *Advertisements for Myself, Good-bye, Columbus, Naked Lunch*—a modern satirical convention: the rude ear, the jaundiced eye, and the shrill, complaining voice. The writer has a grudge against society, which he documents with accounts of unsatisfying sex, unrealized ambition, unmitigated loneliness, and a sense of local and global distress. The square, overpopulation, the bourgeois, the bomb, and the cocktail party are variously identified as sources of the grudge. There follows a little obscenity here, a dash of philosophy there, considerable whining overall, and a modern satirical novel is born. In *Salt . . .*, Mr. Gold modifies these stereotypes of subject, tone, and sensibility with a literary formula of his own: imprecise and unmelodic prose, an angry hipster liberalism, some flashes of genuine humor, and a plot structure that has recurred, like an obsessive refrain, in nearly all his novels.

Birth of a Hero, his first novel, told of two men, uneasy friends—one ordinary (the hero), the other crippled and inscrutable. The hero seduced the cripple's wife, the cripple attacked the hero's wife, and the climax was a fight in which the hero wrested the cripple's knife away. *The Man Who Was Not with It* told of two men, uneasy friends—one ordinary (the hero), the other a criminal and a dope addict. The hero slept with a nymphomaniac former mistress of the addict's, the addict attacked the hero's wife, and the climax was a fist fight in which the hero nearly killed his criminal friend. *The Optimist* told of two men, uneasy friends—one ordinary (the hero), the other an ineffectual failure. The hero took a mistress, the failure took the hero's wife, and the climax was a fight in which the hero kicked his rival in the groin. These three novels were set, respectively, in Cleveland, in a travelling carnival, and in Detroit. Now we have *Salt*, set in New York, and the plot is not altogether unfamiliar. It tells of two men, uneasy friends—one ordinary (the hero), the other cynical and cold. The hero takes the cynic's former mistress, the cynic sleeps with her again, and the climax is a street fight in which the hero kicks the cynic in the groin. In each of these novels, the hero's friend has played the role of mentor and father before the exchange of women and the hero's figurative emasculation of him. As a narrator, Mr. Gold appears to have bogged down in muddled Freud.

The title *Salt* warns us that we are in for symbols: the salt of the author's wit; the salt of the hero's tears; the grain of salt with which the cynic faces life; the salt of the sea, which is Mr. Gold's favorite image for waves of sexual excitement; and the salt of the earth, which the author claims his heroine to be. The oranges that Peter, the cynically detached Don Juan of stockbrokers, juggles in the privacy of his apartment are symbolic of his way of life—risky, flighty, temporarily defiant of the laws of nature. The seed catalogues that Barbara, the heroine, studies in the privacy of her apartment are symbols of her healthy, creative disposition and her frustrated longing for marriage and motherhood. The odyssey that Dan, the divorced hero, must undertake is symbolic of the trials that the artist suffers in a symbolic Sodom that is New York. Employing the plot carried over from his earlier novels and the symbols improvised and mixed for this one, Mr. Gold proceeds to construct a series of satirical tableaux—a bitter tour of the offices, living rooms, basements, and bedrooms of his wicked city. (pp. 31-3)

Mr. Gold does considerable nastiness for his reader, and a lot of rolling in excrement, too. The question is: Why? For the sake, of course, of the modern convention of satire. But surely there are, in any era, certain elementary requirements that true satire must fulfill. It must be inventive, attacking its subjects at a point where they did not know themselves to be vulnerable. It must be telling, with an accuracy of naturalistic observation that makes its subjects convincing and recognizable. It must be funny, with that quality in humor that causes readers to improve themselves with laughter.

On the first count, satirical inventiveness, Mr. Gold is totally deficient. His views on what is deplorable in modern life scarcely constitute a revelation. We knew before we met Dan the hero that divorce is an unsettling experience and that Madison Avenue is uncongenial to the artistic temperament. We knew before we met Peter the cynic that sex between disagreeable partners can be sordid and unsatisfactory. We knew before we met Barbara the heroine that a warm single girl in her late twenties is likely to have a rough time. We knew before reading *Salt* that New York can be a lonely place, that some cocktail parties are appalling, that contemporary global problems are staggering, and that dieting has become an American compulsion. Mr. Gold tells us these things again. And when he attempts to tell us something new, he is generally wrong or unintelligible or pseudo-profound or all three. . . . (pp. 33-4)

With the second requirement, accuracy of observation, the author fares better, but not much. His eye and his ear are occasionally acute, but they, too, can be unreliable. The major figures in the novel slip in and out of character until it becomes almost impossible to recognize a single speaker in two successive conversations. . . . And the author's account of what people do is hardly more dependable than his transcription of what they say. Several characters are made to laugh themselves to tears in private—a familiar device for villains in cheap melodrama but scarcely something that occurs frequently in life. When Mr. Gold wishes, as he almost constantly does, to describe realistically two characters making love, he has them smiling amiably throughout. Often the author's errors of observation seem the result not of myopia but of sheer carelessness. (p. 34)

With the last requirement, being funny, Mr. Gold does best. Some of his lines will probably make the reader laugh. . . . (p. 35)

The trouble with the jokes in *Salt*, however, is more serious than their tendency to be repetitious and overlong; they are burlesque masquerading as satire, low comedy pretending to be high. And in true satire the joke and the moral are inseparable; in *Salt*, when the author wants to be funny, he is (in a fairly slapstick fashion), but when he wants to moralize, he preaches. No genuine satirist would indulge in the self-pity, the nagging, and the homiletics that appear in *Salt*:

> "Let's finish what I was saying. Men used to begin their lives with love and end it [sic] with ambition. Now we begin with love and ambition and finish with ambition and love—no good order to things anymore."
>
> "Do you miss good order?"
>
> "Yes, I do. I do."

Whatever this means, Mr. Gold should not have to say it. The moral should lie in the humorous portrait, and need not be gravely, didactically tacked on.

Not the least of the author's problems is that he seems caught between the naughty-boy fantasies expressed in his inscrutable characters and the righteous indignation of his basically bourgeois heroes. . . . On his cynical side, he repeatedly invents crude horrors—cataloguing imaginary instances of brutality, imbecility, and perversion—and then he points to them, aghast. It is often unjust to identify an author's sensibility with that of his characters, but in this case it is almost impossible not to do so: Mr. Gold has written the very novel that his urban and suburban characters, full of the satirical stereotypes that have long been current even in bourgeois irony, would have written; the clichés are precisely those of cocktail-party conversation.

And he has thrown in a few imaginary scandals that only a bourgeois, essentially puritan fantasy could contrive; most of the sordid jokes are merely those that might be told, with some embarrassment, in an office men's room. It is Babbitt, walking the streets of Manhattan, who has written *Salt,* with glee and shame at the daring of his own imagination.

> Peter felt very cruel and drew obscure satisfaction from this judgment of himself.

So does Mr. Gold. And what is unfortunate is that without his commitment to cruelty and irony he might conceivably write carefully and well. When the author writes of the "spinster tributaries" into which Barbara's life divides after her affair with Peter, or of the "telebachelor nod" that Peter and Dan exchange to communicate Dan's acceptance of her, it seems possible that there lies buried in *Salt* a literary talent that has simply smothered in its own misanthropy, a product of the modern convention which requires that writing, critical or creative, become not a work of art but a line of attack. On Grub Street, as on Madison Avenue, there can be a compulsion to conform, to obtain by the suppression of one's individual talents an assurance of having entered the right circles. *Salt* is an application for membership in the fraternity of fashionable discontents, all of whom would blush to utter an unsarcastic or an unpolemic word in an angry middle-aged Establishment that perennially and tediously preempts the revolution. With clichés, symbols, sordid fantasies, and outraged declamations, Mr. Gold has issued yet another in the apparently interminable series of middle-class bohemian manifestoes. (pp. 35-7)

> *Renata Adler, "Salt into Old Scars," in her* Toward a Radical Middle: Fourteen Pieces of Reporting and Criticism, *Random House, 1970, pp. 31-7.*

FELICIA LAMPORT

"The work of the writer is a way out and a way in, and both at the same time, and that's why this book faces two ways," Herbert Gold writes, justifying somewhat murkily the mixture of fact and fiction in this collection of short pieces of the Sixties. But *The Magic Will* faces so many ways that the reader must go through a close-order drill to stay with it. At its best it is poignant, evocative, ironic, lyric, and witty. At its worst it is turgid, self-enunciatory, righteous, pretentious, and slipshod. Good and bad alternate and intermingle until the result adds another corollary to Gresham's Law: bad writing tends to drive the good from one's mind.

It is a pity. Parts of this book rank with the best writing in the author's ten previous titles—from *Birth of a Hero* to *Salt, Fathers,* and *The Great American Jackpot.* These portions are so fine they might even have been memorable in a collection edited with greater care. But *The Magic Will* is shapeless and uneven; its pieces seem to have been gathered in by a dragnet and strung together at random, with no regard for chronology or any other perceptible principle.

. . . In the course of much rhetoric about the "constant skirmish and fading over and across" between the two forms, Mr. Gold says that his essays are stories and his stories essays. The stories, however, are all clearly labeled, and the essay form is stretched like a vast umbrella to cover a gallimaufry of disquisitions, notes, journals, sketches, homilies, and *aperçus.* The author undertakes to coalesce them into a "cross-fertilization of fiction and fact, true lies and partial perspectives," which will "fix the real within the unreal within the real"; his

style, though, is so high-flown that it outsoars its material. "Style that does not work is mere manner," he writes. If he could make his judgment reflexive he would be his own best critic.

Mr. Gold can succeed brilliantly when he is at his simplest and least intrusive, as he is in several of his stories, most notably in **"Song of the First and Last Beatnik,"** a vivid and compassionate evocation of San Francisco's subculture. But in most of the narrative he suffers from a compulsion to undercut his best effects, shattering a delicate mood with a wisecrack, crushing a valid idea under a ponderous sermon, or mercilessly overworking a line he admires. An aphorism to the effect that absolute powerlessness corrupts absolutely, which appeared in his novel *Salt,* crops up here on the lips of a Haitian poet, and still again farther on in the book, where its familiarity seriously diminishes Mr. Gold's impassioned essay on violence.

A more deliberate repetition undermines his account of the tragedy witnessed at the Paris airport, when the charter plane carrying the Atlanta museum group exploded. He writes that at first he recalled only a concentration of Southern accents, then, "Like cards turning up, one after another of these people showed themselves to me." The image is a poignant one, and "flipped up like silent cards" comes as a poetic echo a few lines later. But a sense of echolalia sets in at the third and fourth repetitions; when these cards turn up for the eighth time, all poignance has vanished. The reader feels only a sick impulse to say, "Shut up and deal."

He is soon won back into Mr. Gold's camp by the touching story **"'I Want a Sunday Kind of Love,'"** about a divorced man's Christmas visit to his daughters. The style is controlled and the impact strong. . . .

Yet, once more, the reader is forced to make an about-face. In the final chapter Mr. Gold outlines several plausible stories that he has decided not to write and explains on the highest literary and moral grounds why each would fail. His critical judgment is sound; it might even seem impressive if one of these stories had not already appeared in the book, precisely as outlined, even to the chatty little introduction about his difficulties with an editor. The reader . . . may be pardoned for thinking that the author, or at least the editor, should have read the material all the way through before recycling it into book form.

Exasperation, however, should wholly blot out appreciation of Mr. Gold's considerable talent. Careless flaws and self-indulgent foibles may threaten him with tenure as dean of the promising young writers, but the promise remains.

> *Felicia Lamport, in a review of "The Magic Will: Stories and Essays of a Decade," in* Saturday Review, *Vol. LIV, No. 24, June 12, 1971, p. 32.*

WEBSTER SCHOTT

Herbert Gold's idea of "magic will" reminds me of prayerful intention. He means, I think, the drive to achieve an end, and he alleges something magic and American-made in it. "What the stories and essays of our time would intend to illustrate," he says, "if they had intentions, is the power and pervasive working of will and its corruptions in some specific cases with the American experience." And a few pages later, "To fix and name forever the sense of the magic will of America is a task for a great philosopher-poet if we ever produce one." Gold offers the 21 stories and essays in [*The Magic Will,* a] collection of 10 years' work . . . as his "personal approximations" of our collective magic will. . . .

Instead of conjuring up visions of magic aspiration, Gold's stories and essays tell us about what his fictional characters, various real people he has encountered, Gold and other writers may want and need. All of which are dictated by the facts of humanity (we must have affection, compassion, forgiveness, a sense of worth and protection from our worst fears) and human requirements altered by conditions of place and time. Above all else, the Biafrans of Gold's two pieces about their barbaric war require food, medical attention, and hope. The dying intellectual entrepreneur of **"A Death on the East Side"** demands and achieves self-control in the face of terminal cancer, and the teller of the story seeks humbling experience. Between these extremes—the desperate struggle for life in Biafra and empathy and dignity in the face of death in Manhattan—fall most of the human drives and their manifestations in *The Magic Will*.

Reading Gold's collection I was struck by a new awareness. He is really a superior writer working within a conventional if attractive tradition. He believes that violence, exploitation, suspicion, are human illnesses, not comedy. When he writes about ugliness he sees it ugly. He has strong convictions about right and wrong, and these convictions will be shared by reasonable men. Something else. Gold's stories drawn from his time in Haiti . . . suggest as much fascination with Haiti's political intrigues and cultural strangeness as his concern for the moral plight of the country and its people. Gold is a romancer, a luxurious storyteller as well as a concerned human being. Thus he is a pleasure to read even when the pleasure leads to no particular illumination.

But Gold does have important things to say. Not especially about the art of letters. The mysteries of form don't engage him deeply. He writes straight, linear prose. It serves the purpose—to describe the conditions of his and our life and times. The telling is less consequential than what is told, which argues for his combining fiction and essays in one book. Gold moves in on the loss of innocence in the Hippie movement of the sixties. He tells us what love may be—a pained longing and sex—among the footloose generation. He cannot name (perhaps no one can) the sources of hostility and hate among the disaffected on our streets, in our restaurants and on our campuses, but he feels the pain of these emotions and makes us feel them too. **"A Survival,"** his piece on the death of 130 Americans aboard a 707 chartered from Atlanta to Paris, fixes on the impersonality of 20th-century death as little else I've read. Death runs through much of *The Magic Will* because life is a swarm of riches before Herbert Gold's eyes. "The condition of mortality is our delight when we defy it and ride with it. And the rest of our days it is our anguish."

The joy for Gold in mortality is the quest. He addresses us and himself as a writer: "He seeks a rhythm which can give meaning to his life. His work and his play are one. He aims to keep the child alive in the man's body, and runs the risk of bearing into old age the soul of a baby which only knows how to bang on his high chair and cry, I want." Gold might prefer to call this the magic will. One might wish he didn't, believing Gold is so much smarter than that. But I expect that he who reads this book will see a part of himself in this passage and elsewhere in *The Magic Will* and be grateful. I am. Gold is an upper—a mature one—and we need him.

Webster Schott, "A Luxurious Storyteller, a Concerned Human Being," in The New York Times Book Review, *July 4, 1971, p. 6.*

LARRY McMURTRY

[*He/She*] is a rather primal novel, but it's not so much a primal scream as a primal moan. Some readers will find it riveting, and others claustrophobic, depending on what stage they're at in their own marriages. Herbert Gold is a deft craftsman, not given to waste. In this book his focus is so tight that one is reminded of those little lights doctors use when they need to peer up a nose or in an ear. We get no panoramas, little social description and only an occasional glimpse of some corner of the city. Apart from he/she only three or four characters are allowed so much as a word, and of these only the black boy who spits acquires any weight in the story. The book is about the tenacity of relationships, as expressed in the breakup of one marriage; the impersonal nature of the tenacity is underscored by the use of pronouns instead of names.

That choice, however carefully weighed, may ultimately have been a mistake. Names would have helped. Without them the report becomes a little too clinical.

Also, this is a modern marriage breaking up, and it is breaking up only a bridge away from Cyra McFadden country (memorialized in "The Serial"). The line between passionate seriousness and outrageous parody is narrower than a cable-car track. Mr. Gold doesn't step across it often, but now and then he wobbles across, and, once he does, it becomes difficult to take the angry woman and hapless man as seriously as we had before. Mr. Gold's problem is probably that he is too aware that the fiction of divorce has long since bred cliché. He tries to beat cliché with heavy seriousness, but it finally swamps him. This is unfortunate. His best books, and best effects, have employed a light, comedic touch that he must have felt was inappropriate for such a visceral story. Had he let a little more silliness loose amid the seriousness he would have had a better book. (pp. 10, 21)

Larry McMurtry, "Marital Problems," in The New York Times Book Review, *May 25, 1980, pp. 10, 21.*

ROBERT G. KAISER

"A story," Herbert Gold wrote 20 years ago, "is first of all what follows when someone holds us near the fire by saying, 'Here is what happened and it's important.'" This is a shrewd definition. Nothing here about a plot or an adventure, just "what happened." *He/She* is a brilliant novel about what happened to a marriage in these wrenching times of female awakening. It is a wonderful story, though the plot is as thin as a homely bridesmaid's smile.

Herbert Gold is a master of time-capsule fiction. His stories and novels are nearly all good candidates for burying away in a lead-plated container meant to be opened 100 or 1000 years from now. He is a gifted reporter, a writer whose characters' dilemmas are rooted in a precise cultural moment that Gold evokes supremely well. *He/She,* for example, could someday provide historians with a vivid explanation of what happened to the institution of marriage in college-educated America in the 1970s.

Gold is one of my favorite writers. . . . I discovered his work 20 years ago. . . .

[Then] Gold wrote richly complex stories, disguised as episodic trifles. . . . I remember vividly what Gold wrote in those days about a writer's ambition. It was to create an impression with words so strong that a reader would sit up and say, "Ahh, now I see what you see."

At his best Gold has been able to evoke that "ahh" from a huge audience. *Fathers,* his most successful book, published in 1977, was a big best seller that made him famous at the time. Four subsequent novels have all failed to make a comparable impression.

In *He/She* Gold has reverted to his early preoccupation with men, women and the love between them. After two marriages and five children of his own, Gold at 56 takes on the subject with clearer vision and a wiser voice. *He/She* is meant to be a universal tale—Gold gives no names to the husband and wife whose story he tells; they remain throughout just he and she. It is a risky approach, but I think Gold has pulled it off. These are universal characters, or at least they evoke universal feelings. I thought of a dozen failed marriages among my own friends as I read Gold's painfully true description of this man and woman who could not stay married, but could not stop loving each other either.

Their marriage collapses after the wife unilaterally withdraws from it. He isn't interested in seeing it end—indeed, he is devastated by the spectacle of its ending. Gold can't help making him . . . a sympathetic figure. Like Gold, after all, he is the man; but he wins sympathy by being vulnerable, by hurting before our eyes, and not because he is the wronged party.

In fact he is a male chauvinist of the kind women must find the most distressing; he thinks he is fair-minded and in his thoughtful moments he is fair-minded, but his instincts and assumptions are not fair to his wife. "He knew, of course, that his passion for his wife was an attachment to an idea about himself," as Gold puts it. Her loving him reinforced—perhaps it created—the image of himself that he liked to live with. But she was also supposed to iron his shirts, be the good vice principal's wife and stand aside for him. For a time—through the birth of a daughter—she could do all this. Then, like so many young and middle-aged American women in the 1970s, she stopped being able to do it: "She had fallen in love; she had climbed out of love."

Gold writes from a position that is much closer to him than to her. The book is narrated in the third person, but the narrator is always beside him, never beside her if he is absent. Nevertheless a strong, clear picture of her emerges. . . .

Gold's novel has the pacing and the feel of a good Buñuel movie, and it is just as much fun. The twists the story takes have the bizarre, unpredictable quality of real life. This is a document of our time, as well as a lovely piece of writing.

> Robert G. Kaiser, *"Climbing Out of Love,"* in Book
> World—The Washington Post, *June 15, 1980, p. 5.*

WALTER GOODMAN

Not all the pieces in this collection [*A Walk on the West Side: California on the Brink*], padded with items from the old scratch pad, are as good as Gold at his best. But even the softer items have bite. The anthropological asides about the denizens of Los Angeles, San Francisco, Palm Springs, and Big Sur pro-

duce a generous complement of zippy lines: "Hey mister," implores the bum in Westwood, "gimme a quarter for a frozen yogurt."

In Big Sur these days, we learn, "space mates" tend to replace spouses, "and there is never a fight, although sometimes an interpersonal conflict will break out." We are let in on the rules of open marriage: No criticisms of one's real spouse or of anyone's sexual performance, and "you must be friendly, kind, reserved, though erotically inventive and scrubbed in body."

Gold tells us of the TV movie-of-the-week producer who calls a filmmaker and anthropologist after seeing their documentary on a poverty-stricken neighborhood of old Jews: "Will you take a meet?" he asks. "The producer tells them he sees magic, he feels it, he can almost taste it. The documentary is wonderful. He smells audience, humanity, ratings. Who could want more? There is only one problem. 'Do these people have to be Jewish?'" And who can go altogether wrong writing about a city, otherwise known as Halloween-by-the-bay, where the sheriff obligingly brings in a homosexual minister to serve like-minded occupants of the county jail.

But the major engagement of this book, the main bout, is between Gold, the hyped up, laid back resident outsider, participant-observer, and those of his fellow Californians who are endlessly breaking out, dropping out, hanging out, acting out, or whatever is in these days. Life on the Pacific is like a television commercial: "Permanent youth, perpetual growth, stalwart adventures, erotic play are long-term possibilities brought to us all with the help of sport, vitamins, hair care and regular exercise."

Gold grapples with some very peculiar people who, the point is, are not all that peculiar in that place and this time: The lovely young dancer who aborts the pregnancy caused by one or another of three recent acquaintances because "I'm looking for some better genes for the father of my child." The six women and one man arrested for running a brothel, who insist that they are therapists "performing a psycho-medical service," helping out clients with premature ejaculation problems, sadism problems, water sports problems, exhibitionism and voyeurism problems. The fellow doing a book on Men's Liberation who is obsessed with the question of whether Gold kisses his men friends on the lips. The blind date who in a former incarnation as a man was the "wife" of the male friend of Gold who arranged the date. (pp. 21-2)

The reporting is done more in anguish than in anger. . . .

These pieces are full of sharp details and good jokes—only Gold isn't laughing. He is at bay on the bay, staving off a society gone amok, where "most marriages seem to be in escrow, most relationships in a state of sustained title search," where "every open marriage I know has dissolved in horrific recriminations." It is not always possible out West to tell the therapists from the panderers, the gurus from the con artists, the perpetual seekers from the lunatics and nitwits. All those human potentialists, chasing their karmas, riding with the flow, on "a nomadic quest for Esalen, Sandstone, Arica, est, brotherhood, sisterhood, selfhood. . . ." Gold sees the singles bars, the polyfidelity groups, the constant quest for an "other," as "a preoccupation comparable to the classic pains of the metaphysically lost." He identifies himself repeatedly as the outsider, Jewish, gray bearded, burdened by the past, a Jeremiah of the drive-ins. How can he connect, and keep on endlessly connecting?

Herb Gold, "scarred veteran of marital wars," places his own disappointments within the prevailing madness and suggests wistfully that raising children really does require two people in the house. "Wasn't marriage made to surround kids with care?" he asks like some middle American moral majoritarian. A courageous question in his neighborhood, a cry from the heart of a freeway father. Maybe the Jewish kid from the East really is ready to go home. (p. 22)

> *Walter Goodman, "Leaving Lotus Land," in* The New Leader, *Vol. LXIV, No. 10, May 18, 1981, pp. 21-2.*

JEROME CHARYN

Herbert Gold's particular strength as a writer is the intimacy of detail that he establishes between himself and the reader. At its best, his language sways with a litany of song, and his characters have a special kind of vulnerability. He writes about growing old in America and the ritual of falling out of love. When he swerves from this intimate connection with the reader, as he did in his novel *Swiftie the Magician,* the writing becomes clever and loses the power of song.

In his very best work—such as the long story **"Love and Like"** and the article **"Death in Miami Beach"** and novels such as *Fathers* and *The Man Who Was Not With It*—he establishes a sad but powerful voice, the wound of isolation, that slow dying within and around us. "The mask of existence fits harshly on your skin," he writes in **"Death in Miami Beach,"** "but it is in fact your only skin; and when harshly your skin is peeled off—beneath it you are naked and your naked isolation is no joy to you."

Family is also about slow dying, and it is a novel that exists almost as pure song.... The pull of dying is with us all our lives. It is only at moments of celebration and joy that we escape that pull....

"Herbert" himself becomes the unifying persona of *Family,* but the novel is not a performance about Mr. Gold's own life. *Family* is never a writer's notebook, a portrait of the artist as a Cleveland boy. It is an homage to the loving and bullying women around him: his grandmother, his aunt Anna, and his own mother, Frieda, whose weapons are silence and the cunning act of feeding a house full of men. The women exist in their own mad frame, caring for men but hardly needing them. Grandfathers, husbands and sons are "visible invisible" facts around the house, "ignored in crisis."

Frieda is the central force of the novel, and Herbert does a long dance with her, even before he is born. (p. 12)

It's not his father, Sam, who is the protector of the family. Frieda even assumes that role....

After Herbert's own divorce, Frieda admits that she had a husband before Sam. "Once upon a time my father was not my mother's first man." She'd married a pharmacist she didn't love. And then she married Sam. She thrived, but her men faltered little by little, immigrants trying to accommodate themselves to this world....

In one of the stories Herbert remembers from childhood, Delilah sneaks up on Samson and bites off his hair. Frieda is like Delilah, but she uses strokes of love. Even after Sam retires and is lost in his "Arctic isolation," Herbert says that "she told my father to shape up at ninety-two." She is "bravely and eternally at odds with language and men."

Still, the portrait of Frieda is never corrosive. She is funny, crazy, full of inventive language....

Preparing food becomes the principal outlet for her energy "Only the deepest feelings would derail dinner." The act of eating consumes every other thing. "It was usually dinnertime in Cleveland, except when it was lunchtime."

The women of *Family* move into "a green delight in survival." Herbert adopts Frieda's attitude about language and love and learns how to survive. As a scribbler, he extends her song onto the page, shares her history with us, comes to terms with Delilah's crazy loving. The delight of *Family* is that Herbert Gold can view Frieda with the poison that the very best writers have to use—that merciless precision of detail—and still not reject her. *Family* is a deeply passionate book. (p. 42)

> *Jerome Charyn, "A Homage to His Women," in* The New York Times Book Review, *December 13, 1981, pp. 12, 42.*

PETER ANDREWS

The novelist Herbert Gold is one of the most reliable correspondents we have in exotic California.... He is forever uncovering the latest totems and odd social byways of the Pacific shore and writing about them with grace and humor.

I confess I am frequently baffled by his revelations of the current life styles of Californians, with their passion for self-indulgence and self-fulfillment.... I also find a wearying voluptuousness in Mr. Gold's characters as they scramble about, risking everything, including herpes, in their relentless pursuit of good forehands, good sex and good karma. But he is such a spirited chronicler that, as long as he is leading the way, I am happy to make one more stab at solving the riddle of the mysterious West....

No one captures the seriocomic aspects of variant sex in the Sun Belt better than Mr. Gold. The sex is fiercely casual, but everyone seems to work very hard at it.... It is small wonder that almost every character in *True Love* is a physical fitness addict. They need every ounce of stamina just to get through the perfervid day.

Although the novel is drenched in sex, the author is never so impassioned that he forgets the little politenesses that elevate the act from the merely functional to the socially meaningful. For example, if you are bathing with someone whom you have met only a half-hour before, who soaps whom and with how much vigor? This is a point of etiquette that I never thought much about until Mr. Gold brought it to my attention.

Nor does he overlook the possibilities for neat social commentary about a part of the country where a man can become a millionaire by breeding a square tomato that can be shipped across the country easily but that is inedible on arrival. In an anthropological note worthy of Margaret Mead, he points out that in California we are seeing the first generation of young people who have never buttoned up a coat. They have never known anything but snaps and zippers.

As long as Mr. Gold was trekking through the labyrinth of California sexuality, I was able to tag along, if sometimes dropping back a lap or two to catch my breath. But then he abandoned this luxuriant material to dart into an examination of the psychobabble of California encounter groups. Here, I admit, I got somewhat lost.... When Californians start discussing the extent of their yangness, I can no more understand what they are talking about than I can comprehend the intellectual processes of a Canada goose caught in an electrical storm. I get a sense of eager, even violent, motivations at work, but they are making connections I cannot fathom. Worse, I often cannot tell if they are being serious or kidding. Even Mr. Gold, who has always been such a mordant observer of such matters, may be starting to believe in the efficacy of solving emotional problems by pounding on the floor with a cloth cudgel. . . .

Still, *True Love* is a delicious piece of work—witty, funny and, at bottom, rather wistful. It is another of Herbert Gold's fine portraits of life and love in California, crafted with the nice detail of a gifted short-story writer. As always, I was glad to be permitted another view of the scene, if saddened by the realization that comprehension continues to elude me.

> *Peter Andrews, "The New Wild West," in* The New York Times Book Review, *December 12, 1982, p. 14.*

MICHAEL J. LASSELL

Three quarters of the way through [*Mister White Eyes*], Herbert Gold sits protagonist Ralph Merian down with his deeply disturbed brother Chaz at a homosexual bar in San Francisco. Merian himself is not homosexual, but he concludes . . . that the dancing couples "were onto a truth, but they had it mixed up with other matters."

Gold, too, is onto a truth. He, too, has it mixed up with other matters, as does Merian, a veteran journalist who refers to himself as the V. J. *Mister White Eyes* is the story of Merian's mid-life crisis.

On assignment in Haiti when the novel begins, Merian is defined by his life-consuming work. He has survived numerous international conflagrations, an unhappy early family life and two unsuccessful marriages. He has sworn off love forever, but meets an attractive Englishwoman named Susan. They begin a romantic affair; Merian is too frightened, too isolated, to admit that it involves love.

The V. J.'s editor sends him to Arizona to cover the story of the Stony Apaches. . . . On the Nation (formerly the "reservation"), Merian confronts himself in the face of history and current reality. He meets Hawkfeather, who directs the full measure of his hatred at Merian, dubbing him Mister White Eyes.

Rendered vulnerable by his fear of loving and then losing Susan, Merian sinks deeper into his confusion. He is suddenly obsessed with the truth and can therefore no longer write.

Gold's writing is rich, insightful, full of the details of a variety of worlds and the minutiae of human existence. This is an intensely introspective book; little actually happens. The prose alone is not sufficient to carry interest. Implicit dangers do not become manifest; the undercurrent of sexuality only rarely becomes explicit.

The focus is on Merian, the journalist as stranger to his own life. He is not, however, particularly likable, or even entirely trustworthy. His thoughts, words and deeds are rarely either rational or necessary to the character the omniscient tattletale narrator has described.

The novel vacillates between inventive literary devices of contemporary fiction and the conventions of pulp. Susan seems far too sensible to put up with Merian. She also seems to have major off-stage personality shifts. . . .

Questions keep nagging: *Why* is Merian having so much trouble loving Susan? *Why* is he so attached to his crazy brother? *Why* so haunted by the overly obnoxious Hawkfeather? *Why* can't he write the Apache story?

The ending, which comes in a sudden gush, is meant to be cathartic—at least for Merian. But it's so tangential as to be inaccessible.

> *Michael J. Lassell, "To Find the Truth, to Find the Self," in* Los Angeles Times Book Review, *October 14, 1984, p. 3.*

GEORGE KNUEPFEL

Mister White Eyes is the story of a journalist who travels the world wherever a story breaks out. The occupational hazard is obvious: Such a person can't possibly maintain any kind of relationship with anyone else. Ralph Merian, a.k.a., the "V. J." (Veteran Journalist, his own prescribed nickname) has been a war correspondent, and a Pulitzer-Prize nominee, for over 27 years. Merian and the V. J. can both be said to be the protagonists of this book. Both the man Merian and his occupational counterpart determine much of the action. A third point of view, the author, is also included, and sometimes, when we see through his eyes, it is actually through the eyes of an elevator operator, an ex-lover, or a waitress. This novel is written in an omniscient third person point of view and it doesn't work to the story's advantage. When Gold writes "The V. J. thought it might be time to return to New York. He didn't want to, and so he wanted to", what has he said?

The idea for this book must have sounded something like this in the beginning: Create a character who is a journalist (a person whose entire *raison d'etre* is to exist in the present tense and record what he sees as he sees it) and make him fall in love with a woman, so that the conflict will be "Can this relationship last to everyone's content?" I am not trying to minimize Mr. Gold's story; I am merely trying to get a handle on it.

At work, it is the V. J. in control. . . .

At home, in New York, it is Ralph Merian who calls Susan, his lover, at her apartment. He has recently returned from a trip to an Indian "Nation" (as opposed to the more derogatory "reservation"). In the Indian Nation, he met two women, Claudia and Sandra, both of whom he became lovers with, and an Indian, Hawkfeather, whose hatred for him stems from the fact he sees Merian as a user, a man who comes to the Nation, gets his story, and leaves. At Susan's apartment, he sees Hawkfeather. The sudden, unexpected meeting of characters from both his worlds in one room ought to have been terrifying. . . . But Gold, speaking as the narrator says: "Merian believed the only thing more difficult to handle than non-negotiable demands was unstated non-negotiable demands," pulls the plug out fast. The language at this moment is wrong, awkward and prosaic. . . . And often, Gold offers an image that simply doesn't work: "A Broom stood in a heap of sand in the corner. The broom had been used in history; it was irregularly worn and eroded, *like the mouth of an old man*." How is a used broom like the mouth of an old man? Late in the book Merian is described as looking "worn out and griefy."

The events in this book which are meant to generate emotion in the reader fall flat. I think the main reason they do not work is because they occur too late in the book, far beyond the point when a reader cares for Merian. When we learn about the succession of his parents' death, father, then nine months later, mother, we ought to be moved. But we're not. For one thing, if Merian has any problems, the V. J. part of him will get him on the ball again with work. Thus, when Merian goes to San Francisco to see his long-lost brother who is a babbling psychotic, it didn't seem right that Gold would have in the last quarter of the book a character so tied up with Merian's past and so far beyond hope that we must see him in the light of a person, who given some attention by his older brother (Merian), might have survived. Having Charles's doctor mimic an Italian accent is beyond belief (''Dat's a da trobble,'' she said.'').

Another reason why the events in this story lose power is because nothing is portrayed in relief. . . .

In Ralph Merian, Gold has created a person for whom love means not having to think, because thinking becomes the first step towards craziness, disillusionment, guilt, and the realization we are, each of us, finally alone in this world. . . .

> *George Knuepfel, in a review of ''Mister White Eyes,'' in* San Francisco Review of Books, *Spring, 1985, p. 12.*

KIRKUS REVIEWS

[In *Stories of Misbegotten Love,* the] prolific Gold (whose nearly 20 books include *Fathers, Waiting for Cordelia, Family,* and *Mister White Eyes*) here collects five of his stories. . . . What links these slickly crafted tales is their numbing evenness of voice and subject. All but one concern middle-aged, divorced (or soon-to-be divorced) California men, whose endless kvetching—they view most women as capricious and manipulative—makes them perfect candidates for Leonard Michaels' *The Men's Club*—familiar territory in post-feminist male fiction. The longest, most compelling piece, **''Stages,''** chronicles a dwindling marriage (alternately seen as a ''risk,'' a ''business,'' and a ''routine'') through a series of short but sharply etched episodes. The final story, **''Bart and Helene at Annie and Fred's,''** reveals Gold at his worst. Here, a woman is rejected because she lacks, it seems, the qualities which matter the most to Gold's self-pitying heroes: she's neither young nor stunningly beautiful. In the end, the only thing ''misbegotten'' about these workmanlike but ultimately distasteful stories is their re-publication. (pp. 807-08)

> *A review of ''Stories of Misbegotten Love,'' in* Kirkus Reviews, *Vol. LIII, No. 16, August 15, 1985, pp. 807-08.*

PUBLISHERS WEEKLY

Gold's stories [In *Stories of Misbegotten Love*] center around the vicissitudes of modern relationships. The men in these stories are typically given to wheel-spinning analyses as they seek to be a ''disgrace to the life of the mind'' and try to achieve ''paternal kink.'' Not surprisingly, the women in the stories jilt them with regularity. Gold's strengths lie in his hard-edged descriptions of the inner workings of people involved in relationships. At times, his dialogue has perfect pitch, but the staccato prose can become twitchy.

> *A review of ''Stories of Misbegotten Love,'' in* Publishers Weekly, *Vol. 228, No. 9, August 30, 1985, p. 418.*

JOHN BARKHAM REVIEWS

Hold [*Lovers and Cohorts*] in your hand and reflect on the fact that the stories between its covers sprang from forty years of talent, experience and craftsmanship. Without Herbert Gold's admission that they cover so long a period it would be hard to accept the wide time-span so little difference is there in the quality of matter and manner. A story like **''Ti-Moune,''** about a little Haitian girl whose mother vainly tries to send her to America with a tourist couple, is understated heartbreak with a finale hard to forget.

Whether this story was written long ago or comparatively recently is hard to tell: its style and emotional impact are timeless. In his introduction Gold admits that his ''passions'' as a teller of tales have remained constant: love, family, Jews, Bohemia, wanderlust, and the meaning of life. Examples of all of these themes are present in this volume. Two stories (Gold doesn't say which) led directly into novels. (pp. 3-4)

Gold's ability to evoke emotion tangentially is everywhere apparent. In **''From Proust to Dada''** an elderly Frenchman is reading aloud his literary memoirs about meetings with Proust, Pound and others, when a young American listener suddenly begins to weep. His companions, not listening to the French reading, wonder why. ''He is moved,'' runs the last line. So was this reader.

At the heart of Gold's best stories are his evocation of character, such as the concentration camp survivor reacting to Christmas in remote Dakar, or the renter of a rundown cottage in Los Angeles, a cottage, Gold tells us, that is probably ''the envy of millions.'' What traveler to Europe will not endorse his line: ''Purgatorial telephone lines are one of the great traditions of French civilization.''

Some of the stories have been overtaken by events. **''Winter of '73''** drew its theme from the oil shortage which then gripped this country. Today, with a global oil glut, its theme is quaintly outdated. . . .

Gold also has a distinctive way with phrases. He lets an Italian speak of ''your sublime buffoon, Marco Twain,'' or the eatery in Italy he calls the ''ristorante da Bing Crosby.'' But these are surface virtues: underlying the best of these tales are deeper emotions like the vain regrets of an old man tired of growing old. Here, as so often in these stories, Gold touches the feelings of his readers as he himself was touched by those of his characters. (p. 4)

> *''Teller of Tales,'' in* John Barkham Reviews, *April 19, 1986, pp. 3-4.*

HILMA WOLITZER

There is no chronology offered for the 27 stories contained in *Lovers & Cohorts* . . . [Herbert Gold] has had a prolific career, producing more than 20 other books, among them a collection called *Love and Like,* whose stunning title story is the most successful one included here. **''Love and Like''** is about the particular agonies of the husband in a failed marriage: the wrench of separation from his children, the relearning of bachelorhood and the ambivalence felt toward the recently beloved. . . .

The pain of love's dissolution is explored further, and very deftly, in **''The Smallest Part,''** where the couple's divorce is described as ''amicable and mysterious.'' The mystery deepens when the husband finds himself seduced into a regular habit of making love to his former wife, without ever spending the night with her. It's as if he's obtained visitation rights to her as well as to their child. This arrangement assuages his loneliness and melancholy for a while, and seemingly hers too. When his buried grief finally surfaces again, it is "because he had loved his wife with the passion of his life. And now he indifferently stroked and played at her body, and waited for her to claw and shudder against him; and then, out of politeness, and also so that he might sleep afterward, he allowed himself the modest shudder of pleasure." He discovers (and shares the discovery with his former wife) that one of the reasons their postmarital sex continues is that he doesn't like her very much anymore. Love and like, again. And again, even when we don't know what the wife is thinking, she is made whole, and even sympathetic, by the husband's perception of her.

But the wives in some of the other stories, and the tenderly observed young women ("girls") after whom the husbands yearn, are not given the vitality that would vault them into life. The wives are only shadowy background figures, and despite some idiosyncratic behavior, the universal blondness and availability of the other women create a sameness in them, and finally in the husbands who desire them. The lust the men feel is convincing enough; it's just not that interesting.

There is an additional and essential ache in "Love and Like" that goes beyond sexual longing without excluding it. The two children who are, to some extent, lost to their father in the divorce are so wonderfully drawn that the reader experiences the father's loss. . . .

Three other favorites of mine in this collection, "A Ninety-Six-Year-Old Big Sister," "Cohorts" and "Ti-Moune," all seem to have sprung from the concept of character rather than plot. The affection Mr. Gold expresses for these characters allows their modest stories to evolve naturally. The first two have the persuasiveness of autobiography, and not just because the narrator of the former is named Herbert. Herbert's elderly aunt is the heroine of this story, as the elderly father is the hero of "Cohorts." Aging is the villain in both. "I want my independence," Aunt Anna says, and means it, but left to herself, she doesn't eat properly. . . . When she breaks her hip, thereby forfeiting her hard-won independence, she simply dies, as if by choice. The confused and terrified Dad of "Cohorts" hangs on long past his autonomous days, reaching out to his middle-aged sons for support and comfort. . . . In the end, the sons can't do much beyond providing an outing to distract and entertain him. Their frustration is nicely understated, as is their chilling vision of their own future.

In "Ti-Moune," the fate of a child is the focus of the story. An American couple and their children are in Port-au-Prince on the husband's State Department fellowship for a year's study of Haitian culture. During that time, they become attached to a charming 11-year-old Haitian girl named Monique and nicknamed Ti-Moune (Little One) by the American wife. The whole family is forced to learn a hard cultural and personal lesson when Monique's mother offers her to them at the end of their year for a kind of indentured adoption. Again the meaning is conveyed with subtlety.

There is the risk of sentimentality in these three stories and the achievement of affecting sentiment. Unfortunately, a few of the others hurtle toward endings that appear to have been preordained, and these stories are slighter and less satisfying. But at his best, Mr. Gold is a fine craftsman, with insight into the currents that draw us together and pull us apart.

Hilma Wolitzer, "First Together, Then Apart," in The New York Times Book Review, *April 20, 1986, p. 11.*

PUBLISHERS WEEKLY

In what may stand hereafter as *the* definitive California novel [*A Girl of Forty*], Gold brilliantly sums up the hedonistic lifestyle and emotional immaturity of the breed. Writing in a perfectly calibrated ironic tone, he captures the lingo and the trendy habits of self-absorbed people forever going on about their bodies or their psyches, living totally in the moment, believing that life should be fun, with no ties and no regrets. And in Suki, the titular "girl of 40," he gives us an indelible character. Suki is charming, beautiful, fey, a free spirit who typifies the sunny California outlook. She is also self-obsessed, relentlessly frivolous, so superficial she is dangerous, and casually, blatantly promiscuous. The narrator, Frank, is her sometime bed partner who remains in love with Suki, despite her infatuations elsewhere. Frank has sat on the sidelines all his life, avoiding emotional commitment, but he and Suki are forced to face reality by Suki's son. Peter, a teenager who is as physically perfect and alluring as his mother, has grown up incubating a deep vein of anger against Suki's sexual flaunting. As the darkness in Peter's soul deepens, Gold's depiction of a destructive mother/son relationship gathers a brutal force. This compulsively readable book by the author of *Fathers* and *Salt* is a zinger, a cautionary tale of real power and truth.

A review of "A Girl of Forty," in Publishers Weekly, *Vol. 229, No. 23, June 6, 1986, p. 57.*

Harry (Max) Harrison

1925-

(Born Henry Dempsey) American novelist, short story writer, editor, nonfiction writer, and author of children's books.

Best known for his work in the science fiction genre, Harrison is a prolific writer recognized for his fast-moving adventure stories. Many of Harrison's novels and short stories are intended as parodies and burlesques of popular literary forms. *Montezuma's Revenge* (1972) and *Queen Victoria's Revenge* (1977) lampoon the espionage novel. *Bill, the Galactic Hero* (1965), *The Men from P.I.G. and R.O.B.O.T.* (1968), in which the protagonist enlists the aid of talking swine, and *Star Smashers of the Galaxy Rangers* (1975) parody the science fiction "space opera." Harrison's popular *Stainless Steel Rat* series, which features a futuristic criminal whose services are required for several dangerous missions on the side of the law, satirizes both the space opera and the espionage novel. While these novels, including *The Stainless Steel Rat* (1961), *The Stainless Steel Rat's Revenge* (1970), *The Stainless Steel Rat Saves the World* (1972), and *The Stainless Steel Rat for President* (1982), have been faulted for their occasionally flawed style, some critics have commended them for their unusual combination of adventure and humor. In a more serious novel, *Make Room! Make Room!* (1966), Harrison addresses problems relevant to contemporary society by depicting a near-future New York City suffering severe overpopulation and food shortages. This novel was adapted for the film *Soylent Green*. In *A Transatlantic Tunnel, Hurrah!* (1972), an example of the "alternative world" subgenre of science fiction, Harrison parodies the nineteenth-century Victorian novel. Harrison's recent *West of Eden* (1985), another alternative world novel, concerns the struggle between dinosaurs, which have evolved into intelligent beings, and humans for dominance of the earth.

(See also *Contemporary Authors*, Vols. 1-4, rev. ed.; *Contemporary Authors New Revision Series*, Vol. 5; *Something about the Author*, Vol. 4.; and *Dictionary of Literary Biography*, Vol. 8.)

© Jerry Bauer

KINGSLEY AMIS

With Harry Harrison's collection, ***Two Tales and Eight Tomorrows*** . . . , we return firmly to basics. The stricken visitor from space, the horrifying toy, the simple, vulnerable alien race are all familiar as they stand. Here they become freshened, give rise to a lament for human helplessness, a warning about the perversion of innocence, an angry but not fanatical polemic against religious indoctrination. Mr Harrison achieves this by being interested in what he's saying; how he said it was secondary. (But I wish he'd work at his punctuation.)

> Kingsley Amis, *"From Monsters to Mannerism,"* in The Observer, *May 30, 1965, p. 27.*

THE TIMES LITERARY SUPPLEMENT

[In ***Bill, The Galactic Hero***], Mr. Harry Harrison seems to have set out to write a sort of picaresque twenty-first century novel, a galactic *Tom Jones* cum *Tristram Shandy*. His first main handicap is that the world of ploughboy Bill, who gets shanghaied in the first three pages into the Empire Space Corps as a recruit, is much more that of Gormenghast, Tolkienland or even of Rex Warner's country over the border in the *Wild Goose Chase*, than any geography related to our present knowledge of Outer Space. In fact this book, which is sometimes wildly funny in a very sado-compensatory way, seems to have had the whole edge of its satirical blade blunted by the temporal/ spatial shift of focus in which it is blurredly set. Perhaps all these strictures could be erased had it been compressed into half of its present length.

> *"Bad News from Galaxia,"* in The Times Literary Supplement, *No. 3341, March 10, 1966, p. 188.*

THE TIMES LITERARY SUPPLEMENT

A few writers are trying to heave science fiction out of the welter of genre cliché and steam age technology. . . .

[A] satisfactory, if limited, approach to the genre problem is to send it all up. This Harry Harrison did a couple of years ago with *Bill, The Galactic Hero,* when he mopped up just about all the old Heinlein-Asimov-Clarke universe; of space/time, only the latter component was spared. He savages it now, in the rumbustious if rather spasmodic *Technicolor Time Machine.*

A cheap-jack Hollywood movie company decides to shoot its Viking epic on the real location, back in the eleventh century. They use a cheaply acquired time machine, much of it built on the set of an old science-horror film called "The Creature's Son Marries the Thing's Daughter", and accidentally make history while making their epic. Hollywood and Vinland backgrounds are unobtrusively well-researched. All good straightforward fun, and one enjoys at least every other word of it. A sort of hairy-chested instant camp SF.

> *"Genreflecting," in* The Times Literary Supplement, *No. 3457, May 30, 1968, p. 560.*

JONATHAN RABAN

Captive Universe is a tricky piece of soc sci fi from the anthropology department. Two cultures inhabit Harry Harrison's cigar-shaped asteroid: a tribe of Aztecs in a sealed valley, and a monastic society of post-electronic men in the surrounding rock. These religious technocrats are called Watchers and Observers and their business is to contain the life of the Aztecs by such nasty devices as building electrically-controlled robot gods to stalk the cornfields at dusk (a good tip, perhaps, for any technically inventive anthropologist worried about the decline of primitiveness in his favourite tribe). The whole scheme is masterminded by the Great Designer, the final architect of all the myths, versions of history, taboos and ideological goals that keep this captive universe afloat in space. It's foiled and brought to a state of chaos by an empirically-minded Aztec youth who begins by outwitting the god, learns to operate the computers and returns in vengeful triumph to his village, riding on the shoulders of the hideous, hydra-headed robot. Rain comes down; the robot short-circuits; an avalanche occurs; the Aztecs and Observers have to face one another as humans, without their protective trappings of myth and technology. Nature has got the better of Culture. One of my pet parlour games is watching *Doctor Who* on the supposition that the script has been written by Edmund Leach, and *Captive Universe* offers the same sort of satisfactions. But it's written in the stiff journeyman prose that characterises too much of the science fiction I've encountered; an engaging drama of ideas without sufficient verbal solidity to make it a good novel.

> *Jonathan Raban, "Corroded Dream," in* New Statesman, *Vol. 79, No. 2031, February 13, 1970, p. 226.*

THE TIMES LITERARY SUPPLEMENT

In *Captive Universe* we appear to be getting more of the healthy outdoor life [Harry Harrison] celebrates in his Deathworld series. But something untoward is happening in an Aztec valley. Coatlicue, the goddess with the serpent heads, walks the fields. And why do all the vultures ascend with their prey to one particular spot on a high cliff? Chimal goes to investigate, and soon is in a very nasty situation.

To addicts of the genre, this nasty situation will not be entirely unfamiliar. However, Harrison brings his usual gusto to bear, and the result is a pleasing and exciting mystery, expertly resolved.

> *"Unreasonably Reasonable," in* The Times Literary Supplement, *No. 3554, April 9, 1970, p. 377.*

THEODORE STURGEON

A bad writer, if he writes enough, will come up with a good passage, a memorable character, a remarkable insight. It is a statistical necessity. What then are we to think of a writer who produces a whole book and never does it—not once? It must be purposeful; there is no other way to avoid random virtue. Given that it is his intention, then—why? I think that it is a matter of conscious posture—the conviction that the rules of the game are that he must write-what-happens, avoiding always—even when writing in first person—those deep areas of feeling, or empathy, of reader participation which mark memorable fiction.

There is in *The Stainless Steel Rat* an embarrassment of scenes and situations, adventures, escapes, encounters, gimmicks and gadgets. The book is, I think, archetypical—not so much of most sf, but of the countless volumes of detective/mystery yarns which pencil in their patterns and then let the reader watch the author go over them with his pen. It's all there—the beginning, the middle, the end; you know who's going to win and who will lose. The protagonist (a super-criminal drafted into the ranks of the super-sleuths in order to catch another super-criminal, who is of course a chick) is as omnipotent as Mike Hammer, and as bruisable, and as indestructible, so where is suspense? And always, always, Mr. Harrison tells me, he does not show me—which is, perhaps, the ultimate delineation of what is fiction and what is not, in any field. (p. 744)

> *Theodore Sturgeon, "The Odd Coupling of Hugo and Edgar," in* National Review, *Vol. XXII, No. 27, July 14, 1970, pp. 743-44.*

JOANNA RUSS

Harry Harrison's *One Step from Earth* . . . is a collection of nine stories bound together loosely (and not altogether truthfully) by the idea of matter transmission. There is another hypertrophied introduction, hypertrophied in this case because it has nothing to do with the stories; in fact, the matter transmitter described in the introduction is of the kind used in only one of the nine. Two of the tales don't really need matter transmission at all. The stories are routine, unoriginal, mildly interesting, and readable.

> *Joanna Russ, in a review of "One Step from Earth," in* The Magazine of Fantasy and Science Fiction, *Vol. 40, No. 4, April, 1971, p. 66.*

JAMES BLISH

Harry Harrison has proven, frequently, that he can be a writer of substance when he has his mind on his work. [*The Stainless Steel Rat's Revenge,* a] sloppy, slam-bang adventure story, however, seems to have been thrown out the window of his VW bus during one of his frequent passages from one country to another, to placate tax-collectors and other such wolves.

The story, like its predecessor . . . [*The Stainless Steel Rat*], deals with and is told by an interstellar operative named Slippery Jim diGriz, whose slipperiness seems to consist mostly in being able to conceal upon his person a bigger arsenal than could be packed into a James Bond automobile. Here, he has been re-recruited from a life of crime for an attempt to find out why interstellar warfare, supposedly an impossibility, has suddenly become a going business.

The opposition is conventionally nasty and rigidly military-minded, making them rather easy to outwit on those rare occasions when the narrator runs out of smoke-bombs. Some of the situations have a certain amount of bounce, as is inevitable in a Harrison story—I particularly liked an escape by ejection-seat, possibly because it was the only escape in the book which I could believe. But the whole has no substance whatsoever.

Okay; authors have to write potboilers now and then, and taken on its own terms, this one is fairly good of its breed. But it certainly doesn't deserve the permanence of hard covers. . . . (pp. 12-13)

> *James Blish, in a review of "The Stainless Steel Rat's Revenge," in* The Magazine of Fantasy and Science Fiction, *Vol. 41, No. 2, August, 1971, pp. 12-13.*

THE TIMES LITERARY SUPPLEMENT

Taking us right off the earth, hurtling from planet to planet in an inter-galactic war, *The Stainless Steel Rat's Revenge* by Harry Harrison, only just in the juvenile bracket, if that, is a truly breathtaking book. Out-Bonding Bond for action and with all the mind-boggling possibilities of SF thrown in, Mr Harrison, with all his usual vigour and directness, keeps attention and imagination strained to breaking point in the attempt to keep up with every new gadget, drug, weapon and brain-washing device which his fertile mind can devise. So realistically does his expert pen describe them that one sends up a prayer that they may not be prophetic—nor, indeed, give anyone ideas. One stretches to follow every sinister twist and unexpected encounter as the Special Service of one, moderately goodie, planet sets out to thwart the universe-dominating plans of another, definitely baddie, one. Impossible to put this book down till the end and equally impossible, when one has got there, not to let loose a sigh. For all their cold-blooded strangeness, their robot-run hotels and teams of servitors, for all their mind-twisting drugs and astronomically fast vehicles, both sides still seem to be sadly recognizable. Will the only things to survive from this civilization really be gauleiters and uniforms?

> *"Three for Speed," in* The Times Literary Supplement, *No. 3640, December 3, 1971, p. 1513.*

WILLIS E. McNELLY

Stonehenge is a mystery, a giant ring of stones that has baffled man for centuries. The latest attempt at its solution has produced a remarkable new novel, *Stonehenge.*

Leon Stover, anthropology professor at Illinois Institute of Technology, and Harry Harrison, novelist and short story writer, maintain that Stonehenge was built as a central meeting place or early day parliament to unify the Celtic tribes that occupied England some 3500 years ago. Its construction was directed they say, by Mycenaean warriors who mined English tin to fashion the bronze that gave its name to an age. Further, say Stover and Harrison, it was designed by an Egyptian architect. How all this came about is told in novel form, with lots of rattling good action and lively narration. Moreover, their Stonehenge thesis seems to grow out of the action, rather than the other way around. . . .

Stonehenge is not for the squeamish reader. It is bloody, hard-driving, direct, elemental. One of the best aspects of the book

is its descriptions of primitive battle which evoke the style of Germanic sagas. In fact, the very blood bath in which *Stonehenge* often seems washed lends verisimilitude.

If the characterization seems slighted to advance the story, that fact simply mirrors the primitive nature of the people who, after all, did leave this genuinely unique circle of stones as their monument. *Stonehenge* may well be a controversial novel. It also deserves to be a popular one.

> *Willis E. McNelly, in a review of "Stonehenge," in* America, *Vol. 127, No. 9, September 30, 1972, p. 242.*

NEWGATE CALLENDAR

[In Harry Harrison's *Montezuma's Revenge*] occurs one of the great lines. The hero, a secret agent recruited by the F.B.I., is enjoying an Italian meal in a restaurant in Acapulco. Suddenly he finds his head lying on the table. "They've . . . they've drugged the spaghetti!" With this one nice stroke, Harrison puts into perspective the absurdity of so many spy stories.

Tony Hawkin handily recovers from being drugged by spaghetti, but must face other ordeals dreamed up by the ingenious author (who has also made his mark in the field of science-fiction). The result is an entertaining spoof. On every other page are ex-Nazis, the Israeli secret service (busily engaged in eating pastrami sandwiches), the Mexican police, the Italian secret police, the Soviet *apparat*, the C.I.A., the U.S. Treasury. The plot has something to do with a rediscovered painting by da Vinci, but forget it. You won't be able to follow the plot. Nobody will be able to follow the plot. But you should have a lot of fun with Harrison's humor and, in some sections, deadly satire addressed to the American bureaucracy.

> *Newgate Callendar, in a review of "Montezuma's Revenge," in* The New York Times Book Review, *October 15, 1972, p. 42.*

AUBERON WAUGH

I had never read Mr Harry Harrison's work, or even heard of him, until happy chance decreed that *A Transatlantic Tunnel Hurrah!* [published in the United States as *Tunnel through the Deeps*] should be the only novel sent for review this week. It is very seldom indeed in a novel reviewer's experience that he has the feeling of Keats on first looking into Chapman's Homer. . . .

The great 'if' of history which Mr Harrison posits as a precondition for the idyllic world he describes is that the Christian armies should have lost the battle of Navas de Tolosa in 1212, with the results that the Iberian peninsula became and remained a Muslim country, part of the Great Caliphate; Christopher Columbus never discovered America, which had to wait for Cabot; the Americans lost the war of independence and America remained a British colony. Other consequences are less easily explained, but Mr Harrison sets them down blithely enough, and it would be boring to demand the full explanation in every case: Germany is still divided into warring principalities; the throne of France survives, so does the aristocratic ascendancy in England; our currency is still undecimalised; aeroplanes are huge, slow objects driven by coal—while trains are nuclear-powered; George Washington bred children and, perhaps most puzzling of all, Lord Keynes is still alive in his nineties and just beginning to exert his pernicious influence on an England which is still beautiful and free. (p. 1046)

The novel's plot is complicated and immensely satisfying. In a world which has not discovered vulgarity or the base appetite for violent entertainment, our hero expresses deep remorse after he has been forced to kill an attacker in his own defence. When the villain is finally unmasked, our hero demands: "What could lead you, a respectable member of the community, to such reprehensible actions?"—before allowing him the grace to shoot himself and save a proud family's name.

It all begins with a scheme to construct a railway tunnel under the Atlantic, for trains running at great speed and supported only by the force of magnetic repulsion in a vacuum. The sadness is that Mr Harrison did not revive Brunel's own original scheme for a vacuum-powered railway as its method of propulsion, but one can't expect everything and the vacuum is only provided as a means of obviating wind resistance in the tunnel. The American engineer put in charge of the whole venture is Captain Augustine Washington, a descendant, needless to say, of the traitor George Washington, shot by the British after losing the Battle of Lexington. Washington nurtures hopes of persuading her Majesty to grant America independence, or at any rate dominion status. He also nurtures a courteous and chivalrous passion for Iris, the beautiful daughter of Sir Isambard Brassey-Brunel, England's greatest engineer and father of the whole tunnel scheme. However Sir Isambard is jealous of the Captain and refuses him permission to woo his daughter, much to the chagrin of both. Iris, being a good girl as well as beautiful, can never leave her father because she is all he has.

There are many adventures and close shaves as the result of sabotage attempts by the wicked French, but I shall not attempt to describe them for fear of spoiling the book. Probably it was something to do with the way Mr Harrison skilfully inserts all the certainties and basic decencies of the Victorian novel into a revised contemporary setting, but I am not frightened to admit, at the risk of making a first appearance in Pseuds Corner, that I cried like a baby at the wedding between the beautiful, good Iris and brave Captain Washington. It is a book which I can recommend with all my heart even to those offensive letter-writers in Cheltenham and Bath who object to my describing less wholesome novels as I find them. (p. 1047)

> *Auberon Waugh, "Tears, Idle Tears," in* The Spectator, *Vol. 229, No. 7540, December 30, 1972, pp. 1046-47.*

DENNIS LIVINGSTON

Harrison's [*Tunnel Through the Deeps*] is straight science fiction, combining both the parallel world and technology adventure themes. Two major historical events create this alternative Earth: Moslems defeat Christians in the 13th century in Spain, hence it is Englishmen who discover the New World, and America loses the Revolution, hence the British Empire remains the most powerful political unit of the 20th century. The story takes place in this alternative 1973 and its hero is one Augustine Washington, a brilliant engineer who wishes to clear the family name besmirched by ancestor George by aiding the completion of a train tunnel being built underneath the Atlantic between England and the American colonies. The tunnel is financed by the British government upon the advice of a 90-year old Lord Keynes as a pump-priming economic device. It is Harrison at his best and quite entertaining, though

readers who get no thrill out of technological problem-solving may be bored. The literary gimmick of the book is that it is written in the style of a 19th century novel and the culture and language of the characters are from that period. The implicit premise here, dubious but necessary for the book, is that technological change need not lead to social or cultural change, which results in such charming anachronisms as gold-plated, atomic-powered locomotives, a sexist and class-conscious Victorian society existing amidst sophisticated technology, electric-powered hansoms, and regally-appointed, gigantic airships. We never see the underside of this society, but as it comes through in the book, we would have been better off if old George had indeed lost. (pp. 504-05)

> *Dennis Livingston, in a review of "Tunnel through the Deeps," in* Futures, *Vol. 5, No. 5, October, 1973, pp. 504-05.*

PUBLISHERS WEEKLY

[In *Queen Victoria's Revenge*] Tony Hawkin, who has appeared in a number of other Harrison spoofs, is an American Indian FBI agent. He also happens to love art and to aspire to nothing so much as a gallery or museum job. Tough luck for him. The FBI keeps throwing him into one zany case after another. This one begins as a plane hijacking, supposedly engineered by anti-Castro Cubans. Before it winds up it involves: Scottish nationalists, Arabs, Israelis, Welsh nationalists, and just plain people who are out for the money. Quite the most delectable part of the story, all the way along, is the description of all the marvelous (really tasty) meals Tony achieves on his progress through Great Britain.

> *A review of "Queen Victoria's Revenge," in* Publishers Weekly, *Vol. 205, No. 21, May 27, 1974, p. 58.*

MARTIN SHERWOOD

I suspect that I may have read and enjoyed more of Harrison's novels than of any other single sf writer; consequently, it pains me somewhat to say that *Star Smashers of the Galaxy Rangers* is drivel. For self-indulgence, it exceeds even Kurt Vonnegut's *Breakfast of Champions*.

Because I have liked Harrison's previous output, I am still wasting time occasionally wondering whether there is some obscure merit in deliberately trying to write a bad novel—as this seems to be what he has done, a suspicion strengthened by a tongue-in-cheek jacket blurb which calls this "the greatest and most pretentious epic saga of space conquest ever conceived among the twisted synapses of a science fiction author".

The Men from PIG and ROBOT is smoother, more enjoyable, and eminently forgettable. But then, novels are not necessarily meant to be memorable. (p. 769)

> *Martin Sherwood, in a review of "Star Smashers of the Galaxy Rangers" and "The Men from PIG and ROBOT," in* New Scientist, *Vol. 64, No. 926, December 5, 1974, pp. 768-69.*

PETER ACKROYD

Harry Harrison is a science-fiction writer and an old hand at the future, but [in *The Men From P.I.G. and R.O.B.O.T.*] he bears the scars of a man hardened by too long acquaintance with its pleasures. **"The Man from P.I.G."** is a refugee from Lil' Abner who has landed on a wild planet with a herd or gaggle of vaguely humanoid pigs; secretly, he is an extraterrestrial agent, his mission to solve new crimes, to take his pigs where no pigs have gone before. The story turns into a spoof of Western films and secret-agent serials, but it carries the indelible marks of imitation rather than satire; it is a high-spirited and occasionally funny narrative but none the less orthodox for that. The second and final story in the book, **"The Man From R.O.B.O.T.,"** concerns yet another secret agent on yet another frontier planet. It is a slight fantasy, with the ironic adventures which have become routine nowadays and with a cheek which may hide its tongue but which does not cover the general thinness of the writing.

> *Peter Ackroyd, "Future Imperfect," in* The Spectator, *Vol. 233, No. 7643, December 21, 1974, p. 797.*

MYRA BARRS

Realism is not the point of Harry Harrison's fantasy *The Men from P.I.G. and R.O.B.O.T.* which, like others of his books, is a magnificently extravagant comedy. The passing-out ceremony of the Interstellar Patrol provides the occasion for two stories of law-and-order operations in space. The man from P.I.G. (Porcine Interstellar Guard) successfully defends the planet Trowbri from mysterious marauders, with the help of his herd of trained pigs. The man from R.O.B.O.T. (Robot Intrusion Battalion—Omega Three) finds out why the inhabitants of the planet Slagter are exhibiting paranoid symptoms en masse. In both cases much of the fun comes from the relationship between the patrolman and his aides. The pigs, with their heightened pig IQ, their fine intuitions and superb strength are the more fascinating characters, and whether all the porcine lore the author gives us is science fact or science fiction, it is infinitely convincing. The proliferating robots, on the other hand, are less immediately credible, but what carries this story is the quality of the exchange between the robots, who are programmed to be unfailingly polite, and the irritated humans. . . .

These are two splendid spoofs which might almost have been written on purpose to provide a justification for the ringing last line: "Hand in hand, pig, robot and man marched solidly into the wonderful future."

> *Myra Barrs, "New Pastures Green," in* The Times Literary Supplement, *No. 3813, April 4, 1975, p. 360.*

PUBLISHERS WEEKLY

It's no knock to say that there seem to be more stories in [*The Best of Harry Harrison*] than the 20 it actually holds. Harrison is a writer of such variety, handling broad parody, somber explorations of the future, indignant treatments of stupidity and injustice, sardonic horrors and straight adventure equally skillfully, that the reader is apt to feel he's had at least two books—and perhaps two authors. **"A Criminal Act," "Portrait of the Artist"** and **"I Have Kept My Vigil"** are outstanding but almost all are top-grade. As usual in this series, the author's prefatory comments on each story add to the interest.

> *A review of "The Best of Harry Harrison," in* Publishers Weekly, *Vol. 209, No. 17, April 26, 1976, p. 57.*

DAN MILLER

In 23 years of writing science fiction, Harrison has distinguished himself as a prolific author of consistently good adventures and parodies. The . . . stories collected for [*The Best of Harry Harrison*], interspersed with Harrison's autobiographical and critical comments, well represent his skills at both. Among the highlights are **"The Streets of Ashkelon,"** a 1962 story that broke one of science fiction's more repressive taboos; **"By the Falls,"** one of Harrison's few forays into horror; and **"Space Rats of the C.C.C.,"** a typically hilarious burlesque of the SF space opera.

> *Dan Miller, in a review of "The Best of Harry Harrison," in* Booklist, *Vol. 73, No. 3, October 1, 1976, p. 238.*

MARTIN AMIS

When a novel reaches the SF reviewer with a circular saying, 'the present book is emphatically not a work of science fiction,' it is bound to make him feel rather hunted and insecure. Is Harry Harrison's *Skyfall* . . . simply too subtle for me, I wondered, reading this humble yarn of space adventure and futuristic cataclysm? Or does the author mean that his book is a work of science *fact,* so prophetic and inexorable that the label 'fiction' mocks its achievement? Or is it that Mr Harrison (a notorious joker) is having a laugh at Faber's expense? For if *Skyfall* isn't SF, then neither is *Star Smashers of the Galaxy Rangers,* an earlier and a more typically unequivocal, Harrison extravaganza.

And pretty good it is too, in the Almost Unbearable Suspense genre. The 'largest piece of space hardware ever launched' (it burns 60 tons of fuel per second) gets trapped in a dying orbit some 85 miles above the earth. It is so large that if it does fall out of the vacuum of space it will not burn up in the atmosphere: it will crash, horrendously. . . .

Unfortunately, however, incidental twists aside—you *know* that at least a section of the ship will crash, because Harrison keeps breaking off from the action to insert idyllic cameos in praise of somewhere called Cottenham New Town: sure enough, the booster engine falls off and crashes—into Cottenham New Town! Later on also—and by the same token—you know that the rest of the ship (with the marooned astronauts in it) *won't* crash, because there are no idyllic cameos in praise of life elsewhere—no 'Yukio Kawabata was pleased with his new car-hire business,' no 'It had been a good day at the tribal festivities for Mbongo Mgoobie.' And, sure enough, the ship doesn't crash.

Yet there are thrills enough, for all that this is an utterly conventional pop SF novel, right down to the unkempt prose ('he had the ability of being able to'), the awful sex ('The waves of the music broke over them') and the toiling toughie dialogue ('you got as much chance as a hound dog winning an elephant farting contest'). At this rate, Mr Harrison's chances of transcending the genre might be similarly computed. I hear of plans for a film, though, and will doubtless find myself in the queue.

> *Martin Amis, in a review of "Skyfall," in* The Observer, *October 3, 1976, p. 24.*

J. G. BALLARD

[Harry Harrison's *Skyfall*] has the merit of dealing with contemporary reality. All the sadder, I think, that he should have sent out a special disclaimer, insisting that *Skyfall* is 'not science fiction'. Presumably this means that he believes SF belongs to the realm of fantasy and the improbable, a view contrary to my own—if one is to write about the present day it is difficult not to incorporate at least some element of SF. Harrison's story is the account of a 2,000-ton satellite fuelled by uranium-235 which moves into a decaying orbit, threatening atomic disaster to those unlucky enough to find themselves in its landing path. The novel is efficiently told but somehow unstirring, its lack of conviction for some reason exaggerated by its careful straining after authenticity. Perhaps the space programmes, after their apparent failure to touch our imaginations in any real way, are now convincing only when presented as out-and-out fantasy.

> *J. G. Ballard, "Package Tours," in* New Statesman, *Vol. 92, No. 2387, December 17, 1976, p. 879.*

GERALD JONAS

[*Skyfall* is a] kind of science fiction in modern dress. The model here is the best-selling "disaster novel" in which a carefully assembled cast of stereotypes, together with a faceless mass of extras, are threatened by: earthquake, volcanic eruption, tidal wave, avalanche (check one). In *Skyfall*, the agent of destruction is a huge multistage spacecraft, known as Prometheus, which has been orbited as a joint U.S.-Russian effort. Touted as a pollution-free answer to the fuel shortage, Prometheus's mission is to suck up energy from the sun and beam it down to earth.

The plot may be described simply as a 270-page illustration of Murphy's Law: "If anything can go wrong, it will." When one booster-stage fails to separate from the spacecraft proper, a Russian astronaut ventures out in a spacesuit to cut it loose—but fails to get back safely. The booster itself fails to burn up in the atmosphere as planned and lands on a small town in Britain, incinerating 20,931 people. Prometheus's main engines fail to ignite, leaving the spacecraft in a decaying orbit that is doomed to end on earth in a massive nuclear explosion. I forget the exact number of people that will be killed if this comes to pass, but I'm sure Harrison mentions the figure somewhere.

The trouble with ever-escalating disasters, of course, is that they soon lose their power to move us. No matter how plausible Harrison's statistics and specifications, I found it easier to believe in the gloriously implausible vision of the golden Tubes of Eron. (p. 25)

> *Gerald Jonas, "Of Things to Come," in* The New York Times Book Review, *February 27, 1977, pp. 24-5.*

JOHN H. MOLE

Harry Harrison can . . . be serious, although he writes with a sense of distance and a self-awareness that barely keeps its irony at bay. Gordon Dickson is a more earnest and wholeheartedly mainstream author. They have collaborated for the first time on *Lifeboat* and one can only hope it is for the last. They appear to have struggled to find a common denominator for their respective talents and to have seized in desperation on the lowest. Earth's society is divided into aristocrats, middle-class technocrats and lumpish proletarians. To make this original proposition quite clear the former are called Adelmen, the latter two classes Arbites. Earthmen have entrusted the task of flying their space ships to an alien but friendly race, more

abstrusely called the Albenareth. The ultimate goal of the Albenareth is to die in space—not the most comforting type to have in the pilot's seat. A handful of unattractive Earthmen and Albenareth are cast adrift from a sabotaged space ship. The story seems to be about their attempts to understand each other until the last few pages which offer not only a surprise ending to a complicated plot but its surprise beginning as well.

> *John H. Mole, "The Full Repertoire," in* The Times Literary Supplement, *No. 3976, June 16, 1978, p. 663.*

PUBLISHERS WEEKLY

[*The Stainless Steel Rat Wants You,* the] latest in a popular series has Slippery Jim diGriz saving the galaxy from the disgusting, lecherous and somewhat simple-minded Bug Eyed Monsters. DiGriz, a former con man, is now agent of the Special Corps, a function he performs reluctantly but with style. Along with his wife and two chip-off-the-old-block sons, he bounces around time and space in a desperate manner, eventually managing to enlist the aid of the sinister Grey Men (who instigated the whole mess in the first place). Persuaded by the logic of Moral Philosophy, they brainwash the Bug Eyed Monsters into dropping their battle plans and going home. This is a broad burlesque that is generally fun reading.

> *A review of "The Stainless Steel Rat Wants You," in* Publishers Weekly, *Vol. 215, No. 24, June 11, 1979, p. 102.*

STEVEN R. CARTER

The concept of "interface," defined by *The American Heritage Dictionary* as "a surface forming a common boundary between adjacent regions," is helpful in considering Harry Harrison's *The Adventures of the Stainless Steel Rat,* a series in which the desire to entertain frequently interfaces with the desire to instruct. These three novels (*The Stainless Steel Rat,* 1961; *The Stainless Steel Rat's Revenge,* 1970; *The Stainless Steel Rat Saves the World,* 1972), although delightful to read, might be dismissed as the literary equivalent of cotton candy if one failed to note the number of interfaces in them and the humanistic viewpoint developed from the interfaces. This humanistic approach stresses the need to search for resemblances between things—for points of touching—and to consider them more important than differences. The humanizing interfaces in this series are so pervasive that they seem to be intentional, but intentional or not, they add a significant dimension to Harrison's novels that lifts them beyond the level of pulp writing.

In *The Stainless Steel Rat,* the first in the series, which lays the foundation for the others, the interfaces begin with the form in which science fiction and crime fiction find common ground. Although the intergalactic setting with its numerous futuristic marvels belongs to science fiction, the plot, which depicts a lawman's duel of wits with a clever thief and murderess, is derived from crime fiction. (p. 139)

In addition to the interface between crime fiction and science fiction, Harrison's Stainless Steel Rat series also joins adventure with humor. The adventures abound and are spectacular; there are robberies, confidence games, murders, individual shootouts, military attacks, revolutions, wars carried out with time machines, spying, plotting, and lots of derring-do. However, it is hard to take seriously a hero named Slippery Jim diGriz or a title like *The Stainless Steel Rat Saves the World.* Obviously, some of this derring-do is mock heroic. Consider, for example, the hero's comments when some men attack him: "'Tell them that Jim diGriz died like a man, you dogs!' I shouted, not without a certain amount of slavering and foaming." Clearly, slavering and foaming are not the best ways to prove oneself a man rather than a dog. Or one might note that when Slippery Jim tries to assert his authority as a male, his wife quietly and sweetly punctures his pretensions by reminding him of a simple means of locating the villain that Jim has neglected to try. . . . Thus, the adjacent regions of action and comedy establish a common border in these novels. In a genre little known for humor, Harrison's ability to mingle it with action is a very special contribution. Although he has written several serious-minded and serious-toned science-fiction novels, such as **Make Room! Make Room!, Captive Universe** (1969), and **Skyfall** (1976), he has also written a substantial number of comic science-fiction adventure novels, such as **Bill, the Galactic Hero** (1965), **The Technicolor Time Machine** (1967), **A Transatlantic Tunnel, Hurrah!** (1972 . . .), and **Star Smashers of the Galaxy Rangers** (1973), which amalgamate these elements as skillfully as the Stainless Steel Rat series does.

The hero of Harrison's series, Slippery Jim, is a confidence man and bank robber whose amoral individualism eventually interfaces with social concerns. At the beginning of the series, he considers himself a rat "in the wainscoting of society" and comments that since society is now "all ferroconcrete and stainless steel there are fewer gaps between the joints, and it takes a smart rat to find them. A stainless steel rat is right at home in this environment." . . . He notes further that "it is a proud and lonely thing to be a stainless steel rat—and it is the greatest experience in the galaxy if you can get away with it." . . . (pp. 141-42)

Slippery Jim does not get away with it indefinitely, however. He is finally trapped by the Special Corps, the most efficient police force in the galaxy, and is offered the chance to join them. Harold Inskipp, the man who makes the offer, had once been known as Inskipp the Uncatchable until the Special Corps caught him. He is now the Head of the Corps and is surrounded by senior officials who are all former criminals. Considering the company he would be keeping, Jim decides to accept the offer, though he never goes completely straight—and never returns to being completely crooked. Between cases, in which he invariably saves the world from some impending catastrophe, he usually vacations on funds newly extracted from highly reluctant banks (as Jim well knows, this money will be repaid by the governmental agency he works for).

Since all the most important lawmen in this future society have been recruited from captured criminals, there is an obvious interface between criminal and police activities. Crime remains crime and the law remains the law, but the two regions touch in the minds of individuals and even of an entire group. In this generally peaceful, stable, and dull society—dull because the "goodness" of the citizens has been programmed, as in Anthony Burgess' *A Clockwork Orange* (1962)—the criminals and lawmen share a love of adventure, an understanding of psychology, and an ability to use their wits. Slippery Jim is willing to become and to stay a lawman (with periodic lapses) because police work provides him with as many chances to exercise these qualities as crime does.

The humanistic impulse behind Harrison's concept of interfacing is evident here in the treatment of criminals. Often, though not always, in the Stainless Steel Rat series, the criminal is regarded not as a unique, totally evil creature to be destroyed

but rather as a warped human being to be salvaged and set in a new direction. If sharp distinctions cannot be made between criminals and lawmen, if good and evil can meet and form a surface between them, then one should not be overly eager to mete out harsh and, even more, irremediable punishments like death, to wrongdoers.

In **The Stainless Steel Rat,** Slippery Jim's first assignment as a law officer involves a female criminal named Angelina who matches him in almost every respect. She is intelligent, cunning, and able to anticipate Slippery Jim's moves as often as he anticipates hers. She differs from Jim in that she uses feminine charms to manipulate men and in that she is willing to kill without compunction when someone gets in her way. However, in general her personality resembles Jim's so closely that he falls in love with her as with a mirror image of himself. At the end of the novel, Jim has the opportunity of turning her over to the law, but hesitates because of his attachment to her and his boss Harold Inskipp has to step in to capture her. As with Jim, Inskipp seeks to convert her to police work rather than to punish her.

In the next two books, Angelina marries Jim and assists him in both his criminal and police activities, thus displaying an interface similar to her husband's, between reckless individuality and social responsibility. In both types of endeavor, she proves to be as ingenious and dangerous as her husband, and she saves his life as many times as he saves hers. If anything, she is even more dangerous than her husband because she is more prepared to kill, in spite of the conditioning by psychologists to remove her murderous impulses.

These extensive parallels between Slippery Jim and Angelina suggest that there is an interface between male and female personality and also between male and female intelligence and ability. There remain sexual differences between them, such as Angelina's far greater concern with their children and Jim's occasional macho posing. However, the two clearly have a great deal in common and stand as equals. In spite of (or possibly because of) Jim's scattered, comic attempts to assert that only he has the right to wear the pants in his family, it is obvious that Harrison is on the side of women's liberation. (pp. 142-43)

Although Harrison has not consistently adhered to this view of the sexes in all of his novels, it plays a fundamental role in much of his work. Regrettably, some of his novels present only stereotyped images of women as sex objects, self-worshippers, empty-headed trinket-lovers, good girls on pedestals, homemakers, and clinging, complaining mothers. Notable among these novels are: **Bill, the Galactic Hero, The Technicolor Time Machine,** and **A Transatlantic Tunnel, Hurrah!** (though the portrayal of women in this novel can be justified to some extent since it deliberately presents, with mocking overtones, a wide range of Victorian attitudes, including those toward women). However, a number of his works present women who are as clever, courageous, and resourceful as Angelina and who yet maintain an intriguing individuality so that none of them could be mistaken for another. Consider, for example, the Arab stewardess Jasmin Sotiraki and the Israeli agent Esther Ben-Alter in **Queen Victoria's Revenge,** the pilot Meta in **The Deathworld Trilogy** (1960; 1964; 1968), and the Soviet astronaut Nadya Kalinina and the black doctor Coretta Samuel in **Skyfall** (a novel that directly addresses the issue of women's liberation by depicting a male chauvinist space pilot who is forced to acknowledge that the woman he loves has an ability and a right equal to his to pursue a life of risk and responsibility as a space pilot). The existence of these characters makes it clear that Harrison's portrayal of Angelina is indeed representative of his most firmly held attitudes toward women.

Several additional significant interfaces are developed before the marriage of Angelina and Jim, when Jim is acting as a lawman and Angelina is still a warped murderess. Since Jim wants very much to understand the pathological side of Angelina's character, he hopes to create an interface between reason and intuition that will gain him access to her mind. To accomplish this task, he employs another interface, psychomimetic drugs. These drugs stimulate states of mind; they artificially induce real feelings. With their help, Jim touches his sanity against Angelina's insanity and finds that he can now easily comprehend her since he has the same capacity for insanity in his own unconscious. As he remarks afterwards, "I have read many times about the cesspool of dark desires that lies in our subconscious minds, but this was the first time I had ever had mine stirred up. It was quite revealing to examine some of the things that had floated to the surface." . . . Since one of the things that floats to the surface is his awareness that he both loves and hates Angelina, in the same way that he both loves and hates certain aspects of his own personality, he becomes less and less sure about what he wants to do when he finally catches up to her. All of this interfacing has made him uncomfortably conscious of the complexity of life, of the large areas of grayness that stand between the blacks and the whites.

Finally, there is a highly important interface between humanistic concerns and technological advances in Slippery Jim's philosophy about killing, a philosophy based in part on his newfound awareness of the complexity of human character:

> Cold-blooded killing is just not my thing. I've killed in self-defense, I'll not deny that, but I still maintain an exaggerated respect for life in all forms. Now that we know that the only thing on the other side of the sky is more sky, the idea of an afterlife has finally been slid into the history books alongside the rest of the quaint and forgotten religions. With heaven and hell gone we are faced with the necessity of making a heaven or hell right here. What with societies and metatechnology and allied disciplines we have come a long way and life on the civilized worlds is better than it was during the black days of superstition. But with the improving of here and now comes the stark realization that here and now is all we have. Each of us has only this one brief experience with the bright light of consciousness in that endless dark night of eternity and must make the most of it. Doing this means we must respect the existence of everyone else and the most criminal act imaginable is the terminating of one of these conscious existences. . . .

This statement goes to the heart of Harrison's philosophy as represented in various works since it offers a key to his ideas about the brutalizing effects of war (as in *Bill, the Galactic Hero*), a key to the dangers of superstition and too great a respect for any type of authority, including religious authority (as in *Captive Universe*), and a key to the need for international cooperation to solve the worldwide problems of overpopulation, poverty, and dwindling resources (as in *Make Room! Make Room!* and *Skyfall*). To make this speech, Slippery Jim diGriz, the Stainless Steel Rat himself, must have had an all-

too-brief interface with nobility. In him, the mock hero meets the true hero to form the most interesting interface of all. (pp. 143-45)

Steven R. Carter, "Harry Harrison's 'The Adventures of the Stainless Steel Rat': A Study in Multiple Interfaces," in Extrapolation, *Vol. 21, No. 2, Summer, 1980, pp. 139-45.*

PUBLISHERS WEEKLY

[In *Homeworld,* set in] the near future, economic and ecological crises have reduced the world to two classes: the privileged elite and the poverty-stricken masses. Most of the elite, insulated from any real information, are not even aware of the situation. Newly tapped energy sources and economic stability have convinced them the millenium has come for everyone. Jan Kulozik begins to understand the true state of affairs when the revolutionary underground sets out to recruit him. He joins them and falls in love with his contact, Sara. Kulozik is watched, bugged, chased and finally caught. But he has something he never had before: a sense of self-worth. Harrison has written a fast-moving political thriller, set in a believable future.

A review of "Homeworld," in Publishers Weekly, *Vol. 218, No. 11, September 12, 1980, p. 65.*

PUBLISHERS WEEKLY

On a far-off planet [in *Wheelworld*], the temperate season is about to give way to the deadly burning summer. The fragile corn crop waits to be picked up, but the ships from Earth are late. Jan Kulozik, political dissident in exile on this world, coordinates the moving of the corn thousands of kilometers over treacherous terrain, and in the process threatens the absolute power of the ruling Families. After their many attempts to destroy Jan are frustrated, the Families try him for treason, a capital crime. But the ships from Earth arrive at the 11th hour, and with them the news that the repressive Earth regime that had kept the Families in power has been overthrown. This is a competently written adventure, but it lacks the scope and excitement of *Homeworld,* the previous volume in the To the Stars trilogy.

A review of "Wheelworld," in Publishers Weekly, *Vol. 219, No. 5, January 30, 1981, p. 74.*

TOM EASTON

The third entry in Harry Harrison's current trilogy is now out. In some ways, *Starworld* is good, a pleasure, a satisfying conclusion. At the end of volume two, *Wheelworld,* Jan Kulozik left his family to represent his adopted world in the councils of revolution. Now we see him, promptly captured and shipped back to Earth, a prisoner to be made an example of. He leads an escape, is the sole survivor of the ensuing massacre, and encounters the underground—in a surprising and suspect form. He returns to space to lead the rebels in the last battle, and he wins.

But the book is also a disappointment. Harrison gave us a pawn, turned him into a man-who-can, and now returns him to his earlier status. In *Starworld,* Kulozik is once more pushed by others, unable to control his destiny in any way. Those who—like me—looked for some apotheosis of heroism will not be satisfied. Yet, I must grant Harrison that what he does does have validity well beyond that of expectation. I've commented before on how the monolithic, in-loco-parentis state may foster adolescent thought and behavior. We may have that here again, with the added thought that when one returns to the home of adolescence, one also returns to the behaviors that were appropriate there.

Tom Easton, in a review of "Starworld," in Analog Science Fiction/Science Fact, *Vol. CII, No. 1, January 4, 1982, p. 135.*

MARTIN MORSE WOOSTER

James Blish once described Harry Harrison as being "the Goth in John Campbell's Roman Empire." This description is quite apt, for, just as the Goths conquered Rome but preserved the form of Roman institutions, so too does Harrison preserve the form of the typical late-Campbellian space opera while using the mode as a vessel for Harrison's special blend of anarchic comedy. Harrison's most recent work of importance, for example, the "To the Stars" trilogy, melded an action-packed plot with a more subtle look at Anglo-American differences. **Homeworld** (1980) commented on English follies, while **Starworld** (1981) looked at the problems of American society. Harrison, then, is that rarity, a specialist in intelligently comic space operas.

There's very little intelligence in **Invasion: Earth,** however, and the only comedy is unintentional. This dreadful, illustrated potboiler concerns the first contact of aliens with Earth, aliens who would like humanity to let them take over Antarctica to battle their deadly foes, who have landed on the moon. Of course, the "foes" speak the same language, so all is Not What It Seems. Battling the aliens are a mixture of cardboard Russians, all of whom are paragons of virtue, cardboard Americans welded out of the clichés of World War II, and, as the two protagonists, a comely-but-unwilling female Russian linguist and a jut-jawed American colonel. The aliens are as believable as rubber-suited villains from monster movies. Harrison has written a self-parody, a bad space opera which Harrison satirized more effectively in his **Star Smashers of the Galaxy Rangers** (1973). Avoid.

Martin Morse Wooster, in a review of "Invasion: Earth," in Science Fiction & Fantasy Book Review, *No. 7, September, 1982, p. 31.*

RICHARD W. MILLER

[**The Jupiter Plague**] is a twist on the threat-from-outer-space theme. It is interesting, particularly since the original was written just as the Viet Nam War was massively escalating, to see Harrison portraying the military as the responsible, socially-sensitive, anti-nuclear-intervention force. Dr. Sam Bertolli, the soldier-turned-doctor, is a sympathetic character. He lives, loves, does his job and suffers at the hands of bureaucracy just like any of us. The remainder of the "cast" tends toward the stereotypes of the '60s instead of the '80s: Nita Mendel is a pathologist, outstanding in her own right, but emotional and submissive to males; Eddie Perkins is officious and willing to cover his errors by risking the extinction of humanity; Killer Dominquez is the Hell's Kitchen New Yorker, concerned only with getting his ambulance where it goes as fast as possible; the list goes further, but the pattern is similar.

I also felt disconcerted when it took 14 chapters before anyone asked how humans from Earth could catch a disease from Jupiter. Bertolli's claim in that chapter that he had suspected

what turns out to be the justification for such a biological improbability seemed inadequate. He had enough intimate and confidential conversations (and periods of solo musing, too) for the solution to have been offered much sooner. It also seems unlikely that Bertolli, who is bright but nonetheless only an intern on ambulance duty, would come up with a solution that no one in the World Heath Organization could suggest.

Harrison is a fine storyteller. His descriptions of Bellvue Hospital, the ambulance service and the disintegration of society in the face of an apparently absolutely fatal plague are realistic and compelling. For anyone who enjoys a good yarn without a lot of subtlety or philosophical soul-searching, **The Jupiter Plague** is certainly worth reading. However, it seems unlikely that it would be worth the time or cost for those who have or are familiar with [the previously published] **The Plague from Space** or **The Jupiter Legacy.** (pp. 22-3)

Richard W. Miller, in a review of "The Jupiter Plague," in Science Fiction & Fantasy Book Review, *No. 8, October, 1982, pp. 22-3.*

DON STRACHAN

It's the 30th Century. Male chauvinist pigs still carry women's suitcases; tourists wear Hawaiian shirts. It's hard to tell whether items like these represent the inventive capacity or attempts at humor in **The Stainless Steel Rat for President** by Harry Harrison . . . , a 31-chapter-long metronome concert between grade-school guffaws and gimmick warfare. Hero Jim diGriz is a boring braggart who shows he's cool by ripping off his employer. A moral man under his steel rat exterior, he chooses ballots over bullets to depose an evil planetary dictator. We long for him to outsmart just one halfway intelligent foe rather than take out a dozen oafs with the latest karate chops.

Don Strachan, in a review of "The Stainless Steel Rat for President," in Los Angeles Times Book Review, *December 19, 1982, p. 12.*

KELVIN JOHNSTON

Strangely, you do care about Troy Harmon, the hero of Harry Harrison's **Rebel in Time** . . . , though on the face of it he's just a Sidney Poitier look-alike. It's a variation on Ward Moore's classic *Bring the Jubilee,* with the polarities reversed. Here a red-necked Southern colonel travels back to 1858 with blueprints of the Sten gun, with which he plans to equip the Confederate Army and change the course of the Civil War. Harmon, a black intelligence agent, is sent on a one-way trip to nail him, which of course he does. It's all very predictable, but in a cosy way, and the stock characters are old chums you're prepared to take in your stride.

Kelvin Johnston, in a review of "Rebel in Time," in The Observer, *February 20, 1983, p. 33.*

TOM EASTON

Harry Harrison's heavily illustrated **Invasion: Earth** opens with a flying saucer landing in Central Park. Two dead and fearsome aliens are at the controls; a third attacks the intrepid humans who enter the ship. A fourth, less fearsome than strange, is a prisoner aboard, and it tells of a brutal war among the stars, coming here. Will humans help? Will they let its fellows mount their weapons at the South Pole? Will they supply fissionables and other necessaries? They will? Great!

Hero Rob Hayward is suspicious. Is there really a war? If so, which side are humans now on? He pushes his suspicions, visits the enemy, retains his suspicions, and finally gets permission for an information-gathering raid. He learns the truth, and humans boot the aliens off the planet. A final grudging admission that solving the problem violently might not have been the best approach seems meant to mollify the post-Vietnam generation.

There's action and wit and good stuff for a B-movie. There's superficiality, and lazy thinking, and pictures, and good stuff for a B-movie. It's a distinct lightweight. Ignore it.

> *Tom Easton, in a review of "Invasion: Earth," in* Analog Science Fiction/Science Fact, *Vol. CIII, No. 11, October, 1983, p. 168.*

CHARLES PLATT

[*West of Eden* is] a big novel in every sense: scope, drama, and heft. It postulates an alternate Earth where dinosaurs never died out, and humanity is a mammalian minority oppressed by an evolved society of intelligent reptiles. It's a good concept, and Harrison develops it with an expert mix of adventure, suspense, and properly researched science. Reptilian society is meticulously visualized, as is the psychology of creatures that hatch from eggs as opposed to gestating in the womb. This, and their social stasis—inevitable, in a space 200 million years old—serves as nicely ironic counterpoint to our own, human, behavior.

Unfortunately, the last quarter of the novel lacks revelations or plot development, and cannot be carried by the characters alone—Harrison is literally better at evoking the personalities of lizards than of people. Nor is the ending very satisfying; it seems contrived to leave room for a sequel, and its lack of resolution precludes the pacifist message that would have been the natural conclusion, as it is in much of his other work.

Nevertheless, *West of Eden* is written with skill and integrity, and is much more accessible than the pompous predecessors after which, perhaps, it was patterned: Aldiss' *Helliconia* trilogy, Silverberg's *Lord Valentine's Castle,* and Herbert's *Dune* chronicles. Not only is *West of Eden* more consistently inventive, it is also more fun.

> *Charles Platt, in a review of "West of Eden," in* Book World—The Washington Post, *July 29, 1984, p. 11.*

GARY K. WOLFE

[*West of Eden*] is a fast-moving, well-structured adventure story of the sort Harrison does well, and that remains its chief virtue. Harrison begins by assuming that dinosaurs were *not* rendered extinct by an ancient meteor striking the Earth, and that one species evolved to develop an urban civilization based on bioengineering rather than technology. Humans survive only in nomadic bands and a few agricultural settlements in the western hemisphere, and when the "Yilane" (the intelligent, humanoid lizards) attempt to colonize North America, the stage is set for an epic battle between humans and lizards.

Kerrick, the protagonist, is a young hunter captured and raised by the Yilane who eventually escapes and leads his fellow humans in war against the lizards. The archetypal plot of the orphaned hero reared among strangers permits Harrison to portray a thoroughly-imagined alien culture and to describe endless escapes, pursuits, and battles, but as extrapolation it raises as many questions as it answers.

Harrison's human society, the Tanu, is a convincing portrayal of a hunter-gatherer society. The Yilane culture is what removes the book from the "cave-man" genre, however; it represents Harrison's most serious attempt yet at portraying an alien culture.

But why intelligent dinosaurs? Why, if dinosaurs remained so thoroughly dominant, would they *need* to evolve intelligence? And why would the Yilane, who have evolved thumbs appropriate for toolmaking, have almost no knowledge of mechanical tools but instead depend entirely on genetic engineering? (The Yilane's living "tools" are ingeniously thought-out—monitor lizards evolved into rifles, for example, or ichthyosaurs mutated into boats.) Most important, why a rigid, class-bound matriarchy rife with vengefulness and jealousy?

The Yilane are both the major strength and major weakness of *West of Eden.* Their fascinating imaginary society raises important questions about evolution, sexuality, and class structure. At the same time, they seem too much like the evil empires of endless pulp science fiction adventures, cold-blooded in the most literal sense and set up to be defeated by a resourceful hero. This, together with Harrison's resolute adventure-saga style, make *West of Eden* a superb action novel that never quite achieves the depth and richness a true epic needs.

> *Gary K. Wolfe, "Boy Raised by Lizard," in* Fantasy Review, *Vol. 7, No. 8, September, 1984, p. 30.*

TOM EASTON

Harry Harrison's latest opus is a massive and admirable attempt to transform evolutionary biology and catastrophism into science fiction. Considered by itself, the fiction is very nice indeed. The science, however, is another matter, for though Harrison credits several experts with helping him, he blew it.

In *West of Eden,* Harrison supposes that the asteroid or comet that 70 million years ago wiped out the dinosaurs (among others) and gave the mammals their chance never arrived. The dinosaurs were left free to continue evolving, eventually giving rise to the Yilanè, a very interesting species whose biology affects their psychology and culture quite reasonably. Over reptilianly slow eons, they have developed a technology of biological engineering to produce countless specialized creatures, from boats to cameras. They have also covered the warm portions of the continents of Africa, Asia, and Europe. When the climate cools, they seek new warm lands and discover the Americas. However, the Americas already hold humans, and when the two species meet, their antipathy is deep and mutual. The Yilanè slaughter a tribe, capture and enslave the child Kerrick, and mount a war of extermination on the humans. Kerrick learns language and culture and eventually escapes to lead the human war against the Yilanè. Harrison portrays his Yilanè characters and Kerrick very well, and the reader has little trouble empathizing, even as he yearns to kick them for their blind idiocies. Harrison gives us a cracking good yarn in which humans stand for an idealized tribal life and the Yilanè stand for villainized urbanites. He trades vigorously on the myth of the noble savage, and he stirs within us all the classic sentiments of the adventure yarn.

But he still blew it. For one thing, he makes his dinosaur-types cold-blooded, despite the case for hot-blooded dinosaurs. He tells us that the site of the meteor impact in our world is Iceland, which is the wildest of guesses (it may be right, but who knows?). He has humans evolving in the American north, even though the evolutionary line that led to humans required the African tropics for its appearance. Further, he tells us that his humans descend from New World primates, since the Old World primates don't exist (their place in biological history having been preempted by the dinosaurs). However, the New World primates are themselves descended from the Old World stock, having split away some 35 million years ago when continental drift separated the Americas from Africa.

There are more gaffes too, in biology, climatology, anthropology, and so on. Some of the problems seem due to simple haste. Others may actually be deliberate inconsistencies forced into play to make the story work. Harrison's humans may be one such, for the only way to escape the difficulty with them would be to posit a very different mammalian intelligence or to suppose that the whole story happens on another world, where human colonists meet saurian aliens. In either case, the result would have been a very different story, and Harrison would have been unable to evoke the richness of double vision.

If you could care less about biological or scientific plausibility, you will enjoy *West of Eden* greatly. If you do care, you will be endlessly irritated. Either way, you have to applaud Harrison's ambition. His conception is grand, if flawed, and he executes it very well. (pp. 145-46)

Tom Easton, in a review of "West of Eden," in Analog Science Fiction/Science Fact, *Vol. CIV, No. 12, December, 1984, pp. 145-46.*

(Mary) Patricia Highsmith

1921-

(Has also written under pseudonym of Claire Morgan) American-born novelist, short story writer, and nonfiction writer.

An American-born author who has resided in Europe for most of her adult years, Highsmith is best known for her suspense novels, which challenge many of the conventional precepts of the genre. She avoids gimmicks and formulaic plots, concentrating on developing the motivations behind criminal behavior rather than on apprehending the villain. The presence or absence of guilt for one's actions dominates Highsmith's fiction, and often the innocent characters suffer more than the guilty. Highsmith employs such dualistic pairings as the weak with the strong, the innocent with the guilty, and the sane with the insane to examine the fine line between possession and loss of one's faculties. Critics generally agree that Highsmith's subtle, restrained style emphasizes her premise that anyone is capable of murder.

Highsmith's first novel, *Strangers on a Train* (1950), sets the tone for her subsequent work. In this novel, Highsmith brings together two unhappy men who, although opposites in many ways, are drawn into a web of murder and betrayal. The protagonist of *The Blunderer* (1954) attempts to copy a murder committed by another man, resulting in his own death and the capture of the other man. *The Story-Teller* (1965) portrays a writer who is falsely accused of murdering his unfaithful wife after he records his fantasies of killing her. One reviewer noted that *The Story-Teller* "demonstrates [Highsmith's] unusual talents because she contrives to hold the reader's interest while dispensing with tricks which few writers could have resisted employing in such a context."

Highsmith's most respected novels are those featuring Tom Ripley. A charming character who always has a logical explanation for his actions, Ripley is nevertheless a habitual criminal—a "sociopathic murderer," according to Marcia Froelke Coburn—who has never been brought to justice. Ripley was introduced as an American confidence man living in Europe in *The Talented Mr. Ripley* (1955). In this book, Ripley befriends and later murders an American heir to a business fortune and assumes his victim's identity. After forging a will which makes him the beneficiary of the victim's estate, Ripley resumes his own identity and enters Europe's high society. Highsmith's subsequent novels featuring Ripley, including *Ripley under Ground* (1970), *Ripley's Game* (1974), and *The Boy Who Followed Ripley* (1980), show him participating in several criminal schemes and reveal his willingness to kill whenever he is threatened. Critics have detected a slight change in Ripley's moral outlook in these novels, although his criminal activities persist.

In her later works, Highsmith has begun to address contemporary social issues while continuing to explore the theme of guilt. *A Dog's Ransom* (1972) comments on urban America and ineffectual law enforcement agencies. *Edith's Diary* (1977) explores the methods by which society forces women into subservient roles. Fundamentalist Christianity and its influence on an ordinary American family is the subject of *People Who Knock on the Door* (1983). Highsmith's recent novel, *Found*

in the Street (1986), according to Anita Brookner, "traces yet again the fortunes of a near-psychopath and his victims who meet by chance and whose madnesses mesh in such a way as to ally them for ever."

Highsmith has also published several volumes of short stories. *Little Tales of Misogyny* (1977) garnered considerable critical attention for its stories about brutalized women. Highsmith was accused by some reviewers of being antifeminist, while others contended that the stories were intended to satirize present-day attitudes toward women. *The Animal Lover's Beastly Book of Murder* (1975) is a collection of macabre tales in which animals turn on their human masters. Highsmith's other short story collections include *The Snail-Watcher and Other Stories* (1970; published in England as *Eleven*), *The Black House* (1981), and *Mermaids on the Golf Course* (1985). Highsmith is also the author of *Plotting and Writing Suspense Fiction* (1966), which offers an analysis of her own works as well as a description of her approach to writing novels. Many of Highsmith's novels have been adapted for film, most notably *Strangers on a Train*, which was directed by Alfred Hitchcock.

(See also *CLC*, Vols. 2, 4, 14; *Contemporary Authors*, Vols. 1-4, rev. ed.; and *Contemporary Authors New Revision Series*, Vols. 1, 20.)

NEW YORK HERALD TRIBUNE BOOK REVIEW

Miss Highsmith's novel [*Strangers on a Train*] is easily one of this year's most sinister items. It has its obvious faults. It is not always credible, and the characters are not entirely consistent. Nevertheless, it is a highly persuasive book. Guy Haines, a young architect, is going back to Texas to persuade his estranged wife Miriam into a divorce. On the train he meets a young ne'er-do-well, Charles Bruno, and for some reason tells him his life story. In his turn, he learns that Bruno has a father whom he hates. . . . When Bruno proposes that he kill Guy's wife, and that Guy in turn kill Bruno's father, Guy turns the proposition down with disgust. . . . Then later, Guy's wife is killed, and in a short while he gets a letter which makes it clear that Bruno is the murderer. It is also clear that he now expects Guy to kill for him. The rest of the novel is Bruno's slow and unremitting campaign to force Guy into carrying out his part of their imagined and deadly bargain. Reduced to its skeleton, the plot is exposed in all its incredibility. But as one reads it page by page throughout a full length novel, one is held by an evil kind of suspense. It becomes more believable than one would suppose—a rarely perceptive study in criminal psychology.

> *A review of "Strangers on a Train," in* New York
> Herald Tribune Book Review, *April 16, 1950, p. 26.*

CHARLES J. ROLO

The heroine of this tale of Lesbian love [*The Price of Salt*] is a lonely 19-year-old. . . . Therese Belivet has been working for two years in New York, trying to save $1,500 for membership in the stage designer's union. . . . When she meets Carol Aird—a beautiful, wealthy, sophisticated woman of 30, who is in the process of divorcing her husband—Therese falls totally in love at first sight. . . .

When the two women take a motor trip to the West, it is Therese who, with purblind innocence, causes them to become lovers. And she thereby precipitates a crisis in which both have to make decisions that will lastingly affect their lives.

Obviously, in dealing with a theme of this sort, the novelist must handle his explosive material with care. It should be said at once that Miss Morgan writes throughout with sincerity and good taste. But the dramatic possibilities of her theme are never forcefully developed. While Therese's rapturous love sometimes gives a glow to the story, the novel as a whole—in spite of its high-voltage subject—is of decidedly low voltage: a somewhat disjointed accumulation of incident, too much of which is pretty unexciting as story-telling and does little to deepen insight into the characters. Therese herself remains a tenuous characterization, and the other personages are not much more than silhouettes. This reader's interest was always on the verge of being awakened—and never quite was.

> *Charles J. Rolo, "Carol and Therese," in* The New
> York Times Book Review, *May 18, 1952, p. 23.*

JAMES SANDOE

Kimmel, after fixing an alibi, killed his wife with conspicuous pleasure [in *The Blunderer*]. Stockhouse, with equal motive, did not. But it was Stockhouse who blundered in a very recognizable sort of way until he and Kimmel and the determined policeman, Corby, were all struggling in a hopeless tangle of lies and belated truths and ineradicable misunderstandings.

Miss Highsmith manages so well with the understandable if mussy Stockhouse that she can trample plausibility and drag us along in spite of it. Her fancy is at once extravagant and acute. She has written a remarkable tale and a far more telling one (for me, at least) than its celebrated predecessor, *Strangers on a Train.*

> *James Sandoe, in a review of "The Blunderer," in*
> New York Herald Tribune Book Review, *September
> 19, 1954, p. 12.*

ANTHONY BOUCHER

[In *The Talented Mr. Ripley*] Miss Highsmith abandons the startling trick plot-devices of *Strangers on a Train* and *The Blunderer* for a more direct, less striking but more solid essay in the creation and analysis of character. Young Tom Ripley is an admirable three-dimensional portrait of what a criminal psychologist would call a "congenital psychopathic inferior"; we see him first engaged in an ingenious and pointless mail fraud, then watch him as intimacy with a wealthy youth tempts him to murder and to—but though Miss Highsmith is relatively less tricky this time, she still has surprises which should be allowed to unfold themselves. A reviewer need say only that this is a skillful, if somewhat overlong, suspense novel with unusual insight into a particular type of criminal.

> *Anthony Boucher, in a review of "The Talented Mr.
> Ripley," in* The New York Times Book Review,
> *December 25, 1955, p. 11.*

ANTHONY BOUCHER

Patricia Highsmith made her debut seven years ago with *Strangers on a Train,* which had one of the most striking plot-notions ever presented in a first novel. . . . [*Deep Water*] marks her coming of age as a novelist; less startling than *Strangers,* it is incomparably stronger in subtlety and depth of characterization. Vic Van Allen, indulgent toward his wife's adulteries but impatient with his role of cuckold, creates the legend that he murdered one of her past lovers. Inevitably the legend has a certain deterring effect upon present candidates for her favors; its effect upon Vic himself is more complex, and admirably worked out in a full-fleshed novel of pity and irony.

> *Anthony Boucher, in a review of "Deep Water," in*
> The New York Times Book Review, *October 6, 1957,
> p. 34.*

JAMES SANDOE

The singular Patricia Highsmith has a cool affinity for aberration. Her treatment is internal, not clinical, and this makes for a sharp immediacy rather than a case history. Of David Kelsey's public life [detailed in *This Sweet Sickness*], we know only enough to be sure that he is outwardly successful. Our time is spent in a long, absorbing account of his real existence, . . . his entirely calm, quite lunatic persuasion that Annabelle is as deeply in love with him as he is with her. Outwardly he is handsome, correct, thoughtful. Inwardly he has the calm of assurance. When it is touched or shaken violence ensues, suddenly and dreadfully. His life is a kind of high-wire performance by a man who thinks he is on the ground. It's not so much that Miss Highsmith makes these proceedings plausible as that she makes them unquestionable. I think the world of

Miss Highsmith because while she has me in her firm grasp, she is quite simply the world.

James Sandoe, in a review of "This Sweet Sickness," in New York Herald Tribune Book Review, *February 7, 1960, p. 11.*

BRIGID BROPHY

[*The Two Faces of January*] is a thriller chiefly in the sense that every good novel is. Its reward for not playing unfairly on the nerve of suspense is that it can end without let-down. Instead of dismissing the characters the instant the outcome is known, you go on digesting their cold-crumpet clamminess. They—the main three of them—are Americans abroad. Rydal is a young intellectual, now seedily coming to the end of the resources on which he has been lounging about Europe. Chester and Colette MacFarland have arrived there in haste and out of season, fleeing from probable detection of Chester's career, which consists of petty but lucrative swindles. In Athens in January Rydal notices the MacFarlands and follows them— simply because the young wife resembles the cousin he once seduced, and the middle-aged husband resembles Rydal's father, who humiliated Rydal by contemptuously condemning the seduction. Chester is interviewed by a policeman and, in panic, kills him. Lugging the body into the hotel corridor, he comes slap up against Rydal—who, without question or explanation, makes himself an accessary both to stowing the body and to getting the MacFarlands out of Athens.

The oedipal ambivalence in Rydal's relation to Chester and the strain of near-incest in his feeling for Chester's wife are established *before* the killing. They motivate Rydal's complicity; all his act of complicity does is bind him into a trio as indissoluble (except by death) as father-mother-son, within which the ambivalence must be worked out. The triangle is tense because two of its points are—brilliantly—weak. Rydal alone is a strong person, and his strength is divided by his ambiguity. Is he saving or planning to blackmail Chester; expressing compunction towards his own dead father or getting the last laugh on the moralistic father by reincarnating him in a criminal; protecting or stealing Chester's wife? (Miss Highsmith subtly sets between Rydal and the wife a sexual attraction which is just not quite overwhelming.) The variations are rehearsed as Rydal runs with, away from and in pursuit of Chester, on an itinerary which ends in Paris and includes Crete. Miss Highsmith evokes but never obtrudes on the reader the seductive dreariness of provincial airports, waterside cafés laying claim to sophistication, and ancient monuments in the off-tourist season. It is the story not so much of a chase as of moving, uneasily, on. Shifts of ground stand metaphor for shifts in relationship; psychology is beautifully interleaved with a gritty *genius loci.* (pp. 335-36)

Brigid Brophy, "Swindler and Son," in New Statesman, *Vol. LXVII, No. 1720, February 28, 1964, pp. 335-36.*

THE TIMES LITERARY SUPPLEMENT

There are not many nastier fictional worlds than Patricia Highsmith's, and soon they sicken, worlds for sadistic voyeurs who get their kicks from seeing the poor worms hooked and squirming. There is not much else to do with her new anti-hero, Philip Carter, but pity him or enjoy his pain, and the first without any kind of catharsis soon comes to feel very like the other.

What is Miss Highsmith telling us [in *The Glass Cell*], apart from a case history? That if a man goes wrongly to prison, is there ill-treated and mildly hooked on morphia, comes out to find his decent wife mildly unfaithful, then he cannot but listen to the tempter, and two murders, with the author's promise of no more, are a just repayment of the debt; "The justice I have received, I shall give back", he thinks to himself, having knocked off the moderately innocent, and about to go home free to live with his wife and child. Is this what Miss Highsmith thinks, too, fair's fair, and now hey for happiness? Or does she just believe in the irrevocability of human deterioration, and like watching it happen?

Objections must be moral, not technical. The book is well made, well told.

"Worse and Worse," in The Times Literary Supplement, *No. 3287, February 25, 1965, p. 154.*

THE TIMES LITERARY SUPPLEMENT

Miss Highsmith's exceptional talent as a writer of suspense stories has been proved in *The Glass Cell* and other novels notable for the unease they induce, and although *A Suspension of Mercy* [published in the United States as *The Story-Teller*] is not so compulsive, it demonstrates her unusual talents because she contrives to hold the reader's interest while dispensing with tricks which few writers could have resisted employing in such a context.

A rather uncomfortably married young couple . . . are the principal characters. The husband indulges in fantasies of murdering his wife; she has her own brand of waywardness and goes off without leaving a forwarding address. The husband enacts disposal of the body by burying an old carpet in the woods . . . and, inevitably, the police become suspicious and the husband finds himself in an unenviable position.

Miss Highsmith's people are convincingly modern and she manages her English backgrounds very capably, creating her particular atmosphere of precariousness in her characters' lives, but for most of the book the element of suspense is lessened because the reader is allowed to know that the wife is alive and also because the husband knows this, too. The author's virtuosity, perhaps, has disdained the obvious plot. The outcome of the story is violent, unexpected and, unfortunately, improbable, but its final mood is in Miss Highsmith's characteristically dispassionate vein.

"Carpetbagger," in The Times Literary Supplement, *No. 3326, November 25, 1965, p. 1051.*

DAVID HARE

[In *Ripley Under Ground*, Ripley is] forced to disguise himself as a great painter Derwatt, who's in fact been dead for years, but who's been posthumously forged by a neurotic admirer called Bernard Tufts. Ripley and a corrupt art gallery have profited from the deception, which is bolstered with the colourful fiction that Derwatt is alive and living in an inaccessible village in Mexico.

This amiable fraud is threatened when an American client of the gallery notices an inconsistency in the work and flies over to England to investigate. To try and satisfy the man it's suddenly necessary to resurrect Derwatt, and Ripley volunteers to leave his comfortable French life . . . in order to impersonate the great man. But the American is not deceived by the false

Derwatt's assertion that none of his work has been forged, so Ripley is driven to a horrifying murder and to burying the American in the grounds of his beautiful French home.

The story so far is ingenious and convincing, tightly written and superbly sustained as long as it keeps its sense of danger. Particularly good is the way you feel the warmth of wealth's embrace, the physical comfort Ripley lives in, and the instinctive way he reacts to its being threatened. But the narrative is strained to contain diversions about the pressure forging puts on Bernard's personality. After all this forging is he truly himself or another man etc? You can imagine. These always elegant inquiries into the nature of artistic personality are basically dull as hell, and the tension of the story is dissipated when the book becomes fascinated with the minds of Ripley and Tufts; for Tufts's mind is dull and Ripley's mind seems numb, jotting little intellectual queries in its margin, but never really coming to terms with what it's doing.

You realise once this investigation is under way that nothing in the story is going to develop and all you're going to get is permutations. Sure enough, the end is determinedly inconsequential. . . . The openness of the story and the closedness of the characters jam. The pity is that in avoiding the patness of a lot of thriller narrative, Miss Highsmith puts in its place an intellectual patness—too simply asking familiar questions. And the way nothing ties up seems as studied as the most ridiculously unlikely examples of detective narrative.

> David Hare, in a review of "Ripley under Ground," in The Spectator, Vol. 226, No. 7440, January 30, 1971, p. 161.

MARY BORG

A Dog's Ransom, though of course accomplished and never unreadable, shows signs of inventive strain. Credibility is stretched to breaking-point at a sequence of events starting with a New York couple paying out a 1,000-dollar ransom for a poodle to a poison-pen nut-case. Their gullibility is equalled by the naïvety of the young cop, Duhamell, who finds the crank and then lets him escape to pen another day. You have to shut your eyes to the glaring unlikeliness of the plot to appreciate Miss Highsmith's brilliant counter-pointing of the relationship between the hunted crank and the initially naïve cop, the ways in which evil is transmitted from hunted to hunter and sympathy turns to shared guilt and thence to dislike and betrayal. The trouble is that to illustrate these themes, the plot is wrenched derisorily; what should have been a chilling progression from trivial normality through unease to terror, never seems remotely plausible, quietly accurate though the New York settings are.

> Mary Borg, "Violent Rations," in New Statesman, Vol. 83, No. 2145, April 28, 1972, p. 571.

THE TIMES LITERARY SUPPLEMENT

Patricia Highsmith's new novel belongs in what is becoming a depressingly substantial sector of her total output—it is a mechanical exercise in self-pastiche, employing all her familiar devices and rehearsing most of her familiar obsessions, but with none of the vigour, inventiveness or intensity which in her best work makes those devices and obsessions seem so rivetting. Just about everything in A Dog's Ransom is ponderous and half-hearted; as if Miss Highsmith could barely bring herself to go through it all again.

Go through it, though, she does. And in fact the book opens rather promisingly, with well-heeled publisher Ed Reynolds (one of those trim, organized and decent types that Miss Highsmith often enjoys undermining) receiving poison pen letters which harp mockingly on his "superiority", his "fancy apartment and snob dog." . . .

But then his correspondent [Rowajinski] goes too far—he kidnaps the snob dog (the light, needless to say, of Ed's childless life) and begins demanding ransom money. Ed plays along, but the dog is not returned. Eventually the police are called and although they are not in general much interested in the case, Ed's predicament does catch the fancy of one Patrolman Duhammel. . . .

All this rather uneventful stuff has taken Miss Highsmith too many chapters to establish. . . .

The main action commences with one of the book's many dubious coincidences: Duhammel just happens to spot Rowajinski in the street and just happens to get suspicious of him. He tracks his suspect to his hotel and confronts him. Rowajinski confesses but does not reveal that the dog has long been put to sleep. . . .

Around the edges of the central action of the novel, Miss Highsmith seems to be wanting to say something forceful about the New York police—characterized here as slothful and brutal. But here again, the details are either too stock or too sketchy for the indictment to catch fire. All in all, one feels that although Miss Highsmith can afford to mark time now and then, even she can't afford to do it as sluggishly as this.

> "Man Hunts Dog," in The Times Literary Supplement, No. 3663, May 12, 1972, p. 537.

CRAIG BROWN

It is a common, obsessional, practice for Patricia Highsmith's novels to feature two characters loathing each other yet incontrovertibly locked together. . . . The more they detest each other, the closer they are bound, . . . the more inexorable becomes their doom. They are like Goya's men fighting in a bog, sinking.

Highsmith's Ripley series has so far remained outside this general pattern: there have been detectives and other nosey investigators but, after his original murder, Ripley has been too independent and dispassionate to be gripped by the manias of guilt or revenge. Other people stay firmly on the periphery of his life. He treats his wife Heloise as a charming piece of furniture. . . . He feels little for friends or enemies: people do not impress him. The Boy Who Followed Ripley combines the Ripley and the non-Ripley books in the most subtle and exciting way.

It is a work of frightening perception and great depth. . . .

At Ripley's house outside Fontainebleau arrives Frank, a sixteen-year-old boy who, it emerges, has murdered his multimillionaire father. Although he has managed to evade suspicion, the boy has run away from America in search of Ripley, whose character and past deeds he has accurately surmised from between the lines of press cuttings and his father's conversation. He comes to Ripley in the hope that his conscience and his life can be resolved. Ripley feels responsibility and affection; the boy's admiration borders on love. The two are opposites. . . .

In most Highsmith books, the two protagonists are in sharp contrast to each other: the oppressor and the oppressed, the hating and the hated. Here, past suggestions that they are two sides of the same character are made stronger by their shared history, their lack of antagonism.

It should not now be necessary to expound on Highsmith's great gift to create excitement out of apprehension. She has an uncanny feeling for the rhythms of terror. . . .

Highsmith never shows off: in this book she presents the city of Berlin in all its strangeness, yet nowhere could you pick out a line and say "How clever!" or "How beautiful!". Like Graham Greene, she knows she has no need to gesticulate. *The Boy Who Followed Ripley* is the major achievement of an endlessly fascinating writer.

Craig Brown, "Perspectives of Guilt," in The Times Literary Supplement, No. 4022, April 25, 1980, p. 462.

MARK TODD

A tense imagination, sympathetically enveloping its central figure, singles out *The Boy Who Followed Ripley,* the latest chapter in the life of the amoral, conscienceless but apparently indestructible Tom Ripley who has fascinated Patricia Highsmith for so long. In the novel, many of the incidents which most excite suspense turn out to be harmless—as when the boy whom Ripley is concealing in his French home waits in his room, hiding while an unexpected guest stays the night. The boy in question has arrived in France and . . . has sought out Ripley and engages his attention—quite spectacularly, by claiming to have been deliberately responsible for the accident which recently killed his own father.

For once Ripley is not, at the outset at least, involved in murder himself, but impelled by a fascination with and desire to help the boy, and in this relationship the author's romantic fascination is caught up, its sexual implication not openly stated but hinted at in small details. American Gothic is transferred to the bland and antiseptic affluence of current-day Western Europe; the setting moves from France to Berlin, as in *Ripley's Game,* though the climax of the boy's mental fight to survive brings Ripley back to New England. Only once, with sinister senile governess Susan, does the novel overstep the mark into Hitchcockian *grande guignol.* For the rest, tension, atmosphere and neurotic identification with the character are compellingly held together. (p. 714)

Mark Todd, "Silhouettes," in New Statesman, Vol. 99, No. 2564, May 9, 1980, pp. 714-15.

BILL GREENWELL

The family mog interrupts a slothful but cosy game of scrabble. It backs through the plastic cat-flap with a pair of puffy human fingers and deposits them proudly on the carpet. This comically sensational event opens the first story in *The Black House,* but thereafter the story, rather than unfolding, folds. Its opening, so hilariously concocted, offers us the prospect of a gloriously improbable plot, but there are no such treats in the offing. Nor are there, in a collection which often twinkles with brilliant artifice, tales which do more than titivate the tastebuds. With a writer of Patricia Highsmith's proven finesse, this is more than disappointing. It's frustration of the first order. There's a clever play on the problems of adoption, in which a couple

take in a pair of poisonous pensioners, which nearly gets there. Otherwise, readers will tumble through the back-door of *The Black House,* slightly stirred but unshaken.

Bill Greenwell, "Novel Flavours," in New Statesman, Vol. 102, No. 2637, October 2, 1981, p. 22.

THOMAS SUTCLIFFE

[Patricia Highsmith's] considerable critical reputation rests largely on the supposed accuracy with which she represents states of mental disease. It's certainly true that her novels are plotted as precisely as graphs (they often have the form of exponential curves mounting through imperceptible gradations) and there is a scientific focus in the way that she characteristically traces one line only, a single obsessive consciousness which disappears beyond the axes of reason and time into derangement or death. She achieves her effects by what amounts to an obsessive notation of every point at which her characters shift from innocence to guilt, and because of the repleteness of her prose, the assiduous provision of detail, from a killer's thoughts as he acts to the quality and origin of the wine he drinks, it's tempting to classify her merits as somehow scientific rather than artistic.

The praise is justified but misses the point, for although her style often has the self-conscious, observant flatness of a case history (it is connected as well with the reservation of moral judgment), she isn't a psychologist; her achievement is one of imagination rather than documentation. The steeper sections of those curves are extrapolated from statistics of crimes we all know. The uneasy, disquieting force of her novels derives in part from an inevitable inaccuracy, from the fact that her account of criminal madness is inspired guesswork from somewhere firmly this side of sanity.

In fact what she observes so truthfully is not the collapse of reason but its persistence in what it suits us to think of as inappropriate conditions. Even Ripley, the least scrupulous and likable of her central characters, has motives for his actions, and though they are venal and vicious they are not irrational. Her suburban killers remain calculatingly evasive until the end (death follows death for the sake of concealment rather than gratification). They don't hear voices and they don't have fun. Indeed in the act of killing their attitude is one of dispassionate detachment, of a sustained attempt to rationalize the intolerable. . . .

In all the books death is contingent and unsought, almost never meticulously planned and very rarely the focus for our moral indignation. Patricia Highsmith discards one of the traditional pleasures of crime fiction, the lingering scrutiny of the techniques of murder (her most ghoulish touches come in the slighter short stories), and she repudiates its traditional certainties: that sin, crime and illegality can be taken as broadly synonymous.

By doing so she is able to write, not about what it feels like to be mad, but what it feels like to remain sane while committing the actions of a madman. At the same time she calls into question the complacent distinction between "us" and "them" which makes it possible to praise her only for a convincing pathology.

The stories in [Highsmith's recent collection] *The Black House* are closer to the themes and methods of her novels than those in earlier collections, the horrid frivolity of *The Animal Lover's Book of Beastly Murder* or the sparse and hateful case histories in *Little Tales of Misogyny.* The short story often has to promise more than it can deliver, and there is, in any case, less opportunity for conveying the retarded drag of time which makes the novels so unsettling (they aren't easy or fast reading). As a result some of the less successful stories have an unsatisfactory portentousness; a confused tale about a lonely boy swept away by a giant kite he has made, or **"The Black House"** itself, which describes the dangers of destroying people's myths, are both stories which finally seem to be puzzles rather than problems.

The best however are brilliant essays on the moral concerns of the longer works: fear and loathing, moral absolutism and culpability. They are located too in the same bleak territory of dissatisfied satiety and doubt, suburbs with swimming pools but no churches. It's significant, in fact, that the nearest thing to virtue in the entire book is the expression of guilt. In such a world crime becomes a matter of personal taste. . . . The characters in **"Something the Cat Dragged In"** are debating whether to conceal or denounce a murderer. What the cat has dragged in, during a game of scrabble, are two fingers and a section of palm hacked from a human hand with a billhook. Amateur detection leads to a decent local farmer who, having killed one of his labourers for cuckolding him, confesses and throws himself on the mercy of those who share his secret. The pursuit and debate are fairly routine but its real power lies in the way a quiet conspiracy grows in the space between public statutes and private emotion. The final line makes it clear that the conspiracy is likely to be successful, and that we needn't hope for a poetic justice to intervene to protect our sensibilities. Crime does go undetected and uncondemned and it does so because of our infinite capacity to offer private pleas of mitigation. . . .

"Not One of Us," the best story in the book, is the reserved account of another conspiracy in which a small circle of friends chivvy one of their number into alcoholism, divorce and unemployment. Their actions never really exceed practical jokes in poor taste, but every misfortune confirms his proper place as victim. Though his death isn't even suicide, but a solitary drunken misadventure, a murder has most emphatically taken place.

On its own this painful and Calvinistically rigorous tale would confirm Patricia Highsmith's ability to demonstrate the fragility of our largely untested moral structures, and the way in which they are weakened by the seemingly unimportant defect of everyday malice. Notions of right and wrong which can't even withstand the breezes of social propriety are unlikely to stand up under greater strain; and yet we sanely commit these little murders all the time.

Thomas Sutcliffe, "Graphs of Innocence and Guilt," in The Times Literary Supplement, *No. 4096, October 2, 1981, p. 1118.*

HOLLY ELEY

This mordant indictment of contemporary middle America [*People Who Knock on the Door*] has much more in common with Patricia Highsmith's *Edith's Diary* than with her Ripley books. Edith's engagement with the moral dilemmas presented by the Vietnam war served to provide a focus for her life and inject hope into the monotony of suburban existence; but in *People Who Knock on the Door* the Alderman family of Chalmerston (Indiana) in the 1980s has nothing to struggle against or on which to pin its faith. That is until insurance salesman

Richard Alderman joins a born-again Christian sect . . . and seeks to impose his new beliefs on his wife and two sons.

The issue which divides the Alderman family, and exposes the fragility of Chalmerston's materialistic society as well as the hypocrisy of fundamentalist dogma, is that of the taking of life. With her usual skill Highsmith produces an apparently clinical, though in fact richly imagined, study of human frailty. The story is mainly that of fifteen-year-old Robbie, who is persuaded by his father to unite with him in condemning his elder brother's girlfriend's abortion. . . .

Most of Highsmith's familiar obsessions and devices are present here. Robbie, when not bible-punching or hanging out with a group of aimless, elderly, poor-white fishermen, drowns worms for recreation. Straightforward, studious Arthur, banished from home after the abortion, is forced to put himself through university on a series of part-time jobs while attempting to turn a love affair into a steady relationship. At the same time he is trying to counteract the blinkered intensity of his father's religion with a balanced philosophy of his own. . . . His thoughts (described in detail and at length) are liberal and serious but, like Highsmith's creepier characters, he's not above indulging his imagination when an occasion presents itself. . . .

By the time Robbie shoots and kills his father one sunlit afternoon in the study we know how his reform school psychological case history will read. It is equally clear that little has changed in Highsmith's suburbia since Van Allen (in *Deep Water,* 1958), having found the gap between reality and his hopes impossible to bridge, drowned his wife's lover in the backyard swimming pool. Highsmith's perspective on this particular landscape has always been a moral one; the absence of a church among the swimming pools is keenly felt. Given her earlier books it's not surprising that the eventual provision of one, far from stimulating moral regeneration, is in itself the immediate source of greater unease, then disaster, and . . . a scared feeling of *plus ça change*.

In the end, unlike the Ripley novels or the collections of stories, this book is not so much concerned with the delineation of guilt—or with the complicated feelings induced when we suddenly realize that our sympathies lie with a psychopath—as with the exploration of a foreign place, one which we might have imagined to be prosperous and predictable, easy to pass through and forget. Instead, it turns out to be frighteningly complex and interesting—well worth understanding, if only to avoid reproducing it elsewhere.

Holly Eley, "The Landscape of Unease," in The Times Literary Supplement, *No. 4166, February 4, 1983, p. 104.*

CLARE COLVIN

The best of Patricia Highsmith's short stories [in *Mermaids on the Golf Course*] are those where ordinary life has gone awry and a normal person is suddenly in an abnormal situation. **"A Shot from Nowhere"**, for instance, is a nightmare that could happen to anyone. A young American artist living in Mexico witnesses the death of a boy, shot by an unknown assailant, and insists on reporting the event to the police. He would have been wise to have kept his head down, as the owner of his hotel advised, for the police react by arresting the only stranger in town, which is he. . . . Anyone who has ever had dealings with police officialdom in a strange country will know how easily a complainant could become the accused.

"Where the Action Is" also has a ring of truth. A freelance photographer snaps a girl running from an alley into the arms of two older people. They are her parents, and she claims to have been raped. The photograph is published nationwide and wins the Pulitzer Prize. The photographer is invited on lecture tours and publishes a book about the incident, in which he examines his conscience. . . . It is a brilliant study of a man bereft of any feeling.

The less successful stories are those dealing with the bizarre. In **"The Stuff of Madness"**, a woman sends all her dead pets to the taxidermist, and then displays them in the garden. I spent much of the story wondering how they stood up to the weather, before Ms Highsmith revealed in passing that the taxidermist treated their skins with a special protective finish. There are violent conclusions to several stories that seem designed as a shock ending, rather than a natural outcome of the preceding events. Why does Simon, an actor, try to kill himself while he is waiting for his old mentor to die in **"Chris's Last Party"**? I haven't a clue—nothing seems to lead up to it. The dramatic ending to **"Mermaids on the Golf Course"** is more believable, in its picture of a press conference given by an American politician which turns into a trial of his sanity. The atmosphere of embarrassment as it becomes clear to the assembled hacks that he has indeed lost his marbles, is beautifully conveyed. But it is a pity that the collection, as a whole, is so uneven.

> *Clare Colvin, "Strange Countries," in* Books and Bookmen, *No. 361, November, 1985, p. 33.*

MARILYN STASIO

The gods seem to be napping in this master storyteller's new suspense novel [*People Who Knock on the Door*]. For all the care with which she examines a Middle Western family in the course of moral disintegration, Patricia Highsmith's group character study is surprisingly dull. The problem could be her focus, which is something of a departure from her usual analysis of aberrant personalities. The Alderman family . . . begins to unravel when Richard Alderman, the upright head of the household, becomes a born-again Christian. The women merely cringe when wild-eyed people clutching Bibles and tracts show up on their doorstep to chat about the rigors of godliness and Arthur's girlfriend's abortion. Young Robbie, however, is drawn to his father's new creed, responding on some subconscious level to its undercurrents of violence. As father, son and assorted church elders converge on Arthur (who stubbornly sticks to his own business of being a good kid), family tensions heat up and violence flares. This volatile situation perfectly suits the author's talents for analyzing the psyche under stress. But here she has deflected her probe from the obvious subjects—Richard and Robbie—to Arthur. Her hound-dogging of this sympathetic yet unexceptional youth should have represented a challenge to a writer renowned for her brilliant insights into criminal psychology; but in this case normality is a bit of a yawn.

> *Marilyn Stasio, in a review of "People Who Knock on the Door," in* The New York Times Book Review, *November 24, 1985, p. 24.*

CHRISTOPHER WORDSWORTH

The loss of a wallet in Greenwich Village and its return intact by the finder is the casual starting point for the familiar Highsmith slither into dark places of obsession and violence, but [in *Found in the Street*] the old rattlesnake instinct has lost some of the sensitivity to infra-red radiations that normally direct it to its prey. Jack Sutherland, who drops the wallet, is a successful commercial artist with a rich languid wife who has her lesbian interludes; security guard Linderman, who returns it with a glow of self-righteousness, is a middle-aged mother's boy who believes it is his pious duty to save vivacious young café waitress Elsie from the big wicked city. The cold thrill of anticipation is still there, the study of obsession as consummate as ever, but we miss those precise provincial locations, there is a hubbub of distractions, the murder itself is curiously inconsequential, and Elsie and her incubation from chippy in a hamburger joint into glamorous cover girl is a rare Highsmith flop.

> *Christopher Wordsworth, in a review of "Found in the Street," in* The Observer, *April 13, 1986, p. 25.*

ANITA BROOKNER

The sentimental Victorian title of Patricia Highsmith's latest novel—[*Found in the Street*] . . .—gives little clue as to what is to follow. With her usual neutrality she traces yet again the fortunes of a near-psychopath and his victims who meet by chance and whose madnesses mesh in such a way as to ally them for ever, although the cleverest twist in this extremely clever novel is to let the protagonists go scot free while another comes to a random and sticky end. The low-key fascination which Patricia Highsmith assigns to the story proceeds from the manner in which the reader is inducted into the mysterious world of other people's lives, their domestic routines, habits of work, meals, entertainments, itineraries, alliances: nothing escapes her scrutiny, everything connects, and her curiously affectless prose conceals tremors of intent and a causal connection none the less frightening for its apparent banality.

Two men living in Greenwich Village have nothing to do with one another and no chance of meeting until one of them drops his wallet on the street and the other finds and returns it with full complement of cash and credit cards. The owner of the wallet is Jack Sutherland. . . . The man who finds the wallet is Ralph Linderman, one of those Highsmith familiars whose mild nuttiness is allied to a strong vein of homicidal fantasy. Linderman . . . lives a life of monumental dullness punctuated by walks with his dog, who is called God. Where a lesser writer might have made Linderman a religious maniac, Highsmith makes him an atheist, but an atheist with a strong sense of old-fashioned puritanism, eager to punish the wrongdoer and reward the virtuous. It is his delight in his own honesty that leads him to return Jack's wallet, and his appreciation of Jack's gratitude that entitles him, in his own eyes, to pursue this apparently upright citizen with telephone calls and four-page letters.

The subject of these letters is Elsie Tyler, a young blonde heartbreaker who never quite comes off the page but who fills her role as a focus of both Sutherland's and Linderman's interest more than adequately. They meet her, separately, in a Seventh Avenue coffee shop where she is temporarily working. Jack is fascinated by her looks, makes a few drawings of her, and falls in love with her in a characteristically tepid manner. Linderman, on the other hand, immediately assumes her virtue to be in danger and takes it upon himself to protect her from the dangers that lie in wait for girls in the big city. . . . He takes to following Elsie in the street in order to warn her. When he sees her leaving the Sutherland apartment he knows immediately what has happened, and alerts both Sutherland and Elsie to the error of their ways.

The clued-up Highsmith reader will now know what to expect: a persecution of the one man by the other, in one of those detailed and nightmarish routines that explore and celebrate the whole logic of pessimism. But Patricia Highsmith is cleverer than her readers and this is only one strand in the plot, the one which she uses to trap the unwary and to lull the unsuspecting into what looks like familiar territory. The charismatic Elsie leaves the coffee shop and with the help of Natalia, Jack's wife, is taken on as a fashion model. Elsie is indeed seen leaving Jack's apartment but as Elsie is gay she is in little danger. Elsie is in fact a mildly unpleasant character, despite Patricia Highsmith's evident indulgence towards her, but perhaps she is no more unpleasant than Linderman. Her blamelessness, like that of Sutherland himself, is mainly a negative affair and consists of not doing a great deal of harm to others. All the characters are flawed, and perhaps Linderman alone represents a lesser degree of venality. But Linderman is a nuisance and a bore. In the country of the laid-back he is an intruder. (pp. 27-8)

The peculiar spell which Patricia Highsmith lays on the reader is one of apparent inevitability. There seems to be no escape from the remorseless logic of what has been set up. In this she is effortlessly superior to other writers of suspense stories because she does not furnish her characters with anything but the most threadbare of personalities: their interaction is like the ticking of a clock. The author does not seem to intervene at any point to establish authorship, and the bare colourless prose and the circumstantial detail contribute to a narrative style so curiously insistent as to instil feelings of genuine uneasiness. There is no one quite like her, although her morbidity may raise the ghosts of some of Simenon's finest novels, like *Tante Jeanne* or *Le Temps d'Anaïs*. She presents terror as something impassive, unnoticeable, almost, an everyday affair.

Her great gift, apart from the mastery of her plotting, is to make one curious about other lives, to restore to them their dimension of strangeness, too often eroded in fiction by the easy process of identification. It is to be hoped that not too many people identify with Patricia Highsmith's characters: if they do they are in more danger than they know, and so are the rest of us. (p. 28)

Anita Brookner, "Terror as an Everyday Affair," in The Spectator, *Vol. 256, No. 8232, April 19, 1986, pp. 27-8.*

Janette Turner Hospital

1942-

Australian-born Canadian novelist and short story writer.

Recognized as one of the more important novelists to emerge in Canada during the 1980s, Hospital is noted for her rich prose style and her experiments with narrative. In her novels Hospital examines the ways in which individuals attempt to shape reality in order to conform to personal standards. Her characters often flout social values and customs in their pursuit of individual integrity. Hospital has lived for extended periods in several countries, including India, Canada, and the United States, and has evoked these settings in her novels.

Hospital's first novel, *The Ivory Swing* (1982), concerns a Canadian woman who encounters various cultural conflicts and is forced to reexamine her beliefs about love, marriage, and freedom while spending a year in India. For example, the woman's attempt to free a young Indian widow from a social code that forces her to spend a year in mourning is viewed by natives as a threat to their ancient tradition. Hospital's second novel, *The Tiger in the Tiger Pit* (1983), is told from the perspectives of the members of the Carpenter family as they reunite to celebrate the parents' fiftieth wedding anniversary. The characters privately reminisce about their personal and family experiences. Their varying interpretations of each other's actions reveal some of the conflicts and misunderstandings that have kept the family apart. Hospital's third novel, *Borderline* (1985), is considered her most ambitious work. This book focuses on two Canadians who discover a Salvadoran refugee attempting to enter Canada from the United States. While relating their efforts to aid the refugee, Hospital creates a story with several layers of meaning by experimenting with narrative structure and by exploring the motivations of her characters. Hospital integrates themes related to politics and personal freedom with philosophical speculations on the nature of art and reality.

(See also *Contemporary Authors,* Vol. 108.)

GAIL PEARCE

[*The Ivory Swing*] is about a professor of Indian studies and his family who spend a sabbatical year in southern India. Juliet, the wife, looks forward to adventure and romance, an escape from the cage of academic life in small-town Ontario, but she finds instead a new set of cages: the debilitating heat and indolence of India and the iron rules of caste and tradition. She and her sister befriend a young Indian widow and try to free her from her restrictive existence; through the disaster that follows, they begin to come to terms with their own lives.

The novel is about culture shock, culture clash and the dangers of imposing one's own standard of morality on other people's lives. However, it is less weighty than it sounds. It suffers from a split identity: a literary intent, evinced by a network of analogies drawn from Hindu mythology, but in a style that is frequently overwritten, lurid and sloppy. Rigorous editing could

have made it very much better and more consistent, removing the scattered bathos, banality and inaccurate similes and giving the genuinely striking images room to breathe.

Nevertheless, *The Ivory Swing* provides compelling and enjoyable reading. The plot is well constructed; the characters are plausible and sympathetic; the dank lassitude of the Indian monsoons and the rigid conservatism of a caste-ridden society are vividly portrayed. It is a book for a good evening's entertainment, though not one for CanLit courses.

> Gail Pearce, in a review of ''The Ivory Swing,'' in Quill and Quire, *Vol. 48, No. 10, October, 1982, p. 31.*

MARNI JACKSON

The annual $50,000 Seal First Novel Award can be a blessing and a curse for an author. It takes a story of genuine craft and innocence to make the reader stop adding up the $75 metaphors, and this year's winner, *The Ivory Swing,* succeeds. It turns the shopworn plot of Canadians in exile into a romantic, intelligent, well-written first novel, and for that combination alone it deserves a prize.

Juliet and David are ''university people'' from a small Ontario town bearing a strong resemblance to the author's home town of Kingston. When David's research takes him to India for a year, Juliet goes with him, bringing along their two children and her own consuming project, the conflict between married love and freedom. "Independence smoldered like sulfur in her gut, but domestic commitment was in her genes, heavy as lead." Prose like this runs perilously close to Ladies' Home Daydream at times, but for every lyrical excess there is a leap of imagination and a commitment to sensual prose that makes the lapses forgivable. . . .

The humid language also suits the setting: a still, hot, dusty village in southern India, where "nonentity is contagious." Before long, the perfumed prose effectively casts a spell through which we watch a woman in a dream, dreaming of reality.

Juliet's fantasies are the old standbys—an apartment alone in Montreal and a former lover named Jeremy. . . . But the dream she ends up living in is a beautiful house under coconut palms. Her landlord considers it rude to refuse servants, so she reluctantly accepts one houseboy. As she tries to make the boy part of her family, Juliet sees that the freedom she imposes on him sometimes makes him suffer more than the rules he understands. In India the notion of independence is more complicated than simply refusing to act like a faculty wife.

All around her, Juliet sees women "who weave with love and resentment the silken cages of their lives." One of them is a beautiful young widow, Yashoda, who longs to escape her forced mourning and vigilant family. . . .

At home in Canada Juliet drifted inside her own arguments about freedom. But in India the question of freedom becomes palpable; she lives with a servant boy who cannot change his caste and she watches Yashoda struggle, like herself, to slip free of her family's embrace. In a number of similarly concrete, graceful ways, *The Ivory Swing* asks the questions that novels used to ask. How are we to live? Which rules deserve to be broken and which protect our bonds? Especially, how do passionate people stay married?

The closest thing to an answer is offered in the title, which refers to an ivory carving of the Indian gods Radha and Krishna, tangled in an embrace on a swing that is frozen in mid-arc. This is how Juliet sees her own "sprained life," caught between poles and going nowhere—or in perpetual motion, depending on your point of view. The ending is rather dark, but the commitment to the ambiguities involved is honest and affecting.

> Marni Jackson, "Exiles in an Exotic Dream," in Maclean's Magazine, Vol. 95, No. 40, October 4, 1982, p. 72.

DOUGLAS HILL

[*The Ivory Swing*] offers a romantic adventure of promising complexity mired in a sludge of overblown prose and emotional cliché. There's intelligence and feeling here, plenty of exciting events, an exotic, detailed setting, but the florid, lifeless dialogue and characterization steal the show.

David, a professional type with wildly predictable hangups, takes a sabbatical in South India, accompanied by his wife Juliet and their two children. The novel is primarily Juliet's story, and told largely from her point of view. Against a murky backdrop of local customs and national politics, the family's safety is threatened and the marriage endangered. The plot is

complicated, and if unconvincing, holds a reader's attention fairly well.

Hospital does well with cross-cultural misunderstandings, both superficial and deadly. And she can create mood—the sensuous oppressiveness of a land "where things which existed in the mind had more substance than the blurred mirage of the external world." But she tends to gush and there's far too much gluey writing. . . . (p. 26)

The Ivory Swing has some powerful scenes, much romantic titillation, one bit of explicit sex. It's expertly researched and not uninteresting, but I can't take with utter seriousness a story that insists on solving what the publishers refer to as the "drama of human interaction" with insights like, "over the years she had come to realize there was no such thing as the right or wrong choice. Only a road taken and a road not taken." (pp. 26-7)

> Douglas Hill, in a review of "The Ivory Swing," in Books in Canada, Vol. 11, No. 10, December, 1982, pp. 26-7.

CHRISTOPHER SCHEMERING

Janette Turner Hospital in *The Ivory Swing* presents contemporary India as a world of indolent beauty undercut by terror. The ostensible heroine of this novel of unusual delicacy and power . . . is Juliet, the ambivalent wife of a Canadian academic. She sees her husband's sabbatical in lush southern India as a chance to escape her conflict. But she finds that it only serves to crystallize and exacerbate her own internal dilemma.

The focus of the moral ambiguity and the novel's true heroine is Yashoda. An exquisite creature whose growing rebellion against the one-year seclusion forced upon widows causes fury and finally violence among the villagers. Yashoda is a free spirit who bathes playfully in a forest pond with an adolescent servant boy (inviting the many peeping Toms of the village). She moves about in the background, a shadowy hedonist who plays off both Juliet and Juliet's husband David for her own ends. Juliet, who gets caught up in Yashoda's intrigues, cannot really help since the Indian men flinch at her every move, upset at every Western *faux pas*. . . . But Yashoda has become a mirror to Juliet's own plight, and Juliet can't even refrain from a twinge of jealousy when Yashoda sets her sights on David.

The Ivory Swing is a disturbing meditation on the clash of cultures and the rebellion and feminine rage in each. Juliet swings back and forth between the odd, heady reality of India and her free-floating memories and fantasies of Canada. David shuttles between his uncertain life with Juliet and a fantasy life. . . . Yashoda dangles in between, inevitably becoming the object of catharsis.

While the imagery which saturates the story is striking and the Indian dialogue is right on the mark, Juliet's aggressive intelligence sometimes has that ring of intellectual over-articulateness that seems arch rather than edifying. . . . But this sharpness combined with Janette Hospital's dream-like prose creates a seamless quality of irony which gives *The Ivory Swing*'s characters a balance they need.

> Christopher Schemering, in a review of "The Ivory Swing," in Book World—The Washington Post, June 5, 1983, p. 10.

MARNI JACKSON

Janette Turner Hospital's second novel seems much like a first one, the sort of flawed, talented debut that critics label "promising." *The Tiger in the Tiger Pit,* which tells of a family reuniting for a 50th wedding anniversary, is definitely promising, but after the passion and poise of *The Ivory Swing* it is also a disappointment. There are too many half-invented characters: the voices sound more like feats of ventriloquism than individual people. Without solid characters to anchor Hospital's lush writing, *The Tiger in the Tiger Pit* turns into an intelligent soap opera, full of unearned intensity.

The strongest voices belong to the two central characters, Edward and Elizabeth Carpenter. At 73, Edward is a cantankerous, embittered father who cannot forgive his son, Jason, and his daughter Emily for disappointing him. His wife's calm devotion infuriates him, and his inability to express love imprisons him. The old man is the caged figure of the title, taken from a T. S. Eliot poem: "The tiger in the tiger pit / Is not more irritable than I." Elizabeth, a dreamy eccentric, draws together the splintered family with a tenacity and wiliness that gives the novel its truly melodramatic surprise ending.

As they converge on their home, each member of the Carpenter family has some guilt to expiate, some sin to atone for. Jason is a New York analyst and a self-confessed "bastard" with women. Emily, a concert violinist with a child born out of wedlock, has made a virtue of distance and detachment. She once found happiness with a man on an Australian sheep station, but left it all behind for a life of celibacy and success in London, far from the tendrils of her family and the gamble of love. Her son Adam's longing for a family—either his surrogate father on the sheep station or the grandfather he has never met—mocks her self-sufficiency.

Despite the global lifestyles that her characters represent, Hospital has provided them all with the same quivering sensibility and the same romantic vocabulary: words like cornucopia and susurration recur like musical notes searching for a song. Indeed, Hospital's writing has more character than the characters themselves. She writes the kind of visceral prose that personifies everything in its path. Sometimes the effect is original and risky; sometimes it simply goes too far. . . .

Much as the modern novel, inhibited by irony, could use more magnificent chaos, there is enough spuming in *The Tiger in the Tiger Pit* to keep a reader drenched. Like the family patriarch, raging with untold tenderness and helpless to express it, the novel's energy remains formidable but strangely inarticulate.

> *Marni Jackson, "A Feat of Ventriloquism," in* Maclean's Magazine, *Vol. 96, No. 39, September 26, 1983, p. 62.*

JUDITH FITZGERALD

Janette Turner Hospital's second novel [*The Tiger in the Tiger Pit*] is an unusual blend of goodness and greatness. On the one hand, it is merely a good novel; on the other hand, it is written by a novelist with a potential for greatness. Bring both hands together and applause does not result.

Set predominantly in Ashville, Massachusetts, the novel examines the traumas and treacheries the Carpenter family endures throughout most of its existence. Edward Carpenter, a patriarchal archetype if ever there was one, displays a perverse

predilection for self-abasement in spite of his better intentions. Incapable of breaking out of an inescapable homage to conventional correctness, Carpenter's emotional paralysis is deftly reflected in the active revolt his 73-year-old body engages in. It refuses to cooperate with Carpenter's image of himself, and throughout the novel Carpenter berates it because its legs no longer support him. . . .

Carpenter, a retired school principal, sees (and dreams) things his way. Elizabeth, his wife of 50 years, sees (and daydreams) things her way. Their three adult children, of course, see things their way. The story is focused in the tension that derives from its several ways of seeing. Victoria, the eldest, has long since lapsed into the refuge of mental illness; Jason, the son in the middle, has lapsed into the refuge of practising psychology; and, to complete the trinity, Emily, the youngest, has lapsed into the refuge of becoming a concert violinist. . . .

Together yet impossibly apart, the members of the Carpenter family move inexorably toward discovery and self-definition. Affairs of the heart, the acts of the past, the tensions of the present all combine to provide the novel with a verisimilitude rarely equalled in family fictions.

However, the novel doesn't succeed, not insofar as it could have. The primary flaw of *The Tiger in the Tiger Pit* can be located in the fact that, as a narrative, it can't compete with the singular talents of its creator. Hospital is an author in search of a subject worthy of her vast abilities. Somehow, the terrors and titillations of the Carpenter family are not that subject. Indeed, 50th wedding anniversaries and family reunions of any kind ought to be left to the manufacturers of greeting cards.

The narrative structure of *The Tiger in the Tiger Pit* bears a resemblance to William Faulkner's masterpiece, *As I Lay Dying.* As well, like the hapless Bundren family, the Carpenters display a perverse tendency for chaos (one of the author's favourite words) in spite of themselves. But ultimately Edward Carpenter's attempts to go ungentle into that good night are not the stuff of which great novels are made; neither is the way the remaining Carpenters, either consciously or unconsciously, sustain his rage against the dying of the light. The individual and collective trials and triumphs could have shone and shimmered had they been showcased in a short story; as they appear here, they do not rise to the obvious talent Hospital has expended in their creation and resolution.

Finally, *The Tiger in the Tiger Pit* might be viewed as a literary tragedy, not unlike the tragic heroes Hospital herself alludes to throughout the novel. Hospital's writing, with the exception of her overdependence on simile, is exceptionally polished, brilliantly executed, and everywhere fraught with such intensity of spirit and sensibility and such richness of style that the results are consistently breath-taking. She has the eyes, the ears, and especially the piercing insights so necessary to the art and craft of great fiction. However, when all is said and undone, *The Tiger in the Tiger Pit* will stand as a testament to great failure which, incidentally, is far more admirable than lukewarm success.

> *Judith Fitzgerald, "Life with Father," in* Books in Canada, *Vol. 12, No. 9, November, 1983, p. 33.*

CLARE COLVIN

In Janette T Hospital's first novel, *The Ivory Swing,* a succession of dazzling images of India disguised an unconvincing story. Her new book, ***The Tiger in the Tiger Pit*** has a more complex plot in the relationships between the members of a far from happy family. (p. 33)

Gradually the different facets of the family are revealed through the eyes of each member. The parents' tensions reflect in their children's emotional lives. Victoria, the highly strung eldest daughter, has been weak in the head since coming across a distressing scene in her childhood. Emily, the concert violinist, flees from one relationship to another, unable to commit herself for fear of being trapped into a bad marriage like her mother's and Jason, a psychiatrist, can deal with his patients' problems, but not his own. Elizabeth, aware that there must be a reconciliation or their lives are wasted, stage manages a coming together of the family fragments at their childhood home.

Ms Hospital portrays the claustrophobic web of family relationships with perception. The revelation of past history, seen in different ways according to the viewpoint of each character, has almost the technique of a detective story. Occasionally, though, the descriptive becomes rather too lush . . . and her writing of the women characters tends to throbbing fecundity. She is at her most effective dealing with the crotchety trapped tiger spirit of Edward. (pp. 33-4)

> *Clare Colvin, in a review of "The Tiger in the Tiger Pit," in* Books and Bookmen, *No. 35, August, 1984, pp. 33-4.*

CLARE COLVIN

Janette Turner Hospital's two previous books promised much for the future. ***The Ivory Swing*** was a highly coloured evocation of India and ***The Tiger in the Tiger Pit*** a brilliant picture of a disturbed family. I wrote then that it was marred only by occasional overwriting [see excerpt above] and looked forward to her third book. Alas, ***Borderline*** has overbalanced into the tricksy traps of a writer indulging in Style to hide lack of content.

Ms Hospital may see ***Borderline*** as a parable of our times, for the current obsessions are there—terrorism, South American politics, brutal secret service agents. It begins with two people waiting to cross the border from the United States into Canada—Felicity, a free-wheeling young woman in an 'excessively blue' car, and Gus, a randy insurance salesman with a rocky marriage and a drinking problem. Ahead of their cars, the immigration officers open the doors of a refrigerated van to reveal, among the meat carcasses, a consignment of refugees from El Salvador. In the confusion they miss a diminutive woman who has hidden in one of the carcasses, and Felicity and Gus, strangers until then, rescue her, smuggle her across the border and hide her in Felicity's country cottage. To them she represents one of the world's persecuted martyrs, but while they are away from the cottage, she disappears, leaving only bloodstains indicative of murder. Is she dead? If so, who has killed her, who was she anyway and are Felicity and Gus irrevocably and dangerously involved in her world?

The novel contains the material of a conventional thriller, but Ms Hospital likes to dig deeper into the psyche and what might have been a straightforward plot in the hands of others is masked by swirls of mysticism. Under the characters' stress, what is reality and what is the product of their fevered minds becomes hard to discern. The story is further complicated by having on onlooker act intermittently as narrator. Jean-Marc, the son of Felicity's lover, describes the events in the same way, he says,

as he tunes a piano. 'I tap, I listen, I adjust the pins. I am priest of austere and inviolable computations.' Jean-Marc is a pain and eventually takes the book into discussions reminiscent of John Fowles at his most wilful—'All right, Mr Piano Tuner, you say. Enough of red herrings. Enough of disarming admissions about dreaming Felicity's dreams and remembering her memories. . . . Confess now. The whole truth. Let us hear you say it: *Felicity herself, c'est moi.*'

The problem of ***Borderline*** is that of a writer thrashing around for a subject. Felicity, living in a safe country, feels guilty when confronted by people who, if they lived in their own countries, would be tortured and killed. It may be that Ms Hospital needs a more stimulating background to draw on, and that Canada lacks, for her, the necessary inspiration.

> *Clare Colvin, "Red Herrings," in* Books and Bookmen, *No. 359, September, 1985, p. 28.*

CHERI FEIN

Erasing the borders that define our lives has fascinated Janette Turner Hospital. . . . According to Mrs. Hospital, disintegrating borderlines cause combustion and, literally, death.

Never has this been more the case than in her third novel [***Borderline***], which is by far her most complex and disturbing. So many borderlines are crossed that the book's title might have been more accurate in the plural. Religion, sex, art, politics, family, imagination, dreams, propriety, trust, truth—none are taken for granted. Questions form the foundation of ***Borderline***: What does it mean to be fully alive? Which of life's collisions aren't absurd? How far is going *too* far? Characters and story serve merely as the method of exploration.

"Even the dreams you dream up are dangerous," comments the narrator, a piano tuner who admits to piecing together the story from a few facts and an active imagination. He is performing this exercise as a way to come to terms with the disappearance of his stepmother, Felicity. She, an art historian with "a quality of absence about her," and Augustine (Gus) Kelly, a guilt-ridden philanderer, are brought together when they impetuously aid an injured South American alien during her attempt to cross the border from the United States into Canada. . . .

Although challenging and engaging, the exploratory nature of ***Borderline*** creates some problems. Mrs. Hospital uses her characters to identify various notions of reality. The attempt is worthy, but the results are caricaturelike. Felicity's husband, Seymour (a.k.a. the Old Volcano), represents the life-gulping genius artist whose boundaries are determined solely by his own needs. Her proper Beacon Hill aunts represent those who use borderlines to contain an indestructibly comfortable reality. As for the narrative, it frequently pulls the reader into the characters' vertigo. This is alternately breathtaking and confusing.

Yet perhaps that's exactly what Mrs. Hospital intends. As the narrator notes: "I know truth is an old-fashioned plant, like sage or thyme. I know the difficulties. But I am steering for the essential rather than the merely literal." So is Mrs. Hospital. In her previous novels she proved herself an able storyteller and a gifted writer. Now she has traveled into uncharted, deeper waters. It is a brave course she is on, and the book is a compelling attempt to go beyond the safe borderlines within which much current fiction resides.

Cheri Fein, "A Quality of Absence," in The New York Times Book Review, *September 1, 1985, p. 8.*

PAUL ROBERTS

Occasionally writers truly surprise you. Nothing Janette Turner Hospital has written . . . gave any indication she could write a book as good as *Borderline*.

With a John Fowles-like structure, which is as convoluted and baffling as it is satisfying, and a poetic prose reminiscent of Malcolm Lowry and D. M. Thomas, *Borderline* is still firmly based in its own dazzling originality, much of which stems from a curious ability to keep shifting from a strong story-line and deeply personal obsessions to a compassionate treatment of themes of universal concern.

Two strangers—Gus, a salesman, and Felicity, (perhaps) an artist's model—are waiting to cross the border into Canada in their individual cars. A refrigerated meat truck ahead of them is stopped by customs officials. Among the swinging sides of beef, in the icy darkness of the travelling freezer, huddle several shivering immigrants from Central America. Chaos breaks out as the truck driver makes a run for it, and the frozen immigrants are herded away. Stepping out, Gus and Felicity notice something in the back of the truck: "They stared at the carcass nearest them. Its unzipped front, wilting in the hot air, curled inwards—a Caesarean wound around a fetus. Something, someone, was *in* there. A woman." This is the beginning. "Felicity was shaken by the face. She knew it from a painting . . . 'Perugino,' she said. 'The Magdalena.' 'What?' Gus crossed himself."

They smuggle the woman across the border, at once regretting the act and realizing that it is the catalyst that will transform their lives. Perhaps Felicity is forced to confess the act to a priest; perhaps the Magdalena is rescued or killed. Once she is gone, however, the bond between Gus and Felicity dissolves and they both imagine they can return to their normal lives.

Of course, they cannot. But what were their lives, and who are they, anyway? . . . Hospital has metamorphosed into a poetic novelist—the novel being where all the poets are hiding these days—and must be treated as such.

The book is clearly about Felicity, although, at times, it seems to be narrated by a piano tuner called Jean-Marc. Jean-Marc knows Felicity well—too well. Perhaps he is Felicity. Certainly he searches for her as intensely as she searches for herself; within a sentence he will become her—but then she will become him. A man called Hunter is also looking for her. If he exists, does he work for the FBI or not? Was the woman, the Magdalena, an immigrant or an agent? Did Felicity take such a risk for nothing? What haunts her? Why is the event so important in her life? Why does it in some curious way contain her life?

Borderline raises more question marks than an empty wardrobe. While most writers are content to tell you what to think, here, it seems, you are being told that you should think. The questions do have answers in the end, but that is most definitely not the point. At its most profound level, the book explores what appears to be a tangential extrapolation of the Christian myth, weaving together a diverse and highly complex series of Indian and Chinese speculations on the nature of divinity within an essentially Catholic theology.

Gus—a sort of Everyman—cannot rest until he knows what really happened to the Magdalena; he sees her face everywhere.

He wants to lay her to rest in the same way a person who has had a deeply religious experience wishes he could return to atheism because it's much simpler than bearing the burden of spiritual responsibility. His life literally falls apart in front of him and no longer means anything at all.

For Felicity, life takes on an intensity of meaning that burns like fire. Ensnared in what may or may not be an intricate plot to destroy her for her involvement in a dark, obscure conspiracy, she constantly plunges back into the moments of her life that have, somehow, led her to this point. But within this storm of madness, like King Lear, she learns how to feel the pain of others. In extraordinary flights of peeled and passionate prose, she depicts the human tragedies of El Salvador, tragedies that go beyond politics, beyond strategy and logic. With these moments of horror, Felicity returns to the fragmented images of her own past, gradually making sense of things that stick like shards in her memory. There is a reverberating sense of revelation, something indisputable yet ineffable, flashing through the prose. This is a fugue in words, wildly pyrotechnic yet never out of control, evocative yet irreducibly precise.

The book, as the author explains in the first lines, is about borders: the lines between country and country, person and person, man and woman, waking and dreaming, past and present, reality and fantasy, good and evil.

With *Borderline,* Janette Turner Hospital has crossed an important line herself.

Paul Roberts, "Hospital's Latest Nears New Frontiers," in Quill and Quire, *Vol. 51, No. 11, November, 1985, p. 23.*

M. G. VASSANJI

"These are violent times," observes Seymour the artist: words that, like Conrad's "the horror," leave a faint but persistent echo in the mind, a grim residue at the end of [*Borderline*]. The violence and terror that in the jumbled flatness of our newspapers acquire the character of the surreal and absurd are too real in their bloodiness and savagery for a segment of humanity. How we cope when our paths intersect with this other world, whether we withdraw or engage, is a function of the ghosts we chase, our private obsessions. This is but one of the strands that run through the rich tapestry of this novel, which is impressive in its achievement and out of the ordinary in its scope. . . .

The story is told by Jean-Marc, Felicity's stepson, a piano tuner and self-styled aesthete, who reads Dante in his spare time. Through his frequent interjections the narrative becomes conscious of itself, thus adding another dimension to the novel. The writing is rich and brilliant, at times aesthetic: images recur and reinforce, words resonate, paragraphs are little compositions. But there are instances when it does not work ("He had no visa for the country of talk"), and the result then is an unintended flippant tone.

There are echoes here of Conrad, parallels in theme and form with Renaissance art, allusions to Indian mythology. "Borderline" is itself a metaphor for other barriers: between Felicity the art curator and Gus the insurance salesman; Felicity the mother and Jean-Marc the lover; Felicity the rich white woman and Angelo the illegal alien. Much of the action takes place in Cambridge. Central Square with its poverty and squalor (exaggerated for effect, I believe) becomes a menacing presence, a Third World, an area of darkness in the heart of Cambridge, a walk away from stylish Harvard Square where Felicity has her gallery.

The book itself, pegged on real incidents, barely stays on this side of the border between the real and the fanciful—or what is dictated by form. With its richly embroidered language, with events, names, past and present fitting tidily into each other (despite claims to the contrary), it becomes itself an aesthetic piece, but for the voice of Jean-Marc the narrator.

The ultimate irony of the novel is that when all is said and done, when Felicity and Gus are canonized by art (one a Magdalen who brings one child close to his Father, the other a St. Augustine in Carthage, N.Y.), the "other world," with its violence and terror, retreats into the surreal and absurd—as it does when we finally put aside the book.

> *M. G. Vassanji, "Art of Darkness," in* Books in Canada, *Vol. 15, No. 1, January-February, 1986, p. 27.*

ELSPETH CAMERON

Janette Turner Hospital is fond of a story by Jorge Luis Borges in which a man dreams that he has a son and then learns to his horror that someone else is dreaming *him*. It is a concept that pervades Hospital's own work: the unreality of some realities, the ways our imaginations impose the self on the world, and, most of all, the bizarre, nightmarish timbre of human existence.... In her haunting third novel, *Borderline,* she insists we look afresh at life and admit the horror of the ordinary. (p. 57)

The idea for *Borderline* originated in a story buried deep in *The New York Times* about three years ago. Some Salvadoran refugees had bought illegal passage across the U.S.-Mexico border in the back of a refrigerated meat truck. Once in the U.S., the driver had inexplicably panicked and abandoned his van. Later the refugees were discovered frozen solid. "I received it visually when I read it," recalls Hospital, who became haunted by the story. "Because I cross borders a lot driving, I couldn't help wondering what would have happened if that truck had been opened at the border. And what would have been the impact on the driver behind the truck." Thus Felicity, the ironically named protagonist of *Borderline,* and her lapis lazuli blue Datsun were dreamed into being. (pp. 57-8)

While contemplating her novel, Hospital began to collect news clippings about refugees. "What keeps someone going?" she asked herself. "What makes a person take that kind of risk: to be frozen in the back of a meat van? And then to arrive in a place where they have no status whatsoever. Where they're deported if they're found...." To answer these questions, Hospital probed the refugee community in Boston, with Kafkaesque results. In an episode that found its way into the heart of her novel and dictated its mode, she looked for a refugee centre address that didn't exist, found herself in a barbershop that made Sweeney Todd seem angelic, and was finally threatened on the street. *Borderline* is permeated by the eerie paranoia that set in when she discovered that even well-meaning sympathizers are swept into that sinister, shadowy world. Are events real or imagined? When "facts" are juxtaposed, must human beings project their idiosyncratic fantasies onto them to force meanings, no matter how wrong? Can fear and paranoia cause events to take place? Are some realities so painful that in self-defence we invoke amnesia and deny their existence? How, in fact, can we *know* anything?

To convey such complexities, Hospital tells her story at two removes. We know the elusive Dolores Marquez only through Felicity and Gus; but Felicity and Gus are filtered through a disciple-like narrator, Jean-Marc, an unassuming piano tuner who likes to work note by note. His attempt to make sense of the "jumble of out-of-sequence information" that remains after Felicity and Gus join *los desaparecidos* (the disappeared ones) draws the reader gently into a story that might otherwise be too intense and bizarre to credit. But Jean-Marc is a suspect narrator at best. His ambivalence toward Felicity (who is simultaneously his resented stepmother, his ideal woman, and his best friend) and his negative feelings about Seymour, his painter father (whom he disdainfully refers to as the Old Volcano), suggest that, like the man in the Borges story, he is only dreaming these people into existence according to his own inner need—just as they may be dreaming Dolores Marquez (whom Jean-Marc has never seen) for reasons he cannot fathom....

[Felicity] is most in character when in transit between parallel but mutually exclusive worlds, a lost soul unable at first to commit herself to any life that involves her whole self. But her instinctive act of compassion in rescuing Dolores completes her as a person (Dolores—meaning "grief"—is the other half of Felicity, or "happiness") and enables her to feel the suffering of those who had never before seemed real. Similarly, the philandering Gus undergoes a Dantean vision of La Salvadora which proves his salvation. Though elsewhere Hospital has explored the destructive effects of instinct, she here offers hope that man's impulse to care for others is as strong as his instinct to gratify himself. But ironic ambivalence prevails. Good Samaritanism results in baffling deaths that are both noble and absurd. (p. 58)

Borderline is a coup for Hospital. She brings to the fore political issues that seemed slight and redundant in her first two novels (though not in some of her stories), and through symbolic parallels integrates their startling relevance with her almost existentialist musings on the nature of reality, perception, and art.

Hospital's sensual style no longer threatens to sink beneath its own weight. Her images—which combine visual and philosophical impact—are often stunning.... Firmly structured on a form of almost mathematical purity, lightened by wit, Hospital's style is enlisted in the service of a reality so grotesque and a story so powerfully animated that it seems the *only* style in which the story could be told. (pp. 58-9)

[*Borderline*] overcomes her earlier tendency to retreat from the political to the aesthetic. So strongly does she respond to art (not just literary art but painting, sculpture, and music as well) that her work has sometimes threatened to become a devotional, disconnected dream. In *Borderline,* she not only points up the danger that art can be mere escape and acknowledges the cannibalistic nature of creative acts, she also dramatizes the responsibility of the artist to take a moral stand. In the silent Dolores Marquez, who first appears framed by ominous swinging carcasses, art and life merge. She is the incarnation of Perugino's "La Magdalena" and Edvard Munch's "The Scream." Janette Turner Hospital reminds us that the world's surrealistic nightmares are all too real. It is our indifference to them that is the dream. (p. 59)

> *Elspeth Cameron, "Borders," in* Saturday Night, *Vol. 101, No. 4, April, 1986, pp. 57-9.*

DIANA ABU-JABAR

[*The Tiger in the Tiger Pit*] is structurally similar to the fugue-like mix of *The Sound and the Fury*. However, while Faulkner's classic derived from an intensely developed and stable sense of place, Hospital's work glances from town to town and country to country. Canada is only one part of this family's second-generational wanderings, especially on the part of Emily Carpenter. The story operates with a Proustian eye for detail, taking signals from such simple cues as a gazebo or a branch of honeysuckle and parlaying these into the rich, rambling associations of personal history.

Emily's 8-year-old boy Adam proclaims: "I'm a citizen of the world . . . I was conceived in Canada and born in Australia and now I am being educated in England." This effectively reflects the stage of *Tiger,* and although the novel does not ever ultimately settle in Canada, Emily's sense of dislocation and homelessness suggests a particularly Canadian sense of displacement. Emily's decision to attend with Adam her parent's 50th wedding anniversary marks an affirmation of the importance of family as the source of personal stability and strength. Hospital's writing vibrates with a sensual imagery, linking ideas to flesh, words to blood. It is a kind of writing that seems to insist that all realities are mediated by physical contact. The symbolic family blood link recurs metaphorically throughout this novel. (pp. 2-3)

Diana Abu-Jabar, "North of the Border," in Belles Lettres, *Vol. 1, No. 5, May-June, 1986, pp. 2-3.*

Anthony Hyde

1946?-

(Has also collaborated with Christopher Hyde under joint pseudonym of Nicholas Chase) Canadian novelist and short story writer.

Hyde elicited critical attention with the publication of his first novel, *The Red Fox* (1985). This book, which contains elements of a murder mystery, an adventure story, and a historical novel, revolves around the disappearance and murder of a wealthy Canadian who had once been a spy for the Soviet Union. Although some critics detected such flaws as weak character development and unresolved subplots, others considered the novel credible and well written, particularly noting Hyde's talent for description and his meticulous attention to interrelated events. Critics also praised Hyde for his political insight, especially his treatment of pro-Soviet apologetics and his examination of the motives behind individuals who spy for totalitarian governments. Under the joint pseudonym of Nicholas Chase, Hyde also coauthored *Locksley* (1983), a retelling of the Robin Hood legend, with his brother, novelist Christopher Hyde.

JOHN NORTH

Remember the last time you finally got a reservation at that "fabulous" restaurant everyone was recommending and the food was pleasant but not outstanding? Or the time you queued for the movie "you had to see" but which left you unmoved? The much-heralded book ***The Red Fox*** provides a similar letdown. . . .

Although Anthony Hyde is a competent and undoubtedly promising thriller writer, he has some way to go before he breaks through to join his brother Christopher in the front rank. ***The Red Fox*** is a well-written and entertaining adventure story with an international background and a complex but not breathtaking plot. Some suspension of normal beliefs and expectations, and the occasional coincidence, are acceptable devices to maintain suspense and keep novels of this type rolling along, but there is also an expectation that clues will be fairly presented and that from time to time the villains will have some chance at gaining the upper hand. Glimpsing people in pitch darkness from a distance of several feet without their being aware (even if you've just switched off a light), being able to trail cars for mile after undetected mile on a deserted road, and stumbling across villains (still unseen) when the trail runs cold can stretch the patience of the reader just a bit too far.

Robert Thorne, a freelance writer and "Russian expert", is quietly living out his mid-30s in a small Virginia university town after abandoning journalism and teaching. The story opens with Thorne's visit to the Pennsylvania grave of his diplomat father whose suicide, two decades earlier, was dismissed as a hunting accident. When he returns home he receives two surprises: a telegram from May Brightman, a former lover now

Photograph by Jim Merrithew

living in Toronto, and evidence that his house has been skilfully searched.

May's problem is that her father, a wealthy furrier who got his start by importing furs from the Soviet Union, had disappeared without a trace 10 days earlier, and she wants Thorne to help prod the reluctant bureaucracy of the justice system and to look into the background of her adoption by Harry Brightman in Halifax in 1940. He agrees. During an exploratory search of the mid-town mansion of the missing man he gets his first sight of another searcher who vanishes immediately but appears and reappears throughout the rest of the book.

After a visit to the Brightman family lawyer, Thorne goes to Halifax to pick up the trail, which leads to a dead end in the Nova Scotian Black community and a confession of a Russian connection by an ageing doctor who assisted in the adoption. The apparent discovery of Brightman's suicide in Detroit causes Thorne to abandon Halifax, collect May, and fly to Detroit to identify the body and take care of the details. . . . With vague hints of a missing fortune and the possibility of May's real parents being significant figures from post-revolutionary Russia, he starts his quest in earnest.

The trek leads from Detroit through libraries and contacts in Washington and New York, a protracted surveillance in the New Hampshire woods, a gory scene at a Quebec fox ranch,

225

houseboats in Paris, hotels and gas stations in Leningrad, the unbroken snow of the Russian wilderness, and eventually back to the Pennsylvania hills close to the cemetery where his father is buried.

Thorne may be one of the most unremarkable heroes ever to be encountered in a thriller. Although he responds instantly to a cry for help from the woman who refused to marry him (and as far as we know, the only woman in his life), he seems remarkably detached from the process. The only true feeling he shows is a nagging suspicion about the reasons for his father's death. Aside from this, he moves through the story with a sort of mechanical tenacity, always showing remarkable restraint, needing virtually no sleep, and evincing a total lack of concern for the violent events and mind-bending possibilities surrounding him. One is left with no clear picture of what he's really like and no desire to encounter him again. . . .

There is a final action-packed showdown before the well-telegraphed denouement that is unlikely to surprise seasoned thriller readers.

It is unfortunate that the book falls so short of its promise-packed publicity. Had it arrived, like most others, virtually unheralded, it would probably have garnered general approval of the "promising start with eager anticipation of future output" type. One can only hope that Anthony Hyde will be able to recover from the dubious benefits of "instant fame" and develop into the calibre of writer his first effort portends.

John North, "The Quick Red Fox Proves Too Fast for Hyde," in Quill and Quire, Vol. 51, No. 7, July, 1985, p. 61.

JOHN GROSS

The Red Fox arrives with a roll of drums—it is shortly to appear, the publishers tell us, in 15 different foreign editions—and it seems reasonable to begin by asking whether the fuss is justified. A few pages, however, are likely to be enough to break down most initial resistance. The book really is a superior and unusually intelligent example of its genre, and—for a first novel—a remarkably assured performance. What has Anthony Hyde been up to until now? . . .

Many of the virtues of *The Red Fox* are of a strictly traditional variety—indeed, I think it is a tale of which that other sometime resident of Ottawa, John Buchan, would have been proud (in my book, at least, high praise). Mr. Hyde knows how to bait the storytelling hook; he deals out his revelations with a shrewd sense of timing; and if most of his characters, from the bony Scotch-Canadian lawyer to the smooth K.G.B. man, only manage to stay one step ahead of cliché, in this kind of writing one step is enough.

He is good at evoking atmosphere, too, above all at capturing the glamour that lurks in supposedly glamourless settings—in back streets, grayness and drizzle, humdrum townscapes. (It has been a long time since I read a book that made me so keen to visit Halifax, Nova Scotia, or Berlin, N.H.) Only Detroit defeats him, though he does have a fine, half-surreal description of a police car pound there. The detail in the Russian scenes carries a high degree of conviction, from the starkness of winter in the remote village to the mingled smell in the cities of cement dust and fumes from the huge trucks "which people will proudly (and truthfully) tell you are the largest trucks in the world."

Mr. Hyde's most valuable asset, however—and it is an unusual one among thriller writers—is his firm grasp of historical and political realities. When he writes about Grigori Zinoviev or Georgi Dimitrov, he knows what he is talking about, and doesn't simply trot out their names to add a veneer of spurious authenticity. (It is the merest slip, though a regrettable one, that at one point he should mix up Bakunin with Bukharin.) He understands the larger forces at work in the background of his story; he has a feel for ideology and the way it can color a life style.

It is this clear-sightedness, I would like to think, that saves him from falling into the trap of overelaboration that is the bane of so much recent espionage and semi-espionage fiction. *The Red Fox* has a complicated plot, but not so complicated that you get lost in it. Nor is it one of those self-defeating spy novels where every horse is a Trojan horse, and nothing is but what is not, and where you are left feeling that one side is as good or bad as the other.

Only at the very end does Mr. Hyde go seriously astray—or so I would submit. The story has a final twist that is both ingenious and adroitly prepared for, and many readers may well feel that this is as much as you can reasonably ask. But it seems to me to be a denouement that belongs to a lower, more lurid order of thriller, and one that is at odds with the book's sharper insights. A pity; still, it doesn't significantly detract from the excitement or interest of what has gone before.

John Gross, in a review of "The Red Fox," in The New York Times, August 23, 1985, p. C24.

JOSEF SKVORECKY

The valuable core of Anthony Hyde's first novel, *The Red Fox,* is its meditation on idealistic Westerners who spy for totalitarian governments. The author unhesitantly defines such idealism as treason—not pure and simple, perhaps, but shameful all the same. To read that lesson in *The Red Fox* is a refreshing experience, given the proliferation of books and films—for example, Robert Littell's novel *The Amateur* or *The Jigsaw Man,* starring Laurence Olivier and Michael Caine—where the fact is in various ways obfuscated. Stripped to its essentials, the argument of such works goes that some British lord or American intellectual was disappointed with democracy (or even with some Government agency), saw the light from Moscow and acted for the enemy in good faith—therefore he can and should be exonerated.

Such aristocratic and middle-class spies required a long series of eye-openers to recognize where their ideals had led them—the Hitler-Stalin pact, the East Berlin workers' uprising, the Gulag revelations, oppression in Hungary, Czechoslovakia and Poland, in Cambodia, Afghanistan and Ethiopia. The eyes of some have remained closed even after these spectacles, but *The Red Fox* is the story of a traitor whose eyes finally *are* opened and who, having acquired knowledge by bitter experience and self-examination, says many wise things on the subject of ideological spying. . . .

I am in no position to judge to what extent Mr. Hyde's fiction moves within the boundaries of reality or, at least, probability on the matter of what the startled narrator at one point speculates is "some sort of wild émigré sect—Russian and religious, anti-Semitic and anti-Soviet." The dangerous treasure chase, however, seems to answer the novelist's rather than the sect's needs. . . . And it indicates a more general ambivalence in Mr. Hyde's authorial intentions: on the one hand, he shows a genuine intent to address the psychological and moral problems of ideological spying; on the other, an ambition to write a best-selling thriller.

As a thriller, the novel displays most of the absurdities of the genre. There are encounters in pitch-darkness and on stormy nights reminiscent of the settings for Sherlock Holmes's struggles with his archenemy, Professor Moriarty, and even of the Gothic novel. There is a barely glimpsed master criminal who eludes the hero as if endowed with miraculous dexterity, yet perishes ultimately in a simple shoot-out in the woods—a variation, known to all practitioners of crime fiction including myself, on what John Dickson Carr called the disappointment of the solution.

There is a melodramatic plot complication involving the family of the last Czar, Nicholas II, that seems meant primarily for readers of Harlequin romances. There are crude improbabilities: for instance, the *dezhurnaya*—the night clerk or, better, corridor watchdog—in the hero's Moscow hotel waves aside his disappearance after a postmidnight trip to the bar by assuming that she has overlooked him, and then does not report his absence from the hotel throughout the night and the following day. There are far too many drives, walks and shadowings of other people's movements through landscapes that contribute nothing more than meaningless atmosphere and slow the tempo we expect of a thriller.

And then there is the Achilles' heel of crime fiction—the lengthy explanation, the gathering around Poirot, who, in spite of his genius, was rarely able to arrive at the solution with the one flash of logic Raymond Chandler demanded. Mr. Hyde simply leaves loose ends. . . .

In the world of thrillers, such concerns are probably more important than matters of political insight. My point is that this book could have been more than a thriller. The betrayal of democracy is no minor matter, and Anthony Hyde demonstrates that he has a better grip of the problem than technically more accomplished authors. One rarely comes across succinct and clear-sighted appraisals of the basic repertory of pro-Soviet apologetics, but Mr. Hyde provides them in abundance. . . .

Mr. Hyde is certainly capable of treating his subject without the distractions of the thriller, a genre in which he seems an apprentice rather than a master anyway. If he does someday write a serious novel addressing the issue, it will no doubt prove much more of a thriller than *The Red Fox.*

> Josef Skvorecky, "On the Scent of Treason," in The New York Times Book Review, September 1, 1985, p. 8.

ANTHONY OLCOTT

The Red Fox is something of a patchwork, stitched up of bits that can be marvelously entertaining, but which fail fully to coalesce; curiously, this thriller's lack of focus may well be the fault, not of author Anthony Hyde's inexperience (and certainly not of lack of talent), but rather of the genre's' limitations, for Hyde attempts to bring to a conventional medium emotions and insights of a complexity uncommon in escapist ·fiction.

True, there are grounds on which to suspect inexperience, as Hyde's publishers stress that *The Red Fox* is a first novel. Perhaps this may explain the occasional creakiness of a plot

turn, or a reliance on coincidence. . . . Such splotches, though, are so infrequent and minor in comparison to Hyde's vivid evocation of person and place, in this story of a search across Canada, the United States, France and even Russia, that it is impossible to believe that Hyde is not an experienced writer, well used to conveying the world in words.

Some of the cause may also be simple timing, since the book concerns secrets of Russian and Soviet history. Hyde's Thorne is an amateur Kremlinologist well-equipped to rummage about in the doings of such arcane figures as Georgi Dimitrov and Bukharin (whom a gremlin has rendered as "Bakunin"), both of whom are caught up in the secret which is the spine of Hyde's book, and Hyde's handling of Russia is sure and convincing. However, both because of certain details which are no longer true (such as that gasoline is no longer sold for cash, so that Thorne could not sneak out of Leningrad as described), and more significantly, because the nature of nationalism and the interagency rivalry between the KGB and the army's intelligence branch, the GRU, have both changed dramatically since Brezhnev's death, the Soviet Union which Hyde portrays as current is in fact history, and thus an obtrusive element in enjoying *The Red Fox.*

Yet *The Red Fox* is not primarily about Russia, nor is it entirely a thriller of plot. Hyde's book begins with an act of kindness, as Thorne agrees to help a former girl friend locate her missing father. . . . [Because] she once agreed to marry Thorne, then mysteriously changed her mind, Thorne feels compelled beyond bounds of kindness to discover why the man has disappeared. Thorne equally is drawn on by the emptiness within himself which came from having watched his own father commit suicide, an act Thorne could neither explain nor forget. *The Red Fox* thus is a story of twin obsessions, with the nature of the woman whom Thorne loves without return, and with the nature of himself and his own history.

These obsessions are not, Thorne learns, as private as they might seem, for both the missing father, then Thorne's own father, prove to have connections with Soviet espionage. . . .

What distinguishes *The Red Fox* from thrillers of lesser ambition, though, is that Hyde never allows [the] more public dangers to subordinate Thorne's private quest. What Thorne learns about himself is as important to the book as what he learns about history, making *The Red Fox* an unusually human and civilized novel. Hyde avoids the colossal (and usually silly) scope of the common thriller, just as he disdains the clinically-described brutality which infests so many modern books. His focus is always on Thorne as a man, his love for a particular woman, his need to balance an understanding of his father as a parent and as a person.

Unfortunately, such concerns seem too intimate for the genre, so Hyde ties them to something of a scale acceptably thrilling, or tries to. . . . [The result is that] Hyde is forced into concocting an ultimate secret, that perhaps the last of the Romanovs was not murdered, that a legitimate claimant to the Russian throne may yet live.

It is this, both the intimation and the genre convention which demands that Hyde make it, which most seriously vitiates *The Red Fox.* . . . Paradoxically though, it is this weakness which also most highlights the strength of *The Red Fox,* and of Hyde, for what in a lesser book would seem ludicrous here seems only unnecessary, something unwisely added to enlarge the audience for what in fact is the story of a man coming to understand himself. . . . [One] cannot help but rejoice at this debut, while hoping too that *The Red Fox* will give Hyde the audacity to shrug off genre, and follow his instincts into the less contrived but equally thrilling arena of real human relationships, intelligently and perceptively described.

Anthony Olcott, "Russian Hide and Seek," in Book World—The Washington Post, *September 22, 1985, p. 7.*

GILLIAN MACKAY

There is more than one red fox in Anthony Hyde's absorbing new spy thriller, which moves from Toronto's Kensington Market to a remote Russian village. Among the candidates is a ruthless Soviet terrorist, a wily old spy and an elderly French Canadian who raises foxes. Animal cunning is the key to survival in Hyde's bleak world of broken promises and compromised ideals. In classic spy novel tradition, the author has fashioned an inventive tale of honor and betrayal. But unfortunately, the suspenseful narrative of *The Red Fox* is sometimes undercut by flabby writing and melodrama. . . .

The Red Fox is at its best when it sticks to straight action. Like a set of Russian dolls that open one by one, each riddle leads to the next, right to the final line of the book. And in an entertaining feat of ingenuity, *The Red Fox* leaves the reader to ponder one last enigma that can never be solved.

Gillian Mackay, "Sleuthing in a World of Spies," in Maclean's Magazine, *Vol. 98, No. 38, September 23, 1985, p. 64.*

CYNTHIA GRENIER

In these days of treason chic, when the Guy Burgesses and other traitors of yesterday are being treated with a kind of gentle indulgence—as witness *Another Country, Pack of Lies, The Jigsaw Man, An Englishman Abroad, The Human Factor*—it is exciting to discover a novel, *The Red Fox,* whose very essence is an examination, and condemnation, of idealistic Westerners who spy for totalitarian governments.

What makes the discovery doubly exciting is the fact that *The Red Fox* is . . . about to be published in fifteen other countries. Which means there is every reason to expect that Anthony Hyde's penetrating analysis of how idealistic men became traitors to the societies that nurtured them is going to reach a singularly wide readership. . . .

While giving us all the usual trappings of a thriller—suspense, high adventure, violence, vivid descriptions of cities as diverse as Detroit and Leningrad—Hyde is a serious novelist with a serious story to tell. As a first novel, it does have its awkwardnesses and moments of implausibility—no more, to be sure, than most exemplars of the genre. But in a sense they serve to set off all the better Hyde's lucid analysis of the standard collection of pro-Soviet apologetics. . . .

Perhaps the most perceptive comment in [*The Red Fox*] comes from the long disillusioned Brightman on the run:

> Do you know what a Communist is, Mr. Thorne? How can you spot him? Pick him out of a crowd. Let me tell you. It's very simple: a Communist is that person who can most skillfully justify the greatest number of the murdered dead. Which makes me a *failed* Communist. Undoubtedly, I can still murder and maim, but I could no longer *justify* it—I've lost the greatest skill I could once claim to possess.

While Hyde's gifts for character and political perception are undeniable, one would now like to see him use these talents in a serious, non-genre novel.

Cynthia Grenier, in a review of "The Red Fox," in The American Spectator, *Vol. 18, No. 11, November, 1985, p. 47.*

Rachel Ingalls

19??-

American-born English short story writer and novelist.

Ingalls has gained critical respect for her fabulistic tales, most of which are classified as novellas or long short stories. Ingalls is particularly noted for her economical writing style and her ability to make the fantastic credible. Her fiction often centers on unfulfilled individuals involved in bizarre situations which serve to underscore their feelings of worthlessness yet offer them a means of escape from their unhappy lives.

In her first collection of short fiction, *Theft* (1970), Ingalls displays her characteristic grim tone, concise prose style, and use of the unexpected ending. The title novella, a contemporary retelling of the crucifixion of Jesus Christ, was regarded as a political allegory denouncing tyranny. In her subsequent collections, *Mediterranean Cruise* (1973) and *The Man Who Was Left Behind* (1974), Ingalls examines such themes as loneliness, friendship, and marriage, often from the viewpoints of male protagonists. One reviewer observed that the stories in the latter volume focus in different ways on "the fact of human vulnerability, the isolation and desolation from which most of us are protected by a few fragile relationships." In her recent collections, *Three of a Kind* (1985) and *The Pearlkillers* (1986), Ingalls examines human relationships within the context of supernatural occurrences involving fortune-telling, angelic visitations, jinxes, and ghosts.

Ingalls's novels utilize fantasy to examine female wish-fulfillment. In *Mrs. Caliban* (1982), a California housewife suffering from an inferiority complex has a brief love relationship with a gentle, human-like amphibian who helps her to overcome her marital problems and achieve a more positive self-image. Hermione Lee noted that "the diplomatic matter-of-factness of the narrative makes us accept the events without laughing at them," and the novel is considered by several critics to be among Ingalls's most accomplished works. In *Binstead's Safari* (1983), an abusive husband and his wife travel to Kenya, where the wife is transformed into a confident, independent woman through a love affair with a legendary lion hunter. After giving herself in death to a lion associated with her lover, she also becomes part of the country's legend. William Scammell described the novel as "a powerful female fantasy about initiation into perfect love and perfect death."

JANET BURROWAY

As political allegory, Rachel Ingalls's first novel *Theft* strikes [deep]. . . . Two brothers-in-law find themselves in the same jail for minor thefts. The position seems a relatively comfortable one at first, since they are looked after by a kind and cagey Greek warder, and outside there's a riot going on. What the riot is about we never precisely learn. The narrator, Seth, speaks of 'them' and 'us,' but 'we' might be black, or just poor, or just too far to the left in a place where martial law has been declared. In spite of this ambiguity, and Seth's na-

ïveté, the two brothers are vividly characterised: the hunger, the fruit-picking, the suspicions they have in common, their very different moral conclusions.

As the evening wears on the riot moves inside, and they share the jail with a moaning murderer, a rotten-toothed religious fanatic, a clutch of young militants who are on 'our' side and whom Seth finds revolting and incomprehensible—how can it help him that they pee on the wall?—and finally an older and tougher group of rioters. It is difficult properly to praise the ingenuity of the author without giving away the climax, which comes as what can only be described as a *literary* shock. William Golding has said that the purpose of his surprise endings is to force a second reading, and Rachel Ingalls might well make the same claim. Details that were merely colourful become part of an ingenious, not facile, pattern. This is a short book, and in some ways a young one. But there is more than promise in a first novel that is not decorated autobiography but a true fiction. (p. 280)

Janet Burroway, "Stark Stony," in New Statesman, *Vol. 80, No. 2059, September 4, 1970, pp. 279-80.*

THE TIMES LITERARY SUPPLEMENT

[In *Theft,* Miss Ingalls is] concerned with the way in which laws of society are weapons of tyranny; suffering individuals caught in the system may be innocent, may be the voice of freedom, peace, or love, yet their fate has been decided in advance. . . .

Miss Ingalls is . . . devious in leading us gradually to her Kafka-country. Jake and Seth, brothers-in-law getting cheerily drunk on beer to celebrate becoming a father, are used to being hungry, used to being bullied by the tax men and the military police who exploit ordinary simple fruit-pickers and farm-workers in this country of theirs (which has no name, no date). . . . Seth, who's scared of risking danger to the wife he loves, keeps out of Jake's political friendships. But both are arrested on trivial charges of theft in the market-place, and their friendly jailer, and expatriate Greek, warns them that things don't look good. . . .

A "religious nut", emaciated and raving of the assembly of the wicked, provides some disquieting entertainment for the guards. There's a lot of talk about the good life Seth and Jake have had despite their poverty, and about the dangers of idealism. But you realize suddenly, before Seth describes being dragged out to carry these great bits of wood, that this gaol is in Jerusalem, and that the "religious nut" is going to hang between them on a hill outside. It's an impressively shattering climax, and because Miss Ingalls doesn't attempt to go beyond it, or to suggest the practicalities of Seth's story, she succeeds in avoiding all the embarrassing tragic irony and self-conscious updated idiom which usually ruins any retelling of the Gospel drama. Seth and Jake may occasionally sound a little like Butch Cassidy and the Sundance Kid, but their bewilderment and beliefs are less incongruously expressed than the efforts of most trendy Christian voices radio listeners suffer. And Miss Ingalls writes with the kind of confidence and economy rare, and hopeful, in first novels by young women writers.

> *"Fables of Our Times," in* The Times Literary Supplement, *No. 3578, September 25, 1970, p. 1074.*

THE TIMES LITERARY SUPPLEMENT

Each of the three stories that make up this excellent book [*The Man Who Was Left Behind*]—the work of an author who is as sensitive as she is accomplished—deals in a different way with the fact of human vulnerability, the isolation and desolation from which most of us are protected only by a few fragile relationships. Once one of these is destroyed, the hairline balance of sanity as well as ordinary well-being is irrevocably upset. This is, however, an over-simplification of the material which Rachel Ingalls handles with the most deft technical assurance. Too often the accolade of "economy" is bestowed on writers whose prose is merely arid or insubstantial: this writer possesses the genuine gift—she assembles and places words with a precision that enables her to achieve her effects with the minimum fuss, so that each story finds and maintains its own pace.

["The Man Who Was Left Behind"] concerns an elderly man who, after an appalling family tragedy, becomes a sad, disorientated tramp in the North American town where he was once a respected and influential citizen. The other two stories are both set on the island of Rhodes and are about precarious marriages, but they are very different in content and approach. It would be no service at all to reveal more of the plots: suffice it to say that each ends with a moving, perhaps mildly surprising, climax that is truly a climax and no mere twist.

Miss Ingalls sets up a scene with skill and speed whether it is a cold Northern town, a Mexican landscape or a Greek village. Brief images . . . are aptly and imaginatively realized. Her characterization is admirable, with central figures as well as with the supporting cast, and here the author's accurate ear for dialogue helps her significantly.

Most important, perhaps, of her many qualities is Miss Ingalls's ability to establish in remarkably few paragraphs the whole complex background in the lives of her central characters, so that they are as fully rounded and credible as those in most longer novels and the piquancy or poignancy of their immediate circumstances in the stories has all the more impact. A thoroughly admirable achievement.

> *"Disorient Express," in* The Times Literary Supplement, *No. 3754, February 15, 1974, p. 149.*

LORNA SAGE

[*The Man Who Was Left Behind* consists] of three stories about the fatal innocence of Americans abroad, mental travellers whose paths are littered with real destruction. Miss Ingalls writes impatiently, as though each time she has to cram the whole of her characters' lives into the one climactic movement. The effect is unhappy: rather like those tragedies that are all fifth act, where the sought-after intensity and concentration are dissipated in ungainly flashbacks that try to smuggle in the missing pieces. What you win on the roundabouts, you lose on the swings, and the conventional proprieties have their revenge.

Nonetheless, the most important meanings struggle through. The story that comes off best, "**Something to Write Home About,**" unfolds a crazy, utterly unexpected pattern behind the stream of bright postcards a young wife sends her mother. There's a distinctive, sinister inventiveness about this sort of revelation that makes Miss Ingalls, for all her overdoing, a force to be reckoned with.

> *Lorna Sage, "Undoing the Past," in* The Observer, *March 10, 1974, p. 33.*

ALAN BROWNJOHN

One of the skilful features of Rachel Ingalls's new novel [*Mrs Caliban*] . . . is its capacity to keep the reader storing clues and hints in the memory in case they all have some relevance to a wider plan to be revealed in its final pages. In the event, most of them do not; and the proliferation of loose ends left untied means that one needs an ability to be charmed or intrigued by weird bits of detail which exist purely for their own sake in order to enjoy the novel. *Mrs Caliban* is certainly not the sort of allegory that appeals to those who want their fictions to work with the efficiency and consistency of an intricate machine, in which everything relates to everything else.

Dorothy and Fred are fully aware that after the accidental death of their only child, and a subsequent miscarriage, their marriage is drifting through inanition towards a break-up. . . . We are in suburban America, and there is sudden and alarming media coverage of the escape of a sea-creature from an Institute of Oceanographic Research. This is "Aquarius the Monster-man", and all six foot seven of him, walking and talking and consuming the sticks of celery she offers, enters Dorothy's kitchen, transforming her life by becoming her house-guest . . . and her lover. The monster, who is soon familiarly known as Larry, is a lost and simple life-force restored to Dorothy, a creature of brutal innocence who gives her a sense of purpose and a new joy in existing.

Larry, unfortunately, ought to bring more symbolic weight and conviction than he does to the action that follows, where perfunctory discussions with Dorothy about nature and nurture, the strange habits of civilized beings, and the purpose of living, fail to prove particularly trenchant or profound. Rachel Ingalls weaves her philosophical comments into a set of episodes involving Larry (he is heavily disguised so that people cannot see he is a huge green frog) and Dorothy in night-drives which take them to the sea, and to a mysterious garden of bamboo trees and elegant sofas. She has Dorothy's daytime activities ... focus on a cool and slightly bitchy friendship with Estelle. Estelle is a decent enough parody of liberated American womanhood, who in turn lifts Dorothy out of her restricted home life with visits to ''the studios'', and uses her as a listening ear for her own troubles. There is a suggestion of gentle satire about their conversations concerning consumer goods, lovers and children, but it remains too elusive to catch. The narrative is altogether rather vague and inconsequential (even dreamlike stories can have more vigour); and is all the time leading to a dénouement in that same bamboo garden, and the revelation of the point which a watchful reader will have guessed for some time.

Several readily identifiable fables lie behind *Mrs Caliban,* supplying it with most of the little power and excitement it possesses as a shot at macabre moral fantasy. But merely blending the ingredients of the frog prince, the beauty and her beast, and Shakespeare's monster from the sea, and stirring them all into a modern setting rendered with scarcely any depth or thoroughness, does not seem enough. Miss Ingalls's prose shows some signs of delicacy and astute organization. Sadly, in this novel it wastes itself in the service of a tale which, long before a predictable conclusion, lapses into the purest banality.

> Alan Brownjohn, ''The Age of Aquarius,'' in The Times Literary Supplement, No. 4110, January 8, 1982, p. 35.

CAROLINE MOOREHEAD

It is eight years since Rachel Ingalls published her last book, a collection of short stories called *The Man who was left behind,* highly praised at the time by critics. *Mrs Caliban* is worth the wait: a delicate and infinitely precise novel, not quite science fiction, but somewhere in the realms of fantasy. It makes a lot of contemporary fiction seem boorish and obvious.

The setting is American suburbia. A young woman, Dorothy, who has recently lost both a small son and an unborn baby, takes in and protects a freak man-frog, a 'monsterman' captured not long before off South America and now escaped from torturing scientists.... Against a background of small town adultery and friendships, beautifully touched on and bitterly accurate, Dorothy and Larry—as the scientists named him— become lovers. She describes to him the deceptions and crises of her life; he tells her about the sea whence he came, and about the way he has been treated by his captors. He is curious about what he sees and hears around him. The explanations Dorothy gives him about human behaviour and customs make touching and absurd reading.

Once you accept the frog, and the obvious metaphors, there is nothing extravagant about *Mrs Caliban.* And since the frog is human in speech and character, and also exceptionally pleasant,

there is no testing of credulity in their fondness and need for each other, nor in the dreadful sense of loss of the outcome.

Rachel Ingalls is a remarkable writer, able to convey, in a single phrase or line of dialogue, an entire rounded scene. Her ear for speech and its context, both inflections and gestures, is faultless. The physical details of life ... are conjured up with a brevity of words that is very powerful. The characters too come complete with past and expectations. This is economy at its best: full of sense and suggestion, never empty or bald. (pp. 20-1)

> Caroline Moorehead, ''Obsessions,'' in The Spectator, Vol. 248, No. 8008, January 9, 1982, pp. 20-1.

MELVYN BRAGG

[*Mrs Caliban*] is very rum indeed. Into the private desperations of the American suburbia of affluent marital warfare [Ingalls] introduces a monster....

The story of the monster's intrusion into Dorothy's life and the consequent mayhem is told with an uncanny lightness of touch. This author, though, has always told her stories with wit but here she excels herself in making the monstrous acceptable. For the monster—a useful contender for any Science Fiction Chamber of Aliens—is tamed by Dorothy's welcoming care. He makes love to her, eats her avocado pears, chats away about the oddities of the complicated society which human beings have made for themselves, goes back to his oceanic habitat for a nightly swim and develops a liking for television, Merce Cunningham and flowers. It all makes you smile but it never makes you laugh. Rachel Ingalls's great gift for language and time keeps you hooked on the end of her line and she reels in the story like an expert fly fisherman.

American adultery as a tortured and tolerated way of life gets a surprisingly lengthy stretch of attention in such a short book. The friendship between Dorothy and the dynamic Estelle is described with ease and that feeling of social authenticity so hard to achieve, so often disdained by modern novelists who simply cannot do it. What suffers is the melodramatic plot. The revelations are a little too heavily signalled, the ending merely disastrous rather than tragic.

That's if you read it for realism. This apparently plain and straightforward Gothic tale can also be read as a total fantasy. The depressed fantasy of a woman left too much alone, conjuring (like Ariel) out of the radio waves the monster of innocence and desire (like Caliban) who will come and restore her. If the monsterman were to be extracted from the story then Dorothy's behaviour and its consequences would still make sense. More *sense,* of course, than the picture of her driving down to the beach with a superhuman frog in dark glasses and over-sized sandals. Rachel Ingalls manages to transmit both possibilities without being clever-clever and without cheating.

It is difficult to imagine an odder or more strangely entertaining novel being published this year.

> Melvyn Bragg, ''The Hulk's Gal,'' in Punch, Vol. 282, No. 7368, February 3, 1982, p. 201.

HERMIONE LEE

Rachel Ingalls writes with complexity and distinction within a ... modest space. *Mrs Caliban,* her last novel, oddly and hauntingly described a gentle love-affair between a suburban housewife and a giant-sized green sea-monster, a kind of grown-ups' E.T. *Binstead's Safari* also risks the subject of an instant, extreme love which edges over into magic. As before, [Ingalls] is not fey or soppy about this, but, rather, grave, careful and sombre.

Stan Binstead, an American folklorist, reluctantly takes his wife Millie, whom he dislikes, to London and to Africa in his research on cults of animal worship. In London, Millie's miserable dependence on Stan drops from her; by the time they are on safari she is popular, adventurous and alive and he is full of anxiety and dread. This marital shift is concisely set up as a preface to the central magic story of Millie's encounters with her hunter/lover/lion and Stan's quest for a lion-cult.

Several levels are delicately sustained: Millie's dream-like transformation takes place inside a 'frame' of ominous offstage feuds and killings, in a world where the idea of lion-hunting as a 'test' is vanishing (Hemingway is ironically invoked) and heroes are no longer useful except in myths. It is an interesting novel about folklore and heroism, and, most strikingly, it is a beautiful and restrained celebration of the happiness of love....

Hermione Lee, "Soap-Operatics," in The Observer, May 8, 1983, p. 31.

ADAM MARS-JONES

Millie Binstead, the central character of Rachel Ingalls's new novel [*Binstead's Safari*], has by the beginning of the book reached a state of tacit marital breakdown. Her husband Stan, an anthropologist whose sensitivity decreases exponentially the nearer he comes to dealing with his own tribe, spends most of his time—with considerable success—trying to make her feel worthless.

[When Stan plans] a trip to Africa, to investigate rumours of a new lion-cult, Millie uses no sentimental manoeuvres; she just says she wants a holiday....

On previous form Millie should have been as cowed and subservient in London, where they prepared for their safari, as she had always been in America; but in fact she started to make a life for herself....

[Millie] has already made a conquest before [she and Stan] leave the city for the wilds; she has met the glance, through a shop-window into which she was absent-mindedly gazing, of an infinitely charismatic and attractive man. He courts her, seduces her, and manages to send messages to her when she is up-country; she finds she is pregnant (something she has never achieved with Stan), and decides quite calmly to divorce her husband and remarry.

Her lover, Harry "Simba" Lewis, turns out to be a legendary figure in the area: his nickname "lion" was given to him when he survived the initiation-ritual of the Masai, which involves single combat with an enraged lion. The suggestion gains ground as the book proceeds that he is also capable of turning himself into a lion at will, and that he is the supernatural source of the lion-cults that Stan wants to investigate.

His supernatural powers, though, have their limitations, and he is killed by poachers. Thereafter a massive lion starts putting in appearances near the Binsteads' party, exhibiting behaviour that baffles experienced lion-hunters, but Millie suffers a relapse into her previous acquiescence to Stan's idea of her. The lion, though, has plans for Millie and Stan, and eventually claims them both.

Without its supernatural element, *Binstead's Safari* would look uncomfortably like a routine novel of marital unease and adjustment, with some oddly old-fashioned assumptions; Millie, after all, gets the strength she needs to reject Stan from another man, and there is cliché enough in the plot-line of the oppressed wife miraculously transformed by romance.

Stan's psychology is likewise none too convincing; he examines his past as the novel proceeds, and comes to realize that he has always felt inferior to his brother, who was killed in the Korean War and is therefore exempt from failure. He has always taken his resentment out on Millie.

But even with its trappings of premonition and eeriness, *Binstead's Safari* fails to combine satisfactorily its *genres*. It has its share of captivating moments—at one point Stan fails to notice that the natives, in their songs about the Lion's Bride, are referring to his once-dowdy spouse—but as a whole it fails to transcend its elements of adventure-story and of novelette.

Adam Mars-Jones, "Lionized," in The Times Literary Supplement, No. 4180, May 13, 1983, p. 481.

WILLIAM SCAMMELL

The setting [of *Binstead's Safari*] is Hemingwayesque, and so are the descriptions of lion-hunting, and the values of the hunter.... But the feel of the novel is very different, rather like that of *Jane Eyre* transposed into a new key: a powerful female fantasy about initiation into perfect love and perfect death.... [Stan Binstead is] an anthropologist out to track down a living oral culture, and with him goes Millie, his neglected and unloved wife. Once in Africa she blossoms, falls in love with Harry Lewis, a charismatic hunter who might or might not be exploiting his own cult amongst the villagers, and goes ecstatically to her death at the hands, or rather teeth, of a 'lion of lions', who is identified with her dead lover. Few male novelists would dare to write such atavistic celebrations of courage, virility, and heroism nowadays, I imagine; it is the very stuff of a Mills & Boon romance, but raised to an almost convincing level. The mechanics of the plot creak a bit—violent deaths occur as casually as cocktails, and the way in which Stan Binstead and his guides blaze away happily at big game strikes me as anachronistic in these conservationist days; but Rachel Ingalls is stalking the irrefutability of dream rather than a slice of life. The fantasy doesn't quite succeed in extricating itself from literary models, perhaps, but it promises interesting things to come, not least a writer who can write. (p. 132)

William Scammell, "One- and Last-Liners," in London Magazine, n.s. Vol. 23, Nos. 5 & 6, August-September, 1983, pp. 129-33.

JACI STEPHEN

In *Three of a Kind* [published in the United States as *I See a Long Journey*], Rachel Ingalls proves her mastery, which has already brought her considerable critical acclaim, over the novella form.

Of the three, *Blessed Art Thou* is the most original, and although there is a serious "message" being preached, at no time does it detract from the sense of the bizarre or the humour of the situation.

In a California monastery, Brother Anselm claims he has had sexual relations with the Angel Gabriel. Subsequent events turn the whole question of sexuality, sexism and the church, upside down. . . .

I See a Long Journey and *On Ice* are as skilled in their consistency of tone, although their endings are more "forced". Most refreshing in all three is the resistance to pass direct authorial judgement and comment when the narrative is at its most ironic.

Jaci Stephen, "Sleepless Nights," in The Times Educational Supplement, *No. 3617, October 25, 1985, p. 56.*

COLIN GREENLAND

Two of Rachel Ingalls's latest novellas [in *Three of a Kind*] feature nasty things happening to American tourists; in the third, an unsuspecting Californian monk embraces a most peculiar miracle. None of [Ingalls's] victims intends to invoke the visitation, nor is it a routine matter of hubris and nemesis. Simply, it seems, the otherworld is there, humming in the unconsidered spaces around the individual life, waiting to strike like lightning. A certain fixity of habit achieved, a certain level of discontent tolerated, and it descends, unannounced and implacable, to take over.

As with Dorothy in *Mrs Caliban* . . . , who fell in love with a man from under the sea, and Millie in *Binstead's Safari* (1983), who found herself betrothed to an African lion-god, it is a displacement of sexuality that first signals the imminence of catastrophe. In *I See a Long Journey,* Flora and James are a wealthy couple from a famous and powerful American family; their equable, taciturn chauffeur Michael is a lifelong friend of James's. After a stormy beginning, Flora has settled down in her role as the "elegant young matron in magazine pictures". Only her secret, groundless infatuation with Michael lingers to indicate that she is not fully resigned to her luxurious lot. Rather than elaborate the mundane, primate geometry of this triangle, Ingalls shifts it to the Far East where, at a countryside temple, Flora seeks the vatic judgment of a juvenile goddess. Something disrupts the triangle: whether it is the casual violence of the streets or something more numinous and savage, Ingalls keeps perfectly unclear. It is not so far from the central situation of *A Passage to India.*

In the opening paragraphs of the second story, *On Ice,* we learn that Beverley from Missouri is going skiing in Austria with her German lover, ten years her senior. By now this is enough to warn us of an avalanche ahead. Ingalls, however, teases such suspicions gently: the boyfriend is a minor character, and the moralizing sentiments that might have prevailed to doom the unwise relationship as told in a romantic novelette are here given to a vacuous, evangelizing preppie called Angela. The villain is someone quite unexpected, Beverley's fate quite undeserved. *On Ice* is like a horror story, without a moral. . . .

The fantastic or violent interruptions Ingalls describes are made especially cogent by the even tenor of her prose. *Blessed Art Thou,* the third story in this volume, is the most overtly playful and satirical. It would be a disservice to reveal anything more of the joke than the title itself does. . . . Ingalls deftly sketches a series of comic portraits: management-oriented Brother Frederick, grimly bigoted Brother Adrian, impressionable Brother Dominic, and laxly transcendental Brother Elmo, who had "received the call, so he said, on a trip". All struggle to come to terms with the spectacular sin of the unrepentant Brother Anselm, ex-surfer. . . . The tone and palette of *Blessed Art Thou*

are quite different from those of the other stories; yet the pattern of sexual digression and subsequent apocalypse persists.

Ingalls is too subtle a writer to confine her fiction to the mechanisms of Gothic or farce. She has been justly praised for originality and precision. Yet her fiction does not always show the economy of structure conventionally practised in the genres she sometimes echoes. *I See a Long Journey* opens with four pages of confusing and quite unnecessary circumstantial detail about how Flora came to marry James; *On Ice* makes a similarly jerky if less dilatory start. Some kind editor should perhaps have lent the author a blue pencil.

Colin Greenland, "The Hum of the Otherworld," in The Times Literary Supplement, *No. 4308, October 25, 1985, p. 1202.*

VICTORIA GLENDINNING

Three of a Kind consists of three stories, "of a kind" in that in each the trusting central character is in a false situation from which only magic or a miracle can save her. Two of the stories [*On Ice* and *I See a Long Journey*] display an appalled distaste for super-rich Americans, cut off from humanity by the need to protect their money and even their lives. The third story [*Blessed Art Thou*] is set in a monastery, where prejudice imposes equally destructive codes. A monk who miraculously conceives after a visitation from the Angel Gabriel makes the author's point that

> Anything could happen in life, and everything did, only most people were so unaware, so lacking in powers of observation, that they did not notice.

That is what Rachel Ingalls's novels have been about too. Her writing is always spare, but in these sketchy narratives there is no space for her unearthly imagination to take a hold on the reader. Though the three stories are full of small brilliant bites they leave you hungry for something more substantial. But she's good, a true original, and we must be grateful for what we get.

Victoria Glendinning, "Lying in Wait for Love," in The Sunday Times, *London, November 3, 1985, p. 45.*

JACK BEATTY

[*Mrs. Caliban* is a] tour de force about a passionate affair between a lonely housewife and a six-foot-tall green monster gifted with a confiding manner—imagine Phil Donahue in the body of an elongated frog. (I know many of you will cease reading at the mention of a monster; I would myself if I were in your place. You must take my word for it: the novel justifies its monster.) (pp. 16, 18)

With a style spare and elegant, and in a quietly compelling fictional voice, Ingalls makes the housewife's love for the monster not only credible but moving. "Dorothy," with the Oz association no doubt intended, is the housewife; the monster she calls "Larry," as if to mitigate the odious marvel of him. Larry has escaped from a local laboratory—we are in California—where cruel scientists, having captured him in the jungle, have tortured him into learning English. . . . In making his escape Larry has killed two of his keepers, and radio bulletins have made their terrible murders known to Dorothy long before the moment when the monster, not yet "Larry," comes through her kitchen door and looks her inscrutably in the face.... A fantastical scene, yet by this point we have learned enough about the dolors of young Dorothy—her dead son, miscarried baby, unfaithful husband—that we understand why she hides Larry. More, we know why she falls in love with him. As in Renaissance tragedy the violation of the natural order made by their interspecies coupling—woman with amphibian—cracks open the moral universe, and betrayals, murders, and ghastly accidents pour out in profusion. By turns droll and erotic for most of the way, *Mrs. Caliban* ends in a blaze of Shakespearean evil. (p. 18)

Jack Beatty, in a review of "Mrs. Caliban," in The Atlantic Monthly, *Vol. 257, No. 4, April, 1986, pp. 16, 18.*

JONATHAN KEATES

[The] four stories in *The Pearlkillers* are possessed by a knowingness that at times is awing in its perspectives.

When, for instance, Carla's great-aunt Regina in **"Inheritance"** offers her a black velvet box containing a blob of shrivelled brown matter, like burned meat, on the end of a gilt chain, the thing becomes ours to play with. It is, maybe, one of those pearls the family skin has a reputation for destroying or, given the ghoulish air of festivity and ceremonial colouring the occasion, something altogether more predictably macabre. She leaves us not merely holding the solution, but with a sense that whichever ambiguity we settle for will disclose something of our own nature.

This is even more apparent in the triumphant inevitability of **"Captain Hendrik's Story,"** to whose sheer formal grandeur it is difficult to think of a modern parallel. After years of absence a Scandinavian explorer returns to his family, armed with an official account of his adventures, which they eagerly accept: the truth, far more luridly grotesque than anything Hendrik could possibly have devised, only emerges when his ravaged, mephistophelean partner in crime turns up to blackmail him. The reader realises that this is what he has wanted to happen, and the tale, without ever losing its grasp, becomes an investigation of all those moral shadowings and veilings that fiction itself involves.

Jonathan Keates, "Archetypes of Ambiguity," in The Observer, *April 20, 1986, p. 24.*

PATRICIA CRAIG

[Blight] is the theme of Rachel Ingalls's pungent quartet of stories [*The Pearlkillers*]. 'Pearlkillers' are people whose skin rots pearls: involuntary destroyers. So, we have Lily, twice widowed in Vietnam ..., finding solace in thoughts of Ancient Egypt and the cult of Isis, and finally making it to Cairo on her third—reluctant—honeymoon. **"Third Time Lucky"** is the ironic title. In **"People to People"** a group of university students, twenty years on, is faced with exposure of the truth about a night of high jinks when one of their classmates met his end. That past death engenders five in the present. In **"Captain Hendrik's Story"**—the longest of the four—a shooting is undertaken, once again, to keep something dark: in this case, the dissipated activities of a Swedish sea captain, who'd been whooping it up in Vienna all the time he was supposed to be lost in a jungle in South America. Ingalls has a calm way of presenting her ornamental imaginings which is highly effective.

Patricia Craig, "Belfast Book," in London Review of Books, *Vol. 8, No. 10, June 5, 1986, p. 19.*

CAROL ERON

In this witty, macabre collection of stories [*I See a Long Journey*], everyone is looking for love. The trouble is the quest for love can be a very long journey, particularly if, like the people in these tales, you do not know exactly who you are....

Fortunately, a lot happens to these rather dull, passive characters, and Rachel Ingalls achieves the considerable feat of writing about dull people without ever being dull. How does she do it? For one thing, these are tales of fantasy and the people are not intended to seem quite real, though they do talk, argue and, occasionally, scream. These characters represent ideas which Ingalls sets deftly in opposition to each other. Also, she knows how to tell a tale.

At first life seems normal. In the first novella, *I See a Long Journey,* a rather ordinary wealthy couple (except that she married a man she does not love) plans a vacation. In the second tale, *On Ice,* a couple takes off for a ski holiday. In the last story, *Blessed Art Thou,* a young monk enters a chapel for confession. But in all three cases the situation starts to slide immediately, though so subtly you feel uneasy without knowing why. Indeed, it is not clear that there is any cause at all for unease until the sudden violent endings.

We move from the improbable in the first story to the impossible in the second to the completely outrageous in the third, where a lonely young monk, Brother Anselm, is visited by an angel. The angel makes love to him—with a truly incredible result. "It isn't possible it could be another divine birth," the director of the monastery pronounces, but the monks furiously debate the phenomenon that has occurred in their midst. Is it a medical anomaly, an evil trick, a monster, a miracle? Holy or unholy? Will it be an ordinary human birth or, as one monk proposes, a phantom pregnancy caused by the brother's neurotic craving to become the object of his devotion, the Virgin Mary? Above all, what to do about it? ...

It is all very funny, though much is said tongue-in-cheek by the man-turned-woman about faith, love, chaos and woman's vulnerability. As those in power close in around him, Anselm ruminates: "He had always imagined that women enjoyed a special kind of freedom ... but now he saw that they were just as trapped as men." This story, like the others, comes to tragedy, though Ingalls is a master at making you laugh right before you gasp in horror.

A sharp observer of the psychodynamics of a certain kind of male-female relationship, Ingalls draws out the "hidden manipulation" lurking behind apparently benign behavior, even a kind word or pat on the hand. Usually the manipulation is perpetrated by men, decent enough types by the way, who in contrast to the women simply know how to get what they want. Yes, these are cautionary tales, but you will hardly notice you have been lectured until later, because the stories work together to deliver their lesson from three very different points of view.

An American who has lived for many years in England, Ingalls is the author of the novel, *Mrs. Caliban,* among other books. She is not well known in [the United States], though she deserves to be. There is talent and energy here, and these stories stay in the mind.

Carol Eron, "Brother Anselm and the Angel," in Book World—The Washington Post, *August 24, 1986,* p. 8.

ANNE BERNAYS

The three novellas in *I See a Long Journey,* by the author of the novel *Mrs. Caliban,* are ice and fire—they take you to places you don't usually go. Rachel Ingalls . . . in at least one of these stories (the last) has managed to supply something Nabokov demanded of fiction, namely, "esthetic bliss." . . .

[*I See a Long Journey*], which leads off the book, is about Flora, who marries James, "the most important of the heirs" to an immense fortune. . . . [To Flora, it] seemed odd that a woman should live in a house as large as a castle, with nothing to do all day but easy, pleasant, tasks, and still need a rest. But it was true." Flora falls into a deep depression.

To coax her out of it, James suggests they take a journey to an unnamed city in the Far East, accompanied by their bodyguard-chauffeur, Michael. . . . James, Flora and Michael visit a strange temple presided over by a child goddess, and it is from this point that Ms. Ingalls leads us farther into the territory of fantasy and actual chaos, mingled and mixed. The ending is a shocker, the sort of conclusion that makes you go right back to the beginning and read the whole thing over again.

The second novella, *On Ice,* is a carefully plotted tale in which events seem to flow or melt into one another. Beverley, a young American woman, and her German boyfriend, Claus (10 years her senior and "already a settled man: a doctor"), go to a Swiss mountain resort for a week of skiing. . . . As in the first story, Ms. Ingalls invites the reader on a seemingly innocent journey and then delivers the *coup de grâce*. But instead of finishing us off, she takes us out the other side and into a world of feelings that are buried in most of us.

The third novella, *Blessed Art Thou,* is an inverted saint's life. It is extremely funny, singular, perhaps a masterpiece. Brother Anselm, a personable monk in a California wine-producing monastery, is visited one night by the angel Gabriel, who gets him pregnant. . . . What happens after this makes up the bulk of the story and is largely a brilliantly dramatized examination of the range of philosophical attitudes toward an "impossible" event, such as "I think we should bring back the old practices and burn you at the stake" and "How can it be unnatural if it's happened?"

Meanwhile, the other monks get drunk on their own wine and discuss politics, religion and what on earth to do about Brother Anselm, who has his enemies as well as his supporters. None of the brothers, however, has the faintest idea how it happened or what it means. . . . Ms. Ingalls maneuvers so skillfully into this fantasy that you simply believe it and want to help make Anselm comfortable in his confinement, along with his friends who bring him pillows for his back and shyly ask to see his breasts. Again, as in the two previous stories, the ending is both unexpected and disturbing.

Ms. Ingalls's prose is crisp, clear and inflected with the kind of ironic overtones that stamp it contemporary. She has married this prose to fictional devices borrowed from an earlier time. The result is rich and wide-ranging. There is something salutary about a writer who rejects what she cannot use—the present tense, minimalism, the ending that trails off into the mist— and uses what she cannot bear to reject—the architectural plot, the surprise narrative spin. Ms. Ingalls is an original. She is right up there with the masters of the novella.

Anne Bernays, "Brother Anselm, in a Family Way," in The New York Times Book Review, *August 31, 1986, p. 9.*

David (Michael) Jones

1895-1974

English poet and essayist.

Jones's work reflects his deep concern with humanity's decreasing interest in the past and with the depersonalizing effects of technology. He created symbolic and highly allusive works by blending his knowledge of history, legend, and literature with elements of the Roman Catholic liturgy. In his best-known books, *In Parenthesis* (1937) and *The Anathemata: Fragments of an Attempted Writing* (1952), Jones interspersed verse and prose passages, lyrical descriptions, concepts from such fields as myth, anthropology, and geology, formal and colloquial language, and the legends of his Welsh heritage. The experimental forms and wide range of cultural references in his works led some critics to link Jones with the Modernist movement. Jones worked in a variety of art forms, and his books are adorned with his watercolor paintings, engravings, and sketches. Many of Jones's writings were published as fragments and drafts; critics generally believe that he intended his artistic output to be a single, unified work that was never completed.

Jones's first book, *In Parenthesis,* is based upon his experiences as an infantry soldier during World War I and draws upon the Arthurian legends of Thomas Malory, the Welsh stories of the *Mabinogion,* and the medieval battle epic *Y Gododdin.* Depicting an Anglo-Welsh regiment and its eventual participation in the Somme offensive, *In Parenthesis,* as Thomas Dilworth noted, is "a profound and shattering disclosure of combat's physical destruction and spiritual outrage, which is sustained by a controlled and variegated tone lacking in the work of the combatant poets who wrote during the war." While most chroniclers of World War I concentrated on the inhumanity of battle, Jones perceived the war as evidence of the continuing decline of Western civilization. This regression began during an era Jones and others termed "the Break," when, as D. S. Carne-Ross explained, "man stepped clear of his past and turned his back on all the previous history of the race." This historical breach, in Jones's opinion, resulted in humanity's growing dependence on technology and alienation from history.

The Anathemata comprises eight interrelated sections that trace the development of civilization since the earth's formation. Crucial to this work is Jones's belief in the artist as "maker" and the concept of art as a gratuitous action made in sacrament to the glory of God. *The Anathemata* is composed as a daydream of a man witnessing the Consecration of the Catholic Mass, which is seen as the archetype of all artistic creation. The book's antiphonal structure and devotional title further emphasize its sacramental intent. Although the esoteric elements and hermetic qualities of *The Anathemata* led some critics to fault it as obscure, others contended that the demanding reading is ultimately rewarding.

In the pieces collected in *The Sleeping Lord and Other Fragments* (1974), Jones continued to examine Western culture through Welsh lore and historical allusions. In "The Hunt" and "The Sleeping Lord," for example, the Welsh landscape is portrayed as the slumbering body of King Arthur, a symbolic Christ figure whose reawakening will redeem Wales. "The

Photograph by Mark Gerson

Tutelar of the Place" concerns a feminine spirit who protects ancient Wales from Roman military advances and encroaching industrialization. Other pieces in *The Sleeping Lord* center on a group of soldiers during the last days of the Roman empire. These soldiers, often speaking in contemporary British vernacular, represent parallels between the decaying regime and twentieth-century Western society.

Interest in Jones's work has increased through the posthumous publications *Introducing David Jones: A Selection of His Writings* (1980) and *The Roman Quarry and Other Sequences* (1981). *The Roman Quarry,* consisting of previously unpublished pieces and unrevised manuscripts from Jones's books, has earned high praise from critics, as reflected by Guy Davenport's assessment: "Scholars are right to publish these fragments, for they make evident the richness and painstaking care of Jones's fertile talent." Jones's essays, collected in *Epoch and Artist: Selected Writings* (1959) and *The Dying Gaul and Other Writings* (1978), further elucidate the themes of his poetry. The sagacity of Jones's essays prompted Joseph Schwartz to comment: "They are the product of a visionary, erudite, highly original, and utterly sincere mind. . . . What [Jones] does so splendidly in them is to remind one of the profound significance of tradition, of what we inherit, of our responsibility for that magnificent heritage, and of our need to be innovative in keeping it lively."

(See also *CLC*, Vols. 2, 4, 7, 13; *Contemporary Authors*, Vols. 9-12, rev. ed., Vols. 53-56 [obituary]; and *Dictionary of Literary Biography*, Vol. 20.)

KATHLEEN RAINE

For David Jones knowledge is inseparable from love; we can only "know" in a living and real sense what we love. The poet must 'work within the limits of love. There must be no muggings-up, no "ought to know" or "try to feel"; for only what is actually loved and known can be seen *sub specie aeternitatis*.' The images the poet uses must be 'significant and warm'; true for the heart as well as for the mind.

For David the "actually loved and known" must therefore be in the first place experienced. In this sense we can only love and know whatever comes to hand; those things we know as children, the soldiers David as a little boy got out of bed to watch as they rode past his parents' house; his mother putting him back to bed afterwards; the tools of his grandfather's craft of boat-building; the Welsh songs his father sang. The first test of what is ours is that it is "given." Although this is arbitrary, yet in a world whose texture is woven without a break from past to future, our own place in that unbroken web is far from arbitrary: it is our situation within a totality common to all. "Nowness" is for David all-important; it is where we stand in our relation to the whole of the past and the whole of the future; it is where past and future meet, are actualised and incarnated. 'I have made a heap of all I could find'—so he begins his preface to *The Anathémata:* 'Part of my task has been to allow myself to be directed by motifs gathered together from such sources as have by accident been available to me and to make a work out of those mixed data.'

Most readers of David Jones find great difficulty in coming to terms with his particular sources. Few know the Welsh language, or even the Welsh mythology; though most of us feel that the Arthurian legends are in some sense our own. Again, the Latin liturgy of the Catholic Church is unfamiliar to most English readers, even those who may be Christian. David's third field of experience is the trench warfare of the first World War; again an experience known at first hand to few of his readers now though still probably—at least superficially—more within everyman's imaginative reach than the other two. And yet he does not insist upon our sharing his particular knowledge or terms of reference: rather he seeks to remind us that we each have our own. This may indeed be the real difficulty; for there are many readers who would rather be given by an author a whole heap of information, however remote, than be quietly reminded, on every page, that everyman has his own unique place in a total mythus; be sent, as it were, in search of his own ways of access into experiences which only so can the author share with us. (pp. 9-10)

It is participation in what David Jones calls some 'cultural mythus' that makes us civilised; barbarism can invade from within any society which allows its traditions to be forgotten. David himself had no illusions about the dangers of our own situation. He saw it as the end, if not of all civilisation, at all events of *a* civilisation, the two thousand years of European Christendom, which itself rests upon two thousand years of Egyptian and Hebrew civilisation. This terminal situation is in a sense the occasion (though not the theme) of all his work.

David, though he often, and with powerful exactitude, gave expression to his fears for the future nevertheless thought it important to build upon such fragments of the living tradition as he himself had inherited. It is by default that the cultural mythus is lost; it must be renewed in a living present. This renewal of an inherited mythus David Jones has surely accomplished. There is about all his work that element of "nowness"—as he calls it—which he saw as an essential mark of all significant art.

The generation which has succeeded that of David Jones and the two living writers he most admired (Eliot and Joyce) seems to have largely lost the historic sense. For David history was not something merely learned but the space within which he lived. For him the past was all contemporaneous; and this not because he or anyone else knew more than a few fragments of the past but because time is an unbroken unity within which we are situated. He never saw any present object—horses or daffodils no less than such human *signa* as Roman inscriptions or the Catholic liturgy—without being aware of its dimension in history; a dimension not of natural science but of human experience. Perhaps a watershed now lies between these three great writers who could still use history as their sounding-board and a generation who seems more at home with ever-contemporaneous nature than with man, to whom alone history belongs. I think of St. John Perse, for whom history was itself a branch of natural history. Have we then already entered the new dark age foretold by Eliot and certainly also feared by David Jones? (pp. 11-12)

David writes as if his range of knowledge were just what for him had happened to come to hand; and in a sense this is so. Had his father's family not come from Wales, he would hardly have incorporated into his work all those Welsh names and place-names which give so much trouble to his Anglo-Saxon readers, who might fairly protest that the author should think of his public. He did also "happen to" serve in the British army; and the Christian religion also "happened" to be his inheritance, though not in its Catholic form. But as David would have seen it, however far some Protestant sect may have deviated, it still remains a branch, or at least a twig, upon the single tree of Christendom, of which the Roman church is the bole. For David Jones, who traced all back to beginnings, it was not a mere personal or aesthetic preference that led him to the Catholic faith, but the indivisibility of history; to have called himself a Christian in a less than total sense; to have dissociated himself from the total past of the Church would not have seemed possible to him. Nor was he (though deeply studious of the Catholic liturgy and of Thomist theology) sectarian; I have more than once heard him speak with familiar affection of those Welsh Methodist hymns which are likewise part of the cultural mythus of Wales.

But David Jones is not a personal writer: he is a national writer, a bard in the strict sense of the word. He invites us to participate not in a private world but in a shared and objective world, to which each of us is attached by the same texture of living strands as is the poet himself. The discovery of these fine, devious, yet living threads of attachment in ourselves likewise is powerfully effected by David's writings. His poetic intention is to make us aware of the whole historic context in which we participate. . . . (pp. 13-14)

It is not necessary that the reader should share the poet's background of exact knowledge: what does matter is that the poet is writing from such a background. The reader is aware, even when ignorant of their relevance, of certain names and allusions that we take on trust in the knowledge that these are firm foundation in a real, and therefore in a shared world. They may or may not awaken our curiosity to follow up the clues the writing offers; in either case they establish a historical retrospect; and because they are pieces of reality they do somewhere link up with whatever similar, though different, pieces we may ourselves possess. The poet does not thrust his own facts upon us, but rather uses these to remind us of our own, often untreasured but none the less precious, fragments of the same totality. (p. 16)

In both his completed works, and also in his wonderful fragment *The Sleeping Lord,* the experience narrated is a collective experience. *In Parenthesis* is the more accessible, for the soldiers who together go into battle are individual persons with names and faces and turns of speech; of whom the central figure, John Ball (to all intents and purposes David himself) is one in that companionship of the army described by the phrase *idem in me*. David himself considered it a less important work than *The Anathémata,* and most of his critics agree, though not perhaps most of his readers. The hero, we feel, should have a human face. The collective central Person (who is a succession of anonymous persons) of *The Anathémata* does not awaken our love in the same passionate way as do the men of B-company of the Royal Welch Fusiliers. . . . Yet it would be wrong to think that *The Anathémata* is a different *kind* of work than *In Parenthesis*. We may read it as a more than usually detailed documentation of an episode in the first World War; but that was not how the author intended us to understand his book. In a sense the theme is the same as that of *The Anathémata,* human life seen in the light of eternity. . . . (pp. 18-19)

To return to *The Anathémata* whose theme is the simultaneity and unity of all human life in the eternal presence of God. The simultaneity of all those "signa" that David Jones found 'down the history-paths' is true not only of all that the mind brings together from past and future and near and far; it is also true for the Catholic Christian because the Mass is not only a memorial of the Sacrifice of the Cross, but an actual perpetual entering into that timeless event, at which all mankind is present; from the Quaternary down to the British Tommies on the Somme, and down to ourselves. Of God the centre is everywhere and the circumference nowhere. . . . The centre which is everywhere is, in *The Anathémata,* situated in David Jones, hearing Mass said, probably at the Carmelite Church in Kensington, sometime before 1952, when the book was published. From this point in time, place and person, the perspectives are created; but what is seen is the single invisible human experience common to us all. This remains true whether or not we are professing Christians; for David—as for whoever understands the Mass aright—the Mass is a sign and enactment of the central human mystery, universal by virtue of our very existence and nature. If for other religions there are other rites this in no way diminishes the all-embracing universality of what the Mass signifies for Christendom. One does not have to be a Catholic in order to share the experience offered in *The Anathémata:* one has merely to be human.

One other very beautiful aspect of David Jones's "actually loved and known" is the natural creation; above all the animals 'who praised God with growl and cry' . . . but also the kingdom of Flora Dea, and indeed the rock strata themselves, the forms of hill and mountain, the 'creature of water' or 'hearthstone creature of fire'. For him man is not dissolved into the cosmic but the cosmos subsumed into the human. I remember his once remarking, about a picture he was painting at the time, on the difficulty of raising every element in a painting to the same degree of transmutation. His sense of the sacred extended to *all* the elements of the real world. It was a cow, I seem to remember, that was giving him trouble. Unless he could transubstantiate, consecrate, "make over" every flower, bird and beast as at once itself and significant of the sacred (and for David as for Blake everything that lives is holy because it is the signature of God) he would not be satisfied. (pp. 21-2)

While so many moderns re-dissolve man into the cosmos, with David Jones it is quite the contrary; for him the whole cosmos is 'made man' when God puts on our human flesh, which is of one substance with the bear and the 'thick-felled cave fauna' and the older and less creaturely dinosaur and 'unabiding rock' and the 'terra-marl' from all which we are made. 'Incarnational' was perhaps for David the most significant word of all. What is 'capable of being loved and known' is God incarnate. (p. 25)

> *Kathleen Raine, in her* David Jones and the Actually Loved and Known, *Golgonooza Press, 1978, 25 p.*

D. S. CARNE-ROSS

Jones's work is difficult, in the way that *The Waste Land* and *Ulysses* were once found difficult, and the *Cantos* and *Finnegans Wake* still are. Eliot and Joyce quickly found their explicators; Pound had to wait for over a generation, until Mr. Kenner turned up. Jones, arriving later on the scene, was less lucky, hence his principal text, *The Anathemata,* still stands before us in almost its first undoctored strangeness. It belongs to the great age of modernism, to what, at a time of diminished ambition when much verse is either costive neatness or self-expressive sprawl, looks like the giant race before the flood. . . .

[Jones wrote] two major books, *In Parenthesis* (1937) and *The Anathemata* (1952), and a thematically related book of shorter poems, *The Sleeping Lord* (1974). These are flanked by two collections of discursive, highly personal prose, *Epoch and Artist* (1959) and *The Dying Gaul* (1978), both bearing essentially on the poetry. For those who have caught a rumor of this poet's quality but hesitate to take the plunge, a very good selection drawing on all three volumes of verse has now appeared, *Introducing David Jones.* . . . My guess is that his reputation is going to depend primarily on his poetry. *In Parenthesis* is clearly the place to start.

"Poetry," because it is best to cut a few critical knots and call *In Parenthesis* a poem, even though many pages are typographically prose and Jones called it simply a "writing." More on this later. The story-line is sufficiently clear, covering seven months of the First World War as Jones himself experienced it, a private in the Royal Welch Fusiliers, from December 1915 to July of the following year. It quickly comes clear that this is and isn't a "war book." There is a full, steady facing of the particular, a rendering of all that made this war perhaps more horrible than any before or since. Jones very exactly catches the feel of it, the trivia and boredom and appalling discomfort, the surrealist landscape known to us from so many sources, in the final section (the start of the battle of the Somme) the terror of an infantry assault against strongly held enemy positions.

But *In Parenthesis* gives us less than we expect, and more. What is largely missing is the note of protest, the sense of war as an aberration, something that must never be allowed to happen again. War is hell, certainly, but Jones never doubted that there is a good deal of hell around and this aspect of the matter did not greatly surprise him.

The stress falls elsewhere, on what we may at first take as formal devices of presentation. The familiar modernist juxtaposition of past and present, for example. . . . Or there is Jones's way of moving in and out of realism, again familiar enough. The fourth section records a single day in full realistic detail, from the moment when the troops stand-to just before daybreak to some time before midnight when a patrol goes out. This section, however, includes a long epic "boast" by one of the company. . . . The speaker, Dai de la Cote male taille (the imposing name is from Malory—his greatcoat doesn't fit), goes on to claim blood-kinship with all the soldiers of all the wars legendary and historical of the past.

And there is another man in this Anglo-Welsh regiment, Corporal Lewis, who "had somewhere in his Welsh depths a remembrance of the nature of man. . . ." His head is full of what Jones likes to call the deposits, and beneath the present military action he sees the shapes of many earlier actions. He thinks of one soldier who "will not come again from his reconnaissance—they've searched his breeches well, they've given him an ivy crown—ein llyw olaf—whose wounds they do bleed by day and by night in December wood." He is thinking of that December day in 1282 when Llywelyn, *princeps Galliae,* the last of a line of native Welsh princes going back 900 years to the Romano-British period, fell in a border skirmish. His head was taken to London, derisively crowned, and henceforth Wales came under English rule. "Lance-Corporal Lewis fed on these things," we are told, and so did David Jones.

Since the history and legends of pre-conquest Wales are hardly part of our common stock of knowledge, the temptation to dismiss this sort of thing as idle antiquarianism is strong. *Not* to do so demands an initial act of faith, faith sustained by nothing except the fact that Jones can obviously write, and that his writing is everywhere marked by what he called "nowness." Nobody writes in this way unless he has something to write about.

"I suppose at no time did one live so much with a consciousness of the past," Jones said of the First World War. Not everyone's reaction, but this is how Jones experienced the war and a lot of past has found its way into *In Parenthesis.* It is full of the immediate English past, military and domestic, and beyond that of Shakespeare and Plantagenet warfare in France, of Arthurian warfare out of Malory, and beyond that of the heroic age of Wales (each section has a quotation from the seventh-century epic lyric *Y Gododdin*), and beyond that of the "loricated legions" of Rome and the foundational trouble at Troy. Jones came in retrospect to see the first of our "great" modern wars (at least up to the battle of the Somme) as the last action of an older world, the last time that the ancient usages still just held, hence it represented what he and his friends called the Break, the point at which man stepped clear of his past and turned his back on all the previous history of the race. "The whole of the past, as far as I can make out," he wrote later in *The Dying Gaul,* "is down the drain." (p. 41)

So Jones, neither passing judgment nor offering remedies for what is beyond remedy (he did not deny that these changes may be inevitable, only insisted that loss be recognized as loss), held firm to what he knew his place to be, the island of Britain and its many-layered historical deposits. He described himself, at a time when the sense of cultural finitude and belonging is fragile or actively resisted, as "a person whose perceptions are

totally conditioned and limited by and dependent upon his being indigenous to this island." He made his stand on the Celtic bedrock over which the Roman, Saxon, Danish, Norman, and successive European waves broke so richly. In pre-conquest Wales he found what he was looking for, "the tradition of the conceptual unity of the Island."

There is a solid enough theme for an epic here (not a word Jones used of *The Anathemata,* perhaps wisely), resembling that of the *Aeneid* and to some extent the *Cantos.* All three poems take civilization as their subject, rather than the self; all three are foundational. But while Pound's subject is the founding of the (that is, any) city and finally a city in the mind, Jones is concerned with a particular, historical founding, whatever the admixture of myth and legend, as Virgil was. Virgil's poem points forward to a founding that, when he wrote, had in one sense occurred long ago and in another was already, if rather desperately, under way. Jones begins at "the sagging end and chapter's close," the apparent collapse of everything whose creation his poem celebrates. Not that the tone is tragic or embittered. His Welsh tradition taught him to be steadfast in defeat.

The simplest account of *The Anathemata* is that it is about the matter of Britain, the buried deposits that make it what it has been and is; and the coming there of the "Mediterranean thing" (thing, *res,* is another key Jonesian word). This is Roman, pagan and imperial Rome and also Christian Rome. (pp. 41-2)

As always in Jones, the meaning is specifically Christian, but there is something here that to an outsider feels larger than Christianity, a sense of natural piety that speaks to all those who are affronted by a world where the sacred has no place. Jones the Christian poet here joins hands with Pound the religious poet, who also has much to tell us about bread. Both in their different ways struggled to recover the sense and substance of our primary creations and both wanted to make the earth habitable once again.

It has to be admitted that the interests at work in Jones's poetry are of this large order. Like Pound he took civilization as his theme, but unlike Pound he wrote no *Pisan Cantos,* nothing that can at least pass as personal poetry. Nor is there any hope of understanding *The Anathemata* in the way the later Eliot allowed us to approach *The Waste Land.* We cannot, that is, take cultural themes as an imposing front masking some private anguish. His themes really are, or were, public property.

This, I suppose, may put some people off. Others are likely to feel that to have to mug up enough of Jones's out-of-the-way lore to make sense of his poetry is more than can decently be asked of them, particularly when they have so little assurance that he addresses our present condition. Perhaps the best course, should one decide to take a few soundings, is to approach him as a craftsman. His mind was in some ways a simple one but his hand was very cunning, capable of strong large-scale design and an intricate joinery of words.

From his principal formal master, Joyce, he learned that the traditional distinction between verse and prose had been dislocated, perhaps fatally, and he set about creating a medium which includes both. (As Celtic saga narrative, both Welsh and Irish, did.) The prose of *In Parenthesis* ranges from everyday colloquialism to great artifice of syntax, cadence, and diction. *Kunstprosa,* that is, often deliberately poetic and highly mannerist ("virid-bright illuminings," "the word of command . . . mischiefed of the opaque air"). This is combined with brief indented speech units which can but need not always be called verse. They may simply be snatches of dialogue. The "verse" is used for such elevated passages as Dai's boast or the mounting terror and tragedy of the final section on the battle of the Somme. The "prose," however, is often no less elevated and intense. In other words, the distinction between the two mediums is not the usual one. It may also be that they are not yet sufficiently distinguished.

The Anathemata shows a clear formal advance. The prose is composed in the long flowing rhythms, arias, sometimes, singing their way through whole periods, which will henceforth characterize Jones's use of this medium. The verse is now far more distinctly verse and the rhythms that in prose can flow so lyrically are here sharply checked. The unit is the brief metrical phrase or colon, very deliberately accented, the movement sometimes almost that of prose. . . . The metrical phrases are usually paired, half-lines balanced against each other on the principle of parallelism. Jones's prosodic model, it has been convincingly argued, is the "antiphonal structure . . . of versicles and responses in the Catholic liturgy and the antiphonal singing of the Psalms."

There is a still further development in his last book, notably in the latest poem there, [the title poem] **"The Sleeping Lord,"** a magnificent treatment of one of Jones's most persistent themes. (The sleeping lord is an Arthur figure who will one day return to his people and whose great outstretched body is in some sense the land itself, now wasted but eventually to be restored.) We find here the same combination of paired phrases or half-lines, mostly of two, three, or four stresses, with or without weak or unstressed syllables. (Jones learned from Hopkins, of course, but the movement of his verse is very different.) . . . Within this regularity there is however room for great variety, since falling rhythm can be balanced against rising, phrases very deliberately accented may be combined with others whose movement is that of ordinary speech, and units as different in rhythm and syllable-count as "they shóvelled aside the shárds & bréccia" and "of wárm-félled greát faúna" are metrically equivalent.

Within his mixed medium or *prosimetrum*, Jones created what amounts to a new principle of verse composition. This I take it is or isn't exciting news, depending on one's literary politics. To those who believe that verse must always possess or imply form, and that when it moves away from forms that seem exhausted it is in order to move toward fresh ones; who hold that the creative experiments of the great modernists have not been followed through and that much remains to be done; who are exceedingly bored both by the relapse into traditional meters and by verse that is verse merely by courtesy of an irregular right-hand margin: to such people Jones's formal innovations are of the highest interest. Taken as a whole his work in fact constitutes a large unexplored territory in modern poetry. One has to assume that in [the United States] too it will find the right readers in time. (pp. 42-3)

D. S. Carne-Ross, "The Last of the Modernists," in The New York Review of Books, *Vol. XXVII, No. 15, October 9, 1980, pp. 41-3.*

THOMAS DILWORTH

The year is 1938. The crowded room falls silent at the sight of W. B. Yeats towering in the doorway. Yeats searches the room, finds the one he wants and, making a profound bow from the waist, intones, "I salute the author of *In Parenthesis*." The author of *In Parenthesis* is David Jones, a modest Welsh

Londoner reputed to be one of the best painters in Britain. He has published nothing prior to this long poetic narrative, which T. S. Eliot will judge "a masterpiece." David Jones subsequently writes *The Anathemata* (1952), which Auden calls "one of the most important poems of our time" and "probably the finest long poem in English in this century."

Few modern poets have been so highly praised by fellow poets. Yet even now, seven years after his death, David Jones is not well known in North America. He is not widely read, even in Britain, because he is not easy to read. His major works are epic-length, fragmented in the Modernist mode, and highly allusive. His allusions to Welsh literature and legend, classical and Norse myth, anthropology, geology, folklore, and the Christian liturgy involve what is, for many of us, unshared background. Realizing this, Jones supplies his own annotations. You may object in principle to poets annotating their own works, but you find yourself reading these notes willingly, because this man is clearly writing about what he knows and loves, and has not merely researched material for use in poetry. David Jones does demand more of his readers than most poets, but he also rewards more than most. Unlike Pound's *Cantos,* for example, the long poems of David Jones are ultimately unified. And few modern poets can touch him for richness of language and breadth of imagination.

By most accounts, *In Parenthesis,* written in the early thirties, is the finest work of literature to emerge from combat experience in the First World War. It is a fictionalized chronicle of David Jones's first seven months at the front, culminating in the Battle of the Somme. The narration is often lyrical, and varies in perspective from vivid, camera-like objectivity to the emotionally charged, subjective view of a participant. Complementing the work's documentary surface is existential appraisal by means of literary and historical analogues that bring to bear on military life a broad range of human experience and aspiration. The result is a profound and shattering disclosure of combat's physical destruction and spiritual outrage, which is sustained by a controlled and variegated tone lacking in the work of the combatant poets who wrote during the war.

The poem is not a pacifist tract. Its ironies are double-edged; they indict war but also stress the essential goodness of the individual combatant. Victimized by an absurdity beyond his control, the foot soldier is an Abel in innocence, a Beaumains in patience and humility. He is Isaiah's suffering servant, who, by interior disposition and participation (whether conscious or not) in a spiritual economy, compensates for the degradation of his circumstances. This is most emphatically affirmed near the end of the poem. . . . During the battle, in a broken woods, the realism and surrealism of combat give way to myth, as the newly dead are visited by the benign feminine archetype who is "the Queen of the Wood." (pp. 437-38)

The Anathemata is a greater and more complex work. Its subject is, initially, western culture from its prehistoric beginnings. The frame of reference moves by impressionistic time-shifting from modern times to the Jerusalem of Christ, to geological prehistory, to republican Rome, to classical Greece, to a merchant ship in the second millennium B.C. The time then shifts to Anglo-Saxon England, to nineteenth-century London, to late-medieval London, back to classical Greece, then to imperial Rome, to early medieval Britain, to papal Rome, back to Jerusalem, and finally back to modern times. All this—the poem is two-hundred pages long—takes place in the mind of a man daydreaming during the Consecration of the Mass.

The Anathemata seems at first to lack coherence, but is unified by a complex symbolic resonance that issues, ultimately, in archetypes. Specific ships of various historical periods evoke the image of a cosmic ship that symbolizes the universal voyage of man. Particular women (divine and human) partake of an archetypal femininity symbolic of the earth, the city, and mankind as the bride of God. Archetypal symbols of this kind universalize the poem beyond the limits of the West. They converge, furthermore, in an ultimate symbol and anagogical center of archetypes, the Christian Eucharist—which, in this poem, fulfills, and is implicit in, all things.

Three selections from *The Anathemata,* comprising one-quarter of the total poem, are included in [*Introducing David Jones*]. The first selection is most of Part I, **"Rite and Fore-Time,"** which concerns the formation of the earth, the evolution of man, and the development of technology and ritual art. The second selection is all of Part II, **"Middle-Sea and Lear-Sea,"** which broadly speaking concerns the spread of western culture by commerce from the Mediterranean. The third selection is a piece of Part VII, **"Mabinog's Liturgy,"** in which Gwenhwyfar—better known outside of Wales as Guinevere—stands stock still at the offertory of a sixth-century Christmas midnight Mass. (pp. 439-40)

The correspondence between the earth in the opening section of the poem and this Celtic queen in the penultimate section illustrates how the work's images give and receive significance from one another. . . . But the work's correspondences are so multifaceted and pervasive that, for an adequate sense of any of its parts, you have to read the whole.

Throughout the fifties and sixties, David Jones wrote what may be considered extensions of *The Anathemata.* These are middle-length poems, of four to thirty pages, concerning the Roman occupation of Jerusalem, the Passion of Christ, and the Celtic resurgence in post-Roman Britain. These shorter works are continuous with his previous work in that they reveal spiritual and cultural dehumanization in technocratic and imperialistic societies—ours, by analogy, included. Dominating the Celtic poems is the figure of Arthur, the leader of a British war-band who embodies tribal memory of a Brythonic fertility god. He is also a Christ-figure and the embodied hope for cultural renewal. In **"The Hunt"** where he rides "for the healing of the woods," he is folklore's Jack o' the Green,

> for the thorns and flowers of the forest and the bright
> elm-shoots and the twisted tanglewood of stamen and
> stem clung and meshed him and starred him with
> variety
>   and the green tendrils gartered him and briary-loops
> galloon him with splinter-spike and broken blossom
> twining his royal needlework
>   and ruby petal-points counter
> the countless points of his wounds. . . .

Here the language aurally traces the variety and interlace of the vegetation. In its complex alliteration, furthermore, it approximates the cynghanedd of early Welsh poetry, which Jones, like Hopkins, read in the original. Its echo here is thematically appropriate. The easiest approach to David Jones for someone wanting to try him out for the first time is probably through these shorter works.

The depth and breadth of resonance in the poetry of David Jones is astonishing. That it is so little read may have spurred Hugh MacDiarmid to Celtic hyperbole when he claimed, in conversation, that "David Jones is the greatest poet, in English,

in this century." I think the limited range and flexibility of syntax in some of Jones's later poetry may disqualify him for that august (and to my mind, unoccupied) position. But Basil Bunting, in a recent letter, is certainly right to regard David Jones as one of the few "poets who have made this century the most fruitful in English poetry since the XVIth." (pp. 440-41)

Thomas Dilworth, in a review of "Introducing David Jones," in The Georgia Review, *Vol. XXXV, No. 2, Summer, 1981, pp. 437-41.*

JOHN B. BRESLIN

[The recent flurry of publishing activity on David Jones] prompts several reflections about Jones himself, his art and the relationship between art and religion, more specifically, art and Catholicism, in the 20th century. For there can be no doubt that Jones's conversion to Catholicism after the First World War and his subsequent friendship with Eric Gill and other Catholic artists and intellectuals had a shaping effect on his own art and his concept of the artist's role in society. . . . Both in his art and his poetry he was idiosyncratic, revealing powerful influences (Hopkins, Joyce, Eliot in the poetry) but forging his own synthesis of history, myth and ritual to make a statement about the condition of Western civilization in this post-modern period.

For his aesthetic theory Jones drew heavily on Jacques Maritain and other neo-Thomists who were popular in post-World War I England. But the thinker who influenced his ideas the most, and who stands near the top of his acknowledgment list in *The Anathemata,* was the French theologian Maurice de la Taille. From his complex study of the relationship between the Last Supper and Calvary and between both and the Mass, Jones drew a "sacramental" principle of art that made of sign-making the central human act and that enabled him to draw direct lines between, for example, the world of Arthurian myth and the experience of trench warfare. Word and deed belong inextricably together if either is to have any meaning. Without the reality of Calvary, the words of the Supper remain empty; without those words, repeated subsequently and ubiquitously, what happened on the hill would have been consigned to history's dustbin. That act of "anamnesis," of creative remembering, is as essential to art, in Jones's view, as to religion. It is only in retrospect which pushes beyond the event itself to include its mythic substratum that we can begin to fathom the real meaning of human life. Thus *In Parenthesis* recalls Jones's own experience of World War I, but its way of "remembering" extends to Malory and Shakespeare, to Homeric epic and Welsh legend, not to dress up the reality but to see it for what it was, both its horror and its heroism.

Jones inveighs against the "fact men," the technocrats, whether of first-century Rome or of 20th-century Europe, because they are reductionists, giving us under the guise of objectivity a stripped down, impoverished version of human experience. What the artist attempts is quite different. He is by Jones's definition a maker, a shaper, not simply a recorder or even a seer. This insistence reveals the importance of the plastic arts in Jones's own development, but it also recalls the ancient Greek tradition that gave us our word "poet" from the verb "to make." Part of the making is remembering. Just as part of remembering, psychoanalysis reminds us, is making (*poiesis* and *anamnesis*), but what principally distinguishes artistic making is its gratuity, its gracefulness. Conceived in contemplation and executed in fidelity to the demands of its medium, the art object exists for itself and its capacity to evoke responses. Ideally, every object of man-the-maker should partake of this sacramental quality, but the growth of technology and mass production has flooded our world with purely utilitarian objects whose ugliness derives from their ''subhuman'' character. One thinks not only of the disposable plastic implements we handle every day, but also of the cleverly phrased words or shaped images whose only object is to solicit a sale. It was a constant puzzle to Jones how man-the-artist could produce such artifacts. . . . He explained it in part by resorting to a characteristic set of images drawn from his wartime experience. The true artist is the infantryman who deals with reality directly and tactually but most of us have become ''staff-wallahs of one sort or another,'' removed from the trenches and dependent on second- or third-hand reports for our understanding of what's happening.

In both his painting and his poetry Jones attempted to bridge that gap by turning the tangible, visible, audible objects of experience into the matter of myth without surrendering their specific qualities. It might be a glass filled with flowers which in the painting ''Flora in Calix-Light'' reminds us that the flora we admire were once reverenced as a goddess; or it might be a snatch of dialogue in *In Parenthesis* or a few words of a liturgical text in *The Anathemata* which suddenly light up the fundamental links that give art its claim on our attention, the connections between what we do here and now and what they did there and then. What makes this enterprise of Jones' especially important for Christians is the synthesis he attempts between the aims of art and religion, two powerful cultural forces that have seldom in this century laid credible claim to the mutual nourishment that was once taken for granted in the West (*Ars fovet fidem. Fides fovet artem*). Like his fellow modernists, Jones gives art a privileged position in his anthropology; indeed by defining man as a sign-making animal he makes aesthetics absolutely central to an understanding of human life. But unlike Wallace Stevens for whom poetry displaced religion, or unlike W. H. Auden who, in theory anyway, maintained a dichotomy between the two, David Jones insists on and demonstrates their complementarity. (pp. 395-96)

The graceful gesture made without, indeed in spite of, utilitarian motives joins poetry and religion here. The skillful weaving of Gospel story and Arthurian myth, together with references to the technical language of theology (anamnesis) and aesthetics (poiesis) and a glancing blow at political ideology (''the party funds''), all of these reflect the diversity of Jones's sources and his belief in the cohesive power of the great Western myths. It was no accident that David Jones developed an abiding interest in geology and archaeology, for both his painting and his poetry are layered works, formed by a process of accretion, often over a long period, and revealing the various deposits he tapped to make his own unique contribution to our common story. Recognition of that contribution has been sporadic, but as interest grows and the recently published material is assimilated, the place of David Jones as a major influence on our understanding of art and religion in the 20th century seems assured. (p. 396)

John B. Breslin, ''David Jones: A Christian Poet for a Secular Age,'' in America, *Vol. 145, No. 20, December 19, 1981, pp. 394-96.*

NICOLAS JACOBS

Of *The Anathemata* (1952) David Jones wrote, 'It had its beginnings in experiments made from time to time between 1938 and 1945. In a sense what was then written was another book. It has been rewritten, large portions excluded, others added, the whole rearranged and considerably changed more than once.' He adds, 'Should it prove possible I hope to make, from this excluded material, a continuation, or Part II of *The Anathemata*'. In the event he spent most of the last thirty years of his life reworking and redeveloping this material; some of it was worked up for publication over the years and is accessible in *The Sleeping Lord and other fragments* (1974) and elsewhere. What remains is from one point of view a draft for a long poem which would never have been completed, but from which passages were extracted and made into pieces to some extent complete in themselves, and from another the quarry of the title of [*The Roman Quarry*], from which material was constantly being abstracted but which was itself being constantly expanded. The sequences now published [in *The Roman Quarry*] represent an edited version of the material left by David Jones at his death in 1974, arranged on the basis of such organization as was deducible from the subject-matter and from the author's own notes. (pp. 168-69)

[*The Roman Quarry* is] a patchwork of fragments, of false starts and abandoned conclusions, with numerous wrong turnings and abortive links between fragment and fragment and with sections of *The Anathemata* and of *The Sleeping Lord and other fragments*. It seems unpromising, though I suppose it might be done, to attempt to restore the entire poem as it might have been, especially as that was plainly a shifting continuum which never took final shape in the poet's mind and would never have done so for all his attempts to reduce it to coherent form—the comparison with Langland, as so often, is attractive—for too much has been taken out of it and given its own subsequent shape to make that possible: yet the recurrent allusions and connexions serve to discourage any consideration of the fragments in isolation. The image of the quarry seems to me felicitous as providing the best means of understanding the structure of the material, though where we go from there remains to be seen. Repeated readings may make the picture clearer. As it is, the order in which the fragments are printed here—''The Roman Quarry,'' ''The Narrows,'' ''Under Arcturus,'' ''The Kensington Mass,'' ''Cailleach,'' ''The Grail Mass,'' ''The Old Quarry, Part One,'' ''The Agent,'' ''The Old Quarry, Part Two,'' with ''The Book of Balaam's Ass'' as a concluding section, is probably the best that can be done, and the amount of editorial labour that lies behind it must have been considerable.

The differing stages of composition represented in the various fragments present an even more serious problem. It is clear that no single critical approach will serve for all the material. Readers of René Hague's commentary on *The Anathemata* will be aware of how a more expansive version often lies behind what eventually appeared in print; they may also have formed the impression that these anterior versions, however interesting their subject-matter, were often diffuse or precious to a degree surprising in the light of the finished work, and that much of David Jones's effort in composition must have been directed towards toning down overwritten passages and pruning and tightening an originally disordered and rambling discourse. His letters, and to some extent his essays also, demonstrate the essentially discursive and digressive, synthesizing rather than systematic qualities of his mind: there, where formality and rigour are not indispensable, those qualities are acceptable and even engaging, to the extent that they are an expression of the writer's personality; but nothing was further from his intention as a poet than mere self-expression, and when, as René Hague remarks of **"The Old Quarry, Part One,"** 'we might almost say—using the words in no disparaging sense—that he puts down the first thing that comes into his mind, almost without reflection', I am inclined to repudiate the qualification. Such a way of composing is not the stuff of poetry of any kind, and least of all of the kind of poetic shape David Jones was attempting to make out of the cultural deposits of the Island of Britain as they manifested themselves to an artist in a late phase of that culture.

There is, accordingly, a fair amount of writing in this collection that one would not wish David Jones to be judged by. In its raw state the digressive and seemingly inconsequential nature of the thought looks uncomfortably like incoherence; even if one knows from experience that there is always an argument somewhere, the unschooled reader cannot be expected to take it on trust. The peculiar·stylistic mix of the colloquial, the florid and the erudite spills over, too, at times, into self-parody. Much of this could have been corrected in due course, though it is probable that the poet's unfortunate macaronic style, in which Latin, as elsewhere Welsh, is used as a kind of superior mumbo-jumbo, would not. . . . Some of the long stretches of unattributed dialogue, with one side of the conversation spasmodically omitted, need tidying up so that the reader may better understand who is speaking. The passage in **"Under Arcturus,"** in which David Jones's thinly disguised speculations regarding Arthur and the development of his legend, already worked out at length in *Epoch and Artist* (1959, begun 1940-41), are represented as the prognostications of a third-century Roman soldier, which . . . I find embarrassingly forced and pretentious. If David Jones is to be taken seriously as a poet (rather than as a cult-figure, to be admired not for the quality of his writing but for his personality and beliefs) lapses like these need to be confronted; and now that we have in print as much of his poetry as we are ever likely to have it is probably the time to do so.

The ideas, of course, remain of interest, and even in the rawest drafts a sudden turn of phrase can give delight. Such pieces as **"The Narrows"** and **"The Agent"** are ordered and refined as much as they ever would have been, and can be read without apology or indulgence. In the middle we have **"The Book of Balaam's Ass,"** the Roman conversation-piece and the three Mass sequences, whose shape is clear enough for them to be understood and enjoyed even as allowance is made for their unfinished state. Time and again there are passing intimations of cultural wholeness. Time and again we find expressed a rueful understanding of the minds and hearts of those who cannot or will not themselves understand: in the inner tensions and confusions of the Tribune or, by a supreme effort of empathy, of Caiaphas and of Judas himself; and, in lighter vein, in the words of the blimpish Roman who says of the Britons, 'It will be a new thing for them to observe (at those rare intervals when the drifting vapours of that zone permit them vision) how it is possible to establish contact between two points other than by proceeding in spirals'. Outrageous patronage and covert cultural vandalism indeed, worthy of a Matthew Arnold; but what an admirable evocation of the poet's own manner of discourse! And, most importantly, time and again the bleakness of reality is confronted only for the indelible radiance of the divine order to be glimpsed through it: 'You give and I gain. That drought and all dead for peculiar splendour of this one withered tree to eke-out a half-line for this poet in his poverty'. (pp. 170-72)

Nicolas Jacobs, "Patchwork Greatcoat," in En-
glish, Vol. XXXI, No. 140, Summer, 1982, pp. 168-72.

GUY DAVENPORT

[Jones], poet, painter, calligrapher, engraver, managed with a stubborn dedication to give shape and a high finish to two books—*In Parenthesis* (1937), a powerful meditation on trench warfare and the plight of the common soldier, and *The Anathemata* (1952), a long poem about the Christian meaning of history. Both these works are fragmentary. *The Anathemata* (the accent falls on the third syllable, and the word means votive offerings, such as those the three Wise Men brought to the infant Jesus) subtitled "fragments of an attempted writing." Aside from his essays (good reading, all) and graphic work, Jones's other small books, like *The Roman Quarry,* are collections of passages worthy of the two longer works; in fact, these passages were at one time parts of the major books but were removed by Jones in his final shaping of the texts. Scholars are right to publish these fragments, for they make evident the richness and painstaking care of Jones's fertile talent. All artifacts are fashioned, he believed, to the glory of God. The singularity of Jones's vision was a saintlike love and respect for all made things, from prehistoric paintings and tools to a page of *Finnegans Wake* or a Welsh miner's well-turned expletive.

Jones was Catholic in both senses, a man of gifted piety and an artist seeking comprehensive symbols for the unity of Creation. . . .

For David Jones art was a sacred act and he expected the reading of his work to be as much a rite as he performed in the composing of it. To those who have never opened his books, one might say, as enticement or warning, that he is conscious of reviving very old traditions of narrative and verse from Welsh, Irish and British sources; there is something of Pound and something of Joyce in him. He likes to range, frequently in one line, from a beautifully formal Latinate diction to the saltiest of vulgar speech. To read him properly requires learning a whole new sensibility—for words, for the historical resonance of Roman army terms, for the flavor of phrases in Welsh and for all sorts of things that we may know in other contexts (such as those of geology, archeology and theology) but that we must relearn in Jones's context. Like Joyce, he has made a total anachronism of all history, so that the Crucifixion is both an event in time, upon which all perspectives converge, and an event throughout time: The purpose of the evolution of the world was to raise the hill Golgotha, grow the wood for the cross, form the iron for the nails and develop the primate species Homo sapiens for God to be born a member of. The paleolithic Willendorf ''Venus'' is therefore as valid and eloquent a Madonna as one by Botticelli, and all soldiers belong to the Roman legion that detailed a work group to execute, by slow torture, the Galilean visionary troublemaker.

To make a Gospel of history, Jones brings into play a complex, metaphysical poetry. His leaps of imagination are daring, and many readers find the dense texture alluring before they begin to find its meaning. His readers are always going to be few but well rewarded, for Jones's Celtic love of convolution and compacted images is always in the service of his love of things and people; and judging from the amount of commentary and elucidation that has been published over the past decade, it would seem that he is emerging as one of the great poets of our time. . . .

What makes him so special? The answer will have to be ''tradition.'' Jones, I think, changed the meaning of this word that has figured so much in modern criticism. He does not use the word quite like Eliot or Pound, though he is at one with them in knowing that tradition is maintained by invention and innovation. Wendell Berry, the poet, has recently defined culture as the means by which dull people can be smart and successful. He was talking about the long tradition of agriculture, but he was applying the principle to all culture—to language, to the arts, to all skills that we inherit rather than re-invent generation by generation.

Every so often there comes along a poet or scientist who can realize for us the new configuration, which only our time can see, into which culture seems to be shaped and the historical processes that shaped it. Jones is one of these.

Guy Davenport, "In Love with All Things Made," in The New York Times Book Review, *October 17, 1982, p. 9.*

PHILIP PACEY

In the Preface to **The Anathemata,** David Jones draws a contrast between the poet who "practises his art in some 'bardic' capacity and as a person of defined duties and recognized status in an early and simple phase of a culture", and on the other hand, the poet of today who is "very far removed from those culture-phases where the poet was explicitly and by profession the custodian, rememberer, embodier and voice of the mythus . . . of some contained group of families, or of a tribe, nation, people, cult". Yet David Jones was, or attempted to be, just such a 'bardic' poet, insofar as the times permitted it; it is evident that he felt continuity with writers of epics and singers of folk songs, which are constantly recalled in his writings; he undoubtedly felt himself to be "a man detailed", as a poet as well as a soldier; his conception of the role of the poet *in any age* was that of a "rememberer", one who ought to avoid the worst indulgences of self-expression and place himself rather in the tradition of popular culture—that culture which can spring out of a people's collective experience and collective creativity, as distinct from modern 'pop' and 'admass' culture, so-called, which is handed out by the media mandarins and which acts on us like a drug. That is not to say that individualism in the arts is to be suppressed; far from it, but rather, it belongs in perspective and in context. . . . David Jones was a public poet, very definitely a "voice of the mythus". . . . And as a public poet he saw his role as both conservative, and subversive. Subversive, that is, of imposed, destructive change, whether brought about by conquest or 'progress': that kind of change which is facilitated if a people can be persuaded to forget their past, to drop their opposition. Not that David Jones is against change *per se:* change, growth through time, is his theme; what he objects to is the kind of change which torpedoes the vessels by which we are accustomed to travel. David Jones is on our side—not in any crudely party political sense but because he is prepared to stand beside us in defence of the things we love and which reflect and augment our identity: our place, our language, our way of life, our songs and stories, our worship. (pp. 50-51)

For David Jones the activity which is 'art'—the making and using of "signs"—is intrinsic to mankind; that is, it is not merely or exclusively the gift of a few. Creative geniuses may not be thick on the ground; but there is creative work to be done, joy to be had, at every turn; only in recent times have "most men . . . been made so *sub*normal as to have no art to practise". "No blame to them, it is the nature of the times". But even today it is well-nigh impossible for anyone to extricate themselves from the human world of signs. . . . It is charac-

teristic that David Jones illustrates his theory of art by the making of a birthday cake; and that he should evoke the destruction of a civilisation, not by conjuring up a picture of ruined palaces, cathedrals, museums and art galleries, but with these words: "when all that is left of the potting-sheds are the disused hypocausts."

Now, a potting shed suggests to me, not merely something relatively humble and workaday, but something *real*—I can see it, smell it. (It is also, of course, a kind of artist's studio devoted to sign-making of a particular kind). Potting sheds may also bring to mind David Jones's paintings of London gardens. . . . It is part and parcel of David Jones's entirely unpretentious philosophy of art, that he insists on the crucial importance of what he calls "the contactual"—tangible reality. Listen to how he expresses this:

> The contactual is essential. You have to have been there. Ars is adamant about one thing: she compels you to do an infantryman's job. She insists on the tactile. The artist in man is the infantryman in man, so that unless the central contention of these pages is untrue, all men are aboriginally *of* this infantry, though not all serve *with* this infantry.

"An infantryman's job"! What could be further removed from the rarefied, Romantic notion of artistic genius? (p. 53)

In his essay **"Art and Sacrament",** David Jones speaks of the bread and wine of the Eucharist, thus:

> The everyday things, the food and drink common to a given civilizational milieu . . . were, in the supper-room, declared to signify such and such.

"The everyday things", David Jones's notion of the sacramental or sign-making activity of Man can be crudely summarised as follows: Mankind is given this world of manifold reality, of bird and beast and stone and flower, as a "sign-world"; it is our unique function as a creative animal to perceive things, not least those things which nourish us, as signs, with our body and mind to span the gap between matter and spirit, to impregnate things with meanings, to represent them in our vision and in our making of works by our own hands, and thus to give them back, to return them *with the addition of our love,* through oblation, to their and our Creator. Martin Buber's words, "Nature needs Man for its hallowing" are exactly right; but Man also needs Nature, needs his own 'nature'; he cannot do what is his to do without his body, his senses. . . . Now, what I am getting at is, not simply that for David Jones art is inseparable from religion, but that what is required of us is no more than what we inescapably are and what we can do; we are not talking of the activities of some high priesthood *only,* or of the gifts of kings. As to the first, there is in fact no opting-out: "None of us must allow ourselves to get away with the idea that we can avoid sacrament". As to the second, the words of the carol can suffice: "what I have I give Thee"—in several passages David Jones is explicit that it is precisely what we have and what we love which is asked of us. Thus David Jones is *a* poet, with you and me, of a religious outlook which is, or ought to be, or has the potentiality to become, ours, and universal, whether or not we can individually subscribe either to Christian belief or to Catholic dogma. If we can, then the specific charge which was laid on Man the sign-maker, by One who had taken on all the attributes of Man, at the Last Supper, has a very special significance; no wonder that the celebration of the Eucharist should occur again and again in David Jones's works, literary and visual, and that the Mass should be a crucial element in the structure of his writings.

But ours is a secular age, and such religion as we have is fragmented. I have tried to present David Jones as a public poet, speaking for us and alongside us, a voice of *our* past, *our* culture, *our* hallowing of the things we love, our spirituality. Why then do we not 'own' him? Ours is a secular age; it is one in which we have severed many of our links with our traditions; an age too in which we have all but lost any sure sense of what is real. David Jones knew this: as a "rememberer" he tried to give us back what is ours, so much as he could within his own limits, acutely aware of the difficulties involved in so doing, and if we realise that he felt himself to be attempting the well nigh impossible then perhaps we need not shy from facing the possibility that in some sense he may have failed. As we have failed him. At any rate the key to the dilemma is surely to be found in what David Jones himself called "the Break". We have been broken off from the things we once loved, from former values: thus we may even resent the voice of a "rememberer" which, however free of self-righteousness or superiority, cannot *not* contain an implicit critique of what we are now, a state of affairs in which we know we are both victims—and accomplices. If we think of the growth of a civilisation—of our growth through civilisation—as a voyage, then what has happened is that we have been shipwrecked; we are like the people on Gericault's 'The Raft of the Medusa'; we have lost our ship and our cultural baggage, and are tossed aimlessly on an indifferent sea. We make matters worse by blinding ourselves to our predicament; we blind ourselves with the facile immediacy of media culture, so that we can no longer summon up the patience required by subtler things. (pp. 54-5)

David Jones may be vague as to exactly how and when "the Break" occurred—and was not the Reformation a kind of 'break', especially if one wishes to regard the Mass as a universal form?—but he is very precise about its effects. "In what sense and to what degree have the last few decades cut us off from the last few milleniums and so from the many milleniums before then?", he asks. "A metamorphosis has occurred affecting the liaisons with our past".... What this amounts to is a loss of the sense of what is real: ... a feeling which is poignantly expressed in the short poem **"A, a, a, Domine Deus"**, unique in David Jones's writings as an entirely undisguised cry from the heart.

All of this created enormous problems for David Jones. In essays, conversations, letters, he constantly wrestled with, in his words, "the almost insuperable difficulties of how to make signs available for today." (p. 56)

"The Break" surely provides a more than sufficient answer to our questions. Ours is not, after all, an age in which *any* poet's is a household name. What chance then for a poet unattracted by contemporary fashions and obsessions; a poet who, in his words, tries to maintain "some sort of single plank in some sort of bridge", so that the past we try to forget may not be altogether lost; a poet whose intense awareness of that past and its diversity so presses into his making of a work of "now" that a dense, thick-textured thing-in-itself, embodying real things and real speech is the inevitable result, possessed of the inevitability of art? How could such work not present difficulties for an age which has achieved its own variety of illiteracy—the technical ability to read minus the patient art of reading,

or at least, minus opportunity to practice that art. And yet, if it is we who fail David Jones, there may be one area in respect of which we may plead that we are let down by a failure which is not ours.

Let me make it clear that I am not pointing to a flaw within the work, but rather, to a limitation in its compass, so that for some it may seem like a plank which falls short, and falls short on *this* side of the gulf. "Poetry", David Jones wrote, "is essentially arrived at by the long digestion of certain conceptions, you can never say 'ought' to it".... For all his recognition of the actual and potential benefits of modern technology—as when he describes carbon dating as "an example of the marvel of our technics put to great use"; for all his realisation that the utile can be wedded to the spiritual, as in the example he cites, that of Chartres Cathedral; can we avoid detecting in David Jones a failure of nerve, an almost neurotic (his word) disinclination to adjust to the "age of technics", and a disregard of the continuity in the history of technology? Though we agree with his general analysis, and sympathise when he talks of candlelight as consoling in a way that neon light is not, is there not, even in **"A, a, a, Domine Deus"**, an extreme, personal alienation from modernity, an implied wholesale condemnation of modern architecture, and artifacture, which differentiates David Jones from us and has the effect, to a degree, of withdrawing his work from the public realm to which I have argued it belongs, rather as he very largely withdrew his person from the world which most of us are obliged to make our way in, like it or not. I have shown that David Jones did not despise everyday things as such; yet, and not without inconsistency (he habitually wrote, not with quill pens or even inoffensive pencils, but with biros, not to *my* mind one of the more sympathetic products of our age), he failed to make contact with the things of today and projected values which could be said to be 'precious' in a contemporary context. I repeat, I do not imply that this is a flaw in his work; it is almost the case that the repeated complaints in the essays and letters draw attention to technology, and indeed to the many humane and creative achievements of modern time, as an absence in the work that would otherwise not be noticeable; it is an absence which does not weaken the work in itself but does perhaps dislocate it a little from its time and people.

Yet how he worked, how he wrestled: **"A, a, a, Domine Deus"** is a confession of failure by one who tried his hardest. If there can be no 'ought' applied to art, David Jones was not one to use this as an excuse for basking within the limits of the comfortable. He was not above self-criticism. . . . Far from creating difficulties for the sake of it, he furnished his poetry with copious notes, knowing not to expect too much from those "chaps" who might read it. And perhaps we need not be too despondent. David Jones himself was certain that Man cannot for ever conceal from himself his true nature, which must mean that "the Break" is not for ever. "The Break" is not identical with the change which David Jones perceived in the conduct of the 1st World War, when "things hardened into a more relentless, mechanical affair", but the War certainly represented for him, within its parentheses, an extraordinary concentration of human experience, from initiation into, through the flowering of, a way of life and a culture, followed by its destruction *and then,* redemption. In a letter published in *Epoch and Artist* under the title **"Past and Present"**, David Jones imagines a "burying-party" or "salvage squad" of the future unearthing relics of our civilisation. And "whoever they are they will find sufficient tokens of us to tell them what were still valid as signs, for some of us, when our whole front was finally rolled up''. . . . Moreover, while many lost meanings require learning and interpretation and decipherment, many of those things which David Jones celebrated, which have been loved, which are loved—places, creatures, flowers, and art itself—have some power to work wonders on us; to recover a sense of the real requires us simply to open our eyes and, though it is not as easy as the saying of it, to believe in what we see.

David Jones's remembering is for us and is ours; it is for those who follow us. We should preserve his work, not simply in cold storage, in libraries or fall-out shelters, but in our hearts and minds so that, in ways akin to the oral tradition essential to the transmission of popular culture in the past, it is carried forward with love, accompanied by our understanding and appreciation of it. I mean, of course, something with a broader base and more down-to-earth than the adulation of a clique; and I believe a particular responsibility rests with David Jones scholars to recognise that his work *ought not* to be the exclusive preserve of scholarship or of an elite, and to be guided by that recognition. Indeed, much has already been done in that spirit— I think of concordances, interpretive essays, introductory volumes and also of the radio version of *In Parenthesis,* a revelation not least in its musical realisations of the 'folk' music embedded in the poem. If this was something 'other' than the 'original', David Jones himself appreciated that for some it might make that work more easily approachable. And if *Finnegans Wake* can inspire a film, why not *The Anathemata*? At least, purism carried to the point of snobbery would be singularly *in*appropriate if used to defend David Jones's work from either explication or from sympathetic re-presentation or ''showing again . . . under other forms''. Nor should interpreters hesitate to make the fullest use of David Jones's work at its most direct and transparent—in the paintings, for instance, or in those passages in which a narrative grips our attention in the manner of a historical novel at its loveliest. (pp. 57-60)

David Jones was never indifferent as to whether or not his work would be understood; yet in his faith he could feel confident that it *would* be understood, irrespective of its reception on this plane of being, and that its intercessions would be blessed with redemption. Mindful of this, let us remember that he made it on our behalf. (p. 61)

Philip Pacey, ''Why David Jones Is Not a Household Name,'' in his David Jones and Other Wonder Voyagers, *Poetry Wales Press, 1982, pp. 49-61.*

ELIZABETH WARD

[David Jones] is regarded as a writer who is not only tremendously difficult to read and understand, but also as a committed apologist for Roman Catholicism and political views which many people consider potentially reactionary. None of these elements is necessarily sufficient in itself to warrant neglect, though each may separately antagonise, as each may separately attract, particular groups of readers: Pound was also difficult, Eliot was also (Anglo-) Catholic, and both, more outspokenly than David Jones, supported right-wing views. It is the specific combination of these elements in David Jones's case—the particular way in which his ideology reacts upon his style—which distinguishes him from writers like Eliot or Pound and continues to limit his popularity. (p. 2)

His attitude of crisis-bound pessimism flowed not from any empirical or objective analysis of history, but from a way of

seeing which can only be described as mythopoeic, a word which means literally 'making, or productive of, myths' . . . , but suggests not only the exploitation of mythological sources but also, in an extended or Jungian sense, the subordination of the interpretative faculty to the imperatives of pre-existing archetypal patterns, or 'myths'. The idea of history as a cyclical conflict between good and evil is an example of mythopoeia in the latter sense, as is David Jones's key, dualistic, Snow-like notion of the 'radical incompatibility between the world of the ''myths'' and the world of the ''formulae''' in the present time. This mythopoeic bent had emotional rather than philosophical origins in David Jones's case, which is why the details of his seemingly uneventful life are of such importance to readers of his poetry. (p. 3)

In *In Parenthesis* (1937), David Jones discovered the First World War to be a subject uniquely commensurate to the scale and intensity of his visionary historical pessimism. Matched in this way with a real historical catastrophe, the sense of civilisational disaster assumes a credibility which almost succeeds in persuading the reader of its general, as of its particular, truth: the function of prophecy. *The Anathemata* (1952), though a far more ambitious work, risks the abandonment of the historical subject, with the result that its abstract 'myth-making' impulse is too openly exposed and the poem's language and structure strained beyond intelligibility in the effort to sustain it. For all its scattered splendid moments, *The Anathemata* is markedly inferior to *In Parenthesis*. *The Sleeping Lord and other fragments* (1974), nine pieces dating variously from 1938 to 1967, represents a partial recovery of the historical perspective. Seven of the nine fragments compose a double sequence introducing the twin themes of Roman imperialism and Welsh subjugation, clearly meant as a joint political allegory. The result is an interesting but uneven body of poetry: on the one hand, the sharp historical focus of each sequence restores a sense of immediacy to the work's familiar underlying myth of confrontation and gives rise to some passages of considerable emotional power. On the other hand, the manipulation of historical material to ends so transparently polemical produces an impression of programmed writing again inferior in quality to *In Parenthesis*. The very fragmentation of *The Sleeping Lord* reflects its willed and unspontaneous qualities, just as these reflect the literal turn taken by David Jones's imagination in his later years. (pp. 4-5)

[*The Roman Quarry*] is of exceptional exegetical importance in that it proves for the first time that everything David Jones wrote, after *In Parenthesis* was published in 1937, was conceived as a single, large-scale, epic poem which he was never able to complete. Not only the pieces included in *The Sleeping Lord* but also *The Anathemata* were salvaged or quarried from this impossibly ambitious continuing enterprise, a fact which sheds a great deal of light on David Jones's use of the term 'fragments' in the titles of both works. *The Roman Quarry* as a whole is a fantastic journey through one man's cluttered and myth-shadowed dream of history; despite its many gleams of beauty and curiosity, it is not, in itself, literature, and should not in my opinion be considered on the same level as David Jones's authorised published works. (pp. 5-6)

As the modern world became in David Jones's eyes, under the pressure of a growing mythopoeic sense, yearly more horrifying and oppressive, so he both withdrew from it personally and turned in his art to abstraction: to the abstract-as-generalisation in his adoption of the essay form, to the abstract in the sense of almost total transcendence of realist conventions in his paintings and poetry. The two impulses are different, though related in motivation. The prose writings represent an attempt to explain the abstract terms and principles of his rejection of contemporary civilisation, marking in this a change in the nature of his imaginative response to the world from 'fiction'—in Frank Kermode's sense—to its temporary opposite, 'myth', the impassioned literalness of the enterprise merely underlining the programmatic quality of the vision. 'Fictions', writes Kermode, 'can degenerate into myths whenever they are not consciously held to be fictions. . . . Myth operates within the diagrams of ritual, which presupposes total and adequate explanations of things as they are and were; it is a sequence of radically unchangeable gestures. Fictions are for finding things out, and they change as the needs of sense-making change.' *The Anathemata* was David Jones's most ambitious attempt to realise the myth itself, not merely to articulate its principles, but to body forth in a concrete verbal shape the essential or abstract form of the vision still only embryonic—or 'fictive'—in *In Parenthesis,* and now brought fully to light in *The Roman Quarry.* The apocalyptic nature of that vision did in fact compel David Jones to an intensification of language sufficiently extreme to modify not merely what the reader sees but his way of seeing—surely, despite *The Anathemata*'s torrent of particularities, abstraction as Klee understood it. That the achievement is at best ambiguous, half-successful, is not only because the vision broached in the poem finally outstrips the capacity of language to realise it in bodily images, leaving a chaotic residue of unassimilated intentions, but because, as *Epoch and Artist* confirms, the vision is itself ambiguous, threatened by contradictions which too readily recall the political ambiguities that confounded David Jones's friends in the 1930s. *The Sleeping Lord,* reverting to abstraction in the polemical sense rather than pursuing a reflexively mythopoeic style in the wake of *The Anathemata,* is at once a less ambitious and a more successful representation than the latter of the great dualistic myth which governed David Jones's life: clearer by virtue of its limited recovery of realism, but by that very token also more irrevocably self-indicting. (pp. 67-8)

[The] study of the interaction of ideology and style in David Jones's work brings to light a theoretical problem—namely, the apparent disjunction between the traditionalist content and the anti-traditionalist form of his poetry—which is not easily resolved through a reading of the poetry alone. . . . David Jones himself recognised as 'one of the marks by which we know a true writing from a false . . . a kind of inevitability—of both form and content'. It is a fact that the mind instinctively presupposes analogy in this way, associating an intellectual apprehension of order with ordered formal expression, or the praise of continuity with enactment of the *principle* of continuity in the celebration, through mimesis, of traditional ways of using language. Conversely, openness or discontinuity of language is taken to indicate a loss of belief in, variously, order, pattern or tradition, or all three. One senses an epistemological relationship between form and content which runs deeper than the poet's conscious intentions in any given instance. But according to these criteria, David Jones's poetry, typically fractured, opaque and allusive, appears to signify dissent from precisely that sense of 'inward continuities' which he was so concerned to affirm in his capacity as artist and polemicist. Given that his conception of the artist's rôle in contemporary Western life was primarily that of a conserver, a 'rememberer', a bridge between past and present, how is the critic to account for the startlingly innovative ways in which

he used and stretched the language? The answer to this question has obvious bearing on one's ultimate assessment of David Jones's poetic achievement. (pp. 205-06)

[The] vaunted obscurity of his poetry, bristling as it is with syntactic and allusive difficulty, is more accidental than substantial, disguising an inner transparency of meaning whose interpretation, as Renato Poggioli has observed of avant-garde art generally, 'is made easy by education and familiarity'. . . . David Jones's mature aesthetic theory is offered not as aesthetic but as historical judgement, as a characterisation of the contemporary 'civilisational situation' in general; poetry is implicated only in so far as unprecedented civilisational changes entail far-reaching linguistic changes, thereby, indeed, affecting the poet's whole position and strategy. But a careful reading of the texts soon reveals that aesthetic and historical judgements are in David Jones's writings indistinguishable or, rather, interchangeable for the purposes of advancing his general argument. The consistency of terminology with which he portrays 'our sort of civilisation' is remarkable, but it bespeaks less the inner coherence of informed historical judgement than the consistent application of abstractly derived formulae. Phrases are manipulated into arguments as one might arrange beads or counters to form a pattern. . . . The vocabulary of rejection remains surprisingly formulaic, even in the context of passages which are highly charged, sometimes passionate, in tone and rhythm. It is notable, for instance, that adjectives like 'technical' or 'technocratic' or 'utilitarian', registered in so negative and self-indicting a way in these essays, are rarely applied to specific objects or phenomena—motor-cars, factories, mechanical devices, even the industrialised city- or landscapes which had used to excite Eric Gill's anger—so forestalling any specific refutation. Thus, although the essays and other pieces jointly develop an argument which adverts to contemporary history and therefore requires to be assessed according to objective historical criteria, it is not essentially an historical argument at all, but an aesthetic and emotional one transposed into an historical key. (pp. 206-07)

[Given] David Jones's apocalyptic, though unsubstantiated, picture of contemporary civilisation as 'anti-symbolic', he both recommends and foresees the strategic *rapprochement* of art and religion, in the service of 'sacrament' or symbol and the maintenance of an organic life. Adherents of both, no matter how irreligious the artist or inartistic the religious believer, are seen to be engaged in identical enterprises, since both defend the 'validity' of 'signs' against the erosive scepticism of the technological mind. (p. 208)

[The] complexity of David Jones's use of language is largely illusory, a result less of conceptual or even syntactical difficulty than of rhetorical, that is, allusive, density. But innovative, in the sense of abandoning conventions of form—regular rhythm and rhyme, typography, punctuation—his language certainly is, albeit along lines already charted by Eliot and, in the field of fiction, by Joyce. (p. 209)

All David Jones's key images flow from the determinant sense of opposites and work in their turn to reinforce it. The metaphors generated in this way dictate almost as much as they express his perception of the 'civilisational situation'. Judgements presented as historically objective are frequently no more than the rhetorical culmination of an eloquent series of images, unaccompanied by concrete historical evidence. The sheer visual impact of David Jones's metaphors of isolation and besiegement, for example, often appears to serve in place of rational exposition as an instrument of persuasion. The fact that a great many of these pieces were composed or begun in London in the early 1940s, in an atmosphere which Stephen Spender has vividly depicted as that of 'a little island of civilisation surrounded by burning churches', no doubt accounts for the apocalyptic colouring of much of this imagery, but scarcely guarantees its reliability on the level of polemic. (pp. 209-10)

In its fusion of mythopoeic traditionalism and formal experimentalism, David Jones's work represents a central impulse in modern Western literature. In differing ways and to differing degrees of intensity, Eliot, Lawrence, Pound and Wyndham Lewis, for example, also developed out of a complex sense of nostalgia and disillusionment a subversive, if not revolutionary, attitude towards contemporary civilisation, accompanied by attempts to restore an ideal *status quo ante,* often with primitivist overtones, whose chief manifestation in practice was the subversion of traditional ways of using language. As an original and sometimes profound contributor to this major stream of creative thought, David Jones will always find his readers and champions. Some, like Eliot himself, or like Auden, will be enabled by the coincidence of their own religious and/or ideological convictions with those of David Jones to take his work as a whole, literally in the spirit in which it is offered. Of the ideas which animated his work David Jones had, after all, observed, 'it must be admitted that to minds which rule out any reference to "absolute values" let alone any notion which implies "God", all of this is unrewarding'. There are however others who, suspending disbelief, take his work partially and metaphorically, finding its powerful anti-technological animus of sufficient interest to override their objections to its ideological implications. From this latter perspective, indeed, David Jones's work can only gain in pertinence, if not in popular appeal, as the problems of mass urban existence in a heavily industrialised society increase; its popularity in terms of the first point of view will depend entirely on the future status of religious or political primitivism in public intellectual life. Meanwhile there remain considerable rewards of a purely literary, if superficial, kind to be enjoyed by any reader of David Jones's poetry—especially *In Parenthesis* and parts of *The Sleeping Lord*—who is prepared to read selectively.

At the same time it is unlikely that David Jones will ever achieve the really widespread recognition sought on his behalf by some critics today, not only because of the, to many readers, disturbing implications of his ideological convictions (a factor which has also limited appreciation of Eliot, Lawrence, Pound and Lewis) but also, and more importantly, because of the peculiarly deleterious effect of those convictions upon his creative imagination, an effect much less seriously evident in the work of the major Modernists, with the possible exception of Lewis. That is why I have sought above all in this study to demonstrate the interaction between ideology and style in David Jones's work, considering its negative as well as its positive consequences; the results are intended to support my assessment of his ambiguous status as a figure at once original, representative and yet of firmly restricted significance in the field of recent English literature. (pp. 223-24)

Elizabeth Ward, in her David Jones: Myth-Maker, *Manchester University Press, 1983, 236 p.*

PETER SANGER

The effort which editing *The Roman Quarry* took, the disarray of its manuscripts and their appearance and semidecipherability (which may readily be judged from six facsimile pages included) offer a cue to the spirit with which this book should be read. Although it is longer than *In Parenthesis* and almost as lengthy as *The Anathemata,* it would be unjust to treat it as their equal. *The Roman Quarry* is essentially a collection of rough drafts, in varying conditions of finish, some clearly superseded by versions in *The Sleeping Lord and Other Fragments.* . . . Even in their often tentative forms, the drafts have the same thematic unity which characterizes all of Jones' work as an artist, poet and essayist. In fact, the dichotomies between the local and the imperial, between the intuitive and the rational, the gratuitous and the predictable, the feminine and the masculine, the Celtic and the Roman, between use and sign, which Jones' work is concerned with as it seeks balance in sacrament and moments when the politics of eternity convert to their advantage the "Happy Fault" of the politics of time, all these are even more apparent in *The Roman Quarry* because they are handled with an incompleted art. For that reason also, the reader cannot bring to this book the same expectations as those formed and met by *In Parenthesis* and *The Anathemata.*

As *The Roman Quarry* shows, Jones achieved artistic balance and unity no more easily or quickly than any other serious poet. His poems began in lengthy premeditation, often followed by outbursts of energy which created not only brilliantly exact solutions to what he wished to say, but also tangles of excessively compressed allusion, repetition, obscurity, tangential miscalculation and plain bad writing which had to be revised, refined, excised, developed. In fact, *The Roman Quarry* exemplifies in places just how crude the first inspiration of a great poet can be. Jones himself was aware of this condition. (pp. 80-1)

If Jones had been a lesser poet, such drafts would have been of little interest, but it is the pertinacity and courage they reveal, "the times," as Jones wrote about his painting, "when you nearly *break* yourself *turning the corner* from a muddle to a clarity, and it takes every *ounce* of nervous effort to be any good . . ." which make them as valuable as the drafts of Yeats. (pp. 81-2)

To summarize, it is difficult to estimate accurately, but approximately half of *The Roman Quarry* has not been published in any form at all, while of the remainder, a good deal has been published in quite different and later versions.

From the points of view of text, form and content, it is obvious that *The Roman Quarry* must be a basis for the re-reading of Jones' later work and for a re-evaluation and extension of existing studies concerning it. Firstly, as a text, the collection offers what will probably remain for many years the only easily accessible source where Jones' revisions and variants can be studied. Secondly, from the formal point of view, *The Roman Quarry* will be needed to make a comparative study of the oddly neglected area of Jones' prosody, one which was at least as complex, as instinctual and as premeditated within the conventions of its time and language as Milton's. Thirdly, the importance of the content of *The Roman Quarry* is far more than can be adequately indicated in this review. Putting it simply, we now can read more poems by Jones which, at their best, are as good as anything in *The Anathemata* and *The Sleeping Lord and Other Fragments.* To speak more specifically, we are now in a position to re-evaluate **"A, a, a, Domine Deus."** It can no longer be regarded as something of a sport in *The Sleeping Lord and Other Fragments*. It must now be seen as part of the pattern of Jones' concern with the dead zone of desecrated humanity and nature, a zone from which *sign,* in Jones' sense, has been evacuated.

"A, a, a, Domine Deus" . . . they were the words spoken by Jeremiah, in despair because of what he knew and in selfdistrust of his ability to prophesy. . . . Against the despair of **"A, a, a, Domine Deus,"** a despair felt increasingly by many of us, David Jones formed and was given significant speech. (pp. 83-4)

Peter Sanger, in a review of "The Roman Quarry and Other Sequences," in The Antigonish Review, *No. 58, Summer, 1984, pp. 79-84.*

Janet Kauffman
1945-

American short story writer, novelist, and poet.

Kauffman's collection of short stories, *Places in the World a Woman Could Walk* (1983), received much favorable critical attention. Kauffman grew up in rural Kentucky and Pennsylvania and lives on a Michigan farm; many of her stories are set in small towns and rural locations. Her protagonists are often strong-willed, independent, intelligent women. Citing Kauffman's background in poetry as an asset to her fiction, critics praised these stories for their imaginative language and perceptive depictions of ordinary lives.

Kauffman based her first novel, *Collaborators* (1985), on "My Mother Has Me Surrounded," one of the stories included in *Places in the World a Woman Could Walk*. The narrator of *Collaborators* is a young girl whose vibrant, domineering mother both fascinates and repels her. When her mother is incapacitated by a stroke, the girl discovers hidden strengths in her own personality. Critics lauded *Collaborators* for its lyricism and narrative power, claiming that Kauffman's novel and short story collection mark the emergence of an important new voice in American fiction.

(See also *Contemporary Authors,* Vol. 117.)

Courtesy of Janet Kauffman

BOB SHACOCHIS

If we are again to embrace the regional in American fiction, as we unfailingly do when our literary experiments outlive their usefulness, then my vote is for story writer Janet Kauffman to commandeer an old pickup truck down country roads, stirring wind and raising dust, to haul such literature back fresh from the heartlands.

I am inclined to believe that on farms of the South, young girls grow up with a kind of magic, some golden power they possess to express themselves. Last year, Kentucky gave us Bobbie Ann Mason and her collection, *Shiloh and Other Stories.* . . . This year the Bluegrass State, in its manner, has another contribution to the chorus of contemporary prose, a Kentucky farm girl now a Michigan farm wife.

Kauffman is, to my taste, more delicious than the usual fare, cherries and figs and exotic soup to the biscuit and peas of other, less visionary, regional writers. Although informed by much the same background, the same values and themes as Mason's work, Kauffman's collection of stories [*Places in the World a Woman Could Walk*] is so strikingly different in sensibility and effect that it must not be considered mere counterpoint delivered by a sister fled north.

The difference between rural South and rural North, as represented by these two fine writers, is not class but consciousness—the power of the individual. Many characters in both collections endure broken lives and deferred dreams, and suffer a stubborn, disproportionate loyalty to place, a fear of change

represented by whatever is beyond the state line, or by a husband taking off across that line.

But Kauffman's characters aren't playacting in a modern culture artificially spread by television, superhighways, and fast-food franchises. They have a solidness that will not be eroded, a graceful self-reliance: a battered housewife teaches another woman to be more generous in spirit, not to be afraid to talk and share. Hearts don't break from brittleness; they swell dangerously from being overstuffed. These are people whose minds are clear as spring water, who know themselves more keenly than their Southern brethren, people who possess a richer awareness of possibility. The reward for such knowledge is freedom—the earned right to be yourself without crippling self-doubt, the inalienable right to seek something better. (pp. 52-3)

[In **"Places in the World a Woman Could Walk"**], Lady Fretts, "an obvious darling and good fat widow" to her neighbors, decides to rise up from the sofa she has been riding for a dozen years, passively mourning the death of her husband, and remake her life. "*You* mourn, if you must," she tells her sister-in-law, Molly, who has been living with her. Kauffman's protagonists do not permit their lives to dwindle and empty, however grave the loss they are forced to assume. . . .

Kauffman occasionally favors a left-behind narrator, stalemated between past and present, taking account of change.

250

Sister-in-law Molly realizes, ironically, that "A woman makes up her mind these days, and life turns right around, pulls out like a cartoon knitting." After twelve years in a house she kept like her personal closet, Lady Fretts, who led a life "like the unblemished blind, by feeling," has re-entered the world, surefooted and powerful.

The gap in Lady Fretts' involvement in life is significant. In these stories, the antidote to a man's devastation in the world of a woman is silence and solitude, a rethinking of the order of things, rediscovery of the elemental—a response not of hatred nor of unrelenting bitchiness. In fact, although men aren't often trusted or counted on, they are dealt with gently, even when they don't deserve it. Rejecting righteousness and alienation for the higher cause of understanding, Kauffman, from a most feminine point of view, is a humanist, a champion of light.

I love Kauffman's stories for their bedrock of optimism. By that I don't mean fairy tales, cheap sentiment, endings that gush honey. What we find in her collection are women, and sometimes men, in circumstances through which they can be unto themselves, pursue their own strength, not despair of their weakness or retreat from confusion. Even when success is denied them, their progress is heroic, toned with dignity.

For all that, there are moments when the separate worlds of men and women combine in glory—moments we have all known yet not risked telling. "**Patriotic**" is such a story, an anthem to all that is right and good among us. Here is a land where no one is overwhelmed by the pressures of responsibility. Women drive tractors with assurance, perform sweaty labor with love, and good-hearted men never deeply offend. Don't think sham or proletarian nonsense. Think equilibrium, for such is the creation of the storyteller. . . .

The language of these stories can be as laconic as that of tight-lipped country folk, bearing a wit you wouldn't dare laugh at open-mouthed for fear of cutting your tongue on the blade of its underside. Or Kauffman's sentences can be all spunk and fancy: she can spit language as accurately as a writer like Barry Hannah, or gulp emotion with as much muscle.

Let us admire smart toughness in a woman as much as we honor calm sensitivity in a man. Kauffman doesn't fool around. She dives for the mystery within each personality, the surprise that jolts every narrative track. As readers, we're never bored or worn out, nor, for that matter, are the lives we witness before us. She grafts country values to the modern world with unprecedented authority, with a sense of destiny for us all.

Of the twelve stories in this collection, only one impressed me as flawed, a rather artsy juggling of perception, as fractured as a cubist portrait. But that idea fits the package, for as much as strength guarantees perseverance, our weaknesses underline our humanity. Kauffman identifies weaknesses, then overlooks them, with all the compassion we expect but rarely receive from each other.

As with the best of the regional writers, Kauffman is a regionalist only in the sense of setting, of stage. . . . When a writer knows herself this well—her voice, her people, her world—we can allow her anything. (p. 53)

Bob Shacochis, "Women Walking Tall," in Saturday Review, *Vol. 10, No. 1, January-February, 1984, pp. 52-3.*

ROBERT TOWERS

The somewhat gawky title of Janet Kauffman's collection of short stories [*Places in the World a Woman Could Walk*] announces its feminist leanings (to say bias would be misleading), leanings that emphatically extend to life on the farm. The men have mostly gone off to find paying jobs or have simply gone off, leaving the women to do the heavy as well as the light work on the home place. In the funny and exhilarating story called "**Patriotic**," the narrator, whose husband works in construction, relies upon a seventeen-year-old boy and a stout neighboring woman, Mrs. Bagnoli, to help her with hay baling. . . .

The story is a celebration of hard work, good nature, and high spirits. It is also, amusingly, about breasts. The boy, Floyd, is shirtless from the start; his "two dark tits" are "flat as stickers." The narrator's breasts under her V-neck shirt are "smallish pegs, with nubbed blueberry nipples"; she informs us that she does not wear a bra to work on hay baling—"it would fill with leaves." As the day heats up, both women remove their shirts. Mrs. Bagnoli, who wears a black bra "big as the top of a swimsuit," tosses her nylon blouse onto the muffler pipe of the tractor. It soon catches fire, threatening the little crew with a gasoline-tank explosion that could blind and deafen them and "stop time just where it is." But Mrs. Bagnoli knows enough to keep driving, and the blouse burns harmlessly to ash. "'No need to tell her a thing,' Floyd says." Later, when the two women are drinking gin-and-tonics around the kitchen table and Floyd, having called his girlfriend, has driven away, Mrs. Bagnoli says, "Wouldn't you say . . . that he is encouraged by what he has seen of womanhood?" To which the narrator replies, "I hope so. . . . Time will tell."

Female solidarity, together with newly perceived female opportunities, figure in a number of the stories, but on the whole the treatment of the other sex is friendly, if a bit condescending. Janet Kauffman's women are extremely susceptible to men, no matter how unreliable (or indeed dangerous) they may be. In "**The Alvordton Spa and Sweat Shop**" a hair stylist named Marabelle lives in a windowless basement (the rest of the house having been left unfinished by her absconded lover-builder, Red) where she offers refuge to various women, including the narrator, who need a few days or weeks of recuperation from whatever is weighing upon them. But at the end, Marabelle is planning a trip to Houston, where the faithless Red now lives.

In her successful stories, which also include "**Harmony**" and the delightful hen-and-rat tale called "**Who Has Lived from a Child with Chickens**," Janet Kauffman achieves her effects with light, deft touches, and a minimum of explanation. She writes elliptically, sometimes quirkily. . . . The remaining pieces in this small collection seem to me slight or teasingly cute or—like ["**Places in the World a Woman Could Walk**"]—too programmatic in their feminism. But their presence does not seriously get in the way of the stories that really work. (p. 35)

Robert Towers, "Good Pix from Stix," in The New York Review of Books, *Vol. XXXI, No. 9, May 31, 1984, pp. 35-6.*

GREGORY L. MORRIS

"New voices" in American fiction—especially American short fiction—seem a dime a dozen these days, almost as common as poets, and more verbose. That's why it's such a pleasure to hear a voice among the babble that's authentic and intriguing and worth one's interest. In [*Places in the World a Woman Could Walk*], Janet Kauffman pushes her way forward through the crowd, sometimes quietly, sometimes with surprising force, but always with a tamed confidence in her private talents. . . . Her stories are of rural people, of rural landscapes (most are placed in Michigan, where Kauffman works her own farm)—a sort of northern agrarian fiction that figures life as a crude dance between earth and laborer, where existence is defined by the quality of one's work and effort. Labor strips people of their pretensions (as in the story, **"Patriotic"**), lays bare the neutrality of the work-hardened flesh. Muscle, toil, the plainness of the honest human soul—these are the elements of Kauffman's fiction.

One of Kauffman's special strengths is the attractiveness of her characters. Many of her narrators are younger women, busy observing and learning extraordinary things from people ordinary in their labors but extraordinary in their elemental knowledge. In **"Breaking the News to Doll,"** a young woman discovers not only that her aged father is the semi-romantic target of an equally aged woman, but also that age need be "celebrated." . . . In **"The Mechanics of Good Times,"** a young man finds himself drawn inexorably in love with a woman "who appreciates minor devotions, attention to the simple mechanics of good times." These "minor devotions," this openness to the world's possibilities for surprise, this desire for "things worth some attention"—these "demonstrations," as a character in **"Harmony"** calls them—are the marks of Kauffman's characters and their stories. And she lets them tell their tales in a language that is true and simple and original, in a human voice shaded with intelligence and imagination. That, it seems, is what good writing is all about, and that is what Kauffman accomplishes here. (pp. 108-09)

Gregory L. Morris, in a review of "Places in the World a Woman Could Walk," in Prairie Schooner, *Vol. 59, No. 1, Spring, 1985, pp. 108-09.*

MICHIKO KAKUTANI

Set down in elliptical, lyrical prose, *Collaborators* is essentially a long tone poem, a dreamlike montage of images describing the exchanges of mind that take place between members of a family. As in a dream, the setting—an Edenic farm, bounded on one side by the ocean, on the other by a prison—is at once real and metaphorical; the actions of the characters, both personal and mythic. Recurrent scenes (a family at the seashore, a woman striding across tobacco fields) and recurrent motifs (blood, water, salt, sunlight and fire) combine to give the story a densely patterned feel, as does Mrs. Kauffman's incantatory language.

[*Collaborators*] is Mrs. Kauffman's first novel, and it apparently grows out of a finely crafted short story contained in the collection *Places in the World a Woman Could Walk*. In that earlier story ("**My Mother Has Me Surrounded**"), a minutely detailed tableau depicting a woman and her daughter at the beach turns into a subtle rendering of their intense and conflicted relationship: as gestures and phrases accumulate, the reader comes to feel the mother's fierceness of spirit, as well as the girl's sense of being overwhelmed by her protective and possessive presence. In the novel, Mrs. Kauffman develops this idea further, sketching in the rarefied world they inhabit and tracing the arc of their emotional transactions, as the girl grows into adolescence and the mother lapses into illness. . . .

[Mrs. Kauffman] possesses a finely tuned ear for the rhythms and sounds of words, and *Collaborators* is dappled with lovely images and scenes: a child's memory of an eighth-grade party with "tables of cupcakes sprinkled with red sugar beads, and cool clouded weather, hanging low"; a woman's plans for a dinner party, in which the guests are as carefully picked and arranged as flowers; a remembered glimpse of a barn, where there was nothing but tobacco "leaves like long dresses hanging over our heads."

Too often, however, the finery of Mrs. Kauffman's language simply results in wordy passages, freighted with ambiguity and a kind of portentous symbolism. What are we to make, for instance, of sentences like, "The difference between you and me, she said, and she meant the difference between Mennonites and her, is that *you* try to keep an eye on the planet, while I, like the trilobite, watch my step"?

Such writing, sustained over pages and pages of minimal story line, tends to suffocate the reader, and while *Collaborators* nicely attests to Mrs. Kauffman's painterly eye and mythic imagination, in the end it collapses from the weight of its own prose—crumpling into itself and vanishing from the reader's mind like a half-remembered dream.

Michiko Kakutani, in a review of "Collaborators," in The New York Times, *February 19, 1986, p. C20.*

ANNE TYLER

When Janet Kauffman published her first book of prose, a short-story collection, it was clear at once that she was not just another of the indistinguishably competent new writers who seemed to be springing up everywhere across the country. *Places in the World a Woman Could Walk* . . . was both deeply felt and bitingly precise. The author's dual professions of farmer and poet gave the stories two gifts: an intimate, gritty sense of life on the land and a skill with language that amounted to alchemy.

Only a couple of stories in that collection seemed less than perfect. One was "**My Mother Has Me Surrounded**"—a description of a woman on the beach as seen by her small daughter. Ironically, it was the story's authenticity that did it in, at least for me. Every last detail of the mother's appearance, every slant of light on her skin, was described at exhaustive length. Of course, you would expect as much from the worshipful young narrator, but it did make for the kind of slow-moving, self-conscious, super "sensitive" piece that often emerges from a creative writing class.

Now "**My Mother Has Me Surrounded**" reappears in toto, with almost no alterations, at the start of Janet Kauffman's first novel [*Collaborators*]. What's interesting is that, here, it works. (p. 34)

A complicated character has been set before us. Well, we knew she was complicated even when chapter two stood alone as a short story. What's been added now is a relationship that's complicated as well—the sinewy, tough, often bitter relationship between the mother and her daughter, Andrea Doria. It's this relationship that gives *Collaborators* its compelling strength.

The plot is simple enough. A child living on a Mennonite farm in Bucks County, Pennsylvania, follows her mother devotedly, drinking in her outpouring of memories and theories and injunctions. Then one day, when the daughter is 12, the mother suffers a stroke. She works back from it inch by inch, relearning how to speak and walk, and everyone is pleased at her progress except the daughter, who refuses to accept the fact that her mother is not the woman she used to be. In the end, the mother suffers another stroke and dies. Simple.

But the mother is so magnificent at the start, so glorious and powerful and outrageous, that the understated and more or less predictable fact of her death comes as a sort of fist-blow to the reader's chest. This is a woman whose favorite topic of conversation with her daughter is a past love affair with three men at once—grandfather, father, and son. . . . When she packs a suitcase, she packs long black Mennonite dresses and a red swimsuit. She packs gauze prayer caps and a box of tampons. . She is feisty and irreverent, she has a personal bone to pick with God, and some of her most casual remarks can take our breath away.

> If all of my loved ones were drowning, she says to me—to the me that is no one—and I had the strength to save one, I'd save Ruth.
>
> You could save two, I say. But I know I am going under.

Picture this woman reduced to ordinariness—talking again, yes, but saying nothing very surprising; walking, but no longer striding or swimming or setting the snow wild with her shovel—and you have some inkling of the effectiveness of *Collaborators.*

But there's more to this book than the mother. There is the daughter, who's a pretty fierce character in her own right. When her mother is incapacitated, Andrea Doria turns "sour," as her family puts it. She takes on a good share of the responsibilities, but she is sullen and resentful. A neighbor points out to her that stroke or no stroke, all mother-daughter relationships eventually have to change. "My mother," the neighbor says, "nearly threw me out of the house when I was fourteen, and this was the same woman who saved me from drowning in Coatesville." Then she asks, "How old are you?" Twelve, the daughter tells her. The neighbor says, "You look fourteen." It's a moment that gives us pause. The mother's stroke becomes more than an arbitrary twist of plot invented by the author. It stands for something inevitable, something that's part of the process of life itself, and therefore all the more moving.

Perhaps it's a sign of the times that mothers are beginning to emerge as epic heroes in fiction. I'm thinking in particular of Jamaica Kincaid's stories, in which the mother is viewed with much the same combination of obsessive adoration and resentment. But in Jamaica Kincaid's work, the mother is all; the daughter is at best a pale imitation. In *Collaborators,* the daughter has it in her to fill the mother's shoes someday, you just know it. That's what makes her story so important, and so painful, and so deeply satisfying. (pp. 34-5)

Anne Tyler, "Daughter's-Eye View," in The New Republic, Vol. 194, No. 16, April 21, 1986, pp. 34-5.

STACEY D'ERASMO

Janet Kauffman made her debut in 1983 with *Places in the World a Woman Could Walk,* a remarkable collection of short stories. Her weighty, spit-in-your-eye rural women and lush imagistic style were a welcome change from the near-anorexia of more fashionable fiction. Kauffman's women rampaged through the countryside, each engaged in hand-to-hand combat with spiritual and material circumstances. These were women to watch, women who made you wonder what they would do next.

Now Kauffman has expanded one of those stories, **"My Mother Has Me Surrounded,"** into a novel. Set in the Mennonite, tobacco-growing country of Pennsylvania, *Collaborators* finds the emotional DNA for the creation of the world in one mother-daughter bond. In telling us the story of a girl's adolescence as it breaks over her childhood, Kauffman turns the myth of Demeter and Persephone inside out to reveal the loss not of the daughter, but of the mother, and from the child's point of view. . . . This story goes to the heart not only of mother-daughter relationships, but of the negotiations between body and mind, character and culture, identity and loss.

"My mother lied to me about everything," begins Andrea. The first half of the book is an aria to that fabulous liar, her mother, the powerful swimmer, the keeper of language, both world and perception of the world rolled into one muscular ball. Although a faithful Mennonite, her mother seems to have struck a private deal with God that heaven is His, but dominion over the earth and its creatures is hers. Andrea says, "When I was with my mother, the earth spun like a planet, always at hand, the flood and the dry air, both, heaven and hell, balled up and thrown together as far from God as my mother could pitch them."

She writes her favorite words in the dust for Andrea to learn: "collaboration," "subterfuge," "mingle," "subvert," "float," "dive." She is a titan of words and their meanings, of actions and their effects, as buoyant in her metaphysics as she is in the nearby lake. She instructs Andrea not to rely on God for favors, because "He never was anybody's lover." Not that Andrea would ask—her deity is her mother. Andrea languishes in a fever of expectation in her mother's shadow, torn between the ecstasy of being noticed and the terror of being left behind. (pp. 50-1)

All at once everything changes. Her mother has a stroke that leaves her fighting to remember a single name, to walk a few steps. For the first time, the weight of language, of explanation, is on 11-year-old Andrea, whose pet name, Dovie, her mother can no longer remember. At this point the novel takes off: where the first part details the unassailable force of the mother, the second reveals the coming to power of the daughter. As Andrea tries to save her mother—repeating simple words for her to relearn, walking her slowly out to the garden—she grasps at great chunks of territory for herself, and in the gaps of her mother's memory her adult heart takes root. This journey from near-invisibility to a surety of presence is as riveting as a good suspense novel, and as carefully plotted.

Although Janet Kauffman, like her protagonist, was raised on a tobacco farm in Pennsylvania, this is more than poeticized autobiography or a moving addition to the literature of "growing up." Kauffman borrows from autobiography the urgency to remember, but subsumes the particulars into a larger myth: how the world is lost and regained through consciousness. (p. 51)

Stacey D'Erasmo, "Daughter Knows Best," in The Village Voice, Vol. XXXI, No. 17, April 29, 1986, pp. 50-1.

X. J. Kennedy

1929-

(Pseudonym of Joseph Charles Kennedy) American poet, editor, critic, and author of children's books.

In his verse, Kennedy frequently adheres to a traditional approach, often using rhymed stanzaic patterns. His work is characterized by emotional restraint and refined wit, and he is admired for his wry satires of American society, education, and religion, in which he employs idiomatic language and expressions. Kennedy's first two volumes of verse, *Nude Descending a Staircase* (1961) and *Growing into Love* (1969), display his predilection for such conventional poetic forms as the elegy and the sonnet. Both collections include poems detailing Kennedy's career as an academician, his Roman Catholic upbringing, and his atheism during his adult years. Kennedy's atheism is again the focus of *Bulsh* (1970), a group of twenty-eight heroic couplets satirizing Christianity. *Breaking and Entering* (1971) contains poems from his first three collections as well as several previously unpublished poems. In *Emily Dickinson in Southern California* (1973), Kennedy mimics Dickinson's unique style while satirizing West Coast culture. In a more serious vein, *Celebrations after the Death of John Brennan* (1974) is an extended poem concerning the suicide of one of Kennedy's former pupils, with extracts from the student's own verse. *Cross Ties: Selected Poems* (1985) includes poems from Kennedy's previous volumes along with epigrams and children's verse. Kennedy has also earned respect for his work as editor of several poetry and fiction anthologies, and in 1971 he and his wife founded *Counter/Measures*, a periodical devoted to traditional verse.

(See also *CLC*, Vol. 8; *Contemporary Authors*, Vols. 1-4, rev. ed.; *Contemporary Authors New Revision Series*, Vol. 4; *Something about the Author*, Vol. 14; and *Dictionary of Literary Biography*, Vol. 5.)

THEODORE HOLMES

Without much question Mr. Kennedy's *Nude Descending a Staircase* will take its place with the most distinguished first books of his generation. Unlike most first books, it will be popularly read and widely sold (I see that it has already won the Lamont prize) because it devolves from those levels of wit, tale, nuance of phrase, and precocity that form the large base of any immediate public response to poetry, to engage us at the level on which the deepest poetry absorbs us. Its personality as light verse is as amusing and full of laughter as anything I know, and its soul is as redolent with illuminations of the human condition—especially the modern—as I have experienced. Mr. Kennedy's originality, the peculiar disjunction in his sensibility that is the source of all wit, his mastery of vocabulary, syntax and the special quality of the American idiom, the purity of his style, the wry just off-tune harmonies of his ear, are too obvious and too well used to need any elaboration here. What I would like to point out to the reader of these poems is the special way (and this is the particular

Courtesy of X. J. Kennedy

genius of Mr. Kennedy's work) his funniness gathers to it and becomes absorbed in his seriousness, lest it be missed in the pyrotechnics of his more superficial effects. Here is a poetry so good its best qualities are in danger of becoming obscured by the lesser, and it being taken and praised for its minimum values.

Mr. Kennedy is never simply funny. His humor, wryness, and irony always enact themselves in a way that serves to open the human condition to the cognitive capacities of the mind. His wit is the source of his creativity and the auspices under which his understanding conducts itself—in short, it provides that groundwork in texture to his work that we call "style". It allows him to go far afield for comparisons that produce insights that would not be possible in different, more serious contexts. . . . In a poem that will last as long as men and women do, a tired floozie sings of her faded beauty and past conquests. In what conducts itself with the good-hearted cheer of a robust drinking song, the whole pattern of the psyche's involvement with sex looks out from apparently accidental allusions taken for the sake of their rhyme:

> All the gents used to swear that the white of my calf
> Beat the down of the swan by a length and a half.

> (pp. 319-21)

This poem, with **"The Man in the Manmade Moon"** and **"B Negative,"** that express the fragmentation, impersonality unto death, and the disintegration of human values Mr. Kennedy sees all about him, with **"Lilith"** and [**"Solitary Confinement"**] crowns his achievement in this book. (p. 321)

Theodore Holmes, "Wit, Nature, and the Human Concern," in Poetry, *Vol. C, No. 5, August, 1962, pp. 319-24.*

THE TIMES LITERARY SUPPLEMENT

[X. J. Kennedy] can see other people as more than aspects of himself. He presents them to the reader not as rungs on a ladder of salvation or as catalysts of an emotional chemistry but as fellow sufferers under the most mysterious of dispensations. In *Breaking and Entering* Mr Kennedy finds the human condition comically purgatorial—desperate but not serious. He deals with it in forms that can only be described as conventional, and he makes that much-derided quality a virtue. Into the humour, wit, elaborate figures and technical mastery demonstrated by his first book [*Nude Descending a Staircase*], Mr Kennedy has steadily infused a moral energy independent of religion and dark with ambivalence. His art and articulateness, the evidence of his control over his rhetoric, add power to the wry insights. One respects the mind of a man who has worked so hard to make it accessible.

In most of his poems Mr Kennedy at least entertains us, drawing on genuinely literary resources. His language, his tune, his meaning are what hold us. . . .

The denser or longer poems like **"Ant Trap"**, **"The Ascent"**, **"Golgotha"**, **"Artificer"**, **"Ode"**, **"Last Child"** have visible structures as elaborate as an espaliered tree, with the same life, growth, and tension. Never relaxing his fondness for wordplay or his compulsion to work out a conceit, Mr Kennedy manages to describe in fear and trembling the alienation of the new young from the new old:

> Minds expanding, on mad creeds
> Nurtured by moon in Katmandu, they bloom
> Like vines that crack their temple steps; burn weed,
> Smoke and explode his sunken livingroom
> And, sooner than believe him, die from speed.

The same kind of power will be felt in the brilliant sonnet **"Nothing in Heaven"**, where the irregularities of the whimsical octave on heaven are opposed by the exactitude of the furious sestet on hell (a city much like our own). This is the power, and these are the irregularities Mr Kennedy would do well to cultivate.

"No Shortage of Satisfactions," in The Times Literary Supplement, *No. 3643, December 24, 1971, p. 1602.*

ALAN BROWNJOHN

Most of the formal, academic, very clever and detached American poetry characteristic of the Fifties and early Sixties has now disappeared under the pressures from confessional, very personal verse, freer forms, and avant-garde experiment. But X. J. Kennedy, one of the most bizarrely resourceful practitioners of the earlier style, still holds out [in *Breaking and Entering*]. His first English volume is a selection of the best poems from his two books, *Nude Descending a Staircase* (1961) and *Growing Into Love* (1969), and some new ones; and its achievement justifies his personal persistence with what might now seem an unfashionable verse manner.

Kennedy is a fantastic. Inside forms of late Augustan neatness and metaphysical virtuosity he works themes deriving from myth and religion, literature and modern urban living, doing it with a kind of quietly hysterical ornateness. There is humour (the manner assists wit in all senses of the word) but it is uneasy, abrasive. Archaic phraseology is made to bite with energetic technical accomplishment, and irony. . . . It is all, undoubtedly, a performance: skilful and alarming, if not often moving. Good and evil, success and suffering, important matters in his verse, are elaborately stylised. . . . *Breaking and Entering* is a lesson in how the whole thing can still be done in this vein, an essay in calculated intelligence. The extraordinary wit and energy startles and hurts rather than touches. But one remembers it. (p. 52)

Alan Brownjohn, "Light Fantastic," in New Statesman, *Vol. 83, No. 2130, January 14, 1972, pp. 52-3.*

RAYMOND OLIVER

To say that X. J. Kennedy is the funniest poet alive is not to suggest, condescendingly, that he is only or merely funny. He might, like Chaucer, have incurred the disapproval of Matthew Arnold for his lack of "high seriousness"; but he has something better than that—low seriousness, which in Kennedy's case implies, along with a certain scurrility, depth rather than height of seriousness.

The comedy [in *Cross Ties*] ranges from broadly farcical situations to the subtlest of effects woven into the very texture of the verse, perceptible in a rhythm or slight nuance of meaning. Occasionally the wit is wet and fizzles, at least for this reader; and the four sections marked **"Intermissions,"** containing various kinds of light verse, children's rhymes, verbal wisecracks, etc., are not clearly differentiated from the chronologically dated sections, because Kennedy's comic muse is both prolific and invasive. But in any case the book as a whole starts very well and finishes even better.

The secret of Kennedy's excellence is his mastery of traditional verse. Because the iambic line allows him to set each syllable into its place, and because he rhymes so expertly, his lines are easy to remember; after all, accentual-syllabic verse in rhyme was originally a mnemonic device, a fact remembered these days by song-writers rather than poets. And because Kennedy, being very talented, knows what to do with these technical devices, his lines are also memorable. (p. 21)

Equally striking is this poet's control over diction. He is so deft that, like Flannery O'Connor, he can merely flatly, factually *state* in such a way as to reveal the true grotesqueness of his subject; thus a poem about a cross-country trip by car itemizes the tourist stops, concluding, "And snake farms where you stood and looked at snakes."

X. J. Kennedy is a close observer of reality, who, in the spirit of Emily Dickinson, can use these details to embody perceptions of the subtlest, most elusive kind. His main literary antecedents are not, however, American but from the English Renaissance—one notes the mark of Herrick, for instance, in the exquisite, poignant **"Little Elegy"** for a girl who skipped rope—and from the French 19th century, especially Baudelaire and Rimbaud (Kennedy's very sharp **"First Confession,"** about a trip to the priest, is his answer to the "confessional" poetry done so messily by Lowell and others).

Kennedy is a man of faith, in the sense that he believes in values that cannot be reached by the methods of induction.

And he is "unreconciled / To a darkness void of all kindness." For all his wit, he is never cruel; he has a remarkable sunniness, of which the many charming verses for children are evidence, but which also shows in a good-humored toleration for all kinds of things including the less exalted aspects of himself (there is a striking "Ode" to his own posterior).

For Kennedy the natural and therefore untidy is good, as in the marvelous **"Nothing in Heaven Functions As It Ought,"** and the rigidly artificial is bad. His variations on this familiar theme are fresh because personal and vivid. And comic, as ever; the poems are inhabited by characters with names like Ool and Bulsh who go around uttering curses and prophecies always to good effect because grounded in humorous concretes.

There are also several poems about poets and poetics, notably the stunning dramatic narrative **"Reading Trip,"** where he confronts a young Turk who demands that he forget about prosody and take up with "Disposable stuff, word-Kleenex." There are also deeply moving poems about people, e.g., **"Schizophrenic Girl."** But I want to conclude by drawing attention to a quiet but technically brilliant poem called **"Old Men Pitching Horseshoes"**; like the best genre paintings suggested by the title, it presents us with the fullness of being. Very few poets can achieve such solidity of art. (pp. 21-2)

> Raymond Oliver, "X. J. Kennedy's Poems Revel in Humor, Humanity," in The Christian Science Monitor, August 7, 1985, pp. 21-2.

LACHLAN MACKINNON

"The Devil's Advice to Poets", according to X. J. Kennedy's limerick, is that "In perpetual throes / Majors metamorphose— / Only minors remain who they are". Kennedy has scrupulously ignored this advice, which means that although [*Cross Ties*] contains poems written from 1955 to 1984 it is impossible to tell early Kennedy from late, and although political events are referred to, the poetry bears few signs of the changes in taste that have occurred since Kennedy started. Yeats and Auden, Lowell and Berryman to the contrary, Kennedy, like Frost, whose voice he deliberately takes on in a light poem, demonstrates the virtues of consistency. The tension which emerges in his best poems is that between extreme prosodic formality and the spoken voice. . . .

Kennedy's five chronological sections are divided by four **"Intermissions"**: those consisting of epigrams and epitaphs and verse for children are too clever to be funny, but some of the **"Light Verse"** and **"Songs"** work well. **"At Brown Crane Pavilion"** translates a Chinese poem of 800 AD, and ends "Sun knows its way down home. Wish I knew mine. / Got the mist on the river, waves on the river blues". The shift from one formulaic set to another is entirely convincing, and Ts'ui Hao is made to feel like a living man. **"Talking Dust Bowl"**, another song, is less even, but in the lines "Had my fill of hanging around this town / Like a picture on a nail waiting to be took down" Kennedy achieves one of a series of striking vernacular similes.

This attachment to the vernacular has its perils, though: sometimes the ghost of Frost is too much in evidence as in the sad **"O'Riley's Late-Bloomed Little Son"**. . . . **"Home Burial"** is only the most obvious of the poems that press in on this suburban scene and make it too stale to be true. Here we see Kennedy's most distinctive note—pathos—in a botched form; **"One-Night Homecoming"** is much more successful, dealing with a man staying with his parents. He notices his father's failing breath, his mother's increasingly slovenly inattention to "yolk stuck to the dishes", and resents being asked why he hasn't brought his own children. . . .

The best poem here is probably [**"Cross Ties"**], where the poet walks along a disused railway track hoping for an intimation from nature. Frost's "The Most of It" lurks behind this, but Kennedy's conclusion is his own. "Out of reach / Or else beneath desiring" he is ignored by hawks, and must

> Walk on, tensed for a leap, unreconciled
> To a dark void all kindness.
>   When I spill
> The salt I throw the Devil some and, still,
> I let them sprinkle water on my child.

The "dark void all kindness" is neither cosy nor cheering. Kennedy is a much more interesting poet than anthologies have suggested and, despite the pressure of his models, he has shaped a rewarding and versatile career out of his fidelity to himself.

> Lachlan Mackinnon, "High Fidelity," in The Times Literary Supplement, No. 4303, September 20, 1985, p. 1039.

R. S. GWYNN

X. J. Kennedy, whose stature as a poet has suffered from neglect, is conscious, in all humility I think, of what a rarity he is, calling himself "one of an endangered species: people who still write in meter and rime." Those who favor neat schisms in their -isms would call him an "academic" poet, though Kennedy's ties to the university are now limited to guest lectures and readings. . . . In both his instructional and poetic endeavors the sense prevails that poetry is a game to be played by certain rules: learn them and be admitted to the circle; ignore them and remain outside in the cold. Such orthodoxy might be deemed classical, harking back as it does to Horace, Boileau, and Pope; but Kennedy continually stresses that it need be neither solemn nor, to anticipate his own pun, an end in itself: "The goose that laid the golden egg / Died looking up its crotch/To find out how its sphincter worked. / / Would you lay well? Don't watch" (**"Ars Poetica"**). Verse like this, in which all the variables of language, style, and content are kept in play, argues strongly for the revival of the long-dormant potentials of regular meter and rhyme.

Kennedy is at his most engaging as a satirist, but this generous selection of his poetry [*Cross Ties*] reveals depths that most readers would not automatically associate with his work. Even the title . . . cleverly puns on the persistence of a Catholic upbringing in the mind of an adult who is badly, to put it mildly, lapsed. . . . Yet Kennedy, for all his outward rejection of the supernatural, cannot quite escape the thought that, just possibly, there are some things a purely existentialist philosophy cannot account for: "When I spill / The salt I throw the Devil some and, still, / I let them sprinkle water on my child." Merely to doubt is one thing; to doubt one's own doubt is far more serious.

Kennedy's poetry reminds us that sanity in a poet is not necessarily the same as blandness. His poems do not look away from modern life: indeed they often describe such ubiquitous horrors as family violence . . . ; despair and suicide in nascent genius . . . , and night-thoughts of a future where all is night. . . . Through all this one never loses the sense that Kennedy has managed to strike a fair bargain between absolute pessimism and sheer escape. What other poet would even *think* of mourning the loss of a world-view, the collapse of the "Great Chain of Being," in the folk-measures of a chain-gang song?

If we count ourselves human and remain ruefully proud of being so, then one measure of the praise we extend to the poet is the degree to which we recognize in his work a fellow member of the species. X. J. Kennedy notes that all of our aspirations to the sublime are limited by our humanity; we are like his "swans in ice," who are "so beautiful, so dumb, / They'd let a window glaze about their feet, / Not seeing through their dreams till time to eat" ("**Poets**"). Lines like these may well shame a generation of younger poets into reinvestigating the further possibilities of formal verse. (pp. lxxviii-lxxix)

R. S. Gwynn, "Swans in Ice," in The Sewanee Review, *Vol. XCIII, No. 4, Fall, 1985, pp. lxxviii-lxxix.*

ROGER MITCHELL

Sound continues to echo sense, so when we read X. J. Kennedy's skillfully metered verses [in *Cross Ties*], we must expect to encounter a certain describable set of beliefs. It would seem natural in poetry so given to its form, its exterior if you will, that little interest in the inner life is shown there. Kennedy is, rather, a social historian of his corner of existence. Ironically, it is the point of the sequence, "**Emily Dickinson in Southern California**," to measure the vapidities of California culture by the work of a woman who had almost nothing but an inner life. That poem, however, and Kennedy's work in general, is much better at rendering the vapidities than it is the spiritual life. He is a satirist, and few poets are funnier than he.

True, Kennedy has made earnest attempts at lyrical soul-searching. "**Daughter in the House**" and "**The Shorter View**" are notable in this vein, if somewhat stifled. He is clearly not here to bare his soul. Indeed, he scoffs at poets who attempt such things in his epigram, "**To a Now-Type Poet**": "Your stoned head's least whim jotted down white-hot? / Enough confusion of my own I've got." Soul-searching here is connected to ephemerality, haste, awkward language, and drugs. Would Coleridge have been a now-type poet? Not only is Kennedy not such a poet, but he is also a poet for whom the modern world is dreary and shallow. His comfort is in pointing this out and in crafting those things which baffle the modern world, namely, carefully wrought poems in a recognizable and outmoded manner. I'm convinced, and this is perhaps only an article of my own faith, that prosody, as he uses it, is telling us to sit down, not be so silly, and pay attention to what matters. It is a demonstration of mental and moral composure in the face of so much sham and slither. . . . The culture does not like what he cares for, so he is reduced to being a kind of monk in the Dark Ages keeping the great poets and their forms alive by copying them into large unread books. Or, into books read only by students who are told to by their teachers. Eliot called it redeeming the time.

Has [Kennedy] dropped out of his time? Yes and no. He came to poetry at a time when wit and the well-wrought urn were in vogue and the poets of the seventeenth century were thought proper models. "**Little Elegy**," "**O'Riley's Late-Bloomed Little Son**," and "**On a Child Who Lived One Minute**" are perfect tributes to the success of that literary moment. All Kennedy has done has been to stick to those ideals. A Romantic revival

has occurred since then, and he, almost alone, has not gone along with it. The integrity of that choice should be better known. It has allowed him to say things verse can't say anymore. But it has also put his work out at the edge of an art that itself barely hangs by its fingertips to the world's awareness. If he is driving a horse and buggy in the age of the automobile, it is an elegant, well-made buggy, and the animal is gorgeous and well-groomed.

On the other hand, his wit, lucidity, simple virtues, and craft may do what they did for Frost, another poet who refused to go along, in his case with the great Modernist revolution. We can turn to these poems, as we can to the poems of Frost's invented, out-dated New Hampshire, and think, "Here is the way we were and are no more." If we want to. The good-hearted Irish Catholic backwater out of which Kennedy writes, to say nothing of the literary tradition he is implicit spokesman for, does not have a comfortable relationship with our world. If we want to know what we are today, let me say "now"— an obligation poetry cannot ignore—we must read elsewhere. (pp. 232-34)

Roger Mitchell, in a review of "Cross Ties: Selected Poems," in Poetry, *Vol. CXLVII, No. 4, January, 1986, pp. 232-34.*

LOXLEY NICHOLS

X. J. Kennedy has referred to himself as "one of the endangered species": His allegiance to traditional verse forms verifies that he is indeed a breed apart from many of his contemporaries. While not all are equally rewarding, the poems in *Cross Ties* are of a range and depth that demonstrate the viability and elasticity of a poetic voice that submits willingly to the strictures of meter and rhyme. In this collection we find the sumptuous and the spare, the raucous and the reserved, the poignant and the sardonic. "**Cross Ties**," "**Schizophrenic Girl**," "**Poets**," "**Daughter in the House**," and "**Old Men Pitching Horseshoes**" are only *some* of the best.

Kennedy's poetry, like Dickinson's and Eliot's before it, is marked by a style of wit and argument characteristic of seventeenth-century metaphysical verse. In "**One A.M. with Voices**" we hear traces of Donne with a New Jersey accent. . . . Sometimes, however, Kennedy goes too far in his intellectual wordplay, and his poems become tangled in conceits that border on the absurd. "**Aunt Rectita's Good Friday**" is ruined by the last lines: "Brooding on sorrowful mysteries, she shoves / Into its clean white forehead-fat the ham's / Thorn crown of cloves." (Or have I missed the joke?)

Yet there is more to praise than to criticize. The mere structure of the book gives an inkling of the precision with which Kennedy writes. Not just an odd lot of poems left over or recycled, *Cross Ties* is a carefully constructed entity itself, a drama of sorts, wherein the poems, arranged chronologically over a span of thirty years, are divided into five sections, or acts, of major poems, with four intermissions of lighter verse for adults and children. In it we find standard Kennedy favorites and poems collected for the first time. That some of the selections from previous volumes appear here in slightly altered form reveals the poet's attention to detail. But more than that, it bespeaks a belief in the inherently organic nature of poetry and the creative process. Such considerations might also illuminate Kennedy's readiness to undertake translations (Rimbaud's

"Ladies Looking for Lice," for example) and parody ("**Emily Dickinson in Southern California**"). In other words, Kennedy proves that what has been made can be remade, not only from the reader's point of view, but from the poet's as well.

Reading *Cross Ties* is a bit like walking through a minefield. Though he moves with soft, slow deliberation through the time and space of these 166 pages, the reader will inevitably detonate missiles of blistering truth, shattering any complacency he may have had. Such a journey is disquieting, to be sure, but well worth the effort. For the poems in this volume are as finely crafted and varied as they are honest. (p. 55)

Loxley Nichols, "Facing the Gorgon," in National Review, *Vol. 38, No. 13, July 18, 1986, pp. 55-6.*

C(hristopher) J(ohn) Koch

1932-

Australian novelist and scriptwriter.

In his work Koch examines Australia's ongoing search for identity in relation to its European and Asian influences and its desire for individuality. He often contrasts Australia with his native island of Tasmania, centering on his homeland's paradoxical yearning for and rejection of life on the mainland. Koch is praised for creating realistic, introspective young protagonists whose search for adventure in foreign lands leads to emotional conflict. Koch's prose is noted for his attention to detail and his accurate presentation of colloquial language.

In his first novel, *The Boys in the Island* (1958), Koch depicts the childhood and adolescence of Francis Cullen, a Tasmanian who seeks excitement and fulfillment with his friends in Melbourne. Francis's experiences do not live up to his expectations, however, and he returns to Tasmania disillusioned yet wiser for his adventures. Koch's next novel, *Across the Sea Wall* (1965), focuses on Robert O'Brien, an Australian journalist who becomes involved in an ill-fated love affair with Ilsa, a European woman, while traveling in Asia. Helen Tiffin observed that "O'Brien's attitude to Ilsa represents the colonial's attitude to Europe and his complex need for it, his yearning towards it, yet his disappointment at what it actually offers and his outright rejection even of those qualities most desired."

Koch's vision of the colonial psyche reappears in his best-known novel, *The Year of Living Dangerously* (1978), which was adapted into a critically acclaimed film. This work relates the ordeals and emotional entanglements of an Australian reporter, a Chinese photographer, and an English woman in Indonesia during the overthrow of Sukarno in 1965. Koch's recent novel, *The Doubleman* (1985), is narrated by a Tasmanian folk musician who achieves success with his band in Australia after coming into contact with a satanic figure. In this book, Koch intersperses romantic, Gothic, and supernatural elements while alluding to the dualistic nature of humanity.

THE TIMES, LONDON

[In *The Boys in the Island*] Mr. Koch is a trifle . . . pretentious in showing how Francis, a sensitive youth who suffers early disillusion in a love affair, is attracted by the thought of the great cities of the mainland, Melbourne and Sydney, and by his friend Lewie whose simple ambition is to be a crook. Neither boy turns out to be quite so tough as he had hoped and, in the case of Francis, disillusion with love is followed by disillusion with cities and their excitements. There is a kind of frustrated lyricism both in Francis and in the writing (where it expresses itself in italicized sentences), and perhaps this is the kind of first novel Mr. Koch had to get out of his system. The way should be now clear for something more satisfying and satisfactory.

A review of "The Boys in the Island," in The Times, *London, January 22, 1959, p. 13e.*

Photograph by Bob Finlayson. Courtesy of C. J. Koch

ANDREW LESLIE

Novels by Australian writers are seldom static. The restless need to search, to find an identity, to comprehend the strange spiritual geography of the subcontinent and its people runs through them like a refrain. With the suburbanite coastal fringe as the starting line, the search sometimes takes them into the bleak and savage interior, back to the roots. Or, as in [*Across the Sea Wall*], the flight from dead respectability draws them away to new horizons (often just as respectable—but no matter; movement and experience are the thing).

Tired of his clerking job in Sydney, the young hero . . . boards a liner for Europe. On the ship Robert gets in tow with a group of night-club entertainers and develops a passion for Ilsa, a strip-tease artist. Pursuit of this big, blonde Brunnhilde of a woman takes him up into the foothills of northern India and through disillusions that take the shine off his innocence.

The author describes Robert's emergence from the cocoon of romanticism with a gentle pen; the irony is nicely soft-pedalled and hindsight is rigorously excluded. After the event the sadder and wiser hero might see the ridiculous side of his attempt to scale that Junoesque mountain of love. But at the time, in golden youth, it all seemed tender, poignant, and pretty desperate.

Andrew Leslie, "The Australian Quest," in Manchester Guardian Weekly, *March 11, 1965, p. 11.*

ANTHONY BURGESS

[*The Year of Living Dangerously*] has various claims on our attention. In the first place it is an Australian novel, and it is dangerous to ignore the writers of that lavish, wilful land. . . . Mr Koch has got through the net and this novel, his third, is a very fine example of what Australian fiction can do. It is intelligent, compassionate, flavoursome, convincing, and well constructed. It is not about Sarsaparilla country or the outback. It is about Indonesia during Sukarno's final year. . . .

The Year of Living Dangerously (Sukarno's own loudly proclaimed name for the year he did not yet know was to be his last in power) seems to be [an] authentic . . . picture of a sick city and a despicable regime. Mr Koch carried out a mission in Indonesia for Unesco. His characters are journalists long-established in Jakarta; they have Mr Koch's intimate knowledge of the ambages of the sordid, hostile, bankrupt capital and their Bahasa (or Indonesian Malay) is as exact as his. . . .

The central story concerns Guy Hamilton, Singapore-English with an Australian passport, radio journalist and new boy in Jakarta, and his complicated relationship with Billy Kwan, Australian Chinese cinema cameraman and dwarf. The East is full of weird mixed personages, unsure of their racial and cultural allegiances, polyglot, half-sane brains crammed with a weird variety of information, their obsessions as intense and capricious as a blowtorch in a child's hand, frantically loyal and as frantically treacherous. In Billy Kwan Mr Koch has created one of the most memorable characters of recent fiction, incredibly eccentric by the standards of Western agonistology but all too convincing in the twilight Jakarta. An English girl, Jill, comes into it, and Kwan is her undemanding protector in a world of drooling pawers. Jill and Hamilton fall in love, and Kwan's response is, inevitably, very complicated—part envy, part vicarious fulfilment. Jill, who works for the British military attaché, has a military secret; Hamilton learns it; Hamilton is pursued by a Russian lady. Filleted like this, the plot sounds conventional enough, but most plots do. The book as a whole has no whiff of the conventional.

For the dwarf Kwan has a quasi-mystical belief that the Indonesian struggle is a kind of *wayang* representing a timeless conflict between the light and the dark. But it is not a clear-cut conflict: Wang sees Sukarno as possessing some of the attributes of a saviour; at the end, as is to be expected, he tries to assassinate him and is himself killed. The strength and originality of the novel lie in the subtle interweaving of the play, the *wayang,* and the reality. Sukarno, we learn, would present variants of the *wayang* to his ministers, their fall from grace hideously prefigured on the lamplit screen. He is himself the *wayang* master, the reality of his rule either augmented or reduced to a nightlong drama of light against dark, and no one sure which is which.

The distinction of this novel, then, lies in its author's capacity to make an exactly caught phase of history symbolic of a larger reality. But on the simple documentary plane the book works extremely well. There are the smells of nutmeg, urine, and human rage and hopelessness. There is also history, with the shoddy pretentiousness of Sukarno's metaphysical capital imposed on Dutch Batavia, the canals when wet public lavatories, when dry arteries of an under-city made of rusting cans and cardboard. And there are the Jakartans themselves, starved but

fed full with the visions of Bung (or Big Brother) Karno. This book is to be prized as a rare fictional record of a bad phase of Oriental history driven out of the world's mind by Vietnam.

Anthony Burgess, "Under Sukarno's Shadow," in *The Times Literary Supplement, No. 3999, November 24, 1978, p. 1359.*

JOHN NAUGHTON

Sooner or later, it seems, everyone wants to get a novel about foreign correspondents out of his system. *The Year of Living Dangerously* is C. J. Koch's effort in this direction. Set in Jakarta in 1965, the year of Sukarno's final fling, it portrays the decay of the régime as reflected in the eyes of a small clique of Western journalists who gather nightly in the Wayang bar, the only air-conditioned watering-hole in town. The action centres on a rookie Australian correspondent, Guy Hamilton, and his curious stringer cameraman, Billy Kwan, a near-dwarf of mixed Chinese and Australian parentage.

Kwan is an enigmatic and interesting figure, someone who is immersed in the teeming life of his adopted city, yet who lives continually at one remove from reality. He is, for example, an obsessive keeper of files—on friends, on topics, on the dangerous politics of a sinister régime. Kwan befriends Hamilton, at one point even 'donating' his girlfriend, and generally makes it possible for the young reporter to make it on his first foreign posting. But in the end it is Kwan, not his protégé, who takes all the knocks.

Mr Koch thus assembles an interesting enough set of ingredients—steamy dictatorial politics, intrigue, sex, death, jealousy, journalism—stirs them conscientiously, and sets them to simmer. Yet somehow it does not quite come off, and the book obstinately remains less than the sum of its parts—highlighting perhaps the danger of deciding that Jakarta (or anywhere else) is 'the perfect setting' for a novel. (p. 865)

John Naughton, "Going Downhill," in The Listener, *Vol. 100, No. 2591, December 21 & 28, 1978, pp. 864-65.*

ROBYN CLAREMONT

Christopher Koch's *The Year of Living Dangerously* has been particularly welcomed after so long a silence. It is an important addition to his work since it not only approaches with confidence a much wider area of experience than he has previously dealt with, but it must also be seen as the inevitable and fulfilling sequel to his earlier work in pursuing and enlarging upon the themes which were opened there.

An appreciation of this continuity may well prompt a reconsideration and a more balanced view of the earlier books. *The Boys in the Island* (1958) has had favourable attention since its appearance, but much of this has been based upon a reading of it chiefly in terms of that well-established theme in all literatures, the sensitive exploration of the child's reluctant progress from youth to experience. As a consequence this specific interpretation of the book has tended to preclude a consideration of the wider implications inherent in this model.

Across the Sea Wall (1965), Koch's second book, was generally seen as marking a declension from the 'promise' of the earlier book; one senses a preconception that, the uncertainties of adolescence dealt with, this book should have had something new and positive to say about destinations rather than turning to a yet more uncertain view of adult life. Critics spoke with disappointment of 'the shallow self-indulgence' of its 'small-time tragic hero' and its 'hardness of manner which refuses to believe in anything'. *The Year of Living Dangerously,* on the other hand, has attracted praise based on a 'maturity' measured largely in terms of its internationalism. (p. 25)

The journey of Koch's work is both form and meaning, providing the organization both of life itself and of the mythic framework for the progressive engagement with experience. Indeed on the most explicit level the continuity of his work can be expressed by its geography, moving as it does from the island of the first book to the increasingly wider scenes of the second and third. In *The Boys in the Island* the preoccupation with place as specific and symbol is given its most concrete and detailed expression. For the boy Francis Cullen, place gives identity to persons, and both partake of a secret life which is elsewhere and other from his own; to enter into the one would be to possess the other.

This sense of seeking the self through the definition of otherness is allowed to arise naturally in the book from the learning process of the child who discovers who he is by carving himself out, separating himself from, the undifferentiated world of experience. But for Francis this process is continued beyond the fantasy of infancy into the dream-search for the Otherland. . . . (pp. 25-6)

His earliest fascinations are with Gooree, the mysterious suburb next door where the bad boys live, and Lutana Rise, home of Terry O'Brien and his wicked uncles, whose existence hints at a knowledge he does not possess and a certainty of identification which he longs for.

The central section of the book presents him with an experience in which dream and reality overlap. In loving Heather Miles and the place that is associated with her—innocent Greendale, country of carnivals and sentimental cowboy music—he is nearest to achieving the identification with both place and person which he desires. But, lacking self-definition, he is susceptible to the menacing power of the adult world and the mysterious evil of Mr Miles and the confident Donnie; the childhood idyll is broken and he returns to the Mainland dream which he associates with Lewie and his gangster fantasies. . . .

The Boys in the Island makes the search for the otherplace a process of the dream of childhood, but such a dreamer is not always a child *Across the Sea Wall* follows the dream itinerary of Robert O'Brien, a twenty-three-year-old escapee from impending marriage, who undertakes a shipboard voyage—the archetype of freedom's desire—in the company of 'those for whom the ordinary life—the comfortable home, the comfortable job—will never be enough . . . the company of us whom I call: international vagrants'. . . . Robert seeks a 'perfect place, repeated in many ways, multiform but always instantly recognisable, because it would be undeniably *other:* existing in a climate of otherness'. . . . (p. 26)

The question of love and responsibility have taken on a bleaker aspect than in *The Boys in the Island.* There Francis's and Heather's love was seen as compelling and serious, but like the love of children, its selfish innocence a natural stage in the evolution of identity. The intention distinguishes the quality of the relationship, as Francis began to recognize in his other, less innocent, involvement with Keeva who is also an exploiter and manipulator, building the self from the fragmentation of others, or, as Robert does with Ilsa, maintaining identity for himself by the wilful estrangement of another. Being still a

child, Francis survives, but Robert, who plays upon the dream of childhood, is returned to his starting-place. Wanting above all to be free, to savour strangeness alone, he is excluded forever from the real journey of life and pays the price of illness and spiritual death.

Across the Sea Wall is an unhappy story. Pursuing the omen proposed by the epigraph from Keats which introduced *The Boys in the Island*—'only the dreamer venoms all his days'— it is a cautionary companion-piece to that book. One can interpret the critical discontent mentioned earlier as a failure to recognize the terms in which the book is conceived: that it envisions the fate of those who refuse to relinquish selfhood as an end. Parallels are suggested in Robert's friend Jimmy who represents the cynical extreme of the traveller who sees and uses only what pleases him, and Michael Maleter, Ilsa's dubious 'manager', who in espousing his own version of existentialism haunts Robert with the fear that love, the acceptance of otherness, means the total surrender of the self. Robert's fixedness in dream, rather than increasing upon the inchoate gains of the child Francis, is shown as perverse in its regressiveness, wasteful and destructive of the journey's promise. Ilsa herself is no easy travelling companion: here awkwardness is continually emphasized. She is large, plain, childishly obstinate and foolish and yet still for Robert mysteriously other and desirable. Her association with the goddess Kali is more than the obvious evocation of the ambivalent female principle: Ilsa is to be the test of Robert's acceptance of the outward life, difficult and demanding, as well as the easier satisfaction of the inward dream.

The Boys in the Island and *Across the Sea Wall* are both very closely-viewed studies; our involvement with the central characters is intimate and continuous. In *The Year of Living Dangerously* Koch enables us to take a more comprehensive view by presenting us with a range of people, all of whom are travellers of a kind, viewed through the neutral gaze of Cook, a confidant and observer professedly untroubled by the kinds of problems that life presents to the others. The Jakarta of this book is an achieved otherplace, a stage in the journey for the group of foreign correspondents gathered there to watch, with the inquisitive detachment of the professional outsider, the last year of Sukarno's rule. For most of them it is a place of licence, a place to dally with dream in a way not permissible in their ordinary lives. Wally O'Sullivan enjoys his brown-skinned boys, Curtis the prostitutes of the cemetery, Condon his voyeurism along the canals. For Hamilton it is the place where careers are made, the troublespot posting where others' disasters are the material of good copy, far from the dreaded Sydney newsdesk, graveyard of married men. All these are exploitative attitudes, and the corollary is quite clearly shown: such a use of others is based upon inherent self-satisfaction and a complacent acceptance of social fragmentation. . . .

Most of the foreigners in the book have as little time for self-examination as for the attempt to see the essential life of the people about them or the forces which are engaged there.

The startling exception is the Australian-Chinese dwarf, Billy Kwan, whose uncertainty of self makes his life a continuing search for the meaning of his own and others' natures. He is the true investigative reporter of the book; his immense curiosity about others' lives, his desire for definitions, is revealed in the dossiers he compiles (which lead some to believe that he must be a paid spy—how else explain such passionate absorption in the otherness of those around him?).

His search is directed, like Francis Cullen's, towards finding someone whom he can recognize as his complement, a resolution of the puzzling incompleteness of the self. He focuses on very dissimilar figures: Sukarno, originally for Kwan the complete man, strong and compassionate, living by a mutual interplay of energies between himself and his people; Hamilton whom he sees as his brother; Ibu, the hopelessly destitute woman whom he identifies with the mother aspect of Durga, the goddess whose faces are good and evil.

The book is the progress of Kwan's disappointment and disintegration as these sources of identification waver and fail. On the widest scale his gestures of understanding and compassion are utterly futile in securing change or reconciliation in Indonesia's injured and divided society. He cannot prevent the death of Ibu's infant son, his passionate appeal to Sukarno is never seen. Finally his only success is in the one-to-one personal relationship with Hamilton, for it is his influence that enables Hamilton to receive an intimation which alters his life. . . .

The scene at the *wayang* is a most important one and illustrates very clearly some ways in which this book differs from the earlier work. What is presented here is a dramatic objectification of themes which previously were approached through the more private world of dream. (p. 27)

In *The Boys in the Island*, Francis's earlier sense of the otherness within is built upon the fantasy life he leads with 'the Lads' who are sometimes the typical imaginary companions of childhood, and are later identified with actual companies of quasi-heroic figures with whom he longs to join. In *Across the Sea Wall* the infrequent and unexplained references to Robert's inner voice—'the master'—come less happily, retaining only some vague noumenal force inaccessible to the reader. A significant shift has occured in *The Year of Living Dangerously* whereby dream is projected outwards into areas of public significance rather than being retained within a personal mysticism.

Several elements have a part in this scheme. One, as suggested already, is the distancing of the narrative itself, another is the historical context, an actuality which can be measured in terms of a 'real' Sukarno, Aidit and so on, a real pattern of events whose significance can be common property. The symbolism of the *wayang* stories which has been part of the continuing pattern of the book is of this kind even though its truth is more intuitive than rational. Its parallel of the inner search for the harmonious self and the desire to make sense of the otherness of experience offers, through the medium of myth and archetype, a generalized and objective force more potent than the private dream suggested by 'the Lads' and 'the Master'. . . .

One notes that in this book the quality of the journeying has changed. In keeping with the growing assimilation of Eastern thought, more emphasis is placed on interplay and process; the ever-renewed struggle between political and social forces illustrates a concept of life as becoming rather than being. . . .

The self and the world, inner and outer, dream and reality, otherness and nearness: how can one term in each of these dualities be absolutely defined and distinguished from the other unless by exclusion, and how, once separated, can they be related except by compromise?

Koch's characters pursue these dilemmas in different ways. Francis Cullen, deliberately rejecting the conventional reality offered by the model of his home and suburb, accepts at first

the terms of his inner dream and seeks its mysterious secret signals in a world which transcends ordinary laws. His return to the island is at the same time an acceptance of the uniqueness of the self (which is another face of his fascination with the strangeness of the other) and a realization that 'growing up' is a passage from freedom to responsibility.

Robert O'Brien's prizing of the separateness of his own selfhood disables him from the identification with the otherness of experience which is his consuming dream. He is not unaware of the claims which others have upon him; because he knows this and still refuses them, he has also to exist with the knowledge of his diminished self.

The Year of Living Dangerously extends and broadens the social implications of these responses by placing the individual's quest for a solution of dualism within a wider pattern of relationship. (p. 28)

> Robyn Claremont, "The Novels of C. J. Koch," in *Quadrant*, Vol. XXXIV, No. 7, July, 1980, pp. 25-9.

HELEN TIFFIN

Like Patrick White and Randolph Stow, Christopher Koch explores in his fiction the post-colonial Australian identity, not in an exclusively political sense, but rather in its spiritual and metaphysical ramifications. While all three novelists have constantly dealt with aspects of this theme, Koch has seemed most conscious of the vestigial European inheritance and the increasing Asian perspectives in shaping the Australian spirit. His interest in and insight into the colonial personality was perhaps a special one because, as he suggests, in his home state of Tasmania, it was much easier initially 'for our great grandfathers to put together the lost totality of England'. The greater the illusion the more difficult the eventual recognition of significant difference. Again, a sense of colonial displacement and remoteness might well be felt more acutely in an environment which sees itself at two removes from the ancestral European 'reality'—a satellite of mainland Australia which in turn is a satellite of Europe. While the relationship of Tasmania to the mainland figures largely in his first novel *The Boys in the Island* (1958), Koch constantly explores the wider implications as well. (p. 326)

It is the pathos of absence . . . that is the central theme of *The Boys in the Island*. Even when it is not articulated in geographical terms, this sensibility manifests itself in the belief that real life, fulfilled, adult life, lies always in the future (although paradoxically what is being sought is really the ancestral past), and always in another place. The colonial mind is disdainful of self, and in the characters, Francis Cullen of *The Boys in the Island* and Robert O'Brien in *Across the Sea Wall,* this issues as an impatience with innocence, while the search for the 'other place' is objectified in the relationships with the different women of the novels. There is an interesting contrast with the *bildungsroman* pattern in which sexual initiation is often an element in the achievement of experienced maturity. In Koch, however, the sexuality is regressive and the pattern of both novels is uncompromisingly circular: the main characters arrive at the point from which they started, and the narrative modes underlie this circularity. *Across the Sea Wall* is told retrospectively from an opening and concluding frame, while *The Boys in the Island* opens with a young boy's dream which prefigures the failure to find satisfaction or fulfilment in the 'other place'.

Francis Cullen's premonitory dream of the Soons not only forecasts the fate of the teenage boys who are drawn to a magic Melbourne only to find it 'a dark city of black and red iron, and chimneys of terrible masters', but also introduces images of questing for something that constantly retreats into the distance or the future. From the perspective of the island the mainland . . . promises discoveries of 'the hidden haunts of vice and excitement' . . . , the objective correlative of which becomes Melbourne. (p. 327)

Throughout the novel, that 'city of a great meaning' has been visible only in signs, and only in the projection of sign and symbol onto naked reality has it seemed momentarily within reach. In the classic *bildungsroman* pattern the hero would learn from bitter experience that this great meaning for which he has been seeking is essentially unobtainable, but the need for such an otherland, the sense of the missing real world is a feature of the adult colonial psyche. Thus the ends and the beginnings of the journey are the same. 'It was as though, across the intervening spaces of the valley, where only the moving red tail-light of a car was definite, like the sullen beginning of some perilous expedition, they dared him to come again. Against that prospect, a wind-tormented young eucalypt in a garden tossed its thin body backwards and forwards, as though trying to break free from its roots'. . . . The novel ends with this image of the colonial psyche. Tormented even when he maintains his roots, yet led on by a sullen and malicious will-o'-wisp, the colonial indeed finds the task of matching up the demands and pulls of two worlds 'the task of a lifetime'.

In Koch's next novel, *Across the Sea Wall* (1965), Robert O'Brien takes up the challenge of the tail light, and pulling up the roots that seem to be attaching him too firmly to class and place, he sets off on that inevitable journey to the ancestral homeland of Europe. With Jimmy Baden he boards the ship, *Napoli*, in Melbourne. . . . On board the *Napoli* Jimmy and O'Brien meet a strange collection of people, Ilsa Kalnins, Carleen Jackson, Michael Maleter, Serge and Sundar Singh. Only Sundar Singh and Carleen Jackson are not Europeans, and only Sundar, who is an engineer returning to India, is not in the entertainment business. After a day in Jakarta, the first port of call, which is almost as magical as Jimmy and O'Brien might have wished, O'Brien finds himself involved with Ilsa Kalnins, and replacing Michael and Serge as the girls' lovers and stage entrepreneurs, he and Sundar leave the boat with Ilsa and Carleen to journey through India to Sundar's home in Delhi.

The proposed journey to Europe is thus aborted in Asia, superficially, because O'Brien has been enchanted by Jakarta and the exotic prospect of India, but on the allegoric level because, in becoming Ilsa's lover, he has already come in contact with ancestral Europe, making the continuation of the journey unnecessary. Two aspects of Ilsa fascinate, obsess and at times repel O'Brien: one is his sense of the vast experience of Europe embodied in her both through her ancestry and through her living there during the war: the second, related to this, is her maternity which to O'Brien seems both mysterious and paradoxical. (pp. 328-29)

After he has returned to Australia and re-established the doomed relationship with Ilsa, [O'Brien] is able to articulate the problem more clearly: 'her homeland has become part of the maddening blank in her, completing the circle of my anxiety'. . . . It is however the maddening blank or what he feels to be the blank in his own experience that he seeks to fill and Ilsa, for all his attempt to project this on her, cannot supply it.

Associated with her appeal as an 'experienced European' is the sense of her sexual maturity and maternity, something O'Brien is drawn to instinctively even before he discovers she has had a child. For O'Brien, Ilsa is the ultimate mother-figure, even if aspects of this motherhood sometimes repel him. Moreover she is not the unequivocal mother-protector that O'Brien would be more comfortable in finding—there are cruel contradictions apparent in her. Though her breasts ache with milk, she has deserted her child, and is, in O'Brien's view, capable of great cruelty as well as sickly sentimentality. Though he literally drinks the milk from her breasts, he can neither absorb the magic experience from her nor find the security that image might suggest. Europe has rejected her 'children' and can never supply the maternal security her colonials expect even as they rebel against being mothered by her. (pp. 329-30)

O'Brien's attitude to Ilsa represents the colonial's attitude to Europe and his complex of need for it, his yearning towards it, yet his disappointment at what it actually offers and his outright rejection even of those qualities most desired. While such patterns and even characters are relatively common in the contemporary post-colonial novel, Koch introduces a new element in his use of India and Indian mythology to elaborate the theme. . . . In using such symbolic underpinning, Koch, like Randolph Stow in *Tourmaline* faced the problem of giving his Western readers sufficient information on Indian thought to enable them to interpret his use of the myths in the novel. Koch does this in *Across the Sea Wall* through the character of the practical Sundar Singh who can reasonably act as teacher-guide to the 'tourists'. It is Singh who gives an account of the goddess, Kali, while the travellers are still on board the *Napoli*, and it is with Kali that Carleen and particularly Ilsa are identified. Kali, in Singh's account is the cruellest god of all—'and yet she's an aspect of Siva, who's good'. . . . Kali too is a 'maternal whore' . . . and here the inherent contradictions in her character (from a Western point of view) are obvious. Kali combines those traits of Ilsa's character which seem contradictory to O'Brien, and whose coexistence in the one personality so fascinate and repel him. Here Koch seems to be indicating that an Indian conception of life and personality is closer to actuality than a Western insistence on consistency within a philosophy which tries to frame experience on polar opposites, but insofar as Ilsa in the allegorical framework of the novel stands for Europe in the colonial imagination, potentially she can reconcile contradictory attitudes in the colonial that fret him.

Another aspect of Kali is important in the allegorical structure of the novel. Kali's destruction and creation is *lila*, 'play—all play!' . . . , and as dancer she is weaver of illusion, of *maya*, creator of the shadowy world in which unenlightened human beings believe they exist. Like Kali, Ilsa is a dancer, weaver of a world of magic illusion, and this is an important correspondence.

In the colonial imagination Europe dances before the colonial to weave the illusion of its reality that in one sense renders the colonial's own world a world of shadows. . . . In *Across the Sea Wall* O'Brien's negative associations with Ilsa's dancing and his unwillingness to see her 'expose' herself in the dance thus have a significance beyond personal sexual jealousy. Kali as dancer weaves the illusion of existence, but is also capable of rending the veil and destroying the illusion. O'Brien is uncomfortable with the illusion, but terrified of the striptease which will expose the void in his idea of existence. (pp. 330-32)

Across the Sea Wall provides a complex treatment of the drama of the colonial psyche where character and narrative are functions of this allegorical exploration. India, Kali and Hindu philosophy generally give the reader (and an unwilling O'Brien) clues to the psychic nature of 'Life's spoilt children' and the complex yearning for the northern world that is part of their essence. O'Brien never consciously learns a lesson or resolves the complexities within himself, but at the end of the novel he is able to adjust to Australian life while accepting as inevitable his yearning for that otherland.

Europe, Asia and Australian identity are again linked in . . . *The Year of Living Dangerously* (1978), a novel centrally concerned with the nature of the colonial psyche and with Australian identity. It is not however that absence, that sense of the missing real world which is stressed in this novel, but other aspects of the colonial personality.

The Year of Living Dangerously deals with a group of journalists in Jakarta and their public and private lives in the months leading up to the abortive 30 September PKI coup which eventually resulted in the downfall of the charismatic Sukarno. The story is told by an Australian narrator, Cookie, a confidant of the other journalists. Apart from President Sukarno who hovers constantly in the background of the reader's mind, the chief characters in the novel are journalist Guy Hamilton, and his 'stringer cameraman', Billy Kwan. . . . [Hamilton and Sukarno are Billy's alter egos] and initially he worships both men. His increasing disillusionment with both Sukarno and Hamilton moves the 'private' action towards its destructive climax as the public order runs 'amok', the title of the final section of the novel.

On the surface Billy's two alter egos seem vastly different from him and from each other, but by a process of character equivalence and allegorical association which Koch pioneered in his earlier novels, the parallels between the three characters are elaborated. Like Kwan, Sukarno is a small man, but a small man with a volcano inside. . . . Sukarno is colonised man, but colonised man apparently asserting himself successfully. Indonesia too is a product of a 'dying colonial world', one where questions of self-definition and identity are important; where various stances and attitudes must be tried out, paraded and asserted as a colonial people seeks to re-form its own identity and style. Former puppet of the imperial powers, Indonesia, led by Sukarno, will change that role, and Sukarno becomes the political *dalang*—the supreme puppet master and creator of postcolonial Indonesia. But like Billy Kwan, who also attempts to arrange and direct other lives, Sukarno eventually cannot control his puppet creations.

Physically, Kwan and Hamilton seem unlikely sides of the one coin but they too are connected as colonials. Both, as Kwan points out, are 'hybrids' and so strong is their psychic association that they even look alike to the narrator Cookie and to Kwan himself. Hamilton, born in Singapore of British parents but resident since childhood in Australia, and Kwan, part Australian, part Chinese, are both uncertain of their identity, destiny or style—Kwan from the beginning of the novel, Hamilton increasingly as former certainties disappear. Initially anglophile through childhood memory of his English father, Hamilton learns through his experience with Henderson just what cold comfort England can offer. Though he is off to London to marry the English girl, Jill, at the end of the novel, he is increasingly certain that Europe is not his world. As he tells Jill, he wants to stay in Europe only 'if I can belong there' and he now shares Billy Kwan's instinct that he cannot. . . .

Billy, too, has shaken Hamilton's belief in the importance of ancestry, and he makes the point that identity is not a going back, a case of choosing which ancestral line to retrace, but a going forward however fitfully. When Hamilton insists on the value of Chinese culture and on Kwan's potential for identifying with it and thus attaining a sense of belonging to a complete culture, Billy replies: 'Ah look, old man, you're being a bit superficial aren't you? Only my father speaks Chinese, and he came out to Australia as a boy. I don't speak it at all. How do I manage to belong to a culture I never grew up in?'. . . . The question is of course a pertinent one for the English-Australian as well, who, until he has more or less become the disadvantaged 'prisoner' of Colonel Henderson, still feels his destiny lies in Europe.

Though dwarfdom and hybridization are important colonial metaphors in the novel, the central metaphor, on which the structure is also based, is that of the *wayang kulit* or Indonesian shadow puppet play. In a shift which itself indicates a significant step towards decolonialization, Koch has used as his symbolic underpinning in the novel the classical *wayang*. . . . Just as the complex characteristics of the Hindu Kali had provided a useful and informative analogue to the colonial's complex attitude to the 'missing real world', so the *wayang kulit* provides Koch . . . with a particularly appropriate base from a number of perspectives. While some aspects of the 'game' he plays may be of lesser importance in terms of their detail than others, the use of the puppet analogy does have a serious and complex function. . . . Notions of colonialism are reinforced in the history of the *wayang* itself, since the shadow plays are colonial versions of the Hindu *Gita*. Perhaps most important of all the idea of the *dalang* or puppet master allows Koch to play cleverly with the idea of character creation and manipulation on several levels where, like an intricate series of Chinese boxes, the supreme *dalang*, Koch, controls the narrator, Cookie, who relates his story and draws his characters from the files of the innermost, would-be *dalang*, Kwan. Although Koch cannot take for granted a knowledge of the underlying mythic story on the part of his readers, the *wayang* offers a way of conveying such information. Traditionally wayang audiences may watch the performance from either of two perspectives: from the front where they see the finished performance or from the rear where they can appreciate both the puppets and the skill of the *dalang*. With the *wayang* then as symbolic underpinning of the novel, Koch is able to draw his parallels with justifiable openness, allowing the reader to admire the artistry of the game while still being absorbed in the narrative itself. (pp. 332-35)

The structure of *The Year of Living Dangerously* follows that of the tripartite *wayang* division of *patet nem*, *patet sanga* and *patet manjura*. Traditionally *patet nem* 'lasts from nine in the evening until midnight; *patet sanga* . . . lasts from midnight until three in the morning; and *patet manjura* . . . lasts from three until the grey dawn around six'. Ending its *patet manjura* with midnight in this novel corresponds to the circularity of the earlier novels, indicating that for the post colonial—Kwan, Hamilton, or the nation of Indonesia—it is not yet dawn.

Although their settings differ, Koch's three novels all explore the peculiar tensions of the post colonial personality through Australian protagonists who are all questers doomed not to find the fulfilment, excitement or promise their sensibilities lead them to seek. Although the allegory is only embryonic in his first novel, it becomes a much more important element in his later work as he experiments with bolder and more complex patterns, turning, like Randolph Stow, to Asian religion and philosophy for his structural devices and motifs. (p. 335)

> *Helen Tiffin, "Asia, Europe and Australian Identity: The Novels of Christopher Koch," in* Australian Literary Studies, *Vol. 10, No. 3, May, 1982, pp. 326-35.*

FLORA CASEMENT

Across the Sea Wall . . . involves a man struggling to escape from the confines of his stifling environment. In this case Robert O'Brien, a young Australian, is seeking a change from his staid, conventional background in the way of a trip to Europe. But the extraordinary Latvian showgirl he becomes infatuated with on the voyage alters his plans. He is half attracted, half repelled by her peculiar and unfashionable beauty and the two are precipitated into an intense but uneasy love affair. But the cultural and moral backgrounds they come from are so different that each is searching for the impossible in the other and the relationship is doomed from the beginning.

C. J. Koch's unusual story is a brilliant portrayal of the cruelty of love; the two main characters are permanently scarred from their brief and disastrous liaison, and the hopelessness of their yearning is delicately and compassionately described. This novel is highly recommended.

> *Flora Casement, in a review of "Across the Sea Wall," in* The Times, *London, August 5, 1982, p. 7.*

RACHEL INGALLS

[The film *The Year of Living Dangerously* is based on C. J. Koch's novel of the same name.] Credit for the screen adaptation is given to Mr. Koch, together with David Williamson and Peter Weir [the director of the film]. . . . Some faults in the film probably have to do with production difficulties. . . . But a much greater fault is the confused screenplay. There are at least four plot-lines running through this work and just when you think they are going to coincide, they sabotage each other.

The main theme of the book is that of the shadow-puppet theatre, the *wayang kulit:* all the characters, all the political figures and events are depicted with ultimate reference to that idea; and there is time and scope to blend the real with the invented. The factual parts of the novel are informed and informative, the fictional characters a good deal more plausible and less prettified than in the film. Mr. Koch is especially good on the world of the foreign correspondent. His Djakarta is a place of fear, suspicion, competition and intrigue. The Guy Hamilton of the film has none of the resilience, persistence or cunning of the original—above all, none of his unwillingness to believe in appearances. In their effort to squeeze the whole book into a screenplay, the writers have had to pare down the characters to stereotypes. This would be all right if we were intended to see only the two lovers against the colourful background blur of a war-torn city. But the film aims higher than that. It aims for everything the book succeeds in, after having abandoned the book's subtle construction.

The book starts out being narrated in the first person by a journalist one assumes to be C. J. Koch. . . . [The] narrative glides easily into the third person wherever necessary. The narrator of Guy's story disappears, so that we read it directly. This ingenious method of story-telling works so well that one does not balk at the frequent change of focus—in fact, it seems

to suit the large canvas. But in the film, Billy takes over the position of author, with the result that he becomes the hero of the piece. He dominates the viewer's imagination. When Billy dies, the audience loses much of their interest in the surviving characters. It is possible that a mere voice-over extract from the files could avoid this difficulty, but probably not, as the imbalance seems intended: the character carries a tremendous authorial and directorial charge. From the first moment of the film, Billy tells us what to think and we trust him. We also admire his restless and poetic mind. Guy's suspicion that Billy is an agent does not impress—we know he couldn't be one; nor does Guy's remark that Jill might be a spy: she is introduced on Billy's recommendation, so she has to be all right. Straightaway we have lost the idea that the political conflict has its echo in the doubts and treachery among the characters. Billy is not to be doubted. There is consequently no sense of Guy's guilt at his failure to trust him. And Billy himself suffers from over-sanctification. Too little remains of his deep need to believe in heroes, of his thwarted sexuality, his voyeurism, his clinical approach to emotions he does not share, his compulsion to control others and incapacity to deal with his own powerful emotions. There is no reason left, except perhaps excessive spiritual sensitivity, why he should be the character who cracks. He makes a grand, romantic gesture that is politically useless, and he knows it. What we are given instead of this interesting man is an idealised portrait of an artist full of understanding and compassion, who is so centrally positioned that he becomes, as it were, the progenitor of all the other people around him. (p. 22)

If the first mistake in the screen adaptation is the decision to make Billy the narrator, the second is the attempt to keep the look of political unrest, while refusing to allow any native statement about it. We are given Billy's education of Guy, but get the Malay point of view only at the very end, when Kumar asks Guy if it is wrong that he should want to help his people: 'Why should I live like a poor man all my life, while stupid people in your country live well?' This is such an important point that it should be presented at the start of the film, where it might help to establish some notion of what all these foreign journalists are doing in the country and why the people who live there are suffering. Kumar, of course, cannot come out from cover till later, but his thoughts and words might have been given to another character. They could, for example, be given to the Communist leader to whom Guy speaks in the interview Billy obtains for him—the interview which is the making of Guy's career as a correspondent and which, for some incomprehensible reason, we are never shown. We see demonstrations without hearing the opinions of the participants, we are told that Guy is a good reporter, but we do not see him actively at work with other people, only passively looking on or caught in the middle of a mob. He and all the other main characters of the film except Billy are isolated from the political events.

The plots, themes or general ideas in the film concern betrayal, conversion, sacrifice, voyeurism, the nature of the artist and of his place in society. They are all supposed to hang together, as in the book, but they tend to bump into each other. Jill betrays her employers, and therefore her country, to Guy. He betrays her trust for the sake of his job. Billy only betrays himself after being betrayed by his idol, and dies sacrificially. Guy sacrifices his tapes, and perhaps an eye, to win Jill back. Jill does not seem to be called upon to make good her betrayal, as it is enough for her to be the future wife of the hero and to forgive him. Her part makes less sense than anyone else's. She considers Guy's latest despatch melodramatic. This appears to turn him on. . . . [It almost seems] as if what she needs from a man is good writing and what Guy has always wanted is the perfect literary critic. This line of thought might somehow have been connected with the later conflict of loyalties over the message about the arms' shipment and a theme that had to do with integrity and trust in one's work. It is dropped as soon as Jill and Guy become lovers. Her criticism of his work merely presents her as a woman who is fairly intelligent and does not go to bed with men as soon as she meets them.

There are many other points where pieces of characterisation and truncated plot are scattered around. The night-town scene with Curtis may link up with part of a pornography or prostitution theme not present elsewhere; it does little to further the plot, but shows that after Guy falls in love, he will not sleep around with other women even when he's drunk, and that he's a better man than Curtis, not just a better journalist. (The book tells us that Curtis is a first-rate newspaperman. That's why he gets the Saigon assignment.) Some scraps of a free-floating equation about love-sex-commercialism-truth appear to be at work here, adding to the narrative sprawl.

The theme most comprehensively explored is, appropriately, voyeurism. It is not worked out completely because of the change in Billy's character and standpoint, but it is frequently present and often implied. Our attention is drawn to the fact that the Western journalists report, photograph and describe scenes as if they were theatrical events of no concern to them. We see Billy taking candid-camera shots of lovers he has brought together. And very late in the game we realise that there are political spies all over the place.

There is also another plot, like a shadow in the story, which has almost nothing to do with the action, but is just a combination of sets of patterns and is in a way more interesting than the pseudo-realistic tale of foreign correspondents in Djakarta. It places each character next to another similar or opposite type and lets the audience draw its own conclusions. Billy is like Guy. 'We even look alike,' he tells him. 'It's true, we've got the same colour eyes.' Billy is trying to make Guy use his eyes to look at the world as he does. Billy is also like Sukarno, who is the creator and puppet-master of his country. And, on the other hand, he is like the dwarf Curtis buys for Guy. Every character has a disguise as another person, and sometimes a double—even the bright swimming-pool of the European community repeats itself as the overgrown pool at the Dutch villa. The madonna-figure of the Malay mother, who is a prostitute out of necessity, is set against Jill, who, if not loved and appreciated, 'could lapse into the promiscuity and bitterness of the failed Romantic' (a gorgeous movie line). Guy, the good journalist, stands in contrast to Pete Curtis, although they could also be congruent personalities. Billy dies in Christ-like sacrifice. Guy, like Judas, betrays his teachings. The Christian allusions apply to West and East alike, the visual images mirror each other. Jill in her swimming-pool resembles the Malay girl in hers, and so on.

Billy counsels Guy to watch the shadows, not the puppets. Certainly this shadow-plot is more successful than the main story. It is possible that if the team of scriptwriters had junked half the realistic plot, they could have made a better picture out of the interplay of the three main characters in all their disguises: the artist who loves the woman he cannot obtain, the woman only satisfied by the man who does not love her enough, and the ambitious, worldly man who is afraid to trust people and refuses his friendship to the man who asks for and

deserves it. It might even have been possible to get away with a happy ending for such a film.

Mr Koch does not give his book a happy ending. His hero and heroine escape on the plane, but she remembers that his reaction to her pregnancy was the phrase, 'Even if it isn't mine,' and he is going to feel out of place in Europe, is guilty about his failure to trust Billy, and is going to be totally blind. They will not have an easy life, in spite of their love, nor is it right that they should, for Djakarta is meant to be the world as it is everywhere—one never escapes it unscathed. And, according to Billy, the only way to alleviate suffering is to do what you can about what you see in front of you, to give and to participate.

What Mr Weir makes of this rather sour conclusion is the hero's adventurous and dashing ride to the airport, escape to freedom and to the arms of his beloved. Approximately five hundred thousand people will be massacred in the wake of their departing aircraft, but we are supposed to think only of this immaculate candybox couple who get out of the mess and will live happily ever after somewhere else. It is easy to imagine how they will be: he in a man-of-distinction eyepatch, she still with her large collection of nice clothes. What is this picture about? It sets us up for wisdom and sacrifice and then hands us a quick get-out, telling us to rejoice despite the bloodshed—with these lovers fled away. (pp. 22-3)

There are still some fine things to look at. All the love scenes . . . are intimate and tender. The political action and crowd scenes are well-paced and exciting. Everything looks right, vivid, attractive. And there is one scene that shows us just how good this film might have been: the scene at the Dutch villa and the dream that reveals his danger to Guy. Everything the snarled-up script pretends to, and fails in, this scene achieves, without effort and without words. It improves on the book, where the events take place as part of a digression concerning Guy's flirtation with a Russian spy who gives him a doped drink after she tries to push him under in the pool. The film has Guy watching the girl scrape away the waterweeds with the 'forbidden' sign. He smiles but she does not smile back. She dives into the scummy water. He is then shown covered in sweat and sleeping, and afterwards comes the dream of being underwater, accompanied by the muffled sound of bubbling water. The encounter with the girl, at first playful and as if about to become amorous, shifts all at once into fear and combat. She pushes him downward. The shot changes, the sound stops, we see her head out of the water, her face grimacing with hatred as she tries to kill him. And he wakes up suddenly. Every theme so disordered in the rest of the picture finds easy expression here: the interaction of West and East, man and woman, light and darkness, the exotic and the homicidal, pretence and truth. The scene is handled with daring, elegance and precision. (p. 23)

Rachel Ingalls, "Getting out of Djarkata," in London Review of Books, *Vol. 5, No. 18, October 6-October 19, 1983, pp. 22-3.*

RICHARD JONES

[C. J. Koch's *The Doubleman,* a foray into that region where psychopathology and the supernatural meet, is] ambitious and draws on a . . . variety of human experience, mood and personality.

The story is told by Richard Miller, a Tasmanian of Irish-German descent, who is slightly crippled by polio as a child, and retreats, with Keats-like fervour, into the realms of Faery. The work of Dulac and Rackham shows him the supernatural agencies behind ordinary surfaces; a height near Hobart is 'not just a mountain' but the 'sign of an amazing Beyond'.

One day, on his way to school, Miller meets a strange older man, Clive Broderick, who eventually persuades Miller's cousin, Bryan Brady, to buy a Ramirez guitar. Broderick teaches Brady how to play it and opens up a musical career for him.

Brady joins Darcy Burr, the nephew of the man who sold the instrument, in professional tours, and Miller, by this time a radio producer, helps to publicise them. In time, Miller's Estonian wife joins the pair as a singer, and later the stepson of Deirdre Dillon, a child-woman whom Miller first knew in Tasmania, becomes the group's drummer. The Rymers have a great success and their special contribution to the folk-music revival sweeping Australia in the 1960s is a haunting sound that evokes the supernatural.

All this may sound a bit glib and fey; but Koch avoids whimsicality by grounding these events in a most persuasive realism that converts Hobart and Sydney into places of greater psychic depth and resonance than they know. They are also wonderfully observed scenes of family and professional life. (pp. 27-8)

The Doubleman is an enjoyable novel, full of surprises, but curiously short on two emotions that such a book ought to arouse: fearful wonder at the menace in ordinary situations, and poignancy when the enchantment fades. (p. 28)

> Richard Jones, "Haunted Hobart," in The Listener, Vol. 113, No. 2907, May 2, 1985, pp. 27-8.

KARL MILLER

It is possible that C. J. Koch's novel *The Doubleman* . . . will be reviewed as a pathfinding contribution to literary psychology. A clever and diverting book it certainly is . . . and it applies to established themes a new ambience and a new geography. It takes the double into a delirious realm of folk music, radio, television and the charts. The inhabitants of a land of Faery cut their discs and their capers dressed in Medieval costume; the Mersey sound is emulated by Sydney's very own elf sound. But this is not a novel novel. It is a Gothic novel, which abides by a tradition of which the writer is learnedly aware, and which can lead him to telegraph his punches. Some of it reads like Bulwer-Lytton's *A Strange Story,* of a long time before, which ends up, as it happens, in Australia, with a kind of atomic-diabolic explosion.

Having recently completed a book on the literature of the double, I read Mr Koch's novel with a pang—compounded of interest and of its dualistic opposite—which may readily be understood. . . . At all events, I swallowed my anxieties and tackled *The Doubleman,* and I seemed to discover there—this, too, may be readily understood—material that bore on conclusions reached in the book I had written. . . . Like other strange stories of the genre, it both embodies and attracts coincidence. . . .

In the literature of romantic duality the most important of all pairs is the one constituted by the author and his principal character, or his narrator: here, if you like, is the primal duplication of the genre. In these fictions doubleness ensues on the singleness of someone's afflicted solitude. The principal character suffers, serves as patient rather than agent, but is capable of wishing to escape from his sufferings. Then there are two of him, or more—a development which expresses his dilemma and attempted escape. The character lacks character, very often, and exercises a negative capability which turns these novels towards the condition of poetry. This is what Goethe, in *Wilhelm Meister,* thought all novels were like, and this is the kind of novel that C. J. Koch—of the suitably German name—has delivered.

The narrator, Richard Miller, is lame, loses his father in the Second World War, is literary, theatrical, passive, longing to be 'at one remove' from everyday life, from Tasmania, where he is looked after by his grandfather, . . . Karl, an architect and alderman of German stock. . . .

Early on, [the] otherworld exists for Richard as a Fairyland whose occasions are derived from the Border Ballads, with decor borrowed from artists like Arthur Rackham. But it gradually assumes a more sinister dimension. As a boy, Richard has met a portentous, learned stranger, Broderick, to whom occult powers are attributed, and then, in the role of producer eventually, he joins a high-flying folk-music venture, in the company of his cousin Brian from the Irish side of the family and of the weird Darcy Burr. Broderick is the Devil, or the magus that trafficks with him, and Darcy doubles for Broderick as a sorcerer's apprentice during the storms and triumphs that come their way when their eldritch folksy pop music transfers to Australia in a welter of guitars, penny-whistles, Tam Lin, Thomas the Rhymer, drugs, inspiration and greed. All this casts a spell on the escapist Richard Miller. Darcy, spokesman for an alternative theology, had learnt that there were 'two people inside me: one who was weak and sentimental; the other somebody who could be strong enough to make himself free'. But Richard shakes the spell, and seems set to persevere as a broadcasting executive on the climb, and as a kind of sentimental Catholic who has been sliding back to Mass by the end of the book. . . .

As a programmatic dualiser among novelists, C. J. Koch is second to none. There are two of everything in his novel. Deirdre, who proves false, is, as Darcy is, 'two people', and the language of her 'shape-changing' might almost be that of Charlotte Brontë's *Villette,* with its interest in inconsistency. This is a tale of two cities, there being 'two Sydneys' on show. According to Darcy, 'Fairyland's double': 'The Faery Otherworld had two aspects: dark and light; Hades and Elfland.' Come to that, 'the universe is double.' . . .

That the novel is orthodox in terms of romantic tradition can't be doubted. Here once more are flight, reincarnation, an authorised solitary enclosed in double talk and in the uncertainty this promotes. The novel is double, and its hero is double, and in quite a familiar way. Richard rejects the black magic and the ghost music that come to him: but the novel can seem to love it, and to suggest that there are two Richards, one of whom is brothering it out with Broderick and Darcy because of a sufferer's wish to remove himself from the world, and that this Sydney sound is something very special. Not since Flann O'Brien has so much been made of Phouka the Fairy. We are meant to half-believe in Phouka, and, for that matter, in Hecate and Hades.

But only half-believe—so that there is something in the book both for the sceptical and for the superstitious reader. . . .

As for Mr Koch's hearty alderman, the concidence of names directs my thoughts less to him than to his grandson, who is meant to command sympathy but doesn't command mine. I can bring to mind mundane explanations which might fit . . . different kinds of coincidence (with accident, presumably, playing rather more of a role in the case of the shared name). But I would like to think that an element of explanation might also be got from the literature of romantic duality, in which victims are oppressors and oppressors are victims, in which the excluded person who nevertheless wants to escape is likely to fall in with his double. This is a literature which is still being written, as I've said; we're not having the kind of time which makes these fantasies redundant, though I don't suppose the aptly-named Tasmania of Mr Koch's romance will persuade many of its readers that the Devil has been causing trouble down under.

> *Karl Miller, "Diary," in* London Review of Books, *Vol. 7, No. 8, May 2, 1985, p. 21.*

PHILIP SMELT

Seven years after *The Year of Living Dangerously,* a political thriller set in Indonesia, C. J. Koch has written *The Doubleman,* a novel about the loves and ambitions of a group of Australian folk musicians in the 1960s, tracing the rise of three young men from their childhood in the cultural outback of Tasmania to musical stardom in Sydney. . . .

Infected by the psychedelia and pretentious spiritualism of an era that is perhaps better forgotten, Koch relies on figurative language that is generally unimpressive and at times quite meaningless. In describing, for instance, his first attack of polio, Koch's narrator plucks a simile from nowhere when he says "Pain struck me in the back like a great silver club." His musical imagination is similarly vapid: "The guitar accompaniment was slow and rudimentary, like water falling on a stone." Endless idle enquiries litter the book. "Is there really some hidden significance in the number seven?" is the question that opens one chapter and leads into a long paragraph which includes the Faery Process, Hind Etin, the Great Silkie, Thomas Rymer and Pythagoras to conclude with "Certainly I had renewed myself by the end of the seven years I spent as an actor in Melbourne."

The dust jacket proclaims Koch's ability "to make an exactly caught phase of history symbolic of a larger reality". No doubt he has captured accurately enough the unremarkable folk music phenomenon of twenty years ago, but what weightier matter Koch is struggling to symbolize is not clear.

> *Philip Smelt, "Dual Otherworlds," in* The Times Literary Supplement, *No. 4288, June 7, 1985, p. 644.*

D. J. TAYLOR

Professor Karl Miller has written on C. J. Koch's *The Doubleman* in *The London Review of Books,* defining it as a text of romantic dualism [see excerpt above]. A more prosaic approach seems in order. Fatherless and crippled by polio, Richard Miller . . . is growing up in post-war Tasmania. Paralysis is crucial in his introduction to the allegorical sub-world which the book extrapolates. Flat on his back, living life at one remove, he notes that "it was now that my interest in the other world began." This interest is reinforced by his encounter with the mysterious Broderick, a sort of Magus figure, who has a sinister familiar named Darcy Burr and who teaches Richard's cousin Brian to play the guitar. But Richard, after a sexual initiation at the hand of unfathomable Deirdre Brennan, decamps to Sydney in the hope of becoming an actor.

It is at this point that the book begins to lurch towards its disconcerting conclusion. Darcy and Brian reappear as Thomas and The Rhymers, a quaint folksy ensemble whose lyrics preach the occultism that enlivened Miller's childhood. And not just occultism. Among the tribe of hobmen, water sprites, bogles and various other fauna of the supernatural, there arises the notion of dualism. "Faery's double", Darcy tells Richard, and indeed reflection assures you that the book contains two of everyone, even Deirdre, whose death—and the splitting up of the group . . . is the novel's finale.

Again the reader is enmeshed in a web of actuality and illusion, of things not being what they seem. The metaphor is music. "In complex music the melodies aren't there at the beginning just for what they are." Apparently not. The quest—for meaning, for one's true associates—is pervasive. "I can always find y' Dick" says Darcy. "there's nothing easier than finding people." I smell Jung. One's first reaction is to assume that this is meretricious tosh, but that would be to deny the book's obvious merit. It is an axiom that within every novel of ideas there is a decent realist fiction screaming to get out. In *The Doubleman* one can detect an interesting novel deflected from its proper path by this accretion of Darcy Burr's "ghost music", the story of a lonely adolescent, proceeding to struggling actor—amid the mincing old queens of the ABS drama department—finding fulfilment in success and marriage to Katrin. Mr Koch is capable of conjuring up sharp and ineradicable images, ranging in a few words over *Mitteleuropa,* when describing Katrin's ancestry, manifesting a keen awareness of the passing of time, a sense of people's lives slipping away, of youthful promise inadequately fulfilled. There is an oddly old-fashioned air hanging over *The Doubleman.* It is very much a book of the 1960s. Dope, tinsel, and misplaced enthusiasm combine to remind one what dull, fatuous years they were. (pp. 52-3)

> *D. J. Taylor, "Down Under with Waltzing Jane," in* Encounter, *Vol. LXV, No. 3, September-October, 1985, pp. 51-4.*

Larry Kramer

1935-

American dramatist, novelist, and screenwriter.

Kramer is best known for his controversial drama *The Normal Heart* (1985), which garnered acclaim for its realistic, socially conscious approach to the subject of acquired immune deficiency syndrome, or AIDS. Kramer's experiences as a founder of the Gay Men's Health Crisis in 1981 inform his approach to *The Normal Heart*. The play is fueled by the protagonist's anger toward the media and public officials who have seemingly ignored the importance of informing the American public about the AIDS epidemic. Often compared to William M. Hoffman's play *As Is*, which stresses the personal and emotional effects of AIDS, *The Normal Heart* instead emphasizes politics and polemic. Several critics also noted similarities between *The Normal Heart* and Henrik Ibsen's play *An Enemy of the People*, which centers on a man who stands alone in his attempt to awaken society to potential health hazards. Although some reviewers faulted the play's didactic tone, most agreed with Clive Barnes's assessment that Kramer's "angry heart is in the right place, his accusations searing, his descriptions of the disease properly harrowing."

Both *The Normal Heart* and Kramer's first novel, *Faggots* (1978), focus on homosexuality and the topic of alternative lifestyles. *Faggots,* which portrays members of the gay community as narcissistic individuals who devote themselves to sadomasochistic, promiscuous sex, is considered by critics to be a sensationalized account of one segment of the homosexual subculture. Kramer also wrote the screenplay for the film *Women in Love*.

Alon Reininger/Contact

BARBARA G. HARRISON

I would like to make it very clear that in reviewing [*Faggots*]—which I might as well tell you I find revolting—I am not reviewing male homosexual life. I don't think Larry Kramer is writing about homosexual life. (Anita Bryant may think so, but that's her problem—and, to a reprehensible degree, Kramer's.) Although Kramer . . . has allowed his publishers to tout *Faggots* as "the inner reality of homosexual life," he is in fact writing about a peculiarly ugly, vicious, perverse, depraved, sado-masochistic subculture in which love does not exist—a subculture that homosexuals have been at pains to say is not representative of homosexual life. . . .

At the end of this book (which leaves nothing to the imagination), there is what is meant to be an epiphany. Fred Lemish, the homosexual whose story this is, tells himself that he "must have the strength and courage to say No . . . , it takes courage not to be a faggot just like all the others. Now it's time to just *be.* . . . I'm here. I'm not gay. I'm not a fairy. I'm not a fruit. I'm not queer. A little crazy, maybe. And I'm not a faggot. I'm a Homosexual Man. I'm Me. Pretty Classy."

Pretty Lousy Writing.

Lemish (I keep wanting to call him *Nebbish*) makes his decision to just *be* (whatever that may mean) after a long Memorial Day weekend, during which he and the hapless reader become intimately involved with nonculinary amounts of Crisco, with urine and excrement, with "fag hags," gallows, whips, leather executioner's masks, ropes and thongs and chains and buzzsaws. . . .

The action takes place in the "meat rack" of New York's Fire Island, in bars and discos and bathhouses with names like The Toilet Bowl and Everhard; it includes fire, accidental death, dismemberment, raids, blackmail, incest. . . .

And a cast of thousands: Lemish says "there are 2,556,596 faggots in the New York City area"; and so many of them turn up in this busy busy novel it's difficult to keep track of who is doing what to whom. . . .

Forty-year-old Lemish, until his belated and unconvincing epiphany—which reads suspiciously like the last-minute inspiration of an editor intent on a moralistic ending—carries on wildly and witlessly and in ripe detail about "secret cavortings in the dens and vicepots and cesspools of the underground faggot world . . . experiencing Everything to the fullest."

But I doubt that he'll have many readers—heterosexual or homosexual—cheering him on his grotesque pilgrim's progress. He's just not a sympathetic character. . . .

On the one hand, Lemish, like every other "faggot" in this novel, considers himself part of a privileged elite minority, a participant in arcane rites and partaker of "narcotic beauty." On the other hand, he, like almost everyone else in the book, casts about for someone to *blame*. . . .

It's worth mentioning that when Fred and his pals aren't busy bartering their bodies, or taunting the "straight" world—and looking for vengeance because they themselves are *not* straight—they are to be found working out in gyms. (Which is boring.) If they're not "thin and gorgeous," it's all over for them. So, are we meant to feel sorry for people who are both narcissistic and self-loathing (and self-justifying)? Are we meant to share Kramer's fascination and revulsion with them?

I can't think what Kramer had in mind. . . . Nor can I think that anybody but Anita Bryant and her crowd will be made happy by this book; it will serve to confirm all their wicked propagandistic nonsense. If Kramer had written with any kind of ironic detachment, or with any compassion, I shouldn't feel obliged to say that this is the work of a cynic who has done the homosexual community an enormous disservice. What makes matters worse is that, through the sensational trash, one sees glimmers of good writing. I wish that that good writer would come out of the closet—minus the whips and chains.

> Barbara G. Harrison, *"Love on the Seedy Side,"* in Book World—The Washington Post, *December 17, 1978, p. E4.*

SAMUEL McCRACKEN

[Once] one erases the line between homosexuality and heterosexuality *simpliciter,* it is not easy to redraw it elsewhere. Just as some of our more enlightened states have been trying to draw it between private acts involving consenting adults and all other acts, some groups advocating the sexual "liberation" of children try to erase it, to be redrawn heaven knows where.

Some lines have, however, been drawn in an extraordinary new novel, *Faggots,* by Larry Kramer. A satire written, like all good ones, from the inside, *Faggots* deals with one large class of male homosexuals, those who live in New York. It holds some positions critical of homosexuality that would be unusual even among the most critical anti-homosexuals: enduring relationships are next to nonexistent among homosexuals; they are far too involved with drugs for their own good; sado-masochism is a pretty nasty business; . . . and most homosexuals are unfulfilled people whose gaiety is desperate rather than spontaneous. Kramer is of course already beginning to be denounced by the activists. (p. 23)

> Samuel McCracken, *"Are Homosexuals Gay?"* in Commentary, *Vol. 67, No. 1, January, 1979, pp. 19-29.*

MARTIN DUBERMAN

[*Faggots*] is a foolish, even stupid book. And not because, as some will argue, it has tried to be an exact transcription of that fatuous segment of the gay male population which defines existence wholly in terms of gyms, discos, orgies and Fire Island phantasmagoria. No, the book fails because it has nothing of discernment to say about that scene nor, in place of

insight, any compensating literary distinction. Announced as a searing indictment of the giddy Fire Island set, *Faggots* merely exemplifies it. And often cannot manage that. The book's wooden dialogue, strained humor and smug disdain are no match for the inventive flamboyance of Fire Island hedonism when viewed from an angle wider than primitive moralizing.

I say this as someone who can't stand the place, who thinks it magnifies the worst aspects of gay male life and lends credence to the standard homophobic equation of gayness with narcissism and mindlessness. A serious dissection of the self-absorbed frivolity of this subculture within a subculture would be well worth having. But it would have to be one capable of seeing that "obsessive triviality" does not encompass the reality of a style whose exuberant, risky raunchiness we may one day realize contained the seeds of a far-reaching social transformation. *Faggots* is not remotely that needed dissection. It is a plastic, trashy artifact of the worst aspects of a scene to which it high-mindedly condescends. (pp. 30-1)

> Martin Duberman, *in a review of "Faggots,"* in The New Republic, *Vol. 180, No. 1, January 6, 1979, pp. 30-2.*

JOHN LAHR

[*Faggots*] flits over the same New York terrain as Mr. Holleran's book [*Dancer from the Dance*] but without an iota of his ability. Where Mr. Holleran honors the sadness as well as the sensations of homosexual life, Mr. Kramer merely exploits them. In *Faggots*, the love that dare not speak its name is hoarse from shouting. Fred Lemish, nearly 40, is in search of Life and happiness; he pursues it in the baths, the discos, the Pines. Here are characters like Randy Dildough, Blaze Sorority, Boo Boo Bronstein, Jack Humpstone, Nicolo Loosh, presented in a jocular, baroque style which is, sentence for sentence, some of the worst writing I've encountered in a published manuscript. "And so they dance, our friends, in various circlets of together and alone." Backward reels the mind! Mr. Kramer wants the book to be a rambunctious farce; but his frivolity isn't earned and so it becomes an embarrassing fiasco. (p. 40)

> John Lahr, *"Camp Tales,"* in The New York Times Book Review, *January 14, 1979, pp. 15, 39-40.*

DOUGLAS WATT

The Normal Heart is an angry, unremitting and gripping piece of political theater. . . . Larry Kramer's episodic drama [is] about the mounting virulence of AIDS in the gay male community, particularly New York's. . . . (p. 279)

[*The Normal Heart*] is unsparing in its attack upon the indifference shown by the media—the *New York Times* is mentioned specifically—and heads of government, both local and federal. [Kramer] doesn't hesitate to name names, Mayor Edward Koch among them.

The play, covering the period from July 1981 to May of last year in this city, is a kind of Living Newspaper with a personal drama embedded in it. Ned Weeks [is] . . . a homosexual reporter unable to get any of his fellow gays on the paper or in the city government to come sufficiently out of the closet to spread the news about the growing death toll and, in the process, put an end to the widespread conviction among gays that "promiscuity is liberating."

One of the work's many shortcomings, almost all of which are swept away by the immediacy and forcefulness of the drama, is the fact that all the male characters but one—Ned's very successful older brother, a lawyer . . .—are gay. The play's only female is the doctor . . . who spins on and off authoritatively in a wheelchair, the result of her having contracted polio a few months before the Salk vaccine came into use. Her disability, and the inferred promise of hope for some future AIDS victims, reflect the poster-art quality of the enterprise, but the explosive nature of the subject and the driving performance keep us engrossed until the very end, a rather stagy scene involving a death-bed marriage between Ned and his fashion-reporter lover . . . followed by an embrace between Ned and his straight brother. (pp. 279-80)

[*The Normal Heart*] is a horror story told with a rage encompassing even the author's lashing out against Jews and Catholics and a federal government that, in his opinion, turned aside from the World War II holocaust itself. You may find a lot to quarrel with in this evening, but there's no denying the factual evidence or Kramer's fervor, and you are bound to come away moved. (p. 280)

> *Douglas Watt, "The Tragedy of AIDS," in* Daily News, *New York, April 22, 1985. Reprinted in* New York Theatre Critics' Reviews, *Vol. XLVI, No. 8, Week of May 20, 1985, pp. 279-80.*

FRANK RICH

The blood that's coursing through *The Normal Heart* . . . is boiling hot. In this fiercely polemical drama about the private and public fallout of the AIDS epidemic, the playwright starts off angry, soon gets furious and then skyrockets into sheer rage. Although Mr. Kramer's theatrical talents are not always as highly developed as his conscience, there can be little doubt that *The Normal Heart* is the most outspoken play around—or that it speaks up about a subject that justifies its author's unflagging, at times even hysterical, sense of urgency.

What gets Mr. Kramer mad is his conviction that neither the hetero- nor homosexual community has fully met the ever-expanding crisis posed by acquired immune deficiency syndrome. He accuses the Governmental, medical and press establishments of foot-dragging in combating the disease—especially in the early days of its outbreak, when much of the play is set—and he is even tougher on homosexual leaders who, in his view, were either too cowardly or too mesmerized by the ideology of sexual liberation to get the story out. . . .

Some of the author's specific accusations are questionable, and, needless to say, we often hear only one side of inflammatory debates. But there are also occasions when the stage seethes with the conflict of impassioned, literally life-and-death argument. When the play's hero, a writer and activist named Ned Weeks . . . , implores his peers to curtail sexual activity rather than risk contracting AIDS, another equally righteous activist vehemently counters that such sweeping measures will negate years of brave, painfully hard-fought battles for the freedom to practice homosexual love "openly" and "without guilt." While the logic may be with Ned—"AIDS is not a civil rights issue but a contagion issue," he says—Mr. Kramer allows the antagonist . . . to give full ideological and emotional vent to an opposing point-of-view. . . .

Ned is a loud, tireless firebrand who favors confrontational strategies in dramatizing the AIDS threat; the mostly timid men who join him in founding an AIDS-awareness organization are often afraid either to risk public exposure of their sexuality or to take on the heterosexual power structure forthrightly. To thicken the conflict further, Mr. Kramer has Ned fall in love with such a weakling—a fictional New York Times reporter named Felix . . . who can't decide how completely to step out of the closet.

The constant squabbles between the radical Ned and his cautiously liberal friends—which often sound like replays of those that divided the antiwar movement of the 60's—can become tiresome. The trouble is not that the arguments are uninteresting, but that Mr. Kramer is not always diligent about portraying Ned's opponents, including the organization's frightened president . . . , in credible detail. Worse, there's a galloping egocentricity that overruns and upstages the play's most pressing issues. The more the author delves into the minutiae of the organization's internecine politics, the more *The Normal Heart* moves away from the larger imperatives of the AIDS crisis and becomes a parochial legal brief designed to defend its protagonist against his political critics.

The writing's pamphleteering tone is accentuated by Mr. Kramer's insistence on repetition—nearly every scene seems to end twice—and on regurgitating facts and figures in lengthy tirades. Some of the supporting players, notably Ned's heterosexual brother . . . and a heroic doctor . . . , are too flatly written to emerge as more than thematic or narrative pawns. The characters often speak in the same bland journalistic voice—so much so that lines could be reassigned from one to another without the audience detecting the difference.

If these drawbacks, as well as the somewhat formulaic presentation of the Ned-Felix love affair, blunt the play's effectiveness, there are still many powerful vignettes sprinkled throughout. Much to his credit, Mr. Kramer makes no attempt to sanitize AIDS; the scenes featuring the disease's suffering victims are harrowing. The playwright is equally forceful—and at his most eloquent—when he passionately champions a prideful homosexual identity "that isn't just sexual."

> *Frank Rich, in a review of "The Normal Heart," in* The New York Times, *April 22, 1985, p. C17.*

MEL GUSSOW

Ibsen described Dr. Thomas Stockmann in *An Enemy of the People* as "muddle-headed," and he is, in the sense that he never learns, he cannot learn, the positive uses of pragmatism. In his headstrong pursuit of truth he consistently ignores political, economic and personal realities. Blunt, outspoken and adversarial, he is an innocent in a land where, in his words, people chase after expediency. He further weakens his own case by proclaiming that the majority is never right, thereby alienating those who could provide a measure, if not a maximum, of support. . . .

With certain alterations, one could be discussing not only Stockmann but also Ned Weeks, the hero of Larry Kramer's *The Normal Heart,* a new play that speaks with passion about a contemporary problem that is not so far removed from the poisoned water of *An Enemy of the People.* The principal problem in *The Normal Heart* is not Acquired Immune Deficiency

Syndrome (a subject that is not mentioned by name in the course of the play), or even the broader question of a bias against homosexuals. As Ned affirms, ''This is not a civil rights issue. This is a contagion issue.'' In common with Stockmann, he is trying to staunch an epidemic. He is a whistle-blower and he is surrounded by people who are worried about their careers, their images and their sex lives. Life itself is at stake.

Both Ned and Stockmann realize that the prime power base in a community is public opinion, and each sees two obstacle-ridden routes to that source: the mayor and the press. In each case, the hero ascertains and assails recalcitrance, but where Ibsen attacks the mayor and the press with satiric humor, Mr. Kramer uses insult, and in most cases there is no one there to reply to the charge. The approach vitiates the effectiveness of his argument on his targets.

The Normal Heart freely mixes fact, fiction and dramatization, somewhat in the manner of a Costa-Gavras movie. The author names names when it suits his thesis. But, as with the best of Costa-Gavras, *The Normal Heart* is a moral *j'accuse,* and it is an indictment with wide dimensions. At one point, Ned tells the fellow members of a health crisis center that is trying to make people aware of the plague-like proportions of the disease, that in their cause they ''will never have enough friends.'' He makes it clear that, depending on the depth of commitment, his colleagues have the ability to become their own enemies. . . .

The Normal Heart is the second persuasive AIDS play of the season. The first, William M. Hoffman's *As Is* . . . , is a movingly personal consideration of the disease, focusing on two men, one of whom contracts AIDS, while the other becomes his sympathetic watchman and nurse. Both works are that rarity, plays that take an immediate, responsive stand on issues of great timeliness and consequence. . . .

Both *The Normal Heart* and *As Is* confront their shared crisis directly and graphically. Though both plays share a milieu and a sensitivity, they differ in temperament. *As Is* is filled with rage, *The Normal Heart* with outrage. In addition, Mr. Kramer's play has a historical perspective both in its treatment of homosexuality and in its attitude toward public apathy. It also has a polemic purpose, one of several reasons why a comparison to *An Enemy of the People* is in order. (p. 3)

The Normal Heart is episodic and overlaid with facts and statistics. It is, however, a deeply felt document. . . . (pp. 3, 24)

Trapped between a reluctant Establishment and a frightened homosexual community, he never stops challenging—and taunting—the status quo. . . . Though the character is apparently the playwright's alter ego—events recounted on stage parallel Mr. Kramer's own campaign to arouse public concern for AIDS victims—the perspective is broadened to include other, divergent points of view. . . .

[The only woman in the cast is] a doctor, crippled by polio, who takes on AIDS as a crusade. Where Ibsen's Stockmann stands alone in his quest, [the doctor] becomes Ned Weeks's comrade-in-arms. In one of the evening's most incendiary moments she attacks public health officials for their neglectful attitude toward what she considers a national emergency. Her impassive antagonist is a contemporary American equivalent of those in *An Enemy of the People* who choose to disregard

Stockmann's warning. They are, in Ibsen's phrase, people who ''didn't dare do otherwise.'' (p. 24)

Mel Gussow, ''Confronting a Crisis with Incendiary Passion,'' in The New York Times, April 28, 1985, pp. 3, 24.

CLIVE BARNES

Both [William M. Hoffman's *As Is* and Larry Kramer's **The Normal Heart**] deal with the health crisis caused by the epidemic known as AIDS (Acquired Immunity Deficiency Syndrome), which is taking a cruel toll of the populace, principally those in the homosexual community.

Both plays are written by homosexuals, about homosexuals, but not, specifically, for homosexuals. They deal with death and suffering—the tragic commonplaces of human experience.

They are politically slanted, in that they wish to awaken awareness of this menace to society, and to ensure that adequate measures, particularly money for urgent, desperately needed research, are taken, and that the growing horror of this plague receives its proper public awareness. . . .

Both plays, but particularly Kramer's, draw comparison with the Jewish Holocaust. There are obvious differences—AIDS needs no Hitler—yet sufficient similarities to give cause for pause. The major lesson here, surely, is that human suffering never goes away simply by being ignored.

The Normal Heart is altogether a less graceful, less well-written, less effective play. It is also more controversial, more annoying, and more disturbing.

Kramer, the man, is spluttering with rage and anguish, which is not much help to Kramer the playwright. Indeed, if one wished to be inappropriately flippant, one might subtitle the play *Kramer vs. Kramer.*

Kramer himself was, in 1981, a founder of the Gay Men's Health Crisis, and, in circumstances fictionally related in the play, was dismissed by the organization's leadership two years later, after they had finally managed to secure a meeting with Mayor Koch.

Obviously the play, and its hero Ned Weeks . . . , has its roots in Kramer's life story—and may be none the worse for that.

But his mixture of fact and fiction has the shaky effect of us never quite knowing whether we are watching a documentary seemingly justifiable, onslaughts against city government and the media alike—or a dramatization.

The writing is often banal, and even more often unconvincingly informative, piling on facts and statistics as if it were journalistic polemic rather than dramatic dialogue.

This hero also has a lover dying of AIDS, in this case a *New York Times* reporter who has had difficulty with his closet door. And Mr. Kramer—in a scene that makes you blush for ever doubting the death of Little Nell—does not flinch from arranging a deathbed ''marriage'' between the two.

Even Ned's principal ally in his battle against ignorance, a doctor specializing in AIDS victims, is a woman in a wheelchair, felled by polio, an unnecessarily melodramatic touch.

But Kramer's angry heart is in the right place, his accusations searing, his descriptions of the disease properly harrowing (except for that deathbed moment, he never romanticizes the sickness), and his political case, aimed at the folly and cover-ups of the homosexual community as much as at the callous indifference of the outside world, made with emphasis.

For the theater, too much emphasis. *The Normal Heart* is more of a tract than a play. . . .

Yet even if it is primarily an essay in pamphleteering, a nobly partisan polemic, that does not mean that what Kramer is saying is not worth saying. And how many people of the thousands who will see the play, and be stirred by its sheer intensity and passionate concern, would ever have read the tract?

Clive Barnes, "Plague, Play and Tract," in New York Post, *May 4, 1985. Reprinted in* New York Theatre Critics' Reviews, *Vol. XLVI, No. 8, Week of May 20, 1985, p. 280.*

Robert Littell
1935?-

American novelist, editor, and scriptwriter.

In his novels Littell portrays the intrigues of the cold war. As a former Eastern Europe and Soviet Affairs editor for *Newsweek*, Littell experienced first-hand the closed societies behind the Iron Curtain. His knowledgeable insights have helped solidify his reputation as a reliable novelist of international intrigue. Littell is praised for the intricacies of his plots, his convincing characterizations, and his realistic descriptions of life in totalitarian countries. James N. Baker noted that Littell's work has "the piercing irony of an insider."

Littell's initial work of fiction, *The Defection of A. J. Lewinter* (1973), won the Edgar Allan Poe Award for best first novel. This book tells the story of an American missile engineer who defects to the Soviet Union and becomes involved in an elaborate power struggle, as both countries attempt to determine the truth behind his defection and his value to their governments. *Sweet Reason* (1974), Littell's next novel, is a black comedy set in an obscure Asian country at war with the United States. *The October Circle* (1976) focuses on several Bulgarian exiles who band together to protest the 1968 Soviet invasion of Czechoslovakia. *Mother Russia* (1978) is a satire of contemporary Soviet life as told by a Russian con artist. With *The Debriefing* (1979), Littell returned to the spy novel and to a plot similar to that of *The Defection of A. J. Lewinter*. In this work, his protagonist is a Soviet defector who seeks asylum in Greece. Littell next produced *The Amateur* (1981), which pits a vengeful United States government worker against the two superpowers. *The Sisters* (1985) portrays two unscrupulous American intelligence operatives who play a major role in President John F. Kennedy's assassination. Littell also coedited *The Czech Black Book* (1968), a collection of translated newspaper articles, transcripts from radio and television broadcasts, and other pieces detailing the Soviet invasion of Czechoslovakia in August, 1968.

(See also *Contemporary Authors*, Vols. 109, 112.)

PAUL H. CONNOLLY

The plot of Robert Littell's *The Defection of A. J. Lewinter* recalls the "Spy-Counterspy" cartoons of *Mad* magazine: an American scientist working on ballistic nose cones accidentally acquires the formulas for the trajectories of warheads and their decoys, and, for various reasons, he decides to defect to Russia. Incredible? Precisely the reaction of the Russians, who, though obviously eager for such information, have no way of testing its veracity. Eventually, they accept both the scientist and his data, and an intricate game of chess commences as the Americans deliberately emphasize the value of Lewinter, hoping the Russians will suspect he is a planted agent, and the Russians deliberately respond with incredulity, hoping that the Americans will credit their disbelief.

It is a clever plot, and the short book offers a very enjoyable evening's entertainment. It would, and probably will, make a quite respectable movie. But it is not a classic of intrigue. A good suspense story should be as intricately knotted as macramé, with no loose threads, no weak links. The texture should be thick and absorbent. But here there are too many accidents, too many irrelevant asides. Lewinter's motives for defection are weakly serio-comic: he both fears the Strangeloves of the military-industrial complex, and he hopes the Russians will rejoice at the solid-waste-disposal system he has engineered as a hobby. The acquisition of scientific secrets depends on a photographic memory. And a number of characters and incidents are scarcely supportive of the plot. (pp. 522-23)

> Paul H. Connolly, in a review of "The Defection of A. J. Lewinter," in America, Vol. 128, No. 21, June 2, 1973, pp. 522-23.

THE SPECTATOR

Many American reviewers have compared Robert Littell's *The Defection of A. J. Lewinter* . . . to [John le Carré's] *The Spy Who Came in From the Cold*. The comparison is unfortunate since, though it may attract to Littell's book attention it would not otherwise receive, it is bound to make for disappointed hopes. *The Spy* is a classical thriller, one of the great masterpieces, and *The Defection* is like it only in intent, not in the quality of its execution. Lewinter, an American scientist, defects to Russia for no apparent reason. Uncertainty about his motives, and about the value of what information he possesses, leads the secret services of both countries to take actions designed to convince the other side to act towards Lewinter in a way that would serve their own interests: thus the Americans, who want the Russians to believe that they have planted Lewinter (so that the Russians will dispose of him), take actions which on the surface suggest that they have *not* planted him, reasoning that the Russians will conclude from those actions that they *have*. Naturally, the Russians work this out and . . . well, you can fill the rest in for yourself. The point of the story is to suggest that all the mayhem of intelligence work relates not to the value of the defector or the interests of his country but to the rules of the intelligence game itself.

The plotting is neat and elegant, but the book is too long. *The Spy* was not long and its power came from the tightness with which each sequence of events was described.

> A review of "The Defection of A. J. Lewinter," in The Spectator, *Vol. 231, No. 7577, September 15, 1973, p. 346.*

CHRISTOPHER LEHMANN-HAUPT

Robert Littell's *Sweet Reason* is conventional insofar as it deals with a destroyer's tour of duty off the coast of some small Asian country. But the captain of the U.S.S. Eugene F. Ebersole is an absurd figure of a Navy man named J.P. Horatio Jones who wears spit-shined Adler elevator shoes and asks, "If war isn't hell, then what the hell is it?" (It's a "career opportunity," says Lieut. (jg) Lawrence Lustig.) And the sorts of action the captain leads his crew into are sinking harmless junks, torpedoing a school of whales and impressing a junketing Congressman with the shelling of a rural village.

Now it's clear enough what Mr. Littell is trying to say about warfare in the mode of Vietnam. He's saying that it's black comedy in which everyone is acting out a sick joke. For in *Sweet Reason,* the cream of American youth is represented by Ensign de Bovenkamp, a basketball star from Yale who is potent in everything except the sexual game. The most sensitive of American youth is a poet who, contra-Eliot, thinks August is the cruelest month because "That's when all the psychiatrists go on vacation . . . leaving their patients stranded without a couch." And Sweet Reason is nothing but the signature on a series of seditious memos whose mysterious source preoccupies Captain Jones even more than executing the war. . . .

And if *Sweet Reason* rises to comic absurdity here and there, its structure and its jokes remind us too much of Joseph Heller's *Catch-22,* while the rest of it recalls every Navy story from Herman Wouk's novel *The Caine Mutiny,* to Neil Sheehan's report, *The Arnheiter Affair.* Subtract these obvious predecessors and you have little left but a tired exercise in gray comedy.

> Christopher Lehmann-Haupt, "Trying to Novelize Vietnam," in The New York Times, *February 20, 1974, p. 35.*

DAVID WILSON

Sweet Reason never makes an appearance in Robert Littell's second novel [*Sweet Reason*]. It is the *nom de guerre* of an elusive subversive who posts seditious leaflets round the decks of the USS Eugene Ebersole, a battered old tub pulled out of semi-retirement to bolster the American war fleet in coastal waters far from home. The war zone is Yankee Station, a thinly disguised Vietnam, and this decayed destroyer is only there because of a clerical slip of the pen. A last-page twist reveals Mr Littell's purpose, and reveals also how the reader has been conned. Sweet Reason is posted missing, presumed drowned: perhaps he exists only in the mind—and in the American military mind has long since been suppressed.

The Ebersole belongs to a navy in which an ensign wins the Congressional Medal of Honor by mistake and a refuelling tanker has "We give green stamps" painted on the hull. *Sweet Reason* is a nautical *Catch-22* or a *M*A*S*H* on the ocean wave. The cast is properly farcical. . . .

While much of the book is sharp and some of it is funny, it adds up to an uneasy blend of dry satire and knockabout farce, occasionally spiced with serious purpose. The one passage which is not intended to be funny gives a bird's-eye view of a napalm attack on a "gook" village whose inhabitants, from the air, look like children and mostly are. The point seems to be that while those who give the orders are foolish knaves, those who obey them are merely fools. Which is an old story, however entertainingly it is told.

> David Wilson, "Below the Waterline," in The Times Literary Supplement, *No. 3817, May 2, 1975, p. 492.*

DIANA ROWAN

Totalitarianism, as Dr. Hannah Arendt has diagnosed it, is the extreme manifestation of the egalitarian impulse in politics. It is the attempt to reduce masses into a single malleable material. It is also total war by the political sphere against the private sphere of life.

Robert Littell's new novel [*The October Circle*], set in Communist Bulgaria during the 1968 Soviet invasion of Czechoslovakia, dramatizes that thesis in chilling detail and ponders a complicated array of problems, couching them in neatly turned metaphors. A woman preens in front of a mirror, and finds no image reflected there; she does not exist, or else the mirror is just painted on the wall. A mime acts out suffocation in a narrowing space, and is later trapped by police between the glass panels of a revolving door.

For all its bitter realism, this is also a witty, even entertaining adventure, steeped in black humor, peopled by a crew of characters ranging from the merely picaresque to the utterly bizarre. Tacho, the Racer, is a record-breaking bicyclist who, twenty years after his victory (back in the Past Imperfect, as the author terms it), is still puzzling over the elusive difference between motion and real movement. Now, in the Present Ridiculous, Lev, the Flag Holder, and Popov, the mad poet, struggle with different facets of the same problem: anonymity and resulting inertia in the face of a monolithic power. . . .

There is more than a touch of the poet in this novelist, as he continues to develop his themes. Octobrina, a painter old before her time ("bone dry and brittle, like a fallen leaf or fallen angel") works with still lifes of animate objects, portraying life, she says, abstracted down to its motionlessness. Things exist not with respect to their movement, but only in the contrast between their stillness and their potential for movement. . . .

Can an assembly of characters this eccentric be reduced to part of a "single malleable unit"? Their ultimate burst of political protest brings suppression as ruthless as it is predictable; and yet, reduced to immobility, by imprisonment or execution, their real movement begins. As an affirmation of that "private sphere of life," communal cooperation, others will carry their story forward. In doing just that, Littell's metaphor is complete.

> *Diana Rowan, "Eccentrics in Noble Protest," in* The Christian Science Monitor, *March 22, 1976, p. 22.*

T. J. BINYON

The October Circle could have been an absorbing political novel or an exciting thriller, but in the event it is neither. Robert Littell imposes a simple, supra-ideological moral scheme on the novel, whereby Dubček and those who sympathize with him are good, and all the rest bad: he shows no awareness of the fact that for dedicated communists—which all his heroes are—the issues are far more complicated; the story is sentimental and whimsical, where it should be harsh and direct; the pretentious rhetoric his characters employ is no substitute for closely knit political argument; and the narrative, written almost completely in the present tense, moves jerkily forward like a series of sub-Shavian stage directions.

> *T. J. Binyon, "Simple Heroes," in* The Times Literary Supplement, *No. 3880, July 23, 1976, p. 905.*

JAMES N. BAKER

Robespierre Isayevich Pravdin is an uncommonly imaginative hustler. As a boy, he bred poisonous snakes and killed one or two a week for a 10-ruble bounty. Later, incarcerated in the medical section of a Soviet prison camp, he received extra goodies for selling a two-minute look at a list of female prisoners with VD. Now Pravdin survives in the 1970s, living in central Moscow, where he sells information to American journalists and plagues the Soviet bureaucracy with proposals that the proletariat be offered such bourgeois luxuries as Classic Comics, vaginal deodorants and Q-Tips. . . . Robert Littell has tackled the absurdities of the police state in his previous novels, but never more effectively than in [*Mother Russia,* a] zany satire on the frustrations of contemporary Soviet life. . . .

[Pravdin's] neighbor, Mother Russia, is a batty old anti-Bolshevik fond of knocking off letters to an American sewing-machine manufacturer—"zingers to Singer." When she senses Pravdin's "closet idealism," she tries to enlist him in a plot to unmask a Nobel Prize-winning Soviet author as a plagiarist. . . . Advised to take on the mission by a mystic mentor who claims to be "the 71st incarnation of God" (and who doubles as a KGB official), Pravdin sets out on a quixotic crusade to destroy the writer's reputation. Here the black comedy becomes steadily more chilling as, for the first time in his life, events slip entirely out of Pravdin's control. Littell perceives a foreign society with the piercing irony of an insider.

> *James N. Baker, in a review of "Mother Russia," in* Newsweek, *Vol. XCII, No. 1, July 3, 1978, p. 79.*

WALTER CLEMONS

The chilling formalities of novels about contemporary espionage are as familiar by now as the rules of the sonnet. We assume at the start that superalert opponents in the looking-glass war will fox each other to a stalemate. All we ask from this gloomy form of entertainment is that the concocter leave us with a bitter taste in our mouths slightly distinct from previous service.

Robert Littell is an expert. *The Debriefing,* his fourth novel since *The Defection of A. J. Lewinter,* presents us with a Russian courier who defects with a briefcase of classified documents chained to his wrist. They turn out, of course, to be of enormous value to the West. But have they been planted? The defector seems sincere: "You think you're genuine; we all agree on that," says the American in charge of debriefing.

To find out whether all is what it seems, it becomes necessary for an American agent to go to Russia to retrace the steps that led the courier to leave his homeland. Here the novel suddenly spurts in interest. Stone, the American White Russian operative, meets an 80-year-old dead ringer for Stalin, who formerly served as his ruler's double at public functions and now lives in happy retirement with his transvestite lover. (pp. 77-8)

Littell plays his cards with clarity and elegance. I count it a definite plus that I was able to grasp the multiple final betrayals without having to flip backward through the book to find out who was who. Littell excels at lucid complication. (p. 78)

> *Walter Clemons, "Playing by the Rules, Deftly," in* Newsweek, *Vol. XCIV, No. 4, July 23, 1979, pp. 77-8.*

NEWGATE CALLENDAR

In 1973 Mr. Littell made a big impression with his *The Defection of A. J. Lewinter.* His new book [*The Debriefing*] follows along that line, in that it is about a Russian defector. But the emphasis is entirely different. The Russian breaks away in Athens. A smart American is in charge of his debriefing. Is the Russian a plant? If so, what's behind it? To find out, the debriefing officer himself penetrates Russia.

Mr. Littell is a smooth and sensitive writer, and *The Debriefing* is a better book than most of its kind. The ending is cold, cold, cold. One problem, though: The author's hand is too much in evidence at the turn-around conclusion; things are moved around to accommodate the idea he had. There is also some clichéd writing. By now we all know about the amorality of Big Government, and Mr. Littell did not have to hit the reader over the head with "But too many promises have been broken. I don't know heads from tails any more. Both sides of the coin look the same to me." Yes, *The Debriefing* is a bit contrived. But it is also superior entertainment.

> *Newgate Callendar, in a review of "The Debriefing," in* The New York Times Book Review, *September 2, 1979, p. 21.*

MICHAEL MALONE

If there's anything tastier to thriller fans than ordinary citizens bludgeoning, gunning down or driving over one another, it's secret agents up to similar shenanigans *pro patria*. . . . In *The Debriefing,* Robert Littell depicted the C.I.A. as a mangled mingling of Wall Street mismanagement with cloak-and-dagger Disneyland. Since writing that story of a K.G.B. defector, and an earlier book, *The Defection of A. J. Lewinter,* Mr. Littell's views of the Company he calls "Byzantium" have not mellowed. Acid etchings of agents and officials fill *The Amateur* with characterizations as graphic and incisive as his evocation of Communist Prague, where much of this Spy Who Stays Out in the Cold story takes place.

Wry, scholarly Charlie Heller, snapped up by the C.I.A. because of a *Kenyon Review* article on the diarist Pepys, is a cryptologist cleared to highest Top Secret. No Bond he, Heller has done nothing racier than tease a crateologist (Russian crate identifier) down the hall, snitch Government Scotch tape and use his computer to try to find the cryptogram in Shakespeare's works that will reveal the plays' "true" author. His passion for deciphering codes, for "spiraling into the core of language" and emerging from "the gibberish with a clear text," derives from his faith in truth, his faith that as patterns fall into place he can discover "where is the why." Heller is, then, an amateur in what proves to be a drab but deadly le Carré-ish world of disillusionment, compromise and banal bureaucratic evil, where truths unravel like rotted cloth. (p. 15)

Sustained by the need for vengeance, Heller survives, learns to kill, learns to live and love again, and even learns who wrote Shakespeare's plays (not the Swan of Avon). *The Amateur* has a taut, chilling plot and a protagonist as memorable as one of Len Deighton's heroes or le Carré's George Smiley. (p. 36)

> *Michael Malone, "Secret Agents," in* The New York Times Book Review, *May 10, 1981, pp. 15, 36.*

MAUDE McDANIEL

Many adults haven't decoded an important message since their Little Orphan Annie Secret Decoders last spelled out "Drink Ovaltine." Robert Littell scratches the old itch with the dedication in *The Amateur,* providing the reader with a cryptogram of one's very own to decipher, which is best saved for last and may incidentally get our minds off the unpleasanter aspects of this clever novel.

Charlie Heller is a CIA cryptologist far more passionately involved in his search for the real author of Shakespeare's plays than in the darker side of his profession until terrorists murder his fiancée abroad. The gentle hero turns into the vengeful Count of Monte Cristo, blackmailing his curiously reluctant superiors into allowing him to train in professional assassination techniques and seek out the killers. . . .

The CIA remains the chilling Frankenstein monster of recent perception and continues temperamentally incapable of admitting this problem: It is not the nature of yellow, apparently, to worry about whether it is a streak or a ribbon, and Littell wastes little time on the matter either. Actually, we're all more interested in who wrote Shakespeare. I can't tell you that here but it's in the book, top secret, for readers' eyes only.

> *Maude McDaniel, in a review of "The Amateur," in* Book World—The Washington Post, *August 2, 1981, p. 10.*

PETER ANDREWS

The Sisters is Mr. Littell's seventh novel and as slick a thriller as they come. Once again, he explores the labyrinth of Soviet and American intelligence activities. This time we meet Francis and Carroll, a pair of old veterans in the C.I.A. who spend their every waking hour hatching plans and plots for covert operations. Dubbed "the sisters Death and Night," from a line by Whitman, the two cook up what Carroll calls "the most beautiful operation that has ever existed in the annals of in-

telligence work." . . . In short, the sisters are able to control a K.G.B. sleeper agent and order him to commit any crime they wish, which the Russians can then be blamed for. Their Russian counterparts, realizing that something has gone haywire, have to construct a countercase that will put the blame for whatever happens on the C.I.A. The forces unleashed by this operation all come together in Dallas on Nov. 22, 1963. . . .

Mr. Littell's suspenseful fiction surrounding the Kennedy assassination is fascinating and strains credulity to the breaking point, but no more than the Warren Commission report did. Do you really believe that Lee Harvey Oswald acted alone and two days later, while in police custody, was shot and killed by a grieving nightclub owner? And what about those puffs of smoke from the grassy knoll? Mr. Littell has provocative answers to all those questions and more.

When he wants to, Mr. Littell knows how to lash a narrative across the page with the insistence of a dog sled driver bringing serum through a blizzard to a sick child. And he rarely gives you time to ask too many questions, which is probably just as well. At one point, he has Feliks Arkantevich Turov, a burned-out Russian secret agent, flee to the West through the washroom at the airport in Moscow in an escape worthy of Edmond Dantès's breaking out of the Chateau d'If in *The Count of Monte Cristo.*

Although he has a nice feel for the devices of the traditional 19th-century adventure novel—he even has "documents" hidden under the floorboards of an old house—Mr. Littell is at his best as a modern and mordant observer of the cold war scene. . . .

There are a couple of sloppy spots in *The Sisters,* which is surprising for Mr. Littell, who is usually scrupulous in not letting the mechanics of storytelling tip his hand. When Turov, who dabbles in ceramics, is preparing to flee Russia and inadvertently slips into his pocket a wire loop used in cutting clay, you get the feeling we may be in for some garroting before long; 10 pages later we are. And although it is clear halfway through the novel that this is a story concerned with the assassination of President Kennedy, Mr. Littell turns fearsomely coy and never actually says so. Kennedy is identified only as a "Prince of the Realm." In a book that relies so heavily on exact detail and verisimilitude, this becomes an irksome evasion.

But such minor quibbles aside, Mr. Littell once again delivers the goods in fine style. If *The Sisters* is not his best spy novel, it is a very, very good one and it would be churlish to ask for much more than that.

> *Peter Andrews, "Freedom Lies Beyond the Washroom Door," in* The New York Times Book Review, *February 2, 1986, p. 9.*

THOMAS R. EDWARDS

Robert Littell's *The Sisters* shows what imagination and decent writing can do for a thriller. The Sisters in question are in fact men, related only by a long and close professional association. Francis and Carroll are the CIA's odd couple, slightly epicene right-wing veterans now thought outdated or even crazy by the rest of the agency. They lead dull bachelor lives in Washington, they always work as a team (Francis is the idea man, Carroll works out the details), their derisive nickname comes from a suitably ominous line of Whitman's: "the hands of the sisters Death and Night incessantly softly wash again, and over again, this soil'd world.'' As the story begins, in 1963, they are plotting an unauthorized "perfect crime" for which they need an agent who won't know, or ask, who his clients are.

The crime is the assassination of John Kennedy. . . . (pp. 13-14)

Littell's appeal to readers of thrillers is both subtler and less satisfying than Ludlum's. All the men in *The Sisters* are hardened professionals (as usual, the women don't much matter); no access is provided for civilians, no faintest suggestion that the fantasy has room for people like us. We see the thing and its considerable artfulness from a clear, disinterested distance. But such purity costs something. Certainly my own feelings about political murder or covert intelligence in general were never exercised as I read Littell's cool, elegant story—in a way, ludlums may be better for the health. (p. 14)

Thomas R. Edwards, "Boom at the Top," in The New York Review of Books, *Vol. XXXIII, No. 8, May 8, 1986, pp. 12-15.*

William McIlvanney

1936-

Scottish novelist and poet.

McIlvanney is respected for his realistic portrayal of conflicts among Scotland's social classes and age groups. In his acclaimed novel *Docherty* (1975), for example, he examines differences between two generations of a Scottish mining family at the beginning of the twentieth century. In his novels with contemporary urban settings, McIlvanney depicts similar conflicts exacerbated by the increasing crime and materialism of Scottish society. Written in a rich English prose style, McIlvanney's novels often contain Scottish colloquialisms that lend verisimilitude to his stories but sometimes make the dialogue difficult to follow. McIlvanney has been praised for his vivid descriptions of Scottish locales and his ability to evoke the beauty and hardships of Scottish life.

McIlvanney's concern with class consciousness informs his first novel, *Remedy Is None* (1966). With a storyline that includes parallels to Shakespeare's *Hamlet,* this novel tells the story of a young university student who, like McIlvanney, is the son of a miner. When his father dies, the protagonist, unable to reconcile his working-class background with his academic career and his mother's new middle-class husband, quits college and eventually kills his stepfather. McIlvanney blends the dark broodings on death and revenge that preoccupy his protagonist with a lively recreation of the local color of small-town Scottish life. In *A Gift from Nessus* (1968), the protagonist is pressured by his job, his status-seeking wife, and his mistress; he is forced to reconsider his values when his mistress commits suicide. *Docherty* details the resignation and hopelessness of life in a Scottish mining town. The Docherty family attempts without success to approach life with a sensitive and intelligent outlook in an environment predicated on hardships and brutality. The protagonist of McIlvanney's recent novel, *The Big Man* (1985), is revered by his community because of his physical strength but realizes that he must reevaluate his priorities when he is recruited by the Glasgow underworld for an illegal bare-knuckle prize fight.

McIlvanney has also authored the novels *Laidlaw* (1977) and *The Papers of Tony Veitch* (1983), which feature Glasgow police detective Jack Laidlaw. More colorful than most hard-boiled detectives, Laidlaw reads philosophy and fiction, which he often applies to his investigations of crimes in the seamy neighborhoods of Glasgow. These novels are noted for their strong plots and sophisticated presentation of complex ideas. In addition to his novels, McIlvanney has published two volumes of verse, *The Longships in Harbour* (1970) and *These Words: Weddings and After* (1985).

(See also *Contemporary Authors,* Vols. 25-28, rev. ed. and *Dictionary of Literary Biography,* Vol. 14.)

IRVING WARDLE

Where novels are concerned, powerful talent generally seems to have two accompanying factors: a firm outer shell with-

© Jerry Bauer

standing great stress from within; and the presence of characters who kill the reader's superior detachment and make him feel that he might not put up much of a show in their company. On both counts William McIlvanney passes with honour.

Remedy is None is the story of a first encounter with death. Charlie, the undergraduate hero, is summoned home to his father's death-bed and arrives in time for a last conversation in which the old man confesses himself a failure and curses the man who took away his wife.

This interview has an explosive effect on Charlie. Death, meaningless to him before, now obsesses him, and he views his previous existence as a distant memory. He does not return to the university, and his speech relapses into Lallans: periodically he is possessed by blindly destructive impulses which find their true victim when his mother revisits the family with her new husband. Charlie picks a fight and kills him.

Although no one mentions it, the parallel with *Hamlet* is too plain to miss; there are even stand-ins for Rosencranz and Guildenstern. Looked at in retrospect, it is a highly schematic novel. Yet at the time of reading, the impression is of uncontrollably violent emotion which might lead anywhere. And just as *Hamlet* presents the riddle of why the hero does not act, so the question here is why he does. It is not an empty question, as the reader is made to share Charlie's sense of compulsion:

to enter into his memories of family life and growing up (there is a beautiful elegy on Saturday nights in the dance hall); to experience the sensation of changing from the typical to the extraordinary; and to feel his own relish in the crescendo of violence that leads up to the murder.

The source of these impulses may be obscure, but there is no doubt of their reality. Nor is Mr McIlvanney thrusting them down the reader's throat. Among other things, this is an extremely funny book, containing brilliant pub conversation and some of the most impressive chatting-up ploys I have ever seen in print. This amplitude is reflected in the style. It is highly correct, but flexible enough to accommodate remote images and ideas and make them relevant.

If one of Mr McIlvanney's aims is to record an extraordinary experience, his second aim is to make sense of it. Eloquent as they are, I don't think the analytic passages succeed in doing this. But it is the tension between emotional and intellectual passion that defines the book's quality. It is a very Scottish combination, but I have rarely seen it operating as powerfully as in this first novel.

> Irving Wardle, "Elsinore Revisited," in The Observer, May 29, 1966, p. 22.

THE TIMES LITERARY SUPPLEMENT

Mr. McIlvanney brings certain primary virtues to [*Remedy Is None*]: intimacy with its background, respect for its people, the ability to make them interesting and a keen ear for the way they actually speak. He also takes for his theme a human situation of primary importance and he explores it with passion and perception. It is that of Charlie, a university student who comes home to Kilmarnock to be at his father's deathbed and learns while he is there something of the true nature of his father's failure and the deep pathos of his life. . . .

Mr. McIlvanney altogether succeeds in conveying Charlie's sense of the intolerableness of death after such a life; and his reaction to those who do not seem to share this feeling—his brother, his sister, his girl friend and others—is quite believable. He sees them and the life around him with the apparent clarity, and actual distortion, of hate and its anguish. The skill with which ordinary life is evoked and commingled with Charlie's contemptuous and despairing vision of it is admirable—as in the scene in which he returns home to find his sister and her young man courting in the sitting room and vents his bitterness on them, whom we know to be innocent and oblivious. In spite of a somewhat cursory ending, *Remedy Is None* is a memorable novel.

> "Father and Son," in The Times Literary Supplement, No. 3355, June 16, 1966, p. 539.

FRANK McGUINNESS

The story of a young man's obsession with the death of his father that finally plunges him into madness and the murder of his mother's second husband, *Remedy Is None* might almost be an updated rehash of *Hamlet* with Elsinore removed to Kilmarnock and the Prince transformed into a brooding pleb. As a blow to post-Freudian vanity, however, it must be admitted that the hero of William McIlvanney's first novel remains as much of an enigma as his courtly predecessor and the true motive of his lunatic crime is no more easily adduced. But this is no criticism. An altogether less absolute author than most of his contemporaries, Mr McIlvanney shows himself remarkably free of those facile influences that would reduce all human behaviour to oversimplified psychological equations and render the modern novel as predictable as any knitting pattern. Where they are only concerned with illustrating their pontifical certainties, he remains open-minded, content to indicate the whole complex of emotions behind any significant act or belief and leave the interpretation of what may be deemed the real truth to his reader. In consequence, his novel is of absorbing interest both as a study of encroaching lunacy and as a cool indictment of a society blind to any values save those of social and material success. Few writers have been able to claim as much at their first attempt.

To compare it with *Hamlet* is not to dismiss Mr McIlvanney's novel as a slavish copy, a jazzed up version of an inimitable masterpiece. Far from it. At most, it simply means that he has exploited a similar theme and in the figure of Charlie Grant created a hero close to Jan Kott's description of Hamlet as 'a young rebel who has about him something of the charm of James Dean'. . . . For his part, Charlie is very much the cool young sybarite of the Sixties, shrugging off the burden of parental dreams as lightly as the struggle it has cost his father to put him through college at all. His attitude strikes an authentic note. A generation removed from that working-class image fostered by the intellectual foundlings of the depression, he is politically apathetic and socially neutral, his carefree life on the campus untroubled by anything but the fear that his girl friend might be pregnant. All this crumbles, however, when he is summoned home to the deathbed of his father, a scene described with a stark power and simplicity that could scarcely have been excelled by Lawrence at his best. His first experience of death, Charlie is shattered by it, the guilt of his own filial neglect swelling up into a massive resentment of the heartless world around him. Haunted by the old man's dying confession of himself as a worthless failure, he becomes moody and violent, shows no inclination to resume his studies and throws over the girl he intended to marry. Worse still, he is eaten up with the idea that there should be some expiation of his father's death by those who misused him in life, a notion that slowly hardens into hatred of his mother, the woman who finally destroyed what little happiness her husband could have found by leaving him for a richer man. The thought of her treachery becomes the focal point of his guilt-ridden grief, compelling him towards the fateful moment in which his mind finally cracks and he exacts his futile revenge, battering her husband to death in front of her. This is the culminating horror of a sequence of events that the writer has cunningly woven into a pattern of tragedy that would seem to lead almost inevitably to one fatal conclusion. It is probably as close to tragic compulsion as the scepticism of our age will permit.

Although the novel is essentially an intense, even painful, analysis of a mind hovering on the brink of insanity, it must not be assumed that Mr McIlvanney's talents are confined entirely to introspection and despair. The truth is that those dark gifts are matched by a flair for comedy that makes his book consistently amusing and occasionally hilarious. But his witty description of youthful priapism and horseplay is more than a comic bonus. Together with his acid commentary on our social and moral deceits, it provides an effective counterpoint to the central theme of the work and prevents it from becoming another glib essay on communal guilt. Yet occasionally, it must be said, he comes slightly unstuck, particularly in his portrait of the mother. This is not to deny that his cameo of a silly, vain woman desperately clinging to her fast departing youth is not meticulously realized and exact. On the contrary, it is because she emerges as such a convincing and elegant expression of middle-class fatuity that one finds it almost impossible to imagine her ever married to Charlie's father or entertaining his robust relatives. But this is merely to seek for flaws in a compassionate and intelligent novel that marks the arrival of a very good writer indeed. (pp. 111-13)

> *Frank McGuinness, in a review of "Remedy Is None,"
> in* London Magazine, *n.s. Vol. 6, No. 5, August,
> 1966, pp. 111-13.*

DAVID HAWORTH

A Gift from Nessus concerns a Scottish salesman, his marriage, and the promotion that is compromised by an affair he's having with a young schoolteacher. He opts for the promotion but his mistress, Margaret, kills herself and, in McIlvanney's hands, Cameron is left at the mercy of fearful self-realisation which is of almost Strindbergian intensity. To have written as strongly as he has a story with a plot which might just be considered as a television play, is not short of remarkable. The style is adroit yet latinate; he can savour more meaning and emphasis in words such as 'performance' and 'dilemma' than any writer I can recall. . . .

The final confrontation between Cameron and his wife is as excruciating as a probe on a tooth nerve and quite extraordinarily dramatic. It's just as well, because if this crisis, subtly prepared for through the book, had not come off, for all its felicities the novel would have failed. The ending is ambiguous, though hopeful. The accuracy, intelligence and its quality of controlled zeal will take some beating—even by the author. (p. 147)

> *David Haworth, "Small Lessons," in* New States-
> man, *Vol. 76, No. 1951, August 2, 1968, pp. 146-47.*

KENNETH GRAHAM

William McIlvanney (his first novel, **Remedy is None,** won an award last year) could well take some lessons from [Emyr] Humphreys's stories. One of the latter, "The Suspect", subtly suggests in 20 pages as much about a marriage, infidelity and a social setting as McIlvanney can expound, with great effort and earnestness, in the whole of *A Gift from Nessus*. The plot (consciously, I suppose) is very secondhand: a travelling salesman, trapped in futility, with ulcers, a harshly ambitious wife and a helplessly loving mistress, slowly moves towards a hope of salvation through agony, assertion, guilt and abnegation. There are a puritanical father, a foreseeable suicide and full ashtrays in dreary hotel bedrooms. What does the author infuse into these familiar ingredients? Sincerity, feeling and a laborious cleverness. It's not really enough. The events are so expected; the ideas, the values, the feelings so estimable, so banal. The Glasgow background is not over-indulged—always a temptation to anyone who has admired and survived that city—but some such solidity might have balanced so much inner anguish. Above all, the style—repartee rather than style—is clotted with forced similes and metaphors. Even the salesman's samples have to be 'the bacilli of persuasion'. And there is a heavy undergrowth of truistic apothegms, like this: 'The seeds of yesterday's casual moments become forests, we wander lost in today. Past oak trees yield themselves into acorns, too small to be recovered.' True, Mr McIlvanney, very true. But do you think we came up the Clyde on a banana boat?

> *Kenneth Graham, "Fumbling," in* The Listener, *Vol.
> LXXX, No. 2054, August 8, 1968, p. 184.*

THE TIMES LITERARY SUPPLEMENT

William McIlvanney's second novel [*A Gift from Nessus*] confirms the reputation he established with **Remedy is None** as a new writer of solid talent and sensitive intelligence. Eddie Cameron, a failure as a salesman, and fearing the first intimations of an ulcer, has been conducting a covert affair with Margaret, a young teacher exiled from her rigorously puritanical home. . . . Cameron's interior monologue of soul-searchings is given in prose of great verve and sensitivity, the arid wastes of business Glasgow are sketched with energetic irony and authenticity, and Mr. McIlvanney's handling of a large group of minor characters is assured and skilful.

Where most new novels assume a context of flip permissiveness, *A Gift from Nessus* makes the moral torments of a self-hater in a staid and Calvinistic society seem convincingly important. Only in his dialogue is Mr. McIlvanney still showing an uncertain touch: the gift of style, valuable in other respects, betrays him into excessive smartness in many passages of conversation—a lot of the characters have a flair for rapid, aphoristic abuse in the vein of John Osborne. But in his treatment of the central dilemmas of his characters—Cameron driven by guilt into causing Margaret's suicide and finally dragged into suburban conformity by the hideously relentless Allison—he shows himself already a writer of unnerving insight and substantial promise.

> *"Moral Torments," in* The Times Literary Supple-
> ment, *No. 3473, September 19, 1968, p. 1058.*

THE TIMES LITERARY SUPPLEMENT

Letting William McIlvanney's [*The Longships in Harbour*] fall open anywhere, we find instantly that he knows what he's doing. . . . This is a book of poetry; and being that, it can be criticized. At present Mr. McIlvanney is far too much concerned with Movement moral preoccupations—supercharged with what sounds like a Presbyterian legacy of spiritual doom—and overactive syntax that out-Larkins Larkin:

> I saw him first. No bigger, going fat.
> Recognition laboured, calved with disbelief.
> Deft at the darts, he made a little moment.
> Taking the kudos of his friends, he came across.

Recognition calves, the world rehearses, Asia bleeds, eyes abdicate and at one point perceptions trudge. If Larkin don't get you then Amis will: those super-verbs are a tip-off. On the whole this is a collection to worry over, quarrel with, grudgingly approve of and shelve until it is joined by his next.

> *"Language on Language," in* The Times Literary
> Supplement, *No. 3570, July 31, 1970, p. 849.*

LEONARD CLARK

William McIlvanney's voice [in **The Longships in Harbour**] is a welcome one. He has already developed an individual technique and writes with deep compassion about social injustices. He chooses his language carefully, making good use of telling images. There is a tautness and toughness about his poems in direct contrast to much of the sprawling prose which passes for poetry today. Yet he always writes clearly and powerfully.

Poems like **"Initiation,"** **"Grandmother"** and **"Old Men at Union Street Corner,"** all evidences of his Scottish upbringing, are genuine poems of our time. (p. 370)

Leonard Clark, "Five Welcome Voices," in Poetry Review, *Vol. 61, No. 4, Winter, 1970-71, pp. 370-71.*

PAUL GRAY

[*Laidlaw*] should surprise those who think that the only Scottish murder mystery is *Macbeth*. Set in contemporary Glasgow, it has not a bonny brae nor a twirling tartan to its name; but it offers an assortment of colorful underworld types who demonstrate that tough talk is not softened when it is spoken with a burr. (p. 68)

[McIlvanney's] novel goes down smoothly and with just the right amount of bite. The identity of the killer is revealed in the opening pages: Tommy Bryson, a young homosexual whose attempt to go straight results in the sex slaying of a Glasgow girl. The question is whether the police can get to him before two rival bands of killers, for reasons of their own, run Bryson to earth.

Although McIlvanney keeps this question hanging almost to the end, his focus is not on suspense but on a close-knit society's reaction to criminal outrage. Detective-Inspector Jack Laidlaw is assigned to catch the murderer, but he resents the assumption—especially rife among his fellow policemen—that this process is just the same as caging an animal. He argues, instead, that "monstrosity's made by false gentility. You don't get one without the other. No fairies, no monsters. Just people."

Yet Laidlaw is no bleeding heart. . . . As McIlvanney pieces him together, Laidlaw emerges as a jumble of contradictions, a sensitive, intelligent soul performing brutal, repetitive work. Indeed, some of Laidlaw's ruminations sound like heavier luggage than a functioning policeman ought to carry: "What's murder but a willed absolute, an invented certainty? An existential failure of nerve."

Such outbursts of bookishness threaten to tip the novel into a treatise. Fortunately, McIlvanney always manages to regain his balance by hitting the streets. His evocations of the old city seem etched in ancient stone and rubbed with coal dust. (pp. 68-9)

McIlvanney captures the speech of his Glaswegians with similarly high fidelity. . . .

Purists may want their crime stories with more matter and less art. But McIlvanney has created a hero and staked out a terrain that justify his techniques. Late in the novel, Laidlaw suggests that he will be back. It will take a few more cases for him to join the ranks of Maigret, Martin Beck or Lew Archer, but there is definitely a promising new man on the beat. (p. 69)

Paul Gray, "Criminal Outrage," in Time, *Vol. 109, No. 26, June 27, 1977, pp. 68-9.*

JEAN M. WHITE

[This first mystery, *Laidlaw*], by Scottish poet-novelist William McIlvanney, who has won fiction awards back home, just may be the start of an absorbing new series. We have had the sagas of Martin Beck of Stockholm, Maigret of Paris, Gideon of London, and Van der Valk of Amsterdam. And now comes Jack Laidlaw of Glasgow, a dour, angry, compassionate, abrasive, moody Scottish police detective.

This Laidlaw is a complex and irritating man. A Scotsman overcast with Calvinistic guilt, he keeps Kierkegaard and Camus in his desk drawer and alcohol that he sips as a form of "low-proof hemlock" in a cache. He believes that the world would be a better place if people would have the courage of their doubts rather than their convictions. A man who inhabits paradoxes—and incessantly broods over them. . . .

What makes McIlvanney's first mystery special is the way that he writes and the way that he handles people and place. Glasgow, with its dreary back alleys and the hard, violent men of its pubs, is as much a protagonist as Laidlaw. McIlvanney, who lives and teaches in Glasgow, has smelled the city, listened to its sounds (be patient with the dialect for its flavor), and felt its presence. . . .

Laidlaw, who "improvised every situation into a crisis," sometimes can be as exhausting to the reader as he is to Harkness, his young colleague, who provides a nice counterpart to his superior's overintrospection. So does Jan, Laidlaw's mistress, who cuts the brooding off with "Good night, Aristotle," observing: "You have to shut the door eventually on that stuff . . . and give yourself room just to be."

Sometimes McIlvanney doesn't shut the door soon enough on the brooding. And the novelist at times overreaches for an excessive, strained metaphor. But it is a small price to pay for a first mystery of such accomplishment and the promise of a superior new series. We certainly want more of Laidlaw, a policeman who doesn't believe in monsters any more than he believes in good fairies and can observe that people often choose guilts that they can handle as a way of hiding from the truth. There aren't too many cops like that in your standard police procedural.

Jean M. White, "Scottish Sleuth," in Book World— The Washington Post, *July 17, 1977, p. K5.*

NEWGATE CALLENDAR

In one respect, *Laidlaw* by William McIlvanney . . . [is] a procedural. The central figure is Detective Inspector Laidlaw of the Glasgow Police Department. But this book has a literary style far beyond that of most books in the genre. Where most authors of police procedurals—and of crime novels in general—deal with stereotypes, McIlvanney has the ability to create real people. Laidlaw, for instance, is well educated, philosophical, unconventional in word and deed. McIlvanney also gets under the skin of his lower-class characters. The father of the murdered girl is a brilliantly etched picture of an Archie Bunker-type from Glasgow, a city the author knows (he lives there) and loves.

There is no great mystery in *Laidlaw*. The identity of the murderer is known from the beginning. McIlvanney achieves tension by the way he manipulates the people associated with the miserable killer. Action is not neglected, and in John Rhodes, a tough, almost Mafioso type, the author has created an unforgettable character. But everything in *Laidlaw* rings true. it is a tough novel, with an exciting ending, and it is superbly written. You should not miss this one.

Newgate Callendar, in a review of "Laidlaw," in The New York Times Book Review, *July 31, 1977, p. 30.*

NEWGATE CALLENDAR

In 1977 William McIlvanney wrote a Glasgow procedural called *Laidlaw,* and it turned out to be one of the best of the year. We have had to wait a long time for its sequel, but here it is— *The Papers of Tony Veitch.* . . .

Again we have Detective Inspector Jack Laidlaw, who this time is informed of the death of a vagrant. The dead man was an alcoholic who had a message to pass to the inspector. So Laidlaw starts an investigation. For one thing, he liked the old boy. For another, he thinks the man was murdered, and Laidlaw is disturbed by the fact that his colleagues are willing to write the case off as an accidental death. The man, says Laidlaw, had led a rotten life, ''so the least he deserves is that we should care about his death enough to understand it.''

Laidlaw talks this way because he is a man determined to see justice done for low and high alike. He is a very tough man in addition to being highly intelligent and sensitive. His investigation leads him to a pair of mob leaders who are on the verge of an all-out gang war. Perhaps it can be averted if they locate the mysterious Tony Veitch, a man Laidlaw himself is just as eager to find.

As in *Laidlaw,* the writing is unusually probing. Mr. McIlvanney shapes phrases like an artisan, with a lavish use of unhackneyed imagery. . . . [The] book's characterizations are all three-dimensional. As a stylist Mr. McIlvanney leaves most of the competition far behind.

> *Newgate Callendar, in a review of "The Papers of Tony Veitch," in* The New York Times Book Review, *June 5, 1983, p. 37.*

JAMES CAMPBELL

''Rough voices, drunken songs of Ireland's suffering in Scottish accents, swear-words in the street.'' The characters in *Docherty* possess a small but personal lexicon. In the West of Scotland mining town where they live their rough voices are the only things they have with which to alert an otherwise indifferent world to their existence. They will inherit nothing, and leave nothing behind them, except a few songs and their own community in the High Street, which is described on page one of this novel as a ''hell''.

Docherty, which won a Whitbread Award when first published in 1975, has all the ingredients of a pot-boiler—heroism, failure, family rivalry, birth, death, unwanted pregnancy, war and catastrophe—except a plot. William McIlvanney's purpose is too serious to admit an artificiality of which he proves himself quite capable in his thriller-writing. In *Docherty,* he means to speak not about his characters but *for* them. This novel is the testament of a warrior who survived to tell the tale.

It begins in 1903 when Tam Docherty's wife is giving birth to her third son and it ends with a funeral in the early 1920s. Throughout, the author's evocation of the shape and substance of the community, and the family's place within it, is rendered with great authenticity. Yet, for all the anecdote and incident, all the legend surrounding ''wee Tam'', there are few occasions when the story moves with its own momentum. William McIlvanney has smothered his characters with love, so that at times we have difficulty seeing them. . . .

If this novel's most impressive feature is its rendering of ''rough voices'', it is also through voices that it comes into a peculiar conflict with itself. *Docherty* is written in two entirely different vernaculars—Tam Docherty's speech and William McIlvanney's commentary—which would not recognize each other if they passed in the street. This technique, of the author taking ten sentences for every one spoken by his characters, is complicated by the fact that McIlvanney, when not writing dialogue, is a writer with a single register: in poetry, journalism and fiction, he tends to write—and more to the point, to overwrite—in the same dazzling fashion. There is an unwillingness in all he does to sacrifice his attention-seeking style to the subject it supposedly attends. In *Docherty,* he writes about his characters in a language they would not understand. . . .

In the end the characters in *Docherty,* like the characters in Dickens's *Hard Times* whom they often resemble, may be suffering from an excess of nobility. Aware of this trap and the sentimentality it reeks of, the author has swerved to avoid it by including a specifically Scottish West coast characteristic: violence. I am worried that McIlvanney enjoys his characters' violent encounters more than a conscientious novelist should; he displays an unwholesome relish for a face transformed to ''a bloody pulp''.

The same suspicion is prompted more than once by *The Papers of Tony Veitch,* a sequel to the earlier crime story, *Laidlaw.* Torn between the toughs and the moralists in his books, McIlvanney has bridged the dilemma by creating characters who are philosopher-hardmen: Tam Docherty, in his own way, is one, and Detective Inspector Laidlaw is another. He reads Scott Fitzgerald and Kierkegaard with one hand and disarms Glasgow's fiercest crooks with the other, occasionally delivering a moral homily while he's about it. Laidlaw loves pure justice more than the ceremony of the law, but he takes himself too seriously, and this book—hingeing on the discovery of the truth about Tony Veitch—is damaged by the lack of a good reason why Laidlaw should be interested in him at all, other than his love for all mankind.

As in *Laidlaw,* the pace is fast, the path strewn with verbal fireworks: the best sections are those featuring Glasgow's underworld and its ugly population, which McIlvanney describes with a total absence of condescension. Fans of the earlier book will enjoy it and immediately look forward to the next, but it is eight years since *Docherty;* perhaps its author should sacrifice the glitter which has become his trademark and put his talents to a new test.

> *James Campbell, "Toughs and Moralists," in* The Times Literary Supplement, *No. 4188, July 8, 1983, p. 732.*

JEAN M. WHITE

For admirers of William McIlvanney's Laidlaw, who appeared to high praise some six years ago, it has been a long wait for a sequel. *The Papers of Tony Veitch* . . . marks the return of Jack Laidlaw, the idiosyncratic Glasgow cop who examines life's meaning and a suspect's alibi with the same skeptical, questioning attitude. . . .

Laidlaw seems to be the only one who cares that Eck Adamson has died, leaving only some confusing last words and a piece of paper with two scrawled names, an address in a section of Dublin where money grew, a phone number to a street booth, and the name of a pub, The Crib, in a tough neighborhood.

McIlvanney uses the police procedural form to write a richly atmospheric novel of place and character. He can capture a scene, a feeling, a person, a snatch of dialogue with a brush-stroke of words.

His wife's carefully arranged social evening with another couple gives Laidlaw "the feeling of being involved in field-work on group sedation." During the questioning of a married couple, one of Laidlaw's fellow cops sees the husband "spending his days attached to his wife like a life-support unit, a human pacemaker."

This second Laidlaw novel doesn't have the stunning impact of the debut book. Then McIlvanney was in control of his material. In *The Papers of Tony Veitch,* the action is not as focused in a confusion of subplots involving warring Glasgow toughs. (Some of the Glaswegian barroom talk "comes cross like Linear B," which is the way Laidlaw describes the last message of the dying wino.)

But a little plot slackness and arcane argot can be forgiven a talented writer and observer like McIlvanney.

> *Jean M. White, in a review of "The Papers of Tony Veitch," in* Book World—The Washington Post, *October 16, 1983, p. 10.*

ED WARD

The close-knit family, the one-industry town, and the interdependencies in each group form the setting of *Docherty,* which tells the story of Tam Docherty, miner, and his four children, in particular the youngest, Conn, who grows up to discover that the rough-and-tumble life of the mines and the town itself may not be for him. This puts the squeeze on Tam's relationship with friends and co-workers, since one of his sons has returned from World War I a cripple, his daughter is married off and out of the house, and the remaining son is the only one who will follow his way of life. In the microcosms that are the Docherty family and the town, small things create tensions that must be resolved delicately lest the social structure tear apart and everyone be cast into chaos. It is hard for Americans to understand this (which may be why the book has never been published here), but McIlvanney's clear, low-key presentation of the story makes the dilemma obvious without condescending to either the reader or the characters.

Docherty also introduces one of the aspects of McIlvanney's work that must have been responsible for his lionization and is certainly something Americans respond to: his impeccable ear for Scottish speech, its vocabulary, its cadence, and even the spaces between sentences that give them their meaning. Formidable at first, it's a hell of a lot easier to scan than Burns's archaisms, and once you get used to its odd words and phrases (to "greet" is to weep, for instance), it goes down easily. Thanks to McIlvanney, I was able to understand the first Glaswegian I spoke to, and most of the ones I spoke to subsequently—no mean feat.

It's obvious why *Docherty* excited people so much when it came out and why it won the Whitbread Award for the best fiction of 1975. He's got the village scene down, and his unsparing look at it, added to his empathy for working-class characters who wouldn't seem "interesting" enough to the average British novelist, make it fairly bold for mainstream British fiction. That the book comes from dour, gray Scotland, a place much disdained by those who live south of it, just makes it all the more unusual. It's a compelling novel, as claustrophobic as the small rooms in which most of it takes place, with humor and drama enough to override all the clichés

that threaten to sink a story like this: sensitive young boy turns his back on the coal pits, epic of man's love and heartbreak as his family wrestles with the changes of the new century. Maybe McIlvanney's Scottishness keeps it terse enough to be right. *Docherty* is a gamble taken and won, but McIlvanney was already looking elsewhere. (p. 14)

McIlvanney's two Laidlaw books are among the best that crime fiction has to offer, novels that can stand proudly on the shelf next to an establishment rave like *Docherty. Laidlaw,* in particular, will startle readers inured to the conventions of genre fiction. A sexually confused boy, the catamite of a local disco-owner with tenuous connections to what passes for organized crime in Glasgow, murders and rapes an 18-year-old girl in Kelvingrove Park. Terrified, he hides out in an abandoned building, where his lover brings him food. Meanwhile, the girl's father has hired a group of thugs to kill the murderer, and Laidlaw, in a brilliant scene he later describes to Harkness as "like hand-wrestling without hands," convinces crime lord John Rhodes that the police won't let up on criminals until this murderer is caught, and it's in Rhodes's best interests to give the police any information his men find. So we have the police looking, Rhodes looking, and the hired killer, a young hood named Lennie, who's trying to ingratiate himself with the local "hard men," also looking. The novel spirals in on the young man, psychotic and alone, still clutching the girl's underpants. It's not your usual thriller tension, and the whole thing hangs on the delicate web of relations between people on both sides of the law. *Laidlaw* won McIlvanney a Silver Dagger from the British Crime Writers' Association, and made him something of an outlaw with the critics and litterateurs who had hoisted him up as the coming thing among Scots letters.

The Papers of Tony Veitch isn't quite the masterpiece *Laidlaw* is, but it's no victim of second-novel blues, either. McIlvanney says, "Although they're two Laidlaw books in people's minds, they're distinct books for me," and perhaps it's better to think of them that way. Laidlaw manages to hit *every* layer of Glasgow society in this one as he tries to figure out who would want to lace a harmless old wino's "bevvy" with paraquat, and why the old man had been carrying around a sheet of paper with the names of an heiress, a "hard man" who had just been stabbed to death, and a criminals' pub, as well as a schoolboyish paragraph of philosophical musings on Good and Evil.

Tony Veitch's problem is that, although it reprises characters from *Laidlaw,* it lacks some of the earlier novel's color. A lot of the moral ambiguities are missing, and there aren't any scenes with the power of Laidlaw talking to the murdered girl's father or his "hand-wrestling" contest with John Rhodes. The characters are nearly all scum: Tony Veitch's wealthy father tries to protect his titled neighbor's daughter while dismissing his own son with a sneer; a contract killer back from exile in Birmingham impatiently skulks through the book, waiting for the moment to do his job. When Laidlaw and Harkness go to visit the wino's aged sister to tell her that her brother is dead, she threatens to take off with the novel for the few pages she's in it.

These reservations notwithstanding, it's still a superior crime novel, and if the idea of wrapping someone in electrical wire and plugging him into the wall seems an unusually sadistic method of getting rid of him, rest assured it's happened. (pp. 14, 17)

It's not that McIlvanney is merely a good crime writer. He's a novelist with a strange gruff affection for the land he lives in, and an attitude that's neither optimistic nor pessimistic, but like the Glasgow sky, which is usually gray, and as likely to break open into glorious sunshine as to burst into rain. (p. 17)

> *Ed Ward, "William McIlvanney Goes Underground," in* VLS, *No. 31, December, 1984, pp. 14, 17.*

DOUGLAS DUNN

Scottish history is likely to prove a far cry from William McIlvanney's future concerns. He is colloquial and vernacular and, in *These Words: Weddings and after,* determined on an earthy, no-nonsense, truth-telling exposure of the woe that is in marriage, the hypocrisies and selfishness of love and its demands.

The Longships in Harbour, McIlvanney's last book of poems, appeared in 1970. At the time it marked him out as one of the most interesting of the younger Scottish talents. A hard and serious interest in verse, for example, suggested that he was reading more widely than in the local magazines and anthologies. Two novels appeared before his first collection of poems, and subsequently McIlvanney's gifts have been put at the service of exploring the seamier side of life through the genre of the crime novel at which, in *Laidlaw* and *The Papers of Tony Veitch,* he excelled.

McIlvanney's new poem is prefaced by a long essay—**"The Sacred Wood Revisited"**—which takes T. S. Eliot to task for his courteous intellectual bullying and a critical trend which has set up all sorts of obstacles between poetry and its potential readers. McIlvanney's argument is neither simplemindedly populist, nor a shrill howl accusing the literary world of élitism. In fact, it is hard to say what it is, other than that it is a view. Where it baffles is in its obtuse avoidance of attention to recent poetry, and the implication is that McIlvanney has not read much of it. An effective way of dealing with the expectations produced by Eliot's criticism is to ignore them; that seems not to have crossed McIlvanney's mind.

McIlvanney's long poem is admirable in its vigour and mystifying in its badness. He is right in believing that rich material for poetry can be found in ordinary life, but he has brought to the expression of that conviction an old-hat rhetoric—"the dark plucks of circumstance", "telekinesis of supportive speech", "the flashing of innumerable smiles", "the cosmic vaudeville of his rant". The reader is at liberty to suspect this of being hollow noise. Habits like these detract fatally from the splenetic energy of McIlvanney's poem.

> *Douglas Dunn, "Embracing History," in* The Times Literary Supplement, *No. 4282, April 26, 1985, p. 470.*

MARGARET WALTERS

[The] hero of *The Big Man* survives by coming to terms with his own anger, and with the way other people look up to him simply because he's a savage street fighter. William McIlvanney's novel is an absorbing study of a man and the small, economically depressed Scottish town that has formed him. Dan Scoular 'meant something in the life of Thornbank and he tried to live inside that meaning as best he could, like a somnambulist pacing out someone else's dream.' . . .

The novel is rather old-fashioned, solid and occasionally stolid; it's a little too carefully plotted, as if McIlvanney were hankering back to his successful thrillers. The scenes in Glasgow—home turf of his detective Laidlaw—seem predictable after the fresh and all-too-credible account of discontinuity and discontent in Thornbank. The exchanges between the unemployed Dan and his wife Betty have the authentic note of love gone sour under the weight of necessary compromise and gradual self-disappointment.

In the pub, in the street, Dan reluctantly lives out a communal dream of physical courage and integrity; yet a fight leaves him queasy and nervous, with 'a dazed sense of having had his self-control mugged by his own violence.' At his best, McIlvanney digs deep and fruitfully into a class unconscious, into the way men dispossessed, not only of jobs but of their belief in past or future, still struggle to make—and un-make—their own heroes.

> *Margaret Walters, "No Hiding Place," in* The Observer, *September 1, 1985, p. 18.*

JAMES CAMPBELL

[The title character of *The Big Man* is] Dan Scoular. His reputation among the people of the West of Scotland village of Thornbank rests as much on his moral as his physical authority. He is already, in their eyes, a champion, and when offered a part in a bare-knuckle fight in Glasgow, the prospective reward seems to include not only a decent purse, and the likelihood of more, but a chance to assert the collective will of the community. . . .

When McIlvanney allows his characters freedom in the lives he has created for them, *The Big Man* succeeds both as moral drama and first-rate entertainment. But readers of the saga *Docherty* and the Jack Laidlaw crime novels (in some ways *The Big Man* is a meeting of the two) will recognize the author's habit—almost a mania—for dissecting the history and conscience of each character in turn, a method which at first provides air for them to breathe but eventually suffocates all and sundry in words. The boxing ring where Dan trains is said to "dominate the dialectic of the room like an irrefutable premise, a bleak simplistic statement the point of which is the abjuration of words". In what could have been an effective, simple scene in which Dan's wife is "putting on her face" before the mirror, the unemployed labourer's wife is assailed by an extraordinary articulacy: "Perhaps what we see in other people, she thought, are the complex stances and tics they have developed in response to the reactions to their original selves."

No other Scottish writer lectures the reader so thumpingly as McIlvanney; not content to show—which he does with skill and immediacy—he insists on telling as well. But in spite of these authorial incursions, the narrative of *The Big Man* is well sustained. The search for identity through violence is a peculiarly urban Scottish fate, which McIlvanney has always made it his business to explore.

The fight itself stands for the reader as a destination in the book, and is no disappointment when it comes. Thanks to a local busybody (the secondary characters in this novel are as well drawn as the leading men) Dan has the spectre of his wife in another man's arms to fight as well as his opponent and the ugly Mason; his chances are never better than even. Big men like Dan Scoular might be defeated in the small ring in a Glasgow field (though I'm not saying) but in other ways they cannot be defeated, which is one of McIlvanney's themes.

James Campbell, "Knuckling Down," in The Times Literary Supplement, *No. 4302, September 13, 1985, p. 1000.*

LORNA SAGE

One of the most straightforward and enduring reasons for writing novels is the conviction that the lives that matter are precisely, somehow, the lives that don't count—that get lost in statistics and stereotypes, or turned into fodder for polemical generalisations. *Docherty* by William McIlvanney is this sort of book: defiant, painstaking, ruminative, it's a memorial to a working-class generation at the turn of the century, whose experience is at once deceptively available to us, and temptingly alien, inviting myths.

Docherty is a remarkable man, not by virtue of stifled talents or extravagant suffering, but because he epitomises the common meanings. Briefly he manages to make sense out of the random, violent patterns of existence in his Scottish slum, so that gambling, poaching, drink, the mystique of physical prowess, become an articulate language, a way of triumphing over all the pressures towards callousness and self-contempt. His slow defeat, though, is inevitable, merely postponed. The war maims his son and makes cruel nonsense of physical pride; his embattled loathing of the mine bosses is revealed as passive habit, and will never be changed, or acted on. He becomes a fantasist, 'a man immuring himself alive in his own past,' and his pointless death confirms his oblivion. Only if values are facts has this life made any difference—this, or something like it, is what the novel is saying.

The story is mostly told through the hopeful, critical eyes of the children, especially the youngest son, Conn, and it's characteristic of the book's tone that though Conn begins by sounding like a portrait of the artist (the one that got away) he too goes down the mine, and faces the old problem of self-respect and self-definition all over again. William McIlvanney is continually aware of the gap between his novelist's prose and the eloquence of his people which has nothing to do with written language, and little to do even with speech. The very means by which they ritualise their lives cut them off from us, just as the ways they find of coping with poverty are, ironically, also ways of sealing off questions and perpetuating their plight. A ceremonial trial of strength at a party, for instance, will spark off this sort of analysis—a measure of the distance between author and character. . . . In trying to be explicit and sceptical, not mocking his characters with pastoral 'simplicity,' Mr McIlvanney is always in danger of distracting attention from them on to his own contorted scrupulosity. *Docherty* does manage a difficult honesty, but it would have been even better if the author wasn't tempted to remind you of it so often.

Lorna Sage, "Coaldust and Granite," in The Observer, *March 16, 1986, p. 30.*

Harry (Kurt Victor) Mulisch

1927-

Dutch novelist, nonfiction writer, short story writer, poet, journalist, essayist, editor, and librettist.

Long recognized in Europe as an important writer and the recipient of many foreign literary awards, Mulisch attracted significant critical attention in the United States with his novel *De aanslag* (1982; *The Assault*). Like much of his fiction, *The Assault* is written in a realistic prose style laced with mythic, historic, and symbolic overtones. Critics praise Mulisch's fiction for its psychological probings, humane sensibility, and keen awareness of the cruel side of human nature.

The Assault follows the life of Anton Steenwijk, a Dutch anesthesiologist who tries to distance himself from the childhood memory of the murder by Nazis of his parents and brother during World War II. Despite Anton's attempts to remain apathetic, many chance encounters with people who witnessed or were involved in the tragedy bring him insight into their motives; this knowledge spurs Anton to meditate on the vagaries of fate and also causes him much grief. John Gross described *The Assault* as "a morality tale, a dark fable about design and accident, strength and weakness, and the ways in which guilt and innocence can overlap and intermingle."

According to Mulisch, *The Assault* contains a number of autobiographical elements. His mother was Jewish and her family was killed by Nazis; his father was a collaborator with the Nazis and was subsequently jailed. Mulisch claims that the ambivalent duality of his childhood loyalties has influenced much of his work. *Het stenen bruidsbed* (1959; *The Stone Bridal Bed*) is generally regarded as Mulisch's finest early literary achievement. The novel concerns an American pilot's return to Dresden, Germany, a decade after he took part in the bombing of that city during World War II. Mulisch examines the effect of guilt on the psyche and makes extensive use of interior monologue to describe the events of the war. Mulisch suggests parallels between Dresden and Troy with flashbacks written in mock-Homeric verse, reflecting his penchant for reworking history and myth into fiction. *Twee vrouwen* (1975; *Two Women*), a best-selling novel which was adapted for film, depicts a tragic lesbian relationship narrated by one of the partners. Critics praised Mulisch's sympathetic and unclichéd treatment of this controversial topic and noted his artful rendering of the myth of Orpheus within a realistic narrative mode.

Throughout his prolific career, Mulisch has shown an interest in an eclectic range of topics and literary genres. He covered the Adolf Eichmann trial in *De zaak 40/61: Een reportage* (1962), championed the anarchist Dutch Provo movement in *Bericht aan de rattenkoning* (1966), scorned the nuclear arms race in *Wenken voor de Jongste Dag* (1967), hailed the early days of the Cuban revolution in *Het woord bij de daad* (1968), and participated in a collaborative opera-project on the life of Che Guevara in *Reconstructie* (1969). For most of the 1960s, Mulisch was a prominent figure in Amsterdam's new political left, but during the 1970s no powerful movements sustained his enthusiasm. He expressed his disenchantment with utopianism of all types in *De toekomst van gisteren* (1972), a hypothetical work which extrapolates European history as if Ger-

Photograph by Pieter Vandermeer. Courtesy of Harry Mulisch

many had won World War II. Mulisch's other works include *Het sexuele bolwark* (1973), which offers an analysis of notorious psychoanalyst Wilhelm Reich, and *De composite van de wereld* (1980), a philosophical study which consolidates his views on human existence and history in a comprehensive structure based on the musical octave.

(See also *Contemporary Authors*, Vols. 9-12, rev. ed. and *Contemporary Authors New Revision Series*, Vol. 6.)

THE NEW YORKER

One of the most brilliant, terse, and bitter novels to come out of the Second World War, [*The Stone Bridal Bed*] tells of a postwar meeting between survivors on opposing sides, and of their shared guilt and revived memories. The scene is unpretentious—a conference on dentistry in Dresden in 1956, during the Hungarian revolution—and the hero is a Jewish Dutch-American dentist whose face was disfigured in the course of a bombing mission over the city. He spends one night with Hella, a Communist guide who was imprisoned in a German concentration camp for years, and he devotes the rest of his time to discovering the identity of Dr. Schneiderhahn, a mysterious figure who is either an ex-dentist once in charge of removing the teeth from corpses at Auschwitz or a turncoat spy for the Western powers. (p. 165)

A review of "The Stone Bridal Bed," in The New Yorker, Vol. XXXIX, No. 14, May 25, 1963, pp. 164-65.

ROGER SALE

Harry Mulisch, a Dutchman, has written a curious, wry, and thoughtful novel, **The Stone Bridal Bed**, about an American flyer who helped bomb Dresden in 1945 and who returns to that city ten years later to attend a Communist congress. We are brought closer to home by the ubiquitous European absorption in the last war and by an interweaving of past and present similar to that of *Hiroshima, Mon Amour* and *The Tin Drum*. Yet nothing creates home as surely as does good prose, and Mulisch is a fine writer apparently blessed in Adrienne Dixon with a superlative translator. **The Stone Bridal Bed,** thus, is that rare thing, a quotable foreign novel:

> He thought, there are two histories. . . . He thought, one is the history of the *spirit,* bloody but spiritual, with a purpose and results: Alexander, Caesar, Napoleon—Battle of Marathon, Battle of Dresden, Bombardment of Berlin, Hamburg. That is time, evolution. But beside it, under it, there is anti-history in the stillness of death, and at certain intervals history sinks away in it. At such times the anti-history of Mao Dun Tanhu, Attila, Tamerlane, Genghis Khan, Hitler prevails. Then there is no more thought, no purpose, no result—only nothingness. There is no lapse of time between the massacres of the Huns and the concentration camps of Hitler. The lie side by side at the bottom of eternity. He thought, *and there lies Dresden.* . . . We smashed up Dresden because it was Dresden, just as the Jews were slaughtered because they were Jews. No further message. . . .

But the idea is not allowed to stand by and for itself. Because the flier is a part of both histories, he wanders through Dresden, cruelly trying to probe the pasts of the two Germans who are kind to him, seeking forgiveness as well as assurance that they are as guilty as he. This is a beautifully done book, evidence that the future for the novel of ideas is both considerable and unlike its past. (pp. 603-04)

Roger Sale, "The Newness of the Novel," in The Hudson Review, Vol. XVI, No. 4, Winter, 1963-64, pp. 601-09.

P. SMYTH

The thirty-six metrically irregular and sporadically rhymed lyrics [in *De wijn in drinkbaar dank zij het glas*] range in length from four to thirty lines, exemplifying a variety of approaches and styles. Many are ironical. The first of the book's four parts has no discernible thematic unity; the circus and childhood are the respective motifs of the next two sections; trite everyday conversational patterns are satirized in the last part, which I find the best. Mulisch's late-blooming interest in poetry still seems unlikely to emerge as a particularly significant facet of his literary personality.

P. Smyth, in a review of "De wijn in drinkbaar dank zij het glas," in World Literature Today, Vol. 51, No. 4, Autumn, 1977, p. 634.

JENNIFER UGLOW

Why did Harry Mulisch choose [a lesbian relationship as his subject in *Two Women*]? A cynic might suggest that as an extremely prolific writer of wide popular appeal he had a keen eye for the trendy topic. But he seems rather to have seized the opportunity offered by a new convention to re-examine an old story. His novel, which avoids voyeurism, is concerned with the links between formal representational modes and "real life", and its underlying subject is Eros, the transcendent yet destructive power of consuming physical love.

Two Women describes an affair between Laura, the narrator, and a younger woman, Sylvia. Their idyllic relationship seems shattered when Sylvia apparently runs off with Laura's ex-husband, Alfred, but it eventually transpires that this is a necessary part of her desire to give her lover an "impossible" gift, the child Laura could not conceive herself. Alfred, having abandoned wife and family to be used simply as a means of insemination is understandably resentful and the book proceeds to a bloody dénouement. The operatic effect of the plot is intensified by a contrived structure whereby flashbacks of the affair are set within the framework of Laura's drive to the South of France where her mother has just died. Fortunately the artifice is offset by a spare but allusive style, elegantly translated by Els Early.

That Mulisch is as interested in love as he is in homosexuality is made clear by the assertion, repeated by all three central characters, that the two women are not habitual lesbians; their relationship is based not on sexual preferences but on their love for each other as individuals. Yet because this love is outside the ordinary pattern, free of the clutter of familiar associations, it can be viewed and described with greater clarity.

The sexual difference means that Laura's passion can be presented as a first love, full of adolescent obsession, and with a devastating effect on this mature, sophisticated woman. She is endowed with all the pathological symptoms attributed to great lovers since medieval romances, from burning eyes to dizzy spells. The romantic tradition is further invoked since love strikes at first glance, irresistibly, and is intensified by surrounding hostility. The lovers' doomed ecstasy, like that of Romeo and Juliet, Troilus and Criseyde, Heloïse and Abelard, makes itself a refuge, a private world. . . .

The characters live out romantic conventions. In the literature of Eros the beloved object frequently almost disappears, dissolves in the flame of desire and remains elusive. Thus Sylvia, partly because of her taciturnity and her natural taste for deceit, remains mysteriously blank, not only to her male and female lovers, but also to the reader. She is a sacrificial victim and emerges, appropriately, from a landscape of chained natural forces: her father is superintendent of three of Holland's great dykes, "the Watcher, the Sleeper, the Dreamer, which kept the tumult outside in its place, and in the antiquated insides of the Dreamer they had installed a nuclear reactor, which was supposed to stop the tumult from within".

Much is made in **Two Women** of metaphors of landscape and geography. Mulisch also conveys well the immanence of the beloved ("Sylvia communicated through the entire world") and the function of passion as escape from the mundane. He suggests that such love is like the ultimate "AWAY" to which children run, yet the escape-road is presented as circular. . . .

The centrepiece of the novel is an all-male version of *Orpheus and Eurydice*, which aims to revive both the acting conventions and the spirit of Greek society. The playwright claims support from the "most ancient story of man, the Epic of Gilgamesh". But can such drama truly be tragic, asks Alfred, or does it remain melodramatic? Do we need the ultimate opposition of male and female to lift it to a tragic dimension?

The question is fascinating but *Two Women* provides no answer. For all its celebration of sensual desire it remains an uncommitted, cerebral work; a cold analysis of the heat of passion.

> Jennifer Uglow, "She and She," in The Times Literary Supplement, *No. 4044, October 3, 1980, p. 1118.*

JOHN NAUGHTON

Some years ago, a survey found that fantasies about lesbian relationships ranked highly in many men's psychic entertainment. If this is in fact what Harry Mulisch is up to, then I've been well and truly taken in [by *Two Women*]. For, having come to scoff at his finely-pared account of a relationship between two Dutch women, I remained to celebrate.

The narrator of *Two Women* is a thirtyish divorcee living in Amsterdam. She is, in some ways, the epitome of the multitude of cultivated, professionally-employed singles which throngs that enchanted city—the people one sees, for example, in the Concertgebouw in the evenings, or the Stedelijk Museum on Sunday afternoons. The central thread of the novel is a chronicle of a passionate love affair which develops after the narrator picks up a young girl called Sylvia one Saturday afternoon.

Sylvia, to put it mildly, is a mystery. Mulisch's image of her is lightly etched; she is seen as waif-like, with the casual indifference to the exigencies of domestic arrangements which one sometimes finds in children. She meets the narrator, walks with her, goes to her flat, cuts her hair, goes to bed with her, moves in. No problems—even though Sylvia is locked into a conventional family set-up in a provincial Dutch town. Her strange acceptance of a new order of things baffles her lover, and eventually leads to an appreciation of a powerful, dominant personality which has emerged without the advantages of education, leisure or social class.

Harry Mulisch has for years enjoyed a substantial reputation in Holland among the kind of people of whom his narrator is an archetype. . . . His style is a classically Dutch blend of irony and sentimentality, the characteristic feature of a culture trapped at the intersection of three great literatures—French, German and English. His tender account of the development of the relationship between his heroines keeps one hooked to the—bitter—end. And his low-key portrayal of societal attitudes towards homosexual women is more effective than a thousand outraged feminist tracts. (pp. 804-05)

> John Naughton, "Strange Encounters," in The Listener, *Vol. 104, No. 2691, December 11, 1980, pp. 804-05.*

JACK BYRNE

Lesbian literature seems to have come a long way from Radclyffe Hall's *The Well of Loneliness*—more humor, more understanding, more drama, more humanity, more exploitation, more confrontation, more resentment, more misunderstanding. . . . Having said that, it is important to note that [Mulisch's *Two Women*] is much more like Moravia's *Two Women*, in that it transcends a mere lesbian relationship. Rather, it describes a desired mother-daughter intimacy that can withstand the onslaught of societal concerns for familial stability. It is the story of Laura, the older woman, who has just lost her own mother and who, having divorced her husband, Alfred, is at loose ends regarding her sexuality. She meets Sylvia, the daughter she never had, and she capitulates to her motherly needs by involving herself in a lesbian relationship. Sylvia offers herself as a daughter to the attractive, independent mother she never had. The publisher's blurb tells us that "this delicate novel is the record of a love affair." Yes, but it is much more than that, for in addition to a plot twist, near the end, that is not all that surprising—Laura's ex-husband has managed to penetrate the ménage à deux in what appears to be a successful attempt to leave Laura in a ménage à une—the actual tragic ending is most unpredictable, justifying, if that is necessary in this decade of open-mindedness, its telling. Mulisch eschews vulgarity at every turn in his attempt to dramatize a story that must end tragically to satisfy the conscience of "Dear Reader 1980s." Radclyffe Hall might not agree that we have come all that far.

> Jack Byrne, in a review of "Two Women: A Novel," *in The Review of Contemporary Fiction, Vol. 2, Spring, 1982, p. 180.*

JOHN GROSS

[*The Assault* begins one] winter night in 1945, [as] a Dutch police inspector called Fake Ploeg is riding home on his bicycle through the outskirts of Haarlem. Much of Europe has been liberated, but the Netherlands is still occupied, and Ploeg is as vicious a collaborator as the country can show, a man infamous for his cruelty. Suddenly, six shots ring out—the Resistance has settled accounts with him. Here, at least, is a case of simple justice being done.

But life is complicated, and in no time at all the shooting has begun to have unlooked-for repercussions. Ploeg falls dead outside a house on the quayside—one of a group of four, the home of a sailor called Korteweg and his daughter. Their neighbors, a family called the Steenwijks, peer out of the window, and to their horror they see the Kortewegs dragging the body in front of the Steenwijk house. . . .

[Their house] is burned down as a reprisal and Mr. and Mrs. Steenwijk are taken away—as it turns out, to their deaths. [Twelve-year old Anton Steenwijk watches] helplessly; then he himself is driven off to the police station. Subsequently he is released and sent to stay with his uncle and aunt in Amsterdam, but not before he has undergone two more searing experiences. He spends the night in a darkened cell with a female member of the Resistance who has been injured—she talks to him about her life and her ideals in a way he can barely understand; and he sees a middle-aged German soldier who has tried to protect him from being killed when the convoy in which they are traveling is attacked from the air.

This is how *The Assault* opens. The rest of Harry Mulisch's remarkable novel is devoted to unraveling the consequences of that first fateful night. Anton grows up determined to put the past behind him. He becomes a successful anesthesiologist (a symbolic choice of career, but the symbolism is handled lightly); he marries, has a child, remarries, has another child, lives a quiet life, adopts a stance of mildly ironic detachment. But in a series of episodes spaced over 35 years, we watch the experience he wants to forget reasserting itself.

Not only are there pent-up emotions that have to be unlocked, and memories that have to be confronted before they can be exorcised. There are also nagging riddles. Why did the Kortewegs, decent people, act in the way they did? Even if they were in a panic, what made them choose to endanger the Steenwijks—a family with children, with whom the Korteweg daughter at least was on friendly terms—rather than dumping the body in front of their other neighbors, the Aartses, a childless couple who had always held themselves aloof? What exactly happened to Peter after he disappeared? And there are other puzzles, too, about the original shooting itself as well as its aftermath.

Anton doesn't actively pursue these questions, on the contrary, most of the time, he tries to keep them at bay. But they force themselves on him, piecemeal, and the urge to get at the truth about them is what gives *The Assault* its narrative thrust. At one level, the book can be read as a detective story, of the superior Simenon variety, with intriguing twists and turns and a definite solution.

It is also a morality tale (though one that doesn't point out any easy moral), a dark fable about design and accident, strength and weakness, and the ways in which guilt and innocence can overlap and intermingle. There are multiple ironies in the drama that binds together Steenwijks, Kortewegs, Beumers, Aartses, Resistance fighters—and the Ploegs, too (for Fake Ploeg has a son). Tragic ironies, with nothing facile or contrived about them; and ironies, it should perhaps be added, that are never allowed to diminish our sense of the pure evil of the regime against which the initial violence in the story is directed.

For a book to have deeply serious intentions, as this one does, is, of course, no guarantee of artistic success. But Mr. Mulisch also brings exceptional skill and imagination to his task. Townscapes and interiors are firmly delineated—cliché or not, you can hardly help being reminded of the clarity of Dutch painting; characters are established with a deft economy; in the opening pages, Anton's small-boy reactions, the stolid humanism of his father, the adolescent impatience of his brother are all equally convincing, and as the story develops, a hundred small touches sustain the effect of psychological truthfulness. There is a particularly strong feeling for the way the past changes as each new layer accrues.

> *John Gross, in a review of ''The Assault,'' in* The New York Times, *May 11, 1985, p. C24.*

HAROLD BEAVER

The Assault is the first novel to appear in America by one of the Netherlands' most revered, award-winning novelists. Published in Dutch in 1982, it is set mainly in Amsterdam and Haarlem. The odd reference to ''the Haarlemmer Hout'' or ''Nieuwe Zijds Voorburgwal'' need not discourage readers; the brick houses, canals and flat meadows are familiar from any tourist brochure.

But *The Assault* holds out no tourist attractions. Nor was it just runaway sales (more than 200,000 copies sold in the Netherlands) that attracted foreign publishers. It is as a parable of war, whose guilts and neuroses reach well into the present, that this novel is so persuasive. Certainly in the Netherlands the book raised again, at a deeply personal level, the problem of national reconciliation. . . .

[*The Assault*] is about the murder of a Dutch policeman—a willing Nazi tool—as he pedals quietly home on his bicycle at dusk past four prim villas on the banks of a canal on the outskirts of Haarlem. It is January 1945, only months before the liberation of Europe. A wheel spins for a moment; the corpse lies inert in the gutter. It is just a Dutch suburban still life, except for one appalling detail. Then a man emerges, followed by his daughter, to drag away the corpse lying before his house and dump it in front of his neighbor's.

One boy from that marked villa survives when it is blown up by the Germans in ''retribution''; the rest of his family is wiped out. It is his narrative. Like Job's messenger, he is alone escaped to tell us. . . .

We may read *The Assault* in part as a thriller. But it is a political thriller that removes the postwar scar tissue protecting society. And it is a psychological thriller probing the moral devastation between neighbors, fellow students, husbands and wives that is still a fading factor, 40 years after the event, in Dutch life.

For the aging protagonist, one question resounds as the past unfolds: who was guilty? Who was ultimately responsible for his mother's and father's and brother's brutal and pointless deaths? The Germans? The resistance fighters who murdered a police bully when most of the rest of Europe was already liberated? Or the hidden Jews, for whose protection the body was dumped in front of the narrator's house rather than one of the other villas? And why move the body at all?

So the debris of memories, of guilt and anguish, is exposed. The neurosis among the older generation in the Netherlands is pervasive to this day. In the wake of such a repressive occupation, the devastation has been psychological. . . . The Dutch still nurse memories of World War II. It was their war. Forty years are as nothing. On the recent anniversary of the liberation, flowers were laid everywhere, below monuments or at street corners where citizens were killed. Tears welled up as families stood solemnly in front of their television sets for taps. The communal secrets and cowardices and terrors of such an occupation are never over.

It is Mr. Mulisch's triumph to have revealed all this—among characters that range from ambassador to anti-Communist thug—with an X-ray cunning. His form is a simple narrative, its chronology that of one life. ''The War is still on; right?'' the protagonist asks. ''Sure,'' a former resistance hero replies. ''Sure.'' If none of the characters (whether plumber or nurse) can ultimately leave the war alone, the war does not leave them alone either. The confusions of a democratic society built on such divisive memories can only—ultimately—be repressed.

> *Harold Beaver, ''A Corpse at the Doorstep,'' in* The New York Times Book Review, *June 16, 1985, p. 7.*

BRUCE ALLEN

Mulisch emerges in this tense and fascinating novel [*The Assault*] . . . as a sophisticated and resourceful craftsman who has much to say about the lingering aftereffects of World War II on his homeland and his generation. (p. 23)

The Assault is about survival, and survival's effects on personality and personal relationships. It is also a mystery story, divided into several "Episodes," of which the first recounts an incomprehensible act of aggression followed by violent reprisal. The last, occuring 36 years later, explains—as well as anything can—why an innocent family was destroyed and an uncomprehending boy made to remain a victim for years thereafter.

Mulisch begins the story with a prologue set in January 1945 in the northern inland city of Haarlem. Although much of the rest of Europe has been liberated, the Nazi presence remains strong and menacing, and families like the Steenwijks—on whom the focus rests—remain apprehensive and keep quietly to themselves.

Then, a dramatic initial "Episode" shatters this cautious calm. The sound of a shot brings the Steenwijks to their front windows; they see on the street the body of local police chief Fake Ploeg—a notorious Nazi collaborator known as "the greatest murderer and traitor in Haarlem"—fallen before one of their neighbor's houses. They watch, unbelieving, as those neighbors, the Kortewegs, drag the body away and dump it on *their* doorstep. Then, before the Steenwijks can rid themselves of this incriminating evidence, the German occupation police arrive on the scene.

Three of the family are executed; only 12-year-old Anton survives. (pp. 23-4)

The subsequent episodes circle back repeatedly to grapple with the events of that night and with Anton's intermittent efforts to understand why his family was so "chosen." . . . In 1956, Anton meets the murdered policeman's son and is disturbed and challenged by the latter's belligerent insistence that innocence and guilt are not as clear-cut as Anton wishes to believe.

The year 1966 brings Anton, now married and a father, to a funeral attended by former Resistance fighters and heavy with echoes of the war years. Here, he learns much more about the night that forever altered his life, measuring his passivity against the tenacious belief that evil must be met with violent resistance. Finally, in 1981, now in his 40s, "plagued by worries and anxieties," Anton attends an antinuclear rally with his teen-age daughter. There, a chance meeting completes his understanding of the complex motives that made the Kortewegs "mark" the Steenwijks' house and leaves him with an unanswerable question—"Was everyone both guilty and not guilty?". . . .

Mulisch builds toward this great climactic scene with masterly patience and rhythm. It vibrates with tension and perfectly rounds off a psychological tour de force that strikes unexpectedly deep. We observe Anton Steenwijk aging and changing, gradually comprehending the depth of a commitment and passion he had never shared or understood, and can scarcely imagine. As we do so, we ourselves begin to understand what it must have been to live this experience. It seems to me that this is the highest kind of achievement of which fiction is capable—and that Harry Mulisch's subtle and resonant novel ranks with the finest European fiction of recent years. (p. 24)

Bruce Allen, "Celebrated Dutch Author's Novel Explores Survival and War's Afteraffects," in The Christian Science Monitor, July 16, 1985, pp. 23-4.

LIZ HERON

As an exploration of memory and the troubling compulsions of the unconscious, *The Assault* is extraordinarily moving, its skilfully constructed narrative inching backwards to explain the past, as it moves forward. But it also suggests the limits of what can be understood in anything other than the metaphysical dimensions of classical tragedy: chance; the smallness of individual lives beside the clash of armies; the many-sided nature of truth.

It seems less successful on the level where [the protagonist] Anton's life itself becomes a metaphor for Western Europe's post-war history, its closing of the door on the trauma of the war while living out its ubiquitous and far-reaching consequences. Whether this is because Mulisch's larger themes are too large for the book's scope, or whether they are just undercut by the apparent resolution of complex political questions in a single coalescing image of antinuclear protest, I am not certain. But if only for the way in which it broaches these themes it still demands to be read. (pp. 28-9)

Liz Heron, "In That Sleep," in New Statesman, Vol. 110, No. 2852, November 22, 1985, pp. 28-9.

NICHOLAS SPICE

Harry Mulisch treats the plight of the Dutch Jews, and of Jews everywhere [during Nazi occupation], with his own kind of delicate irony, giving the matter a crucial structural importance for his story, but bringing it to the surface only once. This single mention of it is like a chink in a dike: through it the whole unspeakable history floods in. Or again, it is like a tiny window, through which for one short moment we are allowed to peep down upon a vast panorama of brutality and blood.

In one sense, . . . *The Assault* takes the Jewish Holocaust as its starting-point. In another, perhaps deeper sense, it grows out of a fascination with chance. Speaking at a party held recently in London to launch his novel, Mulisch referred to the shooting of [Nazi collaborator] Fake Ploeg and its immediate consequence as 'this accident'. He had meant to say 'incident' and quickly corrected himself, but the slip was revealing and quite in keeping with the idea from which he said the book originally grew, an idea which came to him in a kind of vision—a vivid mental picture of four detached houses on the side of a canal. Within this image Mulisch discovered the essential elements of his plot and a succinct summary of his most abstract as well as his most domestic themes. Four houses, containing four separate family destinies, and representing four equal chances in the game of life.

Outside one of them—the one where his protagonist would live—the cosmic dice would roll to a standstill. But which should it be? Mulisch decided on the second house from the left. The afterthought which made him have Ploeg shot outside the second house from the right gave him the twist his story needed, an unanswered question to motivate his plot beyond the initial catastrophe. Why did Mr Korteweg and his daughter move Ploeg's body? And, seeing as they did, why to the left instead of to the right, to the Steenwijks whom they knew, rather than to the Aartses whom no one knew or cared for? Because of this mystery in the events which open the book, and because by the end of it the mystery has been cleared up, *The Assault* has been spoken of by some—by John Gross, for example [see excerpt above]—as, on one level, like a detective novel. The resemblance, however, is weak.

Anton Steenwijk does not seek out explanations for what happened on that terrible January night in 1945, they seek *him* out, unbidden and, consciously at least, unwanted. Anton's first wish is to forget. Fate, however, won't let him, and as the years go by, it throws in his path a number of chance encounters with the surviving actors in the drama, who proceed to press upon him their self-justifications and confessions. Anton's meetings with Mr and Mrs Beumer (who lived in the first house on the left), with Fake Ploeg's son, with Cor Takes, one of the two Communists who shot Ploeg, and, finally, with Karin Korteweg, Mr Korteweg's daughter, carry most of the ethical argument of the novel, as well as being the means whereby the original incident is understood. They are necessary vehicles of exposition and meaning, and as such they do not escape seeming slightly staged. It is as though Mulisch has had to make special arrangements for his protagonist to meet these people. The conversations and arguments that ensue are stiffened by the duty they perform, of covering intense narrative, emotional and intellectual ground efficiently and fast. Part of the trouble with these scenes may be that Mulisch just doesn't write the very best dialogue, but I think the real problem is inherent in the novel's structure and the very powerful message which that structure is designed to put across. The interests of fiction have deferred here to the purposes of poetry.

The episodes which fill up the second two-thirds of *The Assault* do not emerge as the unforced stages in a forward-moving plot, for the simple reason that the plot is moving backwards. A great release of dramatic and descriptive energy occurs in the first 60 pages, which establish and then destroy Anton Steenwijk's childhood world. 'All the rest,' as the book acknowledges, 'is aftermath—the cloud of ash that rises into the strat-osphere from the volcano, circles around the earth, and continues to rain down on all its continents for years.' The final sentence of the novel recalls this image in a context which suggests a far less innocent analogy. Thirty-six years after the incineration of his childhood home, Anton is walking, or rather drifting, through Amsterdam in the middle of a mass demonstration against nuclear weapons. He is pictured 'dragging his feet a bit, as if each step raised clouds of ashes, although there are no ashes in sight'. It is an effectively rhetorical ending, reminding us that *The Assault* is about holocausts, burnt offerings, destructions by fire, reducings to rubble, reducings to ash, of things, people, lives, civilisations, and about the rhythmic and sinister return of these catastrophes under cover of collective amnesia. (pp. 17-18)

The Assault . . . tells the story of someone who has endured the experience of evil, and cannot forget. Harry Mulisch has hinted that there are autobiographical elements in his novel, but if there are, they are subjected to the same creative transformation as the rest of his material. The result is, palpably and throughout, a fiction, and, if it moves us, it does so through the devices of the imagination—by analogy with the reality it supposedly portrays. Mulisch's imagination is of a particularly synthesising kind. He elaborates his ideas through a network of related and interpenetrating images, and he is a master of what Ezra Pound dubbed phanopoeia, 'the throwing of an image on the mind's retina'. When I remember reading *The Assault*, I remember watching a film—and in fact it has already been made into one. It is a book to be read at one go. (p. 18)

Nicholas Spice, ''Ashes,'' in London Review of Books, *Vol. 7, No. 22, December 19, 1985, pp. 17-18.*

Lorine Niedecker

1903-1970

American poet and essayist.

Niedecker's verse is praised for its stark, vivid imagery, subtle rhythms, and spare language, which Kenneth Cox described as "whittled clean." Concerned with the distillation of images and thoughts into concise expression, Niedecker described her work as a "condensery," and several critics have compared her poetry to the delicate yet concrete verse of Chinese and Japanese writers. Although Niedecker's long correspondence with Louis Zukofsky, who frequently published her poems in his journal, *Origins,* and contact with such respected writers as Cid Corman and Basil Bunting, brought her some critical notice, her work was generally overlooked until late in her life. Since her death in 1970, several critics have identified Niedecker as a significant and original voice in contemporary American poetry.

Niedecker was born in Fort Atkinson, Wisconsin, and lived in this wilderness area for most of her life. Her isolation from other writers and the austere beauty of her natural surroundings had a notable impact on her work. Niedecker chose to write in seclusion, and many of her closest relatives and neighbors were unaware that she was a poet. Her first book, *New Goose* (1946), was privately printed, and her second, *My Friend Tree,* which did not appear until 1962, was published in England. Niedecker attracted significant critical attention with *North Central* (1968), a volume which collects several of her best-known poems, including the long sequences "Wintergreen Ridge" and "Paean to Place." Critics noted in *North Central* Niedecker's stylistic affinities to William Carlos Williams, particularly in her use of short lines and colloquial speech, and to Louis Zukofsky. The verse in this volume features terse language, which conveys with precision and vibrancy her observations of the natural world as well as abstract concepts. This duality of substance and thought is strongly present in both of the volumes published shortly before Niedecker's death: *Tenderness and Gristle: The Collected Poems* (1970) and *Collected Poems, 1968* (1970). Also evident in these books is Niedecker's interest in history, which she tends to approach from a personal perspective rather than from a broad, collective viewpoint. Among her later poems are sequences about such historical figures as Thomas Jefferson and Charles Darwin.

Three volumes of Niedecker's poetry have been published since her death: *Blue Chicory* (1976), *From This Condensery: The Complete Writings of Lorine Niedecker* (1985), and *The Granite Pail: The Selected Poems of Lorine Niedecker* (1985). *From This Condensery* collects all of Niedecker's poems as well as reviews and other prose. Evaluating her achievement, Michael Heller observed that "[Niedecker's] gift . . . has been the courage to breach her reticence, to speak simply and accurately as few poets do today. Thus despite their often bitter quality, these poems are peculiarly consoling to the reader, for they offer, above all, the comfort of substance, of authentic possession."

(See also *CLC,* Vol. 10; *Contemporary Authors,* Vols. 25-28; and *Contemporary Authors Permanent Series,* Vol. 2.)

Courtesy of Gail Roub

KENNETH COX

Lorine Niedecker's poems are few and short but their character is not easy to define. Any one of her poems is unmistakably hers yet different from her others, as one element in any of her poems may surprise yet belong. They might be mistaken for sketch notes or diary jottings made on widely different occasions, but this would be to overlook the carefulness and complexity of the writing, hidden under feminine ease.

The poems hold attention by their quiet confidence. Their language is colloquial and elliptical to a degree that registers the feel of a place and the personality of a speaker before meaning. It is the speech of the American people, whittled clean. Many of the poems suppose someone to be saying them and set the immediate human context, the attachments and irritations of domesticity. They catch the inflexion of a voice, establishing relations between persons speaking, spoken to and spoken of. . . .

The prevailing mood of the poems is alert calm. They convey pathos, asperity and affectionate irony: it is rather as if one were in the presence of a close relative from whom little is hid and to whom little needs to be explained. They acknowledge semi-articulate intimacies, their interrupted cadences emitting a shrewd tenderness, a delicate tang. (p. 169)

The world of the poems is that of everyday adult life, but drawing on the continuum of existence lying a little below consciousness. Things familiar and unfamiliar—the weather, common objects, something read, a sudden thought—hang in it together without question, explanation or reason. The tonality of the poem creates a magnetic field in which occasional observations and promptings lie still, imaging depth. . . .

The surréalistes presented incongruous objects to recall, release, amuse, startle or upset. The poems of Lorine Niedecker leave the reader in peace. They resemble more the poems of Pierre Reverdy, whose unexpected conjunctions also calm rather than shock. But Reverdy tended to reduce associated elements to a dim monochrome, like a painter who matches tints by lowering the illumination. Lorine Niedecker domesticates sharp and diverse elements, even upheaval. (p. 170)

The poems gather together a sense of kinship and house, the biological and economic axes of society, with a scope and sense of proportion more often found, writ large, among the novelists. Their real subject is not so much an incident or experience as the relation between this experience or incident and another. Elements unrelated are omissible—hence the apparent sketchiness: sometimes the referents are insufficient. The more divergent they are, the more urgent the need to bring them into relation. The concreteness of things is a function of the relation between them. . . . (p. 171)

To describe the operation of the poems in this way may falsely suggest they hold an objective rigorously in view. The best of them set one experience alongside another, or in relation to its temporal and spatial determinants, not with obvious intent but with the tremulous certainty of a compass needle. They place human life in its domestic and physical setting and with reference to its natural co-ordinates, the succession of the generations and the cycle of the seasons. The order of nature is established with an almost Franciscan quality of affection. . . . (pp. 171-72)

Some of the poems establish relation without making overt statement:

> Paul
>   when the leaves
>   fall
>   from their stems
>   that lie thick
>   on the walk
>   in the light
>   of the full note
>   the moon
>   playing
>   the leaves
>   when they leave
>   the little
>   thin things
>   Paul

The words turn in a slow descent, showing as it were their upper and lower sides. We murder to dissect. Apart from the double meaning of 'leaves', they attain their effect, similar to the effect of playing on open strings, by putting the sound of 'fall' (meaning autumn and an isophone of 'leaf', with low vowel in place of a high one), its rhyme 'Paul' (the boy to whom the poem is addressed) and isophone 'play' against op-

posite sounds like 'thick', 'thin', 'thing'. But the plangency, the recognition of inevitable loss, less concerns a tree shedding its leaves than the corresponding human situation.

By such subtle wordplay, using the cadences and overtones of familiar speech, Lorine Niedecker's poems construct miniature imitations of the world magical in their properties. Their tiny structures shape emotion stored a long time.

It is almost impossible to say how it is done: the poems mostly dispense with means. One device may be noticed, though once the mechanism has been exposed its efficiency may be impaired. A poem recording a physical or moral event in common words may aim at something beyond the event without going outside the words used: it can do this by reminiscence of rhythm, accident of sound or coincidence of sense. The most economical form of expression would be by means of a word which happens to have a double sense. The fulcrum of many of the poems is therefore a concealed pun. . . . (pp. 172-73)

The poem for Paul quoted above equates three shapes: leaf, stemmed note on stave, full moon behind tree-stem. In another of the poems the equation is conceptual, a conceit:

> Now in one year
> a book published
> and plumbing—
>
> took a lifetime
> to weep
> a deep
> trickle

In a poem on Easter it has the sly twinkle of a *double entendre:*

> A robin stood by my porch
> and side-eyed
> raised up
> a worm.

These are examples of a method reducible to a verbal or visual pun and possibly owing something to the Japanese use of a hinge-word, *kake kotoba,* a word working like a two-way switch. But, avoiding faults frequent in translation from the Chinese and Japanese (slack rhythm, insipid diction), Lorine Niedecker imitates *haiku* and *tanka* loosely, not closely, and retains features of English prosody, such as occasional rhyme, to add point. The extreme reduction of content typical of Japanese forms is salted like a Greek epigram or American wisecrack.

But essentially the poems collect and modify experience, pacifying and civilising the mind. . . . (pp. 173-74)

And the best of the poems do without devices altogether. Just as simple in appearance and sparing in expression, they convey a manifold meaning beyond the reach of analysis:

> I've been away from poetry
> many months
>
> and now I must rake leaves
> with nothing blowing
>
> between your house
> and mine

These slight and listless lines convey a feeling of moral backlog, an accumulation of experience unexamined, a sense of being overtaken and left behind, a separation from a salutary influence, an obligation neglected, a need to restore order, inspiration replaced by drudgery: yet nothing so definite as any of these. It is an image which contributes to the collective conscience. (p. 174)

Kenneth Cox, "The Poems of Lorine Niedecker," in
The Cambridge Quarterly, *Vol. IV, No. 2, Spring,
1969, pp. 169-75.*

MICHAEL HELLER

Miss Niedecker's poems [in *Tenderness and Gristle: The Collected Poems (1936-1966)*] are for the most part notations of isolation, of the poet's own and the world's sheer recalcitrance, an inert and almost blind physicality which she confronts in her native landscape (the rural Midwest) and its people: "the folk from whom all poetry flows / and dreadfully much else." The poems are natural and seemingly artless constructions as though mirroring this region of the United States, an area as yet unhumbled by technology, grazed and plowed, yet lying before the eye with its contours basically unchanged. And it is out of its loneliness and austerity that Miss Niedecker speaks. (p. 444)

Yet these poems seem neither self-pitying nor mean, for there is in Miss Niedecker's work an obstinacy, an almost iron commitment to valuing her world, a moral concern for her art that is rare and important. It is a concern for clarity, for the most basic *knowing* of one's own existence. Thus in poem after poem she establishes precisely how it is a human suffers and celebrates there being other humans, other objects in the world. In the book's first poem:

> There's a better shine
> on the pendulum
> than is on my hair
> and many times
>
> ..   ..
> I've seen it there.

the pause between the last two lines ingathers the poet's feelings of jealousy and love of beauty so that "I've seen it there" can bear witness to both, a witnessing which if it took sides would be absurd or banal. This is to derive a power not from human vanity or longing but from disclosure, an ability to render with exactness the totality of a subjective relationship.

To render, to create such summations is to do more than substantiate one's own existence; it is to create through craft a dialectic of words and silences with which the reader can interact. . . . The experience of passing through the poems is mainly sensuous; moving across and down the lines one senses not ideas but complex interplays: rising and dying sounds, imagery as much counterpoint as counterpart to the music. Such tensions and delays function to build the poem into its own justification and release: an articulation that discharges the energy of the poet's perceptions yet never drives one out of relation to the poem.

This articulation, however, hovers precariously on the good faith of poet and reader. The poems are made with such strictness, such rigor, to say no more than what must be said (this "condensery," as Miss Niedecker humorously states it), that they are less in danger of being misunderstood than in being overlooked.

This is to trust one's language—today a decidedly uncommon virtue—as an occasion in which a "world" might occur, in which: "a weedy speech / a marshy retainer" sustains a life or at least offers definition to its isolations. Thus Miss Niedecker relies on the fiercest, simplest powers of ordinary words, those words as Freud put it, in which the sum total of magic is reposited. In this she is a true keeper of the word-hoard, repurifying its contents through scrupulous use, reawakening in us the sheer dignity of human utterance.

Not that this should be mistaken for modesty or restraint; rather, it is usage located in necessity, a poetry (Roland Barthes's term) of a possible adventure: the meeting point of a sign and an intention. For Miss Niedecker it is the courageous intention to experience the world as it is, to arrive disarmed but for her language. Thus the poems are free of conceptions or prefigurations; they seem to be without means. . . . (pp. 444-45)

To experience the tragic, to not accept failure, but to know precisely what failure and bitterness have cost . . . is the imaginative, the artistic dimension that can redeem us from indifferent or redundant fate. This is to obtain to a difficult and courageous beauty: to stay open to hurt and at the same moment subject oneself to an almost classical scrutiny:

> What horror to awake at night
> and in the dimness see the light
>   Time is white
>   mosquitoes bite
> I've spent my life on nothing.
> The thought that stings.

Yet what Miss Niedecker has achieved, and this is what makes her work distinguished, is not to become the poet-victim of her condition but its agency, singing the song of her world and herself *through* herself. It is an objective, yet human magic which makes her poems seem as organic as the experiences they arise from, resonating with pure being rather than with associations. It is as though the linguistic act had been forced to an ultimate and concrete embrace of reflection creating an inviolable structure that could hold the transitory, the evanescent in a perpetually alive form. . . .

That such self-examination seems never merely personal or oppressive is immaculate artistry, a capacity to make of the representations of one's memory the clean outlines of a myth. As poet-maker, Miss Niedecker seeks for the events in her life an absolute justice of words, a supra-literalness of the self which can transform existence (and this is its tragedy) into judgment.

Her gift (now our gift) has been the courage to breach her own reticence, to speak simply and accurately as few poets do today. Thus despite their often bitter quality, these poems are peculiarly consoling to the reader, for they offer, above all, the comfort of substance, of authentic possession. . . . (p. 445)

Michael Heller, "'I've Seen It There'," in The Nation, *Vol. 210, No. 14, April 13, 1970, pp. 444-45.*

GILBERT SORRENTINO

It is difficult to think of a contemporary to whom Miss Niedecker may be compared. The spare and harmonious quality of her work is reminiscent of Sappho, of the anonymous poetess of the Greek Anthology who wrote the beautiful and fragile "The moon has set / and the Pleiades". . . , and of Sulpicia, the 1st-century B.C. Roman poetess who is preserved for us in six brief elegiacs whose plain grace is inimitable. Miss Niedecker's English has the brevity and compactness of classical verse, her syntax carefully balanced in a way usually possible only with highly inflected languages. . . .

For a model of her poetic methods, the reader may examine this small untitled poem written in 1935. The subtlety of the line-breaks that gives the poem its depth of clarity as well as its ambiguity is notable—something achieved only by the best poets. One sees also that the clarity as well as the ambiguity are matters of how the medium is handled, not of meaning or "interpretation."

> There's a better shine
> on the pendulum
> than is on my hair
> and many times
>
> .. ..
> I've seen it there.

If the poem were to end at line three we would have an image; at line four, an image with gloss. The pause, which works as a wordless fifth line, and the flat statement of line six take the poem onto another plane altogether: "and many times," so located, functions so as to turn the poem perfectly on each of three readings, all coherent and absolute.

Blue Chicory reveals these methods still in operation, used, if possible, even more exactly. The last poem of the first section of the book has but one verb; it comes as the last word of the poem and thereby functions as the energy that gives the work its rationale. All the other words wait for the verb to explain them:

> Your erudition
> the elegant flower
> of which
>
> my blue chicory
> at scrub end
> of campus ditch
>
> illuminates

—and when the verb drops precisely into place, we see that it does exactly what it means. The energy that clarifies the poem also illuminates it. There is no fat on these poems and no rodomontade masquerading as feeling.

Miss Niedecker had little attention paid her in her life, none at all by ignorant or malicious arbiters of what is "best" in modern poetry. It doesn't matter much. Her work is here, the product of a true poetic sensibility, faultless and luminous.

> Gilbert Sorrentino, "Blue Chicory," in The New York Times Book Review, *February 13, 1977, p. 27.*

THOMAS D'EVELYN

[Lorine Niedecker] lived almost her whole life on Black Hawk Island on Lake Koshkonong in Wisconsin. There, she stayed out of literary trouble. From the evidence of **The Granite Pail,** Niedecker knew what she was after when she sat down to write.

Among other things, she sought, as she wrote in a sequence called **"Traces of Living Things,"** "the very veery / on the fence." That's her "objectivist" aim, one she never reduced to mere things. The thing in view doesn't eclipse the viewer, as it seems to in some imagistic poetry. Niedecker was, among other possibilities, a most natural nature poet. . . .

Niedecker's wit, the sweet mother wit inseparable now from our mother tongue as it sings in her poems, survived the process of composition. That method, an honorable one, involved con-

densing her experience into an image and a rhythm, bidding goodbye to everything that simply dissolved under the pressure of her art. Only a hardy wit, toughened by many winters on Black Hawk Island, could survive that. For every living line, the process could take years.

Her method recalls that of the late and great Ezra Pound. . . . Pound, the self-appointed master of modern poets, spent the teens and '20s of our century promoting the virtues of *the smallest number of words.* So *condensare* was his watchword. This method can leave one with nothing to say, or with a few, unforgettable lines.

Unlike Pound, . . . Lorine Niedecker could speak of herself with a gentle and accurate sense of how she must appear to others. Still, Pound's intemperance and his certitude, combined with his poetic talent, made him a master teacher, and Niedecker and her poet friends learned much from him.

In brief, I would call Niedecker a good minor poet were she not so at home in her own limits. Her honesty freed her to do her most distinctive work, work that frustrates the critic's job of evaluation. Time will tell. For now, note that her sense of humor never entirely fails her. Note that her long poems (like **"Thomas Jefferson"** and the moving **"Darwin"**) repay repeated readings.

One returns, finally, to her tiny poems for what they tell us about this singularly devoted life:

> Now in one year
>   a book published
>   and plumbing—
> took a lifetime
>   to weep
>   a deep
>   trickle

Behold the morality of poetry, the personal end of Niedecker's taxing art: self-pity transmogrified into good humor and wisdom and self-knowledge. That trickle eroded rock. A torrent of praise for that trickle!

> Thomas D'Evelyn, "A Most Natural Nature Poet," in The Christian Science Monitor, *November 20, 1985, p. 25.*

GEOFFREY O'BRIEN

Poets are constantly exhorted to "find their own voice," but for all the thrashing about and self-searching, the language of most poems comes out flat, generic, interchangeable. In the academies and urban centers and pages of little magazines, the voices overlap and blend. Perhaps the poets listen too much to each other. A truly idiosyncratic voice—a voice with what used to be called *character*—would need some space around it, some silence in which to nurture its distinctive branchings and coilings. Consider Basil Bunting and Lorine Niedecker: holed up in small corners of the universe, far from the markets where reputations are traded, each spending a lifetime to make, line by line, a small durable book of poems. . . .

They were linked by their connection with Louis Zukofsky— who included a somewhat reluctant Bunting among the original Objectivists, and whose 1931 special issue of *Poetry* catalyzed Niedecker's sense of poetics—but unlike Zukofsky, neither had much taste for theoretical formulations. Bunting defined poetry as a "flow of noise," Niedecker as "depth of emotion condensed," and otherwise they left such matters to the more metaphysically inclined. Their writing was local, concrete, and absolutely individual: not the individuality of a confessionalist ego but the impersonal solitariness of a mind wholly given over to its perceptions. They did not simply take up a given language and use it to describe something. In their hands, language itself metamorphosed under the weight of elemental presences: flavors, textures, geological strata, abrupt patches of vegetation. Each of them evolved something like a private dialect of English, a linguistic mode not obscure but gnarled, weathered, worn smooth in unpredictable places.

They approached poetry as a practical job of work, its tools obdurate, its material elusive. Both Bunting and Niedecker on occasion compared a poem to a fishing net, an empty structure trapping what it can of light and air and natural noise. The craftsman's trick is to know just what waters to drop the net into, and when to haul it up: slow, precise work requiring silence, sharp reflexes, wide-awake senses. It's a poetry grounded in this world, not any transcendent other, and its methods and effects are unavoidably material. . . . Niedecker described her conception of poetry in physical terms: "I'd say mostly, of course, cadence, measure make song. And a kind of shine (or sombre tone) that is of the same intensity throughout the poem. And the thing moves."

Lorine Niedecker—a fisherman's daughter for whom net imagery was autobiography rather than metaphor—lived for most of her years in an island cabin on Lake Koshkonong, Wisconsin. Her work might be summarized with the title of one of her poems: **"My Life by Water."** It's all one "sublime / slime- / song," heavy with mud and frogs, periodically submerged by floodwaters. . . . Her marshland is as distinct a poetic landscape as this century has given us, fertile and destructive, its boundaries fluid, its inhabitants prey to a permanent uncertainty in the face of "Springtime's wide / water- / yield." There are no possessions that can't be swept away without warning. The seepage even invades the perimeters of personality: "My life is hung up / in the flood / a wave-blurred / portrait." Momentary fragments of intense knotted interrelation—"mossed / massed quartz / on which spruce / grew dense"—emerge from the water's obliterating rush. . . .

Paradoxically, this clear-eyed poet of nature was at the same time elaborately literary, filling her lines with quotation and allusive wordplay. The writings which most influenced her— she cited among others Zukofsky, Dickinson, Thoreau, Lucretius, haiku—were for her part of nature, an inward extension of landscape. A poem could be built with any materials; her later poems include complex collages constructed from the words of Thomas Jefferson, William Morris, and Charles Darwin. There as elsewhere, she displays a builder's joy in formal placement. Structural integrity becomes a model of happiness, and her patterned surfaces swarm with decorative beauties, with playful echoes of nursery rhymes and folk tunes, with uncanny approximations of the most diffuse and gossamery phenomena. The way the words fit together implies some kind of contentedness. Yet her poems have an emotional force like the breaking of an oppressive silence. Within their elegance, at its core, we become aware of a ragged, raging splendor, neither tranquil nor polite.

Much contemporary poetry takes the form of a discourse among intellectual peers. The mind on the receiving end is in some sense known, a friendly quantity. Niedecker's work differs in function; it's not so much a discourse as a mediation between herself and the speechlessness of what surrounds her. Ultimately she was her own audience, the poem not self-expression

but a space she could inhabit, handmade like her cabin on Black Hawk Island. The problem in her poems is how to make oneself compatible with the sheer blind otherness of the natural world. No matter how graceful her ferns and water lilies, the waters are rooted in death. In the great extended sequences— **"Lake Superior," "Traces of Living Things," "Paean to Place," "Wintergreen Ridge"**—she kept returning to a point of mineral quiescence . . . not in ecstasy but to attain a minimal point of equilibrium, where her mind could bring itself into tune with the mindlessness of matter. . . .

All at once—after years when Niedecker's work was scarcely available—we have two major editions to choose from. *From This Condensery* has (letters aside) all her writing, including apprentice poems, variant drafts, fictional fragments, book reviews, a radio adaptation of *As I Lay Dying*. It reveals much that was unknown, particularly in the intensely political nature of many of the early poems: "We know him—Law and Order League—/ fishing from our dock, / testified against the pickets / at the plant—owns stock." Niedecker may have been localized, but her concerns were from the outset global. This presentation of the complete Niedecker canon . . . ought to (but will probably not) be widely noted as a major event. In one respect, however, the book isn't entirely satisfactory. Over the years she continually rearranged her poems into different sequences, often revising them in the process; the editor has chosen to reprint the same poems each time they crop up, while ignoring the arrangements Niedecker approved for books published during her lifetime. The consequent impression of clutter and double vision sometimes blurs the formal clarity of Niedecker's aesthetic. Cid Corman's selection of her poems, *The Granite Pail*, is a better bet for an introductory sampling, although it hardly exhausts the beauties of her writing. (p. 43)

Geoffrey O'Brien, "Solid as a Rock: Country Poems, Made to Last," in The Village Voice, *Vol. XXXI, No. 3, January 21, 1986, pp. 43-4.*

MICHAEL HELLER

Lorine Niedecker, throughout a literary career of some 50 years, both admired and wrote poems she hoped would stand up against a culture engaged, as she put it, in "the armed avoidance of quiet." She once told the poet Cid Corman, who is the editor of *The Granite Pail,* a selection of her poems, "I want to plant my poems in deep silence." Her masters and influences were meditative men and women—Jefferson, Darwin, William Morris, the botanist Asa Gray and more contemporary strategists of poetic silences like Mr. Corman, Basil Bunting and her sometime mentor and correspondent, the Objectivist poet Louis Zukofsky. From them she learned to use contemplation and the absence of noise not as a defense against the world, nor as a form of withdrawal, but as a compositional element, a way of forcing the reader's attention on the precision and subtlety of her verse. Trees, flowers and rivers, in particular those of her native Wisconsin, are among her favorite subjects partly because their growth and development occur without auditory fanfare. In one poem in *From This Condensery,* a collection of all her poetry and prose edited by Robert J. Bertholf, the poetic act is likened to the soundlessness of a bird in flight:

> I was the solitary plover
> a pencil
>   for a wing-bone
> From the secret notes
> I must tilt

        upon the pressure
        execute and adjust
            In us sea-air rhythm.

Her "secret notes" are her poems, densely compacted verbal performances that accrete nouns and adjectives as they drop like plumb weights down the page. . . .

The poems are structured musically—this she learned, especially from Zukofsky. They seem to demand of the reader a concertgoer's attention as their often monosyllabic words play off assonance and dissonance, fuguelike rather than orchestral.

Niedecker's poetry, as Mr. Corman points out in his preface to *The Granite Pail,* "appropriates voices more than history." She favors the individual account over history's tendency to drown out the single voice. But even more, what she loves about the historical figures who populate her poems is the way silence both enshrouds and energizes their perceptions. She cites Audubon, writing home from England to his wife, "Dear Lucy, the servants here / move quiet / as kill-deer," and also Jefferson, who hoped to "establish / an absolute power / of silence over oneself."

Her favored mode of understanding, also evidenced in all historical personages who figure in the poetry, is observation, as though the act of contemplation thoroughly wedded one with the physical universe. Much of her poetry works from an awareness of interlocked unities, the interanimation of the living with the mineral:

        The smooth black stone
        I picked up in true source park
            the leaf beside it
        once was stone

        Why should we hurry
        home.

For Niedecker the natural world is a "true source." Where everything is somehow related to everything else, there is no need to hurry "home," since home is everywhere, as even the "home/stone" rhyme suggests. The intense brevity of the poem, isolating individual words in the reader's attention, transforms each noun into a large-scale metonymy until what that noun represents is also capable of standing for the world as a whole. This metonymic mode is most apparent in the longer sequences such as **"Wintergreen Ridge"** and **"Paean to Place,"** *collagiste* hymns to interrelatedness that skillfully use enjambment of place, memory and history with witty or comic commentary. . . .

Yet nature and history are by no means her only subjects. She observes herself in her poetry as carefully as she does the natural world. Her insistent terseness can remind the reader of Sappho or Emily Dickinson, as in this line from a poem about a dead neighbor—"Dead / she now lay deaf to death." And like Dickinson, she can be simultaneously comic and grave. . . .

Niedecker referred to her method of composition as "condensery" (hence the title of her collected works). In all her work, the tightness of the poetic line allows the reader almost no time to linger or indulge the sentiment; instead, the sparseness and precision invest the language with magical resonances, the words seemingly wiped clean of extraneous matter so that they may register authentic substance and feeling.

At the time of her death, in 1970, Niedecker's poetry was known only to a handful of other poets. This situation, at least partly due to Niedecker's own diffidence about her work, was somewhat alleviated by the efforts of Mr. Corman, who printed much of her work in *Origin* magazine, and by the poet Jonathan Williams, whose Jargon Society published an earlier collection of her work and the current volume of collected poems, radio plays and prose [*From This Condensery*]. With the issuance of these two books, the sudden availability of her work is a distinctive literary event, for her poems, in their powerful yet nearly mathematical compoundings of language and silence, are among the subtlest of our time.

> *Michael Heller, "Silence Is Musical," in* The New York Times Book Review, *January 26, 1986, p. 25.*

DOUGLAS CRASE

[Because Niedecker] married so late, because for many years before that she lived alone on the river with no telephone, because her primary link to the literary world was her thirty-year correspondence with Louis Zukofsky and because her other correspondents were also Objectivist poets or their admirers, because she wrote short-line poems, and because we really don't know enough about her otherwise, a largely sentimental image . . . [of her has evolved]. According to this image, she was the American bittern of poetry, a Thoreauvian Bashō who somehow got reincarnated female in the upper Midwest but adjusted to the accident with Objectivist therapy. She crafted poems of "nicety" and "discretion" and made them, we have been told, of language "whittled clean"; poems the more emphatically discrete for the silence in which they were said to be contained.

This image is about to become unstuck. For years you couldn't get a Niedecker collection anywhere, and now there are two of them, sufficiently different to demonstrate how truly inadequate our understanding of this poet is. One is a selected poems, **The Granite Pail,** edited by Cid Corman. The other is a complete poems plus creative prose, **From This Condensery**, edited by Robert J. Bertholf. Corman puts together a seductive selection unencumbered by notes or textual variants; some of its pages are almost unencumbered by words, since this is the Niedecker planted in silence, the orthodox version up to now. Bertholf, by contrast, counts more than four times as many poems in his collection; working directly with the poet's manuscripts, he has turned out a Niedecker that is rangy, turbulent and sometimes troubling as well.

Maybe no one is more surprised than these editors, because the result of their contrasting presentations is a disagreement over Niedecker's intentions and methods that amounts, ultimately, to a disagreement over her achievement as a poet. The issue is joined in what is probably her best-known poem:

        There's a better shine
        on the pendulum
        than is on my hair
        and many times
            . . .
        I've seen it there.

                ("There's a better shine")

Even by itself, which is how Corman prints it, this is a complex performance. By itself, it is a subtle reflection on life's vanity, say, on the cycle of personal fate. But when Niedecker first published the poem, in 1936, it wasn't by itself. It was third in a six-part sequence, **"Mother Geese"**, arranged among other poems predominantly concerned with cycles of a more inclusive sort—the economic and political cycles whose reality was vivid during the Depression years when "**Mother Geese**" was written. (p. 309)

So much for the discrete poem. In a manuscript note (included among the "Notes" in Bertholf), Niedecker observes of another poem that "these phrases that look forward and back are fascinating to do but I suppose there's a limit." A limit, that is, unless you can arrange the poem within a longer sequence where poem as well as phrases look forward and back. It's a distinguished strategy, ever since Whitman. The trouble is that Niedecker rearranged her work continually in this manner, so that at the time of her death a single poem might exist in several versions, in more than one position among the sequences, in a sequence and on its own. On the evidence of *The Granite Pail,* which moves smoothly forward with no hint of options, Corman must believe that what Niedecker required was a good editor. Bertholf is inclined to let the manuscripts have their own way (which is how we got "**Mother Geese**"), so that *From This Condensery* is thick with variants and near-outright repetitions. It's impossible to say how many of these Niedecker intended to clean up. . . . Her poem "**Dear Paul: Four Versions**" (as Bertholf prints it) certainly suggests that her conclusion was based on practice. Maybe we have caught up with her, or maybe it's only that our current esthetic validates her indecision, but here is a poem whose ever-shorter alternatives read as a single work, each succeeding version a more daring synecdoche for the first, and the whole thing an affecting commentary on the dubious, time-honored business of leaving things out.

The irony is that Bertholf left so little out of his edition and then chose to call it *From This Condensery.* The phrase comes from one of Niedecker's least satisfying and most self-regarding poems, but its elevation was probably inevitable, since it echoes the Poundian and then Objectivist notion that a poet's job is to condense the raw material until he or she has revealed the discrete poem waiting at its core. Of course Niedecker would sometimes borrow this expression; it isn't easy to find the right metaphor for how you make metaphors. But what is equally clear now is how much she was aware that her own methods differed from those of her correspondents, and that this difference would not be recognized for some time. In the poem "**Otherwise**" she has turned for sympathy to a likewise idiosyncratic practitioner, Gerard Manley Hopkins, addressing him as "Dear friend," and getting in along the way an unusually irreverent pun on the name of the master condenser, Ezra Pound:

> the scanning's plain
> but who will veer
> from the usual stamp and pound
> Other work?—I've not yet found
> the oak leaves' law . . .

Maybe she hadn't codified it, but in her poems Niedecker returns often enough to "the law of the oak leaf" to indicate that here was the law she meant to follow in poetry.

Good enough, but aren't we just out on a limb with another metaphor? It would be better to watch the poet in action, and if you are patient with the perversely unindexed *From This Condensery,* there will be times when you can almost see how a poem took shape. One especially redeeming example is in "**Crèvecoeur,**" a poem written after *Letters from an American Farmer.* Bertholf prints the initial prosy poem in which Niedecker has entered two lines that seem only recently harvested from her reading: "Astonishing how quick men learn who serve

themselves. / At night the fireflies can be caught and used as a reading / light." When this harvest reappears in a more obviously finished poem, the transformation has been dramatic:

> Learn Crèvecoeur and learn fast
> the firefly, two pairs of wings
> and a third to read by
> disappearing.
>
> ("**For Paul**")

Shorter by three words, this is hardly a condensation. The poem has expanded, burgeoned almost—the way (why not?) an oak leaf takes up its mineral facts and unfolds from the bare branch. "True value," this poet has written elsewhere, "expands."

As it turns out, the leaf metaphor was no more wholly Niedecker's own than was the condensery. Oak leaves show up in the first sentence of Zukofsky's famous 1931 brief for Objectivist poetics, and he would later remark to her in a letter that to prepare for a poem you must wait for the fact to die out and come back like a leaf on a branch. Surely, she knew where the metaphor came from. Just as surely, there were bound to be differences in what it would mean to her. At home on the Rock River her father had been a commercial fisherman who sometimes took his daughter along to seine for carp on the lake and river. "I spent my childhood outdoors—," she remembered, "redwinged blackbirds, willows, maples, boats, fishing (the smell of tarred nets), twittering and squawking noises from the marsh." It was a world of natural reality too sensuous for her ever to leave.

> My life
>   by water—
>   Hear
>
> spring's
>   first frog
>   or board
>
> out on the cold
>   ground
>   giving
>
> ("**My Life by Water**")

Yet there was also the world of words, and Niedecker acknowledged in particular the influence of her mother, every day "speaking whole chunks of down-to-earth magic." It must be too simple to say that poetry provided the theater where Niedecker could mediate the tug of war between her father's magic facts and her mother's magic words. Yet in the earliest poem made available by Bertholf, a poem printed in her high-school yearbook nine years before Zukofsky's essay, this tug of war between reality and words is already Niedecker's subject. It was still the subject a year before she died, when she observed in a letter to Corman that a poetic method was successful if it suggested "the reality that may get inside us and fill the subconscious of the future!" If this is what she also understood from Zukofsky about the fact coming back like a leaf on the branch, then we have in Lorine Niedecker a magnificent example of how good poets turn influence to—it's irresistible—misprision.

Misprision, "devoted treason," is the infraction partly illustrated by the poem set off in the preceding paragraph. Yes, those short lines and tripartite divisions are reminiscent of certain earlier poems of William Carlos Williams, who once counted Niedecker, along with Zukofsky and himself, among the original Objectivists. But the alliteration, the assonance, the near-rhymes—these add up to a sensuousness you may rarely associate with Zukofsky or even Williams. And because she could deploy this sensuous magic without getting burned, a skill she had begun to perfect in **"Mother Geese,"** Niedecker could take on subjects sometimes thought too hot for modernist poets to handle:

> How bright you'll find young people,
>   Diddle,
>   and how unkind.
> When a boy appears with a book
> they cry "Who's the young Einstein?"
> Einstein, you know, said space
> is what it's made up of.
> And as to the human race
> "Why do you deeply oppose its passing"
> you'll find men asking
> the man with the nebular hair
>   and the fiddle.
>
> ("For Paul")

Sophisticated in its ambiguities, lucid as a nursery rhyme, this poem is also distinguished by something that makes it highly unusual in recent poetry—you can memorize it. Because of its music, you may even *want* to memorize it: a poem about nuclear extinction that works because it's so subversively joyful.

It also works because, as with the pendulum poem, Niedecker has fitted it into a sequence that greatly expands its context. This sequence, **"For Paul,"** is addressed to a talented child of 6 as a sort of premonitory guidebook to the magical outside world, a vade mecum as concerned with questions of public and private virtue as if Anne Bradstreet had returned to be-queath a state-of-the-art version of her *Meditations* to the children of a very altered Commonwealth. Written for the most part in the early 1950s, and arguably the central work of Niedecker's career, **"For Paul"** was apparently published piecemeal but never as the single work the poet manifestly intended. Its recovery and restoration by Bertholf must rank as the biggest surprise and the triumph of *From This Condensery*. As an arrangement of fifty constituent poems—and more if you include the alternative ending (don't)—**"For Paul"** provides the richest opportunity for Niedecker to indulge her redemptive talent for resonant, subtle and also humorous transitions.

It may seem devious in a review to praise transitions, since you can't exactly quote one. But transition is the element that imparts the unimpeded grace to Niedecker's late and finest sequences: **"Lake Superior," "Thomas Jefferson," "Darwin," "Paean to Place."** Each of these demonstrates that, for this poet anyway, poetry is enlivened during those moments it looks both forward and back. How different this turns out to have been from the Objectivist conceit, at least as expressed by Zukofsky, that no verse should be called a poem unless it conveyed "the totality of perfect rest." For Niedecker, accustomed by her river to fluxes of flood and silt, humans themselves were a transition (a transition of minerals in **"Lake Superior"**), and their cultural evolution likewise a transit of fact as it leafs into words. So nothing could be more important than this unrestful evolution where we in fact *make* our lives and which is, so poets hope, the project of poetry. (pp. 309-10, 312-13)

Douglas Crase, "Free and Clean," in The Nation, *Vol. 242, No. 10, March 15, 1986, pp. 309-310, 312-13.*

Robert Nye

1939-

English novelist, poet, short story writer, dramatist, script-writer, critic, editor, and author of children's books.

A versatile author who has experimented with a number of literary forms during his career, Nye is best known for his imaginative comic novels in which he creates variations on existing myths, histories, legends, and literature. He is particularly noted for his energetic prose style, his intellectual and verbal dexterity, and his wry, manic wit. Through tall tales, scatological humor, and puns and wordplay, Nye comments on the relationship between fantasy and reality. By combining the traditional and the contemporary, Nye seeks to create what he termed in one story "a song both old and new, original and remembered." He stated that his stories arise from "those folk tales which are as it were the dreams of the people coming down to us without the interference of our own identity."

Nye began his career writing poetry for British literary magazines. His earliest poems are collected in *Juvenilia I* (1961) and *Juvenilia II* (1963). Although critics found some of his poems awkward, Nye's interest in myth and legend prompted comparisons with the poetry of Robert Graves. Nye's later collections, including *Darker Ends* (1969) and *Divisions on a Ground* (1976), although considered derivative of baroque nineteenth-century verse, were praised for their refinement of style and evocation of archetypal themes and images.

Mythical lore is again central, although in a purely esoteric sense, to *Doubtfire* (1967), Nye's attempt at the *nouveau roman,* or antinovel. Narrated by William Retz, an adolescent boy suffering an identity crisis during which he assumes the roles of various literary figures, the book resembles poetry in its dense, stylistic complexity and anticipates the direction of Nye's subsequent fiction. Nye began to directly rework the lives of literary personalities in *Tales I Told My Mother* (1969), a collection of fabulistic short stories characterized by puns, wordplay, and prurient humor which critics compared to the work of sixteenth-century French satirist François Rabelais.

Nye's interest in the relationship between fact and fiction finds its most direct expression in his series of comic novels begun during the 1970s. These works are modeled on the medieval morality play and presented from the suspect viewpoints of characters derived from myth and literature. Nye embellishes traditional tales with digressions and statements of questionable validity from his protagonists. He stated that he found his proper "voice and pitch" with *Falstaff* (1976), a novel consisting of the "memoirs" of the comic braggart introduced in Shakespeare's historical plays. As dictated to an unreliable group of scriveners, Falstaff's incredible sexual and heroic adventures take on an extra dimension of untruth. *Falstaff* won acclaim in the United States and England and was adapted for both radio and stage. In *Merlin* (1978), Nye presents the wise man and sorcerer of Arthurian legend, who recounts his story "locked in the present tense" of a fictional reality as the devil's attempt at an antichrist. Determinism versus free will and the illusive nature of freedom and reality, recurring themes in Nye's fiction, are further developed in *Faust* (1980). Nye reworks the legend of Faust by focusing on Christopher Wagner, Faust's

servant, who unwillingly succumbs to superstition and doubts his own reality as he narrates the old man's story forty days prior to the date that Faust's pact with the devil is due to be redeemed.

Nye's tendency toward pastiche and scatological humor is downplayed in *The Voyage of the Destiny* (1982), a speculative historical novel. Presented as Sir Walter Raleigh's diaristic account of his unsuccessful 1617 expedition to South America in search of gold for King James I, the novel contrasts Raleigh's hopes for easy ascension in the royal court with his failure and impending punishment by the king. *The Facts of Life and Other Fictions* (1984), a short story collection, includes Nye's usual variations on myth and legend and his attention to the nature of reality but also features his interest in science fiction, fantasy, and supernatural fiction.

Nye has written several books for children, many of which remain true to C. S. Lewis's belief that such works should also be enjoyable to adults. Many of these works, which include *Taliesin* (1966), *Wishing Gold* (1970), and *Harry Pay the Pirate* (1981), are based on ancient Welsh and Celtic legends. Nye also wrote verse for a dramatic presentation, *The Seven Deadly Sins: A Mask* (1974). Several of his dramas, including *Mr. Poe: A Public Lecture with Private Illustrations* (1975) and the one-act plays and film script which comprise *Three*

Plays: Penthesilea, Fugue, and Sisters (1976), have been adapted for both radio and stage. Nye is also a respected critic and editor.

(See also *CLC*, Vol. 13; *Contemporary Authors*, Vols. 33-36, rev. ed.; *Something about the Author*, Vol. 6; and *Dictionary of Literary Biography*, Vol. 14.)

THE TIMES LITERARY SUPPLEMENT

Mr. Robert Nye, with an energy he shares with Mr. [Peter] Redgrove, presents . . . [a] problem. His present collection [*Juvenilia I*] consists of work written up to his eighteenth year. It contains some of the most dreadful verse ever published, but—at that age—it would be unwise to dismiss him on such a count. What is much more important is that he is developing a new way of handling abstractions, perhaps the most tricky problem facing poets today. Thus he begins a poem on **"The Last Supper"** with the lines:

> We have not knelt down at this table
> To also gorge with the rabble
> Of Giant Treacle,
> Who when blood falls on Haymarket
> Washes both his hands in it.
> Our treason is high treason,
> A crown cast in the beans.

Here, indeed, he is approaching a definition of treason such as has never yet been made.

> *"Problems for Poets," in* The Times Literary Supplement, *No. 3129, February 16, 1962, p. 106.*

THE TIMES LITERARY SUPPLEMENT

[A lyrical poet] was once told by a friend that his poems were no longer "even word-perfect". It turned out that the friend's meaning had nothing to do with the craftsmanship of the verse; he meant that the poet, like a careless or inefficient shorthand-writer, was no longer getting down properly on the page what was being given to him, was no longer being sufficiently passive and receptive, ready to listen and transcribe while postponing full understanding of what he was doing. This is the old theory of inspiration or possession, the theory of the poet as prompted by spirits. . . .

[Nothing] demands more delicate and conscious shaping than a true lyrical poem. The purely lyrical poet tends, therefore, to be a kind of mixture of the medium or shaman or, in more respectable language, the "negative capability" and the craftsman, of the passionately niggling, perpetually self-dissatisfied sort. The notable English poet, of this kind, in our own time, is Mr. Robert Graves, and the wilful, aggressive, polemical masculinity of much of Mr. Graves's prose can be seen as the proper compensation for the suppression of will and aggression in his best poems. One does not know whether Mr. Nye has ever made the pilgrimage to Majorca. Yet he seems in gifts and temperament admirably fitted to be what Mr. Graves would call his tanist, the young rival and successor (who is essentially merely another avatar of) the aging king.

The present climate of criticism makes for excellent handling of novels and plays, kinds of writing that have a coarse, broad relevance to the social scene, but for obtuse criticism of poetry. . . . [Obviously] and innately poetic qualities are likely to be dismissed as "sentimental" or "naive". Mr. Nye's first volume, *Juvenilia 1,* did, however, encounter critics who, worried by what they thought an immaturity of attitude and an elusiveness of meaning, had the sense to recognize "poetic inventiveness and feeling for language . . . a fumbling power" and "the innate poetic gift without which spontaneity—inspirational or otherwise—is futile". It might be said that Mr. Nye's first volume was "word-perfect", but that he often seemed like the good shorthand-writer who does not quite understand the drift of the letter he has taken down, and therefore cannot fill in the gaps, complete it properly, in his own words. There was also a sense of unworthiness, which is natural to the poet as the secretary of Hidden Powers.

All this comes out finely in the dedicatory poem to [*Juvenilia II*]. . . . Here is a poem in which everything, in Mr. Graves's term, admirably "tallies": and in which several traditional modes and themes, the riddling poem, the young poet's invocation of, say, Beatrice and Virgil, the transference of religious awe and courtly love into half-regretful marital affection, are beautifully blended. But it is, of course, a poem of cool decorum, without glaringly striking individual lines or phrases. . . .

The last poem in the book has a similar Gravesian decorum, cool passion and judging concentration. . . . In the in-between poems one has sometimes a sense not only that Mr. Graves's principles are being followed, but also that familiar properties of his are being borrowed a little too freely: the owl, the cold, the whisper, the tight gathering together of dread, love and mystery:

> howlet (she whispers) howlet, owlet, owl
> (kissing the owl-light on the windowpane
> before her breath can shrink from it, a warm fleck
> in freckled glass)
>
> love! (& he burns his lips
> with death no words or kisses plainly speak of—
> laughing to greet his cold reflection coldly)

Perhaps the punctuation there, Blake plus E. E. Cummings, is meant to deflect our attention from the Gravesian derivations. But the craftsmanship in the nearness and likeness and difference of "fleck" and "freckled" is quite individual. Here is a proper poet, though it is hard to see how the larger literate public (greedy for flattery of their own concerns) could be brought to recognize that. But other proper poets—how many of them are there left?—will recognize one of themselves.

> *"Secretary of Hidden Powers," in* The Times Literary Supplement, *No. 3204, July 26, 1963, p. 560.*

MICHAEL WOOD

They are three children: a boy, a girl, another boy. The South-end they live in is a country of metaphor, a fabulous kingdom by the sea. It is Arthur's Britain, it is fifteenth-century France. There is a Beast where the night begins. An ambiguous Grail awaits one of them.

Doubtfire is this one's poem, his version of their childhood. He calls himself William Retz, he sees himself as Gilles de Rais reincarnate. Like Gilles de Rais, he dabbles in witchcraft and fails to evoke the devil. And like Gilles de Rais, he serves Joan of Arc, the girl who was burned at Rouen, and who dies again in a fire on Southend pier. He is Rimbaud too, the "child raped by poetry", "he has had verbal erections and cannot forgive the dictionary." His testament: "Life—I leave it to my poems." Rimbaud went away, became someone else in Africa. William Retz, at the end of *Doubtfire,* swimming in the North Sea, abandoning the purity of suicide, loses his name, needs another.

Other people in the book have only a preliminary reality. They are pretexts, figments in Retz's fiction. He appropriates them, turns them into aspects of himself. . . .

Doubtfire is a cerebral, literate, un-English novel, much richer than my simplifications suggest. Retz is Hamlet, Raleigh and Robin Hood, as well as Rimbaud and Gilles de Rais. Jokes litter the pages. "Intersex." "A man after my own fart." "A portrait of the artist as a Jung man." One thinks of Joyce, who wrote of girls who are jung and easily freudened. Then forgets him and thinks of Rabelais. There are technical echoes (lists, for example) there is a similar obscenity, a similar furious passion for the intellect.

Nye's language fails at times, falls into an unstylish baroque ("Sebastianed with tender commas of probability"), or into an alarming flatness, as where Retz tells us who Joan of Arc was, or how love is two becoming one. Ironies cloak these lapses, but not enough. But otherwise, *Doubtfire* is brilliantly sustained, a book where language is the hero, a poem-novel with careful syntax, proliferating pictures and a strong sense of the concrete.

> *Michael Wood, "A Lady in Southend," in* The Times, *London, January 27, 1968, p. 20.*

MARY SULLIVAN

Doubtfire is an original in need of translation. As it is, it's only half penetrable, yet what is lurking in its thickets is of real interest. It explores the disturbed mind of a boy approaching sexual maturity, wavering between reality and fantasy as he discovers the world and himself. But only the author is in [on] the secret of which characters are drawn from the outer world and which from the boy's confusion, and the reader is left to make what he can of the stylised persons and the shapeless torrent of feelings and thoughts. Of course this is deliberate. . . . But with the best will, all the reader can do is to rest on the moments of recognition, grab the isolated jokes, and regret that so much intelligent sympathy on Robert Nye's part should go for so little in the end.

> *Mary Sullivan, "Visible Men," in* The Listener, *Vol. 79, No. 2031, February 29, 1968, p. 279.*

P. H. POROSKY

Robert Nye, in *Doubtfire,* makes Henry James, John Hawkes or Alain Robbe-Grillet seem like rank amateurs of suspended coherence. In fact, at times one wonders if there is any coherence at all. Or, if so, whether the author has suspended it for too long, making the reader wait until the closing chapters for a few niblets of clarified air to bring a cheer to the lips and a gladness to the mind which has labored through two hundred pages of an allusionary maze. The reader is left with many questions. For a while, nothing but questions. For example: why has a writer of obvious talent chosen such an awkward vehicle to display some of the most indirectly profound insights of the *Situation* ever seen in print? Why does he seem to find

it necessary to ensconce so much sparkling virtuosity behind smoke screens of graduate-school learning? Why is he at times so pointedly clear that he makes the reader bleed in squirming appreciation and at other times so patently vague and cleverly obscure that he blurs his receiver's eyes with yawning exasperation? After trudging through the many deep valleys of Robert Nye's prose only to gain a few breath-escaping peaks, the reader's final question has to be—was it all worth it?

A word of warning to this reader: bring your mind along; it will come in handy.

> I, said William Retz, the "hero" of sorts suffer
> of a vision of the order my own disorder mocks.

If there is a "key line" in the novel, this is it. Author Nye blatantly, almost too audaciously, *tells* us about his characters, then as if guilty from such excess, sneaks back from his conventional expository stance to confuse and confound through disoriented and subjective commentary. (p. 100)

Nye *writes* continuously out of context in this novel. It is in fact his assiduous avoidance of pattern and structure which is most striking. Other authors have fragmented time, subjectivized external reality, switched point-of-view without transition signals, inserted asides in lonely islands of seeming unrelatedness. Nye has done all of these and more. His story pattern gives the effect of watching someone shake a jar half-filled with colored marbles. The effect is never the same twice, yet there are repeated details. He re-mentions a particular act or environmental detail as if to announce, look here, these things are more important than they might seem. The structure of *Doubtfire* is formed, perhaps better fused, by Life itself. There remains no doubt that there is life here, a short but furiously fired particle of life. And we are led to believe that the major character's madness is our madness, his position as victim, our position. In this way, the author gains a kind of grudging sympathy for his character which a different kind of heavy-handedness could not achieve. Time to William Retz, the defeated poet and liver of life, is more than relative; it is meaningless. Meaningless because it is predetermined. . . . In the few days of Retz's life which we are permitted to see, it is not any particular event that matters. It is plain and total Reality that matters most to author Nye, and least to his characters. The book itself, a montage like the old transparent plastic training aides, asks the question of What. . . . Nye's prose strives (most of the time) to give the reader actuality and memory at the same time. It is an unending receipt of Reality filling out, not filled-out. (p. 101)

The Reality of Nye's intricately clever "nowhere somewhere else" is not real because he teaches us that no reality is real. Madness, grotesque bizarreness replace so-called lucidity because, as Nye's characters learn, lucidity is really a fiction, a process of imagination, the mirror image, or finally, as in the case of William Retz, the poem.

One could get too inextricably tied up in the thick webs of literary reference and trickily clever symbolism, such as with the names, Ben Flamel or Joan Dark. But that would be missing the truth for the sake of puzzle-finding fun. A puzzle worth solving, however, is that of the major extending metaphor in the work, for metaphor seems the key to clarity.

The metaphor is fire. As charter members in the Arson Club of life, William Retz and his two friends are ministers of the reality of fire. But to them, and presumably to us, fire is a highly positive if flammable substance. To Nye's characters fire is life itself. Life's process. And it is left for fire to communicate the central point about Nye's unreal reality. He shouts this message loud and clear: Reality once brought out in attempted clarity (through the word spoken or written) becomes no longer reality or truth, but only a mirror image of that reality, that truth left behind somewhere in a kind of creative(ing) concept. There is then the impossibility of anyone (re)creating truth or reality as well as fire creates its own life. As often with Nye when he is at his best, the dimensions of already accepted and acceptable ideas increase multifold, and one is then ready to approach both the book and (Nye perhaps hopes) life as if it were a forever dangling mobile and not a flat wall. He makes this plain: fire is the true reality because it destroys reality (what it burns) and thus itself too AS IT BURNS or lives. . . . Thus the fire (like life) *was,* no longer *is.* And the major issue of the book (one can hardly call it a novel), life and/or love, is brought into Nye's peculiar yet original perspective. Life/love are real ONLY because they are dying while living. Freeze life/love (or pour water on them) and their value disappears, becomes cold, dead, unreal, if permanent. The final lesson is clearer than Nye in his own words would like to believe: in the fury of his doubting self-dialogue he is determined to ignore his audience and thus in the process actually make his work more applicable to it, giving his audience a dimension of life to be shared rather than observed. The reader is more the challenged participant in life, less the passive listener. And as such he yearns to carry away with him at least a few sturdy crumbs of Nye's earnest breadwork.

The reader might wish that Nye would have spared us such obviously contrived and over-conscious usages as

> . . . and by some unseeing unerring *coarse* yet
> vivid instinct it is always his . . .

but he does this seldom enough to make it merely a petty objection. At times he is more adept, as in particular patches of external description. (pp. 102-03)

There is enough here for almost any reader's identification, but he should be warned. This work cannot be read as much as felt. It is not *about* (someone, something) but *is.* Having its own life and force, it bursts and is consumed in its own flame. Its substance can not be reported, but, like Life, must be suffered.

And the reader may be reassured that the author comes forth with his trumpet blast of clarity before it is too late. The saga of the poet-moth fatally drawn into life's flame is not new but here well delineated. Nye's approach to the familiar theme is just fresh enough:

> . . . The burning must be accepted, truth loved,
> as easily as lies are. Then the bright logic will
> be achieved, the poet (eidolon) will have be-
> come the poem (logos), the moth the flame,
> the appearance the reality . . . The poem's sub-
> ject is the poet's need to write poetry to attain
> wholeness.

And in *Doubtfire* one senses that Mr. Nye indeed means this very much. (p. 104)

> *P. H. Porosky, "The Moth Becomes the Flame," in
> Northwest Review, Vol. 10, No. 1, Summer, 1968,
> pp. 100-04.*

DAVID WILLIAMS

A reviewer's duty is to tell his readers what a book is *about.* With Robert Nye's *Tales I Told My Mother* he'll probably get farther if he proceeds by way of similes rather than epitomes. Reading it is like sitting in a fairground coach and being whirled around a priapically painted merry-go-round: startling visions flash briskly by, and then you start seeing them all again, recognizable still but bulgy and distorted because the speed of the motion has given you giddiness.

But I should pause perhaps in order to say that it consists of nine interrelated short stories. Yet no. That won't do either. Perhaps better to borrow from the musicologists and say that here is a rondo with nine themes—*is* it nine?—all chasing each other.

The third piece is called "**Axel**" and I'd advise the reader to start with this because it's around "**Axel**" that Nye's wheel of fire revolves. Then go back to number one, and then straight through to the final "**The Amber Witch**", where most of the spectral fantasticks—Chang the Giant, Rufus Goate, Mary Murder and the rest—are drawn into a sort of twelve toned— or should it be nine-toned?—resolution.

"O Sterne, pray for me. O Carroll, play for me. O Munchausen, pay for me". Nye supplicates at the beginning of "**The Amber Witch**". These are all departed spirits he might appropriately communicate with; and certainly they all contribute something to the exhilarating verbal skylarkings which are an important element in *Tales I Told My Mother.* . . . [Clear influences on Nye's writing include] Joyce and Rabelais. Rabelais I think particularly. Nye shares his liking for an intensive etymological pub-crawl which may end up in the gutter or in Paradise, and sometimes in both places simultaneously.

This book is alive with vivid symbols—the dead man with the half-sovereign clenched between his teeth for example—which appear and reappear with all the accepted rightness we accord to the visions of our dreams. Earlier Nye has talked of the "thermonuclear content of the English language". His book, tight packed with originality and bracing experiment, shows he has the knack of triggering it off.

> *David Williams, "The Nine Theme Rondo," in The
> Times, London, December 20, 1969, p. iv.*

ALAN BROWNJOHN

Robert Nye is nearly surfacing from the misjudgment which led him to collect his early poems into two books called *Juvenilia I* and [*Juvenilia II*]. He was always better, and more adult, than that, and *Darker Ends* (which includes improved versions of some of those earlier pieces) gives a better impression of his strengths. He is still oddly, and unconsciously, derived in places, quaintly metaphysical or even Victorian . . . and there are too many flimsy, imagistic fragments. But his poems about the dissatisfaction and coldness behind the conventional domestic emotions are modestly well-judged; and once, in "**Crowson**", the recurring theme of the evil waywardness in his own nature gains an impressive force. (p. 331)

> *Alan Brownjohn, "Dualities," in New Statesman,
> Vol. 79, No. 2034, March 6, 1970, pp. 330-32.*

PETER PORTER

[*Darker Ends*] would have been unthinkable in the 'fifties. Nye's aestheticism would have seemed precious. . . . His heavy years of reviewing have made Nye prize essence more than body. *Darker Ends* shows the cat of lyricism with just a few of its whiskers and a half-smile visible. Too much has been lost in the pruning. *Juvenilia I* [and *Juvenilia II*] contained poems vastly over-written, but the youthful extravagance and heraldic confidence of it all was very attractive. Nye knows better now, his progress seems to be towards that final refinement of style—giving up altogether. Where once he would fill a poem with medieval tags, picture-book gliding and grandiose bits of history, he is content to make a few frozen gestures. . . . He has observed modernism and been frightened, though the new poems are more in the vein of English pastoral. *Darker Ends* has none of the faults of the earlier poems but none of their exuberance either. There are love poems and domestic poems and poems making short trips into the meaning of existence. . . .

Nye's energies are now given to the experimental novel and *Darker Ends* suggests this is where we should look for his best work. (p. 165)

> *Peter Porter, "A Form of Refrigeration," in* London Magazine, *n.s. Vol. 10, No. 4, July-August, 1970, pp. 160-66.*

THE TIMES LITERARY SUPPLEMENT

Robert Nye is fascinated not only by stories but by what he sees as the story teller's licence to give imaginative body to what is essentially sparse, even skeletal material: memoirs, biographies, letters, argumentative footnotes, police or newspaper reports. Nye's technique in these nine tall stories [in *Tales I Told My Mother*] has a good deal in common with the film director Ken Russell's, and so have some of his preoccupations; the Pre-Raphaelites, for instance. . . . [There] are moments in Nye's book when the games seem there to taunt rather than to amuse or enlighten, when they back away into some private framework of allusion, and this breaks the spell.

In general, though, the freedom Nye allows himself is extended to his reader, or ideally his listener, so that the fantastic developments of his narratives are offered quite undogmatically, as a personal selection from an infinite number of alternatives. The Victorian melodrama, which has a Glaswegian nymphomaniac escape conviction for the murder of her lover to marry a close friend of William Morris and model for Rossetti, is a tour de force of pastiche and ingenuity.

> *"Tall Tales," in* The Times Literary Supplement, *No. 3537, December 11, 1970, p. 1417.*

MICHAEL MOTT

[In *Darker Ends*] Nye shows himself straining against, rather than for, violence. What he is seeking is a method of containing the savagery of his inner vision, not of taming it.

Many of the aids he calls up to help him may seem at first sight archaic and anachronistic. Yet Nye has the odd power to make real once more the ancient substitutes: figures in folklore, savage animals, owls, the presences that haunt children's nursery rhymes. If he asks us at times to believe in something very like ghosts, perhaps as an insurance against worse things still, it is a considerable accomplishment to make the argument sound so valid.

In ["Darker Ends"] Nye wonders why he frightens his son by making shadow pictures on the wall with his hands. . . .

But Nye must sit late and ponder a more terrible vision he will communicate only to us, and then carefully:

> To tell the truth, when he is safe asleep,
> I shut my eyes and let the darkness in.

There are occasional lapses—"Fishing" seems coy, for instance—but, on the whole, these well-made, thoughtfully made, strangely made poems ought to command response and respect.

> *Michael Mott, in a review of "Darker Ends," in* Poetry, *Vol. CXVIII, No. 2, May, 1971, p. 112.*

D. M. THOMAS

Robert Nye's *Divisions on a Ground* is slimmer even than it looks, since many of the pages contain short poems. Not that this would matter, if the poems resonated. On the whole they do not. They are intelligent and polished, but something fails to clinch them. . . .

Mr Nye is successful at undercutting reality with surrealistic atmosphere, as in the urbanely sinister "Henry James", and a poem whose interrelated worlds are implied by the title, "Travelling to my Second Marriage on the Day of the First Moonshot". I enjoy too the genial "Reading Robert Southey to my Daughter". . . . But when the poems try to express the real tangible world, they do not—as Emily Dickinson would say—"breathe". There seems too little pressure generated by the theme; we are less aware of what is being said than of the way the poem is saying it.

> *D. M. Thomas, "Corrected Vision," in* The Times Literary Supplement, *No. 3921, May 6, 1977, p. 548.*

HELEN McNEIL

In Robert Nye's *Merlin*, his second mythic novel (after *Falstaff*), everything calls attention to itself. Taking a revisionist view, to put it mildly, of the matter of Arthur, Nye creates a mockingly devilish babble through which the received story is faintly overheard. How many children had Lady Macbeth? Who were the parents of Merlin? To flesh out a myth usually trivialises it into the merely human. Nye may add genealogy and slapstick anecdote, but his creatures evade the human: instead, they are sounds. Their incessant giggling, scratching, farting, cursing, pissing, birching (lots of that), frigging and fucking only lead one away from any suspicion that these things have ever lived, or that they resemble us. They are just a lot of noise, and that is what *Merlin* is about: the complex noise of itself being told. Merlin the narrator, 'a man locked in the present tense', can only follow what happens as it happens. So the tale proceeds by jolts and leaps and halts. The narrative does not evoke an earlier or deeper magic. Nye's hell, like his Grail Castle, is parodic. What is left are the words which tell all this: aggressive, allusive, slangy and above all self-conscious. Sometimes the words can force perception and disgust simultaneously on the reader, as when each of several characters inhabited by the devil 'smile like a fox eating shit from a brush'. The obscene passages, with their mythic tits and bums, make the most powerful scenes in a book that has few completed actions. The non-humanity of these knighturnal emissions places them in the great reductive tradition of pornography—in which a man may call himself Sir John, but when things get going he is really only a John Thomas. (p. 339)

> *Helen McNeil, "Blind Lives," in* New Statesman, *Vol. 96, No. 2478, September 15, 1978, pp. 338-39.*

PETER KEMP

[*Merlin*], purporting to trade in archetypes and primal patterns, is . . . trivial. Its action skips back and forth between Hell—where an infernal scenario is being devised by a trio of vaudeville demons—and Britain—where various members of the Round Table are on display as the book smirkily observes the coming of Arthur and others. The humour in the nether regions is appropriately diabolical. . . . Satan, urged to impregnate a languorous virgin, is told to 'be a devil': but he's feeling a little queer again', which leads to merriment about choirboys and how funny it is that he's 'the angel of the bottomless pit'.

Every now and then, this limp material rises to a pornographic interlude featuring as its main stand-bys birches, candles and enthralled voyeurs. And there are constant hints that all this titillatory romping has something to do with the Nature of Fiction. . . . [We are] told that 'Alchemy is metaphors,' and the author calls the sections of his novel Black, White, Red, and Gold after the stages of the process reputed to convert base metal to gold. No transformation takes place here, though. Mr Nye's style often gets precious but his contents remain dross.

Peter Kemp, "Wet and Dry," in The Listener, *Vol. 100, No. 2580, October 5, 1978, pp. 454-55.*

JOHN NAUGHTON

[In retelling *Faust*], Nye has to stalk in the tracks of some distinguished forebears—Marlowe, Goethe and Thomas Mann, to name but three. All would no doubt agree that the demonic doctor is no easy prey, despite the fact that a great deal is known about him in a documentary sense. For a man with no personal experience of contractual arrangements with the Devil, Mr Nye does pretty well. Perhaps going to live in Ireland (thereby negotiating a pact with the tax collector if not with Mephistopheles) has been of some assistance?

His method is simple and effective—the portrayal of Faust in his last days, as reported by one Kit Wagner, scholar, companion and occasional purveyor of sexual services to the great man. Wagner hates Faust with a virulent intensity; he loathes him for all the obvious reasons—disgusting personal habits, egocentricity, irascibility and, above all, the fascination that he generates wherever he goes. On the other hand it's hard to avoid the impression that, well, Wagner really *likes* the old guy. . . . [On] Ash Wednesday 1540 . . . it dawns on Faustus that he has only 40 days left before the lease on his soul expires. As ill-luck would have it, the delivery date (Good Friday) falls on the 13th of the month. Faced with this, Faustus does not meekly eke out his allotted span, but instead engages in frenetic activity, and particularly a 'pilgrimage' to Rome with nefarious intent.

There is little point in revealing the niceties of the plot. It is, after all, something of a hackneyed tale. But Mr Nye makes one sit up and take note by his stratagem of forcing the story through the scabrous filter of Kit Wagner's well-stocked mind. Reading it conjures up the fantasy of standing under a cold shower hearing J. P. Donleavy discuss the sex life of Aleister Crowley.

John Naughton, "Fascinating Faust," in The Listener, *Vol. 104, No. 2683, October 16, 1980, p. 513.*

J. B. STEANE

[The narrator of *Faust*] assumes that we have heard of Faust and goes on to introduce himself. He is Christopher Wagner and from time to time Faust calls him Kit. Helen and Gretchen also appear; there are jokes about Luther, "the great constipator"; Calvin preaches asthmatically in Basel while in the front pew Faust takes brandy and Wagner his girl friends. In the form of a chattily intimate diary, mostly telling of the present but sometimes recalling the past, an account is given of those forty days (Faust's last) from Ash Wednesday to Good Friday.

During the course of this account, there is much to irritate and repel, much that fascinates, much to admire. I personally had decided long before the end that it was a book I would not be re-reading—and on reaching the end realized that there was nothing for it but to return and start afresh. There's a certain appropriate devilry in that: witness Nye's Merlin who on the last page grins from ear to ear and crosses himself with his tail. "'Begin', he says. 'Again', he says. . . .

Beginning again, then, this time knowing the story (which we might think we know already, but Mr Nye's story we do not know till the final page): are we to get beyond "plot" and come, just possibly, to wisdom? Certainly there are intimations of wisdom amidst all the bums and balls and the rest of it. Surprisingly, one's impression is not so much of a bawdy romp as of a hovering on the edge of mystery. "That's enough history. I prefer mystery", said Nye's Falstaff, and here, too, Wagner the servant is always tantalisingly at the edge of his master's understanding.

Faust's is the will determining Wagner's narration, and despite his glaring and grinning, his smells and boils, his slurping and falling about, his puppet-mastery and riddling mystery, he is the character who compels attention. Yet in the foreground, as we read, is Wagner's chatter, his ruderies, his single-word sentences and single-sentence paragraphs. He is not quite Marlowe's Wagner, a cheeky little cockney who can run rings round the solemn university students, though Marlowe's surprisingly adroit comic characterization may have been his point of origin (as the "Christopher" and "Kit" also suggest). He has some of the verbal mannerisms of the catcher in the rye; he is in a sense the reader's familiar. And he is uninhibited in his descriptions of sexual experiences.

It might be argued that there is a difference in kind between the sex in Nye's novel and sex in a pornographic film because here are humour and inventiveness rather than lifeless routine and commercialism; but it is a tiresome routine when "come" cannot pass without a pun, and, as for commercialism, the author cannot be unaware that his writing invites the sort of "Warning" which I have seen displayed in a book-club's advance publicity of the novel—"This novel contains explicit sex scenes. And how!". Even more seriously self-defeating than the explicit sex is the untiring liveliness of style. Nye's narrator, with his briskness, his vocabulary that is at once colloquial-common and imaginative-original, is so unfailingly bright that he becomes almost dull.

Fortunately, these defects recede as one remembers the book from a little distance. Into the foreground, oddly assorting with the modern manner of narration, comes the sixteenth century; and at the centre is Faust himself, who has made a spell for Robert Nye as he has also recently (and not such a dissimilar one) for D. J. Enright. "Mr Nye writes like Rabelais reborn": Kenneth Tynan's tribute to the author of *Falstaff* is the kind of label that sticks for life. Nye begins to emerge as himself, I fancy, only after the Rabelaisian guffaw has quietened down. It's not, to my mind, a particularly attractive sound at the best of times.

J. B. Steane, "History and Mystery," in The Times Literary Supplement, No. 4046, October 17, 1980, p. 1161.

CHRISTOPHER NORRIS

It has been said that every artist of genius must eventually prove himself equal to the challenge of transforming, updating or somehow taking over the archetypal legend of Faust. In our own time the tale has been most strikingly retold by Thomas Mann in his grim metaphysical allegory of German culture in the throes of self-destruction, reflected in the life and work of a hell-bent modern composer. Robert Nye's re-telling [in *Faust*] is on a different plane entirely, going back to the historical roots of the myth and treating it with a Rabelaisian mixture of earthy knockabout humour and spoof documentation. He has hit on the ingenious idea of recounting the story from the viewpoint of Faust's young assistant Wagner, an undeveloped character in other versions (notably Marlowe) but here set up as a witty and zestful narrator, striking sparks off the legend at every turn. He is pictured as an easy-going hedonist and sceptic, recording Faust's history right up to and beyond the fatal hour, in order to prove to the world that his master's 'pact with the devil' was the figment of a crazed imagination. The legend is eked out to provide some splendid comic extrapolations, including an attempt to assassinate the Pope and various bawdy adventures on the journey to Rome, related with appropriate relish. Some of the best jokes make a target of Luther, treated (as in John Osborne's play) as a creature driven by bodily lusts and torments, converting them into spiritual zeal by a species of Freudian 'sublimation'. The narrative is peppered with joyful obscenities and gross sexual metaphors which underline the theme of religion as a form of displaced (and perverted) bodily desire. Faust becomes a chronic old lecher and drunken fool, while the Helen he conjures up (and who tags along throughout) seems not so much the dream of Trojan antiquity as a here-and-now lady of ambiguous background and fading charms. . . . The whole book is really a compendium of jokes, some of them told straight off on the flimsiest of narrative pretexts, others having a more subtle relation to the legend and tradition of Faust. The novel is cleverly constructed as a day-to-day transcription of events, written up by Wagner in various moods (from despair to comic disgust) and just keeping pace with each giddy turn of events. The style is a brilliant mixture of pastiche folksy Germanic (shades of Carlyle) and modern colloquial bawdy. Anachronisms, whether of fact or language, are hardly to be grumbled at in such a spirited piece of novelistic daring. A thoroughly enjoyable book, though not one for the squeamish or custodians of moral sweetness and light.

Christopher Norris, in a review of "Faust," in British Book News, December, 1980, p. 760.

MIKE POOLE

[In *The Voyage of the Destiny*, a] flotilla of ships, top-heavy with ordnance and colonising zeal, sets sail for South America on a doomed, deluded mission. Seventeen English men-of-war with names like *Destiny* and *Encounter* spelling out an 'arithmetic of death' for their Spanish-speaking rivals. . . . [This is] Robert Nye's latest excursion into literary myth: a first-person account of Sir Walter Raleigh's failed 1617 expedition up the Orinoco in search of gold for James I.

Nye's Raleigh is a broken man pursuing an El Dorado that doesn't exist in order to placate a monarch who already has him marked out for the block; a lyric poet masquerading as a man of action in an era of high adventure, logging his final voyage for posterity and finding that it also charts a painful voyaging inwards. This double narrative, endlessly tracking back and forth to the promptings of memory and counterpointing present failure with past triumph, is the framework in which the novel unpicks the legend of Raleigh the poet-explorer. It's the story of a meteoric rise to courtly prominence under Elizabeth and an even more rapid fall from grace, and years of incarceration in the Tower, under James. As usual, Nye's version of the past is richly re-worked.

For the most part though, *The Voyage of the Destiny* is a surprisingly restrained affair—the bawdy pastiche of the earlier novels has largely given way to a more sombre tone. Raleigh's meanderings become a sort of philosophical peregrination through which Nye picks up on a post-Renaissance scepticism to discourse on the illusoriness of identity, the pitfalls of history and the treacherous nature of his own art as a novelist. The narrative is peppered with references to its unreliability and Raleigh himself returns again and again to an image of himself as *water:* 'no shape, no form, no meaning'. It's a perfect example of having your cake and eating it: writing a realist novel while doubting realism itself; claiming historical accuracy yet always covering yourself by addressing history itself as 'unknowable'.

Mike Poole, "Task Force," in New Statesman, Vol. 103, No. 2666, April 23, 1982, p. 27.

VALENTINE CUNNINGHAM

Robert Nye's hottest line is doing up, or doing over, old literary properties. With boisterous skill he has refurbished the myths of Falstaff, Merlin and Faust, as now he turns his rumpling hand to the reputation of Sir Walter Raleigh [in *The Voyage of the Destiny*]. . . . What we know of [Raleigh's] life combines bloodletting, sauciness and penmanship much too handily for a novelist of Robert Nye's predilections to pass up.

The Voyage of the Destiny gives us the log of Raleigh's final voyage—the one he was released from the Tower for, his last no-hope hunt for gold in Spanish Guiana. Which is gripping enough. The journal is also, though, an apologia for his life that Raleigh intends for his son Carew: the inside story of Raleigh's risings and fallings in Royal esteem. And this is more gripping still. Knowing he has a strong Rabelaisian reputation to keep up, Nye pulls out all his plain-speaking, lip-smacking, bawdy stops. His Raleigh is keen to tell home truths, to spill beans, to debunk himself and all the others. . . .

The city of London? It stinks. The sweet Thames is in fact an unsavoury running latrine. . . . [King James] liked nothing better than paddling [his toes] in the entrails of stags he'd just killed. . . . Other great men espouse nastiness no less eagerly than their monarch. The big arrangers, the Cecils and the Howards, did for poor Kit Marlowe, stabbed to death through the eyes. They and their like will do for Raleigh. In James's final coup against him Raleigh smells Bacon. At least knife-eyed Marlowe smelled sweet. Which is more than can be said for some of James's foul-breathed emissaries, or even pub-crawling Ben Jonson.

And so, gossipily, rumbustiously, on and on. Raleigh's prose is grimly undeterred by any talk whatsoever: turds and pricks, gallows and pox, the messy slaughterings of Irish Spaniards, the direst racking of poets, it slurps them all up with relish. . . .

Happily, there's more to Nye and Raleigh than mere ribaldry, for all the ribaldry's attractiveness. Raleigh is much given to pious reflections about fathers and sons, and to less pious ones about the function of father substitutes in his story—his own tutorship of James's son Henry, drunken Jonson's relationship with Raleigh's own son Wat, the catamites who call James "Dad". Ironies about unhappy families proliferate, especially around the strife on the European scene: Spain against England, Catholic against Protestant, Christian coven against Christian coven. And Raleigh's consciousness of his story's family meanings is matched by the keen self-awareness of his writing as writing. Alert to current trends in the novel . . . , Nye has made Raleigh the deftest of *nouveaux romanciers.* . . .

Clever stuff. Not, however, in the end, clever enough, perhaps. Irksomely, *The Voyage of the Destiny* doesn't quite hang together. Even its sprightliest rollicking and niftiest raciness don't always help it over the lumpiness and bittiness of its narrative proceedings. Like Raleigh on the scaffold, it can be afflicted by severe bouts of long-windedness. And its bid for ultimate high seriousness is dragged down not just by its eager touch for the sordid and low. The "third Voyage" that the novel seeks to narrate—the one that's somehow beyond and different from the Guiana trip and the journey of Raleigh's life, in other words the mystical quest for Raleigh's, for man's destiny—is not only "difficult" for Raleigh to "define", it remains hard for the reader to grasp. And as Raleigh and Nye keep reaching and fumbling together for this ultimate meaning, they just miss giving one the satisfying sense that this novel is at last really getting the grip it wants on the mystery of Walter Raleigh.

> Valentine Cunningham, "Spilling the Elizabethan Beans," in The Times Literary Supplement, No. 4126, April 30, 1982, p. 481.

JOHN MELLORS

The Voyage of the Destiny purports to be Sir Walter Ralegh's journal, written in the last year of his life for the edification of his wife, Bess, and his only surviving son, Carew. The journal is a voyage of discovery for Ralegh, an expedition into the secret places of his own heart and mind.

Since much of that year, 1618, was spent in sailing back to England from the West Indies, the book has the strong narrative of an exciting sea story to give it backbone. The flesh and muscle are provided by Ralegh's account of his past and his insight into his own nature and motives. . . . Nye's prose provides cuttingly sharp edges and much more besides. He has the zest for fine phrases characteristic of the age of which he writes: Ben Jonson 'has a belly like a hill and a face like a map of the Indies, all boils for islands and pox-marks for sea-currents'. . . .

Ralegh refused to be enslaved or intimidated by King James, and in 1618 he sailed home knowing that without the gold of El Dorado he had no defence against a vindictive monarch. He was no traitor, but on the scaffold he transferred his allegiance. Now, he said, 'I am Death's subject.' This final scene, a touching, dignified climax to a most impressive novel, is told by Carew; in a macabre postscript he says that he keeps his father's embalmed head in a velvet bag, and 'sometimes—not often—I take it out to look at it'.

> John Mellors, "Secret Lives," in The Listener, Vol. 107, No. 2760, May 13, 1982, p. 27.

NEIL PHILIP

Tales I Told My Mother, a collection of nine intertwining stories, is an immature 'experimental' work which nevertheless well repays attention. Nye's prose is dazzling even at its most opaque, and his sheer delight in language is a delight for the reader, too. Beneath a playful surface, Nye explores the mystery of imagination. His narratives follow a logic of association rather than inevitable progression, forcing the reader to come to terms with the dream or fantasy life which unfolds in the mind parallel to 'real' life. . . . 'Without fantasies I could not prevail', says a character in one of the many comic passages; as the last page reveals, 'there are sometimes dreams that more than one person can dream'. Nye's command of language and image compels attention; but for all that *Tales I Told My Mother* is seriously flawed, most notably in the obscurely shifting narrative voice, which seems to manufacture rather than reveal mysteries. This is a problem with which Nye has come to terms in later work such as the award-winning *Falstaff.*

> Neil Philip, in a review of, "Tales I Told My Mother," in British Book News, June, 1982, p. 334.

DAVID MONTROSE

Robert Nye has stated that he does not so much write short stories as tall tales (his novels display the same tendency). Such tales are the most self-reflexive of fictions—the conventional short story is intended as a credible lie, but the tall tale is transparently incredible, the more inventively so the better. Since the form largely dispenses with the traditional components of realism—character, milieu, and so forth—a great deal depends on the teller's ability to contrive arresting plots.

Nye's previous set of fictions, *Tales I Told My Mother,* displayed plenty of ingenuity in this regard. Its nine tales, bizarre enough when taken separately, came together—in a deliberately tangential manner—to produce an unclassifiable whole incorporating, among other people and things, various members of the Pre-Raphaelite Brotherhood, a Chinese giant, a reinterpretation of Chatterton's suicide, the Wandering Jew, and a lost novel by Emily Brontë. Comparable invention is, alas, rarely evident in the unconnected tales of *The Facts of Life,* which has little in common with the dark imaginings of its predecessor. . . .

Everyday life, of course, abounds in tall tales and popular fictions. Nye, though, explores this fantastic aspect of the commonplace only in the ironic title piece, where, in a flurry of euphemism, a father warns his uncomprehending son of the mental and physical debilities engendered by masturbation. Nye prefers artifice for its own sake. In "Adam Kadmon", longest of the sixteen stories assembled here, the narrator pauses to deliver a commentary that could almost be applied to the entire collection. The story, we learn, is "a pack of lies" inspired by "a pure desire to tell lies". It has no other function or meaning.

Half these fictions are steeped in folklore and legend. This public domain of the tall tale provided Nye with the basis for two fine novels, *Merlin* and *Faust,* and there are indeed two tales here that, on a smaller scale and with rather less verve, embroider existing legends of Thomas the Rhymer (**"True Thomas"**) and of the portentous birth—cf *Henry IV, Part I*—of Owain Glyndŵr (**"Glendower"**). Elsewhere, Nye manufactures new legends. **"Adam Kadmon"** is a compendium of counterfeit folk-tales: a kind of Brothers Grimm in miniature, with obligatory appearances by a cruel prince, a beautiful princess, a haunted church. . . .

Nye operates more impressively in other *genres*. His attempt at jocose sf (**"Visakha"**) misfires, but **"Randal"** is a finely-judged tale of the supernatural, and **"The Whole Story"** a delightful fantasy somewhat after the manner of Flann O'Brien. Here, a pair of lovers (Gertrude Stein and D. H. Lawrence) are caught up in an Irish plot—in which Yeats and Joyce are implicated—to rig the Nobel Prize for Literature. . . . **"59x: A True Tale"** also concerns literary detection. It is established that a volume up for auction is, unknown to everyone but the narrator and his bibliophilic sidekick, an extremely rare first edition of *Candide*. Unfortunately, what looks like a slow build-up turns out merely to preface a huge anti-climax: the bibliophile buys the book and that's that. Or perhaps the absence of twist is the twist. The final literary fiction, **"The Second Best Bed"**, is the pick of the volume (and perhaps its least tall tale): a revelation of Shakespeare's sexual proclivities narrated in wry style by Anne Hathaway. . . .

The Facts of Life confirms Nye's wonderful gift for language. Too often, though, the impression is of "mere writing". Even so accomplished a creator of fictions is hard put to it to make more than airy-fairy tales from the stuff of folklore when apparently determined to work variations on conventional themes rather than attempt idiosyncratic transformations.

> *David Montrose, "The Lie Transparent," in* The Times Literary Supplement, *No. 4185, June 17, 1983, p. 622.*

JOHN MELLORS

In *The Facts of Life* there are 16 stories. . . . Those written in the early 1970s are short fragments, the exercises of a poet flexing his muscles in prose. Robert Nye's lively wit is better displayed in the longer stories. A time-traveller from another planet chooses to land in Tibet because it is less contaminated by 'progress . . . an imitative disease endemic' among Earth's inhabitants. Even more fun is **"The Whole Story"**, in which Gertrude Stein has a butler called Kipling, who turns out to be Chesterton. . . . Nye's stories are decorated with snippets of philosophy and theology and advertising slogans, but too many are disappointingly lightweight compared with his novels.

> *John Mellors, "Urban Magic," in* The Listener, *Vol. 111, No. 2843, February 2, 1984, p. 28.*

John (Henry) O'Hara

1905-1970

American novelist, short story writer, dramatist, essayist, scriptwriter, journalist, librettist, and critic.

In his novels and short stories, O'Hara explored America's obsession with power, status, and sex. His chosen milieu was often the small town, and the fictitious community of Gibbsville, the "county seat" of Lantenengo County, Pennsylvania, recurs in much of his work. By focusing on what Edmund Wilson termed "the cruel side of social snobbery," O'Hara's fiction depicts the intense and destructive rivalry between the wealthy establishment and the upwardly-mobile ethnic classes. Matthew J. Bruccoli praised O'Hara's social chronicles as a valuable "record of three decades of American life." Although many critics compared O'Hara's concern with the social process to that of F. Scott Fitzgerald and noted similarities between Ernest Hemingway's sparse prose and O'Hara's hard-boiled, understated style, O'Hara never received the critical recognition awarded some of his contemporaries. However, his popularity among readers remained consistent throughout his career, and many of his novels were adapted for film.

O'Hara was born into a prominent Irish family in Pottsville, Pennsylvania, a small industrial town which Gibbsville closely resembles. While growing up in Pottsville, O'Hara observed the Protestant elite and their disdain of the Irish Catholic community; James W. Tuttleton suggested that O'Hara's novels "[may] be seen as the means by which he worked out his own ethnic resentment against the high and mighty in southeastern Pennsylvania." In 1925, O'Hara was hired as a reporter for *The Pottsville Journal,* where he worked for two years. O'Hara spent a year as a waiter on an ocean liner bound for Europe, and upon his return to the United States he moved to Chicago in an unsuccessful attempt to find work as a journalist. O'Hara eventually gained a position with *The New York Herald Tribune* in 1928 and sold his first short story, "Alumnae Bulletin," to *The New Yorker* that same year. O'Hara soon became a regular contributor to the magazine.

In *Appointment in Samarra* (1934), his first and probably best-known novel, O'Hara illustrates the destructive power of a stratified society. The novel takes place during the last three days in the life of Julian English, a wealthy but insecure man whose antagonistic behavior towards his family, Gibbsville's social elite, and the town's Irish community drives him to suicide. Delmore Schwartz noted that O'Hara's decision to name the protagonist Julian English was "probably neither accident nor intention," for "English is an Anglo-Saxon, he resents the Irish, he belongs to what is supposed to be the upper middle class, and the tragic action which leads to his suicide is his throwing a drink in the face of a man with the choice name of Harry Reilly." O'Hara recounts the events leading up to English's death in intricate detail, evoking both the despair of the concluding days of the Jazz Age and the changing social hierarchy of the United States during the Depression.

Following the critical and popular success of *Appointment in Samarra* and a stint in Hollywood as a scriptwriter for Paramount Studios, O'Hara published his second novel, *Butterfield 8* (1935). The book was based on a real-life scandal in which

a young Manhattan socialite with questionable morals died under mysterious circumstances. While *Butterfield 8* shares several thematic elements with his first book, especially the antagonism between social classes, O'Hara was faulted for creating two-dimensional characters and a contrived ending. Hollywood is the setting for *Hope of Heaven* (1938), O'Hara's third novel. Based on his experiences working in that city, *Hope of Heaven* depicts James Malloy, whom many critics contend is O'Hara's alter ego, and his encounters with several characters who are victimized by the false promises of affluence projected by the film industry. Critics generally regard *Appointment in Samarra, Butterfield 8,* and *Hope of Heaven* as a trilogy portraying the decaying moral fabric of American life during the 1930s.

O'Hara's early short stories, many of which were first published in *The New Yorker,* are collected in several volumes, including *The Doctor's Son and Other Stories* (1935), *Files on Parade* (1939), and *Pal Joey* (1940). These stories were highly praised for their convincing, realistic dialogue and helped solidify O'Hara's commercial popularity. The title story of *The Doctor's Son* is a semiautobiographical account of O'Hara's relationship with his father and is regarded as one of his best pieces. Primarily an initiation story, "The Doctor's Son" relates the emotional growth of James Malloy and his first encounter with hypocrisy and bigotry in the Gibbsville community. Many of the stories in *Files on Parade* are set in New York City and Hollywood and focus on the dark side of human nature. *Pal Joey* consists of loosely-connected vignettes revolving around a small-time nightclub entertainer and his attempts to gain professional and social respectability. *Pal Joey* was adapted into a critically acclaimed Broadway musical, for which O'Hara, who wrote the libretto, won the New York Drama Critics' Circle Award in 1952.

O'Hara described the theme of *A Rage to Live* (1949), his next novel, as the "idea that any social situation is likely to blow up in one's face." *A Rage to Live* is structured as a multigenerational saga centering on the Caldwells, a prominent Fort Penn, Pennsylvania, family who are gradually losing their standing in the community. Like *Appointment in Samarra*, O'Hara depicts the social composition of the town in detail and focuses on the hostility between Fort Penn's leading families and the encroaching Irish middle class. This rivalry is represented by the illicit love affair between the promiscuous heiress Grace Caldwell Tate and Roger Bannon, a socially ambitious Irish contractor whose interest in Grace is motivated by his hatred toward her family and his desire for revenge. While this work generated huge sales, it received largely negative reviews. The most frequent complaints voiced by critics concerned O'Hara's failure to justify Grace's transgressions and the seemingly gratuitous violence he included in the novel. O'Hara's well-documented bitterness over the critical reception of the novel culminated in the termination of his long association with *The New Yorker* after a scathing review written by Brendan Gill was published in the magazine.

In 1955, O'Hara published *Ten North Frederick*, a critically acclaimed novel in which he returns to Gibbsville to focus on Joe Chapin, an aspiring politician who becomes an alcoholic. The novel begins at Chapin's funeral and illustrates through flashbacks Chapin's obsession to become President of the United States. O'Hara contends that Chapin's political ambitions derive from a false and unrealistic faith in the power of his socioeconomic class. When Chapin gives the local Republican party a large sum of money to insure his nomination, the head of the party takes the money and ostracizes Chapin from the political arena. Critics praised O'Hara for his convincing depiction of the futility of Chapin's life and of the predatory nature of society. *Ten North Frederick* received the National Book Award.

In 1960, O'Hara resumed his relationship with *The New Yorker* by contributing *Imagine Kissing Pete*, one of three novellas included in *Sermons and Soda Water* (1960). An aging James Malloy is the narrator in these works; he attempts to come to terms with his own life and describes the anxiety felt by members of his generation. The stories collected in *The Cape Cod Lighter* (1962), *The Hat on the Bed* (1963), and *The Horse Knows the Way* (1964) further demonstrate O'Hara's mastery of the short story form, and critics consider them to be his best later works. O'Hara also continued to write multigenerational sagas, among them *The Lockwood Concern* (1965), *Lovey Childs: A Philadelphian's Story* (1969), the posthumously published *The Ewings* (1972), and its sequel, *The Second Ewings* (1977). Although these novels were less highly praised than his short story collections, O'Hara remained a favorite among the reading public.

The publication of *Collected Stories of John O'Hara* (1985) prompted critical reassessment of his career. While some critics view his work as severely dated, most regard O'Hara's observations as accurate portraits of American life during the first half of the twentieth century. As Joseph L. Quinn stated, for those readers "who are interested both in what their parents and grandparents might have thought and felt and been exposed to during those years, and in being entertained while they pursue that interest, there is no better place to travel to than O'Hara country."

(See also *CLC*, Vols. 1, 2, 3, 6, 11; *Contemporary Authors*, Vols. 5-8, rev. ed., Vols. 25-28, rev. ed. [obituary]; *Dictionary of Literary Biography*, Vol. 9; and *Dictionary of Literary Biography Documentary Series*, Vol. 2.)

EDMUND WILSON

[The essay from which this excerpt is taken was originally published in The New Republic, *November 11, 1940.]*

[John O'Hara] derives from Hemingway, and his short stories sound superficially like Hemingway's. His longer stories, like Cain's, have it in common with Hemingway that the heroes and heroines are doomed. But O'Hara's main interest in life is of an entirely different kind from Hemingway's, and his writing really belongs to a different category of fiction.

O'Hara is not a poet like Hemingway, but primarily a social commentator; and in this field of social habits and manners, ways of talking and writing letters and dressing, he has done work that is original and interesting.... John O'Hara subjects to a Proustian scrutiny the tight-knotted social web of a large Pennsylvania town, the potpourri of New York night-life in the twenties, the nondescript fringes of Hollywood. In all this he has explored for the first time from his peculiar semi-snobbish point of view a good deal of interesting territory: the relations between Catholics and Protestants, the relations between college men and non-college men, the relations between the underworld and "legitimate" business, the ratings of café society; and to read him on a fashionable bar or the Gibbsville country club is to be shown on the screen of a fluoroscope gradations of social prestige of which one had not before been aware. There is no longer any hierarchy here, of either cultivation or wealth: the people are all being shuffled about, hardly knowing what they are or where they are headed, but each is clutching some family tradition, some membership in a select organization, some personal association with the famous, from which he tries to derive distinction. But in the meantime, they mostly go under. They are snubbed, they are humiliated, they fail. The cruel side of social snobbery is really Mr. O'Hara's main theme. (pp. 22-3)

[This social surface] Mr. O'Hara analyzes with delicacy, and usually with remarkable accuracy. His grasp of what lies underneath it is not, however, so sure. His point of view toward his principal characters tends to be rather clinical; but even where his diagnosis is clear, we do not share the experience of the sufferer. The girl in *Butterfield 8* is a straight case of a Freudian complex, somewhat aggravated by social maladjustment; but we don't really know her well. Julian English of *Appointment in Samarra* is apparently the victim of a bad heredity worked upon by demoralizing influences; yet the emotions that drive him to suicide are never really shown. The whole book is in the nature of an explanation of why Julian threw the highball in the face of the Irish climber; yet the explanation doesn't convince us that the inevitable end for

Julian would be the suicide to which his creator brings him. As for . . . *Hope of Heaven,* a story of Hollywood, I have not been able to fathom it at all—though here, too, there seems to be discernible a Freudian behavior-pattern. One wonders whether the personality of the script-writer who is telling the story is intended to play some role of which he himself is unaware, in connection with the conduct of the other characters, or whether the author himself does not quite know what he is doing.

One gets the impression—confirmed by a statement which Mr. O'Hara is reported to have made—that he improvises more or less and never reworks or revises. His longer stories always sound like first drafts which ought to be trimmed and tightened up—which might be turned into very fine little novels, but which, as it is, remain rather diffuse and rather blurred as to their general intention. What is the relevance to the story, for example, of the newspaperwoman in *Appointment in Samarra,* whose career is described on such a scale? The account of her beginnings is amusing, but the part she plays in the drama doesn't seem to warrant this full-length introduction. What is the point of the newspaper reporter who suddenly gets into the picture, and more or less between us and it, at the end of *Butterfield 8*? What on earth is the justification—aside from establishing the atmosphere for a drama of general crookedness—of the long story about the man who stole the traveler's checks at the beginning of *Hope of Heaven*? If Mr. O'Hara has definite ideas about the meaning of these characters in his scheme, I can't see that he has brought it out. He seems merely to be indulging his whims. He happens, however, to be gifted with a clean, quick and sure style, which by itself gives an impression of restraint; and the unfaltering neatness of his writing carries him over a good deal of thin ice. But he appears, in perfecting this style, to have been following, from the point of view of architecture, a line of least resistance. Each of his novels has been less successful, less ambitious and less well-disciplined than the one that went before; but while the long stories have been deteriorating, the short stories have been improving: in the most successful of them he has achieved his characteristic effects as he has hardly been able to do in his novels. The best of his work, in my opinion, consists of *Appointment in Samarra,* the admirable long short story called "The Doctor's Son" in the collection of that name, and the short pieces of *Files on Parade*. . . . (pp. 23-5)

[As for *Pal Joey*], it is funny, well-phrased, well-observed; but, heel for heel, Pal Joey is a comedown after Julian English. *Appointment in Samarra* is a memorable picture both of a provincial snob, a disorganized drinking-man of the twenties, and of the complexities of the social organism in which he flourished and perished. But Pal Joey is merely an amoeba of the night-life of the jitter-bug era; and he is a little amoeba-monster. It is not that one objects to O'Hara's creating a monster—*Pal Joey* is successful as satire precisely because the author is not afraid to go the whole hog; but that he seems to represent a contraction of John O'Hara's interests.

The truth is perhaps that O'Hara has never really had his bearings since he dropped Gibbsville, Pa. . . . He partly retrieved himself by becoming the outstanding master of the *New Yorker* short-story-sketch; but we expected, and still expect, more of him. (pp. 25-6)

Edmund Wilson, *"The Boys in the Back Room,"* in his Classics and Commercials: A Literary Chronicle of the Forties, *Farrar, Straus and Giroux, Inc., 1950, pp. 19-56.*

DELMORE SCHWARTZ

O'Hara is a snob (in the fundamental attitudes with which he regards his characters); he is as sensitive to social distinctions as any *arriviste* ever was, and his snob-sensitivity provides him with inexhaustible energy for the transformation of observation into fiction. It was probably neither accident nor intention which made O'Hara call the scapegoat hero of [*Appointment in Samarra*] Julian English; for English is an Anglo-Saxon, he resents the Irish, he belongs to what is supposed to be the upper class, and the tragic action which leads to his suicide is his throwing a drink in the face of a man with the choice name of Harry Reilly. It might as well have been Murphy, O'Mara, or Parnell. . . . An author like O'Hara is perfect in *The New Yorker* because *The New Yorker* is in the most thoroughgoing way devoted to a sense of the social milieu, the hopes, resentments, frustrations, and fears which the American scene creates or compels. And if there is a persistent nastiness and contempt for human beings in much of O'Hara's writing, that is valuable too, because many people feel like that without admitting it. O'Hara's explicitness is desirable, just as candor is more desirable than hypocrisy, although one might well prefer the compassion of Dostoevsky, or at least Scott Fitzgerald, but let us not be Utopian, difficult to satisfy, and worst of all, *highbrow.* (pp. 294-95)

Delmore Schwartz, *"Smile and Grin, Relax and Collapse,"* in Partisan Review, *Vol. XVII, No. 3, March, 1950, pp. 292-96.*

LOUIS AUCHINCLOSS

[*The essay from which this excerpt is taken was originally published in* The Nation, *November 19, 1960.*]

In the strange, angry world that [O'Hara] describes, the characters behave with a uniform violence, speak with a uniform crudeness and make no appreciable effort to control lusts which they regard as ungovernable. The most casual meeting between a major and minor character will result either in an ugly flare-up or a sexual connection, or both. It is impossible for an O'Hara hero to order a meal in a restaurant or to take a taxi ride without having a brusque interchange with the waiter or driver. Even the characters from whom one might expect some degree of reticence—the rich dowagers, for example—will discuss sex on the frankest basis with the first person to bring the subject up. And in Gibbsville or Fort Penn the first person to bring it up is the first person one meets. A great deal is said about each character's exact social position, perhaps because it is so difficult to determine it from his habits and conversation. Everyone, apparently, does *everything,* and everyone knows that everyone else is doing it. But that does not mean that the shibboleths of an older society are dead. Far from it. The code of an earlier culture, though only dimly remembered, is superstitiously venerated. O'Hara's men and women dance around the Victorian traditions of class distinction and sexual restraint like savages around a cross left by murdered missionaries and now adorned with shrunken heads. The hatred of the immigrant who coughed his lungs out in a coal mine is kept alive in the hatred of the rich Irishman who can't get into the Lantenengo Country Club. And although the O'Hara hero knows that sexual liberty is now the rule, he clings to a dusky little hope that the magic of the marriage vow will somehow safeguard his spouse. Thus Robert Millhouser in *Ourselves to Know,* a man versed in the ways of prostitutes, who has married a nymphomaniac half his age with full notice of her vicious propensities, shoots her dead without a qualm when he discovers that she has been unfaithful to him.

From time to time there emerges from the jungle a superman or superwoman, the darling of the author, to dominate the scene, such as Grace Caldwell Tate in *A Rage to Live* and Alfred Eaton in *From the Terrace*. They differ from their contemporaries in that they have a little more of everything—more sex appeal, more brains, more money, more social position. But, above all, they have more defiance. They look the universe in the eye and spit. They are defeated in the end of their chronicles, but only by accumulated envy; they have not been able to learn that the other beasts in the jungle cannot endure the sight of so many advantages. Grace Tate might have been able to live in Fort Penn with a husband, but as a beautiful widow she is hounded out of town as an unmated lioness is hounded out of the pride by the others of her sex. And Alfred Eaton, for all his brilliant capabilities, is condemned to a life of idleness because he is too plain spoken. The *hubris* of O'Hara's superpeople is not that they have offended the gods. They have offended the grubby little people who share their faults but resent their success.

If O'Hara were consciously trying to describe the chaos of a society where each individual flouts the moral code, yet applies it with brutal bigotry to his neighbor, and where the inhabitants of every town play at being masters and serfs like boys and girls in a school play dressed up in wigs and hoops, he might be a more important novelist than he is. Surely it is a damning picture of the contemporary world. But my complaint is that what he seems to be doing, underneath all the violence and bluster, is to be writing an old-fashioned novel of manners where the most important item about any character is the social niche in which he was born. Each hero must start the race of life with a particular ribbon pinned to his lapel, and he will never be able to take it off, whether he be proud of it or ashamed. To O'Hara, in other words, it really seems to matter if he belongs or does not belong to the Lantenengo Country Club. (pp. 149-52)

When he takes for his hero a Gibbsville aristocrat of the old school, O'Hara, like Marquand with George Apley, writes his most successful novel of manners. Joe Chapin, in *Ten North Frederick,* is a man who has been brought up with high ideals (though this is largely blamed on a passionately possessive mother), and he is unique among O'Hara's characters in that he seeks to live according to his own somewhat fuzzy conception of the old moral code. He is faithful to his wife, conscientious and high-minded in the practice of law and active in civic affairs. The tragic flaw in his character is his irrational belief that he is destined to become the President of the United States. Many men have been so obsessed but few can have suffered from Joe's peculiar delusion that he could attain his objective by the simple expedient of attending meetings of bar associations. The other characters are puzzled as to what Joe is up to, and, indeed, it takes all the genius of Mike Slattery to guess it from the nature of Joe's activity. When Joe, in his late fifties, finally decides that the time is ripe to throw his hat in the ring, he offers Mike a hundred thousand dollars for the nomination of lieutenant-governor. Mike quietly pockets the money for the party, and Joe is left to drink himself to death. It is difficult to be sympathetic with a man so deluded, and it is not clear that Joe's ideals at the end are any higher than Mike Slattery's, but the contrast between the two men is always interesting. We see Joe against a background of privilege and Mike against its opposite; we see the even greater disparity

between their wives; we see Joe fumble, outmaneuvered, and fall into the clutches of his wily and contemptuously pitying opponent, and we learn more about the forces of society that has placed the two in conflict than in a whole volume about polka-dot ties and fraternity pins.

When I turn, on the other hand, to the defeat of Julian English in *Appointment in Samarra,* I can understand it only in terms of a compulsion to suicide. Taken as such, the novel is certainly a powerful description of self-destruction, possibly one of the most powerful ever written. But again I am troubled with the nagging suspicion that this may not be what the author intends. Is Julian meant to be destroyed by himself or by Gibbsville? Does his instinct to antagonize lead him surely to the most dangerous persons, or is their envy of his looks, his breeding, his easy manner and apparent success what makes them hunt him down? Had Julian lived elsewhere than in Gibbsville, that lumberyard of chips on the shoulder, would he have survived? But I suppose such speculations are idle. Julian belongs to Gibbsville, and it is never difficult to find enough hate in Gibbsville with which to destroy oneself. From one end of town to the other the populace fairly throbs with hurt feelings. Al Grecco provides its motto as he drives through Lantenengo Street early Christmas morning and lowers the car window to shout out at the darkened homes:

"Merry Christmas, you stuck-up bastards! Merry Christmas from Al Grecco!"

Perhaps it is the motto of O'Hara himself and of the contemporary novel of manners. (pp. 153-55)

> Louis Auchincloss, "The Novel of Manners Today: Marquand and O'Hara," in his Reflections of a Jacobite, *Houghton Mifflin Company, 1961, pp. 139-55.*

JAMES W. TUTTLETON

John O'Hara's realistic notation of the character of American social life is perhaps the most striking feature of his compendious body of fiction. Few writers of the twentieth century since Dreiser have documented as massively and as realistically as O'Hara, during a career that spanned more than thirty years, "the way it was" between the 1920s and the 1960s. Unlike Fitzgerald, who tried to capture the precise sense of how it felt, subjectively, to be alive at a given moment, O'Hara's method, in writing about what he called "the most interesting subject in the world—the human being," was almost wholly objective and reportorial. He believed that what makes a human being distinctive is the way his sensibility is impinged upon by the pressures of the external world. For O'Hara . . . , the material properties of existence do not merely express character; in a special sense they "constitute" character. Virginia Woolf attacked this theory of characterization in *Mr. Bennett and Mrs. Brown* (1924). In criticizing Wells, Galsworthy, and Bennett, Mrs. Woolf argued that they were "never interested in character itself"; instead, to make the reality of, for example, Hilda Lessways believable, Bennett began "by describing accurately and minutely the sort of house Hilda lived in, and the sort of house she saw from the window. House property," she observed, "was the common ground from which the Edwardians found it easy to proceed to intimacy. Indirect as it seems to us, the convention worked admirably, and thousands of Hilda Lesswayses were launched upon the world by this means. For that age and generation, the convention was a good one." But for the modern writer, she argues, such techniques are not only outmoded but "the wrong ones to use." (pp. 184-85)

The material properties of existence, however, are endemic to the novel, and for O'Hara—as for Balzac, the early James, Wharton, and Lewis—they are necessary for more than mere verisimilitude. Each believed that character is the product of external pressures represented by houses, streets, towns, professions, habits, and opinions. For all of them, a character is what he is because of the vocation he takes up, the kind of house he lives in, the social role he wants to play. As Mrs. Wharton put it in discussing Balzac and Stendhal, the French novelists of manners were first to discover that "the bounds of personality are not reproducible by a sharp black line, but that each of us flows imperceptibly into people and things." O'Hara's stress on the fabric of things, therefore, is not an outmoded *convention of fiction* but rather the expression of a behavioristic conception of character. . . . (p. 185)

The power of environment to shape character is . . . the chief assumption at work in O'Hara's fiction. None of his characters is ever as absolute as Marquand's George Apley in attributing his behavior to the determinism of environment—"I am the sort of man I am, because environment prevented my being anything else." But since O'Hara intended us to see behavior as a function of the conventions of time and place, his novels are not "arranged" like works of art that create a new reality. Instead they are wholly mimetic representations of "life," freed as much as possible of artifice, including—on the plane of style—figurative language. . . . In documenting the effect of convention on character, O'Hara composed seven "Lantenengo County novels" or "Gibbsville novels" (after the county seat). The value of the setting is not merely that O'Hara grew up in Pennsylvania and knew the environs, but also that it constituted a whole world available for social analysis. . . . (pp. 186-87)

If, as O'Hara once argued, "everything an author does, everything, can be made useful," much that happened to him was incorporated into the Lantenengo County novels. They suggest reflections of his own "experience" as man and boy in Pottsville, a town of about 25,000 people (the county seat of Schuylkill County) some ninety miles northwest of Philadelphia. In his Lantenengo County saga—which compares with Faulkner's Yoknapatawpha chronicle in social density and historical scope, though not in artistic excellence—O'Hara's principal method is to integrate a more or less full-length biography of a major character (plus, perhaps, a series of shorter biographies of other Gibbsville residents) into the social history of the town itself. This method often requires O'Hara to do a three- or four-generation panorama in order to show us the forces that produced his protagonist and to reveal the agencies of social change at work in the community during his lifetime. So totally are his biographies integrated into the sociological history that his novels constitute a dramatized record of the community life of southeastern Pennsylvania. (pp. 187-88)

O'Hara's entrée into the social life of the eastern cities—Providence, New York, Philadelphia, Wilmington, and Baltimore—gave him a length's lead on other contemporary novelists of manners. After the death of Marquand, the social life of the cities had few authentic interpreters besides O'Hara. . . . O'Hara is of course no Insider, but his fiction may be taken as a message slipped out to the rest of us describing exactly *how* different the rich are from you and me. . . . (p. 189)

O'Hara is more conscious of the polite manners of this aristocracy than almost any other American novelist of manners. Some of his characters are sensitive to the point of morbidity about the class proprieties expected of them. Arthur Mizener

has suggested that Julian English is intended to represent "the true American gentleman, refined, aware, instinctively gallant, whose bad behavior is a result of his sensitive nature's being driven beyond restraint by the crudeness of the people around him." But Julian's bad manners in throwing a drink in Harry Reilly's face exclude him from the class of real O'Hara gentlemen, like Joe Chapin ("His manners were exquisite even in a day when good manners were the rule"), Alfred Eaton ("Beautiful manners . . . the thoughtful type . . . quite aristocratic-looking . . ."), and Sidney Tate ("He had good manners, and he seemed to me sincerely, genuinely respectful"). . . . While the manners of some of O'Hara's characters may be "Chesterfieldian," O'Hara usually manipulates manners to express individual sensibility and a moral view toward the world. The manners of Sidney Tate, for example, are a perfect expression of his belief that "in this world you learn a set of rules, *or* you *don't* learn them. But assuming you learn them, you stick by them. They may be no damn good, but you're who you are and what you are because they're your rules and you stick by them. And of course when it's easy to stick by them, that's no test. It's when it's hard to obey the rules, that's when they mean something." . . . (pp. 191-92)

The good manners of Sidney Tate are remarkable because most people do not learn any moral rules in this world and do not have a code to express the principles they live by. Or, if they have learned any rules, they cannot keep them and continually fail the test. Those who have a code of manners are remarkable because of the decline, if not disappearance, of polite manners in American society. The informality of social life in the twentieth century has caused a serious loss to the novelist of manners, who is deprived of nuances of form as an index to a wide variety of phenomena—including manners as the expression of moral sensibility, emotional turmoil, absentmindedness, and so on. Edith Wharton suggests the emotional turmoil of a young woman in *Madame de Treymes* (1907) who emerged into a Paris Street *without yet having put on her gloves*. O'Hara knows that such slight deviations from an accepted norm of manners can be a highly significant index to complex inward matters. But such is the loss of form in our time that the meaning of manners is harder for the modern writer to suggest, and the novelist runs the risk of losing his audience if his use of polite manners is too technical. O'Hara ended one of his stories with the protagonist walking out of a room with the bow of his hat on the wrong side of his head. O'Hara meant this obvious lapse to indicate inner agitation. (p. 192)

O'Hara must be criticized for the failure of his novels to embody significant generalizations. He does not penetrate very deeply the surfaces of American life, and in committing himself to the significance of the "insignificant" O'Hara was preoccupied too much with the things of this world. But the absence of ideas in his writing is also the consequence of an indirect method that has often confused and irritated his readers. O'Hara follows Fitzgerald and Lewis in concerning himself with the life of society, but he loved Hemingway's kind of understatement. He does not generalize because he does not want to be caught making a statement. But his Lantenengo County novels are informed by one overriding idea: America is a "spurious democracy" marked by the intense hatred of its rival social classes. (p. 193)

The metaphor which expresses the idea that democracy is a spurious "union of equals" is the Christiana Street gang. In *Appointment in Samarra,* the rich live within two or three blocks of the middle and lower classes. Because there are not enough rich children to make up a football team, they have to go down to Christiana Street to play with the sons of the less affluent. . . . The Christiana Street gang—which is a symbol of the social "contract"— is composed of the sons of a butcher, a motorman, a surveyor, a freight clerk, two bookkeepers for the coal company, a Baptist minister, a neighborhood saloon-keeper, a garage mechanic, and a neighborhood convict. Because of the diversity of religious, occupational, and social backgrounds in the gang, a rule of decorum prevailed: you could not talk about jail because the father of one of the boys was in the pen. You could not talk about drunks because of the saloonkeeper's son. Talk about Catholics was forbidden because of the motorman's son. And Julian could not talk about doctors because of his father's profession. These topics are, of course, talked over—and O'Hara's ear for nuances of class in dialogue is exceptionally accurate—but only behind the back of the boy involved. Despite the social differences that separate them, these Gibbsville boys have developed a code of manners which permits them to get along together well enough to "play the game." Common need and the proximity of rich and poor in the American small town thus make for a "spurious democracy, especially among boys," O'Hara observes, "which may or may not be better than no democracy at all." . . . At least, none of them is deceived by the arrangement. (p. 194)

Democracy presumes a willingness to subordinate private need to the common good and the brotherhood of man expressed in fraternal respect and fellow-feeling. But O'Hara distrusts human nature and calls "the brotherhood of man" "a term that is usually invoked when someone is making a pitch." His portraits of the social process show men and women driven by ungovernable desires—greed, lust, ambition, and savage egotism. Democracy is hardly viable in such a world, and the Lantenengo County novels—with their atmosphere of anger and hatred—chronicle the failure of this egalitarian dream. Jealousy, envy, and hostility separate the classes, irritations are produced by social climbing, frustrations grow out of the arbitrary codes which imprison people in a social class—these are the origins of the hatred that O'Hara sees as the infected core of American social experience. (p. 195)

O'Hara's method of organizing his novels around the twin focus of character and community, in relation to the idea of our "spurious democracy," is aptly illustrated in *Appointment in Samarra*. The period is the 1920s, the community is Gibbsville, and the character is Julian English. The conflict in Gibbsville is revealed in O'Hara's notation of the manners of the various social groups in the town—the aristocracy, the solid respectable middle class, and the underworld of racketeers, bootleggers, prostitutes, and pimps. The aristocrats of Lantenengo County are an upper-middle-class commercial oligarchy composed of families like the Englishes, Ogdens, the McHenrys, the Chapins, the Caldwells, the Stokeses, and the Hofmans. They live on streets like Lantenengo or North Frederick, belong to the Lantenengo County Country Club, are generally graduates of Pennsylvania, Princeton, or another "Ivy League" university. The middle class, more or less excluded from the social life of the rich, is made up of families like the Luther Flieglers, the Dutch Snyders, the Dewey Hartensteins, the Kleins, the Reichelderfers, the Harvey Ziegenfusses, the Rothermels, Benzigers, Fenstermachers, Gormans, Reillys, and Millhousers. This class is constituted of small businessmen, skilled craftsmen, and tradesmen. If college men at all, they have gone to less prestigious schools like Lafayette, Penn State, Muhlenberg, or Lebanon Valley. (pp. 195-96)

If the aristocrats have their exclusive clubs and hotels like the John Gibb and the Nesquehela, the middle class has its own social haunts—like the Stage Coach Inn. The climactic scene in *Appointment in Samarra,* in fact, occurs at this road house, where O'Hara brings together the major classes of the town to dramatize and test the manners of each group. O'Hara's novels are full of such public rituals—weddings, funerals, county fairs, and festivals—where the various classes of the community are brought together in a dramatic confrontation. In his treatment of the special underworld class created by prohibition, O'Hara also documents what it feels like to live at a flophouse like Gorney's Hotel, to eat at a greasy spoon like the Apollo Restaurant, and to guard the boss's girlfriend to make sure that she is not playing around. Though beyond the law, this class has conventions of its own expressed in the interior monologues of Al Grecco and the style of Loving Cup, Packy McGovern, and Foxie Lebrix.

These classes are not rigidly separated. As with the Christiana Street gang, there is enough interaction to permit the desire for social mobility that aggravates class hatred, which O'Hara sees as paramount in the social experience of communities like Lantenengo County. There is a good deal of incidental ridicule of minorities like the Italians, Poles, and Jews—some of whom, like the Brombergs, have "invaded" Lantenengo Street. But the major ethnic tensions occur among the Anglo-Saxon aristocrats and the Irish and Pennsylvania Dutch middle class.

The central action of *Appointment in Samarra* is Julian English's throwing a drink in the face of an unpleasant Irish social climber. . . . A number of Irish Catholics in Gibbsville take it as an insult to their religion, and Pat Quilty, the town undertaker, transfers his automobile business to Julian's rival, Larry O'Dowd of the Gibbsville Buick Company. (pp. 196-97)

In one sense, O'Hara's novels may thus be seen as the means by which he worked out his own ethnic resentment against the high and mighty in southeastern Pennsylvania. This is especially true of *Ten North Frederick,* in which Joe Chapin tries to engineer a political appointment, without taking into account the local political machine. . . . When Joe goes over the head of Mike Slattery, the local party boss, to try to get a federal appointment from which to launch his presidential bid and then offers the Republican party bosses $100,000 for the lieutenant governor's nomination, Slattery takes the money and directs the party to nominate someone else. (pp. 197-98)

The hatred of the Pennsylvania Dutch for these aristocrats is equally intense. There is a paradox in this since a number of Pennsylvania Dutch families like the Reichelderfers go back to the early days of the Revolutionary War, and some of them— like Charlotte Chapin in *Ten North Frederick*—are descended from the German nobility. But the aristocrat's view of them is that they are stodgy middle-class Germans, and despite how rich and established they become, no one ever called them aristocratic. The consequence of their bourgeois stolidity is that the aristocrats ridicule them as "dumb Dutch bastards" and mimic their funny accents. Even Sidney Tate, O'Hara's most nearly perfect gentleman, cannot escape the prejudice of his class. (pp. 198-99)

A second way of defining this hatred among rival ethnic groups is to see it as a struggle between rich and poor. This may or may not amount to the same thing since the poor are often Irish, Pennsylvania Dutch, or another minority. Roger Bannon, the Irish contractor in *A Rage to Live,* runs afoul of the rich Caldwell clan and is virtually driven out of Fort Penn. A part of his hatred for the Caldwells is class structured. The son of a father known for radicalism, Bannon grows up thinking that benevolent local squires like William Penn Caldwell are a greater danger to the workingman than J. P. Morgan and should be combatted by any means, so he seduces Grace Tate. O'Hara's study of Tom Rothermel in *From the Terrace* suggests that envy of the rich may become the energy behind socialist radicalism. In Port Johnson Alfred Eaton grows up in a household where it is bad taste to talk about money and is thus unequipped, in a sense, to handle the fortune he later inherits. Thomas Rothermel, the poor boy with nice manners who grows up holding two or three jobs at once, knows everything about money by the age of eleven. In later years Rothermel argues that the capitalistic system stinks because it deprived him of his childhood. As a union official sympathetic to communism, Rothermel sees World War II as a contest between fascism and capitalism.

In the study of Rothermel's "violent hatred of the rich," some of O'Hara's finest social insights are dramatized. Rothermel knows enough about the very rich not to look for "the thin, cruel aristocrat who would delight in starving the tenantry." And he knows that the Port Johnson Eatons and Van Peltzes are "spurious aristocrats" not really in the same class with New York millionaires. But he has seen the Eatons put on "the airs of the gentry with their coachmen and their condescension as they did their shopping in Lower Montgomery Street," and he hates them doubly for assuming a superiority not even justified by their wealth. Jean and Creighton Duffy, very rich New Dealers in Washington, puzzle Rothermel because they seem to be aristocrats, although they ought to be Irish Catholic outsiders. The episode which crystallizes Rothermel's hatred of the Duffys occurs at a party one evening when he observes Duffy and his butler Barrett in relaxed conversation. Characteristically, the insight involves an expression of manners. Although Rothermel tries to break the butler of his deferential manner, Barrett is coldly precise and impersonally polite toward Tom—"colder than any snub Tom had ever received from one of the society men." . . . Gradually Rothermel comes to understand that in such relaxed moments Duffy and his servant are showing their respect for each other. . . . (pp. 200-01)

What is remarkable about O'Hara's treatment of the rich and poor is his identification with the values of both. Not a little of Rothermel's hatred for aristocrats reflects O'Hara himself, the Outsider from Pottsville. Yet more than any other twentieth-century novelist of manners, O'Hara admired the capacity of the rich to command power. Joe Chapin and Alfred Eaton are about as far removed from O'Hara's middle-class world as they can be, yet O'Hara's understanding of their observable manners is more informed and sympathetic than we are accustomed to find in an Outsider. (pp. 201-02)

A third way to see the hostility pervasive in O'Hara's Gibbsville chronicle is to visualize it as a contest between the established and the intruder. Fort Penn regards Grace Caldwell's husband with suspicion because he is a New Yorker—not a local boy. He never escapes their disapprobation. In *The Lockwood Concern,* Abraham Lockwood's "concern" (in Quaker usage the term refers to an obsession of a religious nature) is to form a dynasty, to raise his sons to be gentlemen. The Lockwood plan requires Abraham to overcome the stigma of his father's being a murderer and to establish himself as "a man of business and leading citizen." . . . Although "murder never disqualified a family from a position in history; it was the method by which kings became kings, barons became dukes," Abraham's scheme

founders because Lantenengo County never accepts the Lockwood outsiders from Swedish Haven. It is crucial that Abraham marry his son George into one of the first families of Lebanon Valley. But Eulalie Fenstermacher's father blocks the marriage because George "did not talk like a Pennsylvanian, he dressed too old for a college senior, he had artificial manners." . . . And when George marries a woman undistinguished in social station, the dynastic dream slides over into nightmare: Penrose winds up a murderer and suicide and George an ineffectual candy manufacturer. Great-grandson Bing becomes a penny-ante whoremaster in the West, and great-granddaughter Ernestine Lockwood, a syphilitic, sterile nymphomaniac, marries an impotent New England homosexual. The causes which destroy the Lockwood dream of an American aristocracy are complex. But one inescapable cause is the opposition of Lantenengo County society to the Swedish Haven Lockwoods.

The reason that Outsiders are excluded, O'Hara suggests, is often based on the illusion of status rather than upon status itself. Middle-class Irma Fliegler in *Appointment in Samarra* hates not only the Jewish Brombergs who have "lowered" Lantenengo Street property values, but a good many aristocrats as well. Her reasons for feeling superior are wholly irrational. . . . No different from most Gibbsville residents, Irma Fliegler is typical of her fellow townsmen in desperately clinging to "some family tradition, some membership in a select organization, some personal association with the famous," from which she tries to derive social distinction.

The theme of hatred, in relation to the "spurious democracy" that constitutes American social relations, is given ironic expression in the Ralph Barton cover of *The New Yorker* described in *Appointment in Samarra*—a picture of "a lot of shoppers, all with horribly angry or stern faces, hating each other and themselves and their packages, and above the figures of the shoppers was a wreath and the legend: Merry Xmas." The perfect motto for the whole Lantenengo County series is given at the end of chapter I of *Appointment in Samarra,* where Al Grecco, the bootlegger, follows Julian English home on Christmas night, and, as he drives down Lantenengo Street, rolls down his window and yells out at the darkened houses: "Merry Christmas, you stuck-up bastards! Merry Christmas from Al Grecco!" (pp. 203-04)

O'Hara is notorious for the cynical and "hard-boiled" treatment of sex in his novels. A survey of his work suggests the fullness of his notation of sexual phenomena—incest, homosexuality, lesbianism, transvestitism, voyeurism, and pederasty, not to speak of the more "normal" sexual pastimes, usually fornication and adultery. The sex drive is the most important naturalistic force, besides environment, operating in O'Hara's universe. If he gives us extensive flashbacks outlining the sexual experience of his personae it is because the individual's sexual history partly makes him what he is in his destructive social relations.

In general, O'Hara presents American society as an arena of competition for social position in which sex means athletic diversion, self-gratification, a means of alleviating boredom, and a method of social revenge. Inevitably sex means trouble. His modest understanding of the emotions, his anti-intellectualism, and his too-ready dependence upon lust to explain his characters tend to weaken the authority of his fiction. His treatment of sex is most troublesome, I believe, when sexual maladjustment is casually explained as the consequence of class antagonism. Jim Roper's homosexuality, for example, is presented to us as the consequence of being jilted by Mary

Eaton when "a rich bastard with a big car came along, and I got the gate." His seduction of Mary is the only revenge he can relish. Lloyd Williams has a brief affair with Edith Chapin simply because she is an aristocrat's wife and he is just a colliery "patch lad." In *A Rage to Live* Grace Tate is the victim of an elaborately planned seduction by a psychopathic Irishman who resents her upper-class snobbery. When she snubs Roger Bannon publicly in the streets of Fort Penn, there is no other way he can get "satisfaction." "Doing it to the rich man's daughter" may be precious little consolation to the snubbed outsider—and a perversion of the act of love—but it is Bannon's mode of revenge. Bannon, Parker Wells, and Larry Von Elm of *From the Terrace,* and George Lockwood of *The Lockwood Concern* all go after the women of the very rich because of hatred—as revenge for the social ostracism they have suffered.... The clearest symbol of the sexual assault motivated by class antagonism in *Appointment in Samarra* occurs when an eleven-year-old boy at the Gibbsville Mission, where Caroline English is teaching, reaches under her skirt and touches her. Characteristically, he is a redheaded Irish brat. (pp. 204-05)

Sex is rarely the expression of love in O'Hara's world, and love rarely survives in marriage. Many of O'Hara's violent death scenes—murders, accidents, and suicides—reflect how the glands degrade men to the level of animals. Penrose Lockwood and Marian Strademeyer, Peter Van Peltz and Victoria Dockwiler, Norma Budd and Joseph Waterford, Julian English, Gloria Wandrous, Anson Chatworth, George Lockwood, and Hedwig Millhauser suggest in their deaths that love is inevitably doomed by the nature of our sexuality. In the parable from which *Appointment in Samarra* takes its name, Death is a woman; in O'Hara's world sex means not life but death.

Norman Podhoretz has observed that O'Hara "draws no conclusions from class" [See *CLC,* Vol. 1]. O'Hara draws conclusions, but they are implied in the experience of his characters. Nothing can be done about heredity and fate. But what can achieve the redemption of society, his novels suggest, is freedom from the antagonisms of class that make American society an arena of social warfare. In short, redemption through love. If goodwill obtained more widely, there would be no social barriers obstructing the fulfillment of love. A Julian English could love his Polish Mary, a George Lockwood could marry his Eulalie Fenstermacher, and an Ann Chapin could marry her Charlie Bongiorno, even if he is an Italian accordion player. But O'Hara knows only too well that love fails because people withhold themselves from each other. His novels therefore suggest no way that love can transform the social order. His skepticism continually thwarted his own effort to visualize redemption through love. His portraits of "great love"—Alfred Eaton and Natalie Benziger, Joe Chapin and Kate Drummond—usually turn out to be simplistic, for when O'Hara moves from the physiology of sex to the emotion of love he tends to fall back on romantic sentimentalism.... Still, O'Hara was right without doubt in believing that people would be a little less miserable and contemptible and the social order a little more humane if the cruel realities and illusions of caste did not keep them from loving each other. (pp. 205-06)

> *James W. Tuttleton, "John O'Hara: Class Hatred and Sexuality," in his* The Novel of Manners in America, *The University of North Carolina Press, 1972, pp. 184-206.*

MATTHEW J. BRUCCOLI

[The] permanence of John O'Hara will be determined by whether he is read—especially by whether he is taught. The professors of English exert great influence by merely exposing students to particular books. In this way classics are made. O'Hara's novels are not on the standard American literature curricula. Professors like works that are susceptible to pedagogical exegesis; but O'Hara's work does not lend itself to that approach, for he set himself the task of eliminating cruces. It is hard to explicate what is clear. Moreover, the professional class has generally been inimical to what it regards as O'Hara's materialism.

What are the grounds for including John O'Hara among the classic American writers? First of all, there is the Americanness of his work: its value as a record of three decades of American life. The unsurpassed accuracy of this record requires that it be accorded respectful consideration for inclusion among the permanently valuable achievements in our literature. Although there are critics for whom "mere accuracy" is contemptible, there also are those who believe that one of the requirements of fiction is to be truthful. O'Hara's detractors employ the tactic of conceding his merits and dismissing them as paltry. A familiar critical cliché is that he achieved only "surface reality"—thereby implying that it was easy to do, and that in devoting himself to "reportorial realism" O'Hara missed the deeper varieties of psychological or spiritual reality. (If "surface reality" is a negligible achievement, perhaps it is worth asking if there is any virtue in its absence.) But "surface reality"—even accepting the condescension of "surface"—is not a mindless reportorial exercise. It presupposes the writer's mastery of his material, for it is mandatory that his meaningful details be really meaningful. John O'Hara was better at using such details than anyone else: he knew exactly what he was writing about. The chief literary benefit of successful "surface reality"—in addition to the pleasure of recognition it affords—is that it conditions the reader to believe in the whole work by making all the other elements more convincing. Good readers learn to distrust writers who are incompetent with details. The more-or-less grudging acknowledgment of O'Hara's "surface reality" is intended to signal the absence of more profound qualities in his work. Fashionable critics look in vain for evidence of his commitment to relevant issues. O'Hara knew that such things have nothing to do with literature. His concern was to write truthfully and exactly about life and people.

It was O'Hara's conviction that readers in the next centuries would turn to his work to find out how Americans lived in the first half of the twentieth century. Nonetheless, there have been objections to his "preoccupation with case histories and social backgrounds," objections which strike at the heart of his method. It is certainly true that "case histories and social backgrounds" are integral to his work; but they are not defects. A writer's preoccupations are defects only when he fails to make them meaningful. Indeed, that is one way to define the writer's chief obligation: that he make his material meaningful to a considerable body of readers. There will always be readers who are indifferent to O'Hara's social history, just as there will be readers who are indifferent to Faulkner's preoccupation with Southern history.

One test of a writer is his ability to create memorable characters. Here again the critics who patronize O'Hara's surface realism assert that his concern with surfaces betokens superficial characterizations. A rebuttal to this charge is the observation that, in O'Hara's own time, he created characters who achieved secure positions in the American literary experience: Julian English, Grace Caldwell Tate, Joe Chapin, Alfred Eaton and even Joey Evans. One surprising flaw in O'Hara's character portrayal is his frequent failure to show his characters actually engaged in their occupations—except for doctors, newspapermen, performers or bartenders. . . . Unlike Cozzens, who presents the work of professional men with an impression of absolute familiarity, O'Hara tends to concentrate on the social and sexual activities of his protagonists. This defect is more serious in O'Hara than, say, in Fitzgerald, because the work of men is a crucial aspect of O'Hara's world. O'Hara has been cited for "the tenuous motivation for the behavior of major characters"—a serious charge in the case of a writer who believed that the creation of convincing characters was crucial to the art of fiction, especially in his own work. In particular, critics as well as general readers have challenged the sexual conduct of O'Hara's characters because of their apparently unmotivated adulteries and infidelities. The only possible defense is that this behavior accorded with O'Hara's observation; and he always insisted that he was dealing truthfully with human behavior as he knew it. (pp. 342-43)

[Another] charge brought against O'Hara's work is that it includes "characters whose presence in the tale cannot be fully justified on aesthetic grounds." This criticism can be answered with Jules Romains' observation that life includes characters whose presence in life cannot be fully justified on aesthetic grounds. The writing of fiction is a process of selecting and ordering the materials of life—mostly a process of omission. The issue of how lifelike realistic fiction should be will always remain open. To the extent that a writer undertakes an exact transcription from life, his work becomes less creative. To the extent that he introduces exact causal relationships into his work, it becomes less lifelike. The concept of absolute realism is, admittedly, a delusion, for all writers *connect*—imposing more order on their material than it had in life. That O'Hara's fictional world is occasionally less rigorously connected than other writers' is intentional, and not evidence of his loss of control.

Another way of judging a writer is in terms of his style and technique—with high marks often given to the writers whose work is complex, and therefore purportedly profound. There is no multiplicity of meaning in O'Hara, no ambiguity or ambivalence. His aim was clarity, which is not a spectacular quality. It cannot be said that he was a stylist, for he did not create a style that was uniquely his. Nevertheless, his prose is always recognizable by what he called his "presentation"— the way in which he prepared his material. He presents a world that is identifiably his. A world that has life of its own. This quality, then, may well be what entitles John O'Hara to inclusion among the company of great writers: his work lives.

Related to O'Hara's realism and presentation is his mastery of speech. Even his most splenetic critics admit that he had a great "ear," suggesting that no art is involved in O'Hara's dialogue. (It was all done by ear.) It is worthwhile to recall O'Hara's injunction that writers who cannot be trusted to get the speech of their characters right cannot be trusted for anything else.

Many critics rate literature according to the author's view of "the human predicament," seeking evidence that he provides an ennobling view of humanity. These critics are antagonistic to O'Hara's work—claiming that his characters aren't worth writing about—because he provides no such comforting message. It has not, however, been established that the expression of such ideals is obligatory in great literature. Some of these "humanists" go further and assert that O'Hara's work offers no standards of conduct, no human values—ignoring the abun-

dant evidence of his strong commitment to the values of love, loyalty, duty, honor, pride. In missing—or suppressing—that evidence, they fail to perceive that John O'Hara approached his work with a Puritan conscience. He believed in his responsibility to his genius. (pp. 344-45)

> *Matthew J. Bruccoli, in his* The O'Hara Concern: A Biography of John O'Hara, *Random House, 1975, 417 p.*

DOUGLAS ROBILLARD

[The publication of **Selected Letters of John O'Hara**] brings sharply into focus the question that we must answer about O'Hara: has he been given his due as a writer? . . . If O'Hara seems at times in his letters to overstate the case for his writings, his justification must be that he never saw them properly evaluated by the critics or the academy. The sorting out of a writer's reputation is always a chancy business. Hawthorne died highly regarded, but Melville died virtually unknown. Hemingway and Faulkner achieved high reputations during their lifetimes, though Faulkner's was withheld until he had completed his best work. Fitzgerald died young, and his enduring reputation has come posthumously, in large part as the result of the loving care of his friends. O'Hara has been dead for nine years and probably his readership has declined now that there are no more new books to sustain it. Because he placed a ban on the printing of his stories in anthologies of American Literature, there are no anthology pieces to call attention to his work and invite new readers to it. Because there are thirty volumes of novels and short stories, his work has a tendency to look blocky in the thick volumes that were published, quickly, year after year, and may seem uninviting to the prospective new reader. The times are propitious for review, analysis, and appreciation.

If we approach O'Hara the novelist, we see at once that he was popular because he was understood by the general reader. A large audience could get through the novels without the uncomfortable sense that they did not know what was going on. The stories are neatly laid out, clear in their development; things happen, and the narrative line is preserved at all times. Characters act, change, age, and die. All is set forth in a leisurely and copious way. Sometimes a conversation will take more pages than appear necessary for the proportions of the book, but the conversation is lively and interesting, and one knows that O'Hara enjoys writing conversation.

A novel like **From the Terrace** (1958), to take an extreme example, displays amply the weaker sides of O'Hara's art as a novelist. It is too long; it goes on and on, rather relentlessly. The reader can see that the author knows very well where he wants to take his hero and the story, but Alfred Eaton is not quite interesting enough to sustain the narrative line for as long as O'Hara wants him to. It is disappointing that O'Hara believed this his best novel; his letters are sprinkled with evidence of his faith in it. For similar reasons, **Ourselves to Know** (1960) does not work well as a novel. The details pile up; the analysis of character goes on; the story moves through the whole long lifetime of a man; but the whole is finally less than the sum of its parts.

This is not to say that O'Hara often fails as a novelist. Quite the contrary. His first novel, **Appointment in Samarra** (1934), is a distinguished piece of fiction. Here he is already a knowledgeable craftsman who can maintain pace and build scenes carefully and sparsely, allowing himself to add nothing that does not contribute directly to the momentum of the story. . . . Subsequent novels like *A Rage to Live* (1949) and *Ten North Frederick* (1955) are fine, strong books, well planned and thoroughly realized. Of their lighter sort, *The Big Laugh* (1962), *Elizabeth Appleton* (1963) and *The Instrument* (1967) are worthy of careful study. They exist meaningfully within their restricted lengths and, above all, they are well-written, for O'Hara is an excellent prose stylist who is not often recognized for this quality. His prose tends to be unobtrusive. It is characteristic of his technique that he makes it work at the jobs of characterization and narration and does not allow it to call attention to itself.

An event of great importance for O'Hara's career was the composition of a trilogy of short novels, published under the collective title of *Sermons and Soda Water* (1960). The three stories find their center in Jim Malloy, O'Hara's favorite character and alter-ego. Two of them, *Imagine Kissing Pete* and *We're Friends Again,* should stand with the best fiction that O'Hara has written. They move swiftly, in a direct and uncluttered manner, and they leave much for the reader to do on his own by way of completing the suggestions and sketches of the text. It is not quite possible to say that writing *Sermons and Soda Water* caused O'Hara to begin on the long series of shorter fictions that graced the last decade of his career. But he does strike his best and most characteristic effects in the shorter tales which he was now to write. He is wholly artistic and plausible in those stories which leave the reader with a residue of unsatisfied interest in the characters and situations he has created. (pp. 74-6)

[O'Hara's] turn to the novel in the late 1940's and a rather bitter argument with *The New Yorker,* the chief publisher of his short stories, had taken him away from the [short story] form for more than a decade. He records his feelings at his return to shorter fiction: "The pleasure was in finding that after eleven years of not writing short stories, I could begin again and do it better." The remark is a sensational example of understatement. The stories that he now wrote were exciting, moving, full of a great storyteller's most polished artistry. Their vitality emerges from the richness of background and context; they are often great character studies that portray, explain, and develop but still leave the essential mystery and richness for the reader to take beyond the limits of the story. Sometimes the title of the story is the name of its subject: "**Arnold Stone**," "**Pat Collins**," "**Andrea**," "**Natica Jackson**," and "**Claude Emerson, Reporter**," are essentially pieces which take one person through a considerable amount of new experience and succeed in revealing subtle mixtures of personality, motives, and deeply aroused feelings. (pp. 76-7)

Even stories that do not telegraph their intention in their titles turn out, at their best, to be character studies. They are of such recent vintage that critical opinion has not yet settled upon some kind of sorting out of the best from the lesser works. . . . A distinguished feature of all these stories and many of the others is that they often open up what, for O'Hara, is a wide-ranging territory; he treats characters who live at all levels of the social scale. The typical, and quite identifiable subject matter of the O'Hara novel is the life of well-to-do people, high up on the economic and social chain of being, who often suffer well-to-do woes, without serious deprivation. This is, of course, a simplification of the world of the O'Hara novels, and it does not, by any means, describe them all. But its orbit encompasses a very large number. There is more variety in the shorter pieces than in the novels. Surprisingly, O'Hara can

write in an engaging manner about low-lifers, a subject he treats only tangentially in his longer fictions. In a novella like *The Bucket of Blood,* he gives a fair slice of the life of Jay Detweiler, a hobo who becomes a person of some small consequence by bartending in, and finally owning, a tough tavern called the "Bucket of Blood." The place is across the tracks, far from the country clubs of the socially ambitious. But Jay Detweiler is a character of substance, capable of turning down an offer to join his fairly respectable enterprise with prostitution. It is a comic story that brings to light some of O'Hara's often submerged talent for that difficult art.

Those stories which treat O'Hara's own special territory, the world of well-off upper and middle-class people, the landowners, bankers, lawyers, doctors, and business executives, imbue them with more life and substance than many of their cousins in the long novels by telling less about them, about their lives, deep fears, and stunting aspirations, by hinting, suggesting, and catching them in awkward poses, vulnerable, lost, and aching. One who comes to mind is the narrator of "**Justice**." After a long calm life of dampened but perfectly acceptable feeling, he falls in love with a young woman and lets his incautious passion cause a murder and the wreckage of two households. The very language of his narration shows his inability to comprehend his own nature; at the end of the story he can only look unbelievingly upon the violent results of his brief sortie into a life of richer feelings. . . . [Another of O'Hara's protagonists], Natica Jackson, a beautiful and successful actress, falls in love with a married man and the result is catastrophe; the injured wife murders his children. The examples multiply in O'Hara's keen and sympathetic probing of the pains of living.

When this great and brief outpouring of short fiction—we are talking about a decade or less of work, done while other large scale projects were under way—is properly assessed and fitted into the limits of our literary history, I believe that it will establish O'Hara in that great storytelling tradition that is very nearly the best thing in American literature. He will then be ranked, as he should be, with the great line of story tellers in the nineteenth century that includes Irving, Poe, Hawthorne, Melville and James, and continues in our time with the great stories of Hemingway and Faulkner, Fitzgerald at his sparse best. A place will have to be made for him ahead of his already highly praised successors, John Updike, Bernard Malamud, Peter Taylor, John Cheever, and Flannery O'Connor.

How O'Hara himself would feel about all of this is a teasing question. . . . He would certainly have ambivalent feelings about any judgment that seems to slight the novels for the short fiction. All of the evidence in the letters and elsewhere indicates that, while he knew and thoroughly understood the quality of his short fiction, he felt that the long novels, those demanding, thoroughly plotted, carefully detailed accumulations of thousands of events, acts, conversations, and secret misdeeds, those books upon which he worked so faithfully and seriously in a heart-straining schedule of genuinely hard nighttime labor, were his central monument. But one turns again and again to the shorter fictions and becomes convinced at last that they are the finest creations of their author. (pp. 77-9)

> *Douglas Robillard, "'A Great Character Study': John O'Hara's Letters and Fiction," in* Essays in Arts and Sciences, *Vol. VIII, May, 1979, pp. 73-9.*

DEBORAH A. FORCZEK

Any reassessment of O'Hara's place in the Thirties must look at the themes and style of his Thirties fiction. During these years, O'Hara wrote three novels: *Appointment in Samarra* (1934), *Butterfield 8* (1935), and *Hope of Heaven* (1938). He also collected his short stories in two volumes, *The Doctor's Son and Other Stories* (1935) and *Files on Parade* (1939). O'Hara took the post-Depression remnants of the Jazz Age and studied them with the skill of a Thirties social realist. As Malcolm Cowley observed, the hallmark of most Thirties literature was its breadth, its desire to capture all facets of American life. For most authors, this meant a microscopic portrait of the lower class, a group ignored in the previous decade's fiction. For O'Hara, it meant a need to chronicle all levels of society, from the lowliest bootlegger to the wealthiest socialite. O'Hara's settings depicted such disparate locations as a sleazy road house in Gibbsville, Pennsylvania, a run-down Chicago night club, or an elegant New York townhouse. When O'Hara was considered at all, critics called him a Pennsylvania author. While this characterized his late works, Pennsylvania was only one part of O'Hara's geographic range in the Thirties. He was equally at home in Hollywood, writing a description of Depression Los Angeles that rivalled the frenzy of Nathanael West's apocalyptic vision [in *The Day of the Locust*]. . . . (p. 52)

[O'Hara] offered a broader view of the 1930's ethos: the Depression not only affected the lower classes but the upper and middle classes of O'Hara's fictional world. It was deceptive to think of the Thirties as only the Southside Chicago streets of *Studs Lonigan*. O'Hara's depiction of the Gibbsville Country Club typified a different side of this complex decade. Although he never ignored the lower classes, his major themes focused on the middle and upper classes—their status anxieties, class conflicts, and political disinterest. (p. 53)

The Depression and its politics affected O'Hara's characters, but they did not view politics as central to their lives. The real aftershocks of the Depression had not yet hit Gibbsville's middle class in 1930. *Appointment in Samarra*'s first reference to it occurred in Irma Fliegler's monologue and was an accurate expression of her class's sentiment: "Next year, according to Hoover, things would be much better all around, and they would be able to do a lot of things they had planned to do, but had had to postpone because of this slump." She referred to the Depression in an off-hand way and believed that the "slump" was only a temporary aberration. What mattered to people like Irma were issues of personal prestige. Should Jews be allowed to live on Lantenengo Street? Will the Flieglers be admitted to the Gibbsville Country Club? Who was entitled to the custody of Grandfather Doane's Civil War medals—Irma or her brother? Irma Fliegler's thoughts revealed the negligible concerns some people had for politics during the 1930's.

O'Hara occasionally treated politics as humorous, as he did in his short story, **"Invite."** The tale, written as a letter to "Betty" from a college boy nicknamed "Chamberlain," alluded to the couple's first meeting place: a hotel in the tense London of 1938. Chamberlain proceeded to his main point—an invitation to a prom weekend at a small Midwestern college. O'Hara succeeded in capturing the incongruous mixture of seriousness and frivolity that would characterize a college junior. . . . This Chamberlain was a snob, whose only interest was in having an Eastern girl attend his prom and impress others with their London conversation. He treated world events with indifference and elevated his prom to a matter of state with his intricate planning. In mimicking the trivialization of politics for some Americans in the Thirties, O'Hara was rewarded with a lowered status in the Thirties canon.

In *Hope of Heaven*, O'Hara reflected an increased concern with the changing political climate of the Thirties. Peggy Henderson, the novel's heroine, was a Hollywood bookstore clerk and political leftist. She religiously attended political meetings, since she was certain that the Fascists were also meeting and growing in strength. When she became depressed over a petty matter, she reminded herself of the plight of the German Jews. She always wanted to support the Scottsboro boys or the Spanish Loyalists, but she never seemed to write any checks. Peggy was O'Hara's most clearly drawn political character, but even her politics were peripheral to her life in sunny California.

Although politics played a minor role in O'Hara's fiction, he shared his fellow Thirties authors' belief that social class distinctions were critical in determining an individual's fate. While Steinbeck and Farrell chronicled the doomed lives of the lower class, O'Hara portrayed equally doomed members of the upper and middle class who had disturbed the existing social order. O'Hara's belief in determinism was as strong as any of his contemporaries. (pp. 54-5)

In the Gibbsville world ruled by status, elites retained their power through inheritance. Money became legitimate through the number of generations born on Lantenengo Street, not the number of dollars spent in buying a home there, as the Brombergs had done. In *Appointment in Samarra*, heritage was more than wealth and a family name, it was family character traits as well. Julian English's grandfather had committed suicide when the town had discovered his financial indiscretions as its banker. Julian's father, Dr. William English, led an exemplary life, repaying his father's debts, yet he was terrified that he would one day inherit his father's "weakness." When the doctor caught his son shoplifting, he thought the trait had appeared in the third generation. People still believed theories about inherited suicide traits in the 1930's. In this novel, they became a self-fulfilling prophecy for the Englishes. Once Dr. English noticed the trait in his son, he stopped "loving" him. This loss of parental guidance pushed Julian away from medicine and undermined his confidence, culminating in his suicide. O'Hara emphasized the lingering belief in biological determinism through the ideas of the small town doctor.

O'Hara continued to explore the theme of determinism in his second novel, *Butterfield 8*. (pp. 55-6)

Although *Butterfield 8*'s main plot centered around another suicide victim, Gloria Wandrous, it differed from his first novel since O'Hara attributed Gloria's death solely to environment. A family friend had molested the young Gloria, and this experience began her promiscuous life as a call girl. O'Hara's fatalism was similar to other Thirties authors, as Farrell's portrait of Studs Lonigan's death demonstrated.

Thus, the themes of O'Hara's fiction reinforced the determinism of his fellow Depression writers: yet he broadened this determinism by surveying all segments of society. . . . While O'Hara varied from his fellow Thirties writers in subject matter, he sympathized with their desire to realistically record their times. O'Hara's critical portraits of the manners and mores of the upper and middle classes added a different dimension to our understanding of the decade.

Nowhere is O'Hara's talent as a portrayer of the 1930's more apparent than in a consideration of his literary style, which displayed many of the characteristics of the documentary. . . . O'Hara also used journalism explicitly and implicitly to strengthen his documentary approach. These techniques enabled the Thirties artist to achieve his goal: a recreation of the "texture of reality." (pp. 56-7)

O'Hara recorded a variety of Thirties sounds for his audience. *Appointment in Samarra* alluded to the top dance songs at a country club party in 1930 ("Oh Give Me Something to Remember You by"), at a road house cafe (Cole Porter's racy, "Love for Sale"), and in a private record collection (Paul Whiteman's version of "Stairway to Paradise"). In the story, **"Invite,"** the young man used the promise of Tommy Dorsey's music as an enticement to a possible prom date. In *Butterfield 8,* a chance meeting between James Malloy and Eddie Brunner, Gloria's one friend, revolved around their love of jazz. They made small talk about Fats Waller, Louis Prima, Bix Beiderbecke, Miff Mole, and Benny Goodman.

Yet O'Hara did more than mention song titles or musicians to record the sounds of the Thirties; he mimicked the decade's speech patterns as well. O'Hara had what critics would later derogatorily refer to as a "tape recorder-like" ear for dialogue. O'Hara knew that it was impossible to reproduce real variations in speech, but he tried to suggest the way different characters would speak. Like other realists, O'Hara depended on the vernacular to impart verisimilitude. But unlike other Thirties authors, O'Hara extended his use of the vernacular to encompass the upper class speech of Orange County's club women as well as Pal Joey's lower class slang. (pp. 57-8)

Like other documentary stylists such as Dos Passos, O'Hara sought to present the feelings of his times as accurately as possible. To imitate the sense experience, writers tried to simulate the camera, especially the technique of the newsreel pastiche—bits and pieces of random news items woven into a whole. One of O'Hara's most effective examples of the pastiche opened the fifth chapter of *Butterfield 8:*

> On Monday afternoon an unidentified man jumped in front of a New Lots express in the Fourteenth Street subway station. Mr. Hoover was on time for the usual cabinet meeting.... A woman named Plotkin, living in the Brownsville section of Brooklyn, decided to leave her husband for good and for all.... Babe Ruth hit a home run into the bleachers near the right field foul line.... Patrolman John J. Barry, Shield No. 17858, was still on sick call as a result of being kicked in the groin by a young woman Communist in the Union Square demonstration.... Gloria Wandrous, taking a warm bath at home, went to sleep while worrying over what she should do about Mrs. Liggett's mink coat.

The catalogue of details suggested a camera panning a large scene of life in the 1930's. O'Hara juxtaposed facts about the well-known (Hoover, Babe Ruth) with the unknown (the subway suicide, Mrs. Plotkin) as a framework for the actions of Gloria Wandrous' world. (pp. 58-9)

O'Hara's use of realistic details owed much to the influence of the documentary style of the Thirties. In *Appointment in Samarra,* he indicated his broader thematic concern of status anxiety with a detailed look at the ritual of choosing a dinner menu for a club party. The Ammermans, for example, needed to shore up their uncertain position in Gibbsville society with the club's best dinner: the filet mignon with Baked Alaska. O'Hara's attention to the minutiae of the dinner informed his

audience of the society's subtle rules and created a context to judge English's later transgressions. (p. 60)

O'Hara's style often relied on journalism for its realistic tone. . . . O'Hara fused this aspect of the documentary style with his personal experience as a reporter. Journalism thus appeared as an underlying motif in his Thirties work.

O'Hara used the reporter in all of his Thirties novels. *Appointment in Samarra*'s opening and closing scenes featured women journalists. O'Hara imitated a "you are there" article on boxing, written by Gibbsville's breathy version of Sophie Irene Loeb, Lydia Faunce Brown. The last person to see English alive was the society columnist whom he tried to seduce. More than stray characters, O'Hara's journalists gave the novel an additional layer of realism. In his next two novels, *Butterfield 8* and *Hope of Heaven,* he employed a single character, the autobiographical Jimmy Malloy, as the reporter figure. In *Butterfield 8,* Malloy played a minor role, serving with his girl friend as a contrast to the doomed lovers Gloria and Weston Liggett. In *Hope of Heaven,* however, O'Hara developed Malloy's character as a reporter-novelist who went to Hollywood as a film writer. (pp. 60-1)

O'Hara's literary style conformed to the Thirties artistic philosophy, best expressed by the social scientist, Paul Lazarsfeld, as a "maximum of concreteness." O'Hara achieved this concreteness in his prose as he portrayed the sounds, feelings, and sights of a different side of this decade. . . . For O'Hara, the documentary style became his tool to achieve his goal: telling the truth about his time.

Often literary historians have a difficult task in retelling the "truth" about their time. In the complicated process of remembering the Thirties, O'Hara has nearly been forgotten. But an author whose self-ascribed task was "to record the way people talked and thought and felt, and do it with complete honesty and variety," deserved a place in the history of a decade whose aims he felt and whose times he recorded. . . . With other Depression authors, he shared a common career pattern, a philosophy of determinism, and a documentary style. As a realist, O'Hara presented a detailed portrait of Thirties life, a portrait all the more valuable since he was one of the few authors during this decade to document the lives of the upper and middle class. (pp. 61-2)

> *Deborah A. Forczek, "'He Told the Truth about His Time': John O'Hara and the 1930's," in* John O'Hara Journal, *Vol. 2, No. 1, Winter 1979-80, pp. 46-65.*

ROBERT EMMET LONG

O'Hara's final decade as a novelist was inaugurated by *Ourselves to Know* (1960), which has the form partly of a family chronicle, but is strikingly different from O'Hara's family sagas of the 1950s in its extraordinary interest in the inner life of its protagonist Robert Millhouser. If *Ourselves to Know* is psychological in its orientation to a degree unwitnessed in O'Hara's earlier novels, it is also more philosophic. It questions the relationship of God and man, the mysterious decrees of fate and limitations placed upon individuals by their psychic makeup. Robert Millhouser's life forms the basis of a meditation not only on Millhouser but also on the condition of mankind. (p. 125)

It comes out rather early in *Ourselves to Know* that Robert Millhouser had murdered his wife, and thus no suspense exists as to what the critical episode was in Millhouser's life. . . .

The murder does not occur until very late in the work, and O'Hara leads up to it only very gradually by focusing upon selected periods in Millhouser's life—his twenties and thirties, his marriage and imprisonment, and the period following his release. Because the reader is informed early of the murder, O'Hara is able to highlight later episodes of Millhouser's life, such as the incidents following the murder, out of chronological order.

What is particularly impressive about *Ourselves to Know* is the psychological atmosphere that suffuses it. From the moment he first appears, Robert Millhouser is evoked as a haunted and solitary man. . . . Rarely, in fact, does he leave his large house "enclosed" by a white paling fence at the edge of town. . . . The house becomes virtually emblematic of Millhouser's haunted mind, and in its morbid atmosphere and sense of a haunted isolation, it makes one think of Hawthorne. (pp. 128-29)

[Three characters] enter importantly into and have an effect on Millhouser's life. The first is his widowed mother, Zilph, a woman so self-contained that she is temperamentally unable to show him love (a role usually assigned in O'Hara to the father). Another is Chester Calthorp, Millhouser's closest college friend, a cultivated young man who wishes to become a painter, as Millhouser does himself, and whom Millhouser looks up to and admires. After college, Millhouser goes to Rome with Calthorp to study painting; but there he becomes homesick, recognizes that he has no gift as a painter, and, what is more, discovers that Calthorp is an active homosexual. Disillusioned, Millhouser returns home, where he lives with his mother until her death in 1902. Essentially he is alone. Years pass in this way until he meets the third person to affect him decisively Hedwig Steele. (p. 129)

Hedda is an extraordinary conception—more depraved in youth than Mary St. John Eaton, in *From the Terrace,* is in maturity. In a striking passage, when the Steeles are traveling by train in South America, Hedda does not occupy herself with picture books but stares brazenly at fellow passengers. She seduces a much older man, who later hangs himself, and in Mexico City, when her mother lets her out of her sight, she has an affair with a Johnny Villareal. When her mother slaps her, Hedda slaps back. Hedda is the "bad seed" the Steeles have somehow produced, and in Lyons they are more than willing to transfer their daughter in matrimony to the much older Millhouser. After the marriage, they move away.

Robert Millhouser is a wealthy man, the director of an important bank, and he has much to offer Hedda. What he gives, she takes. . . . During the first year of the marriage, she has an affair with the crudely physical Bart Vance, who sees her late at night at the house when Millhouser is away on business. These incidents so trouble the servants that they give notice, and finally, learning of her relations with Vance, Millhouser reaches the point where he knows that he must kill her. He shoots her in her bed as she sleeps. O'Hara implies that Millhouser had married Hedda because he had known subconsciously that something terrible would come of the marriage, and that this would bring him out of his isolation by forcing him to *feel*. But even after committing the worst of human acts, the taking of another's life, he remains "devoid of feeling," and in killing Hedda, who represents the passional part of experience, he removes himself forever from life.

Robert Millhouser is presented with such elaborate indirection and is such an elusive figure that one wonders if there is not some trick involved in O'Hara's creation of him. Many indicators in the novel suggest that he is latently homosexual, but if so then at least part of the enigma of his nature is dispelled. (pp. 130-31)

The problem of how Robert Millhouser should be regarded, whether as a man incapacitated for life because he cannot "feel," or as a man who can be explained partly as a repressed homosexual, troubles the novel, although it does not destroy it. Millhouser is a richly evoked character, projected dramatically and memorably against the background of his blighted past and isolation in his morbidly moldering house in Lyons; and even if uncertain of its causes, the reader is wholly convinced of his paralysis. *Ourselves to Know* reveals O'Hara's talent at maturity—in his rich creation of the community of Lyons, his many convincingly drawn characters, and emphasis upon the projection of sensibility over outward events. (p. 132)

The Big Laugh (1962) is disappointing to the point of being dismaying. In this novel, which gives the impression that it was improvised from the opening page to the final one, O'Hara returns to Hollywood, where he traces the career of an actor named Hubert Ward, an unsympathetic antihero. Hubert Ward is a kind of Pal Joey who succeeds, and he is like Joey in that his shallowness and opportunism are matched by the same qualities in the people around him. (p. 135)

At one point only does *The Big Laugh* engage the reader—when Hubert is introduced to the circle of the high-ranking producer Charley Simmons and his wife Mildred. . . . At this point, the novel begins to be *about* something—the social structure of Hollywood society. The parties given at the executive level reveal the status of the various characters who belong to the film industry, and O'Hara notes their differences in status tellingly. Moreover, he has captured these characters in an evocative atmosphere of malaise that lies beneath the surface of their glittering success. . . . But this middle portion of the novel disintegrates before long, and O'Hara returns to Hubert's meretricious success story, an account so artificial that it possesses very little sense of reality. What is striking about *The Big Laugh* ultimately is its hostile view of humanity, its embittered nihilism that also seems O'Hara's.

To move from *The Big Laugh* to *Elizabeth Appleton* (1963) is to come suddenly into the presence of sweet reasonableness. . . . *Elizabeth Appleton* is an "academic novel" of a kind, but not entirely. Its academic setting is less important to the novel than it might seem; and in addition the academics who appear in it are few and faint. Essentially, it is an inquiry into a marriage that is set against the background of a college in Pennsylvania. (pp. 136-37)

Elizabeth Appleton reads in many respects like a novel of manners—without having the social density of one. It contains acute observations and is attentive to the social relationships of its characters, who are frequently defined by the class to which they belong. Elizabeth and her sister Jean, daughters of a Wall Street banker, have been brought up among the affluent on the North Shore of Long Island. Money is an important factor in their upbringing, since it dictates which individuals qualify and which do not. Elizabeth's mother, Amelia Webster, is a great aristo who comments with disapproval on the Prince of Wales's accessibility during a visit, his "extraordinarily democratic behavior on the North Shore." She distinctly does not favor Elizabeth's interest in young John Appleton, who is about to begin a teaching career at Spring Valley College. Her husband, on the other hand, although he has made a good deal of money, has the attitudes of a leisured gentleman who sees beyond mere money-making and the artificial ranking of individuals by their incomes, and he endorses John Appleton as a husband for Elizabeth. Jarvis and Amelia Webster had had a son who drowned one summer in his youth, and Jarvis tends to see Appleton as a son, or as a replacement for the son he has lost. The Websters' marriage is not happy, and O'Hara implies that in securing Elizabeth's marriage to Appleton, Jarvis Webster has also taken revenge on his wife, whose snobbish attitudes have oppressed him. Elizabeth comes to John Appleton partly as the result of a conflict within the Webster family. (pp. 138-39)

O'Hara's structuring of *Elizabeth Appleton* is handled skillfully, but the novel can be faulted in a number of respects, particularly in regard to characters who do not fill out their roles. (p. 140)

The novel has other limitations. Its collegiate background is relatively thin, and in the sequence that deals with the fraternity initiation, and the student demonstration before the Appleton house when it is learned that John is not to be named president, the writing is unconvincing. Troubling, too, is the arbitrary decision of the trustees to find someone from outside, an anticlimax that cancels out the impression the whole novel gives that the outcome will be determined by the complications existing among its characters. On the whole, however, *Elizabeth Appleton* is a rather agreeable, low-keyed work. It contains particularly acute observations of women, who have been more finely felt and are consistently more interesting than the novel's men. The ending is quiet, but one feature of it is striking— the revelation that Elizabeth has chosen to remain with John Appleton because he is weak and needs her even more than does [her lover] Porter Ditson. A faceless, voiceless man of limited vision, John Appleton is something like Joe Chapin [in *Ten North Frederick*], but escapes his fate because the strong woman in his life chooses to spare him. In this respect, *Elizabeth Appleton* is a more smiling version of O'Hara's repeated theme of the man who is dominated or even emasculated by the woman he marries. (pp. 140-41)

The Lockwood Concern (1965) is surprisingly romantic, even at times baroque. As a multigenerational family chronicle, *The Lockwood Concern* might have been one of O'Hara's largest works, but has instead been kept to the proportions of a novel of medium length. It begins in the present, but before long, in O'Hara's familiar manner, goes back in time to the distant past, in this case to the career of the founding member of the family, Moses Lockwood, whose story begins in the period of Jeffersonian democracy of the 1830s. (p. 141)

O'Hara called *The Lockwood Concern* "an old fashioned morality," a fair enough description of it in its continual consciousness of good and evil, and the lesson that runs all through it that the price of moral isolation is death. Death enters thematically into such earlier novels as *Appointment in Samarra* and *Ten North Frederick,* and into many of O'Hara's stories of the 1960s concerned with characters who are aging. But in *The Lockwood Concern* death is a constant presence and comes to seem like the ultimate reality that the Lockwoods, in their hereditary obsession, are attempting to outrun. Death is associated with the line's founder Moses Lockwood, who had killed two men, and with many of the Lockwood women, who are blighted in their lives, or waste away and die. When George Lockwood's house is completed, a boy from nearby who has climbed a tree limb to peer over the wall falls to his death, impaled on the spikes along the top of the wall; and his death seems an ill omen for the future of the house. When his brother Penrose commits suicide, George Lockwood dissociates him-

self from the incident, determined not to let it deter him from his self-aggrandizing ambitions. . . . At the very end of the novel, George Lockwood dies in a fall on the secret staircase. Alone in his death agony in the empty depths of the house he built, blinded and choking on his vomit as he attempts to cry out, he seems like some terrible sufferer in hell.

The Lockwood house is the opening and final setting of *The Lockwood Concern,* but it appears as well in other sections of the novel, and is ever present in the reader's mind. It holds the family's moral history, its egotism, and terrible isolation from others. Human isolation is, of course, O'Hara's great theme; but in *The Lockwood Concern* it has been treated more romantically than elsewhere, and has been given a distinctive psychological emphasis. What lies behind the "Concern," really, is paranoia. The Lockwoods' paranoiac mind can be noticed in their extreme, unnatural suspiciousness of others, the defenses they raise to keep others away from them, and the grandiose schemes and sense of themselves that they nurture. However baroque George Lockwood's life may be, it is focused by a believable "mind set," and to know George Lockwood is to enter memorably into the imagination of paranoia. The fantasia of his mind has been created at a level of excitement that exceeds anything in *Elizabeth Appleton,* and despite its oddness, melodrama, and excess, it is a more deeply imagined novel. (pp. 143-44)

Lovey Childs: A Philadelphian's Story (1969) is distinguished by a disdainful view of humanity. (p. 147)

A pronounced feature of *Lovey Childs* is its concern with lesbianism, which also appears in a number of O'Hara's stories of the 1960s. In *Lovey Childs,* although not in all the stories, lesbianism is treated as if it were a diseased aberration of sexuality. Lovey's mother is revealed as a lesbian, and her mental breakdown, which occurs after her seduction of a young girl in Buffalo, New York, is made to seem directly attributable to her sexual orientation. Another character, Marcy Bancroft, a lesbian student with Lovey at the Hathaway school, is almost preternaturally evil, a character similar in her precocious carnal knowledge to the "imp child" Hedda in *Ourselves to Know.* Moreover, when Lovey is in Reno obtaining a divorce from her first husband Sky Childs, she is stalked and seduced by Virginia Vernon, a confirmed lesbian and a very unpleasant individual. (pp. 147-48)

Sex itself in *Lovey Childs,* in whatever form, seems peculiarly diseased. Sky Childs, the sportsman-millionaire Lovey marries, loses no time in being unfaithful to her with a show girl. The sleazy details of their divorce, splashed across the pages of the New York tabloids, make it clear that the marriage was not made in heaven. In another instance of the unloveliness of sex, Henry Gage, a socialite, has his throat slashed in Harlem, where he had gone one night in search of offbeat pleasure. The novel is set for the most part in the late 1920s and the early part of the Great Depression, and its sexual theme is intended to evoke the bankruptcy of the period. . . . Lovey's story might even have had a certain plausibility if O'Hara had not continually resorted to melodramatic devices. It is incredible, for example, that Lovey's mother, a woman who seems eminently stable when she first appears, should, when the reader hears of her again, be confined to a mental institution as the result of a lesbian strain in her makeup. It is preposterous that Lovey should seduce Father McIldowney when he comes to look at the Lewis home as a possible property for the Church, and that he should later hang himself from a rafter in the sacristy. Such instances of melodramatic plotting as these destroy any claim to seriousness that the work might have, and make *Lovey Childs* one of O'Hara's emptiest novels.

In some respects, *Lovey Childs* reads like a preliminary sketch for O'Hara's last, posthumously published novel *The Ewings* (1972), which also shows a pronounced preoccupation with lesbianism. (pp. 148-49)

The Ewings did not deserve the uniformly hostile reviews it received when it appeared, but it clearly has many flaws. Its structure, for one thing, is not altogether satisfactory. . . . A number of the scenes are concerned with the world of business and finance—with the Cleveland law firm of Hotchkiss, Ewing & Kelley, where Bill Ewing succeeds his late father as a partner while he is still in his late twenties, and with the Cuyahoga Iron and Steel Company, to which Ewing is named to a directorship. Yet it soon develops that the real subject of the novel is Bill Ewing's mother Ada, who takes over the work. (p. 149)

Ada Ewing has been a proper wife of a successful Cleveland attorney, and later as a widow at fifty-two she discovers that her life has kept her in ignorance not only of the world but even of herself. What is conspicuous about Ada is not that she is a dissolute woman but that she is an innocent. There is an odd kind of humor in O'Hara's treatment of her—so odd that it is hard even to characterize. It involves irony, but is not harshly sardonic. "Playful" and "whimsical" are words that come to mind, but they do not quite capture O'Hara's "all-knowing" quality in regard to her, his almost mysterious refraining from expressing an overt attitude toward her. O'Hara always knows much more than Ada does, both about herself and about the different social groups she enters. In Ada's initiation into lesbian sexuality with Priscilla, her responses are almost childlike in their simplicity; she is genuinely surprised that such practices exist and that they give tactile pleasure, and at the same time she remains somehow matronly and well-behaved. (pp. 150-51)

Later, Ada goes to visit her wealthy friend Sophie Cudlipp at Palm Springs and discovers that Sophie, also a widow, keeps a handsome younger man named Will Levering. One night Levering steals into Ada's room to make love to her, obviously a "present" from Sophie, and her horizons are expanded, although she continues to be naive. After she has been back in Cleveland, and scandal begins to spread about her rather marginal relations with Priscilla, Ada finds it best to get away. She visits her old school friend Rhoda Shipley, a wealthy widow in Santa Barbara, and in a scene that is handled with a suave understatement by O'Hara, they find that they have both been lonely and have a common lesbian interest. The two matrons, a little over fifty, find their solution to loneliness in living together as lovers. At the end, her name darkened by scandal in Cleveland, Ada seems every bit as unworldly as she had appeared at the beginning. Ada is an unlikely conception, yet she lives as a character as many of the minor characters do not. . . . (p. 151)

Clarence Kelley is somewhat off to the side of the novel in the earlier part, but in an unpredictable strategy, O'Hara makes him the focal figure of the work at the end. He, too, has had an unfulfilled life. After a relationship with a young man that threatens to become talked about, he marries unhappily, and later forms a platonic fondness for Bill Ewing's father. After Kelley's death, his life is suddenly made more clear to the reader. Bill Ewing enters Kelley's bedroom, which contains his books—including volumes of Freud, Walt Whitman, and

Huck Finn—and, with an irony of which he is not aware, remarks: "What a lonely life he must have led!" He then notices and is puzzled by an old photograph of his parents, taken fifteen years before, on their boat *The Wanderer,* and wonders why Kelley had kept it in his bedroom for years. Suspecting that the admirable Clarence Kelley had loved his mother, he is swayed to think less harshly of her, and the novel ends with a poignant sense of the distances that divide people.

In the 1960s, O'Hara produced a staggering amount of work. . . . He worked incessantly, without revising what he wrote; had he done so, his weakest work at least would surely have benefited. But as it is, the period adds to his achievement. To his superior earlier work in the novel—*Appointment in Samarra, Butterfield 8,* and *Ten North Frederick*—the final period adds two other novels, *Ourselves to Know* and *The Lockwood Concern,* as well as two minor, unpretentious novels that reveal an interest in sensibility, *Elizabeth Appleton* and *The Ewings.* An interest in sensibility and in his characters' inner psychological states distinguishes O'Hara's best work of this period, but O'Hara's themes are surprisingly consistent—as they are, in fact, throughout his career. In each of his phases as a novelist, the settings, characters, and narrative methods are varied, but the underlying vision is always the same one of isolation and loneliness.

So many rehearsals of the same theme suggest at least one of O'Hara's limitations as a novelist. Although resourceful in varying the narrative strategies of his novels and possessing impressive skills as a technician, O'Hara does not give the impression of having a large range of thematic ideas. He did not progress from early attitudes toward man and society to later ones farther along in his career, or develop wholly new preoccupations as time went on, as is the case with many other writers. His development from the early novels—taut, dramatic, and symbolically plotted—to the sprawling, allegorical family sagas, to the psychologically oriented last novels, was largely aesthetic. It has sometimes been said that O'Hara's particular interest is that he was a "social historian," but the pattern of his work, viewed more broadly, reveals him as an aesthetic analyst of an obsessive, prismatic theme. (pp. 151-52)

> *Robert Emmet Long, in his* John O'Hara, *Frederick Ungar Publishing Co., 1983, 197 p.*

FRANK MacSHANE

To say that John O'Hara's stories stand up well, as they certainly do, is to use a physical term in an almost literal way. It means that they are as sturdy and fresh as they were when they were first created. This achievement—one of the most important in literature, since it earns the reader's trust—is due mainly to the way O'Hara used his ear to its best advantage. It was his greatest gift, and he relied on it from the start. (p. v)

The link between contemporary fiction and the oral tradition of epic and folk literature may seem remote, but in fact the two forms have much in common. When people gathered to hear the stories that were later attributed to Homer or collected in the Old Testament, they did so to find out what things were like in the past. They wanted to hear the voices of their ancestors; they wanted to know what people *said.* The bard or priest who told the stories was like Coleridge's Ancient Mariner, who took his listeners by the hand and recited his impassioned tale. He was memorable not for what he said but for how he said it; and for his special gifts, he sat at the right hand of the chieftain or king.

Then as now, authentic storytellers were those who had a good ear. They were able to report the very words that Achilles used when addressing his troops, or the actual lamentations of Job in the midst of his travails. Speech is not mere decoration. Its form and substance come from inner feelings and fundamental beliefs. It is the mark of human personality. Shaw's *Pygmalion* is a comedy about social distinctions, but it is also a commentary on the nature of truth. Professor Higgins and Liza use language in different ways not only because they were brought up in different places but because they have their individual ambitions and needs, and these are reflected in the way they talk. (pp. v-vi)

Talk was, for O'Hara, the beginning of many of his stories. Often he would sit at his typewriter and start by thinking of a couple of faces he had seen. He would put the people together in a restaurant or on an airplane, and they would begin to talk. (pp. vi-vii)

Dialogue was not the only device O'Hara used to get into his stories, but in general he relied on actual things. He was interested in the telling detail, the phrase or name that had some resonance. A Brooks Brothers suit or a Swaine and Adeney's umbrella, the Racquet Club or Palmer Stadium, Romanoff's or the Twentieth-Century Limited, all carry much more than their surface identities. When O'Hara writes about a woman "pounding her Delman heels on the Penn Station floor," he creates a whole person in the phrase, just as he does with the woman who, getting into her car in the parking lot of a suburban railway station, "kicked off her shoes and put on a pair of loafers that lay on the floor."

By using such details, O'Hara invented almost single-handedly what came to be known as the *New Yorker* story. Arranging a brief encounter between two or more people speaking a language appropriate to the setting, O'Hara gives an impression of reality in a few phrases. Often the point is not immediately plain, for O'Hara believed that truth was allusive. But his themes were consistent, and they depended on having real people express themselves in real places.

If Napoleon was right in calling the Piazza San Marco in Venice "the best drawing room in Europe," O'Hara's stories as a whole provide the best conversation in America. Although he was for years associated with the upper-class world of New York, Philadelphia and Long Island, he had a remarkable range of subjects, more so than Faulkner or Fitzgerald or even Hemingway, whose work influenced him in many ways. The central characters of his stories are not only club men and business executives; they are country doctors, movie stars, beauticians, bartenders, schoolgirls, nightclub singers, gas station attendants, telephone operators and bus drivers. America in the twentieth century is what he knew, and in 1960 he said, "It is my business to write about it to the best of my ability, with sometimes the special knowledge that I have. I want to record the way people talked and thought and felt, and to do it with complete honesty and variety."

Behind the modesty of this statement lies O'Hara's vision of America and, by extension, of humanity everywhere. He saw society as a structure that rarely succeeded in covering up the disorders that lay beneath the surface of human intercourse. He saw decency and hope routinely destroyed by selfishness and cruelty, leaving individuals with little solace to face the essential solitude of life and death. Yet O'Hara's vision is not a cheerless one, for he also celebrated individual acts of kindness and imagination, and he does not pass judgment or ap-

portion blame. His stories are peopled with such varied individuals—pretentious, gentle, deranged or simply pensive—that it seems clear that for all his doubts about humanity, O'Hara was in love with life itself. His testament as an artist is that his short stories, covering a period of over thirty-five years in the writing, are still extraordinarily alive.

This quality says a good deal about the short story in general and the reasons for O'Hara's pre-eminence in this form. It is sometimes fashionable to dismiss the short story and to attribute its apparent decline to the greater versatility of the novel and to the rise of nonfiction. But the trouble does not lie with the form but with its practitioners. A really good short-story writer will always find a popular audience. In recent times, J. D. Salinger, John Cheever and John Updike have been remarkably successful, and the reason is that they are all masters of the form. They all have a good ear and an eye for detail. These qualities give their work the same vitality that keeps collections of Chekhov and Poe on the paperback shelves in bookstores across the country.

John O'Hara belongs to this small company of great short-story writers simply because of the quality of his work. His aesthetic purposes were a direct extension of his attitude toward life itself. "Life goes on," he wrote as a young man, "and for the sake of verisimilitude and realism, you cannot positively give the impression of an ending: you must let something hang. A cheap interpretation of that would be to say that you must always leave a chance for a sequel. People die, love dies, but life does not die, and so long as people live, stories must have life at the end."

It is at their endings that O'Hara's stories give their greatest pleasure. Just when the story ends, or perhaps a few moments afterward, when all the pieces fall into place, the reader grasps what it is really all about. A sort of epiphany occurs. It can produce chill or warmth, depending on the story, but it is an organic part of the story itself. It is not a surprise ending like one in a Saki or Ambrose Bierce story, which loses its force once it is expressed. Rather it deepens the feelings that come from beneath the surface of the story. Emerging from the skillful mixture of fact and feeling in the story, it lingers on, like a phrase of music, in the memory. At the end of *We're Friends Again,* one of the novellas in *Sermons and Soda-water,* the narrator speaks of a theme that is paramount in O'Hara's work. "What really can any of us know about any of us, and why must we make such a thing of loneliness when it is the final condition of us all?" Then he adds, "And where would love be without it?"

During his lifetime, O'Hara published eleven collections of short stories and three volumes of novellas, making a total of over four hundred pieces of short fiction. [*Collected Stories of John O'Hara*] contains fewer than ten percent of these, but those reprinted here represent O'Hara's finest work. (pp. vii-ix)

Taken as a whole, his shorter work, starting from the sharp, incisive stories of his early years at *The New Yorker* and continuing into his more relaxed and expansive period in Princeton, represents the growth and maturity of one of the finest short-story writers of modern times. (p. ix)

Frank MacShane, "Introduction: The Power of the Ear," in Collected Stories of John O'Hara *by John O'Hara, edited by Frank MacShane, Random House, 1984, pp. v-ix.*

JONATHAN YARDLEY

This selection of 36 short stories by the late John O'Hara [*Collected Stories of John O'Hara*] is instructive, but not in ways that its editor presumably had in mind or, for that matter, that I had anticipated. . . . He was one of the most popular and admired writers of his day, but *Collected Stories of John O'Hara* says nothing so much as that his day is done.

Arriving at this conclusion gives me little pleasure, for O'Hara is a writer for whose work I once had a great if mistaken affection. His obsessive subject is the manners, both social and sexual, of the northeastern middle class; to a young man growing up in the 1950s he seemed irreverent, penetrating and daring. By contrast with John P. Marquand, whose novels of manners had a measured, reticent (and, as it turns out, far more durable) quality, O'Hara seemed cocksure and, especially in his later fiction, somewhat scabrous, characteristics that often appeal to young readers.

O'Hara's audience, though, was scarcely limited to the young and prurient. His readership was enormous and enormously loyal, though it fell off, just as he did, toward the end. . . . His style was hard-boiled and his eye was cold, though he was certainly capable of a sentimental twist. He described middle-class life with an authenticity that readers immediately recognized—it was their own world, after all, that he was describing—but he embellished the familiar with racy adventures that made them feel they were peeping through their neighbors' keyholes. . . .

But to today's reader all of this seems something from another era: a period piece that has a certain curiosity value but is also impossibly dated. The details for which O'Hara was so celebrated and which he supplied in such profusion . . . arouse more confusion than recognition now, because they are details that no longer mean anything to us. By the same token, the prose that seemed so tough and worldly a few decades ago now seems merely arch and mannered; as for that celebrated ear, the passage of time discloses that it was made primarily of tin.

O'Hara's principal subjects, in these stories as in his novels, are what he calls "the complications of sex" and the "unwholesome human traffic" with which the world is crowded. On the first he is clinical, on the second cynical. He is less clinical in the stories than in the novels, for the stories were written for magazines . . . that shielded their readers from sexual matters. The cynicism, though, is pervasive. He could give a story a sentimental ending if it suited his purposes, but his view of the world was implacably resentful, condescending and sour; apart from a worldly young reporter who appears in many of the stories and who is clearly O'Hara himself, he does not seem to have created a single character whom he genuinely likes or admires.

Nor has he created, in all . . . of these stories, a single one that has any real claim on our attentions or any real chance of surviving in our literature. The first 14, originally published between 1935 and 1945, are for the most part sketchy and formulaic slices from life that, with their trick endings, owe more to O. Henry than to Maupassant and, with their manic recitation of detail, owe more to the newsroom than the salon. . . .

In the later stories, published between 1960 and 1968, O'Hara tended to write at greater length. The best of these is the first, *Imagine Kissing Pete*, which originally appeared as one of the three novellas in *Sermons and Soda Water*, a collection that

did much to revive O'Hara's reputation after a long stretch in which he had devoted himself to rankly commercial novels. . . . Its subject is a marriage that seemed doomed from the outset but eventually is rescued by a combination of inertia and a shamelessly mawkish conclusion that O'Hara tacks on to tie everything together.

Like so much else in these stories, that conclusion smacks less of genuine sentiment than of cynicism. O'Hara's view of his fellow man may have been unceasingly hostile, but he was entirely capable of throwing in a happy ending if that seemed to him what his audience wanted. What we see at work in these stories is not an artist but a manufacturer: a facile and observant writer who saw a great deal but had very little to say about it. O'Hara was a terrific reporter . . . and his gifts for that specialized skill must not be underestimated. But the stories he tells in this book are yesterday's news; today they are merely tired, antiquated and pointless.

Jonathan Yardley, "Appointment with O'Hara," in Book World—The Washington Post, *February 10, 1985, p. 3.*

CHRISTOPHER LEHMANN-HAUPT

It's a satisfying job of picking and arranging that Frank MacShane has done in putting together the 36 pieces in [*Collected Stories of John O'Hara*]. . . . Here is **"Over the River and Through the Wood"** (1934), with its stunning conclusion in which a man is suddenly pushed into the "terror" of old age. Here is *Imagine Kissing Pete,* the remarkable long tale of a bad marriage gone good with which O'Hara returned to *The New Yorker* in 1960 after an absence of a decade.

And here is **"The Girl From California"** (1961), which is so plausible an account of an Italian show biz star visiting his family in Trenton, N.J., that I had forgotten in the years since it was first published that it was actually a work of fiction.

Indeed, I can't offhand recall any favorite of mine that is missing from this collection. But then they've all melted together over the years into a single archetypal O'Hara story—an action set in the author's fictional hometown of Gibbsville, Pa., involving members of the local country club. And this suggests another virtue of . . . [the] collection: It evokes the rich variety of the O'Hara palette. . . . [The stories] hit you hard and they hit you soft. And the passage of time has dated them hardly at all. . . .

[Frank MacShane] attributes this durability to the power of O'Hara's ear for dialogue [see excerpt above]. That power is undeniable, at least so far as O'Hara's gift for mimicry is concerned. The voices are alive in these pages even when they are using dated expressions . . . , and you can usually spot the origins of a speaker no matter how fast he or she may be climbing away from them.

But after reading straight through this collection, I have to question whether it's really their authenticity that makes O'Hara's voices seem so vital. In actuality, nobody talks the way his characters do. I used to think they did. . . .

Reading him now, what I find astonishing is the directness with which his people talk, especially the narrators of his stories. There is never a wasted word or the meaningless hum of social chatter. Whether the subject is sex or business, the characters know what they want and cut to the point with a swiftness that is almost shocking. This lends them an air of knowing, even when what they know doesn't seem particularly worthwhile. They are always on the inside, disclosing secrets, revealing the way things work, whether its small-town adultery or the Hollywood star system. The reader is forever left with his nose pressed against the glass.

So the secret of O'Hara's vitality may be precisely the opposite of what it's generally accepted to be. It isn't that his people sound like us. It's that they tell us things we've never heard before—things that we imagine might be going on in bed or behind locked doors. Does their knowingness reflect John O'Hara's famous sense of hierarchy, his fascination with clubs and honors and rank, his obsession with belonging? It is certainly a clambering world that his people live in, and those few of them who are happy are usually at the top of the heap or some place else exclusive.

Yet in *Imagine Kissing Pete*—surely one of the best stories O'Hara ever wrote, and not just because its unhappy people arrive at a happy ending—there is a remarkable passage that suggests another reason for the sense of worldly wisdom that his characters convey. "We knew everything, everything there was to know," reflects the narrator, who is as close to being John O'Hara himself as any voice in this entire collection. "We knew so much, and since what we knew seemed to be all there was to know, we were shockproof.". . .

In short, as he concludes: "We knew everything, but we were incapable of recognizing the meaning of our complacency."

This is as close to a credo as O'Hara ever allowed himself to utter, at least in his short fiction. It explains the lack of smugness in his characters' relentless habit of knowing. The chilling wind that whistles everywhere in these stories blows just as bitterly at O'Hara's characters as it does at his readers. We are not members of inferior classes or clubs. We are in the same boat, and, reading O'Hara once again after all these years, the chances of our survival seem as precarious as ever.

> *Christopher Lehmann-Haupt, in a review of "Collected Stories of John O'Hara," in* The New York Times, *February 18, 1985, p. C14.*

JOSEPH L. QUINN, S.J.

[*Collected Stories of John O'Hara*] will probably prove to be of most value to today's young readers, among whom O'Hara is relatively unknown—despite the fact that he was incontestably one of the leading chroniclers of American society during the first half of the 20th century. For college students who are interested both in what their parents and grandparents might have thought and felt and been exposed to during those years, and in being entertained while they pursue that interest, there is no better place to travel to than O'Hara country. Even for many readers and rereaders in their mid-30s and beyond, this introduction or reintroduction to O'Hara will hold a special pleasure, and it all has to do with the laundering of a literary reputation. . . .

Almost to the day of his death in April 1970, John O'Hara had been fighting, and losing, a 40-year-running battle with serious critics and virtually all academics. Despite the gratification offered by those millions of readers who were pleased by his books over that period and who paid him more than a

million dollars for producing them, O'Hara found the hostility and, even more, the indifference of what he called the "eggheads" annihilating. . . . Over the past decade, however, delayed recognition has started to come, and from those very precincts that had previously failed either to report favorably or to report at all. (p. 225)

The stories themselves fall into three main categories. Most of the best are situated in O'Hara's northeastern Yoknapatawpha, which biographer Matthew Bruccoli refers to as "The Region," the fictional Lantenengo (Schuylkill) County in Pennsylvania fanned out around the author's own home base of Gibbsville/Pottsville. A related and yet quite distinct world deals with the moneyed or formerly moneyed members of a society spread around Philadelphia, New York and Long Island. These people travel in wider circles—north to Boston, east across the Atlantic, etc.—than do the Gibbsvillians, and they provide scope for the broader aspects of O'Hara's own experience. O'Hara once remarked that "I know every important person in this country, or I know someone close to each of them." This boast strikes one at first as foolish, and perhaps it is, a bit; but the authoritative tone of many of these stories and the verisimilitude of the life and lives depicted therein warns against dismissing the claim out of hand.

In **"Over the River and Through the Wood"** (the title comes from "Thanksgiving Day," a Lydia Maria Child poem that every school child once knew), for example, a young O'Hara shows remarkable sympathy for an aging and once rich roué who is a Thanksgiving guest in a house he once owned. Alcoholic and sexual indulgence have led to near disintegration of the protagonist's life. He is trying to come back, or at least hang on, and at the climax of the story he goes to the room of one of his granddaughter's guests to offer her cocoa. Mishearing "come in" for "wait a minute" he enters the young woman's room to find her nearly naked—and furious at the impropriety. Although he guiltily realizes that he had been thinking about her, he is both innocent and utterly destroyed: "Mr. Winfield instantly knew that this was the end of any worthwhile life he had left."

Among the best of "The Region" stories is **"Zero,"** a winter's tale set in Mountain City (Frackville), Pa. . . . The main character in **"Zero"** is stealthily meeting a former mistress, a younger woman whom he had impregnated and who has just returned from an out-of-town trip and an abortion. They quarrel and he strikes her. He returns home to a suspicious wife, they quarrel, and he strikes her. She angrily threatens to kill him, and his response is simple and strange: "Go ahead, you'd be doing me a favor." Although shocked, she recognizes these words as the truth. He wishes to be dead and free, not only free of her but of the other woman as well. (pp. 225-26)

A third category of stories concerns Hollywood, the setting for some of the most impressive of O'Hara's later work. **"Natica Jackson"** verges on novella length, and the two principals find the search for a passionate and enduring love so exhausting and frustrating that they are willing to settle for less. It turns out to be a good deal less. Natica is a movie star, and single, who initiates an affair with a married man. His wife finds out and takes their two children for a motorboat ride. Stopping in the middle of a large lake, she encourages the youngsters to go over the side and swim, then drives off and leaves them to drown. Haunted by her crime and their own, the two lovers die to one another.

From the first, the sheer volume of his work had been prodigious; but the quality-index was high despite the author's lifelong aversion to revising. Before O'Hara was 45, *The New Yorker* alone had published no fewer than 197 of his stories. . . . The next decade brought something of a concentration on other forms, but in 1960, when the author was at an age (55) when most writers are finished, a second flood began to build. The relaxed and expansive mood of the more mature and on-the-wagon O'Hara was reflected in the greater length of the later stories. At the end there were almost 400 to choose from, and the best of them are all here. (p. 226)

Joseph L. Quinn, S.J., "'What Is Essential Is Invisible to the Eye'," in America, *Vol. 153, No. 9, October 12, 1985, pp. 225-26.*

Raymond Queneau

1903-1976

(Also wrote under pseudonym of Sally Mara) French novelist, poet, editor, dramatist, scriptwriter, essayist, and travel writer.

Among the most highly respected Gallic literary figures, Queneau is noted for introducing contemporary French vernacular into the written language, which he believed had atrophied since being formalized by bourgeois literary circles in the seventeenth century. Labeling his theory "le néo français," Queneau announced his intention to modernize French prose and "rid literature of its various rusts." Generally using light pastiche, Queneau parodied traditional literary forms and devices by phonetically spelling out words, phrases, and sentences to reflect their contemporary usage and pronunciation. In Queneau's hands, according to Maurice Blanchot, language "comes apart, loses the meaning through which it has attained durability, loses the means of its power, loses its syntactical force. . . . But, under the same dizzying influence, another language and another style spring up from the debris of these words."

Inspired by the intricate linguistic and narrative structures of James Joyce and by Louis-Ferdinand Celine's revolutionary use of French colloquialisms, Queneau began his literary career in Paris in the 1920s. He received his bachelor's degree in philosophy from the University of Paris and became associated with André Breton and the Surrealist movement in art and literature. The Surrealists rejected bourgeois literary values and the philosophy of reason and embraced instead subconscious irrationalism. In his fiction, Queneau typically centered upon the ridiculous in everyday life through light, madcap humor comparable to that of French satirist Alfred Jarry. Beneath the whimsical surface of his works, however, Queneau examined serious philosophical concerns. In his experimental first novel, *Le chiendent* (1933; *The Bark Tree*), a servant's death causes a chain reaction of absurd consequences, culminating in the regression of the other characters to their vague, prefictional origins. Both *The Bark Tree* and Queneau's next novel, *Les derniers jours* (1936), reflect his interest in the complex structures of mathematics and the metaphysical discourse of philosophy.

The characters of Queneau's novels are not psychologically complex or realistic but function instead as vehicles for his thematic concerns. Queneau's hero is typically a simpleton who lives entirely in the present, avoiding both hope and disappointment by virtue of his incomprehension and lack of reflection. In the novel *Pierrot mon ami* (1943), Queneau centers on an ambiguous man whose unrealized pursuit of a beautiful, socially superior girl evokes no regrets. A similar character blunders through a series of failures in *Loin de rueil* (1944; *The Skin of Dreams*) before inexplicably becoming a Hollywood film star. In *Le dimanche de la vie* (1951; *The Sunday of Life*), a man for whom war and conflict are unfathomable concentrates only on the present. He eventually becomes a fortune-teller who earns his living by anticipating his customers' immediate needs.

Queneau achieved widespread popular success as a novelist with his satire *Zazie dans le métro* (1959; *Zazie in the Metro*). This work revolves around an outspoken little girl who visits

© *Jerry Bauer*

her uncle in Paris and upsets the adults around her through pranks and foul language. Queneau's theme in this book is the uncertainty and confusion of conventional social roles. In *Les fleures bleues* (1965; *The Blue Flowers;* published in Great Britain as *Between Blue and Blue*), Queneau explores the theme of history. This fantasy centers on a clash between two men, one an artist who cares only for the present, the other a violent Duke who values art for its ability to imaginatively reconstruct reality. *Le vol d'Icare* (1968; *The Flight of Icarus*) is a complex, multilevel work in which the protagonist of a *belle époque* novel escapes the neurasthenic existence created for him by his author, Hubert Lubert. Suspecting plagiarism, Lubert sets a bumbling detective after his character but loses him to Queneau. John Sturrock contended that "the subject of *The Flight of Icarus* is not the freedom of characters, but the freedom of novelists, and how it should be used." *On est toujours trop bon avec les femmes* (1971; *We Always Treat Women Too Well*), a novel Queneau wrote in the mid-1940s under the pseudonym of Sally Mara, mimics James Hadley Chase's *No Orchids for Miss Blandish,* a sadistic but successful thriller published during World War II which George Orwell labeled "pure fascism." Set during the Dublin uprising of 1916 and employing characters from Joyce's *Ulysses, We Always Treat Women Too Well* blurs the distinctions between heroism and brutality in its depiction of a kidnapped woman whose immorality exceeds that of her captors.

Queneau was a highly respected member of France's prestigious literary jury, L'académie Goncourt, and the editor of the multivolume *Encyclopedie de la Pleiade* for more than twenty years. The breadth of his knowledge is also evident in his poetry and other literary experiments, in which he used such elements as paradox, inverted logic, and contradiction. *Exercices de style* (1947; *Exercises in Style*) garnered critical acclaim and is considered among Queneau's most accomplished works. In this book, Queneau restates the same banal occurrence in ninety-nine different versions. In his verse narrative *Petite cosmogenie portative* (1950), Queneau traces the development of the solar system from its early evolution to the computer age. Queneau employs complex experimental forms in *Morale élémentaire* (1975), a collection containing, among other texts, prose and verse poems. These pieces, which are arranged in columns, are identical in structure and may be read in several directions, not only from left to right but also from bottom to top by individual column. *Pataphysical Poems* (1985), which borrows the nonsensical term "pataphysics" from Alfred Jarry, collects verse from Queneau's career. Queneau also wrote a travelogue, *Le voyage en Grece* (1973), contributed dialogue to several film scripts, and adapted his novel *Le dimanche de la vie* for film.

(See also *CLC*, Vols. 2, 5, 10 and *Contemporary Authors*, Vols. 77-80, Vols. 69-72 [obituary].)

V. S. NAIPAUL

I fear I missed the point of *Zazie*. It is a fatiguing piece of French whimsy, just ready-made for one of those ghastly gay French films. It apparently attempts to amuse by its obscenities, its word-play and its phonetic dialogue. Zazie is an 11-year-old girl who uses bad language and knows all about sex. Her mother is a murderess, her uncle dances in a homosexual nightclub. Their simple surrealist adventures I found quite unfunny. There are some aspects of the French genius I can't bear: their journal-keeping, their retelling of Greek myths, and their handling of children in books and films. . . .

> *V. S. Naipaul, in a review of "Zazie," in* New Statesman, *Vol. LIX, No. 1527, June 18, 1960, p. 915.*

LAURENT LeSAGE

When a great Parisian editor pushes aside the pile of waiting manuscripts to write a novel himself the French are bound to take notice. Particularly if he is Raymond Queneau, . . . who is already famous for his comical fantasies in prose and verse. *Zazie dans le métro,* however, exceeded all expectations. Winter before last, . . . this account of a chaste nymphet with a soul as candid as her language is vile became the talk of Paree.

Zazie has come up to Paris with her mother, who—to get rid of Zazie while she herself enjoys a holiday with a new boyfriend—plants the child with Uncle Gabriel. Poor Gabriel, a big easygoing man, is in for three memorable days. . . .

Although Gabriel's milieu is not what you call "drawing-room," he is really not prepared to hear from his niece words that would make mobsters wince. She is too much for Charles, who has offered to drive them sight-seeing in his venerable taxi (Zazie asks if he didn't find it perhaps on the banks of the

Marne); [and] too much for Gabriel's landlord, against whom she stirs up a mob by accusing him of indecent advances when he was only trying to corral her. . . .

The most to suffer though is Gabriel, a sensitive soul underneath his brawn, who has told Zazie a dozen times if he has once that he is *not* a hormosessual. The little love is not quite sure what one is but she has heard him thus qualified because this colossus, although actually quite virile, earns his living as "danseuse de charme" in a fairy joint. Queneau puts no rein on his extravagant fancy in creating this preposterous character and all the other *commedia del arte* figures drawn from the Parisian populace. He lets his story go completely wild after Zazie and her uncle get tangled up with a busload of tourists at the Eiffel Tower. It bounces along like an early Chaplin or Mack Sennett film, with wild romps across Paris, the "satyr" of the morning turning up as phoney policeman, a mad widow popping in and out of the narrative, the whole thing ending at dawn with a dish-throwing brawl in a restaurant.

The antics of Queneau's loony people might well have been enough to amuse the French, but it was their language that made *Zazie* the most scandalously funny book of the season. Nobody takes more delight in words than the learned Queneau, and his dialogue—whole phrases often run together in phonetic spelling—can ape to perfection the verbal habits of the lower classes. As if this were not enough fun in itself, he engages in all sorts of side play such as having Gabriel give Hamlet's soliloquy in argot or larding his text with spoofing commentaries and allusions of an incongruously erudite nature.

The task of rendering all this into another language is nothing short of formidable. The translator must know Parisian speech as well as Queneau himself, catch all his sly jokes, and have at his command, as well, all the resources of his own language. . . . Yet no ability could transfer *Zazie* intact into another language, because the psychology, the humor, the modes of expression remain of necessity uniquely French, and to create its equivalent in English would not be to translate this book but to write another. For French readers, recognition of the familiar under Queneau's distortions made the charm of the book. This, alas, is not for us. But the exotic can have its charm, too, and if Queneau's caricatures are for us bereft of living models, we may find them none the less fascinating for it. Freed of all contingencies, they become pure figures of fun and their story a fantasy taking place on the moon.

> *Laurent LeSage, "A Mischievous Miss in Paris," in* Saturday Review, *Vol. XLIII, No. 42, October 15, 1960, p. 25.*

VERNON HALL, JR.

Zazie, age eleven, is probably the most Rabelaisian youngster in literature. Like all pre-adolescents, she has a rather limited vocabulary and the word that she repeats most often is the three-letter one for her bottom. . . . [With her uncle] and others she engages in a series of surrealistic adventures [in *Zazie*], the most amusing of which concern a busload of foreign tourists. These poor devils are given a run-around by their guide that should evoke bittersweet memories from American travelers. The guide is too lazy to push his bus through Paris traffic so he shows them a railroad station and tells them it is the Sainte Chapelle. The gullible tourists shout "Hurrah" to this glory of French architecture. . . .

Little Zazie has no more luck than her tourist friends. The one thing she wants to see in Paris is the Métro and this is closed because of a strike. When her uncle suggests she see Napoleon's tomb instead she yells, "I'm not interested in that old windbag with his silly hat."

But, after all, it is not the monuments which will interest the readers of this book; it is the vernacular of the natives. As Laverdure, an important character in the book who, by the way, is a parrot, says, "Talk, talk, that's all you can do." For most readers this will be enough. . . .

In 1948 [Queneau] wrote a remarkable *tour de force* entitled *Exercices de style*. In this, by recounting the same banal episode in numerous different styles he revealed himself as a master of rhetoric and a word magician. In *Zazie dans le métro*, also, the real charm lies in his pyrotechnics. Intoxicated with a vocabulary partially picked up from the streets, partially invented, he passes on this intoxication to his French readers. Unfortunately to translate this book's idioms into English is almost as difficult as to translate those of *Finnegans Wake* into French. For instance, Zazie calls an American soft drink "Cacocalo." This is both funny and ironic in French; in English it is neither. . . .

[Even in translation] *Zazie* will amuse and entertain the reader. He would do well, however, if his French is really good, to go to the original, since many of the slang expressions and most of the portmanteau words lose a great deal of their spark when made English.

> Vernon Hall, Jr., *"Girl Who Knows All the Words,"* in Lively Arts and Book Review, *December 11, 1960, p. 36.*

RONALD BRYDEN

[In French, Queneau is] the nearest Gallic approach to Joyce. In translation he comes over altogether lighter and frothier: a blend of Firbank, Warhol and Brendan Behan. *The Flight of Icarus*, like *Zazie in the Métro* a few years back, is less novel than intellectual comic-strip: a daisy-chain of dialogue 'frames' ballooned with puns and in-jokes. . . .

Icarus is a character who slips off the pages of a *belle époque* novel and flees his creator through the streets of Paris. He's pursued not only by his author, Hubert Lubert, and a *bourgeoise* fiancée Lubert invents for him, but by a blundering private eye, Morcol, reminiscent of the preening, beady incompetent who matches wits on children's television with the Pink Panther. The point, such as it is, isn't the conventional maunder round literal and literary reality: 'How extremely Pirandellian!' says Morcol scathingly. Rather, it's a parodic canter through several *vagues* of French literary fashion. Icarus flees Lubert's pages to escape a Fin-de-Siècle destiny of neurasthenia, sensitivity and absinthe, only to find an equivalent 20th-century fate waiting for him in a form which mocks lightly Cocteau, René Clair and Genet.

It's hard to tell how seriously you'd have to take the French original: *Zazie,* you may remember, was taken very seriously indeed, with much talk of its elevation of Parisian street-slang to the vocabulary of art. The pleasure of *Icarus* in translation, I'd say, with its shaggy Marx Brothers dialogue, puns and high-jinks with dead literary modes, is that it needn't be taken seriously at all. It can be read as a grown-ups' equivalent of the Asterix books.

> Ronald Bryden, *"In the Hammock,"* in The Listener, *Vol. 90, No. 2310, July 5, 1973, p. 25.*

JOHN STURROCK

'Napoleon my arse', the very laudable motto of *Zazie in the Metro,* proved two things. The first, rather obviously, was that the unassuming Raymond Queneau does not admire Napoleonism; the second, less obviously, was that language is the great leveller and that a fiction, which, far from representing reality actually suspends it, is the one place where emperors and gamines, the historical and the imaginary, meet as equals.

The Flight of Icarus teaches these same convivial truths and in the same stealthy way; unlike his showier contemporaries, Queneau insinuates his philosophy, he does not browbeat us with it. In the French, the inaugural event of this deceptively comic novel could be traced directly to the title: *Le Vol d'Icare.* Most people spotting the *double entendre* in that familiar caption would find it a dead end: what future could there possibly be in taking the *flight* of Icarus to be also the *theft* of Icarus? Not so Queneau; to him, the cohabitation of two thoughts in a single sound was an ideal, because quite impersonal, cue for a novel. The plot of *The Flight of Icarus* was deduced from an objective accident of the French language.

Hence the peculiar origin of its hero. Instead of being native to Queneau's novel, Icarus is a refugee from another novel, by a novelist with the suspiciously symmetrical name of Hubert Lubert. Ten or fifteen of his sorrily conformist pages and Icarus is off; he bolts into the far more refreshing pages of Queneau, where he can mix with racy *fin-de-siècle* Parisians as well as other fictional truants like himself. Hubert assumes that Icarus has been plagiarised by some envious competitor short of a hero, and sets a detective on his trail. Icarus, however, remains at large until the literally bitter end—the very last line of the novel.

The Paris into which he defects, far from being real, is wildly literary, distilled by Queneau from such revered chroniclers of Decadence as Alfred Jarry. . . . [To] make things stagier still, the novel is written entirely as a scenario: 74 lightning scenes in which the characters alternately soliloquise or converse in every linguistic register from the pleb to the precious.

At first, Icarus lives retiringly and safely on the immoral earnings of his girl-friend, but later he is betrayed by a fad for machinery, or progress—another sombre hint that his own lifespan and the novel's are completely synchronised. He moves up from bicycles to motor-cars, to heavier-than-air machines, which is when he falls traditionally out of the sky. He comes back to reality—the world that resumes once a novel is finished—with a fatal bump. Reality is Hubert, who snaps his manuscript opportunistically shut on his fugitive hero; Icarus's parole is up, determinism has been restored.

The Flight of Icarus is, in short, about escapism. The question is, what kind of escapism? It is certainly not about the ecstatic notion that characters in novels escape from their creators and settle their own fate. Queneau has always shrunk from such permissiveness. . . . He became a lifelong convert to an alternative, classical doctrine that prose, like poetry, thrives on formal constraints, and that new books should be artful syntheses of existing ones.

For all its surface jokiness and whimsicality, *The Flight of Icarus* is, in Queneau's sense, a classical novel, precisely if invisibly programmed by his own equivalents of rhyme and metre, and standing—at a carefully rakish angle—on top of the literary past. It seems disorganised only because Queneau's constraints are purely formal, they are not the public constraints we are more used to: of verisimilitude. The subject of *The Flight of Icarus* is not the freedom of characters but the freedom of novelists, and how it should be used.

John Sturrock, "Free Fall," in New Statesman, *Vol. 86, No. 2208, July 13, 1973, p. 55.*

JOHN UPDIKE

[*The essay from which this excerpt is taken was originally published in* The New Yorker, *October 10, 1977.*]

Serenity, which Jarry so flagrantly lacked, Raymond Queneau exemplifies. His books have a double calm: that of a satisfactorily finished design and that of a pleased acceptance of reality. "The Sunday of life"—a phrase even more lyrical in the French, "*le dimanche de la vie*"—comes, the epigraph tells us, from Hegel, who, in meditating the world of Dutch painting, spoke of "the Sunday of life, which levels everything, and rejects everything bad." There is much bad that the characters of [*The Sunday of Life*] must reject or ignore: death strikes often, greed manifests itself, an ineluctable dissatisfaction and restlessness permeate their moods. A stroke paralyzes the heroine, Julia, and the coming of war threatens the hero, Private Valentin Brû. The years are 1936-40, and in France conversation "always came back to Hitler's innermost thoughts." . . . *The Sunday of Life,* employing the same cavalier touch with which Queneau in *The Flight of Icarus* etched the 1890s, portrays those gray pre-war years when *vin blanc gommé* could still be ordered in cafés and President Fallières (1906-13) could still be remembered. (p. 398)

The plot is scarcely worth retelling. Some of the incidents, especially the needling, coarse, slangy conversations among the sisters and the brothers-in-law, seem scarcely worth reading, their banality is so thorough. . . . Queneau's famous de-Academizing of the French language by means of phonetic spellings like "*Polocilacru*" for "*Paul aussi l'a cru*" and "*Doukipudonktan*" for "*D'où qu'ils puent donc tant*" defies translation totally, as the introduction admits. The nuances of slang, like the nuances of poetry, must be taken on faith. But even to a French reader, one suspects, *The Sunday of Life,* like its characters, has margins of enigma. The novel, that is, is egoistic, and given to the same excessively private contemplations as Valentin Brû, who sits in his unfrequented framer's shop literally clock-watching, trying "to follow time, nothing but time." . . . Brû, ingenuous at first, a simpleton who cannot even recover his suitcase from a baggage checkroom, becomes a monster of introspection and a master psychologist, who as a fortune-teller plays on the innocent egoism of others. . . . (p. 399)

Hegel is the presiding philosopher of *The Sunday of Life,* as Descartes was of *The Bark Tree,* and so, as the book's holiday darkens under the shadow of wartime, there are allusions to History. . . . In a curious way, the novel is about the Battle of Jena (1806). It is mentioned on the first page as Private Brû's virtually only thought. . . . At Jena, Napoleon defeated Prussia and went on to enter Berlin; the battle is thus a mirror image of Hitler's defeat of the French and his occupation of Paris. But the Prussians were to have their revenge, and so were the French, as Queneau knew, though his characters in this novel do not. Jena is a paradigm, perhaps, of momentary defeats, of "everything bad," which human life in its timeless succession

of Sundays outlasts. "The days that pass, which turn into the time that passes, are neither lovely nor hideous, but always the same." So much for history, for Hegel's glorification of history . . . and the state, which was to have such sinister reverberations in the German consciousness. Against the grandiose Queneau posits the quotidian, in the same patriotic spirit in which Wallace Stevens wrote, "Say this to Pravda, tell the damned rag/That the peaches are slowly ripening." Valentin Brû, from one standpoint a cipher, a whisper (his name suggests), is from another a "sort of ascetic," the possessor of an active inner life and a satisfied sensuality: the quintessential Frenchman, mysterious as all egoists are, yet sufficiently tied to his society to volunteer for duty on the Maginot Line. Queneau, like Jarry, is more conservative than his cheerful anarchic manner promises: not love machines nor war machines render human loyalty and decency obsolete. (pp. 400-01)

John Updike, "Human Capacities," in his Hugging the Shore: Essays and Criticism, *1983. Reprint by Vintage Books, 1984, pp. 394-401.*

GEORGE CRAIG

When a clever man translates into humour his fascination with the possibilities of words (and few writers have done so as often and as engagingly as Raymond Queneau) we tend gratefully, if a little too soon, to assume that we know where we are: in the world of what are called language-games. Secure in our knowingness, we set aside all questions of content or charge. This is a danger which Queneau's *We always treat women too well* illustrates with peculiar sharpness.

A post office, carefully plotted on the map of Dublin streets and monuments in the time of George V, has been forcibly taken over by a bunch of characters with strangely familiar names: among them Corny Kelleher, Mat Dillon, Larry O'Rourke and Chris Callinan. But of course: it is Bloomsday a few years on and "anything can happen and probably will" (the very mention of Joyce justifying, for the translator, any and every kind of word-play). Then again, the novelist has chosen as a frame for his fiction the activities of an armed gang which holds prisoner a frightened (although in this case astonishingly resourceful) virgin. It appears, fairly conclusively, that this must be a pastiche of the genre exemplified by *No Orchids for Miss Blandish*—killings, maimings and sexual outrage. There is also, finally, the blank-cheque notion of "black humour".

Queneau's seven armed rebels storm a post office on the corner of O'Connell Bridge. . . . They shoot the commissionaire and the superintendent, driving out the other employees with boot and rifle-butt. The section leader telephones the GPO; the rebel code-word is at once answered; the first stage of the Rising is over. . . . We read the account of the rebels' last stand and of their fading before an assault that comes from in front and from behind, from above and below. Nothing and no-one is left intact.

Assumptions that all this must be "erudite pastiche" or "inspired romp" block access to real difficulties—and real delights. Why Ireland and 1916? Why is the leader of the (rebel) band called John McCormack? And why is its battle-cry "Finnegans Wake!"? Even more to the point, what was the Frenchman Queneau (no great player-for-safety) intending to do in issuing the original under the pseudonym "Sally Mara"? It would not be difficult to invent ugly answers to these questions. But Queneau offers full and disarming answers.

He does this partly by turning the questions back to us: if we can accept that, in order for the misvalued hero of a Western to get the girl in white, a couple of dozen Indians have to be shot off their horses, why can't we do the same or similar with an insurrection? He does it also by exploring the gap between ideological certainty and personal doubt. For if anything is being mocked in the novel, it is the pretension to know. Queneau's wide sureness of linguistic touch and his compassionate tone remind us, humbly and humblingly, that heroism, brutality, devotion and love itself are labels: names that mark a reality all right, but from the outside. The inside, or what these events feel like to their protagonists, asserts a different reality, one which coincides with the other only at moments and as if by accident. . . .

Obscenity and tenderness, subtlety and violence: for readers not immediately put off by that mixture, there is in Queneau's novel the chance of a deliciously fast-moving, enormously funny experience.

> George Craig, "The Accosters' Last Stand," in The Times Literary Supplement, *No. 4064, February 20, 1981, p. 186.*

NICHOLAS SHRIMPTON

[The heroine of *We Always Treat Women Too Well*] is not waiting for her dry-cleaning to be delivered. She has taken her clothes off because, while making love on a post-office desk, her lover has had his head shot off ('the body continued its rhythmic movement for a few more seconds') and her dress has been soaked in blood. In a few moments' time she will be back on the job, and another shell will leave another lover even more cruelly cut off in his prime. 'It was for you', he will murmur, handing over the severed member. And she, with more tenderness than tact, will deliver the impromptu epitaph 'Poor little thing.'

The writer responsible for this bawdy and brutal stuff is, you will be surprised to discover, the distinguished French intellectual Raymond Queneau. . . . He published *We Always Treat Women Too Well* under the pseudonym Sally Mara in 1947, the same year as his masterly *Exercices de style,* and finally owned up to it in 1962. . . .

Revelations of this kind are always intriguing. . . . But the sober truth is that *We Always Treat Women Too Well* was never really a piece of popular art and its failure as pulp could always have been predicted. The book is an elaborate intellectual joke, no less jocular for being in part addressed to a serious concern.

Fundamentally this is a parody of James Hadley Chase's *No Orchids For Miss Blandish,* the sadistic gangster novel which enjoyed such extraordinary success in wartime Europe and which Orwell denounced as 'pure Fascism'. . . . Queneau was echoing that opinion . . . only three months later. By 1947 he had shifted from criticism to mockery, producing a version of Chase's plot in which the humiliated kidnap-victim outdoes her brutal captors in calculating immorality.

If that were all, this might be a tough and telling piece of cultural commentary. Unfortunately Queneau's mandarin playfulness drives him to complicate the recipe. He sets the action in the Dublin uprising of 1916 and borrows his characters from Joyce's *Ulysses.* A few excellent jokes result. But on the whole the consequence is erudite whimsy of a kind which makes it hard to see the book as anything but a literary curiosity.

> Nicholas Shrimpton, "Castrations," in New Statesman, *Vol. 101, No. 2607, March 6, 1981, p. 22.*

CHRISTOPHER SHORLEY

[*The essay from which this excerpt is taken was originally presented in a slightly different form at the Annual Conference of the Society for French Studies at Oxford in March, 1979.*]

[In this essay], discussion will centre on the ways in which Queneau . . . [handles] non-verbal communication in fiction, and the term 'non-verbal communication' itself will be used in a broad, non-technical sense. In recent years, of course, non-verbal communication has become a subject of academic study in its own right, occupying an area bordering on anthropology, sociology, psychology and linguistics. (p. 408)

For much of his career [Queneau] remained an obscure figure, and when he finally acquired a reputation, whole areas of his work were still overlooked. The stylistic originality of his first novel, **Le Chiendent** (1933), was overshadowed by that of Céline's *Voyage au bout de la nuit,* first published a year earlier; the other novels he wrote in the thirties passed largely unnoticed; and **Pierrot mon ami** (1942) and **Loin de Rueil** (1944) were not favoured by the wartime conditions in which they appeared. It was not until 1959, with **Zazie dans le métro,** that he achieved widespread recognition as a novelist. And even then, the image of the progenitor of Zazie, especially after Louis Malle's frenetic film version of the novel, released in 1960, was not a particularly accurate reflexion of Queneau. In so far as he was known in literary circles before **Zazie,** it was above all for his advocacy of something called 'le néo-français'—and this was the result of his own rather exaggerated propaganda. His theory, derived from his reading of *Le Langage* by Joseph Vendryès, was that in French, popular speech had become completely divorced from its written counterpart—to the detriment of the latter, which was tending to atrophy and decay. His declared aim, therefore, was to generate a new written form. . . . All Queneau's novels contain examples of 'le néo-français'—ranging from the extensive borrowings from popular vocabulary, to the regular practice, in **Le Chiendent,** of spelling *monsieur* in such a way as to recall its modern pronunciation—'meussieu'—to the use of the word-order of spoken French—most strikingly in the construction of sentences divided into a first part, based on pronouns and expressing grammatical relationships, and a second part giving the nouns to which the pronouns refer. . . . Despite all Queneau's emphasis on 'le néo-français', however, the linguistic renovations in his literary texts are neither complete nor even systematic. The proportion of 'reformed' orthography is strictly limited: in terms of his work as a whole it serves as a sort of seasoning, but little more. Further, his orthography shows scant internal consistency and little connexion with his attacks on allegedly moribund features of written French. In *Zazie dans le métro,* for instance, the much-maligned mute 'e' is rarely suppressed. And Queneau's modernization of French syntax has been far more limited than some of his theoretical writings might suggest. However striking his variations on traditional grammar may seem, he adheres for the most part to the patterns which this same grammar requires, limiting himself to occasional contrasts.

At all events, in two articles written towards the end of his career, one entitled **"Errata"** and the other, more explicitly, **"Le néo-français en déroute",** Queneau repudiates many of the claims he had previously made about the nature and destiny of the French language. And in doing so he shows that 'le néo-français' is not an end in itself, but simply one literary device among the many he uses. (pp. 410-11)

The language of Queneau's fiction, then, does not constitute a revolution in French usage, or even a wholesale reform. Yet it performs functions which are no less important in linguistic terms, and a good deal more so when considered from a literary point of view. His wide-ranging experiments at once point to the arbitrary nature of linguistic convention and reaffirm the writer's freedom of action. And this in turn is characteristic of his open-minded approach to the whole question of human communication. Queneau's commitment to language in all its manifestations is perhaps the most consistent single element in his works. But commitment is not blind faith. On the contrary, his basic conviction is that no system of communication is completely satisfactory. . . . Yet for Queneau the literary artist this absence of absolutes is a source not of despair, but rather of hope. For if language always correlated perfectly with its referents, it would be merely a mechanical process, and thus devoid of real interest. In Queneau's view, precisely because of its imperfections, language remains endlessly fascinating—an instrument which can be examined and experimented with indefinitely, but never fully mastered. This underlies his whole attitude to the role of the writer of literature. . . . It also helps to explain the fact that although he produced some analytical studies of a strictly linguistic nature, his most interesting and ambitious explorations in communication are to be found in his imaginative works. (p. 412)

The territory Queneau calls 'le langage' is bounded at its opposite extremities by two totally different modes of expression, one written and the other oral. On one boundary lies the aggregate of 'bâtons, chiffres et lettres'—symbols inscribed or printed on the page—which give the title to a collection of Queneau's articles, most of which are devoted to the nature of literary discourse. . . . Within the limits of the printed page Queneau frequently experiments with typography: he varies type-faces, invents new punctuation marks, uses a shortened line to convey the rhythm of a dialogue; he even splits the page into two columns to represent a debate going on in a character's mind. At the other extreme, oral language need be nothing more elaborate than a grunt or a moan. Queneau has even gone so far as to suggest that all language may have originated in cries of pain. (pp. 412-13)

[Contemporary] written language, for all its range and subtlety, can never completely accommodate the non-verbal qualities of what Queneau rather loosely calls 'le langage oral', and the gap between the two is a critical one. . . . (p. 413)

[Queneau's] treatment of 'l'oral' goes far beyond the 'stage directions' to which he specifically draws attention. . . . Characters frequently express themselves as much by their tone of voice and their inarticulate cries of joy, rage or pain as by their words. This tendency reaches its logical conclusion in *Exercices de style,* a series of ninety-nine variations on a banal altercation on a Paris bus. . . . Queneau's characters display a wide range of expression which has no real connexion with speech. Not only do they laugh and cry: sometimes they do both at once. . . . They are also endowed with a remarkable diversity of facial expressions, blushing, smiling, frowning, pouting, turning pale or green or yellow—and sometimes revealing several emotions simultaneously. . . . [Here it is clear that Queneau] does not aim for a systematic transcription of sounds and gestures any more than he seeks methodically to reproduce the orthography or the grammar of 'le néo-français'. Essentially, here again,

the intention is to extend and enhance his literary resources rather than to confine himself to a system of conventions. (pp. 414-15)

Queneau rarely chooses to explore the psychological depths of his characters—if psychological depths there be. Moreover, it is striking that an author of such linguistic and stylistic power should people his fiction with figures who are so often taciturn and even inarticulate. For the most part they are presented from the outside, and their idiosyncratic mannerisms are a convenient shorthand means of characterization. (p. 416)

Almost all Queneau's characters, in fact, have some significant non-verbal element in their make-up. But there is one who seems to exist almost entirely outside the domain of words. This is Jean-sans-Tête, . . . from *Le Dimanche de la vie.* He could be described as a simpleton—or perhaps as the village idiot of the tightly-knit community living in and around the rue de la Brèche-aux-Loups in the twelfth arrondissement of Paris, where Valentin Brû—the central character—sets up his shop. Jean-sans-Tête is one of a number of vagrants who profit from Valentin's charity; but whereas the others are mere beggars, Jean has wares to peddle—and the nature of these wares is a first indication of the importance Queneau attaches to him. For Jean-sans-Tête is a seller of brooms . . . and the broom is one of Queneau's most cherished personal emblems. But Jean has a more fundamental importance. On the verbal level he is barely capable of any communication, for he has at his disposal only a tiny stock of words—or snippets of words. . . . Yet in broader terms his capacity for self-expression—and understanding—is shown to be exceptionally high. He first appears at a time when Valentin is becoming involved in a profound, quasi-Hegelian meditation on the nature of time and history. And despite his lack of words, Jean—and he alone—whether by intuition or by empathy is able to follow Valentin's thoughts, nodding his head 'compréhensivement' and making himself clearly understood by dumb-show. . . . The two sequences in which Valentin and Jean converse together make a telling contrast with the affected gestures, hypocritical exchanges and empty 'bécots sonores' to be found in the rest of *Le Dimanche de la vie;* and Jean-sans-Tête stands as perhaps Queneau's most memorable symbol of the real virtues of non-verbal communication.

It has been clear from the outset that Queneau, in common with most other authors, has little to offer to the academic discipline of non-verbal communication: the non-verbal behaviour he observes and portrays is generally commonplace, and his presentation of it is by no means systematic. Furthermore, within a literary context, many of his devices were anticipated by others—as Queneau, who was acutely aware of his debt to the writers of the past, would readily have appreciated. Nevertheless there remain strong reasons for setting him apart from most of those who preceded him in exploiting the resources of non-verbal behaviour, and for attaching particular importance to his own contribution. (pp. 417-18)

Christopher Shorley, '''Joindre le Geste à la Parole': Raymond Queneau and the Uses of Non-Verbal Communication,'' in French Studies, *Vol. XXXV, No. 4, October, 1981, pp. 408-20.*

JOHN UPDIKE

[*The essay from which this excerpt is taken was originally published in* The New Yorker, *December 14, 1981.*]

Raymond Queneau, that most learned and light-hearted of experimental modernists, in 1947 published, under the pseudonym Sally Mara, a kind of thriller set in Dublin during the uprising of 1916, entitled *On est toujours trop bon avec les femmes*. The book, unlike the American-style novels, sexy and tough, that it burlesqued, did not prove popular with the French public in the Forties; nor has it been popular with the *Queneauistes*. Excluded from the official Gallimard edition of Queneau's oeuvre until 1962, it has been persistently regarded by academics as "an unfortunate but forgivable interlude in a distinguished man's career." . . . Perhaps *We Always Treat Women Too Well* is less funny in French than in . . . translation; the borrowing of its Dublin locale and personnel almost entirely from Joyce's *Ulysses* is certainly a less circuitous joke in English than in French, and the risibility of sex and violence may more readily strike American readers hardened by Hammett and Chandler and Spillane than readers saddled with tender Gallic sensibilities. Queneau himself, in a 1944 essay, attacked the greatly successful thriller *No Orchids for Miss Blandish* as glorifying "fascist" behavior at a time when the Western democracies were battling fascists in war. Yet the sado-erotic tradition in French literature has a pedigree going back beyond the notorious Marquis to Rabelais and Villon, and it seems unlikely that the postwar critics who embraced Genêt and Georges Bataille would snub Queneau's sportive travesty out of mere squeamishness.

We Always Treat Women Too Well, though sufficiently endowed with Queneau's cerebral prankishness, electric pace, and cut-on-the-bias poetry to give glimmers of delight, is a work of casual ambivalence, whole-heartedly neither parody nor thriller, and with a moral by no means as simple as anti-fascism. A group of Irish Republicans, all named from minor figures in *Ulysses,* storm and take a post office at the corner of Sackville Street and Eden Quay; they kill the doorman and the postmaster, who bears the un-Gaelic name of Theodore Durand and cries "God save the King!" in token resistance. The other workers in the post office are expelled, but one female clerk, Gertie Girdle (close verbal kin to Gerty MacDowell, the limping temptress of Leopold Bloom in the "Nausicaa" episode of *Ulysses*), remains in the lavatory, where she entertains a series of Molly Bloom-like interior monologues until her eventual discovery by the rather bumbling and scatterbrained rebels. Once discovered, she, though at the outset a virgin given to inner raptures over her "beloved fiancé, Commodore Sidney Cartwright," embarks with shameless and inexplicable expertise upon a guerrilla campaign of seduction among her captors, eventually making sexual contact via one orifice or another with six of the seven men. Meanwhile, the British soldiery and a gunboat in the Liffey commanded by Sidney Cartwright besiege the post office and at last recapture it. Yet—and this is the curious fact—no connection between Gertie's seductions and the rebel band's defeat is insisted upon, though it would have been easy for Queneau to make connections, and what little he has of a plot would seem to hinge on them. . . . Gertie's sexually active presence among the men functions as a distraction, to be sure, but is never made to appear detrimental to their defense against odds that all come to recognize as hopeless. Cartwright, on the *Furious,* knows that this post office is where his fiancée is employed, and is reluctant, accordingly, to demolish it; so her presence if anything prolongs rather than shortens the lives of the rebels.

Why, then, does this woman, who has no sympathy with the rebellion and "the greatest respect for our gracious King George the Fifth," consort so lustily with her captors? Because, Que-

neau himself might answer, that's the sort of thing that happens in books like this. In *No Orchids for Miss Blandish,* the heroine is beaten, drugged, and raped at the hands of an armed gang, and falls in love with the ruthless leader. . . . The genre of thriller that Queneau is both protesting and imitating construed sex and violence as parts of a single force-field; it assumed that a tension close to enmity naturally exists between men and women. (pp. 401-03)

In a sense, Gertie is the future, bringing death to the past. The Irishmen defend themselves with an antiquated code of honor; doomed to die, they become concerned that in retrospect their heroism will be sullied by their lechery. . . . The final two survivors, Corny Kelleher and Mat Dillon, concoct an ingenious scheme to achieve Gertie's silence: they do something unspeakable to her. . . . In the event, the thoroughly violated Gertie lies to her British rescuers, mildly claiming that the Irishmen tried to lift up her skirt to look at her ankles. The horrified British shoot their captives on the spot, but not before Gertie has stuck out her tongue at them and Kelleher has ruefully concluded, "We always treat women too well."

This farce feels genuinely sexy. Queneau has toyed with the forms and codes of hardboiled fiction without emptying them of content; we are left with an impression of relations between men and women as lawless and predatory. . . . Amid all his cerebration and irony, Queneau hangs tough. (p. 405)

A patent spoof on patriotism, murderousness, seductiveness, Irishness, and piety, [*We Always Treat Women Too Well*] at bottom makes the deeper satirical point that Queneau's fiction consistently makes: the ineluctable banality of existence, as shown by the subtle clumsiness and foreordained triteness of our attempts to render life into words. (p. 406)

> *John Updike, "Thirty-four Years Late, Twice," in his* Hugging the Shore: Essays and Criticism, *1983. Reprint by Vintage Books, 1984, pp. 401-09.*

FLORENCE E. RECHSTEINER

In an early but important article on Cubist activity, Winthrop Judkins states that a primary characteristic of Cubist forms is their "iridescence." Iridescent are those forms which, replayed across the canvas and displayed at different angles, undergo multiple transitions, mutate as they enter into new contexts. Variously lighted or shadowed, sometimes amputated or foreshortened to the glance, these elements—actually fragments of the most common objects: a bottle, glass, piece of fruit, guitar—represent an amalgam of views of a single item or items as well as an analysis of the objects as variously seen or imagined. Frequently, however, the forms lose their specificity, taking on compound or new identities as they align themselves with other shapes in the enframement. Their capacity to change and perform multiple functions is precisely what defines them as "iridescent."

Raymond Queneau's third novel, *Les Derniers Jours,* offers a scriptural display of formal iridescence. A story of student life and times in Paris, 1920-23, it not incidentally takes place in an epoch enthralled with Cubism. Cubism is, in fact, the subject of two discussions in *Les Derniers Jours,* and may well be a concealed model. Like Cubist painting, the novel, although firmly anchored in the quotidian, is clearly a formalist effort displaying the artist's combinatory genius. Its rhymed, fluctuant elements create a rhythmically pleasing aesthetic arrangement. It is equally true, however, that the only immediately visible unity is an aesthetic one, for in Cubist fashion, Queneau eschews a consensual view of reality in favor of an indeterminate view of things: the world of *Les Derniers Jours* is not organized for the reader but fragmented and discontinuous. . . . While fragmentation parallels Cubist procedure on the level of story, iridescence mimes Cubist practice on the level of narrative discourse. In the narrative, it is the units of discourse—lexical items, phrases, sentences—which function as do the fragments or objects in Cubist works, their iridescent effects achieved through verbal and discursive mutability.

We may compare the scattering of objects upon the painterly canvas and their distribution at various points and different angles to the scattering of motifs and phrases throughout *Les Derniers Jours.* The impression of volatility produced by the reeling focus and constantly shifting perspectives in the Cubist painting have been reproduced in the form of verbal mobility. As we move through the text, we have the impression of having seen the same words and images before, but in a somewhat different arrangement. (pp. 3-4)

Several examples of iridescence can be located within a single chapter of *Les Derniers Jours*. In the introductory scene, *le chien* appears in three instances and in three different contexts. It first denotes the animal itself, [the dog]. . . . In its next reference it is compounded, become "le chiendent," a sobriquet given to the Général Faidherbe. Finally, *chien* is used in a metaphorical context, to describe the smell of a cafe. . . . Within this same section is a *mise en scène* of lexical options. . . . The umbrella which first appears as a *parapluie*, then reappears as a *riflard* and finally as a *pépin*. (pp. 5-6)

All references to the umbrella function denotatively. What is notable about their reoccurrence is the typically Cubist treatment of the object. First, there is a display of expressive mutability through lexical change and compounding. Secondly, the object enters into different formal adjustments where it takes on dissimilar and even opposing functions. Associated with Tolut, the umbrella is a shelter under which the character appears to us as a defenseless, anxious creature, threatened by the approach of a truck. . . . Associated with Brabbant, the umbrella becomes an assertive device. Brandishing the object, he uses it as a sexual advance and defines himself for us as an active, extroverted personality. . . .

It is not only single images which are used variably but whole phrases or scraps and bits of scenes. Displaced, slightly or radically transformed, these details enter into entirely different contexts where they may indicate different facets of a same phenomenon. (p. 6)

"Representational iridescence" occurs in *Les Derniers Jours* when entire word groupings appear as movable pieces that can take on a variety of forms and achieve different effects depending upon their spatial arrangement and graphic qualities. Shifting representational modes, that is, lists, dialogues, monologues, and poems appear as formal options through which the image finds alternate expression. While third person narration and dialogue constitute the principal modes of narration, these other forms are evidence of the variety of possible mediating systems. Nearly one-sixth of *Les Derniers Jours* is rendered through monologue. Delivered in the main by Alfred, once by Jules, these "speeches" are in large part repetitive of much of the information supplied through the third person narrator. Devoid, however, of the narrator's irony and delivered in a mechanical, staccato manner, they also provide an alternate stylistic posture. (p. 7)

As a formal procedure, "iridescence"—what we have defined with Judkins as fluctuation of form—works to shift attention away from the allusive subject matter to the manner and means of production. The subject of *Les Derniers Jours* is primarily form and only secondarily student life in Paris during the Twenties. Emphasis on expressive means is not, however, to be confounded with the Parnassian notion of art for art's sake. If this were the case, neither Cubist painters nor Queneau would experiment with fluctuating forms but would work at perfecting a single representational view. What is at stake are the notions of dynamism, of change and perceptual relativity. The integration within a single, architectonically ordered whole of a number of ways of combining and expressing the objects of experience highlights the mediacy of any representational effort and the very arbitrariness of linguistic, literary or visual images. The final product, *Les Derniers Jours,* appears as a new reality (albeit artistic) of iridescent/permuted/mobile elements, one possible combination "out of the thousands upon thousands of natural combinations that have never been composed." (pp. 8-9)

Florence E. Rechsteiner, "Formal Iridescence in Raymond Queneau's 'Les Derniers Jours'," in Romance Notes, Vol. XXIV, No. 1, Fall, 1983, pp. 3-9.

PETER READING

Some artists (like Duchamp, Stockhausen, Joyce) are of interest as much for their innovatory influence as for what they produce. Teo Savory, who has translated [*Pataphysical Poems*] into American, believes Raymond Queneau to be of this class—"What has been overlooked in the English-speaking world as much as his poetry itself is Queneau's linguistic influence, one quite as profound in our times as that of Joyce." Suzanne Chamier shares her opinion; in a preface she remarks that Queneau "introduced language-as-spoken (on the bus, in the street) into language-as-written. This technique, in use by certain experimental novelists, particularly English-speaking (eg, Joyce, Faulkner) . . . became an added dimension of Queneau's 'poetic art'." She suggests that "the French pataphysical heritage may be linked with the contemporary linguistic critique of metaphysics as evidenced . . . in [the works of] Jacques Derrida, Jacques Lacan, Italo Calvino". All this would have been worth elaborating, as would the information on what Pataphysics is ("a term Jarry invented in his satirical farce, *Ubu roi*. . . . Pataphysics purposely defies logical analysis"), but perhaps there was insufficient introductory space. . . .

[*Pataphysical Poems* consists of] poems from six books published between 1943 and 1969. This poet (because of ludic uses of rhyme, the colloquial, the phonetic, the invented word) must present more than average difficulties for a translator. Teo Savory says "As Queneau was not literal-minded himself, and as, therefore, literal translations of his poetry destroy their essence, the translator must try, as far as possible, to enter into and render the poet's own spirit." [One poem translates as]

Ah when I was young
how happy I was! Like
a lizard in the sun
looking at my toenails
at the seaside all tan
and full of the Old Nick
with a lively prick

Here, though, the original tripping iambic trimeter is demolished in part by a stiff literalism, in part by a bizarre incorrectness. Why toe*nails,* rather than just "toes" or "big toes"? Why render *brunir* as the unnecessarily awkward-sounding "at the seaside *all tan*"? Why does my *abencérage,* suggestively raising (erecting, pricking up) its head (cap, top, crest), become the coy/ridiculous "full of Old Nick with a lively prick"? From where, and why, has Old Nick appeared? . . .

One of the consistent concerns (and causes of delight) throughout the rich and varied output of Queneau is the idea of the existence of a number of different possible readings. These may be indicated, as in many of the poems here, by ambiguous wordplay, or, in a more literal way, by physically presenting the reader with alternative possibilities. . . . There is also the sense that the realities of experience and of language are different, creating a unique tension between form and content. Often the starting-point is purposely minimal and the real subject-matter becomes the language. . . .

Savory, writing of the problems besetting these translations, says that certain . . . difficult poems had to be left out "as they would have been, though translatable, puzzling, even meaningless, in English". It is useful to have parallel texts, especially the verso pages.

Peter Reading, "Contrariwise," in The Times Literary Supplement, *No. 4327, March 7, 1986, p. 254.*

ROBERT PETERS

Many features of Queneau's verse [in *Pounding the Pavements, Beating the Bushes, and Other Pataphysical Poems* (published in Great Britain as *Pataphysical Poems*)] should excite American poets. To generalize, American poets are not overly fond of paradox, ambiguous verse discourse, contradiction, and what may appear irresponsible toyings with logic and diction—all qualities of innocence and surprise loved by Queneau. He is, at the same time, a poet of suffering and angst, motifs he shrouds in satire and farce, in a "Pataphysics"—a view of truth revealed via contradiction and exception. The appropriate image is the spiral, or *gidouille,* which, as Suzanne Chamier points out in her preface, "suggests a way of circling around language" in a "spirit of comic-seriousness." . . .

"**Down-and-out**" reveals Queneau's method. He observes a young veteran at a tacky coffee counter—Queneau loves specific details. The vet, who has lost his nose and teeth in war, stirs saccharine into his "black barley" coffee. Though Queneau is "tearful," his heart twisted, and he's "full of spleen," he "can't stand saccharine." He respects his rage, refusing to "sweeten" the soldier's plight with sentimentality. Life is harsh, and he must be observed without eyelids, i.e., without sanitizing or prettifying. In a more playful moment, from the lengthy **"Toward a Poetic Art,"** he celebrates the tiny, casual poem, one seemingly about inconsequentialities. In a delicious pun "poeme" (read "poe-me," or "poor me"), he notes that a poem requires merely a few "well placed well chosen words." As a "little poem" passes by, he grabs and "enpapers" it, "enrhythms, enlyrics, enpegasuses, and enverses" it. Elsewhere, in **"Memory,"** poems are like eggs—one is enough for a chicken, a dozen will produce "ecstasy" for an indigent poet. So, wine turns to urine, eggs are devoured, and bread sours in your gut. . . . Poets who loathe urban life must eschew romanticizing the country. In **"Rural Hazards,"** a gourmet dies from eating a poisonous mushroom ("the despair of this vegetable / has made it indigestible"); another gourmet picks "an innocent nettle dozing" and is pricked for his trouble; yet another pops a plump pear (it has been "napping") into his mouth—there's a loathesome insect buried inside. . . . Queneau loved the Aesopian fable as yet another means to honesty: a frog ("more horned than a dodecahedron") wishes to assume the shape of an egg. He rolls himself into a sphere, not an "exact" ovoid. Distressed, he asks a bull if he wouldn't look great on display in a dairy shop-window. The steer thinks the frog rash. Frog persists, vainly choosing the top of a wall to display himself: and there's the "start of his fatal fall. / To be an egg has its drawbacks." Queneau's poet, typical of the Existential man, like his poems, is "little": he'd like to see his "little life / flourish a little bit / my little life my little life . . ." The sky may at any time collapse: you go "straight on / toward what you don't see." The slow approach of aging is as devastating as an instant explosion, and is a frequent theme. . . . Finally, everything turns black. The sky covers over with "apustulate scum." Yet, humans persist: "A girl embraces the fellow she loves / A paper-boy peddles his news of doom."

Robert Peters, "The Offspring of Jarry and Goncourt," in Exquisite Corpse, *Vol. 4, Nos. 5-8, May-August, 1986, p. 12.*

Mary Robison

1949-

American short story writer and novelist.

In her fiction Robison depicts contemporary American life in a spare, laconic style that frequently features understated humor. Like Ann Beattie, Raymond Carver, and Frederick Barthelme, Robison portrays characters who live uncommitted lives in a bleak, disordered world. Although some critics fault Robison for neglecting to explore her characters' motives or interpret the reasons for their lackadaisical behavior, she is considered a perceptive observer of American idiosyncrasies and is particularly praised for her skill with dialogue. Anne Tyler describes Robison's prose as "stripped, incisive, clear as a piece of glass held up to the light."

Robison's first collection of short stories, *Days* (1979), was generally praised for her use of a deadpan narrative tone that reflects the languor in her characters' lives. *Oh!* (1981), Robison's first novel, centers on a wealthy and eccentric midwestern family. By focusing on the interactions of offbeat family members and their friends, Robison offers a humorous portrait of the absurdities and alienation in contemporary American life. The stories collected in *An Amateur's Guide to the Night* (1983) take place in the midwestern United States and feature such distinctly American venues as fast-food restaurants and convenience stores. The characters are typified by the protagonist of the title story, who attempts to escape the banality of life by studying astronomy. In reviewing this book, Frances Taliaferro stated that Robison, at her best, is "a technician with a sense of humor, a minimalist with a good eye for what can be salvaged from lives of quiet desperation."

(See also *Contemporary Authors,* Vols. 113, 116.)

Courtesy of Mary Robison

ANATOLE BROYARD

Mary Robison's stories [collected in *Days*] seem to me to question our fundamental assumptions about what is relevant in fiction. During most of our waking hours, nothing very exciting occurs, and she appears to be interested in those gray areas. . . .

It is as if Miss Robison was attempting to democratize fiction, as if she were saying that life is a rather pointless or inscrutable business, and we are most authentically alive when we recognize this fact and examine it.

Her stories are a form of affirmative action in defense of the poverty of experience. Life is less a luxury boutique of sensations than a thrift shop of ambiguities and ambivalences.

Some of Miss Robison's stories in *Days* seem to be played out against an implicit counterpoint, as if she were insisting on her view against a ground base of our expectations. . . .

Miss Robison is a scavenger. She consumes what most other writers have ignored as unpalatable. At the very least, she offers a kind of surprise, the surprise of encountering less, rather than

more, than we hoped. Her stories deal in reverse O. Henry twists.

It may take a while for you to get used to the stories in *Days*—that is, if you ever do get used to them. In **"Apostasy,"** for example, a young woman named Donna says to her sister, who is a nun, "They said you're dying."

"Probably," her sister replies. "Your last pal."

"Well, Jesus Christ," Donna says.

"Well, I'm dying," her sister says.

"In a way I envy you," Donna says.

"I'm willing you my St. Augustine," her sister says.

"Goody," Donna says, and then a bee stings her sister.

When I had read this passage, I said to myself, "Now what am I supposed to make of that?" I suppose I could say that I have never read an exchange like that before, and then I would have to wonder whether it is a virtue of Miss Robison to have offered me a novel experience or whether she has simply imposed on me a scale of values that I cannot interpret.

As you can see, Miss Robison makes you think. Perhaps you would prefer to be moved to feel rather than to think, or perhaps you would prefer not to think about why Miss Robison chose to write that eccentric passage. These are contemporary issues between authors and readers of fiction. . . .

As Hamlet said to Horatio, "There are more things in heaven and earth than are dreamt of in your philosophy." I'm divided in my mind whether to be grateful to Miss Robison for calling my attention to the minuscule mysteries that make up the nitty-gritty of our anxieties, or whether to see her as one of those people who root around in trash cans.

Once when I was walking along Park Avenue very late on a cold night, I saw a man fishing in trash cans, and in a sudden burst of sentimentality, I pulled out my wallet and gave him $5. I think some people will react to Miss Robison that way. I don't suppose there's any harm in this, if you don't make too much of it.

> Anatole Broyard, "Affirmative Actions," in The New
> York Times, June 2, 1979, p. 21.

ANNE TYLER

Mary Robison's *Days* is a collection of short stories—or not so much stories as splinters of contemporary life, set under a microscope. They give the impression of having been chosen at random; one moment is no different from another to most of these characters, who look at their bombed-out worlds with perfectly blank eyes. A man describes the death of an acquaintance in a violent foundry accident; his girlfriend responds by suggesting he accept a $100 bid on his motorcycle. A bride and groom spend their wedding night watching quiz shows on television. A man climbs a Cyclone fence, breaks into a house and arrives in his estranged wife's bedroom to announce, "It smells like furniture polish in here."

The humor in these stories comes from their particularity, from the absurd irrelevance of individual events and conversations. People cry and trim their toenails; they study the washing instructions inside their swimsuit bras; they stare at the dishwasher hose; they are introduced to us while turning up a cow's jawbone in a coalyard or while lolling in a utility cart and smoking Russian cigarettes as a Lawn-Boy hauls them through the snow. There is a deadpan exactitude in Mary Robison's voice. Everything is precisely speared, with no wasted motions.

But the flatness can be debilitating. "I don't think you're taking your life seriously," one character tells another. You could say the same thing about nearly all the people in this book. The danger is that gradually the reader himself may cease to take these lives seriously. As each story clicks shut—not so much ending as simply closing back over itself—there's a "So what?" hanging in the air above it.

It's a good idea to read *Days* a few pages at a time, in order to separate from the empty exercises those pieces that really work. Some do work, magnificently. "**Smoke**" is a killer of a story about the payments that a family exacts from its members. "**Relations,**" with its rambling account of the chance meetings of distantly acquainted cousins, only hits after you've turned the last page and supposedly passed on to something else. And "**Pretty Ice**" shows Mary Robison's style at its best: stripped, incisive, clear as a piece of glass held up to the light.

> Anne Tyler, "Two Sets of Bleak Lives," in The New
> York Times Book Review, July 29, 1979, p. 13.

ELIZABETH INNESS-BROWN

Mary Robison's stories [in *Days*] recall those '70s superrealistic airbrush paintings of Chevy convertibles, gas stations, hamburger stands, and other pop Americana: they dwell on the common, making art of it, with that same unrelenting blown-up detail. As a result they're bigger than life, both magnetically attractive and awfully plain, and sometimes frightening, as in this description from "**Care**": "He took out a thin green cigar and set fire to it." The greenness of that cigar, the violence of its lighting—this is the kind of brightness Robison plays with, the kind of image-making that makes her stories intensely satisfying to read, but unmemorable, much like the paintings.

Each of the *Days* is a moment excerpted from someone's longer story, beginning in the middle and ending in the middle, standing like an acronym for the whole. More often than not, the characters are family, the scene domestic, the events mundane but with implied importance. It's also implied that nothing much different happened before or will happen after the story. The rendering is clean, flat, accurate, full of dialogue, and nearly emotionless, and the total effect is what Barth calls a "hard-edged, fine-tooled, enigmatic super-realism."

Though nothing much happens, the incipient draws the reader on. In "**Kite and Paint,**" two men in their sixties await a coastal storm in their beach house; when the storm is imminent, they decide to fly some exquisite handmade kites, sure to be destroyed in the rising winds. The story's ending is typically Robison, typically incisive. . . . Robison shows us everything we need to see, tells us nothing, and we get the point. A beautiful precision. (pp. 281-82)

Always the ruthless surgeon, Robison, when she writes in the omniscient voice, seems almost evil, so cold is the result. But sometimes she risks a warmer point of view, and these stories— "**Pretty Ice,**" "**Camilla,**" and "**Widower**" among them—are the most successful. (p. 282)

Characteristically, relationships and emotions are foggy, sensed rather than known. We're not sure, for instance, if the two men in "**Kite and Paint**" are lovers; Robison carefully omits the irrelevant, no matter how tantalizing. It's as if we're invisible guests in so many strange homes, visitors to whom nothing can be clear, even with all the evidence of observation. Sometimes we're not even sure a "story" is being told; fortunately, the end is always superbly clinching.

Eight of these stories first appeared in *The New Yorker*, where—short and sweet—they read like bolts of lightning revealing ravages of a storm. . . . The stories flatten and give an odd, myopic view of things when they appear side by side, so that it's difficult to read more than one or two in a sitting, but this could well be a good thing. One by one, they quietly attest to the consistency of Mary Robison's ability, and to the design of her art, its clarity and potential. (p. 283)

> Elizabeth Inness-Brown, "Mary Robison, 'Days',"
> in fiction international, No. 12, 1980, pp. 281-83.

ANATOLE BROYARD

Mary Robison is growing on me. When I read *Days,* her recent book of short stories, I was interested but skeptical [see excerpt above]. I saw her writing as a sort of deliberate counterpoint to the actual, just as in certain kinds of jazz singing, the vocalist sings *against* the melody. In Freudian analysis, a dream often means the opposite of its manifest content, and in Miss Robison's fiction, something like this seems to be going on too. It's remarkable what an effect you can get if you look at the world upside down. . . .

He can act so reasonable that he fools you, one character in *Oh!* says about another. There is an implication all through the book that when anyone is reasonable, he *is* acting. We only *act* reasonable. Or as another character says, "I'm just a person trying."

The people in *Oh!* like to watch bad movies on television, and there is a sense in which experimental fiction is like an old, bad movie. Neither is much interested in ordinary reality. Bad movies can't handle it and advanced fiction takes the position that it has already been handled too much. . . .

At any rate, I found myself accepting the characters in *Oh!* When Chris wins $100,000 in a lottery, I was not surprised to learn that he abandoned Maureen and their 8-year-old illegitimate child, Violet. The world is full of abandoners. When he got tired of abandonment, Chris came back to Maureen because he couldn't think of anything else to do. If you consider the question seriously, you'll find that it is quite hard to think of things to do once you've got out of the habit.

Mary Robison is like someone who's got out of the habit of "thinking" of things to write. She has a kind of dislocatedness that sounds authentic. Her writing is like the sawdust that termites leave: you know that something is chewing on something else. When I thought I had termites in my house, my handyman tasted the sawdust and said no. He can taste real destruction.

So can Mary Robison. She's something of a gourmet of various kinds of collapse. A 57-year-old man says of his 40-year-old fiancée that only her neck and her knees are old. Chris loves Maureen not in spite of the fact that she is thin, with minute breasts and badly bleached hair, but because of it. She has pathos, and that's what he needs. Of course she has defiance, too, for pathos without defiance is not sustaining. . . .

A militant woman in *Oh!* argues that while the graffiti in men's public toilets are obscene in silly ways, those in women's toilets are filled with compassion and communication. Under Mary Robison's influence, I'm inclined to believe it. She's right in her choice of title, too: sometimes the only answer to the world and to the question of fiction is *Oh!*

Anatole Broyard, "A Gourmet of Collapse," *in* The New York Times, *June 6, 1981, p. 13.*

GEOFFREY STOKES

[In the collection *Days*] Robison was the Darwin of helplessness. The inarticulate characters and flattened landscapes were a taxonomy of impotence. In their magazine context, these chill observations often acted as a sort of palate-clearer, but when the stories were gathered together, the variations on stasis seemed not quite varied enough. About halfway through that first book, as yet another variety of passivity took its brief turn on stage (and when I was all too sure that a number of substitutes were waiting in the wings), I began to feel like a Robison character. Kind of interested in watching what goes on, but not very. You know? Okay.

So it wasn't exactly your major thrill when the heroine of Robison's newly published first novel, *Oh!,* announced early on, "All I want to do is sleep." The characters in *Days* spent an inordinate amount of time in bed, as though the notion of

life as a sleep and a forgetting had become a positive program, and I feared that left to herself, *Oh!*'s Maureen Cleveland could have curled up unnoticed on virtually any page of the earlier book.

But as the title's punctuation implies, Robison does not leave her protagonist to her own devices. In addition to the torpid Maureen, *Oh!* offers us infinitely tolerant Daddy Cleveland, a more-or-less retired miniature-golf mogul; prissy Miss Virginia, Daddy's intended (who hosts an inspirational TV program for the kiddies every Sunday morning); Lola, the salt-and-pepper of the earth black maid (among other things); Howdy, Maureen's perpetual student older brother; Violet, her nine-year-old illegitimate daughter (Mo had been pregnant at 15); Chris, Violet's father and Mo's sporadic suitor, and a host of lovable walk-ons. There is also a plot of the picaresque variety and a surprising amount of truly batty humor.

[The Clevelands'] literary antecedents are more British than American; Wodehouse's dotty country families come to mind, and even more particularly, the Larkins of H. E. Bates's *Darling Buds of May* series. The Clevelands' universe is self-contained; caught up in it, strangers can only adapt or flee.

But Mary Robison ain't H. E. Bates, and there is something decidedly not charming about the Cleveland entourage. . . . Daddy is tolerant, sure, but only because he's nearly always so drunk he doesn't notice that there are things going on—or not going on—that *ought* to bother him. Lola is leadenly playing out her Stepin Fetchit role, and Maureen is a lump. Violet, alone among the household, acts her age, but that's pretty easy when you're nine and Howdy isn't so much indolent as infantile. Supported by Daddy's limitless money, Maureen does nothing (when she lets Violet wander outside during a tornado watch, one doesn't laugh) and Howdy tries everything (for as long as his attention span lasts). When outside events momentarily threaten their idyll, the only action they can imagine is to go find their long-absent mother.

Enter Chris. Or, more precisely, re-enter Chris. Though he has something of the Cleveland children's divine selfishness about him (he had, of course, decamped promptly on winning $100,000 in the lottery), he is nothing if not a man of action. Too much action, often. When it's discovered that Violet is seriously allergic to wasp stings, Chris tracks down their nests in a nearby tool shed, but instead of spraying or destroying the nests, he burns the entire shed down. Like everything else, Daddy Cleveland tolerates this.

Still, Chris is too much for Maureen and Howdy to handle. Their passive-aggressive style effortlessly routs Miss Virginia's heavy-handed Goodness, but Chris's active aggression overwhelms them. Like "Napoleon . . . or Magellan," he takes over Daddy's position. Things will be different. Violet will be safer. There will be less laughter.

If this review had been written in the Mary Robison mode, it would have ended with the last sentence, for while she classifies and describes varieties of inaction, she seems unable to reach any judgment about them other than that they *are*. This was perfectly appropriate to Darwin in his field researches, but one expects philosophy as well as biology from a novelist. One is disappointed. And one fears that Mary Robison is perhaps a bit *too* fascinated by passivity.

Geoffrey Stokes, "Uh Oh!" *in* The Village Voice, *Vol. XXVI, No. 32, August 5, 1981, p. 32.*

KATHA POLLITT

Like Ann Beattie and Raymond Carver, with whom she is often bracketed, Mary Robison writes about American anomie, seventies style, in a way that mirrors the very attitudes it depicts. Mo's depression and Howdy's solipsism [in *Oh!*] are both reflected in Miss Robison's flat, hip, deadpan voice, in her rejection of certain kinds of narrative approaches—the analysis of motive, for example—in favor of a cool, meticulous description of surfaces and reporting of dialogue.

Sometimes, this attention to surface pays off. Miss Robison has a poet's eye for the unconscious surrealism of commercial America: ''A teen-ager in blue makeup and an orange wig stood in front of Skyway's stream of automatic doors. He was hawking helium balloons stamped with pictures of footwear.'' And she has a playwright's ear for American speech, the things one hears people say all the time but rarely sees written down. The stretches of banal conversation in which no one listens to anyone else may go on too long, but a line as fresh and accurate as Violet's ''Tell me what else about Grandma?'' is almost by itself worth the price of the book.

I confess that I have trouble taking the Carver-Beattie-Robison school of fiction as a profound and searching critique of the way we, particularly the post-Vietnam young, live now, which is what its many admirers and imitators would have me do. Granted, America is a land of Skyways and logo-bearing balloons, a land where tornadoes strike without warning and men win lotteries and desert their pregnant girl friends. But are we really as zonked out as Maureen and Howdy? One could argue that the vision these writers share, of a pared-down, emotionally drained, random world, reflects less the failures of contemporary America than some obscurer failure to connect on the part of the writers themselves.

If, for all that, I found myself enjoying *Oh!* it's because deep down Mary Robison has an offbeat cheerfulness that undercuts her alienated stance and keeps her sodden characters afloat. Unlike Ann Beattie, who lavishes a mournful wistfulness on her upper-crust waifs, and unlike Raymond Carver, with his obsessive violence, Miss Robison seems to think her characters are doing as well as can be expected, under the circumstances. True, I don't quite understand what circumstances she has in mind—That life is painful? That God doesn't exist? That Vanzandt who used to patrol the golf course stepped into the propeller of a pontoon plane in Hanoi?—anymore than I understand why Chris wants to marry Maureen or why Mr. Cleveland never told his kids their mother had died years ago in a mental hospital or why I'm not supposed to agree with Virginia when she says that the Clevelands's problem is a lack of intelligence.

But earned or not, this buoyancy is Mary Robison's saving grace. It makes the novel less pat, the way the exclamation point qualifies the blankness of the title. (p. 14)

> *Katha Pollitt, ''Family and Friends,'' in* The New York Times Book Review, *August 23, 1981, pp. 14, 29.*

JAMES WOLCOTT

Essential to the furnishing of Mary Robison's fiction is a well-stocked liquor cabinet and a crackling cascade of ice. In *Days,* Robison's 1979 collection of stories, her characters seemed to drift numbly through life with drinks glued to their palms— props as dear to their sense of style as the cigarettes so deftly employed by Salinger's Glass family. . . . *Oh!*—Robison's confident first novel—is even more lethally saturated in alcohol, with the characters fishing cubes out of the ice bucket and freshening their drinks with all the desperate giddiness of passengers on a doomed ocean liner. Indeed, *Oh!* could easily be grouped with Kurt Vonnegut's later fiction and Barry Hannah's *Ray* to form a new subspecies of fiction that might be tagged the Bad Chemical novel. In the Bad Chemical novel, characters are not propelled by reason or belief or even desire but by whim, caprice—by whatever strange combination of booze, drugs, and hormonal hoochie-coochie happens to be percolating in their systems that day. (pp. 38-9)

Set in a sweltering sprawl of the midwest plagued by tornadoes and low-buzzing helicopters, *Oh!* is a wiseacre comedy about a family of well-off misfits called the Clevelands. Mr. Cleveland, a widower with controlling interest in a corporation that has a wide range of interests (bottling plants, convenience stores, miniature-golf franchises), isn't reluctant to begin his day with a few stiff ones. . . . Everyone in the Cleveland household seems to swim idly through a pickled haze. . . . The only character in *Oh!* with her feet planted firmly in the sober world is Cleveland's mistress, Virginia, a born-again Christian who hosts a Sunday morning kiddie show and regards the excesses of the Cleveland clan with sniffing dismay. It's a losing battle prim Virginia is waging against the family's sarcasm and wooziness, and she knows it. She eventually packs up her indignation and leaves the Clevelands to their hell-bent ruin.

As a comic look at the muddle and disarray of modern life, *Oh!* is a far more accomplished novel than *Ray* or Tom McGuane's recent excursions into lurching funk. It's also a springing advance over the softly demure *Days.* Comprised mostly of stories first published in the *New Yorker*, *Days* too often displays the limitations of the *New Yorker*'s imprint: the stories are anecdotal and unassuming, meek little mice which peep their heads out into the daylight, then retreat into the sheltering dark. Whatever its shortcomings, *Oh!* doesn't suffer from a case of mousiness. It's a very lean, fleet, assured, sassing piece of work. Though the Clevelands are as awful a nest of reptiles as one would care to meet . . . , *Oh!* isn't an off-putting entertainment. As the Clevelands fiddle away on each other's nerves, the novel takes on the snappy rhythms of a radio comedy—a revamped version of *The Bickersons.* (pp. 39-40)

Like Kingsley Amis in his early prime, Robison is capable of being both amusing and disagreeable—or, rather, she screws up the disagreeable to a piercing comic pitch, making the reader wince with laughter. She also shares Amis's chief flaw: she can be too pettish and lax with her talent, occasionally settling for easy effects. Lola, for example, is a more refined version of the character Amanda Rudolph played in TV's ''Make Room for Daddy''—the spunky black maid who keeps her head while all the white folks around her ditheringly lose theirs. (Lola does have a weird spell or two, but she's still an anchor of sanity compared to the Clevelands.) That Robison's strengths and weaknesses are rooted in media culture isn't surprising. A hair or two over 30, Mary Robison is part of the generation that grew up with the TV humming in the living room, and her fiction reflects the influence of television on her characters' lives—in shaping their speech and wants and attitudes, in reducing their attention span to splinters. History, art, discipline, moral restraints all seem to have evaporated with the dew. Only the aquarium-blue light of the TV remains, and the sound of liquor purring over ice. . . .

Unlike a lot of current writers, who seem anxious to cuddle in the reader's lap and make nice, Mary Robison isn't afraid to light a few hotfoots, tweak a few noses. Seasoned a bit, Robison's flair for brittle talk and catastrophe could result in a comic novel one wouldn't be ashamed to place on the shelf next to the best of Evelyn Waugh. She, too, deals in slapstick declines and falls; in vile bodies. (p. 40)

James Wolcott, "Boozy Lives," in The New Republic, *Vol. 185, No. 10, September 9, 1981, pp. 38-40.*

MICHIKO KAKUTANI

Rootless, alienated and blasé, Mary Robison's characters have problems connecting with anyone or anything. Used to improvising their lives, they live day to day, without hopes or ambitions. They talk, yes—endlessly, but without ever really listening to one another, and their talk is curiously devoid of sincerity or passion. Conversation, for them, is not a way of communicating, but a series of desultory non sequiturs and defensive jokes. It is a way of making the time pass by—like eating junk food or watching horror movies.

Like Raymond Carver and Ann Beattie, whose fictional territory closely resembles her own, Miss Robison has achieved in one novel and two short-story collections a style perfectly adapted to delineating these attentuated lives. The idiom is 1970's colloquial; the voice, cool and flat; the prose, resolutely unadorned. There are few clues to people's motivations, little narrative exposition and a willful resistance to interpretation of any kind.

In Miss Robison's finest stories—in [*An Amateur's Guide to the Night*], "Coach," "Smart," and ["**An Amateur's Guide to the Night**"]—this approach results in strong, unsentimental portraits of contemporary life. Fuller-bodied than the others, these stories supply the reader with enough information to feel the texture of the characters' lives; and as a consequence, we can sympathize with their difficulties, perhaps even admire their thwarted efforts to cope.

All too often, however, Miss Robison's coolness results in stories that seem as attenuated as the lives they portray. Not only is the language impoverished, but a sense of authorial vision also appears to be absent. "**The Nature of Almost Everything**," "**Look at Me Go**" and "**I Am 21**" are little more than mood pieces, depicting an alienated sensibility; the author's attitude in these stories amounts to a kind of shrug.

In other cases, Miss Robison seems so reluctant to impute motive or causality that the stories read like an anthology of random events. In "**You Know Charles**," the following sequence occurs: a troubled young man named Allen goes to visit his aunt; he sees a menacing-looking teen-ager standing outside her apartment building; Allen tells his aunt about his problems; she invites the teen-ager in for a visit; she takes photographs of the two young men; she collapses in the bathroom. What is the reader to make of this? That life is ironic? Or that people are unhappy? In any case, we never know enough about the characters and their dilemmas to want to bother to find out.

Almost all Miss Robison's characters, it seems, suffer from a sense of dislocation. One woman hears voices in her head, another complains about a brain tumor; an accident-prone man totals the family car, then catches on fire while cooking on the hibachi. Others, like Nobuko who hasn't changed out of her pajamas in weeks, are simply afflicted with a nameless anomie.

"What's the matter?" her boyfriend asks. "There are things," Nobuko says. "Many things."

Spaced-out casualities of the 60's, these characters belong to a generation that grew up skeptical about the world around them. The adversary stance of that decade, however, has degenerated into a vague alienation with everything around them; they could care less about politics or ideas. Getting through, coping, is all they aspire to do. . . .

In lieu of any greater order, these characters concentrate on small tasks, such as memorizing the names of the brightest stars or arranging their shirts by color. Larger commitments are beyond them, and their abdication of responsibility leads to families that are shaky and relationships that are confused. . . .

Floating through life, these people tend to shuck off relationships and identities the way a snake sheds its skin. Why bother working at a career or sustaining a friendship, they figure—sure, things fall apart, but something else will always take their place. . . .

As far as such characters are concerned, fate is something in other people's hands, and instead of trying to exert control over their lives, they accept their lot with a sigh. For the reader, this passivity, this sullen willingness to submit to the buffetings of fate, ultimately drains Miss Robison's characters of interest. In one way or another, all of us make concessions and compromises, but it is still the struggle to make sense of the things that constrict our dreams that lends life—and literature—a sense of vigor and purpose. In the end, it's hard to really care about characters who appear to care so little about themselves and others.

Michiko Kakutani, in a review of "An Amateur's Guide to the Night," in The New York Times, *November 15, 1983, p. C17.*

FRANCES TALIAFERRO

Mary Robison's first collection of short stories, *Days* (1979), introduced a skillful, curiously antiliterary writer. Like her *New Yorker* contemporaries Raymond Carver, Ann Beattie and Frederick Barthelme, Mrs. Robison is nobody's acolyte; both in style and subject, she avoids the precincts of high art. Her short stories are snapshots in an album from K Mart, conversations taped at the next table in Jerry's Steak Chateau. Her novel *Oh!* (1981), a portrait of a feckless, funny Midwestern family, is *You Can't Take It With You* revised to suit the free-form humor of the 1970's. In both *Days* and *Oh!* the voice is uninflected and dispassionate.

The temptation is to hear in Mrs. Robison and her colleagues the voice of a generation, the near nihilists in blue jeans who survived the heyday of the counter-culture and now sit passively by while the iron enters their souls. Such identifications are convenient but a little vindictive. In any case, Mrs. Robison's work will not fit cozily into "the *New Yorker* sensibility" or the pigeonholes of social history. She seems to me not so much a maker of cultural documentaries as a free-lance pathologist who takes her little emotional biopsies in clean slices wherever she finds symptoms of unease.

Most of the 13 stories in *An Amateur's Guide to the Night* are more substantial than those in *Days*. There are some very short pieces, however, notably the haunting "**Yours**," a portrait of an elderly husband and young wife in autumn, carving jack-o'-lanterns far into the night as if there were no tomorrow. In fact, there is no tomorrow for the wife, who has cancer. . . . In four pages, the author establishes all the necessary data of time, place and circumstance, suggests the depth of companionship and love between Allison and her husband and provokes the reader to piercing thoughts of life's pleasantness and death's surprises. The unsentimentality is brisk but not unkind; a strong sense of daze and loss rises from unlikely details. . . .

A Robison story characteristically begins and ends without ceremony and starts somewhere near the middle. . . . In this fiction without landscape, the conventional signposts are missing—no dialogue of heavy significance, no set pieces to signal the big scene or climactic moment. Here pleasure and pain are unmodulated; everything happens at about the same pitch and volume.

Readers who do not like to do the work of inference and prefer to be spectators at a literary ceremony will find these stories annoyingly sparse. With their cryptic expositions and spartan absence of figurative language, they take some getting used to, and some of them still strike me as unnecessarily pointless and inscrutable. At her best, however, Mrs. Robison is both wise and entertaining, a technician with a sense of humor, a minimalist with a good eye for what can be salvaged from lives of quiet desperation.

> Frances Taliaferro, "Stories without Signposts," in The New York Times Book Review, November 27, 1983, p. 13.

DAVID LEAVITT

In **"An Amateur's Guide to the Night,"** the title story of Mary Robison's new collection, the narrator's 35-year-old mother refuses to attend her daughter's high school graduation because she's "afraid of the 'going forward into the world' parts of the commencement speeches." At 36, the heroine of **"The Nature of Almost Everything"** tells us, "my goals are to stay sober and pay off my MasterCard bill." Eleanor, in **"Smart,"** is also 36, very pregnant, and loathe to leave her Washington apartment. . . .

Thirty-six is a bad age in the world of Mary Robison's stories. These heroes and heroines are people who can't move, who don't want to move because they're terrified of what will happen to them if they try to change. It's the 17 to 21 year olds who bring *An Amateur's Guide to the Night* alive; with their pluck, their bravery, and their unflagging determination not to sink into the mire which has claimed their elders, they are probably the most generous kids to appear in literature since Holden Caulfield, as well as the most appealing.

Lindy, the narrator of the title story, must contend with a mother who passes herself off as a sister on double-dates, makes Lindy stay up all night watching horror movies with her, sleeps in her bed, and intentionally turns off the alarm clock so that she'll be late for school. To stay sane, Lindy turns to the sky, by means of a telescope through which she charts the stars. Her neighbors call her Carl Sagan and ask her questions about Halley's Comet; Lindy wishes that her mother and grandfather cared too. . . .

The young narrator of **"I Am Twenty-One"** is doing C work in all her courses except "The Transition from Romanesque to Gothic"; on the final exam she writes so much on essay question one that she has no time to work on essay question two. Late in the story we discover a possible explanation for

her shortsightedness; her parents recently died in a car crash. As she "grieves" her exam, she really grieves her loss; when she goes to bed she repeats in her mind her entire, brilliantly detailed answer to essay question one—"word for fucking word." Her knowledge of the barrel vault's effect on 13th century church architecture, like Lindy's knowledge of astronomy, reveals a grim determination not to give in to grief.

Robison doesn't hold out false hope for the young people in her stories; most of them will probably end up failing as dismally as their elders. But through them, she's able to introduce a note of optimism into an otherwise bleak landscape. Their vigor and enthusiasm brighten the stories. . . .

An Amateur's Guide to the Night is Mary Robison's third book. In *Days,* her first collection . . . , Robison showed off her perfect eye for detail and ear for dialogue, and the result was a group of flawless stories, remarkable for the scope of their vision as well as their execution. *Oh!,* her novel, displays Robison's fine sense of humor, though it veers occasionally toward the zany. If there's a particular innovation in *An Amateur's Guide to the Night,* it's her increasing use of first-person narration. Most often, she speaks in a precise, chilly, yet passionate third-person voice which the flap copy of *Days* compares to a recording angel's. Robison's first-person stories are more rough-hewn, the utterances of beasts rather than angels, but what Robison sacrifices in angelic authority she gains in warmth. It's as if her voice, with all its rigor and energy, melds with the spent voices of her characters, and ennobles their sad accounts. When she speaks through her younger characters, her knowledge combines with their exuberance to give us narratives of genuine urgency.

Mary Robison has been writing short stories for several years, but she's never attained the critical acclaim enjoyed by such contemporaries as Raymond Carver and Bobbie Ann Mason. It's my hope that *An Amateur's Guide to the Night* will win her the readership she deserves. No American short story writer speaks to our time more urgently or fondly than Robison. Word for fucking word, her work demands our attention.

> David Leavitt, in a review of "An Amateur's Guide to the Night," in The Village Voice, Vol. XXIX, No. 2, January 10, 1984, p. 44.

DEAN FLOWER

[The stories collected in *An Amateur's Guide to the Night* seem] shockingly narrow, turned in upon themselves. They are meant to be, of course: mere glimpses of domestic life, such as anxious parents talking at the kitchen table while a psychotherapist upstairs persuades their daughter to please eat something. Or an anxious football coach having trouble paying attention to his wife and teenage daughter. Or brother and sister twins, old enough to enter medical school, having problems growing up. Or a young man trying to talk to his alcoholic aunt before his father's impending marriage. These are all conceived as "ordinary people," in the Donald Sutherland-Mary Tyler Moore sense. They enact what Herbert Gold meant by the phrase, "the age of happy problems." Robison, like so many other talented Americans writing short stories these days, does close-ups of white upper-middle-class relatively-affluent well-educated urban and suburban families, with special emphasis on the pangs of growing up. After the likes of Cheever, Updike, Beattie, Paley, Mason, Leffland, Carver, Alice Adams, and so many others working the same vein, cultivating these domestic gardens, one would like to start passing out airplane tickets to the rest of the world.

Robison nevertheless has a fine ear for the odd opacities and queer metaphors of our casual talk. Here is a man called Coach when he is surprised to discover his daughter at home: "You're not home. Aren't you with whoosis? You're supposed to be out. You are *beet* red." As she stomps off to her room, Coach tells her about his new job: "I'll even be on TV. I'll have my own show on Sundays. And I'll get written up in the press all the time. By *real* reporters. Hey! Why am I yelling at wood here?" Another character yanks out the plug of a vacuum cleaner, saying "Come on, you." . . . Robison's stories all proceed by means of these odd, off-the-wall glimpses. If the author steps in to comment at all, she does so in the same spirit: "For Jackie, a newspaper has always meant more physical exercise than actual reading" and we see him "rush through a section, his arms closing and opening, and paper beating like wings." These observant touches are funny, but in the end we are left entirely to our own conclusions. My own is that if these stories are indeed meant to be some kind of guide to the night, Robison has not made it dark enough for us to need one. (pp. 307-08)

Dean Flower, in a review of "An Amateur's Guide to the Night," in The Hudson Review, *Vol. XXXVII, No. 2, Summer, 1984, pp. 307-08.*

Dave Smith

1942-

(Born David Jeddie Smith; has also written under the pseudonym of Cornwell Smith) American poet, critic, novelist, and editor.

Smith has gained critical recognition as one of the most significant poets to emerge in the United States during the 1970s. Although originally known primarily as a regional poet of his native Virginia, Smith has broadened his settings to encompass midwestern and far western locales. Bruce Weigl noted: "Part of Smith's strategy in defining his poetic self and simultaneously developing his public voice takes the form of an intimate association of place." Smith's verse reveals his command of language, his inventiveness with poetic form, and his willingness to examine a wide variety of themes. A highly prolific poet, Smith has sometimes been faulted for unnecessary ornamentation and for publishing careless work. Consequently, some critics maintain that he endangers his growing reputation as a major poet. Nevertheless, many observers have detected in such later volumes as *Goshawk, Antelope* (1979), *Dream Flights* (1981), and *The Roundhouse Voices: Selected and New Poems* (1985) an increasingly accomplished vision and style, a pronounced awareness of the poet as a vital public voice, and an experimental verve that demonstrates Smith's range, industry, and promise.

Critics have noted affinities between Smith's work and the verse of such American poets as Walt Whitman, James Dickey, and James Wright. Specifically, they point to his ability to find mythopoeic relevance in the commonplace and his recurrent focus on the interaction between humanity and nature. Smith is most often compared with Robert Penn Warren, whom he has acknowledged as a major influence. Smith's verse reflects Warren's broad thematic focus, his firm rooting in personal experience, his use of concentrated language, and his southern sensibility. Smith's early collections, *Bull Island* (1970), *The Fisherman's Whore* (1974), and *Cumberland Station* (1976), reveal his belief in the power of language to evoke surroundings and dramatize experiences. Many of the poems in these volumes focus on such commonplace topics as fishing, baseball, parenthood, the transition from adolescence to maturity, and love. Smith's command of tone, his emotive language, and his insight into the universality of ordinary experience helped secure his reputation as an important young poet.

The publications of *Goshawk, Antelope, Dream Flights,* and *Homage to Edgar Allan Poe* (1981), according to Robert Phillips, confirmed that "Dave Smith is a huge talent, one of the best poets of his generation." These works reflect Smith's ability to infuse his verse with a contemplative mood in which the primacy of personal reminiscence, experience, and feeling are empowered by the narration of ordered, eidetic scenes from Smith's life. Robert Penn Warren lauded *Dream Flights:* "Here mingle realism and deep pathos; vernacular language and grandeur of phrase; an ideal of beauty and our common world; the movement of daily speech with elaborate, subtle, or powerful rhythm; originality of imagery and metaphor with shrewd observation." The publication of *The Roundhouse Voices* amidst a still highly active career attests to the significance of Smith's work and affords the reader lasting impressions of a densely

© *Thomas Victor 1986*

layered, evolving poetic output. In an essay on Smith's poetry, Thomas Swiss declared: "[Among] respected writers in general perhaps only Robert Penn Warren writes so much and so well."

Smith has also published works of fiction and criticism. *Onliness* (1981), an allegorical novel, is set in rural Virginia and centers on a working-class protagonist's dreams of fulfillment. Critics applauded the illuminative quality of Smith's lyrical prose style. Smith's collection of criticism, *Local Assays: On Contemporary American Poetry* (1985) won praise for his insightful analyses of the contemporary poets whom he most admires: Warren, Wright, Dickey, and Richard Hugo.

(See also *CLC,* Vol. 22; *Contemporary Authors,* Vols. 49-52; *Contemporary Authors New Revision Series,* Vol. 1; and *Dictionary of Literary Biography,* Vol. 5.)

ROBERT PHILLIPS

It was not until his fourth collection, **Goshawk, Antelope,** that Dave Smith began to receive the wide critical attention his work deserves. Who knows why some connect with a single book, others never do? (p. 432)

That Smith has produced a prose book on the late James Wright [*The Pure Clear Word: Essays on the Poetry of James Wright*] seems fitting. In the American literature of longing and homesickness, of the necessity to recapture one's roots, Wright was our quintessential poet of yearning and mooning. Wright's last collection began with a recollection of a nest of red wings in Ohio decades ago, and concluded with a poem titled "Beautiful Ohio." The Ohio River was Wright's symbol for the beautiful, the sure, the American—all the antiquities of his childhood.

Smith belongs firmly in that tradition. Many of his early poems root in an anonymous Virginia fishing village. Others spring from Fredericksburg and Richmond; Cumberland, Maryland; Muskegon, Michigan; and Parkersburg, West Virginia. *Goshawk, Antelope* strayed far from his Virginia origins, to encompass allegories in Oregon, Wyoming, and several locales in Utah, where the poet was teaching. Yet one of the most memorable works in that book was "**The Roundhouse Voices,**" a boyhood remembrance of baseball and his uncle. Highly personal, it had far more impact than some of the larger, more ambitious addresses to universal fates.

Smiths's two new books [*Dream Flights* and *Homage to Edgar Allan Poe*], one of shorter poems, one of longer, circle back to his beginnings in Tidewater Maryland and Virginia and also restore his relatives and immediate family to the canon. Both books exhibit Smith's extravagance of language. His rhetoric resembles not so much Wright's as Faulkner's or Warren's, circumlocuting about the ancient and the holy and the unpredictable, "the heart-given lowering of a boy's body," and philosophical abstractions such as "He is only something in a dream we are the meaning of . . ." Yet even when Smith is at his most abstract, his humanity brings him back to earth. In this sense the jacket photograph of an angel sculpture, for *Dream Flights,* is more than usually appropriate: her wings are quite ethereal, but her naked body is that of a desirable earth-woman.

Both of these 1981 books collect recent work, but it is impossible to know which is the more recent. (The acknowledgements and copyright pages are no help here.) Of the two, I have a preference for *Homage to Edgar Allan Poe.* These brief poems—many complete on less than a page—seem totally successful and never rush off-center or out of control as do a few of the longer attempts. The domestic poems, like "**Discovering Obscenities on Her Wall**" (*her* being his daughter), and "**Reading the Books Our Children Have Written,**" are exquisite and will touch even a reader who has never had children of his own. The title sequence, in six sections, entwines Poe's personal history with Smith's, and is a worthy addition to his family chronicles and regional studies of *Cumberland Station.* . . . And I was glad to find "**Night of the Chickens, North of Joplin**" collected at last (and heavily revised). It describes the drunken night drive of a character (not Smith), and the language swerves and blacks out. . . . (pp. 432-33)

Dream Flights publishes seventeen poems on seventy-six pages. For the most part they are dreams emanating from Smith's Southern roots. There are several involving relations between blacks and whites. Other contrasts are drawn between the innocent and the jaded, the natural and the perverse, the old order and the new, the appearance versus the reality. These include some of Smith's most personal poems, "**The Tire Hangs in the Woods,**" "**The Pornography Box,**" and poems to his wife on the dangers of marriage and breech birth. Nevertheless, the overall title is significant. There are total fictions here, including an imaginative reconstruction of the life of a travelling photographer, circa 1880, which incorporates haunting details.

The two books are not separate entities. Poe's imagery and persona are found in *Dream Flights* as well. Together these collections confirm that Dave Smith is a huge talent, one of the best poets of his generation. (p. 434)

Robert Phillips, in a review of "Homage to Edgar Allan Poe" and "Dream Flights," in The Hudson Review, *Vol. XXXIV, No. 3, Autumn, 1981, pp. 420-34.*

TOM O'BRIEN

Dave Smith's *Onliness* is a provocative, exuberant, at times hilarious, oddly touching but uneven first novel. It is set in Chapel, Va., a town where people "speak little, and mostly curse." Among the most laconic is Billy Luke Tomson, employed by one of the most foul-mouthed, Tom Zucold, owner of the rundown Bowie Garage. Billy Luke is an innocent giant, 6 foot 10 inches tall, an ex-Army shot putter, naïve and nonverbal, and Zucold is a wizened cynic, but with a heart large enough to love his garage and his protégé, whom he nicknames The Grip for his awesome size and strength. Mr. Smith's achievement is that he has found extraordinary human riches in this wrench-and-fender setting of a father-son tale and transformed an auto-body repair shop into the stuff of myth and symbol.

The plot of *Onliness* is fantastic but compelling. Tom Zucold instructs The Grip in the ways of the world, "learns him some" about cars, and watches in wonder as The Grip hurls shots in a lane formed of discarded wrecks behind the garage's workshop. Inside, in that part of the building that used to be a chicken coop, Tom and The Grip domesticate automobile jetsam into funky hominess, complete with electronically maneuverable Ford Thunderbird bucket seats for furniture, Champion Spark Plug clocks, large supplies of Gatorade and endless hours of "Truth or Consequences" on television. When The Grip meets the delectable Promise Land, who drives him to beach-side picnics at breakneck speeds on her pink Harley Davidson, The Grip's education is complete.

But even in this rusty send-up of a paradise, things fall apart. Tom Zucold is convinced that a Citizens' Committee wants to replace the garage with a shopping center. To pay off debts to a local bank, Tom bets all his savings on a legendary roving pool hustler named "The Carolina Kid," who predictably gets drunk and self-destructs the night of the big match at Chapel's Moose Hall. Smelling conspiracy, Tom arms himself, draws his wrecks into a circle, garrisons the garage and wages war. Unfortunately for The Grip, Promise Land is related to "them" on the Citizens' Committee and the war reduces his Gatorade Eden to a sudden Armageddon. When the smoke clears, like a true picaro, The Grip survives, but without mentors.

The problem with the plot is not improbability, but pacing. Mr. Smith gives so much attention to character and setting at the outset that early hints about what is eventually going to happen fail to work as foreshadowing. The opening half of the book is also difficult to follow because of the number and freakishness of the minor characters. While Tom Zucold, The Grip and Promise Land are developed enough to be believable, the carnival of freaks in supporting roles strikes one as that kind of clichéd and disorganized indulgence in the eccentric that often passes for creativity in modern writing.

In addition, the language Mr. Smith uses, while it endows his story with peculiar power in the long run, is bothersome at first. The Chapel dialect is re-created as faithfully here as other provincial dialects in Southern literature, but the clipped, terse phrasing and odd forms of reference provide an unwelcome challenge for a reader trying to follow an already difficult plot. The narrator's voice adds to the strain: Dave Smith is a poet and often he economizes on words as much as his characters do, albeit with a smooth and regular syntax.

Despite these weaknesses, the climax is powerful and thematically rich. (pp. 14-15)

Dave Smith took his title from Tim Hardin's song, "If I Were a Carpenter and You Were a Lady." He has Promise Land use the word to explain to The Grip that human beings remain separate and unique even when they are in love. But the title could as easily fit Tom Zucold, a defiant battler for individual integrity. Mr. Smith could also have called this book "Sincerity and Authenticity," the term used by Lionel Trilling to describe man's search for the fullest quality of life in a technological world. But then his title would lose the piquancy and whimsicalness that gives his treatment of that search zest and power. If the first half is flawed, the second soars. (p. 15)

Tom O'Brien, "Save the Garage," in The New York Times Book Review, *November 15, 1981, pp. 14-15.*

ALAN BOLD

It is sometimes supposed that good poets are necessarily equipped to become even better novelists. With ten slim volumes behind him, Dave Smith has tested the validity of this theory in his first novel. *Onliness* is no tentative beginning, but an ambitious attempt to write the Great American Novel by bringing myth, archetype, allegory and abstraction to a fluent narrative. The finished product manages to rise above all that that suggests mainly because Smith has such a bizarre sense of humour and a well developed sense of style. The joke is at the expense of the American Dream, for this is the Great American Novel writ ludicrous; not so much a divine comedy as an adult comic, with verbal imagery instead of illustrative frames and events that develop with the surrealistic rapidity of situations in a cartoon. It is a simple tale filtered through a mind high on cultural references.

The title of the book derives from Tim Hardin's pseudo-sacred popsong "If I Were a Carpenter": "Save my love through loneliness, / Save my love for sorrow; / I've given you my onliness, / Come and give me your tomorrow." Appropriately enough, the book is as pre-packaged as a popsong. It has all the ingredients of all-American fiction: the dumb ox, the whore with a heart of gold, the seductive Southern belle, the isolated garage, the doomed dream, the token black, the consumer-orientated fetishism, the obligatory violence. Added to these is a movie-inspired version of the mood of waiting for something (be it Lefty or Godot): we are constantly assured that everything's gonna be all right when someone turns up on cue:

Smith provides all the hints needed to interpret the story on various levels. There is never any danger of missing an allegorical point or a symbolic moment or a realization that each person in the book is also a personification. . . .

At the centre of the novel is the hero Billy Luke Tomson, a moronic giant nicknamed The Grip on account of his bone-crushing handshake. He teams up with Tom Zucold, who owns a garage and has made his work his life by creating an ambience

entirely constructed of spare parts from used cars. The Grip is monosyllabic but nevertheless capable of dreaming dreams suggested by commercial catalogues and television quizgames. His one talent is for shot-putting, so he spends as much time as possible attempting to throw a metal ball further than anyone else has ever done before. All he wants from life, in fact, is "to belong, to be a gentleman and drive his lime green Corvette, to love Promise Land and make a record put." This dream turns into a nightmare involving the little fishing village of Chapel, Virginia, in a local war. The Grip, it seems, is an idiotic Everyman—an archetype who goes on a spiritual odyssey to precisely nowhere. He is the innocent Adam looking for Eve (otherwise known as Promise Land) and he is also made in the image of Christ, as Smith clearly emphasizes. After The Grip has been attacked, a friendly neighbourhood Samaritan observes "them fellows crucified you". Later, when The Grip takes up a defensive position in a tree, a voice explains "Christ in a tree".

If The Grip is a kinda Christ, then his garage-owning friend Tom Zucold is a sorta John the Baptist. Both of them are hanging around in the hope that God will show up in the shape of the Carolina Kid, a legendary pool hustler. Tom tells The Grip that the Kid is coming "to save me and you"; and sure enough, when the Kid, whose poster mesmerizes The Grip, shows up, it is noted that he "Act like he's God hisself". To the dismay of The Grip and the despair of Tom it turns out that the Kid is drunk which, in this novel, is another way of saying that God is dead. . . .

Dave Smith's book is sufficiently full of cerebral fun and games to become the text for an undergraduate cult: the story is designed for readers who pride themselves on being smart, and the prose is so polished it glows.

Alan Bold, "Odyssey to Nowhere," in The Times Literary Supplement, *No. 4104, November 27, 1981, p. 1388.*

STEPHEN SANDY

In the splendid amplitude of his means, Dave Smith embraces everything. His central theme in *Dream Flights* and *Goshawk, Antelope* is twofold: to invent the coast of his present, and through memory to charge his past with meaning. Smith's gift includes an innate largeness of conception, a dynamic capacity to grasp experience and get it right in memory as a headlong drive into the reaches of vision: "the place / deep in my head. It now will be / remembered right. Loved." But what most empowers is a richness of formal organization in a network of "open" forms. It is a delight to behold, then to follow the figure in the carpet. On a small scale or large, poems begin *in medias res,* then move jaggedly through a constellation of images and dramatized events, their progress enriching our apprehension of connections as they extend and proliferate. "**Crab**" is finely typical, moving crabwise among its themes: meditations on death, the home, homelessness, the mind; the wanderer shuttling back and forth across these States from job to job, errand upon errand, like the crab of the epigraph, dizzied among habitats, moving between open sea and estuarine evolutionary home. In "**Crab,**" Smith searches for a resting place, a place to stand—in mind; in the landscape far below his jet—a man high in the air imaging himself: a boy in the midst of mud and water, crabbing. The montage of images works; the rivulets of a tidal mud bank of his youth are seen below him now in the "wiggling rivers that come out in the end / where you always knew they would.'' These are imagined again as the whorls and creases in the gray matter of the brain; in the meaty meanders of Thomas Wolfe's brain—or in the larger sense of the poet circling above his quarry, his quest for the final: unsure, determined, instinctive as the mother crab patiently voyaging between homeless shores. Smith effortlessly engages what I'll call a poetics of total encirclement. The index of vision on his horizon is broad enough to include the mundane; the moral meditations of the title poem, **"Dream Flight,"** nest comfortably in the prosaic frame of a DC-10. Or again in **"Crab,"** the poem neatly includes an emblematic organization by elements: earth, air, fire, water. This drive for richness, to embrace by ordering the true complexity of experience, gives Smith's best poems a range of tenors and vehicles which set up more than a single set of harmonic vibrations.

It's just this expansiveness, the Whitmanian proliferations of *Goshawk, Antelope* and *Dream Flights,* which opens a gate on the pastures of enumeration and reminiscence, which potentially signals a deliquescing spread among occasions. But the easy density and thematic variety of *Dream Flights* matches the abrupt consciousness and lyric fullness of his previous collection, *Goshawk, Antelope,* my favorite among Smith's books to date. In 1974 he changed his professional name from David Jeddie Smith to Dave Smith. The analogy to Walt Whitman is inescapable. His poetry opts for an embrace so wide as to be epic in intent. The poems are set in landscapes across "these States" from Hawaii to the Virginia coast; they confer stature and context upon a whole populace, from many corners and levels of our "classless" society. But mostly the poet focuses on his homeland, on the sights, sounds, and circumstances of Tidewater Virginia. In *Goshawk, Antelope* as in his other books, Dave Smith's childhood is a home plate to which he always returns after touching many bases. Fine dividends from memory, as in **"Waving,"** counterpoint more forbidding promissory notes of now, as in **"In Snow, A Possible Life."**

The degree of action in his language, the incidence of verbs and verbals, make his poems dynamic and give them a robust tempo; something is always happening, there is an army of agents for the actions. Perhaps this very Whitmanian quality combined with Smith's great ease with language, his gleaming articulateness, identify his purpose and his accomplishment as much as anything. But also we may read through a volume, or two, very much as we read in *Leaves of Grass*; it appears ultimately unimportant where one poem leaves off and the next begins; the work is all segments of one long poem. The vigor and trenchancy of his eye's mind astonish, please, and trouble. The attempt is epic; whether a poetics of total encirclement can make an epic of our fractured multiplicity or whether this chant of enactments and enumerations can achieve it—these are larger questions.

Part of the charm of Dave Smith's work is the Southern voice—the loquacious detailed articulations of accretive lyricism. These triumph in the Virginia Civil War battlefields and other settings of *Cumberland Station;* they also invigorate the ordinarily starker panoramas of the West, context and occasion of *Goshawk, Antelope.* So far Smith has placed the grid of his verbal eclecticism over South, Midwest, and West with coloratura success; he needs now only to confront the supposedly entrenched vales of New England and the "Eastablishment" to box his American compass. (pp. 294-96)

Stephen Sandy, "Experienced Bards," in Poetry, *Vol. CXL, No. 5, August, 1982, pp. 293-305.*

PETER STITT

There is a good deal of excess baggage in [*Dream Flights*], and even what seems most necessary in a poem is often carelessly done.

The first poem in the book, entitled **"Crab,"** unfortunately illustrates much of what can, and does, go wrong in *Dream Flights.* Here is the first of its several relatively short sections:

> I read once that when he had opened Thomas Wolfe's
> head,
> the surgeon did not even look up,
> his fingers needling and cradling
> back the deep-hidden meat.
> The books said postules or nodules, I forget exactly,
> and more than once I have caught myself
>
> in the Lazyboy, fingertips testing
> the uneven round of my skull,
>
> and again, then again.
> They must have been something
> gray as bubbles I dream
> in the chittering crab-teeth
> at the bottom of my historical place.

The second line presents a puzzling way to intensify the action; who would expect a surgeon, naturally concentrating on his work, to look up at such a moment? After such praise for Wolfe's brain, for the speaker to go on and draw a parallel between that and his own brain seems a bit strong, especially when he does it "again, then again." The "they" refers to "postules or nodules," though this is far from immediately clear, given the syntax; in fact, it sounds at first as though the speaker is describing the bumps on his own head ("They must have been something"). The last three lines create a simile between these "postules or nodules" (and why couldn't it be one or the other? Why didn't Smith look it up?) and the "bubbles I dream / in the chittering crab-teeth / at the bottom of my historical place." The comparison is decidedly odd, especially since this is the most ambitious metaphor of the poem and meant to carry much of its thematic weight. Crabbing turns out to have been a crucial activity in the youth of the speaker; now that those experiences reside mostly in his memory, he chooses to associate "bubbles . . . / in the chittering crab-teeth" with his own brain. Surely this is an awkward and unpromising image. The section's final infelicity comes in its last line; by "the bottom of my historical place" Smith means something like "beneath the waters of the Chesapeake Bay, near which I was raised."

The action of the poem tells how the speaker takes his six-year-old daughter back home with him from Utah so he can pass on to her his crabbing lore, skills, experiences. There is sentimentality here (as occasionally throughout the book): the speaker describes himself as "a stern dreamer" at one point, and as "a boy ratty-tatty as Huck Finn" at another; elsewhere he speaks of a "butcher, kind as a man can be, / who shook my small hand." . . . The [concluding lines of the poem] are confused, almost chaotic—even when read in context, they resist complete understanding. The reason for this is something that seems characteristic of Smith's style: he weaves concrete and abstract elements together in such a way that they become less and less distinct, less and less clear; the reader ends up tangled in a dense, perhaps impenetrable web.

I wish I could say that the poem is atypical of the volume—but I never would have discussed it were that the case. There is a great deal of what looks like plain carelessness in these poems, as though Smith is writing so much he doesn't have time to go back and revise. Another disturbing pattern is how often, and how directly, one is reminded of the poems of Robert Penn Warren. One of the more ambitious of these poems is dedicated to Warren, and the jacket contains an effusive statement from the elder master. Of course, Warren has developed for himself a distinctive style—surely as distinctive as that of James Wright. . . . In many phrases, Dave Smith sounds very like Robert Penn Warren; for example, a horse becomes a "Hoof-striker"; a girl holds her "mouth open in the sexual O"; we hear a "refrigerator / hum over its meat"; the speaker describes a man who "Is me. / Is." Readers of Warren will easily recognize the pattern of these elocutions. The influence is even more pervasive than this, however. Two entire poems in this volume could almost have been composed by Warren, so close are they conceptually to his way of thinking. "**The Tire Hangs in the Woods**" is not a particularly strong effort, but "**The Traveling Photographer: Circa 1880**" is probably the best poem in the book. The problem is that it virtually reproduces in its pattern Warren's wonderful poem *Audubon*. . . . [In *Dream Flights*, Smith] has returned to the project so wonderfully begun in his early books—recording the communal life as remembered and lived in his native area, tidewater Virginia. Such poems as "**Elegy in an Abandoned Boatyard**" could have been deeply affecting were the writing better. But Smith has used the open nature of these long forms without imposing sufficient control, perhaps forgetting that such freedom demands careful responsibility. We see here the weakening of a considerable talent. (pp. 679-81)

> Peter Stitt, in a review of "Dream Flights," in The Georgia Review, *Vol. XXXVI, No. 3, Fall, 1982, pp. 679-81.*

R. W. FLINT

Dave Smith is blessed with a remarkable memory that serves him like a 19th-century novelist's or landscapist's. The only past that concerns him is his own, or what touches him closely. He shuns the playful impersonations of an Eliot, Pound or Lowell, has no interest in echoing certifiable great styles. The grandeur he likes is "Southern" in the homely way made familiar by Wolfe, Faulkner and Warren—grave, homiletic, dithyrambic—an enveloping momentousness that rises and falls like the coastal tides, sometimes swamping his art, sometimes lifting it to a luminous sheen.

Nothing is harder to criticize than such poetry because so much of it is the casting of a spell. And who can criticize spells? The Dave Smith one treasures has first-rate pictorial gifts; he "paints" scenes and actions that stand quite free of whatever emblematic significance he may want incidentally to give them. His are spacious canvases of fishermen, oystermen, clam diggers in their habitats, dusky country revels, roadside racial dust-ups, old folks' homes, or Cumberland railroad roundhouses to which one may want to return as to the Fenimore Cooper of *The Pioneers*, or to William Sidney Mount or Caleb Bingham.

In Mr. Smith the problem of authentication somehow becomes the problem of how to keep moving, not to sink into an ever-threatening torrid or torpid self-enjoyment. We are rarely treated to the detachment of a Cooper. Down to the sweatiest detail we are expected to want to know exactly *who* is painting the picture and to know it immediately. His early success has made

him as curious about himself and how he got that way as his most avid fans are. He treats his fallibilities as lover, conscience-stricken white Southerner, child of a gun-cradling, hunting, moonshining, sporadically crazy society as if they had reached him from far away, like his weathers and waters. . . .

How does [*In the House of the Judge*] rank with the three precocious books that preceded it? At 40 Mr. Smith has barely reached the age when a secure mastery is looked for in an American. Was it a good idea to desert the windy heights of Utah, his penultimate perch, for the old swamp fevers that might assail him once again in the Florida he now inhabits? Such questions have no good answers. In the *poésie fleuve* that his work has become—a stream much beglamoured by its islands—biographical interest accumulates as fast as his initial contemplative capital thins out. A new source of interest, akin to that in the late Lowell and Berryman, threatens the gifts for which he was first esteemed.

There are still vivid episodes in the new book, especially in the sequence referred to in the title of his book, about an old house in Pennsylvania, rented by the poet and his family, whose late owner ran model trains in the basement while bats chittered in the attic. But in other poems, notably those dealing with his sexual prowess and a lady called Celia, there is a noticeable clenching or seizing up of the ego, like a runner's muscles near the end of a marathon. One expects fine things of Dave Smith, and if this book disappoints, it is not a major delinquency. Every river has its shallows. (p. 38)

> R. W. Flint, "Debut and Continuity," in The New York Times Book Review, *February 13, 1983, pp. 15, 38.*

THOMAS SWISS

It is unusual for an American poet to publish two new collections of verse in a single year, and even more unusual for the same poet to publish a first novel as well as a handful of essays and reviews during that time. But Dave Smith is an unusual writer, and not the least of his many gifts is his productivity. Among his contemporaries I can think of no writer as prolific as Smith; among respected writers in general perhaps only Robert Penn Warren writes so much and so well.

Warren has had a direct and enduring effect on Smith's poetry. Like Warren, Dave Smith has never shied away from large thematic and formal concerns in his writing. He works a full canvas in a sweeping but steady hand that establishes broad historical and psychological boundaries; yet he never fails to illuminate the telling detail, the minute particular. In love with language, Smith is naturally drawn to the particular challenges and difficulties of the long poem, but his largest ambition— to be both a teller and explainer of stories—invites risk: some of these poems are overwritten and underdeveloped, and the novel, by turns, is lyrical and heavy-handed. (p. 483)

[In *Dream Flights*] Smith rearranges the balance of poems found in *Goshawk, Antelope*. There was an emphasis on life in western America in *Goshawk, Antelope,* especially Utah where Smith was then teaching. There were also poems, as there have been in every book he has published, which were rooted in the locales of his childhood in tidewater Virginia. In *Dream Flights* Smith returns primarily to the South, often through imagination or dream, to explore the notion of homecoming in a series of long poems which compose an extended sequence. Even the few poems which are not set in the South focus on the idea of return—physically, psychologically, and, most important, spiritually.

Although some of his poems celebrate the pleasures of his immediate surroundings, Smith usually writes in the voice one expects from a man in exile. There's a quickening energy in these poems, an impatient, heartfelt longing that signals a strong desire to chronicle and connect. The poems are physical and sensuous, but the force that drives them is patently complex and abstract; like a man on a search for something he can't quite name, Smith's journey leads him to write poems which are densely layered, so that even in moments of serenity his persona is compelled to remember Randall Jarrell's words: "There is always something; and past that something / something else."

As the title of this volume suggests, many of the poems use dreaming or that disturbing, self-conscious embodiment of dreaming—remembrance—as a device for connecting what might otherwise seem to the reader a miscellany of images, scenes, and statements. The poems work through association, a complex linking that succeeds because of Smith's gift for creating a rich texture and backdrop for the action of the poem. The reader follows the narrator's flights, tracing the movement of the writer's mind, but does not lose sight of the poem's subject.

Smith's subjects are those of a serious writer: the importance of love, the dark nature of man, the smallness of our historical place. Several of the poems are elegies for those poor, often uneducated characters unable to survive in a world that Smith sees as primarily threatening and stormy. A deep strain of violence runs through Smith's work, and this theme appears in these new poems. Innocence is seldom rewarded: characters who live unguarded lives are inclined to fall prey to the destructive tendencies of nature or of other men. (pp. 483-84)

Smith's strong attraction to violence, to stories of southern life marked by tragedy, is tempered by a vision which is fundamentally romantic. As he explained in an interview in 1976, Smith is interested in "the song of possibility, not the dwindling record of doom." The possibility that most intrigues Smith inheres in spirituality. Even the worst situation, Smith would say, can bring out in us an endurance and grace that are noble, heroic. The poems in *Dream Flights* are, for the most part, celebratory, a feat Smith manages by standing back—if only momentarily—from the immediate tragic implications of events, and by attempting to fit specific situations into a larger perspective: one which allows for sorrow and pain but also for happiness and transcendence. (p. 485)

Although both books are approximately the same length, *Homage to Edgar Allan Poe* contains more than twice as many poems as *Dream Flights*. There are other obvious differences: besides being briefer than many of the poems in *Dream Flights,* the poems in *Homage to Edgar Allan Poe* tend to be shorter-lined, the stanzas more traditionally organized. While the Smith of *Dream Flights* is brooding, searching, deeply reflective, the Smith of *Homage to Edgar Allan Poe* is, by comparison, lighthearted, satisfied, more willing to celebrate the passing moment without guilt or remorse. This is the Smith of the occasional poem; in the first chapter the **"Two Songs for the Round of the Year"** are, in fact, poems on Halloween and Christmas. Some readers will prefer *Homage to Edgar Allan Poe* because it's more accessible.

Some of the poems collected here seem offhand and slight. Perhaps they were written too quickly (any writer as productive as Smith will have this charge leveled against him), or maybe

some are written in such a way that the powerful language—always Smith's strong suit—overpowers the subject of the poem. (pp. 485-86)

Homage to Edgar Allan Poe is not a miscellany: the poems are arranged in five sections, each section having its own design. And Smith's characteristic obsessions and themes are present in these poems, if played out occasionally in a minor key. Smith takes up his argument with the personal and historical past, experimenting with time. Time is seldom a linear process in Smith's work: it's recursive, open not only to new interpretations but to full-scale revision within the context and "artificial" time of the poem. Smith's manipulations render time passive so that memory can play a more active role in getting to the heart of the past, and imagination can take a more active role in the present.

Such a bold technique (one which Dave Smith has been perfecting since *Cumberland Station*) serves him well most of the time. It is an approach that allows, perhaps even demands, the extended breath of the long poem; it works beautifully in the longest and best poem in the book, the title poem. But Smith—with his usual ambition and sense of experimentation—has made this approach work in medium-length poems as well. (p. 486)

Like Joyce and some of his literary heirs Smith risks obscurity when he redefines and enlarges point of view. In many of these poems a more traditional kind of retrospect is evidenced as an adult narrator looks back at himself as a child or young adult. In **"Under a White Shawl of Pine"** the persona develops a scene in which two lovers "came down to the small pier, submerged, where our rowboat/dangled on a tether of rope and gathered water once." As the poem progresses, readers are drawn in by the narrator's own sense of doubt: does he imagine this scene or merely report it? What blend of memory and the powerful nostalgia that alters our sense of the past is at work here? (pp. 486-87)

Like most of the poems in *Homage to Edgar Allan Poe,* this one concerns love. Smith's family has always played an important role in his poems, and several of the finest poems in *Dream Flights* revolve around his son and father (**"The Pornography Box," "Going Home: Ben's Church, Virginia"**); but never has he written so openly to and about his wife and daughters. The poems in the second section of *Homage to Edgar Allan Poe,* **"The Stories of Our Daughters,"** are tender and instructive. Smith is acutely aware of a father's responsibility for his children, and though sometimes that awareness is born of fear for the child's safety (an obsession in the work of Smith's precursor James Dickey), more often it is an awareness born of his earnest desire to be a better parent.

Smith's children wander in and out of these poems. Smith checks his desire to explore dramatic moments and instead offers us children involved in ordinary childhood pleasures: stopping, midsentence, to stare off into the distance, calling up to a nested bird, writing obscenities on the bedroom wall, boarding the bus to school. Smith finds beauty—and often a lesson—in these simple acts; and the writing in these poems is for the most part appropriately spare—as if to say more would be to risk coyness, sentimentality.

Smith does not entirely escape the traditional pitfalls of writing about children, especially when the children are the poet's own. There are weak lines in many of the poems ("her words are shy and sweet"; "The spruce, oh, is blue like her eyes"); and those poems that make an allegorical claim (**"Negative: The**

Little Engine That Could'' and **''The Abused: Hansel and Gretel''**) seem to me overwritten and underimagined.

Smith's novel, *Onliness,* has an allegorical narrative line as well. It's a gloomy story, and one that echoes many of the themes in Smith's poems. (pp. 487-88)

At times the prose sings and the story moves along at a swift pace. Too often, however, the book sags under the weight of stilted dialogue and repetitive aphorisms. Smith's tendency to explain even the least significant action leaves the reader with little or no room for participating in the novel.

It is hard to say what might have saved *Onliness:* a lighter touch or a sense of irony and detachment, perhaps, to balance the stark nature of this emotional and psychological landscape. Although Smith can be a very fine writer, his greatest weakness is to make grandiose that which should be played down.

In Dave Smith's new collection of poetry [*In the House of the Judge*] . . . he writes with mixed results. It seems clear to me now, six months after reviewing his two previous collections, that Smith publishes too many minor or unfinished poems. Still the best poems here, a handful at the least, are fully imagined and beautifully crafted; several are among the best Smith has written to date.

Like sections in his earlier books, especially the extended sequence of poems in *Dream Flights, In the House of the Judge* is orchestrated in such a way that the reader is quickly caught up in the journey Smith undertakes as he explores, once again, his personal history. Characteristically this journey arcs into the larger history of Virginia and then returns, with attendant complications, to the emotional heart of these poems: the lives of loved ones, the shared inheritances he must come to terms with in the ordinariness of daily living.

Geography continues to play a large part in these poems, and Smith is engaged with the literal and symbolic geographies of place—especially Virginia, although he also ventures into Utah and Florida (he has lived in both states) as well as Ohio in a poem which was written, I imagine, to pay homage to James Wright. But Smith has honed his sights in this new book, and his former concern for the larger palette of geography has been partially supplanted by a more focused interest in architecture. Hence a recurring image and metaphor in these poems is the house—that place which allows us to withdraw from the public arena so that we might dream in private and—in Smith's case— take stock of the life of the family. (pp. 488-89)

There is less violence in this new volume, less physical drama as Smith mines his ancestry with a gentler touch than he has in earlier poems. As his chosen metaphor—a house—might suggest, the poems explore interiors, primarily psychological. And, though a sense of loss informs many of these poems, as a hopeful romantic Smith manages to find a place for himself in the present, even if it is as ''only a man wanting to keep the furnace steady, the light on, / the houses whole, the dreamed voice heard.''

At times Smith seems to mistake what Richard Hugo called the ''triggering'' subject of the poem for the real and more complex subject. In **''Building Houses,''** for instance, Smith calls up his dense muscular language in places where under-statement would be more appropriate. . . . Because Smith is prolific, . . . I suspect that it will not be long before we have a first volume of selected poems. We can hope that when that time comes, he will work hard to choose those poems which

are truly ripe, those which accurately represent his formidable gifts. (p. 490)

Thomas Swiss, '''Unfold the Fullness': Dave Smith's Poetry and Fiction,'' in The Sewanee Review, *Vol. XCI, No. 3, Summer, 1983, pp. 483-501.*

FRED CHAPPELL

In the House of the Judge has undeniable felicities. It is hard to resist a poem that begins, ''Everything in the village seemed to dance / all the dances of its kind all day long.'' But it becomes easier to resist when the lines slump into a list of zestlessly rendered details—''doors slammed, dark gone to a green-gold,'' and so forth. The dance is vanished then and a final crush of ridiculous metaphor cancels it forever: ''A plow / grinds through winter's lie like the sun.''

It is not hard to see where Dave Smith has gone astray in this book, but it is hard to see why. The poems are overlaid with a heavy veneer of false elegance, lightened here and there by some blank silliness. It is six miles to Jaynes Farm, the speaker muses in one poem, ''I have run with my body that far.'' (At other times he more intelligibly runs with his dog.) In another poem, children ''lick their lips at the future come / as unlikely as death or birth among them.'' I can believe that children lick their lips, but surely they have more convincing reasons to do so. Many of the lines are burdened with pronouns having unclear antecedents. ''We have no lights. Lightning like a girl's grin / stands me dead center of the parlor. It's maples.'' *What* is maples? The parlor furniture? A girl's grin? Lightning? No, he means the trees silhouetted in the window, a detail awkwardly crammed into the last foot of the stanza.

Unclear antecedents might be the theme of this book, in which ''the convergent dead,'' ''the swirled faces of the dead,'' ''the Yankee dead,'' ''the all-knowing dead,'' and many other kinds of dead show up with soothing regularity. One becomes quite accustomed to them; they are for Smith what roses and robins are for less self-conscious poets, not symbols or images, but merely signals that Smith is composing a poem. There is a hankering here for an allegiance to a living and pervasive past, a seeking after that ironic devotion to a sorrowful history that Faulkner, Allen Tate, and Robert Penn Warren share. But in Smith it is forced and unconvincing, and when he states the theme openly it becomes embarrassing. The speaker of one series of poems has been inhabiting the house of a dead, patriarchal, and largely unjust judge:

> This house, its problems, whose but ours?
> The wiring's unsafe, fuses blow, circuits
> corrupt irrationally . . . how can I
> tell what connects to what, and why,
> unless I summon the unreachable maker?

As flatly importuning as these lines are, one is grateful for them, for they do at least broach a theme, which most of the poems here refuse to do. Too often they wander about, genteel, tweedily presentable, moody, and inconclusive, like university dons in English mystery novels.

It is evident from *In the House of the Judge* that Smith needs a theme, knows that he needs one, and will treat one sweetly when it shows up. His promise is still there, and it is still genuine, though it begins to dim in the fitful glare of a trifling facility. I am confident that he will at last fulfill it in a way his usual admirers have not expected.

Smith's real elegance is to be praised, his phony elegance to be avoided. (pp. 252-53)

Fred Chappell, in a review of "In the House of the Judge," in Western Humanities Review, *Vol. XXXVII, No. 3, Autumn, 1983, pp. 251-53.*

BRUCE WEIGL

Dave Smith's selected poems [*The Roundhouse Voices*] come relatively early in the poet's life—he is only in his early forties—but perhaps deservedly so. Gathered here are parts of six full-length collections as well as over fifty pages of new poems. (p. 245)

Although Smith has been careful in his selections, avoiding his weaker and more ambiguous work, this is nevertheless a thick book, and includes many of Smith's longer, more difficult poems. But the range of Smith's types of poems is great, as are the richness of subject and his powerful consistency and resonance of voice.

The order of poems, with the exception of the opening title poem, is chronological. Smith has, however, avoided the popular structural device of identifying the breaks between books (though an identification of those breaks does seem appropriate to a critical analysis of the work). Instead, the poems are gathered here into one book in an interesting and wise way. Without the identifying boundaries of the individual books, this natural order of poems allows the reader to trace the development (the rises and falls) of a poetic talent as well as of a self, a persona, whose ultimate evolution seems to be towards becoming a public voice.

It is reasonable to regard a "selected poems"—even given the subtleties and ambiguities of that selection process—as the poet's version of himself, so it is no coincidence that Smith opens this book with a poem that comes as close as any to being an extended autobiographical sketch, in the Wordsworthian sense of the autobiography of self. In **"The Roundhouse Voices,"** from . . . *Goshawk, Antelope*, the speaker is trying to tell both the reader and himself who he is. Thus we are introduced to the man whose poetic utterances form this volume. And we can drop the pretense of persona; a poet like Smith does not seek to distinguish himself as a person speaking from the voice in the poems.

Breaking an otherwise chronological sequence, especially with a poem of such lofty intentions as this one, is a risky move. Here baseball functions as an extended metaphor for the rite of passage endured by the man-child of the poem. To gain access to a strange, otherworldly field of play (the inside of a roundhouse) the boy must crawl combat-style under a wire fence and slip past a guard. Eventually he makes his way to an uncle who remains throughout the poem a strange and enigmatic father figure instructing the boy in the fundamentals of more than baseball. By the third stanza we are at the funeral of this uncle, and the boy, grown now, thinks back to the days of the roundhouse lessons. . . . That day in the roundhouse he had managed to escape the guard—who had shouted, *"Who the goddamn hell are you, kid?"*—and slide in the soot and black dust of the roundhouse at his uncle's feet as if into home plate, "scoring." But now, in the presence of the uncle's death, and the much-raised stakes, the grown man has "no one to run from or to" and is suddenly unsure he understood the full weight of his uncle's lessons when the man had tried to show him "the right way to take a hard pitch / in the sun that shudders

on the ready man." It's as if the boy had been blessed but the man of the poem has lost the blessing through time. At this point Smith strikes a chord common in a fair number of poems, the notion of the failure of language to sustain us. The poet longs to go back to a simpler time but the footsteps of the guard

> . . . come pounding into words
> and even the finger I give death is words
> that won't let us be what we wanted, each one
> chasing and being chased by dreams in the dark.
> Words are all we ever were and they did us
> no damn good. . . .

Later, in the next stanza, words are "coal-hard and they come in wings / and loops like despair . . ." and words are "skinned and numbed by too many bricks," observations which lead the reader into the final four lines of the poem:

> I have had enough of them and bring them back here
> where the tick and creak of everything dies
> in your tiny starlight and I stand down
> on my knees to cry, *Who the hell are you, kid?*

It seems clear that in **"The Roundhouse Voices"** Smith wished to define the challenge before him. Waking to a day the speaker "did not want to see," he tries to reach back once again to the past for assistance but there is no answer. There is only his inability to connect vitally with a past cut off by death, and the empty cold rooms of the roundhouse where even hope has become an illusion and language a failed promise. It is with this recognition that the poet and—because of the poem's placement in the book—the reader, venture into the subsequent poems. But the poems, as if on their own, prove another conclusion.

From the forty-eight poems of *The Fisherman's Whore* Smith has selected only five, all from the book's first section, which deals largely with the abiding importance of place, specifically the Virginia coasts. Part of Smith's strategy in defining his poetic self and simultaneously developing his public voice takes the form of an intimate association of place. (pp. 245-47)

Place has remained an essential element in Smith's work and no place has been a richer reservoir for image-making and myth-making for him than the coasts of Virginia. Among the watermen of this area the poet found an inspiring ethic in their stubborn insistence upon living respectfully and quietly among natural elements that are often destructive and always ambivalent. In a poet who sees his role as a combatant against the world's chaos, this appropriate metaphor brings out his best. (p. 248)

Unlike **"The Roundhouse Voices,"** these poems established possibilities of renewal, and in them Smith identified the essential landscape to which he would return again and again for inspiration and for spiritual sustenance.

After the publication of *The Fisherman's Whore*, Smith caught fire and began a sustained six or seven years of writing that would extend through five full-length collections of poems, hundreds of pages of criticism and a novel. As an artist Smith responded well to his success with readers and editors; the more he published the more he wrote and the more he wrote the better writer he became. In *Cumberland Station* Smith is more able to heighten the effects of his sometimes exhausting, winding narratives with deft accentual lines. Also, the version Smith gives us here of *Cumberland Station* is radically different from the book itself. *Cumberland Station* was longer than his first book (over fifty pages) yet he has chosen to include only eight of its poems here. Again his selections are advantageous, from the haunting and beautiful **"On a Field Trip at Fredericksburg"** . . . to the surprisingly unabashed celebration of poetry in the sonnet called **"The Spring Poem."** Also included in Smith's selection from *Cumberland Station* is **"The Perspective & Limits of Snapshots,"** an intelligent poem about the limitations of art's way of capturing life. (pp. 248-49)

In the selection of poems from his fourth book, *Goshawk, Antelope*, Smith has been more indulgent and the reader is thus fortunate. What Smith most dramatically demonstrates in this book and what sets him apart from most of his contemporaries and elevates his work to the level of national importance is simply his ability to get better and better. *Goshawk, Antelope* is a book whose focus is the paradoxical problem of making art out of the muck of the world around us, reinforcing Smith's desire for a public identity. To accomplish this act and to dramatize it for the readers' sake, Smith confronts nature and the irony of man's presence in nature so that each poem represents a struggle, on the page and in the heart, of man "fumbling / for love, for living words / that might be knowledge" (**"Messenger"**). So he works against the bleaker view of **"The Roundhouse Voices."** (pp. 250-51)

Place and the pathology of family are now subdued to larger more universal emotions as the poet gradually assumes his role as public voice. Many of the poems of *Goshawk, Antelope* are difficult and extremely demanding. Because the poet has so unequivocally given himself to the transforming power of language and imagination, he has trouble sustaining the intensity necessary to demonstrate the seriousness of his journey of discovery. But cut back to arguably the best thirty pages of a book of over one hundred pages, the load has been lightened considerably. (p. 251)

Goshawk, Antelope was an important book in Smith's evolution as a poet; perhaps it is even his best book. But in spite of this high level of achievement, or because of it, Smith did not hesitate to continue his experimentation.

Homage to Edgar Allan Poe is largely a book about love and this is made clear given the eight poems Smith has included from it here. He opens this section with **"Halloween Delight,"** which also opens the book. Love in this particular poem takes the shape of a childlike delight in the world. Consisting of six sestets of two- and three-beat lines variously rhymed, the poem is as inventive conceptually as it is formally. The regularity of the rhymes is subdued slightly through the use of frequent enjambment. Most striking in comparison with most of his earlier work is the tone of this poem and others like it included here. Here is a peace with the world seldom seen before, and a letting-down of that fiercely driven intensity *to know*. Here the poet is content just *to be;* instead of fighting to get back to memory, he simply lets memory pour over him. . . . (p. 252)

Similar poems included here are **"Reading the Books Our Children Have Written,"** a touching prose poem about the continuity of family and the easy, unquestionable love among young children and their parents; and **"Pond,"** a poem in celebration of

> . . . the last time you were in love,
> the vertigo, the skidding infinite sky,
> the lily's perfect, opening moves. . . .

These lyrics contrast sharply with the thicker, more conceptually ambitious poems which are sometimes unable to bear the weight of their own lush rhetoric, such as **"Nekkid: Homage to Edgar Allan Poe."** It is difficult to get a fix on the tone of this poem. Because the poet juxtaposes almost whimsical imagery of a young boy's description of his unwanted summer-camp trip with much more serious moments of first, uncorrupted love, it is never quite clear how we are to feel about the characters of the poem. Here our acceptance of Smith's unusual marriage of speaker with dead poet depends largely upon the poem's irony being clear and sharp and direct; unfortunately it is not. **"Portrait of Lady"** and **"Wedding Song"** suffer similarly; despite their rich and inventive language and generous emotions, these poems often feel forced, their conceptual devices too near the surface of the poem, so that the drama does not unfold as naturally as in Smith's best poems of this kind. (p. 253)

But these difficulties are quickly and easily forgotten as we make our way into the next fifty pages, chosen from Smith's sixth full-length collection, *Dream Flights*. These are remarkable, linguistically muscular poems whose honesty and aesthetic achievement are unquestionable. Like much of the book from which these poems were selected, these poems return to the poet's Virginia coastal landscapes, where he was first driven to make sense of the world with words. The time and distance away from his native soil have made his appraisal of his homeland and its ghosts less romanticized than earlier, similar versions, and informed by a maturity of vision that allows the poet to wander his physical and imaginative landscapes freely; from these free-flights comes some of Smith's best work, mostly in the form of longer, meditative poems such as **"Elegy in an Abandoned Boatyard."** . . . (pp. 253-54)

Equally impressive accomplishments are two other long poems, **"The Pornography Box,"** a painful but ultimately affirmative remembrance of a lost father, and **"The Colors of Our Age: Pink and Black,"** a sweeping, 171-line era piece which simultaneously evokes the racially turbulent sixties and the figure of a girl the poet calls Celia who functions as muse for the way her presence in the poem allows the poet to reconstruct this critical juncture of emotional and spiritual development. . . . With these poems—in which Smith has brought together realism and pathos; the hard, gritty language of his native place; grand and lofty phrases; the music of the language which we speak and imagine and finely controlled accentual rhythms— Smith establishes himself as a poet rigorously devoted to his craft and worthy of our close scrutiny and ultimately our high praise.

In the poems selected from Smith's seventh and most recent full-length collection, *In the House of the Judge*, the poet most fully and rightfully realizes his role as public voice. The thirteen poems selected for inclusion here have in common a passionate intermingling of Whitmanesque American mysticism with Smith's penchant for capturing epiphanic moments of personal and universal history and compressing them into vivid cadences. (pp. 254-55)

In these poems Smith begins to achieve a clarity that comes only through a mastery of both poetic formality and a colloquial matter-of-factness. He has shed his tendency to preach to the reader. One hesitates to make these kinds of comparisons, but the poems from *In the House of the Judge* have resonant qualities that recall the poems of Theodore Roethke's *The Far Field*. Both of these works are characterized by a powerful sense of self-acceptance and by a voice unburdened with concerns for the ego. (p. 256)

The last poems are selected from a somewhat hybrid book called **Gray Soldiers** (a homage to the South, to the people of the South, to Southernness), and over fifty pages of new poems written after its publication. The best of the new poems are those whose language is clear and accessible but whose conceptual center is complicated through the process of a layering of consciousness. Again, like the later Roethke, Smith is no longer the combatant against chaos; chaos has not disappeared but it has been pushed into the background by a sensibility wise and patient enough to endure the past and celebrate the modest present. (p. 257)

The selection of new poems also includes a great deal of formal experimentation, sometimes successful, sometimes not, and a point of view that is curiously more distant than before. This distance comes as an inevitable result of Smith's growth and development as a poet. He no longer feels compelled to give the self a starring role in the poems; now all of the poet's energy can be focused on the "other," and the "I" functions mostly as a storyteller, artfully manipulating his tales behind the scenes. . . .

Dave Smith has come so far in search of the right words and has already given us so many daring and memorable poems that he has earned the right to be heard and studied with at least a small portion of the huge passion it took to make these poems. (p. 258)

> *Bruce Weigl, in a review of "The Roundhouse Voices," in* TriQuarterly 64, *No. 64, Fall, 1985, pp. 245-58.*

CHARLES MOLESWORTH

Now that Smith [in **The Roundhouse Voices**] has selected poems from throughout his career, arranged them more or less chronologically and added recent work as well, we have a substantial volume and an occasion to see if the poet has indeed begun to achieve major status.

Looked at individually, Smith's poems are indeed accomplished. He has a distinctive style, a subject matter and a gravity of language and sensibility that is worth our attention. In his best poems, such as **"Elegy in an Abandoned Boatyard," "The Pornography Box"** and **"Tide Pools,"** Smith demonstrates an undeniable honesty and is willing both to display his experience and his values and to test them against the frames of memory and introspection. He is infatuated with narrative and enjoys pointillist description touched here and there with figurative language until it generates a highly expressive atmosphere.

But if we take the volume of selected poems as an invitation to read Smith in a larger context, that is, alongside the other poets of his generation, we may see his work differently. Furthermore, if we look hard at what happens to the speaker in each poem—how he reveals and shapes his psyche through the poem, and how he chooses his words—we will also find some cause for dissent from the critical consensus. First, the generational context. Smith's work is related to that of William Matthews, Norman Dubie, Stanley Plumly, among others. The main affinities are a persistent return to the theme of loss, the use of family relations (especially of fathers and sons) as the framework for all emotional value, and the employment of a dramatized scene as the chief lyric structure. (p. 320)

Of course, some of Smith's concern with loss, family and the dramatized scene comes from his indebtedness to such poets as Richard Hugo, James Wright, Gerald Stern and Robert Penn Warren. Indebtedness is part of every poet's work, and Smith's work is indeed enriched by his models. But each of these older poets is known more for his sensibility than for any innovations in form, scale or technique. Smith's art also avoids experimentalism, and it seldom puts any pressure on the received lyric structure. While not in itself a sign of weakness, this disinclination to test new or widely ranging lyric formats eventually betrays Smith's sentimentality and the vague basis of his emotional claims. (pp. 320-21)

In many of Smith's poems the dramatized scene is recalled, heightened, colored by the poet's sense of frailty (the frailties of love and memory) and then resolved by a sort of wistful longing that things might be otherwise. Often this wistful longing centers on the realization of language's insufficiency: "Words stopped," "'culled / by codes we never know," "It was too odd to explain, and wrong," "a naked silence, / its language wild and shocked." These and other such phrases indicate the emotional aphasia that keeps the poems from enacting any transformation or transcendence. Almost inevitably this limits each poem to the emotional trauma that the poet began with, and thus there is seldom any sense of liberation or expansion in consciousness. . . .

Smith has neither the Enlightenment's sense of rationality nor Romanticism's furious ego-strength against which to pit his sense of loss. As a consequence the poems must rely on a plangent language (in effect, on a highly poeticized vocabulary) in order to develop their emotional authority. In turn, this leads Smith into awkward figures of speech which have neither precision nor plain force. We move, then, from the abstraction of a phrase like "blind miles of light" to the wooliness of a "knife . . . brilliant as mooncla w" to the baroque tangle of "blood-button nipples sudden / as rain in the goblet of wine / we forgot."

But it isn't just that Smith reaches for an emotional intensity that his language can't quite contain. Often his thinking is convoluted. . . . (p. 321)

Another consequence of Smith's reluctance to question models or test new structures is that he blends the prosaic and the mystical in ways that do justice to neither (something that was especially noticeable in the late work of James Wright). The poems proceed as if the poet has every right to claim a special status for his vision without justifying it with some exemplary transformation, some creditable emotional enlargement or even some enchantment through urgent music. . . .

The volume of selected poems also reveals the fact that Smith's work is dominated less by poems of locale than it is by those about domestic anxiety or the traumas of his childhood and adolescence. Smith's work is not unlike that of many of our poets under fifty who have been much praised. Emotional honesty, an interest in domestic subject matter, a trust in the power of the poet's ego to appropriate all areas of personal experience and render them authoritative, and a penchant for the short, straightforward, free-verse lyric are the features singled out for praise. In many senses, such poets form the mainstream of contemporary poetry even though their poems are often derivative and strained. The dominant note of humble irony that frequently characterizes them just as frequently conceals a sort of emotional colonization, a sense that all experience and all language, even if it is marked by loss and failure, is finally in the service of proving how sensitive the poet is. When poetry largely abandons its claim to an alternative or transformed or objective world (or sense of the world) and settles for the thoroughly subjectivized drama of the sensitive individual, it narrows its claims on our attention. Despite his skill, such narrowness threatens Dave Smith's poetry. (p. 322)

Charles Molesworth, "Poetic Relations," in The Nation, Vol. 241, No. 10, October 5, 1985, pp. 320-22.

HELEN VENDLER

In the [critical] work of the two poets, [Robert Hass and Dave Smith], a determined effort toward the colloquial (by contrast to the discursive or written model) keeps asserting itself. Academic writing may seem to the poet too enslaved to the head, too unconscious of the body, too much that of the scribe, too little that of the bard, manifesting too strongly the formal written character, too little the genial social utterance. Both Hass [in *Twentieth Century Pleasures*] and Smith [in ***Local Assays: On Contemporary American Poetry***] want to rehabilitate the personal essay. (p. 54)

Poets [like Hass] feel so keenly that academic teachers dilute the intensity and volatility of poetry that they press ever harder, in their own writing about poetry, to insist on the passional investment that art calls for from its readers.

Dave Smith shares this insistence of tone, especially in urging on us, in two essays, the power of Robert Penn Warren's poetry:

> What terror now not to know what had been certain reality, to have to conjecture "perhaps" and to relive the old contingencies, the old hope of continuity—and what courage to make this choice!. . . For even if the promise of reality will be only the scalding of flesh and the not-knowing, passion is all. Passion is feeling; man is feeling; poetry is feeling. In his self-interrogation Warren rejects his earlier *Tempest* tone and, like Lear, calls on the crack of winds.

The tone heard here—a very American one—is that of the lay sermon, in which the spiritual instruction of a pupil is undertaken by a spiritual initiate. What is odd, in both Hass and Smith, is that this celebratory, initiatory, and hortatory tone coexists, as I have said, with remarks from the sensual life of every day. Smith's essay on Richard Hugo begins:

> I had been rereading Richard Hugo's poems during the 1979 World Series in which the all but trounced Pittsburgh Pirates made a stunning and memorable comeback to win going away. I remarked to a friend watching that last televised game that Hugo was the George Raft of poetry. I meant to imply that Hugo was a player of tough-guy roles. My friend, without blinking, said that Hugo was instead closer to the manager of the Pirates, or would be if he chewed. We were, I think, both right.

A paragraph later, the tone has changed to the academic. . . . A few pages later, we are listening to a lay sermon. . . . (pp. 54-5)

What is implied by such changes of tone, cohabiting in a single essay, is a refusal to take a single position or to accept a single form for critical writing. Is an essay on poetry an anecdotal conversation between friends, or a critical description, or an exhortation to a higher self-scrutiny? Does it descend from the familiar letter, from the gloss on the sacred text, or from the sermon? The control of tone in Samuel Johnson, in Arnold, in Eliot, even in Jarrell, means that they were surer of their authority of position and of the homogeneity of their putative audience. Critical practice in America nowadays suggests that the critics are not sure of themselves or of the audience they address. (p. 55)

Dave Smith, himself a southern writer, argues for the importance of Robert Penn Warren and James Dickey, as well as for James Wright, Richard Hugo, and Philip Levine. These are all "masculine" poets (though in different ways) and they are perhaps less attractive to women (I speak for myself here) than to men. Penn Warren writes in large elemental terms, with a cosmic sense of the degree to which nature and man are pitted against each other and yet constrained to a symbiosis; he reaches for the grandest of words, the most transcendental of symbols, the most ambitious claims of moral vision (even when that vision is despairing or occluded). His poems open themselves out into long, loose-limbed sequences, ranging far in space and time. Smith loves this large reach in Warren, and writes generously about it. . . . As usual, Smith's emphasis—here as in his other essays—is on the poet's repertory of images. Smith is far less likely to examine the poet's words as such—yet this is where an adverse criticism of the poets he admires would begin. Warren's image of the migrating geese in the poem "Heart of Autumn" may in itself be a moving one; but can the same be said of Warren's language about it? In watching the geese, Warren says, he feels himself transformed. . . . (p. 56)

A reader might well be put off by the tough legs with folded feet, by the awkwardness of syntactic difference between the apparently parallel arms and legs, by the phrase "my heart is impacted with," by the unpleasing changes of rhythm, and by the nineteenth-century "sublimity" in the words about inexpressibility at the close. A poem can of course survive such difficulties, and perhaps Warren's poem does. But I would like to see greater recognition of the questionable nature both of Warren's language and of his large moral assertions (Smith quotes approvingly, "Passion / Is all. Even / The sleaziest"). A criticism that loves imagery is likely to slight both phrasing and syntax.

Smith is more willing to concede problems in Philip Levine's writing. His praise reveals some of the qualities he values in a poet, as he says of Levine:

> Though he takes on the largest subjects of death, love, courage, manhood, loyalty, etc., he brings the mysteries of experience down into the ordinarily inarticulate events and objects of daily life. His speaker and subject is the abused and disabused spirit of the common yet singular self. He risks the maudlin, the sentimental, the banal, and worse [in order to be] "A man alone, ignorant / strong, holding the burning moments / for all they're worth."

In poets like Levine and Hugo, a rough confrontation with the ordinary, in order to make it articulate, stirs Smith's admiration. His fine essay on Hugo—the best, to my mind, in the book—sums up in a quick and excellent portrait sketch the way in which the life of one male writer might speak to that of another. . . . James Wright's poetry of the depressed Ohio working class moves Smith to another form of identification; and he can say of Dickey's "wandering hero" that though he is "engaged in motorcycling, hunting, flying, climbing mountains, or making love," nonetheless he is "like most Southern writers, divided in his loyalties to the self as macho realist and the self as intellectual."

It is clear that these were the poets whom Smith depended on in the Sixties and Seventies for spiritual kinship and sustenance. He can read other poets with appreciation—there are commendations here of Sylvia Plath and May Swenson, for instance—but those are admirations from a distance. The question, "How can a man act and yet think, plunge into nature and yet live in the mind?" is the most urgent one for Smith and for the poets he most warmly recommends to our attention; this question generates his canon. (pp. 56-7)

*Helen Vendler, "Looking for Poetry in America,"
in* The New York Review of Books, *Vol. XXXII, No.
17, November 7, 1985, pp. 53-60.*

PAUL CHRISTENSEN

Dave Smith is writing at the head of his own generation; at 43, one would think he had few losses to ponder, but his considerable output (eight books to date) from which *The Roundhouse Voices* is a selection, makes a relentless lamentation over lost innocence. Many poems turn on an event in which he was lured through sexual encounter into the world of adults, parenthood, family, and thus the sorrows of generation and death. Smith's world is one of decaying boats, disappearing towns, deceased relatives and old friends, with few consolations in the here and now. His nearly operatic lushness can sometimes make one feel he is raising more than this one complaint; second readings show him to be an obsessive chronicler of youth crucified by wily country girls. It does not give him much to savor, though he writes volubly of his dilemma. . . .

Smith is deeply troubled over sexuality, and in many poems associates the female with knives, scissors, weapons of all sorts, which he suspects are implements used to bring boys into manhood. This is narrow experience, but it is never monotonous; the sheer powers of Smith's language, his musical lushness, the complex punning—at which he is a master—are all so heaped upon his arguments that one falls under his potent spells and believes what he says. He has a gospel, but it isn't the old familiar one, or is it?

*Paul Christensen, "Notes From the Green World,"
in* Book World—The Washington Post, *January 5,
1986, p. 6.*

PHOEBE PETTINGELL

The art of poetry and the craft of criticism represent a dichotomy even when co-existing in the same person. Dave Smith embodies both in two new books. *The Roundhouse Voices* contains work from seven of his previous collections, together with twenty-two new poems. *Local Assays* includes some of Smith's best reviews, along with several theoretical musings, and an interview in which he answers questions about his own writing posed by Peter Balakian. Smith is talkative. It would be inaccurate to say that, over the years, he has honed his poems. Rather, he has expanded the down-to-earth narratives of his first book, *The Fisherman's Whore* . . . , until they have spread into such sprawling, seductive meditations as the recent

"Winesaps" or "Field Music." His criticism, by turns, woos, exhorts, cajoles, or lectures, with bursts of homely metaphors that compare the poet to an athlete or a hound one moment, then preach on the text of morality and art in the next. What binds these diverse elements together is Smith's manner. He always speaks as to one person—not at an amorphous audience. Passion infuses his inflection; he wants his readers to care as much as he does, and tries to make us see the splendors he perceives by any means at hand. In his poems, the tone becomes more reflective, reminiscent. In both, the voice sounds friendly. Though he can sweet-talk, evangelize, even browbeat his audience on occasion, he never patronizes them. (p. 346)

Smith assays to portray the making of poems as a craft, like commercial fishing, or organizing a football scrimmage (**"Notes on the Responsibility and the Teaching of Creative Writing"**), or hunting with dogs (**"Beagling"**). His eloquent tribute to Richard Hugo searches for a baseball player or manager whose style would correspond to Hugo's propensity for "tough-guy roles." A woodcarver becomes the ideal type of the artist in an early poem, **"The Spinning Wheel in the Attic"**:

> Not for beauty's sake, or art's, this wheel
>   came round in his calloused palms,
>   bent willows and oak,
>
> formed for the work of spinning whole cloth,
>   gatherer of scraps fine and coarse,
>   a tool.

Aesthetes, in Smith's book, toil not, neither do they spin. To his sorrow and indignation, however, "our critics venerate the impenetrable art-poems by John Ashbery, award prizes to James Merrill's *The Changing Light at Sandover,* and develop a nearly Talmudic commentary about Charles Olson." In contrast, "the finest living American poet," Robert Penn Warren, can "fix in our minds an image of man." (This last word connotes gender, not the generic.)

Smith is one of our finest practical critics, himself. His essays on Wright, Hugo, and Levine provide the outstanding analyses of those writers to date. He characterizes the intimacy we feel for many of Sylvia Plath's poems by observing, they "are just . . . like members of our family, the suspicious members"; then concludes electrically, "That is what I feel in [her] . . . *Collected Poems,* the crack and sizzle of lightning that Mrs. Shelley invited down to create life." Smith's acuteness as a reader of poetry communicates itself in the same fresh language he brings to his own poems.

He does have blind spots, however. As a self-proclaimed pastoralist, he distrusts city-slickers—especially poets who hang around art galleries, or talk to dead friends through Ouija boards. Smith does recognize that subjects other than artisans or hunters or good ol' boys can equally fix in our minds an image of man. In his speculative pieces, though, he occasionally falls into denunciations of what regional poets like to call "the Eastern literary establishment." In these moments, he sounds, at best, like a proletarian romantic of the 1930s, at worst, a yahoo. (pp. 347-48)

"I don't think you could be a great poet like Whitman unless you'd written as much as Whitman. And as badly," Smith claims, who has surpassed, in the course of little more than a decade, the output of many poets over entire lifetimes. Smith does not repeat himself, or keep his boat cruising familiar waters. Each of his books has sought out a new direction. One does not sense this clearly from *The Roundhouse Voices,* unfortunately. Whitmanesque in many respects, Smith chose to rewrite a good many of his poems for this volume. Second thoughts are not necessarily better, particularly when they express themselves in conventional language. Examples from the recent *Homage to Edgar Allan Poe* . . . and *In the House of the Judge* . . . provoke a twinge of disappointment at the decline of old friends. As fine a poem as **"Nekkid"** is almost ruined. **"Waking in the Endless Mountains"** once spoke of how "Nobody means to do this, to lie in the village green, / but the earth around me is cool, wet, as if it had just been birthed." In the revised version, that green has become "village dirt," and the ground is sentimentally "waiting like a mother / whispering many names." The magical ending, in which the speaker imagines leaving his sleeping children, "while I try to say softer than the brightest star, Goodbye. Goodbye." now mushily concludes "letting my voice be in their dreams, / saying softly" etc. This makes a different poem, not a stronger one. Over and over again, one notices gaps like missing teeth in a favorite line, or strange new protuberances. Naturally, some things have been changed for the better, but too many of the changes have replaced something rich and strange with a phrase that sounds like just anybody—not Dave Smith.

My other complaint is that this Selected omits too great a portion of each of the author's previous volumes—it could happily have been at least a third again as long. What is included, belongs there. This collection concentrates on Smith's most persistent themes: the people of Virginia's tidewater, how it felt to grow up as a Southerner during the 1960s, Smith's family—especially his three children. Not all his landscapes center in the Southeast. *Goshawk, Antelope* . . . evokes a mysterious West, all the more enchantingly perceived because it is foreign to the poet. The recent poems, hitherto uncollected, seem to justify those selections made from earlier books. *The Roundhouse Voices* is probably best read as something new, not as a retrospective.

"Why is it we keep what we cannot bear / to use, and can't escape?" Smith demands in **"Winesaps,"** and the question might stand as a motto for what he chooses to preserve through his poetry: childhood defeats, adolescent shame, adult despair, each somehow transformed by coming to terms with the human condition. (pp. 348-49)

Phoebe Pettingell, "Dave Smith's Voice," in Poetry, *Vol. CXLVII, No. 6, March, 1986, pp. 346-50.*

Robert (Anthony) Stone

1937?-

American novelist and scriptwriter.

Stone's novels feature intelligent yet rootless and alienated protagonists who struggle to survive in a brutal world of violence, drugs, and alcohol. Jean Strouse noted, "There aren't any good guys in Robert Stone country, but there are people who fight the good fight—unholy innocents." As psychological portraits of struggle and defeat, each of Stone's novels steadily progress toward an apocalyptic climax. While writing with straightforward realism, Stone infuses his work with literary allusions and symbolic and ironic crosscut scenes that contribute to his protagonists' growing sense of quest and failure. According to A. Alvarez, "[Stone] is one of the few writers who are at once culturally sophisticated—full of sly quotes and literary references, strong on moral ambiguities—and streetwise."

Although not overtly autobiographical, Stone's novels reflect his troubled childhood, which included abandonment by his father and his mother's psychological problems, as well as his Catholic schooling and, later, his participation in a drug-oriented counterculture group. Drug and alcohol abuse, psychological probings of his characters, and themes related to Catholicism are among the elements included in Stone's fiction. Stone's highly-praised first two novels, *A Hall of Mirrors* (1967) and *Dog Soldiers* (1974), address contemporary American social issues while portraying intelligent yet despairing characters who attempt to overcome personal miseries. *A Hall of Mirrors* relates the adventures of three drug-ravaged characters within the social, political, and racial turmoil of the 1960s. *Dog Soldiers* follows a disaffected American journalist in Vietnam who becomes involved in heroin smuggling. This novel, which won the National Book Award, is considered a poignant and powerful depiction of the effects on individuals of the Vietnam War and the drug culture. Both *A Hall of Mirrors* and *Dog Soldiers* were adapted for film, the former as *WUSA*, and the latter as *Who'll Stop the Rain?*

In his third novel, *A Flag for Sunrise* (1981), Stone presents both conservative and liberal views of American involvement in Central America through his depiction of a small fictitious country torn by guerrilla warfare. One character in this work, a Catholic nun, questions both her faith and her national loyalties when confronted with human brutality. *Children of Light* (1985) examines how the American film industry contributes to social malaise. This novel centers on an uninspired writer addicted to narcotics and alcohol who undertakes a journey to free himself from aimlessness but encounters a series of obstacles which undermine his intentions. Considered stylistically strong for Stone's effective use of irony, *Children of Light* was faulted by several critics for lacking focus. While Stone's later works have received more negative commentary than his earlier novels, he has secured a reputation as a powerful writer. A. Alvarez stated: "In just four novels in almost twenty years Robert Stone has established a world and style and tone of voice of great originality and authority. It is a world without grace or comfort, bleak, dangerous, and continually threatening."

(See also *CLC*, Vols. 5, 23 and *Contemporary Authors*, Vols. 85-88.)

© Jerry Bauer

JEAN STROUSE

Robert Stone is the apostle of strung out. People in his novels have reached the end of the tether: alone, desperate, scared, doing a lot of hard liquor and drugs, they hit the road. And as they go they keep listening in the dark, against all odds, for something that might be a moral channel marker, or love, or God, or just a way to get through the night.

Critics have compared Mr. Stone to Conrad, Faulkner, Hemingway, Graham Greene, Malcolm Lowry, Nathanael West; all apt enough, but there's a James T. Farrell, Raymond Chandler, Dashiell Hammett strain as well—a hard-edged, lonely intelligence that sets bright promise off against stark failure and deals its mordant hand lightly. (p. 1)

Like his characters, Mr. Stone doesn't stay in one place for long: he has ventured to try something new with each book. *A Hall of Mirrors* (1967) leads a trio of wasted 1960's weirdos into a nest of right-wing fanatics in New Orleans, where America's racial and political conflicts rage to an apocalyptic blood bath. *Dog Soldiers* (1974), spare and cinematic, starts out in Vietnam with an American journalist smuggling three kilos of heroin to the United States, and ends up literally bringing the

358

war home to a bizarre shoot-out in the Sierras. In *A Flag for Sunrise* [1981], his most prodigal, densely textured, and, I think, brilliant book, Mr. Stone turns to American intervention in Central America, tracing the paths of some latter-day pilgrims through Catholicism, alcoholism, liberalism and Gnosticism toward the revolution in tiny Tecan (more or less Nicaragua). (pp. 1, 24)

Now, with *Children of Light,* Mr. Stone shifts his focus from the war-torn third world to sunny California, from soldiers of fortune to dissolute writers, from gun-running and the demiurge to movie making and schizophrenia. The result is a fine, complex, often funny tale, full of lights and shadows, with great dialogue and a sharp sense of character and place. It has some problems, . . . but they measure the daring of trying something new, and the risk proves well worth taking.

Both *A Hall of Mirrors* and *Dog Soldiers* were made into disappointing films, and some of Mr. Stone's best scenes here take steady aim at "the industry." The novel starts in Hollywood, where a burnt-out screenwriter named Gordon Walker is just waking up, still half-drunk, to the reproach of a dazzling California day. In short order Walker throws up, tries not to look in the mirror, contemplates without affection the naked girl from whose bed he's just climbed, helps himself to her Valium and vodka, does a line of cocaine and tries not to think about his kids or recently failed marriage. Instead of writing, Walker has been acting in a Seattle production of *King Lear.* Lines from the play keep coming to mind. Catching his mirrored reflection by mistake, Walker looks, he decides, "like a man in his forties who drank"—and then hears from Lear: "'He hath ever but slenderly known himself.' For the first time in his articulate, thoroughly examined life, Walker wondered if that might not be true of him. Not possible, he decided. He knew himself well enough. It was the rest of things that gave him trouble."

Wrong. Walker keeps blindly trying to figure himself out—and at the same time to obliterate the past—in a fog of drink and coke and quotes. Needing a dream, "a little something to get by on," he takes off for Baja where a former lover, Lu Anne Bourgeois, his "dark angel"—Louisianan, Catholic, schizophrenic—is on location playing the lead in a film he wrote 10 years ago based on Kate Chopin's 1899 novel, *The Awakening.*

On the way, Walker encounters a cast of cameos who deserve a review of their own. He spends a night at a seedy beach hotel called San Epifanio (all double-entendres intended) with another former lover, Shelley—"a clamorous presence, never at rest. Even quiet, her reverie cast a shadow and her silences had three kinds of irony. She was a workout." Looking for something to ease him off drinking and coke, Walker next stops to see Sam Quinn, a former stunt man with too much belly and a gold death's-head in one of his front teeth. Quinn hasn't got any downers—he's just buried an old pal, welded into an oil drum, who OD'd on nitrous oxide—but as he and Walker talk about old times, they spot two hang gliders high over a nearby ridge. "Think that isn't kicks, man?" asks Quinn. "That's the way to do your life, Gordo. Look the gray rat in the eye." . . .

Ten years ago, Lu Anne gave Walker *The Awakening,* and he wrote her into the part of Edna Pontellier, a young Louisianan who finds she can't fully give herself to her children and stifling marriage; Edna tries painting, takes a lover and finally walks into the sea. Ten years ago, nobody wanted the screenplay,

but now, after the book has been "discovered" by academics and feminists, Hollywood has taken it up: "It was all perceived as prestigious, timely and cheap. There was a real possibility that the interests involved might find themselves in control of a well-made picture that would generate good reviews, awards and, with the right handling, a favorable profit line. A vestigial social impulse was being discharged. Somewhere, deep within the Funhouse, they had opted for a calculated risk."

Walker arrives to find Grand Isle, La., reconstructed on a Mexican beach—live oaks trucked in from Northern California, dripping with Spanish moss, a field of flowering anthemis vines, a tiny, antique trolley set on a narrow-gauge track across the sand. He also finds Walter Drogue Jr., the picture's director, who "thinks most people are wienies," wants to grab Walker's writing credit and tells Lu Anne, about to do one of Edna's last scenes: "Take care of it for me, kid. . . . The old nothingness-and-grief routine." . . .

And Walker eventually finds Lu Anne, giving a brilliant performance as Edna, off her antipsychotic medication . . . , beginning to drink and hallucinate. Her psychiatrist husband and children have just left the set—and probably her life. Soon she ends up with Walker in bed, then in his coke stash. . . .

There aren't any good guys in Robert Stone country, but there are people who fight the good fight—unholy innocents who do, as Quinn put it, "look the gray rat in the eye"—and Lu Anne belongs among them. In *Dog Soldiers,* Ray Hicks, a former Marine who reads Nietzsche and agrees to carry heroin to the United States as a favor to a friend, gets intercepted by a group of lethal, crooked narcs; he runs for a while, then settles in to battle with a kind of samurai grace. In *A Flag for Sunrise,* an American nun called Sister Justin (Martyr) loses her faith and her virginity, joins the local revolutionaries, gets captured and hideously tortured by a lieutenant in the Guardia Nacional and manages to take him out spiritually as she dies. . . .

In *Children of Light,* Mr. Stone sets the fight on less exotic ground, among writers and actors and failures of love. Here, art plays tricks with life and Hollywood plays tricks with art; children go wrong; madness and genius walk their fine lines. In order to act, Lu Anne (whose stage name is Lee Verger) stops taking her pills even though without them she hallucinates. . . . (p. 24)

Lu Anne flips quickly from grief to antic mania. She can match Walker quote for quote, but where his main text is Lear, hers cover an extravagant range from *As You Like It* . . . and *Antony and Cleopatra* to Emily Dickinson, Kate Chopin, Kipling, Dickens and Scripture. But literature, like religion and love, can't save her. (It's to her Walker says, "I would die for you"—true but not really helpful.) She's out there by herself, staring down the gray rat, and she makes her own apocalypse. On the top of a mountain, in a wildly sad and clever scene complete with storm, stigmata, Shakespeare, biblical cantation and Gadarene swine, she goes for holiness in a pigsty.

Mr. Stone has a genius for the undercut: he provides no safe places or easy comforts—no clear moral sanctions or oversimplifications. Like Lu Anne (and most of his main characters), he was raised Catholic, and like her he cannot find redemption in the traditions behind ritual and allusion. When Shelley delivers a kind of epilogue with a quote from *As You Like It*—"Men have died from time to time and worms have eaten them, but not for love"—somebody else at the table says, "Great line." And in the mountaintop melodrama, Walker tries to talk Lu Anne back from the edge of death by promising baptism, renewal, rebirth—but she's thrown away his cocaine. "Takes the edge off baptism, renewal and rebirth, doesn't it?" she asks. "When you're out of coke?"

Mr. Stone won't let his narrative rest on Walker's bitterness, and doesn't idealize Lu Anne's pain (his own mother was schizophrenic). The question of motivation here, however, is tricky. In the earlier books, whatever has people so strung out is implicit—the war in Vietnam, racial hatred, United States incursions in Central America would be quite sufficient, at one level, but there's also a lapsed-Catholic ear tuned to the cosmic menace. In an exquisite passage of *A Flag for Sunrise,* a skin diver down too far suddenly sees a shudder pass through showers of bluegray fish, "as if the ocean itself had begun to tremble." Then, "turning full circle, he saw the same shudder pass over all the living things around him—a terror had struck the sea, an invisible shadow, a silence within a silence." That's perfect: no shark appears, no leviathan—just raw terror.

In *Children of Light,* motivations have moved into the narrative. Walker flails around wondering why he does things—and comes up with answers that don't make any difference. That benighted quest is just right in Walker, but Mr. Stone's picture of what makes Lu Anne tick doesn't quite work. It's fine as metaphysics: just before her husband leaves, she tells him that her illness "doesn't have a moral . . . Not of the kind you're comfortable with." "Evil," he agrees, "is not the sort of term I'm comfortable with." But the parallel with *The Awakening* seems heavy-handed, as does Lu Anne's search for her "real" self in mirrors, in Edna, in Shakespeare's Rosalind. Mr. Stone describes key scenes from her childhood, as if to suggest the orgins of her madness, but they feel contrived, called upon to explain too much: her schizy sense of unreality comes through much better in action than in explication. And though what bothers her and Walker most is the damage they've done to their children, this sorrow is somehow abstract, offstage, not really part of the experience in the book. All along Mr. Stone has been updating the 19th-century novel of ideas, and he's more skillful at mythic, apocalyptic narrative than at psychological realism. The extraordinary precision and suggestive force of his writing work best when he gives direct fictional life to his larger ideas and questions, when the story itself carries the weight of its own meaning. (pp. 24-5)

Jean Strouse, "Heebiejeebieville Express," in The New York Times Book Review, *March 16, 1986, pp. 1, 24-5.*

PETER S. PRESCOTT

Robert Stone's fourth novel [*Children of Light*] looks on the surface to be less violent, less cataclysmic than its predecessors. No demagogues this time around, no riots, no revolutions, no gunplay. The man who set most of his Vietnam novel, *Dog Soldiers,* in California has now written a Hollywood novel that's set mostly in Mexico. Such tricks might seem even bolder if Stone's novels weren't really all about the same place: the wasteland of the heart's affections. Drugs, alcohol and insanity loom large in this landscape where the walking wounded are destroyed by forces they can control as readily as by forces they can't. From distant hills we can sometimes hear the faint beat of a religious pulse.

Like the protagonists of [*A Hall of Mirrors* and *Dog Soldiers*] . . . , Gordon Walker and Lu Anne Bourgeois are broken, rootless people, too far damaged at the story's start for the reader to hope they can be saved. Walker is a screenwriter and some-

time actor who, in the opening pages of *Children of Light,* has achieved "a vision of his life as trash—a soiled article, past repair." An alcoholic in his 40s, Walker has just lost his wife— she walked out—but he's acquired a 10-gram stash of cocaine. Now he's looking for some kind of sustaining dream. (p. 72)

Read simply as melodramas, Stone's novels are easy to take. The kind of compelling narrative that he offers his readers, the headlong rush toward an apocalypse, isn't much in fashion with our most serious writers just now. Compared with Stone, writers like Pynchon and Barth, Bellow and Barthelme look like fictional decorators, forever pausing for embellishment, digressions and commentary. Yet Stone's alarming tales are in fact literary, informed by a coherent vision of a predatory, insensate society in which innocence and decency can prove fatal and from which all moral authority has fled.

Central to Stone's vision of America is an idea of innocence. Not lost innocence—a conventional concept—but an innocence like a cancer, both rampant and malignant. Stone's characters come from nowhere in particular and go where they really don't belong: to Vietnam, Central America—even to New Orleans, where the protagonist of *A Hall of Mirrors* seizes a microphone to announce: "The American Way is innocence . . . an innocence so vast and awesome that the entire world will be reduced by it." These characters meddle with things better left alone—drugs, revolution, even Kate Chopin's novel— because they have an absolutely unjustifiable confidence that they can make these things work for them. In the end, the things they meddle with destroy them. (p. 73)

Peter S. Prescott, "A Wasteland of the Heart," in Newsweek, *Vol. CVII, No. 11, March 17, 1986, pp. 72-3.*

STEPHEN DOBYNS

The difference between illusion and delusion is in part the difference between making the dream or being its victim. Gordon Walker, the hero of Robert Stone's excellent fourth novel, *Children of Light,* is in pursuit of a better dream. The old ones are all torn and need to be patched together with alcohol and drugs. He seeks the dream that will quiet his internal voice which tells him his life is "trash—a soiled article, past repair." (p. 1)

There is a Faustian quality to Walker. He'd been successful in the glitter world of Hollywood and he sold whatever real ability he had for the immediate rewards he found there. But as his friend the drug doctor says, "One can't give in too much to immediate reward, you know. You lose something, eh? Have to pay off on one end or another." . . .

Walker seems determined on self-destruction, yet the novel is not mired in its own bleakness. In an interview with Charles Ruas, Stone recently said, "I want to share that sense of the terrifying nature of things with my hypothetical reader and, as a result of our sharing it, produce a positive experience that gives rise to hope and transcendence. That's what I'm trying to do."

And in *Children of Light* that is what he has done. Stone is an amazingly deft novelist who writes with great fluidity as he moves from exact dialogue to interior commentary to precise description. He never uses a wrong word or even a weak one. In describing the harbor at St. Epifanio Beach, Stone writes, "A stiff wind from the bay rattled the wire rigging of the boats at moor, banging stays against masts in a ceaseless tintinnabulation.'' The language seems always effortless and full of grace. Together these skills have made Stone one of our best writers.

This is just as well because too often *Children of Light* skirts the edge of being a ''Hollywood'' novel, lingering perhaps too long on the show biz personalities as if they were interesting for their own sakes, instead of being metaphors of our time: cynics, consumers, non-believers, frauds. Yet when these characters work best, Stone seems to be saying we as a nation have traded the dream of a better world for the illusion that keeps us from thinking of any world. Even the director's wife yearns for the 1960s when life seemed to mean something: ''Everybody shoplifted . . . People handed out flowers. You could get laid three times a day with an ugly body.''

Brilliant and wonderful in its parts, the novel occasionally gets lost as it moves through a landscape of anecdote and colorful personalities, perhaps because ultimately the glitter world that Stone describes is a foolish and self-indulgent place. What pulls the novel back is the haunting and beautiful Lee Verger, victim of her dream or delusion and yet one who transcends it.

In the end, Lee Verger tries to rescue Walker by taking him with her into her delusion, created in part from Walker's screenplay. She calls out to him, ''Come . . . or else save me.'' But Walker does neither. It's too late. He holds back in order to survive, to live not in the light but in the shadow-land. (p. 2)

> *Stephen Dobyns, ''The Underside of the American Dream,'' in* Book World—The Washington Post, *March 23, 1986, pp. 1-2.*

A. ALVAREZ

In just four novels in almost twenty years Robert Stone has established a world and style and tone of voice of great originality and authority. It is a world without grace or comfort, bleak, dangerous, and continually threatening. . . .

Stone has a Hobbesian view of life—nasty, brutish, and short—but is also fiercely contemporary, and not just because he has a marvelous ear for the ellipses and broken rhythms and casual obscenity of the way people talk now. Stone is contemporary because he takes for granted the nihilism that seems to be a legacy of the Vietnam War, that fracturing of the sensibility which began in the Sixties with the disaffected young and continues, in these more conservative times, out there in the streets with the hustlers and junkies, the random violence and equally random paranoia. He is one of the few writers who are at once culturally sophisticated—full of sly quotes and literary references, strong on moral ambiguities—and streetwise. (p. 23)

The characteristic Stone note is a combination of high culture and street smarts, an elegant formality slightly disproportionate to the seedy situation at hand: ''Axelrod was in the process of discovering an unwholesome stain on his sleeve.'' Axelrod, in fact, has just been struggling with an unruly, vomiting drunk, but the slow-motion circumlocution—''was in the process of discovering''—and schoolmasterly disapproval—''unwholesome''—set the moment off as though in quotation marks, as though a man of sensibility were describing a scene that defies all sensibility.

Stone uses this mock formal style to keep his distance from heroes who have in common an unswerving instinct for trouble: stoned Rheinhardt, in *A Hall of Mirrors,* who baits a stadium full of primitive Christian rednecks; Converse, in *Dog Soldiers,* conned by misplaced bravado into smuggling three kilos of heroin from Vietnam to California; Holliwell, in *A Flag for Sunrise,* who shambles drunkenly across Central America, trailing guilt, self-pity, and destruction. All of them, in their different ways, are skilled provokers of violence in others, yet all somehow manage not to be dragged under with their betters. They have this tenacity in common, along with an understanding of the precariousness and unjustifiability of their miserable existences. . . . Each of Stone's heroes has been more half-assed than his predecessor, each concurs in ''the moral necessity of his annihilation,'' and each survives.

Gordon Walker, in *Children of Light,* is the most shuffling of them all. He is an aging actor and screen writer, with a boozer's face, a bad coke habit, and an incurable itch for trouble. (pp. 23-4)

Yet *Children of Light* lacks the narrative denseness and control of the earlier books, in which every figure had his own part in the plan and met his own special fate. Each stage of Walker's journey south [to Bahia Honda] is rich in wit and detail, but each is complete in itself, a picaresque incident on the road that gives another angle on Walker's depression and destructiveness, but otherwise contributes nothing to the scheme of things.

The plot begins to move—and then too quickly—only when Walker arrives at the movie location. Stone has sold his previous books to Hollywood and clearly knows, and loathes, that world. Bahia Honda seethes with malice and vanity, with predators and their prey. The most corrupt and troublesome is Dongan Lowndes, a one-time novelist turned highbrow reporter. . . . Lowndes's rancid ill-will, Lu Anne's madness, and Walker's cocaine-induced fecklessness combine to create a disaster. There is blackmail and a drunken brawl; [Walker and Lu Anne] take off; Lu Anne has her big mad scene, then swims out to sea and drowns.

Although the tragedy is inevitable—given Walker's bad habits and Lu Anne's vulnerability—the payoff seems oddly hurried and unconvincing. Apart, Walker and Lu Anne are subtle and disturbing figures; together, they lapse into actorly whimsy. . . . The plot, in its turn, also lapses into theatrical conceit. Before the book opens Walker has been playing King Lear and he is ''still up on Lear-ness, chockablock with cheerless dark and deadly mutters, little incantations from the text.'' Throughout what follows the mutters and incantations continue and the novel's climax is an updated, topsy-turvy version of Lear's mad scene: a storm, a ruined shelter, Lu Anne naked, bleeding, raving, and wallowing, literally, in pig shit, with Walker as the Fool, trying to soothe her and trying to survive.

Perhaps this shrillness and melodrama make sense in view of the drug. Walker snorts coke as often and as heedlessly and with as little apparent effect as the heroes of Hemingway's later books knocked back whiskey. But in the carefully established, beady-eyed world the lovers have left behind, it seems more like *grand guignol* than *King Lear.*

It also seems far more slanted than anything Stone has written before. He has always kept apart from the current fashion that confuses fiction with the art of the self and is suspicious of anyone with a strong gift for narrative. Stone, who has a strong imaginative grip on the contemporary American scene and writes like an angel—a fallen, hard-driving angel—is also a marvelous storyteller. He does not take sides and is as much at one with

Pablo, the murderous speed freak, as he is with Holliwell, the liberal intellectual.

In comparison, *Children of Light* seems self-indulgent. Walker and Lu Anne are the only characters with whom Stone seems to have any sympathy, and gradually Walker, the zonked-out disorderly writer, takes over the whole stage. Early in the book he is continually overwhelmed by irrational attacks of panic; later everything drops away so that this unfocused sense of disaster can be fulfilled. Even Lu Anne, whose madness has been defined with such precision, delicacy, and restraint, becomes a mere crazy—a flailing, horrifying puppet. Her final mad scene is the exact point where the narrative unravels into histrionics, as if Stone had lost patience with the harsh and unsavory world he has so elegantly created and settled for something more stagy but less demanding. It is a solution on which Lu Anne herself has passed judgment, in a sane moment, while pondering one of the more overblown stage directions in Walker's script:

> So much popcorn, she thought. To get the character you had to go down and inside to where your grief was. The place your truest self inhabited was the place you could not bear.

This is the kind of truth Stone is reaching for in *Children of Light.* But to get at it he has sacrificed the intricate, gallows-humor detachment that has made him, in his previous books, one of the most impressive novelists of his generation. (pp. 25-6)

> *A. Alvarez, "Among the Freaks," in* The New York Review of Books, *Vol. XXXIII, No. 6, April 10, 1986, pp. 23-6.*

FRANK RICH

Is there anyone angrier than a screenwriter spurned? In his first three novels, Robert Stone persuasively mined the brawniest tradition of American letters in the American century. With the thematic grandiosity (and sometimes the overreach) of Dreiser, the moral clarity of Fitzgerald, and the combustible vernacular of Hemingway, Stone synthesized the chaos of the sixties (*A Hall of Mirrors,* 1967), the post-Vietnam hangover of the seventies (*Dog Soldiers,* 1974), and against a presciently drawn Central American landscape, the embattled idealism of the eighties (*A Flag for Sunrise,* 1981). But reading Stone's new novel, *Children of Light,* one recalls that its author shares not only literary ground with Fitzgerald and Hemingway, but also scars from the Hollywood wars. (p. 32)

How bitter is Stone about what William Goldman would call his adventures in the screen trade? Let's put it this way: Walker describes a movie script as "the record of petty arguments lost or won, half-assed stratagems and desperate compromises" and "a graph of meaningless motion like the tube-worm trails in a prehistoric seabed."

At this late date, it's hard to imagine anyone scoring more points off soulless Hollywood, especially those pertaining to the cannibalization of writers. . . . Yet the bitchiest film-colony observations are easily the finest passages of *Children of Light.* It's when Stone takes to heavy metaphysical panting and literary deckstacking—attempting to inflate a film location and its scurvy denizens into a spiritual seismograph of a national malaise, attempting to raise (as he puts it) the Universal Tour into the universal tour—that this novel fails. Although far more honest than backstage Hollywood movies like *The Bad and the Beautiful* or *A Star Is Born* (both of which it echoes)—and much spicier than such classic reportage as Lillian Roth's *Picture* or John Gregory Dunne's *The Studio—Children of Light* never quite transcends itself to become *The Day of the Locust* or *The Last Tycoon.* (pp. 32-3)

The most vicious character . . . is an outsider named Dongan Lowndes, another (if temporarily recovered) alcoholic. The author of one much-admired novel of eight years earlier, he has "turned to nonfiction writing for quality magazines" such as *New York Arts,* which has sent him to cover the making of *The Awakening.* Lowndes is instantly identifiable as the biggest rat in the Hollywood woodpile—"an unhappy writer" out to punish the others in print for his own literary disappointments. (p. 33)

Stone is far too smart and gifted a writer to make the mistake of drawing *Children of Light* along the clichéd lines ascribed to Lowndes. But the coke lines in this book (at least one of them, inevitably, snorted up a $100 bill) become tiresome in a way that the mood-altering substances (from alcohol to heroin) used to create the anomic fog of past Stone novels did not. Walker's endless pursuit and intake of cocaine is presented as a sad form of self-destruction, but it plays as a tedious form of self-indulgence. Lu Anne's bad pharmaceutical trips—she substitutes booze and coke for her prescribed medication—are no more compelling. While this heroine is caught on the same fault line between Catholicism and Gnosticism as past Stone characters, who can care about her stoned-out mystical catharses? Although Lu Anne claims that an absence of coke "takes the edge off baptism, renewal and rebirth," the reader feels the reverse.

Lu Anne and, to a lesser extent, Walker are incompletely realized. When Stone attempts to describe their respective relationships to their estranged spouses and children, the writing goes flat and vague. Lu Anne's mental illness is hokily rationalized by a few crude childhood flashbacks and nearly *Exorcist*-esque visualizations of the graveyard demons (known as the "Long Friends") who populate her hallucinatory fits. Like the novel's narrative and thematic concerns, the characters are too often propelled by self-conscious literary motifs. It's as if Stone is emulating the smug Lowndes, rising to the bait of attempting to play intellectual oneupmanship with the pretentious Hollywood vulgarians. (In that game, the unmoneyed civilian loses even if he wins.)

Thus, Lu Anne, herself a Louisianan, is presented all too schematically in the context of the Chopin heroine she plays, Edna Pontellier. Walker, we're told at the outset, has recently starred in a Seattle production of *King Lear*—a rather inexplicable feat, given his condition—and sure enough, an ominous "line of storm cloud" makes periodic appearances as we wait for Stone to provide his own variation of Lear and the Fool on the heath. *As You Like It* (in which Lu Anne played a memorable Rosalind at Yale) also is plundered, as is *Antony and Cleopatra.* The light and mirror imagery—*Children of Light* takes its title from the same Robert Lowell poem that yielded the title of *A Hall of Mirrors*—is archly employed from the very first sentence. And, like all Stone fictions, this one culminates in a sloppy, bloody apocalypse that is less reminiscent of *Lear,* "The Burning of Los Angeles," or *Heart of Darkness* (which provided the epigraph for *Dog Soldiers*) than Hollywood's own answer to Conrad, the final reels of Francis Coppola's *Apocalypse Now.* Somehow the holocaust doesn't seem worth it for such climactic insights as Walker's dictum that "living is better than dying. Morally."

Those who treasure Stone's corrosive descriptive powers, his perfect ear for low-life diction, and his appalled view of the American condition will still find many isolated pockets of pleasure to go with this novel's larger disappointments. But even at its best, this book is haunted by Walker's observations about how to write movies. "Your flights of fancy," the screenwriter tells the lapsed novelist Lowndes, "are reduced to technical possibility because on one level you're moving machinery." In *Children of Light* the flights of fancy are very much reduced to technical possibility, and we can hear the machinery being moved. It wouldn't be surprising if Robert Stone's first half-heartedly imagined novel yields his first Hollywood hit. (pp. 33-4)

Frank Rich, "The Screenwriter's Revenge," in The New Republic, *Vol. 194, No. 17, April 28, 1986, pp. 32-4.*

ROBERT JONES

One wants very much to take Robert Stone as seriously as he takes himself. [In *A Hall of Mirrors, Dog Soldiers, A Flag for Sunrise*], . . . and in his new novel, *Children of Light,* he has given us a portrait of post-sixties America that chronicles the country's decay through the voices of its burnt-out cases. The figure of the drifter, who appears in different guises in each of his novels, has come to symbolize for him the aimlessness that he perceives at the heart of American culture.

What separates Robert Stone's vision from most other novelists is that he creates America at a distance. Vietnam is the geographical center of *Dog Soldiers,* just as Central America is the heart of *A Flag for Sunrise.* Even *Children of Light,* which is about Hollywood, takes place in Mexico. In removing the action of his novels from the land they address, Stone captures the feeling of geographical impunity that pervades the United States. Its battles are played out on other shores. In this eerie vision of exile, Stone depicts American power as an aftertremor that devastates each foreign place we inhabit, while the country itself remains essentially unchanged. For Stone, the historical difference of the last twenty years is that we are now all part of this devastation. Each new generation born is as much a victim of the unassailable American ideal as the lands we have failed to conquer.

Stone chose Robert Lowell's poem "Children of Light" as the epigraph to his first novel, *A Hall of Mirrors,* and has now returned to the image, from I Thessalonians: "Ye are all the children of the light, and the children of the day: we are not of the night, nor of darkness. Therefore, let us not sleep, as do others; but let us watch and be sober." Stone's characters never sleep, but then, most of them are amphetamine freaks; their watchfulness is a drug-induced paranoia. Stone's obsession with the empty promise each of us inherits emerges through these characters' dissolution. The banner we are meant to carry now brings with it, as Lowell says, "the Serpent's seeds of light," the fake illumination that reveals blindness instead of truth. "Sunrise, hast thou a flag for me?" Emily Dickinson asks in her poem. This plea is somewhere in the minds of each of Stone's characters, the longing to attach oneself to a common ground and be made to feel part of a world that one has in no way been equipped to see.

In Stone's world, the other side of this soullessness is inevitable violence. His characters wait endlessly for something to happen, but they haven't a clue as to what they expect. "I don't know what I'm doing or why I do it or what it's like," Converse

says in *Dog Soldiers.* Violence is the natural response to this short-circuit of emotion, and the most memorable scenes in Stone's novels always involve brutality: for example, Hicks's gratuitous murder of the drug dealer with a needle through the vein in *Dog Soldiers* or the torture of Sister Justin in *A Flag for Sunrise.* Moments like these are written with a heartlessness and clarity that are like nothing else in contemporary fiction. Their vividness is such that you forget you are reading a book and the narrative takes on the power of the best cinematic image.

But Stone's downfall as a writer is that he is not content to stop there. He shares with too many other novelists the cursed desire to be significant. And so he wields ideas about as if they were baseball bats in the hands of one of his more deranged characters. This propensity to tell us everything he learned in school mars all that is good in *Dog Soldiers* and *A Flag for Sunrise,* but it cripples altogether *Children of Light.*

In *Children of Light,* Stone miniaturizes the metaphor of war that has been the foundation of his previous novels. In a recent interview in the *The Paris Review,* he said of the perpetual conflict that defines our lives: "It is the simple truth that, wherever you are, there is an armed enemy present, not far away." Through the characters in *Children of Light*—a schizophrenic film star, a drug-dependent screen writer, and other types of Hollywood flotsam—Stone seeks to personalize this "armed enemy" and show how we are dangerous and careless with each other.

The race wars of *A Hall of Mirrors,* the Vietnam and drug wars of *Dog Soldiers,* and the guerrilla wars of *A Flag for Sunrise,* enable Stone to measure his characters' disaffection against a prefabricated conflict. Amidst all that din, we are less likely to notice the weakness of their motivation. In *Children of Light,* there are no land mines, crazed soldiers of fortune, or drug runners to threaten, so Stone must demonstrate how destruction is a property of the self. But we enter his characters' lives in their middle age, and their madness and drug addiction are presented as if they were a natural state. And so we witness their inevitable decline without knowing how they came to be where they are or caring how much further they have to fall.

Gordon Walker's success has passed by the time we meet him in *Children of Light.* But years before, he wrote a screen treatment of Kate Chopin's *The Awakening,* and now it is being produced in Mexico with his former lover, Lu Anne Bourgeois, as its star. Walker has been edged-out of the production, but it was to have been the achievement of his career. He finds himself deserted by his wife, and with a drug habit instead of a job to occupy his days. And so he insinuates himself onto the movie set, "to make my presence felt," he says.

But by the time Walker leaves for Mexico, Lu Anne already has a loose grip on her chronic madness. She has begun to hear voices and hallucinate figures she calls "the Long Friends." Walker arrives just as she films the suicidal swim that concludes the movie. Her increasing terror, her identification with her character in the movie, and her anticipation of meeting Walker become unbearable pressures. The novel builds to Lu Anne's breakdown as she is once again drawn to Walker's arms.

Walker does not go to Mexico to consciously wreck the production. He goes to see what will happen. He knows only that he has the power to unnerve everything around him. Stone's characters all share the kind of self-absorption that is often mistaken for reflection. They endlessly analyze their feelings, but with no sense of the world beyond themselves or of the responsibility that lies beyond immediate action. Near the end of *Children of Light,* Lu Anne asks Walker, "Can't you help me?" And Walker responds, "'I would die for you.' It was true, he thought, but not really helpful."

Nothing makes a difference. Stone wants us to accept his vision as ironic and tragic simultaneously, but it rarely amounts to more than the worst kind of bogus existentialism. I think Robert Stone's intention in *Children of Light* is much like Joan Didion's in *Play It As It Lays.* Her novel is also about wasted Hollywood victims, but Stone lacks Didion's ability to convey B.Z.'s and Maria's history in a few elliptical sentences, and especially to convince us of their exhaustion. Didion makes us believe that B.Z. has played-out every possible hand, so his suicide seems the natural end of the game. But in *Children of Light,* we never believe Gordon and Lu Anne are worn-out by life. They behave more like children who play with drugs and each other's emotions because all their other toys are broken.

We are meant to be moved by Lu Anne's descent into madness, but Stone has written these episodes with the pitch of a Grand Guignol melodrama. Her "Long Friends" whisper words like "malheureuse" in her ear and remind one more of French nannies than hallucinations. At times their voices mimic the chatter of Quaker maidens or sometimes sound like characters from a minstrel show. Everything is "literary" in the most artificial sense. There is no naturalness to Stone's prose, nothing that makes one feel that this disintegration is happening to a human being.

When Walker reflects upon Lu Anne's madness, he thinks: "It was stronger than he was, and evil. Evil, a word attaching to false consciousness." Stone's habit of sneaking extraneous concepts into his characters' minds undermines any sympathy the reader might feel for them. As exasperation for the author grows, the characters become increasingly charmless. Attaching "false consciousness" to Walker's reflection adds nothing to the story but pretentiousness. But this is how Stone attempts to add depth to his narrative where he cannot create it with characterization or style.

By the time Lu Anne begins her ascent of Mount Carmel and the culmination of her breakdown, Stone has lost the reader altogether. The scene is full of thunder and rain, false stigmatas, and Lu Anne dancing naked before clouds as purple as the prose. And when Lu Anne is ready to die and swims out to sea, she turns to Walker with the words: "Come," she called. "Or else save me." The choices Stone gives Lu Anne are meaningless ones. Walker can die with her or save her; it amounts to the same thing in the end.

Stone wants to mirror our cultural breakdown in Lu Anne's empty act, but he doesn't persuade us that she has lost anything. Her suicide is as pointless as her life. And in drawing this parallel between Lu Anne's madness and the real insanity of the modern world, Stone cheapens the tragedy of our own misplaced dreams and the despair that comes from having lost track of the hopes that were once thought possible. (pp. 305-06, 308)

Robert Jones, "The Other Side of Soullessness," in Commonweal, *Vol. CXIII, No. 10, May 23, 1986, pp. 305-06, 308.*

Ted Tally

1952-

American dramatist and scriptwriter.

Tally is perhaps best known for his drama *Terra Nova* (1977), which is based on British explorer Robert Falcon Scott's ill-fated expedition to the South Pole in 1911. Although grounded in historical accounts, including Scott's own journals and letters, the drama is less a recounting of the journey than an analysis of heroism. Central to this play is Tally's depiction of the rivalry between Scott and Roald Amundsen, the Norwegian explorer who beat Scott to the South Pole, and of their different methods of surviving their dangerous journey. By alternating between past and present, Tally investigates a variety of factors which may have influenced Scott's actions, including his strict adherence to personal ethics and social codes and his desire to bring glory to himself and his country. While some critics expressed difficulty understanding Tally's thematic concerns, most praised his insight into the psychological motivations of his protagonist.

Tally is also well known for his comedies. *Hooters* (1978), praised by critics for its witty dialogue, is about the sexual initiation of a college freshman. In *Coming Attractions* (1980), Tally focuses on a bank robber who becomes a celebrity after he is persuaded by an unscrupulous talent agent to commit mass murder. Tally employs parody, puns, and burlesque routines to satirize publicity seekers as well as those who promote and exploit fame. John Simon hailed the play as "that most desiderated and least available commodity in our theater: purposeful satire." *Little Footsteps* (1985) centers on an upwardly-mobile young couple who are expecting their first child and addresses the anxieties of parenthood in the 1980s. Although critics generally faulted the play's protagonists as one-dimensional, they found Tally's dialogue amusing and praised his timely subject matter. Among Tally's other plays are *Night Mail and Other Sketches* (1977) and *Word of Mouth* (1978).

HAROLD CLURMAN

We are today more eager than ever to discover and, if possible, to hail *new* young American playwrights. There is even a certain factitious hysteria in the impulse. It is perhaps part of a useful anxiety to find things and people to be enthusiastic about: these days very little inspires heartfelt approval.

A new "Daniel" has sprung up in the person of 25-year-old Ted Tally. A student of playwriting at the Yale School of Drama, he unquestionably has talent. His *Terra Nova* . . . is now being presented in alternation with David Mamet's *Reunion*. . . .

I speak of Tally's talent, but I cannot at present determine its exact nature, at least for the purpose of predicting his future. Nor is such definition required at this early date: I am being cautious on his behalf. The immediate point is that his play is an intelligent and effective stage piece.

© Jack Mitchell

Terra Nova was the name of the vessel on which the British explorer Robert Falcon Scott, with four other men, journeyed in June 1910 to Antarctica; it was their hope to be the first men to reach the South Pole. After the cruelest hardships, they did achieve their goal in January 1912, but only to learn that the Norwegian Amundsen had got there ahead of them. And, savage as the journey out had been, it was as nothing compared to the journey back. One man broke down completely on February 10 and died. Scott and the other three perished about a month later. Records and diaries found by a search party furnish the basis for the play. . . .

The play is informed with humor as well as pain. . . . What we do accept, apart from the validity of the people as types, is the narrative itself: Tally has made it credible and interesting.

Still, after having been held by the story, I was left a little vague as to its essential meaning: what did the dramatist really intend to say? There is something puzzling in his objectivity. Does he mean to praise courage for its own sake, to pay tribute to the heroism involved in carrying out an almost impossible sporting task? (For Scott had rejected the use of a train of dogs to pull his sleighs and equipment, as Amundsen had done. It wasn't "cricket!") Was locating the Pole something Scott believed in for its scientific value? Are we to perceive in the expedition an existentialist challenge, a variation on the myth of Sisyphus? Was it a kind of folly, the madness of those who wished to astonish the world by jumping off the Brooklyn Bridge, riding Niagara Falls in a barrel, swimming the English Channel?

All these possibilities are implied, but the play attains no poetic crystallization of them. Perhaps we are expected only to wonder, and that may be sufficient. Still, *Terra Nova* lacks the further dimension, the larger insight, which is the miracle of art. It remains, nevertheless, one kind of "good theatre."

> *Harold Clurman, in a review of "Terra Nova," in*
> The Nation, *Vol. 225, No. 20, December 10, 1977,*
> *p. 638.*

J. W. LAMBERT

It seems extraordinary that a 24-year-old American should write a play exploring the psyche of a long-dead British explorer. . . .

[Ted Tally's] subject in *Terra Nova*—which I hope we shall see [in London] before too long—is Scott of the Antarctic, his character, his motives, the stimulus of disappointment, the impetus of the driving woman who became his wife (and the mother of Peter Scott of Wildlife fame), his powers of leadership, his indecisions, his status as a necessary hero and his awareness of it. Structurally the play is ingenious but not obtrusively so. Only at the end does it lapse into what seems to be becoming a cliché of the drama: the central character left alone on the stage until all the others in his life come and circle round him. Another near-cliché, though, . . . [is] Scott's rival explorer Amundsen, who plays a dual role as some kind of hovering inspiration and as the representative of a less romantic view of adventure, indeed of life as a whole—a towering figure last seen in the prophetic dress of an aviator, as which indeed he was to be lost over the North Pole. . . . All in all, this is a fascinating play in itself, and an interesting indication of a new strain in the attitudes of young America. (pp. 15-16)

> *J. W. Lambert, "Globetrotting Theatre," in* Drama,
> *No. 133, Summer, 1979, pp. 12-20.*

JAMES HARRIS

Seated as far out (stage right) as this reviewer was, a fully objective appreciation of Ted Tally's play, *Terra Nova,* was rendered difficult. . . . (p. 18)

The action [of *Terra Nova*] stayed in the Antarctic with Scott, but every now and again scenes from his past life would be acted out, there and then, on the snow. The effect could possibly have been strange and wonderful and disjointed, as opposed to just disjointed, as it was. To add to the confusion Amundsen himself would stroll on every once in a while and have a chat with Scott, and chide him for being so sentimental as not to take dogs and eat them en route. These scenes were of course imaginary, as in fact Amundsen was way up ahead, reaching the Pole first. My companion, who was not conversant with the details of the story before going to see *Terra Nova,* seemed to be even less conversant with them by the time it was all over.

Stories of extreme courage and hardship should make the audience think two things: one—what on earth would I do if I was in their shoes? and two—thank God I'm not in their shoes, or snow shoes in this case. But *Terra Nova* failed to involve on this fundamental level. So Scott came second because he refused to eat dog. Is that really a dramatic issue? No self-

respecting RSPCA-fearing Englishman would eat dog. Surely the point is that Scott was the first ever non-dog-eater to reach the South Pole, and coming second to a dog-eater like Amundsen is just like winning. (pp. 18-19)

Had one not been on duty, one would have taken a page from Captain Oates's book and absented oneself from the proceedings at half-time. All he had to face was being frozen to death, which is nothing compared to the heroism of this reviewer who risked being bored to death by this irritating production of a curiously pointless play. (p. 19)

> *James Harris, in a review of "Terra Nova," in* Plays
> and Players, *Vol. 27, No. 9, June, 1980, pp. 18-19.*

JOHN SIMON

[Ted Tally's *Coming Attractions* contains] that most desiderated and least available commodity in our theater: purposeful satire. Perhaps the greatest single lacuna on the American stage—indeed, in American life—is the absence of satire. This society, which (say, by pitting a Jimmy Carter against a Ronald Reagan in the presidential race) gets down on its knees in a plea to be satirized, nevertheless keeps eluding its just satirical deserts. Though according to a Broadway adage satire is what closes on Saturday, it is also precisely what a sophisticated, truly civilized society must produce and support. (p. 59)

Coming Attractions must not be expected to fill in this ancient and enormous gap single-handed; it is, however, a long, athletic lunge in the right direction. Actually, it begins somewhat slowly and unpromisingly. A clumsy but publicity-hungry bank robber holding a piddling four hostages (all over town there are others holding dozens or even scores) is signed up by a down-and-out theatrical agent ("The biggest act I ever handled was a cocker spaniel that did poodle impressions") to become first a mass murderer and then, on the strength of that, a chart-storming pop-singing star. He is not jailed . . . ; and his act becomes a popular favorite, based as it is on "two things that never failed—violence and bad taste."

It could be argued that *Coming Attractions* has moments that are not strictly original; that, at times, it does not clearly distinguish between the truly satirical and the merely inconoclastic, perhaps even subversive; and that it sometimes bites off less than it can chew. But, true or not, these are minor considerations when you tally up how imaginative, on-target, and tirelessly laughter-begetting much of Ted Tally's play is. What a show such as "Saturday Night Live" would unsuccessfully strive for week after week, *Coming Attractions* tosses off effortlessly, hilariously, and smack in the eye of its more than deserving victims. I don't often burst into gales of laughter in the theater; here, I found myself rocking with guffaws that refused internalization. (pp. 59-60)

I cannot guarantee you unalloyed merriment end to end, but I can promise you several sequences as exquisitely roguish as anything you have ever delighted in, and the best kind of laughter there is—the thinking kind. Tallyho, Ted Tally! There is something better than heartening—positively therapeutic—about a dramatist who can make a defense attorney persuade a judge that he is dealing with a first offender by pleading: "Your honor, has he ever before killed 28 people?" (p. 60)

> *John Simon, "Loesser Unseated, Satire Enthroned,"*
> *in* New York Magazine, *Vol. 13, No. 49, December*
> *15, 1980, pp. 58-60.*

EDITH OLIVER

Ted Tally's **Coming Attractions** . . . is a bit of extended cabaret with satiric intent, but it is too gleeful and too scattershot for satire, and not shrewd enough in its choice of targets. A musical lampoon is more like it. It's about a humble gunman (twenty-seven victims) who is taken up by a theatrical agent and made into a publicity star. The agent, for lampoonish reasons, persuades him to go to the Miss America contest in Atlantic City, where he is captivated by Miss America, captured by the police, and let out on bail. He appears at a night club in Las Vegas, and then decides to quit show business, to the agent's dismay, and marry Miss America, who insists that he become a born-again Christian. There is an eventual murder trial . . . , and his electrocution becomes a production number over a coast-to-coast network. Mr. Tally's **Hooters,** of several seasons ago, was original and very funny, but this time a lot of the comedy sounds second-hand. (His naming the agent Manny is a give-away.) . . . [I did laugh] at a routine involving a P.L.O. terrorist . . . and his white-wimpled side-kick . . . , but the show as a whole is born-again, flimsy Brecht without the acid. (pp. 80, 82)

> *Edith Oliver, in a review of "Coming Attractions,"* in The New Yorker, *Vol. LVI, No. 43, December 15, 1980, pp. 80, 82.*

STANLEY KAUFFMANN

Coming Attractions by Ted Tally has been called by critics a funny satire. This is not quite true. It's funny, all right, but Tally takes some standard satirizable aspects of American life—TV, celebrity-selling, beauty contests, etc.—and shows that they are now far beyond satire. . . .

The pitch of the story . . . is insane, but it is only dailiness goosed a little higher. **Coming Attractions** isn't a chuckly old-fashioned nudge like Kaufman & Hart's *Once in a Lifetime;* it isn't a grab for titters like Christopher Durang's recent spoof of chic New-Yorkniks, *Beyond Therapy.* These could be called satire, which, in H. W. Fowler's definition, aims at amendment. Tally is describing a condition that *is*—exaggerated to underline a blackly comic reality—without the slightest hope of amendment.

His method is touched-up mimesis. Before you go to the theater, you turn on the TV news and see, in this order, a murder in Northern Ireland, a sexy blonde selling you new cars, deaths by arson in Jersey City. Then you go to **Coming Attractions** and hear Tally's newscaster say: "We interrupt 'Celebrity Funeral' to bring you a news update." Which is the satire?

Tally's ultimate triumph is his initial perception. He sees that most of the usual American subjects for cartooning have now been made corny by life, not cartoonists; and he uses that fact as his launching pad.

From the start of his career, Tally has shown a sense of the *Zeitgeist.* His first play, **Terra Nova,** written in 1976 . . . , is about Scott of the Antarctic. When I heard the subject, before I saw the play, I thought: "The 'Vietnam time' is over. A young man has written a play about courage." Authentically, with no thought of fashion-mongering, Tally had responded to social atmospherics. **Coming Attractions** proceeds from the same core of aptness, confronting some acceptances that have become central in our culture. (p. 80)

Coming Attractions is about repulsions, not attractions, and they aren't coming, they are here. Tally is a Jeremiah disguised, wittily, as a wit. (p. 81)

> *Stanley Kauffmann, "A Witty Prophet of Doom," in* Saturday Review, *Vol. 8, No. 3, March, 1981, pp. 80-1.*

JOHN SIMON

[**Hooters,** Ted Tally's already oft-produced second play] concerns two very young men and two slightly older women in a make-out motel on Cape Cod during a summer weekend in 1972. Ricky is the seemingly tougher, more experienced boy, who now works for his father; Clint, his high-school chum and now a college freshman, is more tentative. Cheryl, who is engaged to a meticulous and unromantic businessman, is a "10," but is accompanied by her fellow bank teller, Ronda, a "dog." (pp. 59-60)

There ensues a sexual game of, not chess, merely checkers, in which the unpredictable predictably comes to pass. The less likely mates are conjoined, the less likely relationship is consummated, and so on, until we switch from predictable unpredictability to predictable predictability. But what saves the play from tediousness is the generally peppy, often genuinely droll, dialogue, and the consistently smile-producing interaction of the characters. . . .

Hooters (a synonym, I learn, for knockers—you always learn something in the theater) is a nice little play, though perhaps, on the whole, a little too little. (p. 60)

> *John Simon, "Even the Kitchen Sink," in* New York Magazine, *Vol. 15, No. 44, November 8, 1982, pp. 59-61.*

FRANK RICH

Mr. Tally, the author of **Coming Attractions** and **Hooters,** wrote **Terra Nova** early in his career. . . . Though he has revised the text for its belated New York premiere . . . it still seems a promising young man's work. The gripping events and literate lines are splintered by the author's attempts to manage too much at once.

In a sense, there are three plays here. The most compelling is the story of Scott's mission. We're also given a speculative psychoanalytic dissection of the hero's inner life—and, interstitched with that, an allegory about the end of the British Empire. While all these ambitions are worthwhile, they don't converge in a single dramatic entity. The investigation of Scott's psyche often interrupts and crimps the recounting of the mission; the historical theme is often poured on with speeches.

Mr. Tally's device for binding his elements together is potentially workable: The white stage serves as the terrain of both Antarctica and the hero's mind. Now and then, Scott . . . will be joined by the wife . . . he left behind in England, and the couple will re-enact their courtship or express the anguish of separation. At other times, Scott is confronted by his rival Amundsen . . . whom Mr. Tally employs both as the hero's spiritual alter ego and, in Act II, as a specter of death.

These free-flowing rambles through Scott's consciousness, though fluidly staged, don't satisfy. Scott isn't dramatized in sufficient depth to let us decide whether he is his altruistic public persona or the selfish private careerist fearful of aging and failure. (His wife, an independent-minded New Woman, is even more vaguely drawn.) Amundsen is over-used as a didactic sparring partner. As Scott is the epitome of the English gentleman—forever talking about fair play and "duty"—so the Norwegian all too symbolically represents the new "barbaric" European who will not only beat the pride of English manhood to the South Pole but who will also destroy that manhood in the real war yet to come.

The time spent on these superficially realized secondary matters leads Mr. Tally to shortchange both the narrative and personnel of the mission. . . . It's only when the play's harrowing Act II tragedies fail to move us that we realize how little Mr. Tally has made us care about these men. . . .

[When the production staff] connect with Mr. Tally at his most potent, they create startling images. We watch Scott's daydream of a festive black-tie banquet at home disintegrate into his ongoing arctic nightmare; we see a celebratory group photograph taken at the Pole decompose into a vision of an entire civilization's imminent extinction. Such moments may not deliver the devastating chill that *Terra Nova* promises, but you'll shiver often enough.

> *Frank Rich, in a review of "Terra Nova," in* The New York Times, *April 26, 1984, p. C18.*

JOHN SIMON

[Ted Tally] is a young playwright full of various evolving talents coming along, if not with giant steps, ever so nicely just the same. He is still feeling his way . . . , and is in no unseemly rush for a blockbuster. Everything he has done so far was enjoyable and deserving of support. . . .

Now comes *Little Footsteps*. . . . This time, the subject is parenthood among the yuppies, and the mode is mixed, not to say scrambled. We start with comic fantasies and sardonic monologues to the audience in the manner of *Joe Egg*; from there we go into straight boulevard comedy, thence into gritty farce, only to end as amiable didacticism. It would be a rocky ride indeed if the four disciplines of this tetrathlon weren't nego-

tiated by an authorial athlete as fit and playful as a fiddle. Though little of *Little Footsteps* is overwhelming, all of it is civilized, literate, mind-stretching entertainment, its tomfoolery leavened with thoughtfulness and taste.

Ben and Joanie, in their mid-thirties and married eight years, as upwardly mobile as a helicopter, are expecting. They are repainting the dining room into a nursery (Joanie is a serious painter *manqué*), covering the walls with propaedeutic frescoes and expecting more than a baby: to be model parents, to become even greater conjugal lovers, and, most daringly, to grow up. Ben, to be sure, has doubts. . . . Joanie is full of bravado, though less than sure about her motivation for motherhood; under her brave, gibbous façade, she is eminently deflatable. . . . The spouses explode, and so does the marriage.

Act II takes place during the christening party at the house of Joanie's parents, whither Joanie has escaped from her soon-to-be-shed spouse. Charlotte and Gil are affluent Wasps, and their typicalness is epic; moreover, they never much cared for Ben, a non-feeling that is wholly reciprocated. What happens is, though predictable, not without its minor surprises and major amenities, especially since Charlotte and Gil are amply realized comic figures. If anything, it is the principals who evince a lack of three-dimensionality. No grave matter; Tally writes well, the jokes come thick and fast, and why expect a frieze to be a statue?

The dialogue perks and prickles wittily. . . . The scene in which the wised-up Joanie tells a Ben bursting with paternal resolve what infant rearing is really like comes off as sustainedly riotous, verbally and visually, as anything the comic muse has granted a *farceur*. (p. 83)

The author of *Little Footsteps* may still have a short distance to go, but do subsidize him with your attendance; such an investment in his future is safer than buying pork bellies and funnier than pig bladders. (p. 84)

> *John Simon, "What Babies Come To," in* New York Magazine, *Vol. 19, No. 11, March 17, 1986, pp. 83-4.*

Walter Tevis

1928-1984

American novelist and short story writer.

Tevis is best known as the author of the novels *The Hustler* (1959), *The Man Who Fell to Earth* (1963), and *The Color of Money* (1984), each of which has been adapted into an acclaimed motion picture. These novels, like Tevis's other work, are character studies concerned with such themes as human alienation, loneliness, and imperfection in the modern world. Tevis provides acute insight into the tragic side of the human condition by exploring such dilemmas as identity and loss. Critics have praised Tevis for creating swiftly-paced fiction distinguished by unusual subject matter.

Tevis's first and best-known novel, *The Hustler*, is the story of Fast Eddie Felson, a talented young pool player who aspires to defeat the legendary Minnesota Fats. After he falters within grasp of his goal and is mercilessly beaten by Fats, Fast Eddie returns to the pool circuit. Through Eddie's transient life, ephemeral successes, and inevitable, occasionally brutal failures, Tevis depicts an intense, bitter struggle for identity and fulfillment in an environment not often depicted in contemporary fiction. *The Color of Money*, a sequel to *The Hustler*, depicts the further adventures of a middle-aged Fast Eddie and his attempt at a comeback.

The Man Who Fell to Earth is a science fiction narrative focusing on Thomas Edward Newton, a humanlike alien from the planet Anthea who visits Earth and, by means of his advanced intelligence and extraterrestrial knowledge, builds a corporate power structure. His secret mission is to transport to Earth the dwindling populace of his war-ravaged homeland. In this novel, Tevis examines the frailties and sufferings of both his alien and human characters. Like Fast Eddie Felson in *The Hustler*, Newton is a gifted individual capable of fulfilling his dream yet dangerously susceptible to self-pity, loneliness, doubt, and despair. This conflict between ambition and personal weakness, between inner resolve and hopelessness, pervades all of Tevis's fiction.

In his later fiction, Tevis examines many of the same themes and character types as in his early work. He followed *The Man Who Fell to Earth* with three more science fiction volumes: the novels *Mockingbird* (1980) and *The Steps of the Sun* (1983) and the short story collection *Far from Home* (1981). In these works, Tevis again creates realistic stories featuring vivid protagonists caught in complex struggles with their worlds and with themselves. This is also true of *The Queen's Gambit* (1983), a novel which focuses on a young female chess player who undergoes physical and emotional crises before gaining the opportunity for a chance at the championship.

(See also *Contemporary Authors*, Vol. 113.)

REX LARDNER

[*The Hustler*] is a tense, jolting trip to the tough, dusty, smoky, ball-clackety, money-filled world of the pool shark (that blood-

Courtesy of Mark Marraccini

less master actor), night-peopled with gamblers, suckers, steerers, B-picture sharpies, hoods, compulsive losers, the placid rich, the desperate broke. Fast Eddie Felson, not a bad guy deep down, has no peer at conning marks into games of one-pocket, jack-up pool, sixty-one, nine-ball, straights (you name it). He awkwardly loses. When the bets jump—marks swarm over a sure thing—he swigs liquor, shoots awkwardly, looks lucky (it's not luck), cleans up, high-tails it.

This is small-time—and Eddie is the best there is, he thinks, not a second-rate hustler. He wants to shoot for big money against Minnesota Fats of Chicago, where the best pool is played. But like the army of cue-carrying *hadjis* before him, he finds he's not ready. A marathon match with the tic-ridden Fats and Eddie staggers out, bone-weary, a busted loser.

He meets another loser—Sarah, a crippled girl, bright, cynical, lonely, love-hungry, a sometime boozehound. Later, he teams with Bert, who looks to Eddie like the prince of steerers, a well-connected man who can lead Eddie to money. He sweats and stiffly practices for a comeback.

Bert has the patient, vicious skill of the successful gambler, patterned on a practical philosophy. Some people get their kicks from losing, says Bert. They like to feel sorry for themselves. Losing, when you have an excuse, is easy. Eddie learns the lesson and wins against stiff competition; other lessons, some learned from Sarah, help him win at other things besides pool. . . .

[Tevis] writes like a streak, making straight pool as exciting as a Stanley Ketchell fight. This is a fine, swift, wanton, offbeat novel.

Rex Lardner, *"Conning the Marks,"* in The New York Times Book Review, *January 11, 1959, p. 30.*

TIME

If Hemingway had the passion for pool that he had for bull-fighting his hero might have been Eddie Felson. The poolroom was Eddie's world in whatever town he happened to be, and such moments of truth as he experienced boiled up behind the eight ball. He was a pool shark, although he hated to be called that; he thought of himself as a pool hustler, a town-to-town drifter who conned strangers into games, looked bad or only fair at first, then turned on his skill when the stakes were high enough to matter. Eddie had the skill and pride of a real pro.

The Hustler has its faults as a novel, but opens the door on a world that books have not yet made commonplace. With his first novel, Walter Tevis . . . joins the company of such authors as Dorothy Baker, whose *Young Man with a Horn* . . . looked steadily at a great jazzman, and Edward Hoagland, who lighted up the life of the circus in *Cat Man*. . . . They too were first novels, and they too dealt with character in unfamiliar surroundings. (pp. 89-90)

The story picks up Eddie at the point where he has become so good a hustler that only the biggest man in pool stands between him and the top. Minnesota Fats makes his headquarters at Bennington's in Chicago. In Eddie's world, Fats's name is spoken with reverence. Huge, lardy and gross, Fats plays with the grace of a virtuoso. Eddie takes him on, and for 40 hours they match their delicate skills. At one point Eddie is $18,000 ahead, and the great Fats seems to have met his master. But it is Eddie who cracks, turns to the bottle for help, and takes the pool beating of his life because, as an onlooker tells him later, he is "a born loser."

Eddie begins to hustle again because it is all he knows how to do. Then one night he outsmarts himself, wins too spectacularly, and the poolroom toughs take him to the privy and break his thumbs. His comeback is slow. At the end he has regained his skill and has also learned that skill is not enough, that in the clutches a man's inner resources may be more important than a missed shot.

The moral of *The Hustler* is obviously sententious, the love story is a cliché, and Author Tevis' writing is sometimes too painfully exact. What remains is a succession of scenes in which a smoky, seedy world becomes sharply alive, and where crises are intense even though the scene is grubby and the game is only pool. (p. 90)

"The Eight Ball," in Time, *Vol. LXXIII, No. 2, January 12, 1959, pp. 89-90.*

KEITH WATERHOUSE

The Hustler is an all-American novel with a straightforward, satisfactory plot. A pool billiard shark, Fast Eddie, comes to town in order to take the pants off a crack poolplayer called Minnesota Fats. He wins, and then loses, thousands of dollars in a memorable—and it is memorable—36-hour marathon game.

Fast Eddie goes down fighting, and stays down until a professional gambler teaches him the philosophy that divides the winners from the losers. Then he comes up again, in a way. This could so easily have been just another magazine story, but Mr Tevis's spare, athletic prose lifts it out of that bracket completely. It's not a polished style but a matt-finish style, completely American and curiously effective.

Keith Waterhouse, in a review of *"The Hustler,"* in New Statesman, *Vol. LIX, No. 1509, February 13, 1960, p. 229.*

NORMAN SPINRAD

Most often, single-entry novels into the science fiction genre by so-called "mainstream" novelists who have made their reputations and perfected their skills elsewhere are dismal flops. Well-written demonstrations of the writers' willful and arrogant ignorance of the *additional* skill and knowledge needed to write speculative fiction above and beyond that needed by the successful general novelist. Such failures are usually a direct result of the hubris with which the successful mainstream novelist greets speculative subject matter. The SF cognoscenti have themselves a good laugh at the expense of such self-defined slumming literary aristocrats as they fall on their faces.

But once in a great while, we see such a single work of science fiction produced by an "SF novice" with first class literary skills which not only succeeds on the genre's own terms but which demonstrates the possibilities of whole new angles of attack through which the conventional SF material may be transmogrified.

Such a novel is Walter Tevis' *The Man Who Fell to Earth*. . . . (p. v)

The plot of this science fiction novel by the author of *The Hustler* . . . is definitely of the "stop me if you've heard this before" variety. A lone extraterrestrial, disguised as a human, lands on Earth secretly to save homo sap from his own assholery and to save his own species from extinction by preparing the way for their migration to our planet, which they will then rule secretly and benevolently. He's superintelligent, he's learned our language and our ways from watching our television, he effortlessly amasses a fortune using superior extraterrestrial technology, which he then uses to build a spaceship with which to ferry the "saviors from the stars" to our benighted planet.

You *have* heard it before, haven't you?

But you haven't read it before as a novel of character.

As far as the conventional SF "action adventure" plot handling goes, there's almost nothing to *The Man Who Fell to Earth.* Newton, the extraterrestrial, lands in Kentucky with a load of gold and diamond rings which he converts into the local currency. Using this capital and a lot of "Anthean" technical specs, he rapidly amasses a huge financial empire via marketing new consumer goods and licensing patents. He then begins his spaceship project and is foiled by the FBI and the CIA. It all runs effortlessly and smoothly without conventional plot complications until the denouement. About enough plot material in the conventional sense for an unmemorable short story.

However. . . .

However, conventional SF plotting is not at all what Tevis is doing in this novel. Despite surface appearances, Thomas J. Newton is not Michael Valentine Smith. And Tevis does not use his "stranger in a strange land" as a device for viewing the antics and foibles of the Earthlings through a Swiftian kaleidoscope.

Anthea, wherever it is, is a light-gravity planet, and from the very beginning, Newton feels tired, weak, and physically ill. He also feels awkward, alienated, lonely, and afraid: "He was incapable of warts; but stomach ulcers, measles and dental caries could affect him. He was human; but not, properly, a *man*. Also, man-like, he was susceptible to love, to fear, to intense physical pain and to self-pity." . . . (pp. v-vi)

The Man Who Fell to Earth is very much Newton's story; he is not simply a viewpoint, he is a feeling, suffering, alienated human. (p. vi)

In short, what Walter Tevis has done in *The Man Who Fell to Earth* is written an utterly realistic novel about an alien human on Earth. Realistic in the way Newton interfaces with human society. Realistic in its portrait of his strengths and failures and confusion. Realistic in its depiction of what it's like to be an alien human. Realistic enough to become something of a metaphor for something inside of us all, some existential aloneness.

Tevis brought a psychological realist's approach to what had become something of a science fiction cliche, and by exploring that cliche from deep within reminded us that the other side of cliche is archetype.

Ultimately, that is the challenge of the science fiction novel in extremis—to take a truly alien consciousness, and render it so realistically that it can connect to the reader's own sense of humanity.

To Tevis' credit, he has recognized that in the science fiction novel, psychological credibility isn't enough. The details of the altered reality must cohere into a believable whole.

Too many good realistic novelists attempting science fiction miss this point. They believe that they can write the stuff without doing their homework. Since the subject matter is unreal, verisimilitude is a contradiction in terms.

Walter Tevis, on the other hand, apparently did do his homework. He has written a psychologically realistic novel about an alien human on Earth that also fulfills all the traditional logical realism required by the science fiction novel. The Antheans and their situation add up and makes sense. The Anthean technology which Newton markets is believably done on a technical and even a commercial level. Newton's biology and especially his medical problems are quite well done. Nothing is fudged for sloppy literary purposes.

He has written a realistic science fiction novel that succeeds on both levels, which we need every once in a while to remind us that speculative fiction at the top of its form shares more with the surrealism of Dali than with abstract exhibitionism. (pp. vii-viii)

> *Norman Spinrad, in an introduction to* The Man Who Fell to Earth *by Walter Tevis, Gregg Press, 1978, pp. v-xi.*

DONALD M. HASSLER

Tevis published [*The Man Who Fell to Earth,* a] finely-wrought parable of the lone alien from Anthea sent to Earth to save both his people and mankind, in the same year that Roger Zelazny published *A Rose for Ecclesiastes* (1963), and the

parallels are striking. Both writers weave literary allusion and superb literary craft over well-worn frame stories of aliens appearing as returned gods; the Zelazny hero comes to save Mars like one of their gods returned, while Tevis's hero, Thomas Jerome Newton, comes from a planet in our system much like Mars, from an ancient race that had visited Earth during our Ice Age and had originally taught mankind language and religion. Both stories carry the tone of world weary belatedness, but whereas Zelazny finally allows his hero to inject possibilities for fertility into a dying world, Tevis builds to a fine tragic ending in which Newton can save neither Anthea nor Earth. Norman Spinrad's introduction [see excerpt above] is good on the character development in the novel of the true alien in any culture, the fallen god and fallen man; and Tevis's denouement gives new meaning to the old Greek ironies of the ways in which an enlightened society blinds its clearest seers. (pp. 125-26)

> *Donald M. Hassler, in a review of "The Man Who Fell to Earth," in* Science Fiction & Fantasy Book Review, *Vol. I, No. 9, October, 1979, pp. 125-26.*

MICHAEL BISHOP

[In *Mockingbird*], Robert Spofforth is "a Make Nine robot, the most sophisticated piece of equipment ever to be fashioned by human ingenuity." In the artificially grown body of a powerful black man he possesses all of the recorded knowledge and some of the haunting residual memories of a dead engineer named Paisley. Virtual dictator of a depopulated, far-future America . . . , Spofforth wants only to die but cannot countermand the programming that prohibits his suicide. Here, then, is a character potentially larger than life, dystopia's answer to Milton's Satan.

For better or worse, however, Tevis chooses to make *Mockingbird* not so much Spofforth's story as that of the lovers Paul Bentley and Mary Lou Borne, who defy the manifold repressive dicta of the state—"Don't ask, relax," "Quick sex is best," "When in doubt, forget it"—first by learning to read and then by conceiving a child. They are Adam and Eve to Spofforth's Lucifer, an angel paradoxically incapable of falling until Paul and Mary Lou have succumbed to the temptation of forbidden knowledge and returned in triumph to grant him his death wish.

Doubleday is touting *Mockingbird* as a literary benchmark comparable to Huxley's *Brave New World* or Orwell's *1984*. Although I found the novel thoroughly engrossing, this well-intentioned publicity push overstates its credentials as a pathfinder or groundbreaker. No matter. I suspect that because of its affirmation of such persistent human values as curiosity, courage and compassion, along with its undeniable narrative power, *Mockingbird* will become one of those books that coming generations will periodically rediscover with wonder and delight. If it violates dystopian convention, it does so by concluding with—well, an *upbeat* dying fall.

> *Michael Bishop, "In Dark Corners of the Universe," in* Book World—The Washington Post, *March 23, 1980, p. 6.*

KELVIN JOHNSTON

Every so often, though by no means as often as optimistic publishers suppose, a science fiction novel emerges which belongs in the mainstream of literature, and Walter Tevis's *Mockingbird* . . . is emphatically one such.

It is pointless to recount its plot in any great detail, because by the conventions of the genre it is almost a stereotype—two members of a dying civilisation (male and female, of course), high on state-supplied drugs, serviced by robots, rediscover the lost art of reading, with unforeseen consequences, etc., etc. But the relationship between Paul Bentley and Mary Lou Borne—notice the significant normality of their names—is unforced, touching and entirely credible, and so is their relationship with Spofforth, the real hero of the book.

Spofforth, the virtual ruler of a North America with a population of less than three million, and amongst other things Dean of New York University, is a black Mark 9 robot. Immensely learned, immortal and almost indestructible, capable of loving human beings and being loved, but built without sex organs, he is programmed not to seek the suicide he yearns for until the last human being has died. He falls in love with Mary Lou, allows her to bear a child (by Paul, of course), then agrees to halt the world sterilisation programme if she will help him kill himself.

The final scene, in which she and Paul push him off the top of the Empire State Building in a deserted, decaying New York, ought to be entirely corny, but like the rest of the book it is infused by an austere, melancholy dignity.

> Kelvin Johnston, in a review of "Mockingbird," in *The Observer*, October 12, 1980, p. 34.

PAUL STUEWE

[*Far from Home* is fantasy] fiction for a mainstream readership, and on the whole pretty dull stuff. Tevis's light touch on the realistic pedal brought him bestsellers in *Mockingbird* and *The Hustler*, but the tepid daydreams retailed in this collection of short stories won't satisfy either the sci-fi or mass markets. The author's track record may attract a large audience, but they'll almost certainly be disappointed by a book with all the impact of a string of dud firecrackers. (p. 34)

> Paul Stuewe, "A Shudder of Poe, a Claw of Cats and a Platter of Records," in *Quill and Quire*, Vol. 47, No. 5, May, 1981, pp. 34-5.

ALGIS BUDRYS

The Hustler was originally a short story. *The Man Who Fell to Earth*—a novel which not enough people are fully aware of . . .—is finally unsatisfactory as a novel to the extent that it is essentially an expanded short story. *Mockingbird*—I know; you're supposed to think it was good; haven't lots of people, me excluded, raved about it for you?—was a pasteup of short stories, whether Tevis thought he was using some other method or not. All right, here is a short story collection, and, sure enough, Tevis is one of those rare writers who should never do anything but short stories. He is a Benet, a Collier, a Knight, a Bradbury, an Ellison. . . .

Far From Home takes its title from the conventional, if memorable and striking SF short story first published here some years ago. Half the book contains reprinted material from the SF magazines and other media in which Tevis has displayed his established talent for doing the conventional uncommonly. But the other half contains new stories, or at least stories from a mode new for Tevis and scarce in our pages. They are a form of writing in which the characters *and* the setting are both

fundamentally unconventionalized . . . meta-SF; the mode in which Calvino, Borges and Strete work.

"A Visit From Mother," all by itself, is worth the price of the book to have read. Mind you, you may not like it—but you will be tickled by it, and you won't forget it. Much the same goes for "Rent Control" and "Out of Luck." Others are not as good. "Daddy" is a counterpart of "Mother," and a weak one. The sense is that Tevis had some stories he wasn't sure of, and some he'd been keeping around until he could trust them, put them all in one box, and send them off to Doubleday.

But that, too, is an engaging feature in this case. What we get the effect of having is a series of events in a writer's evolution. Enough of them are successful on their own terms to be fully rewarding. One or two, as noted, are extraordinary.

> Algis Budrys, in a review of "Far from Home," in *The Magazine of Fantasy and Science Fiction*, Vol. 60, No. 6, June, 1981, p. 51.

JAMES J. J. WILSON

[*Far From Home*] is a collection of short stories published in various SF magazines over the past twenty-five years. Some of the story ideas in the book are very clever and amusing. One of Tevis's major problems, however, is that he doesn't appear to be very well-read in SF and, consequently, most of the stories are rather trite and cliche-ridden.

A few of the stories in this book are real gems. One is "The Apotheosis of Myra", about a dream planet which manufactures the ultimate painkiller. As it turns out, the planet is one singular being. The story itself, turns out rather predictably but it also shows that Tevis is capable of stunning imagery when he really tries.

In all, *Far From Home* contains a few excellent stories but the book, for the most part, is one that any SF reader has read a dozen times.

> James J. J. Wilson, in a review of "Far from Home," in Science Fiction Review, Vol. 10, No. 4, November, 1981, p. 56.

DONALD M. HASSLER

A favorite theme in science fiction is what James Gunn has referred to as "the Frankenstein complex," and even though Gunn's purpose is to dismiss the ambiguities in that complex rather quickly in favor of the directness of Asimovian rationality, which is his topic, the image of Frankenstein will not be denied its suggestiveness. The image extends backward in time, of course, to the edge of the eighteenth-century Enlightenment. But recently it has appeared again in an extremely sensitive new novel, *Mockingbird,* by Walter Tevis, a work that weaves together in an unusual and effective way references ranging from the King Kong image of popular culture through the robotic tradition of Asimov to the most basic Romantic dilemma of human identity and human limits. (p. 75)

Dean Robert Spofforth, the central more-than-human android of Tevis's novel, serves as chief academic officer of New York University as well as manager of the rest of a future Earth populated with drugged, inward-turning hedonists. Spofforth's character, played off against two human lovers, Paul Bentley and Mary Lou Borne, dominates the novel. In a sense, it is a triangle love story with great depth and complexity. The basic turn in the plot, however, is that Spofforth has developed intense suicidal urges that conflict with his basic Asimovian programming that says that he must protect humans and protect himself in order to manage the planet. Each spring Dean Spofforth, the "Make Nine" robot, climbs to the top of the Empire State Building and tries to jump. But his inner directives keep his legs riveted to the platform. His intelligence allows him, however, gradually to violate the directives and to prepare for his death by phasing out humankind. When no more of his human charges remain alive, Spofforth can die. He has quietly arranged for a birth control supplement to be continuously included with the world's diet of drugs, and so the people of the novel are the last generation of humans.

Mary Lou and Paul's accidental avoidance of the birth control supplement allows them to conceive a child, and Spofforth's love for Mary Lou and the baby changes him. He banishes Paul and lives with Mary Lou during her pregnancy. Actually, Spofforth is in love with the memory of a girl he had seen years before, a memory that keeps coming back in his dreams. The fabrication of this most advanced android allowed for a rich memory system and the potential, though hardly the ability, for love. In any case, Mary Lou persuades him to explain why no recent pregnancies have occurred prior to hers, and finally a deal is made whereby Spofforth agrees to modify the birth control supplements so that generation on Earth may continue; in return for Spofforth's promise, Mary Lou and Paul, who has fought his way back to New York and the baby, push this robotic tragic hero off the Empire State Building.

The plot turns are less interesting than the images fused in Spofforth himself. From the snide reference that Tevis, the former academic in a large university, makes to his artificial man as a dean, to the profound exploration of human communication through reading, love, and sex as well as of the common elements in all lonely types such as robots, monsters, and aliens, the novel transcends its immediate tradition in science fiction. Certainly, the Asimovian ironies are there. Spofforth is the most advanced artificial intelligence ever created by technology, and he is programmed never to harm humankind or himself. He need never die. But the irony is that his artificial intelligence has progressed to the stage at which the frustrations and limitations of even his godlike position make him want to die. He has become truly human in this sense, and throughout the novel Spofforth's situation functions as an analog for the human condition. That irony of artificial intelligence progressing toward the puzzling dilemmas of true intelligence is the basic twist inherent in robotics. But unlike Asimov, Tevis . . . will not rest with totally rational androids, nor totally rational humans. (pp. 76-7)

The dystopia in *Mockingbird* seems to have evolved rather conventionally . . . as the result of technology's constructing more and more complex automatic systems which cannot be swayed by emotion. The image that Tevis uses to convey the totality of the controlled systems in the novel refers to the classic eighteenth-century rational system for calculating happiness by quantifying sense perceptions. It is called the "pleasure principle"; theoretically, under such a principle the causes and effects of all activities—from sex to painting—can be quantified and hence manipulated. In the novel, Mary Lou's journal laments that whereas she has heard that there used to be strong, individualistic men in the world now it's "all robots. Robots and the pleasure principle. Everybody's head is a cheap movie show." The dystopia in which Mary Lou, Paul, and Spofforth

find themselves is truly a "brave new world" in which emotions have been repressed or, at least, managed.

The basic malfunction in Spofforth is that his intelligence knows that something in him has been repressed. The manufacturing details are clear. Spofforth's most advanced Make Nine brain was made in Cleveland as "an *erased* copy of a very intelligent person's brain. Erased completely, except for a few old dreams." This slight oversight, and the question concerning what was erased in Spofforth's manufacture and what "old demons" remain, allow for the symbolic suggestiveness of his condition. Mary Lou calls him "Bob" when she is living with him; and in answer to her question of why he had to fall in love with her, Bob—displaying an aspect of personality less prominent earlier—answers with rhetoric that evokes major texts from the Romantic tradition: "I wanted to recover my buried life. This erased part of my memory. I would like to know, before I die, what it was like to be the human being I have tried to be all my life." Concluding this important scene of self-discovery, Mary Lou accidentally—accident could never be so important in a totally managed society—provides Spofforth with the word he has been trying to remember from Robert Frost's poem, "Stopping by Woods on a Snowy Evening," which Tevis runs in counterpoint throughout the novel with the mockingbird image.

The classic and lyric theme of the novel is that of the buried life, the sense of something now lost. The society of the novel itself has lost its humanness to the conventional bugaboo of excessive and controlled rationality. But more than that it is a novel about lost texts and the promise of partial rediscovery— mingled with the profound insight of the structuralists and others about reading and about history, perhaps, that the reality of the experience is always removed from the text. *Mockingbird* is a new story set far in the future of Lost Golden Ages in which the lost Ancients are we and our culture of silent movies and reading, the nearly forgotten Golden Age. The clever gimmick that permits Tevis to introduce old texts and a fairly wide range of literary allusion is the academic affiliation of Spofforth and Paul. A professor of film at an Ohio University, Paul is in New York at the start of the novel to work for Dean Spofforth at deciphering titles and captions on ancient silent films. In their society no one can read, since reading has been outlawed as an activity that could produce private and mysterious, hence uncontrollable, emotion. Paul teaches himself the art of reading and writing and then teaches Mary Lou. As they do this the sense of what has been lost from the past becomes more and more intense. Reading, in fact, leads them to sex, love, and close personal communication, which is the only way, Tevis suggests, to regain any contact with what has been lost in ourselves. Spofforth's real monstrosity, then, is that he can never communicate. He has no sex organs on his artificially made body, will not read, and inevitably feels the pain of love more than the humans do. Spofforth is the embodiment of the lost and buried life, and he knows it.

Paul, especially as he begins to rediscover reading and views twentieth-century films, feels a great sadness at the loss of involvement and the lost emotions that his modern, drugged, and controlled society has suffered during the five centuries of perfecting the pleasure principle. His "modern" ignorance is naive and shallow compared to the unfathomable depths that he perceives in the Ancients. Tevis has both Paul and Mary Lou continually compare what they see to old films and to the bits of literature that they rediscover. Their reactions, though eager, are simple-minded and sometimes coldly automatic. One of the first silent film captions Paul deciphers, the one that will remain his favorite, reads, "Only the mockingbird sings at the edge of the woods." He marvels that this rich sounding little sentence, which means more to him than he knows he can understand, was spoken by an old man to a young girl; he then records in the next paragraph of his journal that he watched the huge ape in *Kong Returns*. These small slices of reference along with the tremendous feeling of lost meanings help to universalize Tevis's theme of aloneness so that the reader senses not just a future dystopia of alienation, but the whole scope of human history in which the Moderns are continuously alienated from some lost meaning of the Ancients.

In this Rousseauesque scheme of movement away from meaning mingled with the scheme of the constant comparison between a modern Iron Age and a lost Golden Age, the monster and the primitive and the alien intelligence are all equally alone. Hence the hint of Spofforth as both lonely Frankenstein monster and lonely ape monster, Kong, seems appropriate to the novel. Certainly Tevis's decision to start the book with Spofforth atop the Empire State Building and to end it with him finally crashing to Fifth Avenue, although in a joyful suicide rather than the beleaguered fall of Kong, suggests this possibility. But the real point is the scope of humankind's loneliness as depicted in the novel—with one touchstone, forward in time, the lonely artificial intelligence of Spofforth and another, backward in time, the earliest lonely ape as superior being. (pp. 77-9)

If humans have always been alone and perhaps suicidal (Tevis seems to reach for this larger theme rather than for the lesser theme of the malfunctioning machine), then the few points of solace and meaning are those that can imply touching across the loneliness. Tevis focuses on the mysteries of reading, sex, and love to suggest this touching. The repressed, automaton people of the novel (both artificial and natural) hunger not only for physical touch but also for the few pieces of suggestive and meaningful language that they can uncover. Small bits of T. S. Eliot, Matthew Arnold, Robert Frost, Margaret Mitchell, and the old films go a long way toward helping them cope. Similarly, the allusions in the novel pull the reader toward more connections, more meanings, so that the reader also can recover lost links. Literature that is about the value of literature is a major product of the Romantic tradition that Tevis continues in this novel. In the scene that concludes Spofforth's most explicit statement about his buried life, Mary Lou happens to repeat by accident Paul's favorite line from the silent films about the mockingbird's singing. "'Say it again,' Bob said. There was something urgent in his voice." She repeats the line from which Bob picks out the word "woods," and then the scene builds. Tevis has the artificial man repeat the opening line from the Frost poem as though he were tasting it over and over. The scene ends with Mary Lou's flat observation that understates beautifully the value of *the word* to these people, "So Bob finally got the word for his poem, after over a hundred years of wondering. I'm glad I was able to give him something."

The end of Spofforth is a fulfillment of sorts as well as a non-Asimovian ending to a mechanical man story. In several ways, the android achieves a greater proximity to the value of humanness in his death than he was ever able to achieve in his buried life. First of all, he is released from the robotic directives and is able to make the arrangements for his own death. As he, Mary Lou, Paul, and the baby climb the steps of the Empire State Building in that final predawn morning in June 2467 (one of the skills the humans rediscover along with reading is how

to count and date), he climbs on ahead, carefully carrying the baby since he is so much stronger. This image of the gentle monster android climbing ahead with an innocent in his arms suggests again both the simple, sentimental Frankenstein monster who never really wanted to hurt anyone as well as King Kong. They must climb because in modern New York the drugged populace never uses the building, and so the elevators have long since ceased to work. When they reach the top and are waiting for dawn so that Spofforth may see New York as he falls, he begins to experience joy at his coming death:

> And the thing that has been coming slowly into Spofforth's mind now seizes it: joy. He is joyful as he had been joyful one hundred seventy years before, in Cleveland, when he had first experienced consciousness, gagging to life in a dying factory, when he had not yet known that he was alone in the world and would always be alone.
>
> He feels the hard surface beneath his bare feet with pleasure. . . .

It takes both Paul and Mary Lou to push the android off the building; and just as he begins to fall he feels Mary Lou gently kiss the strong, black small of his back. His plunge, then, contains some pleasure. Tevis has achieved a sad and yet sublime ending for a story about love and loss. Even though one of the key characters is an artificial man, the values and fulfillments in the tale are richly human. Some machines can teach us at times how precarious it is to be human, and those are the machines we should value most. (pp. 79-81)

Donald M. Hassler, "What the Machine Teaches: Walter Tevis's 'Mockingbird'," in The Mechanical God: Machines in Science Fiction, *edited by Thomas P. Dunn and Richard D. Erlich, Greenwood Press, 1982, pp. 75-82.*

CHRISTOPHER LEHMANN-HAUPT

Forget just for a moment that Walter Tevis's *The Queen's Gambit* is a novel about the game of chess—the best one that I know of to be written since Nabokov's *Defense*. Consider it as a psychological thriller, a contest pitting human rationality against the self's unconscious urge to wipe out thought.

The battlefield here is a mind—the prodigious power to reason of Elizabeth Harmon, whom we first encounter as an 8-year-old in a Kentucky orphanage. The forces for evil in the fight are drugs and alcohol, which Beth at first comes to know because of the orphanage's practice of keeping its children tranquilized. Later on in the novel, Beth's mind will be invaded by extremes of loneliness and inferiority. The fact that drunkenness and an instinct to lose are two of the enemies in *The Queen's Gambit* should come as small surprise to readers of Mr. Tevis's earlier novels, two of which are *The Hustler* and *The Man Who Fell to Earth*.

But the positive force in this story is new and interesting. Beth discovers as a child that she has a mind for chess. An amazing mind for chess. Soon after learning the game from the orphanage's janitor, she finds herself playing out complicated matches on a board in her mind's eye. Before too long, she is memorizing variations from the book *Modern Chess Openings* and spotting an error of strategy in a game once played by the great Paul Morphy.

As Beth grows up, her chess gets even more powerful and she begins to win tournaments contested by players of grandmaster standing. But the armies of alcohol and defeat also make their advances. Sometimes Beth's genius seems to be prevailing. At other times her self-destructiveness appears to be winning out. Which will win? Read on, dear reader, though after sampling the first few pages of *The Queen's Gambit,* you will need no more urging from me. And it matters not even a trifle if you don't know the first thing about chess.

On the other hand, Mr. Tevis's novel does happen to be about chess, and novels about chess inevitably raise certain problems for a writer. How, for example, does one describe the games that are part of the plot without either befuddling the nonspecialist with actual chess notation—as some chess novelists have been known to do—or waxing so vague as to risk alienating any reader with the slightest knowledge of the game?

Mr. Tevis, a class-C player who first learned chess at the age of 7, knows enough about the game to describe Beth's contests dramatically, but without getting mired in minutiae. . . . [Given] Mr. Tevis's skills as a writer and dramatist, one quickly catches the drift of each game without having to understand the technicalities.

A more serious question implied by the story is whether a woman could be constitutionally equipped to be a world-class player. Chess is a game that requires extreme aggressiveness to be played at its best. Some have even argued that it re-enacts the Oedipal drama, with victory being achieved by murdering the king. How could a woman identify unconsciously with such a drama? Mr. Tevis solves this problem convincingly by giving Beth plenty of reason to hate all adults, what with her parents' abandonment of her in childhood (albeit by dying in an automobile accident) and what with the less than solicitous ministrations of the orphanage she is stuck in.

As for any clichés about women not having the stamina for the rigors of tournament play: one of the novel's most satisfying passages occurs shortly after Beth has begun to menstruate. Headachy and nauseous, she finds herself overwhelmed by the complexities of a key game in a crucial tournament. Her solution is to leave the board and withdraw to a stall in "the girls' room."

> She sat relaxing, letting her mind go blank. Her elbows were on her knees, her head was bent down. With an effort of will she made the chessboard with the game on Board One on it appear in front of her. There it was. She could see immediately that it was difficult, but not as difficult as some of the games she'd memorized from the book at Morris' Book Store. The pieces before her, in her imagination, were crisp and sharply focused.
>
> She stayed where she was, not worrying about time, until she had it penetrated and understood. Then she got up, washed her face again and walked back to the gym. She had found her move.

I enjoyed *The Queen's Gambit* so much that I wish Mr. Tevis had found some sort of dramatic wrinkle to account for his ending, instead of making it an inevitable outgrowth of what has led up to it. I also wish that at the end I didn't feel so gloomy about Beth's future. But then a number of chess geniuses have not led particularly satisfying lives. Their time in

the sun is often brilliant but short-lived. Their time in the sun is also normally incomprehensible to most of us. But we can understand Beth Harmon. Which is still another reason why *The Queen's Gambit* is so thoroughly engaging.

> *Christopher Lehmann-Haupt, in a review of "The Queen's Gambit," in* The New York Times, *March 1, 1983, p. C13.*

HAROLD C. SCHONBERG

In the course of [*The Queen's Gambit*] Mr. Tevis reveals a great deal about the world of American chess, with a final glance at how the Russians operate, and it is an exceptionally accurate picture that he draws. The only improbability in this story is the sex of his protagonist. In the long history of chess, there have been very few prominent women players, and none who posed any threat to their male colleagues. . . .

Perhaps it is a matter of physical stamina. Chess is a demanding game, and players have been known to lose 10 or 15 pounds during a tournament. There is the daily 5-hour grind, with its 40 moves in 2 hours and 30 minutes and the brain at a perpetual boil. There are the sleepless nights where players study adjourned games. There are the shocks to the ego, the aggravation of frittering away a winning position through an overconfident move or a lapse in concentration or a downright blunder. In so male-oriented an activity as chess, brilliant women are not welcome. Men do not like to lose to women.

Despite the drama inherent in a woman's facing these obstacles, *Queen's Gambit* does not have much of an actual story line. This is a problem that would arise in a book about most great chess players. They start early, and by 16 or so they have made their mark or the chances are they will never make it. They live in even a more circumscribed world than ballerinas or pianists. Their whole life is devoted to the 64 squares. They constantly play, constantly study, talk an arcane argot, welcome no outsiders into their circle.

Mr. Tevis . . . makes the constrictions of such a life abundantly clear. Beth is incapable of small talk, has no social graces, cares for little but the beauty, infinite complexity and emotional demands of chess. She is dependent on sedatives and, later, alcohol. She has a few unsatisfactory affairs. She knows she is missing something, but something bigger than herself has seized her. . . . She knows only one thing in life. But that she knows supremely well.

One does get involved with this strange, unhappy, gifted heroine. Beth Harmon may not be prepossessing, but she has the dedication of a Biblical saint, a freak memory and an ability to synthesize and create and blow her little world apart with a kind of startling originality that nobody else can match. That is what chess on its highest level is all about.

> *Harold C. Schonberg, "A Whole Life in 64 Squares," in* The New York Times Book Review, *April 3, 1983, p. 12.*

A. ALVAREZ

Walter Tevis seems to be a writer who enjoys stacking the odds against himself. His first novel, *The Hustler,* back in 1959, was about pool—not the most universally appealing topic—and in *The Queen's Gambit* he has raised the ante with two apparently impossible themes: child genius and chess. Genius itself is intractable enough to novelists, not least because so few of them have it and those who do, perhaps by definition, have less time for themselves than for their art. But a child genius is not so much intractable as impenetrable, a phenomenon of nature, like a typhoon, awesome and unnerving. As for chess, it is a world to itself, of a subtlety so intricate that it is simply not available to the uninitiated. It is also static, private, and seemingly without drama in the conventional sense: two people facing each other across a small checkered board, unmoving, unspeaking, rarely even looking at each other. From this obdurate material Tevis has produced a spare and compelling book, exciting even for a reader like myself who does not play the game and barely knows the rules. . . .

Tevis's prose is pure and unemphatic, like Beth's lucid, one-track mind, but he knows how to generate tension. As the book progresses and the games become more and more complex, this sense of excitement, stillness, and silence builds steadily until it reaches an extraordinary climax in Moscow where Beth takes on the grandmasters of the Russian chess establishment. Without any exterior action to speak of, *The Queen's Gambit* is a thriller in the most genuine sense of the term. (p. 26)

Again and again throughout the book Tevis recreates [the] image of the chessboard in the imagination, and the girl's mind brooding on it in silence, as concentrated as a laser beam. It reminds me of Coleridge's famous description of Shakespeare at work: "himself meanwhile unparticipating in the passions, and actuated only by that pleasurable excitement, which had resulted from the energetic fervour of his own spirit in so vividly exhibiting what it had so accurately and profoundly contemplated." According to the blurb, Tevis himself is a strong chess player and, certainly, the novel is animated by a passion for the endlessness and elegance of the game. Whence the tension, the buzz, the "pleasurable excitement." But what makes *The Queen's Gambit* so persistently convincing is an even stronger passion for the mental energy chess demands, and for the indifference and blinding assurance of real talent engaged in its own proper work. (pp. 26-7)

A. Alvarez, "Games People Play," in The New York Review of Books, *Vol. XXX, No. 17, November 10, 1983, pp. 26-8.*

KELVIN JOHNSTON

The hero of *The Steps of the Sun* . . . is that rather worrying cult figure the omnipotent, maverick, basically immature American business tycoon, reminiscent of some of Richard Condon's nasties, who this time is trying to import from the stars a safe uranium to end the energy crisis which has left the USA a weak, decadent power overshadowed by China and Japan. But being a Tevis hero, Ben Belson has grave sexual hang-ups, focused on his mother, which much of his time, in the intervals of frenzied tycoonery, is devoted to curing.

He gets his beef back, of course—in fact, he does a humiliating stint as a stud in a brothel for middle-aged female Chinese party bosses—and he is reunited with his one true love, a rather unlikely Shakespearian actress, in an affecting but rather bathetic scene on top of the Empire State Building, watching the lights go up over Manhattan as the lifts, thanks to electric power from safe Belson uranium, are switched on again. An interesting enough read, but it didn't engage my sympathy, still less my intelligence.

Kelvin Johnston, in a review of "The Steps of the Sun," in The Observer, *March 25, 1984, p. 23.*

PETER BRIGG

Walter Tevis writes *good* novels (if one excepts *Mockingbird*), and *The Steps of the Sun* is further convincing proof of his gifts and his achievement. Moreover, he is engaged in the fascinating task of integrating the science fiction mode with sinuous and exacting studies of contemporary man, finding in the process new images of angst and of the courage to overcome the self through contemplation and action. He is not alone in this pursuit, of course—witness Genly Ai or Frank Herbert's mad geneticist—but Tevis's particular tack is to bring the character into the absolute center, subduing plot and the imaginative devices so beloved of the genre to the study of man.

The Steps of the Sun chronicles the adventures of Ben Belson, twenty-first century billionaire adventurer who ventures illegally into space (illegally because the energy-starved Earth cannot spare the uranium fuel) to find non-toxic uranium, which he hits on the second planet he tries. He then returns to Earth where his immensely valuable cargo is impounded, and he fights to free it, ending up with arrangements with the world-dominating Chinese which will allow his beloved New York City and the U.S.A. to once again turn on its lights in style.

That much is a Heinlein plot and Tevis makes it work well, with a clever, powerful Belson manipulating and gallivanting around the corridors of power and the universe. But beyond the good fun is a man in turmoil, his personal history weighing him down, his relationships in collapse, his self-confidence undermined by the blinding knowledge that he can do just about anything except find personal balance. And Tevis dovetails Belson's necessary searches, so that the discoverer of the uranium sends it home and chooses to stay alone on a planet whose obsidian surface is disturbed only by great flowers and a life-giving grass, where, in a morphine trance he gradually recovers his lost potency and sorts out at least part of his tangled mind. Later, this same 'hero' adopts a new mother as a vital part of his personal search. Benjamin Belson is a complex human and a fascinating one. His inner search is as well wrought as the action story in which it is set, and as exciting.

Peter Brigg, "Tevis' Latest Is Hugo Candidate," in Fantasy Review, *Vol. 7, No. 3, April, 1984, p. 32.*

COLIN GREENLAND

There is something familiar about Walter Tevis's latest protagonist, as he confesses himself to an imaginary policeman [in *The Steps of the Sun*]. "Look here, Officer, my name is Ben Belson, the celebrated millionaire financier, friend to famous and beautiful women, theater buff, prowler of the galaxy and closet Marxist. Big hands, big feet, big prick and a booming voice. And a big, throbbing, empty hole in my heart." We recognize the type. Perhaps we have met him before, in other self-reflecting American novels of the last ten years: male, Caucasian, educated, fifty. Formerly idealistic, he is now alcoholic and impotent, numb with guilt and glumly cynical. He is the symbol of a disillusioned generation. Belson's home is an exhausted America of eighty years hence, but his despair is contemporary enough: even in success, his country has let him down. . . .

Like a Renaissance merchant staking his all on a passage to the Indies, Belson goes looking for uranium. He buys a disused Chinese spaceship, refits the captain's stateroom with antiques and the bridge with beige carpet and consoles ("nothing more complicated than a locomotive''), and blasts off, illegally, into the existential void.

His luck is phenomenal. He finds a planet, bleak beyond compare, but apparently sentient, and wholly benevolent. He calls it Belson. Here he develops a morphine habit. A second world obligingly provides his hill of 86 per cent uranyl nitrate, an unstable but not radioactive isotope. Posting a shipful back to Earth, he decides to return to Belson as a hermit. He meditates upon his past inadequacies as husband, father and lover. When acid rain destroys his supplies, the planet mothers him. Its only shrub yields a perfect analgesic; its grass gives massage and blood-transfusions.

As laconic space-extravaganza, *The Steps of the Sun* is not so far from *The Sirens of Titan;* but where Kurt Vonnegut's quaint universe symbolizes nothing but its own absurdity, Ben Belson's wanderings, like more traditional ordeals, gather meaning to his hollow soul. His mercantile expedition turns into a pilgrimage through a cosmos that is quiet and kind. It is the shrunken, suspicious Earth that is hostile, as Belson finds out when arrested after touching down in Washington. His exile continues, in captivity and on the run through a purgatorial United States in love with its own poverty, to a cold utopian China. Belson, with his cargo of pain-killers and safe uranium, can save both East and West, but only if he can save himself first.

The Steps of the Sun has direct connections with some of the stories in Tevis's collection *Far From Home*.... "**The Apotheosis of Myra**", set on Belson (now Belsin) some years later, makes reference to "that old marauding tycoon" who discovered the planet (but, oddly, not the plant). The Oedipal encounters of Barney with his revenant parents in "**A Visit from Mother**" and "**Daddy**" prefigure Ben Belson's Freudian turmoil. Inexplicably, characters recur: Myra, a neglected wife or daughter who collects Haviland china; a Scottish lover called Isabel, forty-three years old and working in the arts. These correspondences illuminate nothing but suggest that Tevis is working out private preoccupations in his fiction. After the shallow and derivative *Mockingbird, The Steps of the Sun* seems to represent a personal breakthrough. Perhaps this is why Belson's chronicle is thoroughly selfish yet entirely sympathetic, deeply depressed yet ultimately uplifting.

> Colin Greenland, "Breaking Through," in The Times Literary Supplement, *No. 4233, May 18, 1984, p. 557.*

PUBLISHERS WEEKLY

Twenty years after his legendary showdown with Minnesota Fats in *The Hustler,* Fast Eddie Felson is back [in *The Color of Money*]. Once a high roller, he's now playing exhibition matches with Fats in shopping malls for cable TV, hoping to get picked up by "Wide World of Sports". But while Fast Eddie may have faded into the middle class for a time . . . , getting back into the action revives him. The money game, he soon realizes, has changed from straight pool to nine ball, and he reluctantly adjusts his skills to the lesser game, not to mention a new generation of competitors. The writing here is taut and evocative. Tevis is unequaled when it comes to creating and sustaining the tension of a high-stakes game. Even readers who've never lifted a cue will be captivated.

> A review of "The Color of Money," in Publishers Weekly, *Vol. 225, No. 26, June 29, 1984, p. 102.*

DENISE P. DONAVIN

[With *The Color of Money*] Tevis at last provides a sequel to his novel *The Hustler*. . . . The plot is quite similar to the earlier story in its emphasis on Fast Eddie, a no-longer-young but still talented pool player who faces terrible odds, personal troubles, and other disasters on his way to self-esteem, success, and big money. With the money no longer in straight pool, Eddie first tries a more conventional business and then masters the more demanding game of nine-ball, thus setting up a showdown with a younger, cocky crowd of seemingly unbeatable players. Minnesota Fats plays a brief but amusing role in Felson's scrabble toward the top. Although Tevis' writing is plodding at times, Fast Eddie remains a sympathetic, captivating character.

> Denise P. Donavin, in a review of "The Color of Money," in Booklist, *Vol. 81, No. 1, September 1, 1984, p. 28.*

LARRY JONAS

After twenty years, Fast Eddie is back [in *The Color of Money*]. Eddie Felson, the pool shark who made *The Hustler* a memorable story of the mean and sometimes lucrative lives of men who live by their manipulative skills with a cue and fifteen vari-colored balls, had been in seclusion since 1963. More or less, anyway. Since his memorable shoot-out on the baize with the legendary Minnesota Fats, Eddie had married and owned his own poolroom. Neither operation had turned out well. Now it is 1983 and Eddie is 50, and trying to make a comeback. He looks up Minnesota Fats and persuades the over-60 gourmand to hit the circuit with him in a series of exhibition matches. Before the start of the first match, Eddie tells his opponent, "I need to start hustling pool again." Fats looks at him. "You're not good enough, Fast Eddie."

With the years, Eddie's skills have eroded badly. And after the tour with Minnesota Fats that ended on a tragic note, Eddie finds that the game has also changed—the pros are now playing nine-ball pool in the big tournaments—and that the players are younger and much more skillful than in his heyday. Arabella, the cultured lady with whom he now lives, has more confidence in Eddie's hopes for a comeback than he does. And after the folk art gallery they open together is savaged, Eddie realizes that his financial future and his self confidence rest on his ability to hone his past skills and take on, and defeat, the top pros in tournament pool. The best of the lot are Babes Cooley and Earl Bochard, a couple of arrogant kids with mesmerizing skills. When Eddie plunks down his $1500 entry fee to enter the big pool tournament in Las Vegas—top prize $30,000—it is Cooley and Bochard who stand in his way as he tries to prove to himself and to his few followers that when the balls are racked up and the game begins, he is still the best in the business.

Nobody writes this type of story—strong conflict and close competition, whether it be chess or pool—better than Walter Tevis. Even if you've never seen the inside of a poolroom, you'll find this one helluva book. (pp. 54-5)

> Larry Jonas, in a review of "The Color of Money," in West Coast Review of Books, *Vol. 10, No. 5, September-October, 1984, pp. 54-5.*

Peter (Dennis Blandford) Townshend
1945-

English songwriter, short story writer, essayist, and poet.

Best known as the principal songwriter and lead guitarist for The Who, a highly popular English rock group that flourished from the mid-1960s until its breakup in 1984, Townshend elicited critical interest from the literary world with the publication of *Horse's Neck* (1985). The book contains semiautobiographical short stories, poems, and anecdotes in which Townshend examines his restless youth, his years as a musician and celebrity, his alcohol and heroin addictions, and his quest for spiritual rebirth. Critics note similarities between *Horse's Neck* and Townshend's most accomplished work with The Who. For example, his obsessions with adolescent rebellion and the search for identity, which recur throughout the pieces in *Horse's Neck*, are also dominant themes in many of his songs, including those which appear on the albums *Tommy* (1969) and *Quadrophenia* (1973). While some critics regarded Townshend's prose as pretentious, others commended his candor and his ability to evoke vivid images and emotions. Townshend has recorded several solo albums and is involved in projects with a variety of musicians. In addition, he has contributed articles for such entertainment periodicals as *New Musical Express* and *Rolling Stone* and is also an editor at the London publishing firm of Faber and Faber.

(See also *CLC*, Vol. 17 and *Contemporary Authors*, Vol. 107.)

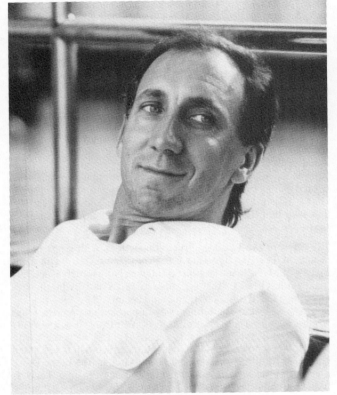

Photograph by Malcolm Heywood. Courtesy of Peter Townshend

PHILIP SMELT

It is well known that rock musicians lead a perilous and degenerate existence, and **Horse's Neck,** a collection of short stories and occasional poems by Pete Townshend, erstwhile guitarist and presiding genius of The Who, reflects all the uncertainty and squalor of his capricious culture. His earliest memory, as related in the opening chapter, is of lying alone on a Northumberland beach while his mother and father gallop across the sand, leaving him feeling vulnerable and isolated and with a life-long fear of horse riding. The next story reveals his fascination with the pantomime horse—in particular the person in the back end which "bloody well followed the front end in darkness and humiliation". Townshend sees this as a model for adult depravity, since "Nothing else in nature behaves so consistently and rigidly as a human being in pursuit of hell."

"Horse" is slang for heroin, but Townshend's much-publicized experience of the drug is apparently not the reason for his equestrian obsession. He observes:

> For a while I was convinced that the horse in
> my dreams and memories was in some way a
> symbol connected with an opium-drenched past
> life. I was wrong. The horse I feared to ride
> was a real giant, not a circus clown's prop.

His literary response to this fear is to saddle up some grotesque, and at times pretentious, constructions. A description of a beach, for instance, is finished off with an unnecessary and jarring observation: "At certain moments you could believe that no one had ever run their fingers through the golden dust, or that no cigarette had ever been discarded. The exploring hand of an inquisitive child would belie that fancy." Elsewhere an amusing story-teller at a party is gently criticized by Townshend for spending "more time on prosopopoeia than denouement". . . .

In **"An Impossible Song"** he sums up the relationship between a divine protector and a faded rock star:

> I still believe in God. I've pushed all thoughts
> of him aside, but he is still on my case. I sound
> conceited but I think I'm special. Why should
> I pretend otherwise? If I'm not special, then I
> must be unusually lucky, and if I'm that lucky
> with no talent and no guardian angel, then that
> makes me special.

What makes Townshend seem lucky and, *a fortiori* it seems, special is the fact that he is still alive. Many of the characters in his stories are dead or dying and Townshend repeatedly reminds himself that he is "a survivor" as he gazes on the wreckage of his generation. If he has survived in order to

378

become a writer, he must, on this luckless and unspecial first appearance, concentrate on developing more talent.

Philip Smelt, in "Lucky but Not Special," in The Times Literary Supplement, *No. 4291, June 28, 1985, p. 733.*

MARTIN BOOTH

Books written by—as opposed to ghosted for—rock musicians are uncommon enough, but to find one of such exquisite excellence is not just a thrill but a revelation that supports the somewhat unfashionable view that rock music does hold in its ranks contemporary artists of genuine genius.

Pete Townshend, leader of The Who and a generation of rock music *aficionados,* has written [*Horse's Neck*], a book that is far superior to anything any of his peers have produced. The contents are a complex amalgam of short fictions, prose-poems, semi-autobiographical pieces and poetry that look at fragments of rock music life, alcohol and heroin addiction, youth and love, all portrayed in a wistfully romantic yet still highly realistic manner that captures the anthemic tone of so many of Townshend's musical lyrics, especially those from his earlier years. In the book one sees not only a private struggle with life but also an entire generation's shiftless discovery of itself. . . .

Townshend has achieved a stark, almost Kerouac-like truthfulness in his writing and the result is stunningly good. Reading this, his first book, one hungers for it to be longer than ninety-six pages and can only anticipate eagerly his next volume in the same genre.

Martin Booth, in a review of "Horse's Neck," in British Book News, *August, 1985, p. 499.*

MICHIKO KAKUTANI

Pete Townshend, of course, is best known as the songwriter and lead guitarist for The Who—the primary author of the rock opera *Tommy,* and the author, too, of those much quoted lines, "hope I die before I get old" (which appeared on The Who album *My Generation,* some two decades ago). . . . In [*Horse's Neck*], his first published volume of prose, he writes, each chapter "deals with one aspect of my struggle to discover what beauty really is."

That vague, pretentious statement probably sums up the experience of reading *Horse's Neck* as well as anything else. Like The Who albums *Tommy* and *Quadrophenia,* the book is an anomalous, idiosyncratic volume, held together more by the author's sensibility, and certain recurrent preoccupations and images, than conventional narrative strategies. It's neither a novel nor a collection of short stories, neither a fully-imagined work of fiction nor a memoir though followers of The Who will doubtless recognize certain themes—and even precise phrases like "exquisite boredom"—from band albums and Mr. Townshend's solo efforts. . . .

On one level, *Horse's Neck* fuzzily recounts the coming of age of a young musician, his problems with drugs and alcohol and his efforts to escape, but it undermines both the documentary interest of such a story and the reader's sympathy for its characters by continuously shifting narrative gears—splitting up individual characters into a handful of incarnations, setting up heartfelt confessions with overly ironic frames and simply confusing the reader with bizarre, dreamlike digressions.

Perhaps Mr. Townshend wants to make the point that reality is so strange that it often seems like a dream or nightmare. Perhaps he wants to argue that fantasy and reality are purely arbitrary divisions. Or perhaps he just wants to convey a sense of the floating derangement that comes with too much alcohol or drugs. Unfortunately, even his objectives are unclear—so muddled and inaccessible are his allusions.

What are we to make, for instance, of the book's title *Horse's Neck* and the repeated references to horses? In one chapter, the narrator sees his parents riding horses by the sea; in the next, he dreams about a horse trapped in the basement of a ruined church; in another, he recounts a sexual obsession with horses, similar to the one in *Equus.* Since we're never given a hint of what this symbolism means or how it connects to Mr. Townshend's other concerns, we tend to come away with the feeling that we've just walked into the middle of a stranger's analysis session—what initially provokes mild curiosity ends up being merely boring.

Clearly Mr. Townshend possesses an instinctive feel for mythicizing the stuff of real life—an ability to take personal emotions, shatter and then reassemble them in more abstract configurations. But while this impulse can result—in such chapters as **"Champagne on the Terraces"** and **"Fish Shop"**—in some dramatic set pieces, it's too often directed toward such adolescent subjects as getting high or having a one-night stand. To make matters worse, the author often slips into the sort of wordy pretention that characterized his lyric writing at its worst. . . . This same windy self-consciousness afflicts the narrator of **"Ropes,"** who announces that he and his buddies "were the frayed rubber band inside the enormous balsa-wood airplane of rock and roll." And it is shared, too, by a character in **"Winston"** who complains that children today "confuse sex with aspiration, violence with fortitude."

There is, in fact, a great deal of such complaining in *Horse's Neck.* Mr. Townshend's characters apparently don't have much tolerance for young people . . . , for women . . . , or for their own spoiled lives. . . . These sentiments, certainly, are not dissimilar to ones expressed by some of Mr. Townshend's lyrics, but at least on the better records, such bitterness and complacency was counterpointed by the music's aggressive and energetic drive.

Michiko Kakutani, "His Generation," in The New York Times, *August 17, 1985, p. 33.*

BRIAN MORTON

Horse's Neck is a painful book, consciously and unflinchingly an exorcism of years of excess. The title refers to a recurring sexual fantasy that is eventually resolved in the final part, and also hints at drink and drugs, the brandy cocktails and heroin that fuelled Townshend's and The Who's headlong rush through the Seventies. . . .

There are few good fictional renderings of the rock musician's world and few coherent fictional accounts of stardom. The best of them—in Polish-American Jerzy Kosinski's novels and in Bob Dylan's maligned and now bowdlerized film *Renaldo and Clara*—focus on the way stardom builds armatures round the self and the need to strip these away to reveal a vulnerable but none the less entire personality within. Townshend is no less brutal and shocking than Kosinski but no less committed to the recovery of the single, separate self.

The last but one section of *Horse's Neck* is entitled **"An Impossible Song"**. It brings together the fears and pressures that lead to the addiction of fame with a kind of chastened recovery of ordinariness that is genuinely moving: "I am very ordinary. I have made mistakes and found it hard to forgive myself, just like you."

Brian Morton, *"Out of the Ordinary," in* The Times Educational Supplement, *No. 3619, November 8, 1985, p. 31.*

HUGH BARNES

The Who provided unlimited material for gossip, like the Beatles and the Rolling Stones who graduated from the British R&B circuit before them. It was, incidentally, as much the lunatic behaviour of their drummer, the late and lamented Keith Moon, as Pete Townshend's songs of adolescent rebellion that won them column inches. Moon was juvenile, a jester from Wembley who delighted in pranks. But the group were remarkable for other things. While the Beatles accomplished a smooth crossing-over into show business, being impish and respectably tuneful, and the Stones were egregious vagabonds, the Who appealed directly to the experience of a generation of fans. That generation has since disbanded, like the group itself, notwithstanding the occasional reunion for charity or nostalgia. Nowadays Pete Townshend frequents headier circles, as a publisher and general source of wisdom. *Horse's Neck* is the first fruit of this latest collaboration: a disguised, disjointed autobiography. (pp. 19-20)

A biography of Townshend would inevitably discuss the pop star's addiction to heroin and his reform. This book eschews the subject, although there is an oblique reference to recent chaos in **"Champagne on the Terraces"**, when a wife says: 'Since you've been on the wagon all you do is sit and dream.' Among the various dreams of childhood and psychosis that make up *Horse's Neck* one resembles documentary. **"Winston"**—this was John Lennon's second name—describes a party the writer attended in New York on the first anniversary of the Beatle's death, and someone he met there. Van Smith-Huntley drunkenly spills pop star secrets to the world. As Townshend points out, ordinary frustration was responsible for his outburst: 'He had lost his band only a year or two before.' But snatches of it resist explanation. Van denounces the inveterate gossips and journalists for their 'high-flown and pragmatic' interpretations: 'It belies the fact that all rock and its so-called stars ever did was stand up and complain.' The remark, however facile, can be applied to The Who, and to the punk rockers whose anger Townshend in some ways anticipated and who settled happily for danceable complaining. Dave Rimmer's *Like Punk Never Happened* charts Culture Club's career and the supremacy of the new idols, like Wham! and Duran Duran, in such a way as to bear out Van's disappointment at the demise of the rebel wave.

In *Horse's Neck* Townshend is at pains to forget his first career. In **"Fish Shop"**, describing a 'giant of a man' recognisable as himself, he achieves astonishing detachment: 'Performing with his band on the stage was my friend Pete, a narrow man with eyes like the eyes a child sees when it stands on its head and looks in a mirror. He was swinging his guitar like a battle-axe, slicing a microphone in two across the stage, its cable curling.' Townshend's past, remote and reproachful, has a habit of intruding into each story. The subject returned to or gestured at is melancholic, turning into inarticulacy or a feeling

of apartness from the everyday world. The collection is marred by waywardness and rambling, despite the odd flourish and lightness of touch. Each scene is presented as an epiphany. The first piece, **"Thirteen"**, sets the mood with a description of a summer's afternoon on the beach at Filey (later recalled as a 'Northumbrian miracle'). The narrator luxuriates in the guilty isolation of a child whose parents have abandoned him. At last the mother and father appear astride stallions, but remain only for a moment before 'galloping off again laughing and waving'. Mothers and horses are ubiquitous in this book, as Townshend explains in his preface: 'My mother features in this book, but her character changes constantly because this "mother" is many mothers, many teachers.' Horses also transform themselves. In another story a young boy longs to stand as the back half of a pantomime horse, to relish the 'darkness and humiliation' it would involve. A dream of a church in a Cotswold village is memorable for the frenzied appearance of a colt among the ruins. The dreamer remembers the beast 'running in a mindless circle'. This, he confides further on, was 'a terrible dream and seemed portentous'. The motif recurs provocatively in the same story, subtly altered, in a house 'devoid of furniture' and life—'except that the tiny room was occupied by another horse'. After much hard work this horse is elevated to the status of 'an oblique warning that I would repeat the same mistake eternally'. It's possible that we are staring up the nose of some ghastly conscience which, like Joyce's, hasn't materialised yet. . . .

Townshend remarks at the beginning of *Horse's Neck* that 'each story deals with one aspect of my struggle to discover what beauty really is.' These are grand sentiments but we are not told whether the 'struggle' continues at the end or has been concluded successfully. We must look elsewhere for an answer—to the book's cover, perhaps, from which a gaunt face stares out. (p. 20)

Hugh Barnes, *"Blue Suede Studies," in* London Review of Books, *Vol. 7, No. 22, December 19, 1985, pp. 19-20.*

SUSAN JELCICH

As guitarist and principal songwriter with The Who for twenty years, Pete Townshend brought a sophisticated lyricism to rock and roll songwriting that today remains unsurpassed and unparalleled. Townshend's work lent initial credibility to the argument of rock and roll as an art form, and he was the first to create lyrics as moving and as hard driving as the thunderous power chords and richly rhythmic drums that accompanied them.

It is with these thoughts in mind that most readers will pick up his first published work of fiction, *Horse's Neck,* a compilation of verse and short stories written over a five-year period. Yet those expecting the kind of richly textured emotions and cathartic identification found both in Townshend's solo work and in his work with The Who will be sadly disappointed.

It is ironic that Townshend's literary work should so strongly emphasize his brilliance as a songwriter. Whereas Townshend's musical work lent legitimacy to the life-long feelings of adolescent frustration and alienation, *Horse's Neck* is filled with weak autoeroticism—obviously inspired by, but not in the tradition of, James Joyce—brutal self-condemnation, and intellectualized self-pity that alienate the reader. . . .

In fact, Townshend's prose is so blatantly ill-disguised that the reader falls into the trap of trying to discover the real-life identities of the characters, a dangerous practice for the reader and a disservice to the writer. However, Townshend has put little effort into fictionalizing his obviously autobiographical material.

The trouble is that Townshend's work contains neither the literary craftsmanship of a finely honed piece of fiction nor the raw urgency or endearing self-deprecation of a thinly veiled, highly autobiographical work, such as Sylvia Plath's *The Bell Jar* or Nora Ephron's *Heartburn*. By wallowing in a pool of personal antipathy and disgust, the author elicits no sympathy on the part of the reader. We simply don't care enough about his characters to share in any of these emotions.

In essence, the bulk of *Horse's Neck* deals with Townshend's ceaseless self-recriminations from his self-destructive days of substance abuse, family estrangement, and extramarital philanderings. In addition, he has never come to terms, musically or personally, with the death of drummer [Keith] Moon, a unique and embraceable man whose death had an unexpectedly devastating and far-reaching impact on Townshend and his band-mates. *Horse's Neck* has most likely served as a catharsis for Townshend—this final attempt to exorcise the demons that have plagued him during the past seven years. However, the reader has neither place nor involvement in the process....

This is not to say that *Horse's Neck* does not have its merits. Not surprisingly, the two pieces that are the most rewarding do not deal with any aspect of Townshend's late seventies/early eighties decline. In **"Thirteen,"** a combination of prose and verse, Townshend examines the mother's role as both nurturer and nemesis, and impressively relates a memory that his mother deems a fantasy, since she can place it at a time when Townshend was barely two years old. . . . It is a warm and comforting piece, a skillful translation of infantile sensations into adult perceptions.

"Fish Shop" concerns a trip back to the old neighborhood, undoubtedly patterned after the Shepherd's Bush section of London, where Townshend grew up. The story concerns the special relationship between the main character, Pete, and Jaco, the owner of the local fish and chips shop, an accomplished flamenco guitarist driven from his native Spain during the time of Franco. It is a tale of fragile beauty threatened by the ignorant bravura of the neighborhood, by those who wish to destroy what they cannot understand. Budding guitarist Pete strikes up a friendship with the shop owner after discovering his name on an old flamenco recording. Once the friendship becomes known around the neighborhood, the young toughs of Pete's acquaintance deem the relationship homosexual. Although Pete is sure of his own motives, the pressure of his contemporaries and his own tender age work against him, and he begins questioning Jaco's intentions. At the end, Pete is betrayed by both the boys he grew up with and the girl he believes he loves. He decides to break with the old neighborhood, and with it, his youthful past.

Although *Horse's Neck* bears strong resemblance to an ill-conceived autobiography in which the names have been changed to protect neither the guilty nor the innocent, it should not become the first and last of Townshend's literary endeavors. As his literary skills grow and his talents develop, it will be interesting to watch this lyrical master channel his efforts into a new genre.

> *Susan Jelcich, in a review of "Horse's Neck," in* San Francisco Review of Books, *Spring, 1986, p. 14.*

Rose Tremain

1943-

English novelist, short story writer, biographer, historian, scriptwriter, and author of children's books.

In her fiction Tremain creates sympathetic portraits of lonely individuals. Her characters typically search for love and acceptance, yet they remain isolated because of their inability to communicate effectively or to change their lives. Critics note Tremain's attention to detail, which lends realism to her work and helps establish complex secondary characters. In several of her works, Tremain focuses on protagonists whose ages and experiences differ markedly from her own. For example, her first novel, *Sadler's Birthday* (1976), centers on a retired butler who lives alone in the manor he inherited from his former employers. Tremain uses flashbacks and an understated prose style to examine Sadler's past and the lives of those with whom he had lived and worked. *The Cupboard* (1981) also focuses on an elderly protagonist. In this work, Tremain juxtaposes the vibrant past of an aged novelist and suffragette with the unhappy life of the young journalist who interviews her. In both of these novels, Tremain explores the psychological motivations of her characters and the ways in which their past experiences have contributed to their emotional emptiness.

In the novels *Letter to Sister Benedicta* (1978) and *The Swimming Pool Season* (1985), Tremain portrays middle-aged couples trapped in unhappy marriages. The former work concerns a woman who is free to reexamine her life after her domineering husband suffers a stroke and her children leave home, and in the latter novel, a man seeks emotional release from his failing business ventures by building a swimming pool when his wife travels to her mother's deathbed. Conflicts between husbands and wives are also explored in Tremain's collection of short stories, *The Colonel's Daughter* (1984), as are conflicts between parents and children and among social classes. Caryn James found "a sense of impending psychic violence" in this collection, adding that "this tension . . . gives the stories their originality and power." Tremain has also written a biography of Joseph Stalin, a history of suffragettes entitled *Freedom for Women* (1971), and several radio and television dramas.

(See also *Contemporary Authors*, Vols. 97-100 and *Dictionary of Literary Biography*, Vol. 14.)

JOHN MELLORS

In her first novel, *Sadler's Birthday,* Rose Tremain has avoided the beginner's temptation to write the story of her life. She has produced an absorbing study of loneliness, the emotional loneliness of an old man who has never aroused in others the love he himself felt, and the separation into solitude of an old couple whose complete lack of sexual rapport has confined their marriage, first, to a tolerant companionship, and later, to a stoical agreement to make good manners the basis on which they can bear to live together. The author's affection for her characters and insight into their problems are as remarkable as

Photograph by Mark Gerson

the skill with which she fixes them in place—East Anglia—and time—mostly 1939.

Jack Sadler, now 76—as old as the century—lives alone in the big house where once he had been butler to Colonel and Mrs Bassett. They are the old couple—dead by now. He spends his time looking back to his childhood when his mother worked as a skivvy, to his adolescence when he was trained as a footman, but above all to the period 1939 to 1953, when he worked as butler in the house he has since inherited from his employers. A decent, upright, hard-working man, Sadler gained the trust of the Colonel and his lady, but never the love of the evacuee, Tom, the one thing he wanted most in life.

This could have been a depressing story, but not as Rose Tremain tells it. She has the knack of using humour, especially in dialogue, to hold the reader's sympathy with her characters in their predicament. *Sadler's Birthday* is funny, sad and accurate; not many first novels combine imagination and discipline to this degree.

John Mellors, "Life without Love," in The Listener, Vol. 95, No. 2454, April 22, 1976, p. 518.

SUSANNAH CLAPP

Rose Tremain's first novel is a study of Englishness and disappointment. *Sadler's Birthday* deals in the sorts of setting which find their way on to calendars and place-mats—a Norfolk country house, a small Suffolk town—and in the kinds of character that American tourists used to find "quaint": a cleaning-woman who bristles with godliness, an aristocrat who treads his orchard in bare feet and tails. Playing with these stereotypes, Mrs Tremain unravels the individual stories behind them with tact, attentiveness and a sure sense of what hurts. . . .

It is one of the triumphs of *Sadler's Birthday* that each of its voices is fully, if briefly, realized: no story is allowed to drown out another. The neatly regulated lives are in turn thrown up against larger events, as if unknowingly jigging to more imperious summonses from upstairs—the chauffeur dies as Hiroshima burns, "as if the bomb had hit him"; on their way to watch the Coronation, the Colonel and Madge are killed in a car crash—and Sadler imagines an open coach, containing a coroneted Colonel, spinning out of control in front of eager crowds. Such parallels, unobtrusively introduced, help to establish both period context and a general tone of wry arbitrariness. They are not buttonholed to serve a moral purpose. Sadler remembers Vera the cook's "Thank God for Tea", and realizes it "was the kind of saying they printed on the front of T-shirts" nowadays, and that "Vera wouldn't have understood that"—but, in general, religion turns out to be of little use to these characters. Everyone, from Sadler's mother to the Colonel's lady, is concerned mainly with getting through his life with as little pain as possible, but they try too, in some degree, to reconcile social performance with what they feel: the novel is excellent at placing different kinds of snub, at pointing to the ease with which people recognize their own "type", and at nailing the kind of nervous giggle which makes a woman wish "she had never learnt to laugh".

One by one characters admit—almost conversationally, certainly without any portentousness on the author's part—to major defeats: Madge to not being "good with people", the Colonel to a lifetime of impotence with Madge. The many ways in which lives can be pinched are shown and left sensibly unannotated. But the very variety of unhappiness gives the novel an odd vitality. No one in *Sadler's Birthday*—not even Vera, who ends up in a "replaceable" geriatric bed—is dispensable, because no one overlaps with anyone else. And if Sadler gets the most extensive knocks, it is because he has the most extensive cares: his concern with getting to grips with things, and the vigorousness with which his search is described, turn what could have been a wan comedy of mannerisms into a rich and informative novel.

> Susannah Clapp, "What the Butler Saw," in The Times Literary Supplement, *No. 3868, April 30, 1976, p. 507.*

JOYCE CAROL OATES

[*Sadler's Birthday*] is a first novel that reads as if it were the consequence of innumerable careful revisions; it is austere, beautifully constructed, an elegiac tribute to the special insights that attend extreme loneliness. . . .

Sadler's Birthday is something of a tour de force. Its subject is the final days of an elderly man who lives in abject loneliness in a grand house he has inherited. Formerly a servant, Jack Sadler is willed his employers' house simply because they have no next of kin to leave it to; his only companion is a dog (105 years old by human measurement). . . . [He] spends most of his time in the past, brooding over his mother and her simple, doomed selflessness, and the single affectionate liaison of his

life, which had been with a young boy decades ago. Time seems to pleat with increasing frequency. Jack hears voices, imagines scenes he has not originally witnessed, relives his most painful losses. His employer, the long-dead Colonel, reappears to drink port with him and to explain this violation of social etiquette: "Never socialize except with equals. Never go up, never go down—cardinal rule," the Colonel says. "But loneliness, old age—same thing—means you have to start breaking rules."

Rose Tremain's characters do not, however, break many rules. For the most part they are quiet, quietly desperate people, intelligent enough to perceive the dreary limitations of their lives but not intelligent enough, and not daring enough, to make any important changes. Though Jack loves the boy Tom as much as he is capable of loving anyone, he accepts the boy's dismissal of him with stoic resignation, much as he has accepted the innumerable subtle and unsubtle humiliations of a life spent "in service." (It is the reader, not Jack, who is likely to feel the injustice of his position, and by extension the position of all servants.) Gentle, Chekhovian in its rhythms and insights, *Sadler's Birthday* is a rather special work, a simple novel that dwells lovingly upon the details of simple lives without condescension or bitterness. In fact, one might wish for more emotion, for more anger. There are times when it seems that the ideal English novel is an artifact of a certain number of cautious, well-crafted pages that manage to offend no one, while stressing the oldest and most conservative of virtues—stability, acceptance, stoicism, a sort of wry self-deprecatory humor that translates into courage. Nevertheless *Sadler's Birthday* is well worth reading, and Rose Tremain a highly promising young novelist. Perhaps her second novel will be more ambitious. (p. 14)

> Joyce Carol Oates, "Four Novels," in The New York Times Book Review, *July 24, 1977, pp. 14-15, 29.*

THE NEW YORKER

[*Sadler's Birthday* is a] sinewy, touching first novel about the old age of a retired English butler. . . . Now shabby, forgetful, and irascible, decrepit Sadler recalls the loyal, impassive, fastidious Sadler he once was with something like amazement. How could he have sustained his role of "perfect servant" for so many years, or tolerated a life that had so little personal gratification in it? Sadler is not without a sense of humor, but he pities himself. And with justification. The bastard child of a timid, kind country girl who was forced to become a servant herself to support him, he was trained at an early age to suppress his own impulses lest they irritate his masters. The story . . . is told with great economy and feeling. This is a short book, but one feels that it says all there is to say about English servants of a bygone era.

> A review of "Sadler's Birthday," in The New Yorker, *Vol. LIII, No. 24, August 1, 1977, p. 68.*

JOHN MELLORS

Letter to Sister Benedicta is about several kinds of love—love of God, sexual love and the love between parents and children. Rose Tremain's narrator, Ruby, feels that she has missed out on all of them, becoming 'so used to half-loving, it's all I can do'. She compares herself unfavourably, not only with the pious nun to whom she is metaphorically confessing rather than actually communicating, but also with her son and daughter, who have dared to break one of society's few remaining sexual taboos and have slept together without guilt and with considerable satisfaction. Ruby, on the other hand, when she has an adulterous affair with a friend of the family, feels 'like a shipwreck under a drowning man'.

Ruby's letter describes the events of a year in which her husband, Leon, gets so angry when he hears what his offspring have been doing that he has a stroke; after lying for months paralysed and speechless, he dies, unvisited by son or daughter. Ruby decides to return to India, where she had lived as a child and been taught by Sister Benedicta in a convent school. From the remarks she makes about India, Ruby seems to regard it as a place where her own inadequacies and wounds are writ large—'a mutilated land . . . a country that is bleeding to death'—and her decision makes a rather unconvincing finale to an otherwise most impressive book. (p. 563)

> John Mellors, "Child Power," in The Listener, Vol. 101, No. 2607, April 19, 1979, pp. 562-63.

FRANCES ESMONDE DE USABEL

[In *Letter to Sister Benedicta,* fifty-year-old] Ruby Constad writes to Sister Benedicta, one of the nuns in the convent school in India Ruby attended when she was a girl, but she is really talking to herself. Ruby's husband, a successful lawyer, has had a stroke, her son seems to have disappeared and her daughter is distraught because her love affair—with her brother—has ended. As she reflects upon the family problems, Ruby dwells upon her own feelings of inadequacy and unattractiveness. But the reader sees beyond Ruby's superficial awkwardness to the capacity for love in this woman who is humorous, unpretentious, and never judgmental. Deceptively modest in its outlines, this novel is a tribute to the human spirit and deserves a wide readership.

> Frances Esmonde de Usabel, in a review of "Letter to Sister Benedicta," in Library Journal, Vol. 104, No. 15, September 1, 1979, p. 1722.

SUSAN KENNEDY

[In *Letter to Sister Benedicta*], Ruby Constad's husband is lying, after a stroke, in a London nursing home, incapable of speech and apparently unwilling to join the fight for life. . . . Leon's illness, brought on, she believes, by the peculiarly cruel desertion of their grown-up children, is Ruby's crisis: what can it tell her, she asks Sister Benedicta, of God and love? What hope can it offer her after the wasted years of an unfulfilling marriage? Its crystalline language gives Rose Tremain's second novel a startling clarity. Ruby is a fat, wistful, vague fifty-year-old; her habitat is Harrods and the streets of Knightsbridge. Miss Tremain gives us a completely rounded portrait. Fleeting suspension of belief comes only with the doubt that someone with so rich an inner imagination, so wry a vision of herself could ever have allowed herself to be defeated by such negative personalities as her husband and son.

> Susan Kennedy, in a review of "Letter to Sister Benedicta," in The Times Literary Supplement, No. 4003, December 7, 1979, p. 104.

SAVKAR ALTINEL

Rose Tremain's first novel *Sadler's Birthday* concerned the efforts of an elderly man to free himself from his complex feelings about his dead mother, and its successor, *Letter to Sister Benedicta,* was about a middle-aged London housewife named Ruby Constad trying to overcome the limitations imposed on her by her upbringing in colonial India and a lifetime of obedience to her husband. Both Sadler and Ruby had symbolic prisons—he, the room where he had tried to lock away his past; she, the convent where she had been educated.

The Cupboard deals with the same theme of freedom and imprisonment. This time, though, there are two central characters: an American journalist called Ralph Pears, and Erica March, an eighty-seven-year-old English novelist and political activist who has agreed to tell him her life story. Ralph, who is, as everyone points out, "short for an American", is literally stunted as a result of a fall from a barn roof which occurred in his early youth, shortly after the failure of his attempt to seduce a black maid. To this humiliating memory is added the barrenness of his present life. He is downtrodden by his bullying editor, and his personal relationships are constantly ruined by his inability to love. . . . What he expects from his encounter with Erica is a renewal of his will to live. . . .

Erica's life as told to Ralph . . . resembles a full basin. We see her first on her parents' Suffolk farm. When she is eight her mother is trampled to death by a bull, and Erica inherits the huge cupboard that used to belong to her. This piece of furniture, which both frightens and soothes her, thereafter becomes the prison she has to avoid. Escape from it and from the restrictive world of the farm comes in a variety of ways. First her Uncle Chadwick, a homosexual vicar turned popular playwright, invites her to London where she joins the Suffragettes. Then she writes her first novel, falls in love with a French painter named Gérard and spends the 1920s and the 1930s in Paris. After Gérard's death in the Spanish Civil War she returns to England, and in the 1950s she is active in the CND movement.

Yet, paradoxically, in the end there is no escape. . . . Everywhere the forces of oppression are victorious. Worse, the cupboard and the farm periodically reclaim her, and throughout her life she suffers from fits of intense depression virtually amounting to insanity, during which she talks to her mother and wants to join her. When Ralph finds her she is an old woman who hasn't done anything for nearly thirty years, and after finishing her story she retreats into her cupboard and kills herself with sleeping pills. . . .

The Cupboard has its defects, but it is a much more ambitious work than the earlier two novels. Both *Sadler's Birthday* and *Letter to Sister Benedicta* were essentially static, and took place largely inside the heads of their protagonists. Here there is an attempt to establish an objective situation, and use it as a basis for narrative. Unfortunately, it isn't easy to believe that an American magazine would really send a reporter across the Atlantic to interview a novelist who hadn't produced anything for three decades, and although the sheer richness of Erica's life necessitates the presence of some sort of editor to impose order on her memories, the questions like "And did you return to London then?" and "Were you very lonely after Gérard's death?" with which Ralph keeps interrupting her have an artificial ring to them, and rapidly become irritating.

A more serious problem has to do with the way in which Ms Tremain uses history. Already in her earlier novels there was an attempt to establish connections between psychological and political freedom, and to draw parallels between Sadler's life as a butler and the servitude brought on him by the memory of a dead woman, or between the liberation of India and the liberation of Ruby Constad. In *The Cupboard* there is an even more explicit insistence that personal and public history cannot be separated, but no real interest is in fact shown in the latter. The book is cluttered with remarks like "There was so much misery in the Thirties" and "We abandoned the French on the beach at Dunkirk" which seem dry and lifeless.

Still, like the Old Masters, about suffering Ms Tremain is never wrong. When it comes to depicting psychological injuries she has few rivals, and the images of human pain she conjures up—Chadwick crying in his bath for his dead lover Robin with his hair dye running into the water, Erica lying on the floor, talking to her mother, a woman going mad and imagining that she is a cat—make this a very moving novel. . . .

> *Savkar Altinel, "All Locked Up Inside," in* The Times Literary Supplement, *No. 4098, October 16, 1981, p. 1206.*

RICHARD BROWN

[In *The Cupboard,* the] life of Erica March . . . is revealed as her memories are prompted by a visiting American journalist. But the journalist and his memories are as much the subject of the novel as she. Together their psychological dilemmas form the basis of a strongly constructed, highly relevant and thoroughly fascinating novel about freedom and the will to live.

> *Richard Brown, in a review of "The Cupboard," in* The Sunday Times, *London, December 27, 1981, p. 41.*

JAMES LASDUN

Rose Tremain's previous books received much serious critical acclaim, so it was disappointing to find in *The Cupboard* little that was not either stereotyped or unconvincing.

Erica March, an 87-year-old literary lady, tells the story of her life to a depressed American journalist who hopes her story will somehow provide a meaning for his own bleak existence.

The trouble, from the reader's point of view, is that Erica's life is simply too wonderfully passionate to be true. Farmyard childhood (her mother died during foreplay with a bull), doll called Ratty May, imaginary friend called Claustrophobia, prison for suffragette-ing with Emily Davison, literary success with allegories about male aggression, Bohemian Paris, glorious romance with temperamental French surrealist in garret—'the reaching out of two dreamers whose only knowledge of morning lies deep in each other's eyes', CND with Bertrand Russell . . . this is a glamourised cocktail of various literary lives, and in its efforts to present an image of vitality in contrast with the journalist's dismal vision of contemporary life, it becomes all too frequently cloying.

> *James Lasdun, "Obliquity and Whimsy," in* The Spectator, *Vol. 248, No. 8008, January 9, 1982, p. 22.*

HELEN ANGEL

Rose Tremain is a promising young writer whose originality and technical cunning have already been demonstrated in two earlier novels. In *The Cupboard* she uses the device of an extended interview to bring together Erica March, octogenarian author, and Ralph Pears, American journalist. . . . [Nearly] the whole novel consists of reminiscences, with only the development of the brief friendship between Erica and Ralph tying the narrative to the present. That friendship is clearly meant to be significant, an encounter that illuminates the meaning of two lives. The reader, however, may well be less fascinated by Erica than Ralph is; her reminiscences seem tediously protracted, and the self-conscious allegorical excerpts from her novels are unequal to the claims made for their importance. Miss Tremain creates some memorably eccentric characters and some vivid scenes. But, in spite of her inventiveness, this novel is laboured and contrived. When Erica's long-anticipated suicide finally takes place, it comes as a merciful release from her monologue. (pp. 185-86)

> *Helen Angel, in a review of "The Cupboard," in* British Book News, *March, 1982, pp. 185-86.*

GRACE INGOLDBY

Rose Tremain goes from strength to strength, more versatile than an egg and a lot more interesting. *The Colonel's Daughter,* her first collection of stories, is a winner—provoking the unusual response of actually wishing it would go on and on. To choose from treasures, there is the unexpectedly violent ripple produced when the Colonel's daughter herself ransacks the family pile, whilst the folks are enjoying a 'heavenly hols'. This moves like a thriller, flipping from one angle to the other and showing clearly Tremain's meticulous attention to detail, as well as the understanding of a varied cast of characters that makes her such a riveting and satisfying read. **"Autumn in Florida"** deals with dignity diminished, when Beryl and George get a taste of all-American fun on the holiday of a lifetime at the Palmetto Village Complex. George loses his golf clubs; Beryl's stomach is upset; both are vigorously insulted but come through. The funniest perhaps is **"My love affair with James I"**, the tale of what befalls the sweetie, Steve, when he is cast (despite baggy eyes and Neanderthal thighs) to play Buckingham opposite the big star Will—who 'crawled onto a stage bent double from his deprived childhood in a Welsh mine, straightened up to do a memorable Hamlet aged twenty' and, though rather diminished by drink, is still an attractive proposition. Steve re-lives the making of the movie, having returned to a life doing lucrative voice-overs for 'Tiggo' catfood—'My voice is my greatest asset . . . it is redolent with depth . . . it reverbs'—and watering the cucumbers on his roof garden.

> *Grace Ingoldby, "Old Scores," in* New Statesman, *Vol. 107, No. 2760, Februry 10, 1984, p. 27.*

DAVID LEAVITT

In *The Colonel's Daughter,* her first collection of stories, British novelist Rose Tremain speaks in many voices. Some of the stories are written with an aristocratic, almost Jamesian elegance, others in a tone that's chatty and colloquial. Most of her characters share, by necessity or choice, a preoccupation with money and status, and almost all exhibit a dazed bewilderment at the situations in which they find themselves. The middle-class characters suffer from a kind of terminal depression; often, the only force that propels them through their lives is the fear that any change will make things worse. The wealthy characters are enslaved by social constraints which ruin them for happiness: all efforts to rebel against "the fearful unkindnesses of genteel lives" come to nothing. When the prim and seemingly contented Lady Amelia Browne tells her husband, "I'd like to die, Duffy," it comes as no surprise; we've already realized that complacency is intimately linked with a despair of which the characters are fully conscious.

"Autumn in Florida," the best of these 10 stories, tells of George and Beryl Dawes, a middle-aged provincial couple who, in a last-ditch effort to achieve a "recovery from mediocrity," splurge on a month's holiday at a plush condominium in Florida. Instead of curing them of mediocrity, the luxury and excess of this new world augment their sense of worthlessness. The plight of the Dawes is best conveyed in their confrontation with Weissmann, a European art dealer who employs an old friend of theirs as his yacht captain. . . .

Weissmann is a European Jew, a survivor, who has become fabulously wealthy in the new world of America. His Europe is not George's country, and like most of Tremain's middle-class characters, George is as intimidated by the decadence and splendor of the European continent as he is daunted by the scale of America. Without sacrificing the incisive detail and humane intimacy which make "Autumn in Florida" so moving, Tremain depicts the global placelessness of the English in the contemporary Western world.

"Wedding Night" tells with similar aplomb the story of twin brothers, half-French and half-English, who in middle age have drifted apart. One of the brothers recalls with grace and conviction the intimacy of their adolescence. When the twins' mother dies and their father remarries almost immediately, they allay their rage by sharing a Parisian prostitute in their bedroom while the father and his new bride sleep next door. Tremain contrasts the shared urgency of that night with the cool distance of the brothers' current relationship. . . . Tremain's tone is both self-assured and a bit ill at ease.

Unfortunately, the other stories don't live up to these two. The heroine of "The Colonel's Daughter" is Charlotte Browne, a famous feminist whose decision to rob her ancestral home sets off a chain of tragic events. Hers is a fascinating tale, but because Tremain tells it from no less than nine points of view, she ends up summarizing when she should be dramatizing; the story reads like a proposal for a novel. "Words with Marigold" and "The Stately Roller Coaster," written as interviews, do little more than expand on Sunday Supplement stereotypes; their "experimental" formats are as tired as their content. "Dinner for One" juxtaposes the domestic harmony of two homosexual restaurateurs with the unhappiness of an elderly woman who, after 50 years of marriage, feels nothing but disappointment in herself and her husband. The conclusion, in which the blissed-out maître d' discovers that his lover is cheating on him, and subsequently communes with the old woman in a moment of spontaneous tears, seems merely predictable. A similarly labored sentimentality weighs down "A Shooting Season"; this brief tale of reunion between an ex-drunk ex-poet and his long-suffering wife ends with the wife declaring, "Yes Marcus . . . there's always tomorrow."

If it didn't include "Autumn in Florida" and "Wedding Night," *The Colonel's Daughter* would be easy to pigeonhole. I could say without hesitation that it was an early work, a testing of wings, by a writer of prodigious talent who had yet to find her

voice. But these two stories elevate the collection; they are remarkable, flawlessly controlled fictions, the work of a master.

David Leavitt, in a review of "The Colonel's Daughter and Other Stories," in VLS, No. 25, April, 1984, p. 3.

CARYN JAMES

At first, Rose Tremain's characters [in *The Colonel's Daughter and Other Stories*] seem to embody British decorum and stability. . . . But beneath their polite demeanors are feelings of jealousy, anger, vengeance and loss, emotions so intense they constantly threaten to break through to the surface. Charlotte Browne, the colonel's daughter of the title story, is a revolutionary who robs her parents' mansion, causing the death of their elderly servant. A middle-aged princess, beauty fading and bank account dwindling, loses a young lover to her daughter. A 20-year insurance policy matures and buys the Daweses one month at a Florida resort, where George discovers his own "profound and unchangeable insignificance." These may look like Barbara Pym people, but they are bitter from years of keeping a stiff upper lip.

Rose Tremain's style consistently reflects this conflict, despite a startling variety of subjects and narrative strategies. She explores relationships between parents and children, husbands and wives, homosexual lovers. Her storytelling devices range from conventional third-person narration to monologues delivered as interviews to a news reporter and a social worker. But always there is a sense of impending psychic violence; this tension, which at any moment might shatter an ordinary conversation about crossword puzzles, turning it into a lament about an empty marriage, gives the stories their originality and power.

In the finest of them, the outburst comes unpredictably and carries the weight of the emotions that have been compounded as they've been suppressed. In "A Shooting Season," a woman's brief loss of composure reveals how painfully she has maintained her well-ordained life. Anna's former husband stays the night, and the couple are awakened the next morning by a shot. She runs out to the river, suddenly crying, not really for the ducks she believes hunters have killed but because she sees her past. . . .

The relationships the author depicts are often twisted because love is tied to money and social class. In the title story, Charlotte steals the family silver and jewels to help her working-class boyfriend, who is so outraged by what she has done that he hits her. It is the one act of physical violence we see and by implication a lower-class response. Charlotte's symbolic attack on her parents is far more typical. . . .

Guy, the princess's kept lover in "Current Account," hates her. Lorna, the daughter of Penelope's first marriage, blames her mother for running off with the wealthy prince. In their vengeful affair, Guy and Lorna share "the glorious knowledge that together they had conquered her, where each had failed to conquer alone"—until the money runs out and he returns to the princess.

While "Current Account" effectively presents the author's cynicism, it also displays the most consistent and serious flaw in her writing. Too often she manipulates her plots and characters. Lorna is dragged into the story, visiting her mother after an eight-year absence in Australia. The result is obvious long before she and Guy walk off into the woods together. The author sets the princess up for a fall; handled less awkwardly, the events would demonstrate that Penelope had brought about her own fate.

Frequently the author sets her characters on parallel courses, only later explaining their connections and drawing them together. "At the very moment Colonel Browne finishes dinner" in Switzerland, an unidentified woman—who turns out to be Charlotte—drives up to his house in Buckinghamshire. Meanwhile, a scriptwriter who will become obsessed with Charlotte is breaking up with his girlfirend in London. The author uses this technique as if it were a bulldozer, as she creates roads that meet only because she has designed them that way.

Still, this is an extremely ambitious and largely successful collection. . . . [Rose Tremain's] stories offer a precise, mature artistic voice.

> Caryn James, "A Sense of Psychic Violence," in The New York Times Book Review, *May 27, 1984, p. 12.*

JONATHAN KEATES

A Russian acquaintance of mine recalls that during the siege of Leningrad she and her brothers were encouraged to read Shakespeare rather than Chekhov, because the former never mentions food while the latter refers to it incessantly. In a national emergency Rose Tremain would be instantly proscribed for precisely the same reason.

The Swimming Pool Season is awash with gastronomy. Not the finicky foodie variety, but the real right French thing which makes you think that Jane Grigson has somehow got at the text en route to the publisher. The book's rhythms and accompaniments are those of masticating, lip-smacking and peristalsis, and the safest time to read it is probably before breakfast.

Any writer as resourceful as Ms Tremain will have her reasons for this. Her characters are propelled by a sort of mournful hedonism, an instinctive enjoyment without pleasure which makes their gloomier moments distinctly Byronic. When, towards the novel's close, viperish Mme de la Brosse invokes local by-laws to have earth shovelled into the swimming pool which Larry and Klaus have so painstakingly built, you feel she only does it to snaffle their furious energy.

That this is almost the only event in the book scarcely matters. Lingering sensually over detail, the author replaces narrative with something like a botanical field-study, throwing down her handkerchief over North Oxford and a French village and scrutinising the forms of life beneath. We watch enthralled as bucolic Gervaise works out a salvation between passive husband and gorilla lover, as Leni, scornful and exploiting to the last, crawls towards death, and as Agnes and Xavier turn incandescent with longing.

Rose Tremain has the rare gift of an inclusive sympathy towards her characters (the mildness of Mme de la Brosse's comeuppance obliquely criticises our more banal expectations) and the ever-rarer talent among English writers of being able to write with absolute conviction about love. At its simplest her knack is that of making us want to cheat by turning to the end of the novel to make sure that everyone we like gets off satisfactorily.

> Jonathan Keates, "Something to Chew On," in The Observer, *March 10, 1985, p. 24.*

VICTORIA GLENDINNING

Rose Tremain seems impressively mature as a writer. There is great confidence in the writing of . . . *The Swimming Pool Season,* and also something surprisingly familiar about its particular kind of excellence. By chance I was rereading an early Iris Murdoch just before picking it up. Not only was the transition from one voice to the other as smooth as silk, but the themes and characters seemed related too. Rose Tremain is writing about chains of unrequited love, involving the middle-aged, the old, the sexless, the inverted, and a troublingly exquisite blond virgin. But her tone is less mythological, and pacier, than Murdoch's and her novel is not dominated by the Murdochian male enchanter. It is two witchlike old women, exercising their residues of arrogance and power before they die, who crank the action here.

One of these is a once-beautiful Oxford don's widow, summoning to her deathbed her 50-year-old daughter Miriam Kendal, who leaves in France a troubled husband. The novel slides between north Oxford and Pomerac, the village near Périgueux where the Kendals are hoping to establish roots and "plant their hearts". . . .

Larry Kendal, temporarily wifeless in Pomerac, is less interested in sexual love than in his rusting red Granada and in the ambitious swimming pool he is building. The pool becomes an emblem of his struggle for achievement, and provides a framework of imagery about flow and change; French plumbing also expresses the inevitability of disappointed hopes, as sewage creeps up from his septic tank. This is an entertaining book, even though it is about universal exile and loss, and the frustrated longing to belong properly to a person or a place. The only person who feels her "plantedness on the earth" unselfconsciously is the skinny, plain peasant-farmer Gervaise, who works her own land and nightly enjoys the extramarital "golden embrace" of the German farm-hand. No one writes about sex, here and elsewhere in the book, more encouragingly than Rose Tremain.

Her secondary characters are all potentially primary. An Oxford bookseller and his pregnant assistant, a sad poet lodging in the Oxford house, a Pomerac widower rotting in one tumbledown room—they all get equal air-space if not page-space, and with her actress-like talent Rose Tremain physically inhabits every one, making the reader peculiarly aware of their bulk, or warm weight, or fragility, or agility. This largeness of focus makes the narrative diffuse; it proceeds by accretion, or seepage. There is no denouement of the tangles of love and longing, just a rearrangement. . . . *The Swimming Pool Season* exhibits every literary talent—except, perhaps, the talent to disturb.

> Victoria Glendinning, "Longing to Belong," in The Sunday Times, *London, March 10, 1985, p. 45.*

LIZ HERON

[In *The Swimming Pool Season*] the landscape of feeling and of social meaning is painted with a delicate attention to the details of food and drink. Food consoles, seduces, betrays; it marks rituals or their decay, intimacy and exclusion; it renders a sense of place and of time passing.

Oxford's eccentric fringes and a somnolent Dordogne village are the alternating locations. Twinning them are the novel's pivotal characters, Miriam and Larry, a middle-aged, middle-class couple who left the Home Counties for France with the failure of Larry's swimming pool business as the long hot summer of '76 came to an end. Larry's swimming pools have become the grandiose dreams of a small man; he begins to build one in the village. All around are lives lost in their own longings, some pushing desperately towards the future, others clinging to memories and outworn talismans.

Repeatedly, the emotional strength of women shelters male dependencies and illusions, and it is the gradations of change (and of viewpoint) in this pattern that create the most interesting tensions: Miriam's late-flowering impulse to independence and achievement as a painter; the stubborn peasant rootedness of Gervaise, heading her ménage à trois; Agnès, the doctor's niece, ruthlessly in pursuit of a sexual self-determination the better to prepare her for a bourgeois marriage; the magnetic Leni, Miriam's mother, now dying.

But the power of individual characters is blunted by the mood of elegiac melancholy; change withers the structures of life and widens the gap between inner yearnings and outward realities. A state of harmony between the two prevails only once, at the centre of the narrative, when a blissful celebration meal, lovingly described, gathers Gervaise and her guests under the perfect mantle of love and friendship into what seems another time.

This is assured writing, enriched by carefully balanced symmetries and counterpoints, although distractingly diffuse in its focus. What makes me uneasy is its overwhelming sense of people dislocated in the present and an undertow of very English nostalgia for a past when life was kinder and more simple. (p. 32)

Liz Heron, "Words & Things," in New Statesman, *Vol. 109, No. 2817, March 15, 1985, pp. 32, 34.*

SHEILA GORDON

The women in [*The Swimming Pool Season*] are stoic, feet firmly planted on earth, a source of maternal steadfastness to their men—who, though grown-up, are not adult. *The Swimming Pool Season* is set in Pomerac—a small French village whose inhabitants have "hard, simple, earth-reared, toil-blinded faces"—and in England during an autumn season. Miriam and Larry Kendal have retreated from Oxford to Pomerac, to live year-round in what was meant to be a holiday home—she to paint wildflowers . . . , Larry to brood over the failure of his

swimming pool business. The Kendals are depressed, the villagers regard them with mocking suspicion, and while Larry dreams and plans to build a swimming pool in the garden . . . Miriam is called back to Oxford, where her mother, Leni, is dying.

The story weaves between the two settings, in and out of the lives and minds of the villagers and of Leni's coterie. The widow of an Oxford don, Leni Ackerman has been a great beauty and has had many lovers; she is described as a sorceress but seems rather to be spoiled, willful, self-indulgent. Leni takes her time dying, and during the forced separation, Miriam and Larry have the space to consider what it is they want from each other, from their lives. Miriam, the plain daughter of a beautiful mother, has broken from the hold of the family by marrying out of their intellectual circle; Larry feels scorned and rejected by them, and by England—which has pronounced judgment on his dream of a swimming pool empire.

"That family can colour whole rooms, whole houses, whole streets and skies with words," one character muses about Miriam's family, and the same can be said about the author. Details—rooms, landscapes, the lives of her broad cast of characters, even their dreams—densely accumulate. . . . People, cows, machines, meals cooked and eaten, the hole being dug for the pool—all have a sense of existing in life. Everyone yearns for love—generally with the wrong person; lovers' couplings are part of the teeming natural order. Miriam, pulled about by the needs of others, weeps in the kitchen because she is "so tired, *tired* of being strong for other people." . . . Everyone is baffled, dislocated by change and breakdown. The women seem to feel as oppressed, now, by the dependence of their men as formerly they have felt oppressed by their authority.

Rose Tremain is a talented writer extravagant, almost, with her gift. Nothing her characters do or think or desire gets past her. She gives us more, perhaps, than we need to know, the very abundance of her imagery diffusing the tension, distracting, leaving the reader groping for the center. The deep insights of even the minor characters into their longings and fears and shame often seem to be the author's insights rather than their own glimmerings of inchoate awareness—she, rather than Leni, is the sorceress; privy to the workings of all the characters' psyches, she, rather than they, determines their actions. What happens with Larry's swimming pool is for the reader to find out. The other resolutions are tied up a little more cozily, more neatly and simply, perhaps, than life generally concedes.

Sheila Gordon, "Miriam, Tired of Being Strong,"
in The New York Times Book Review, *September 1, 1985, p. 10.*

Peter Vansittart

1920-

English novelist, nonfiction writer, autobiographer, and author of children's books.

Vansittart's experiences as an Oxford University scholar and a teacher of history inform much of his work. His novels vividly depict various historical periods and European locales, and his authoritative nonfiction works likewise evidence his knowledge of world history. In his novels Vansittart employs an elaborate style replete with obscure images and allusions through which he recreates a historical period. He often uses the past to comment on twentieth-century moral and political concerns. Vansittart's ornate style has been faulted by some critics as turgid and strained. Others, however, praise his authentic rendering of the past.

Vansittart's historical and political interests have been displayed throughout his career. *I Am the World* (1942) chronicles a dictator's career, and *Enemies* (1947) takes place during the Franco-Prussian War. *The Game and the Ground* (1955), set in a castle in an unnamed Bavarian country, is perceived by many critics as an allegory about Nazism, and *The Tournament* (1958) presents feudal Europe on the brink of the Renaissance. In *The Friends of God* (1962; published in the United States as *The Siege*), Vansittart recreates the Anabaptist reign in Münster, Germany, during the Reformation. Although finding parts of *The Friends of God* overwritten, Richard Winston commented: "[Vansittart] has in fact captured in his prose the phantasmagoria of sixteenth-century woodcuts, the writhing bodies, the strange and bestial physiognomies that the artists of the time saw. He reproduces as much as describes the stench, the filth, the callousness toward suffering, the demonic excesses of the age." *The Lost Lands* (1964), set in medieval France, concerns attempts to regain property lost in feudal wars. *The Story Teller* (1968) borrows its narrative technique from Virginia Woolf's *Orlando* to dramatize one man's life from the Middle Ages to the present. *Pastimes of a Red Summer* (1969) concerns members of various social classes who seek sanctuary in a mental asylum during the French Revolution. In *Lancelot* (1978) and *The Death of Robin Hood* (1981), Vansittart expands on the mythology surrounding two characters of English legend. In *The Death of Robin Hood*, Vansittart portrays the legendary bandit as an archetype of intuition over reason. *Three Six Seven: Memoirs of a Very Important Man* (1983) recounts a year in fourth-century Britain when Rome's hegemony is challenged by raiding tribes.

Vansittart's novels set in the twentieth century include *Orders of Chivalry* (1956), *A Sort of Forgetting* (1960), *Sources of Unrest* (1962), *Landlord* (1970), *Quintet* (1976), and the recent *Aspects of Feeling* (1986). In these novels, Vansittart portrays the effects of the past on post-World War II Europe. In *Orders of Chivalry*, for example, a satire on contemporary London, promoters stage a contest for ideas to restore England to its past glory. In his review of *Aspects of Feeling*, Martin Seymour-Smith noted that Vansittart seeks "to convey the manner in which the present is permeated by the past." Vansittart has also published two volumes of short stories, *The Dark Tower* (1965) and *The Shadow Land* (1967). *The Shadow Land* consists of the traditional legends and tales from the *Mabinogion*

and reworkings of Sir Thomas Malory's *Le morte d'Arthur*. Vansittart's other works include *Green Knights, Black Angels: A Mosaic of History* (1969), a respected history text for young adults, and *Paths from a White Horse* (1985), an autobiography.

(See also *Contemporary Authors*, Vols. 1-4, rev. ed. and *Contemporary Authors New Revision Series*, Vol. 3.)

THE TIMES LITERARY SUPPLEMENT

Mr. Peter Vansittart, whose several earlier books have gradually claimed attention, has taken for the disturbing material of *The Game and the Ground* children with damaged minds: they are the flotsam of the European war which has destroyed their families and orphaned them and sent them roaming the Continent in wild gangs. Now, as Middle Europe tries to reorganize its crippled life, they have been brought, a hundred or more of them, to an old Schloss, where Dr. Eric proceeds patiently to rebuild their sense of order and responsibility by the techniques of "free discipline." Mr. Vansittart finds opportunities to describe, with insight and sympathy, the working of these techniques, and the bafflement, the doubts, the fantasies and the rare but rewarding break-through of light in the minds of the children. In one sense it might be said that he has made it easy for himself to write a novel that has the kind of beauty that startles. The picture of these savage, suffering children must, if it is successful at all, be successful in that way. Yet his success seems, too, to be distinctively his own. There is a passionate abruptness in his writing. He catches fragments of the children's speech, shot with ancient superstitions and myths; he catches their ritualistic observances, best of all the incidental, undeliberate ones, and occasionally something appallingly deliberate, as when he tells how the children sacrifice an old dog.

For these qualities *The Game and the Ground* is memorable, and it has more to add. Dr. Eric's experiment in education is threatened when his brother Nicky returns to the Schloss. Nicky is a romantic, always worshipping some hero, always desiring to be worshipped as a hero himself. The children are impressionable, responsive to every romantic gesture. He cannot resist the temptation to work on them, and under his influence they retrogress towards their old violence. The teachers see the danger, but some are under Nicky's spell, others are paralysed by the knowledge that he can only be deterred by force, which is the negation of their teaching. It is the classic liberal dilemma. Mr. Vansittart works it out searchingly, with a respect for all the contradictions involved in it. As an author he is in fact his own Dr. Eric, probing for a natural, not a diagrammatic, solution. His empiricism gives the book a tension reflected in the prose, which sometimes tears and stays unrepaired, but out of that very rupture comes power.

"Problem Children," in The Times Literary Supplement, *No. 2830, May 25, 1956, p. 309.*

EUGENE BENDER

For close to a hundred years, it has been a minor specialty of British writers to deal with the savage and separate world of children. Some, like Richard Hughes and "Saki," have been content with shock effects: the complexities and malice of adults shown up as tame alongside the innocent cruelties of a child. Others, like Lewis Carroll—who seems, really, to have started the whole thing—have explored in one way or another the shifting and powerful fancies of children—their personal and frequently hellish wonderlands.

Peter Vansittart—a nephew of the Germanophobe peer, with whose ideas he "differs with respect"—has, in *The Game and the Ground,* combined these two approaches, in order to fashion a strong comment on human nature and its distortion. His sixty children are the inmates of a camp, or refuge, at the ancient castle of Kasalten, in a country which doesn't need to be identified as Germany. They are the debris of the war—orphans, wanderers, homeless, some thieves, some murderers. The unnamed narrator and his brother Eric, both ineffective anti-Nazis throughout the previous regime, are owners of Kasalten, and administer the retraining of the children—or, rather, their lack of training. Unable to impose standards that have failed them and the world, they can do nothing but shelter the children and give them a chance to develop free of the intolerable stresses which warped them. . . .

In the broken, fantastic acts and utterances of these children, Peter Vansittart has caught a distorted—and for that reason perhaps all the more accurate—reflection of one sort of modern agony.

Eugene Bender, "Children of the Modern Agony," in The Saturday Review, *New York, Vol. XL, No. 27, July 6, 1957, p. 10.*

THE TIMES LITERARY SUPPLEMENT

Mr. Peter Vansittart has many gifts as a novelist—a round awareness of contemporary history, a brilliant command of metaphor and imagery, an ironic feeling for what is bizarre and fantastic, a steady compassion—and he manages, in a similar manner to Mr. Pritchett, to cram a sentence like a suitcase until it threatens to burst open.

It is all the more pity, therefore, that he has only once—in *Broken Canes*—found a subject solid and direct enough to enable him to dispense with the heavier artillery of his style. Mr. Vansittart is perfectly capable of writing simply and amusingly without loss of gravity, but every page of [*Orders of Chivalry*], which deals with the odd group of people involved in promoting a spectacular Festival of London, is so studded with aphorisms, snatches of rich dialogue, sharpshooting philosophic observations and arresting visual descriptions that the final effect is not only dizzy-making, but obscure and intangible.

The trouble perhaps is that though Mr. Vansittart can create characters swiftly and in depth, he does not really give the appearance of being concerned, in the primary, ultimate sense, with their human relationships. They are heartless abstractions who talk and observe, and whose defence is attack. One would much like Mr. Vansittart to concentrate for a change on two people who feel strongly about each other and who have no need for verbal fencing. It is always what goes on behind the barricades that is interesting, and Mr. Vansittart, when he stops trying to do too many things at once, is well equipped to report on it.

"Sharpshooters," in The Times Literary Supplement, *No. 2925, March 21, 1958, p. 149.*

HERBERT HOWARTH

Although Vansittart draws the line of a story, as a novelist must or forfeit his audience, he is not emotionally focussed there. He is focussed on the images thrown up as he reflects on his characters and their predicaments; the images become, indeed, more important than the inventions which precede their sparking; and especially the images which pose myths. He writes his novels as a poet assembles a poem. His recent works are, technically, simulacra of *The Waste Land;* they gather and dovetale bannerets, scraps of architecture, accoutrement, song from the past, scraps of myth-news from the popular press, stories from the battle-fields of old and new wars, from the chancelleries of ramparts of old and new cities. Over the path of his narrative wave cumuli of memories. An image glints out: "in the yards our long-haired, barely-clad children exchanged finger-nails, blood, spit"; "Saw he in stealth the Grand Bad Man before the mountain. The mountain too was wounded"; "Brixton boys had been fined for jumping out immediately in front of cars, and had tearfully told the court missionary that, could they kill their shadows they would live for ever"; "Had not all the bishops in Westphalia once been struck dumb because of a sudden footprint on the ceiling?"

Two segments of his experience have provided the material for these emotion-charged passages. He has done a great deal of work as a teacher of young children in an experimental school. He has caught the intense, incantatory, initiated intonation of the child when it repeats words which it has picked from talk, story-telling, or print, and which resume a legend for it—resume its intuition of all possible power or all possible hope or dread. Secondly, he is a historian. He has not merely read history for a degree or information, he has lived what he has read. Barbs from the past—or from the history of the present in the columns of the newspapers day by day—are alive and stinging in him. . . . At crucial points of his narrative he foregoes the customary motley of heaped fragments of memory for a careful front-of-the-stage exposition of a historical event that epitomises the vision with which he is struggling. The passion of Vansittart's historical sensibility throws a hush round the passage.

Yet no less at these crucial moments than in the progress through the tangled, glinting imagery around and across the narrative the reader has to use the word "struggling." There is always confusion in Vansittart. It is no more a voluntary confusion than the artificial order of [Rex] Warner's controlled style is voluntary. But though involuntary, the author accepts and enhances it, seeing a possible justification of it: that it is representational. The confusion of the novels mimics the confusion of this and all epochs. Myths light up the chaotic conditions of the avenue of history, the flames dazzle momentarily from poignancies and ecstasies; they do not chart a way through. (pp. 62-3)

[The poet] AE liked to recall, during a stormy messiah-invoking period of Irish affairs: "The gods are never so turned away from man as when he approaches them by disorderly methods." The poet in Warner, like the poet in Vansittart, feels the attraction and the potential of the untranslatable, uncurbable myth, but there is also in him an eighteenth-century classicist, insistent on the use of a rational prose, a curb on the kind of danger that worried AE.

At this point I admit a difficulty. On the theoretical level the last two paragraphs should lead me to conclude that I approve and prefer Rex Warner's technique, two-prongedly irrational and rational at once as we would all like human endeavour to be. But in fact I cannot declare for either the preference or the approval. For both writers are only experimenting; they are achieving something of note while they experiment; but they are both feeling out for what neither has yet found, the secret of the assimilation of the myth into the novel. Either of them may at any moment find it. A concatenation of a new technical idea and the thrust of internal and external circumstance may suddenly result, for either of them, in the subtraction of what is imperfect in their construction and the addition of the unknown essential resource.

I should add that the novel which I regard as Vansittart's best is at present unavailable: a historical novel, *The Friends of God* [published in the United States as *The Siege*]. When I last heard news of it, it was without prospect of printing. Publishers had balked at it, and the author himself was not satisfied with his treatment. I was seared by it, and if I were a publisher would put it in hand tomorrow. But that does not mean that it came any nearer to a solution of the formal difficulties than the other myth-disclosing novels discussed here. (pp. 63-4)

> Herbert Howarth, *"Pieces of History,"* in Critique: Studies in Modern Fiction, *Vol. II, No. 1, Spring-Summer, 1958, pp. 54-64.*

NIKA S. HAZELTON

Peter Vansittart is an upper-class angry young Briton with an excellent subject and, as yet, not enough literary skill to bring

it off. In his morality novel, ***Orders of Chivalry*** . . . , he takes for a ride the whole of English semipublic life: press lords, shady tycoons, cultural climbers, professional wits, TV pundits, and elegant do-gooders. Though his observations are sharp and often funny, the book as a whole does not succeed, because Mr. Vansittart has overloaded it with characters and situations, as well as with metaphors and images.

Orders of Chivalry is about a monumental pageant called "The Festival of London." The principal characters are an ambiguous Hungarian refugee millionaire and his wife, a sensitive siren, who turns out to have Negro blood; a TV funnyman; a professor with a knack for money, and a juvenile delinquent—characters who stand for Violence, Beauty, Frivolity, Deceit, and Anarchy. . . .

The circumstances that lead to the downfall of the shady Hungarian millionaire are rather cleverly developed, but their effect is spoiled by compassion creeping in where it does not belong. The resulting book is neither straight novel nor satire. This is a shame, since Mr. Vansittart has talent, industry, scope, and imagination.

> Nika S. Hazelton, *"Shady Side,"* in Saturday Review, *Vol. XLII, No. 9, February 28, 1959, p. 21.*

V. S. NAIPAUL

A Sort of Forgetting (a currently fashionable sort of title) is very difficult to read and, if only for this reason, must be judged a failure. Its message appears to be that 'one must go on living . . . Life, almost always, retains the capacity of being unexpected. It should never be cut down.' We arrive at this conclusion after following the lives of an American, an Englishman, a Polish Jewess and a German who knew one another at an international school in France after the Great War. They are none of them people. There is no story, only reflection and description; and it seems to me that the Nazi's distorted views are too considerately treated. The whole thing is too fabricated and the writing is unremittingly intense. One is on the side of the author rather than his book.

> V. S. Naipaul, *in a review of "A Sort of Forgetting,"* in New Statesman, *Vol. LX, No. 1536, August 20, 1960, p. 251.*

THE TIMES LITERARY SUPPLEMENT

A Sort of Forgetting is a peculiar, perverse, and fascinating novel. Sometimes it is very beautiful and sometimes it is almost wilfully obscure. But at least the central theme is clear enough.

In memory of the 700,000 dead of Verdun a group of wealthy philanthropists found a school. It is to be international, co-educational, and idealistic, and it is to provide a new kind of aristocracy, leaders for a brave new world. (Contemporary parallels, at Salem and elsewhere, are not difficult to find.) Here we find the four people we are to be chiefly concerned with: Konrad, a German, Ryan, an American, Tony, an Englishman, and Gretta, a lovely young Polish baroness with whom all three are entangled, either romantically or in a vaguely mystical way, but all using her as a never fully explained symbol. In other words they are all young people bright with promise and hope, and it is Mr. Vansittart's purpose to make us see their lives against the facts, against the wreckage of history, the history of their own time and of the past. So the

Second World War comes and goes and the characters suffer their various fates.

Now all this is very well, but the private if representative stories of these four are so entangled with undigested scraps of political theory and pseudo-philosophy, and so presented—sometimes the style is terse, sometimes lush, but most frequently of all it is opaque—that the reader is left gamely struggling after significances which on closer examination are just not there. A fascinating novel, and an infuriating one.

"Stout Heart and Hard Sell," in The Times Literary Supplement, *No. 3052, August 26, 1960, p. 541.*

ALFRED DUGGAN

It could be argued that the shock of the Black Death upset the mental balance of Christendom. For the next hundred and fifty years society was at the same time pessimistic and frivolous, obsessed with morality while seeking only the most empty enjoyment. In some parts of Europe the new emotion of patriotism provided a basis of conduct, but from Paris northward to the Baltic even this satisfaction was lacking. No one could feel an unselfish devotion for guelders or Liège, or even for the brilliant and wealthy Duchy of Burgundy.

This aimless and sensation-seeking futility is described, and exaggerated, in the glittering prose of Peter Vansittart's *The Tournament*. The scene is an imaginary Duchy in the Ardennes, a parody of the real Burgundy. The Duke, though he is only the third ruler of this ephemeral bundle of provinces, has taken to himself some of the attributes of a god-king; at midday he must stand motionless to help the sun, and it is his fault if the harvest fails. A numerous band of courtiers devote their time to helping him in his ridiculous and pedantic imitation of the genuine glories of Charlemagne and St. Louis. . . .

A neighboring prince has announced his approaching marriage to a lady already betrothed to the Duke's cretinous heir, and the Duke must therefore challenge him to single combat. For a few weeks the approaching tournament threatens to bring some purpose into life. With the thinking part of the mind, everyone knows that the neighboring prince will not be such a fool as to appear in the lists, but it is fun to suppose that something real might happen. The combat never takes place. Plague breaks out instead, and the Duke finds real work to do in keeping order and looking after the sick. Then the epidemic dies away, and there is nothing more to be done.

All the gorgeous and meaningless pomps of this idle court are depicted in masterly fashion, with a wealth of religious, chivalric and anthropological knowledge. Here is the early Renaissance, with King Arthur, Joshua, Scipio Africanus and Tancred all equally real and equally legendary. It is a beautiful picture of a way of life much too good to be true; great fun to read about though it hardly fits in with the brutal politics of the genuine fifteenth century, the world of Louis XI of France and Edward IV of England. A sardonic fairy tale, and highly recommended.

Alfred Duggan, "Reluctant Crusaders," in The New York Times Book Review, *May 7, 1961, p. 31.*

GENE BARO

At its best, the historical novel attempts the evocation of a period or a way of life rather than an impossible re-creation of the past. Such a book is Peter Vansittart's *The Tournament,*

in which an unnamed Duchy of the late Middle Ages comes to life in all its variety. It is as if we were drawn through the gorgeous surface of a tapestry to the tumultuous scenes behind, in which the symbolic and allegorical figures caper, grimace, and threaten with raw human energy and urgency.

At the heart of the Duchy is the Duke, almost stripped of his humanity by his consciousness of the demands of power, and by the demand made by his people and his Councillors that his image be larger than life size. A man of sensitivity and of a certain self-doubt, he conforms to the patterns of courtesy, to the ceremonies that bespeak the heroic life. . . .

The story that Mr. Vansittart tells concerns a combat of Princes that never takes place. . . . How the meanings of the Tournament and the influence of its principals are elaborated is the substance of this novel; how the Duke comes, in the context of his plague-torn Duchy, to discover and accept the real test of himself is the meaning of this book.

Mr. Vansittart is a wholly conscious writer. His effects are elaborate and intricate. Perhaps, his high style is occasionally too lapidary. For the most part, it serves excellently the purpose of evocation to which he puts it. The novel moves not as a chronicle, but as a kaleidoscope; it provides a kind of psychological texture against which individual scenes are brilliantly set.

This compelling novel—its effects are sometimes almost hypnotic—puts Mr. Vansittart in the company of such fine writers of historical fiction as Zoé Oldenbourg, Bryher, and Robert Graves, though none of them employs an approach of comparable obliquity and complexity.

Gene Baro, "Chivalry's Red Sunset," in Lively Arts and Book Review, *May 21, 1961, p. 28.*

OLIVIA MANNING

Unlike Signor Calvino, Mr. Vansittart takes a realistic view of the past, but this does not save him from abstruseness. Perhaps some sort of Calvino-caprice could help him to simplify for the reader his theories about the oppressive influence of historical events. *Sources of Unrest* is set in the present but the characters are badgered by bygone tragedies and horrors. Graham, newly divorced and disconsolate, goes to stay with Charles and Barbara on a visit which becomes protracted. He senses a deficiency in the household which makes his presence welcome; at the same time he hopes to contact an old love, Juliet, who is in the district. He becomes attached to Charles's son, Andrew, who, with his adolescent humour, his self-conscious mannerisms and his independence that masks a desperate need, is the best thing in the book. Graham, a damp hero, is the worst. His bedroom scene with Juliet must surely be the anti-seduction of all time. Mr. Vansittart writes firmly, though at times with too great effort ('The room was darker than others, set at an angle averted from the sun which was flaying the roses outside'). He is, one feels, struggling to impart something profoundly felt, but what it is I am not sure that I know.

Olivia Manning, "Historical—Fantastical—Comical," in The Spectator, *Vol. 208, No. 6971, February 2, 1962, p. 148.*

MALCOLM BRADBURY

Sources of Unrest is not without its technical experiment too; its characters speak an elaborate, self-revealing, highly intellectualised prose which enables Mr. Vansittart to analyse in great depth the contest between the generations that is one of the pressing matters of our time. The incidents of the story are plain; most of the characters are seen with too much of a satirical eye for us to believe in them; but this novel confirms Mr. Vansittart's excellence. And two characters, the narrator and the teenage boy Andrew, who are at the centre of the dialectic of the book, are penetrated with great insight. (p. 334)

Malcolm Bradbury, "Novel and Anti-Novel," in Punch, *Vol. CCXLII, No. 6337, February 21, 1962, pp. 333-34.*

HENRIETTA BUCKMASTER

The Siege is not a novel in any true sense. It is an amalgam of medieval superstition, idealism, and apocalyptic vision, of ancient gods and gnostic Christianity, and it moves in a world of half-light. It is long, difficult and allusive.

Saying this, one must then examine the texture since the book is, for better or worse, an extraordinary accomplishment.

Peter Vansittart has created, in a series of verbal cartoons, the city of Munster in the year 1534 when the Anabaptists seized power and attempted to make over the world in their ecstatic image. The Anabaptists were an extreme Protestant sect which believed in the literal application of scripture and in God's reign of justice for the Elect. They spoke in the language of the Apocalypse, of Daniel and Ezekiel. Signs were seen: an angel with one sandal covered the sky over a whole province, a vision of Jesus and Mary blotted out the sun. In a land devastated by the Peasants' War and the terrible retribution that followed, any message that proclaimed kings and priests of the hungry and landless, fell on fruitful ground.

For a time, the Anabaptist "revolution" in Munster brought bread and hope. But the struggle for power among the Council, "God's chosen," who ruled the city, and the advance of the Lutheran and Roman Catholic armies, making common cause, brought panic and anguish. A huge Anabaptist army was forming in Holland to meet the assault, but not swiftly enough....

Human beings are sedulously excluded from *The Siege*. True, there are characters: the tough, brooding Everyman, Count Zimri, the idealistic Manfred and Ruth, but they are merely attitudes in this mystical macabre Dance of Death. The author has, in an uncanny fashion, identified himself with the dreams, the anguish, the nightmare of a stupendous medieval über-mind struggling with demons and reaching toward a terrible vision of a New Jerusalem.

The accomplishment is deeply impressive—and repellent.

Henrietta Buckmaster, "'In a World of Half-Light'," *in* The Christian Science Monitor, *May 3, 1962, p. 7.*

RICHARD WINSTON

"Burnings and catastrophes hung over the land." The place is Germany in the aftermath of the Peasants' War of 1525; the catastrophes were to continue for another thirty years, until the Religious Peace of Augsburg, and to resume in the following century. By the time the religious wars were over, Germany would be shattered, half or more of her population dead, her cities wrecked, her agricultural land laid waste, and the survivors inured to a savagery unparalleled until the twentieth century.

In [*The Siege,* a] turgid, overwritten, but forceful novel Mr. Vansittart presents the beginnings of the fateful chain of events....

The story is told largely from the point of view of Zimri, a lord's son who fights the peasants, then throws in his lot with the revolutionary townsmen of Münster, and in the end establishes a kind of Third Force for the refugees and survivors of the rebellion. Zimri remains fuzzily out of focus throughout most of the novel, and it is hard to determine what Mr. Vansittart intended this brooding onlooker to mean. But we are also allowed brief visits into the minds of Dr. John Faustus, necromancer extraordinary, and of Jan of Leyden, the gay and attractive youth who became king of Münster, introduced polygamy to satisfy his personal desires, and ended his life in an iron cage.

Mr. Vansittart has deliberately tried to render by the very quality of his style the wild superstition, the mystical ecstasy, the mass hysteria of the Germans of the period, and the corruption, self-delusion and religious passion of the leaders of Münster. He has in fact captured in his prose the phantasmagorias of sixteenth-century woodcuts, the writhing bodies, the strange and bestial physiognomies that the artists of the times saw. He reproduces as much as describes the stench, the filth, the callousness toward suffering, the demonic excess of the age. But at a cost. Narrative line is destroyed by glaring contrasts, by headlong pace and abrupt changes of direction. Events and metaphors fall upon the reader like shrapnel. The mannerisms of over-ornate, strained writing ultimately lead to self-parody....

The theme is a tremendous one. Perhaps the intemperate mentality of a fantastic and terrible era cannot be conveyed by employing its own charged imagery. But Mr. Vansittart has indubitably succeeded in writing about his own as well as the sixteenth century.

Richard Winston, "The Top Blew Off in 1525," in Books, *May 13, 1962, p. 4.*

THE TIMES LITERARY SUPPLEMENT

In [*The Lost Lands*] Mr. Vansittart plunges headlong into the thirteenth century. The atmosphere is murky, despite some highly charged writing and the author's zest for historical detail. The novel is concerned with the fortunes of a count of Angiers, the machinations of Templars, Dominicans, Inquisitors, Philip the Fair, and an inhibitedly dualistic sect. But the action is seriously impaired by the ever-elaborate setting, fictionalized history getting the better of historical fiction. There are some interesting speculations about the medieval mind— confusion about time, for instance: are there really such things as years, or are they perhaps inventions of the priests? And about historicity—are King Alexander and Lord Ulysses still alive? There are also orgies, perversions practised out of sheer uncomplicated perversity, and an inclination towards viciousness of a kind sometimes described as English. But the characters never emerge from their background and no plot satisfactorily unfolds. Readers with a taste for the medieval might find it no less amusing to read history.

"Out of the Black," in The Times Literary Supplement, *No. 3267, October 8, 1964, p. 913.*

CHOICE

[*The Lost Lands* is a] sombre, skillfully designed novel of France in the early 1300's. It reveals the interior and exterior worlds of Count Talvas, from an illegitimate and uncared for childhood through illusory power to old age. The quietly savage narration intertwines with Talvas' memories and flashes of puzzled comprehension that his life is wasted in obsession: the lost lands of his father's estate, which he regains by means fair or ill, and which slip away again. . . . Vansittart is no romancer, though this is a gothic tale; he is an evocative historical writer who makes medieval filth, fear, brutality, or religion dark with superstition and Satanism real without resorting to modern equations and psychological concepts. Students of medieval history and anthropology will find this particularly interesting.

> *A review of "The Lost Lands," in* Choice, *Vol. 2, No. 3, May, 1965, p. 161.*

THE TIMES LITERARY SUPPLEMENT

[In *The Shadow Land* Vansittart] retells stories (and translates fragments of verse) from Celtic, Saxon, Viking and Romance sources with tremendous imaginative power. This is a book of dark and light and half-light, of frenzied excitement and despair. But the facts pour out higgledy-piggledy, and in the end the author's lack of self-discipline may nettle rather than magnetize the reader. Mr. Vansittart is like the Sorcerer's Apprentice; he knows the spell but cannot control the flood. If only he could order and restrain the endless welling, he has it in him to become the Sorcerer himself.

> *"Tales of the Middle Ages," in* The Times Literary Supplement, *No. 3431, November 30, 1967, p. 1159.*

DAVID WILLIAMS

The Story Teller is a complicated book. Peter Vansittart has attempted to depict the stages of a man's life by presenting them in historical, instead of personal, human time. Thus Storm's boyhood is passed in the middle ages, his young manhood during the long-drawn-out atrocities of the Thirty Years' War, his active maturity in France during the post-revolutionary days of Barras and the *Directoire,* whilst middle age finds him in the cock-a-hoop Berlin of 1870. In the fifth story he is the elderly *Direktor* of a co-educational college in Sweden during the uneasy pre-war 1930s. The sixth, a short final one, shows him still in Sweden but old now, superannuated—"the body hanging over him like a sack of pains and wrenches" . . . I admired the vigour of Vansittart's historical imagination and (sometimes) the dense, ornate quality of his prose. I had also the feeling of a writer reaching out bravely for some total significance which kept eluding him.

> *David Williams, in a review of "The Story Teller," in* Punch, *Vol. CCLIV, No. 6655, March 27, 1968, p. 472.*

JAMES FENTON

It is doubtful whether authors will ever exhaust the French Revolution as a mine for plots, situations and themes. Peter Vansittart, who is a historian as well as a seasoned novelist, has taken the year 1794, Year Two of the Republic, as his background [for *Pastimes of a Red Summer*], the summer of Saint-Just's victory at Fleurus and Robespierre's death. The action of the novel takes place in a mental hospital near Paris which has turned into an asylum for wanted people of all sorts. Mostly aristocrats who have not the gall to leave France in her

hour of need, the inhabitants set about maintaining certain styles of living, prying on each other's backgrounds and generally passing the time in amusing ways, in the hopes of a new invasion of France by their friends. The young ones fall in love, one unfortunate becomes pregnant and leaves. A new arrival, M. Henri, causes some speculation and later by suddenly leaving and being revealed to be the notorious protagonist of the September Massacres, reduces the inhabitants to a state of hysteria. That is almost all the action of the novel, the main purpose of which is to explore its characters' ideas about and experience of the Revolution. These characters, however, are very much types—the poet, the Lady of court, the antiquarian, etc. One gets the feeling that they must all come from somewhere in French fiction—especially from Balzac, with M. Henri as the Vautrin of the piece. It is true that Mr Vansittart comes some way towards creating a mysterious, half-demented atmosphere of persecution, but he would have done far more had not his woolly, cumbersome, much admired style come in the way: a style which involves the omission of definite or indefinite articles. (pp. 384-85)

> *James Fenton, "Barthist," in* New Statesman, *Vol. 78, No. 2010, September 19, 1969, pp. 384-85.*

KENNETH GRAHAM

With Peter Vansittart the question for the critic is always one of style. In *The Story Teller,* so acclaimed last year, I rather lost my way in a fleshy, airless jungle of words; but *Pastimes of a Red Summer* is (I say it with only a few qualms) something of a triumph. This is no jungle but a magic wood, a language of dense thickets, fierce elisions and sudden metamorphoses, shot through with colour and heat, a game and a spectacle in itself but at the same time an illumination to the mind, a challenge to discovery, a comedy of illusion and identity.

In the middle of such a wood, on the outskirts not of Athens, but of Paris in the year 1794, stands the mansion of St Julien, formerly a mental asylum, and now still, under the enigmatic authority of its Dr Belchamps, harbouring a motley band of refugees from the Terror: aristos, powdered and curled; a stern historian who watches the Roman past re-enact itself beyond the walls of the park; a prophet and interpreter of Nostradamus; a banker, with strange mercantile monsters in his brain; a hapless poet; lovers; the instigator of the September Massacres; and a whole tableau of others.

Caught in the complicated shining prism of Peter Vansittart's prose, these stiff figures act out a gorgeous and terrifying *bal masqué,* full of portent and wit. We almost expect to meet Poe's Prince Prospero—and there is certainly a Red Death outside, in the Place de la Révolution. At times, it becomes an autonomous revolving dreamworld, bred from some horrific marriage of Bosch and Watteau: children act out mythic games on the grass, dressed as an elephant or the Great Turk, while their masked elders, in taffeta and domino, bow, sway, gossip, eat gâteau au Polignac beneath chandeliers; the grounds are patrolled by mysterious mutes; a horse print appears in the garden; roses swell monstrously in the heat of Thermidor. And then the distant sound of the real tocsin, a glimpse of Robespierre or St Just or Fouché in the *bal masqué* of undoubted history, and our standards of proportion are destroyed. Paris and lunatic asylum coalesce. Only Dr Belchamps, aloft in his irony, knows what he knows: that all existence is a dream, identity a perpetual theatre, and revolution, outside or within, only the drama at its absurd apogee.

Obviously, the hazards of all this are preciosity, chicness and an inhuman hermeticism; and indeed at moments I wondered if I was not reading the scenario for a pretentious parkland-by-moonlight film of the old Nouvelle Vague. But I'm almost certain I wasn't. Through the glitter come the recognisable formalised gestures of human feeling, thinking and behaving: a saraband of jealousies, loves, fears and criminality. The aphorisms and the brief intense flashes of speculation open up sudden intellectual vistas that dazzle and convince, even in their occasional mistiness. And the language, once you learn to move at the pace it requires—each packed shorn sentence has the shadow of a dozen implied others around it—shakes off doubts by its originality. and distinction.

> *Kenneth Graham, "Bosch and Watteau," in* The Listener, *Vol. LXXXII, No. 2114, October 2, 1969, p. 460.*

AUBERON WAUGH

Peter Vansittart is one of those heroic people who just go on writing novels in English. [*Landlord*] is his sixteenth. . . .

What, then, has happened to the British Tommy since his days at Agincourt and on the Somme? The blurb talks of 'ribald gaiety', 'lyrical insights' and 'wistful comedy'. I spotted a few lyrical insights, and very nice they were, too, but so far as comedy is concerned, I must sadly report that Mr Vansittart's new novel is far more funny (peculiar) than it is funny (ha-ha). Large parts of it are almost completely incomprehensible which is a great pity, because hidden away in the irrelevant, Pinteresque snatches of conversation, the long and puzzling sociological harangues (puzzling because one is never quite sure whether the sentiments expressed are supposed to be clever and admirable or glib and despicable) the tense quick-flip sentences without subject, verb or object or any discernible bearing on their context—tucked away in all this is the most affecting and delightfully unpretentious love story.

A young man (Bron, as it happens) buys a lodging house, already full of lodgers. He yearns for a girl to love him, but feels handicapped by his enormous height. He hopes that such a girl will appear and ask for a bedroom in his lodging house—this is essentially the purpose of his keeping one. . . .

The tragedy is that genuine emotion and high intelligence not to mention the occasional lyrical insights should be buried in passages of almost total meaninglessness. It would be invidious to quote too many of these passages, when there is so much to enjoy in the book but here is one: 'Love may hitch with summer lights broad and tense on tree, on rose; and the sea is sex too, it's said, and perhaps lights can really be words and music be colour.'

I mean, it doesn't actually make any sense. The book is still thoroughly worth reading, for those who enjoy the funny (peculiar). At one moment, Bron makes an incomprehensible journey to Yorkshire with two burglars. The wife of one then visits him in his bedroom. Why?

But if one has to decide why the book is no more than an entertaining curiosity, when it could have been a red-hot sizzler, one is left once again with a few embarrassingly fundamental rules which have been broken.

In the first place, fantasy must be kept on a much tighter rein linguistically than any other form of writing. In describing a midnight car chase between cops and robbers, the writer can indulge in any amount of impressionistic writing: dropping verbs, changing tenses, jumping in and out of the first person singular—even employing onomatopoeically words which mean something quite different. But readers soon lose interest in fantasy unless events are described unmistakably and with the greatest precision. Two minor points—writers of fiction should always try to avoid the Apocalyptic style, leaving that to Mr Booker, Mr Muggeridge and St John; although Hiroshima and Auschwitz are undoubtedly among the great truths of our time, we must surely (and perhaps for this reason) use them sparingly in novels which are about young men in lodging houses trying to find a girl to lay in 1970.

> *Auberon Waugh, "The Love Life of the Third Bron," in* The Spectator, *Vol. 226, No. 7436, January 2, 1971, p. 23.*

NEIL HEPBURN

Novels seem to aspire less and less these days to the Leavisite idea of literature as a criticism of life, and more and more to direct excitation of easily accessible surfaces of the subconscious. It is as if writers want to use their words as cranially implanted electrodes, on which a quick tweak will, with unfailing precision, give rise to a particular image, emotion, sensation. Symbolism is clearly far from dead; which is bad news for people who look to fiction for the passage of ideas.

In *Quintet*, Peter Vansittart attempts to combine these two modes, using a tumbling stream of imagery on which to float ideas about the way in which we turn the past to our own purposes. Because of its language and style—highly charged, elliptical, staccato—it would be easy to denigrate it as merely overwritten; pages opened at random produce such passages:

> By guiding words I could make caryatids breathe though not yet move, street lamps become harbour lights, the blue and gold sky contract to a Fouquet miniature. Bearded as Lenin, Mother loomed elk grey from a tower. All vanished when words stumbled in too great a hurry. While pylons soared stark over Dungeness, the sky was black before me, blue behind as, still sunlit, it curved over the sea.

This makes not so much for the 'very exciting reading' promised by a puff from Angus Wilson, as for very laborious, difficult reading—ultimately rewarding, but confusing in the babble of sensation that it stimulates in the undermind.

And because of the form it takes—five episodes describe the collapsing orbits of four Oxford friends and the woman, Gillian, around whom they revolve and whose own sun-like beauty gradually burns away—it would be equally easy to dismiss *Quintet* as an Oxonian riposte to *The Glittering Prizes*. There is something familiar about the intertwined fates of Ken, Simon, Innes, Magda and Gillian. But the relationship they are shown to have to the public life of their country both diminishes their individual agony and enhances their symbolic importance. Whether it is Ken, half-disgraced as a colonial administrator, the victim of changing circumstances; or Innes, brilliantly political and the father of a new town; or Magda, inexorable journalist; or Simon, floating outside the ambitions of the others and turning everybody and everything into a scurrilous story; or uneducated, tongue-tied Gillian failing Ken, but ending a *grande châtelaine* at Innes's side—all are in the service of Mr Vansittart's examination of the process whereby ideas become actions, actions become events, and events, in the backward-looking eye of their interpreters, become new ideas.

It is a large and serious theme; and the effort one needs to put into reading the book is repaid, at a high rate of interest. The good things include not only the symbolist quasi-poetry and the satisfying working-out of all the threads of the story, but frequent small bonuses, too, like the discovery that throwaway anachronisms (transistor radios in late-1940s Africa? detergent in early-1950s French farmhouses? student unrest in 1956?), initially irritating, are themselves contributions to Mr Vansittart's discourse on what we do to the past. (pp. 94-5)

Neil Hepburn, "A Quick Tweak," in The Listener, Vol. 96, No. 2467, July 22, 1976, pp. 94-5.

ANNE DUCHÊNE

Peter Vansittart has a fine high-handed way with the novel, treating it like some some kind of heliograph, for flashing messages. The effect [in *Quintet*] is dazzling—sometimes blindingly so, and the messages often need unscrambling. This is partly a matter of nervous tics, such as a marked impatience with the article, but more often indicates a determination to transmit as high a charge as possible through every sentence, with results that often carry poetic shock but equally often seem merely perverse. ("How swift the eagle we kill in bed. Sex limited us, elsewhere wringing out the haggling and servilities we disdained", for instance: a characteristic moment when the code-book seems lost.)

Perseverance is rewarded, however: the messages are serious and passionate, and speak to our condition, with a notable wit and a full flood of astringent imagery. The book is dedicated to the proposition that public events modify private experience, which in turn modifies future events. "History never repeats itself, it doesn't need to", one of the characters says, and it is the peculiar property of modern experience, specifically as it affects middle-class English intellectuals, that Mr Vansittart enjoys trying to define and demonstrate.

His protagonists, friends from Oxford days, move through post-1945 Europe and Africa into today's England. . . . All three, and the two women involved—a scarred writer and a flawless but inwardly faltering beauty who receives the attentions of them all—retire hurt in varying degrees—"bruised".

The gathering darkness is brilliantly lit, by jokes, by sympathy, by memorable images. Often the tide of simile runs dangerously high, threatening to swamp the craft, and the swell of metaphor is not for the queasy. . . . Images of desolation abound—at the back of the uneasy mind, "coins dwindling, the sign that Rome was finished"; "a dreadful grey warmth on the frozen air as waves of mice fled through the German armies, from Stalingrad". But so do good jokes, and single, simple strokes—"Carole used flesh like a bank-account"; an MP's wife in public "like a frost-bitten dahlia"; girls "from manors where tweeded daddies fought taxation as they had the King's enemies".

Mr Vansittart also knows quite as much about domestic stress as all those novelists of whom it is the only stock in trade. His beautiful woman, for instance, is sterile, and "childless women can collapse, nerves and legs lose control. Ragged by new pains they drive cars into gates, tremble on stairs, go blazing hot too quickly, watch men's boredom settle in the woodworm." The concentration is part of the nervous poetic vitality,

the generalization part of a welcome impatience to stay with the larger themes.

Anne Duchêne, "Retired Hurt," in The Times Literary Supplement, No. 3882, August 6, 1976, p. 975.

FRANCIS KING

Any novelist who concludes the last sentence of his book with a semi-colon (the sentence itself consists of a single, enigmatic word 'Grub') and who refers throughout to one of his most important personages merely as 'He', obviously has confidence both in himself and in his readers. In the case of Peter Vansittart, the confidence in himself is fully justified. Though he does not usually appear in histories of the modern English novel, though he has won no literary prizes and though his name is probably unfamiliar to the majority of the general unreading public, he is a writer whose singularity is matched by his strength.

Whether his confidence in his readers is equally justified, the difficulties posed by his latest novel, **Lancelot**, leaves me in doubt. As its title suggests, this is yet another retelling of the Arthurian story, with Lancelot himself as narrator. . . . In his sixth-century *Liber Querulus*, Gildas, looking back over the same period, wrote that 'The subject of my plaint is the general destruction of all things good and the general growth of all things evil throughout the land.' Mr Vansittart's Lancelot deals with the same theme.

This Lancelot is not the son of King Ban of Brittany—even though, fearful of an increasingly threatening future, it is to Brittany (Armorica) that his family, in common with many other Roman-British ones, make their escape, without him. He is not stolen in infancy by the Lady of the Lake and it is not his adultery with Guinevere (here Gwenhever) that leads to the death of Arthur. Mr Vansittart's purpose is to strip away, as though they were layer upon layer of wall-paper, all the fairy-tales pasted over the facts by a whole succession of romancers—the Breton *conteurs,* Geoffrey of Monmouth, Chrétien de Troyes, Layamon, Malory—to reveal the cold brickwork of truth beneath. Arthur is 'This short, doll-headed boor . . . grossly unimaginative.' As 'Dux bellorum' (the description is that of the Welsh Nennius in his *Historia Brittonum*), he is a cunning and daring general, but one totally devoid of the chivalry of the Arthur of legend. Daily life for this leader, his consort and his followers is as remote from Malory's Camelot as the daily life of Idi Amin and his entourage from the Court of the Roi Soleil. Platters are dirty; cups are cracked; frequently Artorius/Arthur indulges in ceremonies of pagan magic and it is during one of them—Gwenhever herself has been shaved bald for it—that Lancelot sets eyes on 'a tree-shaped crystal grail'.

This period—immediately preceded by that described by Kipling in *Puck of Pook's Hill*—was, of course, one of a disorder similar to that in many parts of present-day Africa after the ebbing of another imperial tide. Throughout Mr Vansittart's book one is aware of parallels between life in fifth century Britain and in twentieth century nations such as Uganda and Zaire.

Mr Vansittart compounds this difficulty with, first, the introduction of his mysterious 'He'—a figure who belongs both to the past and to the future, who has magical powers and whom I take to be Merlin—and, second, with a style that, despite its exuberance and freshness, is so allusive and elliptical that one is often obliged to read a sentence or even a paragraph for a second time to confirm exactly what he is trying to convey. He has brought great skill and resourcefulness to his evocation of this misty patch of history; but, though one never doubts that he himself knows where he is going, to follow him is not always easy.

> Francis King, "Unholy Grail," in The Spectator, Vol. 240, No. 7818, May 6, 1978, p. 28.

ELAINE FEINSTEIN

The relevance of Peter Vansittart's **Lancelot** to our contemporary dream-world may seem, at first sight, oblique: though it is certainly even further removed from the legendary figures of the Arthurian Court so long presumed and loved. Vansittart has set his novel in a landscape of decaying Roman rituals, and a growing forest of more primitive beliefs, where blackthorn and ash retain numinous powers. Britain is torn by a confusion of tribal loyalties; and men look for warmth to the hopes of astrological patterns rather than bloodless gods, or the cult of Christus. Among the brutish figures of an omni-sexual court, Lancelot enjoys a certain prestige as a Roman, and a useful strategist. To judge from the brief historical notes at the back of the book, the terrifying vision of a Britain falling into darkness, might justifiably stir a nostalgia for the great Roman peace which will not be regained easily. For all the support of historical detail (where it is offered) we enter the book as we might a nightmare; bewildered by the encroaching thickets and darkness and with some of the fears that haunt the twilight of our own desperate century.

> Elaine Feinstein, in a review of "Lancelot," in The Times, London, May 11, 1978, p. 10.

ALAN HOLLINGHURST

The writing of Peter Vansittart appeals to a specialised taste, one that relishes a view of history as a teeming, vivid, unruly fairground of experience, jostling with brilliant detail and palpable immediacy, while on the other hand liking this material to be co-ordinated by a numinous formal and symbolic arrangement that imposes a deeper portentousness. The reader must relive the actuality of the past as a way of being educated in its relevance to the present. **The Death of Robin Hood** has an extremely ambitious and peculiar structure. Its principal section is set in the reign of Richard I, centring on John and his daughter Eleanor, and the following section deals with machine-breaking in 1812 when another Eleanor (a mysterious recreation of the former one) is arrested for sheltering Luddites. The final section is set in the 1930s. The whole thing takes place in Nottinghamshire and is preceded by a prologue set in Sherwood Forest in primeval times. In all four sections the myth of Robin Hood as a hero, a fertility-figure, a liberator, exerts a symbolic power over the minds of the protagonists. The perpetuation of this myth is strengthened by Vansittart's way of counterbalancing historical accuracy with a fantastic treatment of time; like his reincarnated Eleanor, he sees 'people live for centuries, or merge into each other as they do in dreams, everything constantly reborn . . .' Such a technique makes the creation of historical 'rhymes' between different periods all the easier.

The idea then is highly original and suggestive, but the actual writing, unless one has a taste for it, is an obstacle to its success. In the first section we see uncertainty about nature-myths proliferate in the primitive mind on account of the growth of

words—and this section itself is a nightmare to read, effectively as obscure as the forest and the rites it describes. In the later parts of the book the temptation of words becomes irresistible, and Vansittart uses a dense and highly mannered style to create his tumultuous and compendious impression of history. . . . Things occur too fast for normal description: 'and' and the definite article are largely suppressed, and commas become the weak articulation of clotted sentences: 'Fires inflamed the whole town lit by flash-hatted Brutus, demonic Marat, de-frocked priests, half-naked, blue-trousered Irish.' Literary quotation is richly interlarded as if Vansittart had given up any attempt at kicking the habit, and a quantity of epigrams adds to the self-admiring posture of the performance. We enjoy an uncontested intimacy with historical figures—Kings are Richard, John; Churchill is Winston, MacDonald Ramsay. The tics of a mannered style become insufferable long before the event-lessness of a dull one. Which is a shame, because unless one can surrender oneself to the torrent of Vansittart's prose, a fascinating concept has been irreparably spoiled in the execution.

> Alan Hollinghurst, "Wordy Wisdom," in New Statesman, Vol. 101, No. 2602, January 30, 1981, p. 19.

IAN SCOTT-KILVERT

Much of Peter Vansittart's fiction is inspired by historical or mythological subjects, but the method of its presentation, while strongly idiosyncratic, might be compared to that of Lawrence Durrell's *Alexandria Quartet*. Theme and plot are to a similar extent developed by description and figures of speech rather than by conventional narrative technique, while character is presented through a series of metaphorical statements, which in the manner of an impressionist painting make their effect at a certain distance. [**The Death of Robin Hood**], centred upon the famous medieval outlaw of Sherwood Forest, is divided into four parts. . . . These four distinct historical periods are held together by the powerful amalgam of the author's style, which combines striking descriptive metaphors with proverbs, historical generalizations, magical formulas and fragments of folklore. This novel is not an easy read, but it will certainly reward those who appreciate an unconventional approach to historical fiction and a style which combines wit with a highly imaginative use of language.

> Ian Scott-Kilvert, in a review of "The Death of Robin Hood," in British Book News, May, 1981, p. 312.

MICHAEL WHARTON

In a previous novel, **Lancelot,** Peter Vansittart dealt in a very individual and original way with one aspect of the period, the 'Matter of Britain', the legendary-historical material which concerns King Arthur's resistance to the Saxon invasion and temporary reassertion of Roman-British rule in the western parts of the island. Then in **The Death of Robin Hood,** perhaps his best book so far, he dealt in successive episodes with a connected theme, the persistence through the ages and in diverse forms of that wood-spirit and English archetype up to his disappearance (perhaps not final?) in the suburbanised England of today.

Now [in **Three Six Seven**] this very talented writer takes for his theme the fateful year 367, when Britain, which though in process of transformation was still Roman and indeed, thanks to being an island, still one of the most prosperous and comparatively well-ordered parts of the collapsing Empire, was suddenly assailed on all sides by savage enemies, Picts, Scots, Hibernians, Attacotti, Brigantes, Germans and Scanians from across the northern sea. There was treachery on the Wall, and Picts and Scots, murdering and destroying, poured from the barbarous north to attack the rich, settled lands of southern Britain, with their civilised villas, towns and forts. Was it a concerted attack, an obscure conspiracy or a random outbreak? This is one of the unsolved questions which concern the narrator, Drusus Antonius Muras, a rich businessman with a stake in innumerable trades and enterprises, a man of Sicilian descent, born in Gaul, now living and working in the small town of Calleva Atrebatum . . . , [which was] one of the largest cities of the whole Empire and the richest port of the West. . . .

'A very important man' would be Drusus's own description of himself. Intelligent and ambitious, he is pompous, censorious, cold by nature, devoid of humour though capable of a dry, cynical epigrammatic wit. He is both well-read and efficient and complacently proud of it. Long afterwards, in exile, he writes of the bloody, fantastic and catastrophic events in which he played a part, though not so important a part as he supposes. He believes that history, if there is any, will vindicate his plans for a Britain which could survive, powerful and prosperous, the final wreck of the Empire which he forsees. He is mistaken. Believing in his own acute judgment of men and events, he gets them wrong all the time. This gives the book a pervasive irony which is not the least of its pleasures. But it also presents the author with a problem which he has not completely solved—how to make Drusus tell his story in Vansittart's style.

Drusus is a matter-of-fact man (as he says himself, 'no Muse has kissed my pen'). But Vansittart's style, so unmistakably his own, is the vehicle of a vividly poetical mind: it is at the same time strong and precise yet supple and elaborate. It is intensely visual. This writer delights in the forms and colours of earth, sky and sea, of stones, ruins, trees, ominous birds, weapons, clothes, nuances of human expression, everything in the daedal world. He likes to bring together, somewhat in the manner of Celtic triads, collections of curious images, complex 'word-hoards' worked into intricate forms like jewellery or stained glass, with hallucinatory effect. I can never have enough of this myself, and in Vansittart's two previous books it was wholly fitting. But could sensible, prosaic Drusus possibly have written like that? (pp. 21-2)

Here, flawed though it may be, is a wonderful book, a haunting, many-coloured dream of murderous splendour, an evocation of the past which no other historical novelist now writing in England could rival. When will this writer of extraordinary talent receive his due? (p. 22)

> *Michael Wharton, "Decline and Fall," in* The Spectator, *Vol. 250, No. 8067, February 19, 1983, pp. 21-2.*

NEIL PHILIP

The Bishop of Silchester quotes Plato in Peter Vansittart's new novel. "An immortal soul always learning and forgetting in successive periods of existence, having seen and known all things in one time or another, and, by association with one thing, capable of recovering all".

Vansittart's stance as an historical novelist is captured in that sentence. He is as far from the costume novelist as can be, yet

he is no laboured realist. In a stunning series of novels—recently *Lancelot* and *The Death of Robin Hood,* now *Three Six Seven*—he has reinterpreted our psychological and metaphysical heritage with idiosyncratic, stubborn, poetic verve. He has been compared to John Cowper Powys: though he is intellectually tougher, the leashed sensuality of his work makes the comparison hold. The only contemporary writer with whom he has much in common is Robert Nye.

From the chaste severity of its cover to the plangent, dying fall of the children's rhyme which seals its story of ambition overreached, *Three Six Seven* exhibits a cool control which compels admiration. Subtitled "Memoirs of a Very Important Man", it tells the story of the crucial year 367AD through the eyes of a Romano-British businessman, Drusus Antonius Muras. As the Roman Empire becomes ever more fringed and ragged, threatened by barbarians on every side, Drusus dreams of a strong, independent Britain, no longer drained by the Empire's demands, enervated by the Empire's diseased turmoil. When British tribal rebellions increase, and seem concerted enough to overthrow the Empire's weakened rule, a strong man is needed. Drusus sees himself manufacturing and then manipulating such a leader. . . .

"I shall tell you more evil than good," [Drusus] warns us on page one. The "you" he addresses is the reader today, "posterity" in his terms. The result of this directness is the formation of a powerful double image in the reader's mind, in which the shadow of present troubles falls on the troubles of the past. Drusus complains about the "workshy, grumbling, over-musical, irresponsive Britons"; laments falling standards in every field; pontificates on religion, capitalism, imperialism, immigration, inflation. Yet there is no sense in which his Britain is simply an image of our own, held at a distance for us to see it better. His ways of thinking are alien to us, though the burden of his thoughts is familiar. It is this expression of the thought patterns of someone whose situation is our own but whose world view is not which makes *Three Six Seven* such an exciting and distinguished novel.

There is, perhaps, a sense in which it is too well written. Every cunningly turned sentence bears its full weight of meaning; the prose is very rich, and, in a curious way, shaped so as to keep the reader at bay. One finds oneself at the end of a paragraph with no idea what one has just read; yet, examined, the offending passage proves exquisite, cherishable. Vansittart works largely by the accumulation of phrases, in long sentences devoid of redundant linking matter. . . .

Vansittart offers, to the reader who is prepared to match his breathing, succumb to his rhythms, the sort of intimate, enlarging experience which is only found in the novel at its very best. *Three Six Seven* is the very opposite of the easy, idle read which propels one forward through the pages, leaving no trace; it demands full attention, sends one scurrying back to re-read, lingers in the mind. And—the final test—it leaves me eager to read it again.

> *Neil Philip, "Under Alien Eyes," in* The Times Educational Supplement, *No. 3493, June 10, 1983, p. 26.*

VALENTINE CUNNINGHAM

[Early on, in *Aspects of Feeling*], Peter Vansittart knowingly settles his central cast of three children, Della, Graham and Bayard, wards of smooth, clever Roger Kirkland and his mistress Janet—manipulative presiders over a sort of lesser Cliveden Set—into their task of paying slick tribute to *The Waves*.

As with Virginia Woolf's brood, we follow Vansittart's trio while they grow up—out of pre-war childhood, through the Second World War and the post-war austerities and on into the lusher 1960s. Della becomes a writer, Graham a schoolmaster and assistant to backroom string-puller Kirkland, Bayard a still more shadowy researcher and publicist. But loyalty to the earlier novel amounts to much more than this. Like *The Waves*, *Aspects of Feeling* strives to make its people known by popping niftily in and out of their heads, seeking to couple the world and their impressions of it in an adroit marriage. The result, too, is school-of-Mrs Woolf: the sense that selves and world still evade being known, for all the dazzling insights and glittering scraps the reader is granted. . . .

Aspects of Feeling is, however, more than just a late tribute to Virginia Woolf's brand of modernist scepticism, not least because the questions of how literature interrogates selves and things and seeks to make them known are bolted tightly onto questions of historical epistemology, the knowability of the past.

Vansittart's prose is quite the most greedy for experience and history of any novelist now writing in England. Its efforts to engorge things, places and events are gargantuan. Vansittart's paragraphs will never be a mere collection of decorous annotations. They are richly overdone, stuffed to the gills with overflowing abundance. . . .

Fate-tales in history, the novel insists, easily get trivialized into mere fairy-tales. Historical creeds, like the Christianity of Graham's scathing clerical colleague, collapse into debunkable stories. Those hapless creatures clubbed and bayonetted into the cattle trucks bound for Stalin's East fade, for Graham, into dim, distant and forgettable nightmares.

And yet, for all this kind of despond, Vansittart's efforts to grapple with history and to out-manoeuvre its tendency to opaqueness command admiration, even if his prose is given to such baroque, even Carlylean excesses. What's more, a prevailing indignation with the self-interested secretiveness of politicians—the scowling discontent with the secrecy of their texts, if not altogether with that of Mrs Woolf's kind—is most cheering to watch in its impressively robust action.

> *Valentine Cunningham, "Interrogating History's Secrets," in* The Times Literary Supplement, *No. 4321, January 24, 1986, p. 81.*

MARTIN SEYMOUR-SMITH

In his historical novels, which are by no means typical of the genre (if they were, he would be richer and more popular than he is), Vansittart shares an attitude with the strange Polish novelist Teodor Parnicki. Parnicki does not pretend to be writing 'history' at all: he treats the past as part of his own present, and therefore never even attempts to 'recreate' it. When he feels like it, he freely mixes anachronism, invention and fantasy with meticulously documented fact (usually, let it be admitted, of periods about which no one but himself knows anything). Vansittart has himself said that he is 'unconcerned' with the 'picturesque and antiquarian', and has quoted Croce's dictum that 'all history is contemporary.' The very least of his intentions is to give any kind of 'true' picture of the past. He is instead anxious to convey the manner in which the present is

permeated by the past—and this is one of the many themes of his most recent novel.

But it does prove very hard to place Vansittart in any tradition or group. All the obvious influences are there, as well as a few more unusual ones: Sienkowicz as well as Kafka, the Carlyle of *Sartor Resartus* as well as Dickens—and so forth. But these writers have been thoroughly assimilated. He doesn't resemble anyone at all closely; he reminds the reader of no one of this century. There is sometimes, it seems, a price to pay for this kind of originality. Although markedly eccentric, he is not just that. 'When will this extraordinary writer receive his due?' a critic has asked [see excerpt above by Michael Wharton]; nor is the question in the least surprising. Vansittart himself must be puzzled by the paucity of attention accorded to him. 'Easily upset in life, I am fortunately undismayed by critical neglect, or by reviewers,' he has written. But there is certainly a too personal note about the way in which he handles the 'literary world' in [*Aspects of Feeling*]: the passages dealing with it are the least successful (and the least original) in that very remarkable book. . . . Doubtless British literary life since the war has been every bit as awful and false as Vansittart wants us to think. Still, it has not been so in the way he too irascibly tries to demonstrate; and there has been no publisher remotely like the ones of whom he provides caricatures. This whole exercise reads like that of a person far away from the literary world.

The problem for Vansittart has always been that he is excessive: he wants to achieve too much within the bounds of a single volume. Nor will he give this ambition up—but by now his persistence has become courageous and impressive. He has the aspirations of a poet—he wants to make a brilliant and compressed success, something like a great short lyric—but he lacks the discipline. *I am the world,* published early in the war when he was only 21 years old, is excessive (promisingly so): about the rise and fall of a dictator clearly based on Hitler, it seems to want to say everything that can be said about dictatorship. It is relentlessly and ambitiously unpleasant—the brutal and dark side of Vansittart has not, surprisingly, attracted the attention of reviewers—and is written in a curiously over-rhetorical, almost gushing style which sits very awkwardly with its sombre theme. The earlier successors to it sought almost heroically to correct all of its shortcomings except its excessiveness: its didacticism, its rhetoric, its high melodrama—even its improbability. Perhaps no living English novelist is so relentlessly experimental within his own terms of reference. . . . Yet no contemporary writer is more detached from the actual structures of his creations. He is extremely close to the language he employs, which amounts to a sort of poetry: but he remains detached from 'plots' and all the other devices that are used to take their place. In *Broken Canes* (1957), his worst and most facetious book, he tried to abandon 'rich' prose altogether: the result is a feeble farce about a progressive school. The only interesting aspect of this attempt at a tightly plotted novel is that there is no point of view—the reader is left in the dark as to whether progressive schools are desirable or ridiculous, and the author's desperate ambivalence remains unresolved.

But Vansittart's main impulse in writing is in fact to do just that: to resolve his ambivalence about past versus present, tradition versus progress. A frequent device is to set progressive or humanist types against cynical pragmatists or reactionaries; what is unusual, again, is the absence of a point of view. Yet nothing is resolved. Vansittart's real, unequivocal world is that of a sceptical poet, one in a permanent state of negative capability, immersed in language and what it leads to. But he lacks the capacity to achieve the rhythm of poetry, and such satire as is in him is released, not always very effectively, against all creatures of habit: those whose attitudes are fashionable, false, calculated constructions. The apparently successful but hollow and spiritually dead poetess (this is what she deserves to be called) Della, in *Aspects of Feeling,* is a typical example. One might call Della a novelist posing as a poet. Yet in Vansittart's wistful descriptions of her actual poems (none of which he can quote), there is something of envy of real poetry. Is Vansittart himself a frustrated poet, a poet self-miscast as a novelist?

The 'monster' of this novel is the career diplomat Roger Kirkland, the 'high *sans peur*' without any feelings (even ill feelings), but with many appetites thus made disgusting. His function here is certainly as the focus of disharmony and inhumanity: yet Vansittart is not satirical about him at all, as he is about Della, and he is the only character in the book upon whom is conferred a consistent if cynical wisdom. One simply does not know if the narrator or arranger of this material is for or against Machiavelli . . . Thus we are again teased by an absence of any point of view: is it only because we know (or think we know) that cynicism and lack of principle are wrong that we react unfavourably to Kirkland's talk? We are aware of Della's falsity to herself because the author comes very near to informing us about it through his shrill and improbable description of the manner in which her verses are received by literati. But this may be an unjust criticism, since the surface of almost all Vansittart's prose is corrugated into surreality by his exuberant, sometimes reckless use of language. . . .

[His] most ambitious and interesting novel (until *Aspects of Feeling*) [is] *The Game and the Ground* (1956). This is the only one of his works to bear discernible signs of a single outside influence: but it may be pure coincidence that it resembles Ernst Jünger's uneasy anti-Nazi allegory *On the Marble Cliffs.* The novel is set, in an unnamed country, on an ancient estate that has only recently been in use as a concentration camp. In the dilapidated house that is its centre two brothers are now trying to rehabilitate savage and illiterate children who have been crippled and confused by exposure to the conditions of total war. Then a third brother returns to recorrupt the young people with the vicious hero-myth that has caused that war in the first place. As in George Steiner's novella about a hypothetical Hitler captured in Latin America, the odious false mythology is presented with a gusto that seems dubious. But in this case at least the reason is the author's helpless detachment from what he has simply set in motion: a pessimistic feeling of inability to resist the energy of evil, together with a feeling that he is responsible for all the horrors which fascinate him—just because they do fascinate him. We begin to see that an apparently inartistic surrender to what is felt as natural can be an advantage—and perhaps we see this only in Vansittart among contemporary English writers. He can hardly be accused of being fashionable. But is he, for all that, much more fashionable than he thinks? In *The Game and the Ground* he emerged, for all the vigour of his writing, as a man who was both fascinated and repelled by the immoderateness—the excessiveness—of his own imagination; he also emerged as one who lacked the discipline to discover a structural device by which he might organise a text into coherence. Ultimately I think he has tried to turn this into a strength: by presenting himself as incoherent but truthful. One is reminded of the Spanish novelist Pio Baroja, who claimed that well-

structured novels are not like life (but examination of his [works] demonstrates that they are more cunningly structured than he let on). Vansittart's verbal exuberance is felt by him as amoral: but the reader apprehends this only because, built into the exuberance, is the fact that it bothers the writer. What Vansittart calls his 'didactic tendency' is more precisely a tendency to fall into aristocratic cliché (as exemplified in the sayings of Kirkland, the anti-hero of *Aspects of Feeling*). (p. 14)

His next large book, *The Story Teller* (1968), traced the life of a character from his birth in the Hundred Years' War to his old age in modern Sweden. This was more coherent than any of his previous major novels had been, but suffered from two main faults. The first was that his 'Sweden', intended as 'realistic', was not very convincing. The second was more serious: readers found it hard to sustain their interest in the protagonist because, although his transformations were interesting, he lacked a personality. One great weakness of Vansittart as a novelist is that he pays little attention to character. It is almost as if for him it does not exist, or as if he recognised it as an afterthought. He has a Heideggerian interest in Being as against mere beings, so he cannot make us feel that his beings experience Being (when they do or are supposed to)—he can only tell us, obliquely, how *he* does.

Aspects of Feeling is clearly an attempt to do better in the matter of character, or at least to create more effective illusions; and to exercise a greater power of organisation than heretofore. It is his most carefully plotted novel. But, for all its intrinsic interest and the sheer brilliance of its language, it remains somewhat obscure. Unless, of course, one were not to treat it as a novel at all . . . Where does Vansittart's refusal or inability to systematise lead him—and his reader?

It begins in the 1930s. Roger and Janet Kirkland (she is not his wife) are guardians of three children, whom they are bringing up in their large country house called Dragon House. Kirkland, of the Foreign Office, is young, wealthy, admired and well-connected. The brief section devoted to the adolescence of the children—Della, Bayard and Graham—is ironically presented as idyllic in the traditional sense. It is this, but it is also haunted by past horrors and disasters—pervasive images in all Vansittart's fiction—such as the sinking of the *Titanic* and a picture of a First World War deserter, strapped to a chair and masked, awaiting his execution as his grave is dug. We are thus given a view of menaced innocence presided over by golden-voiced corruption (Kirkland). Between this and the grotesque (and, we take it, contemporary) society wedding of Kirkland and Janet, one of his finest and maddest scenes, he gives a selective account of the lives of the three younger people. Della becomes an empty poetaster whose work is intermittently taken up (she sometimes thinks that this is on its merits or imagined merits, but we learn otherwise). Graham drifts through Army service (during which he is involved in the massacre of the Russians who had worked for the Nazis and who are being returned from Germany to the Soviet Union) and schoolmastering, when he becomes his foster-father's assistant—but he ends as a reluctant, Philip Toynbee-like would-be saint. Bayard, whose name is certainly not accidental, is the mysterious one. Apart from the fact that he is a member of the Crystal Knot, a strange and ancient society which exposes wrong-doing in high places (and thus ferments scandals), we learn little about him. In some ways one senses that Bayard, if Kirkland is the anti-hero, is the hero or 'saved character', the others being merely indeterminate. But if this is so, then in terms of traditional fiction—and Vansittart appears to want to be a traditionalist—it remains unsatisfactorily defined. The lives of Della and Graham are traced in some detail, but that of Bayard is (deliberately) only glimpsed through what the others—to whom he is also a complete mystery—discover. (pp. 14-15)

Vansittart has not here overcome his difficulties with characterisation. But we begin to wonder if he should have done: if characterisation is not, by virtue of where he belongs (without realising it—and I doubt if he could happily grasp the turgid language of deconstruction), an old-fashioned or even a disgraceful concept. It is Being, as I have remarked, in which he is interested—not beings. The portrayal of Kirkland is superb, but it is accomplished through an anthology of suavely wicked sayings. The *mauvaise foi* exemplified in Della's verses is badly handled, though: the literary satire is over-shrill, and the descriptions of the verses make them seem to lack the emptiness of other objects of ephemeral high reputations (for example, Humbert Wolfe or the wartime Pudney). The revelation that what passed for interplay of feeling among these five people was, after all, something else, and something much more sinister, carries less conviction than it should: we are never allowed to view it psychologically. But is that what Vansittart really wants us to do?

What is truly remarkable is the sheer energy and versatility of the prose. Vansittart will not admit to caring about 'what the Novel should be doing'—an attitude that might imply some impatience and even exasperation with contemporary letters.

But he is certainly doing some unusual things with it: *Aspects of Feeling* has the look of a study in relationships strung out over forty years (though no one ages in the least). But is it not instead its author's frenzied prose-poem? Whether the narrator is Vansittart or not, I do not know; I should doubt it. Perhaps he is just a man standing at a crossroads where language meets people . . . This is a sustained interior monologue disguised as an up-market family saga. It is also exceedingly pessimistic—a catalogue of horrors and hopelessness whose only affirmation lies in the vitality of its prose. It requires very close reading, and not, perhaps, reading of an ordinary kind: the real narrative is fragmented—occasionally squandered—amongst the welter of the prose. . . .

Like all his novels, *Aspects of Feeling* leaves a very strong and vivid impression. It is a verbal explosion from a writer who can scarcely believe, intellectually, in the viability of anything, let alone effective self-expression; he is agonisedly convinced that literature really is what the structuralists and post-structuralists say it is: something 'already written' and without origin, its author 'cancelled'. But those critics want the death of the author. Vansittart wants his birth. From that perhaps excessively (for him, too) Modernist position, then, this book makes a fine and loud romantic protest against itself. (p. 15)

Martin Seymour-Smith, "The Strange Case of Peter Vansittart," in London Review of Books, *Vol. 8, No. 4, March 27, 1986, pp. 14-15.*

(Jorge) Mario (Pedro) Vargas Llosa

1936-

Peruvian novelist, short story writer, critic, essayist, journalist, and dramatist.

A major figure in contemporary literature, Vargas Llosa is respected for his insightful examination of social and cultural themes and for the structural craftsmanship of his work. Vargas Llosa is best known for his novels, in which he combines realism with experimentation to reveal the complexities that influence human life and society. He has been particularly praised for using such devices as nonlinear development, rapidly shifting narrative perspectives, and disparate yet converging story lines to mirror the disorder of existence. Suzanne Jill Levine commented on his blend of realism and experimentation: "With an ambition worthy of such masters of the 19th-century novel as Balzac, Dickens, and Galdós, but with a technical skill that brings him closer to the heirs of Flaubert and Henry James, Mario Vargas Llosa has begun a complete inventory of the political, social, economic, and cultural reality of Peru."

Vargas Llosa is often associated with the "boom" in Latin American literature that occurred in the 1960s. During this time, the production of major works by a number of Latin American authors led to international recognition of their important contributions to modern literature. Vargas Llosa first gained attention with *La ciudad y los perros* (1963; *The Time of the Hero*), a satire of life in a Peruvian military academy based in part on personal experience. In this novel, Vargas Llosa focuses on the nature of violence, a recurring theme in his work, by exploring the concept of machismo and its effects on individuals and society. Some readers viewed the military academy as a microcosm for South America and were impressed with Vargas Llosa's observations on how machismo contributes to Peru's violent political and social realities.

La casa verde (1966; *The Green House*), Vargas Llosa's next novel, won wide acclaim and established him as an important young writer. In this work, Vargas Llosa interweaves seemingly disparate stories in a narrative that blends objective and subjective perspectives. Set partly in the jungles of Peru and partly in settled areas, *The Green House* draws upon myths and legends of Peruvian culture. While some critics contended that the multitude of characters in this novel are undeveloped, most praised Vargas Llosa's technical procedures, which convey an ambiguous view of reality and reflect the elusiveness of truth. *Conversacíon en la catedral* (1969; *Conversation in the Cathedral*) was also favorably received. In this novel, as in his previous works, Vargas Llosa subordinates cohesive plot development in favor of a structurally complex narrative. In his presentation of a society torn by corruption and friction, Vargas Llosa uses a montage-like structure with rapidly shifting points of view and settings. While some readers found the novel's labyrinthine structure difficult to penetrate, others lauded Vargas Llosa's use of cinematic techniques and his poignant, often controversial observations on the dynamics of Peruvian society.

With *Panteleón y los visitadoras* (1973; *Captain Pantoja and the Special Service*), Vargas Llosa's satire became less caustic

and more humorous. This work evidences another of his prominent thematic concerns—the effects of social institutions on individual identity—in its examination of sexuality, social order, and human behavior. *La tía el escribador* (1977; *Aunt Julia and the Scriptwriter*), Vargas Llosa's next novel, is one of his most popular and accessible works. While this book is less complicated structurally than his earlier novels, Vargas Llosa's manipulation of point of view is of primary importance. Half of the chapters in the book are overtly autobiographical, relating Vargas Llosa's coming-of-age as a young man who is romantically involved with his divorced aunt and as a journalist who aspires to become a great fiction writer. The alternate chapters are soap opera stories composed by a radio scriptwriter whose elaborate plots and fanatical devotion to his art reflect the circumstances of Vargas Llosa's persona.

In the early 1980s, Vargas Llosa wrote two works that evidence his interest in journalism and in the artist's manipulation of factual material. *La guerra del fin del mundo* (1981; *The War of the End of the World*), the first of these works, concerns a series of battles fought in the Brazilian backlands late in the nineteenth century between a group of social outcasts led by a messianic figure and forces representing the newly established secular Brazilian republic. This work is based on *Os sertões*, an epic account of the backlands war by Euclides da Cunha, who witnessed the battles as a journalist. Some critics believe that Cunha appears in Vargas Llosa's work as a myopic journalist who can offer only an obscured perspective on the conflict. Vargas Llosa reveals how a complex web of social, political, religious, mythic, and economic circumstances and ideas contributed to the violent confrontations. *The War of the End of the World* received international acclaim and won literary awards in several countries. In *Historia de Mayta* (1985; *The Real Life of Alejandro Mayta*), Vargas Llosa conducts a journalistic investigation of the life of the title character, a Trotskyite who led a failed rebellion against the Peruvian government in the late 1950s and quickly faded from public view. This novel focuses on the difficulties faced by the narrator, who attempts to embellish factual material with fictional effects that would enhance the significance of his story. Critics debated the merits of Vargas Llosa's self-conscious examination of fiction writing. However, John Updike praised the work as "the most that political fiction can be: a description of actual social conditions and a delineation of personalities motivated by political concerns."

In addition to his novels, Vargas Llosa has published the short story collections *Los jeffes* (1959) and *Los cachorros* (1967; *The Cubs and Other Stories*), as well as several volumes of literary criticism. He is also respected as a dramatist, journalist, and essayist. The political and social content of his works have earned him an esteemed and controversial position in Peruvian society. In the early 1980s, Vargas Llosa was offered the post of Prime Minister by Peruvian President Fernando Belaunde Terry; he declined, preferring to concentrate on writing. Nicholas Shakespeare commented: "Vargas Llosa's standing in Peru is that of a 19th century writer in Europe. The belief that literature can provide answers to real and important questions means his opinion is sought on social, moral, and, inevitably, political matters."

(See also *CLC*, Vols. 3, 6, 9, 10, 15, 31; *Contemporary Authors*, Vols. 73-76; and *Contemporary Authors New Revision Series*, Vol. 18.)

ROBERT STONE

Mario Vargas Llosa's powerful and haunting historical novel, *The War of the End of the World*, based on events in South America at the end of the 19th century, succeeds brilliantly in penetrating and opening to examination the ancient significance of the millenarian myth. . . .

Mr. Vargas Llosa is a Peruvian, but *The War of the End of the World* is set in the *sertão*, the grim thorny desert backlands of the Brazilian state of Bahia, in the year 1897. As it opens, vast change has come to the enormous Brazilian nation. Approaching the advent of the 20th century, which everyone feels must belong to the Americas, it is at once aflame with the future's limitless promise and burdened by the medieval weight of its past—priestcraft, primitive colonialism, slavery. Personal freedom itself is a new experience for millions of the nation's blacks, for it is less than 10 years since the last Emperor abolished slavery. The republic itself is younger than emancipation, Dom Pedro II of Bragança having abdicated only in 1889. The new republic faces the future under the motto "Order and Progress."

As the century's final decade comes to a close, a mysterious figure, bearded, rail-thin, clad in a purple tunic, appears in the *sertão*. He speaks of love, peace and repentance. He speaks of death and judgment, heaven and hell. The stranger's name is Antonio Conselheiro and he is known to his followers as the Counselor; that is as much as the reader will ever know of his origins or identity. At first examination, his doctrine seems reactionary and ultra-orthodox, more Catholic than the Pope, or at least more conservative than even the unenlightened hierarchy of newly republican Brazil.

As the poorest of the *sertão's* poor—outcasts, the diseased and deformed, murderous bandits, runaway rebel slaves—fall in ever growing numbers under the sway of his intense spiritual force, he preaches his message of millenarian salvation. The republic, he tells the peasants and bandits, the *cangaceiros* of the *sertão*, is not a vehicle of liberty but an abomination born of the union of Freemasonry and Protestantism. Its innovations—civil marriage, the separation of church and state, the metric system—are not measures of progress but the satanic devices of Antichrist, the Great Can. A proposed national census, with its questions pertaining to race and religion, is not an attempt at the advancement of knowledge but a diabolical scheme through which the blacks of Brazil are to be hunted down and re-enslaved, her good Catholics put to death.

At first the few missionaries serving the *sertão* permit the Counselor their pulpits, but very shortly the church condemns him, and only a single disreputable and eccentric parish priest serves as chaplain to his ever more numerous band. The Counselor's disciples repair to the remote abandoned ranch of Canudos, in defiance of the national Government, which is preparing a military expedition against them.

Why this condemnation by the church of so ardent an enemy of the secular state? Because the church is wise and her memory ageless. She knows this man, knows that he brings not peace but a sword and that the sword—wielded down the centuries by the Montanists of Phrygia, by the Anabaptists of Munster, by Cromwell's army—always and without exception is turned against the establishment of which she is now a part. She sees—and here Mr. Vargas Llosa brilliantly elucidates Millennium as the central myth of history itself—that the soldier of Christ who strikes the head from a Stuart king's shoulders serves in the same army as the soldier of reason who will later strike off a Bourbon king's head. Indeed, as we are forced to see, his army will march on through time; his fusillades slay Romanovs in Siberia and bishops in visionary, millenarian Anarchist Spain.

Like Brazil at the dawn of the century, *The War of the End of the World* looks both forward and backward; the forces acted out are eternal and elemental. It is not a multitude of competing ideologies that besets the world, Mr. Vargas Llosa tells us; rather it is one, always the same, calling itself by different names, its hero showing a thousand faces, forever haunting the peace of prelates, presidents, general secretaries and chairmen, threatening their benefices, palaces and chairs in the name of liberty, equality and life more abundant. Espousing the rule of the Messiah, the Christ, the people are in pursuit of an unchanging goal—the final liberation of mankind from evil, the settling at last of the oldest direct question in the world, the question of suffering. A thousand revolutions in the name of that one resolution. (p. 24)

Mr. Vargas Llosa's work is of such scope, his handling of the big questions so confident and intellectually exciting, that one hesitates to fault him. The novel is long and might be shorter, as is true of many ambitious books. His choice of short anti-climactic scenes, a few flickerings after the great explosive ending, might be more considered. But these are small matters. . . .

It is difficult to read a book such as this one, treating as it does the mythic systems of which our beliefs and our history are composed, without being forced to re-examine some of the principles that have served to guide us through their labyrinths. "Consciousness does not condition reality," Marx told us with his common sense; "rather reality conditions consciousness." Incontrovertible, and yet our present world is so replete with intricate palimpsests that a shadow falls across that line between the two that was so clear to him over 100 years ago. . . .

At close quarters with the pathology of history, as a "third world" writer in an age of upheaval, Mr. Vargas Llosa has the temerity to question the uniqueness of the revolutionary mythos. Implicitly, by assigning revolution its place among the ritual dramas of history, he questions its salvific function. Thus he assumes the stance of liberal skepticism, one that should not be confused with pessimism. This, like that of the revolutionary, is a traditional historical perspective and an honorable one. Far from being a posture of despair, it is one of faith and hope, more hope than many of us are capable of. In accordance with Santayana's dictum, it declares that man's capacity to endure is proportional to his historical insight. In an era when, like polar travelers, we move through dangerous terrain, threatened by a sleep that contains not only monsters but the abyss, the clarity of vision and faith in reason implied in Mr. Vargas Llosa's marvelous summoning of the past may represent our surest hope of an awakening. (p. 25)

> Robert Stone, "Revolution as Ritual," in The New York Times Book Review, *August 12, 1984, pp. 1, 24-5.*

RONALD CHRIST

Typically, Mario Vargas Llosa discovers his fiction in some nugget of real-life experience, sometimes reported in an impersonal source like a newspaper, and then develops his find by refracting it through multiple points of view to construct a civic drama where psychological events figure socially, politically. . . . Consequently, the Peruvian author replaces the continuity of introspective character with colliding narrative fragments that clash to isolate and collect figures within a cinematic montage the complexity and scope of which define the ambition of his work. And Vargas Llosa is a very ambitious writer.

Previously he had aimed highest with **Conversation in the Cathedral,** while his last two novels, **Capt. Pantoja and the Special Service** and **Aunt Julia and the Script Writer,** hunkered closer to comedy and games with narrative techniques—almost as if he were holding back a bit, toning up for a really big encounter, and incidentally winning a wider, newer audience with a light-hearted look at himself and some of his past seriousness. The title of his most recent novel [**The War of the End of the World**], however, heralds his renewed aspiration. . . . Nevertheless, this **War,** while offering some exciting skirmishes, is more shadow-boxing than battle, better suited to subway riders needing a long but interruptible read than to admiring fans who still see Vargas Llosa as a laureate lacking only a Nobel crown.

Perhaps the grand subject came too ready-made: the true story of the Counselor, a backland religious leader, who, at the turn of the century in Brazil, established an errant Christian community that challenged the emerging secular republic as the antichrist and nearly succeeded in toppling not only the civil government but also a military establishment unaccustomed to fighting unprofessional wars. Such a conflict of absolutely certain beliefs almost demanded the author's well-known technique: social analysis through clashing views—of the leader and his followers from inside the settlement, from outside by soldiers, politicians, and priests, and from mid-point by natives being won over to the communistic community. But the technique has gone slack, partly because the expansive quality and divided stories inherent in the subject do not require Vargas Llosa's analytic expansion and exploitation, mostly because Vargas Llosa does not edit the sequences so much as merely shuffle them. Few sparks glint when he slams one chunk of the big story into another.

Two principal characters, among the proverbial cast of thousands, contribute to the book's massive hollowness: a journalist who serves as one of Vargas Llosa's surrogate authors, and the Counselor himself. This journalist, nearsighted by Homeric epithet on *every* appearance, breaks his glasses and cannot see anything during the destruction of the religious community. Vargas Llosa obviously intends our necessarily myopic view of historic events, but this man's redundant whining and blinking dwindle to a Dickensian mechanism never properly wound up, losing our interest before earning any. Like the author's insistent little litanies of enumeration and descriptive detail throughout the text, the journalist means more to the author than he ever can to us.

More significant is the void at the center. We hear about the Counselor, about his ability to convert children, legendary criminals, and pathetic misfits into Christian paradigms (with names like The Little Blessed One); but the author cannot get him to say much more than things like "Death is a fiesta for the just man," which sums up his quirky emphasis on proper burial but sounds more like a sophomore's reading of Octavio Paz's *Labyrinth of Solitude.* Worse still, Vargas Llosa withdraws the shadowy Counselor into his citadel rather early on, so we see less of, hear almost nothing directly from him. (pp. 566-67)

Yet, despite an elephantine slackness, **The War of the End of the World** brands our imagination, first with its many small scenes of physical violence—including a rape we should hope to forget—and, second, with its vision of this anomalous war as the beginning of South America's twentieth-century world, the world we watch, through the clouded lenses of our media, being fought over these days. No one aware of the entanglement of church, government, and army in South America can read these pages only as novel, as historical freak. This is a Latin American apocalypse now, and you will shudder in recognition (before sighing with tedium). . . . **The War**'s profound, curious pertinence, which may have overwhelmed the author, will reward you. But never before has Vargas Llosa said less with so much more. (p. 567)

> Ronald Christ, "From El Dorado to Apocalypse," in Commonweal, *Vol. CXI, No. 18, October 19, 1984, pp. 566-67.*

MICHAEL WOOD

The facts are simple and strange. At the end of the last century, on a scrubland plateau in northeastern Brazil, a raggle-taggle band of vagrants, robbers, and ascetics rebelled against the very idea of modern progress. They rejected the recently proclaimed Brazilian republic, and refused to pay taxes or to recognize civil marriages—all of which seemed to them the work of the Antichrist. They were sure the last days of the world were at hand, when the rivers would run with milk, the earth would change places with the sea, and Dom Sebastian, the legendary, long-vanished king of Portugal, would come again to announce the new heaven and to save the just.

The band was led by Antônio Mendes Maciel, known as Antônio Conselheiro, the Counselor, a man who had wandered this wilderness for many years, rebuilding churches, replacing cemetery walls, and preaching odd, brooding sermons stitched together out of the Bible and a book of hours and his own gloomy musings. He was savagely self-denying, hated drink and sex and greed, but he also possessed the weary fatalism of those who know that merely human things are soon to be leveled by the apocalypse. . . .

It is true that Conselheiro burned the billboards notifying a small town of the government's intention to collect taxes; it was said that a group of his men threatened to oust the municipal authorities in another town. But his real crime was conceptual, or ideological. He embodied a form of dissent that civilization, as the Brazilians then saw it, could not accommodate. It was a dissent that had to be stamped out, and was; but only after a series of ferocious military expeditions, of increasing size and might, had learned the lesson that opponents of guerrillas have since learned all over the map: that weapons and drill and scholarly strategy are no match for faith and numbers and an intimate knowledge of the country.

The first small party set out against Conselheiro and his commune in November 1896; the last costly campaign began in August 1897. Conselheiro died in September of the same year, and by October it was all over. The famous Brazilian historian of these events, Euclides da Cunha, says the government's action was a crime "in the integral sense of the word"; a piece of barbarism, he adds, committed by the supposedly civilized against semibarbarians. The rather contorted logic of the thought is worth attending to. A whole delicate diagnosis lies in it. . . .

The story really is baffling. Why did these people flock to Conselheiro's side? What were his motives, his hopes? Was he mad? Was he wilier or more resentful than he seemed? Was there any kind of conspiracy? Why couldn't the government leave him alone, or cope with him in some measured, less desperate and bloodthirsty way? Just what were his enemies afraid of?

Euclides da Cunha has answers for most of these questions—too many answers for his or our own comfort, since they breed new questions before they have settled the old ones, and help, along with his patient, intelligent observation of the land and its inhabitants, to make his book *Os sertões, Rebellion in the Backlands* (1902), a stern and complicated classic, the bible of Brazilian nationality, as it has been called, but also one of the first masterpieces of modern Brazilian literature. Samuel Putnam compared the work to *Leaves of Grass* and *Seven Pillars of Wisdom*. Putnam's translation appeared in 1944, and had a small vogue, I seem to remember, in the later 1960s.

Os sertões is a work of geography and anthropology and of scrupulous military reporting; but it is most profoundly a work of imaginative and thoughtful history, along the lines, I would say, to add another comparison to the pile, of Carlyle's *French Revolution*. (p. 7)

Mario Vargas Llosa's long and impressive novel [*The War of the End of the World*] . . . is in part dedicated to Euclides da Cunha, and contains a character who in many ways resembles him, an unnamed journalist reporting on the campaign against Conselheiro, as Da Cunha did, and permanently altered by his experience of it. But Vargas Llosa's tone and interests are quite different. Da Cunha . . . had the confident, prickly, scientific mind of the turn of the century—a mind not unlike Freud's, say. He was anxious to understand, never wanting for categorical (if sometimes puzzling) explanations. Vargas Llosa has the more modest, less stringent mind of a later time. He would like to understand, but is keener to sympathize, and he knows a mystery when he sees one. . . . If Da Cunha's temptation is a certain harshness of the intelligence, Vargas Llosa's is sentimentality.

The War of the End of the World covers the same ground as *Os sertões*, clings to the same haunting story. But Vargas Llosa insists that the story is "endless," "a tree of stories," and the last words of the novel, in an affirmation that is now almost traditional in Latin American fiction, assert the primacy of passionate fable over unquickened fact. "Archangels took him up to heaven," an old woman says of one of Conselheiro's henchmen. "I saw them."

The point of view moves rapidly, but is always that of the people who participate in the events: various pious or violent followers of Conselheiro; a wild Scottish phrenologist and revolutionary who sees in Conselheiro's teaching a dream of fraternity, only superficially muddled by religion; soldiers and local and national politicians; guides and trackers; the members of a traveling circus; an easy-living priest, who comes to prefer Conselheiro's discipline to the careless tolerance of his superiors in the Church; a feudal landowner and conservative leader, a weary, intelligent, and finally despairing man, whose wife is driven mad by the destruction of their estate. Then there is the journalist I have mentioned, who is left behind by the scattered and retreating army, and gets closer to Conselheiro's inner circle than he ever expected or wanted to be. (pp. 7-8)

There are touches of melodrama in the novel—history in this case is a subtle and economical writer, and we feel a certain bagginess when Vargas Llosa tries to improve on history, or fill it out—and ideas that seem to me dim and reactionary about the relations between sexual and political repression. Rape, for instance, is seen mainly as a mode of male self-discovery ("that sudden, incomprehensible, irrepressible impulse. . . . In anguish, he thought or dreamed: 'How could I have done that?'"). The ugly, unwanted journalist finds love and happiness in the final siege of Conselheiro's battered city (with the same woman the other fellow raped, no less); two male rivals slaughter each other, and lie dying in each other's arms, like figures in a pastiche of Dostoevsky. In all, though, the book's steady and generous concentration, its agility in moving from one angle of vision to another, its deep identification with quite different characters in the somber story, make it thoroughly memorable, likely to stay in the mind for some time.

Sensibly, Vargas Llosa does not attempt to get inside Conselheiro's head, and doesn't even recount his earlier life. He remains opaque, an enigma, although he speaks more gently than in Da Cunha's book, and he makes more sense. He has "quicksilver eyes" and he says, "God is other." We may want to compare this with Da Cunha's: "It was a clownish performance, but dreadful. One has but to imagine a buffoon maddened with a vision of the Apocalypse." Vargas Llosa is arguing, implicitly, that need and faith can't simply be wrong;

that the perceived wisdom of Conselheiro requires sympathetic representation, whatever our skepticism may actually think about it. People are drawn to him, then, not by an obscure social pathology, but by their love, because he has been "able to reach past their abjection, their hunger, their lice, to fill them with hope and make them proud of their fate."

Conselheiro is not mad, merely a forlorn, unworldly saint saddened by the wickedness of the times and the slackness of the established Church. He is not a political man, but he is rapidly caught up, Vargas Llosa insists, in the politics of others, quickly conscripted for scares and machinations. If he is against the republic, he must be a monarchist. In fact, he *is* a monarchist, but his king is not of this world. His revolt is not against life itself, as [R. B.] Cunninghame-Graham suggested [in *A Brazilian Mystic, being the life and miracles of Antônio Conselheiro*], but against life-in-society, the sullied, compromised, unchosen life-with-others that civilization requires of us.

Perhaps such a revolt cannot be explained except as an overriding rejection of what most of us don't think twice about accepting, and Vargas Llosa obviously wanted to leave us with jagged, revealing images rather than theory or analysis: with vultures descending on the ruins of the commune, for example, the whole dream-adventure come to that; with thieves and murderers literally reclaimed, converted into model citizens of their invented country; with honest but rabid military men who despair of the untidiness and corruption of civilian politics and want to make Brazil clean and whole in one fell swoop; with the extraordinary resentment of the ordinary, up-to-date, wheeling-and-dealing world against the practitioners of an ideal. Can it be that we are bound to see people who choose to be different as backsliding or as engaged in conspiracy or treason?

Although the setting of the novel is Brazil at the end of the century, its application is wider and touches more recent matters. Will the lure or the threat of the military ever go away in Latin America? What is the place of religion in those supposedly secular countries? What is the yearning for submission and abnegation that brings back again and again those ever-circling *caudillos*? We need to remember too that the end of the world for Vargas Llosa is not only a promised time but is used more than once in the book as a locution for a far or lost place: the middle of nowhere, the heart of darkness. It is the point where civilization ends, and that, of course, does not need to be a place at all. . . . The road from the backlands leads to Guernica and the arms race and terrorism on all sides. (p. 8)

Michael Wood, "The Backlands Rebellion," in The New York Review of Books, *Vol. XXXII, No. 3, February 28, 1985, pp. 7-8.*

PHILIP HORNE

The War of the End of the World bears a dedication 'To Euclides da Cunha in the other world', and Cunha, who appears in it as the major but unnamed character, acts as the catalyst for Vargas Llosa's reaction to Canudos. Cunha's extraordinary *Os Sertoes* . . . came out in 1902, the year of *Heart of Darkness*, and Conrad's confrontation of civilised and primitive in a remote interior does not so perilously trace the painful raw edge of the topic as does 'this monstrous poem of brutality and force' (as Cunha was later to describe it). *Os Sertoes* is not a composed fiction, but a harrowed piece of testimony by one who accompanied as a journalist the successive military expeditions sent to discipline the back-country; and its text, first treatise and then narrative, moves increasingly into a disturbing quasi-novelistic prose whose violent, ambivalent responses to violent, ambiguous incidents are at the mercy of an overwhelming real predicament. Cunha is imaginatively at full stretch in ordering his feelings under the hardly bearable experience of this increasingly disordered 'war' and it is the presence of 'demons', the anguished struggle between his writing and the world, that attracts Vargas Llosa to him, as it attracted him to the overstrained writer of soap operas Raul Salmon, the original of Pedro Camacho in his earlier book *Aunt Julia and the Scriptwriter*. . . .

Os Sertoes swerves between the accuracy of history and the explanatory power of story: the war of Canudos was generated by monstrous misunderstandings between the two sides, and proved a quite different experience for the Army and for the rebels, so that its true meaning can only be approached by a risky mediation between the clashing fictions of the antagonists. The Cunha figure in *The War of the End of the World* says that 'Canudos isn't a story; it's a tree of stories'; and his original ends up with an image that draws attention to the vertigo produced by his methodical relativism. 'We are like one who has ascended a very high mountain. On the summit, new and wide perspectives unfold before him, but along with them comes dizziness.' Vargas Llosa's genius for dealing with multitudinousness allows him to skirt the same abysses, and scale yet more dangerous peaks, without allowing his adeptness to obscure the giddily dismaying perspectives discovered by Cunha. His multiple strands of narrative—following a highly various group of characters on both sides and neither, most real, some seemingly invented—challenge us to unify this mass of disparate experience (violent, mystical, rationalistic, sensual, military, literary and so on) by some provisional synthesis that yet does justice to the glaring constitutive contradictoriness of the whole business.

One of Vargas Llosa's characters, the politically superseded Baron de Canabrava, caught up reluctantly in a bizarre Faulknerian torrent of bitter retrospection by the Cunha figure, struggles for a moment to suppress the memory of Canudos in the name of sanity:

> It's better to forget it. It's an unfortunate, unclear episode. It's not good for anything. History must be instructive, exemplary. In this war, nobody has covered himself with glory. And nobody has understood what happened.

But the obsessive curiosity which drove Cunha to his equivocal, unforgettable masterpiece is a contagion. People crave stories, stories they can believe. For the Republican Army the explanation of Canudos was a monarchist conspiracy aided by the agents of a European power. For the followers of Antonio Conselheiro the explanation of the expeditions sent against Canudos was that Apocalypse was imminent and that these were the forces of the Dog. Neither of these one-sided accounts still works: the first was baseless propaganda and the date-stamp on the second has long passed. Yet *Os Sertoes* is founded on a tragic sense of the necessity of illusions, a necessity to which it sometimes romantically gives way with a certain self-consciousness. Thus Cunha lucidly notes how the soldiers propagate atrocity stories about the jagunços ('ruffians') who were their opponents. . . . But at intervals in his narrative Cunha's own feelings get written 'up' with a metaphorical profusion and luridness which deliberately exaggerate certain responses in order to find release for others. He goes to town on Antonio Conselheiro's great Temple: 'There it stood facing the east, that stupendous disharmonious façade, without rule or proportion, with its gross friezes, its impossible volutes, its capering delirium of incorrect curves, its horrible ogives and embrasures, a brutish, shapeless hulk, something like an exhumed crypt, as if the builder had sought to objectivise in stone and cement the disorder of his own delirious mind.' Here we detect the melodramatic imagination at work, giving rise at every turn of phrase to what Vargas Llosa's study of *Madame Bovary* calls 'a certain distortion or exacerbation of feeling'. . . .

Cunha's original account, then, already turns fact towards fiction; and when Conrad's eccentric Scots friend Cunninghame Graham came in 1920 to plagiarise *Os Sertoes* in *A Brazilian Mystic* he spun the yarn further by more fictionalisings and distortions. . . . (p. 21)

This real and literary history of distortion superimposed on distortion, this labyrinth of human illusions and perspectives, makes Canudos an ideal territory for Vargas Llosa's preocupations. *Kathie y el Hipopotamo,* his 1983 drama, apparently concerns a ghost writer hired to help a woman tell lies about the past. Its epigraphs announce its subject: Simone Weil's 'Life . . . can only be borne with the aid of illusion' and Eliot's 'human kind / Cannot bear very much reality.' In the preface to the play Vargas Llosa explains the premise, related to these perceptions, which underlies his method: 'The systematic rectification of life that is worked by fiction constitutes the documentary record, faithful as a photographic negative, of some human story.' Our lies, he says, seen from the right point of view, 'express us just as accurately as the more authentic truths we utter'. Canudos itself can be viewed like this, as a systematic rectification, under the influence of Christianity, of the misery of life in the intolerable Sertao (Cunha often looks at it this way). When the world is cruel you may pretend it's about to end. But this is not all, for Vargas Llosa's subsequent use of Eliot and Simone Weil gives us a clue to one special strength of *The War of the End of the World.* Where Cunha mostly invoked the language of science to explain Antonio Conselheiro's religious movement while remaining at a distance, Vargas Llosa's imaginative project involves him in intimate attention to the religious lives of those around 'the Counsellor', in an impersonal narration of their 'different pictures' without ironic signals of sympathy or of respect withheld. Correspondingly, there is no account, as there is in the deterministic Cunha, of the amazing unhappy background of the baffling Counsellor himself. Taking his lead, perhaps, from Flaubert's ''Un Coeur Simple'' (at one point 'a parrot kept frantically repeating: ''Felicity, Felicity!'''), Vargas Llosa lovingly recreates the life of simple faith, the kindness among those in the unique, impoverished, intricately described community of Canudos. The bandits and killers who repent and join the Counsellor fight brutally for him, but the good faith of their conversion is not explicitly questioned, except by them in their conscientious soul-searchings. The lives of these people are—at least subjectively—redeemed by the significance and shape conferred on them by their contact with the Counsellor. (pp. 21-2)

In each of the biographical strands concerning the 'fanatics', we can sense this element of collaborative creative vocation, a transforming interest in their own lives taken by people who seemed destined to the misery of insignificance. Cunha's positivist leanings make the sympathetic intensity of his treatment of Canudos in *Os Sertoes* remarkable: but *The War of the End of the World,* traversing the borderline of fiction and non-fiction on which Cunha trembles, goes imaginatively much further.

Cunha ends his book with the severed head of the Counsellor phrenologically analysed. 'Let science here have the last word. Standing out in bold relief from all the significant circumvolutions were the essential outlines of crime and madness.' His tone—could this be sarcasm?—is hard to gauge. By the end of *The War of the End of the World,* on the other hand, Vargas Llosa's Cunha figure (usually 'the nearsighted journalist') is obsessively recounting official verdicts on the affair in a tone of cool outrage. Characteristics are redistributed—that is, 'distorted'. Much of Cunha's science is passed, not to the Cunha figure, but rather to an invented character, a revolutionary Scots phrenologist with the alias Galileo Gall who battily sees the apocalyptic jagunços as unconsciously fumbling towards the principles of socialism and sets off into the scrublands to help the struggle. The Cunha figure can thus stand more forcefully as 'the writer'. The bewildered experience of Gall, an intriguing if somewhat schematically conceived innocent who is inadvertently involved in a (to him ludicrous and anachronistic) vendetta, becomes an empirical testing-ground for the European materialist framework for rebellion against the injustice of the world—which, it is suggested here, may be more of an illusion (a 'fairy-tale') than the Christian one. As a journalist, too, the Cunha figure moves between two probably invented rival employers: the ex-governor, the Baron de Canabrava, and his successful replacement, the ruthless young Republican Epaminondas Gonçalves.

This fictional world, in other words, is Vargas Llosa's, the plot a cunning embroidery on Cunha's original fabric. He imposes his own wonderfully insidious timings, so that we shift forward and back in time and space with startling equanimity, recognise unforeseen intersections in the characters' lives, have curious instincts constantly aroused, and pick up the book's momentum as it gathers itself for the end of its world. Vargas Llosa packs the book with violence, too: sexual violence, of course, but, most of all, the sights, sounds, smells and sensations of battle and death. The novel's great attraction lies in its combination of the oppressive physical immediacy with which it contemplates the horrific particulars of countless struggles for life in the Sertao and the subtlety with which its scheme makes these remote things matter. Like the best 19th-century novels, it satisfies both our sceptical and our credulous impulses, our preference for true history and our desire for good stories; and almost satisfies our greatest wish in this area—that true history and good story should be one and the same. We might be surprised, then, by Vargas Llosa's daring distortions in the treatment of his Cunha figure, a grotesquely driven romantic artist, racked by chronic sneezing fits, dangerously myopic, an unhappily unloved frequenter of brothels, physically ridiculous: the novel systematically turns the real writer's imaginative captivation by the people of Canudos into a complete realised fantasy of involvement with the rebels, signalled as a rhetorical departure by its location 'in that dreaming that is and is not, a dozing that blurs the borderline between waking and sleeping'. In this later hallucinatory strand of the book the Cunha figure is detached from the Army and swept into the other world, experiences a succession of intensities which one might think 'realities': humiliation, blindness (his glasses broken), terror, pain, hunger, thirst, wonder, comradeship, the tenderness of requited love. . . . Vargas Llosa's complex equivocation between the fictitious and the real only increases the hallucinatory vividness of reading *The War of the End of the World;* it is a paradox of literary experience, and of dreams, that things intensely represented seem to be *there* in a way they're not when we actually see them (which is a different, doubtless a truer way). In this respect *The War of the End of the World* is a perfect nightmare for us as readers, while the war of the end of the world is an appalling reality for the reporters who have come with Colonel Moreira Cesar, 'Throat-Slitter', on the third army expedition, wishing to see things with their own eyes. 'They have not yet recovered from the sight of those throats being slit just a few steps away from them: the meaning of certain words—war, cruelty, suffering, fate—has left the abstract domain in which it dwelt and taken on a measurable, tangible, carnal materiality that has left them speechless.' (p. 22)

Philip Horne, *"Those Heads on the Stakes," in* London Review of Books, *Vol. 7, No. 9, May 23, 1985, pp. 21-2.*

ROBERT COOVER

[There are two stories in *The Real Life of Alejandro Mayta*]—that of the title character and his abortive guerrilla uprising, and that of the unnamed narrator-investigator and his frustrated fictional exploration of this particular but elusive moment in past time that was once hard and now is as embraceable as smoke. The two "failures" parallel and inform one another, each touching each with doubt and irony, and in so doing, effect perhaps a small triumph as well—the sort of triumph experienced, let us say, by the amateur jogger as he completes his morning run (this is the little conceit that opens and closes the novel like whimsical brackets).

The cover story is based on a historical rebellion in the mountains of Peru in the late 1950's, led by a romantic Trotskyite actually named, it would seem, Alejandro Mayta. The revolt itself was crushed before it could even get started, but Mayta apparently survived, and the act itself, for its time, though soon forgotten, seemed original and daring. Mr. Vargas Llosa claims to have read about it in a newspaper while living in Paris and, a young man caught up then in the "revolutionary fervor" of the times (a year or so later, Fidel Castro would march into Havana to the almost universal acclaim of Latin American intellectuals), he was, in spite of its rather pathetic outcome, thrilled by its implications.

Nearly a quarter of a century later, home once more in Peru, his revolutionary enthusiasms mellowed now to a kind of pragmatic and pessimistic humanism, Mr. Vargas Llosa set about interviewing friends and relatives of Mayta—and, eventually, or so we are led to believe, the man himself—with the objective of weaving "a fantasy" (somehow more truthful than the lies that pass for History). "I'm a realist," as the investigative narrator tells one of the characters, "in my novels I always try to lie knowing why I do it. . . . And I think the only way to write stories is to start with History—with a capital H."

This ancient confrontation between art and action, fiction and history (or illusion and reality, as Cervantes would say: the man of letters versus the man of arms), discernible in all of Mr. Vargas Llosa's works, is the central story of *Mayta,* if not its only one: "It is precisely about that," the author has remarked in an interview, "the role of fiction in real life—in individual life, in social life, in historical life. And the kind of symmetry between fiction in literature and fiction in politics."

"Symmetry" is the operative word here. Words and deeds cannot invade one another, but they can cast light (or shadows) each on each, as though they might be separate "languages" with a common but unknowable deep structure. He believes,

for example, that periods of creative vitality tend to precede periods of revolutionary activity, without in any sense causing them to happen, each emerging instead from a kind of shared subterranean turbulence, yet intrinsically unable to cross into each other's territory. Which is why—a narrative artist schooled in radio and newspaper journalism—he is drawn to capital-H History, which does pretend in some manner to bridge this unbridgeable gap and which seems at times to provoke what it writes about. For Mr. Vargas Llosa, the "total novelist," this is something of a scandal. (pp. 1, 28)

For Mr. Vargas Llosa, the central feature of the total novel, aside from its encyclopedic pursuit of an all-encompassing overview, is its unassailable autonomy: its own internal coherence and integrity is ultimately what matters, not its relationship to any supposed "real" world. Indeed, the "real world" disappears altogether, displaced by the perfectly self-enclosed world of the "totalized fiction." The author's singular task is to serve intransigently as chronicler and explorer of that closed world of his own invention or discovery ("Novels that last are those that spring from that transcendental selfishness that puts absolutely everything at the service of literature," he has said), while at the same time withdrawing into Flaubert's God-like remove, omnipresent yet invisible.

His classic presentation of "totalization" is his second and most famous novel, *The Green House,* first published in 1966. Here, the author-deity, himself unseen, omnipotently and suggestively shuffles the elements of five different concurrent plots, remote from one another in time and place, yet each conjoined, as though organically, by the essential givens of the human—and in particular, the Peruvian—condition. Time is telescoped, distant places become as contiguous as film cuts, character dissolves into the landscape, resolution surprises climax, and the book, even while seeming to say more about Peru than any other book ever written, closes in on itself, shutting out everything not within its own pages.

The Green House was so climactic a statement of Mr. Vargas Llosa's esthetic, it might have been a dead end had not a paradoxical element begun to intrude, one evoked perhaps by his early attraction to the work of Albert Camus and Jean-Paul Sartre (see his collection of essays, *Between Sartre and Camus,* in which Camus the artist and humanist seems to win out over Sartre the intellectual radical). Mr. Vargas Llosa lived in Paris at a time when Existentialism was not merely a system of thought, it was an international fashion, a veritable style of life. Its impact on him and other Latin American writers of his generation was the equivalent of the impact of Expressionism and Surrealism on the generation—Jorge Luis Borges, Miguel Angel Asturias, Alejo Carpentier, Juan Carlos Onetti—that preceded his and set the stage for the famous "Boom."

A key feature of Existentialism is the centrality of the perceiving eye/I. For the Existentialists, like the Sophists of Plato's time, "man is the measure of all things," and that man has nothing to start with except the evidence of his own senses. No grand overviews here, no illusion called Being: Becoming is all there is. "Nothing endures but change," as Heraclitus allegedly put it. In such a world of flux, consciousness is a task, not a given, life itself a moment-by-moment invention.

And so, what might happen, Mr. Vargas Llosa seemed to ask himself, should these two enclosures meet—the isolate Existentialist "I" and the closed Platonic world of the "total novel"? What might happen, in effect, should the author-deity send himself—or, like one's only begotten son, something very *like* himself—into his hermetically sealed creation?

Though it can be argued that this second self existed in embryo in Mr. Vargas Llosa's first novel, *The Time of the Hero,* as the cool middle-class cadet Alberto, he begins to take on weight only in the third novel, *Conversation in the Cathedral,* as one of the two principal figures, the embittered editorial writer Santiago Zavala. Santiago, through the novel's unusual montage-like techniques, seems to share not only the author-deity's despairing vision of Peru and some of his private history, but also the power of invading the private lives and dreams of others, at least in Santiago's synthesizing imagination, as dialogue dissolves cinematically into distant thought and action.

This archetypal bourgeois intellectual, enraged at the dictatorship that has stolen his youth and innocence, but paralyzed by inaction, is still clearly an "other," of course. Santiago has a story of his own, a private trajectory which, though it resembles the author's in many ways, differs from it substantially as well—there is a family tale here of corruption, the abuse of power, paternal pederasty and murder, for example, that is presumably not (except perhaps metaphorically) Mr. Vargas Llosa's own. Santiago is still a character. The idea of testing his "totalized" novel by narrowing the distance between the author-deity and his creation seems not yet to have occurred to Mr. Vargas Llosa.

This happens a couple of books later, in the popular and playful (some have said frivolous) *Aunt Julia and the Scriptwriter,* where we are addressed by a first-person narrator who is called "Mario" or "Varguitas," and who, like the book's author before him, works for a radio station in Lima with a crazy Bolivian soap-opera scriptwriter, marries his Aunt Julia and goes to Paris to begin his writing career. His unadorned narration (Mr. Vargas Llosa has no patience with "lovers of surface"), almost cruelly frank in its intimate revelations about friends and family, all forced to bear their own "real life" names, is interlaced with parodies of the scriptwriter's soap operas, wildly imaginative episodes of illicit love and apocalyptic violence. The "invisible" author-deity of the narrator's same name (or has the author hereby somehow shed his name?) emerges only in the creative juxtapositions, the funny space *between* "reality" and "fantasy."

In his next book, *The War of the End of the World,* Mr. Vargas Llosa seems almost to shrink back from these potentially destructive threats to his youthful ideal of the "total novel." As though to purge the work of subjective elements, he moves the action out of Peru across a language barrier into Brazil and into the remote past of the 19th century, there to confront in a kind of abstract purity all those vast social, religious and political forces that have been, from the beginning, his central concern. Even most of his signature techniques of cinematic montage, chronological discontinuity, abrupt cuts, freezes, accelerations and shifts in verb tenses have largely disappeared.

But it's too late. That "second self," once fathered, will not be denied. Here, he turns up as the ugly, ungainly, myopic journalist, "the laughingstock of the office staff," who not only subverts the novel with such self-parodying remarks as, "Whether true or false, it's an extraordinary story" or, "Seeing a flesh-and-blood hero . . . would be like seeing and touching a character in a novel," but who is also one of the two or three most memorable and believable "characters" in a book driven largely by the clash of large social forces.

There remains, however, in the very self-mocking and metaphorical ugliness of this nearsighted journalist something distant and authorially manipulated, just as there remains something artificially "novelistic"—pretended—about the goofy innocence of *Aunt Julia*'s indiscreet young narrator. Both are characters modeled after the author's perception of himself at an earlier age, and not to be confused with that man of 50 now exploiting these "historical" materials.

Now, in *The Real Life of Alejandro Mayta,* the last mask is dropped and we are confronted with an unnamed but famous contemporary Peruvian novelist-narrator who is writing a book—*this* book—about Alejandro Mayta, insisting, as he sifts through the debris of history, interviews living Peruvians and physically traces Mayta's footsteps, that not only is this a total fiction, it is he, the first-person narrator, who is concocting it. A "lie," of course (among many here, as both author and narrator warn us), though an interesting one, for as Mayta's "life" dissolves on us even as it's being shaped, we find ourselves left with the narrator as this book's *only* character, its author-deity's one real creation. The narrator—and perhaps the reader.

For it is the reader in the end who "writes" the story, piecing it together from all the lies and contradictions, the unreliable testimony and historical "data" and openly manipulative narrative strategies, arriving at a knowledge that is finally more like self-awareness than historical certainty about either Mayta or his novelist-investigator. Character, after all, at least in its traditional sense, has, for Mr. Vargas Llosa, long since given way to something more like Sartre's "orchestration of consciousness," a kind of creative interplay between text and reader. Now, in *Mayta,* the author-deity has been absorbed into the same transaction. The static "totalized" space of his impenetrably autonomous world has been subverted by process: not even God the Author is to be trusted—indeed, he, baffled by his own doubling, least of all.

Not that this necessarily makes for a highly entertaining read. There is something plainly irritating about this narrator-character who invents an improbable apocalyptic war (improbable because as a narrator he never even tries to make it convincing), then abruptly calls it off in the last chapter, as though bored with it; who fails to ask obvious questions of his interviewees for no better reasons than those of narrative strategy; who looks down his nose at everyone and everything around him, including his own ostensible subject; and who so insists on—and demonstrates—his own duplicity as to sabotage the very credibility of his quest.

At times, this duplicity has an unpleasant edge of cruelty about it. He cripples his revolutionary hero, for example, with a dizzying weakness for young boys, confirms it by way of his former wife and others, leads us through a sordid seduction or two, then admits in the end it was just a gimmick, a way to "accentuate his marginality," mentioning without comment Mayta's wife and "large family" with whom he still lives. He makes this admission to Mayta himself (if we're to believe anything at all by now), who is hurt and disgusted by the implications of it. Then, having wounded this sick old man, already "destroyed by suffering and resentment," the narrator loses interest in him, and a page or two later (a last-minute deus-ex-machina story about treacherous co-revolutionaries conveniently rescues the narrator from any guilt he might be feeling) ceases his dispassionate plunder, as he would call it (the novelist, Mr. Vargas Llosa tells us elsewhere, is a "vulture," a "cannibal," "a complete egoist" with "an enormous deicidal will for the destruction and reconstruction of reality''), and returns to his morning jogs.

Yet, as can be seen by my own pity and anger, Mr. Vargas Llosa's narrative strategies have in some wise been vindicated. These parallel ''failures''—the 1950's ''revolution'' and the 1980's ''novel''—have generated between them a new kind of space, fragile maybe, impalpable, half-illusory, certainly disquieting, yet oddly immovable. Mayta lives there now with all his contradictions more securely than he does in the slums of Lima. As does the narrator with his contradictions, now less the transient jogger of the Barranco district than this new space's pervasive and imperishable voice. And, once you have visited here, Mr. Vargas Llosa seems to be saying, so too, Dear Reader, must you with all of yours. (pp. 28-9)

Robert Coover, ''The Writer as God and Saboteur,'' in The New York Times Book Review, February 2, 1986, pp. 1, 28-9.

JAY TOLSON

Quite understandably, the novelist Vargas Llosa has at times wished he were free of his region's political turmoil. ''Why is it like this?'' he asked in an essay several years ago. ''Why is it that instead of being basically creators and artists, writers in Peru and other Latin American countries must above all be politicians, agitators, reformers, social publicists and moralists?'' It is something of a surprise, then, that Vargas Llosa would have chosen the loaded subject of revolution and revolutionaries as the theme of [*The Real Life of Alejandro Mayta*]. The choice alone throws him into the center of Latin America's current political debate.

The subject is a daunting one even without its obvious contemporary relevance. What, after all, remains to be said about that quintessentially modern hero—or anti-hero—after Dostoevsky's definitive depiction of the type in *The Possessed?* Consumed by a single passion, the revolutionary, moreover, lacks those complicating ambivalences that make for immediately interesting literary characters.

Shrewdly, Vargas Llosa has made the difficulties of writing about the revolutionary a central part of his novel. He sets his story in a Peru of the not-too-distant future, at a time when everyone is haunted by the specter of revolution. Terrorist violence has erupted throughout the country, and U.S. Marines have been called in to resist an invading Cuban-Bolivian revolutionary force. In the garbage-befouled city of Lima, the narrator, a novelist not unlike Vargas Llosa himself, attempts to put together the true story of Alejandro Mayta, an obscure Trotskyite who in 1958 led an abortive insurrection in the provincial Andean town of Jauja. The narrator wants the facts not so he can write a history or biography but so he can transform them into the stuff of a novel.

But why this minor figure, Mayta? The narrator wonders about that himself. Is it because Mayta's ''case was the first that would typify the period? Because he was the most absurd? Because his person and his story hold something ineffably moving, something that, over and beyond its political and moral implications, is like an x-ray of Peruvian misfortune?''

This search for a clue to the national character, the national destiny, is told in a way that sometimes seems to obscure more than it does to clarify. The narrative technique consists of quick, unsignalled hops between the present (in which the narrator is usually engaged in interviewing Mayta's former

acquaintances) and moments from Mayta's past. This quick-cutting montage forces the reader to wonder whether the scenes from the past are faithful renderings of what the narrator was told or whether they are already the reworked, fictionalized versions of those accounts.

Confusing it is, but at least it serves to make a legitimate, if not altogether original, point: that stories about the past are always reworkings, always fictions. Implicitly, furthermore, Vargas Llosa seems to support the Aristotelian argument that poetry (read fiction here) comes closer to truth than history (or more amateur recountings of events) because it strives after universals, whereas history, a lesser narrative genre, pretends merely to present the facts.

Then, it must be asked, does the narrator of this novel draw a ''truer'' picture of the revolutionary than mere facts might allow? I am not persuaded that he does. And yet here is an irony: I am not sure that Vargas Llosa intended him to.

The Mayta who gradually emerges in the narrator's picture belongs among the great romantics of literature. He is a type, a political Quixote, questing after the ideal society. . . .

But there is something else about Mayta, and this characteristic leads into the novel's all-important twist. Mayta is homosexual. At least that is what several informants say about him, and that is how the narrator chooses to present him. This characteristic, as it is revealed and developed, makes Mayta more vulnerable, complicated, and sympathetic. It doesn't fully explain his revolutionary fervor, although his attraction to a swaggeringly macho young lieutenant lies partially behind his decision to attempt the foolhardy insurrection in Jauja. For the most part, however, homosexuality is a wound that Mayta quietly carries, a wound from which he thinks he might suffer less in a better future world. It is a poignant detail and yet somehow too neat. And Vargas Llosa knows that it is.

That is why Vargas Llosa finally undercuts his elaborate fictional design at the end of the book—or at least appears to. He does so by having the narrator meet the ''real'' Mayta, a much less complicated or sympathetic man than the one we have gotten to know. This real Mayta, now working in an ice cream parlor after having served several jail sentences for crimes which seem only remotely political, is disturbed and disgusted to learn that he has been depicted as a ''queer.'' The narrator-novelist explains that he did so in order to heighten his character's ''marginality.'' But then he confesses that he really doesn't know why he did it.

It is a strange moment in the novel, and one that readers will doubtlessly react to in different ways. But I don't think Vargas Llosa is merely playing games with us. Instead he is attempting to dramatize his views about the problematic relationship between art and reality, particularly in the troubling realm of politics. His novel tells us a great deal about Peru's history, its mixed Indian and Spanish heritages (including the cruel, intolerant streak born of the Inquisition); it tells us much about all classes of Peruvians, from the wretched and hopelessly poor who have no choice but to turn to crime or political violence, to the smugly well situated who, amid national chaos, can worry blithely about the dwindling coffee supply. His novel shows us, in other words, how a sensitive, intelligent man could be driven to the revolutionary faith, and it offers a sympathetic, even somewhat idealized, picture of just such a revolutionary. And yet finally Vargas Llosa draws up short before his own romantic portrayal. Indeed, in a subtle way, he denounces it as just that—as romantic.

Vargas Llosa is too much of a political man to ignore what revolutionaries have brought upon others as well as upon themselves, to ignore, in other words, the disastrous consequences of their romanticism. So he arranges, in his novel, for "reality" (an imagined reality, of course) to puncture the romance. Unfortunately, this obtrusive ploy prevents *The Real Life of Alejandro Mayta* from having what might have been a more pleasing fictional shape. That is the price of writing a disturbing novel, one whose carefully contrived unpleasantness will keep readers from easily putting aside its harder truths.

Jay Tolson, "The Romance of Revolution and the Novelist's Truth," in Book World—The Washington Post, *February 9, 1986, p. 5.*

JOHN UPDIKE

Mario Vargas Llosa, a fifty-year-old Peruvian, has replaced Gabriel García Márquez as the South American novelist for gringos to catch up on; the agreeable impression made here four years ago by the translation of *Aunt Julia and the Scriptwriter* was deepened by last year's awed reception of *The War of the End of the World.* . . . His newly arrived novel, *The Real Life of Alejandro Mayta* . . . , is a dazzling performance—perhaps, it might be offered in cavil, a shade too much of a performance. But never mind; Señor Vargas Llosa has all the moves, and the reader's awareness of the author's virtuosity is in this case woven right into the intricate and suspenseful texture of his tale. In Spanish, the novel is called simply *Historia de Mayta;* the English title reminds one of Nabokov's *The Real Life of Sebastian Knight*—and, whether or not the echo is intentional, Nabokov does keep coming to mind as Vargas Llosa ingeniously, incessantly shuffles past and present, writer and character, "I" and "he," a historical Peru and a futuristic Peru, a mock-documentary manner and the ingenuous camaraderie of the professed fictionist. (p. 98)

Alejandro Mayta was the narrator's classmate at the Salesian School. A pudgy, awkward boy of humble background, he was unduly sensitive to the beggars and other unfortunates of the Lima streets, and once asked the priest of his Communion class, "Why are there rich and poor people, Father?" The question never rests for him; he goes on a hunger strike, loses his Catholic faith, and becomes a Communist revolutionary—for two decades, a purist of the left who finds doctrinal adequacy in a tiny, seven-man cell of Trotskyites, and then, at the age of forty, an incongruous man of action, a leader of an abortive uprising in the Andes town of Juaja, in 1958. (This chronology, we might observe, puts Mayta's birth in 1918, which makes him and his classmate a generation older than Vargas Llosa, who was born in 1936.) Now, twenty-five years after the uprising, in a Peru supposedly racked by guerrilla warfare and turned into a battlefield by a "Russo-Cuban-Bolivian invasion" and American Marines supporting the ruling junta (fiction, though the conditions to make it plausible exist), the narrator decides to explore the life of Mayta, and to compose a novel based upon the violent events long ago in Juaja. He interviews a number of people around Lima, and in the process gives a good walking tour of the once beautiful viceregal capital, now an overcrowded, filthy, and run-down urban sprawl. These interviews—with Mayta's aunt, with former Trotskyite associates, with radical nuns and a former Stalinist whose paths have crossed Mayta's, and with a woman, Adelaida, whom Mayta, a homosexual, had persuaded to be his wife—all alternate, sometimes several times on a page, with scenes from, as it were, the novel in progress, from Mayta's

life in 1958 as the writer imagines it. The double focus is expertly manipulated and sometimes—as when a present-day senator's smooth slanders are interspersed with scenes of his homosexual seduction by Mayta as a young man—provides a stunning stereoptical effect, of lives as they exist in the depths of time. On occasion, Vargas Llosa seems to have too much going all at once, as when the former wife's description of her sham marriage and the fate of the son she conceived with Mayta is played against not only her present marriage, middle-aged self, and dumpy surroundings but an apocalyptic background of the destruction of Cuzco in the imaginary Peruvian war. This science-fiction element, when the plain truth about Peru would be ominous enough, unnecessarily confuses a novel already luxuriantly complex; also, in this chapter the narrator's "I" creeps over into Mayta's consciousness, slipping one more transparency into the overloaded projector. Still, having elected certain instruments, an artist is obliged to use them to the hilt, and all manner of interesting anticipations and retrospections are generated by Vargas Llosa's glinting devices. (pp. 98, 101)

We are invited to admire, as spontaneously as we admire the handsome, pin-striped hidalgo on the back of the book jacket, the imagination that can conjure up, say, the comic fussiness of a tiny left-wing splinter group in solemn session, or the nauseated feelings of a young wife who discovers that her husband is a homosexual, or the numb exaltation of a citified idealist engaging, while beset with altitude sickness, in a gun battle in the Andes. All wonderfully done, though we are disconcertingly reminded that it might have been done quite otherwise, that art is as arbitrary as truth is relative. The last chapter, like one of those Nabokovian endings wherein the scenery falls away and the cocky puppetmaster faces the audience directly, piles twist upon twist and should be left its provocative surprises. The author (it may not be too much to reveal) engagingly confesses to his character, "This conversation is my final chapter. You can't refuse me now, it would be like taking a cake out of the oven too soon."

The question keeps arising, in the reader's mind and on the printed page, why did our hero (the author) take as his subject this obscure and defeated revolutionary, Alejandro Mayta? Because, the answer suggests itself, the subject is political, and it is the proper and inevitable task of the South American novelist to write politically. As the Vargas Llosa persona explains to an interview subject, "I think the only way to write stories is to start with History—with a capital H." Lima, the city founded by Pizarro, from which Spain administered a continent of gold and slaves, certainly has History; the riddle of Latin-American poverty and unrest and crisis has its answer here if anywhere. The physical degradation of the city is far advanced; ubiquitous garbage begins and ends the novel. The proliferating slums, and even the horrors of the dreadfully overcrowded jail, are remorselessly described. Nor is there a rural idyll to offer contrast or relief. The Indians still flock to the wretched shack cities, from Andean towns like Quero. . . . Some reviewers in the United States have taken *The Real Life of Alejandro Mayta* to be a satire on left-wing commitment. It is true, comedy and even farce are found in the ineffectuality of the seven-man Trotskyite cell, utterly isolated with its strenuous jargon from the masses it seeks to educate and liberate, and in the inadequacies of Mayta's uprising, whose main troops consist of seven schoolboys, who, failing to learn the "Internationale," instead sing a school song and the national anthem as they bounce along in the revolution's solitary truck. But, Vargas Llosa seems to say, a revolutionary seed *is* planted that day, amid all the absurdity; and in any case the need for a change shouts out on all sides, in the circumambient misery and disorder. His is a model of the most that political fiction can be: a description of actual social conditions and a delineation of personalities motivated by political concerns. Such motivation, of course, comes mixed with sexual and other intimate, clouded motives; yet it exists. All the political-minded interviewees are left-wingers; there are no junta spokesmen, or intransigent landowners, or fresh-faced *norteamericanos* insidiously urging the virtues of free enterprise. But in his shrewd and lively portraits of Peruvian lawyers and barbers and storekeepers Vargas Llosa catches well enough the tone of the cagey, improvising citizenry that makes do with a system and, having made do, resists sweeping change. The conservative inertia of a society is suggested, while its agitators are dramatized. The dozens of little anticlimactic careers sketched in the margins of Alejandro's own anticlimactic career persuasively imply the limits of human protoplasm and the defeat that awaits each dreaming, idealistic organism. If the novel has a moral, it might be, as a Peruvian bureaucrat tells the narrator, "When you start looking for purity in politics, you eventually get to unreality." (p. 101)

John Updike, "Latin Strategies," in The New Yorker, *Vol. LXII, No. 1, February 24, 1986, pp. 98, 101-04.*

TERRENCE RAFFERTY

Vargas Llosa has never been shy about taking on big themes, or about engineering formal structures elaborate enough to contain all of Latin American history and culture: he seems to want to explain everything, including his own role as a writer. In [*The Real Life of Alejandro Mayta*] he's created a character who's meant to be a representative revolutionary of Castro's generation and a setting that's a stylized version of present-day Lima, overrun with garbage and caught in a crossfire between Cuban-backed terrorists and the American military. The story is told in a series of *Citizen Kane*-like flashbacks, as an unnamed novelist tries to reconstruct the "truth" of Mayta's life from the testimony of those who knew him. This story and this structure, taken together, allow Vargas Llosa to do several things at once: to turn Mayta, who is shown here leading a pathetic insurrection in the Peruvian mountains a year before the Cuban revolution, into a symbol of the old Latin American left, a parodic version of Fidel; to reflect, from the distance of thirty years, on the motives and the ultimate consequences of that first wave of revolution; to introduce, as witnesses, a set of characters who both embody the changes in society and illustrate the subjectivity of memory; and to use the form of an investigation to add an air of mystery and heavy consequence to what's essentially a thin, schematic anecdote.

The novel is absorbing enough for most of its length. The narrator keeps digging into Mayta's past, filling in details, and we feel we're getting somewhere.... All works that arrange themselves explicitly as a search for historical truth create this sort of expectation (as *Citizen Kane* demonstrates), even if the questions are posed in *Reader's Digest*-like terms—"Alejandro Mayta, Visionary or Fool?" This isn't an easy expectation to satisfy: even *Kane* doesn't, quite, and Warren Beatty's *Reds,* which may have been the more direct inspiration for *Alejandro Mayta,* doesn't come close. We realize, as readers or spectators, that the author's conclusions *won't* explain it all, that we'll still have to evaluate, to test his responses against our own—but we want, at least, to be given a statement to argue with. (p. 461)

In the final chapter, the narrator has at last tracked down Mayta, now nearly seventy, and as he asks the ex-revolutionary to confirm or correct the version of his life we've been reading, the character's reality evaporates. Challenged to resolve some of the contradictions in the previous accounts, Mayta responds: "I've forgotten lots of things, and I'm mixed up about lots of others. I'd really like to help you out and tell you about it. But the problem is that I don't know all that happened or even how it happened. It's a long time ago, don't forget." After all that, he *forgot*? (Note for a possible movie: Steve Martin as Mayta.) Furthermore, the narrator reveals that a prominent feature in his portrait of Mayta—his homosexuality—is pure invention. So we've been informed, pedantically, that there's no real Mayta in the sense that this narrative has led us to believe. He's just a blank screen for our projections: whether the real Mayta is a noble, confused idealist or simply a petty crook is unimportant, because all that matters is what we— that is, interpreters like Vargas Llosa's narrator—make of him.

The effect of this stripping-off-the-layers-of-illusion act is to clear the stage of characters and ideas and reveal the real star of the show—the illusionist himself. If everything is fiction and the novelist's reality is as good as any other, why not? Vargas Llosa might like us to believe that he's being ironic about his own activity in re-creating Mayta's life. But this is an awfully disingenuous kind of irony: even though the narrator has admitted that he's a little unreliable, his consciousness now dominates the novel, and, with Mayta reduced to an imaginative construct, there's no reality left to compare it with. In the same year (1984) of *Alejandro Mayta*'s original publication in Spanish, Vargas Llosa wrote an essay called **"Is Fiction the Art of Lying?"** in which he said: "Every good novel tells the truth and every bad novel lies. For a novel to 'tell the truth' means to make the reader experience an illusion, and 'to lie' means to be unable to accomplish that trickery. The novel, thus, is an amoral genre, or rather, its ethic is *sui generis,* one in which truth and falsehood are exclusively esthetic concepts." (pp. 461-62)

Vargas Llosa's work these days—this novel, the **"Art of Lying"** essay, his *New York Times Magazine* pieces on Nicaragua and **"My Son the Rastafarian"**—has the pompous, elevated tone of a man who's writing as a spokesman. Even in his own terms, he doesn't lie like a novelist anymore: he lies like a diplomat, in a glib, self-congratulatory, of-course-you-and-I-know-what-this-is-really-all-about way. Perhaps, at the end of *The Real Life of Alejandro Mayta,* Vargas Llosa feels that his laborious investigation of a single character has given us more of the illusion of "being another" than is really good for us: we might be tempted to draw conclusions, to believe the author too much. (If so, he overestimates the danger.) Or maybe, as seems more likely, he simply decided that Mayta isn't the other he wants us to have the illusion of being—*he* is.

The author is exceptionally coy, in this novel as in some of his others, about his characters' relationship to reality: we can't be certain that the famous Peruvian novelist reconstructing Mayta's life is actually Vargas Llosa, nor that the obscure revolutionary he calls Mayta is based on any historical personage. This isn't all that crucial a question in the case of the narrator: his consciousness survives until the end of the novel, he gets the last word, he can take care of himself. But we do want to know whether a real Mayta existed or not, so we can judge the ethics (as well as the esthetics) of how he's been used here. Vargas Llosa very deliberately builds up the significance of this man's life, then just as pointedly wipes it all out—surely it matters whether he's done this to a human being or a mere invention. The scary thing is that it may not matter to Vargas Llosa. For all the impressive architecture of his earlier novels, none of them demonstrated an especially impressive talent for character. (The most convincing, most lovingly understood person in all his work is the young writer called Marito, and sometimes Varguitas, in *Aunt Julia.*) But none of these novels actively denied the reality of other people, the way *Mayta* does or the way the recent, unforgivable article on his 16-year old son's flirtation with Rastafarianism does. In that piece, Vargas Llosa describes his reaction to his son's appearance by saying, "it wouldn't have been clear to most people that he was actually human," and after several pages of grilling by the father/interrogator, Vargas Llosa still doesn't find any recognizable human impulse in his son's behavior. As in *Mayta,* what the writer doesn't understand can be dismissed as unreal, as if the opacity of a teen-ager's motives or

an old man's memories were a direct affront to him, a license to objectify them as he wishes, novelistically, then let them blow away like the pages of a manuscript. (p. 462)

In another fifteen or twenty years Mario Vargas Llosa will be as old as the feeble Mayta of the last chapter, and there may still be some unanswered questions: was he a serious novelist—a great explainer—or just a smooth-talking candidate for something (Latin American writer most likely to succeed García Márquez)? Perhaps by then, even he will have forgotten what he was up to. Right now, the image of the ambitious, diligent, searching (if sometime ponderous) Vargas Llosa of the 1960s and 1970s is fading fast. He's getting less real all the time. (p. 463)

Terrence Rafferty, "Ambassadorial Fiction," in The Nation, *Vol. 242, No. 12, March 29, 1986, pp. 461-63.*

Derek (Alton) Walcott

1930-

West Indian poet and dramatist.

Walcott is a highly respected poet and dramatist and a leading voice in contemporary West Indian literature. Of mixed African and European heritage, Walcott embodies the cultural dichotomy that provides the major tensions in his work. Employing diverse styles, settings, and subject matter, he explores such themes as racism, the injustices of colonialism, the collapse of empires, and the quest for personal, cultural, and political identity. Walcott's synthesis of French Creole and West Indian dialect with the formal structures and eloquent language of Elizabethan verse, in addition to his tropical imagery and calypso rhythms, creates a hybrid literature that reflects his personal experiences as well as the history and culture of the West Indies.

Walcott's folk dramas, including *The Sea at Dauphin* (1954), *Ione* (1957), *Ti-Jean and His Brothers* (1958), and *The Dream on Monkey Mountain* (1967), are considered to be his most effective work for the theater. *The Sea at Dauphin,* a tale of the St. Lucian fishing community's struggle to survive the forces of the sea, is derived from West Indian folklore and marks Walcott's first use of the native folk idiom. In *Ti-Jean and His Brothers,* Walcott continues the folk tradition of *The Sea at Dauphin* by blending a morality play and a West Indian fable to celebrate the triumph of native resourcefulness over imperialist power. In this play, Walcott also comments on racism and the exploitation of the poor by the wealthy. Walcott's folk drama tradition culminates in *The Dream on Monkey Mountain,* the most highly praised of his dramas and winner of the 1971 Obie Award. This play focuses on a charcoal vendor who descends from his mountain home to sell his wares but is jailed for drunkenness. While in jail, he dreams of becoming the king of a united Africa. Walcott has said that *The Dream on Monkey Mountain* is about the West Indian search for identity and is concerned with the damage inflicted by colonialism on the human soul. Combining dream and reality in the play, Walcott emphasizes what he perceives to be the dangers of replacing the realities of Caribbean cultural diversity with a romanticized vision of Africa in the hope of reestablishing cultural roots. Instead, Walcott advocates introspection and art as the means to rediscover one's personal and cultural heritage. Walcott continues his search for identity in such later plays as *O Babylon!* (1976), which focuses on the Rastafarian rejection of Western culture, *Remembrance* (1979), and *Pantomime* (1981).

In his poetry, Walcott relies more on European literary tradition than on the West Indian folklore so dominant in his plays, although his later poems integrate both Caribbean and European elements. In his first collection, *In a Green Night: Poems, 1948-1960* (1962), Walcott uses traditional forms, including the sonnet, to examine his divided allegiance to his people and to the dying empire that rules them. In *The Castaway and Other Poems* (1965), Walcott extends the themes of his first collection and introduces the image of the shipwreck as a metaphor of the modern world. This vision enables Walcott to examine the synthesis of Western and African civilization that he believes is necessary for the discovery of personal and cul-

tural identity. This volume also introduces Walcott's concern with racism, a theme he explores more fully in his next collection, *The Gulf and Other Poems* (1969). In these poems, Walcott demonstrates his understanding of Caribbean ties to the American continents as his settings move from St. Lucia to Washington, D.C., Cuba, and South America. Just as leaving his homeland figures prominently in many of his earlier poems, the theme of homecoming dominates this collection.

Walcott's long autobiographical narrative poem, *Another Life* (1973), departs from the historical perspective of his earlier verse for a more personal approach. The poem is Walcott's lyrical record of self-assessment and, according to Roger Garfitt, "is an exploration into the past, a work of rediscovery and reconciliation." Walcott continues this personal tone in his subsequent volumes of poetry, *Sea Grapes* (1976), *The Star-Apple Kingdom* (1980), and *The Fortunate Traveller* (1982). In *Midsummer* (1984), Walcott uses detailed visual imagery, repetition, a loose rhyme scheme, and a firm narrative structure in a fifty-four poem sequence that retains the familiar theme of divided allegiance while emphasizing such concerns as middle age, morality, and poetry itself. While some critics concluded that Walcott's emphasis on technical virtuosity resulted in neglect of the poem's subject in favor of a word or phrase to satisfy the structure of the sequence, others applauded his experiment as fresh and challenging. *Collected Poems,*

1948-1984 (1985) documents Walcott's career as a poet by drawing from his previous volumes and reprinting *Another Life*.

(See also *CLC*, Vols. 2, 4, 9, 14, 25; *Contemporary Authors*, Vols. 89-92; and *Dictionary of Literary Biography Yearbook: 1981*.)

SVEN BIRKERTS

[The poems in *Midsummer*] are the meditations of a middle-aged prodigal son, nothing more. The intent is evident. By taking away drama, subject, and any sort of finishing varnish, Walcott is forcing the full weight of scrutiny onto the lines. The poetry has nothing to hide behind—no tricks, no feints. It's an all-or-nothing gamble, and it succeeds.

Poetry in recent years has become more and more bound up with the magazine industry. A poet puts out twenty or thirty separate ''pieces'' and then collects them into a book. The ancient tribal song has been groomed and pomaded until it looks like a whisper. *Midsummer,* ragged-edged and robust, is anything but a magazine book. Its lines are like the links of a chain saw moving through the broad trunk of a life. We are to look at the cloven bole, its rings, whorls, and irregularities. Connections and links have not been engineered—they are implicit and organic. If there are chips and splinters, so be it. Walcott would have it no other way. . . .

Midsummer: boredom, stasis, the harsh afternoon glare of self-assessment. Midsummer equals mid-career, middle age, Dante's *''mezza del cammin di nostra vita. . . .''* The only real narrative prop that we have for any of these numbered poems is given in the first. The poet, comfortably identified with the ''I'' of the speaking voice, is returning by air to his old island home. (p. 31)

It is impossible, of course, to give a fair account of a cycle like this. Walcott is trying to fix, in sharp, living lines, the particular texture of his inner life during the course of two summers. The ambition carries certain hazards in its train. A certain monotony, for one thing. Reading the undifferentiated stanzas from start to finish can be like wandering around in a rain forest. There is something almost vegetal in the proliferation of Walcott's lines. How can anyone produce so many naturally flexed hexameters so quickly?

Walcott is not, of course, blind to the repetitious nature of his project—he wants it to be that way. He tests the constraints of subject that seem to inhere in metric verse, but he does so from within. Like Cézanne, who painted hill after hill because hills were not what he was interested in, Walcott writes poem after poem with little differentiation of subject. His settings and descriptions are, in a sense, pretexts. He would like to throw out as much as possible in order to clear a path to his real subject: language becoming poetry.

Poetry, like speech, is a complex connivance of sound and sense. The lyrical ideal is a condition in which the two are seamlessly joined. Or, better yet, a condition in which it becomes clear that sound is a kind of sense, and vice versa. For as sense is proper to the mind, so sound is to the heart. And the heart, as great lyric poets have always known, is the tribunal before which reason lays its spoils. ''To betray philosophy,'' writes Walcott, ''is the gentle treason / of poets. . . .'' He is

reducing, or eliminating as much as possible, the ostensible subject of the poem, so that the plaiting movement of sound and sense can show itself. This is not an evasion of subject so much as a deeper perception of the poet's function.

Walcott is re-establishing the sound, the music, as a connection to felt and perceived experience. When he writes:

> The oak inns creak in their joints as light declines
> from the ale-colored skies of Warwickshire.
> Autumn has blown the froth from the foaming orchards,
> so white-haired regulars draw chairs nearer the grate
> to spit on logs that crackle into leaves of fire.
>
> *—XXXVI*

he is promoting the status of sound as meaning and is arguing against the notion that meaning is some kind of detachable content. The treason of poets is to believe that sonorousness and rhythmic emphasis establish a body-circuit through experience that reason alone cannot achieve.

Walcott writes a strongly accented, densely packed line that seldom slackens and yet never loses conversational intimacy. He works in form, but he is not formal. His agitated phonetic surfaces can at times recall Lowell's, but the two are quite different. In Lowell, one feels the torque of mind; in Walcott, the senses predominate. And Walcott's lines ring with a spontaneity that Lowell's often lack. . . . (p. 32)

Though Walcott is very much aware of the assaults that modernism has waged upon the metric line, he has elected to work with its possibilities. In part this is a matter of temperament. But there is also the matter of the poet's unique relation to the English language. He acquired in the Caribbean an English very different from that spoken by his counterparts in England and America. Not only is the region a linguistic seed-bed, with every kind of pidgin and dialect, but successive waves of colonization (and oppression) have left phenocrysts of all descriptions. . . .

Walcott's traditional metric is more than a simple act of homage to the past—it is the most expeditious way for him to organize his complex linguistic heritage. Controlled by a firm structure, each element of that heritage can declare itself. And the various distinctions, as anyone in the third world can testify, are not just historical; they are political as well. . . .

There is no one writing in English at present who can join power with delicacy the way Walcott can. He is the outsider, the poet from the periphery, but it may be time to center the compass at his position and draw the circle again. (p. 33)

Sven Birkerts, ''Heir Apparent,'' in The New Republic, *Vol. 190, No. 3, January 23, 1984, pp. 31-3.*

STEVEN RATINER

There is much that is praiseworthy in *Midsummer,* a sequence of 54 lyrics that record one year's passing in the poet's life from summer to summer. . . . The poems focus on the torrid stasis at the heart of summer, the poet's relationships to family and place, and the peculiar perspective of the exile. Immediately apparent is Mr. Walcott's care for language; there is an exuberance, almost a physical pleasure in the construction of his lines that invites the reader to speak the poems aloud.

Two-thirds of the book is set in either the islands of the Caribbean or the tropics of Central America; Mr. Walcott, who is also a painter, offers a wealth of visual detailing in each scene. But the enlivening spark is provided by metaphor—in fact, more metaphor-per-poem than I've come across in a long while. His comparisons are ingenious, wry, bitter, and often provocative.

But I would say the poet's strongest quality is his finely tuned ear and musical sense. Mr. Walcott's composition is essentially musical, and his long free verse lines overflow with slant rhyme, half rhyme, assonance, and alliterative designs. The rhythmical structures and sound patterns propel the reader through each piece with the effortlessness of song and provide a cohesion to the poem's development.

Duly impressed by the technical strength of Mr. Walcott's writing, I found it hard to understand why, in the end *Midsummer* was such a disappointing book. One quality the poet is in short supply of is balance, a sense of proportion that can sustain a tension within the writing and put his strong qualities to their best use. After a time, we are so awash in sparkling language and intricate metaphor, the subject of the poem is all but obscured. We begin to long for the simple declarative line, for unembellished description that holds clear and true. . . .

The real problems begin once you look beyond the brilliance of the oratory; you are surprised by the thinness of the conversation the poet is offering and his acutely myopic vision. The lines rarely carry you further than an arm's length from the poet himself. Too many times the reality of the subject is effaced by the choice of a word or phrase that merely satisfied the cadence or figure of the poem. You are left justifiably suspicious, wondering where the writer's primary commitment lies.

Once you've finished the book, you realize that, despite the progression from one summer to the next, there is surprisingly little sense of movement or development in either time or character. The settings shift dramatically, from the Caribbean islands to Boston and New York, with side-excursions to Great Britain and Central America. Yet there is hardly the feeling of motion and only the barest sense of place. We never come to 'know' Mr. Walcott's territories the way we are given Williams's Paterson, Donald Hall's New England, or James Wright's Midwest. The many landscapes begin to feel like colorful backdrops for what we soon realize is the true subject of *Midsummer:* the mind of the poet.

What we have is one more portentous self-portrait of the poet-at-work—a curious sensibility more at home in the world of words than in any country, more anxious to articulate his psychological responses than any experience he and the reader might have in common. This is the dead-end street in which so many of our contemporary poets have found themselves stranded: language as a performance medium for the all-devouring self, places mere occasions for the exercise of the imagination.

In one characteristic, then, Mr. Walcott is indeed representative of a broad and particularly modern viewpoint, but not necessarily one our society can be proud of. This is the role of poet-as-tourist, the outsider gliding over but not through settings, whose literary concerns outstrip his emotional involvement. This need not have been the case considering the subjects the poet has chosen for himself: the universal significance of the seasons, the racial conflict in America, the confrontation between politics and history in Central America. But curiously we find the head engaged but the heart left in neutral. The image that came to mind was that of a 20th-century Baudelaire, a super-subjective narrator of a society in decline. But *Midsummer* is too careful and self-possessed to incite a revolution

of the spirit, and never achieves the daring and power required to truly expose the outer or inner worlds. Instead we are left with a scrapbook of color snapshots, dramatic but two dimensional, in which too often the figure of the poet is obstructing the view.

Another current runs just beneath the surface in *Midsummer,* the poet's personal speculations at having reached the solstice of his life and career. The poems are rife with uncertainty about the value of his writing. . . . There is a handful of poems in the sequence that ought to soothe his doubts; remembrances of his boyhood in the islands, an apocalyptic vision in Chicago, and several selections from the **"Tropic Zone"** section are substantial exceptions to the book's ruling hypersubjectivity. For me, Mr. Walcott is so splendid a stylist and so talented a craftsman, I can only look forward to a subject that will draw him in this way out from the smothering self-consciousness and give him room for a broader, more vital creation.

Steven Ratiner, "In His Own Way: Derek Walcott," in The Christian Science Monitor, *April 6, 1984, p. B9.*

PETER STITT

Derek Walcott's *Midsummer* is an unpaged, fifty-four part sequence of untitled poems. The book as a whole does not tell a story, and the units themselves rarely even contain narrative elements. What unites these parts is the personality of their speaker, a man of a meditative, enquiring intellect, whom we overhear as he wonders and speculates about a number of loosely related topics. (p. 407)

Though he is obviously sympathetic to the cause of self-rule, and though he can be bitingly, devastatingly critical of the colonialist mentality ("In colonial fiction / evil remains comic and only achieves importance / when the gringo crosses the plaza, flayed by the shadows of fronds"), Walcott still does not like the direction in which the Central American revolutions are moving. In another poem he asks us to "Imagine, where sand is now, the crawling lava / of military concrete." The poem ends with the speaker noticing

> that the smallest pamphlet is stamped with a single star.
> The days feel longer, people resemble their cars
> that are gray as their uniforms. In the millennium,
> most men, at night, sleep with their eyes to the wall.

This speaker seems alienated from both past and future, and lives in a rootless present.

The irony of his position is made clear in poem *II,* which is set in Rome and compares that city with the West Indies. Walcott can describe even so simple a thing as the season in Rome with an allusiveness deeply appropriate to its subject:

> Midsummer's furnace casts everything in bronze.
> Traffic flows in the slow coils, like the doors of a
>   baptistry,
> and even the kitten's eyes blaze with the Byzantine
>   icons.

All of this is contrasted, as the poem ends, with the island:

> Corals up to their windows in sand are my sacred
>   domes,
> gulls circling a seine are the pigeons of my St. Mark's,
> silver legions of mackerel race through our catacombs,

The language and figuration of these lines, of course, indicate the depth of this speaker's cross-culturation; he can no longer see, or describe, the native landscape as it actually is.

James Wright once spoke of Derek Walcott as a twentieth-century man possessing an Elizabethan sense of the language, and I don't think that is much of an exaggeration. *Midsummer* is a magnificent volume, thematically expansive and beautifully written. Because it is so emphatically circular and accretive in its overall structure, I find that my own discussion of it must perforce be circular and accretive as well. Walcott addresses many compelling topics, ranging from the political ironies already discussed to the important moral concern evinced in the meditation on relations between men and women. . . . (pp. 407-08)

Another topic of special interest in the sequence is the sense of spiritual wonderment and longing Walcott occasionally expresses:

> On a light-angled wall,
> through the clear, soundless pane, one sees a speech
> that calls to us, but is beyond our powers,
> composed of O's from a reflected bridge,
> the language of white, ponderous clouds convening
> over aerials, spires, rooftops, water towers.

To Walcott, the circular letter *O* embodies the language of spirituality, and he discovers it both in man's constructions and in nature. By a curious coincidence, we find a remarkably similar passage in Charles Wright's poem "To Giacomo Leopardi in the Sky". . . . Just as the circle symbolizes the concept of spiritual unity, so it is the circular form which—despite the fact that it *seems* to go nowhere—can more closely approach the infinite within poetry. Certainly Walcott and Wright (not to mention their meditative precursors) are in agreement about the spiritual nature of their own aims. (pp. 408-409)

> *Peter Stitt, "The Circle of the Meditative Moment," in* The Georgia Review, *Vol. XXXVIII, No. 2, Summer, 1984, pp. 402-14.*

WILLIAM H. PRITCHARD

I did not find myself challenged by Derek Walcott's sequence of fifty-four poems [*Midsummer*] meant to encompass his ruminations over the course of a year. Each poem goes on for around twenty or so lines of irregular length, and in such a form, unrhymed, you can say just about anything which occurs to you. A typical Walcott opening goes like this:

> I drag, as on a chain behind me, laterite landscapes—
> streams where the sunset has fallen, the fences of
>   villages,
> and buffalo brooding like clouds of indigo, I pull the
>   voices
> of children behind me that die with the first star, the
>   shapes
> entering shops to buy kerosene, and the palms that
>   darken
> with the lines in my mother's hand . . .

or like this:

>   I pause to hear a racketing triumph of cicadas
> setting life's pitch, but to live at their pitch
> of joy is unendurable. Turn off
> that sound . . .

At a number of points I felt like turning off Walcott's sound. . . . Call it Whitmania or elephantiasis, but there's not much modulation. Verbally, the only thing that holds it all together is the ubiquitous word "like": "The floes crack like rifle fire. Then gulls glitter like flakes"; "But now blue spaces open / like gaps in the smoke"; . . . "The moon shines like a lost button"—an so on and on. A lot of Robert Lowell is kicking around in Walcott's unconscious. But surely one Lowell is enough, and *Midsummer* seems to me a mistaken enterprise. (p. 331)

> *William H. Pritchard, "Aboard the Poetry Omnibus," in* The Hudson Review, *Vol. XXXVII, No. 2, Summer, 1984, pp. 327-42.*

THE VIRGINIA QUARTERLY REVIEW

Reading . . . [*Midsummer*] is like walking through a gallery of works by Dutch and French masters—so vivid are the images, including the ones that refer to paintings—the "lemon-rind light in Vermeer," Watteau's "amber spray of trees feather-brushed with the dusk." . . . But it is the way Walcott blends landscape and language that points up his particular genius in this book. Graced with a lyrical voice that adapts in a gravely cadenced trot to the gorse and heather of England or sails without incident to reflect the brilliant water and clear skies of the Caribbean, Walcott is a master of synesthesia. He enables the reader to see movement, feel the flutter of leaves, and give over entirely to the excitement of touching something beyond scrutiny. A native of St. Lucia, Walcott grew up with classical poetry and island patois. The travels of Odysseus are never far from him; they hang like a rich undercurtain for his verbal tapestries. He lives now in both Trinidad and Boston; and while the sirens of the city that "sing" for him are those of ambulances and squad cars, the modern heart is caught and detained indefinitely by them. This, his seventh book, is the best. (pp. 90-1)

> *A review of "Midsummer," in* The Virginia Quarterly Review, *Vol. 60, No. 3 (Summer, 1984), pp. 90-1.*

TERRY EAGLETON

There are few more striking examples of literature's tendency to imitate criticism than the way in which, in the age of structuralism, poets seem recently to have begun modelling their inner and outer landscapes on language itself, writing of the syntax of shrubbery or the dark vowels of desire. Derek Walcott's new collection [*Midsummer*] is rife with such textual or semiotic metaphor: tadpoles wriggle like commas, snakes coil like ampersands, boulevards open like novels and leaves pile "like the dropped hitches of soldiers". The very concision of such metaphors is ironically self-undoing, concluding a spontaneous compact between Nature and writing at the very moment that they gesture sardonically to their own incurable literariness. Metaphor cannot mediate neutrally between mind and world, since, being language, it is already ineluctably on the side of mind. To write like Walcott of Caribbean canefields "set like stanzas" is to be wryly conscious of the rift between Third World agriculture and that other form of cultivation which is poetry. As a Trinidadian who deploys the language of the colonialist a good deal more superbly than most metropolitan speakers, Walcott never loses sight of the productive, disabling gap. To choose an idiom is to choose a politics. . . .

It is nothing as simple, however, as "spiritual exile". To curse your birthplace is the final evil, Walcott writes, and the easy, sensuous eloquence of these poems, written in Trinidad in a deep, empty summer, graces the parched details of the West Indian landscape even as the lawless imagination roams out to the more cosmopolitan circuits where the poet is also at home. A visit to Stratford during the Brixton riots, for example, which also sets poetry and politics in fiercely ironic tension. . . . Language never fits geography, Walcott reflects, and the imagination must therefore weave its own cosmopolitan correspondences, dismantling and reassembling places, playing off one native dialect against another. In the stasis of deep summer, the same seems true of history: the poems raid bits of the poet's past at random, in a calculated resistance to the imperialism of linear time: "my own prayer is to write / lines as mindless as the ocean's of linear time, / since time is the first province of Caesar's jurisdiction." In the culture of colonialism, history and geography are finely blended, so that to move a few hundred yards is to pass from one epoch to another. . . .

One problem for Walcott is how this painfully learned indifference to place and time ("summer is the same everywhere") is not to ape that erasure of local allegiances which belongs less to the cosmopolitan imagination than to the International Monetary Fund. There is a sense in which this is a risk which the poetry has to take, not least since the alternative—cultivating your own garden—is precisely the colonialist critic's fantasy of the "native" writer: "You were distressed by your habitat, you shall not find peace / till you and your origins reconcile; your jaw must droop / and your knuckles scrape the ground of your native place." Since Nature and writing never quite align—"Too rapid the lightning's shorthand . . . too slow the stones crawling towards language every night"—rootlessness is part of being at home, whether in Trinidad or Rome. To accept his licenses a writing at least momentarily emancipated from the burdens of historical responsibility and geographical guilt. . . . But this, of course, is a benediction of high summer; whether it can provide a complete strategy for survival is for this volume a deferred question.

> Terry Eagleton, "Plenty of Life," in The Times Literary Supplement, No. 4258, November 9, 1984, p. 1290.

PAUL BRESLIN

[*Midsummer*] continues Walcott's movement, since *The Star-Apple Kingdom,* toward a less assertively Caribbean, more "international" style. For the first time, one can read from cover to cover without encountering a single touch of West Indian dialect. Not that Walcott's preoccupation with his origins has disappeared: his by now familiar theme of divided allegiance, as a victim of European colonialism and heir of European culture, remains powerfully present. A number of poems take up the metaphor, common not only in Walcott's poetry but also in Seamus Heaney's, of landscape as an indigenous language persisting beneath the acquired colonial language. . . . Walcott seems less concerned with regional history, more preoccupied with such things as middle age, mortality, and poetry itself, than he used to be. Many of the poems are set outside the Caribbean, in Boston or even Rome; more tellingly, there are many poems in which setting is irrelevant.

In abandoning what he has done superbly and trying something else, Walcott inevitably risks a temporary unsettling of his style. At times, his increasingly cosmopolitan voice can sound

uncannily like that of Robert Lowell. . . . For the most part, though, Walcott's voice remains as distinctive as ever, and the occasional echoes of Lowell register as homage rather than unwitting imitation. In *Midsummer,* he has significantly extended his range, with poems that bear his unmistakable stylistic signature, yet modulate to a tone of meditative austerity seldom found in his earlier work, which tends to be more pyrotechnical, more immediately dazzling. The new book is not "better" than previous Walcott, but it is different and comparably excellent. (pp. 173-74)

> Paul Breslin, in a review of "Midsummer," in Poetry, Vol. CXLV, No. 3, December, 1984, pp. 173-74.

PUBLISHERS WEEKLY

In this hefty collection [*Collected Poems, 1948-1984*], Walcott draws on eight previous books of poems and includes in its entirety his long narrative poem *Another Life.* The variety of styles, settings and subject matter in the book is staggering. The mangroves and beaches of Walcott's native West Indies are juxtaposed with the snowy streets of New York's Greenwich Village, while the poems of *Midsummer* take us to Rome, Boston, Chicago. . . . In "A Far Cry from Africa," the poet asks himself how to choose between hatred of British rule and love of the English language. Certainly Walcott's mastery of the language goes unquestioned, whether he evokes the dialect of his homeland or writes lengthy, descriptive narratives or spare, bold lyrics. In these poems, the physical and psychological often merge, as in "The Swamp," where a pithy physical description produces a disturbing vision of chaos. Throughout this impressive volume, Walcott's language is fresh and original, his tone honest.

> A review of "Collected Poems, 1948-1984," in Publishers Weekly, Vol. 228, No. 22, November 29, 1985, p. 40.

MICHIKO KAKUTANI

"I had no nation now," Derek Walcott writes in *The Star-Apple Kingdom,* "but the imagination." It's a statement that succinctly sums up the issues that have preoccupied this eloquent poet throughout his careeer—a career handsomely celebrated, at midpoint, with this magisterial new collection [*Collected Poems, 1948-1984*]. Born in the West Indies to a family of English, African and Dutch descent, Mr. Walcott grew up a "divided child," caught on the margins of different cultures, and from this mixed paternity, he has forged the themes of his verse, as well as that rare thing—an authentic poetic voice.

In such early poems as "Origins" and "A Far Cry from Africa," Mr. Walcott writes of being torn "between the Greek and African pantheon," of having to "choose / Between this Africa and the English tongue I love," and in "Codicil" he describes himself as "Schizophrenic, wrenched by two styles." His search for an identity, both as an individual and as an artist, is amplified further in the lengthy, autobiographical poem *Another Life,* in which he dramatizes his dilemma as "a prodigy of the wrong age and colour," and in the songs of exile contained in *The Fortunate Traveller.*

To be a wanderer between cultures, a prodigal son unable to return home, he implies, is both a blessing and a curse: it means dislocation and cultural disinheritance, but it also means self-reliance and the freedom to invent oneself from "borrowed ancestors." . . .

From the Caribbean, Mr. Walcott has taken the musical rhythms of his verse, occasional samplings of patois and the brilliant tropic-colored imagery of the islands. From England, he has appropriated an old-fashioned love of eloquence, an Elizabethan richness of words and a penchant for complicated, formal rhymes. In fact, in a day when more and more poets have adopted a grudging, minimalist style, Mr. Walcott's verse remains dense and elaborate, filled with dazzling complexities of style. Shakespeare, Hopkins, Marvell, Keats, Auden and Eliot—these are just some of the influences one can discern in his work; Homer, Virgil, Dante and Ovid—some of the allusions.

When Mr. Walcott attempts to invoke the classics to talk about down-to-earth subjects—comparing, say, a prostitute to Helen of Troy—the result can seem artificial and strained, the highfalutin effusions of a willfully literary sensibility, mesmerized by words. . . .

Clearly, Mr. Walcott's at his most persuasive when he's writing about the West Indies, where he grew up and now lives half the year. When he departs the islands, to write about America, his writing tends to devolve into synthetic, if clever, pastiches of other writers, and even overt clichés. **"A Village Life,"** for instance, presents an altogether conventional impression of life in New York City, with people "running the rat race" and living amid "a cemetery of miniature skyscrapers."

It's Mr. Walcott's poems about Trinidad, Jamaica and other islands of the mind that possess a vehement sense of place and an immediacy of expression that makes us feel as though we were seeing something for the first time. In these poems, painterly descriptions of nature (a "moon left on all night among the leaves," leaves on which "the rain splintered like mercury," stars glowing like "fireflies caught in molasses") are combined with literary references and meditations on history and politics to create a compelling myth of the new world: Trinidad as an Eden, once despoiled by slave traders and imperialism, and now redeemed, recreated anew, like Prospero's secret island, in the poet's imagination.

The "leprosy of empire" has taken its toll here and there is terrible poverty and ugliness to be seen ("hell is / two hundred shacks on wooden stilts, one bushy path to the night-soil-pits"), but also the astonishing beauty of a green landscape, illuminated by the bright light of a southern sky.

In an early poem, Mr. Walcott writes of black children "singing 'Rule, Britannia, rule'/ As if they needed practice to play dead"; and in a later one, of friends who "spit on the government," but he refuses to sentimentalize either the collapse of Empire or the noisy prospects of revolution. At the same time, his portraits of the Caribbean remain free of the bitterness and anger that animate the work of the Trinidad-born writer V. S. Naipaul. Indeed there is an elegiac quality to Mr. Walcott's memorializing of the West Indies—as if he regarded its whole history as part of a grander scheme of time.

Michiko Kakutani, in a review of "Collected Poems,, 1948-1984," in The New York Times, *January 15, 1986, p. C19.*

JAMES DICKEY

Derek Walcott's virtues as a poet are extraordinary; both his abilities and his inherited luck-of-the-draw are great. First, he is spontaneous, headlong and inventive beyond the limits of most other poets now writing; these qualities should be obvious at once to anyone who encounters him [in **Collected Poems, 1948-1984**], even at random and for only a few lines. Moreover, at St. Lucia in the Lesser Antilles, between Martinique and St. Vincent, he was quite literally born into a major theme—which again, most poets of our time do not have available with such dramatic urgency as he. . . .

Revering his seamstress-laundress mother and a drunken painter whom the poet named Gregorias ("the black Greek"), Mr. Walcott was from the beginning a "divided child," but one filled with daring, receptivity and invention; and as a result **Another Life,** complete with the book-struck Antillean boy's reimagining of the *Iliad* in terms of his own world and its people, is surely one of the best long poems of our time, a self-sustaining work of real narrative strength, like none other. The mythologizing of island life is unforgettable, and if one were tasked to suggest another piece of writing equal to it in imaginative authority it would have to be Mr. Walcott's *Fortunate Traveller,* in which the poet takes his combustible sensibility out of the tropics and turns it loose in New England, Manhattan, London, Wales and other points that take instantaneous and creative flame from it. It is a good way to burn, wherever you are, wherever Mr. Walcott has been.

To cavil, however: one often has the feeling that words come to Mr. Walcott rather too easily, that, rather than refining to the essential (and with luck and rigor the permanent), he has the tendency to throw in more language and more observations than are needed simply because he has them available.

Straining for effect is the one quality Mr. Walcott's fertile imagination does not need. His endowment is so rich, his writing so effortless, so much a welling-up from the place of his birth and upbringing, from the discovery of other parts of the world and from his essential being, that even literary conventions themselves seem extraneous, and the forcing of metaphor unnecessary at best (and at less than that, ridiculous). Some of his lines can easily take their place among the worst poetry ever written, appearing quite casually, as though they had every right to be there—such as "needles of cicadas stitching the afternoon's shroud" or "and only the skirts of surf / waltz round the abandoned bandstand." The introduction of such commonplace pretentiousness is more jarringly felt in his work than in that of lesser poets, who can find no better way to say what they think they intend.

Reading Mr. Walcott, and

> The grip of winter tightening, its thinned
> volleys of blue-wing teal and mallard fly
> from the longbows of reeds bent by the wind,
> arrows of yearning for our different sky

one reflects on the harm that art may do to original talents, particularly when they feel driven to emulate and when they blindly obey the injunction that the imagination must, to be imagination, set up parallels. Birds fly, arrows also fly—do they not?—an illustration is made possible, an illusion has been created and insisted on. In the case of any poet it may be one of the illusions necessary to sustain life, imaginative life, but it may also be the kind that, habitually indulged in, results in a chronic inability to state, or see, things without allegory. In other words, the teal and mallard fly better without the "longbows of reeds," which have nothing to do with their flight, but are merely parts of a conventional poetic-device engine. If all his work did nothing but stoke this machine Mr. Walcott would simply be another predictable poet, this time with a

Caribbean background; his borrowed contraption would have him where it could throw him flat, in his case flat on the sand.

But fortunately, for him and for us, Mr. Walcott has the energy and the exuberant strength to break through his literary influences into a highly colored, pulsating realm of his own. One says of him, and eagerly, what William James said of the young Kipling: "He has such human entrails!" Though his major theme is exile, the situation of the cosmic castaway, he projects it with unprecedented vigor; one feels that his responsiveness and creativity would save him anywhere he went. In whatever he writes there is a sense of discovery, of openness, Henry James's "accessibility to experience," whether he is drunk in Boston, getting beaten up in New York, disembarking from a cattle boat in England or waiting for his lover and telling her, though she is not there, "I would undress you in the summer heat, / and laugh and dry your damp flesh if you came."

Immersed as he is in powerfully conflicting emotions about his heritage, the history of his region, and in his constant and vitally confused struggle to define his place on earth, he is also, in the best sense, a man immersed in words, not afraid of them, but excited and confirmed by what he can cause them to do. After a few poems the reader is convinced that Mr. Walcott could turn his attention on anything at all and make it live with a reality beyond its own; through his fearless language it becomes not only its acquired life, but the real one, the one that lasts.

James Dickey, "The Worlds of a Cosmic Castaway," in The New York Times Book Review, *February 2, 1986, p. 8.*

J. D. McCLATCHY

Derek Walcott spoke of having been born on an island, St. Lucia, with no ruins, no museum, no dates. "It was," he said, "a country without a history." The task he set himself as a young poet was not to discover his history but to create one, and to make it out of himself, out of his circumstances and his birthright. (p. 36)

From the start, his language and its literature were an available history, a means of composing the self. Actually, Walcott grew up with three languages—French Creole, English Creole, and English. Though he mostly reserved patois for his plays, he has incorporated it into his poems, and some readers have objected. Helen Vendler, for instance, has criticized Walcott's poems in dialect as damp matches, and insists that "mixed diction has yet to validate itself as a literary resource with aesthetic power."

I think Vendler is wrong, and so would readers of Dante and Burns, or of such contemporaries as Tony Harrison in England or Tom Paulin in Ireland. But the real point is that all poetry is written in dialect. As Craig Raine wryly notes, "most bad poetry is written in the dialect of the previous age." Our best poets have created their own. Though we use the term "style" because we more often read than listen to poems, dialect would just as likely describe an Ashbery or a Plath poem whose distinctive accents are unmistakable. Walcott too is a poet who wants to be both read and listened to. His style could be called English speech with a West Indian inflection; or, as he himself might describe it, he thinks in one language and moves in another. Even his "standard" poems have a peculiar loping quality to their lines, a slower rhythm than those of his peers.

Walcott was probably attracted to patois for two reasons. First, at the level of diction and metaphor, as he once told an interviewer, because "the things I saw around me were being named by people in a new language." Second, at the level of gesture and tone, because he associates patois with a native theatricalism: "My society loves rhetoric, performance, panache, melodrama, carnival, dressing up, playing roles. Thank God I was born in it, which made me love live and artificial theater." Walcott tends to use dialect precisely when he wants these extravagant effects; in fact, "artificial theater" is as good a name for it as any. At its worst, it is picturesque. At its best, it can be subversive, upsetting political and cultural habits. And some of his best sustained poems use it. **"The Schooner Flight"** is one. "Either I'm nobody, or I'm a nation," boasts the poem's hero, a mulatto sailor named Shabine, a Caribbean Ulysses. The mixed diction of Walcott's poems eloquently expresses his mixed state, without indulging in either ethnic chic or imperial drag. Here is his gift of tongues, which enables him to speak with intimacy and power.

The dialect he most often used in his apprentice work, however, was the florid grandiloquence of Yeats, Eliot, Dylan Thomas. The experience in, and of, his first few books is largely literary. This was an act both of homage and of assimilation. West Indian literature—its "postcard poetry" and limp tract-novels—simply didn't exist for him, and English literature was his birthright. "Either man is a myth of a piece of dirt," he once said. "Roman, Greek, African, all mine, veined in me, more alive than marble, bleeding and drying up. Literature reopens wounds more deeply than history does. It also releases the force of joy." But in such borrowed robes, his early work is, to use a phrase of his own devising, "fireless and average." Not until his book-length poem *Another Life* in 1973, when he turned his manner into his subject matter, did Walcott use literary history to tap a responding strength in himself.

The poem is the centerpiece of this **Collected Poems,** and remains central in Walcott's career. It is also one of the best long (there are over 4,000 lines) autobiographical poems in English, with the narrative sweep, the lavish layering of details, and the mythic resonance of a certain classic. His story is a simple and traditional one, the growth-of-the-poet's-mind, how "he fell in love with art, / and life began." Love and art are entwined initiations: at the same time he is learning from his painter-mentor Gregorias, he is falling in love with Anna. Because he turns to art as "another life," he turns too toward the body and toward the landscape. Walcott is a poet of vivid sensual and celebratory power. . . . He knows enough to be rueful: "The hand she held already had betrayed / them by its longing for describing her." The tropical landscape also becomes text. . . . His sense of vocation *is* his identity, and what we watch evolving is a personal story of nationalistic dimensions ("a man no more / but the fervour and intelligence/of a whole country"), as well as a major heroic myth with its traditional motifs. The infernal past in Walcott's version is the great fire that destroyed Castries, the capital of St. Lucia, in 1948, the year from which Walcott counts his poetic career. In *Another Life* he calls it his "ruined Ilion." As in Dante, the protagonist is instructed by a master-artist, and inspired by a beloved. And the traditional epic tasks—a reconciliation with the fathers and the founding of a new city—are taken up in a new way.

It is the example of a painter named Gregorias on which the young poet-hero models himself. (In reality, "Gregorias" was Harry Simmons, and his untimely suicide becomes the "stroke" that ends the poem on a troubled note.) In the mature work of the past decade, it is Robert Lowell who has been Walcott's model. One poem not included in this *Collected* is "R.T.S.L.," Walcott's elegy for Lowell, but his influence is everywhere apparent in Walcott's three most recent books, *The Star-Apple Kingdom* (1979), *The Fortunate Traveller* (1981), and *Midsummer* (1984). Like Lowell, Walcott's mode has in these books shifted from the mythological to the historical, from fictions to facts, and his voice has gotten more clipped and severe. There are times when the influence is almost too direct, as in "Old New England," where he paces off Lowell's own territory.... At other times the influence is more diffused, as in *Midsummer*'s diaristic sequence of poems, a format that controls the dynamics of fact and tone. (pp. 37-8)

[Walcott's] style now has a range and a grave radiance that transfigure the smallest detail. And though his poems are built up from details, they have challenged their own fluency by addressing the large intractable problems of modern history— exile, injustice, the lurid terrorisms of the mind, the ordinary treasons of the heart. If art remains his focus and refreshment, sometimes too exclusively, it is because he sees art as that place where the dilemmas of a life have been most urgently portrayed. And it is his warrant for transcendence. (p. 38)

> *J. D. McClatchy, "Divided Child," in* The New Republic, *Vol. 194, No. 12, March 24, 1986, pp. 36-8.*

PETER BALAKIAN

Derek Walcott's *Collected Poems: 1948-1984* is a large selected poems of over 500 pages and includes work from all of his books, beginning with *In a Green Night: Poems 1948-1960*, which was first published in England ... in 1962. Because 1948 marks the public beginning of Walcott's career (his first book, *25 Poems*, was published in that year), this new collection enables the reader to gain a sense of this major poet's growth and evolution. And, because all of his books prior to *Sea Grapes* (1976) are out of print, *Collected Poems* makes available the entirety of Walcott's book-length poem, *Another Life* (1973), and many other important poems from the first half of his career.

The poems from his early books, *In a Green Night, Selected Poems* (1964), and *The Castaway and Other Poems* (1965) reveal his mystic sense of place and a lush imagination which is always poised against a high eloquence. In an extraordinary early poem, "Origins," he is already able to create a language that can contain one of his major concerns—the creation myth of his native place. His ability to discover the sources of a hitherto unnamed place puts him in the company of the lyrical epic poets of the Western hemisphere, especially Whitman and Neruda. Walcott's Adamic ability to embody rhythmically and metaphorically the natural history of his world and transform it into culture-making language is what Emerson called Naming in the highest poetic fashion. "Origins" is a prologue to poems like "The Sea Is History," "Schooner *Flight,*" "The Star-Apple Kingdom," "Sainte Lucie," and his book-length epic, *Another Life*. In "Origins," as in these later poems, Walcott is able to find in the cosmogonic conditions of his landscape a protean identity as a man and an epic consciousness for his culture. The warm Caribbean waters become an amniotic bath for this poet whose memory encompasses, at once, phylogeny and ontogeny.... Out of the Proustian remembrances of his childhood and his deeper racial memory comes a force of imag-

ination in a surging rhythm that defines what he refers to as "the mind, among sea-wrack, see[ing] its mythopoetic coast."... (pp. 169-70)

The selections from *In a Green Night* (1962) show us Walcott's various formal virtuosities. His rhyming quatrains of iambic tetrameter in poems like "Pocomania" and "In a Green Night," or his sonnet sequence, "Tales of the Islands," reveal his ability to mine traditional forms of English poetry without ever compromising his passionate energy or his language's inner music. One senses that the vestiges of form are in the deeper structures of so many of Walcott's later freer poems. For example, the inner cohesion of the lyrical epic, *Another Life*, is in part created by the delicate balance between Walcott's eruptive imagination and the harnessing control of his tradition-bound intellect.

Other poems from the 1962 collection, such as "A Far Cry from Africa," "Ruins of a Great House," "Two Poems on the Passing of an Empire," show Walcott beginning to wrestle with the complex identity that will unfold in his later books— his irreconcilable and pluralistic cultural situation as a transplanted African in a colonial English society. Perhaps he sums up his life's dilemma when he cries out at the close of "A Far Cry from Africa":

> I who am poisoned with the blood of both,
> Where shall I turn, divided to the vein?
> I who have cursed
> The drunken officer of British rule, how choose
> Between this Africa and the English tongue I love?
> Betray them both, or give back what they give?
> How can I face such slaughter and be cool?
> How can I turn from Africa and live?

For his ability to embrace his Black West Indian identity and to accept, with the ingenuity of an artist, the language of his inherited culture accounts for much of the genius and richness of his idiom. Using the English tongue he loves does not preclude his moral outrage at the crimes that the Empire has committed against his people. He hears in the mansion of English culture a death-rattle in each room. In "Ruins of a Great House" he sees clearly "Hawkins, Walter Raleigh, Drake, / [as] Ancestral murderers and poets," and confesses that his "eyes burned from the ashen prose of Donne." Knowing his love affair with English literature, one senses the complexity of Walcott's mind.

For the most part the poems from *The Gulf* (1970) are more personal than the earlier work and bear the imprint of some of Lowell's tone and mood in *Life Studies* and *For the Union Dead*. Travelling between the West Indies and the States, Walcott has acquired a new sense of North-South tension. With his Juvenalian eye, he observes another empire in the midst of its internal conflicts and violence. In the title poem, a flight over Texas provokes his vision of America as "detached, divided states, whose slaughter / darkens each summer now, as one by one, / the smoke of bursting ghettos clouds the glass." In "Elegy," written on the night of Robert Kennedy's assassination, Walcott's sober view of America ends with his recasting of that famous American couple of Grant Wood's "American Gothic": they stand "like Calvin's saints, waspish, pragmatic, poor, / gripping the devil's pitchfork / stare[ing] rigidly towards the immortal wheat."

In *The Gulf* and *The Castaway and Other Poems* (1965), Walcott's luxuriant images and tropes have become so rooted in his nature—in his pathological relationship to the world—that sight and insight, sensory perception and metaphorical meaning merge. In "The Flock," a stunning poem that opens *The Castaway,* his reflection on the imagination and the creative process begins with an image of birds migrating south: "The grip of winter tightening, its thinned / volleys of blue-wing teal and mallard fly / from the longbows of reeds bent by the wind, / arrows of yearning for our different sky." Before the poem is over the birds have become part of the imagination's topography without ever losing their naturalistic authenticity—natural fact and metaphor remain one.

Another Life (1972), written between 1965 and 1972, is an extraordinary leap forward in the evolution of Walcott's work. He has, in this poem of four books and twenty-three sections, "sung," in the epic meaning of the word, a life's story into a mythic journey. Beginning the poem in the middle of his life's journey, he exclaims near the end of the poem, "a man lives half of life / the second half is memory." And the memory in this poem is that of a collective mind and an intimately personal one. The texture, color, tone of the poet's childhood on St. Lucia and his rites of initiation into manhood and art are matched by a language so rich and sensuous that one feels in it that rare balance between the personal life and the fully metaphorical meaning of that life. Consequently, the poem is balanced between its narrative elements—the people, places, and events that have shaped the poet's life (his mother's house, the local townsfolk who become his heroes, his soul-mate the drunken painter Gregorias, his discovery of his history, his metaphorical marriage)—and the lyrical transfigurations of those elements. The poem is at once a paean to the culture of his island and the history of the Caribbean and a dramatization of the morphology of the poet's mind. In his double culture and his divided self, he sees the music of language, the basis of metaphor, and the moral meaning of poetry. For all of the immensely cultured intellect in this poem (I cannot think of a poet who uses the history of Western painting as brilliantly as he does here), there is never anything effete or rarefied in the Stevensian sense. He has managed to do what a modern epic poet must do: encompass history, myth, culture, and the personal life with the realm of aesthetic vision. (pp. 170-72)

Sea Grapes (1976) is in certain obvious ways a quieter and more austere book. After the outpouring of the long poem, it is as if Walcott were forced to retreat in order to examine the troubles of his present life. Poems like "Sea Grapes," "Fist," "Winding Up," and "Love After Love" deal with the tensions between the passionate life of love and poetry and his responsibilities to his domestic life and his solitary self. Nevertheless, the one long poem, "Sainte Lucie," shows us that he is never too far from his tribal self. This five-part poem, which is a kind of psalm to his island; is a mixture of French Creole and even a Creole song, touches of a vernacular speech, and Walcott's inimitable eloquence. In a way the poem looks forward to the continuing epic impulse that defines *The Star-Apple Kingdom* (1979).

Coming to *The Star-Apple Kingdom* after the poems that have preceded it, one becomes aware not only of Walcott's genius but of his stature as a major poet. His ability to renew himself, to revitalize his imagination, to rediscover the myth of his life and his culture, places him among the greatest poets of our century—Yeats, Neruda, Rilke, Williams, Elytis, for example—poets who write out of their obsessions without repeating themselves. Two of his most powerful poems, "The Schooner *Flight*" and "The Star-Apple Kingdom," reveal Walcott's seemingly inexhaustible resources. In "The Schooner *Flight*,"

he unites beautifully a vernacular tradition with his high eloquence so that the reader believes that his persona, Shabine, is both a common man and a speaker of poetry. Shabine, who is trying to escape the woes of his life by fleeing his island as a castaway, is able to sustain a tone that is both autobiographical and mythic. "I'm just a red nigger who love the sea, / I had a sound colonial education, / I have Dutch, nigger, and English in me,/and either I'm nobody, or I'm a nation." He becomes a kind of underwater Isaiah whose vision encompasses his people's history. He sees what it was to be a "colonial nigger," and as the rhythms of the sea provoke Shabine's inner eye ("I had no nation . . . but the imagination"), he relives the Middle Passage, sees the corruption of the imperialist businessman and ministers, and as an angry prophet cries out: "I shall scatter your lives like a handful of sand, / I who have no weapon but poetry and / the lances of palms and the sea's shining shield!"

The language of the title poem, which is set in Jamaica, is able to hold in tension the pastoral munificence of the colonial world and its morally rotten underpinnings. . . . As he recounts the history of the Caribbean, he sees the islands as beads on the rosary—and through this ingenious sacramental conceit he leads us back into history (the Conquistadors, "the empires of tobacco, sugar, and bananas," "the footbath of dictators, Trujillo, Machado," "the alphabet soup of CIA, PNP, OPEC"). But, as so often happens in Walcott's poems, the journey into the darkness of history enables him to validate his identity as a West Indian Black man so that he can "sleep the sleep that wipes out history" and envision, once again, another version of Genesis—what becomes for him almost an imaginative ritual allowing him to reclaim his people's strength. He imagines his "history-orphaned islands" from Cuba to Tobago as turtles coupling, and finds the history of his race in one black woman who sees "the creak of light" that divided the world between "rich and poor," "North and South," "black and white," "between two Americas," as she hears the transcendent silence of the beginning in the "white, silent roar / of the old water wheel in the star-apple kingdom."

Since the ten poems in *The Star-Apple Kingdom* (only eight are reprinted here) comprise a sustained book-length poem, it would seem hard to surpass such an effort in a short period of time. However, *The Fortunate Traveler* (1981) is again a surge forward—another poetic renewal. The book shows Walcott's various selves: an exiled poet writing with ambivalent passion about the North, the Augustan satirist writing in a comic vernacular in "The Spoiler's Return," and the elegist enlarging his familiar theme of exile into a modern vision.

In one of the magnificent poems of the collection, "North and South," the poet confesses his identity as a "colonial upstart at the end of an empire, / a single, circling, homeless satellite." He becomes a modern exiled poet with a global vision of what empire means as he hears "its guttural death rattle in the shoal / of the legions' withdrawing roar, from the raj, / from the Reich, and see[s] the full moon again / like a white flag rising over Fort Charlotte." Like Ellison's Invisible Man or Wright's Bigger Thomas, Walcott finds himself a deracinated Black man wandering through the snowy surreal white streets of the urban North (Manhattan). He is enervated by how far he is from the "salt freshness" of his "raw" culture, and tired of the decadence of America and Europe with its "literature . . . an old couch stuffed with fleas." As the poem shifts to a winter Virginia landscape (amplifying the double meaning of North and South), the poet identifies himself as a slave, and as he imagines that a blue-eyed, red-haired aunt of his might be part

Jewish, he makes a pact with all the oppressed peoples of the world and would rather have "the privilege / to be yet another of the races they fear and hate / instead of one of the haters and the afraid."

He extends this human empathy even further in ["**The Fortunate Traveler**"]. His self-effacing and poignant use of the famous refrain of St. Paul in Corinthians, *"and have not charity,"* is the poem's hymning refrain; it serves as a benediction and an admonition. The poem is borne out of the poet's painful sense of the fissure between the need for a religious ethos and the absence of any moral order in our time. With his savage wit he recasts history so that "After Dachau" supplants "Anno Domini." As he contemplates the 10,000,000 people starving on the earth and the 765,000 skeletons in Somalia, that horseman of the apocalypse—famine—"the leather-helmed locust" stalks his imagination. The beast that Yeats saw "slouching toward Bethlehem" is now among us as Walcott looks at the twentieth century to see "The heart of darkness is the core of fire/in the white center of the holocaust." The poem reminds us of the meaning of *caritas* and the fact that all reform must begin in the human heart. For all the moral advocacy in this poem, Walcott never strays from the richness of his metaphor or collapses his poetic eloquence for the sake of a message. This is the kind of political poem that only a master can write.

The ***Collected Poems*** concludes with a selection of thirty poems from his most recent book, ***Midsummer*** (1984). The collection is comprised of fifty-four short lyric poems, which in their diary-like tone give the sense of a poet charting his preoccupations during the course of a year. Since the collection is a kind of book-length poem, I wish the entire book had been republished. In a certain sense, this is Walcott's most American book (although its personal tone is always ballasted by his sumptuous imagination). Here, he appears more at home in exile, a cosmopolitan poet absorbing the pulse of many cultures; he exclaims "this is the lot of all wanderers, this is their fate, / that the more they wander, the more the world grows wide." He becomes the poet as ethnographer and we see him in the pensiones, hotels, motels, and inns of Rome, New York, Warwickshire, Boston, and even having a nightmarish vision of nuclear winter in Chicago. He has also found a more personal idiom for writing about one of his passions—painting.

His lyrical ruminations on Watteau, Gauguin, Van Gogh, and Chardin show us how Walcott's rich imagination continues to be informed by texture, tone, gradation of color, hard and soft lines, and shifting perspectives—and how much the art of Gregorias's friend is a love-affair with the world. In concluding, it is fitting to mention Walcott's love poems. For they are as full-bodied, erotic, compassionate, personal and mythic at once, as any love poems written in English in this century. "**Bleeker Street, Summer**," "**Goats and Monkeys**," the epithalamion in *Another Life*, "**Egypt, Tobago**," "**Europa**," and the astounding poem about his still-born daughter, "**Early Pompeian**," are poems that embody another dimension of *caritas*.

It is difficult to think of a poet in our century who—without ever betraying his native sources—has so organically assimilated the evolution of English literature from the Renaissance to the present, who has absorbed the Classical and Judeo-Christian past, and who has mined the history of Western painting as Walcott has. Throughout his entire body of work he has managed to hold in balance his passionate moral concerns with the ideal of art. By his fifty-fifth year Derek Walcott has made his culture, history, and sociology into a myth for our age and into an epic song that has already taken its place in the history of Western literature. (pp. 174-77)

Peter Balakian, "The Poetry of Derek Walcott," in Poetry, *Vol. CXLVIII, No. 3, June, 1986, pp. 169-77.*

Arnold Wesker

1932-

English dramatist, short story writer, critic, and scriptwriter.

Wesker is best known for his plays *Chicken Soup with Barley* (1958), *Roots* (1959), and *I'm Talking about Jerusalem* (1960), which were published collectively as *The Wesker Trilogy* (1960). In his plays, Wesker combines personal experience, allegory, and humor to explore such themes as social and familial relationships, the work environment, disillusionment, and individual suffering. Often considered a playwright of ideas, Wesker emphasizes moral values in his dramatizations of social, political, and economic issues. While some critics have faulted Wesker for being overly didactic, others praise the authenticity of his characters' dialogue and his psychological insights into human conflict.

In his trilogy, Wesker examines the effects of political, social, and economic forces on the members and friends of a working-class Jewish family living in London between 1936 and 1959. In the first play of the trilogy, *Chicken Soup with Barley*, Wesker records the gradual disillusionment of the Kahn family with the socialist ideals they once ardently and optimistically embraced. Only the mother, Sarah, retains her beliefs. In *Roots*, Wesker further examines the lives of working-class people, setting this play in rural Norfolk County and focusing on the Bryant family and their daughter, Beatie. Although the Bryants are the principal characters in this work, Sarah Kahn's son, Ronnie, is represented through his socialist indoctrination of Beatie, his former girlfriend. The play ends in triumph for Beatie, as she discovers her own values and beliefs, but her success is muted, for her family persists in their static way of life. Many critics considered *I'm Talking about Jerusalem* to be somewhat anticlimactic in comparison to Beatie's self-revelations at the conclusion of *Roots*. In this play, Wesker returns to the Kahn family, as Ronnie's sister and her husband leave the city in search of an idyllic rural existence. Their dream fades when the husband is caught stealing from his employer and loses his job. As in *Chicken Soup with Barley,* only Sarah clings to her optimistic vision; like Beatie in *Roots,* Sarah's determination to retain her ideals is overshadowed by the pessimism of her family and, by extension, of society.

In *The Kitchen* (1959), Wesker's thematic concerns move away from family and societal relationships to an examination of the work environment. Set in the kitchen of a large restaurant, the play is loosely structured and moves at a frenzied pace, evoking the sounds and rhythms of an actual commercial kitchen. In this play, Wesker is documenting, according to Glenda Leeming, "the fate of the individual personality being shaped by the economic pressures of society." In *Chips with Everything* (1962), Wesker again focuses on society's repression of the individual. This play centers on a rebellious middle-class youth who joins the Royal Air Force yet resists his superiors' attempts to persuade him to follow his father and become a commissioned officer.

Wesker's plays of the 1970s display a shift in emphasis from the examination of the psychological effects of social issues on individuals to the exploration of the psychology of the individuals themselves. In *The Friends* (1970), Wesker is con-

cerned with how people attempt to cope with morality. Regarded as an important development in Wesker's career, *The Friends* demonstrates his concern with issues that can be remedied not only by bettering society but also through self-examination and adjustment. In *The Journalists* (1975), Wesker returns to the *cinéma vérité* style of *The Kitchen* by examining the working environment of a London Sunday newspaper. Just as *The Kitchen* is not about cooking, *The Journalists* is not specifically about journalism but involves the relationships between men, women, and their jobs. Termed a "stage documentary" by one critic, the play moves away from Wesker's concern with individual pain, instead using the characters as representatives of the broader social environment.

In *The Merchant* (1976), Wesker adapted Shakespeare's *Merchant of Venice* into an examination of European attitudes toward Jews and a critique of capitalism by depicting Shylock as a likable bibliophile and a close friend of Antonio. The infamous "pound of flesh" agreement between Shylock and Antonio in Shakespeare's play appears in Wesker's version as a mockery of Venetian law. Although some critics found the play overwritten, Harold Clurman observed that *The Merchant* achieves the effect of "casting doubts . . . on some of the assumptions of capitalist civilization." Wesker has also published the short story collections *Love Letters on Blue Paper* (1974), the title story of which he later adapted for television and the stage, and *Said the Old Man to the Young Man* (1978), as well as several books of criticism and nonfiction.

(See also *CLC,* Vols. 3, 5; *Contemporary Authors,* Vols. 1-4, rev. ed.; *Contemporary Authors New Revision Series,* Vol. 1; and *Dictionary of Literary Biography,* Vol. 13.)

BRENDAN GILL

In *The Merchant,* Arnold Wesker has written an ambitious and very intelligent play.... Not unflatteringly, one could say of it that it is *The Merchant of Venice* as young Shaw might have done it instead of young Shakespeare, with Shylock proving to be a garrulous, lovable bibliophile, Portia a Fabian "new" woman, incandescently certain of her ability to remake the world, Jessica a rebel against the suffocating conventions of family life, and Bassanio a young bounder down from Balliol, his eye already firmly fixed on the main chance. As for Antonio—who, after all, is the merchant for whom the play is named, and who therefore deserves to be taken seriously—in Mr. Wesker's version he is a far more important figure than he is in the original. He is also far more attractive. Instead of despising Shylock for his Jewishness and spitting on his gaberdine whenever a likely occasion presents itself, he dotes upon him. He and the old moneylender are, in a word, chums. One might wonder how on earth the play can survive the transformation of its two chief adversaries into an odd couple. It does so thanks to a witty Weskerian stratagem: the pound of flesh that Shylock is entitled to exact as a forfeit if Antonio should prove unable to repay his loan is a mere prank, mocking the law for requiring that there be *any* sort of formal bond in a transaction between friends. The mild horror of the play lies in the fact that it is affection, and not enmity, that threatens Antonio's life.

Like Tom Stoppard, Wesker enjoys turning received ideas upside down and giving them a good, hard pummelling. Provocative as this exercise was, a little of it went a long way. I admired the many ingenuities of *The Merchant,* but I tired at last of the amplitude with which Wesker spun them out and showed them off to us; he became not Wesker as Shaw-Shakespeare but Wesker as Jack Horner, about whom one always feels that a corner was certainly the ideal place for him. Wesker has written extended passages on, for example, Johann Gutenberg and Aldus Manutius; despite their eloquence, I would have been glad to take a ruthless blue pencil to them.

> *Brendan Gill, "The Odd Couple," in* The New Yorker, *Vol. LIII, No. 41, November 28, 1977, p. 81.*

HAROLD CLURMAN

There is no reason why Arnold Wesker, author of such pungent plays as *Roots, The Kitchen* and *Chips with Everything* should not have written *The Merchant....* It is his retelling of the material contained in *The Merchant of Venice.* Shakespeare himself recast several other plays of earlier times, and was influenced to the contrary by the play of his contemporary, Marlowe.

In the new *Merchant* Shylock, a prosperous broker in love with learning, is a close friend of Antonio, a gentleman weary of trading in goods he has not produced, carried in vessels in which he has never worked. The notorious bond made in connection with the loan of 3,000 ducats between them carries the familiar pound-of-flesh clause, because Shylock refuses to charge any interest on a loan to an intimate, and wishes to mock the law which dictates that no contract between a gentile and a Jew may be made in Venice without stating the terms of indemnity in case of default.

Portia declares herself a "new woman": she is the daughter of a wastrel scion of the aristocracy, and is herself in every way an enlightened person. She does not disguise herself as a lawyer but comes to the Shylock-Antonio trial as a possibly helpful observer and friend to Jessica, Shylock's pleasure-loving daughter, impatient with her father's cultural fetishism. Portia's intelligence sees through the legal nonsense of the disputed contract. Jessica, under Portia's guidance, will not marry the fatuous Lorenzo; Shylock, disheartened by the base prejudice and cruelty of the young Venetian gentry, sets out for Jerusalem, while Antonio reviles the hypocritical venality of the entire society.

The dramatic scheme has provocative possibilities. There are a few witty turns of the screw: at one point, for instance, Wesker introduces Shakespeare's climactic speech, "Hath not a Jew eyes? hath not a Jew hands?" and so on. It is not assigned to Shylock but to the sardonically anti-Semitic Lorenzo, a harangue Shylock scornfully rejects because Jewishness requires no defense or apologetics.

Everyone speechifies at such length that one is inclined to think "less is more," even where there is validity in content and dignity in language. There were moments, particularly in the second act, when I found it difficult to follow what was being said, not because of the excess verbiage and a monotony of rhetoric but because of the lack of clear dramatic relevance. Shylock, for instance, in an elocutionary tour de force, delivers a capsule history of Europe's development from the fall of the Roman Empire to the establishment of the Italian city-states. In this erudite outpouring he does not fail to speak of the signal contributions of Cassiodorous (487-583) who hid in a monastery the classics of pagan culture that were later disseminated through Gutenberg's invention of the printing press. Is Shylock, one wonders, simply evincing once again his enthusiasm for the glories of civilization or is he only shaming the obtuse Christians on stage (also the folk out front) for their ignorance?

We understand and approve the author's intention. He is casting doubts—without blatant polemics—on some of the assumptions of capitalist civilization and doing what his Shylock abhors having done: setting us right on Jewry. In this respect, with the New York theatre public, he may be crashing through open doors.

Yet all the above demurs may be thought wide of the mark. We must allow the author's choice of theme or thesis, even in the studied stylization of its presentation. The essential shortcoming of the new *Merchant* is that as a whole it does not come alive with any but a "mental" impact.

> *Harold Clurman, in a review of "The Merchant," in* The Nation, *Vol. 225, No. 19, December 3, 1977, p. 606.*

JOHN SIMON

The Merchant [is] the worthy Arnold Wesker's response to *The Merchant of Venice.* It seems that Wesker was trying to direct a production of Shakespeare's play in a manner that would make Shylock into a sympathetic character, but found this unfeasible, whereupon he sat down and wrote his own version of the play. . . . The lesson for playwrights, who declare that Shakespeare himself cribbed from all over: literature is like crime—the greater man can steal from the lesser with impunity, but try the reverse and you come to grief.

The Merchant, though not without a certain intelligence behind it, is clearly a polemic, and should have been written as an essay. What we got was a combination of fairly low ghetto comedy mixed with philosophizing full of historic hindsight (this sort of thing is pitifully easy—"No, my dear Columbus, you will never reach Cathay, but what you might discover will be just as good, if not better"; "I know that man can fly, even if he has to be born as two brother souls to discover the secret; if I'm wrong, let my name not be Leonardo da Vinci!") and with bits of Shakespeare sometimes put deliberately into the wrong mouth. Alas, what crept into our ears, as we tried to sleep like moonlight on a bank in Belmont, was the sound, not of music, but of bubbling chicken soup with barley.

John Simon, in a review of "The Merchant," in The Hudson Review, *Vol. XXXI, No. 1, Spring, 1978, p. 154.*

PETER ACKROYD

Pathos—or, more precisely, the gift for conflating sentimentality and reality . . . plays a formidable role in Arnold Wesker's writing. Life is too much with us: enough is enough. The three stories which comprise *Said the Old Man to the Young Man* convey something of this in a flat, but not ungainly, prose which never seems to mean more than it says. The details of contemporary life are skilfully presented but behind them melancholy, brooding, sits. **"The Man Who Would Never Write Like Balzac"** is a bitter account of a young writer whose minimal talents are in inverse proportion to his ambitions. . . . ["**Said the Old Man to the Young Man**"] describes the impasse when two generations of one family confront each other for the first time. **"The Visit"** is a more ambitious and argumentative study of two families who are united only by their unhappiness: one weekend together is enough to raise all of those devils which domestic rituals are supposed to exorcise.

Wesker's book is full of frustration, futility and failure. But on the occasions when he breaks through the pathos, with a sense of human potential and achievement, the book becomes curiously moving and evocative without losing any of its realistic veneer.

Peter Ackroyd, "A Crock of Irish Mist," in The Sunday Times, *London, May 14, 1978, p. 41.*

JACKY GILLOTT

Only three stories appear in Arnold Wesker's collection [*Said the Old Man to the Young Man*]. One about a young man with a name so grand he feels it should be added to the list of literature's other grand names, but he lacks the talent to addend it: and knows he does. One about an unappealingly anti-Socialist young man who suffers the stay of his deaf and tiresome great-uncle, an unhearing upholder of Jewish tradition. And one called **"The Visit"** in which four old friends gather for a country weekend and ponder the fallen aspirations of their lives. All three stories are about facing up to the facts of oneself rather than outdated illusion and all have potentially interesting

moments of confrontation but all, equally, are dragged down by a weight of dialogue that belongs to earnest adolescence.

Jacky Gillott, in a review of "Said the Old Man to the Young Man," in The Times, *London, June 1, 1978, p. 9.*

GLENDA LEEMING

At first sight, the plays by Arnold Wesker that appeared in the 1970s are not radically different from those that made his name in the previous dozen years. For if the plays of the late 1950s and 1960s fall mainly into two groups—the social and family relationships plots of the trilogy; and the work-oriented worlds of *The Kitchen, Chips With Everything* and *Their Very Own and Golden City*—then after 1970 the same two broad areas of interest reappear. *The Old Ones* (1972) and *The Wedding Feast* (1977) return to the trilogy's East End or Norfolk settings respectively, and *The Journalists* (1974) and *The Merchant* (1978), as the titles suggest, pursue further the fate of the individual personality being shaped by the economic pressures of society.

But beneath this recognizable consistency there is change; and what perhaps has changed is the emphasis. To say, as Wesker does, that *The Friends* in 1970 was an attempt to confront the idea of death, and 'Not only death, but a sense of one's mistakes' indicates broadly what could be called the interiorizing of his themes. Of course, in the earlier plays social pressures are also focused through their psychological effect on Ronnie, Beatie, the Simmonds and others; but in *The Friends* and *The Merchant,* particularly, the psychology of the characters, aware and conscious of their sufferings, becomes in itself the arena of the drama. The comedies of this period, *The Old Ones* and *The Wedding Feast,* are slighter in ambition and, though their corrective, satiric purpose is evident, the brushstrokes of this genre are comparatively simple; they have lost the complexity for which the more leisurely development of, say, the trilogy allows scope. These two comedies, then, stand apart from the mainstream of Wesker's less formally comic writing; a more recognizable example of continuity appears in *The Journalists,* which turns to the working life of a group of Sunday newspaper journalists, in a detailed reconstruction reminiscent of Wesker's first play, *The Kitchen.*

It is the different approach to the subject matter, then, rather than its appearance after some years' silence at the turn of a decade, that qualifies *The Friends* as a watershed in Wesker's career. The 'friends' of the title *are* friends—not the extended family of the trilogy, nor the chance collection of workmates of *The Kitchen.* One might say that *The Friends* in fact is less a watershed than a confluence of usually divergent elements in Wesker's work—his growing concern with 'private pain', and his interest in juxtaposing a number of different characters. The relationships of the characters have a new importance, because each is seen as aware of his own sufferings as part of the common predicament. . . . [Now] in their late thirties, they are losing both youthful arrogance and their sense of endlessly available time: and they are the more pressingly aware of their mortality because Esther, the dominant personality of the six, is dying of leukemia there in the house where they have gathered. . . .

So, where the causes of despair and disillusion in *Chips, Golden City* and the trilogy might be removed by human endeavour and a better state of society, the inevitability of death and its impact on the characters cannot be explained away. This is private pain at its most intense, and Roland, Esther's lover, is most affected by sheer animal terror of death—he becomes speechless, literally dumb with fear. Manfred, her brother, is stricken with a despair that reflects on the rest of his life: ageing and the approach of death take away the flavour from all endeavour. Similarly this realization of death illuminates for all the friends the uncertainties and insufficiencies of their achievement so far. . . . Where Ronnie Kahn or even Pip in *Chips* had been defeated by something outside themselves that has affected their character—the behavior of other people, the temptations of the system as it exists—here the friends are faced with one of the insoluble problems of being alive at all. The only alleviation of their anguish must be an adjustment within themselves. (pp. 65-7)

The continuous evolution of the dramatic movement through alterations in tone and mood—rather than through decisive twists of plot—formally corresponds to the subject matter: *how the friends' personalities colour their views* in the substance of the play, which is not concerned with external circumstances, confrontation with outside characters, exposition as such. One can find a similarly free-flowing structure, based on mood, as far back as *Roots,* where there are several sequences of busy or meditative passages reflecting the unfolding of Beatie's character, but a chronologically nearer correspondence can be found in *The Four Seasons,* which not only develops in a series of mood movements, as does *The Friends,* but is an earlier attempt to dramatize private pain. (pp. 67-8)

It is interesting to compare with *The Friends* and *The Four Seasons* the short play *Love Letters on Blue Paper,* although perhaps it should not be discussed on the same terms as other plays, having been written originally as a short story and then adapted for television (later it was adapted for the stage and produced at the National Theatre). It traces the slow sinking into death—again of leukemia—of Victor Marsden, his conversation with a younger friend, Maurice, expressing his memories and fears. These, in turn, are counterpointed by the letters that his outwardly dour, practical wife has started writing to him. As Victor tries to work out, explicitly and through discussion, some suitable way of meeting his death, Sonia, in letters which recall moments of their life together—cherished, trivial or puzzling—is obliquely doing for him what Simone was seeking to do for the friends: affirming the value that his life has had, so that he has a sense of achievement, not of waste, to support his final weeks. The relationship between Victor's diminished physical world and the world outside, including the experiences of the past, is convincing and unforced; there is no oppressive universalizing. Here Wesker is expressing his concern with private pain in its simplest and most economical form (the brevity of a short story and the conciseness required for a television play perhaps promoting this economy of effect). It seems that this theme could hardly be pared down further without losing the balance of interior and exterior worlds.

After the step forward in *The Friends, The Old Ones* is something of a step backwards in its nostalgic return to the area of *Chicken Soup.* In subject matter at least, there is such a strong continuity with Wesker's early work that the play might well be considered as making the trilogy into a quartet. (pp. 68-9)

On the other hand this feeling may be unfair or inappropriate to the kind of play that *The Old Ones* is: it is a comedy, where the similar trilogy plays, for all their incidental humour, are not. The comic form requires that questions raised should mostly be resolved, and *The Old Ones* can reasonably be seen as a

comedy with a sting in its tail, rather than a drama diluted with too much comedy.

The same distinction can be applied to *The Wedding Feast,* which followed the intervening play, *The Journalists. The Wedding Feast* derives by way of an unproduced filmscript from an adaptation of Dostoevsky's story "An Unpleasant Predicament." But Wesker's play is set in Norfolk, and his central character is Louis Litvanov, a paternalistic, socially conscious, rich Jewish shoe manufacturer. Louis's earnest wish to behave well and be on terms of equality with his employees (while retaining his profits, power and control as their employer) inspires him to arrive unannounced at Knocker White's wedding reception. Here his ambivalent social expectations produce alternating frozen embarrassment and excessive familiarity from the disoriented wedding guests, so that the feast (unlike the conclusion of *The Old Ones*) is very far from uniting the participants in harmony, let alone social unity. (p. 71)

Again, then, there is a sting in the tail of the play, but again the comic effect is different from the sting of a straight drama. (p. 71)

The Wedding Feast is a comedy with a fair amount of slapstick—Louis falls into the blancmange twice, and the newly-married couple's wedding couch collapses under them—and although the party includes a menacing Pinteresque sequence in the 'shoe game', in which the blindfolded Louis is beaten with shoes, at first in fun, then with increasing hostility, nonetheless the moments of discouragement and conflict rise only to submerge in the flow of comic incident. The implications and complications are not pressed further. No pause for a 'tableau of misery' here. So, while *The Wedding Feast* succeeds within its own terms as a socially satiric comedy, it is unable, because of the limitations of the comic form, to develop the introspective subject matter that Wesker had elaborated in *The Friends.*

This is not the case in *The Journalists,* which, for all the number of jokes and anecdotes swapped by the characters during the action, is not to be seen as a comedy. Moreover, for all its return to the work environment of *The Kitchen* or *Chips, The Journalists* is not concerned with the 'effects of work' theme in quite the same way as the earlier plays. As Wesker says in his introduction to the text: *The Kitchen* is not about cooking, it's about man and his relationship to work. *The Journalists* is not about journalism, it is about the poisonous human need to cut better men down to our size, from which we all suffer in varying degrees. But because this poisonous human need is here embodied in the journalistic profession, *The Journalists* is also a work-relationship play as the effects on the characters show. Amost all the action takes place in the offices of the fictional *Sunday Paper,* and the physical environment is stressed with all its multiplicity of different pressures and influences. The offices are represented on stage by small, possibly raised, areas around the stage, and the scenes, which are on average shorter than in Wesker's other plays, shift from area to area, the action being plotted to move the audience's attention across the widest possible area of the stage. At the same time as a scene is taking place in one area, the characters in all the other offices are to continue unobtrusively busy, so that individuals are always seen in relation to the rest of the newspaper team.

From this point of view it becomes clear that the characters are, as one would expect, affected by their daily work, some more than others: Tamara's coverage of wars and massacres for foreign news assignments is pushing her to the verge of a nervous breakdown, a photographer is becoming more and more obsessed with the gruesome scenes he is required, and increasingly prefers, to photograph. More subtly, the dominant character Mary Mortimer, a star columnist, has a professionally destructive approach to topics and people, which is at odds with her own liberal and tolerant, even idealistic, beliefs. Mary's obsession is with cutting people down to size, puncturing pretences; her grown-up children say she has elevated the gutter question 'who does he think he is?' to a respected art form. (p. 72)

Mary's indiscriminately suspicious attitude, her refusal to be impressed, is obviously destructive of the exchange of ideas between people, but it is also one manifestation of the general levelling off of the flow of news as it is received and absorbed by the journalists. Tamara's reactions to her horrific material is an exception; the contrast is the more striking given everyone else's matter-of-fact acceptance of these horrors—this callousness being a more common effect of this particular work situation. When a massacre of intellectuals in Bangladesh proves the final straw for her strained nerves, her colleague Gordon admonishes, 'For Christ's sake, you're a journalist. Is this any worse than your reports on the Eichman trial?' and adds briskly 'Don't be a bloody fool. Men have been slaughtering their thinkers for centuries.' . . . And this tends to be the effect on the reader too. (p. 73)

The absolute need for a system of values but the confusion, the sense of being overwhelmed by the outside world, when no such system of values is in operation, is, in fact, a recurrent theme of Wesker's plays. What Cynthia says about the information that comes through journalistic channels presents the same problem that Manfred in *The Friends* expresses: '. . . each fresh discovery of a fact or an idea doesn't replace, it undermines the last; it's got no measurement by which to judge itself, no perspective by which to evaluate its truth or its worth.' . . . and to go back further, this is the same uncertainty that means Beatie Bryant can't answer the question . . . 'What make that [song] third rate, and them frilly bits of opera and concert first rate?' . . . In *The Journalists* there is an inevitable levelling of values by the methods and demands of presentation, and 'lilliputianizing' is a manifestation of this virtual denial of values.

However, though *The Journalists* pursues its theme to considerable depth and does not simplify the conflicting points of view involved, it is true that the plot moves in the public rather than the private sphere (deliberately so, it seems, as Wesker changed the title to the plural from a singular which would have given individual importance to Mary Mortimer) and, as such, is to be grouped with *Chips with Everything* and *Their Very Own And Golden City,* which it resembles in its episodic form as well as in subject and seriousness, rather than with *The Friends.*

However, Wesker's later play, *The Merchant* (1978), both fully explores its chosen issues and places strong emphasis on the interior worlds of its main characters. Here, as in *The Kitchen,* the pressures of society curtail the individual's scope for development and distort human relationships. Based, as the title suggests, on Shakespeare's *The Merchant of Venice,* the play retains most of the familiar names from Shakespeare, but the characters have rather different personalities and this, in turn, contributes to different themes and emphases. Beginning from the premise that, in the trial scene, when Shylock loses his claim to a pound of Antonio's flesh, 'the kind of Jew I know would stand up and say, 'Thank God', Wesker extends this idea further and makes Shylock and Antonio close friends, so that the course of the play shows the social pressures that turn a joke into near murder. Shakespeare's Shylock is motivated by racial hatred in requiring the pound of flesh from Antonio if his debt is unpaid: Wesker's Shylock makes the same condition as an irritable joke against the anti-semitic laws of Venice that insist on a bond—ridiculous laws, he considers, forcing the formality of a legal contract between friends, when he would prefer to *give* the money or, if Antonio will not permit that, at least to lend without interest.

The point made here is the central one of the play: no free trust, or any other relationship, is allowed between the Jews and Gentiles in Renaissance Venice, because the fragility of mutual tolerance, like the fragility of verbal promises in business, is undermined by anti-semitic theory—the Jews deserve no trust, they are exempt from the common duties of humanity. Only the written Venetian laws, then, however irksome, protect the Jews from self-righteous exploitation. Therefore, inexorably, when the debt is not paid, the bond *must* be fulfilled—any waiving and consequent weakening of the law might be used next time as a precedent against the Jews. Shylock has involved himself not as an individual, a friend, but as 'the Jew', the representative of this race. After the trial, when Wesker's Portia intervenes as Shakespeare's does (and Wesker's Shylock *does* cry 'Thank God!'), the court takes the opportunity to confiscate Shylock's goods, including his precious books, and he, embittered and impoverished, banishes himself to Jerusalem. Antonio, who had counted his friendship as the blessing of his life, finds that blessing withdrawn. A brave relationship ends in defeat; it is not unlike the conclusion of E. M. Forster's *A Passage to India* where the Englishman and the Indian discuss friendship: 'Why can't we be friends now? . . . It's what I want. It's what you want' but the circumstances, the surroundings even of inanimate nature, the temples, the birds, the countryside, 'said in their hundred voices, 'No, not yet,' and the sky said, 'No, not here.' For Wesker, characteristically, the responsibility is not mystically placed on the alien landscape, but on the men who make up a divisive society, of Venice or elsewhere.

Again, the continuity of *The Merchant* with the previous half dozen plays appears in other characteristic themes: Shylock himself draws together the concerns of several earlier characters; his contempt—'I am sometimes horrified by the passion of my contempt for men' . . .—mirrors Manfred's contempt for the Englishman, but his naîve enthusiasm is like Louis Litvanov's, and he unites the complementary sides of the brothers in *The Old Ones,* manic Manny and gloomy Boomy, concluding his 'contempt' speech with the words 'Take those books, one by one, place on one side those which record man's terrible deeds, and on the other their magnificence. Do it! Deed for deed! Healing beside slaughter, building beside destruction, truth beside lie. Do it! Do it!' . . . And Shylock is a strongly enough drawn character to sustain the weight of these Weskerian complexities, and carries the momentum of the play by his driving energy.

Less convincing is the character of Portia, who declares herself the 'new woman' who can 'spin, weave, sew,' and reads 'Plato and Aristotle, Ovid and Catullus, all in the original!' and moreover, 'conversed with liberal minds on the nature of the soul, the efficacy of religious freedom, the very existence of God!' . . . She is not, however, given much opportunity to live up to this awesome catalogue within the play. In short, she is perfect, and has little to do but comment on the imperfections of others until it is time for her to intervene at the climax of the trial scene. It seems that Portia's experience should parallel Shylock's, since she also has to suffer the attentions of fools—particularly her complacent and opportunist suitor Bassanio—while, thematically, her surviving confidence at the end ('Bassanio will come to know his place, accept it, or leave it') . . . is a positive balance to Shylock's defeated exile. This theme is not, however, fleshed out dramatically, and when Portia finally admits to Antonio that 'something in me has died struggling to grow up' . . . (though we have noticed her critical reactions to Bassanio) the inward development of this disillusion has to be taken on trust.

Shylock's daughter Jessica, on the other hand, is a fully realized major character. Having given Shylock a sympathetic personality, Wesker has to re-motivate Jessica's elopement with a gentile, which in Shakespeare's play was an understandable escape from a miserly and obviously repulsive, if affectionate, tyrant. The father-daughter love-hate relationship admirably supplies this motivation, in that Shylock's very pride and love make him, too, an affectionate tyrant, here a sympathetic trait but intolerable to the similarly proud and self-willed Jessica.

The Merchant, then, has the plot mechanics of elopement, courtship, and trial scene inherited from Shakespeare's play, which means that there is far more classic, eventful, plot development than in any other Wesker play. But for all this *The Merchant,* just as much as *The Friends,* is mainly concerned with the developing awareness of the characters. Antonio, Jessica, Shylock himself, are unsuccessfully trying to force their ideas upon resisting circumstances, and learning and suffering as a result. Shylock is crushed by what he knew, intellectually, already, but would not accept emotionally; Jessica finds that her romance has been mere romancing; and Antonio endures, lonely, picking up the pieces of Shylock's catastrophe. Compared with them Beatie Bryant, whose character is also examined in depth, and who learns from experience, is for most of her appearance bewildered and not really conscious of the issues confronting her. Shylock, Antonio, Jessica and even Portia, on the other hand, are fully aware of what is involved in their defiance of circumstances, though they also make mistakes. Antonio looks back with regret on the life he has been part of: 'Those books. Look at them. How they remind me what I am, what I've done. Nothing! A merchant!'. . . . (It could be Manfred or Tessa speaking.) And when Shylock's exuberance breaks out in his long set-piece speech on 'the scheme of things' and the immorality of knowledge, he is still aware of the narrow-mindedness of Renaissance man, as he reaches for his compulsory and humiliating yellow hat, symbol of other, greater persecutions; he 'shrugs sadly, as though the hat is evidence to refute all he's said. And yet . . . he defiantly places it on his head . . .'. . . . Both Shylock and Antonio taste the full bitterness of the situation when Antonio's ships are lost and the joke bond becomes deadly earnest. (pp. 73-6)

Five plays in some ten years is a reasonable rate of production, roughly that of Wesker's contemporaries among the 1950s 'New Wave' dramatists, Osborne, Pinter, and Arden. Again, like his contemporaries, Wesker's later plays have had mixed theatrical success, though the hazards of theatrical production and audience reaction are no real guide to the value of the works. In the event, the comedies were the best received, but it is the other plays—*The Friends, The Journalists, The Merchant*—that show a consistent advance in carrying themes familiar from the previous decade, themes of disillusion, the need for values, the interrelation of character and work, into situations where

the conditions are more complex and the characters more articulate and aware. The characters in *The Friends* and *The Merchant* are self-analytic and intelligently speculative—as indeed they are in *The Journalists,* though the nature of that play precludes any full-length study of a single individual. Thus, after the digression of *The Four Seasons,* which explores private pain for its own sake in something of a vacuum, we find Wesker including the dimension of individual suffering, not for the first time (for it has provided the crisis point of all the earlier plays) but as a far more weighty and influential element in the 'pattern' that his characters are trying to make of their lives. (p. 77)

Glenda Leeming, "Articulacy and Awareness: The Modulation of Familiar Themes in Wesker's Plays of the 70s," in Contemporary English Drama, *edited by C. W. E. Bigsby, Edward Arnold, 1981, pp. 65-77.*

JOHN RUSSELL TAYLOR

The reappearance of Arnold Wesker after ten years' absence from the London stage (though not of course from drama) with *Caritas* . . . made me think again about social subject-matter in the theatre and what had happened to it. And realize that if one looks around there is really quite a lot of it about. Not so much, any more, in Wesker—or so it would seem from this new play. It is in many ways unfair that it should have so much weight laid on it because of the long gap since we last saw a new Wesker play in London, since it is only short (about an hour and a half) and would not seem in any way exceptional if we had meanwhile been seeing the four major plays by Wesker which have been done in Scandinavia and elsewhere. I do not, truth to tell, think that *Caritas* is up to much: Wesker never seems quite to decide what he wants to say by recounting the story (or his simplified version of the story leaving out the most interesting bits) of a fourteenth-century Norfolk anchoress Christine Carpenter. Something about prisons we make for ourselves, I suppose, but the case seems so extravagantly special. And not too interesting either. Christine has the urge to sainthood, but is maybe too bedazzled by the image to take full stock of the reality. By the time she realizes fully what it is to be walled up for the rest of her life, without any visionary gleam to illuminate her cell, it is too late: she has made her vow, and must abide by it. Meanwhile odd messengers rush on with thumbnail sketches of the Peasants' Revolt, and then for the last half-hour the set swivels, putting us inside the cell with Christine, while she goes through phases of hope and despair and self-deception and grinding comprehension of the truth. A big chance for an actress, . . . but to little ultimate effect, since the long monologue does not go anywhere or build to anything, and might just as easily be cut off after two minutes or run on for two hours.

John Russell Taylor, in a review of "Caritas," in Drama, *No. 143, Spring, 1982, p. 38.*

SEAN FRENCH

Faced with the united opposition of audiences, critics, directors and actors, most playwrights would seek an easier form of employment, but Arnold Wesker is made of sterner stuff. For the most part [*Distinctions*] is a symposium written in honour of Arnold Wesker and his works with the unusual feature of being entirely written by Wesker himself. If he's anything, Wesker is now a poet of failure, and his accounts of the time when the Royal Shakespeare Company actors revolted and refused to stage his play *The Journalists* or when Zero Mostel collapsed and died on the day before the Broadway opening of Wesker's *The Merchant* (in which he was going to star) have a gloomy fascination. Some of his criticisms against critics are valid; but what would he replace them with? For the rest—sterile debates about the responsibility of art and the artist, naive, self-serving polemics—a long, weary read.

Sean French, "The Perils of Paul," in The Sunday Times, *London, June 16, 1985, p. 45.*

J. K. L. WALKER

Arnold Wesker's *Chicken Soup with Barley* sent a thrill through my generation when we saw it at the Royal Court in 1958.

The loquacity and pugnaciousness that lit up *Chicken Soup with Barley* permeate *Distinctions,* a collection of Arnold Wesker's miscellaneous journalism, notebook entries, interviews and lectures covering the period 1960-83. Addressing a writers' conference in Finland in 1971, Wesker observed that "Self-confession is rarely honoured. Mostly it is abused." *Distinctions* contains a great deal of self-confession: self-analysis, self-revelation, self-justification in the face of critical indifference. One theme which recurs throughout this collection (although Wesker, understandably, claims to be weary of it) is the faltering in his reputation after the success of the early plays—*The Kitchen,* the Trilogy, *Chips with Everything.* In a long interview he gave to *Theatre Quarterly* in 1977 he comments wryly on the struggle to get his later work staged "when at the same time there's an educational system using my plays as required reading". Both here and elsewhere in the book Wesker makes out a strong case for the later plays, from *Their Very Own and Golden City,* first staged . . . in 1965, to *Caritas,* produced . . . in 1981. His reputation for using the stage as pulpit, he argues, fails to take account of the many other elements, "lyrical, absurd, musical, farcical", in his work.

Critics, of course, have given Wesker a bad time, and *Distinctions* assembles a number of stinging and forcefully argued rejoinders. Journalism's self-appointed censors, Wesker complains, can negate months or years of work by playwright, director and actors by depriving them of a paying audience. . . .

The powerful, if sometimes ingenuous, special pleading which makes the "Critics" section of the book such lively reading is evident throughout. Wesker is hard-hitting and fast on his feet when it comes to defending his work, his reputation and his ideas. This combativeness in defence of his created world may be not unconnected with its close association with that of Wesker's own experience, for, as he notes as early as 1960 on completion of the Trilogy, all his writings are "attempts to continue more lucidly arguments I had with my family, my friends and the people with whom I worked". In these pieces there is a sense that he is trying to bludgeon the reader into loving his plays and characters *ex post facto.*

Wesker's position as a spokesman of the Left is also interestingly documented, in particular his retreat from dogma to what he now, it appears rightly, sees as the humanist core of his idealism. "There does exist a body of humanist thought, a roll call of rational, sound, sane actions." An increasing concern with political liberty finds an analogue in a discussion of the nature of "the free spirit", which appears in an essay entitled **"The Two Roots of Judaism"** (1982). The free spirit characterizes a certain kind of Jewishness, Wesker claims; it pervades his own work and is embodied in his recreation of Shylock in *The Merchant.* Art, which contains the dual elements of journalism and poetry, he sees as echoing the dual nature of Jewishness.

Distinctions is crammed with the intelligent, vigorously argued views of a writer who knows what he has set out to achieve and believes, despite the chorus of faint praise over the past twenty years, that he has largely achieved it. The common critical view that plays such as *The Friends, The Old Ones, The Journalists* and *The Merchant* mark a collapse into sentimentality and stasis, and that Wesker's moral urgency continues to drive him into a preachiness and didacticism that were masked by the lively characterization of the early work, may seem unfair in the fierce light thrown out here by Wesker's counter-barrage: at times one seems lifted back to those far-off exciting evenings in Sloane Square, when the air seemed to glow with bravery and honesty. A re-reading of the plays may dim this a bit. They should be read, though; as should *Distinctions* by anyone interested in the post-war theatre.

J. K. L. Walker, "Combative Defence," in The Times Literary Supplement, *No. 4301, September 6, 1985, p. 978.*

Phyllis A(yame) Whitney

1903-

American novelist, short story writer, nonfiction writer, critic, and editor.

Whitney is a highly prolific and popular author of romantic suspense fiction for both adults and young adults. In her formulaic but skillful mysteries for adults, Whitney often centers on characters whose secret or criminal pasts are revealed through the dramatic resurgence of family conflicts and intrigues. Her heroines are usually young career women or brides-to-be who are forced by circumstance to return to threatening family estates and other Gothic settings. They must overcome various dangers and uncover past mysteries before transcending personal crises.

Whitney wrote *Red Is for Murder* (1943), a conventional murder mystery for adults, early in her career, but she was so successful writing young adult mysteries that she did not return to writing adult novels until the mid-1950s. She received Edgar Allan Poe awards in the juvenile mystery category for her novels *Mystery of the Haunted Pool* (1960) and *Mystery of the Hidden Hand* (1963). In her adult mystery *The Quicksilver Pool* (1955), a historical romance set on Staten Island during the Civil War draft riots, Whitney introduced a mystery/romance format similar in style to Emily Brontë's novel *Jane Eyre*. Her other works in this mode include *Skye Cameron* (1957), which takes place in New Orleans at the close of the Civil War, and *Thunder Heights* (1960), which is set in the early twentieth-century Hudson River region. Whitney's novels of the later 1960s are more often contemporary in theme and setting and deal increasingly with family issues and female identity. These works include *Black Amber* (1964), *Columbella* (1966), *Hunter's Green* (1968), and *The Winter People* (1969).

Whitney's adult novels since 1970 center on the rivalries and interdependencies between mothers and daughters while often dealing peripherally with absent or divorced fathers. These works include *Lost Island* (1970), *Listen for the Whisperer* (1972), *The Turquoise Mask* (1974), *The Golden Unicorn* (1976), *The Stone Bull* (1977), *The Glass Flame* (1978), *Emerald* (1982), and *Dream of Orchids* (1984). Whitney has also written two nonfiction works, *Writing Juvenile Fiction* (1947) and *Writing Juvenile Stories and Novels* (1976).

(See also *Contemporary Authors*, Vols. 1-4, rev. ed.; *Contemporary Authors New Revision Series*, Vol. 3; and *Something about the Author*, Vols. 1, 30.)

© Jerry Bauer

WILL CUPPY

[*Red Is for Murder* is] a nicely written and sufficiently exciting yarn about two murders at Cunningham's, a Chicago department store, told by Miss Linell Wynn, sign promotion expert. First in deadly danger was Michael Montgomery, Linell's fiance, a window-display manager. He ran off with Chris Gardner, an illustrator, then returned to face hatred from several directions. Linell took the jilting all right, but it was her hard luck to find a dead body behind one of the fancy windows; and we can't help thinking it would have been better for all concerned if she had shrieked for the cops immediately, instead of trying to keep out of it. Employees to watch include Sondo Norgaard, a genius at cutting paper into odd shapes; Owen Gardner, distressed father of Michael's bride, and Tony Salvador, a hot-tempered decorator—though we're not saying that any of them did it. . . .

Conclusion is tall and startling. This is one of those background stories, of course, but Miss Whitney is no slouch at handling the mystery routine in general. Moreover, she has a natural and likable way of conducting herself in dangerous territory.

Will Cuppy, in a review of "Red Is for Murder," in New York Herald Tribune Weekly Book Review, November 28, 1943, p. 34.

HARNETT T. KANE

[For *The Quicksilver Pool*], Phyllis Whitney has chosen a rich and fruitful historical setting—New York in a period of Civil war crisis, when weariness of the bitter conflict had led Copperheads and others to lift voices and raise plans against the northern effort.

Mrs. Whitney has made good use of her factual data, presenting convincing details of the raging ''counter-war'' during which Unionists divided among themselves in episodes which might have changed the American story. Yet the author has made her history subordinate in the main to a domestic tale, a family drama of interconnected, clashing relationships.

Her Lora Blair . . . lived in a southern border town, which was soon all but wrecked by opposing forces. . . . After she rescued a Union soldier under necessarily romantic conditions, Lora realized that the man still seemed to love only his dead wife. Still she married him and accompanied him to Staten island to take up her life there.

As a former resident of rebel territory, Lora Tyler found more than sectional troubles—a harsh mother-in-law, sick and dominant; a tragic son of that first marriage, and, not least, a political lady rival with an interest in Lora's husband that was not confined to the public platform.

Lora carried the day, and Mrs. Whitney has made her story quick moving, sympathetic, and sometimes moving. If Lora is a bit overidealized, a trifle pat, that fact will not alienate many of the readers of what may be called a wholesome, family type novel.

> Harnett T. Kane, ''Civil War Setting in Old New York,'' in Chicago Tribune, *Part 4, April 17, 1955, p. 5.*

SIEGFRIED MANDEL

Every so often in current novels and plays we meet the blue-blood dowager who by virtue of name and fortune terrorizes a whole clan until some defiant youngster battles her to a standstill. This is pretty much the situation in Phyllis A. Whitney's **The Trembling Hills**. . . . Alternately confused and determined, Sara Jerome Bishop starts rummaging around in the family closet. . . . Part of her persistent rummaging stems from the fact that her mother is a hired housekeeper whose husband has left for parts unknown and Sara hopefully suspects that behind her mother's secrecy there lies a family connection that promises the kind of social station she yearns for. Naturally, Sara suspects right, and the clue-strewn trail leads to . . . a domineering old woman who had made Sara's mother miserable in her early married days. Will history repeat itself in 1906 as dowager Varady takes Sara into the fold? It almost did, but Sara, unlike her mother, fought for the man she loved despite some antagonistic engineering on Aunt Varady's part and gained her respect and undying enmity. Miss Whitney gives her readers their money's worth, expertly weaving an ever-thickening plot and providing a satisfying amount of depth to its characters, all of whom are in perpetual conflict. (pp. 16, 25)

> Siegfried Mandel, ''The Housekeeper's Daughter,'' in The Saturday Review, *New York, Vol. XXXIX, No. 39, September 29, 1956, pp. 16, 25.*

JESSIE REHDER

Set in New Orleans after the close of the Civil War, Mrs. Whitney's romance [**Skye Cameron**] begins on a high note, with the arrival of her heroine, accompanied by a Creole mother willing to flirt with any man who is attracted to her daughter. In the picture, too, is Skye's father, Bruce Cameron, paralyzed and despondent. In New Orleans the family, setting up house-

keeping in the establishment of Uncle Robert Tourneau, become instantly enmeshed in a web of intrigue that is guaranteed to hold the reader's attention for the distance.

For this reader's money, the most rewarding pages in the novel—and, happily, they are many—are those devoted to a re-creation of New Orleans as it was in the Eighteen Eighties. Locales range from the levee to the Pontalba Apartments; from pastel houses with iron fretwork to hidden courtyards fragrant with flowers. There is ruin: a house with a shutter hung awry, a crumbled wall, a street that stands deserted. . . .

The people of the book, Justin Law with his curly thatch of yellow hair, Courtney, his weak brother, and many others including Delphine the servant, her dark eyes veiling scorn, appear in scenes of somewhat contrived melodrama—but it is a melodrama that suits the setting. The plot sets brother against brother, sweetheart against one-time lover. The mother-daughter entanglement, presented on the level of ''I-am-lovelier-than-you-and-I-will-get-your-man,'' is one of the prime sources from which the climax—or rather climaxes—of the novel derive.

These climaxes whirl the reader through a battle for power between Justin Law and Robert Tourneau with the fate of two families resting on the outcome. Skye Cameron, freed of her jealousy of her mother and almost sure of herself, finally manages to turn the battle.

Held together by Skye's growing sense of her own power, the book ends with the heroine in a moment of clarity feeling close to her father—who had gone down to dark shores after his illness and then turned his back and walked away. Before the reader turns away, he will have worked through a spicy narrative set in one of the most charming cities of America just after its glory days, a story ripe with the adventures of a flaming-haired heroine who is at least kissing-kin to Scarlett O'Hara.

> Jessie Rehder, ''New Orleans Rigadoon,'' in The New York Times Book Review, *September 29, 1957, p. 41.*

JENNINGS RICE

[**Skye Cameron**] is another story of New Orleans in the 1880s, of lacy ironwork, shadowy courtyards and the heady scent of jasmine.

When Skye Cameron, twenty-two and red-headed, suddenly found herself transported from a small New England town to the home of her aristocratic Uncle Robert, in the Vieux Carré, she realized that the changes in her life had only begun—but would they be for the better or for the worse? To her mother's warnings regarding the character of her uncle she paid little heed—Uncle Robert had received them most graciously. . . . [Besides], here was young Courtney, her uncle's law clerk, who was already paying her compliments.

On the other hand, as Skye was soon to discover, customs in New Orleans differed from customs in New England, and the tall quadroon servant, Delphine, was destined to be to her more of a duenna than servant. Then, too, a young lady of twenty-two was highly marriageable, and marriage, to the Creole mind, had much more to do with family fortunes than with romantic love. And it was about this time that Skye got her first glimpse of Justin Law, the man with the shadow over his past.

The author of this tale is a practiced weaver of romances, and the story moves along at a good pace toward an artfully prepared climax. Unfortunately, it seems always to hover on the border line between teen age and adult fiction, as if Miss Whitney, experienced in both fields, could not quite make up her mind which one she was working in. The events too have a familiar ring, as do the characters, and the latter are so superficially realized that they fail to arouse much interest in the reader's mind as to what is going to happen to them.

> *Jennings Rice, "New England Girl in Old New Or-*
> *leans," in* New York Herald Tribune Book Review,
> *December 22, 1957, p. 8.*

ANNE ROSS

There is a genre of novel ranging from *Jane Eyre* to *Rebecca* which is always satisfactory. It tells the story of a young woman who is introduced into a wealthy family and discovers a dark mystery in its past. Phyllis Whitney, giving her latest book [*Thunder Heights*] a Hudson River setting during the turn of the century, follows this pattern. Her heroine is the orphaned Camilla King, who has been summoned to Thunder Heights to attend the deathbed of her grandfather Orrin Judd. Camilla's mother had incurred Orrin's displeasure by her marriage and Camilla had never seen the family home. But Camilla's mother had returned on a visit years ago, and had died there mysteriously. And now Camilla finds herself . . . in a strange house, full of hostilities.

Moreover as Camilla remains in the house, she begins to follow a certain pattern which apparently her mother had followed before her, on the visit which caused her sudden death. There are clues which would alarm anybody. Why had cousin Booth painted a picture of her mother taming a wild horse? Was there anything suspicious about the herbs which Aunt Letty brewed and offered as panaceas for all ills? . . .

Miss Whitney maintains suspense and pace in her novel, although it has the smoothness, the gliding over of implausibilities of an old formula. Someday the heroine is *not* going to venture out alone in a dangerous situation. But until that day, Miss Whitney's books will continue to satisfy the reader who likes a fillip of mystery and romance.

> *Anne Ross, "Family with a Dark Mystery," in* New
> York Herald Tribune Book Review, *April 10, 1960,*
> *p. 6.*

SILENCE BUCK BELLOWS

Atmosphere is one of the strongest factors in Phyllis Whitney's new mystery novel [*Thunder Heights*]. The characters are cast in a traditional mold—a beautiful daughter of a wealthy family, disinherited because of a willful marriage; her orphaned daughter, a wrap-up of all the desirable qualities for a story-book heroine; a repentant grandfather, who doesn't live long enough to see his good intentions carried out; a jealous family; and two almost disconcertingly eligible young men, to keep romantic readers on a pleasurable seesaw.

When Camilla King comes to Thunder Heights, at the summons of her grandfather, and finds that she has been made his heiress, she runs into mystery upon mystery, extending as far back as her mother's unsatisfactorily explained demise, and running forward to her own future, which becomes increasingly beset by lethal danger. In an exciting and violent culmination, the mysteries are cleared and the future secured.

Although this is classed as an adult novel, it has earmarks of a girls' mystery-romance. The author has made effective use of the turn-of-the-century period and the Hudson River locale, and she knows how to handle suspense and how to make eeriness convincing. But mystery fans who demand good rationalization and legitimate clues will not find it strong enough fare.

> *Silence Buck Bellows, "Fortieth-Floor Fiction; Lith-*
> *uanian Stories; Mystery Tale: 'Thunder Heights'," *
> *in* The Christian Science Monitor, *May 26, 1960, p.*
> *17.*

BEVERLY GRUNWALD

[*Blue Fire*] cannot be taken seriously as a picture of South Africa because it is a superficial cliché of the attitude some Americans have toward it. Miss Whitney is an American author who makes trips to the locales of her novels for authenticity, but she might just as well have never gone to the Union. *Blue Fire* is an incredible book—incredibly poor—about a Chicago girl who returns to the scene of her birth, Capetown. It combines juvenile mystery and soap opera with simplified sketches of black-white relationships. (p. 25)

> *Beverly Grunwald, "Shapes and Shades of the Dark*
> *Continent," in* Saturday Review, *Vol. XLIV, No. 23,*
> *June 10, 1961, pp. 23-6.*

ANTHONY BOUCHER

Phyllis A. Whitney does quite nicely with contemporary Istanbul in *Black Amber* . . . , in which an American girl, trying to solve the death of her sister, plunges into a web of Turkish intrigue. This one is a bit thin and wordy, but it has lots of local color and the interesting use of such off-trail plot-ingredients as *tespihler,* a kind of irreligious rosary used as a tranquilizer.

> *Anthony Boucher, in a review of "Black Amber," *
> *in* The New York Times Book Review, *February*
> *23, 1964, p. 28.*

LUCILLE G. CRANE

Jane Eyre as a prototype has been successfully used again by Phyllis Whitney in her latest novel [*Columbella*]. The governess-cum-mystery is set in St. Thomas, Virgin Islands, and has all the necessary ingredients of interesting characters, exotic setting, and fast-paced story.

When Jessica Abbott accepted Maude Hampden's request to be a tutor for her granddaughter, she had a two-fold purpose: the one was to detach herself from a past spent caring for her invalid mother, now deceased; the other to help Leila Drew, (the granddaughter of Mrs. Hampden), whose mother was using her as a pawn against her father. Jessica entered the beautiful Hampden mansion, a seething environment that led to violence; but her persistence also led to a satisfactory denouement which must not be divulged here.

The characterization is secondary to the story, which keeps the reader suspensefully alert. The portrait of Catherine Drew, (Leila's mother), as an embodiment of evil is unconvincing; she is a spoiled willful woman who makes life miserable for her family, but she is too shallow to be more than a pest. Jessica is her antithesis in quiet efficiency and stability. Leila is a typical 14-year-old. Kingdon Drew, the father of Leila, has strength but his weaknesses seem more apparent. (pp. 55, 60)

Columbella may be recommended to anyone who likes a romantic mystery. It is almost certain to become a best-seller. Phyllis Whitney fans will not be disappointed and Mary Stewart readers will like her American counterpart. *Columbella* is a most pleasant diversion. (p. 60)

> *Lucille G. Crane, in a review of "Columbella," in* Best Sellers, *Vol. 26, No. 3, May 1, 1966, pp. 55, 60.*

ANTHONY BOUCHER

Phyllis A. Whitney does not have the light bright touch of humor and originality that marks a Mary Stewart; but I guess she writes the straight conventional gothica about as well as anyone going. *Silverhill* . . . is an especially good example. . . . [It's] all very neat, professional, and especially skillful in achieving a unity of time of under 36 hours—which may be a record for the romantic mystery.

> *Anthony Boucher, in a review of "Silverhill," in* The New York Times Book Review, *July 2, 1967, p. 22.*

SR. M. MARGUERITE, RSM

[Phyllis Whitney] has been hailed as the American counterpart of Mary Stewart and Virginia Holt. *Hunter's Green* is another gothic story with all the details of the required ingredients: an ancient and history-crammed English estate; a gruff, dedicated and misunderstood owner; an elderly woman; a few characters that may or may not lead the reader to guess which one is the villain; and of course, a newcomer, an outsider, innocent and victim of intrigue.

Yet one must admit that though the pattern is in general as unvarying as the rules for a sonnet or the recipe for a cake, there are always fresh approaches and the reader's attention is held. The story is very much up to date: there is a "Twiggy" sort of model, Cockney and assured; there are modern conveniences even though the house is cold; and that gruff hero has dedicated his obstacle-crammed activity to producing . . . a fireproof fluid which will propel a crash-and-collision proof car—noiselessly.

There is one good thing about a narrative in the first person. One knows that the heroine isn't going to be killed, even though only four pages from the end of the book she is being driven at a murderous rate for a drop into a lethal quarry. She certainly has to live to tell the tale!

The conversation is good, distinguishing as it does the American from the Bahamian from the Cockney model from the aristocratic English. I would object somewhat to the title of the book: it does not do justice to the very clever scheme of the topiary with its yew tree carvings of chess pieces. . . .

Miss Whitney's smiling promise has been satisfactorily fulfilled.

> *Sr. M. Marguerite, RSM, in a review of "Hunter's Green," in* Best Sellers, *Vol. 28, No. 3, May 1, 1968, p. 61.*

ALLEN J. HUBIN

[In *The Winter People*] Whitney seeks to create that mood of impending doom characteristic of gothics. She does so fairly well, without much recourse to the idiotic behavior common to heroines of the genre. Dina Blake, still bemused by a teenage love, is swept into marriage by sculptor Glen Chandler, and bundled off to the Chandler mansion (sound familiar?). There gather father Colton Chandler, famous portraitist, and Glen's twin sister Glynis. . . . Dina is ready to make allowance for artistic sensitivities, but it is quickly evident that the sister's psychological twinship with Glen is malevolently, preternaturally Siamese—and woe betide the wife who comes between.

> *Allen J. Hubin, in a review of "The Winter People," in* The New York Times Book Review, *May 18, 1969, p. 31.*

MARTIN LEVIN

When Lacey Ames returns [in *Lost Island*] to the old plantation on Hampton Island, a private duchy off the coast of Georgia, she feels "a pervading sense of evil." In a Phyllis Whitney melodrama, such apprehensions are not to be taken lightly, as a couple of sudden deaths prove. You see—9-year-old Richard, the son of Lacey's cousin Elise, is really not Elise's son at all. And Aunt Amalie, who is Elise's mother . . . , is interested in keeping the secret of Richard's paternity. Lacey, for her part, is secretly in love with Giles—even though her emotional needs should be fulfilled by her job as associate editor in a New York publishing house. At the annual Camelot Ball, amid the scent of lilacs and miasma, Miss Whitney tidies the loose ends of a gothic plot as intricate as a lace antimacassar.

> *Martin Levin, in a review of "Lost Island," in* The New York Times Book Review, *November 22, 1970, p. 61.*

BEST SELLERS

[In *Listen for the Whisperer,* Whitney] comes through as a masterful writer of romantic suspense. Laura Worth was a famous movie actress of the past who had suddenly fled Hollywood after a murder had occurred on the set of her last film. Leigh Hollins, born out of a love-affair between Miss Worth and Victor Hollins, a novelist and screen writer, follows her to Bergen, Norway, many years later, after the death of Leigh's father. Miss Worth is still haunted by the unsolved crime; Miss Hollins bitterly seeks revenge against her mother for running out on her and her father. . . . The story is fast-paced and exciting right to the end where the murderer is uncovered and the other sub-plots reach satisfactory conclusions. For those who like character development and detailed description of background and environment, there is much in this novel that will please them. All in all, a good piece of work. (pp. 493-94)

> *"Spies and Sleuths," in* Best Sellers, *Vol. 31, No. 21, February 1, 1972, pp. 493-94.*

NEWGATE CALLENDAR

[In *Listen for the Whisperer,* girl] goes to Sweden to get interview from mother, an ex-film actress. Mother still bothered by old murder on film set. Girl gets interview. Girl hears whispers in the night. Girl gets into a bit of trouble. Reader has to follow girl through such prose as "Her face began to crumple—like that of a child who has been rudely hurt. . . ."

At the end of the book a character says: "Everyone has suffered enough." Amen.

> *Newgate Callendar, in a review of "Listen for the Whisperer," in* The New York Times Book Review, *February 20, 1972, p. 27.*

RICHARD CONLIN

[In *The Turquoise Mask*] Amanda Austin has lived with her widowed father from the time she was five years old. She was brought up in New England and in ignorance of her mother's death "from a fall." Her grandfather, Juan Cordova, lives near Santa Fe and has written to her asking her to come there to visit him before he dies. She finds the Cordova hacienda surrounded by adobe walls and full of a bewildering tension and of relatives—her mother was Dorotea Cordova—who all want her to leave as soon as possible.... Amanda is terrified but resolute in her determination to remain even in a hostile atmosphere until she can clear up the cause of her mother's death. Doro Cordova Austin was supposed to have shot Kirk Landers to death and thrown herself down the steep arroyo as a suicide. Amanda is certain that her hardly remembered mother was capable of such an action. Gradually, the past clears, by reason of small clues here and there, among them an ugly mask painted a turquoise blue and inlaid with turquoise and silver. Miss Whitney's nineteenth novel is full of suspense and beautifully appreciative of the New Mexico scene.

> *Richard Conlin, in a review of "The Turquoise Mask," in* Best Sellers, *Vol. 34, No. 2, April 15, 1974, p. 51.*

CARTER RATCLIFF

[In *The Golden Unicorn*] Courtney Marsh is led by the death of her adoptive parents to wonder who she really is. She can no longer identify with her image as a successful young career woman when she watches her appearance on an important late-night talk show. Among her adoptive mother's papers she finds an old newspaper clipping, a reproduction of a painting in which a moon is obscured by a unicorn-shaped cloud. Mrs. Marsh has written on the clipping, "Is this the unicorn in Courtney's life?" The unicorn painter is Judith Rhodes. She ... is a Magic Realist, one who is often compelled in her endless nocturne/marines to replace the moon with disembodied dolls' heads.

Now, when the Marshes took Courtney in, she was wearing a golden unicorn pendant. Courtney decides to visit Rhodes at the artist's spooky old family house, The Shingles, in East Hampton. Posing as that which she no longer wants to be, a famous journalist, she runs into all sorts of unpleasantness—drawers full of dolls' heads, a vicious Great Dane, the peculiarities of the reclusive Judith and her daughter, Stacia.... Someone driving a Mercedes tries to run Courtney down. Courtney herself drives a Volvo, which shows how well she was doing before she got caught up in all this—though the car isn't much help when she tries to get away from The Shingles. At one point she can't help thinking she "was right about the evil, after all. It *was* abroad in this house—not merely in the person of Stacia, but somewhere else as well. Hidden, invisible, yet always there."...

The Golden Unicorn has as happy an ending as could be imagined, given the ingredients of the story—yet this is never in doubt. The novel employs all the devices of the gothic genre without ever creating a scary atmosphere. Courtney was *wrong* about the evil. There were never any dark, inexplicable forces at work either in people or in the fates. There was just a big house full of neurotics, and when one of them gets bumped off, the sluice gates of normalcy are opened and a beneficent happiness floods the scene. *The Golden Unicorn* is a secular gothic. Ghosts have been replaced by emotional problems as sketched in a pop version of life-adjustment psychiatry. The painter Judith Rhodes and her daughter Stacia have drawn all the gothic weirdness into themselves by virtue of being high-strung creative types. They are ultimately peripheral to the story, which has to do with Courtney coming to find out who she really is and getting romantically entangled with a marine biologist....

The Golden Unicorn deprecates art—it is something strange, to be suppressed, as the gothic novel comes to terms with ordinary life. That's not nice for art, but a novelist full of respect for creativity can produce something a lot less nice.

> *Carter Ratcliff, in a review of "The Golden Unicorn," in* Art in America, *Vol. 64, No. 4, July-August, 1976, p. 29.*

IRENE R. HILL

[Courtney Marsh, the heroine of *The Golden Unicorn*], loses her adoptive parents in a train accident in Rome. She finds a few clues to help her locate her natural parents, principally a chain on which hangs a golden unicorn, found on her neck when Gwen and Leon brought her home. She also discovers a yellow clipping showing a badly reproduced painting by an artist named Judith Rhodes, with clouds outlined in the shape of a unicorn.... Courtney writes Judith Rhodes, requesting an interview for the National Weekly, for which she writes. (pp. 215-16)

At the estate, Courtney finds a family living in fear that their sins will find them out, so they put up a solid front. Starting with her unicorn, other proofs pile up to show that Courtney will inherit under Grandfather Lawrence's will, which provides that his estate go to his first grandchild when she attains twenty-five. At this point all hell breaks loose, with tragedy playing a leading role. It becomes difficult to absorb the relationships within this family, and more difficult to understand how greed dominated their actions.

To reveal any more would spoil the astounding climax. (p. 216)

> *Irene R. Hill, in a review of "The Golden Unicorn," in* Best Sellers, *Vol. 36, No. 7, October, 1976, pp. 215-16.*

IRENE N. POMPEA

[In *The Stone Bull*] Jenny Vaughn feels that she has finally been released from her sister Ariel's shadow and has found happiness on her own. And yet she feels that somehow she could have prevented her talented sister's death.

When she and her husband Brendon McClain come to Laurel Mountain, a Catskill resort estate which has been in the McClain family for generations, she finds that Ariel has been there before her. Brendon has suppressed all mention of Ariel, because he was and still is in love with Ariel.

Though there was a love/hate relationship with her look-alike older sister, Jenny wants to clear Ariel's name when it is whispered that Ariel might have been instrumental in the death of Floris, wife of her lover, a sculptor. In trying to uncover closely guarded secrets, Jenny finds her own life threatened. Because she is Ariel's double, she finds those who loved Ariel looking askance at her for living. . . . [Slowly] she evolves into a person in her own right.

Phyllis Whitney has a knack for painting pictures with words that punctuate the action of this fast paced gothic mystery. Her detailed description of the flora and fauna of the Catskills brings the freshness of the woods to the reader. Guilt flickers from character to character and the climax explodes like a fire-cracker. The cast of characters is so real that the reader will feel he knows someone just like them. Combining mythology, drama, and botany, once more Phyllis Whitney has given her public an experience of genuine suspense. (pp. 173-74)

> *Irene N. Pompea, in a review of "The Stone Bull," in* Best Sellers, *Vol. 37, No. 6, September, 1977, pp. 173-74.*

PUBLISHERS WEEKLY

[*The Glass Flame* is a] nicely atmospheric suspense-romance set in the Great Smoky Mountains of Tennessee. Karen Hallam has just been widowed. Her husband, David, an arson expert, had been asked by his architect brother, Trevor, to investigate some fires set in a new and beautiful housing development that Trevor has designed. David dies, victim of a devastating blaze in one of the nearly completed homes. . . . Karen feels obli-gated to solve the mystery of David's death and goes to Ten-nessee to do so. She stays with Trevor and his family in a beautiful mountain-top home and begins her search. There she finds the situation infinitely complicated—strange family cross-currents, perplexing motivations and threatening events. Whit-ney builds her atmospheric Great Smokies Gothic to a stirring and surprising conclusion. Good entertainment from an old pro. (pp. 61-2)

> *A review of "The Glass Flame," in* Publishers Weekly, *Vol. 214, No. 1, July 3, 1978, pp. 61-2.*

FRANCES TRACHTENBERG

We readers of romantic suspense ask so little of a book—a little romance to stir the sentiment, a heroine, a hero, enough suspense to keep us from returning to the humdrum. Alas, [*The Glass Flame*] makes housekeeping seem exciting.

The story line is that of a marriage ended but not totally severed . . . and arson which is destroying the "dreams" of the male protagonist (I cannot say hero because he has no personality). Ms. Whitney may have been very tired or bored when she allowed this book to go to press. Certainly her rep-utation has been achieved over the years on better writing.

Not only is there no hero, there is no heroine. In fact none of the characters has substance. Nor does the twist ending have any shock effect on the reader: it has been used before, and was telegraphed in the early chapters.

> *Frances Trachtenberg, in a review of "The Glass Flame," in* Best Sellers, *Vol. 38, No. 10, January, 1979, p. 309.*

MARLENE S. VEACH

[In *Domino*] Laurie leaves the East to answer a call from her grandmother who, after no contact for many years, has issued a cry for help from Colorado. Accompanied by her friend and protector, Laurie returns to the dying town of her past and its silver mine, but the family homestead is carefully preserved, both in appearance and tradition. The formidable grandmother is overpowering, and perhaps is Laurie's one true link to yes-terday, which affects her as much as her present. Only learning the truth of her early years can unlock the mysteries that have gripped her in a personal crisis of her own, when the flash of light returns and she is left alone and terrified, a victim of what memory fails to provide, in great turmoil about the events of her past and what sort of future she can expect.

The path of clues is sprinkled with confusing elements that cast doubtful lights on everyone involved in the inexplicable events of today and yesterday. Who is the villain? Who the friend? Her grandmother's challenging nurse? A dashing spec-ulator? Her childhood friend, now disappointingly passive? . . .

Phyllis Whitney has continued in her grand tradition of the romantic novel to weave a delightfully suspenseful tale that will keep you turning pages, undergoing many pleasurable twists and turns of imagination.

> *Marlene S. Veach, in a review of "Domino," in* Best Sellers, *Vol. 39, No. 10, January, 1980, p. 370.*

BARBARA MERTZ

Whitney's devoted readers know what to expect from her, and *Emerald* will not disappoint them; it is romantic suspense writ-ten by one of the most skilled craftsmen in the business. Whit-ney's heroines are liberated women; they may—and do—end up in the arms of the hero, but they have to solve their own problems before they get there. Carol Barclay, the heroine of *Emerald,* faces a tragically contemporary danger: her brutal, powerful ex-husband is trying to kidnap their small son, though the divorce proceedings awarded her custody of the child. . . . Carol must not only protect the boy from his father, but solve a mystery involving two legendary screen lovers of film's golden age before the happy ending can be attained. As usual, Whitney uses the geography and history of the area effectively in work-ing out the denouement, and there are loving evocations of the Hollywood of the past, plus a surprise-twist ending that will catch most readers off guard.

> *Barbara Mertz, in a review of "Emerald," in* Book World—The Washington Post, *January 2, 1983, p. 4.*

MELANIE EIGER

[The opening scene of *Emerald* takes place] in a car. Unfor-tunately, the feeling of being in transit between the past and the future, and never truly in the present, continues through the book.

Carol Hamilton Barclay, a New York writer, flees with her son from her violent ex-husband, and seeks sanctuary with her aged, movie-star aunt, whom she has never met. Carol sets about writing the memoirs of her reluctant benefactor, and becomes embroiled in unravelling the mystery of her aunt's seclusion, leading to revelations of revenge and murder. Car-ol's objectivity is acceptable in the reporter and interviewer, but she seems cold and remote when she is deterred from the efficient pursuit of her "story" by the danger of her own situation and the threat to her son.

The characters in this 1940's Hollywood mystery-romance are too one-dimensional to be involving. On the other hand, the contemporary suspense yarn of divorce and child-snatching is too peripheral to the action and too skeletal in its execution to fill the gap. The modern tale seems to be designed to root the old-fashioned story in the present, but, instead, it distracts from the flow of the plot. Although both crises are worked out to the heroine's satisfaction, the resolution is predictable and doubly anti-climactic.

Emerald would make a diverting teleplay for a soap opera. . . . It is not, however, what one expects or deserves from a respected writer like Phyllis Whitney. The evocative descriptions of the desert milieu were a lonely reminder of what a Whitney work can be. (pp. 458-59)

> Melanie Eiger, in a review of "Emerald," in Best Sellers, Vol. 42, No. 12, March, 1983, pp. 458-59.

CAROL VERDERESE

Hollis Sands, the narrator of Phyllis A. Whitney's *Rainsong,* is the young widow of Ricky Sands, a famous popular singer found dead of a seemingly intentional drug overdose. Hollis, having written many of her husband's hit songs, becomes a target for the press and Ricky's bereaved fans. This prompts her to accept a mysterious offer from her father's old girlfriend to take refuge at a rambling Long Island estate. . . . She tells her story in flashback, describing her terror, lingering grief, depression and subsequent triumph in a detached, guarded tone that tries our sympathy and renders the dubious convolutions of plot and character more improbable. Are we to accept, for instance, that a woman as determined and spirited as Hollis seemingly believes herself to be would allow her husband to exclude her so completely from his work that she would not recognize a member of his band when he later turns up at the estate? Or that Hollis, on the advice of Ricky's manager, would subject herself to a humiliating confrontation with her husband's mistress to dissuade the desperate woman from "going public"? Surely it is unrealistic of her to expect sympathy from her rival, yet this implausible meeting is one of the story's linchpins. When a character conveniently appears from nowhere to move the plot along, Hollis explains, "I didn't ask how he happened to be around at this particular time. I didn't care." Evidently, Phyllis Whitney didn't either. (pp. 18-19)

> Carol Verderese, in a review of "Rainsong," in The New York Times Book Review, February 5, 1984, pp. 18-19.

JANE STEWART SPITZER

The latest novels of Victoria Holt and Phyllis A. Whitney, two established authors in the romantic suspense field, illustrate some disappointing changes in this genre brought about by the onslaughts of current permissive attitudes toward sex and drugs and by competition from the currently popular romance genre. . . .

[The] modern world, with its pervasive social problems, is intruding on this genre and destroying its magic. This is disappointing because romantic suspense novels are read purely for entertainment and escapism. . . .

[Whitney's *Rainsong*] has a contemporary setting. The contemporary aspects of the plot and some of the characters' involvement in the music industry, in drug use, and in illicit sexual relationships are superimposed over the traditional elements—assumed identities, a past tragedy, a brooding mansion, and a heroine in distress. The effect is jarring, and *Rainsong* simply doesn't work. The contemporary aspects rob the story of any possible fairy-tale qualities the traditional elements might provide. To top it off, the heroine, Hollis Sands, a songwriter and widow of a famous singer, is so incredibly naive, unwise, and unperceptive that she fails to elicit the necessary sympathy in the reader. . . .

Names such as Victoria Holt and Phyllis A. Whitney were once synonymous with good quality romantic suspense fiction. That, unfortunately, seems to be changing.

> Jane Stewart Spitzer, "Demystification of Romance," in The Christian Science Monitor, April 6, 1984, p. B5.

SUSAN DOOLEY

In *Dream of Orchids* we are in the hands of Phyllis A. Whitney, whose masterful mixture of one part mystery to one part romance has produced a formula which has served her well for 30 books. With the plot bouncing along at such a happy pace, it would be quibbling to demand depth, though we do drop down full fathom five in search of buried treasure. It is modern day Key West, and Laurel York has come to meet the father she hasn't seen since she was three. The author greases our slide into fantasy with a bit of information about orchids [and Key West] . . . but mostly we are drawn into the mysterious death of the stepmother, the strange behavior of Clifton York's secretary, the odd way the greenhouse door jammed shut and, oh love, sweet love, will Girl get Boy?

> Susan Dooley, "The Loves of Learning," in Book World—The Washington Post, January 6, 1985, p. 11.

ANN GALLAGHER

Set in Key West, *Dream of Orchids* is a wholesome adventure story that begins on a March afternoon when a tall, handsome stranger appears in Laurel York's Long Island bookstore, presents her with a breathtaking orchid, and urges her to go to the islands with him.

This reviewer wouldn't have needed another word of urging, but there are complicating factors here. The stranger, Marcus O'Neill, is doing research for Laurel's father, a famous suspense writer. Clifton York left Laurel and her mother years ago to marry a woman named Poppy, never sending his daughter so much as a birthday card. Now, Marcus tells Laurel, her father needs her. The flamboyant Poppy has died in bizarre fashion among the orchids she cultivated, leaving Clifton and their two daughters distraught and in possible danger.

And so, battling her own long-festering resentment of the father who abandoned her, Laurel goes to Key West where she is quickly immersed in the domestic turmoil of his household. Laurel meets her two half-sisters: the flibbertigibbet Fern; and the cool beauty Iris, determined despite Poppy's passionate disapproval to marry a local Errol Flynn nearly thirty years her senior. Laurel probes the source of Poppy's opposition to the match, and begins to wonder about the circumstances of the woman's death. (pp. 15-16)

This novel has a nice old-fashioned feel to it, a certain propriety and emotional reticence which is a refreshing change when it's become so much the rage to plumb the nasty depths of the human psyche. Most psyches will only bear so much plumbing, just as most people look better with their clothes on. The book reminded me, in its comparative innocence, of Carolyn Keene's wonderful Nancy Drew stories.

The story is told in the first person from Laurel's perspective, which works well. Laurel makes the sort of modest, intelligent narrator whom the reader immediately likes.

Among the acknowledgements in the front of the book is a list of people who provided details to authenticate the Key West setting. Some passages seem to display this reportorial harvest rather obviously, and the text, at moments, can read a little like a tourists' guidebook.

But the story is enjoyable. It incites the rapid turning of pages which is the sign of a suspense novel's success. And besides, when the winter drags on and you navigate to and fro in ankle-deep slush, you just can't have too many tall, handsome strangers in your literary landscape. (p. 16)

> *Ann Gallagher, in a review of "Dream of Orchids,"*
> in Best Sellers, *Vol. 45, No. 1, April, 1985, pp.*
> *15-16.*

Hugo Williams

1942-

English poet, travel writer, editor, and translator.

Williams's poetry is commended for the honesty and imagination with which he approaches his subject matter. His poems, some of which explore the darker side of human relationships, are usually based on personal experience. Williams's early poems were directly influenced by the *Review* school, a movement consisting of young English poets whose work was first published in this journal and whose verse is noted for its controlled, minimal focus on everyday life. After the *Review* school's prominence faded during the mid-1970s, Williams developed a perceptive personal voice, and he is praised for his ability to address his innermost concerns without resorting to confessionalism.

Williams was hailed as a promising poet for his first collection, *Symptoms of Loss* (1965). This volume was highly regarded for the directness and originality Williams achieved in many of the poems. However, the understated, taciturn verse included in his subsequent volumes, *Sugar Daddy* (1970) and *Some Sweet Day* (1975), received less favorable attention, as critics generally found Williams's impassive style ineffective. In these volumes, Williams also experiments with rhythmic patterns and longer sequences. Williams's poems in *Love-Life* (1979) are more personal and reflect the joy and disillusionment of romantic and sexual love. *Writing Home* (1985) consists of overtly autobiographical pieces, some of which recreate Williams's childhood, while others examine his relationship with his father, the late actor and dramatist Hugh Williams. Critics praised Williams for his deft, moving portrait of his father.

Williams has also written two travel volumes. The first, *All the Time in the World* (1966), relates his travels in the Middle East, India and Pakistan, Southeast Asia, Japan, and Australia. The second, *No Particular Place to Go* (1981), garnered considerable attention for Williams's humorous and candid account of his visit to America for a series of poetry readings during the 1970s. In this work, Williams describes his adventures with the women he befriended and other people he met on his bus trips through the United States.

(See also *Contemporary Authors*, Vols. 17-20, rev. ed. and *Dictionary of Literary Biography*, Vol. 40.)

IAN HAMILTON

There are some signs in Hugo Williams's first book [*Symptoms of Loss: Poems*] that he may soon not need the sort of hedging, neatly self-defensive mannerisms on which most of his poems depend and for which they are most likely to be mildly praised and then forgotten; here and there, but especially in the book's second section, he starts to write out of experience which he clearly can't afford to be clever with or hold too expertly at bay. Where his subject matter arrests rather than diverts him he has been able to achieve something sufficiently direct and individual for one to see the elaborate evasiveness that else-

Murphy/Williams

where dominates as some kind of necessary schooling. It is in these terms, at any rate, that the book can be described as promising.

The opening poem, **"Still Hot from Filing"** is fairly typical of what he must abandon if this promise is to be fulfilled. It sets off, in perfect Movement style, from the trivial and workaday—the gaining of a freshly minted key—and takes pride in tracing out an analogy between inanimate key and animate owner:

> I turn and, keylike, feel an itch
> To press my sharpened faculties once
>   more
> Upon more malleable stuff
> To watch my influence unlock a door.

Cleverly enough contrived, but what is the poem really supposed to be about? If the dramatic experience of holding a new key is meant to seem absorbing enough for such introspection to have been *demanded* of the poet, then surely lines like 'Sterile within the wards of flesh', or 'Silver against skin like an arrowhead / And sharp' are hardly up to communicating even the primary tactile excitement that such a fiction needs if it is to be persuasive. Or is the key itself unimportant, the eccentric agent of large feelings that the poet needed anyway to grant expression? But what feelings? There are vague intimations of indecisiveness and loneliness but these are so harassed by the demands of the analogy and are of such generalized proportions that we just don't care about them. As for the 'daring' of the conceit, the ironic distance between thing and person: we have had enough of all that to last at least a century.

Denying abstract, asserted feeling any concrete growth beyond what can be offered by the game or the parable is to imply not just superior control but superior wisdom; too often, though, in Hugo Williams's poems the point is grindingly familiar—redeemable by passion or imagination but not, certainly, by a new set of analogies. A poem like **"An Anonymous Affair"** decorates the notion that there are gulfs between people with a lot of leisured comment about our poignant reasons for giving names to animals: . . .

> Names allow them humanity,
>   make us
> Blood brothers. . . .

[This] just isn't a very profound insight; indeed, it borders on the self-evident, the not worth mentioning. The rhymes and stanzas, far from endowing the perception with some new sharpness, merely give it a shaming dignity. In a similar way, the poem **"Girl on the Beach"** which is about the 'procreative' power of the eye and sets up an example of it, could only have worked if the actual observation had been very strong indeed; as it is, we get:

> Thighs
> Like soft curling
> Beaches, breasts
> like dunes, licked
> By the salt tongue
> Of the surf.

In fact, Williams does have a very sharp eye, but this only becomes clear when he is more interested in what he is looking at than in what he can say about having seen it. The travel poems prove this, and so do the handful of character sketches. **"The Pool Player"**, for instance—though it comes perilously close to just mimicking the toughly sentimental idiom of the Hollywood movie it is based on . . . and is fitted out with a too solemnly instructional last stanza—does involve just that intent, detailed effort of identification that is so clearly missing from, say, the much more condescending compassion of a poem like **"Realities"**. In his excellent **"The Coalman"**, Williams takes this a stage further so that one gets not just a sympathetic accuracy but a rather more subtle interpenetration of responses; the dialogue between coalman and customer is watched over with an eye that is benign, saddened and faintly pitying, but there is no finality, no contented judging. The poem settles quietly on the small, strange indifferences that lurk between the man who brings the coal and the man who burns it. It is the discrepancy between two lonely versions of the one act that provides the basic tension and in this sense the poem brings to life all the abstract notions about the centre of Williams's more cerebral pieces.

The best poems in the book are the two that end it; in these Williams seems to have travelled the full distance from mannered anonymity to an unembarrassed self-awareness, a willingness to write directly out of important personal experience; his voice is still discreet and reticent and there is the sense that much is still withheld, but there are no disguises. . . . It is on the strength of this kind of sensitivity, rather than the book as a whole, that one can confidently single Williams out as a

young poet whom it would be foolish to dismiss as clever or accomplished. He is clearly going to be much more than that. (pp. 95-7)

*Ian Hamilton, in a review of "Symptoms of Loss,"
in* London Magazine, *Vol. 5, No. 12, March, 1966,
pp. 95-7.*

GRAHAM MARTIN

One would like to be . . . enthusiastic about Hugo Williams's first collection [*Symptoms of Loss*], which certainly includes successful and distinctive poems, but the total impression is of a low-spiritedness, of a careful, but bleached-out language, of a quietness scarcely explained in the inept blurbist's metaphor 'His poems are still those of someone listening intently in the audience rather than speaking from the stage'. But what is he listening for? The love—perhaps it should be the non-love—poems, do create a satisfactory bleakness . . . and some of the earlier poems show a neat wit, as if they had developed in ways that also surprised the poet; but those based on his travels in the Far East (**"Scars"**, **"The Hitch Hiker"**, **"Aborigine"**) are strangely unnerved, competent versifications from the diary of a humane traveller, but to what point?

*Graham Martin, in a review of "Symptoms of Loss,"
in* The Listener, *Vol. LXXV, No. 1928, March 10,
1966, p. 359.*

STEPHEN WALL

Many of [Hugo Williams's poems in *Symptoms of Loss*] take off from some quotidian situation and are modulated into abstraction or summary in a way that is often dessicating. . . . The poems which impress most are not those sustained by progression of argument, or conceit and teased metaphor, but those which get across some sense of the shape and feel of people's lives—**"The Actor"** to some extent, **"The Pool Player"**, despite its prosaic tendencies, much more so. The second half of *Symptoms of Loss* owes a good deal to travel and has much more physical exactness, but there is still a reaching for conclusions, a careful, staid quality in the language. But the last two poems, **"The Stage is Unlit"** and **"The Butcher"** (the latter first published in *The Review*), use an idiom that is markedly terser, more convincingly related to the line, and more concerned to let observation tell than to make telling observations. Here significance isn't struggled for, but is released by the language, and one is at last convinced of what had previously only been fitfully hinted at, that here is 'a mind in possession of its experience'. (p. 39)

Stephen Wall, "Pipe and Slippers," in The Review,
No. 16, October, 1966, pp. 36-9.

THE TIMES LITERARY SUPPLEMENT

"You can either stay still and write about other people, or you can move about and enjoy yourself. I doubt whether you can write about yourself moving about and enjoying yourself." Thus Hugo Williams broods in a Nara café, about halfway through his two-year journey round the world. It is one of the few passages in *All the Time in the World* in which he pauses to take stock of what he is doing. . . . There is no feeling that he has burned his boats, "chucked up everything and just cleared off"; there is a home to go back to, friends in England to whom he writes. . . . The blurb says that the book "describes the author's increasing awareness of who he is and where he is going".

Luckily it does no such thing. When motiveless bumming like this is combined with such existential stuff it quickly turns into pretentious Kerouackery; and one of the most refreshing things about Mr. Williams's book is its complete lack of pretentiousness. When he does or says something foolish, or responds inadequately, he knows it and says so. He likes being on the move but realizes, too, what he misses by catching everything on the wing. Yet in fact he catches a great deal, in a succession of bizarre but circumstantial snapshots of natives and expatriates in the Middle East, India and Pakistan, Malaya, Thailand, Japan, Australia, and on a long sea journey through the Pacific islands. What emerges is a young man who is fresh without being gauche, open but not soft-centred.

Mr. Williams is also a very funny writer in a casual off-hand way, with a certain wry and economical ruthlessness. . . . But he is not a sort of embryonic Anthony Carson, because when he is moved or appalled he does not duck behind an ironical mask but lets the reader catch the rawness of his mood, as in his description of his brief encounter with Lily, a Thai girl.

The world today, as Mr. Williams found, is full of young Europeans and Americans having a *wanderjahr* or two. One imagines that few of them have his sharpness of observation and skill in putting it down. He has not written a great travel book; such a book needs either a more dangerous grapple with adventure or a deeper sense of place than *All the Time in the World* offers. But he has achieved the end which he doubted: he has written about moving around and enjoying himself, and the bloom has not rubbed off his enjoyment.

"On the Road," in The Times Literary Supplement, *No. 3393, March 9, 1967, p. 200.*

ALAN BROWNJOHN

Small areas of experience, precise and rather detached selection of subjects for poems, and of images within poems—Hugo Williams's refined, sensitive approach, by these means, to the larger issues of living is not necessarily destined to fail, as a poetry like that of Ian Hamilton proves. But it requires a special blend of delicacy and toughness to work well. The poems in *Sugar Daddy* tend to be briefer and more intimate than in Williams's *Symptoms of Loss* . . . , the ideas a little more casual, the central personality rather more bemused and elusive. There are some agreeably original angles, but a kind of casual, submissive quality seems to be draining energy away. . . . Developing an idea with resource and energy serves him much better, as in **"February 20th Street"**, **"Withdrawal"** and the title-poem. (p. 94)

Alan Brownjohn, "Masquerades," in New Statesman, *Vol. 80, No. 2053, July 24, 1970, pp. 93-4.*

THE TIMES LITERARY SUPPLEMENT

In *Sugar Daddy* the deadly seriousness of the business at hand—mainly the loss of love, partly an alienation accepted and even wooed—is punctuated flashingly by confessions of ambition:

> Washing my hair and dreaming of fame,
> I thought you came into my room.

> Were you saying something?
> I was in America, attending my new
> > play.

But this is a train of thought as valid as any of the others, and bringing it in makes the others clearer. In Hugo Williams's poetry there is usually only the one man speaking, but that one man is many-selved: despair can slip abruptly towards delight, even a delight in (and this is a rare thing in these days of high speeds) making poems. In the first part of a poem called **"Motorbike"** the determinedly deadpan reportage gets engagingly sick of itself in the last line and the pose (which is to have no pose, in fact hardly even to be there) breaks down into the kind of solitary snort of laughter we emit when we catch ourselves daydreaming. . . .

Throughout *Sugar Daddy* there are small moments of information about a smashed marriage. Hamilton-style, the information is pushed at you one piece at a time, each piece with one flat edge so that finally you can assemble the perimeter of the jigsaw puzzle. With Ian Hamilton the expanse of tabletop inside this frame leads straight to the unutterable abyss. With Hugo Williams it remains a trifle wooden. He is at his best when most unguarded, consciously the poet making a poem, finishing his book with an unashamed flourish:

> We move singly through streets,
> The last of some sad species,
> Pacing the floors of zoos.
>
> Our luck homing forever
> Backward through grasses
> To the brink of another time.

"Flights and Depths," in The Times Literary Supplement, *No. 3576, September 11, 1970, p. 994.*

RAYMOND DURGNAT

Often in [*Sugar Daddy*] everyday urban detail suddenly sideslips into the sinister. The effect is of sudden incursions by an overtly alienated and ultimately evil oceanic feeling. One shuttles to and fro between bedsitterland and a psychic world as eerie as *Fellini-Satyricon,* 'glassy with deep-sea monsters', eerie with psychic transmutation . . . , with unknown languages and animated, incomprehensible conversations.

The cover photograph poses the author as a Warhol Superstar, and **"In the Vacuum"** impinges on that world, but the references remain for the most part within the orbit of the domestic and the overground. Williams moves with wary and tactful expertise across the zone between the older, and beat, poetry, settling in neither, although his bland, correct economy of means suggests that his spiritual allegiances belong, finally, to the former. It is, perhaps, the continuous pressure of the libidinous which makes Fainlight the most compressed, the closest to nineteenth-century lyricism. Williams's style hovers just outside the edge of that class, but has its own complexity, provided by his extraordinarily deft and resourceful expansion of perceptual detail into emotional 'epiphany'. Perhaps, though, his commitments remain too elusive for the poetry to achieve its fullness. (pp. 368-69)

Raymond Durgnat, "Men of Two Worlds," in Poetry Review, *Vol. 61, No. 4, Winter, 1970-71, pp. 366-69.*

COLIN FALCK

In *Some Sweet Day* there is poem after poem where the net comes up empty, or almost empty, where the imagistic short-ness of breath and rhythmic inertia is uncompensated for by any kind of magical resonance. In "Synopsis", for example (the title itself seems a bit of a try-on):

> People are taking sedatives in boats
> Going to America.
> Their names drift back to me—
> Hollowed out, unpronounceable.
> I walk through the crowds in the
>   arcades
> And on the sands.

One looks for deeper resonances in that last line but there aren't very many to be found. Even the longer poems in *Some Sweet Day* sometimes have difficulty in keeping going and run out of energy before they get to the end. In the few that don't, where there are longer sustained rhythms, it's no coincidence that the poet has (as we say) something to say, some suggestion of an intellectual content. These poems are always the best. Perhaps the best of all is "The Water Bearer", about a longed-for and entirely imaginary girl, but there's also a short poem called "Century Oaks" that seems to say a lot in its six lines for the very reason that it actually does say something:

> The trees are emptying.
> The cold young days rush through them
> On their way to power.
>
> Down here
> We sweep the dead leaves into bonfires
> Lest they betray our sympathies.

However glancingly, the poem takes in both private and public worlds, and at moments like these one feels the pressure of an actual life with its hopes and longings rather than a life merely in abeyance before its own perceptions.

Williams's verse badly needs an infusion of the muscularity that came across in his first book along with its more imagi-native qualities. The emotions that dominated *Symptoms of Loss* were such normally human ones as ambition, lust and curiosity, but if some of these now seem to the poet to be illusory there are perhaps others he could rely on to build up the structure and rhythmic power of his verse. Almost anything—even (to take a hint from "Century Oaks") perhaps shameless nostal-gia—might do. Or despair: the last poem in *Sugar Daddy* ends with the superb lines

> We move singly through streets,
> The last of some sad species,
> Pacing the floors of zoos,
>
> Our luck homing forever
> Backward through grasses
> To the brink of another time

but Williams has never developed this line in intensely hu-manitarian desolation anywhere else in his verse.

One unnecessary, but perhaps paralysing, difficulty Williams makes for himself is what often looks like an excessive avoiding of obviousness—obvious ideas, obvious emotions, things that have been said before. Instead, we get becalmed in an orien-talishness of unnoticed aspects, interesting trivialities and vaguely wistful longings. . . . Some of the most important things in life undoubtedly have been noticed before and the poet who brightly tries to avoid noticing them again may be in danger of con-demning himself to marginality. Perhaps Williams should root out this tiresome cliché about being original and get deeper into the despairs and disillusions he shares with the rest of us. He's one of the truest poets we have and ought to be saved from his self-imposed poetic malnutrition. (pp. 70-1)

Colin Falck, "Don't Look Down," in The New Re-view, *Vol. 2, No. 16, July, 1975, pp. 70-1.*

GAVIN EWART

[The poems in Hugo Williams' collection *Some Sweet Day* are] very ambiguously dedicated 'To Murphy' (is Murphy a man, a woman, a child, or a dog?).

This kind of verse can be very hit or miss. The unintended rhyme can cause a miss. . . .

Other faults include a very unlooked-for hint of sentimental-ity. . . .

A typical poem, of the so-what? kind, leaves all questions unanswered. . . . But there are also virtues. In his world things are people: 'Our holidays look back at us in surprise'. Places too have a special idiosyncratic identity:

> I want you to shield its light from Syria
> The way you would hide your knowledge
> from a child.

These are lines about a candle. The same offhand quality occurs in such a line as 'We'll bury Mary later, in a rush or gradually.' (p. 99)

The marital or domestic situation has inspired some of Wil-liams' best verse in the past: "Tavistock Square" and "Bed-room of Music" are good examples here. Notes on everyday life ("Beachcombers", about commuters), on Nature ("Em-pires": plant life is purposeful), pieces of empathy like "Hem-lock" and pure imagination like "Dust", are all successes. "The Nestling" is a perfect dream poem.

Perhaps not many poems in this book are as satisfying as individual poems in the last one, and his experiments with rhyme and extending his poems to a greater length haven't yet paid off; but there is still a lot to enjoy and admire. (p. 100)

Gavin Ewart, "A Handful of the Best," in London Magazine, *n.s. Vol. 15, No. 4, October-November, 1975, pp. 97-100.*

DOUGLAS DUNN

Hugo Williams's extraordinary imagination [in *Some Sweet Day*] is open to the sort of carping which these days is reserved for the short lyrical poem of experience. On the page, his poems do look wistful, stray, floating on the warm ice of the paper. That he writes like a young poet invented by Chekhov, a young poet exiled to his uncle's country estate for some unspeakable social gaffe, probably doesn't make his acceptance any easier. His lyricism creates a fragile, haunting beauty that a reader might find difficult to catch. In "The Expatriates", he writes

> The vineyard where we live
> The one we draw about us on summer nights
> Has influenced our poetry
> The way it flavours its watermelons with silence.

Although the poem reflects the *chinoiserie* of its influences, it is hard to deny its beauty, and its simplicity, or, for that matter, its surprise.

For the gentle pace with which Williams unfolds his perceptions, he is, I think, unrivalled among contemporary British poets. **"The Stampede"**, a poem about water buffalo "knee-deep in centuries", ends—

> From underneath their feet,
> From underneath the clouds they are standing in,
> A ripple is spreading
> Which will muddy the stars.

The poem shows the originality of his imagination, which works at the level of converting what might have been seen into the poetic world where phenomena are not so much perceived as reinvented.

While his imagination is entirely eccentric, but personal, refusing to share itself with concerns external to what it is naturally attracted towards, and certainly not theoretical, there is something *avant-garde* about Williams's poems. They have the sense of a thought dawning on a person, not in the terms of intellect, but in the language of how, uniquely, they are seen in the imagination. (p. 81)

> *Douglas Dunn, "Mañana Is Now," in* Encounter,
> *Vol. XLV, No. 5, November, 1975, pp. 76-81.*

BLAKE MORRISON

Ask most readers of contemporary poetry what they remember about the writers associated with Ian Hamilton's *Review* and they will probably come up with something about 'toughness'. . . . [The] typical *Review* school poem had a pretty mean look about it: within its confined space (half-a-dozen lines was the norm) violence and brutality were always threatening to erupt. And yet many of the poems published in the *Review* (and this is rather less well remembered) also looked pitifully vulnerable: the predominant note was one of sadness and failure, the predominant imagery of a conventionally romantic kind—flowers, hands, tenderness and tears. Take away the curt mannerisms and you were left with a poetry that was always soft on 'sincerity' and has now come to prize 'feeling' above anything else.

On the face of it, Hugo Williams's *Love-Life* is the most extreme example to date of such naked declaration of feeling. In his early work Williams showed some attraction towards leather-jacket-and-dark-glasses coolness about emotions: poems such as **"Symptoms of Loss"** and **"Driving on the A 30"** sounded very much like Thom Gunn. . . . But over the years he has acquired a voice of almost childlike directness, and in this, the most intimate and innocent of all his collections, writes with a seemingly artless candour about first meetings and final separations, romantic love and pained marriage, loneliness and guilt. Reading it is at times like being forced to hear the life history of someone you've only just met: it's embarrassing to be told all this, but touching and fascinating too. It is a world in which literary influence seems not to exist, and in which wit, humour and irony would be a betrayal or invasion of the authenticity of the feeling. *Love-Life* is thin, and would be thinner still had not Williams reproduced a number of poems from his last collection. . . . Hardly a substantial collection then, but the poet appears to lay himself so open, to bemoan his lot with such unashamed soppiness . . . , that you'd have to be a sadist to want to put the boot in.

In fact, though, *Love-Life* is not so straightforward, nor so confessional, as it first seems. Whenever he's at his most naively literal, Williams is likely to turn up something which subverts, or complicates, or changes what has so far been said. **"Holidays"**, for example, begins as if written by a ten year old—'We spread our things on the sand / In front of the Hotel'. But what about the last four lines?

> Our holidays look back at us in surprise
> From fishing boats and fairs
> Or wherever they were going then
> In their seaweed head-dresses

Does that 'they' in the penultimate line refer back to 'holidays' or 'fishing boats and fairs' or something else? How can holidays look back? What is the logic behind 'or'? What exactly are 'seaweed head-dresses', and can they have anything to do with the 'seagirls wreathed with seaweed red and brown' in Eliot's "Prufrock"? The poems in *Love-Life* often work in this way: the real suddenly shifts to the surreal, the literal turns into a literary allusion. The cupboard which 'contain(s) the sea' in **"Impotence"** may be the same one which holds a glacier in Auden's "As I Walked Out One Evening"; the rhythms and insistent questioning of **"Bachelors"**—'What do they know of love / These men that have never been married'—take us straight to the similarly haranguing opening of Larkin's "The Old Fools"; **"Love at Night"** ends with a paradox which might have been used by Donne or Sidney—'Merciless angel, it has been your task / To teach me how to live without you finally'. Also complicating and enriching the collection is a motif of drama and of playing to an audience. As titles like **"Once More With Feeling"** and **"Along These Lines"** suggest, Williams is very conscious of *using* his suffering, and of putting it on display. . . . In the end, for such a seemingly confessional collection, there's a surprising lack of hard fact sincerely given away. And this makes us, as readers, more than simply voyeurs: . . . the faces of Williams's protagonists remain slightly blurred and ambiguous, waiting to be filled in by our own experience. (p. 472)

> *Blake Morrison, "On Display," in* New Statesman,
> *Vol. 98, No. 2532, September 28, 1979, pp. 472-73.*

ALAN BROWNJOHN

Hugo Williams represents the change to a different, Sixties way of exploring the most vulnerable emotions: in brief, confiding yet cryptic, free verse structures, asking the furniture of everyday living (cigarettes, carrier-bags, teacups) to carry a considerable weight of feeling. . . . [In] one of the best poems in his new collection [*Love-Life*], **"Your Way Home"**, senses the impotence of hope and stretches out to a distance he can picture only too clearly:

> Your gestures have withdrawn
> Almost to the horizon, while the rain, filed thin,
> Floats in across the miles of flood-fed earth
> That will come between us. I can see your car
> Move up the slip-road into the London lane.

End of poem. And Williams knows where to stop. Yet the emotional charge may have evaporated before the end is reached: **"Bar Italia"** starts poignantly, and finishes in a kind of vague ruefulness. When these poems are moored more securely to the objects they order, the impact is greater: in **"The Ribbon"**, the obsessive gesture of struggling with the knot you don't have to untie actually achieves the significance and pathos the poet wants. (pp. 68, 70)

Alan Brownjohn, "An Unprovincial Province," in Encounter, Vol. LIV, No. 1, January, 1980, pp. 64-8, 70.

VICKI FEAVER

Omit one poem, eliminate a few titles and Hugo Williams's latest collection *Love-Life* could be read as a continuous narrative sequence. Throughout the poet is both raconteur and participant. In a series of poignant vignettes he explores obsessively and at first hand the fragility of modern marriage. The location shifts from kitchen . . . to bedroom, from "old hothouse" to "crowded coffee bar", from "rural slum" to "streets at night". It's the territory of Bergman's *Scenes from a Marriage* or of a sophisticated home-movie, but never boring.

Hugo Williams can ring as many changes with the stuff of unsatisfactory love as a good dress designer with similarly ordinary material. The deceptively simple, the witty, the elegant, the little black numbers follow in succinct and memorable fashion.

> My voice breaks
> And I know it must be time

To pour out my heart to you again, he announces in the opening poem **"Once More With Feeling"**. But, as the irony of the title implies, it's not a cue for a stream of artless confessions. Williams selects his scenes with care, edits and rewrites them. The result . . . is both private and public memento. . . .

In general, though, *Love-Life* is slightly disappointing. Even with its padding of several poems from previous books it is on the thin side. And Jessica Gwynne's illustrations do not add much: Hugo Williams's poems make their own pictures.

Vicki Feaver, "Performances in Feeling," in The Times Literary Supplement, No. 4010, February 1, 1980, p. 112.

BLAKE MORRISON

In 1882 Oscar Wilde arrived in New York for a lecture tour he hoped would allow him to "gather the golden fruits of America". Having nothing to declare but his genius, he had the effrontery to think that more than enough: in exchange for the aesthetic refinement he brought them, he expected the Americans to shower him with financial favours. Which as it turned out they did. . . . Since then a whole fleet of English writers have followed in his wake, disembarking for their reading tours with no less immodest ambitions. Hugo Williams, almost a century after Wilde, is the latest of them, and *No Particular Place to Go* recounts his travels from New York up to Toronto down to Houston over to San Francisco and all the way back to Go.

Acutely conscious of his travelling predecessors, Williams gleefully undermines conventional wisdom about the States being a lap of luxury for English writers. . . .

He travels not graciously but by Greyhound, those buses on which you confess your innermost secrets to strangers and wake with adjoining passengers asleep on your lap. He mixes not with the rich and famous, nor even with Faculty Deans and their wives, but with a stream of bums and drifters. He stays at the seediest hotels in rooms where the air-conditioner takes the clean air out and pumps dirty air in and where you have to keep your shoes on for fear of catching something between your toes. Or else he telephones the friends of friends of friends who've found their way into his address book and pleads with them to put him up.

They mostly do, women especially. For *No Particular Place to Go* is a sexual odyssey as well as a Grand Tour, with a lady at every port-of-call and not a few in-between. Here too Williams's book is a grotesque parody of the legend of sexual excess which Dylan Thomas and others established. Williams has his experiences all right, and they run to double figures, but what a glum record of staunched pleasure or outright failure they turn out to be. . . .

For those who know Hugo Williams only through his poetry . . . , *No Particular Place to Go* will come as a surprise. For although the poetry likes to dramatize its creator as a drifter, "sperm drying on his thigh" as he moves on to another town, it hasn't exactly been renowned for its humour: Williams has been a kind of sad heart in the supermarket, his verse always on the brink of shedding prosaic tears. Prose has allowed him to find new satirical powers, whether directed against fashions in interior design . . . , or against fringe theatre . . . , or against himself. There are many hilarious vignettes as Williams makes his down-and-out way through "B-movie, back-lot America", sending home Martian picture postcards (factories and industrial plants "scattered haphazardly beside the river as if a child had left his things out to rust") and offering useful tips for tourists as if compiling an "alternative" Fodor's Guide. . . .

But there is also something wayward and fragmented about the book which no amount of tolerance for "imitative style" will quite wish away. Banal or pretentious when venturing general comment on the state of the nation, it becomes manic in its accumulation of random touristic impressions and bizarre jottings. Relentless in its surprises, it is finally not surprising at all. . . . His desire to be the wide-eyed drifter as well as the knowing traveller makes for an odd mix: Jack Kerouac and Studs Terkel are gleefully alluded to one minute, but the next he becomes the old Etonian, rubbishing American vulgarity as scathingly as did Evelyn Waugh. Another way of putting this would be to say that his loyalties are divided between Thom Gunn and Philip Larkin. . . . Williams idolizes the cool, leather-jacketed Gunn as someone who made it early to the States, and he sets off to see him in San Francisco (the episode ends in typical frustration). Larkin stands at the other extreme, having once sent Williams a postcard questioning the whole point of travel. . . .

Travel, Hugo Williams briskly ripostes at one point, "is a test to the imagination". Certainly his own imagination is vigorously engaged here, to the extent that we suspect he may be making things up. . . . But we'd be wise to take at least some of the book with a pinch of salt: like Clive James's, these are unreliable memoirs that throw a good portion of fiction in among the fact. Whether Hugo Williams will now take his place among those writers who have won academic prestige by radically challenging our notions of the fictive is more doubtful. But he deserves to be read as an inventor as well as documentor, a writer who has made the most of not making good in America.

Blake Morrison, "Poetry in Motion," in The Times Literary Supplement, No. 4100, October 30, 1981, p. 1254.

ROY FULLER

[Hugo Williams] seems to me to be a poet who has got better and better, though by no means starting from an inferior mark. But nothing so far has quite prepared us for the authority of *Writing Home*. . . . His last book of verse, *Love-Life* (1979), was a private press book, restricted to a sequence of twenty-six love poems. His last general collection, *Some Sweet Day*, previously his best, is now ten years old. The new volume is once again a sequence with a unity, but this time of substantial length. In a marvellously subtle way it brings back the poet's childhood and adolescence, and, above all, his dead father. . . .

Hugo Williams has avoided all the pitfalls in writing of a father-son relationship, and also in the revelation of his own past. There is great feeling in these poems, but it is most adroitly varied and depicted. There is fun, too, but it is miles above the usual clichés of family life and schooldays remembered. . . .

Several [of the poems] are more extended as well as more complex pieces than Hugo Williams has previously written: for instance, there is a six-page poem cunningly constructed out of the actor's letters home from wartime North Africa; and the fine **"Death of an Actor"** is almost as long. The latter well illustrates the slight formalities Williams uses to give his work shape and discipline—a mere repetition of the word "Now", extremely effective.

Throughout there are such devices as internal rhymes and assonances, equal-lined stanzas, even a double "sonnet"—reassuring in the consistent free verse. Williams wrote a while ago . . . that he greatly admired "the technique of certain English light comedy actors who can weigh lines on a scales inside their heads which tells them the exact tone of voice with which to drop them cold, or otherwise. It's the aureole, the echo, the haze of a line which counts, not its specific gravity." Those words are very much apropos the present collection, the most entertaining and haunting I have read for a long time.

Roy Fuller, "Domestic Echoes," in The Times Literary Supplement, No. 4304, September 27, 1985, p. 1054.

PETER PORTER

The Hugo Williams who writes so directly and warmly about his childhood and his actor-father [in *Writing Home*] is the same Hugo Williams who has appeared in print praising the arcane poems of Neil Rennie and the doings of the proto-stylish pop group Dr Feelgood. It's wise therefore to look for some avant-gardish touches in his poetry, something to remind you that Williams was a taste-maker before *The Face* was heard of. It's there in the importance Williams attaches to the right clothes for each memory, the archivist's talent with collage, the sheer stylishness of his simplicity.

Fortunately, the fastidiousness of the poetry in *Writing Home* is enriched by a keen sense of the absurd and tinged with middle-aged regret. He is not just the son of a famous boulevard actor and playwright recalling a childhood. . . . Here, with memory advising on the script, he comes into his inheritance and composes poems with a sure eye to their dramatic effect.

There is plenty in *Writing Home* of the statutory misery of boarding school: up-dated L. P. Hartley has never been in short supply. But ballooning above this field of sensitivity is the figure of his father, Hugh Williams, one of the last of the actor-manager breed which looked equally at home in uniform. Whether invented or quoted from life, the following passage has just the right swagger:

> Three and a half years last night,
> since we walked out of the stage door of
>   the Queen's Theatre
> into the Queen's Westminsters.

This is from a sequence entitled **"An Actor's War."** It made me think of James Agate's Ego books, with their atmosphere of pre-war luxury recalled amid grumblings about austerity, and the incongruity of the artist doing his bit for the war effort. Further on, post-war, Hugo is older and having trouble with girls. His father has his trouble with health and bankruptcy, and the final parting of son and father is soberly and touchingly described in **"Death of an Actor."** Although the book is dedicated to Hugo's mother, . . . only his father emerges from these poems in full regalia.

Except, that is, for the figure of the youthful poet. I say the figure, because Hugo Williams, the crypto-playwright, has written a good part for himself involving trouble getting his hair right and failure at everything (including ties and proper dressing) supervised by his father. . . . [Childhood] memories roll inexorably out of the past into the terrified hands of the present. . . .

Peter Porter, "A Performer Waiting in the Wings," in The Observer, October 6, 1985, p. 25.

ROBERT SHEPPARD

Much currently established British poetry focuses upon the poet's own childhood and parentage. The formulas employed for dealing with this include the use of it as 'interesting material', though without much feeling (Craig Raine), and as an opportunity for regret and self-definition (Tony Harrison). Hugo Williams's *Writing Home* joins this limited crowd but rises above it. Williams has a reputation as an author of minimal narrative poems and, while his work remains terse and accessible, his voice as clipped as ever, with this volume he has successfully achieved longer poems of distinction.

One of these, **"An Actor's War"**, which uses his father's letters home from the last war, is the masterly dramatic monologue of a committed hedonist caught up in a war towards which he remains ambivalent. . . . Even the aftermath of battle is seen as though through an after-party fug: 'there is an atmosphere / of emptying the ashtrays and counting the broken glasses'.

What makes this so attractive is that it is free of the Oedipal struggle documented in other poems, the young Hugo repeatedly trying to outwit his father's 'forty-seven suits'. . . . It is also free of a mawkish tone that spoils the sometimes moving elegy **"Death of an Actor"**. . . . Generalisations about death—it 'takes men on from where they were / And yet how soon / It brings them back again'—reveal a weakness in this elegy. Williams is not adept at statements on the Condition of Man—he shares something of his father's aestheticism—although he is superbly skilled at manipulating dramatic incident, whether it involves the disregard of logic in childhood perception and language . . . or the smouldering recalcitrance of adolescence. . . . The whole book adds up to a fragmentary biography and autobiography, in which the personal and childlike impinges upon the public world of the theatre and *Who's Who*. . . .

Many readers will, doubtless, eagerly consume the anecdotal, the wealth of 'interesting material' here (which is a pity, not least because they will find the two excellent, but uncharacteristic, **"Sonny Jim"** poems disappointingly irrelevant). For the author, however, the book has partly involved the foraging of an 'out of bounds' past for purposes of self-definition. . . .

But the poems are not merely personal, since they recognise the miracle of memory. In an apposite image, memory is presented as a childhood marble dropped through an inkwell: 'then a thirty year gap as it falls through / the dust-hole into my waiting hand.'

Robert Sheppard, "Growing Up," in New Statesman, *Vol. 110, No. 2846, October 11, 1985, p. 36.*

William Carlos Williams

1883-1963

American poet, novelist, critic, nonfiction writer, autobiographer, and dramatist.

Williams is regarded as an important and influential poet for his development of distinctly modern poetic forms free from the influence of tradition. He experimented with language, form, and content and concentrated on recreating American idioms in his verse, believing that language is a reflection of character. In order to match the language spoken by Americans, Williams stressed the importance of allowing a poem to take shape during the creative process and based his verse on the natural pauses, cadences, and inflections of speech. Often praised for its vivid imagery, Williams's poetry focuses on objects rather than directly expressing sentiments or ideas. His famous dictum "No ideas but in things!" announced his belief that the reader can understand and empathize with Williams's thoughts and feelings and be affected by the tone and descriptions in his poems. While Williams received only mild attention for much of his career, the publication of his five-volume epic *Paterson* (1948-1956) secured his reputation as a major poet. As well as a prolific author of verse, fiction, and nonfiction, Williams was a practicing physician, and much of his literary work is based on the people with whom he came into contact in and around his hometown of Rutherford, New Jersey. John Ciardi commented on Williams's lasting significance: "The fifty years of Dr. Williams's great productivity were the years in which American poetry threw off its last colonial dependence on England and came securely to rest in the American language. In that literary revolution . . . Dr. Williams played a powerful part as the maker not only of his own poems, but of the heritage of American poetry."

Williams's first volume of poetry, *Poems,* privately printed in 1909, is uncharacteristic of his later work. Described later by Williams as "obviously young, obviously bad," the verse in this book is composed of formal language and conventional rhyme patterns. The volumes which followed, *The Tempers* (1913), *Al que quiere!* (1917), and *Kora in Hell: Improvisations* (1920), contain poems set in distinctly American surroundings which are characterized by precise imagery, spare language, and colloquial speech. *Spring and All* (1923) further exemplifies these qualities: it combines poetry and prose and, according to Dickran L. Trashjian, "dramatized Williams's concern for the possibilities of poetic creation arising out of a dialectic with the destruction of tradition and convention." *Spring and All* contains the much anthologized pieces "The Red Wheelbarrow," a minimalist poem which reflects Williams's concentration on images, and "At the Ballgame," in which Williams draws material from a representative aspect of American life.

With the rise of the Objectivist movement in the 1930s, Williams's work gained wider recognition. Williams was a leading force in Objectivism, which expanded upon the Imagist concern with sight and sound by also emphasizing thought and feeling. In 1934 the Objectivist Press, operated by such poets as Ezra Pound, Louis Zukofsky, and George Oppen, published Williams's *Collected Poems, 1921-1931* (1934). Many of the poems in this volume celebrate life and are centered on the desirability

© *Rollie McKenna*

of growth and change. Following the publication of *Complete Collected Poems* (1938), Williams began to develop a more dynamic form to accommodate his complex aims and ideas. The three-line form, or "triadic stanza," which dominates his later poems, makes its first appearance in *The Wedge* (1944), a volume infused with intense imagery reflecting the social conditions of the World War II era.

Many critics consider *Paterson* to be Williams's greatest achievement. In this work, Williams juxtaposes scenes, images, characters, and other aspects of modern life to form a portrait of both an American city—Paterson, New Jersey—and an artist—Noah Faitoute Paterson. Williams stated that "a man in himself is a city, beginning, seeking, achieving, and concluding life in ways which the various aspects of a city may embody." Williams employed both poetry and prose, drawing from such sources as letters, notes, and local histories to develop a work which would mirror the complexity of his subject. This montage structure is similar to techniques used by contemporary painters. Among the themes explored in *Paterson* are the relationship between the artist and society, loss of innocence, love, marriage, and the physical and intellectual desolation of modern life. While the first four books of *Paterson* are firmly rooted in the actual world, Book V centers on the imagination and is written in a more lyrical and meditative style. *Paterson* has been referred to as the crowning achievement of Williams's poetic career. Kenneth Rexroth called it "an extraordinary synthesis, a profoundly personal portrait of a man as the nexus of a community, which expands out from him and contracts into him like the ripples from a cast stone moving in both directions simultaneously."

In his later poetry, Williams paid increasing attention to lyricism and to more personal concerns. The pieces in *The Desert Music and Other Poems* (1954), *Journey to Love* (1955), and *Pictures from Brueghel and Other Poems* (1962) evidence a more relaxed approach than those in previous volumes. The poem "Asphodel, That Greeny Flower" in *Journey to Love* is frequently cited as an example of his later style. A long, meditative love poem addressed to Williams's wife, Flossie, this work is composed in triadic stanzas with lines of varying length— the "variable foot" Williams is often credited with identifying. The variable foot reflects Williams's belief that the measure of poetic language is relative and is formed in the process of composition rather than being preconceived. According to Williams, he sought "the division of the line according to a new method that would be satisfactory to an American." Marilyn Kallet stated that "Asphodel, That Greeny Flower" "is the result of traveling in unknown, uncharted metrical seas, the lyrical place discovered as the result of sustained willingness to improvise in a disciplined manner." Called by W. H. Auden "one of the most beautiful poems in the language," "Asphodel, That Greeny Flower" is lauded for its emotional immediacy.

Recognized primarily for his poetry, Williams also published several works of fiction. Like his verse, Williams's novels and short stories usually revolve around the lives of ordinary people within the context of experimental structures and devices. *The Great American Novel* (1923), *A Voyage to Pagany* (1928), and *A Novelette* (1932) are written in an improvisational style that tests the limits of traditional fiction. In his best-known novels, collectively called *The Stecher Trilogy,* Williams depicts the people and circumstances of his wife's youth to create a saga of an American family. *White Mule* (1937) introduces Joe Stecher, a hardworking, goodhearted man; Gurlie, his socially ambitious wife; and their daughters, Lottie and Flossie. *In the Money* (1940) recounts Joe's efforts to establish himself in business and examines his marital problems, which arise as Gurlie encourages him to strive for greater material success. In *The Build-Up* (1952), Joe reaches the top of his profession yet remains dissatisfied and unfulfilled, while Gurlie continues to seek social prestige. The book's final section focuses on the romance and marriage of Flossie and Charles Bishop, a young physician and poet who strongly resembles Williams.

The pieces in Williams's short fiction collections, *The Knife and Other Stories* (1932) and *Life on the Passaic River* (1938), dramatize the plight of the New Jersey poor. Similarly, the pieces in *The Doctor Stories* (1985) present a realistic, unsentimental account of a doctor's work during the first half of the twentieth century. Neil Baldwin summarized Williams's fiction: "His poems show us Williams the pointillist. His novels and other short fiction show us the documentarian, engaged in the endless record of his life with others; the social being against an historic backdrop."

Williams's critical work, while neither as prolific nor as highly regarded as his poetry, provides insight into his poetics. *In the American Grain* (1925), a collection of essays on American history, displays his interest in the people and events which shaped American society. The essays Williams contributed to various books and periodicals are collected in *Selected Essays* (1954), *Imaginations: Collected Early Prose* (1970), and *The Embodiment of Knowledge* (1974). Williams's other nonfiction works include *The Autobiography* (1951), *I Wanted to Write a Poem: The Autobiography of the Works of a Poet* (1958), and *Yes, Mrs. Williams: A Personal Record of My Mother* (1959).

After spending much of his early career in relative obscurity, Williams was firmly established as a major poet at the time of his death. Because of his experiments with language and form and his firm knowledge of contemporary trends in art and music as well as literature, Williams has been linked with such movements as Modernism, Imagism, and Objectivism; he was also highly regarded by writers associated with the Beat movement. Williams's dedication to his craft and his independent and enthusiastic approach to life and literature have earned him an honored place in American letters. Williams won numerous awards, including the National Book Award for *Selected Poems* and *Paterson,* Book III, in 1953, the Bollingen Prize in poetry in 1952, the Pulitzer Prize in poetry for *Pictures from Brueghel,* and the National Institute of Arts and Letters gold medal for poetry in 1963.

(See also *CLC,* Vols. 1, 2, 5, 9, 13, 22; *Contemporary Authors,* Vols. 89-92; and *Dictionary of Literary Biography,* Vols. 4, 16, 54.)

LINDA W. WAGNER

For Williams, speech was identity. He had listened carefully through a lifetime to the diction and the inflection of his patients, his friends, his culture; he had used language signals as a means of making diagnoses; most important of all, he had based his own poetics on theories of speech rhythms. . . . (p. 115)

For the earnest young doctor of Rutherford, poetry was his most important activity. He was a pediatrician, yes; he loved being a pediatrician (and a general practitioner as well: sixty years ago a doctor was a doctor, no matter what his specialty); and his care for his patients surfaces often in both his fiction and his poems. But Williams knew, early, that he wanted a literary life. He worked as a physician so that he might write what he chose, free from any kind of financial or political pressure. From the beginning, in the early 1900s, he understood the trade-offs: he would have less time to write; he would need more physical stamina than people with only one occupation; he would probably demand more from his family. But Williams, with the help of his wife, the remarkable Flossie, was willing to live the kind of rushed existence that would be necessary, crowding two full lifetimes into one, juggling experience and meditation, learning from the first and then understanding through the second. (pp. 115-16)

Judging from his more than forty published books, from his position today as one of our most innovative and generous modern writers, we must conclude that Williams's sometimes frantic lifestyle did work successfully. . . . [It] may be that the combination of careers worked for him at least partly because it was in basic agreement with Williams's personal aesthetic position, even in the groping years when he scarcely had one.

Contact with people—happy people, troubled people, excited and nervous people—meant contact with language. Williams's most consistent principle in sixty years of writing was the use of natural speech rhythms, the line divided and spaced so as to suggest rhythmic breaks in the language as spoken. His hatred of prescribed forms like the sonnet and the influence of formal, British English stems from the same root: he considered such formality inimical to American English. . . . Williams chose to stay with what he was convinced *were* the true materials of his art—American people, American life—and create a poetics that could accommodate his multiple subjects. (p. 116)

Paterson is that remarkable mixture of poetry and prose, loose-lined poems cut by shorter-lined tercets, quasi-formal rhetoric, a section of verse play, and—superimposed—the montage of quotations from stodgy histories of Paterson, notes, and impassioned letters from other struggling writers. A hodgepodge, the American version of Pound's more famous "ragbag," *Paterson* grew from Williams's need to express his fascination with country/man/language; to put it all together instead of fragmenting it—this huge, stirring emotional nexus—so that it would fit into the tidy poems that he was then writing. (p. 117)

Amazing—Williams and the writing of this five-book poem. Completely abjuring any traditional form or genre, he began with what were for him central thematic issues—marriage and divorce, virtue, modern life, and man's search through it all for "a redeeming language." . . . [He] somehow wrestled from an already bewildering lifetime of experience (the quantity of materials he wanted to include is staggering in itself) a few characters, selected scenes, chary images to create the effective poem. But in the process of writing, he confronted again and again the problem of using real speech so that it was more than local color. There was a great difference between Williams's concept of "using" speech, of *finding* the character through his speech, and of just mixing in flavorful slang or idiom as relief in more formal poetic diction. Here is the most important difference, I believe, between Williams and poets like Vachel Lindsay, Sandburg, Cummings, the earlier Eliot, and even Whitman, who—for all his interest in the American character—always managed to write in the same heavily traditional vocabulary.

For Williams, any person's identity rested on his spoken language. Many of his short stories open with a character speaking; we hear the words with no introduction or setting given. . . . In *Paterson,* Williams continues this tactic of preserving natural speech. Whole pages from letters he had received appear unchanged in the poem; speech here, through arrangement, is raised to art. Earlier, in the Cotton Mather section of *In the American Grain,* Williams had used the same approach, by letting Mather's own language and phrasing "create" his personality. The device, for Williams, was not new. In his poetry, however, because of the intrinsic formal differences between poetry and prose, his reliance on this speech identity took on a new ramification. As he pointed out [in *I Wanted to Write a Poem*],

> The rhythmic unit usually came to me in a lyrical outburst. I wanted it to look that way on the page, I didn't go in for long lines because of my nervous nature. I couldn't. The rhythmic pace was the pace of speech, an excited pace because I was excited when I wrote.

Speech as the origin of form, of shape: set against T. S. Eliot's very moderate view of a poet's use of tradition, Williams ex-

plodes: "A false language. A true. A false language pouring—a language (misunderstood) pouring (misinterpreted) without dignity. . . ."

It is not that Williams opted entirely for innovation. Pound chanted "Make it new" for sixty years; Williams's parallel cry was "the American language." As Williams wrote, "Free verse was not the answer. From the beginning, I knew that the American language must shape the pattern." (pp. 118-19)

But Williams was looking for more than a technical ploy, and perhaps that is another reason his insistence on the use of the natural idiom is important. For he was throughout his life, even though he fought Wallace Stevens's designation, a great Romantic.

> All this—
> was for you, old woman.
> I wanted to write a poem
> that you would understand. . . .

And he did. Williams really wanted to reach a public, a public at least partly comprised of actual people, and part of his anger with the academic establishment resulted from its ignoring him. (If no one anthologized his poems, how were the common readers to find them?) Williams wanted to reach people because he saw so many sterile, impoverished lives; poetry, art, beauty might somehow ease those terrors. . . . The theme occurs over and over in Williams's poems: he sees the poem as a way to self-knowledge, the poem as a means of reaching, of communicating, of—in simple—speaking. (pp. 120-21)

As poet or as doctor, Williams was fascinated with "the poem that each is trying actually to communicate to us." To his credit, he heard, unearthed, a good many of those inarticulate poems, and he made new shapes where none existed before, to embody the particular—and particularly American—beauties of his townspeople and their language. (pp. 121-22)

It could well be that in the future, Williams will be compared more often with those other great innovators of modern American literature—Stein, Hemingway, Dos Passos—than with his fellow "poets." And perhaps that will be just as well, for "speaking" in itself knows no *genre* distinctions. It is an act of voice—a human act—and its purpose is, and has always been, to reach. (p. 124)

> *Linda W. Wagner, " 'Speaking Straight Ahead . . .',"*
> *in her* American Modern: Essays in Fiction and Poetry, *Kennikat Press, 1980, pp. 115-24.*

CHARLES DOYLE

For criticism, the important question is: what criteria are we to apply in judging Williams's poems? Many American poets, of the past two decades in particular, have signified their approval of his work either by imitating it or advancing it. Critical difficulty is encountered not so much in characterizing his discoveries concerning 'the poem' as in deciding which among his typical poems are successful, and good, poems, and why this is so.

At the beginning of his career, and by now the point has been made often enough, Williams's poems were highly literary, modelled on approved masters in the English tradition, both in diction and measure. When he broke away from this stale sense of poetry, it was first through the influence of Pound and Imagism. As he suggests in the Preface to *Kora in Hell*, Williams, at this period, escaped from a common mental attitude of the literary poet—considering, or thinking about, one thing in terms of another. Simile, analogy and metaphor he rejected as inappropriate to his sense of 'the poem', preferring to assert the necessity of keeping one's eye on the object. . . . Such insistence on the specific individuality of the object, as opposed to its likeness and relation to other objects, is distinctly American, as is the aim for 'vividness' rather than propriety.

Seeing clearly was, for him, the great virtue, as it was for his painter friends Demuth and Sheeler. Throughout Williams's career we encounter the isolation of the moment of clear perception or experience as if it were hard won from the ever-encroaching flux. In a constant state of alertness the artist makes his discoveries, but he is also active, and morally so, a selector, who 'must keep his eye without fault on those things he values, to which officials refuse to give the proper names.' . . . Genuine contact is made through concentration on the object with great intensity, to 'lift it' to the imagination. An object lifted to the imagination yields up its 'radiant gist'. Sometimes this is simply discovered, while at others (given that the field of energy does not stop at the skin or outer envelope of the human being), the process is completed by the poet by means of invention or structuring. In poems such as **"The Red Wheelbarrow,"** Williams draws our attention simultaneously to the world out there and to our relationship with it, which must be fresh, now. Here is one significance of his assertion that 'Nothing is good save the new,' . . . which is far from claiming that a thing is inevitably good *merely because* it is new.

'Nothing is good save the new' because what is important is here and now, our immediate experience. In the face of centuries of traditional poetic form, which had run into the nineteenth-century mire of 'moral homily' (seeing the poem as aiming for perfection in long-established verse-forms along with the expression of edifying or uplifting material), Williams had the insight to see that the significance of the poem is not in its subject-matter (which is nearly always 'phantasy' or 'dream'), but, as he asserts over and over again in many different ways, in its form. Given his deep convictions on the need for contact and that 'the local is the only universal' it is natural that he should have rejected traditional forms and measure, since these are not local, nor have Americans direct access to their sources. Where to look, then, for new form?

Seen in this way, Williams's position is both perceptive and sensible. A poem is made with words and possesses whatever reality it may have through 'the shapes of men's lives in places'. What more natural than to use the language of those men? When, in his 1948 essay **"The Poem as a Field of Action,"** Williams, looking back, observed that 'Imagism was not structural: that was the reason for its disappearance,' . . . he meant that it did not derive purely from the speech-patterns of its day. Having recognized the vital link between poetry and speech, he then had to work for most of a lifetime before achieving a sound technical base (the variable foot), which could incorporate the American idiom on all occasions without strain. (pp. 169-70)

Only the tradition-bound will by now find it hard to accept Williams's innovations in the line. From *Al Que Quiere!* on, he largely escaped the tyranny of quantitative measure, employing instead a measure based on phrasing. A difficulty in making categorical assertions about Williams's measure (and therefore codifying it) is that his practice varies somewhat. Occasionally it is purely 'musical'. In this early, Imagist period it depended considerably on the syntax and phrasing of written

statement. Very often, at its strongest throughout his career, it related to speech. Sometimes (as in **"Struggle of Wings,"** for example) it can be criticized as too long, or heavy; but even length is no sure criterion, as witness some writing in **"The Clouds."** . . . Generally, however, it can be said that the longer line is most successful when deployed to create a forward verbal flow. Much of the work in *Collected Later Poems* (**"The Mind's Games,"** for example, or **"Aigeltinger"**) is not easy to classify in terms of the line. Almost all of it is natural in flow, which saves it from the charge of being 'chopped-up prose', but a great deal of it is not far removed from prose. Sometimes (as in **"Aigeltinger"**) one suspects a deliberate tinkering with quantitative measure. Ultimately our bases for judging Williams's line must be broad ones: its energy in the specific instance, its 'naturalness' (which, almost inevitably, depends on the spoken word). (p. 171)

Traditional prosody is fixed, while for Williams measure in the poem is always relative. He never insisted on establishing a new set of rules, beyond observing the (for him) undeniable relationship between American measure and American speech. 'The only reality we can know is MEASURE,' . . . but different worlds call for different measures, each consonant with its own time and place. (p. 172)

Williams's basic short line was established in *Al Que Quiere!* Poem after poem in that volume, some quiet some less so, shows surprising tautness and strength of line. Much depends on the energy in the specific line, used with great range and subtlety:

> When I was younger
> it was plain to me
> I must make something of myself.
> Older now. . . .

Here, and in numerous other instances, the line disposition entirely suits the action of the poem (an obvious example here is the muting of line 4). Beyond this everything depends on the articulation of lines throughout. Hence, the poem is 'a field of action', and hence Williams's recognition of the rightness of Olson's theory of composition by field, rather than through accumulating well-turned lines.

Part of the outcome of this new sense of measure as 'relative' is a new respect for the individual word, accepting it freshly not as a label but as an alternative reality, an object in its own right. The word is a 'thing-in-itself', but it derives energy (usually in the form of 'meaning') through contact with other words. Much can be understood concerning Williams's use of the line if we recognize the range of his sentence structures. Vividness is gained very often by employment of the present tense, but he can (through syntactical arrangement) create a sense of immediacy without it. . . . Frequently Williams's poems begin with a question or an exclamation or exhortation, all indicating his eagerness, wonder, curiosity, and usually transmuting his excitement into the energy of the poem. Typically, throughout his career his language is simple and, despite subtle sentence variation, clearly and directly organized. In much of his verse of the late 1930s, early 1940s, which makes *Collected Later Poems* disappointing compared with *Collected Earlier Poems,* he allows himself discursive sentence structures, employing pause, parenthesis and qualification to a greater extent than he had earlier. Seen in the perspective of his whole development, it may be that much of the work of that period is preparatory for *Paterson,* an effort to extend his means deliberately in the direction of discursiveness, which bore fruit not so much in *Paterson* as in the assured, relaxed statement of many poems in *The Desert Music* and *Journey to Love*. Meantime, to the extent that he forgot Pound's dictum that the good writer 'uses the smallest possible number of words', Williams's work of that period lost distinction. (pp. 172-73)

Like Pound, Williams employs the technique of juxtaposition, but where Pound juxtaposes literary or cultural 'echoes' or apparent correspondences, Williams (until *Paterson*) tends to place together things-in-themselves. Even his juxtapositions in *Paterson* are treated so, not intended to suggest analogies, but to present the quality of American experience direct and without interference. Sometimes his juxtaposed objects possess 'one-thousandth part of a quality in common', but often they deliberately (or carelessly) clash. Therefore, in some sense, juxtaposition is 'suggestive', but the reader is not necessarily led through a thought process, almost certainly to a flash of recognition which is an energy-discharge linking the juxtaposed items. Not that Williams is against activity of the intelligence. Traditional metaphor means the positive presence of the writer, in the text, directing his reader, contrary to Williams's belief that the artist should be 'remote from the field' and that art is created through 'concrete indirections.' . . . (p. 174)

Not the artist's autobiography, but the quality of his experience is important. To prevent his experience from being trammelled by convention it must be 'open' and not preconceived. A sense of form must be allied to a willingness to descend to the 'formless ground'. Williams's advice to 'write carelessly' is not really at odds with his insistence on accuracy of observation and rendering. What must be avoided is 'thought about' the object or experience, and (again from Williams's point of view) before *Paterson* evidence of deliberate thought in the *details* of a poem (like over-attention to 'subject-matter') would constitute a weakness in that poem. Perception and the imaginative disposition of perceptions, these are primary to the poem. Verbal and causal connectives, any verbal arrangement which is based on the structure of thought, these adulterate the poem, diminishing its purity and effectiveness. Apart from escaping the tyranny of quantitative measure, this must have been Williams's pre-eminent consideration in his search for, and development of, the variable foot.

All these criteria, and others, are positive and reasonable. Nothing can bridge the hiatus between Williams's intentions and those critics who cannot accept his major requirement—the rejection of quantitative measure for contemporary American poetry. However, almost everywhere the variable foot and composition by field have been accepted at least as legitimate, valuable extensions of the poetic means. Given this, Williams's own requirements for the poem offer adequate tools by which to assess his work, up to the mid-1940s.

Paterson poses fresh problems for the critic. What are to be his evaluative criteria for it? One is the valuable notion of the metamorphic poem implicit in the work, put forward by Sister M. Bernetta Quinn [in *The Metamorphic Tradition*]. Williams's own 'theory' of 'interpenetration' accords well with the metamorphic technique. His use of 'raw material' in the form of a variety of prose passages is of a piece both with his rejection of the 'anti-poetic' and his belief in the thing-in-itself.

To consider Williams's poetic development progressively is to wonder, at times, if he was sidetracked by Imagism and Objectivism. Although 'not structural', Imagism certainly persuaded him of the value of intense concentration upon the object. Objectivism may have intensified this in two ways: by

emphasis on the removal of self from the poem and by (consequently) drawing the attention to the speech or music in which the objective experiences presented themselves. . . . (pp. 174-75)

Both Imagism and Objectivism are in the same theoretical line as Poe's insistence on the poem as a striving for a single effect. In its very name each of these 'movements' suggests a concentration on noun or thing as opposed to 'an easy lateral sliding' through a statement of abstractions easily divorced from reality. His insistence on the value of the thing-in-itself is important in Williams, but even more important is his sense of process. . . . Perhaps the crucial clue in the *Paterson* headnotes is 'by multiplication a reduction to one.' . . . Implying, as it does, movement, activity, this categorically shifts the emphasis of Williams's poem from thing to process, a passing through. His central means is in the metamorphoses of Paterson himself/itself. How are we to judge the value or success of this means? If the nature of Paterson, the man-city, becomes very clear at any one point in the poem, would not this be distracting? Would it not limit the range of possible response? Quest, perpetual change, fluidity, instability—these are characteristic of *Paterson,* giving it vitality. All objects in the poem are instantaneously there and are instantly gone. They are *here and now. Paterson I-IV* is a search for order. As originally conceived, the poem is search only, process only, and the failure of Paterson, the man-city, is comparable with that of, say, Père Sebastian Rasles in *In the American Grain,* a failure which has its own kind of success, in recognizing that *'La Vertue est toute dans l'effort'*. Notably, *Paterson V,* which concerns itself with the tapestry, the relationship of art to life and Williams's lifelong Kora-Venus preoccupation, has a greater immediate clarity, concentration upon the object, and a more obviously discursive point.

The earlier books of *Paterson* are sustained, paradoxically, as much by the fragments of 'experience' or 'thing' as they are by the necessarily fluid central metaphor. Curiously, metamorphosis *invites* discourse, while the 'gathering up' of its own weight has, at times, an effect opposite to the 'taking up of slack'. If one has any reservation about *Paterson V,* it is that the appeal to art, to imagination, is obvious rather than new, or penetrating, or decisive. Yet as a 'resolution', it confirms the tendency of Williams's whole career and is very much of a piece with all the work of his last phase.

Williams's late concentration on the imagination, his alignment of imagination and love, his self-searching, these are not narcissism. Rather his belief in the imagination is similar to his lifelong sense of the local. Emphasis is not on *his* locality, or imagination, because they are *his*. Imagination works from material in one's own experience (whoever one may happen to be). That experience differs from one phase to another, so constant reference to it is simply carrying devotion to 'the new' to its ultimate conclusion.

From his Objectivist period onward all Williams's work implies a sense of the self other than the merely autobiographical or egotistical. In 1947 he observed: 'The objective in writing is to reveal. . . . The difference between the revealer and others is that he reveals HIMSELF, not you.' . . . Again, this stems from a realization that, just as the place a person can truly know is his own locality, so the only self he can truly know is his own. Avoidance of falsification, pretence, is at back of this and of the finally developed sense of imagination. In the long run, love is the important emotion in human experience. What keeps man alive (or kills him, for that matter) is his own imagination and how it relates to the world. Imagination has the power of transforming or maintaining the world, and is the chief metamorphic agent. . . . Williams's latest work is generally discursive in comparison with his pre-*Paterson* poems. Interestingly, this is due at least in part to his metrical experimentation. The stepping of the three-tiered line, which he had used first in 'The descent beckons' (*Paterson II*), has the effect of casting aside the static, fixed-object presentation of many earlier poems. To suggest that Williams was never discursive in his earlier work would be inaccurate. Even though expressed negatively ('No ideas but in things!'), Williams's awareness of the 'idea' in poetry is about as long as his career. His late development of 'the variable foot' allowed him to be discursive without abandoning the cadence and rapidity of natural speech. The order of speech, of prose statement, has replaced a repetitive, metronomic pattern, as the *expected* element in Williams's line. By and large, the line units are dictated by speech, but they have a flexibility and offer a range of possible discovery far exceeding those of traditional meter. Looking for criteria to judge 'the variable foot' we may suggest: (a) is it natural, true to speech? (b) are the variations vital and interesting? For Williams the anti-poetic would be aping of traditional literary forms or copying the speech and/or measure of others.

As an innovator, Williams shared many of his positions with Pound, but he may in the long run prove to be more influential. Pound to a much greater degree applied himself to, and found his material in, art and literature. Williams, likewise interested in simultaneity and interaction rather than causality, suggests his own far different sense of experience in chapter 54 of *The Autobiography*. He refers to the exciting secrets of the 'underground stream' of human experience itself, unselected. Attending closely to it, 'there is no better way to get an intimation of what is going on in the world.' . . . His whole objective, as it ultimately became clear to him, is to lift the 'inarticulate' up to imagination. A sense of the common people as prime source of life, shared in the early years with Eliot, seems never to have left Williams, despite a discouragement made plain at least as late as *Paterson II*.

A 'lifetime of careful listening' to the speech arising from his daily tasks and contacts, convinced him that poem and life, also, are one—and that each person is trying to communicate to the world the poem of himself. In many works, but particularly in *Kora in Hell, In the American Grain, Collected Earlier Poems, Paterson* and the late poems, he demonstrated the informing need for imagination, having realized early that 'The imagination transcends the thing itself.' . . . An explorer and discoverer, always conscious of the handful of men who had contributed positively to the shaping of the American spirit, he takes his place alongside them. (pp. 175-78)

Charles Doyle, in his William Carlos Williams and the American Poem, *St. Martin's Press, 1982, 209 p.*

MARVIN BELL

William Carlos Williams is, arguably, our most American-American poet—as distinguished from such hybrids as Stevens (French-American), Eliot (British-American) and Pound (Italian-American). "Americanism," for Williams, meant that the circumstances of poetry are local, the tone of poetry is personal, the process of poetry is improvisational, and the subject of poetry is reality.

"Dedication for a Plot of Ground" is one of those one-of-a-kind poems, almost a "found" poem, a poem that is notable

for its strategy and organization and one or two key "moves" amidst content that insists on its preeminence. I would understand if the reader were to think it artless. For its artistry resides, in large measure, in such seemingly unartistic "skills" and "talents" as personal energy, a belief that reality may be the content of a poem, feeling deeply without blurry eyes or fuzzy thoughts, and (above all!) strong values—local in origin, stated without irony.

Williams' writing stands in evidence against what most poetry is and even against what most people say *his* work is. Amidst the merely fanciful that dominates the poetry of any age, it stands out still for its sense of worthy content. By example, Williams' poems oppose the mind-set of literary convention in general, and the notion, in particular, that the naming of objects, the accomplishment of literary forms, or the geometries of the imagination are the actual subjects of poetry. Their method tilts toward improvisation: an abandonment of the daily, reasonable and restrained self to force, need, momentum and invention. (p. 16)

Because of such ideas and methods, Williams is sometimes carried by his writing to a moment when words fail. That is, it takes him to the point where poems accomplish what is most rare and most worthy: they enlarge the silence. Hence, his work stands in forceful opposition to that poetry of any time which consists of lies, playful or weighty, which is based on theory, guesswork or manners, which is essentially entertainment, and which only fills up the silence. . . .

Williams' work is badly misunderstood—of course. From those poems of his we can only consider to have been finger exercises, many readers have decided that his is a poetry of cadence and object. Didn't he say, in *Book One* of *Paterson,* "Say it! No ideas but in things."? Yes, but by *Book Two,* he has already amended it to read: "No ideas but / in the facts"; and in *Book Five,* he writes: "You can learn from poems / that an empty head tapped on / sounds hollow / in any language!"; and one has only to read such poems as **"These"** and **"The Descent"** to see that he is a poet of intelligence and ideas. His poems, graphs of a mind, are as good as they are because his mind is as good as it is.

As for the "variable foot," the "triadic stanza" and the "American idiom"—these were all ways to beat the conventional poetic modes of his age and certain prevailing assumptions (still with us) about the nature of poetry. The foot, he said, not being fixed, must be variable. That was a way of using the vocabulary of the other guys to get away with something, since the foot, not being fixed, is not a foot. The triadic stanza—that was genius!—derives, I believe, from Williams' sense of his strength in writing—improvisation, taking the form of wildly various syntax—and his need to use the poetic line with and against whatever sentences energy, rapid association and "impure" diction might throw up. His genius lay in having sensed so definitely that prose can be poetry; that, indeed, it may be the prose of one's time that furnishes the language and strategies for what emerges later as the new poetry.

As for the American idiom, on the surface that means using the language as it is, where you live. Underneath, however, it signals a fundamental position on the nature of content. For if the common lingo is fit for poetry, so is the common man and woman. We are what we say. (pp. 16-17)

It is the actual, the thing or event which is its own best image and metaphor, which engages Williams. And so [in **"Dedication for a Plot of Ground"**] he begins to take stock of his grandmother's life. Just the *outer* events, you might notice. She was born, married, widowed, transported, remarried, and a second time widowed. She lost children, raised motherless grandchildren, and tended her lawn here for fifteen years.

Sure, when the facts by themselves begin to lose their distinction in the general welter of a life, he adds a little something to them: for example, "lived *hard* / for eight years in St. Thomas," or "*defended* herself," which are the additions of language; or "against flies, against girls / that came smelling about," which are the additions, also, of imagination; or "against the growing strength of the boys," which is the addition, *in addition,* of feeling and thought.

And so Williams arrives, by means of memory, association, momentum and improvisation, near to that silence where no more can be said because everything which needed to be said has been. What can he do, then, but return to the physical circumstances of the poem—the ground where somewhere she lies buried, the ground right here which still bears her life. He begins again from the plot of ground, and says what little is needed to conclude the story. When the end is in sight—*before,* that is, it has been stated—he merely interrupts the long litany of facts to say what he has thought all along: that this plot of ground is dedicated, not to a corpse, not to knowledge of death, not to fear, not to lush wonder or pained beseeching of the infinite, but to the *living presence* of one who lived, lived hard, and fought for her values. She was not just a carcass. Hence, if you can bring nothing but your carcass to this place (without bringing, say, intelligence, values and feelings), you might as well stay away. She was better than that.

It is worth noticing the free verse of this poem. Lines three, twenty and thirty-four end with the preposition "of," line seven with "with," lines thirty and thirty-five with "against." Line twenty-two is nothing more than the words "mothered them—they being." Stanza one is seven times as long as stanza two, and each stanza consists of only one sentence. Everyone knows why these things are unacceptable, right? What everyone knows, no one knows. Truisms are false. People are wrong. Williams is alive. If you can bring nothing to his work but your carcass, never mind. (pp. 18-19)

> *Marvin Bell, "Williams and 'Dedication . . .',"* in Field: Contemporary Poetry and Poetics, *No. 29, Fall, 1983, pp. 16-19.*

CARL RAPP

One of the persistent clichés in the recent critical commentary on William Carlos Williams has to do with the idea that Williams' work represents a radical departure from tradition and that Williams himself was an enthusiastic champion of all things new and modern. Particularly since the appearance of J. Hillis Miller's influential essay on Williams in *Poets of Reality* (1965), we have been told, in one way or another, that Williams was a poet of immediate experience, who somehow managed to eradicate from his poetry all traces of belief in a transcendental reality not in accordance with that experience. Thus James E. Breslin has written that, for Williams, "only the moment is real. The present is the beginning, and it contains everything: the seed of all life." And Joseph N. Riddel insists, in his book *The Inverted Bell,* that Williams refused to have anything to do with the Orphic myth of an apostasy from original unity, preferring instead to indulge, with a pure Nietzschean joy, in that happy freeplay of interpretation which is the only appropriate response to the world in which we live, "a world without

truth, without center or origin." As a corollary of this view, it has also been rather widely assumed that Williams wholeheartedly endorsed the experiments of "modernism" in both art and literature, provided, of course, they were not associated with the reactionary conservatism of T. S. Eliot.

It seems to me that this view of Williams is mistaken, partly because it minimizes or ignores an important motif in his writing but also because it apparently derives from an erroneous conception of modern philosophy. Despite appearances to the contrary, Williams strongly adhered to one of the many modern versions of the myth of the fall. He believed, in other words, that the present time is essentially unsatisfactory by comparison to the remote past and to the future and that it is so because, for the moment, we have lost an original vitality or innocence which we must struggle to regain. Indeed, Williams took a very dim view of his own American culture, and he often spoke of the modern period, especially with respect to art and literature, as though it were "an age of darkness" (*The Embodiment of Knowledge*), with only occasional flashes of promise. Immediacy was not for him a certain fact of experience; it was an ideal, a goal, the elusive alternative, as he states in one essay, to "the unformed intermediate worlds in which we live and from which we suffer bitterly." There was a time, it seems, when "the word" (as he calls it in Book II of *Paterson*) lived in the ancient divisions of the poetic line, but now it has crumbled to chalk. This complaint is heard so often in Williams' work that it might almost be said to constitute a sort of *leitmotif* which never wholly disappears even in those instances when Williams' comments on his contemporaries are seemingly most generous. (pp. 82-3)

[The] project of restoring our awareness of the past lies at the very heart of Williams' essays on American history in *In the American Grain.* The truth about the past, Williams claims in this book, remains distorted even in the original records, so that it must be ferreted out and reconstituted in new writing in order to be apprehended. In his attempt to get back to "the strange phosphorus of the life" which precedes every effort that has been made to record it, he repeats or imitates the action of his own heroes, who essentially abandoned the advanced culture of Europe in order to go back to the beginning again, back to the forces and conditions which precede culture. From Williams' point of view, the New World was really the old world brought back. It was the Golden Age all over again, "a beloved condition . . . in which all lived together," "in its every expression, the land of heart's desire." With the passage of time, says Williams, this beneficent condition is invariably lost. The Europeans had lost it in Europe long before they came to America, and now the Americans have lost it as well by refusing to study their origins. Just as the "true character" of the American past is obscured by the very documents which are supposed to preserve it, so the true character of the New World spirit has been virtually obliterated by the emergence of modern culture. . . . Almost from the beginning of our history, from colonial times at least, a cultural inertia has been building, which is manifested in "the niggardliness of our history, our stupidity, sluggishness of spirit, the falseness of our historical notes, the complete missing of the point." "In the confusion," it would seem, "almost nothing remains of the great American New World but a memory of the Indian."

But, if Williams was skeptical about the quality of life in general in modern America, he was even more skeptical about the arts, especially the art of poetry. While it is true that he endorsed the experiments of the modernists, he did so not so much because he regarded them as magnificent achievements in their own right but mainly because he felt that they were salutary thrusts in opposition to the spirit of the age. There had been a time when all was well with the arts, but now, he supposed, they were sick, and drastic remedies were needed to revive them. . . . Perpetually haunted by a sense of failure, Williams could never bring himself to admit that even the best efforts of the modernists were really satisfactory. He always thought of them as a sort of preparation for good things to come.

In 1921, he declared that America was "an artistic desert," a judgment which returns again and again in his work, despite his enthusiasms (usually temporary) for particular artists. In *The Great American Novel,* for example, he complains that we have "no art," "no words," and in *Spring and All* he observes that "the greatest characteristic of the present age is that it is stale—stale as literature." In 1929, although it seems that poetry is "just at the brink of its modern development," language itself is still "in its January," as though James Joyce, Gertrude Stein, Ezra Pound, and all the rest had never lived. However, part of the blame for poetry's arrested development must be shared by the modernists themselves, according to Williams, because none of them seems to have been able to find an adequate poetic form. . . . [As] Williams describes them in the 1930s, the modernists seem like prophets in the wilderness, preparing the verbal way "long before the final summative artist arrives."

In the 1940s and the 1950s, as everyone knows, Williams' search for an adequate form focused more and more on the attempt to define a new conception of the poetic line based on a "new measure." . . . He wrote to Kenneth Burke in 1947: "For myself I reject all poetry as at present written, including my own. I see tendencies, nodes of activity, here and there but no clear synthesis."

In the early 1950s, however, the long-awaited breakthrough seemed imminent. Williams seized upon a small passage of verse in the second book of *Paterson,* professing to see in it at least the rudiments of what he had been looking for. "Only now," he wrote in his *Autobiography,* "have we begun to catch hold again and restarted to make the line over." Nevertheless, despite these glimmerings of hope, he went right on talking to the very end as though the new line or the new measure remained to be discovered. Almost a year after he published *The Desert Music and Other Poems* in 1954, he was still lamenting, to John C. Thirlwall, that "the measure by which the poem is to be recognized has at present been lost," and, in his "statement" on measure for Cid Corman, he referred to his poems using the triadic line as "a few experiments," not to be considered final: "There will be other experiments but all will be directed toward the discovery of a new measure." In 1958, that measure is "beyond our thoughts." In 1961, it is "what we must get to in the modern world." Little wonder, then, that toward the end of his career Williams seriously considered the possibility of collecting all his poems under a new title— not the *Collected Poems,* or the *Complete Poems* but *The Complete Collected Exercises Toward a Possible Poem.*

Clearly, unless we are willing to ignore what amounts to a major motif in Williams' letters and essays, we cannot agree with Miller and Breslin that Williams' work as a whole is grounded in the belief that only the present moment is real or valuable. It is not immediacy that rules Williams; it is the myth of immediacy, the myth of an original state of mind or condition of being from which we have grievously departed and to which

we must return at any cost. For it is only by returning to this state or condition that we can extricate ourselves from "the vague and excessively stupid juxtapositions commonly known as 'reality,'" "the world of make-believe, of evasion," in which, as Williams never tires of telling us, we most certainly spend the greater part of our lives. (pp. 83-8)

Nor can we agree with Professor Riddel that, just because Williams cannot attain the ideal, he therefore dispenses with it altogether *as an ideal.* The evidence shows plainly that he does not dispense with it. On the contrary, it remains an ideal from beginning to end and constitutes both the *archē* and the *telos* of Williams' work as a whole, the standard against which he himself chose to be measured.

It is obvious, I think, that the myth of immediacy bears a striking resemblance to the myth of the fall, which is usually associated with a certain aspect of Platonism or with Christian theology. That is why it has been so important in recent years to deny that Williams had anything to do with the myth or that it has any bearing on his work. To claim that it does have a bearing would be to imply that Williams does not participate in the rupture in Western thought or the revolution in human sensibility which is supposed to be the most significant event in modern thought. It would mean that in some way he secretly retains the concept of a transcendent reality or a point of origin from which we have apostasized and to which we must reunite ourselves. Indeed, Williams' work cannot be understood apart from such a concept, but neither can modern philosophy itself be understood apart from it.

The myth of the fall is still the central myth of our Western culture, though today it is primarily operative for intellectuals in the form of Wittgenstein's "ordinary language" philosophy, or in the phenomenology of Heidegger or Merleau-Ponty, or in the deconstructionist philosophy of Jacques Derrida. Each of these otherwise very different philosophies rests on what amounts to the same myth, and that is the myth that we are just about to emerge from a long and deeply engrained tradition of fundamentally erroneous thinking which is roughly equivalent to the entire Western intellectual tradition. Virtually every participant in this tradition, from Plato to the present, may be said to have fallen into the error of conceiving of reality in terms of metaphysical principles which we now know to be fictitious. Not only do we know that these principles have no validity, we also know how they came into being, what caused them to occur to us in the first place, so that now we can almost say that we have emancipated ourselves from them, or, more importantly, that we have emancipated ourselves from the kind of thinking that produces them, in a manner unprecedented in the history of recorded thought. Indeed, Western man *is* metaphysical man, and metaphysical man is "fallen" man, but we ourselves have the unique opportunity, coming as we do at the "end" of Western thought, of returning to the innocence (or is it the violence?) that precedes the fall into metaphysics. (pp. 88-9)

Nevertheless, while each of these thinkers would insist that a fall into metaphysics can be traced back to a basic misapprehension or misconception of a linguistic or experiental activity which we must finally learn to accept as a sort of given, none of them assumes that this is easy to do. For one reason or another, we are prone to metaphysics. It comes almost naturally to us. Therefore, we find that we can never quite get to the end of separating ourselves from its errors. Or, rather, we find that the process of continually disentangling ourselves is as close as we can come to the end. Ultimately, the goal of philosophical enlightenment turns out to be just as elusive as Williams' immediacy. In one sense, we already possess it, but in another sense it is something which is always evermore about to be possessed.

The myth of the fall in its modern form does not appear to involve an apostasy from God or a forgetfulness of the Platonic Forms, but it does involve the idea that we are estranged from our deepest selves, that we are somehow no longer in contact with that with which we are, by definition, in contact. It is the continuing presence of this very traditional predicament that gives new life to the concept of ''transcendence,'' both in Williams' work and in that of the modern philosopher. For it makes little difference whether we suppose ourselves to be in a flight from the apparent Many toward the real One or in a flight from the apparent One toward the real Many (as is now fashionable). In either case, we have necessarily committed ourselves to a distinction between reality and appearance, or truth and error, the persistence of which makes it difficult to believe that a rupture or a revolution in Western thought has occurred at all. (pp. 89-90)

> Carl Rapp, ''William Carlos Williams and the Modern Myth of the Fall,'' in The Southern Review, Vol. 20, No. 1, Winter, 1984, pp. 82-90.

PAUL MARIANI

[The essay excerpted below originally appeared in the Spring 1984 issue of Sagetrieb.]

Williams's *Paterson* is so large and so complex an achievement that we have tended to overlook the body of shorter poems the man wrote during the years he was in the midst of that hurricane of activity. When we think of the highlights of Williams's career as a poet, we think naturally of groupings, of certain mountain configurations rising out of the surrounding foothills and plains. We will probably think first of terrain like *Spring and All* and *In the American Grain* written in the 1920s, then of *Paterson,* whose most virulent phase of activity occurred in the 1940s, and then—at the last—of those experiments from the 1950s gathered into Williams's last book of poems: *Pictures from Brueghel.*

But such an overview leaves out of the varied terrain whole river valleys, moraines, islands, and peninsulas which make up the continent that is Williams's achievement. During the years when he was working through the formal implications of the modern epic, Williams was also rethinking the transformative possibilities of the lyric poem itself. Perhaps this was inevitable, since Paterson itself could not go forward until Williams could find a new kind of lyric poem upon which to build his epic. One sees these moments of lyrical crisis in Williams's theory and practice in 1938, when he approached the problem with his **''Parody for the Poem Paterson,''** the title itself revealing the anxiety Williams was feeling as he seriously approached the borders of his epic for the first time. And one sees the same thing happening again in 1942 and in 1944: the need to find a new lyric form supple enough, fluid enough, to carry the weight of the territory he was exploring for the first time. (pp. 74-5)

From the time he published *Paterson 1* until the time he suffered his first stroke in the spring of '51, Williams seems to have composed sui generis a new poem—a new kind of poem— each time he wrote. And yet, this extraordinary, extra-*Paterson* activity has yet to be adequately mapped by anyone to my

knowledge. In fact, we do not have an accurate enough chronology of the order in which or the order by which Williams composed these poems. Ironically, it is these same poems, gathered along with *The Wedge* into Williams's *Collected Later Poems,* that have been used and reused by poets too impatient to wait for the critical cartographers to tell them what they have known was there all along. Years ago they learned the way to the secret source and have been drinking from its waters for a long time now.

My instinct, for example, would be to point to the poems of Frank O'Hara, Robert Creeley, and Marvin Bell which use a recognizably colloquial voice moving easily and even randomly from idea to idea, while the poems themselves actually establish a surprisingly complex grid of oblique analogues and equations, all pulling eventually in the same direction. These are poems in which we the reader must make constant adjustments to see how the vivid, talky fragments do cohere. Such a poem seems to look at you and say, well, I'm not after the big philosophical formulations, I'm not going to talk with that deep crescendo voice that seems to incorporate and implicate the great tradition and the past. No, I'm just going to talk about a few things on my mind right now.

If we believe that is all the poet is doing, however, we are in danger of being taken in by the mask of easy intimacy, for the poet's designs on us are every bit as serious as the voice of a Milton, a Shelley, a Stevens. When we think of a poetry of ideas written by a twentieth-century American, is it not Stevens who first comes to mind? But in Williams one senses an engagement with the specifics of things, the flux of names informing the surface of the text, so that the intersections of loci established by this naming grid act as so many points of energy to be accounted for in understanding the text. To read a poem by Williams demands a new measure of the inclusive capabilities of the poem. With Williams we really are on new ground and, unless we realize this, we are in danger of being like those early explorers in the new world who did not understand where they were and so passed on incommunicado. (pp. 75-6)

It is true, as Hugh Kenner has said, that one often gets the sense in Williams of a man gesticulating with his hands to something out there that keeps eluding him: the mystery of a poetry so good, so exacting, that it had yet to be written. But that is only part of the story, for most serious poets must understand that feeling: not satisfaction for what has been achieved, but a desire for what remains absent and elusive and teasingly just beyond one's reach. If Williams desired the Perfect Woman, if he desired to realize in the common, overused, misused language of one's time and place the dream of the perfect poem, he still managed to make a body of poetry, and it is that body—the habeas corpus of that achievement as Williams might have said—that must finally be judged.

The work goes on. The early period has received a great deal of attention in the past decade. And so have the poems of the late period—from **''The Desert Music''** up through the poems in *Pictures from Brueghel.* But this is not so of the poems that Williams wrote just prior to his late flowering, poems every bit as good as those that followed. They are, in fact—in spite of much critical opinion to the contrary—more intelligent and ultimately more satisfying poems as well. And this, I think, is the secret the poets have known.

Shortly after World War II ended, Williams began composing again with the speed and voluminosity of a man for whom time is running out. He was approaching seventy and still believed his best work lay before him. We can feel something of the urgency and despair he was feeling in the second, third, and fourth books of **Paterson**. The same is true of the tenor of his essays, lectures, and letters written during this period as Williams tried to determine what the poem in its post-Modernist phase would look and feel like. He talked about it—some would argue he talked too much about it—but, more important, he wrote new poems as well, not only for the vast mural of **Paterson** in lyrics like "I remember / a *Geographic* picture," or the extraordinary interweaving of voices that begins the second part of **Paterson 1** and goes on, uninterrupted by prose, for several pages, or the "Without invention" section of **Paterson 2,** but in dozens of sketches and cartoons, some of them meant most likely for **Paterson** itself, but which Williams decided to detach and to publish separately as poems, where the themes that were preoccupying him in his own version of "The Prelude" might assume their own resonances.

And many of these "exercises"—if you will—rivulets from the activity of the Great Falls washing over Williams—are extraordinary poems, written in a number of styles that show some of the directions in which post-Modern American poetry has moved. And this they have done so skillfully and so transparently that many critics are still not aware of the new directions Williams's poetry took as he continued to experiment in poetry like Picasso with his painting, breaking new ground and beginning again with the building materials of the poem in his sixties.

Consider, for example, three poems from this period ["**The Birth of Venus,**" "**The Hard Core of Beauty,**" and "**All That Is Perfect in Woman,**" all reprinted in *The Collected Later Poems*], each dealing with the erotics of the imagination worked against a profoundly felt absence. Each of these poems has at its core the figure of the Perfect Woman (whether evoked sympathetically or with fear and loathing) which is itself a symbol of that desire that moves the speaker to the use of words. And yet the tone, the rhetorical strategies, the formal components of the poems themselves, are different in each poem and branch off into different directions in the history of post-Modernist American poetics. (pp. 76-8)

During the late 1940s Williams continued his experimentation with a wide variety of line lengths and stanza forms, ransacking the anthologies and the current little magazines to discover from his predecessors and his contemporaries forms—syntactical forms, stanzaic forms, metrical forms—he could use in the creation of a new poetry. A quick survey of *The Collected Later Poems* itself reveals at least the following: the three-line, four-line, five-line, and variable-line stanza, all cutting across the poem's syntactical patterns and thus creating a musical counterpoint. There are verse paragraphs shaped according to the arc of the thought expressed, sonnets or antisonnets of eleven, twelve, and fourteen short lines, lines of seven and even more accentual stresses, very short lines, alternating long and short lines, lines that are as four-square and compact as if they were in pressurized containers, and lines that seem to drift free of any formal anchoring. There are lines with medial and even initial caesurae (the latter introduced by a colon), and there are refrain lines. In short, there is a sense of the new here everywhere, the sense of a beginning over and over again. Only the iambic pentameter, it would seem, has been avoided.

In looking through these poems, then, one comes away with the sense of a great energy expended, as if Picasso were to pick up and discard a dozen styles as the imagination moved

him. And, as with Picasso, we will not discover in these texts any immediate or easy order. (p. 78)

Paul Mariani, "William Carlos Williams," in his A Usable Past: Essays on Modern & Contemporary Poetry, *The University of Massachusetts Press, 1984, pp. 17-104.*

HUGH KENNER

Eliot had striven for a mid-Atlantic style, not to be identified as either American or British. Even Henry James, with "a mind so fine no idea could violate it", had admitted perhaps one Americanism per sentence, not blemishing his pages with "ain't" and "gimme" but assuming transatlantic nuances in words that look neutral. "That was the real way to work things out" is a Jamesian sentence that employs an unEnglish shading of "real". Williams went much further, exulting in what he came to call "the American idiom", something identifiably *local,* backyard-local. It was everything Eliot felt he had put behind him in acquiring ("by great labour") a Tradition, something that (he told us) "cannot be inherited". . . . And Williams claimed to be making poetry of what Eliot had put behind him. . . .

[Eliot's "The Love Song of J. Alfred Prufrock"] illustrates what was until a lifetime ago a working definition of American poetry: English poetry that had chanced to get written somewhere else. (Whitman? Oh, yes, Whitman; what an eccentric.) Anything written in the English language presupposed the English tradition by default. But by 1910 English was becoming, for complex reasons, the language of International Modernism. . . .

Along with International Modernism, we can now distinguish at least three regional literatures, Irish, American and British. Seamus Heaney has recently cited, in connection with early verses by Yeats, the old poet's apposition between minds that remember the Thames valley with its mildness, and his own need to have things "knit by dramatic tension": almost as though two literatures stemmed from two weathers or two geographies, as William Carlos Williams would have said they did. . . .

It is not misleading to call William Carlos Williams the American Yeats, even to Yeats's eagerness for theory, though without the spooks and gyres. Like Yeats, though less ably, he commenced in imitation of sanctified models; he had a long Keats Period in which he was unreadable. And like Yeats, he swerved suddenly away to something utterly idiosyncratic, validated, he said, by the usages of his native New Jersey, usages at least as authoritative as any you'll hear in Sligo. (p. 451)

He wrote poems to be looked at, and at the same time to be spoken and heard. They need a tense, urgent voice, greeting line after line with astonishment. That is so unEnglish that with the best will in the world many English ears cannot *hear* Williams. Read with English inflexions, his cadences go awry, and the skill of letting lineation guide voice to approximate American inflexions seems not to be widely possessed. Lineation—what constitutes a line—was his tireless obsession. He would type the same short sequence of words over and over, dividing it into lines differently, seeking out a visual notation for what he *heard:* for what musicians, not grammarians, call "phrasing". The results grow too intricate to codify, but one hint may be useful. American voices tend to give prepositions a rising inflexion. Williams tended to break lines at prepositions. These two facts are related.

> so much depends
> upon

—so begins his most famous (notorious?) poem, **"The Red Wheelbarrow"** of 1923, and you have to hit "upon" like a local climax to get the cadence working. That's natural to an American voice, forced to an English one. Many English readers don't perceive the nature of the effort they must make. (pp. 451-52)

Still, browsing will yield unstrained rewards. He published **"A Sort of a Song"** in 1944:

> Let the snake wait under
> his weed
> and the writing
> be of words, slow and quick, sharp
> to strike, quiet to wait,
> sleepless.
>
> —through metaphor to reconcile
> the people and the stones.
> Compose. (No ideas
> but in things) Invent!
> Saxifrage is my flower that splits
> the rocks.

The assonances and alliterations of the first stanza are as intricate as you could wish. . . . Gerard Hopkins might have been pleased. Then the second stanza shifts its base of attack from phonic weavings to audacities of diction: "to reconcile the people and the stones", the stones being the rocks split by "Saxifrage", exactly named. . . . There's much formal invention in those forty-seven words. The snake, what has he to do with the saxifrage, save alliterate? He waits like it, the one to strike suddenly, the other to break up into showy five-petalled blossoms in good time: into, as it were, Williams poems.

And does the Saxifrage truly break rocks? Only, it seems, in its etymology, It does grow among rocks and up through the clefts of rocks. "No ideas but in things", says the poem, yet its climaxing idea is a lexicographer's invention.

Or examine the lineation. What is "sharp" doing at a line-end, separated from the rest of its phrase? . . . To find out, read the poem as Williams heard it, with a rising inflection at "sharp". Repeat that inflection, seven lines later, at "splits".

And who before this has hymned saxifrage? Williams delighted in celebrating the "weeds" poetic diction disregards. . . .

His *annus mirabilis* was 1922, the year he wrote a cranky little book, **Spring and All**, that declared war on the Eliot of that same year's *Waste Land*. The waste land he'd have us regard is something you could photograph:

> Beyond, the
> waste of broad, muddy fields
> brown with dried weeds, standing and fallen
>
> patches of standing water
> the scattering of tall trees

—in April, cruellest month, these are burgeoning:

> Lifeless in appearance, sluggish
> dazed spring approaches—

> They enter the new world naked,
> cold, uncertain of all
> save that they enter. All about them
> the cold familiar wind—. . .

"The new world": yes, New Jersey. Poems too are arriving there, as surely as "the stiff curl of wildcarrot leaf":

> One by one objects are defined—
> It quickens: clarity, outline of leaf

Clarity, outline, those are Williams hallmarks. . . .

Williams kept up the war on Eliot all his life, often pointlessly. In old age he could be heard decrying something he'd misunderstood, the relationship of "The Hippopotamus" to Gautier's "L'Hippopotame". "That he'd pass off a translation as something of his own"—the voice broke in incredulity. And he once asked a perfectly amazing question: could one talk to Eliot, "animal to animal"? No one else has ever entertained such a notion.

Yet it's to Eliot we owe **Spring and All** and the tremendous development that followed it, and very likely we also owe him **Paterson**. That long poem (1946-58) is Williams's *Four Quartets,* even to its original four books (he later added a fifth). Though he'd pondered it for years, it seems to have been the talk of Eliot's new achievement in the 1940s that spurred him to commit himself to it finally. Like the *Quartets* it meditates on named ground, though not on four different grounds (three of them English) but always on the same ground, on American ground: on Paterson, a city in New Jersey not far from his native Rutherford. In 1965 *The Times* (yes, the one in London) paid him the supreme compliment of thinking Paterson "an imaginary town . . . which Williams created as his symbol of America". He'd have liked that: he had lifted a grubby city to the domain of the imagination. . . .

Most of his lifetime American opinion repeated itself with recurring deadliness. It left no space in which he could exist. He was in his mid-fifties before a collection was issued by a publisher you could trust to stay in business. Soon thereafter the New Critics began prating of Wit and Tension, which they couldn't discern in the quirky vivacity he'd derived from hard-edge painters and from looking and listening. For years there were no terms in which he could be discussed. It's not only in England that William Carlos Williams has been without honour. That he's now a principal mentor of the principal American poets is something to be attributed to the tenacity of poetic intelligence. (p. 452)

Hugh Kenner, "The Minims of Language," in The Times Literary Supplement, *No. 4230, April 27, 1984, pp. 451-52.*

HARVEY SHAPIRO

Williams, besides pursuing a prolific career in poetry while making his living as obstetrician, gynecologist, school doctor, pediatrician and general practitioner, also published a clutch of novels and more than 50 short stories. Thirteen of those stories are direct accounts of his experiences as a doctor. They are collected [in **The Doctor Stories**] with some related poems, a chapter from his autobiography that describes his debt as a writer to his work as a doctor, and a note by a son, also a doctor, on his famous father. . . .

There is no elaborate conceptualizing in these pieces about the nature of disease or the role of the doctor. These are bare transcriptions of uninteresting (in a medical sense) cases, but the doctor who set them down is quick to understand his own mind-barriers that stand between him and the right diagnosis.

He comes to acknowledge in these stories his prejudices, his tiredness, his concern about money (this is the Depression and his patients can rarely pay the requisite $10). As Robert Coles says to his young doctors in his introduction: "He prompts us to examine our ambitions, our motives, our aspirations, our purposes, our worrying lapses, our grave errors, our overall worth."

For the general reader, what comes through most strongly in these stories is the nobility of the down and outers the doctor has to treat. Maybe "nobility" sentimentalizes them and Williams doesn't. What he does is this. In **"A Night in June"** he goes to deliver the eighth child of an Italian woman he has known for years. There is no light in the bedroom because the electricity is turned off, so the delivery is by candlelight. Freights rattle past the house. The husband and the woman's sister help as they can. Mostly the doctor waits, dozes off, wakes: "The peace of the room was unchanged. Delicious." The poetry of this poverty and the stoicism of the people are what get to him. When the baby comes he goes to work with the patient: "Go ahead, I said. Pull hard. I welcomed the feel of her hands and the strong pull. It quieted me in the way the whole house had quieted me all night."

There is a famous poem by Wallace Stevens (he and Williams once dominated American poetry and maybe, through their competing influences, still do) called "The House Was Quiet and the World Was Calm." It's about the same peace Williams speaks of. Stevens gets it from conjuring up a picture of a reader at one with the text he reads; Williams gets it from getting close to people.

Almost all the stories have a simple form. They begin with a telephone call for the doctor or the doctor entering the house of the sick. The concentration is on the action. The dialogue is given without commentary or quotation marks. The story moves rapidly. As the people disclose themselves to the doctor, the diagnosis is made and the story abruptly ends. But hidden in that process is a revelation for the doctor and the reader: Through coming to see others clearly, he comes to see himself.

The famous story in the collection, one much anthologized, is **"The Use of Force."** Williams is called in by anxious parents to examine their young daughter, age unspecified, who is running a constant fever. He immediately suspects diphtheria because that's what is going around. He asks if she has a sore throat. The answer is no. He wants to examine her throat but the child refuses to grant him entry. A struggle ensues. In the course of it, Williams comes to despise the parents who are afraid to use force, is enthralled by the tenacity of the child, notices his own more than objective participation in the action. He has his way. The diagnosis is confirmed, the child is left in tears. It is an acute rendering of the way the writer tracks his own mind as it observes and is acted on by the world. In this, it is one with his poetry.

> Harvey Shapiro, "A Physician's Stories," in The New York Times, *October 20, 1984, p. 11.*

GILBERT SORRENTINO

[The material of **The Doctor Stories**] is, as the title makes clear, centered on Williams's medical career. It is not a bad idea to construct a book on these arbitrary lines, but the new reader

of Williams should be warned that this collection is as representative of the author's *oeuvre* as a collection of "mistress poems" would be representative of the work of Baudelaire. That caveat aside, we may turn to the text.

What is most striking about these stories is that they reveal, on a small scale, almost all of Williams's formal fictional devices, devices that were, in effect, extensions of his poetic practice. For instance, in **"The Use of Force,"** a narrator speaks in the first person, but although he is the center of the story, the point on which it is balanced, he is oddly remote, as if he were telling the story not to the missing second-person "you" but to himself: he observes himself as if the "I" is a "he." **"Old Doc Rivers"** is a masterpiece of shifting tones that employs both first- and third-person voices, varying levels of the objective and subjective, and data put together in a seemingly haphazard pastiche of eyewitness account, hearsay, dialogue direct and indirect, and written document—all of it existing on a temporal plane that ignores sequential chronology. And in **"Jean Beicke"** the hoary "truth" that a story's resolution should be delayed as long as possible is shattered when Williams permits the central character to die halfway through the narrative.

In each story, there is a total lack of sentimentality, a lack so pronounced that it makes the neutral stance of much objective fiction seem exotic and romantic. Remarkably, this is done in stories that are told either in the first person or in a third person that constantly intrudes. It can be argued that Williams achieved this "flatness" of tone and language because of his belief that the "artist must for subtlety ascend to a plane of almost abstract design to keep alive." The word "design" is key here, for Williams was not so much telling stories as he was making forms.

Williams was virtually alone in his early rejection of the received idea that a story should "show, not tell." Because he acted on this belief, his fiction bluntly contradicted a basic tenet of modernist ideology; work such as his seemed inept, unrealized, unsophisticated. I had a professor years ago who told me he couldn't read Williams's fiction because the author would not only not allow him to draw his own conclusions about the characters, the characters themselves were two-dimensional. Not once did he question why the writer would fly in the face of "good fictional practice." He was content to think that Williams was ignorant of his own compositional methods.

Such opinions as that of the professor are nowadays quaint if not aberrant, but they are still with us. Our "readers" apparently yearn for traditional fiction, whatever that may be, and rush to embrace the silly pronouncements on the "death of the avant-garde." . . . They have missed the famous boat. As Williams might say, and often did, so be it.

> Gilbert Sorrentino, "A Dose of Strong Medicine," *in* The New York Times Book Review, *October 21, 1984, p. 9.*

CHARLES TOMLINSON

It was Ezra Pound, that indefatigable discoverer of talent, who first seized on the essential elements in Williams's poetry. Introducing Williams's second, still tentative, volume, **The Tempers,** in 1913, Pound quoted one of Williams's similes where he speaks of a thousand freshets:

> ... crowded
> Like peasants to a fair
> Clear skinned, wild from seclusion.

Pound has instinctively isolated here elements thoroughly characteristic of this poet's entire venture—poetic energy imagined as the rush of water; not so much Wordsworth's "spontaneous overflow of powerful feelings," but feelings "crowded," forcing and yet constrained by their own earth-bound track; a certain rustic uncouthness whose end is a celebration and which wears the stamp of locality. "The only universal," as Williams was to say later, "is the local as savages, artists and—to a lesser extent—peasants know."

The most interesting of Williams's early volumes, *Al Que Quiere!,* appeared in 1917, the same year as T. S. Eliot's *Prufrock and Other Observations.* Pound was there to salute the arrival of both volumes and to differentiate them:

> Distinct and as different as possible from the orderly statements of an Eliot . . . are the poems of Carlos Williams. If the sinuosities of Misses Moore and Loy are difficult to follow I do not know what is to be said for Mr Williams's ramifications and abruptnesses. I do not pretend to follow all of his volts, jerks, sulks, balks, outblurts and jump-overs; but for all this roughness there remains with me the conviction that there is nothing meaningless in his book, *Al Que Quiere,* not a line . . .

Perhaps Pound overstates the "roughness" of Williams, but, in pointing out the "jerks, balks, outblurts and jump-overs," he has arrived at one of the earliest and most accurate formulations of what Williams's verse was about. Not only is "locality" (a sticking to New Jersey when Pound and Eliot had chosen European exile) the geographic source of Williams's poetry, but "locality," seen as the jerks and outblurts of speech rendered on to the here and now of the page, is the source of his lineation. In the imaginative play of Williams's poems, where the attention is frequently turned upon outward things, the sound structure of the poems which embody that attention is an expression of strains, breath pauses, bodily constrictions and releases. Thus Williams's "locality" begins with a somatic awareness, a physiological presence in time and space, and this in quite early poems. (pp. vii-viii)

The relation between subject and object appears in Williams in a series of images of physical strain—a poem from *Al Que Quiere!,* **"Spring Strains,"** . . . feels out its own balks and resistances against those of the scene outside where the swift flight of two birds is challenged, as:

> the blinding and red-edged sun-blur—
> creeping energy, concentrated
> counterforce—welds sky, buds, trees,
> rivets them in one puckering hold!

At the close, the birds exert their own counterforce of speed and lightness, breaking out of the riveted landscape

> flung outward and up—disappearing suddenly!

—the poem imparting a verb-like force to its combined prepositions, "outward and up," and ending, as so often in Williams, on a dangling clause that pulls the main clause towards incompletion and asymmetry.

This predilection for the open-ended and asymmetrical leaves Williams free to accept the suggestion of his surroundings with their evidence of overlap and relativity—

> roof out of line with sides
> the yards cluttered
> with old chicken wire, ashes,
> furniture gone wrong;
> the fences and outhouses
> built of barrel-staves
> and parts of boxes . . .

Instead of wishing simply to reform the poor ("It's the anarchy of poverty / delights me . . ."), he senses there is a point where the imagination, partaking of this anarchy, could dance with it, could "lift" it to an answering form, but a form fully responsive to the waywardness and inconclusiveness of daily realities. The broken fringes of the city in **"Morning"** . . . witness a sort of heroism among "diminished things," humorously absurd. . . . Williams hears in all this, and in the profusion of natural fact, a kind of music—"a vague melody / of harsh threads," as he says in **"Trees"** . . . where the tree which first catches his eye is "crooked," "bent . . . from straining / against the bitter horizontals of / a north wind," the jump-overs at the line breaks enacting the pressure of that straining. There is no romantic fusion of subject and object possible in this nature poem: the voices of the trees may be "blent willingly / against the heaving contra-bass / of the dark" but the contra-bass remains contra, the crooked tree warps itself "passionately to one side" and the poem still presses forward as Williams adds "in [its] eagerness," the poem like the tree dissociating itself from a blent music for that "melody / of harsh threads." "Bent" puns and rhymes eagerly against "blent" in this piece.

When Williams in his turn paid tribute to Pound, he saw the poet—himself and Pound included—as seeking a language which "will embody all the advantageous jumps, swiftnesses, colors, movements of the day . . ." He was praising the collage element in the poetry of Pound's *A Draft of XXX Cantos,* but the terms of his praise ignore those other elements of archaism and of the *musée imaginaire* that Williams distrusted in his friend. Both Pound and Eliot, or so Williams felt, had lost contact— it was a word whose meaning he was to go on exploring— with their American roots: they had sold out to Europe that American renaissance of which Pound himself had spoken, one which he had prophesied would "overshadow the quattro-cento." (pp. viii-x)

Williams's poetry and novels explore an America his two most powerful contemporaries . . . left behind, in the raw merging of American pastoral and urban squalor. He described his struggle to make articulate that world, in *Paterson,* as "a reply to Greek and Latin with the bare hands." Williams exaggerates, of course, and as he himself well knew his insistence on "contact" and "locality" needed for its completion an awareness that was also European—the kind of awareness he recognized immediately in the reproduction of a painting by Juan Gris, with its cubist sharpness, its almost fastidious handling of a world of broken forms. "Contact" had been Whitman's word: "I am mad for it to be in contact with me," says Whitman of nature in *Song of Myself.* So is Williams. The difference lies in the *eruditus* of that *tactus eruditus* he speaks of in one poem. "A fact with him," says Kenneth Burke, "finds its justification in the trimness of the wording." Whitman is a great poet, but he is never trim. Trimness was something Williams could recognize and applaud in Juan Gris's "admirable simplicity and excellent design."

When he speaks in the prose parts of *Spring and All* (1923) of Whitman, the company he puts him into is that of two great Europeans, Gris and Cézanne, announcing that "Whitman's proposals are of the same piece with the modern trend toward imaginative understanding of life." At this point, the imagination for Williams was identified with the cubist re-structuring of reality: modern poetry with its ellipses, its confrontation of disparates, its use of verbal collages—a device both Pound and Eliot had used—provided direct analogies. (pp. x-xi)

On the face of it, the inheritance Williams brings to cubism seems to be very close in spirit not only to Whitman but also to Emerson and Thoreau. If "contact" is re-explored, so is Emerson's attachment to the vernacular: "the speech of Polish mothers" was where Williams insisted he got his English from. "Colleges and books only copy the language which the field and work-yard made," said Emerson. Williams's famous "flatness" comes not from the field, but from the urban "work-yard" of New Jersey. (p. xii)

Emerson seems to have prepared the ground for Williams's other war-cry, "No ideas but in things" with his "Ask the fact for the form." Thoreau sounds yet closer with: "The roots of letters are things." Again Emerson tells over things—"The meal in the firkin; the milk in the pan; the ballad in the street; the news of the boat . . ."—in the shape of a list very like Williams's "rigmaroles," as he calls his poems. "Bare lists of words," says Emerson, "are found suggestive to an imaginative mind." When Williams, long after Emerson and after Whitman's application of this, constructed "list" poems, he came in for suspicion, as in the interview which he prints as part of *Paterson 5* and in which, defending what amounts to a grocery list that forms the jagged pattern of one of his later poems, he concludes: "Anything is good material for poetry. Anything. I've said it time and time again."

Paterson 5 came out in 1958. Years before, Williams had formulated his kind of poem made out of anything and with a jagged pattern, in the 1920 preface to *Kora in Hell,* when he wrote that a poem is "tough by no quality it borrows from a logical recital of events nor from the events themselves but solely from the attenuated power which draws perhaps many broken things into a dance by giving them thus a full being." He was often to return to the idea of poem as dance. If, as with Emerson, Williams seems to "ask the fact for the form," the form, once it comes, is free of the fact, is a *dance above* the fact. After *Kora in Hell,* he had another shot at the formula in the prose of *Spring and All,* where he concludes of John of Gaunt's speech in *Richard II* that "his words are related not to their sense as objects adherent to his son's welfare or otherwise, but as a dance over the body of his condition accurately accompanying it."

J. Hillis Miller in his book *Poets of Reality* has argued that Williams marks an historic moment for modern poetry in that his work sees the disappearance of all dualism. If it is not from dualism it is yet from a duality that much of the interest of his work arises: the words "accurately accompany" a perception of the forms of reality, they dance over or with these forms, but it is the gap between words and forms that gives poetry its chance to exist and to go on existing. Williams's most truncated and Zen-like expression of this fact comes in the tiny ["**The Red Wheelbarrow**"]. . . . What depends on the red wheelbarrow for Williams is the fact that its presence can be rendered

over into words, that the perception can be slowed down and meditated on by regulating, line by line, the gradual appearance of these words. The imagination "accurately accompanies" the wheelbarrow, or whatever facets of reality attract Williams, by not permitting too ready and emotional a fusion with them. When things go badly the imagination retreats into a subjective anguish. . . . But when the dance with facts suffices, syntax, the forms of grammar, puns, the ambiguous pull between words unpunctuated or divided by line-endings, these all contribute to—accompany—the richness of a reality one can never completely fuse with, but which affords a resistance whereby the I can know itself.

One has in Williams's best verse a vivid sense of what Olson calls "the elements and minims of language," down to the syllabic components or "the diphthong/ae" ("**To Have Done Nothing**"). . . . It is this drama of elements, played across the ends of frequently short lines, which gives to Williams's "free verse" its cohesiveness, and intensifies what Olson calls

> The contingent motion of
>   each line as it
>   moves with—or against—
>   the whole—working
>   particularly out of its immediacy.

Williams insisted that he did not write free verse, of course. As early as 1913 he was saying: "I do not believe in *vers libre,* this contradiction in terms. Either the motion continues or it does not continue, either there is rhythm or no rhythm." In the same essay ("**Speech Rhythm**" . . .), Williams writes that, in an Odyssey, "rightly considered," "no part in its excellence but partakes of the essential nature of the whole." . . . (pp. xii-xiv)

This intuitive conception of the kind of poetic writing he sought gets closer to essentials than Williams's later and self-defeating attempts to define the "variable foot," that "relative measure" which ends by being what Williams said *vers libre* was, a contradiction in terms. It is "the contingent motion of / each line" and what Robert Creeley has referred to as the "contentual emphases" of each line that give life to Williams's verse, rather than any prosodic notion of feet. These emphases are brought to bear most consistently perhaps in relatively short poems. *Paterson* has its incidental finenesses, but there are stretches when one feels, as in others of the more lengthy pieces, that the dance has broken down. (p. xiv)

Williams may not have been capable of the unity of *The Waste Land,* but, as Octavio Paz insists, introducing his translations of Williams in *Veinte Poemas,* "The greatness of a poet is not to be measured by the scale but by the intensity and the perfection of his works. Also by his vivacity. Williams is the author of the most *vivid* poems of modern American poetry." And the vivacity arises, one might add, from the unexpectedness of Williams's apparently wayward forms. (p. xv)

Williams's attitude to form rather resembles his attitude to friendship, which should be, he says, "dangerous—uncertain—made of many questionable crossties, I think, that might fail it. But while they last, give it a good cellular structure—paths, private connections between the members—full of versatility." This passage comes from Williams's *Autobiography*—Chapter 49, "Friendship." In Chapter 50, "Projective Verse," it is silently transfigured into an ideal of artistic form, and this ideal is seen as part and parcel of Williams's conception of locality. Chapter 50 is, in many ways, pivotal to the book, for, in using Charles Olson's conception of "composition by field,'' Williams does so—and very tactfully—against an implied background of why his forms were not readily understood in his own country or ours, why ''The Criterion had no place for me'' why Eliot's *The Waste Land* had seemed to him ''the great catastrophe to our letters . . . Eliot had turned his back on the possibility of reviving my world.'' That world seemed to Williams to receive its recognition in Olson's ''Projective Verse'' essay, with its preference for an explorative, syllable-based verse and its invitation ''to step back here to this place of the elements and minims of language . . . to engage speech where it is least careless—and least logical.'' (pp. xv-xvi)

Of all the American modernists Williams was the most tardy in receiving recognition. His writing lifetime was dominated by the literary criteria of T. S. Eliot and the New Criticism, in neither of whose terminology was there a place for the kind of thing Williams was concerned with doing. (p. xvi)

To name what possessed no name, to avoid surrendering oneself ''into the inverted cone of waning energy . . . [and] fly off at last into nonentity, general deracinate conclusions,'' were the tasks that Williams had recognized early on—earlier, in fact, than the 1913 essay, **''Speech Rhythm,''** quoted above. *How* early one realizes in his accounts of his undergraduate poem (which he burned) about the prince who is abducted and taken to an unknown country—Williams's inarticulate America—to wake confronted by all the problems of language and cultural identity that Williams himself was to face: ''No one was there to inform him of his whereabouts and when he did begin to encounter passers-by, they didn't even understand, let alone speak his language. He could recall nothing of the past . . . So he went on, homeward or seeking a home that was his own, all this through a 'foreign' country whose language was barbarous.''

This myth would seem to lend itself to a long psychic alienation. But one sees Williams breaking through by meeting the demands of day-to-day existence, never too involved in himself to feel the ballast of place, people and things. (pp. xvi-xvii)

The myth of the prince and the necessity of a counter-statement to it underlie Williams's work. In his *Autobiography,* the counter-statement reappears in the final pages when he drives out to look at the site of the poem, *Paterson:* ''The Falls let out a roar as it crashed upon the rocks at its base. In the imagination this roar is a speech or a voice, a speech in particular; it is the poem itself that is the answer.'' (p. xvii)

> *Charles Tomlinson, in an introduction to* Selected Poems *by William Carlos Williams, edited by Charles Tomlinson, revised edition, New Directions, 1985, pp. vii-xvii.*

GEOFFREY O'BRIEN

[In compiling *Selected Poems*] Charles Tomlinson invites us to read William Carlos Williams again, as if we were just starting out. I for one hesitated a moment before accepting his invitation. There are places so freighted with cherished perceptions that one fears to revisit them. ''No whiteness (lost),'' as Williams himself wrote, ''is so white as the memory / of whiteness,'' and not every return to an old poetic neighborhood restores the anticipated thrill. It's literally as a neighborhood that I've always thought of Williams: his name evokes not books or lines of verse—not symbols or metaphors or even meanings—but physical spaces, structures at once airy and bracing. Reading him was like learning to read for the first time, to read not just with mind or eye but with the whole breath and body.

This full sense of the body's weight makes fresh demands on our engagement with a text, though I experienced them not as demands but as gifts, the sudden lifting of a pervasive tension. For all the pleasures of reading, it does have its aftertaste of claustrophobic malaise. If we don't play our part, or unexpectedly forget how to, the words can turn oppressive. In one sense, poetry is the art which resolves that unease, and so finally we measure its success or failure at gut level. A line of verse, once it gets past the ears, travels through spine as well as brain; caesurae and vowel tones, not as simple sounds but as agents of meaning, resonate to the farthest nerve-endings. This could be said of any poet, but Williams dragged it into the open, made texts that couldn't be read without that level of awareness.

''Poems, to exist at all,'' he wrote in 1934, ''must be and are essentially sensual,'' and the direct knowledge apprehended by the senses manifests itself in ''slight variations, slightly displaced emphases in the line structure.'' Theoretical description hardly conveys the initial shock of Williams's poetry. I remember the way the page opened up, like an accordion or a jack-in-the-box. There was an uncanny feeling of stepping into a different kind of depth—uncanny because the page was so plainly flat, and indeed Williams was doing all he could to emphasize that flatness. The white space around the words was like an ether, expressing as much with its silences as the words themselves. Isolated within that surrounding blankness, the most ordinary words penetrated as never before, as if an obscure barrier had dissolved and we could finally see what our thoughts were made of. . . . It was like a cleansing of the mind.

At the core of the poems, between and under and around the words, a profoundly refreshing emptiness pulsated. Returning after a long absence, I'm overjoyed to find it still there. . . . Williams's contraption, his angular, tacked-together ''machine made of words,'' shows no sign of running down. Its very ricketiness, its traces of impatience and spontaneous enthusiasm, have an air of eternity: a moment of real time—not the idea or memory of it—kept alive in the hyperspace of poetry.

Williams has too often been reduced to a poet of humble commonplaces, a sentimental diarist of red wheelbarrows and plums in the icebox; in tribute, his imitators offer up inert snapshots of puppy dogs and garden tools. But surely ''no ideas but in things'' means that the things are suffused with ideas. Although Williams has sometimes been labeled a Buddhist or Taoist, he's more like a Shintoist: the rocks vibrate, waterfalls are animate, the visible universe harbors deposits of magical energy. The ordinary is *not* ordinary; it's violent, explosive, outrageous. . . . He would not—and this was his great quarrel with Eliot—commit the indignity, the sacrilege, of turning the world into a religious symbol. The world was to be engaged on its own terms, representing nothing but itself.

In Eliot's writing we're conscious of deciphering an abstract code, and as with any coherent code we must pass through a series of numbered steps. A Williams poem, however, grounded in perception rather than logic, comes to us one point after another but all at once, the way the world does. Our eyes can move up or down his columns of words just as they would roam among the undulating slopes of a Chinese scroll. That is the wild freedom of his words—they seem to have escaped from syntax, from the strictures of argument, in order to shine out in their own sheer existence. . . . That illusion of freedom is curiously heightened by the rigorous structure—not implicit but blatant—which forces itself on the view. The ideal Williams poem resembles a multi-dimensional mobile, a perpetual motion machine that would chug away whether anyone looked at it or not. The page writhes:

> All along the road the reddish
> purplish, forked, upstanding, twiggy
> stuff of bushes and small trees
> with dead, brown leaves under them
> leafless vines—

Even after a hundred readings the hallucinatory energy of those lines persists, the concentrated force with which they ambush the senses. The eye takes in the words in one gulp, just as it would a view of road and bushes and vines. Yet the passage isn't really visual at all; it's pre-visual, like a newborn's unsorted sense-impressions. A chaos of perceptions overwhelms the brain's picture-making faculty. . . .

Tomlinson's *Selected Poems* displaces a collection put together by Williams himself [*Selected Poems* (1949)], which leaned heavily on early lyrics and tended to obscure the chronological development of his art. The new book is commendable for its mapping of breakthrough points, those surges of technical invention which dot Williams's oeuvre. Tomlinson, a fine poet whose work has been deeply influenced by Williams, shows special sensitivity to the crucial influence of the visual arts on a writer who was also a frustrated painter. Tomlinson's lucid introduction certainly makes a change from the grudging preamble by Randall Jarrell that disfigured the earlier volume, a paean of faint praise which concluded: "That Williams's poems are honest, exact, and original, that some of them are really *good* poems, seems to me obvious." The humiliation for Williams was that in 1949 he desperately needed even the left-handed endorsement of a critic of Jarrell's stature.

Today the situation has been reversed, and Williams suffers from an academic canonization strangely at odds with his qualities as a poet. . . . A backlash is probably inevitable, so it's not altogether surprising that James Breslin, in his introduction to *Something To Say: William Carlos Williams on Younger Poets,* refers to him as a "poetic fashion whose time has gone," and drags in a parodistic jest of Marvin Bell's on the subject of Williams's disciples: "no ideas but the in-thing." Too many poets have believed that if you stack the nouns just so, chop your lines short, throw in enough white space, and keep your phonemes curt, you can produce instant Williams. No poet is more deceptively imitable. . . . (p. 17)

But even Williams couldn't figure out how he managed it, and he drove himself half nuts concocting a theory to account for what his typewriter gave birth to. The creator of the most sublimely articulated modern poems was often haltingly inarticulate as a critic. For him, clarity could be wrested only at great cost from the heart of the poetic process; the farther he gets from that central energy, the foggier and more obfuscated his prose tends to become. The criticism collected in *Something To Say*—designed to portray Williams as teacher and encourager of younger writers—displays at best an awkward and intermittent frankness, without a trace of aphoristic brilliance. . . . Nothing suggests that he took pleasure in writing these pieces; the utilitarian connotation of book reviews and introductions apparently crimped his imagination beyond endurance. Only in the unharnessed and triumphantly nonfunctional riffing of *Kora in Hell* and *Spring and All* and *The Descent of Winter* could he talk about poetry in his real voice.

The publication of *Something To Say* is of course an aspect of Williams's enshrinement which insists that no scrap of work, no matter how marginal or half-finished, shall go unpublished—even if the net effect is to tarnish the poet's aura. . . .

Williams's transient enthusiasms—for the poetry of Sydney Salt, Merrill Moore, Marcia Nardi, Eli Siegel, George Semsel—serve mainly as a springboard for one more reiteration of his standard sermon on poetics: "What we have wanted is a *line* that will allow us room in which to develop the opportunities of a new language." "In poetry . . . the line and the sense, the didactic, expository sense, have nothing directly to do with one another." "Poems are the effects of engineering skills in poets." Williams's polemics were chiefly, and understandably, a form of psychic self-defense; he had to wait until his last years for the recognition he craved as much as any writer. The stridency, the wan generalizing, the reduction of complex and delicate matters to rigid positions, often seems an echo of others to whom such bellowing came more naturally. In the short term it was a self-defeating ploy, since his chip-on-the-shoulder crankiness provided a perfect excuse for the tastemakers to brush him aside. One wonders, despite his current status, if it might not happen again. The neo-conservative rumblings in journals like *Commentary* and *The New Criterion* show a clear desire to topple Williams's poetic heirs and restore the classicist dynasty represented by John Crowe Ransom and W. H. Auden. Turning Williams into a safely embalmed museum piece could be one way of defusing his influence.

Tomlinson's *Selected Poems,* by directing us away from theoretical commentary and back to the poems themselves, may restore a sense of their continuing fecundity. We may have exhausted some of Williams's identities—as camera eye on New Jersey or homespun recorder of local speech or standard bearer for modernist metrics. But beyond them, and especially in the radical work of the '20s and '30s, further unsuspected recesses keep turning up. His insistence on the bare flatness of writing as writing . . . resurfaces in current language-preoccupied poetry. **"It Is a Living Coral"**—that still life of history as petrified in the dome of the Capitol—implies an approach to decoding artifacts which other poets might well explore. Williams's feeling for history as intrusive presence ("a trouble / archaically fettered") lets him trace the contours of a chiseled narrative as if it were just another kind of vegetation:

> It climbs
>
> it runs, it is Geo.
> Shoup
>
> of Idaho it wears
> a beard
>
> it fetches naked
> Indian
>
> women from a river

Characteristically Williams was most concerned not with what happened in the past but with the raw surfaces through which we learn all we can know of that past.

The day which, to shocking effect, "blows in / the scalloped curtains to / the sound of rain" at the end of **"On Gay Wallpaper"** remains as mysteriously and violently alive as ever. It's the mysteriousness of the actual, that sudden awareness of an empty pause in which all possibilities are latent. Perhaps Williams's years of delivering babies predisposed him to the viewpoint of someone just emerging into the world. The newness of these poems is, in effect, built into them: ''The fragility of the flower / unbruised / penetrates space'' in a syntactic eternity, a fountain trickily rigged to pour out endlessly. Considering the centuries it took for poetry to evolve toward this fine edge of immediacy, it seems a bit soon to consign Williams to nostalgia. An art doesn't get reborn every other day; we shouldn't be in too much of a hurry for this particular springtime to start showing its age. (pp. 17, 21)

Geoffrey O'Brien, "William Carlos Williams and the Relativity of Theory," in VLS, No. 40, November, 1985, pp. 17, 21.

MARILYN KALLET

William Carlos Williams' long poem **"Asphodel, That Greeny Flower"** is beautiful in itself, without ''irritable reaching after fact''; it sings of love, time, death, art, and the life of the imagination—crucial themes which the poet treats with tenderness and courage. By acknowledging the work leading to the poem, by listening to the echoes of a lifetime of struggle that shuttle through the lines while the poem's music rises above struggle, the reader can appreciate the complex simplicity of **"Asphodel"** all the more. The apparent ease and gracefulness of the poem are the more striking when we are alert to obstacles the poet had to overcome. **"Asphodel"** was especially hard won; Williams worked all his life to reach the ease of tone, to achieve the metrical skill that makes the poem sing so fluently; he struggled also to affirm his love for his wife, Flossie. The poem reaches into the depths of Williams' being for this assertion of love, which is also a defiance of speechlessness, of dying ''incommunicado.'' Set last among the late poems that Williams called *Journey to Love* (1955), **"Asphodel"** contains the memory of how hard it was to get there, to the ''desirable place'' in poetry and personal feelings where ''contradiction no longer does any harm.''

Williams' fifty years of work at craft are buttressed with theoretical work and reflections on ''measure''; for most of his life the poet sought in a disciplined way to mark out the rhythm of a new American verse. The new lines must be cut with mathematical precision, for what is at stake is the life of the mind, the imagination captured in its time and locale as ''the radiant gist,'' the ''common language'' of poetry.

Williams listened for the sound and rhythm in the speech patterns of the American language that would reveal our experiences to us. Music hovers in our distinctive landscapes, stirring the poet to his work.

> A music
> supersedes his composure, hallooing to us
> across a great distance . . .
> wakens the dance
> who blows upon his benumbed fingers!
> (**"The Desert Music"** . . .)

The poet's fingers were literally ''benumbed''—Williams had suffered his first stroke in March, 1951, and composed **"The Desert Music"** shortly thereafter. The poem sings ''a music of survival,'' as the words reawaken the poet's faith in his resources. The poems in *The Desert Music* and *Journey to Love* are songs of healing as well as love songs, whose lines restore the aging poet and his world with an affirmation of creative powers. **"Asphodel,"** written for the most part after the poet had suffered a second debilitating stroke in August, 1952, also invokes reintegration and healing. The poet writes to save his

marriage, his sanity, and his life, though the urgency of **"Asphodel"** is tempered by the triadic line, a measure that unfolds gradually. (pp. 1-2)

The great themes that Williams embraces in **"Asphodel"**— love, time, destruction, and the powers of the imagination— are held together by the poem's music, its sound, lines, and resounding images. Williams' use of his special tercet, the triadic line with its variable foot, creates a pleasing effect to the ear.

> Of asphodel, that greeny flower,
> like a buttercup
> upon its branching stem—
> save that it's green and wooden—
> I come, my sweet,
> to sing to you. . . .

Here is an epithalamion, a stately air, lightened by its directness and by the syncopation of the three-ply line. The music of Williams' late poetry, its actual sound, conveys a sense of timelessness and continuity not found in most of the earlier works, however daring those poems are. Breaking ground makes noise. An atmosphere of quiet begins subtly to permeate the late poems, intermingling through the spaces created by the triadic lines with the music of the lines. A ''desirable place to be,'' aesthetically.

"Asphodel," written in 1952-1953, published in 1955 when the poet was seventy-two years old, is, in its sureness of form and richness of content, a summation of Williams' work at life and craft. The poem is no longer pure improvisation such as we find in *Kora in Hell: Improvisations* (1920), a collection of surrealistic exercises attentive to the fleeting passages of the poet's life, notes stolen away from the time Williams spent at his medical practice. **"Asphodel"** is the result of a lifetime of traveling in unknown, uncharted metrical seas, the lyrical place discovered as the result of sustained willingness to improvise in a disciplined manner. . . . The discovery of ''love, abiding love'' and of clarity of form comes only after many years of marriage and of work at craft.

Uncertainties did not deter the poet from starting out: Williams enjoyed the momentum of traveling, exploring. . . . (pp. 3-5)

As a physician, Williams spent time in the car traveling hurriedly from place to place; he used the experience of being on the road as a theme for some poems; the kinetics of his lines reflect the poet's delight in pure movement. Driving can also offer a more leisurely kind of traveling, a ''purposiveness without purpose,'' that leads on one journey not to a precipice, but to a deep and secret place [as in **"The Avenue of Poplars"**].

> I ride in my car
> I think about
>
> prehistoric caves
> in the Pyrenees—
>
> the cave of
> *Les Trois Frères*

In **"Asphodel"** Williams returns to the theme of images found in prehistoric caves; he goes deeper toward the sources of art. . . . Even in the late poems ''traveling'' produces the unexpected; precipices and roadblocks must be avoided to get to the new destination. (p. 5)

In the process of writing or ''traveling'' in a state of awareness, one might even seek to produce contradictions, rather than to avoid them. "But why not e.g. in order to show that everything in the world is uncertain?" One might be "anxious to produce contradictions, say for aesthetic purposes." Surely in *Kora in Hell,* where "imagination but delights in its own seasons reversing the usual order at will," contradictions are the order or disorder of the day.... *Kora* predicts the magical reversal of seasons that occurs in **"Asphodel,"** where the sick and aging poet recreates the certainty of springtime for Flossie, loving her "always for the first time."

Those who seek out contradictions, as Williams did, may not find them practical or useful, but they "still would be glad to lead their lives in the neighborhood of a contradiction." Contemporary poetry is a "neighborhood of contradictions"; Williams lived all his life in that neighborhood, from *Kora* to *Paterson,* until settling down there in the late poems. In **"Asphodel"** Williams has control over his contradictions: we hear the "stress and counterstress" of the powers of art and of the great discoverers pitted against the destructive powers of recent history.... Yet in **"Asphodel"** creation triumphs, the contradictions of loving and not-loving (betrayal), of creation and destruction are "rendered harmless" by the poet's clarity of design and strength of feeling. **"Asphodel"** is Williams' great poem of reconciliation. At least, the poet hopes that he may render harmless the contradictions of his lifetime, by convincing Flossie of his late but good intentions.

"Asphodel" contains the memory of how hard it was to get there. Begun at a time when Williams was physically weak (March, 1952), worked on when he was virtually incapacitated and restricted to his memories (1953), the poem contains a sea of personal and literary memories to voyage on, a garden of specific images from boyhood and adult life, which, like pressed flowers, trigger again the awakening of creative life. Embedded in the poem is the structure of a descent myth as well. As Williams speaks of his journey to hell, we follow him in his memory down through the subway toward an elusive image of his father, down to the prehistoric artwork in caves. **"Asphodel"** has the depth charge of myth, the most profound and comprehensive kind of memory. While the waves of the poem's lines glint on the surface, its deeper treasures wakened are more complex; the lines are no more the work of a child than the drawings on the walls at Lascaux, or the paintings of Paul Klee. The poem remembers how hard it has been for the poet and for human consciousness to come to creation in the face of personal struggles and brutal communal histories.

The poem is the flower that Williams had awaited blossoming in his imagination. **"Asphodel"** becomes a design for meditation. Throughout his literary career Williams gathered images of flowers for his poetry, among them Queen Anne's lace,

locust flowers, the mustard flower, and finally, asphodel, violets, and roses. As in tribal poetry, praise poems like the Navajo "Night Chant," incantation collects the world. Images gather like petals to the imaginative core, to the poet's final expression of self. Finally, the song, the flower, stands for the singer and his world. **"Asphodel,"** the flower of local meadows and the mythic flower of Hades, crosses worlds, as do Yeats' dolphins. The poem is a preparation for death as well as a love song.

"Asphodel" contains its own memories, but there are also memories that we can bring to the poem to enrich a reading. A study of earned simplicity requires a look at contexts: how did Williams manage to write about a life redeemed by memory, about abiding love, at a time when imaginative freedom in America was being shut down? The early 1950s with its Cold War and persecution of intellectuals and artists had to be a difficult time in which to generate warmth. And though Williams thrived on risk, the suspiciousness and intellectual oppression generated in Washington caused him to suffer deeply.

Not everyone can use a journey to hell—in this case a physical and mental breakdown—as a source for poetry. Williams faced obstacles like his illnesses and his persecution by those in Washington by overcoming these personal hells in his poetry. "Nothing is lost" on the poet. As a physician Williams had practiced healing all his life. Self-healing was part of his strength as an artist. The use of hell as a source of song and new life is a shamanic trick, the work of an Orphic poet.

"Asphodel" is a love poem to Flossie, and a poem of self-healing; it also represents a long-sought-after metrical accomplishment. Recognition of Williams' work on metrics helps us to appreciate measure in practice in the poem.... Williams' theories and reflections on metrics have a substance and validity of their own, the way his poetry does. (pp. 6-9)

The surface of the text and an analysis of its unifying action, "to journey towards love," lead to the deeper structure of the poem, to its mythic pattern. Williams' descent into memory allows him to restore to Flossie an image of their wedding, an image charged with gratitude and light. **"Asphodel"** uses the past to create a timeless image. Williams restores the past through his poetry, as Proust did in his great novel, though the differences are striking. Though he uses memory as a source of renewal, Williams loves the *actual*—the present, and the future outside him. (p. 9)

Marilyn Kallet, in her Honest Simplicity in William Carlos Williams' "Asphodel, That Greeny Flower," *Louisiana State University Press, 1985, 163 p.*

Paul Zweig

1935-1984

American critic, poet, autobiographer, translator, and editor.

Zweig is best remembered for his critical biography *Walt Whitman: The Making of the Poet* (1984). In this book, Zweig presents a comprehensive account of Whitman's poetic emergence. Critics praised Zweig for his sensitive portrayal of his subject and his insight into Whitman's life and work. Zweig was also commended for his writing style, elements of which were compared to prose poetry. In an earlier nonfiction work, *The Adventurer* (1974), Zweig offers a historical overview of the role of the hero in literature. He argues that the exotic journeys and exploits of the protagonists of such ancient and medieval works as the *Iliad,* the *Odyssey, Beowulf,* and *Sir Gawain and the Green Knight* were undertaken for the universal good of humanity, while the adventures of the modern literary hero take the form of a personal search for identity. Critics praised Zweig for the originality and enlightening perceptions he exhibited in this book.

Zweig's poetry has received less substantial attention than his nonfiction but has garnered favorable critical commentary. In his first collection of poetry, *Against Emptiness* (1971), Zweig makes frequent use of symbolism and metaphor and attempts various styles. The poems included in his second volume, *The Dark Side of the Earth* (1974), are melancholy in tone, as Zweig contemplates his feelings of loneliness and his preoccupation with death. In his final collection, the posthumously published *Eternity's Woods* (1985), Zweig seeks spiritual comfort and significance in his life while coping with the knowledge of his cancer and his impending death. Critics expressed discomfort with the emphasis on death in some of Zweig's poems, but they praised the sincerity, sensitivity, and candor with which he articulates his innermost concerns.

Zweig also wrote an autobiography, *Three Journeys: An Automythology* (1976), which recounts three significant periods in his life. The first section consists of a journal Zweig kept while traveling alone in the Algerian Sahara desert in 1974; the second part is a remembrance of the rebellious years he spent in Paris as a politically active student; and the final segment describes his spiritual awakening achieved through the teachings of an Indian guru. All three of these "journeys" are manifestations of Zweig's lifelong self-probing.

(See also *CLC,* Vol. 34 and *Contemporary Authors,* Vols. 85-88, Vol. 113 [obituary].)

BILL ZAVATSKY

Paul Zweig's struggle for a poetic presence is more characteristic of French poetry (beginning on Mallarmé's blank page, on up to the current "Tel Quel" poets) though of late writers such as W. S. Merwin and Harvey Shapiro have joined combat on their own terms.

© *Thomas Victor 1986*

Zweig has drawn most noticeably upon the Neo-Imagist esthetic of Robert Bly, without choosing to employ Bly's Surrealist tactics. The spector of Lautréamont flits through *Against Emptiness,* but none of Ducasse's lucid animal energy. Zweig's exploratory thrusts into the unconscious and into memory are inhibited by a hazy *symboliste* vocabulary and a stilted phraseology. He leaves me willing but suspended by lines like: "Angry shapes, shadows of the fear / She mends with cold, innocent color." Lines that in English are too abstract to evoke the implosions I take Zweig to be seeking.

Another difficulty throughout *Against Emptiness* is an apparent clash of concept and image. Too many of these poems . . . are transparently "idea" poems. And what Mallarmé said to Degas still holds: "You can't make a poem with ideas. . . . *You make it with words.*"

Yet there are remarkable moments in this book: for example, from **"The Red Flower Poems":**

> A flower shot through the head
> Comes to life again, despite
> Our principles.
>   When we talk,
> I know I am looking at you.

Zweig also has two wonderful songs—one by lilies, and one by a sloth (reminding me of Roethke's ditties in "I Am! Says the Lamb"). (pp. 6, 15)

Against Emptiness bubbles with enough indications to make me want more from Paul Zweig. By working against the grain of language, the kind of verse to which he seems to aspire has broken new verbal paths. And made other poets very, very uncomfortable. (p. 15)

Bill Zavatsky, *"Breaking In and Out of Self," in* The New York Times Book Review, *December 26, 1971, pp. 6, 15.*

JAMES NAIDEN

[*Against Emptiness*] is strangely titled, but the contents range widely, from familiar concerns and speculations to a neo-surrealistic experimentation—a range that indicates a variegated intellect. Zweig's use of imagery and ring of metaphor are accomplished and sure; he is a poet whose talents are quite diverse, despite . . . a continually shifting focus.

James Naiden, in a review of *"Against Emptiness," in* Poetry, *Vol. CXX, No. 2, May, 1972, p. 116.*

JOHN GARDNER

It's frequently pointed out that there are no longer heroes in literature, only anti-heroes and spoof heroes like 007, and that the reason for this is that writers and readers can no longer believe that there are heroes in so-called real life. In a world in which everything seems to have gone wrong, we long for heroes, secretly wish we could be heroes ourselves—that by some incredible act of intelligence and daring we could make everything noble, as it used to be—and on the slightest provocation we turn some quite ordinary moral mediocrity into a godly ideal. . . .

Optimists tell us our general despair is an effect of Vietnam and the Nixon Administration, but Paul Zweig's important book, *The Adventurer,* suggests that the trouble is much deeper. The idea of the true, unselfconscious hero—"the adventurer"—went hollow long ago, and went hollower and hollower, stage by stage. The object of his study is to trace and explain those stages. . . .

He begins with the shamanistic element in epic poetry, mainly *Gilgamesh* and the *Odyssey*—tells how the adventurer (in this case the shaman) went away to such places as the country of death and brought back wisdom and power, helps to humanity; how the heroic adventurer was half maniac wild man, as dangerous to his friends as to his enemies, not yet shackled by ethics or common sense, an elemental force; how the adventurer-shaman brought health to the whole community, gave life meaning. All this Zweig elaborates with talk of the *Iliad, Beowulf* and *Sir Gawain and the Green Knight.* Throughout this discussion of things ancient and medieval, Zweig's thesis is somewhat harmed, I'm afraid, by his fairly complete misunderstanding of the poems; but distracting as Zweig's misinformation may be, the thesis is a sound one, and a true argument badly argued may nevertheless be significant.

When he turns to the adventurer in modern times, Zweig's book takes wings. In a series of brilliant analyses which touch on most of the important modern European and American writers but focuses mainly on Defoe's *Robinson Crusoe,* Casanova, the gothic novelists, Edgar Allan Poe, Nietzsche, Malraux and Sartre, he traces what happened to us: how the adventurer's flight and fight turned inward, so that where once monastic or castle walls held out the dangerous wilderness the adventurer

brought news of, there were now the thicker, far solider walls of Protestant morality. . . .

But alas, the walls of decency themselves become a prison, and as that fact began to be recognized clearly, new forms arose—the gothic novel of impotent evil and bungling good, the frivolous attempt at escape in Casanova, the monstrously stupid transvaluations of the Marquis de Sade, as well as things healthier, what Zweig describes as "the new mythology of adventure" in Edgar Allan Poe, and the transvaluation of Nietzsche. On all these Zweig writes with splendid originality and insight, such a set of analyses as we haven't seen in years. To report his conclusions, it seems to me, would be like giving away an earned surprise ending. Part of what's surprising about Zweig's book, in fact, is that he can think of so *much* that's new and true to say about so *many* old chestnuts. His piece on Poe is the best, maybe. Someone has finally managed to explain why the mysterious ending of *The Narrative of A. Gordon Pym* is so terrifying. . . .

In the end Zweig leaves the reader—wisely, perhaps—to write his own final chapter, a chapter that would get down beneath the surface of one interesting remark in Zweig's introduction: "We are faced with an interesting paradox. Oriental traditions discourage adventure because they consider the vigorous individuality of the adventurer to be an illusion, a trick of Maya. Modern traditions in the West have been even less hospitable to the adventurer . . . Yet vigorous individuality is precisely what our culture has come to value most."

Zweig's explanation of our present state is that we in the West have gone inward completely, to drug literature, anti-realistic "fabulation" and so on. That sounds like a grim and terrible *finis,* but I wonder if it is. The shamans took drugs and created fabulations. Out of their discoveries and symbolic tales writers like Homer made highly conscious, social and religious works of art like the *Odyssey,* the story of a man (not a shaman but a man) who fights his way back to the duties he loves, his kingship and family, and purges his island of people who scorn "hospitality" in the highest sense—ordered community, glory of Zeus and the Chinese. . . .

I might never have noticed if it weren't for Zweig's book, but it seems to me that as far back in time as we can trace the mind of man, the idea of the hero has always rung hollow—for all its appeal—and that the stages of the adventurer's decline are nothing other than alternative ways, after old ways have failed, of desperately snatching at the heroic ideal we stubbornly refuse to live without.

John Gardner, *"Where Have All the Heroes Gone?" in* The New York Times Book Review, *December 22, 1974, p. 7.*

VERNON YOUNG

The photograph of Paul Zweig in full closeup on the cover of his book [*The Dark Side of the Earth*] is accurately designed to illustrate the content of his poems: the determination to walk, eyes a-glitter and haunted, into a heart of darkness. . . . Zweig, inching his way towards a viable subject, like a caterpillar after a green leaf, improves with every publication, yet one does feel compelled to question the reality of his compulsive negations, since they don't wholly convince. . . . Actually, there seems to be little "self-knowledge" in these poems at half-mast; nowhere in them do we find a comprehensive basis, a lived justification, for the poet's *weltschmerz.* I don't mean that a poet should submit his credentials for suffering in a slip-case with his poems, but if the poems don't entirely ring true, my complaint has bearing. Zweig has a knack, bred from a necessity for distinguishing himself from the insensitive others, of evoking characters without specifying them; they are not in fact characters, they are the character of his perspective. . . . His title poem, **"The Dark Side of the Earth,"** suggests a humane, outraged identification with the bombed and forgotten, yet it fails to account for the fact that everything Zweig touches becomes warped or turns gray: perhaps a translator of Lautréamont is already a hostage to the discontinuous image and to abdication from a rational identity. (pp. 606-07)

> *Vernon Young, in a review of "The Dark Side of the Earth," in* The Hudson Review, *Vol. XXVII, No. 4, Winter, 1974-75, pp. 606-07.*

JUDITH MOFFETT

I have a deep prejudice against writers who, in their own work, call themselves "poets" and make reference to their "poetry"; these always seem embarrassingly immodest things to say for oneself. But Paul Zweig, who offends me in that regard as in others, *is* a poet and **The Dark Side of the Earth** is poetry too. Zweig is poetry's answer to Quentin Compson, and this, his second book of poems, has been aptly titled. The jacket blurb quotes David Ignatow as saying: "The feeling I always come up with about Zweig's work is of a most paradoxical luxuriousness in the treatment of death, and it always leads to the realization that this is a poet affirming his pleasure in living, even at its most extreme, which is the act of dying. Here is a poet who is willing to go to the edge of life, the more intensely to express his joy of it. . . ."

Maybe this makes sense to Ignatow, Zweig, and Harper & Row. To my mind the poems in this volume reveal, more unremittingly than those in his first book did, a *fascination* with death (and death's confreres, war, aging, solitude, muteness, nightmare)—and furnish almost nowhere any words to live by, with or without joy. Zweig may indeed get pleasure out of life, but as a poet he shows little interest in the state of being alive. (p. 168)

Mine is a bias widely shared, I think. Zweig knows himself that people expect more than death of him; a poem in his earlier volume, **Against Emptiness,** opens: "Get the world into your poems, / They tell me, as I try to explain / My confusion." What's disquieting is the feeling that he doesn't try to be against emptiness anymore. Humanity is absent from the earth's dark side; human figures are abstract and cold: a shadowy wife; an estranged friend; a randily surreal "Robinson Crusoe" who observes to his notebooks that silence and solitude are sex (!). The only personal warmth allowed to creep into these pages is for, of all people, Isidore Ducasse, Comte de Lautréamont, addressed here as "my vampire, / My exile", and a century dead, about whom Zweig has written a book. A few such poems at a time might be bearable, even enlightening. Taken all together they are overwhelming, all the more so because there seems no reason to question Zweig's technical competence: these effects can only be the ones he meant to make. His is an ambiance of paradox and nightmare, of elements disconnected, like those flat figures, from the world and one another, like the many fragmented sentences and elements of the poems themselves, set down episodically, items in a list, where nothing flows into anything else. . . . The disparate elements are associated connotatively, but having been selected are left alone

to make whatever meanings they may, as though to name a thing were sufficiently to evoke it. Satisfied—apparently almost comfortable—in solitary, Zweig contemplates easily a world in which "the sperm of lonely men / Lie jewel-like on the leaves" of a tree on Riverside Drive. Nature for him is a rich mold in which mushrooms and beetles are at home, a forest "like a rotten quilt" to cover the rotting corpses folded within. The few poems where one thing leads to another in ordinary narrative fashion come as a great relief—yet there too the theme never changes: a churchbell tolls for a death; a poisonous mushroom sprouts after rain. . . . (p. 169)

What to say, finally, about a good and by no means frivolous poet barely aware of ordinary life, more interested in death—the dark side of the earth—than anything else? Since reviewers probably have no business taking issue with any writer's vision or his choice of subject—if there ever is a choice—better give Paul Zweig high marks for word-masonry and let it go at that. (p. 170)

> *Judith Moffett, "Life More and Less Abundantly," in* Poetry, *Vol. CXXVII, No. 3, December, 1975, pp. 164-75.*

FRANCINE DU PLESSIX GRAY

In 1974 the American poet Paul Zweig loaded tinned sardines, Pernod, tea, spark plugs, a car jack and other items of physical survival into his 2CV auto and set out for a solitary journey into the African desert. He was led to undertake this voyage by that Faustian need for rebirth, that melancholic search for meaning which often assails men in early middle age blessed with all the material trappings of success. How often have we heard words similar to his! "I loved my wife; I had a reasonable job; several of my books had been published and acclaimed . . . but somehow it wasn't good enough." . . .

The first chapter of Zweig's very beautiful new book [**Three Journeys**] consists of the daily journal he kept during this month-long journey in the Algerian Sahara. It is an account of ironic self-probing rather than heroic enterprise, for Zweig comments constantly on the gap between the desert myths he has been brought up with—bandits, fabulous towns—and the dour secondary vestiges of civilization which comprise its reality: bistros called "Café des Amis" that resemble disaffected outhouses, the chronic misery and undernourishment of the oases, grumbling government officials to whom a post in the Sahara represents exile and failure. And from the beginning of **Three Journeys** one is struck by the spiritual and existential analogue it offers to Zweig's earlier book, **The Adventurer,** a critical work in which he elaborated on the notion of the voyaging hero. There, Zweig had argued that the traditional heroic adventurer of Western literature—who once braved death, oceans, dragons, castle walls to bring wisdom and power back to his community—had gradually turned his journey inwards, finding during the 20th century his chief battlefield in the solitude of the human psyche, in the final inwardness of "drug trips" and anti-realist fabulism.

So are Zweig's three journeys trips of total inwardness. He experiences the desert not as an objective material entity in which to fight for survival but as a "personal space" in which to struggle for heightened self-awareness, in which to meditate on that space's spiritual associations: The desert as the embodiment of all the givens of the contemplative life—asceticism, detachment, a ripening awareness of the One. The desert as matrix of the monotheistic revelations—Judaism, Christianity, Islam—that forged the fate of the Western world. The desert as intensified revelation, where all men must go veiled to protect themselves from the gaze of God. The desert in whose mythology the saint and the nomad are apposites. The desert, finally, as a kind of magnifying lens that enlarges and clarifies the meaning of the two other inner journeys which Zweig describes in his book: his decade as an alienated young intellectual in Paris and his startling recent conversion to the teaching of the Indian guru Swami Muktananda. . . .

Notwithstanding my great wariness about the instant Orientalisms that have recently captivated so many Americans, I found Zweig's last chapter, in which he finally fills his life's inner desert by becoming the disciple of an Indian guru, the finest of the book. The desert blooms in this most inner of the three adventures, and so does Zweig's transluscent prose. (p. 5)

What struck me about the last chapter of Zweig's dazzlingly honest work is that most panaceas we are finding these days—be they Zen, Sufi meditation, Tibetan gurus, a return to the Catholic or Jewish trappings of our childhoods—are involved with demanding and severe ritual practices without which the transcendence Zweig writes about cannot be achieved. The bright white, blue and yellow flashes of light that suffuse Zweig's vision and flood him with ecstasy will be attributed by some to the long periods of kneeling, chanting, gesturing and meditation demanded by his teacher. Such causal factors, I believe, are irrelevant to the issue of human happiness. However Zweig's splendid book suggests some more awesome implications:

Crucial to the manifestations of the "new spirituality" we have witnessed in the post-Vietnam decade is a search for surrender, for submission, for rigorous belonging, above all for authority. Could it be that in an age afflicted with a famine for meaning, the searcher recognizes meaning, as Paul Zweig did, in great part by what it *costs* him? (p. 18)

> *Francine du Plessix Gray, "Adventures of a Poet,"*
> *in* The New York Times Book Review, *May 2, 1976,*
> *pp. 5, 16, 18.*

QUENTIN ANDERSON

[*Walt Whitman: The Making of the Poet*] is no ordinary book on Whitman; it is the first successful attempt to show the nature of the chrysalis *Leaves of Grass* burst out of. The admiring and wondering Emerson first put the question: What could account for this fresh and startling voice? Floyd Stovall, in *The Foreground of "Leaves of Grass,"* and others have patiently hunted out answers, but Paul Zweig is the first to take imaginative possession of the whole body of premonitory evidence in Whitman's stories, letters, notebooks, journalism, poems in draft, and has picked out what stirred the poet in his reading and in the world around him.

Justin Kaplan's highly accomplished *Walt Whitman: a Life* (1980) placed Whitman in his period as a man one might have known. Mr. Zweig starts from a different point. Himself a poet, in addition to being a professor of comparative literature, Mr. Zweig is drawn to his subject above all because he prizes Whitman's work; he moves from his experience of the poems to their connections with the man and his times. He wishes to discover how a "drab, excitable journalist" became, not simply the author of these poems, but the "new man" called for by "Song of Myself" in the first edition of *Leaves of Grass* of 1855.

For Mr. Zweig "Song of Myself" is "an engine of self-making." This, he says, is "the clue we must follow to unravel its story," and, as he later puts it, "What is being made here is a man, and a man's name," in a book "intended to erase the boundary between art and life." (p. 1)

Mr. Zweig's selection of aspects of the culture that played into Whitman's hands is highly persuasive. He stresses the "instantaneousness" of the newspaper, which abolishes everything but the present moment, and the grandiose assumptions common to the press and orators about the high destiny of the United States as moral and political lawgiver to mankind—at the very time, Mr. Zweig notes, that it was being pulled apart over the slavery issue, and Whitman himself was being pulled apart by confused erotic impulses and a threatened sense of identity. Phrenology, publicized in books and journals by the distributors of *Leaves of Grass,* Fowler & Wells, offered Whitman an assurance that one could remake one's chart of bumps by manful effort; the firm's slogan was "Self-made or never made." Mr. Zweig shows that the most important of these influences were vocal, were uttered—the public performances of actors, opera singers and orators. They alone truly succeeded in uniting the "clashing but free" atoms of the democracy.

Mr. Zweig's book, however, is not just an assemblage of evidence about the genesis of Whitman's greatness. Its structure reveals that it is altogether more ambitious. The introduction is a remarkably good essay on Whitman in which the book's chief motifs are marshaled; it provokes the question, what more is there to do? Given what Mr. Zweig wishes to accomplish, the answer is, almost everything. Mr. Zweig is not simply writing criticism but something approaching a prose poem. The prose is lucid and nowhere abstruse but it achieves Mr. Zweig's purpose somewhat as poetry does. (pp. 1, 43)

We must credit Mr. Zweig not simply with the best account of Whitman's genesis as a poet, but with great success in rendering the reader's experience of the movement of Whitman's verse. In writing about "Song of Myself" Mr. Zweig manages to represent a quality even more intimately persuasive than our sense of Whitman's presence, a notation of the movements of a mind trafficking with the world it perceives. He cannot, any more than anyone else, solve the question as to how Whitman contrives to give apprehensible shape to such delicate matters, but he uses all his skill to make us press our noses against the impermeable pane of Whitman's genius—perhaps the shrewdest way to enforce his conviction that one cannot do what much current criticism attempts, divorce the maker from the poem. (p. 43)

But Mr. Zweig's sense that Whitman's significance for us terminates in particular poetic achievements, as if poetry were not involved in any history but that of poetry itself, sometimes misleads him. One fact deserves more emphasis than Mr. Zweig gives it. It was not *Calamus,* the group of love poems, or that splendid torch song "Out of the Cradle Endlessly Rocking," all of which appeared in 1860, that have sunk deep into a wide company of readers; it was the presence Mr. Zweig describes as a "capacious 'self'" who lorded it over the world in 1855 and 1856, and who was belatedly recognized as our national poet in the 1950's. Whitman knew how he had brought his strength to bear. When he helped John Burroughs to write a chapter on his poems in 1877 the two of them gave first place to the poems of 1855 and 1856.

Mr. Zweig steps back on occasion to place Whitman in the context of Western literature. These interventions seem too brief, too glancing, to carry much weight. But one must consider them as they affect Mr. Zweig's perspective on Whitman. In his penultimate paragraph he writes: "Whitman's work assaulted the institution of literature and language itself and, in so doing, laid the groundwork for the anti-cultural ambition of much modernist writing. He is the ancestor not only of Henry Miller and Allen Ginsberg but of Kafka, Beckett, André Breton, Borges—of all who have made of their writing an attack on the act of writing and on culture itself." (pp. 43-4)

Mr. Zweig conveys brilliantly a sense of how "Song of Myself" goes as a poem, but he seems to have missed the coherence and specificity of Whitman's assault on the ascendant culture of his time. This is of course the very thing that engages Henry Miller and Allen Ginsberg. . . .

Mr. Zweig's book will hereafter be indispensable, and should be greeted with gratitude, but his "epic of self-making" fails to give Whitman his due as a force in the history of our culture. (p. 44)

> Quentin Anderson, "When the Singer Found His Song," in The New York Times Book Review, May 6, 1984, pp. 1, 43-4.

RAYMOND NELSON

The best achievement of Zweig's [Walt Whitman: The Making of the Poet is the] . . . creation of a personality. There are other achievements, too, in the frequently brilliant historical and critical writing, but they have been anticipated by other commentators and are not so spellbindingly analogous to Whitman's own peculiar genius. Zweig's openness to the dialectical energies of Whitman's life and times, his feeling for the charm, edginess, and grit of the man, may well be the greatest contributions a biographer of Whitman can now make. We need to rescue him from monumentalism as others have had to rescue him at various times from attributions of barbarism, outlawry, boosterism, or complacency. Zweig's is one of those books that periodically rediscovers how original and untranslatable Whitman—man and book—truly was. His recovery of the elusive person is thus an important and welcome triumph. (pp. 727-28)

> Raymond Nelson, "The Knot of Contrariety," in The Virginia Quarterly Review, Vol. 60, No. 4 (Autumn, 1984), pp. 723-28.

PUBLISHERS WEEKLY

[Paul Zweig] was better known as a literary critic than as a poet, despite two volumes of verse that preceded this one. As a posthumous work, [Eternity's Woods] invites an unavoidable pathos. Technically unassuming, if not uninteresting, the collection derives its interest from its theme of the spiritual quest—the poet's search among the particulars of his own life for its meaning. But because Zweig's assertions of faith are never entirely persuasive as either poetry or philosophy, the book is extremely disquieting. His vision of a God who is part Jehovah, part Hindu "cow-mother," part universal light, seems jerry-built, sad and desperate. . . . Eternity's Woods is the poignant final monument of a writer who served the cause of letters well

in his public life, but whose inner life failed him badly at the confrontation with death.

> A review of "Eternity's Woods," in Publishers Weekly, Vol. 227, No. 4, January 25, 1985, p. 92.

JOSEPH PARISI

Known for his excellent critical biography, Walt Whitman: The Making of the Poet . . . , the late Paul Zweig was likewise a skilled and sensitive practitioner of the art of poetry. In [Eternity's Woods], his third and final volume, the perennial and ultimate questions of life are addressed in affecting lyrics that trace the poet's early life and outline his perspectives on death. In reviewing the past, he focuses particularly upon the influences of family: a beloved aunt, a complex father with whom relations . . . were often difficult though intense. Moving to the present, the poet places his life within the context of the larger cosmos, wondering in the presence of a marvelous world where the actual and the eternal meld in the objects of our experience. . . . Much of the charm in this work comes not so much from the intelligence and insight of the poet as from his humility, expressed with candor, calm, and a quiet, accepting love. A sad but noble testament to a life too soon completed.

> Joseph Parisi, in a review of "Eternity's Woods," in Booklist, Vol. 81, No. 22, August, 1985, p. 1625.

ROGER MITCHELL

Posthumous collections are almost always disappointing. They are often put together by close friends or critics with vested interests whose affection for the poet or the work often interferes with critical detachment. The poet almost always leaves behind poems which look finished to someone else but aren't. Such poems often have a high burnish, but the poet would probably have rewritten or discarded them if he had lived. It is even possible that a poet, knowing he was to die soon, might write hastily, hoping to get it all down before the end. All of these harmful pressures were brought to bear on [Zweig's] Eternity's Woods. It is therefore remarkable that the book is as good as it is. (p. 242)

["The Esplanade"] is one of the best poems in the book, a long, tortured reaching toward his father with many bright passages in it like this:

> But now the broken slabs, the color of bread,
> And the prongs of wrenched iron, like crawlers
> Weeping rust onto the eroded pavement,
> Are a zone of permanent ruin along the water's edge.

This is a sensuous, comprehensive image of the son's perception of his father and of their relationship. The wrenched rhythms and sounds match the feeling exactly. Zweig writes this way often, but more often he shows an impatience with images, or he simply feels that they do not do the job well enough. There is an urgency to say things which fights against the urge to write poems. Perhaps it is a condition of the contemporary poem that perfectly ordinary things and bland language have equal access to it with the most rare and dazzling. If this is not true, a like effect is achieved in Zweig's poems by a pervasive desire to be morally earnest. Sincerity comes before craft, and it is difficult to fault this in Zweig's work. . . . Stubborn will and the imperfect gift of speech are strengths in Zweig's work, as well.

This is a book of death, of course, and the richest image Zweig has of it is the house he purchased in France. Two of the best poems, **"The House"** and **"Eternity's Woods,"** concern themselves with buying, repairing, and living in an old farmhouse in western France. "The beautiful indifference of this land," **"The House"** announces, "The brittle weeds in fields still half ploughed / From when he climbed into his bed, and never left it," foreshadow Zweig's unfinished life in the French farmer's. The farmhouse is ancient, made with stones and twisted oak beams, and **"The House"** concerns the choice he made between the continuities it represented to him and his marriage.... A poet this serious and sensitive might have gone on to write some of our best poetry. Though, maybe he did. (pp. 243-44)

Roger Mitchell, in a review of "Eternity's Woods," in Poetry, *Vol. CXLVII, No. 4, January, 1986, pp. 242-44.*

Appendix

The following is a listing of all sources used in Volume 42 of *Contemporary Literary Criticism*. Included in this list are all copyright and reprint rights and acknowledgments for those essays for which permission was obtained. Every effort has been made to trace copyright, but if omissions have been made, please let us know.

THE EXCERPTS IN CLC, VOLUME 42, WERE REPRINTED FROM THE FOLLOWING PERIODICALS:

America, v. 145, December 19, 1981 for "David Jones: A Christian Poet for a Secular Age" by John B. Breslin; v. 153, October 12, 1985 for "What Is Essential Is Invisible to the Eye'" by Joseph L. Quinn, S. J., © 1981, 1985 respectively. All rights reserved. Both reprinted by permission of the respective authors./ v. 127, September 30, 1972; v. 128, June 2, 1973; v. 130, April 20, 1974. © 1972, 1973, 1974. All rights reserved. All reprinted with permission of America Press, Inc., 106 West 56th Street, New York, NY 10019.

The American Book Review, v. 4, January-February, 1982. © 1982 by The American Book Review. Reprinted by permission of the publisher.

American Literature, v. 56, March, 1984. Copyright © 1984 Duke University Press, Durham, NC. Reprinted by permission of the publisher.

The American Spectator, v. 18, November, 1985 for a review of "The Red Fox" by Cynthia Grenier. Copyright © 1985 by the author. Reprinted by permission of the author.

Analog Science Fiction/Science Fact, v. LXXXI, June, 1968; v. LXXXV, July, 1970; v. LXXXV, August, 1970. Copyright © 1968, 1970 by The Condé Nast Publications, Inc./ v. CII, January 4, 1982 for a review of "Starworld" by Tom Easton; v. CII, March 1, 1982 for a review of "The Ghosts of Forever" by Tom Easton; v. CIII, October, 1983 for a review of "Invasion: Earth" by Tom Easton; v. CIV, December, 1984 for a review of "West of Eden" by Tom Easton; v. CVI, April, 1986 for a review of "An Edge in My Voice" by Tom Easton. © 1982, 1983, 1984, 1986 by Davis Publications, Inc. All reprinted by permission of the author.

The Antigonish Review, n. 38, Summer, 1979 for "Reflection on the Young Faludy" by Alexandre L. Amprimoz; n. 58, Summer, 1984 for a review of "The Roman Quarry and Other Sequences" by Peter Sanger. Copyright 1979, 1984 by the respective authors. Both reprinted by permission of the publisher and the respective authors.

The Armchair Detective, v. 11, July, 1978; v. 19, Winter, 1986. Copyright © 1978, 1986 by *The Armchair Detective.* Both reprinted by permission of the publisher.

Art in America, v. 64, July-August, 1976 for a review of "The Golden Unicorn" by Carter Ratcliff. Copyright © 1976 by Art in America, Inc. Reprinted by permission of the publisher and the author.

The Atlantic Monthly, v. 257, April, 1986 for a review of "Mrs. Caliban" by Jack Beatty. Copyright 1986 by The Atlantic Monthly Company, Boston, MA. Reprinted by permission of the author.

Australian Literary Studies, v. 10, May, 1982 for "Asia, Europe and Australian Identity: The Novels of Christopher Koch" by Helen Tiffin. Reprinted by permission of the publisher and the author.

THE EXCERPTS IN CLC, VOLUME 42, WERE REPRINTED FROM THE FOLLOWING BOOKS:

Adler, Renata. From "Salt into Old Scars," in *Toward a Radical Middle: Fourteen Pieces of Reporting and Criticism*. Random House, 1970. Copyright © 1963 by Renata Adler. All rights reserved. Reprinted by permission of the author.

Bruccoli, Matthew J. From *The O'Hara Concern: A Biography of John O'Hara*. Random House, 1975. Copyright © 1975 by Matthew J. Bruccoli. All rights reserved. Reprinted by permission of Random House, Inc.

Chénetier, Marc. From *Richard Brautigan*. Methuen, 1983. © 1983 Marc Chénetier. All rights reserved. Reprinted by permission of Methuen & Co. Ltd.

Crawford, Gary William. From "Urban Gothic: The Fiction of Ramsey Campbell," in *Discovering Modern Horror Fiction*. Edited by Darrell Schweitzer. Starmont House, 1985. Copyright © 1985 by Starmont House, Inc. All rights reserved. Reprinted by permission of the publisher.

Deane, Seamus. From *Celtic Revivals: Essays in Modern Irish Literature, 1880-1980*. Faber & Faber, 1985. © 1985 by Seamus Deane. All rights reserved. Reprinted by permission of Faber & Faber Ltd.

Doyle, Charles. From *William Carlos Williams and the American Poem*. St. Martin's Press, 1982, Macmillan, 1982. © Charles Doyle 1982. All rights reserved. Reprinted by permission of St. Martin's Press, Inc. In Canada by Macmillan, London and Basingstoke.

Foster, Edward Halsey. From *Richard Brautigan*. Twayne, 1983. Copyright 1983 by Twayne Publishers. All rights reserved. Reprinted with the permission of Twayne Publishers, a division of G. K. Hall & Co., Boston.

Gallagher, Edward J. From "The Thematic Structure of 'The Martian Chronicles'," in *Ray Bradbury*. Edited by Martin Harry Greenberg and Joseph D. Olander. Taplinger, 1980 Copyright © 1980 by Martin Harry Greenberg and Joseph D. Olander. All rights reserved. Published by Taplinger Publishing Co., Inc., New York. Reprinted by permission of the publisher.

Grant, Steve. From "Voicing the Protest: The New Writers," in *Dreams and Deconstructions: Alternative Theatre in Britain*. Edited by Sandy Craig. Amber Lane Press, 1980. Copyright © Amber Lane Press Limited, 1980. All rights reserved. Reprinted by permission.

Hassler, Donald M. From "What the Machine Teaches: Walter Tevis's 'Mockingbird'," in *The Mechanical God: Machines in Science Fiction*. Edited by Thomas P. Dunn and Richard D. Erlich. Greenwood Press, 1982. Copyright © 1982 by Thomas P. Dunn and Richard D. Erlich. All rights reserved. Reprinted by permission of Greenwood Press, Inc., Westport, CT.

Hayman, Ronald. From *British Theatre Since 1955: A Reassessment*. Oxford University Press, Oxford, 1979. © Oxford University Press 1979. All rights reserved. Reprinted by permission of A. D. Peters & Co. Ltd.

Heaney, Seamus. From *Preoccupations: Selected Prose, 1968-1978*. Farrar, Straus, Giroux, 1980, Faber & Faber, 1980. Copyright © 1980 by Seamus Heaney. All rights reserved. Reprinted by permission of Farrar, Straus and Giroux, Inc. In Canada by Faber & Faber Ltd.

Kallet, Marilyn. From *Honest Simplicity in William Carlos Williams' "Asphodel, That Greeny Flower."* Louisiana State University Press, 1985. Copyright © 1985 by Louisiana State University Press. All rights reserved. Reprinted by permission of the publisher.

King, Bruce. From *The New English Literatures: Cultural Nationalism in a Changing World*. St. Martin's Press, 1980, Macmillan, 1980. © Bruce King 1980. All rights reserved. Reprinted by permission of St. Martin's Press, Inc. In Canada by Macmillan, London and Basingstoke.

King, Stephen. From *Danse Macabre*. Everest House Publishers, 1981. Copyright © 1981 by Stephen King. All rights reserved. Reprinted by permission of Dodd, Mead & Company, Inc.

Knepper, Marty S. From "Dick Francis," in *Twelve Englishmen of Mystery*. Edited by Earl F. Bargainnier. Bowling Green University Popular Press, 1984. Copyright © 1984 by Bowling Green University Popular Press. Reprinted by permission of the publisher.

Leeming, Glenda. From "Articulacy and Awareness: The Modulation of Familiar Themes in Wesker's Plays of the 70s," in *Contemporary English Drama*. Edited by C. W. E. Bigsby. Edward Arnold, 1981. All rights reserved. Reprinted by permission of the publisher.

Long, Robert Emmet. From *John O'Hara*. Ungar, 1983. Copyright © 1983 by The Ungar Publishing Company Inc. Reprinted by permission.

MacShane, Frank. From *Collected Stories of John O'Hara*. By John O'Hara, edited by Frank MacShane. Random House, 1984. Copyright © 1984 by Frank MacShane. All rights reserved. Reprinted by permission of The Aaron M. Priest Literary Agency, Inc.

Mariani, Paul. From *A Usable Past: Essays on Modern & Contemporary Poetry*. University of Massachusetts Press, 1984. Copyright © 1984 by The University of Massachusetts Press. All rights reserved. Reprinted by permission of the publisher.

Literature Criticism Series
Cumulative Author Index

This index lists all author entries in the Gale Literary Criticism Series and includes cross-references to other Gale sources. For the convenience of the reader, references to the *Yearbook* in the *Contemporary Literary Criticism* series include the page number (in parentheses) after the volume number. References in the index are identified as follows:

Author Index

Author Index

Author Index

Lucas, George 1944-..............CLC 16
See also CA 77-80

Lucas, Victoria 1932-1963
See Plath, Sylvia

Ludlum, Robert 1927- ....CLC 22
See also CA 33-36R
See also DLB-Y 82

Ludwig, Otto 1813-1865......... NCLC 4

Lugones, Leopoldo
1874-1938................. TCLC 15
See also CA 116

Lu Hsün 1881-1936............. TCLC 3

Lukács, Georg 1885-1971........CLC 24
See also Lukács, György

Lukács, György 1885-1971
See Lukács, Georg
See also CA 101
See also obituary CA 29-32R

Luke, Peter (Ambrose Cyprian)
1919-........................CLC 38
See also CA 81-84
See also DLB 13

Lurie (Bishop), Alison
1926-......... CLC 4, 5, 18, 39 (176)
See also CANR 2, 17
See also CA 1-4R
See also DLB 2

Luzi, Mario 1914-...............CLC 13
See also CANR 9
See also CA 61-64

Lytle, Andrew (Nelson) 1902-......CLC 22
See also CA 9-12R
See also DLB 6

Lytton, Edward Bulwer 1803-1873
See Bulwer-Lytton, (Lord) Edward (George
Earle Lytton)
See also SATA 23

Maas, Peter 1929-...............CLC 29
See also CA 93-96

Macaulay, (Dame Emile) Rose
1881-1958.................. TCLC 7
See also CA 104
See also DLB 36

MacBeth, George (Mann)
1932-.................... CLC 2, 5, 9
See also CA 25-28R
See also SATA 4
See also DLB 40

MacCaig, Norman (Alexander)
1910-........................CLC 36
See also CANR 3
See also CA 9-12R
See also DLB 27

MacDiarmid, Hugh
1892-1978...........CLC 2, 4, 11, 19
See also Grieve, C(hristopher) M(urray)
See also DLB 20

Macdonald, Cynthia 1928-..... CLC 13, 19
See also CANR 4
See also CA 49-52

MacDonald, George
1824-1905.................. TCLC 9
See also CA 106
See also SATA 33
See also DLB 18

MacDonald, John D(ann)
1916-.................... CLC 3, 27
See also CANR 1
See also CA 1-4R
See also DLB 8

Macdonald, (John) Ross
1915-1983...........CLC 1, 2, 3, 14,
34 (416), 41
See also Millar, Kenneth

MacEwen, Gwendolyn 1941-.......CLC 13
See also CANR 7
See also CA 9-12R
See also DLB 53

Machado (y Ruiz), Antonio
1875-1939.................. TCLC 3
See also CA 104

Machado de Assis, (Joaquim Maria)
1839-1908.................. TCLC 10
See also CA 107

Machen, Arthur (Llewellyn Jones)
1863-1947.................. TCLC 4
See also CA 104
See also DLB 36

MacInnes, Colin 1914-1976..... CLC 4, 23
See also CA 69-72
See also obituary CA 65-68
See also DLB 14

MacInnes, Helen (Clark)
1907-1985........... CLC 27, 39 (349)
See also CANR 1
See also CA 1-4R
See also SATA 22, 44

Macintosh, Elizabeth 1897-1952
See Tey, Josephine
See also CA 110

Mackenzie, (Edward Montague) Compton
1883-1972...................CLC 18
See also CAP 2
See also CA 21-22
See also obituary CA 37-40R
See also DLB 34

Mac Laverty, Bernard 1942-.......CLC 31
See also CA 116, 118

MacLean, Alistair (Stuart)
1922-.................... CLC 3, 13
See also CA 57-60
See also SATA 23

MacLeish, Archibald
1892-1982.............. CLC 3, 8, 14
See also CA 9-12R
See also obituary CA 106
See also DLB 4, 7, 45
See also DLB-Y 82

MacLennan, (John) Hugh
1907-.................... CLC 2, 14
See also CA 5-8R

MacNeice, (Frederick) Louis
1907-1963.............. CLC 1, 4, 10
See also CA 85-88
See also DLB 10, 20

Macpherson, (Jean) Jay 1931-......CLC 14
See also CA 5-8R
See also DLB 53

MacShane, Frank 1927-..... CLC 39 (404)
See also CANR 3
See also CA 11-12R

Macumber, Mari 1896-1966
See Sandoz, Mari (Susette)

Madden, (Jerry) David
1933-.................... CLC 5, 15
See also CAAS 3
See also CANR 4
See also CA 1-4R
See also DLB 6

Madhubuti, Haki R. 1942-.........CLC 6
See also Lee, Don L.
See also DLB 5, 41

Maeterlinck, Maurice
1862-1949................... TCLC 3
See also CA 104

Maginn, William 1794-1842....... NCLC 8

Mahapatra, Jayanta 1928-........CLC 33
See also CANR 15
See also CA 73-76

Mahon, Derek 1941-..............CLC 27
See also CA 113
See also DLB 40

Mailer, Norman
1923-......CLC 1, 2, 3, 4, 5, 8, 11, 14,
28, 39 (416)
See also CA 9-12R
See also DLB 2, 16, 28
See also DLB-Y 80, 83
See also DLB-DS 3
See also AITN 2

Mais, Roger 1905-1955.......... TCLC 8
See also CA 105

Major, Clarence 1936- .... CLC 3, 19
See also CA 21-24R
See also DLB 33

Major, Kevin 1949-..............CLC 26
See also CLR 11
See also CA 97-100
See also SATA 32

Malamud, Bernard
1914-......CLC 1, 2, 3, 5, 8, 9, 11, 18,
27
See also CA 5-8R
See also DLB 2, 28
See also DLB-Y 80

Malherbe, François de 1555-1628..... LC 5

Mallarmé, Stéphane
1842-1898.................. NCLC 4

Mallet-Joris, Françoise 1930-.......CLC 11
See also CANR 17
See also CA 65-68

Maloff, Saul 1922-.................CLC 5
See also CA 33-36R

Malouf, David 1934-.............CLC 28

Malraux, (Georges-) André
1901-1976..... CLC 1, 4, 9, 13, 15
See also CAP 2
See also CA 21-24R
See also obituary CA 69-72

Malzberg, Barry N. 1939- ....CLC 7
See also CAAS 4
See also CANR 16
See also CA 61-64
See also DLB 8

Mamet, David
1947-.............CLC 9, 15, 34 (217)
See also CANR 15
See also CA 81-84
See also DLB 7

Author Index

Author Index

Author Index

CLC Cumulative Nationality Index

Nationality Index

Nationality Index

CLC Cumulative Title Index

Title Index

Title Index

Title Index

Title Index

Title Index

Title Index

Title Index

Title Index

Title Index

Title Index

Title Index

Title Index

Title Index

Title Index

Title Index

Title Index

Title Index

Title Index

Title Index

Title Index

Title Index

Title Index

Title Index

Title Index

Title Index

Title Index

Title Index

Title Index

Title Index